About the cover:

The image is a stylized art piece representing variety in both behavior and organization. The various borders can be viewed as an array of behaviors each unique to the whole piece. Each of the three individual sections represents a different organization. One might consider that the piece with frayed edges does not represent effective behavior as there are too many stragglers or loose ends – it is not complete. On the other hand, does an organization need to be a solid structured behavioral piece as is represented in the smooth edged uniformly shaped metal ring?

As organizations vary from one to another so too do the behaviors that make a particular organization effective. Out-of-the-box, on-the-spot effective behavior works very well for the piece that is shown as the bottom layer. Highly structured, uniform behavior is represented in the metal ring. A variety of behaviors are represented in the lighter and darker areas of the middle piece – all of which are most certainly effective to that particular piece/organization.

What do you see?

SEVENTH EDITION

Effective Behavior in Organizations

Cases, Concepts, and Student Experiences

ALLAN R. COHEN
Edward A. Madden Distinguished Professor of Global Leadership

Babson College

STEPHEN L. FINK
Professor of Management

Whittemore School of Business and Economics

University of New Hampshire

For Previous Editions:
HERMAN GADON
Retired from the University of California, San Diego

ROBIN D. WILLITS
Professor Emeritus of Administration and Organization

University of New Hampshire

with the collaboration of
NATASHA JOSEFOWITZ
Adjunct Professor

College of Health and Human Services

San Diego State University

Boston Burr Ridge, IL Dubuque, IA Madison, WI New York San Francisco St. Louis
Bangkok Bogotá Caracas Lisbon London Madrid
Mexico City Milan New Delhi Seoul Singapore Sydney Taipei Toronto

McGraw-Hill Higher Education

*A Division of The **McGraw-Hill** Companies*

Effective Behavior in Organizations

Published by McGraw-Hill/Irwin, an imprint of The McGraw-Hill Companies, Inc. 1221 Avenue of the Americas, New York, NY, 10020. Copyright © 2001, 1995, 1992, 1988, 1984, 1980, 1976, by The McGraw-Hill Companies, Inc. All rights reserved. No part of this publication may be reproduced or distributed in any form or by any means, or stored in a data base or retrieval system, without the prior written consent of The McGraw-Hill Companies, Inc., including, but not limited to, in any network or other electronic storage or transmission, or broadcast for distance learning.

Some ancillaries, including electronic and print components, may not be available to customers outside the United States.

This book is printed on acid-free paper.

1 2 3 4 5 6 7 8 9 0 KGP/KGP 0 9 8 7 6 5 4 3 2

ISBN 0072877235

Vice president/Editor-in-chief: *Michael W. Junior*
Sponsoring editor: *John Biernat*
Editorial assistant: *Dana Dorn*
Marketing manager: *Ellen Cleary*
Project manager: *Kimberly D. Hooker*
Production supervisor: *Michael McCormick*
Coordinator freelance design: *Mary Christianson*
Freelance designer: *oversat paredes design*
Supplement coordinator: *Susan Lombardi*
New media project manager: *Barb Block*
Compositor: *GAC Indianapolis*
Typeface: *10.5/12 Garamond Regular*
Printer: *Quebecor Printing Book Group/Kingsport*

Library of Congress Cataloging-in-Publication Data

Cohen, Allan R.
    Effective behavior in organizations: cases, concepts, and student experiences / Allan R. Cohen, Stephen L. Fink.--7th ed.
        p. cm.
Previous ed. entered under title.
ISBN 0-07-239670-9 (alk. paper)
Includes index.
1. Organizational behavior. I. Fink, Stephen L. II. Title.

HD58.7.E35 2001
658.4--dc21   00-037002
www.mhhe.com

Preface

Accelerating Change

We are in the midst of a managerial and organizational revolution. The old rules about how to treat people, how to organize work, and how to lead are all crumbling. A new magazine, *Fast Company*, came from nowhere to chronicle this new world; the first issue of 2000 featured the tension between companies built to last and those built to "flip"–sell or go public in a few years. It is no longer just behavioral scientists who are interested in exploring the intricacies of behavior and change. Even traditional "my way or the highway" managers are forced into seeking better ways to get work done. They are pummelled by new competition, new technology, new regulations, new workforce demands, and clear evidence that without the enthusiastic commitment of employees at all levels, mighty businesses rapidly decay.

We are living in an age when rapidly accelerating technological advances are driving major organizational changes, and major business transactions take place in seconds, across thousands of miles and without any direct face-to-face contact among the players. The speed of such transactions not only drives organizational restructuring but also drives individuals toward the edge of information overload. With access to word processing, spreadsheets, and the Internet, students and managers feel pressure to think and act more quickly than ever. What does this do to the need for careful analysis and planning, to engaging in the kind of reflective thinking required in this course? There's the rub! Managers need to learn to work fast and intuitively and also to disengage from the rapid tempo of everyday activity, literally forcing themselves into a reflective mode. Students have a chance to get ahead of the game by practicing these critical skills.

More than Theory

There has never been a more exciting time to be studying organizational behavioral. Students deserve to learn from a book–and course–that conveys the excitement and challenge of trying to understand and be effective in complex, difficult organizational situations. They must learn to act on their knowledge–even when they cannot be certain of the outcome. This hard work has never been more important, so we have designed a book that engages students in the interplay among analyzing, doing, and conceptualizing from their experiences. A textbook should not be a trunkful of unrelated theories and research findings. A good textbook must recognize the value of focusing on complex *situations* and making the social science findings *serve* the *analysis*. In this way, students are met where they are: eager to learn how to be effective in their work rather than how to memorize social science jargon and findings.

Students also deserve to have a text that consists of practical concepts and guidelines that can serve them throughout their working lives, a volume that becomes an ongoing reference source for action, not just a packages of pages to be discarded after the grades are in.

Thus, we have based this book on the assumption that students best learn effective organizational behavior by practicing it on realistic problems or dilemmas and then reflecting upon their efforts, using concepts, theories, reasoning, and guidance. By playing back and forth between action and analysis, students develop the ability to conceptualize and learn from their experience. In our efforts over the past 35 years to implement our ideas in the classroom, we have dealt with the following general issues:

1. Students have to be persuaded to solve problems using behavioral science theory as a way of going beyond common sense, even while recognizing that theory is seldom sufficient to ensure desirable outcomes.
2. Students need help in preparing for the ambiguity and uncertainty of organizational life without being overwhelmed by complexity.
3. Students have to be taught to increase both their analytical abilities and their interactive skills.

4. Classroom teachers have to convey to inexperienced students the reality of the behavioral difficulties with which all members of organizations must cope. Students with little work experience tend to view organizational behavior as irrelevant or unnecessary. This is true despite repeated surveys made several years after graduation that indicate that, in retrospect, business students value behavioral courses highly and wish they had taken more.

5. Students need help in learning to live with the uncertainty that accompanies subject matter in which the "right answer" depends in part on the values of the manager seeking the answer.

Our Methods

This book is the result of our struggle with these knotty dilemmas. Our approach is a balanced one: Concepts and cognitive material are applied to actual problems–cases and exercises–using classroom processes that reinforce and illuminate the conceptual material.

The Classroom as Organization

We introduce the idea of the classroom as a real organization with genuine problems of leadership, structure, motivation, social pressure, misunderstandings, interpersonal friction, and diversity of backgrounds, goals, and assumptions, among others. These problems parallel those in companies and elsewhere. Therefore, in addition to the textual material, we provide the instructor with ways to immerse students in ongoing classroom experiences in analyzing cases, participating in simulations and exercises, working in groups, taking directions from a "supervisor," and on so.

Written for Students

To foster the integration of concepts and experiences, we have written the text material in an informal, personal style. We use examples and illustrations from the students' world of classrooms and campus organizations, as well as from business and nonprofit organizations. Similarly, we have chosen cases that represent a cross section of organizational life, especially those situations with which students can readily identify, whether in the university, industry, health field, government agency, or other educational institutions. Students themselves have written many cases about their organizational experiences, furthering ease of identification. In addition, the cases were chosen with the book's central conceptual scheme in mind so that there is sufficient data for students to practice using the analytical tools presented.

Theory and Research as Propositions

Sometimes it is difficult for students to grasp or retain theory in ways that permit easy application. Simply describing research findings or presenting a theory as developed by its author may leave students on their own to find ways of translating the ideas into more useful forms. Thus we present as many concepts as possible in the form of situational *propositions* about behavior, all highlighted and screened. We have found that propositional statements are more easily remembered and applied than unconnected strings of references, and that students readily adopt this format as a way of articulating their own insights and concepts. Rather than focusing on controversies in the research literature or treating theory as received wisdom, we offer insights from research in a tentative form that the student can immediately test on a problem being faced. Most propositions, however, are referenced in the Endnotes so that interested readers can pursue the ideas in depth. While trying to ensure that no major concepts were omitted or oversimplified, we selected those we believe most useful in the analysis of actual problems. We also worked to integrate propositions with a central conceptual scheme, *relating all chapters and topics in the book to one another,* so students can see that the field is more than a series of disconnected topics.

Integration of Classroom Experiences, Cases, and Concepts

In general, we have organized the book and course material so that a student can *experience* in the classroom a genuine organizational problem with real consequences while *analyzing* other people (through a case) in a similar dilemma using *concepts* or *research findings* about such problems. In this way, we hope to make the "medium" a reinforcing part of the conceptual "message."

Balancing Openness and Trust with Realistic Toughness

Another way in which we have tried to demonstrate that the course is indeed relevant to *any* manager, present or future, is by the inclusion of more than the usual amount of material on power, influence, and conflict in organizations. These often-neglected areas generate strong student interest and maintain perspective when the book focuses on collaboration, listening, or cohesion. If we expect students to adopt contingency thinking, choosing behavior appropriate to the situation, we must acknowledge those unpleasant aspects of organizations that call for defensiveness or "political maneuvering" as well as the more congenial territories with which organizational behavior has usually been concerned. We have often had to fight our own unintentional tendency to sound as if openness and trust were always appropriate managerial behavior; in doing so, we believe that we have made the book more balanced and theoretically sound.

What's Happening: Managerial Bulletins

Students have always enjoyed the reality of the material we introduce from the business press; we have cited many reports from the firing line and feature them as *Managerial Bulletins* throughout the text. Action-oriented advice to students is similarly featured and called *Managerial Tools*. To help students experience and apply central concepts, each chapter closes with a *Personal Application Exercise*.

Special Features of the Seventh Edition

In an increasingly diverse and global world, the need to understand more about individual, group, and cultural differences has become imperative, so we have extended this material, both in separate sections and throughout the chapters. More international (including Canadian) and gender-related cases, several with women managers as central figures, have been added.

Availability of More than Printed Cases

Some cases are timeless while others must be very contemporary, featuring virtual teams, women in leadership roles, international/cultural issues, and so on. We not only have 17 new cases, but have made others available to instructors through the McGraw-Hill web site. Furthermore, we have expanded the leadership sections to include some new concepts about influence and ways to build employee commitment. New macro-OB material on organizational design and new organizational forms has been added and the material reorganized to be more useful. The discussion of motivation is also enhanced.

Finally, in the spirit of listening to the customer, we have responded to student requests to tighten the writing, making the book flow more smoothly and crisply without sacrificing sophistication.

Sequenced for Classroom Learning

The new edition of the book continues the unorthodox sequencing of the earlier editions, starting with a focus on groups, then the individual, two-person relationships, etc. We chose that sequencing to parallel unfolding classroom phenomena; we found that early in the course students worry about finding their place in a group. The text thus provides timely concepts that help the student understand what is being actively experienced in the classroom organization. Once secure in their group, students are more ready to look at themselves and to explore together aspects of their personal systems. Consequently, we discuss individual behavior after the section on groups.

Integrated, but Rearrangeable Chapters

Nevertheless, over the years, some instructors have said that they would prefer to *start with the individual as the basic building block* and move from there to the larger systems. Thus we have edited the chapters to allow an instructor greater flexibility. This makes it easier to rearrange chapter sequences to focus on the individual, the pair, then the group. The chapters can readily be sequenced as follows, 1, 2, 7, 8, 9, 10, 3, 4, 5, 6, 11, 12, 13, 14, or in other ways that fit instructor preference.

With only a brief lecture on the social system conceptual theme preceding the assignment of Chapters 9 and 10, the instructor can follow alternative sequencing. As with any complex subject matter, all prior discussions enrich subsequent ones, so that a different chapter sequence merely alters which case discussion will have the benefit of students' constantly developing sophistication. It would be wonderful if a method could be invented that would allow students to already know all later topics before studying early ones, but unfortunately no one has been able to devise a way to defeat this shortcoming of the human mind! All we can do is periodically revisit earlier topics with our newly acquired perspective—and learn to live with the perennial feeling that we could have been far more effective if only we had known "then" what we know now. Whatever the sequence, tens of thousands of students have found the *action-oriented learning methods* embodied in this book to be interesting, challenging, and useful. We hope you do too.

Allan R. Cohen
Stephen L. Fink

Acknowledgments

During the course of seven editions, many people have helped in all sorts of ways. We are extremely grateful to each of them. We especially want to thank our now retired colleagues, Herman Gadon, Natasha Josefowitz, and Robin D. Willits, whose extraordinary contributions to the first six editions live on in our words and thoughts. For this edition, the extensive comments of the following academics were invaluable: Terry Gaston, Donald Malm, Rich Sebastian, and Jann Freed (Central College).

Helpful in the preparation of previous editions were all of the following reviewers and colleagues: David Bradford, James Cashman, Tom Chase, James D. Conant, Curtis Cook, Elizabeth M. Coote, Larry Cummings, Neville Duarte, Jann Freed (Central College), Terry Gaston, Gerald A. Gluck, Dorothy Hai, Elliot Kushell, Erik Larson, Donald Malm, Mary Jane Maxwell, Gregg Northcraft, Steve Obert, Joseph O. Pecenka, Sam Robinowitz, Lynne Rosansky, Rich Sebastian, Rodney Sherman, Dayle Smith, Patricia Trow, Bobby C. Vaught, Fran Waller, Kirby Warren, and Rita Weathersby.

Among those who helped us develop the first edition, seven of our colleagues, most of them former students in earlier versions of the course for which the book was written, tested rough drafts in the classroom and gave us valuable feedback. For this help we thank Pat Canavan, Cotton Cleveland, Harry Noel, Richard Pastor, Mary Anne Sharer, Randy Webb, and Mike Williams. Tom Law, Tom Maran, Stephanie E. New, and Paul Samuels were helpful research assistants, courtesy of the Whittemore School.

Numerous deans have been unstinting in their support for our efforts over the years, and we are grateful for their willingness to further the educational process: Carol Aldrich, Jan Clee, Mel Copen, Lyndon Goodridge, Dwight Ladd, Michael Merenda, Gordon Pritchett, Ken Rothwell, and Charles Warden.

Perhaps more important than the deans and colleagues was the patient crew of secretaries who coped with our impossible handwriting and minuscule marginal notes before we mastered our own word processors: Linda Bloom, Marylou Chag, Pamela Dyson, Beri Ellis, Linda Fitzgerald, Susan Gilman, Marjorie Kurtzman, Jennifer McKinnon, Madeline Piper, Mildred Prussing, Lee Rudenauer, and Darlene Thorn. We also thank Rich Sebastian and Anne Cunliffe for their fine exam questions, and Marlene Gorelow for her assistance preparing the Instructor's Manual manuscript.

Finally, we want to mention our wives and children. They are a living part of this book, and their contributions to it and us could never be fully catalogued. In each of these small organizations, countless observations, propositions, complexities, and analyses unfold and develop. For letting us be ourselves even when that entailed long absences for writing and meetings, our thanks and love.

We have continued to learn from the devoted O.B. teachers who attend the O.B. Teaching Conferences and write for *The Journal of Management Education* (formerly *Exchange*). We are proud to be in an academic field that still manages to value teaching and hope that our efforts in this book contribute to the tradition.

A. R. C.
S. L. F.

Brief Contents

Contents

Chapter 8

Chapter 9

Chapter 10

Chapter 14
Initiating Change   347

Cases

Introduction

MANAGERIAL BULLETIN

To Win the Loyalty of Your Employees, Try a Softer Touch

With turnover near 20-year highs, companies are pouring millions of dollars into efforts to increase employee loyalty. The payoff is clear: Replacing an employee costs roughly 1.5 times a year's pay. Also, companies with highly committed employees tend to post sharply higher shareholder returns, says a Watson Wyatt Worldwide study.

Hewitt Associates, Lincolnshire, Illinois, cites trusting, respectful on-the-job relationships as a factor. Watson Wyatt Worldwide says trust in leaders is one of the two most powerful drivers of employee commitment. But many employers have a hard time believing these soft issues really matter to workers, and they're stumbling on this front.

SOURCE: Sue Shellenbarger, "To Win the Loyalty of Your Employees, Try a Softer Touch," *The Wall Street Journal*, January 26, 2000, p. B1. (Copyright © 2000, Dow Jones & Company, Inc.)

"This book is about the human drama in organizations: the sweat-it-out, keep 'em engaged, what does it take to create productive, satisfied, and, above all, growing employees?"

An Introductory Essay

Once upon a time, students had to be convinced that organizational behavior, the people side of business, was a worthy subject, not just soft-headed and touchy-feely, but as worthy as finance and marketing. They saw this important area as just common sense and hoped to get by if they could reel off a few buzzwords, survive a group project, and, at least for a few hours a week, act friendly. But that was in another millennium—ancient history (some three or four years ago)—when companies moved at glacial speed, when getting ahead was possible by keeping one's nose clean (and waiting), and when a college degree was the passport to a better and more comfortable life. A few political maneuvers here, a few breaks there, and you could work your way up the corporate ladder so that you could enjoy life in your suburban home—when you finally got the time to be with your family.

Now, less than one Internet generation later, work life is at once more exciting and more dangerous. You can advance rapidly, maybe even strike it rich working for (or helping to start) a new dot.com company, but you can just as quickly end up without a job, without valuable stock options, and without the network of colleagues who can help you move on.[1] And what if you decide that you do not want life in the fast lane, that you would rather go back to a slow-moving organization with only modest expectations? It's just possible that while you are deciding to join, that company will disappear, swallowed by a competitor that has figured out how to shorten supply lines, eliminate middlemen and other superfluous layers of cost, utilize technology to eliminate warehousing and storage, and automatically bill the customers so that the accounts receivable department is 5 instead of 500 people. The work world is changing, and you will need to be ready for it.

As a result, the study of behavior in organizations is more exciting than ever. Old models of leadership are crumbling, and it is no longer news that people can get more done if they can work well with others who have differing views, expertise, and backgrounds. No one is surprised to hear about the potentials of teamwork nor shocked to discover that in many organizations, people feel "meeting'ed" to death because getting together is so important but so difficult to do well. *Empowerment* has come—and just about gone—from the daily vocabulary of managers because there are so many educated and specialized employees that only a fool (or someone in a rare old-fashioned, uncompetitive, and unchanging business) would argue that the best employees are those with strong backs and silent tongues. Not many bosses still claim that they have all the right answers, although many are uncomfortable with their dependence on others and long for the chance to know it all and be the unquestioned authority.

This all makes the material in this book and course stimulating and challenging. It is about the human drama in organizations: the sweat-it-out, keep 'em engaged, what does it take to create productive, satisfied, and, above all, growing employees? How can you learn to be more effective and more able to use your talent and tap that of those around you? What kind of behavior can actually make a difference, get people to pull together, gain acceptance for your best ideas, and keep you open to learning?

And what about learning these days? There's a nasty little secret in this brave new world: No matter how much you learn in this course, and in your academic career, you will only be acquiring a license to continue learning on the job. There is no one point in time when you will finally know all you need to; graduating is truly only the beginning. So if you keep hoping that with a few more requirements you will finally be there and can start coasting, get a new fantasy. You are just warming up.

"May you live in exciting times!" In China, this statement is hurled as a curse; centuries of upheaval, revolutions, and counterrevolutions have created a longing for stability and predictability in daily life. Whether excitement is a curse or

Off the Ladder: Want to Be a Manager? Many People Say No, Calling Job Miserable

They Cite Stress of Handling Bosses and Subordinates, Ending Up in the Middle

The Dilbert Factor at Work

Listen to these recurring reasons:

"I hated all the meetings. And I found the more you did for people who worked for you, the more they expected. I felt like I was coming in every day and people were expecting me to meet their needs. I was a counselor, motivator, financial adviser, psychologist."

"You're a backstop, caught in the middle between upper management and the work force. I was told 50 hours a week was not enough and that I had to work my people harder. Major philosophical disagreement! I am not renting strong backs; I need people to think and to want to participate. The few dollars more were not worth the pain."

But in today's global, more competitive arena, a manager sits on an insecure perch. Restructurings have eliminated layer after layer of management as companies come to view their organizations as collections of competencies rather than hierarchies. The result: far fewer rungs on the corporate ladder for managers to climb. In addition, managerial jobs demand more hours and headaches than ever before but offer slim, if any, financial paybacks and perks. For many managers, salary increases have been smaller than those going to senior executives and to their own subordinates. And while many companies have eliminated executive perks such as country-club memberships, they increasingly award stock options and bonuses even to hourly workers.

Furthermore, managers now must supervise many people who are spread over different locations, even over different continents. They must manage across functions with, say, design, finance, marketing, and technical people reporting to them. If their employers set up workplace teams, managers must play an even murkier leadership role. And they must be agents of change, champions of the latest reengineering or reorganization, even if they have had nothing to do with creation of the plan or disagree with it.

SOURCE: Timothy D. Schellhardt, " Off the Ladder: Want to Be a Manager?" *The Wall Street Journal,* April 4, 1997, p. A1. (Copyright © 1997, Dow Jones & Company, Inc.)

---

a stimulant, you are studying management in exciting times. Dramatic changes in global competition, government regulations, workforce composition, and employee expectations have led to an explosion of experimentation with leadership and organizational methods. Some of the forces altering traditional assumptions include the following:

- Tough competition from Japanese and European companies, some of which are successfully operating plants in the United States, and increasing competition from companies in South Korea, Taiwan, and Singapore with even lower wage rates. Global markets are expanding rapidly.
- Crumbling boundaries between industries as new technologies, loosening government regulations, unprecedented mergers, acquisitions, and spin-offs create opportunities. For example, banks and insurance companies are increasingly in competition to provide financial services, while Sears and others have entered the credit card business.
- More competition, based on the speed of bringing products or services to market, with organizations searching for ways of utilizing new technologies before they become obsolete.
- Women entering the workforce in increasing numbers, occupying (or deserving) jobs that formerly were held only by men. More than half of all married women

MANAGERIAL BULLETIN

Up with People

"BMW's workplace will be operated by intelligent, well-trained individuals, not by nonthinking, noncaring robots. We must have intellectually flexible associates empowered to contribute to the process."

SOURCE: Dr. Helmut Panke, "Reinventing America," *Business Week*, 1993.

with children now work full time, and increasing numbers of women have aspirations to rise in management, rather than just provide supplementary income. The trade-offs between work and family are a source of tension.[2]

- A renewed entrepreneurial spirit, leading to greater numbers of startups, new sources of competition, and rapid shifts in which companies are dominant.
- Members of minority groups, some of whom do not speak English, making important contributions to the workforce and becoming increasingly ambitious. They bring their various subcultures' attitudes and behavior to their organizations—or are assumed to, by unknowledgeable or biased whites.
- Employees becoming more educated, bringing with them expectations that their jobs should be challenging and meaningful. A sense of entitlement to important, fulfilling work and to a voice in decision making is a frequent by-product of higher education. From blue-collar workers to specialized-knowledge workers, these beliefs are now widespread, and unresponsive organizations can no longer count on automatic company loyalty to hold employees who are frustrated at blocked opportunities to contribute.[3]
- Increasing consumer demands for the highest levels of quality in goods and services for lowest prices—easily checked by using web sites—and for reliable, convenient delivery.
- Many winner-take-all sectors of the economy, where the winners gain dominant market share and high valuations from the stock market, enabling easier acquisitions, while the losers get left out or are overlooked.

As a result of these forces, the work world is changing rapidly. For one thing, everything moves more quickly. Decisions are made faster, without being able to wait for all the data; careers shoot up or flame out, hours are extended, and everyone's contributions are needed. Companies gain or lose market share, rapidly expanding staff or contracting ("downsizing") in sudden spasms. There are far fewer places to hide and just go through the motions.[4]

For many, this has meant the end of automatic loyalty. Seeing how quickly companies can get rid of people—and for several years benefiting from a very strong economy (currently, the longest peacetime expansion ever)—people are quicker to change jobs, leaving for better pay, for a greater chance to strike it rich through stock options or bonuses, for a preferred location, for new challenges, or for glitzier products. In a recent survey, barely more than half of employees reported feeling committed to their companies, despite evidence that companies with more committed employees perform better.[5] In turn, the growing companies are working much harder to attract and keep the people with the necessary skills, setting off what the consulting company McKinsey calls "The War for Talent."[6] The need to keep the right people has pushed many companies to do a lot more to satisfy employees, adding services such as dry cleaning pickup, subsidized day care, and stock options at lower levels.[7]

Gray Expectations: A Middle Manager, 54 and Insecure, Struggles to Adapt to the Times

Young Colleagues Make Fun of His Computer Skills; No One Else Wears a Tie

"I've Peaked in My Career"

Middle-age managers are still plateauing, but there is no resting. They must keep changing–reinventing themselves, learning new skills, mastering new technologies–even as nothing much changes for them.

To stay afloat, Chris Joal, a 54-year-old software company manager, has reinvented himself again and again. Once specializing in managing production, he learned marketing, then purchasing, then finance. He gets up at 5 every morning and doesn't get home until

8 P.M. Yet he still does essentially the same job he did 10 years ago: overseeing a small staff, making revenue projections and supervising expenses in the sales division and resolving disputes over salary compensation. Only this year did he get back to earning the salary he made in 1989.

"I just can't keep up," says Peter Bent, 50, a salesman of medical equipment for Nikon Corp. "The products keep changing. The pressure to produce is relentless. To sell this last product, I had to learn more in a few weeks than I ever learned in college biology class."

SOURCE: Jonathan Kaufman, "Gray Expectations," *The Wall Street Journal,* May 5, 1997, p. A1. (Copyright ©1997, Dow Jones & Company, Inc.)

For a growing number of people, these changes have encouraged a willingness to think of themselves as almost temporary freelance professionals, creating their own personal "brand" and selling their services to the latest and highest bidder.[8] This makes managing more of a challenge; it is seldom enough to give clear, detailed instructions, monitor closely, and be confident that what is needed will be done. Gaining commitment to the organization's goals, showing the benefits from contributing, finding ways to support learning, and so on, become much more important than it used to be. The dilemma most companies face, therefore, is how to generate and maintain employee commitment in times when downsizing is a part of doing business.

For the best and most skilled professionals, jobs are judged largely by how much they create an opportunity to learn, to build one's personal resume so that the next job or project can be even more learningful. Those who are uncomfortable with this kind of continuous stretching are quickly relegated to the dull work, if any remains. There is a great premium on being comfortable with change, ambiguity, and uncertainty; with changing direction on a dime; and with being able to quickly grasp opportunities and take initiative. Organizations are straining to create a more inviting atmosphere for entrepreneurial initiative and seeking those who have it. This puts a premium not only on those who can generate ideas, but who are skilled at influencing others to get things done.

The old rigidly bounded organizations, the "silos" or "stovepipes," are being broken down and flattened so that people who can figure out how to get things done, link across organizational lines, and find supporters for new initiatives are the new most valuable players. The move toward designing organizations by key processes rather than by old departments makes the important action more horizontal (across many units) rather than vertical, with the emphasis on pleasing one's boss. In this new, more fluid world, steely determination to accomplish difficult projects, coupled with great flexibility, is the winning combination.

Because work has become so complex, there is an ever-greater number of teams, task forces, tiger teams, hot groups, and the like,[9] some of which are comprised of people not physically in the same country, let alone the same building. Imagine the challenge of trying to learn to collaborate with people who are in another time zone, have very different specialties, and may not even speak the same first language.

Even high-level executives are discovering the benefits of teamwork, driven by the speed and complexity of current conditions:

> Richard Vancil, a professor at Harvard Business School, noted the increasing popularity of the "office of the chief executive officer." By 1984, he found, 25 percent of American companies used this arrangement, which melds three to six top officers into a team led by the chairman; that's up from only 8 percent in the 1960s.
>
> Others predict that the trend will continue. "It's getting tougher to run a big organization," says Delta Consulting Group's David Nadler. . . . "There are fewer places where one brilliant or two brilliant people will have all the answers."[10]

Top managers must learn new styles of managing, better suited to the increased challenges. Not all of the changes are comfortable for managers. Middle-management jobs are not only being eliminated, but top managers are finding that increased use of information technology lets lower-level workers make decisions, because they have access to information—and the managers are having to learn to share control.[11]

In this more fluid, talent-short world, it is not surprising that some of the old barriers to women and minorities are coming down. It is increasingly important to be able to get along with, include, and learn from those who are apparently different in various ways. Old prejudices and hurdles have a way of hanging around long after they are completely outmoded, so new skills are required both from the majority and the many minorities at work.

All of these trends have generated a far more demanding work life for many, so it is not surprising that there is now far more attention being paid to work and life balance and to spirituality at work. The people who are busiest are often on the edge and want to find ways to enjoy the challenging work but not have it drive personal life or personal meaning out of their waking hours.[12] In turn, this places even more pressure on organizations and managers to balance their demands and to take the whole person into account.

All of this activity and experimentation can be highly unsettling, knocking cherished assumptions and beliefs askew, but it can also provide a tremendously stimulating challenge. Although this book (indeed, any book) cannot provide you with all the answers to the behavior dilemmas facing managers today, it will provide you with a way to understand and address the issues and to practice some of the key skills needed. We urge you to plunge into this course. More than ever before, your career success will depend upon your being able to effectively manage the behavior of others—and yourself.

What Does a Manager Do?

We have been looking at the way in which this book tries to reflect some of the complexities inherent in the manager's job. But just what do managers do? How do they spend their time? What makes the job so difficult?[13]

Interpersonal Functions (Building Relationships)

Although some students think of managing as primarily involved with financial calculations, the thing to note is that managers interact with a great number of people. Because they have been assigned a managerial position, they automatically are expected to form relationships in many directions: with those who work directly for them (subordinates), with their boss or bosses (superiors), with others in comparable positions in the organization (peers), and with a variety of outsiders such as customers, board members, and attendees at industry or professional meetings. Every

Why I Am Not a Manager

Here's What You Get: Pressure from Above and Resentment from Below; Who Needs It?

In 1997, reports the Labor Department, there were 18 million executives, managers, and administrators in the United States. I am not one of them. I have never "managed" anyone or anything. No one works for me or is supervised by me. . . . At various employers, no one has ever hinted that I deserved greater power and responsibility. Perish the thought.

All this may explain why I have a certain grudging respect for managers. I am obviously unfit to do whatever it is they do. They seem to relish responsibility, while I dread it. They have, or feign, confidence . . . What also baffles me is why people want to be managers. Granted, some rewards are tempting: power, money, status and (possibly) the respect of co-workers. But the drawbacks seem as plain: resentment from below; pressure from above; loud criticism of failures; silence over successes. No thanks. . . .

Perhaps managers could once succeed—or at least survive—on status and technical competence. There was a chain of command. Authority was respected or feared. Machines regulated production jobs. This era has ended. The almost-universal task of managers today, in our culture, is to serve twin masters, each of whom has grown more demanding. There's the Organization with its imperatives; and there's the Individual—each with "needs." This is a tough job, and somebody's got to do it. But not me.

SOURCE: Robert J. Samuelson, "Why I Am Not a Manager," *Newsweek,* March 22, 1999, p. 47

manager is in a boundary position between the unit he or she supervises and other parts of the organization or the organization's environment. In that position the manager is a symbol of the unit as well as the one ultimately responsible for inspiring or leading the unit's members to high performance. Thus, managers are forced into relationships with many people whose goodwill they need in order to be successful.

> Outplacement counselors claim most of their assignments involve competent executives who lost their jobs because of personal incompatibility, political in-fighting, or corporate reorganizations. Of all the major reasons for terminating a competent manager, problems resulting from interpersonal relationships is by far number one on the list
>
> Carl W. Menk, President
> Boyden Associates, Inc.

Informational Functions (Giving and Receiving Information)

Relationships with others are needed for the manager to acquire information for sensible action. The manager must know what is going on inside and outside the organization—who is performing well, who is having troubles, what competitors are doing, what projects are proceeding well, what opportunities are available, and the like. While some of this information may be available from written material or reports, most managers find that the best sources of current, useful information are through face-to-face or phone conversations. This kind of information requires careful interpretation, since others may be reluctant (or unable) to say exactly what they mean. Thus, the relationships which managers automatically form as a result of their position need to be open and mutually satisfying for acquiring timely information and for passing that information on to others who need it.

MANAGERIAL TOOLS

New Roles for Managers in Today's Learning Organizations

Successful organizations will need to be "learning organizations" (i.e., systems that exist in a never-ending cycle of adaptation and creative change in meeting environmental demands). The learning organization requires new kinds of leadership roles. First, leaders and/or managers will have to be *designers* of the future, with an ability to articulate a vision and core values that set the direction for others. Second, they will need to be *teachers* in the sense of providing guidance and

inspiration to the learning of organizational members, thereby empowering them to grow and achieve at their highest levels. And third, they will have to be *stewards* (i.e., willing and able to serve the organization and its members in ways that extend well beyond their own self-interest).

SOURCE: Peter Senge, "New Roles for Managers in Today's Learning Organizations," *Sloan Management Review,* vol. 32, no. 1 (Fall 1990). Also see *The Fifth Discipline,* New York: Doubleday, 1990.

Decisional Functions (Making Decisions)

The information is needed, in turn, for the manager to make appropriate decisions. Managers have to decide how available resources—money, people, materials, and time—will be distributed throughout the unit being managed. Even more important, the manager must be a source of, and support to, new ideas, projects, methods, and opportunities. The effective manager cannot wait for innovation but must take the lead in ensuring it.

Another important set of decision-making activities arises from problems that others in the organization can't solve. Whether the problem is deciding what to do about a large canceled order or settling a dispute between two other managers who disagree about the potential for producing a new product, managers are frequently called on to handle disturbances or deviations from the usual routine.

Finally, managers must often serve as negotiators on behalf of their organization. If they are managers of a unit, they must try to persuade higher management to approve their budget request so they may acquire what they believe to be sufficient resources. They may have to negotiate salaries or working conditions with individuals or groups of employees, contracts with important customers, priorities with other units, and the like.

The activities of the manager can be summarized in the Managerial Tools box on the next page, "Mintzberg's Categories of Managerial Functions."[14]

As you can see, managerial work is demanding. The manager must be good at building relationships, gathering information, and making decisions—all of which affect future relationships, access to information, and future decisions! As noted earlier, the manager acts on but is also a part of the organization, and people in organizations have feelings that affect how they respond. They are more likely to provide accurate information or carry out organizational tasks well when they trust their manager.

Needed Managerial Skills

We can identify crucial managerial skills by looking at the activities described above and spelling out what it would take to do the manager's job well.

Think about the kinds of skills necessary to do these activities. In order to carry out the interpersonal activities, for example, a manager would need public speaking skills, a sense of how to dress appropriately relative to the expectations of others, the

MANAGERIAL BULLETIN

*Tricks of the E*Trade*

In his drive to create a Net Powerhouse, Christos Cotsakos is building a culture that's edgy, a bit bizarre—and often brilliant.

It's a weird way to say "welcome," even by Silicon Valley standards. Soon after Arthur Havers joined on-line brokerage E*Trade Group Inc. as vice president for international business development, Chief Executive Officer Christos M. Cotsakos subjected him—as he does every new hire—to the company's initiation rites. At one of Havers' first staff meetings, Cotsakos asked him to stand on a chair and reveal something about himself to more than 40 people who were watching. For a moment, Havers, who described himself as a "proper" Englishman who shuns the spotlight, felt his mind go blank. But then he did something completely out of character: He pulled out a penknife and sliced off the expensive Hermes tie that he was wearing. Cotsakos' game had awakened his wild side.

Think of it as being put in the E*Trade hot seat—one of many far-out tactics used by Cotsakos in his quest to build a powerhouse for the Internet era. Like other Web chieftains trying to make it big, Cotsakos pours his energy into technology, brand-building, and distinctive offerings for the online masses. But, like entrepreneurs of yore—Hewlett-Packard Co.'s Bill Hewlett and David Packard in the 1940s and Apple Computer Inc.'s Steve Jobs in the 1970s—Cotsakos believes that a remarkable corporate culture is just as crucial for catapulting a company to success.

That's why he's spending gobs of time crafting a culture for the Internet Age that at times seems downright bizarre, and at other times brilliant. But it's always pure Cotsakos: edgy, out there, theatrical, and bursting . . . with enthusiasm . . . To create a loose atmosphere, he has employees carry around rubber chickens or wear propellor beanies. And to bond his team, he had his managers attend cooking school . . .Such antics link employees together emotionally and foster an air of openness, says Stanford professor Charles A. O'Reilly III. "If you're open and honest with each other, you're more willing to propose things that are out of the box," he says. Company rituals also help employees grasp strategic objectives so that they take their own initiative and make decisions quickly—a must for any Web company.

SOURCE: Louise Lee, " Tricks of the E*Trade," *Business Week*, February 7, 2000, p. EB18.

MANAGERIAL TOOLS

Mintzberg's Categories of Managerial Functions

Interpersonal (Relationship) Functions

Symbolic figurehead (represents organization to the world).

Liaison (contacts with others outside the unit).

Supervisor (hiring, training, motivating subordinates).

Informational Functions

Monitor (collecting data within and outside the unit).

Disseminator (circulating information to unit employees).

Spokesman (circulating information outside the unit).

Decision Functions

Innovator (initiating and designing changes).

Disturbance handler (dealing with nonroutine problems).

Resource allocator (parceling out time, money, materials).

Negotiator (seeking favorable conditions from others).

ability to talk easily with others and to build trusting relationships so that many people will be open with him or her, the willingness to exert power when cooperation is lacking, a sincere interest in others and in listening to them, the ability to inspire others to work for organizational goals, good judgment of others' personalities and capacities, a knack for sizing up new situations, and so on.

To perform the informational functions well, the manager needs to be able to extract information from conversation, observations, and reading; must be able to judge who has the needed information and to whom it should be circulated; and again, be articulate about organizational goals. These, in turn, require that the manager be able to ask good questions, be observant and attentive to what is happening around him or her, and be skillful at reading between the lines, as well as realizing what is not being said or discussed.

The decisional roles call for imagination, openness to ideas, willingness to take risks, courage under fire, analytical ability, logic, intuition, bargaining skills (including the ability to bluff, sense others' positions and boundaries), and a sense of timing.

The list of required skills can be easily expanded; it is undoubtedly easier to name needed skills than acquire them! Yet at the heart of these skills are very human qualities that involve making relationships with many different people. Without good relationships the manager cannot carry out many of the other functions that constitute managerial work.

At this point it might be useful for you to assess some of your own managerial skills, using the various abilities noted above as the criteria. You could take each item (e.g., public speaking, knack for sizing up new situations) and rate yourself in terms of both ability and confidence (or comfort) in that skill. You might even repeat the process from time to time to measure your development in those skills relevant to this course. Finally, you could check out your own observations with those of others to provide more objectivity.

Managing Time: A Key Skill

Forming friendships is not enough, just as merely being technically competent is not enough. The person who wishes to advance in an organization needs to be aware of the implications for action inherent in the job of the manager.

For example, one of the fundamental issues for managers is where to spend their time. There is almost always an abundance of work, especially since so much time must be spent interacting with others. The manager has to decide with whom to talk,

Managing Your Career: Learning to Manage in a Global Workpladce (You're on Your Own)

As researchers ponder the qualities needed in effective global leaders, a profile is emerging. It is someone who can handle more complexity and uncertainty than domestic managers are typically accustomed to, who relates well with diverse groups of people, who listens more than talks, who craves adventure over the status quo, and who accepts that there is more than one way to skin a business problem.

As one executive put it, good global leaders like getting up in the morning and saying, "I have no idea what's going to happen today."

SOURCE: Hal Lancaster, " Managing Your Career: Learning to Manage in a Global Workplace (You're on Your Own)," *The Wall Street Journal,* June 2, 1998, p. B1. (Copyright © 1998, Dow Jones & Company, Inc.)

MANAGERIAL TOOLS

15 Time-Saving Managerial Practices (Can You Apply These to Student Life?)

Clarify Goals

1. Develop and use clear, long-range goals.
2. Clearly establish what to accomplish each month, week, day, and by each task.

Plan Ahead

3. Use a Daily "To-Do" List to plan and prioritize each day's activities.
4. Before meetings, review agenda, clarify your objectives, get information, anticipate events, and plan actions.
5. Set deadlines for major tasks.

Manage Daily Activities

6. Do important tasks first. Avoid trap of "getting small items out of way." Do tough jobs at your best times.
7. For big projects, divide task into manageable parts and sequence.
8. Handle each piece of paper only once, or note next step.

9. Stick to your agenda. Include restricted moments of relaxation and socializing.
10. Bring work to use during unavoidable idle time while waiting or traveling.
11. Limit interruptions. Close office door, reschedule drop-in visitors, ask secretary to hold phone calls, schedule "thinking time," and honor it.

Organize Your Workplace

12. Clear desk of clutter and other distractions.
13. Develop usable filing system and tickler file.

Spend Time Efficiently

14. Use 80/20 rule: 80 percent of the results are determined by 20 percent of the decisions. Concentrate on those.
15. Review actions to learn from past mistakes, but don't pick at imperfections and waste time on regrets.

SOURCES: Alan Lakein, *How to Get Control of Your Time and Your Life* (New York: David McKay, 1973); and R. Alec MacKenzie, *The Time Trap* (New York: McGraw-Hill, 1975).

for how long, whether to pursue particular individuals or wait for interactions to happen, and so on. Managerial work is fragmented and variable, with many interruptions. The phone rings, subordinates want answers, attention, and approval; the boss wants the same; colleagues need help. Research on managerial work shows that managers average less than nine minutes on half of all the things they do in a day.

Should the pressing deskwork be completed, or would a walk through the plant reveal something important about operations? Or perhaps a meeting with a friend who works at a bank would uncover some useful information about future interest rates. Or a chat with an unhappy employee might save a valuable person who will be difficult to replace. And the phone keeps ringing with "urgent" calls.

Somehow the effective manager has to learn to manage time, rather than be managed by it. Self-discipline and conscious attention are necessary, as is a definition of "work" that includes a lot of relationship building with a variety of people.

Many managers, especially new ones, think of their work as only the technical decision-making part of the day. They see all the people contacts as intrusions getting in the way of real work. But as we have tried to show by carefully examining what managers do, connecting with other people is an essential part of the job, and not necessarily the first thing to eliminate in order to "save time."

Therefore, effective managers learn how to make activities fold in on one another and serve double purposes. For example they use lunch time and short coffee breaks to chat informally with people they might not otherwise easily see, yet who have useful tidbits about the company, the market, projects, and the like.

That Team Spirit Can Lead Your Career to New Victories

Teams, teams, teams. Whether you love 'em or loathe 'em, they're all the rage these days, so learn to live with them. Your career may depend on it.

Teams come in many flavors, but let's concentrate on the most common one: temporary units, usually with members from different departments and job levels, formed to make policy, reengineer operations, or design products, among other tasks. Team members may or may not leave their old jobs.

Working in a team environment can be tricky. On the one hand, you get to showcase your skills to team members from all corners of the company, often including influential senior executives. And team assignments tend to be critical and closely watched.

But that also means that if the team flops, you flop, whatever the reason. Meanwhile, while you're focusing on your new team duties, some young gun in your department is showing how easily you can be replaced. And because teams often challenge traditional departmental roles, the potential for a political tug-of-war is high.

Shaunna Sowell's team experiences at Texas Instruments led to promotions and a better career path than she ever envisioned. But she also burned some bridges with a boss. Mary Kinnear feared she risked her career at Boston Gas by joining a reengineering team. The gamble paid off, but not without some uncomfortable moments. Their stories demonstrate the power—and peril—of teams.

Ms. Sowell was leading a plant design team in 1988 when she was tapped for a product-quality steering committee that was loaded with bosses. She was intimidated at first but her confidence grew with her experience.

"I left one meeting thinking, my God, I've ruined my career," she recalls. "I'd just told a guy four levels above me he was wrong."

Actually, she impressed an executive on the team who was casting about for a vice president of corporate environmental safety. "You have to be a great individual contributor," she says, "that's how you get picked for the next team."

Her team involvement, she says, earned her recognition, jobs, and mentoring from senior executives she never would have gotten in the days before teams.

But the experience also created friction. "My visibility was getting wider than my boss's," she says. "It was pretty uncomfortable." The relationship cooled and eventually, she moved to another position, while still working on teams.

In leading a team charged with redesigning Boston Gas's distribution operation, Ms. Kinnear, a human-resources specialist, also knew she risked offending some influential executives whose turf was being threatened. Some already voiced skepticism about her abilities to do effective work on the team, she said.

Continued

Organizational Politics and Getting Ahead

Similarly, when asked to serve on committees or task forces, alert managers look at the assignment as an opportunity, rather than as a burden. Serving on a committee brings them into contact with people from other parts of the organization, and they use the contact to establish relationships and gather data (often during the "holes" in a meeting—when people are just arriving or leaving, or when a few go to the bathroom during a break, and so on).

Furthermore, managers who want to get ahead realize that committee work allows them the opportunity to "show their stuff," to demonstrate to people who might be their direct boss or subordinate in the future that they are competent, reliable, hardworking, and easy to work with.

Thus, as simple an activity as going prepared to a committee meeting serves several purposes—relationship building, data collection, visibility, creation, and the formation of a good reputation, which might lead to future promotions.[15]

Another way in which managers, especially those new to a particular organization, can create alliances is by observing what social activities, interests, style of dress, and the like are valued by high-level managers in the organization. They can then adapt to those things that do not violate their sense of themselves. Those who

"We were all assured there would be some kind of amnesty for team members," she says. "But there were no guarantees."

When the project ended, however, she was eventually named general manager of one of the eight regional operating divisions created by the project team. Absent the project team, she says, she wouldn't have had the experience or the exposure to land her current job.

Sometimes the fears are real. Deloitte & Touche consultant Boris Lukan was part of a joint reengineering team working with a client, when animosity over cutbacks proposed by the project team forced one team member from the client company to leave. "For people who want to be recognized, projects that drive change are great places to be," he says, "but you've got to be ready for the potential impacts that could come out of upsetting how other people do work."

Still, such influence became so seductive to Margaret Colquhoun, who was on a team reshaping the work processes at her hospital, that she found it difficult to go back to the humdrum routine of her manager's job—even after a promotion. She left to join a consulting firm that specializes in team development.

Ponder these additional points.

Be an expert, not an advocate.

The team needs your specialized knowledge, but doesn't want an obstructionist who continually says, "You just don't understand how we do things in finance."

Research the team as you would any job opportunity.

Are there cliques? Is there one person who dominates? What happens to team members after they leave the team? How strong is management support?

Make sure you keep up your performance in your department.

"You cannot fail at your core hierarchical work, succeed at your team work and be successful overall," Ms. Sowell says. Also, she urges, keep your department boss informed of your team activities. In most companies, that person still has the most influence on your career.

Stay balanced.

"Overload and burnout are more of a problem in teams," Ms. Sowell says. Being sought after for influential teams is flattering, but you must be careful about overcommitting. Each year, Ms. Sowell drafts a contract detailing what she's committing to do that year and shares it with her staff.

See yourself as an equal.

Be diplomatic, but don't hold back your opinions. This is your stage, with an audience that often includes some of the company's most influential people. Don't waste it.

SOURCE: Hal Lancaster, "Managing Your Career; That Team Spirit Can Lead Your Career to New Victories," *The Wall Street Journal,* January 14, 1997, p. B1. (Copyright ©1997, Dow Jones & Company, Inc.)

MANAGERIAL BULLETIN

Inside P&G, a Pitch to Keep Women Employees

The company that pioneered selling products like Tide and Pampers to women reached into the same bag of tricks to sell them on a career at P&G. Starting in 1993, a task force of seasoned brand managers attacked the problem just as they would rescue a troubled detergent or toilet paper: They conducted "customer" surveys among current and former female employees. They set "market share" goals for women in management. They created new workplace "products" and "repackaged" others—such as female-friendly benefits. And they launched internal "advertising" campaigns to help sell women on working at P&G.

After five years, the effort has shown surprising results: Women now account for nearly a third of the vice presidents and general managers in the company's advertising and brand management ranks, up from just 5 percent in 1992. And today some of the company's most important businesses are run by female vice presidents and general managers.

SOURCE: Tara Parker-Pope, "Inside P&G, a Pitch to Keep Women Employees," *The Wall Street Journal,* September 9, 1998, p. B1. (Copyright ©1998, Dow Jones & Company, Inc.)

Look Who's No Longer Missing the Links

Trends: Through a Glass Ceiling with a Golf Club

For women, golf's dividends are burgeoning . . . they get out on the lesson tee and find out they're standing next to a VP of marketing who could be a very attractive client . . .

   The faster women find their golf legs, the better. In a time when one of eight execs who play says the sport is more important than sex, employees who golf are in demand . . . For years, women have gotten ahead in a male-dominated corporate world by working hard at the office. Now, many are realizing, they must also play hard away from it—preferably on a golf course.

SOURCE: Paul O'Donnell, "Look Who's No Longer Missing the Links," *Newsweek*, March 14, 1994.

do what others in the organization value are likely to more easily form relationships around shared interests and to seem more trustworthy.

The true test of somebody who's really good at power is that nothing interests him or her more than other people's problems, because it's an opportunity to be decisive and to exert authority over another person.

Michael Korda

Of course, all of these things do not make up for lack of ability, but their absence can make those who have the power to help advance one's career uncomfortable. Furthermore, there is no law that demands that you try to get ahead. Many people, including some who study administration, do not place high value on career advancement. But should you want to get ahead, it helps to know how to do so intelligently.

Many organizations today encourage a mentoring process, in which a senior manager takes special responsibility for helping a junior person learn the ropes and more effectively move through (and up) the system. This is a special role for a manager and one that takes both interpersonal skill and commitment to the interests of the person being mentored. In the absence of such a relationship inside the company, some individuals turn to external advisors or coaches for help. Interestingly, in our highly technological world, we even find computerized mentors.

There are indications that the familiar career paths of yesterday may be disappearing as traditional hierarchical structures flatten and become more team centered. It may often be up to each individual to create his or her own path, based solely upon knowledge and value to the organization.[16]

Problems of Women and Minorities

Even in the new millennium, women or members of various minority groups are often at an automatic disadvantage in organizations traditionally run by white males, because their visible physical "difference" from the majority makes some majority members uncomfortable or less trusting.[17] The fewer the minority members in the organization at managerial levels, the greater the difficulty they are likely to have in being perceived as trustworthy—that is, as similar enough to be "one of us" where there are sensitive issues. As unfair as this is to those who are seen as "different" in

MANAGERIAL BULLETIN

How to Get Ahead as a Middle Manager by Being Ruthless

Executive Strategies Monthly Offers Tips, but Its Editor Truly Is a Kindhearted Soul

The essential message communicated by the 65-year-old Mr. Weyr (pronounced Wire): Be as ruthless as you must toward subordinates and rivals while toadying to the higher-ups.

How brutal do managers have to get? . . .

–August 1992: "Make a visitor stand in front of your desk . . . Lean back and look at him coldly through a frozen smile. The body language of contempt can cut your opponent like a razor."

–October 1992: "Tantrums should be sudden, scary, and seemingly irrational . . . Throwing a tantrum can be fun."

–January 1993: "Everybody cheats at one time or another in order to advance their careers . . . Dirty tricks are part of the game." . . .

"Everybody wants to get on the good side of the boss, but only the truly savvy know how to do it. One secret is to know when not to try."

SOURCE: Brent Bowers, "How to Get Ahead as a Middle Manager by Being Ruthless," *The Wall Street Journal,* March 23, 1993.

MANAGERIAL BULLETIN

The Crying Game

"[Men] expect you to cry, they want for you to cry, they even irritate you so you will cry—so don't cry," said Peggy Tishman, the philanthropist, from the audience at a workshop on leadership, after members of the panel disclosed that they had learned to save their tears for private offices, bathroom stalls, and other safe zones.

At lunch, Ms. Fairstein, chief of the sex-crimes prosecution unit of the Manhattan District Attorney's office,

said she broke down and cried at her desk 20 years ago as she faced the prospect of her first summation. Her boss found her and sputtered: "Stop crying. Go to the bathroom and throw up like a man."

That, she said, was the last time she cried publicly.

SOURCE: Barbara Presley Noble, "A Few Thousand Women Networking," *New York Times,* March 27, 1994. © 1994 by The New York Times Company. Reprinted by permission.

whatever way, it is useful to understand that in organizations social judgments of individuals are made as well as technical judgments, and these evaluations are often based on such things as dress, sex, color, "style," and the like. It is not accidental that, as more women decided to attempt to move upward in organizations, articles and books began to appear for them on such subjects as "How to Dress for Success," "Office Politics," and "How to Avoid Threatening Your Boss." Even if it is not true that only women who wear tailored blue suits can get ahead in business organizations (as one advisor claims), women, just like any others who choose to try to get ahead, need to be aware of what they can do to inspire comfort and confidence in them by the organization's decision makers. Trusting relationships are not a nicety of organizational life—they are fundamental to managerial work.

The Dangers of Gamesmanship

This can sound like having to "play politics" constantly or play a phony game. It certainly can, and sometimes does, become insincere and manipulative. But it also can be a matter of doing what will avoid surprises, reduce misunderstanding, increase trust, and encourage cooperation—that is, facilitating good decision making and making it easier for people to work together. The line between effectiveness and "gamesmanship" is vague, and every manager at times must make some concession to playing the game. You alone will need to decide where to draw the line, but we want to emphasize that it is not necessarily all phony and can be both functional and genuine. In fact, since most people can spot insincere and artificial behavior quite easily, getting ahead through relationships usually requires that you be genuinely interested in others. Otherwise, they will be cautious toward you, which is exactly the opposite of what is necessary. Furthermore, in a highly competitive organization, the so-called games can even be dangerous.

> We get rid of anyone who starts in with office politics, plotting, or backstabbing. If you have to keep looking over your shoulder, you can't play the game well!
>
> Senior Vice President,
> Fortune 500 Company

> The secret of life is sincerity and integrity. If you can fake that you've got it made.
>
> Groucho Marx

Nothing Is as Simple as It Seems

As should be clear by now, if you long for a job in which people never get in the way, all problems are easily defined with their causes clear and known, decisions are simple, future events are quite predictable, and you can almost immediately find out whether you made the correct decision, you probably ought to think again about a managerial career. Organizational life is much too complex for a handful of rules, theories, or slogans to be automatically applied to every problem. While the behavioral science theories and concepts in this book should be helpful to you in figuring out what is going on, or even in guiding an action, they are by no means sufficient for all problems you will encounter, nor easy to apply. They are more helpful than common sense alone, but they do not come with 10-year money-back guarantees.

> For every problem there is a solution which is simple, direct, and wrong.
>
> H. L. Mencken

Multiple Causality

For one thing, most behavior of any significance has multiple causes and multiple consequences. For example, how can you explain why extremely intelligent, caring managers at NASA decided to proceed with the *Challenger* shuttle launch on a cold January 28, 1986, when, as tragically proved true, the rubber rocket seals would not hold in temperatures below 50 degrees? Although it is an all-too-human trait to want to find a single villain—a simple cause that explains everything—a combination of many factors allowed NASA to send astronauts to their deaths while millions watched on TV.

Key NASA officials were warned the night before the launch by Morton Thiokol managers and engineers but discounted the data. They thought the evidence was not conclusive. The many delays in this and previous launches had created a sense of urgency about pushing ahead. National media had begun to belittle NASA delays. The string of successful missions may have engendered overconfidence that somehow things would work out as they always had; NASA culture reinforced managers for a "can do" attitude and for cool unflappability. As in other large organizations, mid-level personnel were used to withholding "bad news" from higher-ups, and communications often became distorted as they passed up and down the organization. Internal politics and rivalries probably helped shape what managers and engineers told one another.

At Thiokol, the contractor for the rocket boosters, similar pressures impacted key players. Furthermore, the company was competing vigorously with several other corporations to get future shuttle contracts. It is difficult to continue to say "no launch" to a customer who says, "I am appalled," as NASA official George Hardy did, or to another official, Lawrence Malloy, who reacted to Thiokol's reservations by saying, "My God, Thiokol, when do you want me to launch, next April?" Thiokol's engineers, who fought the decision but were overruled by their managers, backed off out of doubt about how certain they could be, natural fears of continuing to argue with their bosses, and even personal distaste for conflict.

Undoubtedly there are other reasons for the foolhardy decision; the ones listed are just some of those made public after the disaster. If you had been asked right after the explosion to "solve the problem once and for all," think about how easily you could have missed the complexities and focused on "firing the incompetent guy who said to launch" or "replacing the lousy contractor." Though either or both of those actions might ultimately be part of a solution, if that's all you did, the other complex forces would undoubtedly cause similar problems to occur in the future. *Oversimplifying your diagnosis of the cause(s) of problems almost always leads to incorrect or insufficient remedial action.* This kind of leap to hasty, oversimplified conclusions happens all the time in organizations; dramatic events like the *Challenger* explosion are just rare public glimpses of what happens when diagnosis misfires.

> Seek simplicity; then distrust it.
>
> Alfred North Whitehead

Here's another dramatic example: One of the world's largest consulting firms was approached by a manufacturer of tubing made from a rare metal. The manufacturer said that its problem was the *measurement of faulty tubing*; the tubing came out of the extruding machines so fast that, by the time they could examine it, too much product would be wasted if the diameter and tensile strength were off. Could a gauge be devised that would constantly monitor quality as the tubing was extruded? The consulting firm eagerly took on the project, since its quality control division could utilize very advanced technology to devise an entirely new kind of measuring gauge. One year and several hundred thousand dollars later, a new gauge was perfected, to everyone's delight. The new gauge was installed but, unfortunately, within another year the manufacturing company went broke, because such an extremely high proportion of the tubing produced had to be scrapped. Although with the new gauge they were immediately aware of quality problems, the *real* problem was that the extruding machines were inadequately designed. The scrap problem was not primarily one of measurement but one of *faulty production* in the first place due to poor equipment design! An improper problem definition led to an elegant but not very relevant decision.

As a manager you will have to learn to see many, often interconnected, causes for behavior. Let's say you encounter a work group that is not performing well. How will you decide ways to improve its performance? More important than the "perfect, latest, and greatest technique," which may not fit the particular problem, will be to trace backward from the problem to find its overlapping and reinforcing causes (see Figure 1–1). Behind any important problem is a tangled web of forces that together form a fabric of causes. In the case of the poorly performing work group, some of the causes might be a combination of (a) poor leadership, (b) inadequate training and knowledge, (c) a change in quality of materials, (d) improper procedures, (e) members who are bored by their work or overwhelmed by it, (f) pay that doesn't seem fair to members, or (g) lack of penalties for poor performance or lack of rewards for excellent performance, or both.

Although the problem may stand out clearly, its components will require careful analysis. If all the causes aren't identified, it will be easy to overfocus on one cause, make the same kind of mistake as the consulting firm, and "go down the tubes." *In analyzing cases in this course or in actual organizational problems, beware of the temptation to oversimplify your explanations.*

Uncertainty

Another problem facing managers is that they must make decisions under uncertain conditions, often before all the desired data are in. Quite often there is insufficient time for thorough study or the roots of the problem are not accessible to the person who must decide. For example, employees are often afraid to tell *any* boss all they know, especially if what they say might include criticism of the boss. And even if they were to be completely open, they might not fully know their own motivations or other necessary information. Finally, the conditions at the time of the decision can change by the time it is implemented, so that what looks sensible at one time may seem foolish later. Because it takes more than three years to design, build, and market a new car, for example, numerous automobile manufacturers have built gas-guzzlers when consumers had turned to mostly economy, or produced compact cars just as family-size was preferred.

Living with Consequences of Decisions

Managers must also live with the consequences of their decisions. They do not have the luxury of leisurely tinkering with something inside a sealed vacuum flask and being able to put aside the experiment when it is not going well. As suggested earlier, even deciding to do nothing is a decision that can affect a manager deeply, since that will not stop a chain of consequences from following, including changed perceptions of him or her by subordinates, colleagues, and boss.

FIGURE 1–1 *Many Possible Causes for Any Given Problem*

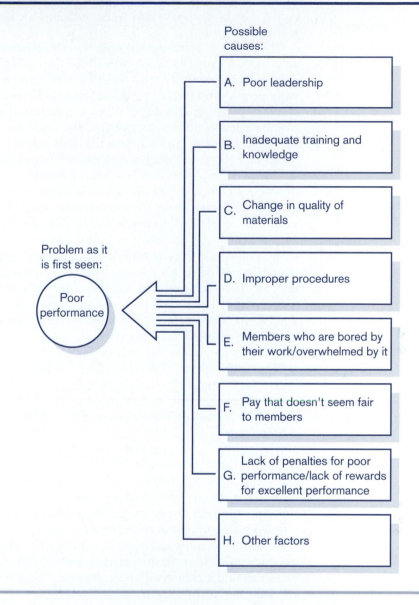

Possible causes:

A. Poor leadership

B. Inadequate training and knowledge

C. Change in quality of materials

Problem as it is first seen:

Poor performance

D. Improper procedures

E. Members who are bored by their work/overwhelmed by it

F. Pay that doesn't seem fair to members

G. Lack of penalties for poor performance/lack of rewards for excellent performance

H. Other factors

> I can live with doubt and uncertainty. I think it's much more interesting to live not knowing than to have answers which might be wrong.
>
> Professor Richard Feynmann
> *The Economist*
> December 26, 1981

Because the manager lives in a complex world of multiple causes and effects, makes decisions under time pressure and uncertainty, and must live with the consequences of decisions made under imperfect conditions, a specific ability is needed. It is the knack of thinking in terms of probable outcomes, rather than certain ones, of figuring and playing the odds. Anything managers can do to predict likely outcomes more accurately, to increase the possibility of correct action, even when they cannot be *sure* about what will happen, is a great asset. If even "no decision" is a decision, the ability to take risks when outcomes are not certain becomes an important managerial attribute.

The pressures of managerial work lead to a relatively high degree of stress for managers as they struggle to cope with all the demands placed upon them. For some, the stress leads to physical or psychological problems. Yet successful managers are apparently people who thrive on the challenges inherent in their work; they consistently report in polls a greater degree of job satisfaction than, for example, hourly workers, who have less control, responsibility, and challenge in their work. In studying organizational behavior, you will have the chance to practice being a managerial decision maker and also to see whether you enjoy being in the hot seat that managers sit in.

You may be placed in a position of having to act and live through the consequences of each action or decision. For example, you may be asked to participate in group projects; if you decide not to say anything to the members of your group who shirk their responsibilities for fear of hurting their feelings, you will be one of those who will live with the outcome. And conversely, should you decide to confront them, you would have another set of consequences to cope with. Which way you choose to handle such a dilemma and which consequences you are willing to accept depend upon your *own* personal values; no one else can tell you what is worth living with. Even in a class discussion or case analysis, you must decide whether to express your views, and you must live with the consequences (both good and bad) of the choice you make: for learning, clarifying your ideas, gaining credit for contributing to class discussion, or for your relationships and reputation with other students.

When you analyze cases, try to think of the people in them as being, like you, real individuals struggling to do the best they can in accordance with their values. The more you can project yourself into their positions, imagine yourself to be in their shoes, the better you will understand why things are happening—and the more interesting the cases will be.

Through this continual process of being placed in organizational situations where you must make decisions about how to behave and then see what happens, your skills and organizational effectiveness should be improved. Most often you will find that there is no *one* correct answer to the dilemmas or situations you face. Because one person's meat can be another's poison, the correct solution will be quite different depending upon the values of the decider.

Almost any course of action, as a manager or in daily life, will entail costs as well as benefits. In assessing alternative courses of action, the effective manager does not expect to find a choice with no costs, but seeks the choice that on balance involves the least net cost or the maximum net benefit. By identifying in advance all the likely costs, the effective decision maker can also identify steps to minimize the costs that become a reality. There is no one best way to manage. What is best depends on the situation and the values of the decision maker.

The rest of the course should give you ample opportunities for practicing. The text, cases, exercises, and your instructor will try to help you clarify your own values and make better estimates of how well they will be served by what you do in a variety of human situations. While practice may not make perfect, it should increase the probabilities of your being able to make sensible decisions that get you what you want and enhance your ability to learn from experience.

Basic Premise: Learning to Learn about Organizations, Everywhere

Even if you have not yet worked in a complex company you have a considerable amount of relevant experience on which to draw. Much of what you can learn about organizational behavior is quite accessible; it goes on around you all the time. You are a member of a family; may live with other people; belong to some clubs, teams, or committees; have a job involving others; eat and shop where people work; and so on. The university itself is a large organization containing many smaller organizations: the fraternity or sorority, academic departments, business and other administrative offices. Even the classroom is an organization. You are in a position to see many of the main ingredients of organizational life in your everyday contacts. All these groupings have implicit, if not explicit, goals, structures, and policies. These, in turn, seek to direct behavior in certain ways. They shape people's interactions with each other, and they are potentially a major source of an individual's productivity, satisfactions, and personal learning or development. In short, you have many ready-made opportunities to study organizational behavior. This book will help you learn to look at and understand more of your living and working experiences, as well as prepare you for your career.

Throughout this book you will be asked to analyze your own behavior—at work, in the classroom, and in your interactions with others. Analogies will be drawn with other organizational settings, through either student experience or the use of case studies. Theories and concepts will be introduced as tools for helping you make sense out of your observations and experiences. The objectives of this book and the course for which it is designed are aimed at enhancing your ability to learn from experience, to test what you learn against new experience, and to extract new learning in a continuing fashion. In that way the organizational challenges of the 21st century will be approachable.

Central Theme: Learning through Doing and Reflecting—The Manager as Involved Actor

A central theme throughout the book is the idea of "learning through doing and reflecting." To learn how to *behave* effectively, rather than just *understand* behavior, it is necessary to be active and engaged, as well as reflective and thoughtful. This calls for a different educational model from what you may be used to. Most college classrooms are not organized to give practice in action and conceptualizing skills, but, rather, to enhance acquisition and understanding of material that may not have immediate direct application. In such classes the professor does most of the talking and grading; students listen, individually write notes and papers, take exams, answer some questions, and address most of their comments to the professor. But just as in a biology lab, where you have to *practice* dissecting a fog to learn the relevant skills, in a course designed to improve your organizational *effectiveness,* a more active student role is necessary.

This means that you still need to master ideas, theories, and concepts; but then practice using them in complex, unique situations, step back and observe how well you achieved your intentions, think about how to modify your ideas or your behavior, or both, then try again in new situations. Therefore, in a course in organizational behavior, the classroom needs to become a learning laboratory in which you, the student, have the opportunity to test out, practice, experiment with, and utilize the variety of concepts and ideas that are the subject matter of the book. Look for connections between what you are learning and your own behavior, as well as the behavior of individuals around you. Differences in class size and duration may limit the opportunity for such experimental learning during regular class hours. Nonetheless, when taking part in any organized activity, you can make observations and apply your conclusions to those relationships important to you in the classroom and outside. (See the learning-model questionnaire at the end of Chapter 1 to diagnose your own preferred style of learning.)

Part of what makes this course exciting—and occasionally frustrating—is that students, like managers, are highly *involved actors,* an internal component of the situations they are trying to understand and manage or change. It is like trying to run and tie your shoe at the same time. Managers cannot call time-out or say "pay no attention to me while I watch and decide what is going on"; their presence and the way people feel about bosses means that even no action or no decision has a powerful impact.

Suppose, for example, that two students in a class begin to argue over a point. No matter what the instructor says, including saying nothing, as the classroom manager he or she will have an effect on the class members. The class members' reactions will depend in part on whether they perceive the instructor as approving or disapproving the open conflict between students, on which side they think the instructor believes is correct, on how well the instructor appears to handle the disagreement, and so forth. Managers have nowhere to hide. A manager's behavior is an inherent part of the problem, no matter how "innocent" the manager feels!

In this course your actions, your classmates' actions, and the instructor's actions are all likely to be factors in any problem that may arise.

> It is an inherent property of intelligence that it can jump out of the task which it is performing, and survey what it has done; it is always looking for, and often finding, patterns.
>
> Douglas R. Hofstadter, Gödel, Escher, Bach:
> *An Eternal Golden Braid*

One dilemma you will certainly face is the struggle to remain appropriately detached or objective while you are personally involved in the learning experience. Sociologists call this role *participant-observer*; it poses a dilemma, because of the natural tendency of people to become *less* detached or objective as they become more involved in a given situation. The fine line is difficult to maintain: *Too much detachment can minimize one's appreciation and understanding of another person or a set of interactions, but too much involvement can bias (even distort) one's perspective.*

> The field cannot well be seen from within the field.
>
> Ralph Waldo Emerson

The learning process you will use—alternating between experience and conceptualization—will also provide plenty of practice in struggling with this dilemma. You will have to maintain openness to learning and a scientific attitude toward situations, some of which you are part of. What we mean by a *scientific attitude* in this respect is the process of (a) sorting out what is going on in one's relationships, (b) increasing the ability to predict likely outcomes of one's own and others' behaviors, and (c) thereby making more informed choices, which can (d) be checked for results against expectations. *It is the act of comparing the intent of any one of our actions with the effect of that action, and then learning from it.* Such an attitude requires that you constantly question, examine, and evaluate the consequences of your actions so that you learn from both your failures and your successes.

A word of caution is in order. Although careful and rigorous analysis is important for managers, reasoning is not a substitute for intuition. Recent research on how even scientists work has revealed the important part hunches, guesses, and wild leaps of intuition play in forming theory. Managers also require the use of this less analytical capacity. Because most problems do not come in neat, orderly pieces, managers need to be tuned into what their instincts signal them as much as to formal deductive reasoning. Overdoing it in either direction, however, can lead to disaster.

Seat-of-the-pants decisions can be brilliant—or merely a reflection of the manager's prejudices and blind spots. Rigorous analysis can prevent stupid mistakes or freeze the manager into analysis paralysis. Mintzberg summarized research on the human brain and argued that some managerial functions, such as planning, required use of the left half of the brain (which controls logical, abstract reasoning) while the more people-oriented parts of managing require the more wholistic, intuitive right brain.[18] In general, as a manager you will have to use all of your capacities to sort out what is going on and to formulate sensible action plans.

> In nearly all the important transaction of life, indeed in all transactions . . . which have relation to the future, we have to take a leap in the dark. . . . When we are to take any important resolution, . . .—we have to act for the best, and in nearly every case to act upon very imperfect evidence.
>
> The one talent which is worth all other talents put together in human affairs is the talent of judging right upon imperfect materials, the talent if you please of guessing right . . .
>
> Sir James Fitzjames Stephen (1829–94)
> Excerpt from "Liberty, Equality, Fraternity: And Three Brief Essays"
> *New York Times,* March 15, 1992

The complexities involved can be demonstrated by an example. Suppose you had never seen a sport played and were asked to make recommendations about a strange new activity, the rules for which you did not know. Can you imagine, for example, what the first tennis match you ever saw might be like? Some people dressed in abbreviated white costumes dash around hacking at a fuzzy sphere with a lollipop-shaped stick, shouting about "love!" Yet sometimes when the sphere comes near them, they step aside and do not wave their sticks but appear to stare intently at some white lines on the ground. The participants stop and start quite suddenly, changing positions, throwing the sphere in the air and batting at it, crouching carefully, or running rapidly toward the long, webbed object hanging between the participants. Before you could ever offer sensible advice, you would have to *watch* carefully for any *patterns* to the game, *deduce the rules* (How long would it take you to figure out the scoring rules, that "love" meant no points, a certain number of points make a "set," and so forth?), *test your assumptions* about how the game works *by predicting what will happen next* ("The first hitter aims for the opposite forecourt, so if I am correct about service rules, the second try must hit in that area or a point will be lost"), and slowly begin to *see the order in the apparent chaos.*

As you become increasingly sophisticated, you could begin to draw conclusions about the internal workings and strategy of the game, making connections between when to rush the net, when to lob over an opponent's head, and so forth. Whether you systematically dissected the components of each stroke and its relation to the opponent's weaknesses or just observed until you had some hunches about what was likely to be effective, you would have to operate as a kind of scientist or detective—gathering data, asking questions of it, forming tentative conclusions based on apparent patterns, testing those by more observation, and so on. In that way you would establish an order to the buzzing confusion you first experienced.

> I'm not smart. I try to observe. Millions saw the apple fall, but Newton was the one who asked why.
>
> Bernard Baruch

MANAGERIAL BULLETIN

When Good Will and Bewilderment Go Hand in Glove

Si Frumkin tells of his experiences after his World War II prison camp was liberated and transferred to a displaced persons' camp:

> Then there were the one-handed American boxing gloves. The children's camp to which I was transferred later got a shipment of American athletic equipment. There were pingpong sets, soccer balls, boxing gloves, and basketball nets. There were also strange elongated leather balls, shaped something like large brown cucumbers, that bounced strangely and unpredictably if you tried to play soccer or basketball with them. They were completely useless. We had never seen American football, and eventually we simply gave up, assuming that there must be a sport in America that somehow utilizes these strange leather gourds.
>
> There was, however, another mystery. In one of the boxes there were gloves, but very strange gloves. On their back they had a kind of pocket that was obviously designed for a hand. There were spaces for fingers and the whole thing fit like an enlarged, padded, expanded palm. The elongated fingers were attached to one another by a system of strings and, furthermore, the gloves could be worn on one hand only—there were no pairs. We tried everything—there was nothing that made any sense. Finally, frustrated, we decided that in America boxing was done one-handed, palm open, and by trying to slap the opponent's face while wearing one of these gloves. We even tried to stage "American boxing" contests, but it never really caught on.
>
> It was many years later, after coming to America, that I went to my first baseball game and solved the mystery of the completely misunderstood—by us—baseball glove.

SOURCE: "When Good Will and Bewilderment Go Hand in Glove," *The Wall Street Journal,* August 10, 1992. © Dow Jones & Company, Inc. All Rights Reserved Worldwide.

MANAGERIAL BULLETIN

Charge to Graduating Seniors

The real world is not arranged for my convenience or yours. It is rarely arranged for my knowledge or yours. It is indeed rarely arranged.

SOURCE: G. Armour Craig, acting president, *Amherst College,* 1983.

Trying to make sense out of an organization can be equally confusing and even more challenging, because you are at the same time a part of what you are observing, affecting it and affected by it. People at work don't often hold still for examination by impartial, detached observers, and they seldom behave by such explicit, preagreed rules as tennis players do.

Whatever may be the context of your role in an organization now or in the future, you will need the skills of searching for patterns and connections, making predictions, testing out the consequences of an action or decision that you make, collecting information as to success, and modifying your actions accordingly. You will need to adopt and maintain an attitude of tentativeness—that is, a readiness to change your mind, to modify your views, to change your theory, to acknowledge your mistakes, and to take corrective action. Don't be like the boss who is so concerned about being right and so closed to feedback that he or she makes inappropriate decisions, saying in effect, "Don't confuse me with the facts."

Propositions

As you progress through the book, examining and learning from your observations and experiences, you can build your own managerial model in the form of hypotheses and concepts—what we call *propositions*—that will help to guide your actions. An example of a proposition is the authors' belief that: Experiencing and analyzing behavior is likely to produce more learning of organizational skills than merely reading or hearing about it. A proposition can be tested and modified if necessary, then applied to other situations. The process of making propositions will aid in your development as a more effective manager and as a more competent individual. You have a chance to develop a way of looking at people in organizations that goes beyond any specific information you acquire; managers who have internalized a way of learning from experience should be able to continue learning in the changing situations facing them at work.

Throughout the book, we have used the propositional format as a way of highlighting major concepts. These propositions serve to integrate various findings from the research and experience of organizational experts. The endnotes at the end of the book contain references that the interested reader can pursue. Also see the suggested readings that appear at the end of each chapter.

Some propositions were derived by the authors from their own experience and knowledge in the field. Specified sources for these propositions could not be provided, but we did include references to closely related literature for students interested in pursuing a given topic.

In summary, then, this book is concerned with the preparation of students who plan to become either managers of people or effective organizational members possessing skills in the following areas: (1) identifying problems, (2) understanding their origins, (3) predicting their consequences, (4) considering gains and losses of those consequences for the short and long run, (5) possessing the willingness and capacity to choose well from among alternatives, and (6) extracting useful learning from experiences in which they are also part of the action and have an investment in the outcome. Thus, this book seeks to cultivate the rare qualities of insight, analysis, and judgment. Its emphasis is on knowledge utilization, the marriage of theory to practice, and the development of managerial skills, and not just on the acquisition of knowledge for its own sake.

Learning Styles

A course that demands active participation and application of concepts to actual complex situations can create some difficulties. We have already noted our assumptions about the interplay of experience and conceptualization, moving back and forth among doing, formulating conclusions, and testing them on new situations. We believe that such a process most closely replicates the process that managers (and other organizational members) go through at work.

Some individuals are not accustomed to learning in such active experimenting and conceptualizing modes. They are more used to passive learning, in which they are most distant from the phenomena being studied. While that mode of learning is valid for mastering some subject matter, it is less appropriate for studying organizational behavior, especially where there is an emphasis on developing managerial skills.

Furthermore, because the work of managers is so fundamentally intertwined with other people, it is desirable to add some collaborative modes of learning to the individual competitive modes more common in other kinds of courses. Learning from and with others is an important part of mastering skills needed for working effectively in organizations. One need not abandon the desire to do well in comparison to others in order to practice mutual teaching and learning. Your classmates will have sufficient diversity of experiences, skill, opinions, attitudes, and values to ensure that someone in the course or task groups will have a different way of seeing the issues raised by the cases and concepts. Indeed, you may be shocked to find that no matter how well you prepare a case and how certain you are of your views, class discussion will reveal many angles you never thought of, along with viewpoints with which you profoundly disagree—held by students equally prepared and certain of their correctness! Learning to bend and reconsider when there is something new, yet be convincing and persuasive when you can help others gain perspective, is difficult to master.

What complicates issues of differences in learning style is the fact that individuals are at different stages in terms of their basic views of the world. Researchers have identified stages of development that individuals pass through or get stuck at, depending on their capacity to learn from making choices and experiencing new circumstances. The stage at which an individual is makes a great deal of difference in how that person approaches education and new learning[19] as well as how he or she thinks about other organizational issues, such as power, authority, work, goals, and interpersonal relationships. People at different stages tend to respond somewhat differently to leadership opportunities, and they often make different decisions about priorities based on how they understand the world (see Figure 1–2). Sometimes communication problems are the result of people genuinely trying to talk to each other from different stages. You may find it helpful to locate yourself and others you know on the chart in Figure 1–2 and also to use it to set some goals for your own learning and development.

> We basically do not know what the world of tomorrow will really be like except that it will be different. That means that organizations and their leaders will have to become perpetual learners.
>
> Edgar Schein
> *Organizational Culture and Leadership*

There is nothing inherently good or bad in any of these stages; they simply identify important issues with which we all struggle as we learn and grow. Furthermore, the issues represented at any given stage may actually be lifelong—that is, they never really disappear and in some way may always influence your perception of a given situation.

As you approach and move through this course, it could be valuable for you to examine your own learning style; how the stage you are at (as best as you can assess it) affects your perceptions of the course, the instructor, and other students (especially those who are at a different stage), and, most important, your way of learning the material presented. Remember, your future skills as a manager might depend in part on your ability to understand and appreciate the differences among your employees and how these will affect their perceptions of you and how you manage.

> We are apt to think that our ideas are the creation of our own wisdom, but the truth is that they are the result of experiences through outside contact.
>
> Without studying or being taught by others, we cannot formulate even a single idea. Therefore it can be said that a person who can create ideas worthy of note is a person who learned much from others.
>
> If we are willing to learn, everything in this world can be our teacher.
>
> With sincerity we hope to absorb wisdom from all people and all things. It is from this attitude that fresh and brilliant ideas are created. The sincere willingness to learn is the first step toward "Prosperity."
>
> Konosuke Matsushita

FIGURE 1–2   *Educational Attitudes and Life Stages (Development over Time)*

Life Stage	Educational Attitudes
Opportunistic: Self-protective; competitive with and ready to blame others; likely to think in only vague general terms or either/or concepts; breaks rules for personal gain; modest self-understanding.	College is a thing you do after high school; it's a drag but important. Professors are the people in charge of a course who show you what to do and keep you on track. Grades are what count; you work for the grade more than for "learning."
Socially oriented: Concerned with belonging and acceptance; typically friendly and nice toward others (except outsiders); often relies on stereotypes and clichés; concerned about rules and with what one "should" do.	College is where you get the education that helps you get a better job and prepares you for the future. Professors are the experts who provide the facts and the answers. They tell you whether or not you understand the material. Grades are important as a means to a good job and are the reward for hard work and ability.
Goal oriented: Achievement oriented, has long-term goals; focused toward mutual responsibilities in relationships; increased conceptual complexity; has self-evaluated standards; greater understanding of self and others.	The point of college is for you to grow as a person, developing your potentials, skills, and awareness for a more meaningful life. Professors' knowledge, competence, and standards of excellence give them authority. One can learn by exchanging ideas and modeling their way of studying issues. Grades are important to show if one has mastered the standards in a course. They don't always represent the amount one learns. In some courses I gain a lot even though I don't get a good grade.
Self-defining and relativistic: Concerned with individuality and self-fulfillment, yet also justice and humanity; desires autonomy in relationships yet is tolerant of others; thinks complexly, seeing issues from multiple points of view; lives with conflicts in personal obligations, needs, and roles while striving to resolve them.	College is a major step in a process of emotional and intellectual development that will continue throughout life. Professors are an important resource that students can draw on as makes sense. In the end, though, I'm the one who is really responsible for my learning. Grades are a measure of performance in the classroom. Their primary importance lies in giving information about how one is doing in the professor's eyes, which is only part of the story.

SOURCE: Table developed by Rita P. Weathersby, adapted from the work of Jane Loevinger and Rita Weathersby.

All of this means that some students may find the book and course for which it is intended rather disconcerting at first. However, we do hold to the belief that as potential managers it is ultimately necessary to be able to use all modes of learning—active, passive, cognitive, affective, collaborative, competitive, concrete, and abstract—and that the modes inherent in using cases and treating the classroom as an organization often need reinforcement. Therefore, practicing them in and out of class even when they feel awkward is a worthwhile way of expanding your ability to learn in situations that call for active participation.

At the end of this chapter is the first of the Personal Application Exercises included to help you personalize and consolidate your mastery of the book's concepts. It is a self-scoring instrument that measures a person's learning style. Complete it, score it, and use the intrepretation guide to understand and assess your own style of learning. That can help you determine what kinds of learning activities you might want to explore in this course and elsewhere. (Your instructor has additional information on this instrument if you want or need it.) We have also included a variety of ideas, set off in boxes called *Managerial Tools,* that can help you be more effective.

The learning process we are suggesting that you use in this course can serve you throughout life. The cases and exercises are all designed to put you in the postion of a manager or organizational member who has to decide what is going on, what the

MANAGERIAL BULLETIN

Common Learning Issues in This Course and Possible Solutions

1. Finding it uncomfortable to speak, particularly in the full class, but also in small groups, because others appear more knowledgeable.

   Try viewing the course as an opportunity to experiment with bold behavior. There's not a lot to lose, and you'll help others who feel equally certain they are the only ones who do not know.

2. Finding others saying what you were about to say before you have had a chance to speak and, therefore, usually being silent.

   Try saying, "Summarizing what Irene said, '...'" You'll probably find that you have added something and helped others reconsider the idea in new ways.

3. Finding it easy to learn a lot from listening and, therefore, being content to just listen.

   Listening is an important skill. Try expanding on what you hear or try summarizing the thrust of the discussion.

4. Finding case discussions frustrating, because they seldom seem to arrive at a "right answer," and every alternative seems as good as another.

   Since most situations, in fact, can be handled in several ways, focus on finding an alternative that feels best to you, one that you could support.

5. Finding that an emphasis on a careful definition of the concepts and terms makes the course seem like "just a matter of semantics."

   While clearly defined concepts and terms can increase precision in expression, practice restating concepts in your own words, so the ideas become "yours."

6. Finding that you disagree with a concept or that it is not valid in a particular situation you have experienced.

   Great! Concepts should be questioned. Share your thoughts with others and plan to utilize the concept where it does apply, or restate the concept so its limitations are clearer.

situation calls for, what alternatives exist for resolving the problem(s) or dilemma(s) faced, and ultimately what consequences your values will permit you to accept. In the book, as in life, we do not expect easy solutions to present themselves very often; the chance to practice sorting out complexities and making informed choices can nevertheless be enjoyable if you plunge wholeheartedly into doing it.

> The mind is a fire to be kindled, not a vessel to be filled.
>
> Plutarch

KEY CONCEPTS FROM CHAPTER 1

1. We live in a constantly changing world.
2. Basic premise: Much of what you can learn about organizational behavior goes on around you all the time.
3. The scientific attitude is the act of comparing the intent of actions with their effects and then learning from the process.
4. The manager, by virtue of position, has relationships that are necessary to acquire information in order to make decisions.
5. Managing requires:
   a. Awareness of multiple causality.
   b. Decisions under uncertainty.
   c. Living with consequences of decisions.
6. Central theme:
   a. Learning through doing and reflecting.
   b. The manager as involved actor.
7. Learning styles: The desirability of active, collaborative learning.

PERSONAL APPLICATION EXERCISE

The Learning-Model Instrument–Kenneth L. Murrell[20]

Instructions: For each statement choose the response that is more nearly true for you. Place an X on the blank that corresponds to that response. This instrument can be automatically scored by filling it out at the following web site: **http://eval1.crc.uiuc.edu/cqi-bin/lmodel.cqi.**

1. When meeting people, I prefer
   _____ *a.* to think and speculate on what they are like.
   _____ *b.* to interact directly and to ask them questions.
2. When presented with a problem, I prefer
   _____ *a.* to jump right in and work on a solution.
   _____ *b.* to think through and evaluate possible ways to solve the problem.
3. I enjoy sports more when
   _____ *a.* I am watching a good game.
   _____ *b.* I am actively participating.
4. Before taking a vacation, I prefer
   _____ *a.* to rush at the last minute and give little thought beforehand to what I will do while on vacation.
   _____ *b.* to plan early and daydream about how I will spend my vacation.
5. When enrolled in courses, I prefer
   _____ *a.* to plan how to do my homework before actually attacking the assignment.
   _____ *b.* to immediately become involved in doing the assignment.
6. When I receive information that requires action, I prefer
   _____ *a.* to take action immediately.
   _____ *b.* to organize the information and determine what type of action would be most appropriate.
7. When presented with a number of alternatives for action, I prefer
   _____ *a.* to determine how the alternatives relate to one another and analyze the consequences of each.
   _____ *b.* to select the one that looks best and implement it.
8. When I awake every morning, I prefer
   _____ *a.* to expect to accomplish some worthwhile work without considering what the individual tasks may entail.
   _____ *b.* to plan a schedule for the tasks I expect to do that day.
9. After a full day's work, I prefer
   _____ *a.* to reflect back on what I accomplished and think of how to make time the next day for unfinished tasks.
   _____ *b.* to relax with some type of recreation and not think about my job.
10. After choosing the above responses, I
    _____ *a.* prefer to continue and complete this instrument.
    _____ *b.* am curious about how my responses will be interpreted and would prefer some feedback before continuing with the instrument.
11. When I learn something, I am usually
    _____ *a.* thinking about it.
    _____ *b.* right in the middle of doing it.
12. I learn best when
    _____ *a.* I am dealing with real-world issues.
    _____ *b.* concepts are clear and well organized.

13. In order to retain something I have learned, I must
   _____ *a.* periodically review it in my mind.
   _____ *b.* practice it or try to use the information.
14. In teaching others how to do something, I first
   _____ *a.* demonstrate the task.
   _____ *b.* explain the task.
15. My favorite way to learn to do something is
   _____ *a.* reading a book or instructions or enrolling in a class.
   _____ *b.* trying to do it and learning from my mistakes.
16. When I become emotionally involved with something, I usually
   _____ *a.* let my feelings take the lead and then decide what to do.
   _____ *b.* control my feelings and try to analyze the situation.
17. If I were meeting jointly with several experts on a subject, I would prefer
   _____ *a.* to ask each of them for his or her opinion.
   _____ *b.* to interact with them and share our ideas and feelings.
18. When I am asked to relate information to a group of people, I prefer
   _____ *a.* not to have an outline, but to interact with them and become involved in an extemporaneous conversation.
   _____ *b.* to prepare notes and know exactly what I am going to say.
19. Experience is
   _____ *a.* a guide for building theories.
   _____ *b.* the best teacher.
20. People learn easier when they are
   _____ *a.* doing work on the job.
   _____ *b.* in a class taught by an expert.

The Learning-Model Instrument Scoring Sheet

Instructions: Transfer your responses by writing either *a* or *b* in the blank that corresponds to each item in the Learning-Model Instrument.

ABSTRACT/CONCRETE		COGNITIVE/AFFECTIVE	
Column 1	Column 2	Column 3	Column 4
1._____	2._____	11._____	12._____
3._____	4._____	13._____	14._____
5._____	6._____	15._____	16._____
7._____	8._____	17._____	18._____
9._____	10._____	19._____	20._____
Total circles _____	_____	_____	_____
Grand Totals_____		_____	

Now circle every *a* in Column 1 and in Column 4. Then circle every *b* in Column 2 and in Column 3. Next, total the circles in each of the four columns. Then add the totals of Columns 1 and 2; plot this grand total on the vertical axis of the Learning Model for Managers (see below) and draw a horizontal line through the point. Now add the totals of Columns 3 and 4; plot that grand total on the horizontal axis of the model and draw a vertical line through the point. The intersection of these two lines indicates the domain of your preferred learning style.

Interpreting the Learning-Model Instrument

The cognitive-affective axis or continuum represents the range of ways in which people learn. Cognitive learning includes learning that is structured around either rote storing of knowledge or intellectual abilities and skills, or both. Affective learning includes learning from experience, from feelings about the experience, and from one's own emotions.

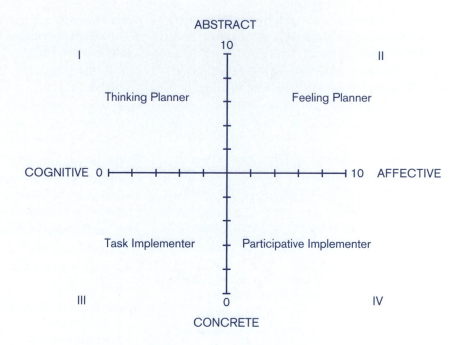

The Learning Model for Managers

The concrete-abstract axis or continuum represents the range of ways in which people experience life. When people experience life abstractly, they detach themselves from the immediacy of the situation and theorize about it. If they experience life concretely, they respond to the situation directly with little subsequent contemplation.

The two axes divide the model into four parts or domains. Most people experience life and learn from it in all four domains but have a preference for a particular domain. Liberal arts education has typically concentrated on abstract learning (domains I and II), whereas vocational and on-the-job training usually takes place in the lower quadrants, particularly domain III.

Occupations representative of the four styles include the following: domain I, philosopher or chief executive officer; domain II, poet or journalist; domain III, architect or engineer; domain IV, psychologist or personnel counselor.

Managerial jobs require an ability to learn in all four domains, and a manager's development depends on his or her ability to learn both cognitively and affectively. Thus, management education and development demand the opportunity for the participants to learn how to learn in each domain.

SUGGESTED READINGS

Adler, N. J. "Women Do Not Want International Careers, and Other Myths about International Management." *Organizational Dynamics,* Autumn 1984, pp. 66–79.

Chatman, J. A. "Improving Interactional Organizational Research: A Model of Person-Organization Fit." *Academy of Management Review* 14 (1989), pp. 333–49.

Cohen, A. R. "Beyond Simulation: The Classroom as Organization." *The Teaching of Organization Behavior Journal,* Spring and Summer 1976.

"Corporate Women." *Business Week,* June 18, 1992, pp. 74–78.

"The Cracks in Quality." *Economist,* April 18, 1992.

Fisher, Anne B. "When Will Women Get to the Top." *Fortune,* September 21, 1992, pp. 44–56.

French, J. L., and A. R. Rosenstein. "Employee Ownership, Work Attitudes, and Power Relationships." *Academy of Management Journal* 27 (1984), pp. 861–69.

Gilligan, C. *In a Different Voice: Psychological Theory and Women's Development.* Cambridge, MA: Harvard University Press, 1982.

Grasha, A. F. "Observations on Relating Teaching Goals to Student Response Styles and Classroom Methods." *American Psychologist* 27 (1972), pp. 144–47.

Jacob, Rahul. "More than Dying Fad?" *Fortune,* October 18, 1993.

Kohlberg, L. "Stage and Sequence: The Cognitive Developmental Approach to Socialization." In *Handbook of Socialization Theory and Research,* ed. D. Goslin. Skokie, IL: Rand McNally, 1969.

Levering, Robert, and Milton Moskowitz. *The 100 Best Companies to Work for in America.* New York: Doubleday, 1993.

Levine, Jonathan B. "Quality: Overview—It's an Old World in More Ways than One." *Business Week,* October 25, 1991.

Louis, M. R. "Surprise and Sense Making: What Newcomers Experience in Entering Unfamiliar Organization Settings." *Administrative Science Quarterly* 25 (1980), pp. 226–51.

Mintzberg, H. *The Nature of Managerial Work.* New York: Harper & Row, 1973.

———. "The Manager's Job: Folklore and Fact." *Harvard Business Review,* July–August 1975.

Moran, Robert T., and John R. Riesenberger. *Making Globalization Work: Solutions for Implementation.* New York: McGraw-Hill, 1993.

O'Reilly, Brian. "Your New Global Workforce." *Fortune,* December 14, 1992, pp. 52–66.

Perry, W. G., Jr. "Cognitive and Ethical Growth: The Making of Meaning." In *The Modern American College,* ed. A. W. Chickering. San Francisco: Jossey-Bass, 1981.

Peters, Tom. *Thriving on Chaos.* New York: Knopf, 1991.

Peters, T., and S. Waterman. *In Search of Excellence: Lessons from America's Best-Managed Corporations.* New York: Harper & Row, 1982.

Port, Otis. "Quality." *Business Week,* November 30, 1992.

"The Quality Imperative." *Business Week,* January 15, 1992.

Rose, Frank. "Now Quality Means Service Too." *Fortune,* April 22, 1991.

Shamir, B., and I. Salomon. "Work-at-Home and the Quality of Working Life." *Academy of Management Review,* July 1985, pp. 455–64.

Sheppard, Blair; Roy J. Lewicki; and John Minton. *Organizational Justice: The Search for Fairness in the Workplace.* New York: Lexington Books, 1992.

Ueno, I.; R. R. Blake; and J. S. Mouton. "The Productivity Battle: A Behavioral Science Analysis of Japan and the United States." *Journal of Applied Behavioral Science* 20, no. 1 (1984), pp. 49–58.

The Total Organization and the Concept of Systems

A New Model for the Nature of Business: It's Alive!

Forget the Mechanical–Today's Leaders Embrace the Biological

Until recently, businesspeople saw their worlds through the Industrial Age metaphor of the machine and built their organizations accordingly. Now, in irreversibly increasing numbers, they see business more as a living system. And in the process they are leading business back to its roots as a natural and fundamentally human institution. . . .

Mechanical Model	Natural Model
Strategic Objectives	
Optimum design	Adaptation
Consistency of operation	Continuous improvement
Leadership Implications	
Command and control	Autonomy for employees
	Articulation of vision
Management Objective	
Economies of scale	Unity of purpose
Structure	
Hierarchies	Self-organizing teams
Organizing Principles	
Division of labor	Synthesis of minds

In an era when change arrives without warning and threatens to eradicate entire companies and industries overnight, organizations can survive only by engaging the eyes, ears, minds, and emotions of all individuals and by encouraging them to act on their knowledge and beliefs. Second, and far more importantly, the new, more enlightened way of business will persist because it hews more closely to what we are as humans.

SOURCE: Thomas Petzinger, Jr., "A New Model for the Nature of Business: It's Alive!" *The Wall Street Journal,* February 26, 1999, p. B1.

"As organizations struggle to preserve the advantages of size with the speed and flexibility of smaller groupings . . . many have begun to experiment with a different way of organizing."

Organizations evolved as a consequence of people attempting to solve complex problems. When a problem requires the efforts of more than one person, some kind of organization is necessary in order to get the work done. Whether the problem requires a few or many to work together–a pair of lumberjacks sawing logs or several hundred thousand employees providing national telephone service–the existence of an organization raises a series of fundamental questions or dilemmas, which must be resolved in order to accomplish the organization's goals. Imagine what it takes to get any complex job done:

1. Goals must be determined, agreed upon, and disseminated (goal setting).
2. Some way of making decisions about goals and all subsequent tasks must be found (decision making).
3. The various tasks necessary to achieve the goals must be divided and allocated (division of labor).
4. People who are willing and capable of doing the tasks must be found, employed, trained, and assigned to the tasks (recruiting).
5. Somehow timely information must be conveyed to those who need it to do their tasks (communications).
6. A way must be found to get organizational members to do the necessary work (motivation).
7. A way must be found to ensure adequate performance of the tasks (control).
8. A way must be found to ensure coordination of the tasks (coordination).
9. A way must be found to measure and modify all of the above when the conditions leading to the original goals change (environmental scanning and organizational mission).

The problems of trying to decide what an organization should do, who should do it, and how they should divide work, coordinate efforts, and so forth have provided challenges for thousands of years. Imagine the organization required to build the pyramids in Egypt or the aqueducts in the Roman Empire. Even the first primitive hunting band had to decide who would do what; where it would hunt; what would happen to the hunter who was disabled, less skilled, or uncooperative. Much of this book is devoted to exploring aspects of the broad issues listed above primarily as they affect the small work group. The goals of each work group in an organization should reflect and contribute to the goals of that organization. The group's membership will be determined by the organization's recruiting policies, and the behavior of individual group members will be influenced by the organization's controls and rewards.

As you proceed through this chapter you should keep in mind the fact that, as a student, you are affected daily by the overall organization of your college or university. Your awareness of *how* you are affected can be useful both as a source of learning for this course and as a way to help you manage yourself during your years in school. At the end of this chapter, you will find a Personal Application Exercise that addresses this notion; check it out before you read further.

The Traditional Organization

Over the centuries, many ways of organizing people have been imagined. Early organizations were often quite simple, with a boss or owner-manager and employees with more or less specific jobs. As the organizations grew, the need grew for subunits with supervisors. Until these organizations became fairly large, they could remain quite loose. As long as the entrepreneur was around and could personally know and supervise everyone, relationships, job assignments, and communications could be informal. Even today, young recently formed companies that are growing rapidly and managed by an entrepreneur who founded the organization are often only

FIGURE 2-1 *Pyramidal Organization Chart*

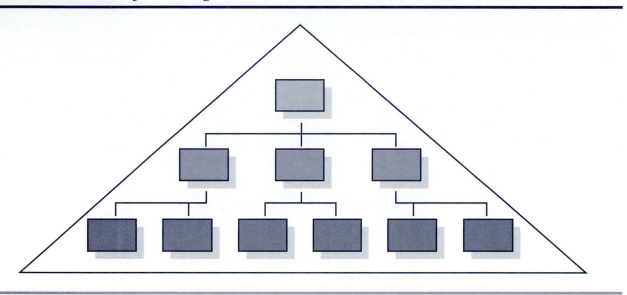

loosely structured. There is so much to do that little time is spent worrying about spelling out boundaries, roles, and rules. Such fast-moving organizations can be very effective, especially when the entrepreneurial leader is charismatic and inspires commitment from employees.

Nevertheless, as size increases something more systematic is needed. Things start to fall through the cracks, causing mistakes and lost opportunities. Employees want equitable and less arbitrary treatment.

As with many elements of organizational behavior, the appropriate response—structure, behavior, policies—is *contingent* on the new situation. As we have been stressing, there is seldom one right answer. The loose, informal organizational forms used successfully by startup companies depend upon small size, charismatic leadership, and markets that provide new opportunities for companies that can spot a need and respond quickly. But what works under those conditions may not work under another set of conditions. When firm size increases, markets stabilize, and technology becomes more predictable, a different type of structure becomes more effective.

In large organizations the most frequent form is the bureaucratic hierarchy, usually represented by boxes and lines in a formal organization chart. The traditional organization chart often looks like a pyramid, with many people at the bottom of the chart and increasingly fewer at the top. See Figure 2–1, which pictorially represents certain guidelines for how the traditional large organization is supposed to go about its work:

1. Decisions are made by specified people in a hierarchy, which gives increasingly broader powers to those who are higher in the organization.
2. There is a set of explicit rules governing the rights and duties of employees.
3. Labor is divided into carefully prescribed jobs by specialty.
4. A set of procedures governs how to deal with problems as they arise from the work.
5. Relationships are impersonal, objective, and fair.
6. Selection and promotion are based on technical competence.
7. Coordination of the work is done through the chain of command (hierarchy).

MANAGERIAL BULLETIN

Principles of Modern Organizational Design

- Organize around outcomes, not tasks
- Value-adding is more important than management
- The contributor must be empowered to act
- Decisions about work should be made by those performing the work

- Do as much work as possible before handing off
- Organizational capability, especially the ability to change, is the basis

SOURCE: *Indications* (a publication of CSC Index) 10, no. 2 (1993).

8. Disagreements between units at the same level are referred up the chain for resolution.
9. Rewards tend to be formalized and uniform.

Such a chart implies who has direct powers over the work activities of others, who is responsible for certain activities, and, therefore, who should talk to whom and about what. The pyramidal model assumes that most problems can be foreseen in advance and logically dealt with by rules and regulations, and that positions higher in the chart indicate greater knowledge and competence as well as greater rights and powers.

Along with such formalized relationships among people, most organizations develop explicit methods of rewarding people's behavior. By means of pay, fringe benefits, stock options, opportunities for advancement, and so forth, organizations seek to attract and hold employees, get high levels of performance out of them, and stimulate initiative and commitment to organizational goals. Similarly, through the use of planning, budgetary constraints, production schedules, and the like, organizations attempt to exercise control over employee behavior to ensure the efficient attainment of their goals.

In traditional (sometimes called *classical*) organizations, it is generally assumed that carefully spelled-out duties, hierarchical structures, procedures, rules, rewards, and controls will create in advance a system that can handle most, if not all, the important decisions and problems inherent in their operations. The idea is to "preprogram" the organization's response to any contingency. This is usually done by predetermining procedures and action choices; otherwise, it is done by referring the matter to a designated authority, higher up the hierarchy, for action on the (presumably few) exceptions. This can work well in stable, unchanging conditions.

The world, however, has not always arranged itself to fit this neat but oversimplified set of assumptions. Problems are not always predictable; greater expertise about particular issues does not always reside in the person with the highest position in the organization. Necessary information may be possessed by those not directly connected on the chart, and yet they must interact directly or action will be unreasonably delayed.

Most organizations today are faced with a world full of uncertainties. These uncertainties can be reduced at least in part through availability of information, which, in turn, requires flexibility in organizational structures.

One of the early departures from the traditional model of an organization was the emergence of informal coordination and the settlement of disagreements among departments through direct unofficial contact, often without any involvement of people higher in the chain of command. Sometimes, as the value of such direct contact became more and more evident over time, this form of working relationship was legitimized and even formalized in job descriptions and in the creation of special roles, such as expeditor or liaison person. But every organization has both a formal and an informal organization. While the formal organization is intended to define the boundaries and proper roles for members of the organization, the actual work that is done usually depends upon people's abilities to take actions when a situation calls for them. These cannot always be prescribed in advance by the formal organization, thus requiring the informal organization to pick up the slack, to compensate for what has not been anticipated. As long as the two systems complement each other, the total organization can be effective; when informal activities begin to disrupt or block the formal objectives, managers get concerned and need to correct something in either the formal or the informal organization.

The Linking-Pin Model

Rensis Likert, for example, proposed that organizations be viewed as a set of interrelated *groupings* of people, arranged in a hierarchy with managers serving as link-pins connecting the groups.[1] A given manager, according to this conception, is both a member of a peer group of managers with comparable responsibilities and a leader-member of his or her own department or group. This role typically involves leading subordinates in *group discussions and decision making,* and then *representing* the group's needs and views in meetings of the higher (peer manager) group—which also is oriented to reach decisions through group discussion and consensus. In addition, the manager might be part of one or more cross-functional task forces. Figure 2–2 depicts the manager's multiple group memberships and link-pin position between groups.

Thus, managers link the various subparts of the organization in ways that serve to keep important information flowing through the system, maintain a sense of total organization, and minimize the kinds of problems and errors often associated with the strictly bureaucratic way of operating. While not a major departure from the traditional model, Likert's approach contains profound implications for the managerial roles and functions described in Chapter 1.

The Bases of Departmentalization

Most traditional organizations divide groupings by management functions—sales, operations, finance, accounting, service, research, and so on. This is called a functional organization, and it works reasonably well in relatively stable environments where problems are predictable and expertise develops with experience. But as organizations are faced with changing conditions, the basis for creating units becomes more problematic. Coordination needs increase, problems are less predictable, and greater focus on different groups of customers is needed. Eventually, organizations struggle with alternate ways to cluster activities into departments: By function? By product? By customer or service? By geographic area?

Each of these groupings brings together new collections of people with their particular perspective and expertise. Each can provide greater focus on something—and inevitably less focus and coordination about other things.

There are no simple answers to how to group people; there are costs and benefits associated with any given way of organizing. For example, an organization that has a sales function and a production department will almost certainly be faced with some inherent conflicts. Salespeople inevitably want to serve the customer quickly, to be able to respond to changing market demands, and to build a high level of credibility with their clientele. From the point of view of sales, any product should be produced whenever the customer wants it. Production people, however, want to standardize as much as possible, reduce costs, and make operations as predictable as possible. They would like to produce only one product for long periods of time so as to reduce setup and errors. The former think in terms of change and flexibility, the latter in terms of stability and long-range continuity. Disagreements and even

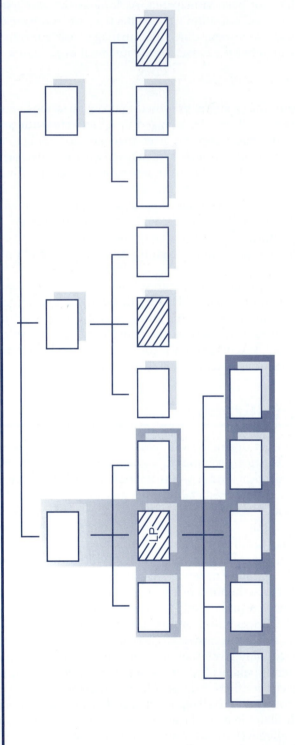

FIGURE 2–2

Organization Chart with Linking-Pin Model

LP

Shows link pin and other members of cross-functional task force

conflicts are inevitable, although not necessarily to the detriment of the company. Can you imagine if either sales or production had exclusive control over decisions and commitments? The company would either be overstretched or totally unresponsive to reasonable customer requests. It is the *balance* that actually leads to the best decisions for the company.

When the functional groupings become out of line with customer or other needs, managers seek regroupings. For example, as a company increases its product lines, it begins to see new markets. But if those markets require a different channel of distribution or different sales approaches or products that are modified to fit the requirements and cultures of other countries, the traditional sales department gets in the way. People know what has worked in the past, and they resist making needed changes. So the top management tries to find a more congenial form of organization. Perhaps reorganizing into product groups would help. Then each group would handle only similar products sold to similar customers. But what if some of the products cross into different customer groupings?

Polaroid cameras, for example, are sold through camera shops, discount houses, and department stores to individual consumers. But they are also sold to large organizations, such as insurance companies, to be used in claims adjustment. And the Polaroid instant ID system is sold to state governments to use for drivers' licenses, and so on. Each type of customer may need different sales attention, pricing, service, product features, and the like. But the cameras are sold all over the world. Shouldn't the company take into account local preferences for advertising, size, and feel of the cameras, where people shop, not to mention taxes and requirements for local manufacturing? Perhaps geographic units make sense.

There are times when an organization can operate best through its functional units, times when it needs the product, the region, or the service as its structural format. There are also situations where no single basis seems appropriate. Instead, a combination of bases seems to serve system goals better.

Variations from the Traditional Organization

Modern organizations have introduced variations on the original pyramidal model in order to accommodate the infinite variety of, and often unpredictable, interconnections that are required for any complex system to cope with its problems. While it is not the subject of this book to discuss the broader questions of organization theory and management (sometimes referred to as a *macro*perspective), it would be useful to note some ways in which large organizations have attempted to create structures that are more adaptable to today's problems.

Strategic Business Units (SBUs)

In recent years, large corporations have experienced increasing demands to be highly flexible and responsive to rapidly changing and often unpredictable market forces. The highly centralized arrangement of the classical organization became a dinosaur in such a market environment. Linking-pin organizations were much more responsive, but too often failed to deliver the right combination of resources or expertise when and where it was needed. Instead of rapid action, decisions would be paralyzed by endless discussion, or balance among considerations would be lost.

Another way of organizing to get the proper focus and bring together the right people is to *divisionalize*–that is, to create whole, relatively autonomous divisions that act like separate businesses. These divisions, often called *strategic business units* (SBUs), define a "market" (region, product line, service) that they will serve. The total organization is structured around such units, each operating as a semi-independent company, but all coordinated by common policy dimensions from a more centralized corporate unit. As you might imagine, the SBU structure has the

MANAGERIAL BULLETIN

The Corner Office Is History

One more step and Joseph D. Reece would have been the plant manager. Now 40, he started as a machinist at GE and, after earning a degree in manufacturing engineering, ascended in the hierarchy. He reached the level of operations manager of GE's ill-fated factory of the future, with 11 people and more than 20 lathes reporting to him.

But Mr. Reece was swept into the "delayering" strategy of the corporate reorganization imposed by GE's chairman, John F. Welch, Jr. Today, all the rungs between machinist and plant manager have been removed. Mr. Reece is called the production leader of Plant 3.

It is a senior staff job overseeing procurement, production control, shipping, and supplies. He says he has kept his salary, but no one reports to him. Everyone, including the sole clerk who works with him, reports to the plant manager, Jerry Labadini.

Rather than supervise the shipping crew now, for example, he advises it. "We break the schedule down for the guys," he said. "We say, 'Here's what's on the book for next week.' From that point on, the guys manage the shipping." And if Peter Baglioni's team feels a need to bypass Mr. Reece to procure some forgings, he said, "It's fine by me. We've never been burned."

He said he has put the pecking order behind him. "You have to look at the big picture," he said. "You can drive yourself crazy if you get hung up on 'Where am I in the organization chart?' and 'Who's reporting to me?' The only reason for managers is to give directions and orders. You don't need that anymore."

Mr. Reece now works at a desk inside a crowded cinderblock structure in the middle of the production floor. In his last job, he had a corner office on the second floor of the plant and an adjacent conference room. Except for Mr. Labadini, and his secretary, Joan Lattanzio, the floor today presents an eerie gray vista of vacant offices and cubicles with unattended computer terminals.

It was harder, Mr. Reece said, to lose another emblem of authority. "I stopped wearing a necktie in January 1992," he said. "That was tough." He had been wearing neckties since his days in Roman Catholic schools. "I got real comfortable with a necktie on," he said. But shedding the tie, like the office, has helped production by bringing the staff closer to the real work of the plant. "We were just isolated from each other," he said.

SOURCE: Peter T. Kilborn, "An American Workplace, after the Deluge; at a Shrunken GE Complex, Life Has Become Challenging; That's Good and Bad," *New York Times,* September 5, 1993. Copyright © by The New York Times Company. Reprinted by permission.

strengths of a large integrated centralized entity along with the responsiveness of the smaller, more entrepreneurial business entity. With major corporations becoming increasingly global, the SBU may turn out to provide the most effective answer to the turbulence of the business environment for the near future.

Nevertheless, there are costs of duplication in setting up autonomous "companies." Each unit having its own facilities and staffs can be very expensive. Some functions such as finance may thus be reserved for headquarters, creating a kind of matrix, with many tensions. And autonomous divisions don't readily cooperate or learn from each other.

Matrix Organizations

One of the more complex organizational forms, designed to obtain simultaneously the advantages of two groupings, is called the *matrix model.* In this model two (or more) groupings are set up to represent competing needs and interests and are coordinated or balanced by a great deal of interaction at the lowest level where expertise resides. An individual or a work group is thus structurally subject to the direction of two bosses, one typically representing a functional concern (e.g., manufacturing) and the other a product, customer, service or geographical concern (e.g., the project office) as depicted in Figure 2–3.

FIGURE 2-3

Matrix Organization

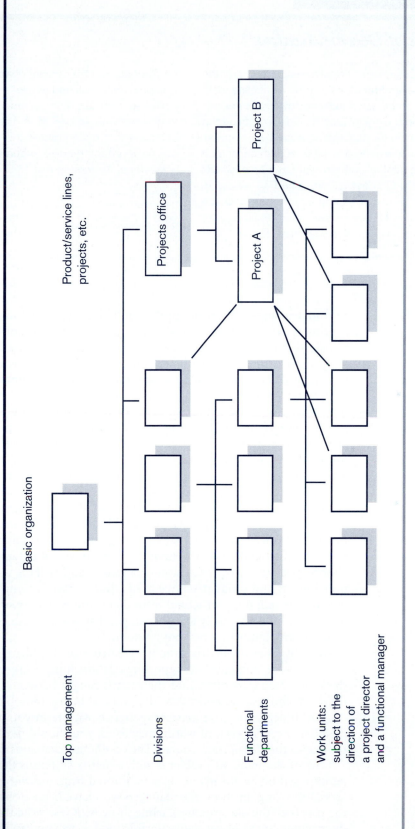

Top management

Basic organization

Divisions

Product/service lines,
projects, etc.

Projects office

Project A

Project B

Functional
departments

Work units:
subject to the
direction of
a project director
and a functional manager

41

MANAGERIAL BULLETIN

Challenges of Decentralization

While [Alcoa Chairman] O'Neill's plan is perhaps the most aggressive and rapid attempt by an old-line manufacturer to push decision making down to lower levels, it isn't the first. General Electric Co. Chairman John F. Welch has thinned management from as many as nine layers to as few as four in the past decade, and he maintains direct contact with each of GE's 14 business groups. Du Pont Co. last fall abolished its executive committee, which had overseen every major decision for 87 years, so its 19 businesses could report directly to a five-person office of the chairman. Since 1985, Du Pont has cut 50 percent of its executive jobs at the vice president level and above.

These changes can speed decision making, but they aren't without risk. M. A. Hanna Co., a Cleveland company that decentralized . . . found initially that its business groups tried to undercut each other. "There was a lot of mistrust at first."

SOURCE: Dana Milbank, "Changes at Alcoa Point Up Challenges and Benefits of Decentralized Authority." Reprinted by permission of *The Wall Street Journal,* November 7, 1991. © Dow Jones & Company, Inc. All Rights Reserved Worldwide.

A matrix organization attempts to build into its formal structure a great variety of legitimate connections, vertically, horizontally, and diagonally. Many of the relationships that might out of necessity occur informally in a classical organization are depicted in a matrix as legitimate aspects of the formal organization. The philosophy behind this is to facilitate in the most efficient way possible the flow of critical information and expertise to places where it is needed. It is presumably a way of minimizing so-called red tape and the danger of important decisions being hung up in the limited channels of a pyramid. Furthermore, the matrix model is flexible enough to accommodate the introduction of temporary groups (task forces, committees, and the like), is effectively able to move resources to the scenes of action where they are needed, and, in general, introduces changes without running into the kinds of long-standing vested interests so often found in more fixed forms of organization. It is most needed when external conditions are rapidly changing.

Finally, the matrix organization provides the kinds of structure that can include functional units and product/service/geographical units under the same hierarchical roof, thereby building on the strengths of each way of organizing without having to choose one way to the exclusion of another, and striking a balance between functional needs and product/service needs. But as you can imagine, a matrix structure is not a cure-all; it is a structural form that is not easy to operate successfully. People have to be interpersonally competent, good at dealing with conflict, and able to tolerate the ambiguity of a two-boss system.

In many cases the matrix structure created more problems than it solved. Because of its inherent ambiguities in reporting relationships, decision making can stall. Furthermore, managers often find themselves caught between conflicting demands of their "two bosses," sometimes to the point of being immobilized.

As a student, you have matrix experience; each term you have four or five faculty member "bosses," each of whom may think you should devote a greater percentage of time to their important course. The conflicting demands can create great tension.

One of the frequent problems with a matrix system is that it may have been superimposed on an already existing traditional structure without a clear shift in managerial thinking. In short, the managers who have been around for years just stick to the past (i.e., the old structure), while those with less vested interest in the past readily gravitate to the newer, more flexible model. As you can imagine, some chaos ensues. This dilemma illustrates that organizational structures are like maps; they are ways of *thinking* about something in an organized way so you can get from point A

MANAGERIAL BULLETIN

Shrinking to Grow

Everyone knows what happened to the dinosaurs that once ruled the earth, and no one more so than the International Business Machines Corporation, which last week pressed ahead with its attempt to evolve into a sprightlier, swifter life form.

IBM, the biggest dinosaur in the computer industry, split off its personal computer operations into a separate operating unit . . .

"The structure is now more reasonable, but what counts is not the structure but the products." . . . Reorganizations in themselves don't do anything, it's what you do after the reorganization. The keys are good products, aggressive pricing, and a well-known name backed by service and support.

SOURCE: Pete H. Lewis, "Be It a Whale or a Dinosaur, Can I.B.M. Really Evolve?." *New York Times,* Sunday, September 6, 1992. © 1993 by The New York Times Company. Reprinted by permission.

MANAGERIAL BULLETIN

Using Structure to Achieve Results

Douglas N. Daft, [new CEO] . . . announced a plan to push worldwide decision-making at the company down to the local level—a plan requiring the layoff of 6,000 workers, including nearly half of those at Coke headquarters in Atlanta. He said the company would embrace local brands and flavors more than it had in the past . . . .

"To me it was so natural and logical," Mr. Daft said . . . reflecting on the way his restructured Coca-Cola will let local managers make decisions about products, advertising and other functions that previously were controlled from Atlanta. "It's something I've always lived by."

SOURCE: Constance L. Hays, "Learning to Think Smaller at Coke," *New York Times,* February 6, 2000, Sec. 3, p. 1.

to point B most effectively and efficiently. If different people working together have different maps, not only will there be some "travel" problems but there might be some question about where they are going.

Horizontal Process Organization

As organizations struggle to preserve the advantages of size with the speed and flexibility of smaller groupings, and address problems of meeting customer requirements (or even exceeding them to "delight" customers) while lowering costs, many have begun to experiment with a different way of organizing. Influenced by the total quality management (TQM) movement and its emphasis on understanding and controlling processes, instead of grouping by departments, whatever their basis, the organizations identify their core processes, such as order fulfillment, materials acquisition and processing, or accounts payable and receivable, then create teams to carry out those processes. Such teams are expected to be highly focused on the internal or external customers or recipients of the outcomes of a process and are normally more self-managing than has been traditional. The members are expected to organize, monitor, and evaluate each other as peers, utilizing the designated process champion less as a traditional boss than as a coach, problem solver, facilitator, and resource acquirer.

This is a very attractive way of thinking about organization, but has not been fully worked out yet in practice. Questions remain about how processes relate to

Seven of the Key Elements of the Horizontal Corporation

Simple downsizing didn't produce the dramatic rises in productivity many companies hoped for: Gaining quantum leaps in performance requires rethinking the way work gets done. To do that, some companies are adopting a new organization model. Here's how it might work.

Organize around Process, Not Task

1. Instead of creating a structure around functions or departments, build the company around its three to five "core processes," with specific performance goals. Assign an "owner" to each process.

Flatten Hierarchy

2. To reduce supervision, combine fragmented tasks, eliminate work that fails to add value, and cut the activities within each process to a minimum. Use as few teams as possible to perform an entire process.

Use Teams to Manage Everything

3. Make teams the main building blocks of the organization. Limit supervisory roles by making the team manage itself. Give the team a common purpose. Hold it accountable for measurable performance goals.

Let Customers Drive Performance

4. Make customer satisfaction—not stock appreciation or profitability—the primary driver and measure of performance. The profits will come and the stock will rise if the customers are satisfied.

Reward Team Performance

5. Change the appraisal and pay systems to reward team results, not just individual performance. Encourage staffers to develop multiple skills rather than specialized know-how. Reward them for it.

Maximize Supplier and Customer Contact

6. Bring employees into direct, regular contact with suppliers and customers. Add supplier or customer representatives as full working members of in-house teams when they can be of service.

Inform and Train All Employees

7. Don't just spoon-feed sanitized information on a "need to know" basis. Trust staffers with raw data, but train them in how to use data to perform their own analyses and make their own decisions.

SOURCE: "The Horizontal Corporation," Reprinted from December 20, 1993, issue of *Business Week,* by special permission. © 1993 by McGraw Hill, Inc.

each other and change over time, and just what activities need to remain centralized and hierarchical. But the skills required of employees—teamwork, conflict resolution, initiative, openness—are increasingly likely to be required of all employees and will enable organizational development not yet imagined.

Future Organizational Forms

It is difficult to say what organizational form might emerge beyond what we already know, but it will probably be driven to a great extent by information technology. As we develop more and more sophisticated means of moving information through and around our organizations, natural groupings of "users" might emerge to utilize that information. Some experts talk about "networks" as the basic units of organizational structure, envisioning a total organization as a complex arrangement of interconnected networks of people carrying out their work both independently and interdependently. These networks might link independent specialized companies that are each very good at one thing—market research, product design, manufacturing, advertising, sales, distribution, and the like—through a very small central coordinating group. Perhaps the metaphor of a giant brain might be a way to picture

How about No Structure at All?

Imagine yourself being hired by a company which said, "Go find yourself a job someplace in the company and don't worry about a job description or a title or any of that stuff." Would you be excited or scared out of your wits? You certainly would have to depend upon your wits (among other things) to survive in such a system. But there are places where such a free-form structure exists and actually works. As reported in the August 1982 issue of *INC. Magazine,* W. L. Gore and Associates is a company where you create your own job; there are no existing niches, "no titles, no orders, and no bosses." Founder Bill Gore's philosophy was to encourage people to manage themselves; he depended upon voluntary commitment. It has worked successfully for this manufacturer; would it work for everyone?

For some the lack of written rules, the reliance on emergent roles and status, as well as the lack of formal titles would be too ambiguous for comfort. Many would find it difficult to exert the initiative necessary to be effective at Gore. Others would find the opportunity to "try their wings" without the constraint of written job descriptions and within a system where everyone is invited to speak up and take initiative regardless of formal rank appealing and exciting. What would be best for you? Under what system, more of a traditional structure or more of a Gore structure, would you be most satisfied and likely to grow and develop? This is a question worth considering. Research shows that young graduates do better in the long run if they are neither underchallenged nor overchallenged in their first jobs. Gore would be too challenging for some; a bureaucratic organization not enough for others. The more you can know yourself and so pick an organization and position that will challenge you but not overburden you, the more likely you are to learn and develop.

Online Pioneers: The Buzz Never Stops (CEO Roundtable)

Q. What's the difference between running the kind of company you run and running a big company?

Candice Carpenter [CEO, iVillage]: Speed. Leading in conditions in which speed is a very big factor. It puts a lot of additional pressure on all the systems. And you have a lot of very young people, and you're teaching them to be managers at a very accelerated pace without a lot of formal programs.

Stephen J. Paternot [Co-CEO, TheGlobe.com]: Tying into that is just the idea of keeping your entrepreneurial spirit. Things are shifting fast enough that you need to be able to jump into any new idea, shift your company into it and move at light speed.

Fernando F. Espuelas [CEO, StarMedia Network]: I would say the absence of a road map. Not that any business is particularly easy, but when there's nothing that you can follow except your instincts and the little bit of data you're able to gather in this context of a lot of speed, I think there's a lot of intuition that goes into these kinds of very fast-moving environments. . . .

Q. What's the first thing that's sacrificed in the name of speed?

Kevin O'Connor [CEO, Double Click]: Facts . . .

Espuelas: I travel all the time. And I try to talk to as many people as possible. We do monthly all-hands meetings and we actually Web-cast them simultaneously and have people call in and try to have an ongoing dialogue. And now we're doing things which I never thought we'd ever do. We're going to create an employee newsletter. We're doing a lot of things that I used to scoff at when I worked at other companies.

SOURCE: By Judith H. Dobrzynski, "Online Pioneers: The Buzz Never Stops," *New York Times,* November 21, 1999, ©1999 New York Times Company.

Lessons from Silicon Valley

FREEDOM TO FAIL   Encourage all levels of management to try new ideas with no penalty for failure—that's how the Valley stays on the cutting edge.

CHAOS TOLERANCE   Develop a culture that's built for change. The most successful companies have done about-faces and cannibalized their own products before rivals could eat into their markets.

SKILLS FOR THE LONG HAUL   Don't stick with an entrepreneur past his or her time. In the Valley, there are few founders still running their billion-dollar babies. When a company grows past $1 billion, get seasoned help.

READY MONEY   Compensation plans should reward success fast. Stock options may be the ticket for employees to work at Net speed. Watch out, though. They may retire young or use their bankroll to fund a startup.

GENEROSITY BEGETS PROSPERITY   Use the Internet to distribute your products free to millions. That gets them to market fast and builds a customer base. Great for feedback and brand recognition.

BUYING INTO IDEAS   Stay in the vanguard by investing in startups. Valley giants do this to stay plugged into what's cooking in new labs.

SOURCE: Ira Sager, Sidebar to "Cloning the Best of the Valley," *Business Week*, August 25, 1997, p. 146.

such an organization. And like the human brain, there would be many centers of activity going on but all coordinated by the higher "cerebral" centers. A few companies are already using this kind of organization.

The Need for a Common Language of Relationships

No matter what model one chooses for a given organization, the dynamic interconnections and interactions among organizational members are not shown on most organization charts and, particularly, are missing from the traditional pyramidal chart. Though a picture may be worth a thousand words, the snapshot of one aspect of an organization frozen into a chart can never capture the vibrant movement and groupings among members in an actual ongoing organization.

While numerous creative charts have been devised to represent the variety of organizational forms invented to overcome some of the coordination problems described above, it is still necessary to find a way to discuss the interrelationships among organizational members. We need to see how individuals connect with one another to form groups, how groups interact to form the organization, and how the organization interacts with its environment.

In order to talk about organizational subparts and their relationships, we will need a special language enabling us to see the parallels between the workings of groups and organizations of various sizes, purposes, and membership. We will want to talk about commonalities (and differences) among a group of 12 assemblers in a factory, an entire insurance company, a team of teachers devising a curriculum, or a small group of fanatics creating an Internet startup. Though we do not want to throw out the everyday words like *group, company,* and *organization,* we need a language that can incorporate all of these when necessary and not be limited to the images associated with particular words. For example, the word *company* may imply private ownership, profits, and either heartless capitalists or efficient management, depending on one's orientation. Yet even government-owned companies, such as municipal transit systems or those operating under public regulation (e.g., the phone companies), or a commune making candles as a means of support must still deal with the same kinds of organizational issues outlined above.

Therefore, we shall utilize the language of social system analysis, which allows us to interchange the most general word *system* with *group* or *organization* when we wish to emphasize the similarities in diverse groupings. Furthermore, the word *system* emphasizes *interdependencies among subparts,* an advantage we will explain more fully in the rest of the chapter.

The Elements and Boundaries of a System

A system is *any set of mutually interdependent elements.* Mutual interdependence means that a change in any one element causes some corresponding change in the others. In turn, those changes will have an impact back on the original changed element. An example of a simple physical system is the heating system in a house. It consists of a source of heat, a thermostat, and a means of delivering heat to various parts of the house. Drops in temperature below a preset level cause the thermostat to send a signal to start the furnace, which delivers heat until the temperature rises in the house; this registers on the thermostat, which then turns off the furnace until the temperature drops again, and so on in a repetitive cycle. The constant interplay among these elements, mutually adjusting to maintain a roughly constant temperature in the house, demonstrates a system achieving *equilibrium,* in which the system parts are constantly tending toward a particular steady state.

> The organism always works as a whole. We have not a liver or a heart. We are liver and heart and brain and so on. We are not a summation of parts, but a coordination . . . all these different bits that go into the making of an organism.
>
> F. S. Perls
> *Gestalt Therapy Verbatim*

To achieve equilibrium, the system depends upon various *feedback* mechanisms. The thermostat cannot make the "decision" to turn the furnace on or off without "information" from the surrounding air (note Figure 2–4). Imagine, for example, if a member of the household hung a warm coat over the thermostat in a cold and drafty room. The feedback cycle would be disrupted; the thermostat would receive inaccurate information ("the room is very warm") and would signal the furnace to shut off irrespective of the actual temperature of the air (now blocked off by the coat) in the room. *The control mechanisms that maintain equilibrium in any system are dependent upon accurate feedback from various parts of the system and its surrounding environment.*

It is usually easy to identify the *boundaries* of a physical system in relation to the environment in which it exists. The heating system's three components are affected by external factors, such as weather, quality of insulation in the house, temperature desired by the inhabitants, and cost of fuel, yet can be easily identified as separate from these other factors. Nevertheless, the heating system can also be seen, depending on one's interests, as a subpart of other, larger systems that include these external factors: the lighting-heating-plumbing (support) system of the house, the house relative to other houses, a contributor to human pollution systems, and so forth. Thus, how broadly or narrowly we bound a system is a strategic decision based on what will work for the problem(s) needing solution.

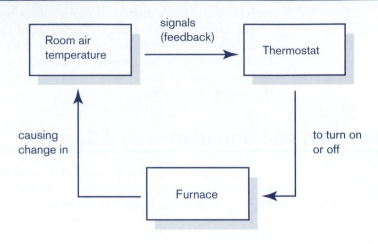

FIGURE 2-4   *Heating System in a Home*

These issues (equilibrium, boundaries and subsystems) are even more complex when looking at *human* social organizations.

A social system also can be seen as consisting of a set of mutually interdependent elements that, when viewed together as an organized whole, can be given a boundary separating the interrelated elements from their environment. For social systems the elements are *behavior* and *attitudes*. An interrelated set of behaviors (interactions and activities) and attitudes (perceptions, feelings, and values) comprise a social system.[2] Because interactions, or exchanges between people, are assumed to be connected with all other elements (by definition) and are observable and countable, they can be used to help draw boundaries around social systems. *Boundaries can* thus *be* operationally *defined by the relative number of interactions among any set of people.* For particular analytical purposes, *a social system is any number of people who have relatively more interactions with one another than with others.*

Implicit in this definition is the notion that virtually any system is a subsystem in some larger system(s), since the system is delimited by *relative* numbers of interactions. Just as the house heating system can for some purposes be seen as the total system (say, if checking out the accuracy of the thermostat) but for other purposes is a subsystem in a larger system, any group of people can be viewed from several perspectives. All the vice presidents in a bank are a social system in that they interact more with one another than with the tellers; but vice presidents and tellers together form another system, since all employees interact with one another more frequently than with, for example, the employees of other banks in the same city.

And like the physical system, which tends toward equilibrium, social systems tend to develop self-adjusting behaviors, which stabilize relationships, make the behavior of those in the system more predictable to members than it would be to others, and perpetuate the system's goals.

As you might guess, the larger the system in question, the more tenuous are the interdependencies. If we speak of the American people as a social system, it may well be true that the way you relate to classmates is affected by and affects the way parents treat children 2,000 miles away, but the connections are not readily traceable and may be unprovable anyway. For our purposes in this book, we will focus on social systems with clearer boundaries and with more easily observable interconnections.

A familiar example is the class scheduling system in a university. Each decision involves and affects numerous people—students, professors, the registrar's office, advisors, building custodians, secretaries, and so on. A professor decides to limit enrollment in a course that normally draws large numbers of students; one result is that students find their options limited and are forced to select other courses, which increases demand for space in the other courses, which may require a change of room to accommodate more students, which bumps another class out of a room, and so on and so on. What seemed to the professor like a simple change causes headaches for many and may well result in pressure on the professor from the dean to accept more students in the course. You can probably think of numerous examples in this same context where attempts to change something at one place in the system result in all kinds of reverberations, good and bad, in other parts of the system. What helps some people may generate problems for other people in the same system.

> The entire ocean is affected by a pebble.
>
> Blaise Pascal

Functional and Dysfunctional Aspects of a System

As you can see, a given action or decision can be functional for some members of a system and dysfunctional for others. The real challenge of managing an organization lies in finding ways to maximize the functional consequences of decisions, minimize dysfunctional effects, and work creatively with situations that inevitably (and often usefully) involve both.

Similarly, because most people are members of more than one social system, it is important to recognize the ways in which the same behavior may be functional in one system and not in another. To illustrate, in most organizations those who reach executive ranks do so not only because of technical skill or knowledge but also because their behavior "fits"—that is, makes other executives comfortable to be with them. Knowing how to behave at the country club, on the golf course, or in the executive dining room is often an important consideration in attaining promotion. Selecting executives by how they fit socially into the higher echelon's particular pastimes can in the short run be highly functional for maintaining harmony. Especially where the potentials for conflict and disagreement are great, as they always are at the top of a large organization, it is much more comfortable to limit fights to those who are "one of our kind," whatever that kind happens to be.

> When Old Boys Ruled
> * The executive should take all the steps he can to ensure that he is personally compatible with superiors.
> * The executive should take exceptional care to find subordinates who combine technical competence with reliability, dependability, and loyalty.
>
> Robert McMurray, "Power and the Ambitious Executive,"
> *Harvard Business Review,* November–December 1973.

Yet the consequences of using such criteria as part of the selection process can be, and have been, extremely dysfunctional for many groups shut out of the top ranks by color, sex, ethnicity, or background. There are surely many more talented leaders among African-Americans, women, Hispanics, Jews, Asians, and non–Ivy League graduates than appear, for example, among the top ranks of most U.S. banks and insurance companies. Not only is the organization ultimately deprived of vast pools of talent and different points of view, but each of the groups is disproportionately kept from advancing, obtaining higher salaries, and power.

Thus what is, at least for awhile, quite functional in one system can be dysfunctional in others, because they have different objectives or purposes. And, as is hinted at in the executive example, *the same behavior can be both functional (promoting harmony) and dysfunctional (reducing talent and diversity available) within a system.* To illustrate, a university sent all secretaries home when the air conditioning failed one excruciatingly hot, humid summer afternoon out of a sense of concern for people's feelings and comfort. Unfortunately, this kindly action backfired in other parts of the system. The university administration sent the secretaries home but not the ground crews working out in the hot sun or the maintenance workers in the various shops across campus. These groups felt discriminated against and unfairly treated. Their morale and attitude toward management were hardly improved. What was functional for one part of the system was dysfunctional for another.

Any act can be analyzed in terms of how well it serves to sustain over time, in relation to surrounding environments, the system(s) in which it occurs. The value one places on whether an act is dysfunctional or not depends on one's point of view. A functional behavior in a system one disagrees with can be considered "bad" (e.g., teaching more effective motivational techniques to recruiters for the Ku Klux Klan), and a dysfunctional act in a system one disagrees with can be considered "good" (e.g., a new assembly worker refusing to go along with cheating in her work group and reporting it to management).

The Supervisor

The supervisor provides an illustration of the difficulty of being functional in all systems. The supervisor is often called the person in the middle. This means that on the one hand management expects him or her to "get the work out from the workers" and push for higher production, while on the other hand the workers (some of whom the supervisor has probably worked with as an equal) expect him or her to be "one of the gang" and understand their problems in attaining, or reasons for not wanting to attain, higher production. Using the language of social systems, the supervisor has membership in two different systems with conflicting goals and finds this a difficult position. Often it can only be solved by withdrawal from the workers—in effect, by giving up membership in their system. Or the supervisor may become extremely permissive with and protective of the workers—in effect, conspiring with them to keep undesirable information from flowing upward. In this case, he or she has forfeited membership in the management system or has at least tried to. Management may not be quite so willing to lose the supervisor and may, in fact, put on even more pressure to increase production. Their efforts feed back on him or her and perpetuate the problem.

But besides the two group systems, management and workers, and the larger system—management, supervisor, workers—the supervisor's personality system is also involved. The supervisor has some views of personal integrity, goals, and ambitions. One kind of person would be concerned about getting ahead in the organization and would respond to the pressure from management by transmitting the pressure to the workers. Leaving aside for a moment the possible negative consequences this pressure might have on his or her ability to secure cooperation from the workers, we can say that the action "pressure on workers" would be functional both for the management system, insofar as it maintains it, and for the supervisor's personality system. By conforming to management's desires, the supervisor can also satisfy his or her own.

However, the supervisor who values highly the friendship of those worked with may reject management's pressure completely and behave as if his or her position were no different from that of the people below. In this case the pressure, which is functional for management, because it maintains management's beliefs about "the nature of workers" and "management's right to manage," is dysfunctional for the

Amherst Has Young Coach in Its Arena

Last year Arena played hockey for Amherst ... This year Arena is the head coach at Amherst and his club is off to a six-game winning streak in Division 3. And, at 25, he's also the youngest hockey coach in the country.

Arena had to change his philosophy. He couldn't pal around with players he had been so friendly with for three seasons.

"I don't hang around with the players as I did in the past," said Arena. "You just can't do it. I'd have a hard time correcting players if I were too friendly with them.

"So, what we did was to agree on a feeling that we're all in this program together and we all want to do the job well. I really like the guys, but most of the time I just see them at practices and games. The players really understand, and we got off to a great start.

"So, instead of being friendly friendly, we're thinking more team friendly, and it has been working."

SOURCE: Bob Monahan, "Amherst Has Young Coach in Its Arena," *Boston Globe,* January 1, 1984. Reprinted courtesy of the *Boston Globe.*

supervisor. To behave that way would not be consistent with his or her own values. Thus, the same act might be functional for one system, yet dysfunctional for another.

Here, however, as elsewhere, the situation may be complicated even more by *unintended and unanticipated consequences,* which can follow from any particular act. In the example above, management's pressure may be functional to the maintenance of what it believes about good managing but may also be in part a *cause* for the need for pressure. Pressure applied repeatedly may cause workers to feel mistrusted, therefore resentful, therefore less cooperative, therefore "requiring" more pressure. The pressure becomes part of a larger system of interdependent relationships, in which management behavior toward workers is both cause and effect of worker behavior and vice versa. Though the pressure may reinforce management solidarity by "confirming" its beliefs about workers, in the larger system presumably designed to make profits for the enterprise as a whole, the pressure may not be as useful as it appears to management (see Figure 2–5).

In short, there may be functional and dysfunctional effects of the same behavior; whether or not the behavior is functional depends on the system in which one judges the behavior. Consequences unintended by the person often occur because too few or wrong systems are considered when anticipating results. One of the manager's key tasks is to ensure that behavior that is functional for particular subsystems but dysfunctional for the organization as a whole is somehow modified so that the total organization does not suffer. This is easier said than done, and much of this course will be aimed at giving you practice in making changes that do not backfire.

We create the city and the city creates us.

Winston Churchill

Openness of Systems and Transformation Processes

Throughout this discussion of social systems we have only referred in passing to the environment of the system. In effect we have talked as if the various systems used as examples were sealed off from their environments, more or less *closed* to outside influences. That was necessary to simplify discussion of a complex subject; but, now

FIGURE 2-5   *Example of Self-Reinforcing System with Functional and Dysfunctional Behavior*

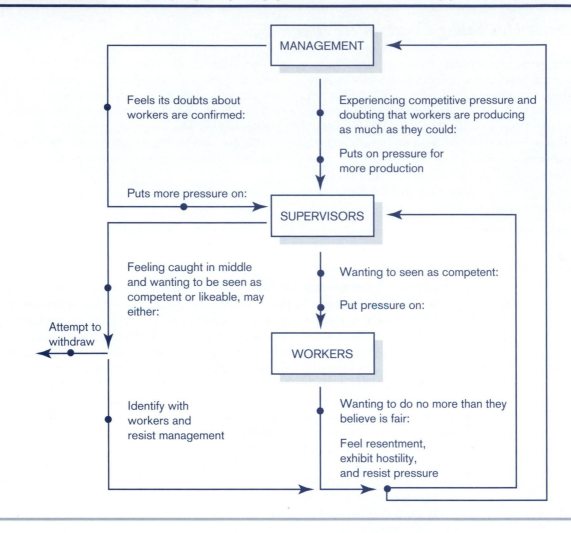

that you have completely mastered the systems concept(!), we can go on to complicate matters a bit.

Ultimately all organizations are open systems—that is, engaged in constant transactions with their environments, which usually consist of a number of other systems. An organization receives *inputs* from its surroundings in the form of finances, raw materials, people, ideas, equipment, and so forth. It then does something to the inputs in a *transformation process,* such as machining pieces, assembling parts, processing information, calculating numbers, building facilities, or treating patients. After these *internal operations,* it sends some kind of finished *output* back into the environment, ranging from tangible products like automobiles and refrigerators, to changed people like recovered patients or educated students, to idea products like reports, analyses, or announcements. The outputs, in turn, become inputs to other systems (see Figure 2-6).

Since organizations are so interrelated with their environments, to remain in equilibrium they must make constant adjustments in the way they operate in order to take into account and cope with changes in inputs and demand for outputs. For example, when wool shortages send prices soaring in the carpet industry, substitutes, such as Acrilan, must be found and developed in order to stay within the price range

FIGURE 2-6   *An Open System*

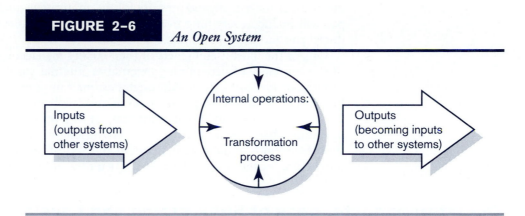

of most consumers. A marketing research firm might collect new data on attitudes from carefully defined groupings and even redefine its sampling group as income levels and population movements shift. A government agency responsible for promoting foreign trade might stay in touch with changes in congressional laws, presidential policy, and foreign government attitudes in order to provide useful guidelines. On the output side, organizational systems need to stay aware of changes in demand, whether for low-mileage cars, liberal arts graduates, or rented warehouse space. Drastic decreases in demand can easily threaten an organization's survival.

All of these environmental changes can and do affect the internal transformation process. *Any system will make adjustments in policies, rules, regulations, and other operating behavior in order to attempt to survive and maintain itself in relation to its environment.*

A hen is only an egg's way of making another egg.

Samuel Butler
Life and Habit

Although organizations often make mistakes, either in interpreting environmental changes or in attempting to compensate for them, the organization will attempt to do what is functional for its survival. One classic example was the March of Dimes organization shifting to other childhood diseases when polio, its original reason for existing, was conquered. Similarly, open *social* systems in organizations are very much affected by the environment around them. The attitudes members bring with them from the wider culture, the particular people who are available to join the system, and economic conditions and their effects on member alternatives for employment are all factors that affect behavior within the system. For instance, when (1) jobs are readily available, (2) young college graduates are the main groups of employees, and (3) there is widespread disillusionment with companies in general, the ability of managers to successfully give direct arbitrary orders without explanation is likely to be considerably diminished. Conversely, when jobs are scarce, employees tend to put up with many forms of treatment they would actively resist in better times.

Further, the demands and standards of whoever receives the social system's output will also affect internal operations. If the system is a total organization, the customers or clients will have considerable influence over the end products, and their response will often force internal adjustments fostering greater chances of survival. If the system is a subsystem of an organization, like a work team on the shop floor or a group of nursing administrators, its "clients" will be other parts of the organization, including management, and pressure for the appropriate quality and quantity of output will include everything from general disapproval and loss of privileges to reduced pay and threats of firing.

One of the most useful tenets of total quality management (TQM) is the notion of the centrality of determining external or internal customer requirements, then meeting or exceeding them. Although customer importance has always been given lip service, TQM forces rigorous analysis and feedback.

In general, then, any system must make at least minimal alterations in its internal operations, based on feedback from its environment, in order to survive. To increase the effectiveness of the system, frequent and delicate adjustments are necessary; the more complex the system, the more difficult the adjustments.

The Interconnectedness of Subsystems and Levels

While much of this book treats environmental facts as givens, or constants, in order to focus on internal relationships and their consequences, it is important to be aware of the connections of any of the systems we look at (small groups, individual, interpersonal, leadership, and intergroup) to the systems and subsystems surrounding them. *The power in systems thinking lies in remembering to trace through what is connectable to what to check to see if (1) a behavior that does not at first make sense survives because it is functional to some other system(s) and (2) a change in one aspect of a system will lead to other changes that are in the desired direction.* Many a manager's greatest difficulties occur when he or she starts to solve a problem in one subsystem without seeing its connections and roots in a wider setting. Managers who forget to test if they are addressing the right problem are like Americans traveling in a foreign country who speak English to a non-English-speaking resident and, when not understood, repeat the same phrase over again, s-l-o-w-e-r and LOUDER.

For example, we have seen managers, excited by a management development tool like stress management, try to solve symptoms of stress resulting from unclear or overloaded job responsibilities by sending all their subordinates off to learn meditation and relaxation techniques. After the executives have learned to relax in the off-the-job training session (often conducted at a plush resort hotel), they return to work and soon find themselves more upset than ever, because higher-level management still fears delegating authority, demands high performance, and has still not clarified what is expected of the subordinates. Not only do the original problems remain unsolved but a potentially useful training tool for some situations gets a bad name.

It is important, therefore, to shift focus periodically from problem relationships within a subsystem to the links of that subsystem with others. There is a saying that a fish is the last one to discover water, exactly because water is "always" there. The fish can spend its time worrying about its food and digestion as long as it is in the water and breathing automatically. Only when it is yanked out of the water does it notice its absence. With people, as with fish, it often takes a catastrophe (or an outside observer) to make visible the fundamental interconnections between the system and its environment. It is helpful, then, occasionally to take a detached view of puzzling behavior and ask *what function it is serving for whom*, rather than too quickly judge it harshly as irrelevant, wasteful, immoral, or foolish. Systems thinking encourages *understanding and acceptance of others' behavior*, at least as a first step in viewing organizations.

Equilibrium versus Change in Systems

As indicated earlier, every system has a tendency to maintain a state of balance, or *equilibrium*. When the flow of raw materials into a manufacturing firm is balanced by the flow of products out of the company, that system can be described as maintaining a state of equilibrium. Should machinery break down, workers go on strike, poor planning occur, and so forth (all transformation processes), the system is thrown out of balance; management then devotes its attention to the reestablishment of equilibrium (repair the machinery, settle the strike, revise schedules). The process is similar to the way the human body works when it experiences stress from disease or accident. One or another subsystem (such as circulatory, autonomic, and respiratory) or a combination of them mobilizes to reestablish the balance of survival-related processes.

Similarly, inputs to the system may cause disequilibrium—flawed raw materials, shortages of critical supplies, misleading or erroneous information about demand, an inability to hire people with needed skills, and so on. Again, management will attempt to establish a new equilibrium by seeking alternate sources of supply or substituting raw materials, more market research, redesigned jobs, or whatever can help gain a balance between inputs and outputs.

Equilibrium does not mean that nothing ever changes; it is more a *dynamic* process in which the various elements adjust to each other to maintain the system's performance and viability in relation to its environment.

While the integrity of a system depends upon its ability to maintain a basic state of equilibrium, its *development* and long-run survival often depend on the ability to realign aspects of its subsystems and modify its transformation processes; this makes disequilibrium at times inevitable and desirable. If a system for too long resists fundamental environment changes, it will eventually decay; if it is too responsive, it may lose its ability to sustain its coherence and identity. A company, for example, can get into trouble if it does not adjust to consumer interests, but it can also lose money if it tries to cater to every whim. In short, every system works toward an internal state of equilibrium by maintaining its existing balance of forces (the status quo); at the same time, every system struggles to respond to the pressures for change as the surrounding environment demands it.

> In any organization, large or small, there must be a certain clarity and orderliness; if things fall into disorder, nothing can be accomplished. Yet orderliness, as such, is static and lifeless, so there must be plenty of elbow room and people for breaking through the established order.
>
> Therefore, any organization has to strive continuously for the orderliness of order and the disorderliness of creative freedom. And the specific danger inherent in large-scale organization is that its natural bias and tendency favor order at the expense of creative freedom.
>
> E. Schumacher
> *Small Is Beautiful*, p. 229.

While you need not accept the status quo just because you understand its function better, we suggest that you maintain a healthy respect for the resistance of systems to change, as well as for the ability of system members to reestablish equilibrium when new inputs are attempted by managers. If every system changed continually, life would be just too confusing and unpredictable to act. One confirmation of this emerged from Freud's work; it was the realization that even neurotic behavior causing great pain to an individual will be clung to as long as it is providing more satisfaction to the person than the uncertain rewards of giving it up. In systems terms, if one of the interdependent elements gives at least partial satisfaction to the personality system, it may persist despite its partially dysfunctional consequences for the total system. In fact, the individual system may be sustaining or integrating itself by the very tension that exists between the functional and dysfunctional consequences of various elements.

Larger social systems, like individual systems, can persist for long periods of time with some dysfunctional elements; remember the managing system of pressuring supervisors that was partly causing worker resistance as well as trying to overcome it? Groups, as well as individuals, may persist in behavior that is less than fully functional for the maintenance of the total system if partial satisfaction of some needs is being derived from the behavior. Present partial satisfactions are often preferred over uncertain future ones, because the costs involved in attaining new satisfactions may not seem worth the risk involved.

Understand the many functions of any behavior you observe before judging it as right or wrong, good or bad. And when you do act, watch for the connected reactions you didn't expect, so that you can adjust your plans.

KEY CONCEPTS FROM CHAPTER 2

1. Fundamental issues for any organization to accomplish its work:
   a. Goals.
   b. Decision making.
   c. Division of labor.
   d. Recruiting.
   e. Communications.
   f. Motivation.
   g. Control.
   h. Coordination.
   i. Environmental scanning and organizational mission.
   j. Rewards.
2. The form of an organization can vary widely.
   a. Entrepreneurial organization.
   b. The traditional pyramidal structure..
   c. The linking-pin model.
   d. Departmentalization, by product, by customer or service, by function, by geographic area, or by some combination of each.
   e. SBU.
   f. The matrix model.
   g. Horizontal process organization.
   h. Future forms.
3. A system is any set of mutually interdependent elements. Every system is composed of subsystems and is itself a subsystem of a larger system. Changes in one part of a system are likely to lead to changes in other parts.
4. The boundaries of a social system are defined by the relative number of interactions among any set of people.
5. Any action can be functional for one (or more) system(s), but dysfunctional for another.
6. Any act can be both functional and dysfunctional for the same system.
7. All organizations are open systems, and:
   a. Take in inputs, transform them into outputs, and exchange those outputs with their environment for new inputs.
   b. Seek to maintain equilibrium by resisting changes in their environment.
   c. Adjust to environmental changes or decay.

PERSONAL APPLICATION EXERCISE

Assessing the College (or University) Structure of Which You Are a Part

- What is the formal structure? What areas/specialties are grouped together? How are programs (like undergraduate, graduate, part-time) managed? Do faculty members belong to program groups, departments, or both? How are the administrative activities structured and grouped? How, if at all, are they connected to the academic groupings? Who evaluates whom in the structure?
- Draw a picture that represents the structure. Is it traditional? Is it some mixture of forms? (You may need to talk to people in order to develop your picture.) Don't worry about getting all the details or even getting it "right." There may *be* no "right."
- What's good about it (i.e., what makes it work well in relation to college/university goals?)? Where do you fit in? What impact does the structure have on you? Does it support your learning? Your satisfaction?

- What's bad about it (i.e., what are the problems and bottlenecks that impede goal achievement?)? Are there negative effects for you?
- Try to create a *new* picture that you think would reflect an improvement over the old. Why is it better? Does it look like anything discussed in Chapter 2?

SUGGESTED READINGS

Ashforth, B. E. "Climate Formation: Issues and Extensions." *Academy of Management Review,* October 1985, pp. 837–47.

Ashmos, D. P., and G. P. Huber. "The Systems Paradigm in Organization Theory: Correcting the Record and Suggesting the Future." *Academy of Management Review* 12 (1987), pp. 607–21.

Beckett, J. A. *Management Dynamics: The New Synthesis.* New York: McGraw-Hill, 1971.

Benedetto, R. F. *Matrix Management.* Dubuque, Iowa: Kendall/Hunt, 1985.

Bertalanffy, L. von. *General Systems Theory: Foundations, Development, Applications.* New York: George Braziller, 1968.

Churchman, C. West. The *Systems Approach.* New York: Dell Publishing, 1968.

Davis, S., and P. Lawrence. *Matrix.* Reading, MA: Addison-Wesley Publishing, 1977.

Drucker, P. F. *Technology, Management, and Society.* New York: Harper & Row, 1970.

Fink, S.; R. S. Jenks; and R. Willits. *Designing and Managing Organizations.* New York: McGraw-Hill/Irwin, 1983.

Forrester, R., and A. B. Drexler. "A Model for Team-Based Organization Performance." *Academy of Management Executive* 13, 3 (August 1999), pp. 36–49.

Galbraith, J. *Organization Design.* Reading, MA: Addison-Wesley Publishing, 1977.

Kanter, R. M. *When Giants Learn to Dance.* New York: Simon & Schuster, 1989.

Katz, D., and R. L. Kahn. *The Social Psychology of Organizations.* New York: John Wiley & Sons, 1966.

Keidel, R. *Game Plans: Sports Strategies for Business.* New York: E. P. Dutton, 1985.

Lawrence, P. R., and J. W. Lorsch. "Differentiation and Integration in Complex Organizations." *Administrative Science Quarterly* 12 (1967), p. 2.

———. *Organization and Environment.* Boston: Division of Research, Graduate School of Business, Harvard University, 1967.

Lewis, P. S., and P. M. Fandt. "Organizational Design: Implications for Managerial Decision Making." *Advanced Managerial Journal.* Autumn 1989, pp. 13–16.

Likert, R. *New Patterns of Management.* New York: McGraw-Hill, 1961.

Miles, R. E. *Theories of Management: Implications for Organizational Behavior and Development.* New York: McGraw-Hill, 1975.

Pascale, R. *Managing on the Edge: How the Smartest Companies Use Conflict to Stay Ahead.* New York: Simon & Schuster, 1990.

Schein, E. H. *Organizational Psychology.* 2nd ed. Englewood Cliffs, NJ: Prentice-Hall, 1970.

Seiler, J. A. *Systems Analysis in Organizational Behavior.* New York: McGraw-Hill/Irwin and the Dorsey Press, 1967.

Townsend, A. M.; S. DeMarie; and A. R. Hendrickson, "Virtual Teams: Technology and the Workplace of the Future," *Academy of Management Executive* 12, 3 August 1998), pp. 17–29.

Weick, K. E. *The Social Psychology of Organizing.* Reading, MA: Addison-Wesley Publishing, 1979.

Wenger, E., and W. M. Snyder. "Communities of Practice: The Organizational Frontier." *Harvard Business Review,* 78, 1 (January–February 2000), pp. 139–45.

Woodward, J. *Industrial Organization: Theory and Practice.* New York: Oxford University Press, 1965.

The Work Group

Designing for Teams

[At P&G] Project groups were the central design theme. Members of teams work in open cubicles, grouped together, and can all see each other, regardless of rank. File cases are literally on wheels, and offices are designed in "bricks" that can be reconfigured in short order if a team needs to get bigger or smaller. P&G personnel travel between floors by escalator, instead of conversation-zapping elevators. So-called huddle rooms are strategically placed where teams can come together to brainstorm. P&G also equipped spaces within the building, such as lunchrooms and lounges, with electronic whiteboards that can convert scribblings to e-mail. Corridors are deliberately wide and have couches where workers can stop for a quick chat. The building opened last July, and Jones is thrilled. He's convinced it will deliver 20 percent to 30 percent productivity gains because "data sharing is immediate, and higher-quality decisions are made faster."

SOURCE: Joan O. C. Hamilton, Stephen Baker, and Bill Nasic, "The New Workplace Walls Are Falling as the 'Office of the Future' Finally Takes Shape," *Business Week,* April 29, 1996, p. 106.

"The demands of the task, technology, or management style can often pull behavior from a group regardless of who the particular members are."

Teamwork and Empowerment on the Rise

A majority of American employees are involved in work teams and feel empowered to make important decisions pertaining to their jobs, according to a Gallup Poll conducted for the American Society for Quality Control. Eighty percent of employees surveyed say some form of team activity occurs in their workplace. Of those, two-thirds say they actively participate in team activities themselves . . .

"Teamwork is becoming firmly rooted as a way of life and a vehicle for employees to feel more empowered," says Jack West, ASQC president. "Quality improvement is proving to be an effective catalyst for this change."

SOURCE: *Quality Digest,* November 1993.

One of the most important subsystems in any organization is the work group. Although many students and managers think of organizations as consisting of a collection of individuals, each doing a separate and distinct job, a large and increasing portion of the world's work is actually done in some kind of group. Even when the individual employee is not formally assigned to a clearly defined group of people, much of his or her work will likely be carried out in conjunction with a particular set of other people, and feelings of "being part of a group" will emerge. Even executives who often like to think of themselves as rugged individualists seldom work alone or in isolation; they are members of a top management team, committees, task forces, study groups, and so forth, which directly affect their success or failure in the organization.

Yet it is not easy to work effectively in a group. Anyone who has ever had to coordinate activities and come to decisions in conjunction with other people will remember at times having felt something like, "If only I could get rid of the others, I could do this job much better myself and save a lot of time, too!" Working together, at least in most Western individualistic cultures, is not easily or automatically accomplished.

God created the world in 6 days—but had the advantage of working alone.

C. Roland Christenson
Commencement Speech,
Babson College, 1987

Why Groups?

Why then is group work so recurrent? Perhaps the most important reason is that few jobs can be done alone. Only when it is clear that one person has much greater expertise than the combined efforts of others could yield, the task requires a creative synthesis and individual intuition, or when solo work will be good training, is work best done by lone individuals. As organizations become more technologically complex and require ever greater numbers of experts, it takes more than one person's energy, knowledge, skills, and time to get most complicated jobs done. Furthermore, when tasks are even the least bit complex, a division of labor makes it possible to use individual efforts more systematically and to take advantage of different talents and skills. A committee studying ways to cut fuel consumption in a company, for example, could have all members engage in the same research and discussion activities, but the complexities of the task make it desirable to divide up the work. One member might review technical literature, another survey the existing heating/cooling system, a third investigate what other companies have done, another check costs of conversion to alternate fuels, and so forth.

Yet in such a committee, as in other group activities where participants have different assignments from one another, activities must somehow be coordinated in order to not duplicate efforts, leave something undone, or work at cross purposes. Thus, a group must find a way to allocate work, coordinate activities, define and agree upon goals, and then gain the commitment of members to carry out the group's work in a manner consistent with its objectives.

Groups also exist for another, more personal, set of reasons. Even where a task does not call for coordinated effort, people working near one another often form relationships to fill social needs for conversation, companionship, or friendship. Human beings are social animals and seem to need human association as much as they need food and drink. So groups often form for reasons above and beyond needs for task coordination. Indeed, for many members of work groups, individual needs for social relationship may be even more powerful in affecting behavior than organizational objectives.

Long before getting jobs, everyone has developed considerable experience with groups; they are the primary units of all social systems. Most people are born into a group—the family—and spend the greater part of their lives living, working, and playing in a wide variety of groups. When young, they belong to cliques, gangs, or clubs. As they grow up, they tend to move into social settings where group belonging gives support and provides avenues to do things they could not do by themselves. Thus, it is not surprising that, in the work world, people continue to find groups to be a principal vehicle for carrying out tasks, not solely to seek superior organization goals through collective effort, but to meet individual needs as well.

What is more surprising is how difficult it is for groups in organizations to be effective and satisfying to their members. Occasionally this is caused by groups being utilized to do what could better be executed by one individual, as implied in the old joke: "A camel is a horse designed by a committee." More often, however, groups are just not run effectively; members do not know how to help the group take fullest advantage of its potential. We will address this issue in depth in Chapter 6, because we believe that the ability to help make a group function effectively can be learned and is worth learning. Thus, we aim to help you improve both your *understanding* of how task groups work and your *skills* at getting what you want from the work groups of which you become a member.

Although many of the concepts we will introduce apply equally well to nonorganizational groups, we will focus on those that are task oriented, because at least half of an adult's waking life is spent at work and most education does not give emphasis to this important area of concern. Nonwork applications of what is learned can be a personal bonus for mastering the course materials.

We can call upon your past experiences to bring to life the several concepts we need to build on. For example, you probably remember groups in which you played a dominant part and others in which you were more on the sidelines, times when you were part of the "in group" and times when you were on the "outs." Think about some of the groups of which you currently are or have recently been a member. How are they organized? What is your place in them? Who controls them? Is there equality among members or a "pecking order"? These are the kinds of questions we will be addressing throughout the next few chapters.

As we go along, we encourage you to use your own immediate and past experiences to validate the theories and concepts that will be introduced. Most of these concepts will also be directly applicable to the classroom setting and will help you understand various aspects of your own experiences as the course unfolds. You should come out with a better sense of the consequences of your own membership in various groups, how your sense of individuality is affected, and how you can strike a balance among (1) your needs, (2) those of other individual members, and (3) the needs of the group as an entity.

How Do You Know When A Group *Is*?

What exactly do we mean by a "group"? Is it any collection of individuals, like strangers at a bus stop, or is it something more? As explained in Chapter 2, any social system is defined by the relative number of interactions among its components. Although the boundary can be drawn anywhere, depending on one's purpose, work groups often are clearly identifiable to others and to their own members. From now on we will use the word *group* to mean small face-to-face groups, consisting of more than 2 people and usually no more than 12 to 15. Such a group has an existence over an extended period of time, tends to see itself as separate and distinguishable from others around it, and has members who are mutually aware of their membership. As noted in the beginning of this chapter, some organizational groups are not formally defined as such but function nevertheless, as distinguishable units.

If a group appears to its members as a useful vehicle for meeting individual needs, then keeping relationships going among members of any group becomes an end in itself. This is why the size of the group is an important factor. If a group becomes too large, it is difficult for the members to maintain direct personal relations, and there is an increasing chance of fragmentation into subgroups.

In summary then, we can determine the existence of a group by noting its *size*, its *degree of differentiation from other groups*, the *existence of personal relations that have some duration, identification of the members with the group*, and often some *common goals*.

Thus, a small collection of people waiting at a bus stop would not be a group by the definition we use in this book. While every individual presumably has the same goal, namely to catch a bus, it is not a common goal in the sense of being a goal that will result from joint effort. While a few individuals might be friends, most would be strangers or, at best, "nodding acquaintances" from the same neighborhood. Furthermore, individually they would not think of themselves as an identifiable group.

By defining groups as stated above we include the following types:

1. Groups that are ongoing parts of an organization, like departments or work teams.
2. Temporary task groups, like a committee or special problem-solving group whose life is compressed into a defined span of time. (Note the differences from ongoing groups in the Managerial Tools box.)
3. Groups that are voluntarily formed purely for friendship or other social needs as noted earlier; these will not be our focus but must be considered since they exist within and across types (1) and (2) above and directly influence these formal system groups.

The Need for Some Concepts

Students have often asked us why it is necessary to have a fancy conceptual scheme for analyzing groups. Isn't common sense enough? Unfortunately, common sense can carry you just so far—and usually not far enough. Social science has given us some valuable organizing principles that fortunately help to sort out what otherwise might be an undifferentiated mass. Everything that one sees can appear equally important—and there are many things one is not likely to notice without some kind of guideposts. The ultimate object of analysis is action: doing something to solve problems or to sustain good results. But action is too risky without good analysis of *why*

Differences between Ongoing and Temporary Work Groups

Ongoing Groups	Temporary Groups
Conduct most organization work that is predictable, continuing, regular.	Used for unusual projects or problems when diversity of opinion, talent, or expertise needed. Task forces, committees, project teams.
Job surrounded with a sense of permanence; a presumption that, with satisfactory performance and the absence of unforeseen catastrophe, the group will continue indefinitely.	Job is temporary, to be worked on until done; then members are expected to disperse to some other task(s) with some other group(s).
Existence of a common identity (as a member of this department or work group) and the sense of a common purpose. Can result in too little diversity of opinion or in forced conformity, or in both.	Member primary loyalty is elsewhere to ongoing "home" group; often act as "representatives," not independent problem solvers. Difficult to achieve common purpose. Can result in maneuvering for advantage, defensiveness about home group, hidden agendas to settle old scores. Members less committed to temporary group, may withhold their time, energy, expertise.
History of working together often results in considerable knowledge about one another and patterned role relationships; makes working together comfortable. Danger of freezing others into existing behavior roles.	Sense of working with "strangers"; need to develop skills of building effective relationships rapidly and being effective in dealing with emergent process problems promptly.
A recognized boss; focal point for resolving issues and making decisions when all else fails. Also a recognized source of organizational rewards.	Likely to be self-governing or led by a chairperson with less clearly defined authority and less power; rewards for effort unclear, while home-group work piles up; individual members may see opportunity of contact with people from other parts of the organization (sometimes in higher positions) as way to make good impression. Can lead to "grandstanding"; focus on audience, not problems.

things are as they are. We all need ways of figuring out just what factors have led to the particular behaviors we find in groups of which we're a part or which we somehow have to manage.

Although in actuality no social system sits still while you hold different parts constant, for analytical purposes we will take the liberty of talking as if various components of a work group can be separately examined. Only then can you begin to improve your ability to understand and affect the behavior of the groups of which you are a member.

We will start by introducing a basic social system conceptual scheme, which will help you to organize the pieces and put together the puzzle that explains why a group has developed in its particular way and what might be done to alter its development.

The scheme we have chosen identifies four essential factors: (1) everything that individuals and the organization bring to a group, (2) what the job itself requires, (3) what behavior and feelings result from (1) and (2), and (4) the consequences of what is actually happening. The scheme is a systematic way of identifying what is going on, why it is going on, and what difference it makes.

A Closer Look at Social System Concepts: Factors Affecting Group Behavior

In Chapter 2 you were introduced to the concept of a social system consisting of two mutually interdependent elements: *behavior* and *attitudes*.[1] We now look at groups in depth, expanding on the concepts to heighten their analytical usefulness.

Behavior

The most directly observable aspect of a social system is the *behavior* of its members—that is, their *interactions* and *activities*. *Interactions—exchanges of words or objects among two or more members*—are particularly crucial types of behavior, since their frequency helps determine system boundaries, friendships, and other feelings. Other types of behavior can be categorized as *activities—that which members do while they are in the group except for their interactions with other people*—such as operating a machine, writing on paper, and issuing a license. In addition to these kinds of work-related activities, there are likely to be a variety of nonwork activities, such as drinking coffee, listening to music, or straightening papers on the desk.

Attitudes

Attitudes constitute the other category used for sorting out the parts of a social system. These can include neutral *perceptions* ("Whenever I help Charley, he smiles"), *feelings* ("I like my job"), or *values* ("Nothing is more important than being honest in my dealings with the people I work with").[2] When all three are combined, the result is reflected in the unique way in which each individual perceives a given situation or reacts to others. We look at such issues in depth in Chapters 8 and 10 when we discuss the importance of the self-concept and the complexities for interpersonal communication. For now, keep in mind that these are important elements of any social system.

Norms

Perhaps the most important type of attitude is that which members of any group inevitably develop about how members in good standing *ought* to behave in that group. These attitudes we call *norms*; they are the cement that holds a group together, because they tell members exactly what behavior is believed desirable to foster the group's goals and maintain its existence. *Norms are unwritten rules, shared beliefs of most group members about what behavior is appropriate and attainable to be a member in good standing.* Behind every norm is the implicit statement: "Follow this norm because, if you don't, the group will be harmed somehow." For example, some common norms in student groups are: "Don't act as if you're trying to impress the person with authority" (as in, "Don't brownnose the teacher"), "Don't act like a big deal," "Participate at least a little, but don't dominate the conversation," "Try not to say anything that will hurt other members' feelings." Can you see what members of a student group might perceive as the dangers if these norms were not followed? Here are a few norms of an executive group at the head office of a national company: "Executives do not bring their lunches," "Eat or take coffee only with your own group, unless you have specific business with others," "Always wear your suit jacket when going in or out of the building, no matter how hot it is," "Carry only a thin zipper briefcase, not the three- or five-inch one the company gives out."

Norms such as these are not always explicit; often they are understood implicitly (or assumed to be understood). Frequently, the only way a norm is observable is by inadvertently breaking it and seeing others' reactions. If a norm has been broken, members will usually react in some kind of negative way—with a dirty look, a sarcastic comment, a "joke" that has a cutting edge, even a physical punishment, such as a "friendly" punch on the arm, or some other negative response. Those who consistently violate norms and cannot be pushed into going along will usually be given the worst punishment of all: They will be ignored and considered inferior. Norms are not written on all members' foreheads; they can only be inferred from watching actual behavior, since they are not the behavior itself but the *beliefs* in most members' minds about what behavior should be.[3] While behavior common to all members of a group usually indicates existence of a norm, it may also be just coincidental or customary. Some checking out of what members believe, or observing whether a nonconformer is punished, may be necessary to establish a norm's existence.

Because norms are not universal—in some executive groups, for example, it may be considered phony *not* to try to impress the boss or weak *not* to dominate conversations—each group develops its own norms, which give the group its particular character. And very often groups feel not only that their norms are useful ways of guiding members' behavior but are inevitable, correct, and better than any possible alternatives. Thus, violation of the norms by current members or even members of other groups is judged quite harshly even though an outside observer might be puzzled at the intensity of the group members' beliefs in its own ways.

> The longer I was in the world of managers, the more I missed my union buddies, their ribald spirit, our singing together, their sensuousness, their sexuality. By comparison, managers were a deadhead lot who had traded humor and sensuality for the role-playing Kabuki world of the corporate headquarters. I have met more people having fun as clowns on one plant floor than in all of the many corporate headquarters I have gone in and out of.
>
> [From an Interview of a Manager, Bob Schrank]
> Bob Sales
> *Boston Globe*

Have you ever entered a new group and found, quite accidentally, that you have violated members' notions of "proper" behavior? Here is an example of a new employee discovering a powerful norm:

> A young business student got a summer job working at a bank as a credit trainee. He arrived on a hot Monday morning in a suit and tie and reported for work on the 16th floor. As the air conditioning had been off during the weekend, the open office where all trainees sat was quite warm. Noticing that others had removed their jackets and hung them over the backs of their chairs, the new employee did the same. At 10 A.M., everyone got up for coffee break at a wagon brought to the floor. Afterward, the eager newcomer returned to his desk and resumed studying the material he had been given. Soon his neighbor was motioning to him to put on his jacket. "Thanks, but I'm comfortable this way," he replied. A few minutes later the neighbor cleared his throat and said in a whisper, "It's time to put on your jacket." Enjoying being in his shirtsleeves, the newcomer smiled but continued as he was. A few minutes later the neighbor, now looking irritated, said, "Really, we all put our jackets on now; you should too!" Genuinely bewildered at his apparently irrational ignoring of the temperature but not wanting to create problems with strangers, the puzzled student put on his jacket and resisted no more. But his initial enthusiasm for banking diminished. It wasn't until many years later that he realized that putting on jackets after 10 A.M. was probably a reflection of public opening hours at the bank and that the trainees did what the loan officers were doing down on the first floor.

Norms can be useful in helping facilitate the group's work or they can hinder it. And they can be highly conscious and explicit or unconscious and automatic. Occasionally, norms can even take on the quality of *magic,* as in the bank example. That is, behavior that may once have been productive continues to be enforced even when there is no longer any use for it (except to bind members together). But whatever their degree of helpfulness and consciousness, when norms are agreed to by most members and strongly held, they have a powerful impact on behavior.

Norms tend to develop around particular subjects of interest to group members. Among other areas, most groups have norms about how much effort and output is expected of members, how to dress (as at the bank described above), the use and meaning of time, the degree to which expressions of feeling are allowed, how to handle conflict, and so forth. The longer groups work together, the more likely they are to develop elaborate sets of norms to guide behavior. One of the difficulties faced by temporary groups is the need to establish shared norms among members who may have quite different ideas about appropriate behavior, based on the norms of their various home groups. Can you generate a list of norms from any group(s) of which you are a member? Which norms are task-related? Which serve personal interactions of members? Which are counterproductive? Answering these questions can give you valuable insights into the group and your behavior in it. It can also be the first step in changing norms that are not useful or desirable.

Sources of Norms

Where do these powerful guidelines for behavior come from? Some are derived from the general culture of the country or region in which the group exists. Although not everyone from a particular culture will have the same norms, making generalizations dangerous, the wider culture can be one influence on group norms.

Most Americans, for example, are raised with great consciousness about the value of time, and a high percentage of adults wear watches. Thus, these general attitudes about time often carry over into organizational groups, which emphasize being on time, getting right to work, and so on. In many Asian and Latin American cultures, time is not seen as a continuous line that is running out, and its value is different, so that being on time for meetings is less likely to emerge as a group norm.

Some norms originate in the culture of the particular organization (i.e., in the general practices and attitudes of the wider organization) and then are carried into particular groups. To illustrate, IBM for years stressed that male executive employees should wear white shirts and dark suits. There was general acceptance by IBM employees that this mode of dress was proper so that in most IBM executive groups formal dress readily became the norm. Even at offsite training programs held in resort hotels, IBM salesmen were likely to be wearing dark suits and white shirts even when groups from other companies using the facilities dressed in casual clothes.

> The new president of a conservative company that did not especially welcome him used his understanding of norms to test how well he was doing in winning other executives over to his side. Noting that all executives wore a tie and jacket in the office, he began to take off his jacket as soon as he got to the office and would walk around all day in shirtsleeves. By observing which executives started to take off their jackets at work, he had a quick and visible indicator of "converts" and could tell at a glance whether he was making progress in gaining allies.

Other norms may be carried into a group by members with a common background and common interests—ethnic, educational, or religious. For example, work groups with a majority of southern Europeans may tend to expect members to be readily expressive of feelings, while a group of northern Europeans may expect restraint and understatement from members. Similarly, groups composed of women or minority members may be more likely to value expressiveness than groups of white males, reflecting the expectations of the wider society. Student groups in a classroom are likely to reflect the norms of the school itself. A large-city business school may encourage one to be aggressive and competitive, while a small rural liberal arts college may be more likely to encourage one to be polite and avoid conflict.

Finally, some norms arise from critical incidents or events in a group's life, which cause the group to learn "the way things ought to be." Perhaps an angry fight between two members over the correctness of a work procedure led to a reprimand from a supervisor for fighting—and from that experience the group developed a strong norm that insists "no one should air his troubles or disagree with a fellow member in front of anyone from management." Sometimes norms come from over-reactions or overgeneralizations from one or two experiences—and then remain untested because "everyone knows" that dire consequences will follow if the norm is violated.

Values

Another important type of attitudes is *values*. While *norms are shared ideas of "correct" behavior in the group, values are more fundamental notions of ideal behavior, usually unattainable but to be striven for.* Values are seldom explicit but very much shape how members interpret events and form expectations about behavior.

For example, in some groups members believe that it is "right" that individuals should always put group needs ahead of their own personal interests. Individuals are expected to subordinate their desires for the betterment of the group. An extreme version of this value is found in the traditional families in India, where even marriage and career choice are made by elders with overall family benefit in mind. The opposite of such values might be found in a contemporary American family where each child is taught from an early age to listen to his or her conscience and make choices accordingly.

In a work setting, such group values as work before pleasure, friendship and loyalty above all, the customer is always right, or everyone should look out for his or her own interests, strongly determine how members behave, even though they are not always attainable.

Quite often, however, conflicting values may be held by various members of a group or even by one member, and this can cause serious tension at crucial times. For instance, telling the truth is a commonly held value but so is avoiding hurting others. These two values are not always compatible. In groups there are often value differences underlying questions of how important it is to talk through strong disagreements: "majority rules" (so outvoted members should accept defeat gracefully) versus "everyone gets his day in court" (so dissatisfied members must somehow be placated).

In general, it is important to look and listen for underlying values even though groups do not always make their values explicit.

Rank or Status

Finally, an important set of attitudes has to do with perceived relative standing within the group. Few groups can (or even want to) sustain complete equality among members; over time some members are seen as better at providing what the group needs, while others are perceived as less able or willing. We discuss the evolution and impact of differential status within groups in more detail in Chapter 5; for now, it is useful to note that groups informally recognize different rankings among members, even when group members may adopt "equality" norms that forbid discussing such differences.

The Basic Social System Conceptual Scheme

With a more developed picture of the elements of any social system, we are now ready to present the basic conceptual scheme of this book (summarized in Figure 3–4). The material that follows is designed to help you sort out the *causes* of behavior from the *symptoms* you can observe. It is hard enough to observe accurately what is going on, since people do not hold still for leisurely study, do not always say why they are behaving as they are (or do not know), or change their behavior when an outsider is watching. But even seeing accurately may not explain why a group is acting as it is—holding down production, sabotaging quality, voluntarily working extra hours without complaint, protecting one another, fighting about everything—in

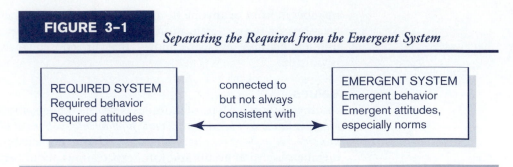

FIGURE 3–1   *Separating the Required from the Emergent System*

short, behaving in ways that are functional and should be preserved or dysfunctional and should be changed. The difficulty is in being able to analyze *all* the factors that together account for or cause the behavior. Since most behavior is caused by many interwoven forces, it is critical to identify more than just one or two. This will ultimately allow for sensible action.

Required Behavior

A helpful conceptual distinction in tracing the source of behavior and attitudes is to separate out that part of a group's behavior and attitudes which is *required* or *given* by the larger system (organization) of which it is a part and that which *emerges* from the interactions of the group (see Figure 3–1). *The required system is what the organization requires of group members as part of their jobs.* It consists of the behavior and attitudes that management has determined to be required of some group of employees in order to successfully meet the organization's objectives. The requirements usually sound logical—especially to the managers who have created them—and specify what people are supposed to do.

The behavioral requirements include both activities and interactions with others. These requirements usually begin with (1) *required activities,* tasks assigned to the group, such as assemble so many parts per hour, sell so many contracts per month, make so many loans per week, and so forth. The required activities may be further broken into much more detail, such as pull necessary parts from bins, visually inspect them as you go, assemble them in this prescribed sequence, test the assembled product, then place it on the finished goods rack. (2) In addition, there are likely to be some *required interactions*: "Get the forms from Clerk A, inquire if there are any more, and after checking them over give Agent C an assignment." (3) Finally, there will usually be some *required attitudes,* such as: "Don't be insolent when receiving instructions," or "Be loyal to our products," or "Don't make fun of the clients."

These requirements are developed by the organization and are frequently called the "formal system." They are usually contained in job descriptions and organizational rulebooks and in directions from superiors, though sometimes they are just seen as "part of the job" and are not spelled out. Written procedures, regulations, and rules—about what to do, with whom to talk, and how to feel—are a formal framework intended to guide the behavior of employees.

The Leader's (Supervisor's) Style and Expectations

Sometimes job requirements are not written down but are conveyed by the supervisor or other supervisors as demands or rules about what is supposed to happen. The supervisor's style, based on assumptions about how to lead or manage, also will create required activities, interactions, and attitudes. A boss, for example, who thinks that subordinates will try to get away with murder will require many written reports, frequent meetings to check up on progress, considerable deference, and pledges of loyalty. While none of these requirements may be written down, they are nevertheless part of the required system for members of that task group.

Furthermore, a boss, as a member of management, tends to behave in keeping with the norms of his or her own reference group (other managers at the same level). These norms may then be translated into job requirements for his or her subordinates. One fairly high executive in a pharmaceutical company started out allowing his managers the freedom to govern their own working hours (within reason). Later, when he discovered that this practice was not consistent with what his peers did (even though there was no company rule about managerial hours), he made it a formal requirement that his managers all come to work at 7:30 A.M. Interestingly enough, the source of this 7:30 custom was the founder of the company, who happened to enjoy starting work early!

For analytical purposes we treat the group's supervisor, creating and passing on requirements for job performance to group members, as outside of the group, even though, from some points of view, the boss could be considered a group member.

The boss's style in passing on demands also has an effect on the group's responses and must be taken into account. Although leadership style and its effect on performance are examined in greater detail in Chapters 11 and 12, for now it is sufficient to call attention to possible variations in the major elements of style—how controlling, task-oriented, person-concerned, explicit, and cautious the boss is—and to suggest that you include a look at it in tracing behavior that emerges from the group.

Emergent Behavior

Inevitably, because people are social beings with needs greater and more complex than those of machines, a variety of unanticipated behavior and attitudes that are not required will begin to *emerge* and over time take on relatively stable patterns. On a smaller scale, this parallels the way in which the informal organization (Chapter 2) supplements the formal organization. Making frequent appointments through a secretary leads to small talk and slowly to some kind of relationship in which a greater amount of information, ideas, and feelings are exchanged than a few informational questions about the boss's availability. The worker at the opposite bench with whom coordination is necessary ventures opinions and complaints, suggests having a coffee break together, slowly becomes a friend, and perhaps visits you when you're sick. In these kinds of ways, a social system elaborates itself, leading to *emergent* and lasting behavior and attitudes that go way beyond what was originally required just to do the job. Some of what emerges will be norms—a key form of attitudes—on how to do the task, how much to produce, and so on, while other norms will be related to purely social relationships, such as who has coffee with whom and who likes whom. *In both cases, it is this emergent (informal) system that gives a group its particular identity,* its view of who should do what, who should have influence, and how close members should feel.

Even the actual leadership of a group may emerge as different from the designated leader. It isn't always the formally named supervisor of a group who has the most influence over decisions and group activities; members with special expertise or skill may well become the most respected or influential persons. The member(s) who emerge with leadership influence may support or oppose, supplement or undermine, the formal supervisor. Group members may or may not be explicit about who provides the real leadership of the group, but they will usually recognize the informal leader(s) in some way—by being extra respectful, deferring slightly, or just by addressing questions or requests for help to them.

The emergent system often influences the performance of a group as much as or more than the required system. It is important to understand the significance and potency of emergent systems, since they can outweigh even formal orders issued from above. Emergent social systems acquire their own life, which is connected to but goes beyond what is required by the formal organization.

It is important to note that a well-developed emergent system with strong norms for behavior can feel to any member as if the group-approved behavior is "required" of him or her. For example, if there is a strongly enforced emergent norm that "each member must produce at least 80 parts per hour but no less than 20," this may feel like a "requirement" to the new group member, even though management may not formally require any particular hourly output. For our purposes behavior "demanded" by a group of its members is still called *emergent* provided that it is a result of group ideas, rather than formal *organizational* requirements imposed from outside the group.

When examining a required system and trying to predict likely emergent behavior, some of the questions you might ask are the following:

1. What tasks are required? What is it people have to do when they are working? How are they likely to feel about the tasks?
2. Who is required to interact with whom, and what relationships are likely to result?
3. What attitudes are required, and are these attitudes likely to cause resentment or enthusiasm?

Individual and Organizational Background Factors

But how can we connect what emerges to what is required? Don't personalities and personal preferences make more difference than the requirements of the job? That indeed is a question worth exploring; while individual personalities matter, and are not readily changeable, the organizational situation outweighs them more often than many people realize.

Personal Systems

People do bring something of their history with them when they enter a group. The values and feelings they have about what kind of behavior is proper, desirable, or possible are carried with them and influence how they react to what happens in the group, as well as whether or not they will choose to accept what happens. While we explore in the chapters on individual behavior more about how individuals influence, and are influenced by, the world around them, at this stage of analysis we take personality characteristics as *givens* in each group. That is, the person arrives at the group with some set of attitudes that, when mixed with those of others, help create whatever emerges.

For our purposes, the individual in the group is also the "carrier" of the wider culture, insofar as he or she brings along norms, values, and perceptions that are introduced into the group through the members. For example, there are widespread beliefs in the United States about the desirability of democratic procedures, especially among peers. If several members of a student study group carry these widely held beliefs, someone is likely to suggest that the group work without a formal leader or make decisions only by informal consensus. Because many members share such beliefs, it is easy for the attitude from the wider culture to be accepted and adopted as a norm in the study group. What individuals have learned from the broader culture and their experiences in it becomes a (background) factor in determining the social system that will emerge in the group.

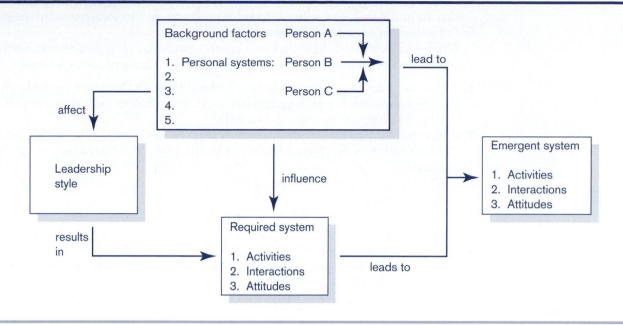

FIGURE 3-2   *Connections of Personal Systems to Required and Emergent Systems*

Of course, as the work force becomes more diverse, there is a greater likelihood of group members bringing diverse attitudes, backgrounds, and assumptions to the work setting. And any given group could have members from different countries, ethnic or racial subgroups, economic backgrounds, and so on.

As suggested earlier, of special significance are the values, feelings, and attitudes of formally designated leaders, as these aspects of personality determine their leadership style. Remember that the style of a leader can have important consequences for what emerges.

The set of attitudes a person brings to the group, the way the person sees him or herself and sees what is proper behavior, we call the *personal system*. The sum of all the individual members' personal systems, plus that of any supervisor or designated leader, is an important background factor needed to understand what emerges in a group. All these personal systems combine with the job requirements to affect the emergent system (see Figure 3–2. Personal systems—what is commonly called personality—can be a powerful influence on the way a group develops. Values, especially, are a deeply entrenched part of each person. The attitudes each person brings shapes what he or she notices, responds to, cares about, and style of interaction. Mismatches in personality can affect communication in every direction.

"[Ralph Waldo] Emerson's long dream of a cooperative assemblage of gifted individuals" failed because of "their inability to get along with one another." [Bronson] Alcott and [Margaret] Fuller had mountainous, clashing egos; [Henry David] Thoreau was by nature quarrelsome about every nit-picking thing; [Jones] Very was a true paranoid; [Ellery] Channing was surly and disagreeable; and [Nathaniel] Hawthorne stood agape at the Concord Sage's blithe dismissal of the moral reality of sin and guilt.

James W. Tuttleton, "The Discord at Concord," review of *Emerson Among the Eccentrics: A Group Portrait*, by Carlos Baker, *The Wall Street Journal*, April 4, 1996.

Nevertheless, job requirements and the group's emergent system often can be so powerful and overwhelming that even people with quite different personal systems will behave similarly when placed in a job. There is a tendency in organizations to overcredit individual personality defects for problems and to underestimate the effect of job requirements and the surrounding situation.

When trying to trace the source of a group's particular emergent system, some questions you might ask about the personal systems of members are as follows:

1. How do individual members see themselves? How do these views combine to help explain the choices the group has made about how to make decisions, produce, relate to one another, and so forth?
2. Why have members accepted or rejected the group's norms? What makes individual members receptive or resistant to the group's accepted way of doing things?
3. Why do some members respond differently to the same set of requirements and leadership style?
4. Do the backgrounds of various members help explain why they initiated key or prominent events?
5. What is the fit between the required system and the members' personal systems? Are the requirements likely to be accepted as proper by the people who happen to be group members?

External Status

In addition to individual personality, another aspect of people that tends to be overlooked as an influence on what emerges in a group is each person's position or status in other settings—home community, social groups, organizations. People's status outside the group influences how they see themselves and how others in the group see them.

To illustrate, if a student task group is formed in a course and one member is president of student government and widely respected on campus, other members are likely to turn to that person for leadership. In turn, the person is likely to begin to take on leadership functions even if he or she is not the most suited to be leader for the given task. Similarly, in an organizational task force or committee, the member who has the highest position or title in the organization is likely to become chairperson of the group. While this does not always happen, position outside a group initially tends to affect position within it. In general, the higher a person's status outside a group, the higher a position or rank he or she will be accorded in a new group, at least at the beginning.[4] Does this fit with your experience?

In tracing the sources of the emergent system, you might ask

1. How does a member's external status relate to his or her position within the group at different times? (Chapter 5 looks in greater detail at member positions in the group.)
2. Is a valuable contributor being ignored because of low external status relative to other members?
3. Are some people getting more influence than their actual contribution merits because of high external status?

Organizational Culture

Culture is a catchall word summarizing the way things are generally done, the prevailing atmosphere or climate, general notions (sometimes explicit but often just understood and taken for granted) about how members of the organization are supposed to act and feel, what is rewarded, and so on. The term *organizational culture* here refers to the culture of the wider organization of which the group being analyzed is a part. One way to think of organizational culture is in terms of the social context or environment in which the work group is located. Another way of thinking about organizational culture is that just as small groups develop norms for behavior, larger organizations tend to develop general norms that apply to every member, regardless of position.[5]

For example, in one insurance company in New England, many employees have noted that the norms within the company included such things as "Don't make waves," "Avoid conflicts by joking or shutting up," "Be informal and on a first-name basis with everyone," "Work long hours and don't be a clock watcher." Whether an organization's climate is friendly or hostile, organization members in general are trusted and assumed to be motivated or suspected and considered irresponsible, disagreements are buried or encouraged, individuality is suppressed or fostered, and so forth, all make a difference to what people bring to their work group. The organization's usual ways of handling such issues affect the beliefs and feelings with which members will approach a group. Every organization has general norms of some kind, and every group in the organization is subject to those norms and is likely to reflect them in some way.

However, the reflection may not always be a clear one because every group tends to develop its own unique character—partly a reflection of its particular membership. Consequently, a group's norms will be an *elaboration* of, a *distortion* of, and a direct *reflection* of the culture (customs) of the larger organization.

In addition, the cultures of the region or country in which the organization is located may shape beliefs within the organization, as suggested previously in the discussion about the sources of norms. For example, a student task group will develop its emergent system in part based on the culture of the college as a whole, and probably in part on the culture of the region or country from which most of its members come.

In tracing the sources of the emergent system, you might ask

1. What is the organization's culture as reflected in generally held beliefs about the way things ought to be?
2. Do any of the group's norms reflect the wider organization's culture, and how its influence was transmitted?
3. Are the group's norms and procedures consistent with or in opposition to the wider organizational culture? The region or country culture?

Technology and Layout

Technology refers to the means by which work is done. It can include the machines, tools, and materials used; the sequence or flow of operations; the way in which work arrives and is processed (continuously or in batches); the pace and timing of work as controlled by machine speed or customer demands; deadlines and interdependencies with other parts of the organization; noise level; and procedures, processes, and forms used in doing work. It can also include the level and kind of expertise or technical skill needed to do the work.

In a group at a manufacturing job, the technology will usually include some machines that have to be operated by group members. In a group working in service jobs, the technology may not utilize machines but may involve meetings, discussion, and deskwork and require a few tools, such as pens, pencils, paper, forms, telephones, and a place to sit. As you can see, the technology of a service group, *when it calls primarily for talking with others,* is almost identical with the required system—that is, in describing the technology, it will be necessary to include a description of many of the required activities and interactions. But this overlap should serve as an indicator of how important the technology is for explaining eventual emergent behavior.

In addition, *the way in which space is used and equipment is laid out can be considered part of technology.* Where machinery is located; the height of walls, desks, cabinets, or machines; the placing of seats, workstations, or offices; and general size of the spaces utilized can all affect behavior.

MANAGERIAL TOOLS

The Concept of Corporate Culture

Corporations develop complex and powerful cultures (like any society) that influence the behavior patterns of employees at all levels. Five elements of culture:

1. *Business environment*–a company's place in the business world as defined by its products, competitors, customers, technology, etc.
2. *Values*–the basic concepts and beliefs of an organization, as well as its standards for achievement.

3. *Heroes*–the people who personify the culture's values and serve as role models for employees.
4. *Rites and rituals*–the systematic and programmed routines of day-to-day life in the company (including ceremonies).
5. *The cultural network*–the "carrier" of the corporate values and heroic mythology. It includes "story-tellers, spies, priests, cabals, and whispers."

SOURCE: Terence Deal and Allan Kennedy, *Corporate Cultures* (Reading, MA: Addison-Wesley Publishing, 1982).

MANAGERIAL BULLETIN

IBM Goes Casual, Drops White Shirts, and Plans a Woodsier Headquarters

IBM brass worked out of a sterile concrete box in suburban New York, where, like capitalist drones, they never varied from an unwritten but ironclad dress code of starched white shirts, baggy dark suits, and boring ties.

No more.

In a move almost as drastic as eliminating IBM's lifetime employment practice, IBM's first outside chairman, Louis V. Gerstner, Jr., has now cut what may be the final links to the old regime: He's doing away with the dress code and building a new, more casual headquarters. . . .

But employees at several other IBM locations that have gone casual seem simply to have embraced a new dress code every bit as rigid: chinos, but no jeans;

loafers, but no deck shoes. And socks are all but mandatory.

IBM actually never had a formal policy mandating white shirts and dark suits. But it's had an unwritten dress code "that's as effective as if it were engraved in steel–or as if it had a loaded gun behind it." . . .

One IBMer, upon learning of the new dress policy, lamented yesterday that he had just received half a dozen white dress shirts from relatives at Christmas, and now he will have to equip his closet with colored shirts–a sign that ever-loyal IBM employees will feel pressure to conform as well to the new casual policy.

SOURCE: Bart Ziegler, "IBM Goes Casual, Drops White Shirts, and Plans a Woodsier Headquarters," *The Wall Street Journal,* February 3, 1995, p. A3.

Both technology and layout are important background factors because they determine many things for people in the organization: amount of individual attention, involvement and judgment needed; degree of interaction, communication, and cooperation necessary to complete work; numbers of people who must be present; and the like. In turn, these constraints affect who is likely to, must, or cannot interact with whom, and when. Thus, both technology and layout set limits on what social interactions and emergent behavior are possible, and cause various interactions to occur. They also affect what behavior can be required.

For example, it is difficult to form a relationship with someone who must constantly tend a machine on the other side of a thunderously noisy nine-foot-high stamping machine; on the other hand, a quiet, open office with desks placed side by

The New Workplace Walls Are Falling as the Office of the Future Finally Takes Shape

Alcoa is eager to solve an increasingly urgent workplace problem: After having downsized, reengineered, customer-focused, shattered old hierarchical structures, and reorganized work around teams—all the things that were supposed to make companies more responsive and competitive—corporations such as Alcoa aren't getting the results they expected. They are, quite literally, running into walls, because the new work styles don't work in buildings designed for the old top-down corporation. "Companies feel work processes need to change, and physical environments can get in the way," says Karen Lalli, senior associate with the Hillier Group, an architectural firm based in Princeton, N.J. . . .

While they may not look vastly different from conventional offices, the new workplaces repeal rules that have governed corporate office design in the past. No perk has been more sacrosanct than personal space, no status symbol more significant than big, heavy mahogany doors sweeping across deep-pile carpet and sealing executives into remote lairs with a smug ka-chunk. In many companies, when employees congregated in

neutral zones such as lunchrooms, hallways, and patios, managers cast a dim eye and mentally added names to their list of slackers.

New workplace design reverses all that. . . .

[Inhale] CEO Robert B. Chess served as a White House staff member in the Bush Administration. He observed firsthand the ultimate form of "office politics." His colleagues were obsessed with their "proximity to the President," he recalls. From the beginning, Chess decided Inhale couldn't afford such nonsense. Everyone—which includes his 65 employees and himself—sits in large cubicles that he calls "bullpens" with four other people of various ranks and functions—no walls or barriers of any kind between them. It forces everybody to talk to each other all the time," he says. Chess says the lack of private space also limits gossip, reduces the need for memo writing, and gets top managers scattered among the troops. Every nine months or so he even stirs the pot, reshuffling everybody.

SOURCE: Joan O. C. Hamilton, Stephen Baker, and Bill Nasic, "The New Workplace Walls Are Falling as the Office of the Future Finally Takes Shape," *Business Week,* April 29, 1996, p. 106.

side makes conversation with neighbors easy. Three people sitting next to one another and feeding cashed checks into a microfilm machine so that the bank will have a record of transactions can easily talk with one another while working. The machines are quiet, do not require close attention, and are located physically near one another. Contrast this with boiler loaders standing in front of roaring furnaces, shoveling coal in as needed, working intensively for half-hour bursts, then resting in a cooler area for 15 minutes. At the least, if there is conversation, it will come in short snatches and have to be shouted to one another over the roar of the furnaces. It's not hard to see that different norms and ways of working together are likely to emerge.

Similarly, the timing of when shift members report and leave can be an important factor in communications and, therefore, important in the emergent system. Organizations that need around-the-clock coverage and high sharing of information (like hospitals) schedule differently from organizations that only work a second shift when there is great demand, and when the second shift's work is self-explanatory.

All of these factors, loosely grouped under technology, shape what is and can be required and are usually fixed or determined in advance or outside of the group's existence. In turn, this will affect the emergent system.

When trying to trace what emerges to technology, you might ask questions such as

1. What is the effect of the technology on what activities and interactions are required to do the work?
2. What is the nature of the group's technology in terms of numbers of people needed, when they must be in certain places, how much latitude they have in

physical movement, variations of work methods used, judgment? How does all this affect how members feel?

3. What kinds of interactions and activities are made easy or not possible, because of the layout, noise level, flow of work, and so forth?

4. What kind of expertise is required by the technology, and how does that affect who group members are, how they see one another, how they will be supervised, and so on?

Reward System

One of the best ways to predict behavior in any work group is to look at what behavior is actually rewarded. Most people tend to do what will get them rewarded. This can be a bit tricky because organizations (or managers or parents) don't always actually reward what they say they will; subordinates do not always correctly interpret what is going to be rewarded; and groups of people sometimes refuse to value the organization's rewards, because the benefits of acceptance by peers outweigh those of management.

Nevertheless, it is very useful to identify the formal and informal reward systems in an organization when trying to understand group behavior. Just as technology is often determined apart from the particular members of the group, the organization's formal reward system (pay, recognition, praise, opportunities for advancement, responsibility, and the like) is usually established before the group exists. Informal reward systems, on the other hand, are often not so explicit. The particular leader, supervisor, or manager of a group may have his or her own ideas about what behavior should be rewarded. The leader's assumptions about what motivates people in general, what kind of people are in the group being led, what kinds of behavior demonstrate hard work, competence, promise, and loyalty all can affect what rewards are available to a group.

The combination of formal and informal organizational rewards is a background factor that affects what is required and what emerges, as well as whether or not employees fully respond to offered rewards and punishments. It is important to remember that sometimes a group's emergent system will be in opposition to the organization's reward system, or at least not fully consistent with it. Workers, for example, can become quite skeptical about incentive schemes, believing fervently that if they increase output they will soon be required to produce the new higher amount regularly and that the incentive pay or bonus will somehow be taken away or so altered that they end up worse off than when they started. Some groups will decide that to "protect" themselves they should perform only to minimum expectations, rather than respond with full effort to the organization's rewards. And occasionally individuals or groups will produce much more—and try much harder—than the organization is able or willing to reward. Thus, it is necessary to probe carefully when analyzing the effect of the organization's reward system on emergent behavior.

In tracing emergent behavior to the reward system, you might ask how pay is determined and what effect that has on behavior, whether the pay system encourages competition or cooperation among members, what the available rewards are besides pay, whether good performance can be easily measured and rewarded or bad performance measured and punished, and how that will affect emergent behavior.

Summary

All of the above factors—personal system, external status, organizational culture, technology, layout, and reward system—can be thought of as background factors, preconditions to the group's existence that help determine what will be required of members and also what emerges in their behavior (see Figure 3–3). Note that these factors usually affect one another; it is by their particular combination that behavior will be determined.

Rewarding Teamwork, Hollywood Style

. . . Deborah Miller spent 15 years hoarding Hollywood intelligence. "Information was gold," she recalls. Then, not long ago, Ms. Miller left the mammoth William Morris Agency for the tiny Metropolitan Talent Agency, where the rules are radically different. Agents were actually sharing information! Even more unthinkable, they were eagerly collaborating on deals!

You hear a lot of platitudes about teamwork these days, even in Hollywood. But rarely will you see it practiced with the precision used at Metro Talent. Although created for the entertainment industry, it's a teamwork model with relevance anywhere. The chief elements: compensation rules that foster collaboration and data systems that make intelligence communal. . . .

For each commission dollar coming in from a deal, 30 percent is scored for the agent who originally brought in the client, no matter how long ago. The next 30 percent goes to the employee currently representing that talent. The final 40 percent goes to whoever had landed the deal in question. The same employee frequently performs all these functions, but many deals link two, three, or more agents.

At bonus time, everyone receives a set percentage of the agency's revenue that has been attributed to him or her—usually about one-quarter of the sum, more in a few cases. The remaining revenue stays with the house, going toward overhead and, thereafter, to Mr. Barrett [the owner].

SOURCE: Thomas Petzinger, Jr., "Talent Agency Shows Stellar Teamwork—in Hollywood No Less," *The Wall Street Journal,* January 26, 1996, p. B1.

FIGURE 3–3   *The Connection between Background Factors and the Required and Emergent Systems*

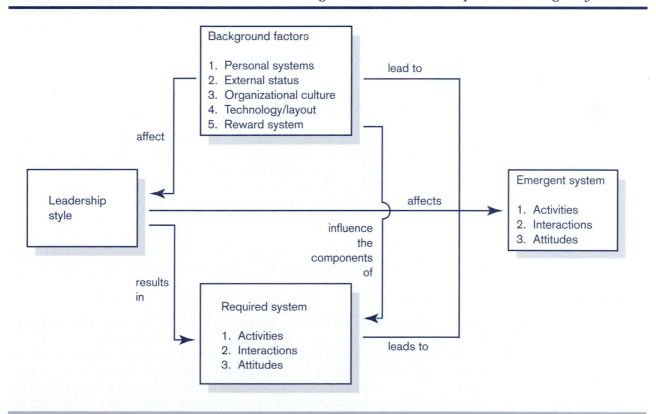

An Expert Cereal-Making Team at General Mills

They do just about everything middle managers do, and do it very well: Since General Mills introduced teams . . . productivity has risen up to 40 percent. [Three members] operate machinery to make . . . Oatmeal Crisp. Denny . . . is a manager but he doesn't supervise in the traditional sense. He coaches the team on management techniques and serves as their link to headquarters.

[Two members] help maintain the machinery, which [another] operates. Team members like the added responsibility, but also feel more pressure. . . . "I work a lot harder than I used to. You have to worry about the numbers."

SOURCE: Brian Dumaine, "Who Needs a Boss," *Fortune,* May 7, 1990. © The Time Inc. Magazine Company. All Rights Reserved.

Key Events and the Emergent System

Key events that occur during the life of a group also influence the emergent system. The background factors and the required system set the direction in which the emergent system is likely to develop, but that process of development is dynamic and interactive. Events may reinforce, modify, or undercut that ongoing direction. As we discussed earlier, norms are often created by a group's reaction to some dramatic event, such as a quarrel among members, a scolding by management, or a breakthrough on a tough issue yielding a sense of accomplishment and a norm to henceforth confront issues early. Other events may make it clearer to members that either a certain norm exists or it is really fairly unimportant and not likely to be strongly enforced. Still other events, such as one member doing an unusually good job, may determine who ends up in particular roles or who has more influence than one might have predicted from knowing the background factors alone. The emergent system is constantly evolving as time passes and *events* occur.

The Consequences of Emergent Systems

All of what has been discussed so far in this chapter must be seen from the perspective of final results. The connections among background factors and required and emergent systems are important primarily in terms of the functionality or dysfunctionality of the consequences for the organization and its members. How does the behavior of any person or group help the larger organization *sustain its competitive position*? In the long run, that is what really matters. Does the behavior create needed products and services; build customer loyalty; keep costs competitive; attract, train, and keep people with the needed skills? We can assess the consequences for sustaining competitive position of whatever emergent system develops along several broad dimensions.

Productivity

Any work organization will be interested in overall *productivity*: how well the group does its required tasks, cost per unit of output, ability to meet deadlines, quality of output, and so on. Productivity is more than a narrow economic measure; it can be used to measure how well the group performs its required tasks to satisfy its customers inside and outside the organization. Although many managers, particularly in small private companies, maintain that productivity and, in turn, profits are all the consequences they care to know about, in fact few people with managerial responsibility actually operate only on this dimension.

TEAMS RULE, *According to U.S. Manufacturers*

Some companies attribute huge gains to abandoning assembly lines in favor of teams. Honeywell Inc.'s defense-avionics plant says on-time product delivery improved to 99 percent in the 1996 first quarter from below 40 percent in the late 1980s. Dell Computer Corp. says teams mesh with its build-to-order business, with a single team following each unit from order to delivery for maximum quality. . . .

Some workers find teams are a double-edged sword. Electrosource Inc., an Austin, Texas, battery maker, adopted a team strategy. Within 12 months, productivity per employee doubled. But jobs were slashed to 80 from 300.

SOURCE: Paulette Thomas," A Special News Report about Life on the Job—and Trends Taking Shape There," *The Wall Street Journal*, May 28, 1996, p. A1.

Satisfaction

For a variety of reasons, managers also are interested in the satisfaction of members of their organization. It can affect employee commitment to the job and organization, their willingness to do more than is required, their creativity and flexibility. It can also affect absenteeism and turnover, the degree to which talented people stay with the organization. Both are costly and affect profitability. While there is *no necessary connection* between satisfaction and productivity (a subject we explore later), the actual satisfaction people derive from their work and membership in a particular group is important enough in its effects on the people involved as well as on their productivity to merit close examination in each situation we study. In fact, in some work groups, achieving satisfaction (close friendship, comfortable relations) may be the only dimension *members* are interested in regardless of management's concerns or the effect on productivity! (If you are in a class task group, you might like to check this.)

Development

A third important dimension is that of individual and group development/growth/learning. Except in those rare situations where the supply of employees is unlimited and they are instantly replaceable, organizations need members who are learning new skills and are flexible enough to solve problems as they arise. The knowledge of employees is an increasingly valuable asset in the information age. A group may be reasonably productive and satisfied but preventing its members from developing, from learning anything that will increase (1) their individual skills or abilities, (2) the range or resources available to the group, or (3) their ability to function effectively as a group in changed circumstances. For example, a student task group may be dividing up the work in a way that produces good reports or papers but teaches members no new skills. An expert report writer may be doing most of the work, using already developed abilities but leaving other members underutilized and unstretched.

Not only would this diminish individual member learning, but it would also mean that the group is giving itself less opportunity to learn to function effectively as a whole. This can easily happen to a classroom group that does well on its first project, then becomes fixated on that successful approach and never tries alternative ways of functioning.

Just as production is not necessarily correlated with satisfaction, group development can be independent of either. Development or learning can be occurring even when productivity and satisfaction are low. For example, even dissatisfied misfits in

MANAGERIAL BULLETIN

Teams of Women

"The theory that Anson has," said goalkeeper Tracy Noonan, a fifth-year senior from North Andover, Mass., "is that any practice we have will be tougher and more physically challenging than any game we play. Our fitness is the key to why we do so well."

But it is more than physical fitness. There is a mental toughness that Dorrance says comes not naturally but with some sweat, some blood, and a lot of tears from those who fall by the wayside.

"Obviously there are things about motivating women that are different," said Dorrance. "But demanding things from them and expecting things from them is exactly the same. We are very demanding here and every year we crank it up another notch.

"It's difficult to motivate women to compete against other women in practice. We understand that. They have an understanding that their relationship to their teammates is superior to the game itself. They are not going to jeopardize their relationship by beating up their best friend in practice.

"With men it's different. If you and I are best friends and play basketball, we will knock the crap out of each other during the game, doing whatever we have to do to win. Once it's over, it's over. We'll still be best friends. Women are not like that. . . .

"I think men have an innate competitiveness," he said. "I don't think with women the competitiveness is universal. In my opinion, they have a very sensible hierarchy which says that my relationship with you is more important than who wins this game. I think it's a wonderful compliment to women because they feel their connection with each other is more important than something as ridiculous as a soccer game and I credit them for that.

"[Men] are more neanderthal. We'd rather win, but our relationship is not jeopardized. When women compete against women, their personal relationships are tied up in the competition. They are forced to reach down and find that competitive anger. It is critical to find the fury that great athletes have."

SOURCE: Mark Blandschun, "The World at Their Feet," *The Boston Globe,* November 14, 1995, p. 85.

MANAGERIAL BULLETIN

Already Known for Product Quality, Motorola Is Ballooning Its Commitment to Employee Learnings

[Motorola's leaders] believe the most crucial weapons in the coming decade will be responsiveness, adaptability and creativity.

> A new campaign built around lifelong learning . . . will dramatically increase training of all employees, from the factory floor to the corner office. The goal is a workforce that is disciplined yet free-thinking. . . . If

knowledge is becoming antiquated at a faster rate, we have no choice but to spend on education," [tough guy CEO Gary Tooker] says. "How can that not be a competitive weapon?" . . . Training is also the *sine qua non* for Motorola's team approach to manufacturing.

SOURCE: Kevin Kelly, "Motorola: Training for the Millennium," *Business Week,* March 28, 1994.

a job may be developing valuable skills; disgruntled employees often leave to start their own ventures, fueled by discontent and what they have learned from the job and from others. The dimension of development and learning is important to assess along with the other two dimensions of productivity and satisfaction. Administrators who are concerned about the long-run enhancement of their organization's human resources will especially value this dimension. However, some managers, feeling under pressure for immediate results, may push productivity at the expense of satisfaction or development.

Why Your Workers Might Jump Ship

Data from the 1999 Emerging Workforce Study show that 35 percent of employees who don't receive regular mentoring plan to look for another job within 12 months. But just 16 percent of those with good mentors expect to jump ship. And don't even ask about training and development. Among employees who say their company offers poor training, 41 percent plan to leave within a year, versus only 12 percent of those who rate opportunities excellent.

High turnover isn't cheap. The survey pegs the cost of losing a typical worker at $50,000. So a 1,000-worker company with poor training could lose $14.5 million, while nonexistent mentoring could cost $9.5 million.

SOURCE: Jennifer Reingold, "Why Your Workers Might Jump Ship," *Business Week,* March 1, 1999, p. 8.

Success Breeds Liking

"Winning seems to cure a lot of things," Kevin Gamble said. "When we weren't winning, there was a lot of tension and everyone was pointing fingers at somebody. That's very unhealthy. Now guys have smiles on their faces again."

SOURCE: Peter May, "Celtics Keep Miami at Bay," *The Boston Globe,* January 27, 1994.

It is important to note again what was stated in Chapter 2, that it may not be possible in any given situation to achieve high performance on all three dimensions. An individual or group may make or have to make trade-offs among these dimensions. What to sacrifice for which benefits is determined by the values of the person(s) choosing. Our concern is to make any action's likely consequences along all three dimensions more explicit in advance so that choices can be more informed. But we offer no magical or easy solutions guaranteeing wealth, happiness, and growth to everyone.

We can complete Figure 3–3 by adding what we have just described. Whatever the emergent behavior and attitudes of a group, their functionality should be assessed along at least three broad dimensions: productivity, satisfaction, and development (see Figure 3–4).

These consequences will then be judged by those members of an organization who feel responsible for performance; as you might guess, should they judge the consequences negatively, they are likely to make some changes in the required system and/or background factors. If productivity, for example, is seen as too low, changes might be made in the type of equipment used, the pay system, the closeness of supervision, the personnel, or whatever those responsible assume to make a difference. Can you see that changes in the required system might in turn affect the emergent system with new consequences for productivity, learning, or satisfaction? Adjustments in one area will lead to responses in other areas until a new equilibrium is reached in the balance among the various components of the group.

All too often, unfortunately, the consequences of change are not those anticipated by the changer; tightening up on supervision might lead to sabotage rather than more productivity, for example. But that is worth closer attention and will be looked at again in the book's final chapter. For now we suggest you begin to get in

An Example of a Work Group on a College Campus

If several college students were hired by a college to be a grounds crew for the summer, the kind of work group they become can be explained and even predicted by references to the interplay of who they are (personal systems), other background factors, their boss's style, and the behavior required of them by the college. Let us assume the following:

- The students have similar interests, all have a strong sense of responsibility, need the job, and view outdoor work as a desirable summer job.
- The crew boss is an older, full-time college employee who takes pride in the college grounds, has led summer crews before, and relates well with college-age people.
- The college is a prestigious institution with a tradition of maintaining a lovely campus and has a reputation for being a good place to work.
- The grounds crew is paid by the hour at a reasonable rate. Its results are highly visible to the general public, as well as to the crew boss.
- The work required of the crew includes cutting grass, raking clippings, picking up trash, spreading loam and wood chips, planting and watering flowers, etc. A certain amount of coordination and cooperation among the crew members is necessary for efficiency. Some care is required not to damage the shrubbery or equipment. Because the campus is in use throughout the summer, the crew is expected to exhibit courtesy toward any pedestrians and not spray them with water, etc. Finally, the college expects the crew to work steadily and give a full day of work, but does not demand an unreasonable work pace.

Given these background factors and requirements, it would not be surprising if the crew developed into a hardworking and satisfied group. It's likely to develop a norm of getting the job done, even if it means working a little bit beyond the normal break time. Talking while working and even some occasional horseplay might go on, but not to slow efficiency or endanger equipment. Overall, the consequences probably would include satisfactory productivity in the eyes of the college, general job satisfaction for the crew, but only a modest amount of learning of new skills by the crew members. These results are particularly likely if the interplay of background factors and requirements are reinforced by a few key events early in the life of the crew, such as the president of the college happening upon the crew just as it is finishing planting flowers under the flagpole and warmly expressing appreciation for a job well done.

Change a few of the factors described above and the emergent behaviors and consequences could be quite different. What if the job were a last-resort job for the students, and the college had a reputation as a low-paying, insensitive employer? What if the college's budget led to the hiring of a crew so small that the workload exceeded what it could reasonably be expected to produce? What if the president saw only the one flower out of alignment and criticized the crew for that while ignoring their overall good work? While one change in the overall array of background factors, requirements, and key events might not make a big difference in what emerged, new conditions would yield quite different norms and results.

the habit of sorting what you observe in groups, as best you can, into the five categories we have suggested: background factors, required system, leadership style, emergent system, and competitive consequences. Then try to trace the connections among them: What causes what? What seems to be associated with what? What seems unexplainable and needs more investigation?

The Relationships between Required and Emergent Systems

It is important to note again that what emerges in groups will not necessarily be supportive of the required system; in fact, emergent behavior and attitudes may well be in conflict with the required tasks imposed from above or by the situation. Sometimes

FIGURE 3-4

The Complete Basic Social System Conceptual Scheme

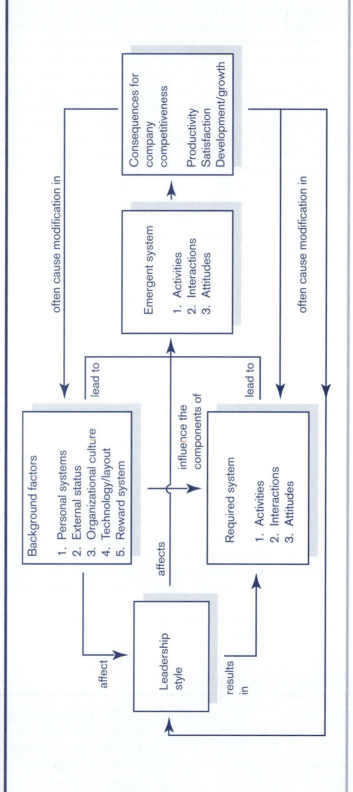

work groups elaborate on ways to improve their performance, inventing improved methods, informally helping one another, and so forth. They even may develop an emergent system that compensates for deficiencies in the required system, as when norms develop in a paper mill that the nearest person to a paper break, regardless of formal position, immediately will start to rethread the paper to minimize waste. At other times, however, groups develop norms of limited production, holding back effort, or even sabotaging the product. Anyone who has ever had an unfixable rattle in a car knows that auto workers may have said "nuts to you" when feeling negative and done things like toss some bolts into a panel as it was about to be permanently sealed.

A key challenge for you will be to attempt to develop a series of propositions (hypotheses, generalizations) to predict when emergent systems are likely to be in conflict with the required system and when not. Can you trace what the relationships are between leadership style, technology, task requirements, member backgrounds, and so on, and the kind of system that emerges? The more useful the generalizations you can formulate, the more effective you can be in making informed managerial choices. And, of course, you need to be ready to modify your propositions when you come across contradictory evidence.

It is often possible to predict likely emergent behavior if what is "given" by the situation—the background factors, leadership style, and required system—are known in advance. Many students are surprised to learn that the particular individuals in a situation may make less difference to what happens than the situation and its requirements. The demands of the task, technology, or management style often can pull behavior from a group regardless of who the particular members are. This is often referred to as the "office making the person," elevating its occupant and forcing growth in whoever fills the leadership role. Recent history with respect to the presidency of the United States has proven, however, in a painfully glaring way that occupying even the highest political office in no way *guarantees* particularly elevated behavior. The pulls are there, however, just as in any organizational situation, and often have induced more noble and strong behavior from presidents than they had exhibited earlier in their careers.

As you move through the course, try to notice if you are increasingly able to anticipate the kinds of behavior, norms, productivity, satisfaction, and so forth, to which a given set of requirements and background factors lead. We try to help you improve your predictive abilities by what follows.

As an aid in helping you get started—to analyze cases, your own classroom group, the group you work in—the next chapters contain a series of propositions (tentative hypotheses) based on research, empirical observation, and experience. We have tried to build them up in a logical sequence and have also attempted to show how you can connect various pieces of what is observable. That type of analysis goes beyond just using the concepts as fancy labels for behavior; it is a way of trying to *explain* what happens by referring to other connected happenings. In that way, possible choice points where your decision as a manager can make a difference to outcomes should become visible.

KEY CONCEPTS FROM CHAPTER 3

1. A group can be defined by its:
   a. Size.
   b. Degree of autonomy.
   c. Differentiation from other groups.
   d. Interrelationships of some duration.
   e. Identification of members with a group.
   f. Common goals and symbols.
2. Behavior in group.
   a. Interactions.
   b. Activities.
3. Attitudes in group.
   a. Perceptions.
   b. Feelings.
   c. Norms.
   d. Values
4. The basic social system conceptual scheme.

a.　Background factors:
　　(1)　Personal systems.
　　(2)　External status.
　　(3)　Organizational culture.
　　(4)　Technology/layout.
　　(5)　Reward system.

b.　Required system.
c.　Leadership style.
d.　Key events.
e.　Emergent system.
f.　Consequences for competitiveness: productivity, satisfaction, and development.

PERSONAL APPLICATION EXERCISE

Imagining Your First/Next Full-Time Job

- Draw a set of empty boxes representing the social system conceptual scheme.
- In the Required System box, fill in the job requirements for your ideal job–the tasks, the kinds of interactions, the rules, and so on.
- In the Background Factors box, fill in a list of your traits–abilities, preferences, outstanding personality characteristics, and the like. Also, list some of the aspects of the workplace, the rewards, the technology, and so forth that would be important to you.
- In the Emergent System box, list the norms and the kinds of behavior and interactions that you would expect to occur, given the contents of the first two boxes.
- Finally, describe the outcomes in terms of *your* productivity, satisfaction, and development.
- Save this product for future reference.

SUGGESTED READINGS

Bradford, L. P., and D. Mial. "When Is a Group?" *Educational Leadership* 21 (1963), pp. 147–51.

Cartwright, D., and A. Zander. *Group Dynamics: Research and Theory.* New York: Harper & Row, 1953.

Hare, A. P. *Handbook of Small Group Research.* New York: Free Press, 1962.

———.*Handbook of Small Group Research.* 2nd ed. New York: Free Press, 1976.

Homans, G. C. "Social Behavior as Exchange." *American Journal of Sociology,* May 1958, pp. 597–606.

———. *Social Behavior: Its Elementary Forms.* New York: Harcourt Brace Jovanovich, 1961.

Jones, G. R. "Task Visibility, Free Riding, and Shirking: Explaining the Effect of Structure and Technology on Employee Behavior." *Academy of Management Review,* October 1984, pp. 684–95.

Lincoln, J. R., and J. Miller. "Work and Friendship Ties in Organizations: A Comparative Analysis of Relational Networks." *Administrative Science Quarterly,* June 1979, pp. 181–99.

Luft, J. "Living Systems: The Group." *Behavioral Science* 16 (1971), pp. 302–98.

Napier, R. W., and M. K. Gershenfeld. *Groups: Theory and Experience.* Boston: Houghton Mifflin, 1973.

Orth, C. D., IL. *Social Structure and Learning Climate; The First Year at the Harvard Business School.* Boston: Division of Research, Graduate School of Business, Harvard University, 1963.

Pettigrew, A. M. "On Studying Organization Cultures." *Administrative Science Quarterly,* December 1979, pp. 570–81.

Shaw, M. E. *Group Dynamics: The Psychology of Small Group Behavior.* New York: McGraw-Hill, 1971.

Smith, P. B. *Groups within Organizations.* New York: Harper & Row, 1973.

Thibaut, J. W., and H. Kelley. *The Social Psychology of Groups.* New York: John Wiley & Sons, 1969.

Trice, H. M., and J. M. Beyer. "Studying Organizational Cultures through Rites and Ceremonials." *Academy of Management Review,* October 1984, pp. 653–69.

Wholey, D. R., and J. W. Brittain. "Organizational Ecology: Findings and Implications." *Academy of Management Review,* July 1986, pp. 513–33.

Zander, A. *Groups at Work.* San Francisco: Jossey-Bass, 1977.

Cohesiveness in Groups

Cockpit Teamwork

Research has demonstrated that in the great majority of crashes and lesser accidents, the aircraft is mechanically functional and crew members are well-trained and healthy. It's the team that goes on the fritz.

Cockpit crews given fairly demanding simulated flight tests after flying together for several days made fewer errors, even when tired, than fresh crews just assembled. Other research has shown that the majority of the trouble crews get into comes on the first leg of the first day of their time together. Ideally, crews would remain intact for a long time. Typically, however, the lifespan of a crew is a mere one or two days. When highest performance counts and money is no object, some military organizations, such as the Strategic Air Command, do approach the ideal, using "hard crews" that stay together. "Everybody agrees that it would be better to have hard crews," says [Professor Richard] Hackman, yet airlines and pilot unions prefer the system the way it is.

SOURCE: Christopher Reed, "Cockpit Teamwork." *Harvard Magazine,* September–October 1997, p. 13.

"...if a group lacks cohesiveness, individual and group learning may be inhibited."

A crucial emergent factor in any work group is the degree to which members turn out to like each other and the group as a whole. A group that is close and unified will behave differently, for better or worse, than one that is distant and fragmented. In this chapter we will look at *what* makes a group stick together. The consequence of sticking together for productivity, satisfaction, and development is ultimately a more important issue, but let us first try to understand what pulls a group together. With a better understanding of the factors that lead to closeness, a manager is more likely to succeed in efforts to increase or decrease this important emergent characteristic of groups.

In an effort to spell out the propositions about closeness, we begin with some elementary "building blocks" of relationships. While the first proposition looks obvious, it is often overlooked and is important to those that come later. Remember from Chapter 3 that technology, work layout, required interactions, and the arrangement of space affect the chances of people talking with one another; we can restate that idea more formally:

The greater the opportunity/requirements for interactions, the greater the likelihood of interaction occurring.[1] That leads directly to the next proposition, which is fundamental to all human relationships:

The more frequent the interaction among people, the greater the likelihood of their developing positive feelings for one another.[2] And, in turn:

The greater the positive feelings among people, the more frequently they will interact.[3] In other words, if you like someone, you will probably choose to spend more time with him or her than with someone you do not like.

People tend to approach other people they see as attractive and to avoid those they see as unattractive. Although most people have general ideas about what kind of people they do not like, these general feelings are often easily overcome when they actually interact with and get to know a particular person or group of people. While knowing someone does not guarantee liking, it is rather difficult to like someone you do not know. In fact, people are often surprised to find how likeable others are once they've had the opportunity to interact with them.

> It is easier for a man to be loyal to his club than to his planet; the bylaws are shorter and he is personally acquainted with the other members.
>
> E. B. White
> *One Man's Meat*

> I know I don't like it because I've never tried it.
>
> Ad for Guinness Stout

These propositions must be modified or at least qualified under certain conditions. For example, when there are strong prior negative feelings on the part of one or more interactor or when there are extreme status differences between those interacting, interaction may only increase prior feelings of dislike or distance and may lead to avoidance or superficial contact. When interaction reveals strong value differences, individuals may decide to avoid one another for fear of getting into heated arguments. Furthermore, even positive interactions cannot increase indefinitely; at some point they will level off and reach a kind of equilibrium where both parties are either interacting enough to satisfy their needs or are prevented by task requirements from interacting further.

While there are exceptions, these propositions are surprisingly applicable to many different situations and have potent implications for managers. Consider different ways in which you might use them to design an organization: To resolve conflicts? To help make work more interesting? These simple propositions, when combined with others that follow (and which you develop yourself on the basis of your observations) can help explain the variety of emergent systems you will encounter.

Factors That Increase Cohesion

Required Interactions

The previous propositions suggest that, once there is a work reason for people to interact, they will begin to do it more often and will develop some liking for one another beyond the original task reason for their interaction. Thus, The more frequent the interactions required by the job, the more likely that *social* relationships and behavior will develop along with task relationships and behavior.[4] This is another way of describing the relationship between required and emergent interactions discussed in Chapter 3.

When members of a group begin to like one another and like being in the group, then the group will have attraction for the members, and acceptance from the group will be seen as desirable by them. In other words: The more attractive the group, the more *cohesive* it will be.[5] As the emerging social relationships form, the group will develop norms—ideas about what behavior is expected of group members. The more cohesive the group, the more eager individuals will be for membership, and, thus, the more likely they will be to conform to the group's norms. Another way of saying this is: The more cohesive the group, the more influence it has on its members. The less certain and clear a group's norms and standards are, the less control it will have over its members.[6]

From the point of view of a total group, finding ways of getting members to feel attracted to and willing to be influenced by the group is extremely desirable; a group can best reach its goals when it has everyone's allegiance and willingness to sacrifice personal desires on behalf of the group. From the individual's point of view, however, cohesion may be a mixed blessing in that there are personal costs in return for whatever may be the satisfaction of being an accepted member. The individual may have to forgo preferred ways of relating to others, put out greater effort than is desired, or give more time and concern than is comfortable. In Chapter 7 we explore more of the dilemmas faced by the individual trying to decide how much to give up for the closeness offered by the group; we want to note for now, however, that while membership has a price for the individual, insofar as the participation of all members is necessary or valuable for achieving the *group's* goals, the creation of group cohesiveness is important.

Common Attitudes and Values

We have already shown how cohesion is increased by frequent interaction, but a number of other factors can affect it. For example, if members of a group come to it with similar attitudes and values, cohesion is much more likely to occur rapidly. The greater the similarity in member attitudes and values brought to the group, the greater the likelihood of cohesion in a group.[7]

We would caution you against assuming that cohesion based on these kinds of similarities is necessarily desirable or even easy to generate today. As discussed in Chapter 1, workforce diversity related to gender, race, and national origin is increasing both naturally and deliberately as organizations globalize and as issues of social justice become paramount in the norms and policies.

A Most "Proper" Manager

A manager was offered a job at an investment banking firm in Boston. The firm's executives were all "proper Bostonians," educated at Ivy League schools. The manager was subsequently told he had been hired because the firm wanted greater diversity among the people employed, and during interviews he had revealed how different he was (despite his technical competence):

1. He owned a power boat (and did not sail).
2. His MBA degree was from the University of Massachusetts, not Dartmouth or Harvard.
3. He wanted to leave early one afternoon each week to coach Little League (not play squash).

Superordinate Goal

Along the same lines, when there are differences among group members, if there is some kind of overarching goal to which group members subscribe, cohesion is likely to increase. For example, a product invention group at a large consumer goods firm consisted of members with very different backgrounds: a chemist, a marketing expert, a production engineer, and a nutritionist. Whenever they met, they argued about how to proceed, feasibility of ideas, desirability of particular products to consumers, the capacity of the company to produce certain items—even what technical language to use when discussing ideas. But all members knew that their reputations and ultimately the company's future depended on their success in coming up with profitable new products. This commitment to the shared overall goal of new product creation pulled them past their frequent disagreements and made them fiercely loyal to their team. They prided themselves on their creativity and their collective practicality. Thus, Group cohesion will be increased by the existence of a superordinate goal(s) subscribed to by the members.[8]

A Common Enemy

Similarly, you probably have had experience with another kind of superordinate goal: dislike for a common enemy. If people have the same enemy, they are likely to feel a kinship; this general notion has long been used effectively by politicians in a number of countries to try to create a sense of national cohesion that overrides the variety of self-interests among different groups. In a smaller group as well, Group cohesion will be increased by the perceived existence of a common enemy.[9]

The common enemy may not necessarily be a hated enemy. Even friendly competition among groups usually has the effect of pushing group members to feel closer to one another. If by the time you read this you have already done a class exercise in groups, you may have noticed how the presence of other groups working on the same tasks seemed to cause people in your group to like one another more and, perhaps, even to begin to make joking comments about how much better your group was than the others. In Chapter 13 we look more closely at relationships across groups, but for now it is important to note that the presence of competing (or even potentially competing) groups often makes members within groups feel closer to one another. In some situations, especially in competitively oriented Western society, this phenomenon is so powerful that, even when a multigroup activity is conducted in which groups are *not* being compared with one another, group members still act as if it were a competitive situation and seem to feel cohesive just by being near other groups visibly working on a similar activity.

Success in Achieving Goals and Group Status

Another factor that can lead to greater feeling of liking among group members is for the group to be successful in achieving its goals. If a group seems to be successful at getting what it wants, that makes the group more attractive to members and seems to carry over in the way that members feel about one another. Thus, Group cohesion will be increased by success in achieving the group's goals.[10]

A connected factor affecting group cohesion has to do with the relative position of the group in relation to other groups in the same overall organization. As you might expect, the higher the status of a particular group in relation to other groups, the more attractive it will seem to members. This is apparently true for everyone but Groucho Marx, who once said, "I wouldn't want to belong to any club which would have me as a member." But for others of us less witty or perceptive, Group cohesion is increased in proportion to the status of the group relative to other groups in the system.[11]

Low External Interactions

A related issue from a somewhat opposite point of view has to do with the amount of time that group members are required to spend away from the group. If group members by the nature of their job have to relate to many outsiders (including others in the same organization but not in the group), they are less likely to feel strong allegiance to their own group. This is very often true of certain kinds of professional employees who spend a good portion of their time dealing with the problems of nonspecialists in their organization and who also spend time at professional meetings with people from other organizations in order to keep up-to-date in their specialty, whether it is engineering, medicine, law, or whatever. Similarly, an organization's purchasing agent will often have to spend more time dealing with outsiders than fellow organization members, leading to reduced loyalty to his or her own department and organization. Thus, Group cohesion will be increased when there is a low frequency of required external interactions.[12]

Resolution of Differences

Every group will at times have differences of opinions; how they are resolved affects cohesion. If a group has repeated problems with resolving differences among members, because of strong differences of opinion, values, or working style, the members' liking for one another will tend to decrease even when the group manages to be successful. Thus, The more easily and frequently member differences are settled in a way satisfactory to all members, the greater will be group cohesion.[13] Nevertheless, success, even if arrived at by a cantankerous process, can soothe many bad feelings. A winning group usually overlooks its differences; a losing group often finds fault with its members.

Availability of Resources

Finally, the way members feel about each other is frequently affected by the availability of resources to the whole group. When resources, such as money, supplies, prestige, or recognition, are scarce, group members are likely to feel competitive with one another. Conversely, when there is an abundance of whatever resources the group needs, members are likely to see each other more charitably and, therefore, like each other more. Group cohesion will increase under conditions of abundant resources. For example, when the staff of an innovative health center saw government grants rolling in, the members felt close to the other "pioneers" on the staff. When government money dried up and even weekly paychecks were in jeopardy, dissension and anger toward one another broke out.

The preceding propositions all relate to group integration. The cohesiveness or attractiveness of a group and the power of its norms to regulate behavior are major aspects of emergent systems and are important factors for diagnosing and predicting group behavior. As explained, cohesiveness is influenced by background factors, such as similarity in member attitudes, and by attributes of the required system, such as the necessity for interaction. By carefully tracing what is brought to the work group and what is required of it, it is possible to make sense of the degree of closeness that emerges. But keep in mind that "nothing is as simple as it seems" (see Chapter 1). Cohesiveness is the result of many factors; a careful analysis requires that you think in terms of multiple causality.

While all of the above propositions have been phrased in terms of what positively increases cohesion, they are also intended to be reversible in terms of what decreases cohesion. As a manager you may wish at any given time to increase or decrease cohesion among a particular group and may be able to affect differing aspects of the conditions cited by the propositions. Deciding in which direction cohesion should be pushed and then how to do it requires a careful assessment of existing conditions.

> The manager of a large department store was faced with customer complaints about waiting time for service. Upon investigation, he found that many of the full-time salespeople congregated near the fitting rooms for conversation. They enjoyed one another's company so much that they found it difficult to interrupt the gossip and joking to go wait on customers. The manager had to find a way to decrease the group's cohesion without creating major resentment that would interfere with selling enthusiasm. How might such a problem be approached? Would it be wise to crack down and prohibit all social talk? What would be the effect of physically rearranging the work area?

Consequences of Cohesion for Productivity, Satisfaction, and Development

Productivity

Since a cohesive group is one in which members adhere to the norms, it should not be surprising that in such a group norms are likely to develop not only in regard to general behavior but also about member productivity. The group will usually arrive at a strong sense of how much each member should produce and how much variation from that level will be tolerated, and then encourage the members to produce at or near that level. Whether production is measured in widgets/hour as in a manufacturing group or in "sufficient hours spent preparing an analysis" as in a student task group, The more cohesive the group, the more *similar* will be the output of individual members.[14]

Another way of looking at the effect of cohesiveness on productivity is in terms of how much effort members will make to see that the productivity norms, high or low, are followed. As you might expect, The more cohesive the group, the more it will try to enforce compliance with its norms about productivity. Cohesive groups will work hard to get members to increase output if it is lower than the group thinks appropriate and also will supply pressure to hold down the output of members who embarrass the group by producing "too much." Cohesiveness does not cause *high* productivity, merely similar levels of it among group members.

You may remember from Chapter 3 that a group's idea of what is the proper amount to produce may be only vaguely related to higher management's or the rest of the organization's ideas of the proper amount. In general, if the group feels in sympathy with or supported by "higher management" (or those who define good performance), it will have a tendency to enforce a fairly high level of productivity on

MANAGERIAL BULLETIN

"Revolution at Corning Ceramics Plant"

Everyone is assigned to a team of about six workers, who together set goals and schedules, and even assign each other jobs. And although that method is proving efficient, it's also the source of numerous conflicts.

"People problems are the issue," says a . . . kiln operator. For instance, some teams have felt pulled down by one lazy member. "If there's a conflict, . . . we're expected to resolve it" instead of turning to a supervisor. "If someone isn't feeling well or pulling their weight, we can't let it go on or it'll just be a bigger problem," she adds, noting how it's difficult to confront a co-worker.

SOURCE: Alecia Swasy and Carol Hymowitz, "The Workplace Revolution," *The Wall Street Journal,* February 9, 1990.

its members and vice versa. Since a cohesive group will bring member productivity into line, The greater the cohesion of the group, the higher productivity will be if the group supports the organization's goals, and the lower productivity will be if the group resists the organization's goals.[15]

A cohesive group that wants to produce more will pull even its weaker members along quite effectively. But the group that sticks together can thus be irritatingly resistant to effort to increase its productivity when, for whatever reason, it does not wish to raise output. What does this suggest to you, as a future manager, about your relationships to task groups reporting to you and about the conditions under which their cohesiveness might be desirable?

Another way in which cohesiveness may not lead to higher productivity arises when members come to like each other so much that they prefer to socialize rather than work, as was the case with the department store salespeople mentioned earlier. Conversely, a group that is not cohesive could still be productive if its members were highly individualistic and driven to work hard by their needs and values—and the work itself did not require great cooperation and interdependence. In some respects, it's like the difference between a basketball team and a baseball team. The former depends on constant teamwork while the latter requires individual effort on behalf of the team.

Group cohesiveness can also either enhance or stifle productivity, depending on the members' willingness to be open with one another. On the one hand, in a cohesive group members feel close enough to one another to be able to discuss issues and problems frankly. Closeness should make explorations of issues easier, because all members can presumably be trusted with information and with members' feelings.

On the other hand, when people feel attracted to a group, they may see the risk of offending someone they like as greater than if the others didn't matter. Holding back opinions, feelings, or ideas, because the approval of others is so important that it can't be tested, can lead to unproductive decisions.

When cohesiveness is a result of great similarity in member attitudes, values, and external status, it can lead to decreased productivity over time.[16] The similarities apparently act as a filter against disconfirming information and events, so that the ease of working together is overwhelmed by the problems of collective resistance to disconfirming inputs. While managers often fear that heterogeneity in a task group will lead to conflict among members and to low group productivity, it is important for them to realize that too much homogeneity can eventually result in mediocre group performance. Some diversity in points of view can increase creativity in problem solving.

Quality Circles and Productivity

The Quality Circles approach—voluntary groups of about 10 workers who meet with a supervisor to make suggestions about how to solve shop floor quality problems—provides an excellent example of how groups of workers can become highly productive as a result of having common goals, achieving success, and having frequent required interactions. While this technology was developed for the purpose of improving product quality on the production floor, extra benefits—increased worker commitment, higher morale, lower turnover, and the like—are predictable from the propositions about

cohesion and realized when the results are supported by the organization. All of these outcomes benefit productivity. Indeed, companies such as Toyota, where almost all employees participate in QC programs, report greater numbers of useful suggestions per worker than companies without formal programs. Many companies have found that equivalent "problem-solving teams" among white-collar workers (technicians, administrators, sales support, and so on) can yield similar benefits if managed well.

Groupthink

Where groups become very cohesive, there is danger that they become victims of their own closeness.

Symptoms

1. Illusions of the group as invulnerable.
2. Rationalizing away data that disconfirm assumptions and beliefs.
3. Unquestioned belief in group's inherent morality.
4. Stereotyping competitors as weak, evil, stupid, and so on.
5. Direct pressure on deviants to conform.
6. Self-censorship by members.
7. Illusions of unanimity (silence equals consent).
8. Self-appointed "mind guards"—protecting group from disconfirming data.

Prevention Steps

A_1. Leader encourages open expression of doubt.
A_2. Leader accepts criticism of his or her opinions.
B. Higher-status members offer opinions last.
C. Get recommendations from a duplicate group.
D. Periodically divide into subgroups.
E. Members get reaction of trusted outsiders.
F. Invite trusted outsiders to join discussion periodically.
G. Assign someone the role of devil's advocate.
H. Develop scenarios of rivals' possible actions.

SOURCE: Adapted from Irving Janis, *Victims of Groupthink* (Boston: Houghton Mifflin, 1972).

Very cohesive groups run the risk of falling victim to "groupthink."[17] Groupthink is a mode of thought and behavior that occurs "when the members' strivings for unanimity override their motivation to realistically appraise alternative courses of action." As a result, the group easily overestimates its own capabilities, cuts itself off from new information, and becomes smug about its own views and judgments. Even very high-level groups of managers can fall prey to this avoidance of discomfort from disagreement; Janis studied President Kennedy and his advisers making the disastrous decisions to invade Cuba at the Bay of Pigs, finding that the few with dissenting opinions were ridiculed and treated as weaklings, until everyone went along.

The Need for Conflict

The NT leader doesn't believe in bottling up emotion. "The way you let off stress is to let it out," he says. He means it. Mr. Shannon points to a circle drawn on the wall near the door; it marks the spot where Mr. Cutler once unleashed a violent kick, cracking through the wall and injuring his toe. For his 50th birthday a few months ago, Mr. Cutler's team gave him a framed piece of his office wall, which he had destroyed in a moment of rage ignited by the failure of a new build to run on his computer.

[I]nnovation, in an age of technological complexity, usually requires dogged system-building and an ability to hold large teams together while allowing—even cultivating—conflict. Conflict lies at the core of innovation "because there isn't always a unique way to solve a problem," says Emanual R. Piore, a former chief scientist for International Business Machines Corp. "When there's no conflict, a lab is no good."

SOURCE: G. Pascal Zachary, "Agony and Ecstasy of 200 Code Writers Beget Windows NT; Badgered by a Driven Guru They Fight Fatigue, Fear, to Build Grand Synthesis," Reprinted by permission of *The Wall Street Journal,* May 26, 1993. © Dow Jones & Company, Inc. All Rights Reserved Worldwide.

The Pledge of Allegiance in Japan

Change in Japan, says sociologist Akira Fujitake, is "stopped by a barrier called 'the group.'" Groupthink, he says, "places harmony over rationality, and therefore acts to reject change." The Japanese like to say that playing it safe is a habit that arises from the country's "agrarian culture" and abiding village mentality. Even people who crave real change "tend to run away when confronted with the opportunity," says Mr. Fujitake.

SOURCE: Michael Williams, and Yumiko Ono, "Japanese Cite Need for Bold Change, but Not at the Expense of 'Stability,'" *The Wall Street Journal,* June 29, 1993.

Fortunately, Kennedy learned from the experience and handled the Cuban Missile Crisis more effectively. In fact, he used some of the "prevention steps" outlined in the Managerial Tools box on page 94. Overcohesiveness can be stifling to a group's effectiveness if members hesitate to risk offending someone—or the group has fallen into groupthink.

A variation on groupthink, in which fear of displeasing others leads to a poor decision, has been dubbed "The Abilene Paradox," from one family's decision to spend the day in Abilene when no individual member actually wanted to go.[18] Yet each, thinking he or she was the only one who did not want to go, never spoke up. In many organizations, cohesive groups end up making equally poor decisions, because no one tests the apparent agreement for fear of being odd person out or of disrupting "harmony." Cohesion does not always lead to effectiveness.

Satisfaction

A cohesive group will by definition have a high overall level of satisfaction; presumably, a group attractive to its members is satisfying. Individual members, however, may very much feel that the norms of the group call for behavior that is not easily given. Belonging to a close cohesive group can be a warm supportive experience; but,

Misguided Friendship Helped Create the Edsel

Of course, business often gets in the way of friendship. But there are times when friendship moves in the way of business . . . One of the revelations I came upon is the behind-the-scenes tales of how Ford launched its infamous Edsel plan—regarded to this day as one of the biggest commercial product disasters of all time. It will shock many to learn that the friendship among the Whiz Kids was instrumental in leading to the disaster. Several of the men were opposed to the huge investment from the start. One even predicted, with chilling

accuracy, that it would be suicidal to take on GM: the assumptions behind the numbers were foolish; they verged on fiction. Yet, the Whiz Kids failed to assert their opposition because the plan was hatched and promoted by their colleague, Jack Reith. As Arjay Miller put it, "We didn't want to rain on Jack's parade." Friendship and ambition do not always mix.

SOURCE: From *The Whiz Kids* by John A. Byrne, Copyright © 1993 by John A. Byrne. Used by permission of Doubleday, a division of Bantam Doubleday Dell Publishing Group, Inc.

Peer Pressure in Japan

Most everyone knows, for example, that the Japanese work long hours and attend corporate outings on weekends. "Does this reflect the fabled company loyalty of the Japanese worker?" Mr. Yoshimura and Mr. Anderson ask. "Hardly; although such activities are formally voluntary, everyone knows that failure to participate is socially unacceptable. Only a complete idiot would make such a blunder. . . . Deviation from the appropriate model is accompanied by penalties that most Japanese

are unwilling to endure." It is anxiety that compels employees to work even when sick, or during a child's graduation. Many American companies have tried to borrow the notion of team spirit from Japan without realizing the system of social controls at work underneath the surface.

SOURCE: Steven R. Weisman, "Peer Pressure," *The New York Times,* March 16, 1997, p. 31.

for some, the embrace of the group may feel suffocating. Should that happen to many members of the group, its cohesiveness may well begin to suffer as members struggle to assert their own individuality. An individual whose values and other attitudes are contrary to those that the group has come to share can feel very uncomfortable and out of place. But the positive feelings from being a member of a cohesive group can be sufficient for some people to offset even low pay, unpleasant physical conditions, harsh bosses, and so forth. That is why commitment of members to the group, leading to lower turnover, follows from cohesion. And this can occur even without commitment to the organization as a whole.

Development and Learning

A cohesive group can provide excellent opportunities for members to help and learn from one another. In fact, that can be part of what attracts members. The sharing of knowledge, skills, and experiences can be very rewarding and growth-promoting. Some groups, however, achieve cohesion only at the expense of individual growth. The group becomes so anxious to maintain a certain kind of harmony that it suppresses individual knowledge and differences for fear of making some members feel unequal or inadequate.

No Mistake about It: Trust Is Key in Learning

[Professor Amy C.] Edmondson found that members of teams with higher levels of psychological safety (those characterized by greater mutual respect and trust) were more likely to ask thoughtful questions, request feedback and help, and admit errors. These teams were also judged to be better performers by nonteam members assessing their work. In addition, they were better able to overcome roadblocks to success such as lack of material or financial resources. "The team members who were comfortable taking risks were free to engage in the behaviors necessary to learn and perform well, and they appeared to be less constrained by outside factors."

SOURCE: Judith A. Ross, "No Mistake about It: Trust Is Key in Learning," *Harvard Business School Bulletin,* February 1999.

Cohesion achieved in this way may not hinder the group from producing adequately and may be reasonably satisfying to members who want the security of minimal competition and differences among peers, but it can serve to "freeze" growth at a particular point. A student task group can, for example, see to it that everyone does his or her share of assignments, warmly socialize in and out of class, and support all members with liking and warmth, yet still prevent maximum individual learning. A quieter member who would learn valuable debating skills from being prodded to defend his/her ideas may be allowed to make contributions behind the scenes and thus never be forced to practice new skills. Or an argumentative member with a unique point of view might be cajoled into "not pushing so hard, for the good of the group," and thus never really be faced with the consequences of such a style or have a chance to think through and persuade others about his or her views.

On the other hand, if a group lacks cohesiveness, individual and group learning may be inhibited. It often takes at least a minimally supportive environment for members to take any risks in expressing ideas, defending unpopular views, and so forth. Also, if a group lacks cohesiveness, it will probably have difficulty looking at its own process or confronting conflicts and thereby be less able to "learn" as a group or develop its capacity to function effectively. Therefore, the degree of cohesiveness in a group can have either positive or negative consequences for development; it takes careful analysis of the particular situation to assess the effects.

The next chapter explores further the connections between group cohesion and effectiveness by looking at the other side of cohesiveness, those forces that separate and differentiate group members. Even the most cohesive groups have differences among members that must be dealt with and that impact the group's productivity, satisfaction, and development.

KEY CONCEPTS FROM CHAPTER 4

1. Propositions on group cohesiveness:
    a. The more interactions, the more positive feelings.
    b. The more positive feelings, the more interactions.
    c. The more attractive the group, the more cohesiveness.
    d. The more cohesive the group, the more eagerness for membership.
    e. The more eagerness for membership, the more conformity to group's norms.
        Therefore:
    f. The more cohesive the group, the more influence it has on its members.
    g. The less clear the group's norms, the less control it has over its members.
2. Group cohesiveness is increased by:
    a. Similarity in attitudes, values, and goals.

b. Existence of a common enemy.
c. Acceptance of superordinate goals.
d. Success in achieving goals.
e. High status relative to other groups.
f. Low number of required external interactions.
g. Differences settled in satisfactory way to all members.
h. Conditions of abundant resources.

3. High cohesiveness correlates with productivity, satisfaction, and development:
   a. Members' productivity similar in a cohesive group.
   b. Group productivity high if the group values productiveness.
   c. Dangers of groupthink.
   d. Member satisfaction high, by definition.
   e. Member development may be high or low.

PERSONAL APPLICATION EXERCISE

Think of a group to which you really enjoyed belonging, where members felt close to each other and wanted to be a part of the group. Which, if any, of the following factors contributed to the cohesion?

Similarity in attitudes, values, or goals? ☐
Existence of a common enemy? ☐
Acceptance of superordinate goals? ☐
Success in achieving goals? ☐
High status relative to other groups? ☐
Low number of required external interactions? ☐
Differences satisfactorily settled? ☐
Conditions of abundant resources? ☐

Did the cohesion feel stifling in any way? Did you see any examples of groupthink? Can you think of an example of when it caused a poor decision to be made? What were the outcomes of the cohesion for:

Productivity?   ☐ High   ☐ Medium   ☐ Low
Satisfaction?   ☐ High   ☐ Medium   ☐ Low
Development?   ☐ High   ☐ Medium   ☐ Low

If any of the outcomes were less than high, what could the leader of the group have done to improve them?

SUGGESTED READINGS

Ashforth, B. E., and F. Mael. "Social Identity Theory and the Organization." *Academy of Management Review* 14, no. 1 (1989), pp. 20–39.

Feldman, D. C. "The Development and Enforcement of Group Norms." *Academy of Management Review,* January 1984, pp. 47–53.

Harvey, J. B., and C. R. Boettger. "Improving Communication within a Managerial Work Group." *Journal of Applied Behavioral Science,* March–April 1971, pp. 154–79.

Mudrack, P. E. "Group Cohesiveness and Productivity: A Closer Look." *Human Relations* 42, no. 9 (September 1989), pp. 771–85.

Schacter, S. *The Psychology of Affiliation.* Stanford, CA: Stanford University Press, 1959.

Seashore, S. E. *Group Cohesiveness in the Industrial Work Group.* Ann Arbor, MI: Survey Research Center, Institute for Social Research, 1964.

Smith, P. B. *Groups within Organizations.* New York: Harper & Row, 1973.

Steele, F. I. "Physical Settings and Social Interaction." In *Physical Settings and Organization Development.* Reading, MA: Addison-Wesley Publishing, 1973.

Whyte, G. "Groupthink Reconsidered." *Academy of Management Review* 14, no. 1 (January 1989), pp. 40–56.

Differentiation in Groups

Building Internal Structure as a Basis for Productivity

No Free Ride

Downeast Technology in Westbrook [Maine] promises a bonus to software engineers before they complete a project. Once the work is over, company officials ask each team member to recommend how the bonus should be divided.

Last year, after collaborating on a complex project and meeting a tight deadline, seven employees recommended how a $5,000 bonus should be parceled out. "In a perfect world, all seven would have gotten one-seventh of the pot," said Poliquin. "As it turned out, one person got zero. Another person, who was considered the hardest worker on the team, received a high of $1,050.

"Personal issues made one person unable to contribute to the project the way management, and the person's compatriots, expected him to contribute," said Poliquin, "which is why he did not receive a portion of the award. . . .

"It's not intended to [cause hard feelings]" Poliquin continued. "The goal is to share equally in providing excellent job performance. So, only those who perform are rewarded.

". . . most of the work that people are doing now is being done in teams. So, at one time there was a movement afoot to link team pay to performance. But some people felt it wasn't fair. Why should a team member who contributes very little receive the same bonus?"

SOURCE: Diane E. Lewis, "A Team Decides Who Gets Bonus," *The Boston Globe,* January 27, 1998, p. C4.

"Over time, a group will develop relative positions or 'ranks' for its members—that is, members acquire different status from one another."

After looking at cohesion—what it is that makes a group stick together and be attractive to members—it is important to examine the way groups differentiate their members in terms of value to the group. Few groups have total equality among all members; some individuals obtain more respect and influence, some more liking, others less of one or the other. Over time a group will develop relative positions or "ranks" for its members—that is, members acquire different status from one another. In this chapter we will look at three key factors that determine the relative positions of group members: (1) status brought to the group from outside, (2) individual adherence to group norms, and (3) group-related roles assumed by members. These factors contribute to individual member influence, which ultimately influence group productivity, satisfaction, and development.

The notion of status differences as something to observe and discuss often makes North Americans uncomfortable because of their widespread professed beliefs about everyone being created equal and that differences among people working together should be minimized or ignored. The United States is one of a handful of countries where such beliefs are widely espoused. In most parts of the world, the ideas that some people are more worthy and esteemed than others, and that everyone has a rank or status that can be precisely identified relative to all others, are accepted as obviously true.

While Americans acknowledge broad differences in status—doctor (professional) higher than garbage collector (blue-collar), professor higher than student (sometimes?)—the idea is resisted in groups of peers or those who see themselves as "about the same." The sameness usually refers to broad categories, such as students, middle managers, or board members, and there is often resistance to the possibility that, in fact, even in a group of peers differences in status emerge, are identifiable, and have important consequences for the group and individuals in it.

For example, one of the most common norms students bring to task groups is "we are all equal," which means that no one student member is supposed to be able to dominate others, tell others what to do, or give orders. Yet it is clear that it would be extremely unlikely for all members to possess equal skills in generating ideas, organizing, analyzing, writing, or interacting socially. As a result, once the group takes on some tasks, various members emerge with different status in the group.

> No two men can be half an hour together but one shall acquire an evident superiority over the other.
>
> Samuel Johnson
> Boswell's *Life of Samuel Johnson*

Just which attributes of members will result in high ranking depends on the norms and standards of the particular group; in some groups, status goes to those who help most with the tasks, while in others status goes to those who make members feel most comfortable and at ease. But inevitably groups do develop some informal ranking of members even if they do not discuss it directly. Although each group must be separately studied to determine the basis for status in that group, in general, Members who contribute most to task accomplishment are accorded the most *respect* in the group, while members who contribute most to social accomplishment (development of relationships) are accorded the most *liking* in the group.[1] One's position on these two dimensions (respect and liking) determines a person's overall status in the group, with the weights attached to each determined by the group's emergent norms and values.

Poor Image for Casual Dress in Japan

The new casual dress code at IBM is no hit in Corporate Japan, where traditional business suits are expected. When Vice-President Tatsuyuki Saeki of IBM Japan appeared before the press in a sweater and slacks recently, commentators raised eyebrows. After Saeki approved relaxed sartorial rules for his personal-computer division in January, fellow IBM Japan units didn't follow suit.

Ditto other companies. Casual wear, once anathema at Big Blue, is still a heresy among the Japanese, to whom appearance (tatemae) is paramount. "In the U.S., the blue-suit image was a drag on us," says an IBM Asia spokesman. "But here, no one ridicules the blue suit. You'd be laughing at the entire nation." Even plumbers don ties to commute, then switch to work clothes.

At game-software companies and research centers, dressing down is accepted. But even their techies are expected to spiff up when they're out and about. A newscaster once tweaked a visiting Bill Gates by pulling up the billionaire's pants leg on camera to reveal threadbare socks and scuffed shoes.

SOURCE: Edith Updike, "The Land of the Rising Eyebrow," *Business Week,* March 27, 1995.

Just Playing Doctor? Shorter Coats Make Residents Feel Naked

Young M.D.s at Duke Battle Dress Code; Hemlines Are Vital Sign, They Argue

A three-decade-old department policy restricted the use of knee-length white coats to veteran doctors. Internal-medicine residents had to wear blazer-length white coats—though residents in other departments, including surgery and pediatrics, had recently switched to the longer coats.

Anyone arguing that medical residents haven't earned a knee-length white coat must answer—or dodge—the question of what butchers, barbers, and cosmetics clerks did to earn them. "At Duke, sometimes even managers in environmental services wear long coats . . ." Environmental services is the custodial department. . . .

You're a Doctor?

When first-year resident M. Angelyn Bethel, 28, went to take care of a patient and the woman got a look at her short coat, she said, "'Are you certain you're a doctor?' I told her I was, but she would have none of it. I eventally had to leave the room to find someone in a long coat to tell her I was OK."

To other traditionalists, the long-coat envy seems adolescent. "If you're a teenager, you're going to want to dress like the people older than you," says vice dean of education for the medical school.

Some residents say a foot or so of fabric can make an amazing difference. Dr. McClure, the third-year resident, says a neurosurgeon whom she declines to name never acknowledged her when she wore a short coat. But the first day she wore a long one, the neurosurgeon said hello. "I said, 'Oh, you see me now' "

SOURCE: Calmetta Y. Coleman "Just Playing Doctor? Shorter Coats Make Residents Feel Naked," *The Wall Street Journal,* February 2, 2000, p. A1.

Bases of Differentiation

Initial Ranking: External Status and Status Congruence

While over the long run each member's status in a group will be based on the member's contribution to whatever the group values, early status in a group is usually related to the status of each group member outside the group. In a company task force

A Vice President by Any Other Name Still Might Leave Some People Confused

Bank titles bewilder most outsiders, who assume that anybody at the bank not wielding a mop is an assistant vice president.

Now the titles are changing. . . . How does "group executive," for example, improve on "executive vice president"? And how do you reply when somebody introduces himself as "vice president, branch manager, individual banking, Memphis"? . . .

The original purpose of bank titles was to give officers the authority to make loans and approve other transactions . . . however, the titles proliferated since they were increasingly used to confer status . . . "to make customers feel they were dealing with an important person." . . . "And pretty soon, a vice president wasn't such a big deal."

SOURCE: Helen Cogan, *The Wall Street Journal,* June 11, 1985.

Good Looks Can Mean a Pretty Penny on the Job, and "Ugly" Men Are Affected More Than Women

Beauty, it seems, earns considerably more than the beast.

A new study on how good looks pay off in the workplace has found the rewards to be substantial . . . education, experience, and other characteristics being equal, people who are perceived as "good-looking" earn, on average, about 10% more than those viewed as "homely." And, surprisingly, men are more likely than women to pay the penalties of a bad appearance.

Attractive people, the study said, tend to earn roughly 5% more than people with average looks. "Ugly" people tend to earn about 5% less than average-looking people. However, differences emerge between men and women.

Men who are uglier than average tend to make 9% less, while below-average women make only 5% less.

The phenomenon isn't limited to occupations where looks play a big part, such as modeling, acting, or working directly with the public. The study found that looks also count for higher earnings in jobs where appearance presumably plays no role, such as bricklaying, factory work, and telemarketing.

The findings suggest another type of workplace bias in addition to race and gender prejudice.

SOURCE: Lucinda Harper. Reprinted by permission of *The Wall Street Journal,* November 23, 1993. © Dow Jones & Company, Inc., All Rights Reserved Worldwide.

set up to investigate ways of awarding bonuses to outstanding performers in a group, for example, a senior vice president will usually be given more respect at first than a personnel department assistant, despite the possibility that the personnel assistant may indeed know more about alternative bonus systems and their consequences. The higher the background factor of external status, the higher the initial internal status of a group member.[2]

But it is not always obvious what attributes group members will use to rank status in the world outside the group. What some people consider high-status attributes might not be seen that way at all by others, particularly if an attribute is not judged to be relevant to the group's purposes. For example, in the bonus system task force just mentioned, being a senior vice president would probably yield a higher rank than being a personnel assistant. But within a group of workers trying to decide how

MANAGERIAL BULLETIN

A Difference in Societies That Can Give United States an Edge in Talks

American officials and students of trade negotiations say that foreign officials, who are not used to dealing with career women in their own countries, often feel awkward when face-to-face at a negotiating table with American lawyers, economists, and other professionals who happen to be women. It's a situation that tends to favor the United States . . . "Are they going to react to her as a man to a woman, as a man to a foreign woman, as a man to an American woman, as a man to a representative of the US government?

SOURCE: Clyde Farnsworth, *New York Times,* July 4, 1988.

to request a change in working hours, the personnel assistant's knowledge of rules and procedures, plus his or her membership on the bonus task force, is likely to result in high status there. Similarly, a high-status judge might be given little respect in a group that has crashed in the desert if his or her survival skills are comparatively low. A mechanic might be given higher status in this situation even though he or she would be seen as lower status in other circumstances.

Furthermore, many other factors may go into setting a person's status. We have been talking about profession and, by implication, income as two important factors, but there are others that often make a difference: age, sex, education (where and how long), ethnicity, marital status, and even the region of birth. In student task groups, class standing, major subject, and work experience are often important determinants, too, since careers are not yet established. Some of these factors, such as education and profession, are achievable by work and ability, while others, such as age, sex, and ethnicity, the person is born with or gets by just existing. Although the rankings may in no way be fair or just, especially to those who are low status, some kind of ranking exists everywhere. In many cultures higher status goes to those who are older, male, married, highly educated, have high incomes, and are members of the dominant ethnic group. In any particular group, however, some of these factors might be reversed, as in these examples you may recognize: "dinosaurs," "yuppies," "ivory-tower pointy-headed intellectuals," "nerds," "fat cats," "male chauvinist pigs," and "white trash."

In general, The higher a person is on external dimensions (or other valued ones), the higher his or her emergent status within a group, and vice versa. To any particular group, however, one factor may be seen as overriding all others; in certain organizations, for example, if you aren't a WASP (or whatever the dominant ethnic background), being high status on all the other factors will not make up for lack of status on that dimension.

Not only can we look at how high a person is on several status factors to estimate likely internal status, but we can also make some predictions about emergent behavior based on how consistent a person's status ranking is *across* factors. For example, some people are high or low in status on all factors; we call that *status congruency.*

If the senior vice president in our example were a 60-year-old male, married, had an MBA, and was descended from someone who came over on the Mayflower, he would be congruently high status on all factors. Conversely, in New Hampshire at least, if the personnel assistant were female, 20 years old, French-Canadian, unmarried, new to the company, and had not gone beyond high school, she would be congruently low status on all factors. But suppose the senior vice president was a 28-year-old African-American woman who was completing a part-time MBA program. Or suppose the personnel assistant was a 40-year-old former philosophy professor who had changed careers and was showing great promise and potential. Can

Person	Age	Sex	Education	Ethnicity	Profession	Income	
A	High	High	High	High	High	High	= High status, congruent
B	Low	Low	Low	Low	Low	Low	= Low status, congruent
C	Low	Low	High	High	High	High	= High status, incongruent
D	...	...	...	...	...	...	= and so forth

you see in these examples how the status factors of each would then be inconsistent with one another, "out of line," or *incongruent*? (See Figure 5–1.) Can you imagine how difficult it might then be for the bonus system task force members to "place" or rank each one? What might be their reaction?

Conformity to Norms as a Determinant of Emergent Status

We previously looked at the way norms emerge and how cohesiveness increases conformity to group norms. But no matter how attractive a group is and no matter how much members wish to belong, it is almost never possible for every member to go along with all of a group's norms. Sometimes norms call for behavior beyond the capacity of individuals in the group, as, for example, "Everyone should make creative contributions to the group's efforts." Some people have more of the skills needed by a group than do others, and when the norms call for those particular skills, they are at a natural advantage. If a student task group desires high grades and must produce excellent written analyses to get them, the individual member who is good at performing such analysis and at writing clear conclusions will naturally be better able to conform to norms about contributing to the group's goals. Another member might be an excellent amateur carpenter, but not be valued as highly in the group, because such manual skills are not necessary for achieving high performance.

Other norms ask individuals to do what goes too strongly "against the grain," irritating the person's fundamental values and personality. To illustrate, some groups ask that all members act humbly even to the point of denying any needs for individual recognition. To a person raised with strong emphasis on individual competition and a belief in sinking or swimming on one's own best efforts, being modest about successes may be either impossible or seem too "wrong" to be tolerated, let alone tried. For such a person, conformity to a norm of "humility" is a virtual impossibility, even if other aspects of the group make membership attractive. In a more gentle, unjudging world, the inability or unwillingness to conform to what are, after all, only one group's particular idiosyncratic norms would go unpunished. The desirability, for example, of false humility has not been proclaimed from on high as the one true way; in fact, just around the corner (perhaps in our competitive individual's family) sits a group with equal conviction about the rightness of savoring glory when it is earned!

Conformists and nonconformists are not absolute personality types; all people have some group or groups to whose norms and values they conform, even when they are physically present elsewhere. The question is only whether a person will (or can) conform to a *particular* group's norms while a member. Nonconformity in that context is usually a sign of subscription and conformity to some other group's standards. If when in Rome a person does not "do as the Romans do," it is usually because he or she thinks that "doing as Americans/Thais/Germans (select your own category) do" is better, nicer, or more comfortable than going along with the present company.

Yet despite the fact that particular norms about productivity and other kinds of behavior can vary sharply from group to group, each group's ideas about proper behavior often become enshrined or "sacred," as if there were no other possible way to

MANAGERIAL BULLETIN

Unusual Norms at Salomon Brothers; Groveling for Jobs

Jobs were doled out at the end of the [training] program . . . Contrary to what we expected . . . we were not assured of employment . . .

Each trainee had to decide for himself . . . Those who chose to put on a full court grovel [to the managing directors who selected] from the opening buzzer found seats in the front of the classroom, where they sat, lips puckered, through the entire five-month program. Those who treasured their pride—or perhaps thought it best to remain aloof—feigned cool indifference by sitting in the back row and hurling paper wads at managing directors.

SOURCE: Michael Lewis, *Liar's Poker* (New York: W. W. Norton, 1989).

behave and still be a good person. Once a group has clear ideas about proper levels of productivity, for example, it will expend considerable energy trying to bring members who deviate from them (hereafter referred to as *deviants*) into line. Thus: The more an individual group member fails to conform to the group's norms, the more frequently negative sentiments will be expressed toward him or her.[3]

The particular form of expression for negative sentiments can vary, depending on the general style of group members and the particular norm being enforced. Some groups may use sarcasm, irony, and indirect hints to let a member know he or she is not conforming properly, while other groups may use nods, winks, facial mugging, or "gentle love-taps" to admonish deviating members. In the classic Hawthorne experiments,[4] where the relationship between social relations and productivity was first explored, one work group was observed in which deviants who produced "too much" were hit on the upper arm with the fist, a process called "binging." This was a crude but effective way to see to it that no one person produced so much that management would start to ask why all workers could not do the same each day.

Whatever the particular medium of expression, every group will have ways of "punishing" its deviant members, and most will have at least some members who cannot or will not conform to its norms, leading to differences in rank. When the group expresses dislike for a member who isn't conforming, it often produces defensiveness or aggression in that member, which in turn can lead to greater punishment by the group and to new attempts to bring the member into line. After awhile, however, the group will begin to ignore the deviant as if to punish him or her by withholding what the group sees as desirable relationships. The person will then become an *isolate,* attached to the group by work assignment but essentially cut out of nonwork interactions. The less a member conforms to a group's norms, the greater will be the interaction directed at him or her for some time. Should the interaction fail to bring the member into conformity with the norms, interaction will sharply decrease.[5]

While the idea of being a deviant in a group seems to have a negative connotation, there often are times when the behavior of a group violates the personal values of a member and may force that member to make a choice between conformity to group pressure for the sake of harmony and standing up for one's convictions. Going along is usually easier and is likely to be supported by the other group members. The cost that is paid is paid primarily by the one member. The choice to deviate by being true to personal values is the tougher decision but at least helps the individual to retain a sense of integrity. Furthermore, it is this sense of doing what is right that motivates *whistle-blowers,* those brave people who are willing to speak up and tell the truth even when they are pressured to just go along. It may, in the long run, even help the group by establishing a norm that supports individual integrity. Therefore, when you use

| **FIGURE 5-2** | *Individual Conformity to Norms and Status in Group* |

the term *deviant,* be careful not to prejudge it negatively; it is a relative matter that can only be judged in context—that is, by what the person is deviating from.

Conversely, the more closely a person conforms to the group's norms and carries out the group's ideas of proper behavior, the better the person will be liked by other group members and become a *regular* member of the group. In short, the greater a member's conformity to the group's important norms, the greater the group's liking for the member.[6]

The people who are best able to conform to the group's norms—because of skills, attributes, resources possessed by them, earned or otherwise—are likely to emerge as informal leaders in the group and be the most respected by other members. Just *what* the group does value varies from group to group and may not be fairly distributed among members. In one classic study, the most important attribute a work group member could have was being Irish, an attribute not easily acquired by non-Irish aspirants but possessed by enough group members to make it crucial.[7] The member(s) who conform most closely to a group's norms have the highest probability of emerging as informal leader(s) to the group.[8]

Interestingly, the informal leaders of a group can end up also having the most license to break the group's norms occasionally without punishment. It is as if a person builds up credits in the "liking and conformity-to-norms account" and thus can be the most free to "spend" the accumulated credit when he or she desires to. Thus, we have to add the counterproposition, Informal group leaders may occasionally violate norms without punishment, provided that they have earned their leadership by general conformity to the group's norms.[9]

Many task groups, however, also have some members who refuse to follow the group's norms. Some students, for example, violate student norms by preparing for every class, reading all the suggested readings as well as the required readings in the course, challenging the teacher, and filling up class time with questions and arguments. They are seldom swayed by any punishments their classmates can generate. What normally happens after the other members give up all efforts to bring the deviant around is that he or she ends up being isolated from the group. In Chapters 7 and 8 we examine individual motives in a way that might help explain why a person would resist peer pressure. However, you can see that those who choose, for whatever reasons, to resist the pressure of group norms often start out as deviants and end up as isolates. (See Figure 5–2 for a summary of the link between conformity and status.)

MANAGERIAL BULLETIN

Packing Off the Peanut Packer

Elizabeth Kovacs was until recently employed by the firm of Q Peanuts as a peanut packer. She was in the habit of arriving at work up to 90 minutes before her 8 A.M. job. She used the time to sit in the canteen with newspapers and coffee and "get myself into the mood for a day's hard work."

Miss Kovacs' fellow workers, though, did not like this one bit. They prevailed on management to issue a warning to her about the insidious practice. When the warning produced no change in the lady's habits, she was fired.

SOURCE: *The Wall Street Journal.*

External Status: How It Relates to Acceptance of Group Norms

Insofar as having a certain ethnic background, age, educational attainment, and so forth makes it likely that a person will share particular attitudes with others of the same background, external status allows group members to quickly "place" new group members. Of course, not *all* middle-aged male second-generation Lithuanian-American engineers, for example, are the same in all of their beliefs, values, and behaviors, nor are *all* Chicana women in personnel jobs the same. But within each category of people, common experiences and background can and often do lead to common tendencies, especially as compared with other groups. Most female human resource employees are probably more like one another than they are like male engineers. Even when there are genuine differences among people within any one category, many outsiders *assume* commonalities—often by stereotypes. But apart from stereotypes, most people's values are based on how they were raised and their experiences thereafter, and various status factors do give shorthand hints at what a person's beliefs are *likely* to be. Thus, although external status may not *accurately* reflect a person's beliefs, and may even sometimes be misleading, groups in their early phases seem to rely on it to place members.

When a group's norms are strongly held, it is often extremely difficult for anyone who was raised from childhood with different beliefs to go along. A Maine native, taught Yankee independence from birth, is likely to be upset and uncomfortable in a work group of first-generation Italian-Americans who believe in helping one another on and off the job, freely borrowing and lending money, tools, and even food, and frequently stopping work to laugh and joke loudly together. The worker from Maine will probably not want or be able to go along with the others' norms and thus will be isolated, while the member of the Italian subgroup who is most spontaneous and generous will probably be most respected. In some other group the exact opposite could be true, and the independent Downeaster would be most respected.

It also has been observed that men and women often have different ways of expressing their ideas; men tend to be impersonal, abstract, and fact-oriented, while women tend to be more self-disclosing and to speak more from direct experience. It is easy to see how women might be perceived as violating a norm of "impersonal rationality" in a predominantly male environment, despite being no less practical (see Belenky et al., 1986, *Women's Ways of Knowing*).

Whatever attributes a particular group treats as high status, external status and status congruence appear to have the following consequences for internal membership rank:[10]

1. High external status congruent members tend to become regular members. It is as if a group coalesces around those whose status is uniformly high when they

come to the group. Perhaps the people who come with lower external status look to those with greater status to see how things are supposed to develop, thereby helping the high-status congruent members become central.

2. Relatively high status but incongruent members tend to end up as isolates. Those who do not "fit" easily into one category create some confusion in others, causing neither respect nor liking. The ultimate result is often isolation, perhaps because the basically high-status person will not as strongly "need" that particular group's approval.

3. Low external status members, regardless of congruence, tend to become deviants. Those whose overall status is low when they enter a group seem to find difficulty in breaking free from the group but cannot fully follow norms to become regulars. They are thus likely to perpetuate within the group the low status they arrive with. Some low-status people who don't care about the group for one reason or another may become isolates, perhaps because they perceive little to lose from ignoring the group.

Roles as Differentiators of Group Members

Can you imagine what life would be like if there were no predictability to anyone's behavior? How would you behave, for example, if you could never be sure of your father's reactions? Suppose you never knew which friends you could count on for cheering up, or blowing off steam, or talking through serious problems, or playing your favorite sport? Wouldn't life be chaotic if you had to make anew every single choice of behavior every time you saw another person? It would be similar to entering a foreign culture every day of your life. While the spontaneity of it all could be exciting, it might paralyze many and wear out the rest.

As people interact, however, individuals slowly arrive at patterned behavior, where each party begins to learn the other's likes and dislikes, needs, sensitive areas, and so forth and can begin to accommodate to one another. A person comes to expect certain behavior and attitudes from others, and they come to expect particular behavior and attitudes from him or her. When you know the types of behavior or pattern expected of you in a particular situation, you have learned a role and automatically know what to do when in that situation. The way you then behave is not necessarily how you always are, but it is likely to be repeated whenever you are with that particular group of people or in that situation. This kind of "specialized" behavior is another way of differentiating members, resulting in a consistent place in the group for all who take on a patterned role. As with other kinds of deviance, behaving in ways not expected by others will cause discomfort in group members and lead to attempts to force the person back into the role. This can be uncomfortable for the individual trying to expand the role as well as for group members affected by the changes.

Thus, while our various roles are convenient they restrict our possible behaviors insofar as we choose to continue in them. Role behavior makes life more predictable and constrained by differentiating people according to particular behaviors expected of them and then reinforcing each role occupant for consistently taking that role. We expand on this in Chapter 10.

Although the patterns may vary to a greater or lesser degree, work group members inevitably acquire roles bringing their own styles and preferences to the group's requirements. Members respond to the needs of the group with their own personal styles and fairly rapidly begin to develop repetitive patterns of behavior. As group members notice one another's emerging patterns, they acquire expectations of how each person will behave, which reinforce whatever behavioral tendencies were exhibited, and soon a whole network of expectations is created, which helps make each person's participation predictable.

Few people have either so limited a repertoire of possible behaviors within them or so clear a notion of what they will not do that they can completely resist responding to others' expectations of them. Whether the behavioral pattern originates from within or from the strong expectations of others, when a person is treated as if he or she were *supposed* to act in a certain way, frequently that person will begin to do so, that is, produce the expected pattern.

Conformity to expectations by others is not inevitable, of course, and sometimes people resist being drafted into roles that do not fit. In our classes, for example, we often see athletes, treated at first as if they are only "jocks" uninterested in learning, struggle to not accept such a demeaning role and to become contributing group members. Roles assigned on the basis of external characteristics like sex, age, or appearance are probably less difficult to resist than those based on actual behavior, but they are by no means easy to escape. It takes a very determined person to continue to refuse to be what others expect, and such determination is rare. We explore this question more closely in Chapters 8 and 10, especially in relation to conditions under which refusal is most likely. At present we can say that, for most people concerned with readily finding a comfortable place in a group, acceptance of particular roles is likely if the roles are not too incongruent with how they view themselves.

For example, early in the life of a new group, there will often be some uncomfortable silences because members do not know one another and feel cautious about risking opinions without being sure of reactions. Inevitably some member will become uncomfortable enough to think up something to say just to ease the tension. It only takes a few such events to initiate expectations of the silence breaker. In some groups that member will then usually be expected to be an idea initiator and be appreciated for that. In another group with different needs, the silence breaker might be seen as bidding for leadership and be "assigned" (often implicitly) the role of "aspiring leader." Of course, the style and particular words used by silence breakers make a difference about how they will be perceived. If it is done with some humor, that member may come to be seen as a great tension releaser and be expected to take that role, to fulfill that function whenever the atmosphere in the group becomes tense. On the other hand, the person who breaks silence by nervous chattering may not be so appreciated even when members notice and expect it.

In general, *roles in groups can be categorized by whether they serve to (1) help accomplish the group task (task-oriented), (2) help maintain good relationships among members (socially oriented), or (3) express individual needs or goals unrelated to the group's purposes (self-oriented).*

Any role behavior reflects the person's personality and needs, but from the group point of view, the behavior will be seen as more valuable if it also fulfills a need of the group for getting the job done or for sustaining satisfying relationships.

Furthermore, one person might take on several of these roles or at different times several members might perform in the same role. How widely distributed and firmly established roles are is an interesting indicator of the degree of crystallization or fluidity of a group's structure. Sometimes particular individuals acquire a "monopoly" on a role, and no one else can take it even though for the task at hand the other(s) would be best suited. A group will be less effective if some or many capable members are prevented from taking needed roles.

The following roles have been found useful and common in successful task groups:

Roles relating to accomplishing the group's tasks:[11]

1. Idea initiator: Proposes tasks or goals, defines problems, suggests procedures or ideas for solving problems.
2. Information seeker: Requests facts, seeks information about a group concern, asks for expression of feelings, requests statements or estimates, solicit expressions of value, seeks suggestions and ideas.
3. Information provider: Offers facts, provides information about a group concern, states beliefs about matters before the group, gives suggestions and ideas.
4. Problem clarifier: Interprets ideas or suggestions, clears up confusion, defines terms, indicates alternatives and issues, gets group back on track.

Some Dysfunctional Group Roles

Most people have had experience with group members whose behavior seems to serve mainly as an obstacle to getting anything done. In moderation their role behavior may be, and often is, helpful to the group; in excess it blocks progress. Below are listed a few of these roles (you can probably add to the list yourself):

- *Nitpicker*: Argues endlessly about the meanings of words and dwells on nonessentials.
- *Endless talker*: Unable to let go of a topic and move on, going over the same points repeatedly.

- *Group humorist*: Uses every opportunity to make a joke, fool around, and distract group from its task.
- *Over-organizer*: Spends more time talking about what the group should be working on than working on it.
- *Topic jumper*: Cannot seem to stick to the point, goes off on tangents, jumps ahead, or goes back to a point already adequately discussed.

5. Summarizer: Pulls together related ideas, restates suggestions after the group has discussed them, offers a decision or conclusion for the group to weigh.
6. Consensus tester: Asks to see if group is nearing decision, sends up "trial balloons" to test a possible conclusion.

Roles related to the group's social relationships:
1. Harmonizer (joker or soother): Attempts to reconcile disagreements, reduces tension, gets members to explore differences.
2. Gatekeeper: Helps keep communication channels open, facilitates everyone's participation, suggests procedures that permit sharing of what members have to say.
3. Supporter: Exudes friendliness, warmth, and responsiveness to others; encourages, supports, acknowledges, and accepts others' contributions.
4. Compromiser: When own idea or status is involved in a conflict, offers compromise, yielding of status, admitting error or modifying position in interest of maintaining group cohesion.
5. Standards monitor: Tests whether group is satisfied with way it is proceeding, points out explicit or implicit operating norms to see if they are desired.

The variety of self-oriented roles is endless. Some (like "group clown") may be tolerated or neglected, while others (like "wet blanket," "playboy," "dominator," "self-confessor," or "bragger") may prove to be extremely annoying to other members and hinder group functioning. In an effective task group, there will be a relatively low amount of self-oriented role behavior and a balance between task- and social-related roles as necessary.

Sometimes self-oriented behavior may be quite functional for a group, serving to release tension or to smooth over differences. Reactions of group members to the self-oriented behavior of a "fight picker" or a "show-off" will depend on the frequency of the behavior and its timing. For example, a good wisecrack in the presence of a disliked authority figure may be gratefully appreciated, but constant joking when others want to work can become quite irritating.

The various roles that members take on become part of how they are ranked by the group. In some groups, idea initiators are most valued. As pointed out previously, high task contributors are usually respected, while high social contributors are usually liked; but each group will weight the value of these patterns by its own standards and goals. In general, The more a member fills both the task and social roles, the higher will be his or her status in the group. Members who only take either task or social roles tend to become overspecialized; their emergent status then depends on how highly the group values their "specialty."

At times you may find yourself playing multiple roles in a group, some of which may even conflict. For example, if you happen to be the best-informed member of a group working on a specific task, you are likely to be both an idea initiator and an information provider with little difficulty, but you could find it hard to also be a gatekeeper. The first two roles supplement one another, but the third one requires a different orientation toward the other members of the group. However, if you *can* learn to master a combination of roles, it can certainly enhance your status as a group leader as well as a contributing member.

Behavior as a Result of Status Differentiation

The status or rank of a group member may not be explicit or directly discussed by group members, but it is usually inferred from observing member behavior. In general, Lower-status members defer to higher-status members, allowing higher-status members to (1) initiate interactions, (2) make statements without being challenged, and (3) administer informal rewards or punishments. Higher-status members will usually talk more, talk "for the group" in public situations, make more contacts with outsiders, and usually have the widest number of connections within the group.[12] Even body posture and seating arrangements can reflect status differences: Higher-status members sit at or near the head of the conference table (or where they sit becomes the head); if the group is talking informally, they will be at the physical center of the grouping; they are looked at when others are speaking; they tend to sit more erectly or confidently. They are more likely to interrupt others or change the subject.

In general, at least in the United States, there are strong expectations about how high- and low-status people are supposed to behave. People who are clearly higher status are expected to be "nice" and not lord it over others. It is a form of noblesse oblige, with expressions of the person's higher status being subtle and designed not to make others feel bad even though they are lower status. In turn, lower-status people are expected to "know their place" and not presume on the privileges of those with higher status; those who do not properly defer are considered "uppity." Because of the democratic ideals in the United States, little of this is talked about directly; but if you have trouble believing it, try testing it in a social or work situation.

> A principle of organization [necessary for] advanced social life . . . in higher vertebrates is the so-called ranking order. Under this rule every individual in the society knows which one is stronger and which weaker than itself, so that everyone can retreat from the stronger and expect submission from the weaker.
>
> Konrad Lorenz
> *On Aggression*

Influence

No matter how egalitarian the ideals of a work group, it is unlikely that all members can contribute equally along those dimensions—task or social—that the group values. Even where external status is roughly equal, as the group interacts some members will have better ideas, warmer personalities, or whatever is seen as desirable. As others perceive these differential talents, their possessors will be allowed more say about what the group should do, directions it should take, how decisions should be made, and so forth. *This ability to affect the behavior of others in particular directions is defined as influence.*

Whether it is explicitly acknowledged or not, as a result of external status, adherence to norms, and roles taken, every member will have some differential degree of influence on others in the group. Some members will be more listened to or taken into account than others; and, in most groups, after awhile everyone knows reasonably accurately the relative standing of members in terms of influence. In student and other peer groups, these differences are often denied, or at least talking about them is seen as taboo for fear of hurting feelings. Nevertheless, differences inevitably exist and can be documented by an observer. Since internal influence in a group correlates with internal status, it can be noted by the same kinds of behavior: deference, assertion, physical spacing, and so on. Just as the thoughtful manager will want to know about status differentials in groups, so will he or she want to be a careful observer of influence differentials and of how influence is acquired within a group.

In general, we can predict that When members have congruently high external status, conform to the group's norms, and fulfill task and social roles, they will be accorded high emergent status and, therefore, have high influence within the group (see Figure 5–3). If some of these factors are different, an altered proposition would be necessary to predict amount of influence within the group. Can you assess the relative influence of members of task groups to which you belong and then trace the influence to the factors discussed in this chapter?

The process of sorting out member influence and status is so important to a group's development that everything can be viewed from this perspective.[13] A group can be visualized as beginning with members sizing one another up and jockeying to find a satisfactory position in the group. The work of the group will become the means for jostling or infighting until each member has a relative position or rank with which he or she is satisfied.

For three or four days each summer, full-time academics at all institutional levels, from doctoral candidates to the professoriat of Ivy League universities meet at the Academy of Management in their thousands to see and be seen . . .

Doctoral candidates, looking for university positions, are glaringly obvious in the hotel lobbies. The males dress in blazers and grey trousers, the women in blue suits. Prestigious professors dress in Bermuda shorts and sandals. One's position in the hierarchy therefore is marked by dress, so the "smarter" the attire the lower is one's standing.

John Hassard and Martin Parker,
Postmodernism and Organization, Sage Books
(div. of Swallow Press at Ohio Univ. Press, Athens, OH) 1993.

Although not everyone can be simultaneously at the top in terms of influence, stability can be achieved when all members accept the rank allotted them. If anyone is unhappy with his or her emergent position, new struggles will break out. The efforts to alter status then surface through attempts to conform more closely to norms, to change them, or to shift roles.

When you join a new group, you have some choice about the nature and degree of status you achieve. While you cannot change your external status, if you are willing to go along with group norms, take on task and social roles, and avoid self-serving behavior, you are likely to gain status and influence. Furthermore, while at first it may seem difficult to take initiative and speak up, a failure to do so will certainly limit your influence. On the other hand, talking too much can shut people off, and while it makes you visible for the moment, it may hurt you in the long run.

A group will not reach a stable equilibrium, where all its energies can be focused on its task, until its internal rankings are essentially accepted by all. Then a kind of cohesion can be reached. In this view, a group cannot be fully productive until it has arrived at a somewhat "crystallized" or accepted structure. Until differences of opin-

To Be a Star among Equals, Be a Team Player

You aim to become the Michael Jordan of business: a corporate superstar who stands at the center of your organization's firmament.

But at a rapidly growing number of companies, corporate stars are being rewarded for their cooperative talents—and not their competitive ones. Teamwork is in . . .

[Consultant Darrel Ray] recalls one Bell Atlantic team member who took extra time to train her new colleagues, helped resolve team conflicts and did extra research about a customer's problem. "She was always looking for ways to enhance her team's performance. By not grandstanding or taking a Michael Jordan role,

she became Michael Jordan for her team," Dr. Ray says. The result: She won a promotion as supervisor in another department, without teams.

Your ability to share information with teammates also may influence your success. "If you don't share information, out of fear that someone might use it to get ahead of you, then you and your team are destined for trouble," says Dr. Ray. He adds: "A true team member doesn't get anywhere without a team."

SOURCE: Timothy D. Schellhardt, "Managing Your Career." Reprinted by permission of *The Wall Street Journal,* April 20, 1994, © Dow Jones & Company, Inc. All Rights Reserved Worldwide.

FIGURE 5–3   *Determinants of Group Status and Influence*

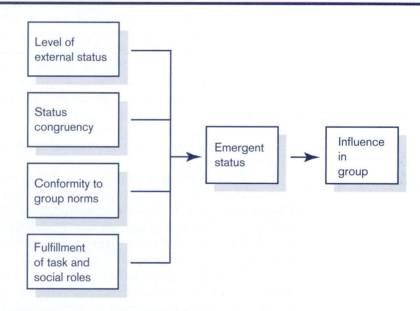

ion about "proper" ranking are settled by the members of a group, it is less likely to be fully productive since so much energy and attention must go into coping with individual restlessness.

On the other hand, A structure that is too crystallized, where everyone "knows his place" only too well, can also have difficulties in producing, especially when tasks are changing and quick responsiveness is needed. You might find comfort and security in knowing your niche in a group, but you might also find it somewhat limiting when it comes to challenge and new learning.

When a member tries to change rank, his or her influence is tested; a successful alteration of position indicates that the person had more influence than he or she was being credited with, while an unsuccessful attempt confirms or lowers the person's position. However, it can often be worth the risk of testing your influence; you lose little and you might discover that it is greater than you thought.

Subgroup

If group members are differentiated by how closely they adhere to group norms, there is a good possibility that they will form subgroups based on their degree of conformity to the norms. In addition, other kinds of subgroupings often emerge on the basis of mutual personality attractions, previous friendships, common interests outside the group, shared positions on crucial issues, and so on. In a classroom task group, for example, subgroups may develop among those who are serious scholars, those who are fraternity/sorority members, the athletes, the campus activists, and others.

As soon as more than two people are in a group, the possibility exists of some of them joining up and then taking sides. The greater the numbers of people in a group, the more likely is subgroup division. It is rare that a group does not develop some cliques.

> The worst cliques are those which consist of one man.
>
> George Bernard Shaw

For the manager the important issue is not whether subgroups exist but the basis for their formation and the consequences for group functioning. If the subgroups exist because of differing but complementary task abilities, they may be quite functional for accomplishing group goals. Even if based primarily on social considerations, they may or may not hinder communications among members, foster cooperation or conflict, prevent or facilitate accomplishment of tasks, increase or decrease satisfaction, and so forth. Although it is certainly easier to assess the consequences of subgroup formation than do anything about it, it is an important factor in determining member standing and resultant productivity, satisfaction, and development.

One of the most serious subgroup problems rises when the smallest subgroup has only one member who is made to be a "subgroup" because he or she is visibly different from the others. The lone woman in an all-male group or the lone person of color in an all-white group—whom we can refer to as the *token* when the person is treated as a symbol rather than as an individual—often has special problems exactly because he or she has no (or very few) other subgroup members who are obviously alike and therefore appears to be even more different from the others than may actually be the case. While members of the dominant subgroup sometimes may actually have more in common with one another than with the token, often it may only be an untested assumption that the token is significantly different. In either case, their attitude can make it difficult for the token to know how to behave. When a joke is made about Speedy Gonzales, does the only Puerto Rican laugh, become angry, or pretend he hasn't heard it? None of these responses is very satisfactory, so even if the token has many other things in common with the others, he or she often has a hard time establishing the common bonds.[14] This can lead to communication and cooperation barriers, which affect the group's ability to coordinate its work.

It could be important and useful for you to test some of the above notions in groups of which you are a member. Often such problems exist just below the surface and need to be brought into the open.

MANAGERIAL BULLETIN

Jeans Therapy: Levi's Factory Workers Are Assigned to Teams, and Morale Takes a Hit

Infighting Rises, Productivity Falls, and Employees Miss the Piecework System; "It's Not the Same Company"

Teamwork, Levi's felt, would be more humane, safe and profitable. "This change," Max Cowan, Levi's operations vice president, wrote to workers in September 1992, "will lead to a self-managed work environment that will reduce stress and help employees become more productive." Instead it led to a quagmire in which skilled workers . . . found themselves pitted against slower colleagues, damaging morale and triggering corrosive infighting . . . Threats and insults became more common. Longtime friendships dissolved as faster workers tried to banish slower ones . . .

Beyond the contention, the team concept simply didn't help Levi's accomplish key business objectives . . . the quantity of pants produced per hour worked plunged in 1993 to 77% of pre-team levels.

SOURCE: Ralph T. King Jr., " Jeans Therapy: Levi's Factory Workers Are Assigned to Teams, and Morale Takes a Hit," *The Wall Street Journal,* May 20, 1998, p. A1.

Consequences of Member Differentiation for Productivity, Satisfaction, and Development

In Chapter 4 we looked at how cohesiveness is connected to a group's production, pulling individual member output toward what the group's norms define as appropriate. Even noncohesive work groups, however, develop at least rough ideas about what is too much work and what is too little. Different groups have particular nicknames, richer than *deviants* or *isolates,* for people who don't carry their own load or for those who are so gifted or willing to work so hard that they make others look bad by their output. Those members who produce "too much" are often seen a "rate busters" or, as they are known in student circles, "curve breakers." Conversely, "freeriders" or "goof-offs" are those who just cannot or will not produce at a pace satisfactory to the particular group's members. In general, then, a person's standing in a group is partly determined by how closely he or she conforms to the group's norms and is particularly affected by adherence to norms about individual output. Conversely, once a person's rank is established, a particular level of output is likely to follow. Of course, the degree of required task interdependence will affect individual freedom to vary production, with jobs that can be done alone more easily subject to individual variation.

An interesting irony of the above observations is that In a high-producing group the isolates and/or deviants are likely to be low producers, while in a group that holds down productivity, the isolates are likely to be high producers! A person may choose not to conform to avoid working so hard or so little, or may be pushed into isolation out of inability to produce near the group's desired rate. Similarly, a person who desires to be an accepted member will, if possible, adjust productivity upward or downward to meet the group's norms. Whatever the cause, there is no doubt that rank within the group is connected to productivity.

A dramatic example of just how powerful a force is exerted upon members to produce according to group norms was reported in *Street Corner Society,* a detailed study of a group of young underemployed men who "hung around" together.[15] One of the valued skills in the group turned out to be bowling ability. But other qualities, such as social skills, intelligence, and power of self-expression, were dominant in giving

Airline Cockpits Are No Place to Solo: Crews Taught That Teamwork Improves Safety

The idea is to create "a superb, self-correcting team, so if an individual does make a mistake and screw up, the team is working well and corrects it" . . . There is case after case where the aircraft technically was able to fly out of trouble, and the crew members individually were able to, and yet they got into trouble" . . .

Teamwork, however, doesn't come naturally to many pilots. They often enter commercial aviation after years in the military, flying fighter jets solo—no cockpit crew or scores of passengers to contend with. If something happens, "their attitude is, 'Get those other pilots out of here and I'll take care of this,' . . . It's understandable, but it's not the optimum response."

SOURCE: Judith Valente and Bridget O'Brian. Reprinted by permission of *The Wall Street Journal,* August 2, 1989, © Dow Jones & Company, Inc. All Rights Reserved Worldwide.

Work Teams Chart Alternatives to Top-Down Performance Appraisals

Every week, team members at Somanetics Corp. vote on bonuses ranging from gift certificates to vacation time for top-achieving peers. The company periodically grants group awards—including company-sponsored outings and cash. Saturn Corp. doesn't evaluate employees individually, but teams can impose sanctions on problem workers—including three-day suspensions.

Perkin-Elmer Corp. says peer pressure suffices to motivate team members. And Corning Inc. notes that teammates judge each other more critically than managers would. Six hospitals managed by Quorum Health Resources Inc. reverse hierarchical performance reviews; employees collect feedback on their performance from customers and co-workers and then discuss the findings with supervisors.

SOURCE: "Labor Letter." Reprinted by permission of *The Wall Street Journal,* September 7, 1993, © Dow Jones & Company, Inc. All Rights Reserved Worldwide.

members status; as you might expect, bowling expertise is not perfectly correlated with ability to argue well or talk to many people. One of the lower-status members of the gang was the "best" bowler when measured by scores attained when bowling casually; but whenever the gang bowled competitively, his scores would inevitably fall below those of the gang's leaders!

The low-status expert bowler may not have been fully aware of why he didn't do as well when competing with the others, but the pressure and razzing from the gang to have his "productivity" fall into line affected him enough temporarily to alter his ability to produce. In general, under competitive stress the gang's bowling scores almost always perfectly reflected their relative status, even though some lower-ranking members had more ability than they could deliver when being "kept in their places" by the others.

In a work group some of the differentiation of members will follow from the task requirements. If various members are required to do different tasks, some group valuation of the respective worth of each task will probably emerge. Those who do jobs that the group sees as crucial to its success will probably be given higher status than others.[16] When the group ranks members by the difficulty of the task each performs, the group is likely to be relatively high in output. Thus: The more that member differentiation is based on task requirements, the more productive the group is likely to be.

On the other hand, if member rank is largely based on external status, the group is only likely to be high producing if by coincidence the factors that determine external status are also those that would determine genuine contributions to the group's tasks. The more that member differentiation is based on external status, the less productive the group is likely to be (unless external status happens to coincide with needed group skills).

Summary Productivity Proposition

Differentiation, of course, need not be inconsistent with group cohesion. Although cohesive groups sometimes cling together and enforce false equality, even when differentiation would be appropriate, as in the case of groupthink, a group can be both differentiated and attractive to members. A highly differentiated group can be quite cohesive if all members believe that their positions accurately reflect their contributions, satisfy their needs, and lead to effective performance. In fact, if the group's tasks can best be done by each member *first* working on different aspects of the tasks and *then* coordinating individual efforts, the more differentiated *and* the more cohesive the group needs to be in order to produce at a high rate. Furthermore, if the group supports the organization's goals, it will pull the highest possible productivity from its members. The greater the differentiation *and* cohesion of a group with norms supporting the organization's goals, the greater its productivity is likely to be.[17]

Satisfaction and Development

As suggested earlier, a group that is highly differentiated but in which each member accepts his or her status can be highly satisfied. Where differentiation, however, is a result of factors that some members do not accept as appropriate, considerable dissatisfaction can result. For example, if a work group automatically assigns low status to its female members, forcing them to do all the menial tasks and ignoring their contributions to the important jobs, there can only be general satisfaction if the women accept their lower ranking. If as increasingly is the case, however, they want to be accorded whatever status they earn by merit rather than automatically being given low (or high) status merely because of gender, the group will have dissension and low satisfaction.

When group members take on roles and ranks that restrict them to merely doing what they know well, growth will naturally be limited. A group highly differentiated on the basis of adherence to norms that support maximum productivity can be very efficient but can limit chances for members to learn new jobs, try new skills, or be creative about work processes. If the group's tasks are routine, a rigid structure may be most productive but least growth promoting. Tasks calling for creativity and responsiveness, however, are not likely to be performed well by a rigidly differentiated group. Furthermore, as we indicated with respect to a crystallized group, rigid differentiation is likely to be quite frustrating to members who want to learn and grow. For example, a group trying to think up a new commercial product, like a labor-saving small appliance, would have difficulty being imaginative if only the marketing person could give input on what customers might like, if only the production manager could comment on how items can be built, and so forth. A free flow of ideas is called for regardless of the members' status and position in order for the group to be creative.

On the other hand, an insufficiently differentiated group may be highly productive at creative tasks, stimulate great learning by members, but be anxiety provoking at the same time. The lack of clear positioning can cause considerable uncertainty and nervousness for some members, even while allowing them maximum opportunities for growth.

Finally, as you might expect by now, an underdifferentiated group will probably be quite ineffective at performing routine tasks, thereby dragging down morale when results are poor, and probably leading to little growth except for those few members who can take advantage of the looseness to pursue their own ends.

The degrees of differentiation and cohesion in a group, then, are important emergent outcomes of the way the group works together. They greatly affect a group's performance, satisfaction, and learning. While we have tried to show how cohesion and differentiation come about, a more detailed look at how groups function as they go about their business can be useful in assessing their effectiveness. In the next chapter we examine more closely the working processes of groups to help you more readily judge what is effective group behavior as it is occurring in the emergent system.

KEY CONCEPTS FROM CHAPTER 5

1. Overall status in group determined by:
    a. Respect: accorded to high task accomplishment.
    b. Liking: accorded to high social accomplishment.
2. Initial ranking.
    a. The higher the background of external status, the higher the initial internal status of a group member.
3. Status affects behavior.
    a. The higher a person is on dimensions valued by the group and the more norms are conformed to, the higher his or her status within the group and vice versa. Members who conform are regulars; the greatest conformers become informal leaders who may violate group norms. Consistency of relative positions on dimensions determines degree of status congruence.
    b. Deviant: member who does not conform to group's norms; most negative attitudes expressed to that member.

    c. Isolate: conforms even less to group's norms; interactions with isolate very infrequent.
4. Roles determine status and group effectiveness.
    a. Task-oriented.
    b. Socially oriented.
    c. Self-oriented and other dysfunctional group roles.
    d. The pressure of balancing multiple roles.
5. The greater the number of people in a group, the more likely is subgroup formation.
6. Influence.
    a. The ability to affect the behavior of others in particular directions.
    b. Affected by rank.
7. Differentiation and cohesion are related to productivity, satisfaction, and development.
    a. Relation to task requirements.
    b. Relation to external status.
    c. Relation to support of organization's goals.

PERSONAL APPLICATION EXERCISE

Looking at the Structure of a Group

Most students in task groups tend to view all members as equal, even when it is obvious that there are differences in many respects. There is a simple exercise, which has been around for many years, that you might try with a group of which you are a member. It involves a series of lineups.

You begin with everyone lined up according to height. It is quick and nonthreatening. You might follow that with a lineup of weight—not as simple as height, but also not very controversial. Then try a lineup on who talks the most. This provides some useful feedback. Then move to dimensions like degree of influence in the group, closeness to the group norms, contribution to group goals, supportiveness of other members, and so on. The important thing is to make sure you choose dimensions that are relevant to the group and will help the group to get a better understanding of its structure. Furthermore, the exercise usually gives members feedback that can help them improve their contributions to the group.

Even though this exercise is fun, it does generate important data.

SUGGESTED READINGS

Bales, R. F., and F. L. Strodtbeck. "Phases in Group Problem Solving." *Journal of Abnormal and Social Psychology* 46 (1951), p. 485.

Belenky, M. F.; B. McV. Clinchy; N. R. Goldberger; and J. M. Tarule. *Women's Ways of Knowing: The Development of Self, Voice and Mind.* New York: Basic Books, 1986.

Benne, K., and P. Sheats. "Functional Roles of Group Members." *Journal of Social Issues* 4, no. 2 (1948), pp. 41–49.

Earley, P. C. "Playing Follow the Leader: Status-Determining Traits in Relation to Collective Efficacy across Cultures." *Organizational Behavior and Human Decision Processes* 80,3 (December 1999), pp. 192–212.

Earley, P. C. and E. Mosakowski. "Creating Hybrid Team Cultures: An Empirical Test of Transnational Team Functioning." *Academy of Management Journal* 43,1 (February 2000), pp. 26–49.

Eisenhardt, K. M., J. L. Kahwajy, and L. J. Bourgois III. "Conflict and Strategic Choice: How Top Management Teams Disagree." *California Management Review* 39,2 (Winter 1997), pp. 42–61.

Elsass, P. M., and L. Graves. "Demographic Diversity in Decision-Making Groups: The Experiences of Women and People of Color." *Academy of Management Review* 22 (1997), pp. 848–973.

Hambrick, D. C. "Fragmentation and Other Problems CEOs Have with Their Top Management Teams." *California Management Review* 37,3 (Spring 1995), pp. 110–127.

Hollander, E. P. *Leaders, Groups, and Influence.* New York: Oxford University Press, 1964.

Hopkins, T. H. *The Exercise of Influence in Small Groups.* Totowa, NJ: Bedminster Press, 1964.

Jacobs, T. O. *Leadership and Exchange in Formal Organization.* Springfield, VA: National Technical Information Service, U.S. Department of Commerce, 1970.

Jehn, K. A., C. Chadwick, and S. M. B. Thatcher. "To Agree or Not to Agree: The Effects of Value Congruence, Individual Demographic Dissimilarity, and Conflict on Work Group Outcomes." *International Journal of Conflict Management* 8, (1997) pp. 287–305.

Jehn, K. A., G. B. Northcraft, and M. A. Neale. "Why Differences Make a Difference." *Administrative Science Quarterly* 44, 4 (December 1999), pp. 741–763.

Kahn, R. L.; D. M. Wolfe; R. P. Quinn; and J. D. Snoek. *Organizational Stress: Studies in Role Conflict and Ambiguity.* New York: John Wiley & Sons, 1964.

Lau, D. C. and J. K. Murnighan. "Demographic Diversity and Faultlines: The Compositional Dynamics of Organizational Groups." *Academy of Management Review* 23 (1998), pp. 325–340.

Maier, N. R. F. "Assets and Liabilities in Problem Solving: The Need for an Integrated Function." *Psychological Review* 74 (1967), p. 244.

———. "Male versus Female Discussion Leaders." *Personnel Psychology* 23 (1970), pp. 455–61.

Thompson, V. A. *Modern Organization.* New York: Alfred A. Knopf, 1961.

Developing Group Effectiveness

Emergent Processes

MANAGERIAL BULLETIN

Teamwork the Specialty at a Great Restaurant

. . . an unusual recipe for success: generous portions of learning and a heaping scoop of teamwork. . . .

Greatness at Radius starts with great teamwork, and great teamwork starts in the kitchen. . . . Two people work at each station, and they have full responsibility for their part of the meal. In other words, the team at the meat station not only cooks the meat but also butchers it and seasons it—a sharp departure from the standard procedure at most restaurants.

Radius has also developed a series of meetings in which both the spirit and the practice of teamwork get reinforced. . . .

What has resulted from this unusual commitment to learning and teamwork? A loyal following—and a growing reputation among the industry's rising stars.

SOURCE: Gina Imperato, "Their Specialty? Teamwork," *Fast Company* 31 (January/February 2000), p. 56.

"It takes greater effort and more formal procedures to make sure that everyone in a large group is fully informed in matters concerning them."

Do you think you could tell from observing a group how well it is working? What criteria would you use? We have suggested that you judge by the outcomes—productivity, member satisfaction, and development. While these are the ultimate criteria of group effectiveness, it would be hard for a group to improve its operations as it went along if this were the only way to make judgments. To wait for the final outcomes to occur can be too late. Nor is progress toward those final outcomes necessarily an adequate basis for corrective action, because progress may become visible only when it is too late to take such action. Therefore, it is important for a group to have some basis for evaluating its emergent processes as it carries out a given task. The group needs to raise such questions as: "Are we working in the right way?" "Does everyone adequately understand his or her job?" "Are we avoiding important issues?" and "How do people feel about the objectives of the work?" To the extent that a group has available some set of criteria by which to assess its processes, it is in a stronger position to improve the way it goes about a task.

The effectiveness of any group depends on several factors. Appropriate human and technological resources are background factors that establish both the possibilities and the limits for productive outcomes. Further, the policies and directives that make up the required system have direct influence over the effectiveness of a working group. Accordingly, most managers pay a great deal of attention to both background and required aspects of a work setting; they take great pains to select the right people for a job and to spell out job requirements and specifications. Yet the emergent processes of a work group, which are equally important, are often overlooked except when they overtly disrupt the work. Even when managers recognize the importance of dealing with emergent processes, they often lack a useful set of criteria by which to judge.

> For example, the top planning group of an aerospace firm was having a great deal of trouble producing useful plans. Their meetings often wandered from their stated agenda to rambling discussions of new books about youth in America, psychological interpretations of current events, and so on. In the meantime corporate profits were steadily declining. Though the vice president for planning was not happy with the way the group worked, he would not risk pushing the group to examine its own processes, partly because he did not know how to judge them himself. Meetings got worse and worse, frustration grew, and finally individual members began to quit for other jobs.

As major corporations experiment with the use of self-managing work teams and incorporate them into their means of production, the demands on managers and workers alike to develop their skills in group process will increase. Such companies as General Electric and Corning Glass are among many to move in this direction.

While Chapters 4 and 5 examined the emergent *properties* of a group (its structure or state of integration/differentiation at any point in time), this chapter focuses on the emergent *processes* (the dynamics) of a group as it functions. In short, the chapter uses a kind of social-psychological "microscope" to examine *how* a group operates.

As a starting point, we look at issues faced by every working group, how these issues determine the criteria by which to evaluate the appropriateness of a given group's process, and how these evaluations need to take into account the particular situation of the group (e.g., its purpose, size, composition, surrounding circumstances, and so forth). While it is not possible to cover all the varieties of situations and show how the criteria apply in every case, we give you a general sense of how to fit the two together. One section of the chapter uses two contrasting case examples to demonstrate how to consider situational factors when evaluating a group's process.

Testing Self-Managed Teams, Entrepreneur Hopes to Lose Job

Eric Gershman, president and founder of Published Image, has an unusual career goal: He wants to eliminate his job.

Mr. Gershman set it last summer when he organized his small Boston concern into four "self-managed teams," a hot concept in which workers largely operate without bosses. Today, the newsletter publisher's 26 employees set their own work schedules, prepare their own budgets and receive group bonuses based on their team's performance. Managers, renamed coaches, primarily play advisory roles.

In recent years, self-managed work teams have become very popular among big corporations as a way to eliminate middle managers while improving morale and boosting productivity. But such teams remain rare among small businesses. Most small-business owners don't see how the idea could benefit them and their enterprises.

But Mr. Gershman says creation of the teams has halted chronically high employee turnover, helped the company keep customers, and increased profit. It also has helped Published Image Inc. to manage its rapid growth by better focusing on clients' needs, he adds . . .

SOURCE: Michael Selz. Reprinted by permission of *The Wall Street Journal,* © January 11, 1994, Dow Jones & Company, Inc. All Rights Reserved Worldwide.

Issues Facing Every Work Group

Every work group has to deal with the same general issues regardless of whether it is a group of machinists on a shop floor, surgeons and nurses in an operating room, executives at a strategy meeting, or students on a project. It is the *way* in which a group goes about dealing with each of these issues and resolving the accompanying dilemmas that constitutes the group's emergent system and, thus, its effectiveness. While the dilemmas are similar for all groups, there are many possible ways of resolving them; and while groups vary in what the members consider desirable or preferable, different circumstances call for different approaches.

Figure 6–1 shows 11 issues facing every work group.[1] Corresponding to each issue, we have listed sets of questions with which a group must cope. We suggest that you study the chart carefully, see how it applies to any group of which you are a member, and evaluate how well that group has gone about dealing with the issues. Even before we go into detail on these 11 criteria of an effective group, you can probably discover some useful ways to apply them for yourself.

Every one of these issues can be related to some key aspect of a group's activities, interactions, attitudes, and norms. In examining group process, you might be looking at who is doing what, how he or she is doing it, who is interacting with whom, what seem to be the prevailing feelings, what kind of norm(s) has emerged in relation to a given issue, and so forth. Which of these questions demands attention depends entirely upon the particular situation, its complexity, and its history. For the sake of convenience, throughout this chapter we will use the word *process* as a general term referring to any one or more of these emergent aspects of a group. It will be your job to determine *which* aspect of group "process" needs evaluation in any given set of circumstances. However, it is important to pay particular attention to group *norms,* since these govern the internal workings of a group. Because norms are difficult to change, their functionality needs to be examined as they emerge and before they become set in concrete. In fact, the 11 issues can be thought of as a classification system for group norms and therefore serve as a systematic guide to their evaluation.

FIGURE 6–1   *Issues Facing Any Work Group*

Issue	Questions
1. Atmosphere and relationships	What kinds of relationships should there be among members? How close and friendly, formal or informal?
2. Member participation	How much participation should be required of members? Some more than others? All equally? Are some members more needed than others?
3. Goal understanding and acceptance	How much do members need to *understand* group goals? How much do they need to accept to be *committed* to the goals? Everyone equally? Some more than others?
4. Listening and information sharing	How is information to be shared? Who needs to know what? Who should listen most to whom?
5. Handling disagreements and conflict	How should disagreements or conflicts be handled? To what extent should they be resolved? Brushed aside? Handled by dictate?
6. Decision making	How should decisions be made? Consensus? Voting? One-person rule? Secret ballot?
7. Evaluation of member performance	How is evaluation to be managed? Everyone appraises everyone else? A few take the responsibility? Is it to be avoided?
8. Expressing feelings	How should feelings be expressed? Only about the task? Openly and directly?
9. Division of labor	How are task assignments to be made? Voluntarily? By discussion? By leaders?
10. Leadership	Who should lead? How should leadership *functions* be exercised? Shared? Elected? Appointed from outside?
11. Attention to process	How should the group monitor and improve its own process? Ongoing feedback from members? Formal procedures? Avoiding direct discussion?

What the Work Situation Requires

Many factors can be used to determine differences in what kind of group process is appropriate to the job. We focus on *five* that tend to have direct and important consequences:

Size of the work group.

Distribution of resources (expertise) in the group.

Complexity and/or diversity of the task.

Time pressure on the group to produce.

Degree of task interdependence required.

As we discuss each of these factors, we generate propositions that describe the effects that each factor has on a work group. After discussing the factors, we look at two examples that represent sharp contrasts in relation to all five of them. Then, using the examples as a point of reference, we discuss each of the 11 criteria (Figure 6–1) and see how they describe effective working groups of very different kinds.

Size of the Work Group

From your experience in groups of varying sizes, have you noticed how small groups have a different "feel" than large groups? The small group allows closer relationships, a deeper knowledge of the members, and a better sense of the whole picture at any given time. These are seen as advantages by many people, and consequently they

A Better Way in Basketball?

Companies "must move from the football to the basketball model of organization," Mr. Avishai [of Monitor Consulting] said. "The quarterback represents division of labor, command, and control. Any company is only as good as its quarterback. Only the quarterback sees the whole field. On a basketball team, everybody is pretty good at everything."

Also, football has plays decided in huddles, often with the clock stopped, whereas most basketball plays happen in real time, more like what happens in business, . . . "Companies should not go looking for Joe Montanas. . . . A great CEO could pull you out of a mess 25 years ago. Today you are looking for teamwork and flexibility."

SOURCE: *New York Times,* January 23, 1994.

prefer working in a small group. Others are happier in a less intimate atmosphere, prefer the greater anonymity of the larger group, and like the security of knowing there are more people to do the work and carry out necessary group maintenance tasks.

Obviously, there has to be a trade-off in the various advantages of large versus small groups, many of which are primarily a matter of personal preference and many a matter of the inherent constraints posed by size. For example, it takes greater effort and more formal procedures to make sure that everyone in a large group is fully informed in matters concerning them; it also takes more time and effort to coordinate the work of more people. While these issues influence the ease of conducting the group's operations, they may or may not detract from its ultimate effectiveness. Remember, our primary concern here has to do with the utilization of resources in carrying out a task. In this regard we can say that, in most instances, The smaller the group, the fewer total resources there are available for work; however, it is easier to obtain full participation and coordination of individual effort.[2] There may be rare exceptions to this proposition. John F. Kennedy once joked at a dinner of outstanding contributors to American life, "Never before have so many brains and talents been present in the same room at one time with the possible exception of the day when Thomas Jefferson dined alone!" Normally, however, fewer people mean fewer work resources, with the result that each carries a greater burden.

Distribution of Resources (Expertise) in the Group

Suppose an instructor assigned you to a group of students to work on a problem involving the use of quantitative analysis. It's likely that you would depend upon the group member(s) who knew such methods best to take the most active part in the task. If the relevant abilities were evenly distributed among the members, the load would not fall upon any one or two individuals but could be shared by all. The more evenly distributed are the resources (levels of expertise) of a group among its members, the more appropriate is total member participation. This does not rule out the option of assigning specific jobs to only one or two members; it indicates only that the degree to which the assignments can appropriately be spread around depends on the distribution of resources. It can be as wasteful to give specific work to members who are unable to do that particular task as it is to ignore the most expert member. It also can be appropriate at times to have someone other than the most expert member carry out a task, in order to develop the individual's skills and, thus, enhance the group's development.

Complexity and/or Diversity of the Work

Suppose the task assigned in the example above were simply to determine the probability of occurrence of an event using some clearly specified information. While it would certainly take some ability to complete the assignment, it is likely that any one person who had studied probability could do it. If the assignment were much more complicated (like determining various production costs for a given product based on information on personnel turnover, salary levels, overhead rates, market demand, and fluctuations in availability and costs of raw materials), the task might better be handled by the combined talents of several people. The proposition that follows from this is: The greater the task complexity/diversity, the more appropriate it is to utilize the resources of a number of people.[3] It allows for the handling of a greater *amount* and *diversity* of information and in more complicated forms. Simple tasks call for simple information and fewer resources for completion.

In developing a plan of action for completing a complex task, groups are sometimes unable to work out every specific step ahead of time and to anticipate every contingency that might arise. Under such circumstances it becomes important for those who are implementing different aspects of the plan to "make the plan work" by adjusting and adapting to the contingencies encountered and coordinating their alterations with those responsible for other parts of the plan. Yet this kind of creative and responsible behavior is likely to be impossible if the individual lacks knowledge about the rationale behind the plan, nor is that person likely to be attentive to "making the plan work" if lacking in commitment to the plan. Thus, another important proposition is, The more likely it is that unexpected contingencies demanding immediate adaptation will occur in carrying out a task, the greater the need for members to have full information about the work plan's rationale and be committed to the objectives of the plan.[4] Because the commitment to a course of action often rests on involvement in the development of the planned action and a consequent sense of ownership of the plan, a corollary proposition follows from the above: The greater the need for individual members to make adjustments to a plan of action, the greater the need for them to share in the original planning and decision making.

Time Pressure on the Group to Produce

This factor poses a paradox. When the time pressure is greatest, very often decisions are most critical. When decisions are most critical, the multiple resources of a group are most needed, and, thus, the working process of that group is of greatest import. Yet the pressure to produce often makes it impossible to take the time to examine group process even if it is operating poorly. Failure to take the time to look at process perpetuates that dysfunctional process; stopping to work on process eats up valuable time and can increase the stress with respect to the task. While either option is costly, the easiest time to work on group process issues is when there is adequate opportunity to deal with them fully; under pressure this is not likely to occur. Therefore, the proposition we suggest in this instance is that The greater the time pressure, the less appropriate it is for the group to work on process issues.[5] One implication of this statement is that, when time demands are at their lowest levels, the group should examine its ways of working to prepare itself to deal more effectively with the periods of high pressure. When there are impending deadlines, a group needs to function well reflexively, although it is often only under pressure that group members realize what they have not settled! Thus, it seems most useful to work on group processes early and on low-risk tasks where time is not crucial, then build on this base for key tasks or time constraints, or both.

Time can also affect decision making and leadership. When time pressure is great, there is often insufficient opportunity for the whole group to talk things through

Team Selling Catches On, but Is Sales Really a Team Sport?

A growing number of companies follow the lead of DuPont, Digital Equipment, Data General, and Tandem Computers in putting sales reps, engineers, technicians, and production managers on teams to serve customers and win new accounts. "One person can't do it all anymore." . . .

Industries such as furniture and apparel are slow to embrace the idea, though. "Salespeople typically work best as the Lone Ranger without Tonto." . . . With big egos and lots of drive, the best salespeople "are competitors, not cooperators."

SOURCE: "Labor Letter," *The Wall Street Journal,* March 29, 1994.

thoroughly to a consensus. A quicker means of reaching a decision may be needed. The proposition that follows is, The greater the time pressure, the more appropriate it will be for a group to make decisions by vote or even by the unilateral action of its designated leader rather than by consensus. (We have more to say about the effect of time on leader behavior in Chapter 12.)

Degree of Task Interdependence Required

A group of auto workers assembling a new car probably has its individual tasks pretty well routinized. They may talk a lot to each other, but it is not required to do the work. Their interactions depend more on personal preferences, mutual attractions, interests outside the task, and so forth—what we have called *emergent factors.* There is some degree of interdependence among the tasks each is performing, because some jobs cannot proceed until others have been completed. However, the bases of the interdependence are clear-cut and require relatively little exchange of information in an ongoing manner. By way of contrast, a group of friends playing touch football constantly needs to exchange information on strategy, weak spots in the other team, mistakes in their own play, and so on. These exchanges are demanded by the nature of their task almost from moment to moment. The player throwing a pass needs to be able to anticipate where the receiver will be and who will be blocking the onrushing opponents. Whether or not the auto workers ever develop any degree of friendship, mutual understanding seems only peripherally related to task accomplishment. In the case of the touch football team, it is extremely useful for the members to know a great deal about each other's abilities, as well as to develop a sense of confidence in and support for each other. The degree of required interdependence leads to what we might call a *team,* which goes a step beyond what we call a *group.*

The proposition that applies in this instance is, The greater the degree of task interdependence required, the more important it is for group members to maintain continuing exchanges with and have knowledge of each other as persons. The proposition refers primarily to task-related information. Whether or not personal friendships as opposed to working colleagueships develop in the course of the interactions is again a matter of member preferences and opportunities. It is not critical to the group's success, though likely when there is high interdependence. Think, for example, of firefighters, whose very lives depend on one another's skill, knowledge, and performance. It is not surprising that while they work together their families become close, spend time together, and form relationships beyond what is directly required by work.

New in Defense: Teamwork

Much of the impetus for the integrated product teams being used to build the F-22 came from Gen. James A. Fain Jr., the Air Force's program manager for the aircraft. General Fain is credited by industry executives with a willingness to abandon the military's traditional arm's-length approach and commit the Air Force to the teams.

General Fain says the major advantage of the team approach is better communication. The traditional process leaves each function—engineering, manufacturing, etc.—too isolated, a special danger for a complex, interdependent product like an airplane.

"You've got to do it right the first time, and thereby control your costs," General Fain said. "That takes bet-

ter communication," he said; the team concept "lets you take in the whole picture, the challenges you face from all sides." There is no doubt that teams will be widely used on other programs, he said.

"Since you don't have unlimited resources and can't afford the luxury of underemployed people, you have to motivate each person to do their damnedest by empowering them as a member of an integrated product team," he explained. "It shouldn't be hard because it's their survival at stake, too."

SOURCE: Richard W. Stevenson, "General Fain, the Team Player," *New York Times*, December 22, 1991.

When You Put All the Factors Together

It is not easy to manage a group well. (For some ideas on how to manage a single meeting, see the next Managerial Tools box.) Each of the five factors can vary and can yield a tremendous variety of possible combinations. You find small groups with an imbalanced distribution of resources, working on simple tasks under high pressure (as in a group monitoring an automated chemical process) or large groups with high task interdependence working on complex tasks under little pressure (as in a corporate research lab). There are obviously too many possible combinations to explore each one. It might be useful and fun for you to generate different combinations to see if you can think of groups that fit; or you might take a look at some groups you know and see if you can describe them in terms of these five factors. Later, as we discuss the kinds of group processes that are appropriate to a given set of circumstances, you can determine how those processes apply to your own examples. For illustration, we utilize two case examples of a highly contrasting nature. In this way we can highlight the importance of considering the situation when you determine what kind of group processes are appropriate.

The Case of the Strategic Planning Team

Imagine that you are observing a group of five senior corporate executives who are developing a long-range plan for the company. Each individual brings equally important but special expertise to the team, and they share the goal of making sure that the plan reflects their different perspectives in a balanced way. One executive is a marketing specialist, another has financial expertise, a third deals with human resource allocations, a fourth is in charge of manufacturing, and the fifth heads up research and development. Clearly, the plan must pay attention to all aspects of the situation, requires an integration of ideas, and must be formulated in a way that allows for many future uncertainties. There is little time pressure on the group, so it can explore issues in some depth.

Guidelines for Running a Meeting

Most people resent poor meetings that waste time. Careful advanced planning and preparation can help, especially when time pressures mean that attention to process during a meeting will be inappropriate. Some tips on improving meetings.

I. Plan for the meeting (chairperson).
    1. Define objectives.
    2. Think through who should attend: diverse viewpoints, knowledge, degrees of commitment.
    3. Develop agenda and estimate time for each major agenda item (all necessary resources, no unnecessary resources).
    4. Make clear what is expected from the group on each item: information sharing, advice, exploration, or decision.
    5. Schedule unimportant items last.
    6. Avoid regular meetings lasting more than 1½ hours.
II. Facilitate attendee preparation.
    1. Provide sufficient notice and directions about time and place.
    2. Circulate agenda.
    3. Circulate, as appropriate, background materials (handouts).
    4. Contact selected attendees beforehand to cultivate preparedness, interest, and so on. On major issues, it is useful to talk to everyone ahead of time, to anticipate clashes, avoid hopeless battles, and the like.
III. Provide suitable physical facilities.
    1. Adequate space and furniture.
    2. Necessary equipment (flip charts, markers, projectors with extra bulbs, blackboard).
    3. Appropriate location ("neutral" territory, away from telephone, freedom from interruption, near data files, and so on).
    4. Refreshments, if appropriate.
IV. Conducting the meeting (chairperson).
    1. Start on time.
    2. Set stage: review purpose, introduce new members, and the like.
    3. Exercise control.
        a. Follow agenda
        b. Prevent one or two from hogging "air time."
        c. Manage time (seek decision when appropriate, move on to next item, and so on).
        d. Cut off side conversations.
        e. Appoint someone to take notes.
        f. Define issues.
        g. Ask many questions.
    4. Manage process.
        a. "Gate keep"—ensure everyone gets a chance to speak.
        b. Stop interruptions.
        c. Initiate a "stretch," open windows, and the like.
        d. Clarify misunderstandings.
        e. Don't take silence as agreement; do not force early consensus.
        f. Stop to find out why discussion is not going well when that occurs.
        g. Summarize.
    5. Speak more to group than to individuals.
    6. Finish on time!
V. Participating in meeting (members).
    1. Prepare self for meeting (read handouts, and so on).
    2. If can't attend, inform chairperson.
    3. Be on time.
    4. Exercise self-discipline (stick to topic, do not interrupt).
    5. Practice "active listening."
    6. Contribute to managing the meeting's process.
    7. Carry out, subsequently, responsibilities assigned.
VI. Concluding the meeting.
    1. Summarize decisions reached.
    2. Review responsibility assignments and clarify next steps (who, to do what).
    3. Take time to assess the meeting's process, if necessary.
    4. Schedule next meeting (if appropriate).
VII. Follow-up.
    1. Prepare and distribute notes.
    2. Follow up on carrying out of assignments.

The Case of the Restaurant Staff

Let's look at another group that differs from the first. It consists of 25 members of the staff of an upscale restaurant (*not* Radius, the restaurant in the Managerial Bulletin opening this chapter). The group includes various levels of expertise from the head chef and maître d' on down to the dishwashers and bus staff, as well as wide variations in experience in a food service industry. The tasks themselves are not very complex, except for the chef's; each person has a clearly defined job with a very limited range of diversity. The restaurant has an excellent reputation to maintain, and every member of the staff is under pressure to be on his or her toes at all times, paying attention to the quality of the food, the service, the cleanliness of the tables and floor, and so forth. While the job that any one person performs, especially at such levels as chef or maître d', can affect the whole operation, each person's work is sharply enough differentiated so that much of it can be performed independently of the other employees. However, key points where coordination is needed are such matters as preparing orders in time, picking up food as it is ready to be served, getting tables cleared off fast enough to prepare for the next customer, and so on. But once a system has been devised, these are routine matters and do not require elaborate or intensive discussion and analysis by the staff at the time of execution.

How the Criteria Apply to Each Group

The Planning Group
The executive team working on the strategic plan can be described as follows:

A. A small group with:
B. Evenly distributed resources,
C. Dealing with a complex and diverse task,
D. Under little external time pressure,
E. But requiring a high level of interdependence.

Under these circumstances, the appropriate group processes would tend to be as follows:

1. Informal atmosphere with close, friendly relationships.
2. Full participation of all members equally.
3. High level of goal understanding and acceptance on the part of every group member.
4. Complete sharing of all information, with every member listening to every other member.
5. Disagreements discussed and resolved, not set aside.
6. Decisions made by group consensus.
7. Criticism of performance open and direct among all group members.
8. Feelings about task expressed openly and directly.
9. Task assignments made and accepted through discussion and negotiation; as voluntary as possible.
10. Leadership shared freely and changed along with corresponding changes in situational demands.
11. Group devotes significant blocks of time to the discussion of its own process.

The Restaurant Staff
The staff of the upscale restaurant can be described as follows:

A. A large group with:
B. Highly differentiated resources,

C. Dealing with simple and narrow tasks, except for a few highly skilled jobs like chef,

D. Under a high level of time pressure,

E. With a relatively low level of task interdependence except at a few key points.

Under these circumstances, the appropriate group processes would tend to be:

1. Formal atmosphere with task-relevant relationships.

2. Participation in discussions based upon expertise.

3. Understanding and acceptance of goals related to level and scope of job responsibilities.

4. Members obtain information from and listen to those other members possessing greater relevant knowledge.

5. Only those disagreements directly interfering with task are dealt with; final resolution determined by those members with greatest expertise.

6. Decisions made by those with relevant level of knowledge and expertise.

7. Criticism of work made by those members with the requisite knowledge and experience.

8. Feelings expressed through prescribed procedures.

9. Assignments made by those members with greatest level of knowledge and expertise.

10. Leadership on any given aspect of task determined by the relevant knowledge and experience.

11. Very little time devoted to examining group process; procedures are devised by higher-level members and carried out in a formal manner.

As you compare the two pictures just drawn, you might have some personal reactions to them. The first one portrays a kind of setting that many but not all people prefer, while the second has the ring of a small bureaucracy and may not be quite as attractive to you, although there are people who do prefer working in more structured, defined settings. What actually happens in any given situation is not just a matter of what the nature of the situation requires or calls for; it is also a matter of what other options are possible and what the members of any group might consider most desirable for them. The staff of the restaurant might very well *choose* to operate in a manner similar to that of the planning group, but it would be fighting an uphill battle in the face of what the task situation demands. For instance, try to imagine 25 people struggling to resolve all the disagreements that can occur in such a large group. How feasible would it be for such a group to arrive at a consensus on all issues? What would be the costs of ignoring the many years of experience and the levels of expertise that some individuals possess, in order to widen and maximize member participation? And what would happen if everyone criticized everyone else and freely expressed all their feelings about every aspect of their work? Though such a set of choices might be made to work, it would consume extraordinary energy, and in the long run it would be unlikely to get the work done effectively.

What both situations have in common is that they are maximizing the use of group member resources. They appropriately differ from each other in *how* they use their resources, but they can be equally high in the outcomes of productivity, worker satisfaction, and development.

Process Can Be Changed

Sometimes a group can improve its process by direct examination of how its members are working together (i.e., by reviewing the criteria of an effective group, discussed earlier). This can be done through informal discussion or by a more formal procedure, such as the use of an instrument. The process thermometer in the Personal

Social Loafing (The Free-Rider Problem)

How many times have you found that some individuals, perhaps even yourself, put forth less effort on a task when it is carried out in a group than when it is conducted individually? When this occurs it is called *social loafing,* the tendency of an individual to exert less effort when working in a group than when working alone. In a well-functioning team, sometimes called a high-performing team, this tendency is not evident, since the level of collective commitment is high. The consequences of social loafing include resentment of the nonperformers by the performers, especially if the rewards (grades, bonuses, etc.) go to the group as a whole, a tendency for the overall level of performance to suffer, and the erosion of cohesiveness and team spirit. A similar set of outcomes can occur if the rewards are related solely to individual performance and, consequently, produce doubts about the value of group effort in the minds of the members. Social loafing tends to be greater in relation to group size. It is easier to "hide" in a big group than in a small one.

So what can you do about it? From a manager's perspective the most important thing you can do is make sure that there is a balance between individual and group rewards for performance and that work groups have a system of individual accountability. With respect to the reward system, it is important that the group itself has some control over who receives what, as well as a fair system for determining that. Similarly, it is important that the group norms and sanctions around performance are understood and supported by all members.

For more information on this topic, see the Suggested Readings at the end of the chapter.

Application Exercise at the end of this chapter is an example of the more formal approach. It clearly has the advantage of making sure that the group addresses all the important issues, but some groups are not comfortable with its tight structure. You might find it useful to experiment with the Process Thermometer in one of your own groups, even if not all the dimensions fit your situation.

Another way a group can change its process is by restructuring itself. A large group can subdivide into smaller groups, each of which can utilize effective small-group process criteria. Further, if the subdivisions equalize the levels of expertise in each subgrouping, then other criteria begin to change in their applications. At the restaurant, for example, it may be that wait staff in each area can usefully meet to discuss possible areas of cooperation; or chef, maître d', and key wait staff might periodically examine the way orders are transmitted. Factors like task complexity and required interdependence may be less subject to change, but even these allow the possibility of exploring various forms of innovation and work variation. For example, individuals normally assigned to one kind of task can exchange jobs with others in order to learn a wider range of tasks and also gain appreciation of one another's role.

We do consider it critical, however, for a work group to remember to utilize its full range of resources in order to be effective. If the task calls for differentiated levels of expertise in a group, then the effectiveness of that group's process will depend upon the degree to which it gives influence to appropriate members. By way of contrast, If the task calls for evenly distributed resources among the members of a group, then the effectiveness of the group's process will depend upon the degree to which influence is equally shared among the members.

Task Group Effectiveness Develops over Time

In taking steps to diagnose the appropriateness of a group's process and to change that process, one must not only consider the work situation as discussed above but also one other aspect of the group: its phase of development as a task group.

Technology Can Change the Process

Computer-Aided Meetings Are Speedy, Honest, Anonymous—and Silent

There's a bloody meeting going on. "This company has no leader—and no vision," says one frustrated participant. "Why are you being so defensive?" asks another. Someone snaps: "I've had enough—I'm looking for another job." Rough stuff—if these people were talking face-to-face. But they're not. They're sitting side-by-side in silence in front of personal computers, typing anonymous messages that flash on a projection screen at the head of the room.

SOURCE: "At These Shouting Matches, No One Says a Word," *Business Week*, June 11, 1990.

An Electronic Message?

Pros

Speeds the process, as everyone talks at once.

Fosters honesty through anonymity.

Gives participants a sense they played a role in decision making.

Creates a printed record of results.

Cons

Requires thinking at a keyboard.

Gives equal time to bad ideas.

Does not give credit for brilliance.

SOURCE: "Business Meeting by Keyboard," *New York Times*, October 21, 1990.

No group can expect to be instantly effective. Groups are known to go through developmental phases or periods during which certain of the 11 issues are central and require resolution before the group can move on to deal with other issues and eventually establish its best working process. You as an individual can probably remember some stages you went through during your life when certain issues were dominant. For example, before you became an independent adult, you may have had to work through a period of counterdependence, in which you were struggling to prove yourself. Similarly, groups typically have to resolve membership issues before they can focus on issues of confrontation and reach full working expectations. The time it takes for a group to work through the phases will vary with the backgrounds of its members. If the members have had little experience working in groups, the process is liable to be slow and even cumbersome. While groups composed of members who have had experience can usually proceed more rapidly, if the range of experience is great and some become impatient with the needs of others, the process may also be slow.

Furthermore, just as counterdependent feelings can be rekindled in individuals from time to time throughout life by the actions of teachers, bosses, and others, so, too, groups do not necessarily leave a given phase of development permanently. From time to time they must recycle to rework old issues that were not fully resolved or to modify their resolutions in the face of new events or new members.

Consequently, a manager who assigns people to a committee or task force needs to understand that it may take some time for that group to reach its full effectiveness. Similarly, as you seek to diagnose the groups of which you are a member, try to consider what phase they are in and what steps you can take to facilitate their appropriate movement to the next phase. Also do not be surprised if at times you and the group need to recycle and work some more on an issue that was previously resolved.

In the next section, we discuss the phases of group development. There have been many different models proposed over the years; one of the most popular is B. W. Tuckman's because the names of each stage are catchy:[6]

1. **Forming.** The initial period during which members get acquainted with each other and try to establish some basis for membership and acceptance into the group.
2. **Storming.** The period during which members try to establish their influence and often conflict over issues of control and status in the group.
3. **Norming.** A phase when the group establishes some ground rules and norms related to both tasks and relationships, usually as a way to resolve many of the conflicts from the previous stage.
4. **Performing.** The stage when the members understand and appreciate each other's contribution to the group's goals, share in the leadership roles, and commit themselves to operating interdependently to accomplish the goals.

We find a five-phase variation developed by Steven Obert more useful.

Five Phases of Group Development[7]

Phase 1—Membership

When a group is newly formed, the members typically wonder about whether they will have a place in the group and will find acceptance in it. They wonder whether others perceive the goals of the group as they do and whether the goals of the group that emerge (are clarified) will be ones to which they can give commitment. Will the price of membership in terms of expected behavior (norms) and the benefits of membership (support, acceptance, goal accomplishment) warrant their psychological joining of the group? In short, members tend to be concerned with their own safety and place in the group, rather than with collective efforts toward the task. Issues of participation and membership, goals, and (in a covert way) evaluation are important.

The atmosphere is likely to be strained, leading to superficial and polite interaction conducted with caution. While some individuals may respond to the ambiguity of the situation with an extra amount of activity and talk (in an attempt to establish some definition), others will tend to be hesitant and reserved.

Members are likely to feel quite dependent on the designated leader if there is one (as usually is the case in business) or look to the wider organization for clarification if there is not. Members often approach tasks with high energy but little coordination.

Any attempt to diagnose who ultimately will exert leadership is prone to great error, although early "activists" sometimes may be propelled into leadership positions that they ultimately cannot sustain. Listening may be quite intense, as people have their antennas out to discover the rules of the road; but distortion is likely (hearing what one wants to hear for safety), and there is little sharing and testing of understanding and interpretation.

Members need to get acquainted and begin to share expectations about goals and objectives. Efforts to rush this process by demanding that people reveal intimate facts about themselves can be disastrous; but full attention to the task, with no effort to get acquainted and no sharing of self, can also be inhibiting. The need is to become acquainted with one another and begin the process of goal clarification.

Similar attempts to establish norms about handling conflict openly or allowing full expression of feelings, while given lip service, are generally premature and therefore ineffective during this phase. Those issues come up later.

Phase 2—Subgrouping

As members begin to get acquainted and identify others who share some of their expectations, pairing and other subgroupings occur. The issue of relationships begins

Group Effectiveness Requires a Balance between People Issues and Task Issues

Meetings are too often a poor way to get the best out of people and . . . one of the most destructive forces in a group can be the participant who is trying harder than everybody else.

Groups can work well . . . when there is a balance between a sense of solidarity and a focus on the task at hand and when the task is appropriate to the group.

SOURCE: Daniel Goleman, "Recent Studies Help Explain Why Some Meetings Fail," *New York Times*, June 7, 1988.

to come to center stage as individuals focus on similarities and dissimilarities and seek out others for friendship, acceptance, and support (allies on task issues).

Relationships may tend to be clinging, as members hang on to those who seem similar among potentially dangerous others. Members begin to express some feeling of warmth within the subgroupings, and the overall atmosphere can become more relaxed, even though information flow will still be somewhat guarded.

A person in the authority position is likely to be resisted regardless of what he or she says; and if there is not a designated leader, then there will be resistance to anyone who tries to take charge. Group members complain to one another about the impossible task that the organization has given them or about aspects of the wider organization. Energy for working on the task tends to sag, and, while members begin to cooperate (at least with their newfound allies), there is little planning of task activities.

Sometimes groups in this phase develop a sense of unanimity of purpose and cohesiveness that may, in fact, be phony, based on a tendency to avoid conflict and withhold evaluations.

One danger is that pairings and subgroups form so quickly after people gain some knowledge of one another in Phase 1 that there is a lack of linkages across subgroups. Knowledge of and some linkage with all group members can be most important for pooling resources and resolving the nearly inevitable disagreements and conflicts that typically emerge in Phase 3.

Another danger during Phase 2 is that the subgroups develop spokepersons, so total group discussions are conducted by only a few members, and a pattern of narrow participation is established irrespective of the requirements of the work situation. This, too, can inhibit conflict resolution in Phase 3.

Phase 3—Confrontation

During this stage, relationships between subgroupings come to the fore along with leadership and the handling of disagreement, as members seek to influence the direction and operating practices of the group. Struggles for individual power and influence are common. Questions of member roles and division of labor often emerge, along with issues of relative contribution and member evaluation.

Listening is often likely to reach a low ebb, with heated exchanges revealing feelings that may have previously been avoided, suppressed, or denied.

One danger is the temptation to avoid conflict by patching things over prematurely before the issues are fully explored and by establishing norms against rocking the boat or raising controversial subjects. When this happens, the disagreements and any associated bad feelings among members go underground, ready to affect future business in often indirect and insidious ways.

A second danger is that disagreement and conflict are dealt with strictly through power, so one individual or one subgroup "wins" and others "lose"; the issue remains unresolved. Someone emerges as a loser, often resulting in either withdrawal or warfare. Withdrawal reduces the group's resources and is hardly a source of satisfaction and growth for the individuals involved. Warfare, which is typically carried over to the next task facing the group, is a sure way to guarantee lowered productivity and energies devoted to attack and self-defense, rather than growth. A third danger is merely a continuation of the struggle and a lack of energy for any new projects.

There is also great opportunity in this phase. When groups are able to resolve differences (whether interpersonal or task-oriented) successfully, the payoff can be immense as the group moves on to Phase 4. Resolution can be accomplished through finding a new, integrative solution, an open discussion of differences leading to clarification of misunderstandings, or the assistance of an outsider in helping the group listen better and improve its process. Success in dealing with disagreement and conflict can build group cohesiveness, members' skills, and confidence in the group's ability to deal with future issues.

Phase 4—Individual Differentiation

During this phase, the issues of division of labor and member evaluation are likely to be dominant. Members begin to become more accepting of differences among themselves, and there emerges a deeper and genuine concern for one another. Task assignments are based on skills, interests, and desires to grow. Roles and status become differentiated, but members respect one another's contributions. Such a division of labor often rests upon a more open, yet supportive, level of member evaluation than existed during the earlier stages. As time progresses and differentiation occurs, this stage may be marked by a kind of euphoria as group members realize that it will be possible to belong to this group without having to fight to the death or totally give in to majority wishes.

The atmosphere during this period is likely to involve cohesion, satisfaction, and trust as a result of having successfully overcome the conflicts of Phase 3 (yet include some underlying tension over the process of member evaluation and differentiation); there is an overall feeling of confidence and progress.

Leadership may have evolved, with one or two individuals having dominant roles, yet without a sense of imposed domination. Instead, members see the pattern as functional. In addition, there is likely to be effective listening, so even the least influential member has the potential to exert influence and, thereby, share leadership.

Phase 5—Collaboration

Too few groups reach this stage. In it, members focus on ways to complement one another's strengths and weaknesses and find that they can honestly level with one another without its leading to disruption. Members support one another when they genuinely agree, and they argue with one another when they genuinely disagree. Responsibility is distributed among members on the basis of individual competence, and leadership passes around the group on the basis of competence to do particular activities. The entire group achieves a cooperative and interdependent relationship with the rest of the organization, providing input to the organization as needed and taking the organization's needs into account when doing work and making decisions. The group learns how to balance individual and group efforts on tasks, allowing individual members to do tasks alone when they have highly differential expertise and doing tasks cooperatively when many opinions and points of view are needed. Learning activities are geared to optimize individual contributions, so each individual can work toward his or her higher potential.

Several Ways Groups Make Decisions; Each Appropriate at Times

1. By the unilateral action of one dominating member or designated chairperson (autocratic).
2. By the unilateral action of a dominant subgroup acting as a power bloc by imposing its will.
3. By assumption, with silence taken as agreement, a ploy often used by a subgroup to exert dominance.
4. By default (inaction). Inaction is a decision to either stay with the status quo or allow "fate" to decide.
5. By democratic vote (dominance of the majority).
6. By unanimous agreement, perhaps resulting from a thoughtful, open discussion and exchange of ideas.

7. By consensus. *Note:* Consensus is not the same as unanimity, in that some members will still not be in agreement even after prolonged discussion; but they will be willing to go along and allow the group to act as most members see appropriate. Such willingness to go along with the majority under true consensus is an outgrowth of those in the minority feeling that their views have been heard, understood, and actively considered, and that the common goals of the group can be served best by action, rather than by further discussion.

The issue of process is central as the group seeks to maintain the effectiveness developed as a result of its successful progress through the preceding stages. There is always potential need for a group to reexamine its process as it faces new task problems and as members individually grow and develop. Furthermore, as working conditions change, aspects of issues bypassed on the way through the five stages may become important. Consequently, a typical group recycles through aspects of these five phases again and again.

Figure 6–2 outlines typical ways in which the 11 issues facing a group manifest themselves as operating characteristics during the five phases of group development.

Helping Group Movement toward Greater Effectiveness

We started this chapter by asking how you can tell how well a group is working without waiting for the ultimate outcomes to occur. Implicitly we also were asking what a group could do to improve its way of working. We suggest that you begin by observing the group's emergent system, noting how it has resolved the 11 issues that any group faces, and then evaluating whether that process has been appropriate given the group's situation (size, resources, task, time pressure, and degree of task interdependence). Such a diagnosis sets the stage for taking corrective action if and where it is needed.

In general, the way to move the group along is to pay careful attention to the underlying concerns of group members and then either discuss these directly to allay fears or take actions that will deal with the concerns indirectly. For example, say that a group you are in is having difficulties coming to decisions because each of three subgroups insists on its own point of view. One approach is to comment on the deadlock, ask if others agree that the struggle is between subgroups each wanting its way, and then talk about how to reach a decision that would not make one or two subgroups feel defeated.

The less direct approach might include such suggestions as asking members to restate others' arguments before making their own; proposing that the group divide in half, with each half composed of members from each of the subgroups so that freer

FIGURE 6–2	*Common Operating Characteristics during Stages of Group Development*

	STAGES	
Issues	**1** **Membership**	**2** **Subgrouping**
Atmosphere and relationships	Cautiousness	Greater closeness within subgroups
Participation	Superficial and polite	In subgroups by subgroup leaders
Goal understanding and acceptance	Unclear	Some greater clarity, but misperceptions likely
Listening and information sharing	Intense but high distortion and low sharing	Within subgroups, similarities overperceived
Disagreement and conflict	Not likely to emerge; if it does, will be angry and chaotic	False unanimity
Decision making	Dominated by more active members	Fragmented, deadlocks
Evaluation of performance	Done by all, but not shared	Across subgroups
Expression of feelings	Avoided, suppressed	Positive only within subgroups, mild "digs" across groupings
Division of labor	Little, if any	Struggles over jobs
Leadership	Disjointed	Resisted

discussion might take place; proposing that the group stop trying so hard to decide among the existing alternatives and begin to brainstorm new solutions that might integrate the opposing viewpoints; or arranging a break from task activities, with lots of informal interaction.

All of these steps are designed to allow a group to improve on its emergent processes and to get past a development phase in which it may have become blocked. One caution, however: A group should not try to rush too rapidly through Phases 1 to 4 in the hopes of avoiding all difficulties. Groups need time to develop, and any suggestions you make will be accepted most readily when others feel stuck and want help in moving. Also remember that circumstances change. A periodic reassessment can provide a group with the data by which to ensure that its processes continue to serve its goals and objectives.

It is important to note that groups sometimes evolve without direct action by the manager, or in a way not anticipated by the manager, as a result of key events. A crisis forces the group to work long hours and deal with its problems; a higher-level executive comments publicly on the group's performance; a member lets the group down by not delivering what was promised—such critical events, as mentioned previously, can propel a group backward or forward in its development.

By the time you have read this, you may have had sufficient experience in a classroom task group to be able to apply the various criteria to your own experience. Can you correlate how well your group has done on group assignments with the way you have been operating? What should you change? What seems to have worked well? Why?

The performance of your group depends on your ability to analyze the task demands, determine the appropriate set of processes, discuss how they vary from what you have been doing, and make whatever changes are necessary (consistent with your desires). As awkward as it may feel to discuss openly the way you have been making decisions, talking and listening to one another, handling disagreements, and so forth, it is in your collective interest to do so if you haven't already. The ability to find ways to correct a group's (or organization's, or individual's) process is a crucial one that can serve you well throughout your organizational career.

3 Confrontation	4 Individual Differentiation	5 Collaboration
STAGES		
Close within subgroups, hostility between subgroups	Confidence and satisfaction	Supportive and open
Heated exchanges	Individuals come in and out based on expertise	Fluid, people speak freely
Fought over	Agreed upon	Commitment
Poor	Fairly good	Good
Frequent	Based on honest differences	Resolved as it occurs
Based on power	Based on individual expertise	Collective when all resources needed, individual when one expert
Highly judgmental	Done as basis for differentiation but with respect	Open, shared, developmental
Coming out, anger	Increasingly open	Expressed openly
Differentiation resisted	High differentiation based on expertise	Differentiation and integration, as appropriate
Power struggles common	Structured or shared	Shared
Used as weapon	Attended to compulsively or too uncritically	Attended to as appropriate

SOURCE: Adapted from Steven L. Obert, "The Development of Organizational Task Groups," Ph.D dissertation, Case-Western Reserve University, 1979.

KEY CONCEPTS FROM CHAPTER 6

1. Group effectiveness related to emergent processes.
2. Process issues faced by every work group:
   a. Atmosphere and relationships.
   b. Member participation.
   c. Goal understanding and acceptance.
   d. Listening and information sharing.
   e. Handling disagreements and conflicts.
   f. Decision making.
   g. Evaluation of member performance.
   h. Expressing feelings.
   i. Work assignments.
   j. Leadership.
   k. Process evaluation.
3. Factors affecting appropriateness of group process:
   a. Size.
   b. Distribution of resources.
   c. Task complexity/diversity.
   d. Time pressure.
   e. Degree of interdependence.
4. The smaller the group, the fewer total resources and the more appropriate is participation by all.
5. The more evenly distributed the resources (expertise), the more appropriate is total member participation.
6. The greater the complexity/diversity, the more resources needed.
7. The greater the time pressure, the less time for process.
8. The greater the task interdependence, the greater the need for continuous exchanges and knowledge of each other on the part of group members.
9. The greater the member participation, the greater the level of commitment to goals.
10. Evaluation of group process needs to be made relative to the group's phase of development. Five phases are described.
    a. Membership.
    b. Subgrouping.
    c. Confrontation.
    d. Individual differentiation.
    e. Collaboration.

PERSONAL APPLICATION EXERCISE

The Process Thermometer

The instrument below can be used by all members of a group to assess members' perceptions of how well the group is working together. To use as a group, first, individually check the one space that most closely expresses how you would describe the group on each characteristic. Then, tally the combined perceptions and jointly discuss their implications.

THE PROCESS THERMOMETER
GROUP SELF-ASSESSMENT QUESTIONNAIRE

	1	2	3	4	5	

1. **Atmosphere and relationship:**

	1	2	3	4	5	
Supportive	___	___	___	___	___	Competitive (self first).
Personal (warm and close)	___	___	___	___	___	Impersonal (cool and distant).
Energetic	___	___	___	___	___	Lethargic.
Cohesive	___	___	___	___	___	Fragmented.

2. **Member participation:**

	1	2	3	4	5	
All equally	___	___	___	___	___	Primarily just a few.
Easy to get "air time"	___	___	___	___	___	Hard to get "air time."

3. **Goal understanding and acceptance:**

	1	2	3	4	5	
Clear (understood)	___	___	___	___	___	Unclear (vague).
Supported by all	___	___	___	___	___	Unsupported by many.

4. **Listening and sharing of information:**

	1	2	3	4	5	
Members listen carefully	___	___	___	___	___	Members don't really listen.
Members usually understand one another	___	___	___	___	___	Members often misinterpret what others say
Everyone knows what's going on	___	___	___	___	___	Only a few are "in the know."

5. **Handling disagreements and conflict:**

	1	2	3	4	5	
Alternate views explored	___	___	___	___	___	Alternate views brushed aside.
Tensions confronted, dealt with	___	___	___	___	___	Tensions avoided.

6. **Decision making:**

	1	2	3	4	5	
Influence is widely shared	___	___	___	___	___	A few exert a lot of influence.
Reflective of a full discussion	___	___	___	___	___	Quickly by majority rule.

7. **Evaluation of member performance:**

	1	2	3	4	5	
Feedback open and constructive	___	___	___	___	___	Feedback avoided.

8. **Expressing feelings:**

	1	2	3	4	5	
Expressed openly	___	___	___	___	___	Kept bottled up.
Personal concerns accepted	___	___	___	___	___	Only task concerns allowed.

9. **Division of labor:**

	1	2	3	4	5	
Roles clearly defined and stable	___	___	___	___	___	Roles vary with individual interests.

10. **Leadership:**

	1	2	3	4	5	
A clear leader(s) exists	___	___	___	___	___	Leadership functions (acts) are done by all.
Member differentiation appropriate and accepted	___	___	___	___	___	Jockeying for position is occurring.

11. **Attention to process:**

	1	2	3	4	5	
Considered legitimate	___	___	___	___	___	Not considered legitimate.
Process often discussed in the whole group	___	___	___	___	___	Process seldom discussed in the whole group.

12. **Consequences:** The group—

	1	2	3	4	5	
Is very productive	___	___	___	___	___	Is very unproductive.
Gives me satisfaction	___	___	___	___	___	Gives me little satisfaction.
Facilitates my learning and development	___	___	___	___	___	Restricts my learning and development.

It is also possible to use the instrument for your own personal assessment. Fill it out as you see the group. Next to your ratings, try filling it out with what you would expect to be the *average* response of the rest of your group. Compare your personal score with the "average group score." Where are there differences? What do you think accounts for those differences? Could you talk with your group about your perceptions? Ask them if they agree with your diagnosis? Suggest possible changes in the way your group operates? Initiate a group discussion of how to change the group's processes?

These are all ways of opening discussion that can lead to healthy changes. If the group is willing to all fill out the questionnaire and then discuss the tabulated results, so much the better. But if not, you can still use it for your own diagnosis and action planning.

SUGGESTED READINGS

Albanese, R., and D. D. Van Fleet. "Rational Behavior in Groups: The Free-Riding Tendency." *Academy of Management Review,* April 1985, pp. 244–55.

Amason, Allen C.; Kenneth R. Thompson; Wayne A. Hochwarter; and Allison W. Harrison. "Conflict: An Important Dimension in Successful Management Teams." *Organizational Dynamics,* Autumn 1995, pp. 20–35.

Argyris, C. "T-Groups for Organizational Effectiveness." *Harvard Business Review* 42 (1964), pp. 60–68.

Bales, R. F. *Interaction Process Analysis.* Reading, MA: Addison-Wesley Publishing, 1950.

Barton, Ronald B. "Group Dynamics." *CIO,* September 1, 1991.

Bennis, W., and H. Shepard. "A Theory of Group Development." *Human Relations* 9 (1956), pp. 415–37.

Brown, K. A. "Explaining Group Poor Performance: An Attributional Analysis." *Academy of Management Review,* January 1984, pp. 54–63.

Campbell, J., and M. Dunnette. "Effectiveness of T-Group Experiences in Managerial Training Development." *Psychological Bulletin* 70 (1968), pp. 73–103.

Carr, Clay. "Planning Priorities for Empowered Teams." *Journal of Business Strategy,* September/October 1992.

Denton, D. Keith. "Multi-skilled Teams Replace Old Work Systems." *HR Magazine* 37, no. 9 (September 1992), pp. 55–56.

Dumaine, Brian. "Who Needs a Boss?" *Fortune,* May 7, 1990.

Earley, P. C. "Social Loafing and Collectivism: A Comparison of the United States and the Peoples Republic of China." *Administrative Science Quarterly* 34 (1989), pp. 565–81.

Earley, P. C., and E. Mosakowski. "Creating Hybrid Team Cultures: An Empirical Test of Transnational Team Functioning." *Academy of Management Journal* 43 (2000), pp. 26–49.

Elmuti, Dean. "Sustaining High Performance through Self-Managed Work Teams." *Industrial Management,* March/April 1996, pp. 4–9.

George, J. M. "Extrinsic and Intrinsic Origins of Perceived Social Loafing in Organizations." *Academy of Management Journal,* March 1992, pp. 191–202.

Gersick, C. J. G. "Time and Transition in Work Teams: Toward a New Model of Group Development." *Academy of Management Journal* 31, no. 1 (March 1988) pp. 9–41.

Guzzo, Richard A., and Marcus W. Dickson. "Teams in Organizations: Recent Research on Performance and Effectiveness." *Annual Review of Psychology,* 1996, pp. 307–38.

Hackman, J. R., and C. G. Morris. "Improving Groups' Performance Effectiveness." In *Perspectives on Behavior in Organizations,* ed. J. R. Hackman, E. E. Lawler, and L. W. Porter. New York: McGraw-Hill, 1977.

Hamson, Ned. "Organic Teamwork in Personnel." *Journal for Quality and Participation*, June 1990.

Hollenbeck, John R.; Daniel R. Ilgen; Jeffrey A. LePine; Jason A. Colquitt; and Jennifer Hedlund. "Extending the Multilevel Theory of Team Decision Making: Effects of Feedback and Experience in Hierarchical Teams." *Academy of Management Journal,* 41 (1998), pp. 269–82.

Jackson, J. M., and S. G. Harkins. "Equity in Effort: An Explanation of the Social Loafing Effect." *Journal of Personality and Social Psychology* 49 (1985), pp. 1199–1206.

Jassawala, A. R., and H. C. Sashittal. "Building Collaborative Cross-Functional New Product Teams." *Academy of Management Executive* 13, and no. 3 (August 1999), pp. 50–63.

Katzenbach, Jon R., and Douglas K. Smith. "The Discipline of Teams." *Harvard Business Review,* March–April 1993, pp. 111–20.

Kerr, N. L. "Motivation Losses in Small Groups: A Social Dilemma Analysis." *Journal of Personality and Social Psychology* 45 (1983), pp. 819–38.

Kirkman, Bradley L., and Rosen Benson. "Beyond Self-Management: Antecedents and Consequences of Team Empowerment." *Academy of Management Journal* 42 (1999), pp. 58–75.

Kirkman, Bradley L., and Debra L. Shapiro. "The Impact of Cultural Values on Employee Resistance to Teams: Toward a Model of Globalized, Self-Managing Work Team Effectiveness." *Academy of Management Review* 22 (1997), pp. 730–57.

Krantz, J. "Group Process under Conditions of Organizational Decline." *Journal of Applied Behavioral Science* 21, no. 1 (1985), pp. 1–18.

Lau, Dora C., and J. Keith Murnighan. "Demographic Diversity and Faultlines: The Compositional Dynamics of Organizational Groups." *Academy of Management Review* 23 (1998), pp. 325–40.

Lipman-Blumen, Jean, and Harold J. Leavitt. "Hot Groups 'With Attitude,' A New Organizational State of Mind." *Organizational Dynamics,* Spring 1999, pp. 63–73.

Luft, J. *Group Processes.* 3rd ed. Palo Alto, CA: Mayfield, 1984.

Maani, Kambiz E., and Campbell Benton. "Rapid Team Learning Lessons from Team New Zealand's America's Cup Campaign." *Organizational Dynamics,* Spring 1999, pp. 48–62.

Mankin, Don; Susan G. Cohen; and Tora K. Bikson. "Teams and Technology: Tensions in Participatory Design." *Organizational Dynamics,* Summer 1997, pp. 63–76.

McCann, D., and C. Margerison. "Managing High-Performance Teams." *Training and Development Journal* 43, no. 11 (November 1989), pp. 52–60.

McGregor, D. *The Human Side of Enterprise.* New York: McGraw-Hill, 1960.

Owens, Thomas. "The Self-Managing Work Team." *Small Business Reports,* February 1991.

Pacanowsky, Michael. "Team Tools for Wicked Problems." *Organizational Dynamics,* Winter 1995, pp. 36–51.

Petrock, F. "Five Stages of Group Development." *Executive Excellence* 7, no. 6 (June 1990), pp. 9–10.

Rice, A. K. *Productivity and Social Organization: The Ahmedabad Experiment.* London: Tavistock, 1958.

Salem, Mahmoud; Harold Lazarus, and Joseph Cullen. "Developing Self-Managing Teams: Structure and Performance." *Journal of Management Development,* 1992.

Schein, E. *Process Consultation.* Reading, Mass.: Addison-Wesley Publishing, 1969.

Schriesheim, Chester A.: Linda L. Neider; and Terri A. Scandura. "Delegation and Leader-Member Exchange: Main Effects, Moderators, and Measurement Issues." *Academy of Management Journal* 41 (1998), pp. 298–318.

Seeger, J. A. "No Innate Phases in Group Problem Solving." *Academy of Management Review,* October 1983, pp. 683–89.

Shaw, M. E. *Group Dynamics: The Psychology of Small Group Behavior.* New York: McGraw-Hill, 1981.

Shepperd, J. A. "Productivity Loss in Performance Groups: A Motivation Analysis." *Psychological Bulletin* 113 (1993), pp. 67–81.

Shrednick, Harvey; Richard Shutt, and Madeline Weiss. "Team Tactics." *CIO,* February 1992.

Simmon, John. "Starting Self-Managing Teams." *Journal for Quality and Participation,* December 1989.

Simons, Tony; Lisa Hope Pelled; and Ken A. Smith. "Making Use of Difference: Diversity, Debate, and Decision Comprehensiveness in Top Management Teams." *Academy of Management Journal* 42 (1999), pp. 662–73.

Simons, Tony, and R. S. Peterson. "Task Conflict and Relationship Conflict in Top Management Teams: The Pivotal Role of Intragroup Trust." *Journal of Applied Psychology,* 85, no. 1 (February 2000), pp. 102–11.

Steckler, Nicole, and Nanette Fondas. "Building Team Leader Effectiveness: A Diagnostic Tool." *Organizational Dynamics,* Winter 1995, pp. 20–35.

Tuckman, B. W. "Developmental Sequence in Small Groups." *Psychological Bulletin* 63 (1965), pp. 384–99.

Wageman, Ruth. "Critical Success Factors for Creating Superb Self-Managing Teams." *Organizational Dynamics,* Summer 1997, pp. 49–61.

Waller, Mary J. "The Timing of Adaptive Group Responses to Nonroutine Events." *Academy of Management Journal* 42 (1999), pp. 127–37.

Wanous, J. P.; A. E. Reichers; and S. D. Malik. "Organizational Socialization and Group Development: Toward an Integrative Perspective." *Academy of Management Review,* October 1984, pp. 670–83.

Basic Human Needs and Rewards

Overworked and Overpaid: The American Manager

Managers Are Miserable, and This Does Their Companies No Good. If Paying Them More Does Not Solve the Problem, What Can Be Done?

With most companies having thinned the layers of corporate bureaucracy, most managers work longer hours. . . .

Managers have been forced to give away power to semi-autonomous teams. Firms have also outsourced operations that managers used to regard as part of their fiefs. Status-enhancing perks, such as executive dining rooms, have long since disappeared; now some companies expect their managers to be on the road so often that they are forced to "hotdesk" and share offices. . . .

Thanks to flatter management structures, the old reliable ladder of career advancement has gone. . . . Above all there is the danger of losing your job. . . .

Pay does not top the list of managers' priorities . . . the two things that senior managers cite most often when discussing loyalty are corporate pride ("I'm with ABC Corp.") and trust in their chief executive's ability to take decisions. "How you are treated"–a category which is as much about respect as it is about pay–comes third. . . . As long as pay is not seen to be insultingly out of line, other things matter much more in keeping good managers. . . .

Naturally, the best answer is to pay people well *and* look after them–if you can afford to.

SOURCE: "Overworked and Underpaid," *The Economist,* January 30, 1999.

"Organizations today are finding it increasingly difficult to sustain the motivation of employees toward high levels of performance when the uncertainties about job security pervade the atmosphere."

Ted, a member of a student task group, attends all meetings but inevitably sits silently through the discussions. Though his grade depends partly on the contribution he makes to solving problems in the group and he has clearly done the necessary reading, he cannot be enticed or bullied into talking. He responds to all questions aimed at drawing him out with brief yes or no answers. When pressed for an opinion, Ted mutters something like, "I agree with Ellen." How would you explain and deal with his behavior?

Joe Wexler is a 40-year-old machinist who keeps getting fired from jobs.[1] In his current job he is once again heading for trouble. He keeps posting notices on the shop bulletin board, criticizing the company and its management practices, quoting poems, and citing chess problems in order to "broaden horizons" among fellow workers. As chess champion of the city, he is clearly intelligent and able to see that his actions are provoking his boss; why does he continue to defy the requests to keep his notices down?

Throughout your life you have seen examples of people behaving in ways that do not make sense to you, that seem wrong, foolish, self-defeating, or totally incomprehensible. Sometimes you can shrug your shoulders and walk away; but as an organizational member, particularly one with managerial responsibilities, you cannot avoid dealing with difficult behavior. Furthermore, you can undoubtedly remember times when you were behaving in a way that seemed perfectly clear and logical to you but was totally baffling to, or misunderstood by, your parents, boss, or friends. How to understand what is happening inside yourself or in another person is one of the most challenging yet important abilities you can acquire.

In this chapter we focus our attention on what is desired by individuals themselves, quite apart from what is called for by the total organization or immediate work group. One of our core premises is that, *for individuals, much of organizational life requires balancing personal needs and desires with those of the organization.* Sometimes it is possible to satisfy the person and the organization with the same action; occasionally it is totally impossible to meet the needs of both. More often people at work must somehow find ways to be true to themselves while still meeting organizational or group demands.

As we pointed out earlier, the behavior approved in one situation may be frowned upon in another; what we are interested in now is what makes an individual respond in his or her particular way, given the external system's norms and values. For example, how the group might deal with Ted's behavior depends on its norms and values. A group that places a high premium on active participation is likely to pressure Ted to be more forthcoming. How Ted would handle that, in turn, would depend on the strength of his need to remain silent in the group. Similarly, Joe Wexler could give in or continue to defy the pressures to change his behavior; it would depend on what was at stake for him.

How does a person choose whether to go along with the group or organization or even with another person? What motivates one person to accept willingly some group members doing almost nothing to contribute to solving group tasks, while another responds to the same problem with confrontation of the slackers, and still another fumes privately but only smiles in the group? How can we understand individual differences and similarities? With which of the following two quotes do you agree?

What is most personal is most general.[2]

Behavior is determined . . . by a personal, individual way of perceiving which is not identical to that of any other individual.[3]

We will proceed on the assumption that *both* of the above contradictory statements are true. In some ways we are all the same, and we can understand particular behaviors through universal feelings and motives. In other ways each of us represents a unique combination of elements, which adds variety to life but makes prediction of behavior much more complicated.

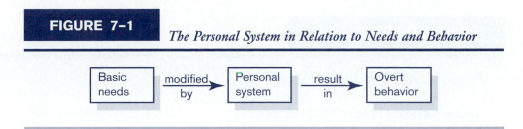

FIGURE 7–1   *The Personal System in Relation to Needs and Behavior*

For the manager as involved actor (discussed in Chapter 1), the problem is one of finding some useful concepts to guide generalizations about people, other concepts to help understand the uniqueness of each person, and some guidelines to help know when to use which. That is not an easy task. There are a variety of theories about motivation and many schemes for categorizing behavior. Some are catchy but shallow; others are sophisticated but so complicated that they confuse, rather than illuminate.

With today's increasing emphasis on teamwork, especially in companies that are creating self-managing teams, it is especially important to managers to understand what motivates individuals and how being part of a team effort can meet those needs. Usually the ultimate success of a team depends as much on the members understanding and respecting individual differences as it does on sharing common goals.

During periods when a company is restructuring or downsizing its workforce, employees normally find themselves more concerned about their own welfare than about the interests of their team or the company as a whole. Organizations today are finding it increasingly difficult to sustain the motivation of employees toward high levels of performance when both new job opportunities and uncertainties about job security pervade the atmosphere. In Chapter 8 we expand on this problem in the context of dealing with stress on the job.

Chapters 7 and 8: From the General to the Particular

In this chapter we introduce you to some theories about human needs in general. Psychologists have many ways of categorizing human needs; we emphasize those most useful for understanding individual behavior at work. However, such theories tend to be quite broad and include wide variations in behavior. For example, we refer to the "need for recognition" as a concept for understanding some aspects of behavior; while that notion might provide a possible insight into someone like Joe Wexler, the chess champ, it will fail to capture the particular *individual's* way of meeting that need. To understand the latter requires other frames of reference that tap into the individual's own world. Chapter 8 is devoted to a concept we have found useful for understanding an individual's behavior: the *personal system*. It is suggested as the stepping stone into the world of another person, the key mechanism that modifies needs and produces particular behavior (see Figure 7–1). Through it we can come to understand and appreciate more fully the actions and attitudes of those around us.

Fundamental Human Needs[4]

Survival Needs

The most uncomplicated behavior is found in infants. When they are hungry, thirsty, or uncomfortable, they cry; when they are happy, they smile or giggle; and when they are sleepy, they sleep. How simple a set of rules for predicting behavior! Through observing and studying infants, psychologists have learned a great deal

Tough Love for Techie Souls

Silicon Valley's Latest Fad: Rebooting Crashed Execs

Kepler displayed some of the classic signs of what [executive coach] Hollands calls a Controller. At Advanced Micro Devices Inc., where Kepler is now director of technology development, he was great at working with his own division but got territorial and defensive when it came to dealing with other groups. He had no idea that his emotionless demeanor was intimidating people and destroying rapport. . . . Hollands says she often runs up against four other personality types wreaking havoc in the Valley. The Intimidator stifles creativity in his staff, inhibits communication across departments, scares the hell out of his peers, and sabotages his boss. The Withholder omits essential information, leaving people out of the loop and never building a team. The Stressor prevents action, shifts blame, and wastes time. The Techno-bound focuses solely on technical issues and writes off people problems as illogical and a waste of time.

SOURCE: Michelle Conlin, "Tough Love for Techie Souls," *Business Week,* November 29, 1999, p. 164. Copyright 1999 McGraw-Hill, Inc.

about the universal forces governing behavior; the infant's life is much less complicated than the adult's. Not many adults cry when hungry or thirsty; whether or not they cry when in pain depends on what was learned as children. But at least people still smile and laugh when they are happy, and some people even go to sleep when they are sleepy. Although people tend to complicate the ways of meeting basic human needs, the needs must still be met; *survival* depends on it.

To survive, one must have enough air, water, food, protection from physical dangers, and so forth. The infant obviously is dependent upon others to have survival needs met; the best it can do is give some signals of hunger, thirst, or discomfort. Fortunately, as mentioned above, the range of adult responses to the infant's signals requires little thought about the uniqueness of the individual infant. Survival needs can be met in fairly universal ways. Even as they grow and mature, people develop fairly similar methods of meeting these needs. Tastes and preferences develop, but the basic ingredients for survival are more or less universal.

Another characteristic of survival needs is that they demand relatively immediate gratification. The human organism will not tolerate deprivation of basic needs for very long without experiencing some level of threat. While you personally may not have had to endure prolonged periods of hunger or thirst or physical discomfort, can you see that even the fear of deprivation, let alone the experience of it, can act as a strong motivator?

One reason people work, and probably the most universal reason, is to survive—that is, to provide themselves with all the means necessary to guarantee adequate nourishment and protection from harm. And knowing this, it is possible for managers of organizations to expect people to exchange work effort for contribution to survival. While human motivation to work is certainly not governed solely by survival needs, it does seem to be based strongly enough upon them to account for the success of wage incentives, fringe benefits, pension plans, health benefits, and the whole myriad of programs typical of modern industry.

Increased competition, pressures to cut costs, demands for greater efficiency in the use of human resources, and technological advancements all pose threats to employee survival. Downsizing (or rightsizing) is pervasive and may be characteristic of organizational life for some time. People who have lost or anticipate losing their jobs look at employment in survival terms. Students who anticipate a limited job market

Setting the Tone: A CEO and a Professor Offer Their Insights on How to Keep the Troops Motivated

In T. J. Rodger's neighborhood, money talks.

The president and chief executive of Cypress Semiconductor Corp. routinely suspends several vice presidents' paychecks until they complete subordinates' performance reviews. He halted his own paycheck during 1996 for the same reason. He once hired a Brink's truck to deliver newly minted gold coins as part of a profit-sharing plan for everyone at the San Jose, Calif., international distributor of semiconductors.

WSJ: . . . money matters a lot down at the bottom. People move in a minute for money.

Mr. Rodgers: I will agree with you for direct labor and for technicians. But you get all the way down to, say, a $60,000 engineer, and I believe my generalization holds.

WSJ: They don't work for money?

Mr. Rodgers: Where they work is not determined by money as long as they feel they are fairly compensated. When an engineer quits, sometimes it is for money. The story is always the same. "I have this problem. I want to buy a house." Real estate is expensive. But basically if they are not being hassled by money, money is not the primary motivating factor for them coming or going.

SOURCE: Joann S. Lublin, "Setting the Tone," *The Wall Street Journal,* April 8, 1999, p. R10. Copyright© 1999, Dow Jones & Company, Inc.

upon graduation find themselves in a highly competitive situation relative to their peers and are likely to grab the first opportunity that comes along. In short, your perspective on how you weigh your options is directly related to the level of needs operating at the time. Survival needs can be very powerful even in a wealthy country.

Those of you who have had to work can undoubtedly remember how important your paycheck was to you. People who are threatened about their survival will put up with almost any work conditions in order to earn the money necessary for food and shelter. Can you imagine yourself, however, spending your entire life in a job that satisfied only your basic needs? Most people seek something more from their work. What are some of the other sources of motivation?

Social Needs

Again we look to the developing infant for some clues. So far the little person has survived; he or she is adequately fed, clothed, and protected. Not enough. We have already spoken of the human being as a social being; infants deprived of some basic minimal level of human contact do not grow in healthy ways. Normally the family provides the primary context for meeting the social needs of the infant, the needs for human contact and affection. This important ingredient is a kind of support base that provides a sense of belonging and the beginnings of feelings of personal worth. While the individual might survive the absence of such a support base, it is not likely to be a very healthy existence and can set the stage for a lifetime of desperately seeking a state of social belonging or of apathetic withdrawal from human contact.

Like the survival needs, the social needs do not just disappear from the scene once provided for. They continue to exert important influences on individuals' behavior throughout their entire lives. Also, when threatened, they tend to prompt people into some kind of definite action. Think about those times when you have felt alone, isolated, deprived of the kinds of warmth and support that human contact alone can offer. You seek out your friends or your family or even casual acquaintances. When it gets really bad, you may hang around a public place just to be in the presence of others, or you may even approach a total stranger to strike up a conversation.

> No more fiendish punishment could be devised, were such a thing physically possible, than that one should be turned loose in society and remain absolutely unnoticed by all the members thereof.
>
> William James
> *The Principles of Psychology XII*

Unlike the survival needs, the social needs do not seem to demand immediate gratification, at least among most adults. When necessary, a person can await the return of a valued friend, although a letter or even just thinking about the other can provide some degree of comfort. Also, the social needs are expressed and satisfied in a greater number of ways than are the most basic survival needs. Look at the variety of social systems people live in, the differences in family relationships, and the varying patterns of friendship and social groupings. In short, the social needs of people seem to have some relation to survival but not quite the critical character of the needs for air, water, food, safety, and so forth. And while they exert a powerful influence on all our behavior, they are subject to wide variations in style.

For many years organizational managers paid little attention to the social needs of people. It was assumed that the economic reward of "a fair day's pay" would elicit a fair day's work and that worker needs required no more attention. That assumption is only valid under certain limited conditions. Most people simply need more than just the pay for work, especially if they feel reasonably sure that they can get their needs for survival met elsewhere if necessary.

Over the years it has been discovered that workers' productivity is usually governed to a great extent by their social relationships, a point we have already discussed in detail in earlier chapters. What we wish to bring out here are the motivating forces behind those social interaction patterns. When permitted or encouraged, or both, and when the physical setting does not constrain it, the social needs will make themselves visible. It is a process as inevitable as eating when you are hungry. When managers attempt to constrain social behavior beyond certain limits, the need does not disappear; it only becomes coupled with frustration and seeks alternative outlets. For example, one factory erected a barricade between women employees seated opposite one another so as to discourage "distracting" conversation. This resulted in a significant increase in the number of trips the women made to the washroom! The thoughtful manager is careful to look at the ways in which social behaviors may be functional or dysfunctional to the work effort. That distinction makes it possible to provide ways to encourage the former and eliminate the latter.

Many of the cases you are studying in this book address problems of worker behavior involving a mix of work-related and social-related activities. It is often tempting to treat all social behavior as dysfunctional and, consequently, to recommend a hard-line approach to eliminate it. We have already raised this issue with respect to the notions of a group's required and emergent systems, the latter generally involving social behavior of one sort or another. Here we are reemphasizing the same issue but focusing on human motivation. Arbitrarily curtailing all social behavior of workers not only overlooks the significance of emergent behavior but goes counter to the very foundations of human needs.

When workers are organized into teams, we find a wide variation in the level of social needs of the members. Some thrive on the opportunities for frequent interactions, but others, who are less inclined to interpersonal interaction, may find the team

Great Expectations?

Is your job living up to its promise? Is your boss the kind of leader that you thought you'd have? Is your work living up to the new economy's bold new compact? FC-Roper Starch Worldwide survey looks at the gap between promise and performance.

In an online poll of 1,122 college-educated, working adults, we probed the proposition that work is, indeed, personal.

So what's the cause, and what's the effect? One reasonable hypothesis: Some workers go into their jobs less prepared than others to invest the time and effort that success demands. They lose ground to colleagues who know that achieving greater rewards requires greater effort—and they get stuck working long hours just to survive. When you think about it, that sounds like ample grounds for resentment.

Pay people poorly, and they'll grumble a bit. Treat them unfairly, and they'll scream "Betrayal!"

. . . [T]he notion of finding community at work is another new-economy myth. If anything, many people appear to be disengaging themselves from the social aspects of their work, seeking a balanced life in which personal fulfillment doesn't depend so completely on their job.

We asked respondents to characterize their relationships with colleagues at work. More than one-third (36%) say that they would be friends with their co-workers "even if we didn't work together." Those who develop such bonds tend to be younger. Among people in their forties and fifties, just 30% view their colleagues as friends. In any case, slightly more than half of all respondents (50.3%) agree with the statement "My co-workers and I make a good team, but we're not friends." And 9% say that while they tolerate their officemates they "would rather not work with them."

Most people go into a new job expecting empowerment, and whether they actually get it largely determines whether they gain a sense of fulfillment from their work.

The workplace isn't a perfect substitute for community. The ideal of being paid according to one's value still gives way to more conventional (and less democratic) reward systems. And people don't always get the autonomy or the respect that they deserve.

Work is important and meaningful, but not crucial. It can be fulfilling, but it's more likely to be so when it is balanced with outside interests and other meaningful pursuits.

SOURCE: "Great Expectations," *Fast Company*, November 1999, p. 212.

pressures to be difficult to handle. You may observe these differences for yourself in student task groups.

So far we have talked about two fundamental sets of needs, those that affect survival and those that are of a social nature. Now we go on to areas of motivation that appear a little later in the individual's developmental years. These areas are of major significance for the learning and growth of the individual.

Higher-Level Needs

Most people are motivated by a range of needs that go well beyond survival and social belonging. They begin at a very early age to seek the approval and recognition of others and to seek a sense of personal respect that tells them that they are achieving something in this world, that they are leaving their mark on it in some way. For some people the route to self-esteem is through being productive, for some it lies in achieving higher and higher levels of prominence and recognition, and for others it comes through achieving power, authority, and responsibility. It is through the satisfaction of these needs, particularly through work, that people feel adequate and can grow and develop into fuller human beings.

Even beyond needs for achievement, recognition, responsibility, and so forth, there seems to be something more human beings each strive for, something that in some way reflects the inner potential inherent in each person. Such terms as

MANAGERIAL BULLETIN

Top Management Incentives Can Work with the Rank and File

According to a recent survey of 644 companies conducted by Sibson & Company, Inc., human resource consultants in Princeton, New Jersey, nearly half the companies with variable pay plans–bonuses, profit sharing, and the like–include hourly employees in those plans.

"Companies are recognizing that they must motivate and reward top performing employees at all levels," said Charles Cumming, a Sibson principal.

SOURCE: "The Trickle-Down Effect in Perks," *New York Times,* November 4, 1990.

self-realization or *self-actualization* have been used to identify this level of needs. Whatever one calls it, the reward for fulfilling any need at this level seems to be in the process itself and not necessarily in the responses of others. It is the doing, the engaging in the act itself that carries its own reward.

Another way of thinking about these kinds of accomplishments has been called the need for competence or mastery. Even very young children may spend hours attempting to master skills, aptitudes, and abilities that are not directly connected to any safety or social rewards. Have you ever seen a baby repeatedly practicing pulling itself upright? As adults we still have the need to master new areas, whether work related or not. The intrinsic pleasure of conquering a complex task can be a powerful motivator quite apart from the pay or praise received. Hobbies can give pleasure just from engaging in them. Some people have jobs that involve high levels of creativity, imagination, and problem-solving ability–jobs that drive them to work very long hours without their even seeming to notice the effort. They can acknowledge the importance of the rewards that satisfy other needs, such as security of income, recognition by their organization, and so forth; but many insist that the overriding satisfaction is in the creative process itself. Can you think of activities, work or otherwise, that tend to absorb your time and energy for no other reason than the job of engaging in them?

Other ways in which people meet needs for self-realization include learning and expanding knowledge, developing a philosophy of life, pursuing religious interests, and similar activities yielding a sense of self-expansion and growth. In recent years many people have "gone back to the soil"–that is, they have discovered the sense of personal satisfaction and joy that lies in the process of raising plants, flowers, and crops of various sorts. It may be that the development of a total sense of appreciation for life and all its potential is the ultimate in self-realization.

If you examine the kinds of learning experiences you have had that have been the most personally rewarding, they are likely to be the ones that tap into the widest range of your needs, especially higher-level ones. For some the most satisfying learning (when they feel most engaged and alive) happens during a course or school experience. For others it is in their jobs. The satisfaction related to that kind of experience may be self-realization, a sense that you are realizing some inner potential for learning and growth.

Individual Variations in Human Needs

While all of the needs discussed–survival, social, self-esteem, mastery, or self-actualization–appear to be universally operating for everyone some of the time, each person has different intensities of each need, and these intensities change in different situations. Some people, for example, are so preoccupied with gaining social acceptance that they hardly acknowledge or act on their other needs; it is as if they are "frozen" at one level of need and cannot unthaw enough to use the full range of human responses in them. Could that, for example, be a clue to understanding the silent group member, who perhaps so fears rejection that it becomes almost impossible to say anything that might be ridiculed? The need for social acceptance might be driving out behavior that would satisfy needs for learning, mastery, or recognition.

There is controversy among psychologists about whether the needs discussed above all exist simultaneously in people or are indeed arranged in a hierarchy of importance. This controversy seems to reflect the principal difference between the points of view of Maslow and Herzberg—the former proposing the hierarchy model, the latter insisting that survival needs ("hygiene factors") and growth needs ("motivators") exist along independent dimensions. (See Suggested Readings for references.)

On the one hand, there is considerable evidence that a hierarchy does exist and that the lower-level needs (i.e., those that are more survival oriented) must be satisfied before the individual is able to devote energy to higher-level needs. A frequently cited example is the starving man who is not likely to be concerned about his self-esteem until his belly is filled, as in the Indian company cited earlier. There is also evidence from the area of child development that supports this concern. Children who are deprived of basic satisfactions during the early years are often found to be limited in their degree of total psychological growth; they tend to remain insecure and survival oriented even as adults.

On the other side of the issue are the many exceptions: examples of people who pay little attention to their basic needs, devoting their energies to intellectual or creative pursuits. There is also evidence from studies in organizations indicating that higher-level needs may exist separately and alongside the survival needs. It has been shown that workers who are very unhappy with pay, working conditions, fringe benefits, and so forth, can still respond positively to improved opportunities for responsibility and advancement, as well as to a broadening of the work tasks themselves. Some researchers argue that the notion of a hierarchy is not especially relevant to the manager; the important thing to recognize is the significance of higher-level human needs as critical motivators for work. They stress that an organization is seeing only a limited picture of human needs when it pays attention solely to such items as pay and working conditions (survival issues) to the exclusion of worker esteem, achievement, and opportunities for self-realization.

We can look at this issue in still another way. Whether or not *all* employees could potentially respond to work that is more challenging, complex, and engaging, there are many who are prepared, for whatever reasons, to settle for low responsibility and autonomy if pay is adequate and working conditions decent. Managers can choose, therefore, to seek out such people for routine work, see that they are well paid, and ignore any unmet needs at work. Conversely, they can find those who are most concerned with self-realization to do the more inventive complex tasks and then give them scope for creativity. This kind of thinking fits the notion of appropriateness to the situation, at least in terms of short-term productivity.

But there are problems inherent in this approach. Even if sufficient people of each type could be found (and that is becoming increasingly difficult as younger people come to expect more fulfillment from work), there is still the question of long-term development of the human resources of the organization. Is it possible that the managerial assumption of low worker motivation, leading to jobs that are purposely kept routine, forces workers to set their sights only on pay and other survival rewards? Is that reaction likely to be seen by managers as confirmation of low motivation, which then locks in the very behavior that causes the problem? To what extent is this a *self-fulfilling prophecy*? Is it important for employees to learn new skills and aptitudes or to just perform routinely what they already know? Is it desirable, ethically and pragmatically, to keep satisfaction at the lowest acceptable level, ignoring social and higher needs, which may be less visible? Will that gain the desired level of commitment, imagination, loyalty? Is it healthy for an organization to have most of its employees just going through the motions, leaving all responsibility and decisions to a few "higher ups"? Do not an increasing number of organizations have tasks that demand employees to be dedicated and willing to go beyond the minimum requirements?

If you want more than a short-term adequate fit, then there are many ways to explore the design of work to meet a greater range of human needs. Jobs requiring only robot-like, repetitive activities can be automated or redesigned to be more challenging. Parts of various jobs can be combined to enrich the work of any one employee. Jobs can be rotated to provide variety and change of pace. Workers can be given more responsibility and autonomy through more delegation of decision making and through opportunities to set their own working hours, work pace, and work methods. (See Chapter 14 for more detail about possible changes.)

It is important for a manager to recognize the ways in which the characteristics of a job (i.e., how the work is designed) play a significant role in the level of motivation of the employee. The work of Hackman and Oldham[5] attests to the proposition that The greater the role a worker plays in the design and management of his or her own work, the higher will be the level of motivation to perform that work. The most important characteristics of a job, according to their research, and the observations of many managers, include

1. *Skill variety*: Tasks that require a wide range of skills and talents on the part of the worker.
2. *Task identity*: Tasks that possess wholeness, that require a total effort that leads to completeness.
3. *Task significance*: Tasks that make a difference to others and to the organization as a whole, and possibly even beyond the organization (e.g., the community).
4. *Autonomy*: Freedom to carry out tasks with minimal supervision or external control and in a manner that works best for the individual him/herself.
5. *Feedback*: Frequent opportunities to get information about the outcomes and effectiveness of one's performance as a means of learning and improvement.

As a student you probably find that these same characteristics apply to the work assignments in your courses. The most engaging and rewarding experiences you have from your courses are likely to involve variety, wholeness, meaning, autonomy, and feedback. Remember these principles when you manage a work environment.

All of these methods have costs associated with them and are partly dependent on the availability of employees who want to engage themselves in work, rather than just put in time to get the money to satisfy needs elsewhere. Some jobs do not lend themselves to redesign or would be too expensive to change. Cost considerations will surely play a part in deciding whether to try to find security-oriented employees to fit existing routine work or to change the nature of the work itself. But money (or short-term profits in profit-making organizations) is not the only consideration when looking at the fit between motivation and work. The satisfaction and learning of organizational members have important consequences, too.

Again, there are differences related to gender. Strong evidence supports the notion that men tend to place greater emphasis on the importance of control, hierarchy, and rationality than do women, while the latter tend to emphasize the importance of relationships, lateral connections, and intuitive judgment. The fact that organizations are moving in the direction of team-centered management suggests that what may be the more natural style for many women might well be useful learning for many men. It is also worth mentioning that, as organizations hire increasing numbers of people from diverse cultural and national backgrounds, there will be much to be learned about the variation in ways that human needs are satisfied.

One final point worth mentioning is the fact that human beings have an incredible ability to accommodate themselves (perhaps even resign themselves) to unpleasant or adverse conditions. Coal miners, boiler tenders in the hold of a ship, and the like, somehow seem to accept the unhappy conditions as a normal part of their existence. Perhaps much of the sense of discomfort—even outrage—to which social scientists allude in describing these work environments may not exist all that

Some Theories of Motivation

Theorist	Principal Concepts
Maslow	Viewed human motivation in hierarchy beginning with basic needs related to *survival* and developing into higher-level needs related to growth. Specific need hierarchy included: a. Physiological. b. Safety (physical and psychological). c. Love d. Esteem (by self and by others). e. Self-actualization. Although not developed from research in work environments, concept valuable in understanding behavior at work.
Herzberg	Identified higher- and lower-level needs; former labeled *motivators,* latter *hygiene factors.* Two-factor theory developed from research in industry; discovered that attempts to reduce dissatisfactions among workers by increasing pay, adding benefits, improving working conditions, and so on, failed to sustain motivation to work. Found that long-term satisfactions in work stemmed more from achievement, opportunities, recognition, and the like; things built into work, not just added on. Job enlargement and enrichment came from Herzberg's work; are ways of strengthening motivators.
McClelland	McClelland's early work concerned *need for achievement* and *need for affiliation,* both considered important sources of motivation in work environment. Research on need for achievement provided important insights into growth of industrial societies and showed a link between need for achievement and entrepreneurial behavior. More recent work pertained to *need for power.* Provided insights into behavior of leaders and their impact on society. Distinction between *personalized power* and *socialized power* may be critical step in removing negative connotation of power.

Theorist	Principal Concepts
White	Suggested that desire for *competency* is a powerful force behind much of human behavior.
Festinger	Experience of *dissonance,* being psychologically uncomfortable, viewed as source of motivation. Person acts to reduce dissonance either by avoiding dissonant situations or by acting to change source of dissonance. If source is discrepancy between internal idea and external situation, person will either modify idea or attempt to change situation.
Alderfer	Proposed a motivational model that essentially reduced Maslow's five levels to three levels, as follows: • *Existence needs*—related to basic survival. • *Relatedness needs*—pertaining to social and interpersonal relationships. • *Growth needs*—related to the development of one's potential. In contrast to Maslow's concept, Alderfer's theory as does Herzberg's suggests that individuals tend to pursue more than one need level at a time.
Skinner	B. F. Skinner devoted his entire professional life to the study of how people learn. Focusing exclusively on observable behavior, this theory states that learned behavior occurs as a result of reinforcement. If a particular action is rewarded, then the chance of that action being repeated increases. Absence of any reward lowers the probability that the action will be repeated, as does punishment; but the latter also tends to produce fear or anxiety and, consequently, avoidance behavior.

strongly in the minds of the workers in the situations. Therefore, one should think twice before automatically assuming that what appears to be a repetitive, unstimulating job is in fact so to a person in such a job. Enrichment might best be defined by the potentially enriched.

In general, however, most often a worker's commitment to the job can be enhanced by allowing that worker to shape or reshape the way the work is carried out. If a manager wants more than just compliance from employees, this kind of improvement is essential.

Summary Propositions

Regardless of whether or not we assume a strict hierarchy of needs, we can state that There are a wide variety of human needs operating at work. To motivate organizational members, some diagnosis must be made of which particular needs are most important and then a system of rewards (pay, responsibility, and so forth) developed to fit. (1) The closer the fit between member needs and organization rewards, the

Punt, Pass, and Ponder the Questions

In the N.F. L., Personality Tests Help Teams Judge the Draftees

Dave Heine, senior vice president of Personnel Decisions International, a testing organization in Minneapolis, said tests of all types, including cognitive and behavioral, are proliferating in corporate America, with more filtering down to lower-level workers. The trend, though, is toward simulations that put people in realistic work settings and see how they respond.

Like the football teams, corporations have focused over the last four or five years on whether someone will be a good fit with an organization, not on the person's raw intellect, said Pat Hauenstein, vice president of Development Dimensions International, a Pittsburgh testing company.

SOURCE: Timothy W. Smith, "Punt, Pass, and Ponder the Questions," *New York Times,* April 20, 1997, p. 11.

higher productivity will be. (2) The higher the level of needs, the more varied the rewards necessary to achieve productivity, satisfaction, and individual development. Conversely, the lower the level of needs, the less varied rewards have to be.[6]

The Manager and the Reward System

A social system maintains its existence by virtue of its ability to meet the needs of its members. The behavior of the members that contributes to the system must be reinforced—that is, rewarded, encouraged, and supported. In an organization the manager exercises primary control over the reward system; yet many managers fail to appreciate how their own behavior and decisions may reinforce or discourage desired behavior on the part of employees.

Behavior Is Governed by Outcomes

It seems fairly obvious that: People tend to repeat behavior that is rewarded, avoid behavior that is punished, and drop or forget behavior that produces neither.[7] In other words the outcomes of one's actions play a major role in determining one's future actions. If one knows that putting in extra hours leads to more money, one is likely to put in the extra time if more money is a current goal. If one knows that his or her pay will be docked for being late to work, the alarm clock is likely to be set with time to spare. If extra hard work goes unrewarded, it will probably soon fade from a person's repertoire in that situation.

As a manager, one is in a position to reward, punish, or ignore many different kinds of behavior. The manager's choices will have important effects upon worker productivity, satisfaction, development, and ultimately upon the overall climate of the work environment. Given all the complexities of human behavior, some guidelines would be useful for improving your skills in managing behavior. While by no means exhaustive, the following represent seven key principles:

1. Rewards usually work better than punishments.
2. Intrinsic rewards usually are more effective than extrinsic rewards.
3. The timing of rewards is important to their effectiveness.
4. Conflicting sources: Behavior that results in both reward and punishment produces conflict.

The Bonus Isn't Reserved for Big Shots Anymore

[T]he portion of Fortune 1,000 companies that offer bonus pay plans for hourly employees has risen . . . to 34 percent . . .

Bonuses are also thought to be better for promoting teamwork. . . . Bonuses can be distributed in a slew of variations to meet specific company needs . . . the trend was to award small groups so people felt they had contributed. . . .

But bonuses can backfire. Companies can inadvertently encourage the wrong behavior in employees by tying compensation to increased sales. . . .

Sears . . . used to reward auto-shop employees according to the size of the repair bills. The upshot? Over-billed customers and lawsuits.

SOURCE: Barbara Bucholz, "The Bonus Isn't Reserved for Big Shots Anymore," *New York Times*, October 27, 1996, p. F10.

5. Avoidance of negative outcomes and their associated feelings and perceptions are important determinants of behavior.
6. Feelings and perceptions become associated with outcomes.
7. Rewards are perceived in comparison to others'.

Reward versus Punishment

Although managers may give lip service to "the power of positive thinking," they often become more concerned about controlling than rewarding employees. For example, can you think of instructors who always seem to worry about students getting away with something? They are likely to offer more punishment for doing something wrong than rewards for doing something right. Such a pattern may or may not be very effective in bringing about productive behavior in either workers or students; it normally is not very satisfying or conducive to development.

While behavior that is ignored tends to disappear, behavior that is punished—either directly or by withholding anticipated rewards—is more likely to go underground, particularly if it is related to some important need. Imagine working at a routine, monotonous job and being punished for even talking to your co-workers. Does it eliminate your social needs? When the "punisher" is not present, the behavior is likely to appear and may then be rewarded by the response of others, by the satisfaction of meeting the social need, and even by the joy of "getting back at the boss."

For example, in a state prison where the prisoners make automobile license plates, it had been the usual practice for the guards to impose very tight control over the behavior of the prisoners and to punish infractions of the rules severely. Despite (or perhaps because of?) this punitive control, the prisoners managed to outwit their guards by printing letters upside down, putting foul language on plates, and even making ashtrays out of the metal.

You can see how a manager can become trapped by building a control system based on punishment instead of a reward system based on positive incentives connected to basic needs. The fact is you may be able to reduce the frequency or strength of some behavior through punitive measures, but you are not likely to eliminate the chances that it will occur again.

Often you can get people to do what you want by using the threat of punishment for not doing it. It may only work, however, as long as you have a "captive" group of employees—that is, workers whose options are limited. If the shoe is on the other foot and you are forced to compete for good workers, rewards may be the only basis by which you will be able to retain your employees, much less get high productivity from them.

In short then, the use of punishment to manage behavior *can* produce desired outcomes under certain conditions and may even be appropriate (e.g., when the behavior poses an immediate threat to the system). However, Most behavior is more effectively managed by the use of rewards and positive incentives than by the use of punishment.[8] In addition, punishment frequently results in other undesirable outcomes. Managers who have used "behavior modification," which is built on Skinnerian principles, as a way of dealing with difficult employees (see Managerial Tools, page 153) have reported mixed results. Rewards have worked well, punishments have not. The concept works best with less complex behavior and jobs.

Intrinsic or Extrinsic Rewards

Rewards that occur apart from the work process are called *extrinsic*. Pay, benefits, bonuses, special privileges, and so forth are examples of extrinsic rewards. *Intrinsic* rewards are those that are built into the work itself, including such factors as a sense of accomplishment, a chance to be creative, or the challenge of the work. Extrinsic rewards require constant attention and revision on the part of management, while intrinsic rewards are more immediate outcomes of an individual's efforts. If you are taking a course in something you enjoy, one reward lies in the learning process itself. If the course is required and irrelevant to you, the only reward may be the grade, which is clearly extrinsic.

In most cases, Intrinsic rewards are more effective and long lasting than extrinsic ones.[9] Job enrichment and enlargement seem to be methods of increasing the intrinsic rewards of work. The basic survival needs are appropriately met by extrinsic rewards, but the social and higher-level needs are best met through intrinsic rewards. Look at the difference between a situation in which social interaction is a legitimate part of the work process (as in the assembly teams at Cummins Engine) and that in which it is treated as a "fringe benefit" of getting the work done (e.g., a coffee break or company social event). The former tends to be more effective in terms of making multiple rewards intrinsic to the work; the latter forces a separation between the task rewards and the social rewards, consequently reducing the payoff directly associated with the work.

Obviously, extrinsic rewards are part of any organization's performance incentives, and under certain conditions (monotonous work, nonchanging technology and work patterns, and so forth) management needs to depend upon extrinsic factors to motivate employees. In general, when an extrinsic reward system is necessary, it is most likely to be effective under the following conditions:[10]

1. Rewards that are important in the eyes of the employees can be tied to performance.
2. Information pertaining to *how* rewards are given is open and public.
3. Management is willing to explain the system to employees.
4. There is adequate variation in the rewards to match varying needs and performance.
5. Performance can be measured.
6. Meaningful performance appraisal occurs.
7. A high level of trust exists between management and employees.

The absence of these conditions tends to breed lack of interest and suspicion about "the name of the game."

One final point needs to be made here. Since many jobs have both intrinsic and extrinsic rewards, it is important to consider what happens when you combine them. Logic tells us that it is a simple additive relationship: The more rewards present, both intrinsic and extrinsic, the stronger will be the person's work effort. However, some research findings[11] suggest that this logic is not necessarily valid. There is evidence that in some instances extrinsic and intrinsic rewards are negatively related—that is, can work against one another. More specifically, in a situation that is already intrinsically rewarding, the addition of extrinsic rewards may actually reduce the effectiveness of the intrinsic rewards. The explanation for this is in terms of the *perception* of the person receiving the rewards. We will say more in Chapter 8 about individual variations in responses to common rewards; but for now it should be noted that a person perceiving an activity as rewarding in itself might, if overpaid (in some form) for engaging in that activity, tend to devalue the intrinsic worth of the activity. A competent musician, for example, might tend to perceive less intrinsic reward in performing as the payment for performing increases. That's why "going commercial" is feared. Obviously other factors may affect the person's perception, but it is important to be aware of a not-so-simple connection between types of rewards on a job and what will be seen as rewarding.

On the other side of the argument is evidence that supports an additive relationship between intrinsic and extrinsic rewards. For example, entrepreneurs, who are high in the need for achievement, tend to find success rewarding in itself and money, while a less important reward in its own right, serving as a symbol of that success. Thus, the two kinds of rewards reinforce each other.[12] Consistent with this is support for the notion that the two kinds of rewards tend to be additive when they occur close in time and when both are clearly contingent upon performance.[13]

The Timing of Rewards

While intrinsic rewards are built into the work itself, extrinsic rewards normally occur some time after the task has been accomplished. *How much time* lapses between effort and reward and *how regular* the time intervals are can have important effects on behavior. As a student you must have experienced wide variations in the time intervals between exams and grades. Most students seem to prefer the shortest possible intervals. Can you see how your study habits may also be related to the timing of exams? As long as you know in advance when tests will occur, and assuming that a good grade is a relevant reward, you can plan to do most of your studying just prior to the exams and put in the least effort just after them. But suppose the instructor uses surprise quizzes throughout the semester and you cannot predict when you will be tested? Chances are you will maintain a moderately high level of effort all the time, in part to maximize the odds of receiving a decent grade but also to avoid the chance of being punished by failure.

Different organizations have different patterns of dispensing their rewards. While promotions, raises, bonuses, and the like tend to occur at regular long-term intervals in most places, some organizations make these more or less directly contingent upon job performance: The rewards are timed to reinforce their connection to performance. Where the connection is vague, which can occur when the rewards are poorly timed, employees can easily begin to wonder about the payoff for hard work.

Wages and salaries in most cases are governed by many more factors than just individual work output. However, where a person's income *is* a direct consequence of work produced (products sold, services provided, and so forth), then the timing of the income can have strong effects upon the work output. Regular predictable return encourages a high level of productivity; delays and uncertainties about payments can easily result in reduced performance. A salesperson working on a commission basis usually counts on receiving that commission within a short time of having earned it. Can you see how important it can be for a company that depends upon high sales (and uses a commission system for its salespeople) to minimize the lapsed time between a sale and a commission?

While there are many ways to schedule rewards both in the classroom and in a work environment and while there are considerable variations among people and circumstances, you may find the following guidelines useful:[14]

1. Predictable frequent rewards that are directly connected to work behavior tend to result in a high overall level of performance.
2. Predictable but infrequent rewards that are directly connected to work behavior tend to result in peaks and valleys of performance; the peaks occur as the reward time is approached, and the valleys occur just after the reward is received.
3. Unpredictable rewards that are directly connected to work behavior tend to result in moderately high overall levels of performance but also in some dysfunctional anxiety.

The first principle seems to be especially important when people are concerned about survival, as might be the case during economic hard times. Regular, frequent wages or salaries tend to be most functional for survival needs. A business that is struggling to meet its payroll or forced to owe its employees back pay is faced with an uncertain reward system. Depending on the loyalty of the employees, the history of the company, and the potential threats to its survival, management will need to pay special attention to alternative rewards in order to maintain productivity.

Conflicting Sources of Rewards

Think how easy it would be to manage people if all you had to worry about were simple connections between behavior and rewards. However, as you well know from all the previous chapters, not all the rewards and punishments are in the hands of the manager. Peer relationships and a variety of personal factors also come into play. For example, a worker may be rewarded by the boss for being productive and punished by co-workers for being a "rate buster." What happens then is that he or she is caught between conflicting outcomes, which definitely complicates choices. The two sources of reward seem to be mutually exclusive and contradictory. The worker's final choice will depend on the relative strengths of the rewards and punishments related to each choice and the relative strengths of the needs involved.

A manager who is aware of potential conflicts of this kind has many options for dealing with them. In most respects his or her choice must consider the given situation. However, we can say in general that It is better to add attractiveness to desired outcomes than it is to add threat to undesired alternatives.

It seldom takes more than one burn to teach a child not to touch a hot stove. Even the sight of the stove can conjure up a strong enough fear to make the child avoid a second contact. In many ways, adults behave like burned children; a bad experience with some behavior leads to avoidance of that behavior and any circumstance associated with it. Of course, one person's bad experience may be another's pleasure; some few people (called *masochists*) learn to consider particular types of pain as rewarding. Regardless of what causes discomfort, however, if there is no way to avoid an unrewarding situation, then the person is forced to live with his or her anxieties. If, for example, your past performances on exams have not been rewarding, you probably would like to avoid future ones. Just the thought of another exam can raise your anxiety to an uncomfortable level.

> The lion and the lamb shall lie down together in peace. But the lamb won't get much sleep.
>
> Woody Allen

One of the interesting aspects is the fact that: Avoidance behavior is itself rewarding; it reduces one's tensions and makes one feel better—at least for the moment. Did you ever put off studying until the last moment, preferring to take your chances with how you might feel later? What about the shy man who is afraid to ask the boss

MANAGERIAL BULLETIN

Individual and Group Rewards Can Work Together

The group approach helps avoid one problem with individual incentives: sometimes a factory slumps even as individual workers excel. "If I get paid on the number of units I produce, why the hell should I help you if it reduces my production?" says Jan Muczyk of Cleveland State University. "If we're doing it as a group, it's in my interest to help you. The sooner you come up to speed, the sooner my paycheck increases."

SOURCE: *Newsweek,* November 14, 1988, p. 46.

for a raise? He goes as far as the boss's door and then, with a sigh of relief, returns to his desk.

The price you pay for avoidance behavior is that you often lose out on something else that you want. The employee mentioned above may never get that raise until he or she has pushed open the boss's door and asked for the raise. Can you think of different people or experiences that attracted you but generated such anxiety that in the final analysis you gave in to avoidance? What price did you pay? What effect did your behavior have on your feelings about yourself?

You probably know people who tend to make others anxious. Sometimes, a manager is a source of fear for employees simply because of the power he or she possesses. If the manager's behavior tends to be punitive, then he or she is likely to generate avoidance behavior in employees. Many executives have been known to say, "My door is always open to my employees," only to wonder why few pass through that door or, worse yet, only to assume that the employees have no problems.

As a manager you will often be in a position to affect your employees' tensions and fears in conscious ways; how you choose to do so can be a very important matter. You can maintain a high level of control through the use of punitive and withholding behavior. You may get people to do what you want but at a price for you and for them. Avoidance behavior tends to develop consequences leading to a climate of mistrust and secrecy, which is not very conducive to the development of human resources.

Feelings about Outcomes

When you are rewarded for your behavior, it usually makes you feel good (except when you have done something you are ashamed of just to curry favor; then rewards may bring guilt). Generally, however, rewarded behavior itself becomes associated with good feelings. These feelings can be secondary rewards for the behavior and increase the chances of its occurrence. The more positive the feelings one associates with a given kind of behavior, the more firmly entrenched that behavior becomes.[15] If you do something that gets you respect, liking, money, and advancement (multiple payoffs), you are likely to place a high value on that behavior; it becomes associated not only with the positive outcomes but also with a range of good feelings about yourself. Your feelings about various aspects of a situation (including people, surroundings, and so forth) with rewarding outcomes tend to become associated with the rewards. You tend to view the setting as a good place to work, the boss as a nice guy, and your co-workers as good people to work with. Out of these feelings grows your judgment about the climate of the organization. Can you think of ways in which getting a good grade on a paper can generalize by association to other aspects of a course, including the instructor, the text, other students, and even the attractiveness of the classroom?

Rewards in Comparison with Others (Equity Theory)

It is also true that our feelings about a given reward are affected by what others receive. You might feel relieved to receive a B on a paper after worrying about getting a lower grade; but then, after learning that a classmate received an A on a paper you thought was no better than yours, your relief may change to resentment. We all tend to view things comparatively and make our judgments on the basis of relative fairness. It is a matter of *equity*[16]—that is, the relative worth of what we receive when compared with what others receive for the same (or similar) work.

A blatant example of a current uncorrected inequity is the difference in salary levels of women versus men in the same occupations. Feeling underpaid is not an absolute judgment; it is a *relative* matter. Even if women's salaries were raised substantially, the sense of inequity would not change until the *differential* was eliminated. You can probably think of examples when your perceptions and feelings about a given reward (pay, promotion, special benefits, and so on) were affected by what others received. Anyone's general attitude toward a place of employment (or school, for that matter) is strongly affected by perceptions about fairness.

Circumstances can also affect one's feelings about an inequity. When Chrysler Corporation was close to bankruptcy, the workers were willing to accept lower wages relative to their counterparts at GM and Ford; the company's survival and consequently the workers' very livelihoods were at stake. Then, when Chrysler began to show profits again, the workers became more and more conscious of the $2-per-hour difference between their wages and those at the other companies. Whatever the reasons—self-esteem, sense of fairness, need to be repaid for earlier sacrifices—the differential was no longer acceptable, and it became a powerful determinant of the workers' behavior and attitudes.

Complicating the issue of equity even further is the possibility of making comparisons with many different kinds of groups. Does a machinist working for a medium-size manufacturing firm in semirural Ohio compare her wages to assemblers and supervisors or secretaries and managers, to other female employees in her firm or in town, to machinists in nearby firms, to machinists in comparable firms in Cleveland and Cincinnati, or to her husband, who is a high school teacher in Akron? Many managers have run into serious difficulties because the comparisons they made about rewards to employees were different from the groups used by their employees as a reference point. And, of course, not all employees and not all employees in a given category, may agree on the standard of comparison. Although you will need to investigate carefully before you just assume to whom any individual or group compares itself, people generally compare first to those closest to home—within their own job category and with others in the firm who work nearby. You neglect easily visible comparisons at your peril.

Procedural Justice

Just as you might think, after learning about the grades of other students, that you have unjustly received a lower grade in a course than you deserved, you might also feel that the way in which the grade was determined was also unfair. You might believe that the instructor favored some students over others for the wrong reasons: they were more outspoken or they somehow managed to obtain special attention from the instructor. In other words, it was not so much the outcome (i.e., the grade itself), but more the procedure that was used to determine the grade that you judged to be unfair. Similarly, in a work setting employees need to trust that the performance appraisal system is a fair one, treats all employees equally, and is comprised of procedures that are just.

The examples above illustrate *procedural justice,* which links a worker's (or a student's) motivation to his or her *perception* of the fairness of the procedures used to

MANAGERIAL BULLETIN

Pitting Workers against Each Other Often Backfires, Firms Are Finding

To prod branch managers to perform better, a European bank encouraged them to compete against each other to produce the most improved results.

The winner was promised a bonus. But the outcome was disappointing. The bank discovered that a greedy officer had steered a customer to a rival bank, rather than help another branch manager win the bonus.

Companies often pit manager against manager in the hope that the race will bring out the best in both. When monitored properly, internal competition can boost employees' egos and help them feel they control their own destiny. "It's healthy," says organizational psychologist Raf Haddock. "There's a human drive to compete and to strive." But the competition can get out of hand when the stakes are too high or supervisors get careless.

Sales Contests

Sales contests, a widespread form of competition, have also produced some awkward situations for the companies that sponsor them. Data General Corporation, a Westboro, Massachusetts, computer maker, caught its salesman for the Texas area poaching on Oklahoma's turf. An office copier salesman for another company asked a Lawrence, Kansas, customer to sign up for a copier even though the customer wasn't going to go through with the purchase. The salesman "just wanted to win his trip to Hawaii," says the customer, who refused to help him out.

What Works

Just posting performance rankings hurt the efficiency of a Los Angeles-based workman's compensation insurance company. It ranked offices according to how frequently they distributed disability payments on time. But a former employee recalls that when one office got a claim that was meant for another, workers frequently used the mail, rather than the telephone, to reroute the information in an attempt to lower the rankings of competitors.

Some companies embarrass workers to goad them on, but humiliation can backfire. Data General used to award a statue of a horse's rear end to the region with the worst quarterly record of meeting its goals. The company thought the award worked fine. "It became a real rallying point," says William D. Jobe, a former vice president who created the award. "Nobody wanted to take that home with them." . . .

Some Drawbacks

Management consultant Reed Whittle sees significant drawbacks in automatically pushing promising employees to compete. "The idea is to put them all in a dark room with a knife, and the guy who comes out is the best guy," he says. But "while they're in there slicing each other up, the competition is out there slicing you up." . . .

To head off problems from competition, consultants recommend issuing formal performance evaluations regularly and rewarding all producing employees in some way. . . .

Long Term versus Short Term

In many cases, instinct alone will lead to competition. Some time ago, Hewlett-Packard Company told its managers to stress inventory control and posted rankings of how each division was doing. Pretty soon executives vied for the best ideas. "We used to stand around in the halls and say, 'Hey, I've got an idea,'" recalls Douglas C. Spreng, a manager whose division sliced its inventory in half.

For their efforts Mr. Spreng and several other manufacturing managers were named general managers, posts previously dominated by marketing executives. "Those promotions haven't been lost on our people," says Mr. Spreng. "The manufacturing manager who came up underneath me picked up the ball and carried it on."

evaluate that performance. To the extent that the individual perceives the procedures to be fair, his or her desire to perform will be greater than if the procedures are perceived to be unfair. Think of the times when you felt that your efforts at work or in school went unrecognized or were undervalued because the person evaluating you was biased against you, tended to favor others, or did not even have appropriate

MANAGERIAL BULLETIN

Incentives Work Best When There Is a Challenge

BankAmerica also redesigns its elaborate performance-pay system every year to take account of changing circumstances. For example, employees can earn bonus pay by issuing a certain number of mortgages. As interest rates drop and their job gets easier, the bank raises the target.

SOURCE: "Grading 'Merit Pay,'" *Newsweek*, November 14, 1988, p. 46.

information about you to make a valid judgment. Organizations are political entities where some people are "in" and some are "out." Your perception of where you stand in the scheme of things will have a powerful effect on your behavior. Furthermore, there is no way to avoid personal feelings and, consequently, personal preferences on the part of bosses or teachers. However fair one attempts to be, there is usually some element of personal bias that creeps into our perceptions and judgments of others.

As a manager it will be essential for you to be as explicit as possible in your expectations of your employees and encourage feedback from them regarding their perceptions of the fairness of your judgments and how you arrive at them. This is not an easy task; in Chapter 10 we discuss the importance of the interpersonal feedback process, and provide you with some concepts and tools for managing it.

Individual Variations

While the principles discussed so far tend to have general applicability, their relative importance may vary with people and circumstances, and there may also be exceptions to one or more of them. Some people, for example, seem to have a high tolerance for uncertainty and are not bothered by unpredictable rewards; and some people show little concern about pay differences (equity).

As a future manager, you will need to understand a variety of other people's preferences in order to make sure that your reward system leads to the highest levels of productivity, satisfaction, and development. Even such a simple matter as the timing of rewards can make a critical difference in your success.

The Importance of Individual Expectancies

You can see that managing rewards in an organization is no easy task. It may be that in general some people respond mostly to intrinsic rewards (perhaps people with higher-level needs) and some more to extrinsic rewards. But in the final analysis, it is very likely that the individual's own assessment of a situation and expectancies about his or her behavior in relation to valued rewards will be the most relevant way to understand behavior.[17]

How much effort would you put forth in order to obtain a given reward? Obviously, your answer to that would depend on how *attractive* the reward is to you and the extent to which you really *expected* to receive that reward for a given effort. How often have you heard students say things like, "Getting an A is not that important to me; it just isn't worth the effort in that course," or "You can break your back for an A in this course, but the chances are you won't get it anyway"?

It is just these kinds of individual *expectancies* that make it difficult for a manager to predict how strongly motivated a worker will be, even with an excellent reward system. In the final analysis, you cannot really understand the effects of the rewards and punishments you dispense unless you understand how these are *perceived* by their recipients. After downing an enormous meal, one witty Irishman proclaimed, "Thanks be for that little snack; some folks might have called it a meal!" To understand which is which and for whom, you will need to look within individuals, into each personal system.

KEY CONCEPTS FROM CHAPTER 7

1. Group processes and individual dilemmas:
   a. Accepting the group's way of doing things.
   b. Trying to change it.
   c. Refusing to go along with particular behavior.
2. a. Basic needs (survival, social, higher-level needs) modified by . . .
   b. Personal system result in . . .
   c. Overt behavior.
3. The hierarchy of needs is individual; however, there are tendencies which exist universally.
4. The closer the fit between member needs and organization rewards, the higher the productivity.
5. The higher the level of needs, the more varied can be the rewards to achieve productivity, satisfaction, and development.
6. Behavior is governed by outcomes.
   a. Rewards better than punishments.
   b. Intrinsic rewards more effective than extrinsic.
   c. Importance of the timing of rewards.
   d. Conflict is produced by behavior that results in both reward and punishment. This sometimes leads to avoidance behavior.
   e. Feelings and perceptions associated with outcomes.
   f. Avoidance of outcomes is important determinant of behavior.
   g. Comparison to rewards received by others (equity theory).
   h. Procedures for making judgments (procedural justice).
7. Individual variations and the importance of expectancies.

PERSONAL APPLICATION EXERCISE

How Do You Decide Which Needs to Satisfy?

List five or six of your most important needs (i.e., those things that motivate most of your behavior). The list might include such things as having fun, learning new skills, getting friends to appreciate you, solving a challenging problem, and the like. Then rank the list from the most to the least important. You may have to force yourself to make some difficult choices, but try to do it anyway.

Now reflect on a typical day and how you spend your time. List all the activities you engage in and how much time you spend in each. At best you may only be able to estimate the times or just categorize the activities in such general ways as "a great deal of time," "some time," and "very little time."

Finally, match the two lists in such a way as to reflect the extent to which you are spending the most time on the most important needs, and vice versa. If the match is not a very good one—that is, you find that you are spending a lot of time on less important needs and little time related to more important needs—then it may indicate that you should try to figure out why that is and whether or not you can make better choices on how you spend your time and, consequently, how you might meet your needs more effectively. You might also want to reexamine your list of needs; perhaps you have not accurately reflected your actual priorities.

This little exercise can have important implications for your future role as a manager. Many, if not most, managers have a difficult time managing their time in such a way that they feel satisfied and fulfilled in their jobs. Many important needs go frustrated because of the time that gets eaten up on less satisfying activities. Granted that managers often have less than complete control over how they spend their time, but most have much more control than they exercise, partly because they do not take the time to engage in the kind of "exercise" suggested above.[18]

SUGGESTED READINGS

Alderfer, C. *Existence, Relatedness and Growth.* New York: Free Press, 1972.

Ball, Gail; Linda K. Trevino; and H. P. Sims, Jr. "Just and Unjust Punishment: Influences on Subordinate Performance and Citizenship." *Academy of Management Journal* 37 (1994), pp. 299–322.

Blau, G. J., and K. B. Boal. "Conceptualizing How Job Involvement and Organizational Commitment Affect Turnover and Absenteeism." *Academy of Management Review* 12 (1987), pp. 288–300.

Broedling, L. "The Uses of the Intrinsic-Extrinsic Distinction in Explaining Motivation and Organizational Behavior." *Academy of Management Review,* April 1977, pp. 267–76.

Bullock, R. J., and E. E. Lawler. "Gainsharing: A Few Questions and Fewer Answers." *Human Resource Management* 23 (1984), pp. 23–40.

Cummings, L. L. "Compensation, Culture, and Motivation: A Systems Perspective." *Organizational Dynamics* 12 (1984), pp. 33–44.

Eden, D. "Self-Fulfilling Prophecy as a Management Tool: Harnessing Pygmalion." *Academy of Management Review,* January 1984, pp. 64–73.

Festinger, L. *A Theory of Cognitive Dissonance.* Stanford, CA: Stanford University Press, 1957.

Guest, R. H. "Quality of Worklife—Learning from Tarrytown." *Harvard Business Review,* July–August 1979, pp. 76–87.

Hackman, J. R.; E. E. Lawlor III; and L. W. Porter. *Perspectives on Behavior in Organizations.* New York: McGraw-Hill, 1977. In particular, see the following therein:

Dowling, W. F. "Job Redesign on the Assembly Lines: Farewell to Blue-Collar Blues?" pp. 227–42.

Hackman, J. R. "Designing Work for Individuals and for Groups," pp. 242–56.

Hamner, W. C. "How to Ruin Motivation with Pay," pp. 287–97.

Nadler, D. A., and E. L. Lawler. "Motivation: A Diagnostic Approach," pp. 26–38.

Wanous, J. P. "Who Wants Job Enrichment?" pp. 257–63.

Herzberg, F. *Work and the Nature of Man.* Cleveland, OH: World Publishing, 1966.

———. "One More Time: How Do You Motivate Employees?" *Harvard Business Review* 46 (1968), pp. 53–62.

Herzberg, F.; B. Mausner; and B. Snyderman. *The Motivation to Work.* New York: John Wiley & Sons, 1959.

Kerr, S. "Organizational Rewards: Practical, Cost-Neutral Alternatives That You May Know, but Don't Practice." *Organizational Dynamics,* Summer 1999, pp. 61–70.

Kiggundu, M. N. "Task Interdependence and the Theory of Job Design." *Academy of Management Review,* July 1981, pp. 499–508.

Locke, E. A.; G. P. Latham; and M. Erez. "The Determinants of Goal Commitment." *Academy of Management Review* 13, no. 1 (1988), pp. 23–39.

Londom, M., and G. R. Oldham. "A Comparison of Group and Individual Incentive Plans." *Academy of Management Journal,* March 1977, pp. 34–41.

Luthans, F.; H. S. McCaul; and N. G. Dodd. "Organizational Commitment: A Comparison of American, Japanese, and Korean Employees." *Academy of Management Journal* 28 (1985), pp. 213–19.

Machungwa, P. D., and N. Schmitt. "Work Motivation in a Developing Country." *Journal of Applied Psychology* 68 (1983), pp. 31–42.

Major, B., and E. Konar. "An Investigation of Sex Differences in Pay Expectations and Their Possible Causes." *Academy of Management Journal* 27 (1984), pp. 777–92.

Maslow, A. *Motivation and Personality.* 2nd ed. New York: Harper & Row, 1970.

McClelland, D. C. *Power: The Inner Experience.* New York: Irvington Publishers, 1975.

Mitchell, T. R. "Motivation: New Directions for Theory, Research, and Practice." *Academy of Management Review,* January 1982, pp. 80–88.

Morris, J. H., and R. M. Steers. "Structural Influences on Organizational Commitment." *Journal of Vocational Behavior* 17 (1980), pp. 50–57.

Nadler, D. A., and E. E. Lawler III. "Quality of Work Life: Perspectives and Directions." *Organizational Dynamics,* Winter 1983, pp. 20–30.

Pate, L. E. "Cognitive versus Reinforcement Views of Intrinsic Motivation." *Academy of Management Review,* July 1978, pp. 505–14.

Randall, D. M. "Commitment and the Organization: The Organization Man Revisited." *Academy of Management Review* 12 (1987), pp. 460–71.

Roberts, K. H., and W. Glick. "The Job Characteristics Approach to Task Design: A Critical Review." *Journal of Applied Psychology* 66 (1981), pp. 193–217.

Roethlisberger, F. J., and W. Dickson. *Management of the Worker,* science ed. New York: John Wiley & Sons, 1964.

Scholl, R. W. "Differentiating Organizational Commitment from Expectancy as a Motivating Force." *Academy of Management Review* 6 (1981), pp. 589–99.

Shipper, F., and C. C. Manz. "Employee Self-Management without Formally Designated Teams: An Alternative Road to Empowerment." *Organizational Dynamics,* Winter 1992, pp. 48–62.

Steers, R. M., and R. T. Mowday. "The Motivational Properties of Tasks." *Academy of Management Review,* October 1977, pp. 645–58.

Stonich, P. J. "The Performance Measurement and Reward System: Critical to Strategic Management." *Organizational Dynamics,* Winter 1984, pp. 45–57.

Thomas, K. W., and Betty H. Velthouse. "Cognitive Elements of Empowerment: An 'Interpretive' Model of Intrinsic Task Motivation." *Academy of Management Review,* October 1990, pp. 666–81.

Tosi, H., and L. Tosi. "What Managers Need to Know about Knowledge-Based Pay." *Organizational Dynamics,* Winter 1986, pp. 52–64.

Vroom, V. *Work and Motivation.* New York: John Wiley & Sons, 1964.

Weckler, D. A., and A. T. Lawrence. "Creating High-Commitment Organizations through Recruitment and Selection." *The Human Resources Professional,* Spring 1991, pp. 37–43.

Weisbord, M. R. *Productive Workplaces.* San Francisco: Jossey-Bass Publishers, 1987.

White, R. W. "Motivation Reconsidered: The Concept of Competence." *Psychological Review* 66 (1959), pp. 297–333.

Wofford, J. C. "A Goal-Energy-Effort Requirement Model of Work Behavior." *Academy of Management Review* 4 (1979), pp. 193–201.

The Personal System

Know Thyself—and Work Downhill

A few common personality traits usually determine how a person performs . . .

Am I a reader or a listener? . . .

How do I learn? . . . Some people learn by doing. Others learn by hearing themselves talk. . . .

Do I work well with people or am I a loner? . . .

Do I produce results as a decision maker or as an adviser? . . .

Do I perform well under stress or do I need a highly structured and predictable environment? Do I work best in a big organization or a small one?

. . . do not try to change yourself—you are unlikely to succeed. But work hard to improve the way you perform.

SOURCE: Peter F. Drucker, "Managing Oneself," *Harvard Business Review,* March–April 1999, pp. 65–74.

"A person does not always see his or her own competencies as others do."

If, as a potential manager, you wish to understand the behavior of another individual, you will have to go beyond concepts that simply apply to "most people" and to needs in general. It is necessary to develop some insights into the unique ways in which each person operates from his or her own frame of reference. To understand someone whose behavior is puzzling, surprising, or contrary to your expectations requires a way of getting inside that person, seeing the world as he or she does. From within, an individual's behavior makes sense, is understandable and reasonable, even when not clear from outside.[1] We discuss the various components of a personal system that seem to be most useful in understanding a person's behavior.

Many psychologists—following Skinner—argue that we should stick to observables and leave alone the "black box"—that is, what goes on inside the person. To them, inference is, at best, crude speculation far removed from real measurable data. They claim that it does the human being an injustice to fill up the black box with vague concepts, insisting that it is enough to study overt behavior and to make our predictions from that.

There is validity to the position of such behaviorists, and managers cannot afford to overlook it. The best predictor of future behavior *is* previous behavior. When you hire somebody for a job, the key questions you ask pertain to *prior performance.* When you decide to promote someone, you are usually making a prediction that his or her future behavior is likely to be consistent with past behavior. It is possible for managers to hire, fire, promote, and make job changes quite effectively using only performance data (observable behavior) as their criteria. Whether or not they ever *understand* the behavior—that, is, can explain *why* it occurs—is another matter entirely, one that requires developing some ways of explaining what goes on inside that so-called black box.

We do not expect to turn you into a psychologist, nor do we think that a manager must be an expert on all the intricacies of human behavior. Individuals are so complex anyway, perhaps even more than the social systems they create, that even experts seldom lay claim to all "the answers." What we do hope to provide for you is a way to appreciate some of the inner workings of a person (including yourself) and some tools for organizing your picture of an individual so that you can understand and explain and more effectively predict behavior, not just classify it. While it is not easy to make useful inferences about things that cannot be directly observed, people tend to do it anyway. They interpret the motives of, or label, people in categories based on quick observations; motives are *attributed* to others based on their behavior. Using some of the following concepts, you will improve your ability to make such judgments or, perhaps more important, slow down the process of coming to conclusions that tend to filter future inputs and lock in false definitions.

It is not easy to see how the world looks to someone else; few of us have been very well trained in such empathic skills. Fortunately, there are some ways of getting clues about how people see themselves and how that affects their behavior.

In the pages that follow, we take a careful look at the personal system as an important modifier of human needs. We begin by providing an overall scheme, showing where the personal system fits into the total sequence of events that determine the behavior of an individual. We already have covered the topic of basic human needs and have pointed out that the connection between needs and actions is a very complicated one, involving all the variations of individual personality. Without going into detail just yet, we can say that the general sequence is that shown in Figure 8–1. While the personal system is only one factor in this sequence, it is the most complex one and carries the key to understanding individual behavior. It is that critical link to understanding a person's expectancies regarding his or her actions in a given situation; the expectancies are then the immediate preludes to actions.

FIGURE 8–1 *The Connection between Needs and Actions*

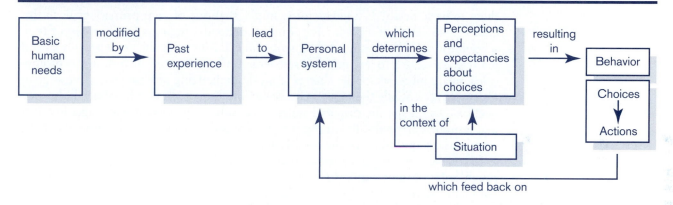

Structure of the Personal System

The personal system is structured around four basic subsystems plus a derived subsystem that exerts a unifying force on the others. The basic subsystems are

Personal goals.
Competencies.
Beliefs.
Values.

The unifying force is the *self-concept.*

It is important to keep in mind that we are still thinking in systems terms—that is, we recognize that the various aspects of an individual are all interrelated. Growth and change in any one component of the personal system always affect the others. Let's examine each of these components (see Figure 8–2).

Personal Goals

Goals are those objects or events in the future that we strive for in order to meet our basic needs. A given goal (e.g., a high income) may be related to several needs (such as security, prestige, and achievement). Also, several goals (e.g., success as a manager, generating new ideas, and studying art) may all be related to one basic need (perhaps to actualize creative potential). Can you identify some of your goals as a student and relate

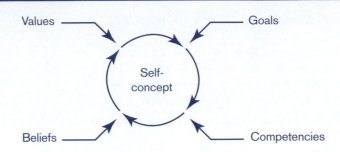

FIGURE 8–2   *The Personal System*

them to basic needs? Is it likely, for example, that one of your primary goals in this course is to get a good grade? For some students the high grade means security in school, for others it means achievement, and still others see the grade as only one of many goals related to learning and self-actualization. At work such things as promotions, salary increases, or the change to tackle challenging new projects serve as goals for employees. While these goals clearly tap into one or another basic need, the connections vary from one personal system to another. The task of a manager involves maintaining compatibility among the goals of individuals, those of subparts of the organization, and those of the total system.

If you were to list your various goals, you could probably arrange them in some rough order of importance. Like the hierarchy of universal needs, a person tends to have a hierarchy of personal goals. Having a hierarchy helps one to set priorities and to resolve internal conflicts between goals. An example of an internal conflict might be the person whose goals include both rapid advancements in a career and also having a close family. Both require high levels of commitment but frequently pull a person in opposite directions. Currently, women are increasingly faced with this particular dilemma; and, for some, priorities are changing dramatically. Many men experience the same pulls.

If you knew only a person's goals, you could probably explain significant aspects of that person's behavior. From the outside, it's often fairly easy to infer a person's goal(s) by observing the person's behavior (although it's not a bad idea to ask!). As a manager you will almost always be concerned about the individual goals of those you work with, in particular as they pertain to your own goals and to those of the larger system.

One of the paradoxes of life is that people sometimes don't know what their goals are until they've reached them. Have you ever had the experience of realizing how much you wanted something only *after* you got it—or failed to get it? One's concept of oneself often makes it difficult to recognize certain aspects of one's own personal system. Later in this chapter, we examine just how the self-concept can both include and block out parts of a person's total personal system.

Competencies

Competencies are the areas of knowledge, ability, and skill that increase an individual's effectiveness in dealing with the world. People are not born with competencies; they must *learn* them, although each person has varied natural capacities in different areas. Since the learning process is time and energy consuming, people tend to have a great investment in their competencies. While one may at times be willing and able to modify one's goals in a given situation, it is more difficult to alter competencies; new learning and change take time. Each person tends to be good at particular activities and strives constantly to reinforce these by engaging in behaviors that uti-

Self-Efficacy and Performance

Do you have confidence in your ability to perform a task? It depends on the nature of the task, your previous experience of success or failure with it, your mood at the time, and other situational factors that you cannot predict. To the extent that you believe that you can perform a task well, it may be said that you have a high level of *self-efficacy* with respect to that task. Clearly this is an essential aspect of your self-concept; it is a way of defining your sense of competency with respect to both work and school.

From a manager's standpoint, a high level of self-efficacy on the part of employees can make a significant difference in the overall performance of the enterprise. Ways to build and enhance employee self-efficacy include

1. Making sure that the individual's personal system, especially competencies, is a good match to the required system and to the organization's culture, with special attention to the norms of the group to which the individual is assigned.
2. Providing opportunities for self-development and for increasing autonomy in managing their own work.
3. Providing a support system through your own coaching efforts, as well as through team memberships, where others can recognize and appreciate an employee's worth.
4. Creating opportunities for employees to experience success in a task early on, keeping in mind that success usually breeds further success.

SOURCE: For more information on this topic see R. Wood and A. Bandura. "Social Cognitive Theory of Organizational Management," *Academy of Management Review,* July 1989, pp. 361–84.

lize them. When circumstances either block one from doing what one is good at or require one to do things one is not well qualified to do, then a person experiences some degree of threat.

A person does not always see his or her own competencies as others do. Managers often "surprise" their employees by telling them what a fine or poor job they are doing. Recent research even suggests that the least competent people have the most over-inflated views of themselves.[2] While it is possible to predict performance from an external assessment of a person's competence, to *understand* behavior usually requires knowing that person's *own* view of the competencies.

It is not uncommon for individuals to underestimate their own competencies and to withhold potentially valuable contributions to a team effort for fear of looking foolish. Others, not knowing what is going on inside the noncontributor, may tend to label him or her a "goof-off" and useless to the team. Such an attribution, while understandable, is not an accurate reflection of what is really going on. This is why knowledge of someone's "self-concept," which is discussed later in this chapter, is vital to understanding that person's behavior.

In general, we can say that competencies form an important part of the personal system. To the extent that an individual can find ways to translate competencies into effective behavior, the individual experiences reinforcement of them. The wider the range of one's competencies, the more likely one is to find avenues for their fulfillment. The narrower the range, the more limited one feels in coping with the world, and the more limited one is in the possible range of goals one can attain in life.

Beliefs

Beliefs are ideas people have about the world and how it operates. Everyone has beliefs about people, human nature, what life is all about, what the business world is like, what professors are like, and so on. A person brings beliefs into every situation and seeks to

MANAGERIAL BULLETIN

Can Charm School Help?

[The head of Defense Advanced Research Projects Agency (DARPA)] gave one of his managers an ultimatum: Go to "charm school" and learn to deal less brusquely with people, or look for another job. Craig I. Fields took the advice and spent weeks acquiring more social polish. It made a difference, Fields's friends say—but evidently not enough. . . .

"Raw Deal"

Part of the problem is that old bugaboo, people skills. [A] former MCC program director says he resigned 10 months after Fields arrived because he "had zero touch for people or how to motivate them." Combine that with a 22% cut in staff . . . and "morale is subterranean," says one former manager who was asked to leave.

SOURCE: Otis Port and Peter Burrows, "R & D with a Reality Check," *Business Week,* January 24, 1994.

confirm those that fit the situation. Sometimes events do not support one's beliefs, and one is surprised (pleasantly at times, unhappily at others). If the disconfirmation is very strong, one becomes defensive, disparaging, resistant, and so forth. People like to have events support their beliefs; it makes them feel "right" and helps them to maintain a stable "fix" on the world. Can you think of some beliefs that you brought into this course? Did you believe, for example, that organizational behavior is all common sense? Was that confirmed or disconfirmed? Did you have some preconceived ideas about how groups function? What happened to these ideas?

One of the dilemmas posed by a person's beliefs is the fact that they often become *self-fulfilling prophecies*: Somehow people have a way of making things happen (even bad things) that they believe "always happen." Have you ever failed in a task mainly because you expected to fail? When you're sure you can't do something, you normally lose the very drive it takes to succeed in a difficult task. Of course, there is the satisfaction of knowing that you were right in the first place, which is a small but concrete consolation.

Managers can trap themselves into a set of beliefs that are dysfunctional but self-confirming. Some years ago Douglas McGregor (whom you already know from Chapter 6) described two distinctly different sets of managerial beliefs. One set[3] which he labeled "Theory X," includes such assumptions as

1. The average human being has an inherent dislike of work and will avoid it if he can.
2. Most people need to be coerced, controlled, directed, threatened with punishment to get them to put forth adequate effort toward the achievement of organizational objectives.
3. The average human being prefers to be directed, wishes to avoid responsibility, has relatively little ambition, wants security above all.

Think about how a manager with such beliefs might react if he or she noticed two employees lingering past the normal lunch hour. Would the manager bother to find out if they were discussing something work related? Many managers would be prone to assume otherwise and would reprimand the employees, who in turn just might "prove" the manager to be correct by reacting negatively and by figuring that they

End of the Road: Firing of Executive Gives Rare Glimpse of Intrigue inside GE

[Industrial psychologist] Mr. Smart met with [eventually fired vice president] Mr. Russell in Chicago and later wrote a memo for him listing his strengths: "Far above average intelligence . . . very hard worker . . . professional appearance . . . can be very warm, supportive and caring." But Mr. Smart . . . was told by midlevel managers at Superabrasives that Mr. Russell was "insecure, paranoid, indecisive . . . utterly lacking in strategic vision or leadership capability." Employees . . . also expressed deep concern about Mr. Russell's sometimes violent temper, viewing him as a "loaded cannon." . . .

SOURCE: William M. Carley and Amal Kumar Naj. *The Wall Street Journal,* November 23, 1993.

might just as well be what the boss thinks they are anyway. The other set of assumptions[4] which McGregor labeled "Theory Y," includes the following:

1. The expenditure of physical and mental effort in work is as natural as play or rest.
2. People will exercise self-direction and self-control in the service of objectives to which they are committed.
3. Commitment to objectives is a function of the rewards associated with their achievement.
4. The average human being learns under proper conditions not only to accept but to seek responsibility.

Managers very often confirm their assumptions by treating people in ways that bring out the very behavior they expect, thus confirming what they believed in the first place. Have you ever had your parents treat you "like a child" and then find yourself behaving like a child? What about the teacher who believes that students will cheat if they are not watched carefully? That often leads to extensive controls, which students resent. Thus, the minute the teacher stops "watchdogging," cheating will occur. On the other hand, the manager who is willing to delegate more responsibility often discovers, lo and behold, that people are capable of taking it. Obviously this is not always the case; there will always be people (workers, students, and others) who do seem to operate best under Theory X assumptions and others who do best in a Theory Y setting. *No one set of beliefs is valid for all situations.* Competent, flexible managers are open to all possibilities, all kinds of people, and all kinds of situations. Their beliefs remain tentative, always subject to testing and revision.

One way of looking at the concept of "theory" is to view it as a set of beliefs, but ones that have been developed from systematic observation and research. Just as any beliefs tend to guide a person's behavior, managers use theory to guide their behavior in relation to members of an organization. And just as the validity of many beliefs depends upon the circumstances, the theories of a manager are most useful when they are open to the *contingencies* of the situation.

In the next section, we discuss the core of people's beliefs, namely values.

Values

Values tend to form the foundation of a person's character. While some of one's values may change over the course of a lifetime, they do tend to remain fairly deeply entrenched in one's personality. A person develops a sense of right or wrong, good or bad, beginning quite early in life. Many of our ideas change through the teenage years, but as mature adults, we tend to hold on to and defend some basic core within us, which tells us *what is really important in life and basic to one as an individual*. Examples of values would be such ideas as the following:

   a. Always being honest with others.
   b. Always standing on your own two feet and not burdening others with your problems.
   c. Never deliberately hurting another's feelings.
   d. Never letting anyone feel you have not lived up to your responsibilities.
   e. Always doing your best at any activity you try.

These are the kinds of attitudes that a person normally refuses to violate; they determine people's integrity as individuals. Following one's values enhances the basic sense of personal worth; failing to follow them causes guilt, shame, and self-doubt.

Values also tend to exist in a hierarchy of importance. Some are likely to be more central than others. When people experience value conflict, this hierarchical arrangement often helps them to make a decision. To illustrate, an accountant needs help solving an audit; she believes in standing on her own two feet, so she does not want to seek help. But she also believes that it is even *more* important to be fair to clients, so she goes beyond her independence values and consults with an expert colleague.

Internal value conflicts are often very hard to resolve. For example, imagine yourself in a position where you must fire an employee for being absent too much due to alcoholism. One of your values is to always be honest and another is to always be kind. How would you balance these values against one another? Can you find a way to honor them both? For some people, being honest with the person might be felt as an unkind act or being kind to the person as a dishonest act. Perhaps you can think of examples in your own life where you found yourself in a values conflict. In situations like that, the way one sees oneself not only guides behavior but is also *forged*, making future choices more consistent with one's most deeply held values.

It is not unusual to find yourself in circumstances where your values conflict with your needs or goals. Suppose, for example, in order to be successful, advance, and be recognized by your superiors in an organization, you had to engage in behavior that you considered unacceptable (e.g., political backbiting, concealing information about a defective product, using the rumor mill to make a rival look bad). Your goal of advancement—perhaps even your need to survive in an uncertain job market—could push you to behave in ways that conflict with your values, at least your *intended* values. What you end up doing might then reflect your *adopted* values. Can you think of current or recent situations in your life that illustrate this dilemma? You might explore the issue of student cheating in these terms, looking at the pressures to survive, compete, be honest, get high grades, all as potential sources of conflicts between students' goals and values.

In short, we can say that the area of personal values serves as the principal governing body of the personal system. The individual is enhanced by behavior that reinforces values, less affected by behavior that is not value laden, and violated by behavior that is not consistent with deeply held values. The value component of the personal system can limit the range of goals, competencies, and beliefs allowable, and it tends to evoke the strongest defensive behavior when under threat or challenge.[5]

Rationalizing: An Easy Escape

By and large, most people try to act in ways that move them toward their goals and also conform to their personal values and sense of right and wrong. Thus, most individuals will work hard to gain a desired promotion yet not engage in deceit and underhanded actions to gain that goal. Nonetheless, humans are all too skilled at justifying their behavior even when, from an outside perspective, it looks like a clear violation of their values. We say, "How on earth could you have done such a thing?"

MANAGERIAL BULLETIN

When the Signal Is "Move It or Lose It"

The economy is rotten. Revenues are down, layoffs are up. Costs and corners are being cut as performance demands accelerate. People are coping with all this new stress on the job by doing things they normally wouldn't do. . . .

Saying that a command is unrealistic or impossible is likely to trigger a retort like: "You're paid to get it done, so do it," or "If you can't do it, we'll find somebody who can." Indeed, a decision to stand one's ground may be tantamount to putting one's job on the line. It should be no surprise that unethical behavior creeps in. Most cases of unethical management practice I have seen occur when basically decent people get caught in the move-it grind.

SOURCE: Barbara Ley Toffler, *New York Times,* November 17, 1991. Copyright © by The New York Times Company. Reprinted by permission.

and they say, "I had no choice," or "It wasn't my responsibility; I was just following orders," and so forth. Most reasons that people invent to justify their behavior sound reasonable and help reduce some of the "dissonance" they feel. (See Chapter 7 reference to Festinger in the box on motivation.) But the rationalization process only serves as a defense against the potential pain from violating one's own values. Remember the *Challenger* explosion and the comments made by NASA officials mentioned in Chapter 1?

The Nuremberg trials confronted many people with gross violations of human values and established, at least implicitly, a precedent for holding individuals responsible for their own choices. However, living by one's principles can sometimes be very difficult. The B. F. Goodrich experience is an excellent example of how an essentially honest person, when faced with a threat to basic security (e.g., keeping a job and providing for family), may end up violating a fundamental value (in this case, honesty).[6] An engineer in the company was ordered to report inaccurate information on tests of brake linings for an air force plane. He did so and then justified his action as a way of protecting the financial security of his family. Is this an acceptable course of action or not? Do understanding and compassion justify the violation of "what is right"? Would that such choices were simple and clear!

In our discussion of leadership in a later chapter, we return to this issue in the context of ethics in business decisions. In the meantime, it is important for you to be conscious of the values and ethics that affect your personal choices; these establish the foundation for the kinds of decisions you may make in the future as a manager or leader.

The Self-Concept

The general consistency of the personal system is organized by the individual's *self-concept—the way the person sees himself or herself.* The self-concept reflects the person's own unique way of organizing goals, competencies, beliefs, and values. Competencies are normally developed in order to meet goals, which in turn must fit with beliefs and values. For example, a man who decides to become an accountant is likely to be someone who sees himself as methodical, believes in the fallibility of people, and is dedicated to the values of being orderly and cautious. His manner of behavior is likely to be quiet and sober, his dress fairly inconspicuous, and his car somewhat conservative. In short, A person's self-concept generally has enough internal consistency so that it is possible to infer various aspects of the person from other known aspects.

MANAGERIAL BULLETIN

Businesses Crack Down On Workers Who Cheat to Help the Company

Alan J. Russ considers what he did cheating for his boss.

As manager of a division accounting department at TRW, Inc., the 45-year-old Mr. Russ would inflate the number of hours spent making fan blades for military planes, thus raising the price of the blades. Mr. Russ maintains that such "ballooning" was condoned by his immediate supervisor. "It wasn't cloak-and-dagger," he says. "It was standard operating procedure."

So it came as a jolt to the 18-year TRW veteran when, 18 months ago, he was ushered into an office at quitting time and fired for what he had been doing. The Cleveland-based electronics and automotive parts company subsequently dismissed or disciplined 29 other employees for "irregularities and unethical behavior." TRW denies that cheating was an accepted part of anyone's job.

In many ways, Mr. Russ's experience reflects the increasing attention being focused on workers cheating for their companies. While it's unclear whether such cheating is actually on the rise, it has become more visible as both the government and businesses crack down on practices like ballooning, particularly among defense contractors. Those found cheating—even at their boss's request—are now more likely to be fired than merely reprimanded. Some of them, like Mr. Russ, are in turn taking their bosses to court.

SOURCE: Gregory Stricharchuk. Reprinted by permission of *The Wall Street Journal*, © June 13, 1986. Dow Jones & Company, Inc. All Rights Reserved Worldwide.

People strive to maintain their concepts of themselves by engaging in behavior that is consistent with their goals, competencies, beliefs, and values as they see them,[7] even to the point of pain or failure to achieve stated goals. Insofar as people succeed in confirming their self-concepts, they experience a basic sense of adequacy and worth. Sometimes people become so highly invested in protecting their self-concepts that they begin to have difficulty in seeing themselves as others do. This can lead to defensive behavior and to interpersonal conflicts, issues that we go into later in this chapter and again in Chapters 9 and 10.

People also strive to enhance their self-concepts by learning and by developing themselves toward some "ideal self."[8] This tendency can often pose a dilemma for the individual. To enhance one's self-concept may mean change in some aspects of it; to change one's self-concept runs counter to the tendency to maintain and/or protect it. It is a struggle between the security of knowing what one is and the risk in becoming something more. However, while a person may often feel comfortable with the idea of simply "being what he or she is," most people do strive to live up to their ideal selves as much as possible. To the extent that the ideal self is not too discrepant from the perceived self, it serves as an incentive to learn and grow. When the discrepancy is too great, the person is likely to suffer from a lack of self-acceptance, which in turn leads to self-doubt and then to behavior that, sadly enough, tends to confirm the low self-concept.

In general, Behavior that appears illogical or self-defeating from an outside perspective usually makes sense when viewed from inside; people generally make choices that are consistent with their self-concepts.[9]

Self-Concept and Perception

One of the major issues in understanding others lies in the nature of all human perception. Organizational reality—what others and the organization expect, reward, or demand—can only be known by an individual through his or her *own* perceptions.

Who Am I Really?

Compulsive

Disorder disturbs me, no question.

I don't like unwashed dishes in the sink

And am ashamed of such silliness.

I arrive earlier and earlier for planes

And don't admit it to all of my colleagues

Because it looks a bit wimpy.

I seek and respect flexibility in others, but I know in my heart

That my own flexibility is slipping away, and I fight to keep it.

Naive

Naive has served me well.

I really believe that one comes out ahead by trusting people.

They sometimes let one down but not often.

Failure to trust people spreads waves of caution and fear, and I find that is bad.

Sometimes I get fooled, and sometimes I feel like a fool,

But, overall, being naive has served me well.

It may bring me down one day.

Sense of Humor

Somehow, a sense of humor has always been central to me.

It has served me well.

To divert conflict, ease situations, and make life better.

Sometimes whimsy gets the better of me,

But irony, word play, and punning all come naturally

And have made up a lot of my life.

Integrity

It sounds corny, but to me it is central.

It is what we come into the world with, and that's about all.

I really believe it cannot be fully replaced if compromised.

To me, integrity and honesty are core issues.

I hate it when businessmen are nailed for being corrupt,

And I do not think it is necessary.

Maybe this is pompous, and

Maybe I have not been "put to the test,"

But I like to believe that I will go out as I came in—

With my integrity intact.

To Summarize

For me, life seems to consist of finding out what one will not be (not a great athlete, an opera singer, or a scientist)

And what one might be (a successful businessman, a father, and a husband).

One can keep learning (and that is fun and rewarding),

Continue to broaden one's horizons (and that is good),

Create one's own future (and that is a privilege).

One can be a decent human being.

And that's what it's all about.

SOURCE: Robert Saldich [now retired president] of Raychem Corporation in Menlo Park, CA. Written for the 25th reunion yearbook of his MBA class at Harvard Business School.

Although it makes many people uncomfortable to acknowledge this, what a person sees and hears tends to be selective and to involve a degree of distortion shaped by the person's self-concept; *one perceives what one needs or expects to perceive.* For example, a good accountant can glance at a page full of figures and almost see mistakes "jump out." The correct numbers are barely seen; those that don't fit are noticed. An organization having difficulty will be seen differently by the production, marketing, and research managers; each is likely to perceive the area he or she is most familiar with as needing the most resources but doing the best job.

This selective process can be functional; it saves time, allows people to concentrate on what's really important, and can help them perceive the meaning in incomplete messages, words, and so forth. On the other hand, distortion and selection can be dysfunctional; expecting the boss to be aloof and distant, for example, can make his nervousness or shyness seem cold and "confirm" what is expected. When natural perceptual processes keep people from seeing what would be useful to see, they can create real difficulties.

In addition, because any mental concept is an abstraction and therefore a simplification of reality, distortion is an inevitable part of committing experience to memory. Human beings fit experience into preexisting conceptions, discarding details and lumping things together. This can be functional (just as is selective perception); it allows the creation of a degree of order from chaos. By equating new experiences with old ones, previous experiences can be utilized. But this efficient sorting method also has potential dangers: The new can be overly distorted to fit preexisting concepts, ignoring important details, failing to discriminate differences, and resulting in stereotyping, rather than accuracy.

In short, a person's self-concept—the way in which his or her goals, beliefs, competencies, and values come together—alters how everything is seen. What one person would perceive as a rotten break, another sees as a golden opportunity. Comments that one person sees as unbearable pressure from others to conform to the group's norms about preparing well for meetings, another dismisses as just joking around. What one student sees as a smile on the professor's face, another sees as a smirk.

The extent to which people perceive events as threatening will depend on their past history with similar events. Because each of our histories has been uniquely different, it becomes difficult to anticipate just how someone else will react to a situation. In general, The more emotionally loaded an event is (for whatever reasons) for an individual, the greater will be the tendency for perceptual distortion to occur.

Fortunately, much of what occurs on a day-to-day basis in most organizations can be viewed by many without strong feelings and therefore with relatively low distortion or disagreement. But most of the important challenges for managers involve emotionally loaded situations—such as confronting resistant subordinates or peers, trying to please or move the boss, or struggling to pull a meeting together to reach a decision to which all will commit—and arouse just the kinds of reactions that strongly affect perceptions.

Attribution Theory

While we have emphasized the fact that all behavior is a product of the individual and the situation and that it is important to understand someone's behavior from that person's own vantage point, it is difficult to assess the extent to which a given action is being pulled by the situation or determined by the person's own tendencies. Human beings are meaning-makers; we attribute *causes* to events, especially to people's behavior. We cast blame, find fault, or construct seemingly reasonable explanations for what we observe in others and in ourselves. Unfortunately, we tend to take credit for good intentions and blame the intentions of others for bad outcomes, even when the behavior we see may be caused by events that are not visible rather than evil motives or incompetence. Managers who look for quick solutions to problems tend to attribute the causes of those problems to employees, without stopping to consider the influences of situational factors. Deming, the famous pioneer in statistical quality control, insisted that over 80 percent of the problems in the workplace were caused by a combination of poor management practices and poorly designed systems, not by the workers themselves.

Attribution theory[10] provides a way of diagnosing a person's behavior in a situation to determine the balance between internal and external causes. In essence, the theory suggests that there are three important factors to consider: consensus, distinctiveness, and consistency. Consensus is the extent to which others would act the same way in the given situation; the stronger the consensus, the more the behavior is situationally determined. Distinctiveness is the extent to which the person behaves differently in other situations; the greater the distinctiveness, the more the behavior in the particular situation is situationally determined. Consistency (the opposite of distinctiveness) is the extent to which the person behaves in the same way whenever faced with the same situation; the greater the consistence, the more the behavior is personally determined.

Let's look at an example. A student disagrees with a point made by the instructor. The instructor gets irritated and criticizes the student for making a stupid statement. Is the instructor essentially an authoritarian person who tends to get angry when challenged? Or was the instructor feeling stressed by personal problems and just happened to get upset at that moment? It would be easy to make the first assumption and draw some conclusions about the kind of person that instructor is. But if the second assumption were more accurate, then the conclusions would be invalid. And yet, how often do we make that error? Learning from others, for example, that usually the instructor welcomes challenges and that the given behavior was very unusual for him or her in that kind of situation (distinctive) would support the situational attribution, as would finding out that the behavior was inconsistent with his or her behavior at other times and in different situations. And it might not be unreasonable to assume that other instructors might behave similarly under the same circumstances (consensus).

In short, before making any attributions regarding the causes of a person's behavior, it is important to ask yourself the three critical questions suggested by attribution theory: Would others behave in the same way under similar circumstances? Is there a consistent pattern of behavior here that occurs every time this person is faced with this kind of situation and/or other kinds of situations? Even in answering these questions, always keep in mind how important it is to view the situation through the eyes of the individual experiencing it, which in turn is affected by that person's self-concept.

Rosabeth Kanter,[11] in her pioneering work on gender issues in the workplace, discovered that behavior patterns attributed to women were actually characteristic of people in low power positions in an organization, irrespective of gender. It just so happened that these low power positions tended to be occupied by a disproportionate number of women. Men in those same positions tended to behave in exactly the same way. This is an example of how stereotypes play into our attributions and can lead to serious misperceptions of the causes of behavior. It is easy to see how stereotypes about race and national origin can produce attributions that have little or no basis in fact. As our organizations become more diverse and multicultural, it will become increasingly important for managers to be sensitive to the traps that attribution theory warns us about.

Defensive Behavior

In many cases the maintenance of the self-concept depends on the retention of certain beliefs, even when these are no longer valid by external standards. The following case illustrates vividly the way in which a strongly held set of beliefs about self can prevent disconfirming data from being accepted:

> Frank had been a supervisor in a manufacturing plant for over 20 years. As part of a total quality effort, involving the implementation of self-directed work teams, the company had instituted a program to train all supervisors in team leadership and facilitation skills. Although Frank was ambivalent about the changes and felt that he was already managing things well, he did cooperate and participate fully in the program.

One portion of the training involved having pairs of participants gathering data on how their partner was perceived by others on the job, including their manager, their co-workers and their subordinates. Each partner took all the data, created a composite picture, disguising the sources, and then shared it with the other partner. In general, the participants found the exercise very useful, generally positive, but often with some surprising revelations.

Part of the feedback that Frank received was that he tended to be overly controlling and did not give his workers enough latitude in how they performed their jobs. This upset Frank. He thought of himself as helpful and supportive, as someone who offered ideas and guidance without trying to control others. His reaction to the feedback was very defensive. He insisted that others misperceived his intentions, that the data were not really valid and must have been given by only one or two people. Frank's anger at the feedback seemed unusually strong to his partner, who was puzzled that Frank did not accept it in a more constructive way.

What Frank's partner failed to realize was that Frank felt extremely threatened by the feedback. It said, in effect, that Frank was not as competent as he believed, and even more deeply perhaps, that he was not living up to some basic beliefs and values about proper management.

This example illustrates how data that appear to another as pertaining only to someone's expectancies may, in fact, cut very deeply into the core of that person's self-concept. The information not only challenged the executive's goals, it also implied to him that he was violating his own beliefs and values as well as behaving incompetently as a manager. This illustrates the capacity of individuals to block out disconfirming data that are too threatening to the self-concept.

When people encounter data that do not gibe with their self-concept, defensive behavior is likely. The data may be denied, projected onto someone else, twisted to have a more acceptable meaning, or attacked as not valid. People's defenses protect them from being too uncomfortable, from having to change too rapidly, from too easily letting go of the self-view they have built up. Yet insofar as defenses prevent new data from being incorporated, evaluated, and responded to, they keep people from learning and growing. The problem for you as a manager is how to recognize defensiveness in yourself and others and how to respond to it in a way that increases the likelihood of learning and decreases the rejection of new information.

In summary, we can offer the following propositions:

1. *The greater the threat of information or events to a person's self-concept, the greater the likelihood of a defensive response and vice versa.*
2. *The more defensive a person's response, the less the likelihood of learning and growth.*
3. *Refusal to consider disconfirming data, regardless of the form the refusal takes, is an indicator of defensive reactions.*
4. *Attempts to tear down the defenses of another are likely to increase defensiveness; learning and openness to new experience are more likely when the defensive person feels safe and can lower his or her own defenses.*[12]

This last proposition circles back to the first; responses that do not threaten another's self-concept are most likely to reduce defensiveness. If you can sense what other persons value, what is important to how they define themselves, you can back off from whatever is threatening the self-concept and allow them more elbowroom.

The Self-Concept and Behavior

In the remainder of the chapter, we discuss how the personal system as organized around the self-concept determines the behavior of the individual. We first examine the ways in which the norms and role obligations of a given situation can combine with an individual's self-concept to exert powerful influences over behavior. Then we discuss the effects on actual behavior of a person's expectancies (positive and negative) regarding the probable consequences of his or her choices. Finally we discuss some of the broad implications of an individual's choices with respect to careers, lifestyle, and the development of a basic sense of one's own adequacy and worth in this world. Our intent is to help you gain some insights and perspectives on yourself, as well as to facilitate your knowledge of others, whether as a future manager or as a member of any social system.

The basic proposition that underlies this section is that All other things being equal, the behavior most likely to occur in a given situation is that which the individual expects to best maintain and enhance his or her self-concept.

Norms and the Self-Concept

One reason a group may become cohesive is because it confirms the members' self-concepts; its *norms* (unwritten rules governing member behavior) are congruent with the members' values and beliefs, provide for the exercising of their competencies, and support the achievement of personal goals. Obviously, one of the reasons a group's norms are what they are is because of its members' self-concepts, which were brought to the group in the first place. However, because of variations in member needs and self-concepts, it is very unusual to find a group in which *all* the norms support *all* self-concepts at *all* times. Also, because people tend to be members of many different groups during their lives, they experience wide variations in the degree to which their self-concepts are supported by the norms that are present in a given situation. While a person may seek out settings that are likely to be self-confirming, it is very difficult to completely avoid situations in which there is pressure to conform to norms that conflict with some aspect of the person's self-concept.

You have undoubtedly experienced times when those around you seem to be pressuring you into behaving in a way that runs counter to some aspect of your self-concept. For example, in task groups it is not uncommon for some kind of norm to develop in relation to having a beer after work. Your goal may be to stick to soft drinks, but if you have no basic value opposed to drinking alcohol, the chances are fairly good that you will give in to the pressure of the norm. If, on the other hand, your feelings run deeper, then your resistance to the pressure will obviously be greater.

> What a dependency if you want everybody to love you!
>
> F. S. Perls
> *Gestalt Theory Verbatim*, p. 36

The dilemma with respect to resisting norms is likely to be greatest when your livelihood is at stake. It may be important to your survival to remain a "member in good standing" of a work group. Norm pressures that go only against goals tend to result in conformity, while pressures that go against competencies, beliefs, and/or values are likely to result in deviance or isolation. The norms and values of a group are equivalent to the values of the individual; they are the respective "oughts" of their system. As such they are resistant to change. Conflicts between groups and individuals at the values level tend to be irreconcilable, at least without major sacrifice on the part of either the individual or the group.

In one classroom work group, a norm had developed to do the least work possible yet still get a "decent" grade. All of the students in the group liked the idea and supported the norm except one. Her goal in the class was to learn as much as possible, and she believed it important and right to give an all-out effort on every project. The rest of the group members were afraid that she would have enough influence (since she was the most knowledgeable member) to change the developing norm. They put more pressure on her, only to get back more resistance. She went from

And I Don't Do Windows!

[The *Times* of London's drama] critic, finding himself in a theater that is burned down in the course of a play's first night, turns in a perfectly straightforward critique of the performance, remarking only that he cannot comment upon the ending, because the theater burned down during Act Three. The editor sends him a gentle note next day, suggesting that if such a thing happens another time, he might perhaps contribute a brief report on the calamity to the news pages. "My dear editor," the critic replies, "you seem to be under a misapprehension as to the nature of my employment with the *Times*. I am your Dramatic Critic, not your *newshound*."

SOURCE: Jan Morris, *Pleasures of a Tangled Life* (New York: Random House, 1989), p. 102.

group deviant to group isolate, eventually not attending meetings of the group and doing most of the coursework on her own. Her concept of herself as a "good student" was so basic that she could not bring herself to violate it, even though the situation called for her to attempt exerting influence on the group.

Therefore, The willingness to conform to group norms is a product of the closeness of the norms to one's self-concept.[13] The costs and benefits of conforming must be weighed against the costs and benefits of deviating. Sometimes the choice will be obviously toward conforming; sometimes it will involve a hard struggle; and sometimes individuals reach a point beyond which they cannot comply.

Roles and the Self-Concept

A role is made up of a particular set of behaviors and attitudes that accompany a given position in a social system. Roles are shaped by the expectations others have about the person occupying the role. Roles serve to confirm or disconfirm the self-concepts of those who occupy them, as well as provide ways for individuals to broaden their self-concepts. To illustrate, in most task groups in which leadership is allowed to emerge freely as the group develops, it is those individuals who see themselves as leaders among their peers who most readily take on the leadership roles. Insofar as the group supports this, the individual is able to reaffirm his or her self-concept via the behaviors associated with the role. The role is likely to be consistent with the person's goals ("I want to be a leader"), beliefs ("A group needs leadership"), competencies ("I know how to pull a group together"), and values ("It is of the utmost importance to get the work out; I know how to do it so I should take the initiative"). In other cases individuals who might wish to be leaders but doubt their competencies can—with some help and a little push—try out leadership roles until they have broadened their self-concepts to include that kind of role, at least in some situations.

No matter how a particular role is defined by a boss, peers, tradition, and so forth: The individual's own unique perception of the role obligations determines his or her reaction to the prospect of adopting the role. To the extent that a role is perceived to be congruent with the self-concept, the individual is inclined to adopt it; to the extent that a role is perceived to be incongruent with any aspect of the self-concept, the individual is inclined to reject it.[14]

An example with important implications for society relates to women and the roles they choose. As more and more women reject the self-concept of constant "supporters of men," they increasingly resist the kinds of roles that accompany such a position in society. The issue goes well beyond a matter of goals; it clearly pertains to the competencies of women as compared with men in almost all fields of work, and it is without doubt a basic matter of beliefs and values, especially in a society that espouses equality.

This issue has appeared more frequently in the classroom as more women students enter courses in management and administration. Tradition tended to draw the female students into various secondary roles in task groups. They often fell right into the "secretarial role" and into other roles of a supportive and maintenance nature, including, sometimes, making sure that the group was well nurtured. Somehow it was never a male student who determined that the group needed homemade brownies at its meetings. Now many women students overtly reject the secretarial role, some with more vigor than others. Even though someone taking such a role is highly functional for the group, it may be equally dysfunctional for the person asked to fill it. Obviously, this issue is not clear-cut, especially for many women who have built major aspects of their self-concepts upon supportive role behaviors that, while not fostering their own growth, have been important sources of self-confirmation. It is not easy for anyone to give up behaviors that are comfortable, even if limiting.

Because roles are important vehicles for giving order and consistency to a person's behavior in a social system, they often serve as a source of support for a person's basic sense of adequacy. People derive their sense of adequacy by doing the things at which they are competent and by learning to be competent at the things they value. Every time people are faced with a situation that goes beyond their competence, they feel a blow to the self-concept, to a sense of personal adequacy; every time individuals experience success in some activity, they enhance their sense of adequacy and confirm their concept of themselves as competent.

To the extent that individuals can build their lives around roles that enhance competencies, they will develop a basic sense of adequacy. To the extent that individuals find themselves cast into roles that conflict with or fail to utilize competencies, they will tend to develop a sense of inadequacy. Problems occur when people feel pressured to do things that do not fit with their competencies, at least as seen from inside, or when they feel constrained by circumstances from exercising the competencies they possess. Imagine yourself in a job in which all your previous training has little use. You see others in the organization doing things that you know you could do as well or better, but the role you are cast into in the system does not allow you to engage in any of those activities. That can be more than frustrating; it could even be degrading. People in dead-end or low-ceiling jobs often feel this way. Then again, imagine what it might be like to be assigned to a job long before you are ready for it, only to perform at a mediocre level. This is hardly conducive to developing a sense of personal adequacy. Employees in rapidly growing firms sometimes find themselves in this position, swept upward in a series of promotions until they reach a point where they lack the requisite knowledge to perform adequately. Then they spend a great deal of time worrying about being "found out."

Sometimes a role conflict can go very deep and hit on matters of personal worth. This happens when a role calls for a kind of behavior that the person believes is wrong. Since most positions in an organization entail multiple roles, especially as one moves up the hierarchy of the system, most people at one time or another are called upon to adopt a role that goes against their personal values. For example, at some time an executive may be assigned to be the "hatchet man" in a situation needing strong action. On the other hand, while his or her values as related to the total system might support such a decision, a concern for employee security might not support it. Although learning to live with that kind of problem may be a useful aid to executive success, the price that is paid for violating one's own values may appear later as insomnia, ulcers, nervous conditions, and so forth. Or it may lead to a shift in the violated values. It depends on how deep they and the beliefs that support them are. In either case, tension between values and role obligations is a major source of stress. The important thing for you to look at now is the relationship between your values and the ways in which various roles may call upon you to behave

Old Self-Concepts Never Die

One of the authors interviewed a 50-year-old man who had once been president of his own company but was now one of a number of executives in a small manufacturing firm. He still had a concept of himself as "top man" and frequently made decisions that were later countermanded by the chief executive of the company. Making his own decisions reinforced the concept he held of himself in the old role as president but created problems in his present situation. Being overruled reinforced his subordinate role in the firm. He had a great deal of difficulty accepting that role because the behavior that went with it violated his own sense of competency as a manager, resulting in a loss of his sense of personal adequacy. This once high-level executive spent a great deal of his time telling stories of the good old days when he made really tough decisions.

inconsistently with your self-concept. To the extent that individuals adopt roles that support their values, they experience themselves as worthwhile; to the extent that individuals violate these values, they doubt their personal worth.[15]

Rewards and the Self-Concept

Just as roles can call for behavior that violates an individual's values, so can the organization's formal or informal reward system. In Chapter 7 we referred briefly to the idea that different individuals might perceive the same reward differently. Having added the construct of the self-concept, we can now expand on the relation between rewards and individual responses to them.

Rewards will be viewed by each individual in terms of

1. How valuable the reward is, given the person's goals and values. To the individual who wants group acceptance above all, for example, cash incentives for extraordinary performance may not be perceived as particularly valuable. Any rewards requiring getting ahead of peers would be undervalued by such individuals.
2. How compatible the activity required to gain the reward is with the person's goals, values, beliefs, and competencies. A chance to receive a bonus and have one's picture in the company newsletter may be seen as quite valuable, but if to get it the introverted financial analyst would have to start selling new accounts, the reward may not induce the requisite behavior.
3. How the rewards offered compare with those available to relevant others, and who is seen as relevant, will also be influenced by the person's goals, beliefs, and values. Individuals who are ambitious will tend to compare their rewards to those higher in the organization and to those in highly successful organizations. Individuals who desire acceptance will compare themselves with their immediate peers. Individuals who are competitive will also compare themselves with peers and will struggle for even very small relative advantage. In one group of up-and-coming managers, there was intense interest in what the boss did about pay raise differentials that netted less than a $3 per week spread against base salaries of $40,000 to 50,000 per year! Clearly, symbolic differences were at stake.

Expectancies and the Self-Concept

The influence of the situational factors discussed above (norms, roles, and rewards) and of other factors on individual behavior is ultimately mediated by the individual's expectancies. This was mentioned in Chapter 7, but it warrants emphasis now that we've developed a more complete picture of the personal system.

Why Apple's Guru [Steve Jobs] Struck Out with NeXT

[T]he personal traits required to launch a high-tech company can [and did] doom an enterprise. There is a fine line between what is extreme and what is merely dynamic and determined. Ideas ahead of their time can become ideas whose time will never come. Superconfidence can turn into arrogance that leads to stubborn adherence to an unworkable plan. Attention to detail can become stifling perfectionism and excessive control. "Doing things right" can be an excuse for extravagance. Creating an image of success in order to inspire confidence in customers and investors can lead to half-truths and distortions.

SOURCE: Ed Zschan, *The Wall Street Journal,* © December 10, 1993, Dow Jones & Company, Inc.

Before you make a choice, you usually appraise the situation and decide which alternatives are likely to result in self-enhancement. Few people like to waste their efforts, and even fewer wish to engage in behavior that goes against their goals, beliefs, and so forth. To deal with the matter of choosing the best course of action in a situation, your appraisal takes the form of a kind of prediction: "The chances are that if I do thus and so, I will achieve what I want." You make a statement (implicit or explicit) of your expectancy regarding the probable outcome. It's like being your own personal scientist, making hypotheses, testing them out, revising them when they prove wrong, and holding on to the ones that prove accurate. As discussed in the previous chapter, outcomes that are rewarding tend to create and reinforce the expectancies that are positive. By the same token, outcomes that are nonrewarding or punishing lead to expectancies that are neutral or negative.

Guideline Propositions for Predicting Individual Behavior

1. The greater the strength of expectancy that a particular behavior will have a positive outcome, the more likely it is that the behavior will occur, and vice versa.
2. To the extent that a particular behavior is perceived to be positively related to the maintenance and enhancement of the self-concept, the behavior is likely to become an ongoing part of the individual's repertoire.[16]
3. The more limited an individual's range of competencies, the more likely is an existing competency to be used regardless of situational appropriateness.

Figure 8–3 shows the ways in which behavior and self-concept are linked; it also summarizes the concepts we have discussed in this chapter.

Situational Determinants of the Self-Concept

Have you ever seen a person you had experienced as knowledgeable, decisive, and confidence unexpectedly become hesitant, unsure, and almost shy? One young woman who was poised, confident, and often an initiator (leader) in student activities worked in a retail store for three years after graduation and then joined the Peace Corps. While overseas she appeared tentative, diffident, and was slow to deal with problems. How might one explain this contrast in behavior?

She felt that her usual pattern of behavior would elicit negative outcomes and reactions that would disconfirm her self-concept. Instead of seeing herself as knowledgeable, competent, and legitimate to exert leadership, she saw herself as a

FIGURE 8-3 *How Behavior Results from Perceptions and Expectancies as Influenced by the Self-Concept*

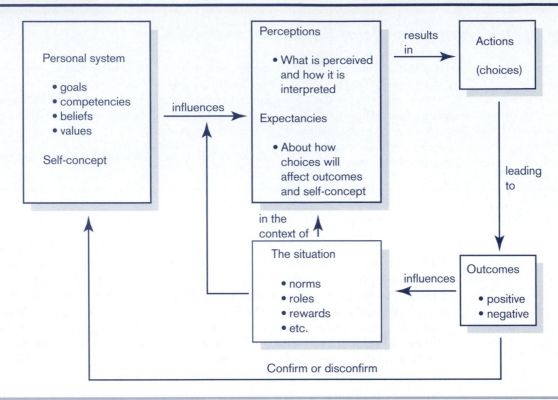

neophyte, lacking knowledge about the situation, and as such obligated to act more as a "guest" than a "member of the family." She also lacked the support systems she had at home. In a sense, her self-concept was different in the two situations.

Thus, in seeking to explain or predict someone's behavior, we need to remember that, while an individual's self-concept develops slowly and is relatively stable, it is also partly situationally dependent. People vary their behavior in each situation to maintain and enhance their self-concepts, and each situation can influence how they see and feel about themselves.

Structuring the World around Us

When you study, do you focus on details or look at the larger picture? When you take a trip, do you get sidetracked and pay attention to all the points along the way or focus on "getting there"? When you shop, are you quick to make a decision, or do you feel compelled to check out every possibility so that you *know* you've made the right decision?

Among the things that make people different from each other, one of the most interesting is the way in which each person organizes or structures his or her world. And this is often a source of puzzlement. Jane wonders how Jack can get anything done with such a disorganized approach to tasks and a desk that looks like a tornado hit it. Jack wonders how Jane can enjoy her work since she is so compulsive, makes a list of activities for the day, and arranges the papers on her desk in neat piles. Jane goes crazy trying to keep Jack focused on an issue or problem; Jack loves to explore all the implications or related issues as they pop into his head. Jane tries to control Jack; Jack tries to loosen Jane up. Sound familiar?

Psychologists have long studied differences in the ways people structure their worlds—that is, the *thinking* processes people use in managing their lives. How people organize their thinking affects what they are likely to *perceive* in a given situation, what they are likely to remember most readily, and how they plan and organize work for themselves and for others.

In the example above, Jack was a *divergent* thinker and Jane was a *convergent* thinker. Although that is not the only difference between them, it is clearly an important one that can either be a source of conflict or a basis for building a *complementary* work relationship, one that capitalizes on the differences as *strengths*. Most decisions by managers are complex enough to require some ability to look at implications and consequences (a divergent thought process) as well as move things to some conclusion and action (a convergent thought process). Some people can do both, but usually because they have consciously developed the side of themselves that was not a natural tendency in the first place. Some successful managers have been smart enough to surround themselves with people who *collectively* are both divergent and convergent thinkers.

In recent years, a conceptual framework for understanding individual differences has become very popular among organizational behavior teachers, students, consultants, and managers. It is rooted in the personality theory of Carl Jung but has been translated into a set of concepts and tools that have very practical applications. The principal proponent of this work, Isabel Briggs Myers, published a widely used instrument and series of supporting texts designed to help people understand themselves and others better. Although we do not describe this approach in detail, we provide a summary of the basic theory and its applications in a way that should give you some insights into people, including yourself. If you are interested in studying the approach in greater depth, a useful place to begin is with the book *Gifts Differing* by Isabel Briggs Myers.[17]

The Myers-Briggs Model

The model describes people in terms of four dimensions:

1. Introversion–Extroversion.
2. Sensing–Intuition.
3. Thinking–Feeling.
4. Judging–Perceiving.

Let's look first at each dimension separately and then discuss what kinds of pictures emerge as they combine. Keep in mind as you consider this approach that these dimensions do not represent fixed traits in people, but rather they identify *processes* that everyone is capable of using, even though each individual has a propensity for operating at one or another end of each dimension. Furthermore, keep in mind that people change as they grow, developing skills that broaden their abilities to engage in behavior that may not have been "natural" or preferred in earlier stages of life. Also, circumstances often pull out of us capacities heretofore untapped.

1. Introversion–Extroversion

Where do you get your cues for making decisions or taking action? From inside yourself or from other people? If your tendency is to be a kind of "loner," mostly responding to your inner world, you are probably an *introvert*. If you tend to be highly social and responsive to other people in your world, you are probably an *extrovert*. These terms are not intended to reflect lifetime labels; you may tend to be more introverted than extroverted, or vice versa, or you may even be somewhere in the middle. As a manager, it will pay you to be sensitive to cues both outside and inside yourself, sometimes responding more to one than the other but always looking for an appropriate balance. The research engineer whose style is highly introverted may find the demands of others to be a source of tension when promoted to a managerial role. Sometimes the dilemma results in poor management; hopefully, it can be an opportunity for the individual to broaden his or her way of structuring the world.

2. Sensing–Intuition

Jack says, "Let's go with it; I have a hunch we're on the right track." Jane says, "I need more information; it all seems too ambiguous for me to go ahead." Who's right? Either? Neither? Both? Probably all of the above. Jack trusts his past experience and the intuitive sense that he has built from it; Jane trusts real data, what she can *see*, or *hear*, or *touch*, and so on, as the correct means for making decisions. Again, maybe some combination, some balance of the two approaches, produces effective decisions. Furthermore, some situations demand a thorough search of facts, while others are better suited to hunches that are not easily explained.

Sherlock Holmes usually approached a case by building pieces of information into a careful, logically deduced conclusion. Hercule Poirot was not so "logical," depending more on his ability to make leaps in thought, to fit pieces into a whole in a sudden flash of insight. Are you Holmes or Poirot? You may need to become a little of each. In fact, even Sherlock Holmes at times acted on pure intuition, and Poirot was always careful to pay attention to details. The world of a manager demands a combination of intuitive and sensing abilities.

3. Thinking–Feeling

A good manager uses both mind and heart. Did you ever hear the conjugation "I am firm, you are stubborn, he is pig-headed!"? You tend to view yourself as a rational, thinking person; somehow that's considered a "good" way to be. Other people—especially those who don't see things the way you do—are less rational, more emotional; and that's not so good. Yet *all* people are a combination of rational or nonrational, or, as defined in the present context, *thinkers* and *feelers*. At one time the business world had the norm, "Keep your feelings out of people decisions." That is much less the case nowadays. It is recognized that how you feel about a decision can determine the success of its implementation just as much as the logic of that decision. The realities of organizational life often evoke emotions that play a dominant role in a manager's behavior. Fear of failure, fear of the boss, excitement about a new product, compassion for an employee, anger at another person, and so forth, are but a few examples of emotional forces that appear in the day-to-day life of a firm.

Even though you may tend or prefer to use thinking as your way of dealing with the world, you would be unrealistic to believe that your feelings don't enter the process. Or, if you trust your feelings more than your logic, you may find that your actions lack consistency and coherence. Thinkers (forgive the label) see feelers as soft-headed do-gooders; feelers see thinkers as cold hard-noses. These stereotypes generate conflict; the differences could be useful complements to one another if understood and appreciated. The implications for male–female work relationships should be obvious, especially with the history of stereotyping in that arena.

4. Judging–Perceiving

The distinction here is similar to the one made earlier regarding convergent and divergent thinking. A tendency toward *judging* means a preference for getting things finished and settled, not leaving loose ends, using a structured plan to do work, and a low tolerance for ambiguity. This is a different use of the term; it does not refer to passing judgment on something or someone, in the usual sense of "judging." A tendency toward *perceiving* means a preference for exploring many routes, leaving things open, seeking change, starting a variety of activities (which often remain unfinished), and a high tolerance for ambiguity. To be effective as a manager, over the long run you'll need to operate at times in a perceiving mode—for example, when you are trying to understand a problem—and at times in a judging mode—for example, when you are trying to move people to act on the solution to a problem. The tensions that develop between "perceivers" and "judgers" can, as in the previous dimensions, be sources of irreconcilable conflict or effective problem solving.

Combining the Dimensions

There is a well-researched instrument designed to help you understand your "type." It measures your preferences or tendencies along the four dimensions and generates a picture that combines the dimensions into 16 possible categories. If you are interested, your instructor may be able to help you obtain access to the instrument, but its use is carefully controlled through professionally trained people who can administer, score, and interpret the data. In the absence of this, you can at least explore for yourself, possibly with the help of people who know you best, how the four dimensions fit together for you.

An awareness of these differences in ways of dealing with the world and an awareness that each process can contribute to solving a concrete problem can help you to:

1.   View someone else's approach simply as "different," not bad or inferior, with its own potential to contribute, however frustrating it may seem.
2.   Consider trying a different "tack" if you find yourself stuck in dealing with some situation.
3.   Recognize the need to supplement your own natural pattern by consulting with others and seeking to broaden your own repertoire of approaches.

One way in which the Myers-Briggs model has been used effectively is for team building. As members of a team learn to understand and even appreciate differences among them, they are better able to build on complementary strengths and ways of dealing with problems. Intuitive types have the ability to make creative leaps in thinking, but often need the more sensing types to make sure that all the facts are being considered. Similarly, perceivers will tend to engage in endless explorations of alternatives and really need to be balanced by judging types, who are more inclined to move quickly to a decision, often too quickly. An effective team learns to build on these differences; in fact, an absence of diversity along the Myers-Briggs dimensions, while it can produce an easy harmony, might limit the creative potential of a group. This is something for a manager to consider when composing task teams, especially if they are to be self-managing.

Life Phases and Life Choices

The kinds of career and relationship choices you make and the commitments involved are very often a reflection of the period of life in which you find yourself. Unique as you might see yourself, there is no doubt that many of the things you have and will experience are also experienced by others. In fact, there are some fairly predictable phases of life that most people go through. This is fortunate, since it can help you to understand yourself and others better. And each of these phases seems to contain some new needs, struggles, and choices along with some old familiar ones that somehow were never completely "put to rest."

> When choosing between two evils, I always like to take the one I've never tried before.
>
> Mae West
> In *Klondike Annie*

Combatting Stress—With the Help of High Tech

For some time, researchers have related stress to a variety of physical ailments, including high blood pressure, heart disease, colitis, ulcers, migraine headaches, insomnia, back injuries, and eczema. The American Heart Association estimates that recruiting replacements for executives who die of heart disease costs American industry $700 million annually. . . . "Many executives would rather pay [*for stress management training*] out of their own pocket than admit to a 'weakness.'" But the need for ways to channel pressure is still there. "You can be as competitive as you need to be. We don't attempt to change anyone's life or personality. We teach people constructive ways to deal with that stress."

SOURCE: Marilyn J. Cohodas, *Boston Business Journal*, March 24, 1986.

Figure 8–4 shows examples of life phases in terms of key events and typical issues that characterize them. Study the chart and see where you fit in. Also see if it gives you some insights into people you know—parents, friends, co-workers, your boss, and so on. Can you see how the things that motivate them are a result of both their unique personality and the place or places they are in their lives? These insights can help you as a manager to understand your employees and help them to plan career paths consistent with their life phases. Keep in mind that these phases are very general, can vary a great deal from person to person, may even occur in a different sequence for some, and, in rare instances, might not even apply to a person whose key life events have been extraordinary.

One phase deserving some special attention is the forties—the period that is often referred to as the midlife (or midcareer) crisis. In the same way that people at age 22 might be carefully considering the kinds of career and life choices they are making, many people find themselves reexamining those choices against the backdrop of experience after 20 or 30 years in a career. This often leads to a major change of direction—an upheaval of sorts. It feels like a crisis in that it can mean letting go of a very familiar, secure state of existence and entering a very unknown state often full of risks and anxiety. At times a fear of disappointing oneself and others prevents a risky choice, but a willingness to push past that fear can be the very thing needed to generate renewed commitment to life, to work, to oneself, and to others. The feared disappointment very often reveals itself as a myth. Unfortunately, the struggles you currently face do not magically disappear after age 21 or 25 or 30. They usually reappear in new (and sometimes old) forms, only to challenge you again.

Understanding and Managing Stress

At any stage of life, stress can be a factor affecting performance. Those who experience too little stress may not call into play their best attention and energy; those who experience too much stress may become immobilized, repeat useless behavior, or scatter their efforts. Some of the recent attention to stress reduction ignores the utility of stress for accomplishment. Moderate amounts of experienced stress generate focus and mobilize a person's resources. Performance is actually enhanced under moderate amounts of stress.

Compounding the problem is the fact that individuals vary enormously in their tolerance for externally caused stress. The same situation can be perceived as excruciatingly overbearing or as wonderfully challenging by individuals with different

FIGURE 8-4 *Adult Life Phases*

Age	Key Events	Characteristic Tensions
Late teens	Leave home, new roles, and more autonomous living arrangements; college, travel, army, job. Initial decisions about what to study, career, love relationships.	A balance between "being in" and "moving out" of the family. For women, career versus marriage. Search for identity. Testing limits. Struggle with authority.
Early to mid-20s	Provisional commitment to occupation and first stages of a career; being hired; first job; adjusting to work world. Marriage, decision to have a child.	"Doing what one should." Living and building for the future. Dreams versus reality. Struggle for opportunity. For women, struggle to find place in male work world versus security of socially accepted woman's role.
Late 20s to early 30s	Change occupation or direction within an occupation. Go back to school. Marriage, parenthood, part-time job (for married women)	"What is life all about now that I'm doing what I should? What do I want out of life?" For women, awareness of unfulfilled needs either as wife/mother or as career woman, desire to start career, or desire to have children ("last chance").
Mid- to late 30s	Pursue family activities. Children old enough for mother to return to school. Important promotion in work. Plateau reached in career.	Concern to establish order and stability in life and with "making it," with setting long-range goals and meeting them. Awareness of passing youth. Fear of "settling in," having missed something. For women, struggle to enter or reenter career or go back to school. Self-doubts versus self-confidence.
The 40s	Change in activities from realization that life ambitions might not develop. Change in career; empty nest; a second career for women whose first career was in the home. Death of parents.	Awareness of bodily decline, aging, own mortality; emergence of feminine aspects of self for men, masculine aspects for women. Feeling of stagnation. Need for renewal, to prove self, to reaffirm youth. For women, recognizing the tougher side, fear of being a "beginner" in a career, feeling of being out of place in a youth-oriented culture, and discomfort with own success in career. Fear of lacking an identity.
The 50s	Last chance for women to have a career or vigorously pursue a deferred life goal or interests. Reaching highest level of status in career or settling for less.	An imperative to change so that deferred goals can be accomplished—"It is perhaps late, but there are many things I would like to do in the last half of my life." A mellowing of feelings and relationships; spouse is increasingly important. Greater comfort with self, or fear of never living up to own aspirations. Renewed sense of purpose, self-acceptance, and vigor *or* Feelings of doubt and self-pity. For women, achieving sense of wholeness through integration of both sides of self; for those who entered career late, a struggle similar to that of men in the 40s.
The 60s (and beyond)	Retirement of self and spouse; aging; health problems. Loss of stamina.	Review of accomplishments. Eagerness to share everyday human joys and sorrows; family is important; death is a new presence. Concern about having made one's mark on the world. Desire to grow old gracefully. Renewed need to belong, but fear of being dependent.

SOURCE: Based on Rita Weathersby, *Developmental Perspective on Adults' Uses of Formal Education* (doctoral dissertation, Harvard University, 1977); and G. Sheehy, *Passages: Predictable Crises of Adult Life* (New York: E. P. Dutton, 1976).

self-concepts. Thus, there is no way to create universally appropriate levels of stress. It is sometimes possible, however, to identify signals that individuals are experiencing so much stress that their performance is impeded. It is important to know how to "read" them in yourself and in others, especially when you are responsible for the performance of others.

Signs of Stress

How do you tell when someone is feeling a high level of stress and may need some relief from it? Fortunately, some symptoms are fairly overt and readily recognized. Unfortunately, the person feeling the stress is often the first to *deny* it! In other words, *you* may be the one to recognize another person's need for help before that

MANAGERIAL BULLETIN

Stress Is in the Person, Not in the Situation

Whether stress will escalate into something more seri- ous seems to depend on a number of factors, including the severity and duration of the stress and the individ- ual's ability to cope. "It's the frame of mind that's im- portant rather than the stressful event itself," says Alan Breier, clinical director of the outpatient program at the

Maryland Psychiatric Research Center in Catonsville, Maryland. "What matters is whether the stress leaves a person feeling helpless and out of control."

SOURCE: Sara Sinolop, "The Crippling Ills That Stress Can Trigger," *Business Week*, April 18, 1988.

person does. Or vice versa! You may notice that the other is irritable, not concen- trating on work, missing deadlines, not socializing, and so on. If these things are pointed out, the response may be "I'm fine, thank you, just need more sleep" or "I don't know what you're talking about!"

Some signs of stress are *covert* or have very subtle overt aspects. Feeling anxious may or may not be very visible to others; upset stomach, headache, exhaustion, and many other physical symptoms are likely to be known only to the person experi- encing them. Even feeling distracted and unable to stay focused on a task may re- main hidden from others for a long time.

Given the many indicators that can signal stress, is anyone every *free* of it? As a manager, it is difficult to judge when a situation is serious enough to warrant some action. After all, anyone can show some of these symptoms at almost any time in a given day.

Here are some guidelines for knowing when to pay special attention to someone (including yourself) who is showing signs of stress:

1. If the signs persist for a prolonged period of time (weeks or months), then they should be judged serious and potentially damaging to the health and welfare of the person.
2. If *many* signs of stress are occurring at the same time, it is probable that the *level* of stress is unduly high and is not likely to subside quickly.
3. If the *behavior* of the person is out of character, that is, represents a departure from what is *normal for that person*—and *it persists,* then the level of stress is likely to be unhealthily high. A person's behavior in this context should not be judged against a "most people" standard, nor should it be compared to your *own* behavior. Everyone is different, and those differences need to be appreci- ated. An exuberant, socially active salesperson who has become consistently quiet and withdrawn is probably in trouble. By contrast, a laboratory researcher who normally works best alone may be showing signs of stress by becoming loud and boisterous at social events.

No simple magic formula exists for making these judgments, especially since they are so personal in nature. There is a fine line where personal and managerial concern crosses the other's right to privacy. However, part of managerial responsibility is to develop people, not just supervise task completion, so a delicate balancing act is re- quired. People develop as total individuals, not just as performers of tasks.

Some Organization Sources of Stress and Ways to Cope

People move through many different contexts: work, family, school, social activities, and so on. Each has its own stresses and strains. It isn't always possible to keep the stress from one area of life totally separate from the other areas. A conflict at home

The High Cost of Stress

It sounded like an offer you'd better refuse. General Motors Corporation gave a fiftyish manager the option of early retirement. Many of his colleagues had accepted similar offers. But four of them killed themselves shortly after.

When J. C. Penney Company announced it was moving corporate headquarters from New York City to Plano, Texas, employees were so upset that the company expanded its counseling staff from 1 to 12. Four years after the court-ordered split-up of American Telephone & Telegraph Company, managers still suffer. Morale is at rock bottom and they react to layoffs in other departments as if their own jobs are on the line.

SOURCE: Emily T. Smith, "Stress: The Test Americans Are Failing," *Business Week,* April 18, 1988.

can easily be displaced on an employee at work—and vice versa. Therefore, whatever the source of stress, its effects are often played out in other contexts.

Nevertheless, as a manager, you won't be in a position or have the responsibility to deal with an employee's home life, even if problems there sometimes spill over into the workplace. But you can help your employees organize and carry out their jobs in ways that minimize unnecessary stress.

Here are four major sources of job-related stress:

1. Uncertainty or ambiguity.
2. Unfinished tasks and intrusions.
3. Role expectations.
4. Growth and development.

Uncertainty or Ambiguity

The greater your confidence, the better you perform; the more certainty you have in a task, the greater confidence you feel; the more information you have about a task, the more certainty you have and the greater confidence you feel. By contrast, situations in which you lacked the information you needed created uncertainty, and you probably felt less confident about your performance.

The failure of a manager to provide employees with the information they need to carry out a task creates a gap of uncertainty, which inevitably produces stress. If a manager is consistently amiss in providing available and needed information, high uncertainty and, consequently, high stress are likely to be created. The world is inherently uncertain, and there are a great many sources of uncertainty over which managers have no control. However, a conscious attempt to reduce the uncertainty as much as possible can at least minimize the level of stress and help maintain performance. At the same time, cautious individuals, especially those overstressed by uncertainty, may not make every effort to gather information, ask questions of their boss and peers, or fill in the gaps as much as possible before and during the execution of a job. Guesswork can then compound the uncertainty with bad decisions. If you are in a situation where you are unsure about how to proceed, take the initiative to inquire. That doesn't always produce the desired answers, but forging ahead blindly doesn't either.

Because some people have a greater tolerance for ambiguity than others, relatively turbulent work environments can be stimulating and challenging, rather than a source of stress. But those who prefer a more structured, less ambiguous setting ought to pursue work—or be helped to find jobs—in a relatively stable and controllable arena.

MANAGERIAL BULLETIN

Why Executives Look for New Jobs

A 1992 survey based on 3,581 managers and executives presents insights into how executives view their work.

Factors most likely to cause stress on the job.	Percent of Respondents
1. Degree to which politics, not performance, affects organizational decisions	41%
2. Lack of job security	28
3. Degree to which my career has stalled	25
4. Volume of work that must be accomplished in an allotted time	21
5. Amount of red tape I must go through to get my job done	21
6. Number of projects and assignments I have	20

Average Number of Hours a Week Spent On

Work	56 hours
Leisure	13
Household obligations	10
Dependent care	5

All things considered, are you happy with your present job?	Percent of Respondents
Yes	60%
No	33

Estimate the percent of time you feel satisfied, dissatisfied, and neutral about your present job.	
Satisfied	54%
Dissatisfied	27
Neutral	19

Number of Nights a Month Required to Be Away from Home	Percent of Respondents
0 night	11%
1 or 2	26
3 or 4	23
5 or more	42

SOURCE: Paul Ray Berndtson; Center for Advanced Human Resource Studies at Cornell University. Reprinted in *The New York Times*, December 5, 1993. Copyright © 1993 by The New York Times Company. Reprinted by permission.

A major effect of the trend toward sustained downsizing in organizations is the creation of ambiguity and uncertainty about security and survival. Few people are at their best under these circumstances, much less able to perform their jobs at a level acceptable to their bosses. Ironically, the pressure for high performance is often self-imposed, in the hope that it will ensure one's survival through the next round of lay-offs. While it is difficult to predict how long and to what extent the practice of downsizing will continue as a way to maintain a profitable enterprise, its psychological effects on both the victims and survivors are likely to last for some time.

Unfinished Tasks and Intrusions

Do you recognize this scenario? No matter how hard you try, it seems as though you can never fit all your tasks into the time available. Some things take longer than expected, you keep getting interrupted, a critical piece of information isn't there when you need it, something else comes up that takes precedence, and so on and so on and so on. The net result is that you carry around a lot of unfinished business. That plays on your mind and intrudes in other activities: You can't sleep, are distracted at home, and unable to focus your energies on immediate tasks at work.

An accumulation of unfinished business can easily become a major source of anxiety and produce enough stress to immobilize even the most competent person. It can become so overwhelming that the person begins to feel helpless and hopeless, unsure where to begin or even if it's worthwhile to *try* to begin.

(If you belong to the International Society of Procrastinators, you recognize this all too well. Of course, you probably never got around to sending in your dues, so you're no longer a member of that esteemed group!)

What can be done about all this accumulated unfinished business? First, start somewhere: set *priorities*. One option is to start with the quick and easy tasks, creating a sense of making progress. Some people have to start with the most important and pressing jobs—big or small, difficult or easy—and, once the jobs are completed, feel a great burden removed. Wherever the start—and it may not make a lot of difference—the tension release will be its own reward.

Part of setting priorities is deciding whether or not some tasks can be ignored or done poorly. Stanford professor David Bradford's law number 8 is "Any job worth doing may be worth doing mediocrely." It is remarkably releasing to deliberately *decide* to slide by on low-consequence tasks. Deliberate choice is necessary, however, because some tasks poorly done can come back to haunt you and make things worse.

Some people create unfinished business and, consequently, a great deal of stress for themselves by not knowing what to let go of. A need to be involved in everything can be an awful burden. For any given task, or part of a task, ask yourself, "Do *I* have to be the one to do this? Do *I* even have to be involved at all?" It may be difficult for many people to let go of control, but doing so can certainly help to reduce stress.

Some find that distancing themselves from their work setting for even a short time can help them get a better perspective on what seems overwhelming. Being *in* the setting that's generating the stress only serves to heighten the stress and to impede clear, constructive thinking. A "breather" reduces the immediate tension and helps to mobilize personal resources more effectively.

It is worth mentioning the value of proper diet and exercise in preparing people for dealing with stress, whatever its source. Many people under pressure fail to take care of themselves, generating a cycle that results in poor sleep, fatigue, and low tolerance for doing the tasks that would relieve the feelings of stress. This physical aspect of coping with stress is easily attended to, once recognized.

Role Expectations

At times the expectations associated with fulfilling a role can produce major stress. There is not enough time to finish an assigned project; unexpected changes occur that require some rethinking about a task; several tasks are being demanded, and are all called "top priority"; the list is endless. Many people push on and try to fulfill the expectations by working harder or putting in more time, sometimes only to end up with a situation that is totally out of control. While embarrassment may be a barrier to going to your boss and asking for more time or for help, it clearly makes sense to do so. It makes sense to *renegotiate* the role expectations before disaster occurs.

An effective manager will learn how to spot the signs of stress that signal "overload" and will initiate a process of renegotiation, sometimes even before the employee does. Mutual expectations will be established that will encourage subordinates to initiate such contacts when the occasion calls for it. This can be a useful way to prevent burnout, avoid losing some good people who simply leave in order to get away from the stress, and, in general, promote productivity in employees.

Growth and Development

Most people are attracted both to growth and to preserving things as they are. There's a side of everyone that likes the security and comfort of the status quo. You know what you're good at and where your support comes from. It's a comfort zone that gives you a solid base in life. However, living only in that comfort zone can

80s Stress Graduates Can Advance—to Anger

The Full-Blown Emotion Seems Apt for the 90s and, of Course, There's a Workshop

And now, from the folks who brought you stress-cutting seminars for the 1980s, anger-busting workshops for the 90s.

"Everyone knows that stress causes problems for executives, both on the job and off," said Gilda Carle, a $2,500-a-day organization development specialist whose clients include IBM, General Foods, Mobil Oil, and Pitney Bowes. "It's time to focus on the anger that

lies beneath. It's finally OK to mention the emotion by name." . . .

In general, . . . male executives vent their anger more easily than their female colleagues. "Men become outraged, while women become enraged," she said. "Men play a sport, release their frustration. Women sit on it, think about it."

SOURCE: Nancy Marx Better, *New York Times*, December 22, 1991. Copyright © 1991 by The New York Times Company.

eventually become boring and even lead to restlessness for something different. Therefore, people decide (or are pushed by circumstances) to venture forth into new areas, stretching in new ways. This leads to inevitable uncertainty, getting into skills never before attempted. It also means living with the stress that accompanies such steps. There's always the chance of failure or of making a fool of oneself. While in the learning process, it isn't always great consolation to know that, whatever the outcomes, you will eventually feel stronger for having taken the risk, or that disaster fantasies often exceed the eventual realities. While it may not always be true that there is "no gain without pain," growth is seldom completely comfortable.

A fulfilling life, then, necessarily involves stress of one kind or another. But as today's new venture becomes part of tomorrow's comfort zone, you learn to seek change and growth, and you build an increasing tolerance for the stress that goes along with it. You may even become addicted to growth and development, and that's not a bad addiction to have.

How to Deal with Stress

As already mentioned, there are steps one can take to manage the stress that tends to creep into any job:

1. Cultivate self-awareness so as to recognize stress symptoms.
2. Assess your tolerance for ambiguity, and seek to move into a situation that doesn't chronically exceed your limits.
3. Monitor your diet and exercise schedule, and practice good health activities to enhance your physical capacity to handle stress.
4. When faced with too many tasks, try to get started and focus on them one at a time.
5. Set priorities for each day's work. (See Managerial Tools on time management in Chapter 1).
6. Delegate by asking yourself if a particular task really requires your involvement.
7. Check on whether you are doing a task unnecessarily well; try to avoid being a perfectionist when "perfect" isn't necessary.
8. Don't overconcentrate. Take a break occasionally, or even "sleep on a problem."
9. Renegotiate role expectations.

KEY CONCEPTS FROM CHAPTER 8

1. *a.* Basic human needs, modified by
   b. Past experience, lead to
   c. Personal system (in the context or a situation), which determines
   d. Perceptions and defensiveness.
   e. Expectancies regarding choices result in
   f. Behavior—choices—actions, which feed back on the personal system.

2. The structure of the personal system:
   a. Personal goals.
   b. Competencies.
   c. Beliefs.
   d. Values.

3. All organized around the self-concept.

4. Rationalizing: An escape from the pain of violating one's values.

5. Perceptions: Everything interpreted through individual filters.

6. Attribution: Assuming internal motivational causes for behavior that may be situationally determined. To distinguish, examine:
   a. Consensus, whether others would act similarly in all circumstances.
   b. Distinctiveness, the extent to which the behavior varies with each situation.
   c. Consistency, the extent to which the behavior is the same in varied situations.

7. Defensive behavior:
   a. The greater the threat to a person's self-concept, the greater the defensive response.
   b. The greater the threat to a person's self-concept, the less learning and growth.
   c. Important to attempt to find a nonthreatening alternative.

8. Self-concept and norms:
   a. The willingness to conform to group norms is a product of the closeness of the norms to one's self-concept.
   b. Costs and benefits of conforming weighed against costs and benefits of deviating.

9. Self-concept and roles:
   a. To the extent that a role is perceived as congruent with the self-concept, inclination is to adopt it.
   b. To the extent it is seen as incongruent with any aspect of the self-concept, inclination is to reject it.
   c. To the extent roles are adopted that support values, one experiences self as worthwhile.
   d. To the extent that one violates these values, one doubts personal worth.

10. Self-concept and rewards:
    a. Worth of rewards determined by goals and values.
    b. Activity acquired to gain reward must be compatible with goals, competencies, beliefs, and values.
    c. Reaction to rewards influenced by what relevant others receive.

11. To predict behavior, one would have to know:
    a. Strength of the goals directing the particular behavior.
    b. Expectancies regarding the positive and negative consequences from the environment.
    c. Expectancies regarding the positive and negative consequences to the self-concept.

12. *a.* Expectancies—regarding choices (positive versus negative outcomes)—result in
    b. Behavior—choices (actions, learning defenses), which confirm or disconfirm the self-concept.

13. The ways in which people organize and structure their worlds provide important clues to understanding individual differences.
    a. The Myers-Briggs Model as a category system.

14. Life choices are influenced by life phases.

15. Understanding and managing stress:
    a. How serious depends on number and persistence of symptoms in context of what is normal for the individual.
    b. Sources of stress related to: ambiguity, unfinished tasks, role expectations, and personal growth.
    c. When managing stress, attend to physical psychological, and social factors.

PERSONAL APPLICATION EXERCISE

Becoming Aware of Your Own Personal Propositions

Since the way you see yourself determines your behavior, it is useful to make explicit how you are viewing yourself. Not only can that ease your decision support, it can help you understand better the implicit personal propositions by which others operate. Finally, assumptions that are specifically spelled out are more easily evaluated; sometimes, when you see your own assumptions clearly, the need for minor alterations becomes apparent.

One way to become more aware of your own personal propositions is to use a series of incomplete sentences. Make a list of phrases that represent the kinds of situations you frequently face. For example, you might use such phrases as:

- Whenever I have a job to do that I don't like, I tend to . . .
- When I am in competition with others, I tend to . . .
- When I want someone to like me, I tend to . . .
- When I am afraid of failing, I tend to . . .
- If I try my hardest, I tend to . . .
- If I am true to my own values in a group, I will . . .

If you just let your thoughts fill in the incomplete sentences without any censoring, you can get to some of the ways in which your self-concept is determining your expectations and, thus, your behavior in both positive and negative directions.

Another way of approaching clarity about your working propositions is to try to state the underlying assumption behind each of your most frequent concerns as a person. For example, if you avoid informal interaction with group members, because you worry about being hurt in relationships, the underlying premise might be: "If I am vulnerable and let others get too close, they will hurt me."

If you always act warm and friendly to everyone, whether or not you mean it, the premise might be: "If I don't make people feel I like them, they may attack me."

Another kind of premise, related to feelings of competence, could be stated, "If I ever let myself be caught unprepared, I will be extremely embarrassed." The opposite might go: "If I try my hardest and then don't do well, I will be more disappointed than if I do just enough to get by."

Underlying most of your behavior will be propositions of the sort just mentioned. List those that most frequently seem to control your behavior. Once stated, it can be useful then to assess under what conditions each statement is likely to be true and under what conditions it may be inaccurate.

SUGGESTED READINGS

Adams, J. D., ed. *Understanding and Managing Stress.* San Diego: University Associates, 1980.

Allport, C.; P. Vernon; and G. Lindzey. *Study of Values.* 3rd ed. Boston: Houghton Mifflin, 1970.

Bazerman, Max H.; Ann E. Enbrunsel; and Kimberly Wade-Benzoni. "Negotiating with Yourself and Losing: Making Decisions with Competing Internal Preferences." *Academy of Management Review* 23 (March 1998), pp. 225–41.

Beehr, T. A., and J. E. Newman. "Job Stress, Employee Health, and Organizational Effectiveness: A Facet Analysis, Model, and Literature Review." *Personnel Psychology* 30 (1978), pp. 665–99.

Bhagat, R. S. "Effects of Stressful Life Events on Individual Performance Effectiveness and Work Adjustment Processes within Organizational Settings: A Research Model." *Academy of Management Review,* October 1983, pp. 660–71.

Brief, A. P., and R. J. Aldag. "The Self in Work Organizations: A Conceptual Review." *Academy of Management Review,* January 1980, pp. 75–88.

Brief, A. P., and S. J. Motowidlo. "Prosocial Organizational Behaviors." *Academy of Management Review,* October 1986, pp. 710–25.

Brown, M. "Values—A Necessary but Neglected Ingredient of Motivation on the Job." *Academy of Management Review,* October 1976, pp. 15–23.

Brunson, B. I., and K. A. Matthews. "The Type A Coronary-Prone Behavior Pattern and Reactions to Uncontrollable Stress: An Analysis of Performance Strategies, Affect, and Attributions during Failures." *Journal of Personality and Social Psychology* 40 (1981), pp. 906–18.

Charles, A. W. "The Self-Concept in Management." *Advanced Management Journal,* April 1971, pp. 32–38.

Cohen, S. "After-Effects of Stress on Human Performance and Social Behavior." *Psychological Bulletin* 88 (1980) pp. 82–108.

Cooper, C. L., and J. Marshall. "Occupational Sources of Stress: A Review of the Literature Relating to Coronary Heart Disease and Mental Ill Health." *Journal of Occupational Psychology* 49 (1976), pp. 11–28.

DeFrank, R. S., and J. M. Ivancevich. "Stress on the Job." *Academy of Management Executive* 12, no. 3 (August 1988), pp. 55–66.

Diamond, M. A., and S. Allcorn. "Psychological Barriers to Personal Responsibility." *Organizational Dynamics,* Spring 1984, pp. 66–77.

Dozier, J. B., and M. P. Miceli. "Potential Predictors of Whistle-Blowing: A Prosocial Behavior Perspective." *Academy of Management Review,* October 1985, pp. 823–46.

Dyer, W. G., and J. H. Dyer. "The M*A*S*H Generation: Implications for Future Organization Values." *Organizational Dynamics* 12 (1984), pp. 66–79.

Edwards, Jeffrey R. "An Examination of Competing Versions of the Person-Environment Fit Approach to Stress." *Academy of Management Review,* April 1996, pp. 292–339.

Felson, R. B. "Ambiguity and Bias in the Self-Concept." *Social Psychology Quarterly* 44 (1981), pp. 64–69.

Frankl, V. *From Death Camp to Existentialism.* Boston: Beacon Press, 1959.

Gioia, D. A., and P. P. Poole. "Scripts in Organizational Behavior." *Academy of Management Review,* July 1984, pp. 449–59.

Gist, M. E. "Self-Efficacy: Implications for Organizational Behavior and Human Resource Management." *Academy of Management Review,* July 1987, p. 472.

Gist, M. E., and T. R. Mitchell. "Self-Efficacy: A Theoretical Analysis of Its Determinants and Malleability." *Academy of Management Review,* April 1992, pp. 183–211.

Greer, C. R., and M. A. D. Castro. "The Relationship between Perceived Unit Effectiveness and Occupational Stress: The Case of Purchasing Agents." *Journal of Applied Behavioral Science* 22, no. 2 (1986), pp. 159–76.

Guth, W. T., and R. Tagiuri. "Personal Values and Corporate Strategies." *Harvard Business Review* 45 (1965), pp. 123–32.

Jansen, E., and M. A. Von Glinow. "Ethical Ambivalence and Organizational Reward Systems." *Academy of Management Review,* October 1985, pp. 814–22.

Jick, T. D., and L. F. Mitz. "Sex Differences in Work Stress." *Academy of Management Review,* July 1988, pp. 408–20.

Jones, T. M. "Ethical Decision Making by Individuals in Organizations: An Issue-Contingent Model." *Academy of Management Review* 16, no. 2 (1991), pp. 366–95.

Jourard, S. *The Transparent Self.* Rev. ed. New York: Van Nostrand Reinhold, 1971.

Karasek, R. A. "Job Demands, Job Decision Latitude, and Mental Strain." *Administrative Science Quarterly* 24 (1979), pp. 285–308.

Levinson, D. *The Seasons of a Man's Life.* New York: Alfred A. Knopf, 1978.

London, M. "Toward a Theory of Career Motivation." *Academy of Management Review,* October 1983, pp. 620–30.

Manning, Michael R.; Conrad N. Jackson; and Marcelline R. Fusilier. "Occupational Stress, Social Support, and the Costs of Health Care." *Academy of Management Review,* June 1966, pp. 738–50.

Manz, C. C. "Self-Leadership: Toward an Expanded Theory of Self-Influence Processes in Organizations." *Academy of Management Review,* July 1986, pp. 585–600.

Mihal, W. L.; P. A. Sorce; and T. E. Comte. "A Process Model of Individual Career Decision Making." *Academy of Management Review,* January 1984, pp. 95–103.

Morse, J. J., and J. W. Lorsch. "Beyond Theory Y." *Harvard Business Review,* May–June 1970, pp. 61–68.

Nelson, D. L., and J. C. Quick. "Professional Women: Are Distress and Disease Inevitable?" *Academy of Management Review,* April 1985, pp. 206–18.

Peak, Martha H. "Cutting Jobs? Watch Your Disability Expenses Grow." *Management Review,* March 1997, p. 9.

Rhodes, S. R., and M. Doering. "An Integrated Model of Career Motivation." *Academy of Management Review,* October 1983, pp. 631–39.

Sandberg, J. "Understanding Human Competence at Work: An Interpretive Approach." *Academy of Management Journal* 43 (2000), pp. 9–25.

Schuler, R. S. "Definition and Conceptualization of Stress in Organizations." *Organizational Behavior and Human Performance* 2 (1980), pp. 184–215.

Shapiro, E. C. *How Corporate Truths Become Competitive Traps.* New York: Wiley, 1991.

Shaw, James B. "A Conceptual Framework for Assessing Organization, Work Group, and Individual Effectiveness During and After Downsizing." *Human Relations,* February 1997, pp. 109–27.

Sheehy, G. *Passages: Predictable Crises of Adult Life.* New York: E. P. Dutton, 1976.

Stead, B. A. *Women in Management.* 2nd ed. Englewood Cliffs, NJ: Prentice-Hall, 1985.

Terkel, S. *Working.* New York: Pantheon Books, 1974.

Tharenou, P., and P. Harker. "Moderating Influence of Self-Esteem on Relationships between Job Complexity, Performance, and Satisfaction." *Journal of Applied Psychology* 69 (1984), pp. 623–32.

Weathersby, R. *Developmental Perspective on Adults' Uses of Formal Education.* Doctoral dissertation, Harvard University, 1977.

Whetten, D. A. "Coping with Incompatible Expectations: An Integrated View of Role Conflict." *Administrative Science Quarterly,* June 1978, pp. 254–71.

White, R. W. "The Process of Natural Growth." In *Organizational Behavior and Administration,* ed. P. R. Lawrence and J. A. Seiler. New York, NY: McGraw-Hill/Irwin, 1965.

Diagnosing the Two-Person Work Relationship

Job Requirements and Background Factors

MANAGERIAL BULLETIN

Does Anyone Here Speak Business?

[Channelware's Gord Larose] had a clear-eyed understanding of his own strengths—and his own limitations. From the beginning, he knew that he only wanted to run the technical side of the project. . . .

"I have trouble behaving myself when I'm around a lot of executives," says Larose, "which is true of most technical people. Jeff Dodge . . . is slightly more presentable." As Dodge himself says, "I'm housebroken. I can go into a room crowded with customers, translate engineering terms into English, and put those customers at ease."

[Larose explained:] . . . "Jeff has strengths that complement mine, which is why we have a stronger team."

SOURCE: Ron Lieber, "Startups: The Inside Stories," *Fast Company,* March 2000, p. 284.

[Opposites attract] . . . "when the opposite qualities are complementary to one another—when one person's skills fill vital gaps in the other's repertoire of skills, or when the values of one . . . somehow suggest a way past the other's flat sides."

> If it weren't for the people around here, we could get some work done.
>
> Manager's Lament

"I've got to find a way to get Endrunn off my back," complained Mark Buckley, six months after becoming president of Vitacorp. "I'll be damned if I'll let him charge into town and interfere in this company as he does in the others he's responsible for. Our business is very different from all the other ones he supervises and, until recently, the parent company left us alone. None of them, including Oliver, really understand our business. If I give him any encouragement at all, he's ready to bolt into all kinds of operating areas. And he's dangerous with any information, because then he thinks he can be a hero. He impulsively leaps to conclusions and starts making promises or giving orders to my people. He alternates between being too political and too quick on the trigger, so I give him absolutely no information he doesn't have to know. He sees my quarterly financial results, which ought to be enough."

Buckley was adamant about Oliver Endrunn, group vice president for the conglomerate that owned Vitacorp. He was convinced that the best way to keep an aggressive, outgoing, self-confident financial whiz like Endrunn safely at bay was to avoid supplying him with "ammunition."

For his part, Endrunn was equally frustrated with Buckley. "Mark's very clever, but too political. He plays everything so close to his vest! Must be his training as a lawyer. . . . I don't want to interfere with his operations, since he knows his business better than I do; but I can't be uninformed when my boss wants to know what's going on. And until I get to know Mark well enough to be sure that he's going to keep doing things right, I've got to stay on top of the action. After all, my tail is on the line. So I've had to cultivate my own sources of information in his organization; when I'm in town, I just chat with people to get an idea of what's going on. I almost never want to take action on what I find out, and I certainly don't tell his people what to do, but he can't expect me to fly blind. If he were more open, things would be a lot easier."

Wherever two people get together to do a job, the outcome depends on how they get along. If they bicker, backbite, build grudges, or avoid one another, they are less likely to be productive, satisfied, or growing than if they enjoy being together and are mutually supportive and appreciative of one another's abilities. In a work setting where you may be *required* to work with somebody not of your own choosing, you may have added difficulties with which to cope. Even sophisticated executives like Mark Buckley and Oliver Endrunn can find it difficult to work together. We refer to them throughout Chapters 9 and 10 to illustrate the concepts for diagnosing and repairing work relationships.

You can learn to understand and improve your work relationships, even with people not of your own choosing. It goes without saying that interpersonal relations occur at all levels in an organization; in fact, an organization can be thought of as consisting of a *network* of interconnected relationships.

While some jobs are carried out in relative isolation and remain little affected by interpersonal factors, most work either requires or encourages interaction among individuals. The more a job requires two people to work together, the more important is the kind of working relationship that develops. Even where the interaction is only peripheral to the task, the relationship can still become a source of satisfaction or frustration and thus affect the total work effort in important ways. Think about some of the jobs you have held. Often the most important memories will be the people you worked with, either because they were a source of help and enjoyment on the job or because they got in your way and made life miserable for you. These

Do You Have What It Takes?

"There are lots of brilliant people who can't relate with others," says Robert LoPresto, an executive recruiter. "We replace that kind of person every day."

SOURCE: Kurt Sandholz, *National Business Employment Weekly,* Fall 1987.

issues are often just as critical in an organization as the nature of the work itself. Good interpersonal relations support the work effort; bad ones can kill it.

In this context the usually bitter observation, "It isn't what you know, but whom you know (and who knows you) that counts," is accurate. Being interpersonally competent, able to make effective relationships, *is* indeed a skill that an organization member should have. In a network of relationships, the person who cannot meet others and build working relationships carries a heavy handicap. In contemporary organizations more and more jobs require the ability to work effectively with diverse individuals.

Managing Interpersonal Relationships

If you are a manager, the interpersonal relationships among your employees can have a major effort on your ability to achieve goals. You try your utmost to get a job done, and two of your key people can't seem to work together. Why? What do you do? Is it some kind of personality conflict? Is there something about the job that's creating the problem? Did you as a manager fail to do something?

Similarly, as an organizational member, you may find that there is someone you are supposed to work with who bothers you. Ed jokes when you are serious, is never on time when you pride yourself on punctuality, and uses 50 words where 3 would do. From his point of view, of course, you're too sober, can't relax, and never seem to enjoy exploring all the interesting byways of problems. As a consequence, both of you avoid one another whenever possible, and when you have to talk to one another, both of you walk away dissatisfied. Is it Ed's fault? Does he have a personality defect? Are your joint assignments impossible? Could you do anything to improve the relationship if you wanted to?

Trying to sort out all the possible reasons why people do or don't work well together can be frustrating. There are some concepts that can help you to do the sorting out, can provide some semblance of orderly thinking, and can even offer some clues to managing these kinds of problems.

In many ways the two-person relationship is simply the smallest form of a group. Both involve communication processes, role relationships, status differences, expectations for behavior, degrees of liking and respect, and, ultimately, consequences for productivity, satisfaction, and development. In examining two-person relationships, therefore, we focus on the fit between personal systems and job requirements, because these two aspects most strongly affect interpersonal relationships.

Job Requirements

Many, if not most, interpersonal difficulties arise less from personality differences than from the demands of the job. This is especially so when the two people work for different parts of the organization. With different bosses, different jobs, and therefore different demands on them, what looks like personality clashes may just be responses to quite incompatible job requirements. Even within one unit, incompatible job demands can lead to difficulties.

A job's required activities, interactions, and attitudes have an important effect on relationships because they so directly determine what a person does, with whom it is done, and what feelings will be brought along. There are several questions we can ask to get at the impact of job requirements on relationships. First, to what extent and in what ways does the job require that two people *interact* in order to do their work? Second, are the required *activities* spelled out in such a way as to make it easy or difficult for the two people to cooperate? And third, are the *attitudes* required of each such that they will be able to work toward a common goal, resolve disagreements, share information, and so on?

For example Harry and Betty are product managers, each reporting to Ben. Each is expected to increase sales every year while holding down expenses. In many geographic areas, they use the same salespeople because sales of neither of their products are large enough to occupy the full time of a salesperson. Ben asks them to make their best case at budget time for why each should get a larger share of the department's budget. He posts their monthly sales and profit figures on a big chart over his desk. Each can only increase sales by getting salespeople to spend more time on his or her product. The products at times require calling on different customers. In such a situation it will not be terribly surprising to find that Harry and Betty are very competitive with one another, say nasty things about the "selfishness" of the other, and firmly believe that the personality of the other is unpleasant if not downright sickening. Yet, with a more compatible set of job requirements, they might both find that they enjoy each other's drive and scrappiness and even admire one another.

The fundamental issue is how psychologically close or distant two people are required to be in order to carry out a given task. Some simple jobs located near each other require no relationship between any two people in them. The only exception might be when a new worker comes on; then it would seem to be appropriate for one of the other workers to familiarize the new person with the task and to serve as a temporary helper.

Contrast such jobs with those of Mark Buckley and Oliver Endrunn, introduced earlier. Buckley is a company president reporting to Endrunn, who is responsible for several other companies. At the least, Buckley is expected to make many decisions in Vitacorp and must provide Endrunn with sufficient information about results to satisfy Endrunn that all is well. Oliver has to make judgments from a distance about Mark's success; to do so, he must interpret ambiguous "soft" data. Financial results are important, but they don't reveal everything. Is Buckley making the right investments for the future? Are appropriate new products being created? Is he developing future executive talent? Are relationships with key customers being strengthened? These are questions that require subjective interpretation and predictions about the future; Endrunn needs some way to interact enough to get a feel for the state of the business, without offending Buckley, who needs to feel he's really in charge to lead his business.

Clearly this kind of work situation requires a broad range of possible interpersonal relationships. Jobs can be assessed along several dimensions, including

1. How simple or complex the task is.
2. The degree to which the people involved in the task possess differential expertise.
3. The extent to which human factors (feelings, attitudes, behaviors of people) are involved in the work, as opposed to technical factors alone.
4. The frequency of human interaction or contact fostered by the task situation.
5. The degree of certainty with which the outcomes of actions can be predicted.

Quietly, Dot-Coms Rewrite Rules on Office Romance: As Work Becomes Life, Barriers Fall

Not content with redefining other aspects of workplace culture, dot-com companies, often populated by the young and dedicated, are throwing out corporate rules that discouraged dating and fraternization among employees. But they are finding that writing the new conduct codes, which often allow relationships between a boss and an employee, is not so easy.

People have always found romance on the job. . . . Among the dot-com set, workplace dating is almost de riguer. . . .

At Excite@home, . . . "You really get to know people and you're working toward the same goal and it fosters romance. People work 10 hours a day in some cases. Your work becomes your life."

SOURCE: Abby Ellin, "Quietly, Dot-Coms Rewrite Rules on Office Romance," *New York Times*, December 26, 1999, p. 8. © 1999 The New York Times Company.

Normally, a work situation that is simple, is equally familiar to both workers, is low in human factors, demands little interaction, and has high certainty of outcomes calls for a *minimal task relationship*. In contrast, a work situation that is complex, calls for different knowledge from each person, is high in human factors, demands a great deal of interaction, and has a high degree of uncertainty with respect to outcomes calls for a much broader type of interpersonal relationship, something closer to a *colleagueship*. Obviously, there is a range of situations between the two extremes and therefore a range of relationships that might fit the different situations.

A Range of Required Work Relationships[1]

In the *minimal task relationship,* each person's behavior and the exchange of information are determined by the specific demands of the task and its accompanying roles. Although minimal task may characterize a great many required work relationships, in an age of complex technology we find that most work relationships demand interactions beyond just minimal task. For example, consider two workers on a paper-making machine; the feeder at one end needs to know how the paper is coming out at the other end so that appropriate adjustments can be made. Various hand signals or brief phone conversations (the machine is long and noisy) are exchanged to get the proper thickness and tensile strength of paper.

Perhaps one of the most familiar kinds of work relationships is the superior/subordinate relationship, which usually occurs when one person possesses greater knowledge, experience, or authority than the other. Consequently, some element of *control or influence* is being exerted over one person by the others. For example, one person may be training another (perhaps a newcomer) or supervising someone with less expertise.

With the element of control present, we often find some of the more difficult management problems, primarily because different people—like Endrunn and Buckley—have different needs for control or to be controlled. They may even disagree about how much relative expertise each has.

You can see that each element we have added beyond the simple minimal task level makes the relationship more complex, demands more frequent interactions among the parties, and increases the degree of task interdependence involved. As already indicated, the ultimate in a complex work relationship seems to be the *colleagueship,* in which two individuals collaborating on a complex task need to develop

FIGURE 9-1   *Summary of Connection between Job Requirements and Kinds of Task Relationships*

ideas freely as well as concern for each other's welfare. Ideas must bubble back and forth as a result, work goes on during some social occasions, and social talk sometimes occurs during work.

Some managers insist that one can never mix business with friendship; others take the opposite view that one cannot work successfully with another person unless close, friendly relations are maintained. As you might suspect, both points of view contain some grain of truth, but neither is valid for all situations. No one type of interpersonal relationship is appropriate to every work situation, even though the minimal task aspect of relationships will almost always be one component. Figure 9–1 summarizes the connection between job requirements and the type of task relationships that may be required.

Each aspect of work relationships leads to different outcomes. The result of a good *minimal task* relationship is competent performance, which is normally a principal objective of the organization. A poor relationship of this type leads to very visible output problems that demand direct attention. The outcome of an effective *controlling/influencing* relationship is *improved performance* on the part of the person being influenced and *satisfaction* on the part of the controller. An ineffective relationship in this area tends to result in less than adequate competence on the part of the worker (subordinate) and increasing dependency of that person on the controller (superior). With respect to *colleague relationships,* effectiveness leads to all the above outcomes, as well as to *solidarity,* which can serve as an important support base for both people. If the colleague relationship fails to develop well, the outcome often includes alienation, hostility, and ambivalence on the part of one or both persons (See Figure 9–2).

Background Factors

While job requirements are important determinants of interpersonal relationships, we cannot leave out the powerful influences of certain background factors, including the organization's culture, its technology, its reward system, the external status of the individuals in the relationship, and (perhaps most important of all) the personal systems of those individuals.

Organizational Culture

Just as the general climate and ways of doing things affect work group behavior, they also affect interpersonal relationships. Some organizations discourage anything more than distant impersonal relationships. People say or believe things like "familiarity breeds contempt," "let's keep personalities out of business," and so forth. Other organizations have cultures where closeness is encouraged, as reflected in attitudes like "I can't work with somebody I don't know," "we're like family here," "you can't treat people like machines," and so on.

FIGURE 9-2 *Work Relationship Outcomes*

Work Relationship Outcomes

Type of Relationship	Positive	Negative
Minimal Task	Competent performance	Output problems
Controlling/ Empowering	Improved performance controller satisfaction	Less than adequate performance and increasing dependence by person influenced
Colleague	All of above, solidarity	Alienation, hostility, or ambivalence

---

FIGURE 9-3 *Contrasting World Views—European American and Indian American*

European American	Indian American
Linear thinking	Circular thinking (no beginning or end)
Orchestrate-specialize	Collaborate—generalize (everyone is weaver, no specialists)
Leader-boss	Leader-father (nurturing, has less material)
Hierarchical	Egalitarian
Innovative	Adaptive
Change as progress	Change as adaptation
Majority decision	Consensus decision
Resolves cognitive dissonance by action	Tolerates cognitive dissonance—wait and see
Speak up	Keep quiet
Revealed religion	Religious ethnicity (born in)
Do own thing: but conform	Be unique: but community comes first
New situations: take bull by horns	New situations: hold back till sure
Power, control: based in possessions, material	Power, control: based in secrecy, initiation, age
Ethnocentricity: self-conscious, inclusive, "my way for all"	Ethnocentricity: take for granted, exclusive, "others can't do it my way"
Status: achieved	Status: ascribed
Dualities: good versus evil	Yin/yang: all parts of same thing
World: all one space	World: "we" space and "they" space

SOURCE: Adapted from Margorah Maynyama, "Epistemologies and Esthetic Principles," *Journal of the Steward Anthropological Society* 8, Spring 1977, pp. 155–67. In *Case Research Journal*, Spring 1993, p. 72.

The culture of a particular organization is often a reflection of the wider culture from which its members come. The general culture may emphasize not revealing feelings or weaknesses, keeping problems to oneself, avoiding crying when upset; or it might encourage openness and expressiveness, close relationships, and the like. Many national cultures, for example, emphasize relationships over tasks and discourage any kind of direct conversation that would make colleagues uncomfortable; a few, such as the United States, encourage more of a focus on getting work done. See, for example, Figure 9–3.

Think of the organizational culture that affects Mark Buckley and Oliver Endrunn. There appear to be little openness and trust, a rather distant style that makes efforts to get information informally appear to be spying. Buckley and Endrunn complain about each other, but not directly to one another.

Fighting for Fun and Profit at Motorola

Motorola makes a cult of dissent and open verbal combat. Each employee is entitled to file a "minority report" if he feels his ideas aren't being supported. The reports are read by bosses of the workers' bosses. Unlike at other firms that have such devices, retribution at Motorola is considered "un-macho" or craven. Engineers say they are encouraged to dispute their superiors and one another vigorously at open meetings.

The ferocity of conflict can be shocking, especially to newcomers. "It gets wild," says Mr. Fisher, 52, a PhD in applied mathematics who came to Motorola from AT&T's Bell Labs in 1976. "I was amazed when I came here. The discussions get violent—verbally, fortunately."

Two legendary protagonists are John Mitchell, Motorola's vice chairman, and Ed Staiano, the respected head of the company's cellular operations. In one case, Mr. Mitchell taunted Mr. Staiano for allegedly failing to meet the business goal of Motorola's cellular phone segment. Enraged, Mr. Staiano defended his performance, screaming obscenities at his superior. Some of these scenes have been played out before a bemused board of directors. Mr. Staiano admits to some "embarrassingly conflictive dialogues" but says that "good

ideas end up surviving." Messrs. Mitchell and Staiano manage to remain friendly after the fireworks.

Mr. Fisher says he himself was "uncomfortable" with such conflict as a younger manager, but now he is convinced that "out of conflict comes catharsis."

Gems in the Junk Pile

More specifically, the cult of conflict quickly identifies and fixes mistakes, unmasks and kills weak or illogical efforts, keeps top managers fully informed, and sometimes unearths enormous opportunities. . . .

Sometimes, however, the infighting leads to missed opportunities, because one better-entrenched team can overwhelm a newcomer. . . .

There is some question as to how much Motorola can be emulated. It has a totally nonunion work force and a macho culture uniquely suitable to its professional class of highly trained engineers.

SOURCE: G. Christian Hill and Ken Yamada, "Staying Power: Motorola Illustrates How an Aged Giant Can Remain Vibrant." Reprinted by permission of *The Wall Street Journal*, © December 9, 1992. Dow Jones & Company, Inc. All Rights Reserved Worldwide.

The more open the usual interpersonal style in the organization, the greater the likelihood of any two members being open when interacting; the greater the general politicking, competitiveness, aggressiveness, and hostility in an organization, the greater the likelihood of any two members being cautious with one another; and the more sociable and personal the climate, the greater the likelihood of two persons sharing nonwork information and feelings along with the minimum necessary task exchanges.[2] People take their cues from what is going on around them and usually respond, at least in part, to what they perceive are general expectations.

It is not just in Rome that people "do as the Romans do." For example, in one big-city hospital, backstabbing, yelling, and dramatic power plays were the general rule. Individual executives who were warm, charming, and considerate outside of the hospital would regularly interact with knives flashing when at work. "That's what I have to do in that crazy place to survive," they'd say, and then go after fellow executives in ways they would never think of doing elsewhere. Thus, the organization's overall culture can have a powerful influence on relationships (both required and emergent) as they occur within its environment.

Technology and Layout

The primary interpersonal effect of technology and layout comes from the way in which machine or desk placement, work sequence, and physical barriers create the *need* and *opportunity to interact*. A fundamental proposition of this book is that greater interaction tends to greater liking, and this is true for pairs of people just as it is for groups. People who, for whatever quirk of layout, share a confined space, or have to

Business Travelers Would Prefer to Fly Quietly, and Away from the Boss

Given the choice, most business travelers would rather sit next to a co-worker than the boss on flights–as long as their colleagues do not talk too much.

Of business travelers expressing a preference, 58 percent said they would not mind sitting next to the boss, but 87 percent preferred a fellow employee as a seatmate, according to the survey commissioned by United Airlines' Shuttle by United.

Fifty-four percent of travelers between the ages of 18 and 29 strongly favored a seat far from the boss, while 64 percent of those age 30 to 49 preferred a seat near the boss. On a gender basis, 65 percent of women favored a seat near the boss versus 56 percent of men.

The survey showed that 54 percent of business travelers prefer a quiet seatmate, while just 31 percent like a chatty seatmate. But 59 percent of East Coast travelers preferred a silent seatmate versus 47 percent for West Coast travelers.

SOURCE: Reuters Limited, January 29, 1998.

talk to one another to coordinate something, or even find themselves consistently waiting in line next to one another to pick up materials, are likely to begin talking. Once talking, they tend to speak of more than task issues and from there start a positive relationship.

If, however, the technology or layout consistently forces one person to be dependent on the other, greater potential for trouble exists. Dependence often leads to dominance in one and resentment in the other. Forced interaction thus can lead to negative feelings.

On the other hand, it will be difficult for any relationship to form between people who are physically separated, have no need to interact, are given their breaks at different times, and can barely hear one another because of noisy equipment. Buckley and Endrunn, for example, are in different cities and have no opportunity to bump into one another without special effort. Their only required interaction is quarterly to discuss financial results, or when there is a crisis. Occasionally, however, when individuals share a particularly unpleasant job in unpleasant surroundings, they band together to commiserate, and positive feelings result.

In these ways, technology and layout can affect the emergence of positive and negative relationships, even *require* a minimal task relationship, or prevent a relationship from developing at all.

Reward System

Reward systems can affect relationships by two mechanisms: (1) emphasis on individual competitiveness versus emphasis on collaborative effort and (2) public versus private payoffs. Reward systems that pay (in any currency, including money, recognition, or promotion) only for individual effort do not encourage positive relationships between potential competitors, especially where the system allocates a relatively fixed amount of reward. Since it would be hard to be friends with someone whom you have just beaten out of a larger share of the pie, individuals in such situations tend to keep their distance from one another. Mark Buckley is probably judged by Oliver Endrunn on overall results and in competition with the heads of the other businesses Oliver is responsible for. Mark and Oliver probably have some joint goals, however, because Oliver's overall results depend partly on how well Mark does in his business. Thus, some reward systems encourage working together toward common goals and induce relatively positive mutual feelings as long as the other is trying hard and carrying his or her load.

The effect of public knowledge on individual rewards is harder to assess. Where everyone's salary is different and known, potentials for mutual jealousy abound. On the other hand, guessing at how others are doing may also lead to suspicions and jealousy, although some people might prefer not having to think about differences. In general, rewards openly given, except when they are group rewards, probably decrease potential intimacy between individuals and reinforce some distance, even if a polite distance.

External Status

When any two people have to work together, they are likely to be influenced by the external status of each other. If from different parts of the same organization, the person with the higher organizational position is likely to expect to take the initiative, be deferred to, speak for the pair when talking to others about their work, and have the last word. If their external status is roughly equal, each will probably expect both of them to act more like colleagues—speaking frankly, able to argue and interrupt one another, sharing responsibility and visibility if there is any, alternating the lead in a spontaneous way, and not trying to score points at the other's expense.

One of the problems between Buckley and Endrunn is that their external status is not settled. Endrunn is "higher," but Buckley is president of a whole company. They don't agree about who should be deferred to.

The same rough expectations are likely to hold for two people from different organizations. If a person of lower back-home rank does not "properly defer" to one of a higher back-home rank, the lower-status person is likely to be seen as "uppity and pushy." Between roughly equal-rank people, if one starts to dominate, that person will be seen as "too big for his or her britches" or as "putting on airs." And in turn, higher-status people who are especially open and friendly may be seen as gracious but run the risk of coming across as weak. In short, when analyzing two-person relationships, external status should be examined for its effect on attitudes and, in turn, on the relationships.

Of course, all of the background factors discussed are only general pressures or influences on relationships. Any one individual with a unique personal system may override these background tendencies.

Personal Systems

We have already devoted considerable attention to the importance of personal systems as background factors in group behavior. In Chapter 8 we discussed in detail the various components of a personal system, in particular the self-concept. In the present chapter *the respective personal systems of two people are viewed as major determinants of their emergent relationship,* particularly in the context of the required system. This "fit" between their respective goals, competencies, beliefs, values, and self-concepts is an important basis for explaining the quality of interactions between any two individuals.

It should not be surprising that, when given the opportunity, people tend to build relationships with those who have similar values, beliefs, abilities, and goals. Birds of a feather do flock together; the chances of speaking "the same language" make communication easier and more comfortable. In some circumstances, however, opposites attract. This is especially true when the opposite qualities are complementary to one another—when one person's skills fill vital gaps in the other's repertoire of skills, or when the values of one are attractive because they somehow suggest a way past the other's flat sides.

Consequences

The most desirable kind of relationship permits the exercise of choices, generates feelings of competence, and produces confirmation of cherished values. Anyone would prefer relationships that reinforce all aspects of the self, although each aspect

The Odd Couple in the Citicorp–Travelers Merger?

These two men, who elected to rope themselves together in an attempt to scale a merger of Alpine proportions, are the most unlikely of soulmates.

Mr. Weill, a self-made billionaire, is the Brooklyn-born son of immigrants from Poland. He began his career as a shy Wall Street messenger, and after decades of voracious deal-making emerged as the portly and jocular head of Travelers and a fixture in rarefied Manhattan social circles.

Mr. Reed, who was raised in Argentina and Brazil, is by training a cerebral and methodical engineer who spent his entire career at Citicorp, ascending to chief executive in 1984. By nature as reserved as Mr. Weill is effusive, Mr. Reed survived Citicorp's near-collapse several years ago in part because he is abundantly skilled in the sometimes vicious art of corporate politics.

Mr. Weill is a homebody who has cultivated a coterie of loyal executives, while Mr. Reed is a globetrotter and, for the most part, has operated as a loner. Yet the two men seem to authentically enjoy each other's company. And they are clearly determined to make their merger a success; among the goals they have set together is a doubling of Citigroup's profits by the end of 2002, from $6.7 billion last year.

"John's incredibly intelligent, and he has decades of experience in this global marketplace that I do not, so I learn a lot from him," Mr. Weill said. "He doesn't take any of my space, and I don't think I take any of his. He has a real interesting thought process that he goes through to come to a decision. I'm maybe more intuitive, but 99 percent of the time we come to the exact same place."

Mr. Reed countered: "He always says 99 percent. I haven't hit the 1 percent yet. One of these days I'll have to find out where we differ."

In fact, Mr. Reed readily cites one clear difference: "He gets things done through a web of people relationships, which is very different than the sort of process orientation that I've had." In addition, Mr. Reed said, "He's an instinctive manager, and I probably hadn't fully appreciated that, so I've learned to listen to some of his instincts, which are pretty good."

SOURCE: Timothy L. O'Brien, "The Honeymooners Amid the Storm," *New York Times*, November 15, 1998, p. 1.

usually has a different priority. Goals are open to compromise; it is usually possible to accept alternative ways of doing things in a relationship, providing that they don't seriously threaten either the sense of competence or fundamental beliefs or values. Competencies are less open to compromise, but they are learnable—again provided that they are consistent with values. Values and beliefs normally are not negotiable; they go very deep and pertain to the integrity of the individual.

Mark Buckley and Oliver Endrunn see themselves as very different. Mark, trained as a lawyer, is quiet, cautious, and controlling. He values autonomy. Oliver is more outgoing and aggressive and wants to feel expert. He values being informed. Their roles force them to work together, but they probably wouldn't choose each other as friends.

In all probability, the most rewarding relationships in your life gave you self-confirmation, while the least rewarding ones had the opposite effect. In any current relationship in which you are experiencing problems, try diagnosing the levels at which the problems exist. Are they primarily goal conflicts? If so, the chances are fairly good that you can work them out. However, if they reflect more basic differences in beliefs or values, the problem is likely to be harder to settle. Resolution of conflict in any work relationship depends upon the level of the personal system the conflict taps into.

The required task relationship can be another source of difficulty. An individual having a limited concept of his or her abilities, for example, may find any relationship beyond minimal task somewhat threatening. Or someone who is used to seeing him- or herself exclusively in the role of "boss" may have problems with a colleague type of relationship, preferring to be the superior member of a controlling/influencing relationship. Therefore, it is important for you as a manager to pay attention to the kinds of working relationships you demand of your employees and how your requirements fit with their personal systems. While you cannot constantly redefine work relationships just to suit workers' preferences, some awareness of these contingencies may save you a great deal of aggravation in the long run.

Gender Differences: The Male–Female Relationship at Work

Gender and our expectations because of gender are another aspect of the personal system that shapes relationships. This factor is becoming increasingly important for relationships in the work setting.

In many societies females and males tend to have been brought up differently, steering toward different social roles and careers, and encouraged to develop different aspects of their personal systems. For example, with which gender do you associate each of the following roles: secretary, engineer, homemaker, manager, physician, elementary school teacher, community volunteer worker, and truck driver? Is one gender predominant in some roles? Similarly, with which gender would you associate each of the following personality traits: forceful/assertive, competitive, nurturant, unemotional, rational/logical, and intuitive? Whatever differences you see are partly the result of how you were socialized, and research has shown that this differential socialization starts at birth. Parents and adults treat baby boys and baby girls differently (dress, toys, gentleness in handling, emphasis on appearance, and the like). Consequently, while there is great variety among women and men—so that some women are more forceful than some men, and some men more intuitive than some women, and so on—many have been channeled toward different roles and personal traits.

This has meant that certain jobs and professions have been populated predominantly by men and others by women. It has also meant that women tended to take on the supportive roles in life, such as secretary or nurse, which meant that women were often in the less powerful positions in the work world. Even in elementary school teaching, where women predominate, the principals have typically been men. This also meant that individuals get criticized when not exhibiting expected attributes of that gender. Thus, women who are forceful and assertive may be criticized as being aggressive and unfeminine, and men who exhibit sensitivity and perceptiveness to the feelings of others may be seen as weak.

But this pattern has been changing as more women work and pursue careers, as members of both genders insist on a wider choice of lifestyles beyond that dictated by societal stereotypes, and as people have begun to value growth as a whole person capable of a wider range of personal traits than suggested by the gender stereotype. Women are moving into jobs as managers in what has been a male world; men are opting to be less workaholic; and many couples are dealing with the pressure of balancing dual careers and raising children. As a result of these changes, men need to learn to work with women as peers and bosses, while women need to learn to work with men as peers and subordinates. Both need to learn to work with the other as work colleagues, not just as dates, lovers, neighbors, and spouses of business acquaintances. In other words, everyone can deal with others more as unique individual human being and less as gender role stereotypes.

Specifically, this means that many men must learn to be comfortable and nondefensive in dealing with women who are assertive, who are no more supportive than male colleagues, and who respond as equals. Men may also need to learn how to bargain and even "fight" with women, as well as to take orders from a woman. Above all, many men must learn to treat women as fellow professionals regardless of their sexual attractiveness, and to give up behaviors that many women find demeaning (e.g., being called "honey") or sexually harassing (comments with sexual innuendo, overly familiar touching, and the like). Similarly, women must learn to

Deportment Gap: In Today's Workplace, Women Feel Freer to Be, Well, Women

Floppy Bow Ties Give Way to More-Alluring Attire; Sex Banter Has Its Place; Flirting—or Good Business?

One young woman thinks of it as the Attractiveness Card. An older gentleman calls it the Cheerleader Promise. Either way, it's responsible for a fair amount of the electricity—and confusion—in the office air these days.

A whole lot has changed in the workplace in a very short time. When an earlier generation of women marched to work 25 or 30 years ago, they found their best strategy lay in pretending their home lives didn't exist and in covering up their sexuality. Remember those awful suits and silly bow ties?

Their daughters are joining a very different work world. There are plenty of talented, able women around. Young people work around the clock and have little interest in erecting barriers between their social and work lives. Women are far more relaxed. They are wearing tank tops to interviews and Capri pants around the office. They are also less inhibited about using the personal tools at their disposal to get ahead professionally.

This, of course, is something competent businessmen have always done. For example, attractive and athletic men have long drawn on their business skills, but also on their charm and golf game to help them get to the top. The difference now is that young women feel more comfortable doing the same thing. And their style has a decidedly female bent to it.

Sometimes it is unabashed flirting. Other times it is teasing, bantering, a direct look in the eye. Just like the men, these women are confident about their business skills and not shy about showing it. Just as men feel no need to mask their masculinity, women are letting their femininity show.

The shift is noteworthy in an era in which women such as Carly Fiorina, chief executive officer of Hewlett-Packard Co., and Jill Barad, who resigned last week as CEO of Mattel Inc., are making it to the top of their companies. The number of women between the ages of 25 and 34 in managerial and professional jobs has increased 14.6% to five million in the last five years, according to figures compiled by the Bureau of Labor Statistics. Everywhere, it seems, young women are climbing off that bottom career rung and working alongside guys 20 and 30 years their seniors.

SOURCE: Ellen Joan Pollock, "Deportment Gap," *The Wall Street Journal*, February 7, 2000, p. A1. (Copyright © 2000, Dow Jones & Company, Inc.)

utilize and exert power, develop personal support systems, and deal with men (who have a lot yet to learn about dealing with women as professionals) in ways that are firm and educational yet don't create resentment unnecessarily. Both are likely to need to develop their own personal systems toward being comfortable and competent in a wider range of behaviors.

Finally, more often today women and men must find ways to build marriage relationships as dual-career couples, where sharing housework, balancing career demands, and mutual supportiveness, along with careful time management, are essential.

Some men and women will find adaptation to a multigender work world more difficult than others; some may choose to move into careers where more of the older patterns apply; but all can benefit from being aware of the changes that are occurring in our society, and all must consider the implications for work relationships, applying the concepts of the next chapter to build and maintain good work relationships with both genders. The same requirements apply to dealing with any colleagues who are different in fundamental ways.

Other Differences: Demographic Diversity

When you are in college, you usually are dealing with people of similar age and even of similar socioeconomic backgrounds. Most older people with whom you will be in contact are likely to be instructors and administrators, rather than peers (fellow students). This is not likely to be true in the work world where diversity is common and dramatically increasing. As employees and as managers, relationships must be built with a wide variety of people of diverse backgrounds: age, race, religion, socioeconomic class, education, and occupational orientation. You will need to continue to develop your ability to relate to many different individuals.

Interpersonal Styles

Yet another aspect of personal systems that shapes relationships is *interpersonal style*, the general way in which each person tends to interact with others.

> I've been working for Mr. Whiting for more than five years, and he still is stiff and formal with me. It takes getting used to—I think I'm getting there, but I confess that I wish he'd loosen up once in awhile. I've never seen him express any anger, at least not openly. I can usually tell when he is mad about something. He doesn't show much joy either, though I really believe he likes his job. And I think he likes and respects me—I hope so, anyway. Sometimes, when we're working on a report together, he really gets into exploring ideas. But that's the most I get. As for me, I prefer to get in there and mix it up with someone. I think I pick my own people so I can do more of that. It's not as quiet in my area as it is in Mr. W's office, but you know you're doing something.

This manager eventually changed jobs, and he attributed that decision to his frustration in dealing with his boss. He liked and respected the man, but he could not interact with him satisfactorily. It is important for managers in their various interpersonal roles to be aware of *how* they interact with others and the effects of their style on others' performance.

Some Styles of Interaction

Almost no one behaves in exactly the same way in every situation; some settings and people call forth different behavior than do others. Only a very brave or disturbed person would treat his boss, mother, and lover with the same kinds and styles of interactions. But almost everyone does have a preferred or dominant interaction style of some sort, one that fits his or her self-concept, and with which he or she feels most comfortable. When given the opportunity, that style will be used for interaction with other organizational members. For example, a female school principal saw herself as ambitious, confident, extremely capable, and honest. When at school board or other community meetings, she related to others in an open, challenging way. She did this even when others were more cautious and guarded in their styles and responded to her with fear.

While it is difficult to describe interaction styles, we will use a few general categories to make discussion manageable.[3] As you consider each of the styles, try to picture yourself in various settings that pull that particular way of interacting from you. Some people are very different at home, at work, with friends, on a date, and so forth. Others show only slight variations from their "usual" style. See where you fit in.

One style involves *conventional-polite* forms of exchange, those that are governed mainly by social convention and what is normally considered "acceptable and polite" behavior. When any two people meet for the first time, they are likely to start in this style; some people, however, prefer to keep as many relationships as possible that way. Their conversation tends to remain at an impersonal and cordial level and its content stays within the bounds of what is easiest to talk about.

A second style of interaction is *speculative-tentative*. The person who prefers this kind of interaction examines, questions, and evaluates everything and everyone in a careful manner, usually with the intent of trying to learn and understand. Conclusions tend to be tentative and open to modification, with fixed positions seldom taken. What is discussed this way may be anything from the task at hand to the rela-

Corporate Therapy: The Latest Addition to Executive Suite Is Psychologist's Couch

Personality Clashes Prompt Companies to Seek Help of Shrinks Like Dr. Smart; Meeting of Managers' Minds

When two General Electric Co. officials clashed over management styles, GE brought in [a] psychologist to reconcile them. At Ameritech Corp., he is helping an executive soften a personality that has alienated subordinates and peers.

Increasingly, companies say that in today's fast-changing markets and intensified competition, person- ality clashes or leadership flaws at the top can be costly. At DSC Logistics Inc., for instance, clashes between two senior executives three years ago were so heated that even their secretaries skirmished. The impact was so pervasive that managers "failed to meet business goals at a time the company was trying to expand."

SOURCE: Amal Kumar Naj, "Corporate Therapy," *The Wall Street Journal,* August 29, 1994, p. Al.

tionship itself. The main quality of the interaction process generated by this style is an open flow of exchanges that are seldom emotionally loaded or threatening. This style has some of the low-key quality of the conventional-polite type of interaction. It is what might be expected in a discussion about future careers—for example, where exploration of a great deal of data, thoughtfulness, generation of alternatives, and their consequences are all appropriate.

A third style of interaction is *aggressive-argumentative*. This occurs when a person vigorously takes fixed positions on issues and pushes his or her own arguments. The person's feelings tend to be strong, while listening tends to be poor. This style often results in dominance. Interactions with such a person can be stimulating or frustrating, depending on your preferences; either way, the interactions are seldom dull and require high-energy responses.

A fourth style of interaction is *expressive-confrontive*, in which thoughts and feelings about situations and people are expressed openly and directly. People who relate in this way often develop very close working relationships and intimate friendships. The range of feelings expressed is very wide and varies from anger to tenderness—whatever is actually being felt. People who find expressive-confronting interactions personally rewarding vary considerably as to how often and with whom they consider such interactions desirable, but they usually try to get there in a relationship as rapidly as possible.

These four categories do not exhaust the possible ways of viewing interaction styles, but they can be useful in understanding some of the sources of friction in two-person relationships.

Apart from what is called for by the job itself, people who prefer one style may fit compatibly with some styles but generate friction when with others. For example, the person who naturally prefers conventional-polite forms of interactions will probably be made exceedingly uncomfortable by the person who loves an expressive-confronting style, but may feel quite at ease with a speculative-tentative person. The confident female principal, for example, often intimidated teachers who preferred that interaction with women remain "proper" and "polite." Buckley and Endrunn were a bad combination of conventional-polite and aggressive-argumentative. They clashed, but not openly.

Keep in mind that you interact with many other individuals whose styles may be similar to or different from your own preferred style, and therefore your sense of interpersonal competence can be very strongly affected by the *range* of interaction styles of which you are capable. It could be useful for you to assess your competence in this area by looking at your ability to deal with a variety of people and situations that require you to interact in different ways, sometimes not in the manner you prefer.

While almost anyone will respond partly to the situation (as when two strangers meet and both use a conventional-polite style), when there is *ambiguity* in the situation, people see and define it largely from their own respective frames of references. Thus, to a proper New Englander, the fifth year of knowing someone may be too early for open warmth and expressiveness, while to a Southern Californian, five minutes of polite but friendly conversation may be seen as enough to begin some self-revelation.

Similarly, the same desires and feelings may be expressed quite differently, depending on the preferred styles of those involved. Two "expressives" might show genuine liking by grand and sweeping statements, strong pledges of caring, and lots of hugging or back-slapping, while two "conventionals" might never use the actual words "I like you" but show it through thoughtful gestures like remembering to send a birthday card, inquiring after a sick relative, and so forth.

Nevertheless, much behavior is affected by the situation and its requirements, as well as by the desires or preferences of those in it. To better understand what interpersonal behavior is appropriate under which work conditions, we turn now to task requirements and their effect on relationships.

When Interaction Styles Meet Job Requirements

What happens when you take a job in which you are required to interact with others in a manner that does not match your preference? How can you know in advance whether or not the job requirements are likely to fit your style? From a manager's point of view, is there a way to match interaction styles with required work relationships?

We cannot offer any specific guidelines without risking an arbitrary classification of people. There are no pure types; most people show a blend and a variation of styles that fit different situations. However, as in the example of Mr. Whiting discussed earlier, some people's preferences or comfort zones are narrower than others. Therefore, the thing to keep in mind, as you look at your own interpersonal competence and its development, is the issue of *range* of styles. When you want to, can you adjust your style to fit task requirements and the desires and styles of others?

In general, The more complex a required work relationship tends to be, the wider the range of interaction styles needed by the individuals in that relationship.[4]

This is critical for many managers who aspire to higher positions in an organization. So often a person trained to do a specific kind of work (e.g., accounting) that may require little interaction with others beyond a minimal task level is promoted to a managerial position, only to be confronted with his or her limited range of interaction styles. A high-pressured negotiating session, for example, may require aggressive-argumentative behavior, and the person simply cannot do it. He or she may attempt to handle things in the accustomed polite or speculative manner more characteristic of "the old job."

Of course, the opposite extreme is also possible. Have you known people who seem to be expressive and confronting no matter what the circumstances? It's as though they have an overdeveloped need to *relate!* Even the most routine impersonal tasks are converted into rituals of personal intimacy.

It should be obvious that no one style of interaction is suitable for all work relationships. Having a wide repertoire of styles can help you to adapt effectively to the demands of a complex work environment. However, even with a wide repertoire, you are likely to prefer to relate to others in certain ways more than in other ways. Note this experience of a young man working for a summer as a plumber's helper:

> I was assigned to an older, very experienced man who was used to working alone. The boss assigned the man to teach me whatever skills were needed on the job. I

MANAGERIAL BULLETIN

Coke CEO Douglas Ivester Falls Flat, Resigns

Tone-deaf. What went wrong? In hindsight, Ivester's go-for-the-jugular style and knowledge of the numbers made him the perfect second banana to [former CEO] Goizueta, a master strategist. But as CEO, Ivester proved incapable of managing Coke's most treasured asset: its image. An accountant by training, Ivester knew the math, but not the music, required to run the world's leading marketing organization. . . .

Ivester was viewed by staff as a tough, unapproachable taskmaster. . . . "Ivester understands it's important to build relationships, but [to him] it's just an intellectual exercise."

SOURCE: "Is Douglas Ivester the Real Thing?" *Business Week,* December 20, 1999.

was eager to learn; he did not know how to teach or help me and preferred not to try. I tried to be friends with the man; he felt that friendships had no place in a work setting. At times when I thought he had overlooked something on the job, I pointed this out. It only made him angry; he thought I was questioning his ability to do the job. I finally settled for doing simple jobs that I could figure out for myself. I initiated very little conversation with him, except at lunch or over coffee when it was "all right." He was satisfied; I was not.

The relationship illustrates an incompatibility between the job requirements and the preferred interaction styles of the two people involved. We can also see how different levels of the self-concept were affected. The rejection of friendship or colleagueship at work by the older man was a matter of beliefs or values and probably was unchangeable. The assistant's desire for colleagueship was probably less a matter of values than a goal; thus, he was able to adapt. The plumber's lack of competence to teach and be helpful was a matter that could not have made him feel good about himself. Similarly, the assistant must have felt inadequate, wanting to be shown what to do so that he could gradually undertake more interesting assignments and not be totally dependent.

The issue of respective goals was something for the two individuals to negotiate. It is possible that if the older man had had the competence to teach the assistant, then he might have been more open to the latter's observations and "trouble shooting." While the younger man was not specifically assigned to that role, it was one that might have been both helpful and desirable in the relationship, though not strictly necessary.

In summary, we can offer the following propositions:

1. To the extent that a required work relationship is compatible with the preferred interaction styles of both persons assigned to it, the relationship will be accepted.

2. To the extent that a required work relationship is incompatible with the preferred interaction styles of either or both persons assigned to it, the relationship will be resisted; the degree of resistance will depend on the level of the personal system or self-concept affected in either or both individuals.

In either event, the actual relationship that emerges is likely to vary from that required, either elaborating on it toward the colleagueship or pulling back toward a less involving type.

In Chapter 10 we examine what actually happens in a relationship once the two people begin to interact. Before proceeding, however, we suggest that you examine Figure 9–4 as a way of reviewing what we have covered so far. The left-hand side of

FIGURE 9–4   *Job Requirements and Background Factors' Effects on Interpersonal Relationships*

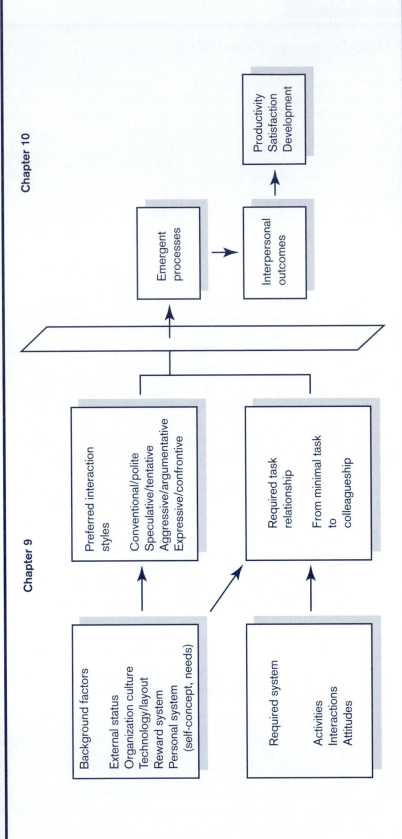

the figure is filled in with the concepts of Chapter 9; the right-hand side will be completed in Chapter 10.

KEY CONCEPTS FROM CHAPTER 9

1. An organization is a network of interpersonal relationships.
2. Social system schema applied to interpersonal relations.
    a. Required system.
        (1) Ways in which two people are required to work together.
        (2) How close or distant they need to be to carry out the task.
        (3) Nature of task.
            (i) Simple or complex.
            (ii) Differential expertise.
            (iii) Human factors involved.
            (iv) Frequency of required interactions.
            (v) Degree of certainty in outcomes.
        (4) Range of required work relationships.
            (i) Minimal task to colleagueship.
            (ii) Control in relationship.
    b. Background factors.
        (1) Organizational culture.
            (i) Supportive, open climate fosters close, trusting relationships; climate of suspicion fosters distance and mistrust.
        (2) Technology and layout.
            (i) Opportunities versus barriers to interaction.
        (3) Reward system.
            (i) Importance of rewards for collaboration versus rewards for competition.
        (4) External status.
            (i) Differential status creates barriers to colleagueship.
        (5) Personal systems.
            (i) Compatibility versus incompatibility in goals, competencies, beliefs, and values.
            (ii) Gender differences: The male-female relationship at work.
            (iii) Role of interpersonal styles:
                Conventional-polite.
                Speculative-tentative.
                Aggressive-argumentative.
                Expressive-confrontive.
            (iv) The more complex a required work relationship, the wider the range of interpersonal styles needed.
            (v) Importance of compatibilities among required work relationship and the preferred interaction styles of both parties.

PERSONAL APPLICATION EXERCISE

Understanding the Best and Worst of Your Relationships

If you could do the following for an actual work relationship, it would be ideal, but if you have to apply it in a nonwork relationship, it will still be useful.

Consider the relationship you have with someone you like and with whom you work well. Make a list of the similarities and differences between you, including backgrounds, values, beliefs, competencies, goals, and interpersonal styles. As you list these, note whether the similarities are what draw you to the other person, whether the differences are sources of conflict or sources of attraction, and in general, how your interaction styles fit.

Repeat the process with reference to someone with whom you do not get along. Contrast the two relationships and try to diagnose the basic reasons why one works and the other doesn't. Finally, see if you can identify some ways you might change the negative relationship into a more positive one.

SUGGESTED READINGS

Athos, A, and J. Gabarro. *Interpersonal Behavior.* Englewood Cliffs, NJ: Prentice-Hall, 1978.

Bowers, D. G. "What Would Make 11,500 People Quit Their Jobs?" *Organizational Dynamics,* Winter 1983, pp. 5–19.

Cowill, N. L. *The New Partnership: Women & Men in Organizations.* Palo Alto, CA: Mayfield, 1982.

Crary, M. "Managing Attraction and Intimacy at Work." *Organizational Dynamics,* Spring 1987, pp. 26–41.

Fisher, R., and W. Ury. *Getting to Yes.* New York: Penguin Books, 1983.

Goffman, E. *The Presentation of Self in Everyday Life.* New York: Doubleday, 1959.

Hill, W. F. *Hill Interaction Matrix.* Los Angeles: Youth Study Center, University of Southern California, 1965.

Hocker, J. L., and W. W. Wilmot. *Interpersonal Conflict.* 2nd ed. Dubuque, IA: Wm. C. Brown, 1985.

Homans, G. *The Human Group.* New York: Harcourt Brace Jovanovich, 1950.

————. *Social Behavior: Its Elementary Forms.* New York: Harcourt Brace Jovanovich, 1961.

Johnson, P. B. "Women and Interpersonal Power." In *Women and Sex Roles,* ed. I. H. Frieze, J. E. Parsons,

P. B. Johnson, D. N. Ruble, and G. L. Zelman. New York: W. W. Norton, 1978.

Leader, G. C. "Interpersonally Skillful Bank Officers View Their Behavior." *Journal of Applied Behavioral Science* 9 (1973), pp. 484–97.

Levinson, H. "The Abrasive Personality." *Harvard Business Review,* May–June 1978, pp. 86–94.

Miramontes, D. J. *How to Deal with Sexual Harassment.* San Diego: Network Communications, 1984.

Quinn, R. E., and P. L. Les. "Attraction and Harassment: Dynamics of Sexual Politics in the Workplace." *Organizational Dynamics* 12 (1984), pp. 35–46.

Schutz, W. C. *FIRO: A Three-Dimensional Theory of Interpersonal Behavior.* New York: Holt, Rinehart & Winston, 1958.

————. "Interpersonal Underworld." *Harvard Business Review* 36 (1958), pp. 123–35.

Steckler, N. A., and R. Rosenthal. "Sex Differences in Nonverbal and Verbal Communication with Bosses, Peers, and Subordinates." *Journal of Applied Psychology* 70 (1985), pp. 157–63.

Improving the Two-Person Work Relationship

Processes and Outcomes

Racing Onto the Web, One Manager's Secret Is Simple: Listening

Lisa Simpson is a hard-driving Harvard M.B.A. who puts in 14-hour work days and is known as a tough negotiator. Her management style has never been very touchy-feely. But as president of Sony's Online Entertainment unit, she has had to find ways of dealing with some of her staff's sensitive personal issues: an increasingly blurred line between work and home, a warp-speed work schedule, and a frenetic job market that has her employees in high demand. . . . one of her most valuable skills is a rather touchy-feely one that's often ignored . . . She knows how to listen.

SOURCE: Carol Hymowitz, "In the Lead," *The Wall Street Journal,* February 8, 2000, p. B1. © 2000, Dow Jones & Company, Inc.

"A positive relationship leads to good outcomes for both task accomplishment and member satisfaction."

In Chapter 9 we looked at the background and required factors that affect interpersonal relationships. Now we turn to an examination of what emerges from the interplay of these factors. Any two individuals are likely to have appreciable latitude to establish a type of relationship that is to their liking and to adopt an interpersonal style that fits their preferences. Nevertheless, much can happen in a relationship that can lead to misunderstanding, disagreement, and friction. Mark Buckley and Oliver Endrunn, whom you met in Chapter 9, are intelligent, high-level executives who have to work together, yet they irritate each other. Thus, what emerges takes "working at," both to develop it in a positive direction and to maintain it once it has been developed.

In discussing steps individuals can take to build and maintain positive relationships, we need to look at several *interpersonal processes* that are crucial for any relationship, namely:

- Adaptation to what is required and to one another.
- Communication.
- Reciprocity.
- Trust and other feelings.
- Dealing with blind spots (need for feedback).

We discuss each of these processes in some detail and indicate steps the individuals can take to foster a positive relationship. A positive work relationship is, first, one in which the required task gets done properly and with reasonable efficiency. Second, the relationship must at the same time be reasonably satisfying to both parties and foster, or at least not hinder, individual growth and development. What constitutes satisfaction will depend on what is desired and also on what is expected in that situation. For example, you may be quite satisfied by a polite but distant relationship if it were with the elevator operator in your building, but quite dissatisfied if it were with your direct supervisor. Satisfaction will also depend on the relationship enhancing, or at least not disconfirming, each member's self-concept. Finally, any continuing relationship will need ways to deal with the frictions that almost inevitably arise. A positive relationship leads to outcomes good for both task accomplishment and member satisfaction on an ongoing basis.

Adaptation to Requirements and to Each Other

When individuals first enter into a work relationship, there may be some discrepancy between what is required and what is expected or desired by one or both individuals. For example, Buckley wants autonomy and control, while Endrunn wants information and reassurance. To the extent that each party can diagnose the situation accurately and adapt to what is required and to what the other expects and desires, relationships will develop in a positive direction. In some cases, this may mean that one party must make all of the adaptation, as in the case of the plumber's helper discussed in Chapter 9. In most cases, both must adapt, such as when two engineers of equal experience are working on a joint design project. To blindly ignore the issue or refuse to adapt is to ensure the emergence of a less than positive relationship. To adapt within the range of what is at least tolerable is the way to move in a positive direction. If, however, the degree of adaptation is so great as to violate either person's self-concept, then the participants will need to openly confront the issue and find a resolution or else try to leave the situation. Finally, throughout the life of a relationship, there may be times when either individual will need to adapt his or her interpersonal style to fit a particular event. Thus, adaptation is usually required early in a relationship, to build in a positive direction, and also to a lesser degree throughout its existence.

One factor that can make it difficult for individuals to adapt to one another is differences in how each structures the world around them. Consider the possible difficulties individuals at different places on the four dimensions of the Myers-Briggs model discussed in Chapter 8 might have:

Introversion–Extroversion

An individual at the extroversion end of the scale, who might instinctively make it a point to touch base with many others before acting, might be seen by someone at the introversion end of the scale as indecisive, overly political, or wasting time socializing. Conversely, the former might view the latter's tendency to go it alone and avoid opportunities to interact with others as a sign of aloofness and even snobbishness.

Sensing–Intuition

Similarly, the individual who always seeks facts before acting (sensing) may easily view someone who relies on intuitive insight as "impulsive" and as acting on mere whim without "doing proper homework." The latter, in turn, might view the former's care in getting all the facts before deciding as a case of worrying excessively about details or even as decision avoidance.

Thinking–Feeling

Thinkers are likely to see themselves as capable of making the hard decisions based on a logical analysis of a situation and see Feelers as tenderhearted, given to irrational judgments, and too easily swayed by emotions and compassion. By contrast, Feelers will see themselves as sensitive, considerate, and responsive to people's needs and see Thinkers as hardnosed, distant, and insensitive.

Judging–Perceiving

The differences here are especially interesting since they bear directly upon the problem-solving aspect of a manager's job. Perceivers see themselves as good at uncovering all the diverse implications of a problem, and they enjoy exploring these. They see Judgers as pushing too rapidly toward solutions and unwilling to spend the necessary amount of time really digging into a problem. The Judgers tend to get impatient with the Perceivers, seeing them as never able to arrive at a solution, always going off on tangents, or getting sidetracked. Judgers see themselves as decisive and capable of getting quickly to the heart of the matter and on with the business at hand.

Implications for Working Relationships

Awareness of the differences described above can be very helpful in understanding two-person work relationships. For one thing, the two people can learn to understand and even appreciate their differences. For another, it provides a way to look at *complementarity* in work relationships. Most situations call for a variety of managerial approaches, including the ability to use thoughts, feelings, intuition, judgment, and perceptions. Mutual adaptation can facilitate drawing on one another as sources of information.

Communication

In any relationship, people must communicate, which is always subject to distortion and misunderstanding. Even what may be a fairly simple and straightforward exchange of factual information in a minimal task relationship is subject to miscommunication. The likelihood of miscommunication becomes greater when the information being exchanged is more complex and emotionally charged. Misunderstanding can block the development of a relationship and create tension in an otherwise positive relationship. Unless the parties involved have the skill and the

FIGURE 10-1   *Four Levels of Exchange between Speaker and Listener*

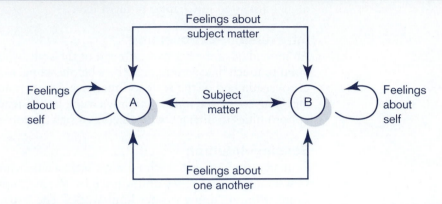

FIGURE 10-2   *Other's Statements Are Modified by Receiver's Self-Concept*

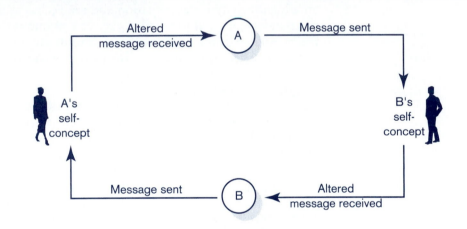

inclination to minimize miscommunication and to correct misunderstanding as it occurs, a positive relationship is not likely to develop or be maintained.

What happens when one person talks to another? The process is so complicated that it is a wonder that anyone ever understands and is understood. This section includes a description of the communication process and the factors that ease or hinder understanding.

Communication between people involves an exchange of (1) the content of what is being discussed, (2) feelings about the subject matter at hand, (3) feelings about the other person, and (4) feelings about self (see Figure 10–1).

The same exchange can be seen another way: what Speaker A says is modified by B's self-concept (which includes how B interprets A's self-concept). For example, A is B's boss. B has had many troubles in the past with people in authority–parents, teachers, bosses. He sees himself as having been misunderstood and unappreciated by them. A is in a hurry, doesn't know B's background, so calls over his shoulder on the way by, "Hey, lend a hand, will you?" B hears this as a criticism, reddens, and mutters to himself at the "attack" (see Figure 10–2).

FIGURE 10–3 *Self-Concepts and Perceptions of Other Filter Messages In and Out*

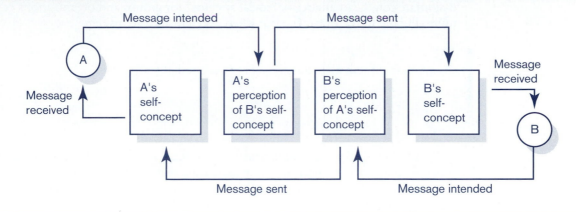

This gets even more complicated as the self-concept of each alters the way messages are sent as compared with the actual feelings of the speaker. That is, A is feeling angry at B's apparent uncooperativeness and wants to reprimand B; but A sees himself as a kind person, so he tries to soften the blow through indirection. Instead of saying what he feels—"You infuriate me when you sit there doodling while I work hard"— he says, "Isn't it amazing how some people just can't cooperate with others?" B—who sees himself as an intelligent person, eager to be helpful when he gets an original idea, but sees A as typically aggressive and impatient—feels puzzled about where A's remarks concerning cooperation come from, misses the feeling, and replies to the content, "Well, it depends on the people involved, but I don't think cooperation is so difficult." A starts to steam; B senses it but doesn't know why. The relationship begins to deteriorate (see Figure 10–3).

The potentials for difficulties are great. Let's take a closer look at the barriers to communication, above and beyond the perceptual ones already discussed in Chapter 7.

Barriers to Communication

Characteristics of Language
The very nature of language constitutes a barrier to communication. Many words are imprecise. The meaning of *level* to a carpenter is quite different than to a landscape contractor who is putting in a new lawn. How many is "a few"? Does *right away* mean drop the bucket with molten metal, or first pour it and then start the next job? In the sentence "Where do I begin?" is *where* a location or a procedure?

Many words have multiple meanings; miscommunication occurs when the two parties apply different interpretations. Does "There's a bug in my computer" require a software fix or a brush that can blow a gentle puff of air? *Write, right* (correct), *right* (not left), and *Wright* all sound the same, right? Sometimes words have different meanings to different subcultures of the country. Have you ever ordered a milk shake in Boston? To get ice cream in it as in other parts of the country, you must order a frappe. Once you taste it, do you say "That's wicked awesome" or "That's b-a-a-d" when you like it?

The fact that words are imprecise and have multiple meanings has become an ever greater threat to communication as society has become more interconnected and mobile. The possibility has increased of contact with someone of a different background or culture and hence a different way of using words. The fact that words are imprecise and have several meanings is also one reason why jargon develops. Jargon at its best is designed to avoid ambiguity, and when used for this purpose, it can be helpful. On the other hand, "P. req." for purchase requisition, "MI" for myocardial infarction (heart attack), or "social systems" for groups and organizations can be unintelligible to the outsider, even when efficient for the insider.

> I'm willing to discuss it; I just don't want to talk about it.
>
> Mr. Fairly Bear
> a Shari Lewis Puppet

Finally, words have an emotional coloring that influences the communication process because they trigger mental associations and emotional responses. Consider the following: "I want a large slab of slaughtered cow" versus "I would like the king-size cut of prime roast beef"; "let us be bombarded by the egghead's theories" versus "let us be informed by the expert conceptualizer." The words *slaughtered cow* conjure up many distasteful images that do not enhance people's appetites even though they may, in fact, be more precise than the term *prime roast beef.* Often the emotional color is communicated rather than the intended meaning.

Multiple Channels

Messages are transmitted by more than words; content and especially feelings are transmitted by gestures, voice intonations, facial expressions, body posture, and so forth. All these media (elements) for messages go into the same communications package. The package is clear when the messages sent are consistent with one another. This occurs when everything fits together; when the nonverbal enriches the verbal, when the "music" fits the words. When a facial expression or a gesture or a tone of voice doesn't seem to match the words, "static" is created. Have you seen someone get red in the face, pound the table, and declare, "What do you mean I'm angry?" The words and music don't go together; it's like a love song sung to a march tempo. Since nonverbal messages tend to be ambiguous in meaning, thereby leaving room for interpretation by the other person, misunderstanding is likely. An embarrassed smile can easily be seen as implying agreement when it really means, "I'm too embarrassed to say how ridiculous I think your idea is." Frowns of concentration may be seen as disapproval, and so forth. In Chapter 13 we discuss how communication across cultural boundaries can create serious misunderstandings.

The State of Mind of the Two People

When a person is feeling strong emotions (anger, fear, defensiveness, and so forth), it is very difficult to *listen* to another person. *Both* parties are subject to perceptual distortions. What usually happens is that A's emotion triggers emotions in B; then each has trouble listening to the other. For example, an aggressive-argumentative exchange often contains emotionally charged, defensive kinds of messages. Effective communication becomes blocked, the tensions increase, and the whole cycle escalates. It is likely that everyone has faced similar problems and could benefit from learning how to change the quality of a communication process when it is blocked, defensive, and nonsupportive of the participants.

When possible differences in mental set, emotional state, channels used, words chosen, and so forth are added together, it becomes apparent how difficult it would be for the message sent to be the same as the message received. How many times have you argued about what was "really" said in a conversation? Each person "*knows* what I said" and each "*knows* what I heard," even though both are sure the other is wrong. Some degree of distortion seems inevitable in communication.

Some Steps to Ensure Effective Speaking, Listening, Understanding

If you want to communicate effectively, try some or all of the following:

Choosing Your Words

1. Use words that are likely to have meaning and clarity to the other person (e.g., "speak in the language of the listener").
2. Anticipate different ways your message could be interpreted, try to speak unambiguously, be alert to evidence that what you meant isn't what it meant to the other.
3. Allow yourself to be spontaneous and open. Express your feelings. Speak your mind, but consider talking *about* what you are feeling, instead of emoting, if the other person is likely to be put on the defensive by your expressiveness or is basically uncomfortable when faced with strong emotion.

Listening to Nonverbal Messages

1. Pay attention to tone of voice, facial expressions, body posture, hesitations, etc. What do they communicate in addition to the message in the words? (Listen to the music as well as the words.)
2. Pay attention to your own manner. Does your tone, pace, etc., fit your words and reflect your inner feeling?
3. If you sense something is bothering the other person besides what is being said directly, consider raising that to the surface by some such statement as: "Is _____ also at work here?" "Are you also concerned about _____?" "Is there something else beneath the surface here?"

Timing and Situation

1. Don't raise "heavy" issues when the other person is preoccupied or there isn't time to deal with them properly.
2. Consider the setting when you raise a topic for discussion. Is it too public? Will it be distracting? Will it cause misinterpretation (e.g., be seen as really unimportant or said for public consumption only)?
3. Ignore small points you may differ with and focus on the main theme. Don't digress or argue over minor errors or points of disagreement.
4. Deal with issues and tensions early. Try to handle problems while they are still small.

Testing for Understanding

1. Invite the other person to restate what you've said in his/her own words and test whether you've been clear.
2. Restate what the other said in your own words and thereby test that you have fully understood.

Preserving the Relationship

1. Don't hog the air time—give the other person an opportunity to be heard.
2. Be careful you aren't so busy preparing your response that you don't really pay full attention.
3. Don't interrupt.
4. Acknowledge what is of worth in what someone is saying, even if you disagree with the basic message.
5. If the other person makes an especially good point, say so. Give positive feedback when you can do so sincerely.

Gender Differences

Larry and Susan are driving through an unfamiliar section of town on their way to a party. It becomes obvious to Susan, after they seem to have driven in circles, that they are lost. She says, "Larry, why don't you stop and ask someone for directions?" Larry keeps driving. Susan says, "Didn't you hear me?" Larry says, "Yes, I heard you," and keeps driving, obviously getting tense. Susan remains silent for awhile, her tension rising. The pattern repeats itself to the point where both are angry, Susan shuts up, and Larry tunes out. Sound familiar? It turns out that such a pattern is not unusual and reflects some differences in the way men and women tend to view and handle the same situation. Larry's need to prove that he doesn't need help and

Hands-On Approach Can Get Sticky

Sexual harassment cases have men walking on eggshells, feeling inhibited and resentful around women. Men complain that women are creating problems where they don't exist—and if there is a small problem, women blow it up out of proportion. But women don't deserve all the blame for the proliferation of sexual harassment accusations.

While conducting a seminar for an accounting group in San Diego last summer, I wanted to make a point about the appropriate and necessary use of touch in a business environment. I asked a member of the audience to stand and told the audience to imagine that I was a manager leaving for a six-month sabbatical and that the man standing was my temporary replacement. "While I'm gone, Joe here will be in charge," I said. "Any questions or problems, look to Joe."

I then reached out and firmly placed my hand on his shoulder and held it there. I wanted to show how to convey a sense of trust in an employee in front of other workers. The audience immediately saw the positive effect of the good way to touch. Talking, while simultaneously touching, showed I had passed the baton of authority to Joe.

I followed up with what I thought was an acceptable and humorous example of inappropriate office behavior. One of the men in the audience happened to be wearing Bermuda shorts. His legs were crossed and one knee was sticking out in the aisle. Saying, "Of course how and where you touch is very important," I touched the man's bare knee. As I walked away, I heard him say, "I'm a happily married man." I smiled in acknowledgement, assuming he was just making a follow-up remark to generate a little more audience laughter. I then went on to the next subject.

Two days later, I received an overnight express letter from the director of the accounting group. Attached to it was a letter of complaint from the man in the audience. He complained that he and his wife (who had not attended the seminar) felt sexually harassed and were calling for my resignation.

The letter started a chain of correspondence and phone calls from the accuser and his legal counsel. The director pleaded for my defense. Since there were 50-some witnesses (other audience members) who could speak about the situation, I was ultimately cleared of any wrongdoing. But the male accuser wouldn't leave it alone.

Because I was innocent, I refused to do anything more than write a note of apology assuring the man and his wife that I had no interest in him whatsoever. However, as the old saying goes, "The squeaky wheel gets the grease." Before it was over, I was fired from my seminar contract of seven years. The reason was documented as budget cuts, but the real cause was the "victim" of my harassment. . . .

Continued

won't make himself dependent on someone else conflicts with Susan's comfort in seeking help. The result of the differences is that they stop communicating, each ending up feeling isolated.

Since males and females are often treated differently from childhood, they tend to develop different perspectives and attitudes about life. These differences can distort communication and lead to misunderstandings. Men often talk about impersonal topics like sports or the economy, whereas women more readily discuss personal matters and their feelings. This can easily result in a tendency for members of the same sex to gravitate to each other and avoid attempting to hold conversations with the opposite sex. In a work setting, communication problems often occur because of this difference; men see themselves as objective and women as too subjective, while women see themselves as direct and personally honest about their feelings, and men as cold, distant, and competitive. Even though truly effective decision making involves a blend of the so-called male and female mentalities, too often the result is a domination of one over the other, most often with the male viewpoint on top.

There are organizations where women have not been promoted beyond a certain level, in part because they were seen as not "strong" enough to handle the combative

The benefits awarded in sexual harassment cases in 1992 totaled $6,242,512–an average of less than $850 per suit. Although not a large dollar figure, it was still double the benefits awarded in 1991. The real cost is in the additional legal fees, decreased productivity, and poor morale. As one employer currently tied up in such a case says, "It's very depressing trying to get anything accomplished. You never seem to get away from the controversy." This comment has become all too typical, and the cost, both actual and accrued, will only be going up.

So how do you create personal bonds and camaraderie in business without ending up in court? After my own experience, this is something I've thought long and hard about. Here are some suggestions:

- *Stick to the boundaries you, or your company, have set.* Don't think a person or situation is the "exception to the rule." It won't be. For most companies the policy is straightforward and concise—if any action is perceived by anyone as harassing, embarrassing, or threatening, it should be addressed immediately.

- *If you suspect your actions, whether overt or subtle, have offended, ask the other person about it right then and there.* The innocent have the courage to address a potential problem immediately. The guilty often hope it will be unnoticed and go away. It won't.

  Ask your questions in a nonthreatening way. "Did I do something inappropriate or make you feel uncomfortable?" Then be quiet and listen. Whatever the person says, listen and ask a follow-up question. "Is there anything else you would like to say?" Be quiet and listen in a way that invites an honest response. Even if his or her answer lets you off the hook, you should still express your regrets with something such as, "If in any way I offended you, please accept my apology." Don't mumble or minimize it—or blow it out of proportion. State your regret clearly and sincerely. To prevent any fallout, inquire: "Is there anything I need to do to correct this situation?"

- *If you think the situation still might come back to haunt you, go tell your manager.* "I made a mistake and here's what I did to correct it." It pays to bring up the bad news before someone else does.

The key for both the accuser and the accused is to slow down and reason out the situation before making a move. We must not follow the pattern of popular thinking and overreact. Both sides need to recognize when to call it quits. Either sex can readily and wrongfully make public harassment charges. But if these are made thoughtlessly, it's just one more hindrance to America's productivity.

SOURCE: Debra Benton. Reprinted by permission of *The Wall Street Journal*, © March 22, 1993. Dow Jones & Company, Inc. All Rights Reserved Worldwide.

tough style that characterized the organization. While such differences are not always the case, and the situation may be improving in many organizations, be sensitive to the fact that gender can be a source of rich interpersonal communication or a barrier to it.

Other Common Problems of Communication

Ambiguous Communications: The Mixed Message

This occurs when several channels are in operation at the same time and they are not completely in tune with each other. One channel may be sending a message that is different from or contradictory to another, making the message difficult to understand. To illustrate, the words are polite or even friendly, but the tone of voice is angry or hostile (as might be the case with sarcasm). Another example is when the words are a question, but the manner of expression is an assertion. Have you heard someone say, "Wouldn't it be a good idea to . . . ?" when he or she really means, "You'd be a fool not to . . . ?" Such ambiguous communication is likely to occur when a manager is trying to behave in a participative manner with subordinates but really wants to maintain absolute control over outcomes.

Incomplete Communication: The Throwaway Line

This occurs when enough of a message is sent to indicate the presence of an issue, but not enough to make clear what the issue really is or how serious it is. For example, in the middle of discussing one issue a reference is made to another problem, but it is off-hand and passed over very quickly. This kind of communication tends to raise anxiety and leave the recipient in the unfortunate position of having to fill in the rest of the message with his or her own fantasies, which are often worse than the actual situation.

Nonverbal Signals: The Person's Emotional State

Watch a busy executive going about his or her business; note the speed of movement, facial express, posture, and so forth. It doesn't take much to interpret rapid pace, furrowed brow, and thrust-out chin as, "I am harassed and under pressure; don't bother me with trivial matters." At times, such nonverbal behavior can become a part of a person's everyday style to the point of constantly appearing harassed even when not. If one is unaware of the unintended message, the reactions of others to it can be puzzling. Are you aware of the kinds of signals expressed in your nonverbal behavior? Does your characteristic body posture say "I like myself" or "I feel insignificant"? Does your facial expression usually suggest anger, fear, curiosity, or what? Do you sit in a way that says "don't approach me" or "I am receptive to new relationships and ideas"? This may be an area worth exploring with your fellow students or co-workers. Although you can sometimes guess at how you are seen by observing the way others react to you, asking for feedback is probably the best way to find out, though not always the most comfortable.

So don't listen to the words; just listen to what the voice tells you, what the movements tell you, what the posture tells you, what the image tells you.

F. S. Perls
Gestalt Theory Verbatim, p. 57

Nonverbal Signals: The Secret Society

While nonverbal communication goes on all the time, people who are close develop "special" signals to each other, such as a knowing look, nod, or smile, a warning of threat, or a smile of support. These forms of communication can be very handy or convenient, and they also tend to confirm the solidarity of the relationship. However, they also may convey a sense of a "secret society" that walls off others. In some situations this type of communication is very important. For instance, in negotiation sessions it is important to know how others on your side feel about things as they happen without openly conferring. But even in these situations, it heightens feelings of exclusion and can have negative consequences, too.

It Takes Both People for Communication to Work

One person alone cannot establish effective communication; he or she has no means of checking out whether or not the intended message was the one received.

Guidelines for Active Listening

Objective: To help others gain clear understanding of their situations, so they can take responsible action. To demonstrate your appreciation of meaning and feelings behind others' statements, of worth of the other person, and of your willingness to listen without passing judgment.

Do

1. Create supportive atmosphere.
2. Listen for feelings as well as words.
3. Note cues—gestures, tone of voice, body positions, eye movements, breathing, and the like.
4. Occasionally test for understanding: "Is this what you meant?"
5. Demonstrate acceptance and understanding, verbally and nonverbally.
6. Ask exploratory, open-ended questions.

Don't

1. Try to change others' views.
2. Solve problem for other.
3. Give advice (no matter how obvious the solution is for you).
4. Pass judgment.
5. Explain or interpret others' behavior.
6. Give false reassurances.
7. Attack back if the other is hostile to you—understand the source of the anger.
8. Ask questions about "why" the feelings.

SOURCE: Cohen et al., *Effective Behavior in Organizations* (New York, NY, McGraw-Hill/Irwin, 1976). Based on Carl Rogers and Richard Farson, "Active Listening."

Because of the probability that some distortion will take place, good communication requires an exchange of messages, a two-way process. For A to disclose something to B without knowing how it was received is only half the process. And the more important the disclosure is to A, the more vital it is for A to check out its reception.

Think about the relationship between Buckley and Endrunn. If Buckley decided to tell Endrunn that he didn't want him to talk to Buckley's subordinates, what would Endrunn hear? Given his view of Buckley as political and closed, he might interpret it as a power grab, rather than a concern for the position in which this could put the subordinate. That could lead to a downward spiral in the relationship. Many exchanges, especially around work routines and the like, require a minimum amount of checking out; they are least subject to distortion. But even these communications can, if badly managed, lead to misunderstandings that may become more significant and require a great deal of clarifying. *An accumulation of little miscommunications often builds into a major source of conflict between two people.*

We can summarize with the following working proposition: The greater the (a) complexity of a subject, (b) importance of a subject to the parties involved, and (c) feelings aroused by the subject, the greater the possibilities for distortion, and therefore the greater the need for each to check with the other on what has been heard and said.[1]

I only wish I could find an institute that teaches people how to listen. After all, a good manager needs to listen as much as he needs to talk . . . real communication goes in both directions.

Lee Iacocca
Iacocca: An Autobiography

This is not to suggest that every message you send to another person requires a response or acknowledgement from that person, and vice versa. Often a simple nod of the head or observing the subsequent behavior of the other person is enough to complete the process. But, As a task becomes more complex, as a relationship requires more avenues and frequency of communication, it calls for more attention to whatever processes ensure accuracy of communication. This principle becomes doubly important when there is some degree of tension in the situation. The key to more effective listening is the willingness to listen and respond appropriately to the feelings being expressed as well as to the content.[2] An acceptance of the existence of feelings and the legitimacy of the other person having them, even when you don't agree, usually eases the tension created when a person feels misunderstood or put down by the listener and also allows a focus on whatever is generating the original feelings.

You can probably understand by now why so many managers tend to classify human relations difficulties as "communication problems." While the phrase is often just a catchall to reduce things to their simplest possible form and can cover up the problem more than illuminate it, the observation is not too far off the mark. It is hard for people to understand one another. And while accurate understanding in no way guarantees agreement, there is little advantage in trying to sort out relationships through the additional static of unclear messages. It is worth the effort to practice listening to feelings as well as words and to check out meanings when clarity is not certain. Effective communication is a basic step in building relationships. Just be certain that when you see a problem between two people you don't automatically blame everything on communication processes when other factors may be at work, as described in Chapter 9.

Reciprocity

Throughout this chapter we have raised questions about the connection between what one person wants and how that affects, and is affected by, what another person wants. For a relationship to continue, there needs to be some kind of mutual accommodation of each to the other, some *reciprocity* between what each gives and gets. Just as roles develop among group members to fulfill particular group functions and are selected by individuals in line with their self-concepts, people often develop interpersonal role relationships at work.

The norm that it is obligatory to "pay back" roughly what one has "received" is almost universal and operates between individuals, groups, organizations, or even societies. Although disputes can arise about whether what one party offers is sufficient to repay the other's original "gift" (How many "thank you's" does it take to satisfy your friend of the opposite sex that you really liked the sweater?), virtually everyone accepts that everything should somehow be repaid. Gratefulness for help, dinner invitation for dinner invitation, warmth for kindnesses; whatever the currency, mutual satisfaction of debts over time is necessary to sustain an equal relationship. And failure to repay leads either to breaking off the relationship or to continued obligations and status differentials.

"Noblesse oblige," or taking care of those who are less fortunate, is a way of dealing with unequal abilities to repay, though even in that type of relationship deference, loyalty, and gratitude are expected in return for more durable goods.

> Friendship is seldom lasting but between equals . . . Benefits which cannot be repaid and obligations which cannot be discharged are not commonly found to increase affection; they excite gratitude indeed and heighten veneration but commonly take away that easy freedom and familiarity of intercourse without which . . . there cannot be friendship.
>
> Samuel Johnson
> *The Rambler* No. 64

This universal *norm of reciprocity* serves to stabilize relationships, to bring them into a steady state, which allows predictability and continuity. You may remember that the taking of *roles* serves much the same function. When behavior becomes patterned, meeting the expectations of others in a particular social system, everyone has a clear idea of what to expect and how to treat others. Each person develops a set pattern of behavior that provides something for the other; as long as what is provided is desired, the relationship is easy to maintain. Accepting a position will reveal that others have expectations about the type of relationships deemed appropriate for someone in that role. Just as the plumber had some ideas about what kind of interpersonal behavior a plumber's assistant should exhibit, and as Buckley and Endrunn had ideas about how a president and group vice president should relate, organizational members develop expectations that the role occupant cannot easily ignore despite personal preferences that might be different. It takes a while for each party to alter expectations and preferences to fit the other.

To build and maintain a relationship, one needs to fulfill the norm of reciprocity; yet the currency of "exchange" is often rather subtle. (It is not always as easy as, "You bought lunch yesterday; today I will buy.") For example, if you and another manager had occasion to assemble your teams for joint meetings sometimes in her conference room and sometimes in yours, and it had become customary for whichever one of you was on home turf to sit at the head of the conference table, it could violate expectations of reciprocity if you were to quickly move into that seat in her conference room. If the seating has come to mean a recognition of one another's status, breaking the pattern could easily be seen as an attempt to dominate and a failure to properly reciprocate her usual recognition of your status. It may not be possible to fully avoid failures of reciprocity, but you need to be alert to what is expected of you in return for what others have done for you, and to choose consciously whether or not to honor the expectations. Conversely, if you eventually want something from another person, you can utilize reciprocity by doing something useful—helping the other to meet his or her personal or organizational goals—and asking for a "return on your investment" when necessary. This need not be done in a harsh, demanding way; since most people recognize when they "owe you one," they will naturally want to pay you back.

In any ongoing relationship, there are usually mutual expectations; as long as they are honored, the relationship remains stable. Often, however, the expectations are unclear or unrealistic, or one of the parties finds it difficult to live up to them. If so, it is best to discuss the issue with the other and attempt to modify the expectations in line with reality. All too often people are prone to let a situation build, perhaps because of embarrassment or a feeling that "one must always honor a commitment," until things have gotten out of control. Then, unfortunately, the relationship might end or require a major effort to rectify. If there is a lesson in this, it is that *every relationship needs nurturing, and continuing attention to mutual expectations is essential to the maintenance of reciprocity.*

In short, as needs and circumstances change, people may need to renegotiate their expectations of each other, a process that takes time and effort but pays off in mutual growth.

Trust and Other Feelings

Every relationship has the potential for confirming or disconfirming the participants' self-concepts. Whatever is sought in the relationship—whether it is liking, respect, or influence—a satisfying relationship confirms people's view of themselves and makes them feel good about who they believe they are. When two people agree in their goals, it makes them both feel supported; when they affirm each other's competencies, they feel a sense of adequacy; and when they reinforce each other's beliefs and values, they each feel worthy. A relationship that makes each person feel supported, adequate, and worthy will generally lead to mutual feelings of closeness, warmth, and trust. By way of contrast, a relationship that makes each person feel unsupported, inadequate, and unworthy will generally lead to mutual feelings of distance, coldness, and suspicion.[3]

The terms *closeness* (versus *distance*), *warmth* (versus *coldness*), and *trust* (versus *suspicion*) take on different meanings in different kinds of relationships. Closeness and warmth are mainly a matter of degree. For example, a minimal task relationship would certainly not draw two people as close or generate as many warm feelings as would a colleagueship; the stakes are different in each case. But even a minimal task relationship in which each person experiences self-confirmation can lead to some degree of closeness and warmth.

Trust

With respect to trust, the situation is more complex; trust is a central issue in all human relationships both within and outside of organizations. Trust can refer to several aspects of a relationship: (1) how much confidence you have in the other's competence and ability to do whatever needs doing, (2) how sound you believe the other's judgment to be, (3) your belief in the extent to which the other is willing to be helpful to you, (4) how certain you are that the other has genuine concern for your welfare rather than any desire to harm you, and (5) how confident you are that the other will deliver on any commitments made.

Because trust can refer to any or all of these areas, it is useful to be clear about which area you mean when you use the concept and helpful to check what others mean by it. "I don't trust you" is a very different statement when it means "your lack of carpentry skills make me doubt whether you can build that chest" than it is when it means "I think you would drop it on my toes at the first opportunity." Remember Theory X and Theory Y from Chapter 8? They are sets of beliefs that express greater or lesser trust in the motives of others.

> Trust is the lubrication that makes it possible for organizations to work. It's hard to imagine an organization without some semblance of trust operating somehow, somewhere.
>
> W. Bennis and B. Nanus
> *Leaders* (New York: Harper & Row, 1985)

While deep and all-encompassing trust may not be called for in a work situation, when it does emerge it can make work easier. It does this by forming the basis for greater *openness* in the relationship on all fronts. For example, two close friends probably will feel greater freedom to be open and honest in task-related areas than would two relative strangers. The two friends are more likely to be willing to take *risks* with one another, that is, to say things that may be critical or revealing in the belief that the other person will hear it accurately and not use it in a destructive way. While the level of trust in a relationship can develop gradually over time, through the course of interactions, very often it takes some kind of risky behavior in relation to the other person to build trust at the deepest levels. To deepen a relationship requires that someone take initiative in trusting the other—say, to do a really tough part of a joint task—before he or she can be certain of the consequences. If neither will take the risk of trusting at least a little, the relationship remains at the same level of caution and suspicion. Note the way Buckley and Endrunn cannot improve their relationship unless one or the other is willing to take the initiative and be more open.

On the other hand, when someone violates trust (especially when it has involved some personal risk), the relationship is usually damaged. The effect may be temporary

CEOs Find That Closest Chums on Board Are the Ones Most Likely to Plot a Revolt

With friends like these, a chief executive officer needs help.

The "friends" are retired chief executives sitting on the CEO's board. Though often handpicked by the CEO, these outside directors have been turning on their pal in a spate of recent corporate coups.

Indeed, a pattern is discernible in these deposings: The person mostly like to plot the CEO's doom is an outside director who formerly ran his or her own company. Armed with powerful leadership skills and the credibility of a formidable business background, this director rallies other directors and launches a boardroom coup. . . .

Ironically, chief executives commonly see retired chief executives as their closest chums on a board.

They were cronies who had experienced the CEO's problems first-hand—and who heartily agreed that corporate chiefs were worth a lot of money. But now, "Good-old-boy directors are out." . . .

Many directors clearly are placing this duty above friendship. Despite a close friendship with Mr. Akers, outside director James Burke gently convinced the IBM chairman that he should step down as the company's woes widened.

SOURCE: Julie Amparano Lopez. Reprinted by permission of *The Wall Street Journal,* © March 26, 1993. Dow Jones & Company, Inc. All Rights Reserved Worldwide.

or permanent, depending upon how deeply the violation affected the self-concept. It is easier to forgive a co-worker who goofed up some piece of the job or whose interpretation of a task was grossly in error than it is to forgive a close colleague for deliberately taking an action that puts you in a bad light with others.

In general, then, The greater the trust one has in another's competence, judgment, helpfulness, or concern, the more open one will be about matters relating to that aspect(s) of the relationship. In turn, the more one feels trusted, the easier it is to be open.[4]

But how can we go about building and maintaining trust? As just implied, in part one must act with integrity and not violate whatever trust exists. This requires meeting commitments made to the other person and maintaining such confidences as may occur. Even where you have information that was not given you "in confidence," you need to use common sense about raising issues in public that put the other person on the spot unnecessarily or unexpectedly. If the organization's culture is one where everything is open and above board, there may be very little that can't be brought up at any time, but in most cultures there are some constraints. In general, people do not like to be caught by surprise, especially high-level managers in front of their bosses or even peers. Consequently, common sense usually suggests raising issues in private or at least alerting an individual ahead of time. A person who exhibits such common sense will be seen as more trustworthy than someone who shows no sensitivity to another's feelings about not being caught off guard or embarrassed in public.

Still another way to build trust, apart from doing your own job well, is by being open about your own actions and intentions. It is not easy to trust someone who is secretive and who "plays the cards close to the vest." Keeping others informed not only avoids surprises but reduces the threat that the unknown entails. In part this means being sensitive to others' needs to know what is going on, and in part it means making yourself more vulnerable.

Come Out of the Shade

"[Arthur Watson, president of NBC Sports, was] the only man in this business I ever knew who told the whole truth. All the rest of us try to shade things at least 10 percent."

Dick Ebersol

SOURCE: Jack Craig, "Watson Got Results, Not Publicity," *Boston Globe,* June 30, 1991.

Fooling some of the people some of the time is not enough for sustained success in to-day's interdependent organizations. Those who lie to get their way are almost inevitably found out, and then frozen out of the action by peers and bosses who do not trust them. Repeatedly, we have found that authenticity works, not only because it gets on the table the most data to work with, but because it helps to build trust. A reputation for shady practices, or even for constant self-interest at the expense of others, is corrosive; colleagues and bosses resist the influence attempts of those they don't trust.

David Bradford and Allan Cohen
Power Up

Dealing with Blind Spots: The Need for Feedback

The development of a relationship involves the behavior of both parties; to make it easier to look at the interconnection, see Figure 10–4. It shows the relationship from the perspective of each person and also what the combinations of their separate perspectives produce. From each person's vantage point there are aspects of the relationship that are *known* (that each is aware of) and aspects that are *not known*. What both persons are aware of (upper left box) are those things that have been shared openly; what neither person is aware of (lower right box) are those things that have not made their appearance in the relationship, the future unknowns that may or may not emerge. The other two boxes determine the direction in which the relationship is to develop, if at all. They include those aspects of the relationship that one person or the other is aware of, but not both. What person A alone is aware of (has not shared with person B) in the relationship we call B's *blind spots* (and vice versa). The blind spots can be positive or negative in nature, but as long as they remain hidden from one person or the other, they tend to serve as obstacles to the development of a mutually enhancing relationship. The fewer the number of blind spots one has, the greater the understanding of one's impact on others, and the greater the opportunity to choose alternative behaviors.[5] It is discouraging and a handicap to be misunderstood or misjudged on the basis of some behavior or mannerism of which you are not aware; you can't change what you do not know about.

In order for anyone to improve performance, please another, or change self-defeating behavior, it is necessary to be aware of the effect one is having on the other(s). Because people can best alter mistakes or unintentional consequences *with* information on the effect of their behavior, rather than without it, telling others how they are coming across is a kind of gift. It is the feedback of data, which cannot be

MANAGERIAL BULLETIN

Surround Sound: Managerial Feedback at GE

If you can't operate as a team player, no matter how valuable you've been, you really don't belong at GE. **To embed our values, we give our people 360-degree evaluations, with input from superiors, peers, and subordinates. These are the roughest evaluations you can get, because people hear things about** themselves they've never heard before. But they get the input they need, and then the chance to improve. If they don't improve, they have to go.

SOURCE: Tichy and Sherman, "Jack Welch's Lessons for Success," *Fortune,* December 13, 1993, excerpt from *Control Your Destiny or Someone Else Will.*

FIGURE 10–4   *Model of a Two-Person Relationship*

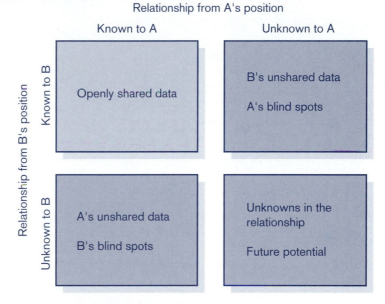

Relationship from A's position

	Known to A	Unknown to A
Known to B	Openly shared data	B's unshared data A's blind spots
Unknown to B	A's unshared data B's blind spots	Unknowns in the relationship Future potential

Relationship from B's position

Note: This model is a modification of the "Johari Window," a concept presented in J. Luft, *Group Processes* (Palo Alto, CA: National Press Books, 1970).

acquired nearly so effectively, if at all, in any other way. The feedback process in which information is given on the consequences of certain actions is central to any human relationship in which learning is desired or necessary. For example, if a group member's constant jokes bother you, making it hard to take even his valuable contributions seriously, you prevent him from learning how to be more effective if you do not tell him.

But there is a dilemma in all of this. If trust is required for openness and feedback is a form of openness that can be risky (because the receiver may not welcome it as intended), how can you get others to give you the feedback you need? How can you build sufficient trust toward you to allow others to take the risk of telling you how you come across? Declaring your trustworthiness does not often work; the person who feels a risk will not easily accept testimonials! Usually it requires that you go

MANAGERIAL BULLETIN

Reviews from Peers Instruct—and Sting

Still at many companies, the notion of giving helpful criticism clashes head-on with the corporate culture. [Consultant] Mr. LaMountain worked with a manufacturing company whose middle managers were so used to attacking each other that their meetings were "kind of like the old Roman games," he says. "Somebody got in the middle of the arena, and another played lion and tried to gobble them up. They thought that made people tough."

In fact, though, Mr. LaMountain says, most employees were afraid to open their mouths.

SOURCE: Sue Shellenbarger, "Reviews from Peers Instruct—and Sting," *The Wall Street Journal,* October 4, 1994, p. B1.

MANAGERIAL BULLETIN

How to Boss the Boss: A Six-Step Plan

One tool for making the workplace more productive is the 360-degree evaluation, in which superiors, colleagues, subordinates, customers, and suppliers all provide feedback about someone at a company. But this can be deadly for subordinates. Bosses aren't stupid. They can usually figure out which subordinate rated them low in communication skills or the ability to take criticism. And they will get even—maybe not immediately, but eventually.

SOURCE: Robert L. Dilenschneider, "How to Boss the Boss: A Six-Step Plan," *New York Times,* September 21, 1997, p. 16.

first, taking the risk of disclosing something about yourself—your perceptions, feelings, concerns, and so forth. Self-disclosure builds trust. But self-disclosure can also be risky; it may not be received as intended, or it may be used against the discloser. Consider the following example.

> The production manager and sales manager of a computer manufacturer must write a joint report to their boss on whether or not to produce new DVD drives. The sales manager's job will be made easier if the model is added to the line; her salespeople want to be able to meet competition with up-to-date models even though sales will not at first be too high. The production manager's job will be made more difficult if the newly designed drive is put into production, since there are already problems with the existing level of production. If the wrong decision is made, it will be costly to both of them. Do they work together to examine all aspects of the problem, or does each hold back information unfavorably to their respective positions? If the sales manager admits that she has doubts about the market potential of DVD and suspects the sales staff is only using the lack of them as an excuse for poor efforts, will the production manager pounce on that and force a negative decision? Conversely, if he tells her that a special assembly line could be set up to minimize disruption to present production, will she take advantage of that to force a positive decision? Would either use the other's revelation to look good to the boss? Can they build sufficient trust to be able to share all the needed inputs and come to a sensible decision in which each does what is best for the company regardless of personal inconvenience? The degree of trust, openness, and closeness between them will have crucial ramifications for the company—and for their relationship in the future.

MANAGERIAL BULLETIN

Annual Agony: It's Time to Evaluate Your Work, and All Involved Are Groaning

Employees Dislike Reviews, Even if Favorable; Bosses Wonder How to Do Them; Some Prefer Frequent Talks

In almost every major survey, most employees who get job evaluations and most supervisors who give them rate the process a resounding failure.

Performance appraisals are a growing issue in corporate America. As companies shrink their management ranks, many supervisors find they must manage and evaluate larger staffs, and they are overwhelmed. As companies develop work teams, they wonder how to assess individual team members. And as companies— especially high-tech companies—reshuffle their troops frequently, they are finding that the rapid changes can render annual performance reviews almost useless.

So, companies are spending many millions of dollars annually to overhaul performance-review systems. A 1995 survey indicated that 44% of 218 companies with evaluation systems had changed theirs in the previous two years and that another 29% expected to do so. AT&T Corp., for example, is adopting a global appraisal system. PepsiCo Inc. instituted a new system last year that replaced 37 appraisal forms that a manager might have to use with one form accessible via the Internet.

Performance management, as it is called, has become a lucrative, fast-growing business for consulting firms, even though many clients still become disenchanted with new systems in a few years. Although consultants won't disclose actual billings, Development Dimensions International Inc., of Pittsburgh, says revenue for its performance-management services has doubled in the past two years; similar billings at William M. Mercer Inc., of New York, have climbed 25% just this year.

Theoretically, a performance review should benefit both employee and employer. Its aims: to inform workers of their strengths and weaknesses on the job, tell them how to improve and lay out career-development options, and to give supervisors a chance to underscore the company's business goals and show how the employee fits into them. Managers generally use an evaluation form to numerically rate employees in several categories and then give them an overall rating.

"Most of the time, it's just a ritual that managers go through," says Winston Connor, recently retired vice president of human resources at Huntsman Chemical Corp. in Salt Lake City. "They pull out last year's review, update it and do it quickly." He also says many managers use the annual review "to dump out all the negatives collected over an entire year" on an employee.

Adds Jean Gatz, an employee-training expert in Baton Rouge, La.: "Most of us don't like to sit down and hear where we're lacking and where we need to improve. It's like sitting down with your mom and dad and they're telling you, 'We know what's best.'"

Research results point up the inadequacy of appraisal systems. The "we're-more-confused-than-enlightened" finding originated in a survey of 200 big companies by Psychological Associates Inc., a St. Louis consulting firm. A survey by the Society of Human Resource Management, of Alexandria, Va., concluded that more than 90% of appraisal systems are unsuccessful. And a 1993 survey by Development Dimensions International of 1,149 human-resources managers and others found overwhelming dissatisfaction.

Researchers at Temple University and Rensselaer Polytechnic Institute found that 98% of 151 Philadelphia-area managers encountered some type of aggression after giving employees negative appraisals. More than two-thirds of the bad reaction was verbal rather than physical. But a Los Angeles city technician killed four of his bosses last year shortly after getting a poor review.

SOURCE: Timothy D. Schellhardt, "Annual Agony," *The Wall Street Journal*, November 19, 1996, p. A1. (Copyright © 1996, Dow Jones & Company, Inc.)

In general, we can say that

1. The greater the extent of openness in self-disclosure and feedback, the greater will be the resulting level of trust.
2. The greater the level of openness that is required, the greater the level of risk experienced.

Guidelines for Giving Feedback

Giving feedback should be analogous to holding up a mirror where individuals can see themselves as others see them and learn how their actions have been affecting others. It is *not* telling others what is wrong with them or telling them how they *should* change. It is offering your perceptions and describing your feelings in a nonjudgmental manner as data that recipients can use as they find appropriate.

1. Examine your own motives.

    Be sure your intention is to be helpful, not to show how perceptive and superior you are, or to hurt the other. Be on the other person's side.
2. Consider the *receiver's readiness* to hear your feedback.

    In general, feedback is most useful when it is sought, rather than when it is volunteered. When possible, wait for signs of the other wanting it; nevertheless,
3. Give feedback promptly.

    Feedback given soon after the event, except when the individual is upset or otherwise not ready to listen, is better than that given when details are no longer clear in anyone's mind.
4. Be *descriptive* rather than evaluate.

    Describe what the person did and any feelings it aroused in you, but do not label or evaluate it. ("You interrupted me and that frustrates me because I lose track" is descriptive; "You were rude" is evaluative.)

5. *Deal in specifics,* not generalities.

    Describe concrete events. ("You interrupted me when I was reviewing . . ." versus "You always try to hog all the air time.")
6. *Offer* feedback; do not try to impose it.

    Give information as something the receiver can consider and explore, not as a command that he/she change.
7. Offer feedback in a *spirit of tentativeness.*

    Offer feedback as one person's perceptions, not as "the truth." Being dogmatic usually puts people on the defensive.
8. *Be open to receiving feedback yourself.*

    Your actions may be contributing to the other's behavior; not everyone may feel the same as you do about the other, which reflects on your perceptions as well as on the other's behavior.
9. *Avoid overload.*

    Focus only on what is most important and changeable.
10. *Highlight costs of the behavior to the other.*

    If you can, help the other person see how the behavior in question costs him/her, or prevents meeting his/her objectives.
11. Watch for any behavior of the other while receiving feedback which confirms or disconfirms the feedback; using the reaction to illustrate your points is a potent reinforcer.

---

3. The greater the level of risk required, the greater the level of trust that is needed for openness.
4. The closer that self-disclosure and/or feedback come to the core of the self-concept, the greater the level of risk that is experienced and the higher the level of trust necessary for openness.[6]

You need trust to take the risk of being open. But it is hard to develop sufficient trust until you do take that risk. If the risk is positively responded to, the first critical step in building trust is established; if not, then you are left only with the satisfaction of knowing that you had the courage to take the risk. Risking mistakenly can be disastrous; risking too cautiously can be isolating.

Furthermore, it is occasionally necessary to work with someone whom you do not trust; finding a way to get the job done without either making yourself vulnerable or offending the other person is a valuable skill to acquire. While open, trusting relationships are freeing and satisfying, plunging into acting as if the person will respond in kind just because you would prefer it is like diving into a new swimming

MANAGERIAL BULLETIN

Can't We Just Get Along?

[Calgary hockey coach Pierre Page]: "I said to Phil [Housley], 'I've heard from everybody that you're a pain in the [butt]. Is it true?' and he said, 'I can be.' I said, 'You've probably heard I can be a pain in the [butt],' and he said he'd heard that, too. We never had a problem. So often, it's a perception. You have to try as much as you can to listen to what he wants, and hopefully he'll listen to you, and if you both want to win, you'll make a deal."

SOURCE: Nancy L. Marrapese, "Star System Can Work," July 21, 1996, *Boston Globe*, p. F7.

MANAGERIAL BULLETIN

Turning the Tables: Underlings Evaluate Bosses

Robert E. Allen, AT&T [former] chairman and chief executive, . . . changed his ways. . . . His lieutenants didn't like the passive way he ran the management executive committee.

Mr. Allen says he now spends more time drafting the committee's agenda, airs his opinions freely during its meetings, and pushes the group harder to make clear-cut decisions. Still, getting written feedback from his senior executives made him uncomfortable initially. "Nobody likes to be told that they are not performing at the maximum level," he concedes.

Over the past year, nearly 68,000 AT&T managers have received upward appraisals.

SOURCE: Joann S. Lublin, "Turning the Tables," *The Wall Street Journal*, October 4, 1994, p. B1.

place without checking for rocks beneath the surface. Conversely, assuming that *all* water is loaded with rocks can rob you of a great deal of pleasure.

Unfortunately, it is almost impossible to develop guidelines for judging when it is worth risking openness and trust. As in other human situations, you have to decide whether the expected gains are sufficiently greater than the potential losses to be worth the possibility of a failure. Keep in mind that trust is usually built a little at a time. Pushing too hard or too fast, or both, can scare off the other person and also may be too risky for you; not pushing at all, however, is not likely to produce any change. Normally, though, your own willingness to *begin* being open will result in a reciprocal response.

Mark Buckley, for example, needs to gently initiate discussions with Oliver Endrunn about ways of effectively striking a balance between being informed and being unnecessarily interfering; blasting Endrunn for bypassing him would only make Endrunn defensive and angry. From his side, Endrunn can talk with Buckley about what information would help him relax so that he wouldn't have to seek it all the time; attacking Buckley for being too political would simply lead to further guardedness.

Negotiations

A common relationship situation involves negotiation, where each party (sometimes representing wider constituencies) wants something from the other party and cannot automatically get it, but both are willing to discuss it.[7]

FIGURE 10-5   *Alternative Negotiation Strategies*

Is the Substantive Outcome Very Important to You?

		Yes	No
Is the relationship outcome very important to you?	Yes	**Trustingly collaborate** when both types of outcomes are very important	**Openly accommodate** when the priority is on relationship outcomes
	No	**Firmly compete** when the priority is on substantive outcomes	**Actively avoid negotiating** when neither type of outcome is very important

They may have a conflict over preferences, priorities, or resources, both tangible results and intangible psychological objectives. Getting a raise is a *tangible objective*; feeling pride because you got the boss to give more than he wanted to is an *intangible objective.*

Negotiations have outcomes in two dimensions: substantive results and the resulting relationship. Thus, sometimes "winning" can be losing because the relationship is badly harmed and desirable options in the future are foreclosed. These two dimensions lead to four alternative strategies for negotiation (Figure 10–5).

Many negotiations within organizations are with others whose ultimate good will is critical so that relationships must be a critical dimension. That calls for a collaborative negotiating style, even when the other is acting competitively. To go for the jugular in such situations is remarkably short-sighted. When a long-term relationship is less important, however, acting in a fully collaborative, trusting way can leave you vulnerable to being suckered. The core dilemma of negotiations is that openness is necessary for creating the best win-win results, but openness can give the party being negotiated with an advantage. Managing this dilemma and learning how to build in the other party the necessary trust and willingness to collaborate are great arts.

Negotiating either way still calls for thorough preparation and a number of important factors that enhance the ability to get what you desire. These include having the information you need about the situation and the other's likely interests and reputation; the full endorsement of your organizational unit or constituency if one is involved; the power of the organization's rules, policies, and procedures to back you; good options to reaching this agreement; no deadline by which you have to have an agreement; and a strong reputation for being persuasive, tenacious, and honest. The more of these factors on your side, the better your negotiating position.

Once you have assessed the importance of the outcome and relationship, done your homework, and lined up the support you need, the approach to negotiations should vary by whether you choose to negotiate competitively or collaboratively; although negotiations with colleagues generally call for collaboration, you should know both styles. Figure 10–6 shows the differences in approach.

A Recap

In summary, individuals involved in a relationship can steer it in a positive direction by being adaptable to the requirements of the job and the desires of the other person, by developing and practicing good communication skills so as to minimize and

FIGURE 10–6	*Comparison of Assumptions, Strategies, and Tactics: Competitive versus Collaborative Negotiation*

Assumptions	**Competitive Negotiation**	**Collaborative Negotiation**
Goal perspective	Short-term	Long-term
	Perceived as incompatible	Perceived as compatible
	Emphasis on tangibles only	Emphasis on tangibles and intangibles
Perceptions	Mistrust, suspicion, defensiveness	Trust, honesty, openness
Orientation to issues	Extreme demands and positions	Satisfy mutual needs
Orientation to relationship	Ignore and exploit relationship	Build trust; preserve and enhance relationship
Orientation to rationality	Emotional, irrational	Rational, reasonable
Orientation to concession making	Keep concessions few and small	Concede as necessary; work toward mutual agreement
Orientation to authority	Limited or no authority	Controlled authority
Orientation to time	Ignore deadlines; use time as tactic	Follow deadlines; use time for problem solving

deal with misunderstanding, by honoring and utilizing the norm of reciprocity to maintain a balanced exchange, by acting with integrity in a manner that keeps the other informed about actions, intentions, and expectations, and by seeking to reduce mutual blind spots through self-disclosure and feedback. These practices will also be useful in building a reputation for the future, as well as in doing the maintenance work to keep a positive relationship from falling into decline. If careful attention is given to these interpersonal processes, the result should be a good relationship leading to productivity, satisfaction, and even individual development. We close this chapter with a look at some other outcomes that are related to productivity, satisfaction, and development.

Outcomes of Interpersonal Relationships

Liking and Respect

It's possible for two people to work together, even productively, without developing much liking or respect for one another. In a minimal task relationship, this probably poses little problem, at least for getting the work done. However, as discussed in Chapter 7, most people have more needs than those that pertain only to the task; therefore, few people would find very desirable, for long, a work relationship that lacks liking and respect.

Liking is normally related to the personal and social aspects of a relationship. If the quality of communication between two people is such that feelings of closeness, warmth, and trust develop, the outcome will obviously be liking. Even when the task does not require such interpersonal communication, if the individuals themselves desire it, if their backgrounds are compatible, and if the opportunities for interaction are present, then the chances are good that their relationship will result in liking. Any one of these factors, however, can affect the outcome. For example, in one company two members of a management team had very similar styles of interacting—both were aggressive and argumentative. Their interpersonal process was terrible; neither could listen to or understand the other. Consequently, they maintained a kind of distance, coolness, and mistrust, which resulted in mutual dislike. While they did, in fact, respect each other's abilities in the job, their dislike made work unpleasant for the entire team.

In a work relationship, mutual respect normally occurs as a result of the recognition of one another's competencies. Can you think of people you hold in esteem because of their abilities? Are they all people you also like? As discussed in Chapter 5, feelings of respect may not be consistent with liking. Furthermore, co-workers may develop a high level of task-related trust but never feel close or warm on a more personal level. And while their processes of communication may be poor when feelings are involved, the two people may be perfectly capable of exchanging needed information about the work as the situation requires it. In short, we can say that

1. In a minimal task relationship, liking and respect need only be minimal in order to get the task done.
2. The degree of liking needed in a task relationship depends upon the preferences of the individuals but also tends to be more appropriate to relationships that extend beyond the minimal task level.
3. The degree of respect needed in a task relationship increases as task interdependence increases and as the differentiated abilities of each person are required for satisfactory completion of the job.
4. To the extent that personal closeness, warmth, and trust emerge, liking will result.
5. To the extent that task-related trust emerges, respect will result.[8]

While it may at times seem difficult to be both liked and respected, the two outcomes are not necessarily mutually exclusive. The assumption that they are can, in fact, result in a manager saying, "I'd rather be respected than liked; at least I'll get the job done." What is unfortunate is that this limits the range of the manager's interpersonal competence and consequently may reduce responsiveness to the needs of many employees. Insofar as a job requires more than a minimal task relationship, the development of *both* liking and respect can have important consequences for productivity, satisfaction, and development. Let's examine these consequences in the form of some propositions.

Propositions Linking Liking and Respect to Productivity, Satisfaction, and Development

While the connections are neither simple nor direct, since many other variables need to be considered, there does (except for minimal task) seem to be some very general relationship between liking and respect on the one hand and productivity, satisfaction, and development on the other. We will list the propositions without elaboration; you ought to be able to apply them to your own experience and to examples you may study.

1. When liking and respect are both high, productivity, satisfaction, and development tend to be enhanced.
2. When liking and respect are both low, productivity, satisfaction, and development tend to be reduced.
3. When liking is high and respect is low, productivity tends to be reduced, satisfaction tends to be enhanced, and development may be affected either way.
4. When liking is low and respect is high, productivity tends to be enhanced, satisfaction tends to be reduced, and development may be affected either way.

Keep in mind that these statements represent very general tendencies; that is, when all other things are equal, then the factors of liking and respect can provide predictive guidelines to productivity, satisfaction, and development. A deeper understanding of the connection, especially in regard to development in a relationship, can be obtained by examining the quality of the patterned role relationships that emerge between two people.

Patterned Role Relationships

For a work relationship to be sustained at anything more than the absolute minimum required by the task or for a nonrequired relationship to continue, a mutually satisfactory role relationship has to emerge.

The role relationships people establish with others become important sources of stability in their lives; they count on them to help maintain personal identity, a basic sense of adequacy, and a sense of worth. Yet, once established, role relationships become very difficult to break out of even when they are no longer fully desired or are preventing needed growth and change. For example, think about the kinds of role relationships you have with members of that familiar organization, your family. How much have these changed as you have grown older? Do you find yourself being drawn into some of your "old behavior" every time you visit your parents? Well-developed role patterns are very hard to break. They tend to determine and shape a great deal of our behavior, and when they are outmoded, they serve to constrain a great many more satisfying possibilities in the relationships.

> We tend to take for granted those to whom we are the closest. Often we get so accustomed to seeing them and hearing from them that we lose the ability to listen to what they are really saying or to appreciate the quality—good or bad—of what they are doing.
>
> W. Bennis and B. Nanus
> *Leaders* (New York: Harper & Row, 1985)

Here is an example observed at a large urban hospital:

> The director of nursing, an attractive woman, had allowed the male administrators to treat her as a "dumb blonde," pleasant but not very smart. Their discomfort at the possibility that she might be beautiful *and* competent led them to treat her that way; her discomfort at upsetting their expectations and possibly being seen as an "aggressive bitch" led her to play along.
>
> At a training session with her female assistant director, she was confronted about this behavior and began to practice using her considerable analytical abilities. Shortly after, she was at a meeting of her peers, male directors of other departments. Someone made a snide comment about something in her jurisdiction; she came back with a fast, concise, and powerful rebuttal. When all the dropped jaws were restored to the astonished faces, one of the men said, "I'm glad to see that your nice legs haven't been affected by your brains," a not very subtle attempt to get her back in role. She had to struggle hard to continue making contributions; eventually she left the hospital for a similar job where she could start fresh.

Have you experienced a similar dilemma? It is a problem that frequently occurs, exactly *because* the relationship is reciprocal, when you attempt to change your behavior toward another person. You can decide, "From now on I'm going to be different with so-and-so." Then when you try it, "so-and-so" either resists the change, thinks you're crazy, or simply overlooks your new behavior as a temporary phenomenon. Psychotherapists struggle with this issue when they seek to bring about change in a client's behavior and other key people in the client's life continue to cast him or her into the old roles. As a gag song put it, "I Can't Get Adjusted to the You That Got Adjusted to Me." Sometimes, even when a person changes in ways that you find desirable, it can be difficult to begin treating that person in new ways! It means building a whole new role relationship, which also requires changing some of your own behavior to match the other person's. That isn't easy.

Can you see the implications of this problem for individuals who want to move upward in an organization? Every promotion or job change calls for new or altered role relationships with former colleagues and superiors. It can create great problems to become the supervisor of someone who formerly trained or managed you; how does one change from "promising young trainee" to "responsible executive"? Not everyone can easily let go of established patterns.

Don't You Dare Be Intimidated!

At Sun Microsystems . . . , Scott McNealy is the intimidating and outspoken chairman, president and chief executive. He says that he has an open e-mail policy, just like his open-door policy. This allows workers who might wilt under his glare to zip carefully crafted complaints directly into his desktop computer. He says he receives two or three suggestions a day.

[He] says it's tough for him "to get unfiltered data" from subordinates. He realizes that his style gets in the way. When he asks workers for their feedback, "I think I actually get them a little intimidated. Then if they won't give me the answer, I get a little aggressive, and that gets them a little more nervous," he says.

To offset this, Mr. McNealy tries to send a clear message that he does want criticism. He says he makes it known that "I can't stand a 'yes' person or someone who won't tell you your fly is down. What good is someone who won't tell you your fly is down?" The result: Some salesmen do tell him when he's said something "dumb" during sales calls.

Mr. McNealy says he does get defensive "because CEOs are defensive. But I'll walk away and it will register and I'll never do it again. Then I'll go back to the person and say, 'Thanks for the feedback.'"

SOURCE: Joan E. Rigdon, "Managing Your Career," *The Wall Street Journal,* August 10, 1994, p. B1. (Copyright © 1994, Dow Jones & Company, Inc.)

Self-Sealing Reciprocal Relationships: A Pattern of Conflict

Even more difficult than changing one person's role in a relationship is addressing the problem of mutually reinforcing limiting patterns. When two people have trouble working together, it is often because each produces in the other the very behavior that most irritates the counterpart, reinforcing the original behavior and keeping the pattern going. For example, Buckley wants autonomy and resents Endrunn's interference, so he withholds information, which induces Endrunn to poke around for information, reinforcing Buckley's conviction that he must give less information, which reinforces Endrunn's conviction that Buckley is closed and, therefore, won't voluntarily give information, and on and on. (See diagram of the self-sealing loop.)

This kind of endless loop can be called a *self-sealing reciprocal relationship*. The more each tries to deal with the other in the usual way, the worse the problem gets. This is often the source of continuing interpersonal struggles.

It is very difficult for one party in such a closed relationship to bring it to a halt; once inside a self-sealing loop, it is hard to see the pattern and to see how you are contributing to the problem. It's always crystal clear to each party what the *other* is doing wrong. A fellow worker, however, can often see the pattern. Once someone points it out, the involved parties can much more easily see how to break it. Mark Buckley could decide to supply Endrunn with much *more* information, and point out that he's willing to continue if Endrunn will stop jumping in with instructions to Buckley's subordinates. Or Endrunn could say to Mark, "In order to be comfortable I need to feel informed. If I interfere as a result, let me know. I want you to be able to be effective."

One party's admission of what he or she is doing to perpetuate the problem is often enough to break the sealed reciprocal pattern and lead to problem solving. In general, when you're having trouble with someone else, it's useful to look for what *you* might be doing that contributes to the problem. Poor relationships are seldom caused completely by one side. And since reciprocity is likely to be the tie that links related roles together, *changing your own behavior may indeed be likely to induce changes in the behavior of another*. If you start treating your parents as if they were serious adult

Self-Sealing Loop

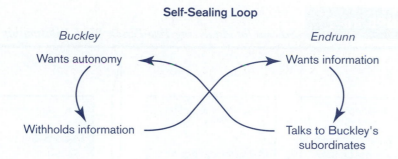

friends and as if you were also a mature adult, they will have to accommodate somehow the alterations in your behavior. If the co-worker who avoids responsibility is treated responsibly and expected to come through when needed, he or she may in fact be less likely to let you down than otherwise.

Insofar as a relationship exists in which both parties feel connected to one another, there is potential leverage for affecting the other's behavior by altering your own. Though the pulls are likely to be great to get back into the old roles, it is worth exploring whether a role relationship that is giving you trouble can be redefined into a new set of reciprocal roles through your own initiative. When that works, it can be very freeing and can lead to greater influence over the work environment you are in.

Summary

In short, the patterned role relationships that emerge in a work environment have important consequences for productivity, satisfaction, and development. While certain kinds of fixed patterns can enhance both productivity and satisfaction, as when the various aspects of two people's jobs are reciprocal, the developmental aspects of a relationship normally pertain to learning and change. When two people learn from one another, when they are able to create new role patterns as tasks and needs demand them, then the relationship will enhance all three outcomes, especially development. While work relationships of this kind may be rare and difficult to build, they are indeed worth the effort in the long run. We hope that the concepts and examples offered in this and the previous chapter will aid you in your own quest for growth-promoting work relationships.

Figure 10–7 illustrates the total picture we have covered in Chapters 9 and 10. It should be obvious by now just how complicated a two-person relationship can be; we hope to have provided a coherent picture by following the sequence of factors shown in the chart. For your own practice, you might attempt to trace some relationships with which you are familiar through the sequence; you can go in either direction. For example, you might begin with the outcomes and try to analyze how they came about. By working your way back through processes, looking at the required relationship (if it's a work context), and considering the backgrounds and circumstances, you might be able to explain the relationship in some depth. Were the outcomes predictable from any of the factors identified in the scheme? Possibly you can use this approach in a forward direction—that is, to predict the probable outcomes of some current interpersonal relationships as you see them emerging.

By developing your diagnostic skills in this fashion, you can identify ways to alter the interpersonal processes to improve the relationship. If you can develop such interpersonal skill, you can't help but become a better manager of your own relationships and, if it's ever required of you, a better manager of other people's work relationships.

FIGURE 10-7   *Schema for Analyzing Two-Person Work Relationship*

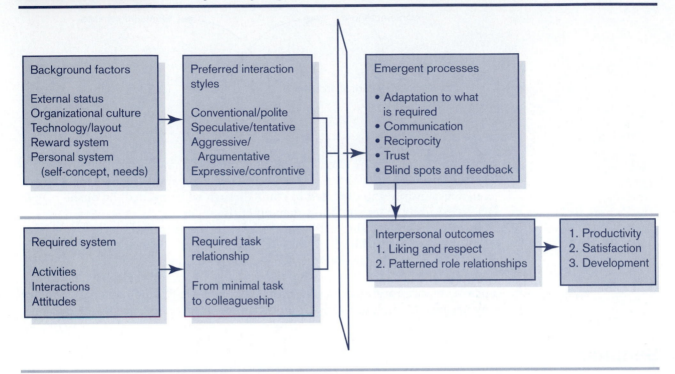

As stated earlier in this chapter, interpersonal competence is a basic ingredient of effective management; it makes a critical difference in how much *influence* you may exercise in relation to peers, superiors, and subordinates. In the next chapter, we will show just how the leadership in an organization is fundamentally a process of influence. You will be able to judge for yourself just how the interpersonal factors covered in this chapter constitute important background factors for leadership effectiveness.

KEY CONCEPTS FROM CHAPTER 10

1. Interpersonal processes.
   a. Adaptation to:
      (1) What is required.
      (2) The other person's expectations and desires.
   b. Communication.
      (1) Levels of exchange between speaker and listener:
         (i) Feelings about subject matter.
         (ii) Subject matter.
         (iii) Feelings about one another.
         (iv) Feelings about self.
      (2) Self-concepts and perceptions of other filter messages in and out.
      (3) Barriers to communication:
         (i) Imprecision of language.
         (ii) Multiple channels (verbal and nonverbal).

         (iii) State of mind.
         (iv) Gender differences.
      (4) Common problems of communication:
         (i) Mixed messages.
         (ii) Incomplete communication.
         (iii) Unconscious nonverbal signals.
         (iv) Conscious nonverbal signals.
         (v) The greater the emotional involvement with a subject, the greater the likelihood of distortion.
      (5) It takes both people for communication to work.
   c. Reciprocity.
      (1) To maintain a relationship, one must fulfill the norm of reciprocity.
   d. Trust and other feelings:

(1) Feeling supported, adequate, and worthy leads to closeness, warmth, and trust in a relationship.

(2) Trust:
   (i) In the other's competence and ability.
   (ii) In the other's judgment.
   (iii) In the other's willingness to be helpful.
   (iv) In the other's concern for your welfare.
   (v) That the other will meet commitments.

(3) Trust is easily destroyed, unless you:
   (i) Act with integrity.
   (ii) Maintain confidentialities.
   (ii) Do your job effectively.
   (iv) Avoid inappropriate secrecy.
   (v) Keep others informed.

e. Dealing with blind spots (the need for feedback).
   (1) Openness and self-disclosure reduce blind spots.
   (2) Openness often means taking a risk, but can build trust.

f. Attention to interpersonal processes is necessary to
   (1) Build a positive relationship.
   (2) Maintain a positive relationship.

2. Negotiations are a special but common form of interpersonal relationship.

a. Can be over tangibles or intangibles.

b. Substantive results and relationship impact are outcomes of any negotiation.

c. Strategy depends on the importance of each outcome.

d. Situation and personal style affect negotiator's power.

e. Major differences between competitive and collaborative negotiations.

3. Outcomes of interpersonal relationships.
a. Liking and respect.
   (1) To the extent that personal closeness, warmth, and trust emerge, liking will result.
   (2) To the extent that task-related trust emerges, respect will result.
   (3) Correlations of liking and respect with productivity, satisfaction, and development.

b. Patterned role relationships.
   (1) A source of stability in people's lives.
   (2) Can become self-sealing.
   (3) To break the pattern requires both to change; either can start.

4. A positive relationship is one in which:.
a. The required task gets done properly and with reasonable efficiency (productivity).
b. The parties involved are reasonably satisfied (satisfaction).
c. The growth of both is fostered, or at least not hindered (development).

PERSONAL APPLICATION EXERCISE

Reducing Your Blind Spots

One of the greatest handicaps of a manager is the existence of blind spots. Unfortunately, managers often don't know how to reduce or prevent blind spots, even if they suspect they have some. You might do well to discover your own, even before you become a manager. There are a variety of ways to do this, short of creating a potentially awkward but rewarding situation by just asking others to tell you what they think of you. The following procedure could be valuable to you, even though it may not feel comfortable at first.

In most relationships there are things you do that people wish you would stop doing, things you don't do that they wish you would start doing, and things you are doing that they like and want you to continue. Pick someone you trust and ask that person to interview a half dozen or so of your other friends (or co-workers), using the framework described above (i.e., "stop, start, continue" categories). That person should then put together a composite of all the interviews in order to mask the sources of the comments. Any words or expressions that would identify the source should be changed or deleted. What you will receive is a fairly clear picture of the impact of your behavior on others in a form that you should find useful. Although you might expect to find a lot of negative comments, this usually does not happen. In fact, you will probably be pleasantly surprised.

Finally, in the spirit of reciprocity, you might offer to do the same thing for the other person.

SUGGESTED READINGS

Antonioni, David. "Designing an Effective 360-Degree Appraisal Feedback Process." *Organizational Dynamics,* Autumn 1996, pp. 24–38.

Athos, A., and J. Gabarro. *Interpersonal Behavior.* Englewood Cliffs, NJ: Prentice-Hall, 1978.

Beier, E. G. "Nonverbal Communication: How We Send Emotional Messages." *Psychology Today* 8 (1974), pp. 53–56.

Bouty, I. "Interpersonal and Interaction Influences on Informal Resource Exchanges between R&D Researchers across Organizational Boundaries." *Academy of Management Journal* 43, no. 1 (February 2000), pp. 50–68.

Caudron, Shari. "Spreading Out the Carrots." *Industry Week,* May 19, 1997, pp. 20–25.

Collins, E. G. C., and T. B. Blodgett. "Sexual Harassment . . . Some See It . . . Some Won't." *Harvard Business Review,* March–April 1981, pp. 76–95.

Cox, Taylor H., and Blake, Stacy. "Managing Cultural Diversity: Implications for Organizational Competitiveness." *Academy of Management Executive* 5, no. 3 (1991), p. 47.

Edwards, Mark R., and Ann J. Ewen. *360 Degree Feedback,* New York: AMACOM, 1996.

Fidler, L. A., and J. D. Johnson. "Communication and Innovation Implementation." *Academy of Management Review* 9 (1984), pp. 704–11.

Hall, E. T. *The Silent Language.* Greenwich, CT: Fawcett Publications, 1959.

Halperin, D.; C. R. Snyer; R. J. Shenkkel; and B. K. Houston. "Effects of Source Status and Message Favorability on Acceptance of Personality Feedback." *Journal of Applied Psychology* 61 (1976), pp. 85–88.

Hayes, M. A. "Nonverbal Communication: Expression without Words." In *Readings in International and Organizational Communication,* ed. R. C. Huseman, C. M. Logue, and D. L. Freshley. Boston: Holbrook Press, 1973.

Hequet, M. "Giving Good Feedback." *Training,* September 1994, pp. 72–77.

Jacoby, J.; D. Mazursky; T. Troutman; and A. Kuss. "When Feedback Is Ignored: Disutility of Outcome Feedback." *Journal of Applied Psychology* 69 (1984), pp. 531–45.

Kiechel, Walter, III. "The Art of the Exit Interview." *Fortune,* August 13, 1990.

Kosicki, George. "Interpersonal Comparisons and Labor Supply: An Empirical Analysis." *Economist,* Spring 1993.

Landler, Mark. "Everything from IPOs to S-E-X." *Business Week,* February 17, 1992.

Larson, J. R. Jr. "The Dynamic Interplay between Employees' Feedback-Seeking Strategies and Supervisors' Delivery of Performance Feedback." *Academy of Management Review* 14, no. 3 (1989), pp. 408–22.

Lewicki, R. J. "Negotiating Strategically." In *The Portable MBA in Management,* ed. A. R. Cohen. New York: Wiley, 1993.

Reese, Jennifer. "The Decline of Office Manners." *Fortune,* May 31, 1993.

Reilly, Richard R.; James W. Smither; and Nicholas L. Vasilopoulos. "A Longitudinal Study of Upward Feedback." *Personnel Psychology,* Autumn 1996, pp. 599–612.

Rice, Faye. "How to Deal with Tougher Customers." *Fortune,* December 3, 1990.

Sinetar, M. "Building Trust into Corporate Relationships." *Organizational Dynamics* 16, no. 3 (Winter 1988).

Sitkin, Sim B.; Denise M. Rousseau; Ronald S. Burt; and Colin Camerer, eds. "Special Topic Forum on Trust in and between Organizations." *Academy of Management Review* 23 (July 1998).

Vinson, Mary N. "The Pros and Cons of 360-Degree Feedback: Making It Work." *Training and Development,* April 1996, pp. 11–12.

Yammarino, Francis J., and Leanne E. Atwater. "Do Managers See Themselves as Others See Them? Implications of Self-Other Rating Agreement for Human Resources Management." *Organizational Dynamics,* Spring 1997, pp. 35–44.

Zaleznik, A., and D. Moment. *The Dynamics of Interpersonal Behavior.* New York: John Wiley & Sons, 1964.

Leadership

Exerting Influence and Power

MANAGERIAL BULLETIN

The Power of Personal Commitment and Vulnerability

So how do you motivate people? Not with techniques, but by risking yourself with a personal, lifelong commitment to greatness—by demonstrating courage. You don't teach it so much as challenge it into existence.

SOURCE: Peter Koestenbaum, Philosopher and Consultant to Top Executives, quoted in Polly Labarre, "Do You Have the Will to Lead," *Fast Company,* March 2000, p. 222.

"The core problem for leaders is getting others to do what is necessary to accomplish the organization's goals."

The topic of leadership has fascinated people through the ages. After much discussion and research, the pursuit of a universal definition of effective leadership is still intriguing but elusive. The world awaits definitive answers to such questions as: What makes a good leader? Who can be a leader? Can anyone be a leader? Can leadership skills be taught? What makes followers follow? What are the limits to leadership?

Social science researchers for years pursued the notion that there must be some common qualities shared by all leaders. Many long lists of sterling qualities (aggressiveness, wisdom, charisma, courage, and so forth) have been generated but have not been found to apply to all leaders in all situations. To be effective a leader's qualities must relate somehow to the situation he or she is in and to the nature of the followers. This view is consistent with the situational approach taken throughout this book, yet is barely widely accepted. The belief does not easily fade away that General Patton, Mahatma Gandhi, Vince Lombardi, Golda Meir, and Martin Luther King—or the heads of AOL, GM, Microsoft, and John Hancock—must have had exactly the same qualities.

Throughout this and the next chapter, we will be using the terms *manager* and *leader* interchangeably, even though customarily there is a distinction. A manager is usually considered to be someone who makes sure that work is carried out properly, while a leader is considered to be the person who decides on what the work ought to be (i.e., the direction to be taken). The two roles are increasingly hard to separate, since most managers today do have some responsibility for setting direction, and few get to just carry out routine work.

As you might expect, insofar as there are common components to the manager's or leader's job, a few traits appear to be consistent requirements. In Chapter 1 we induced from Mintzberg's analysis of a manager's job some of the skills required by a manager. Recall that a manager needs interpersonal skills to acquire information needed for decision making. Leaders need to have the ability to influence other people's behavior, a readiness to absorb interpersonal stress, the capacity to structure social interactions to task needs, some self-confidence, and the drive to exercise initiative in social situations, all of which are directly related to the nature of managerial work.

> The role of the CEO is to produce poetry and plumbing.
>
> James March

Effective leaders also have a strong drive for responsibility and task completion, energy and persistence for accomplishing goals yet a willingness to tolerate frustration and delay (since working with and through others does not always result in immediate action!), some willingness to take risks and be original in solving problems, and, perhaps most important, a willingness to accept the consequences of making decisions and taking action.[1]

In general, you can see that these traits are closely related to the kinds of situations in which virtually all leaders find themselves, having to build relationships in order to accomplish tasks and having to take responsibility for their system's performance.

The *particular* requirements for effective leadership in each situation, however, may well outweigh all of these traits or make only certain ones critical in importance. As we will show in Chapter 12, different kinds of tasks, different kinds of subordinates, and differing leader characteristics all affect what leader behavior will be effective. Thus, possession of the qualities listed does *not* guarantee that one will become a leader, nor does the absence of any one of them rule out the possibility of

MANAGERIAL BULLETIN

In the Lead: Some Managers Are More than Bosses—They're Leaders, Too

Managers "know how to write business plans, while leaders get companies—and people—to change," says Carol Bartz, chief executive of Autodesk Inc. When she was recruited six years ago to head the Silicon Valley software company, profits were flat, and sales growth was slowing dramatically. New software releases were way behind schedule. The prior CEO had left amid open rebellion by the company's young and undisciplined programmers, who viewed top management as an overbearing evil. Ms. Bartz didn't hesitate to impose her views. She rounded up employees she determined were "opinion leaders" and persuaded them that no matter how inventive they were at 3 A.M. dreaming up new software, they wouldn't get anywhere if they didn't deliver products on time. The new version of the company's flagship product made it to market just four days late.

Within six months, she dumped marginal businesses, made an acquisition and reassigned programmers, ignoring those who advise new CEOs to respect the past. "That's a mistake," insists Ms. Bartz. "If you just do what's already been done, how do you show your value? You have to make tough decisions." She also impressed employees with her personal courage. On her second day at Autodesk, Ms. Bartz, a former Sun Microsystems executive, was diagnosed with breast cancer. Figuring that as a new CEO it wasn't the time to disappear, she refused to let her illness distract her from her job. She had a stopgap lumpectomy, then worked a month before getting the radical mastectomy she needed.

Straightforward and unpretentious, with a hearty laugh, Ms. Bartz links her leadership strength to knowing that "you constantly have to reinvent yourself." Since 1992, she has more than doubled Autodesk's revenue to more than $600 million. "Human nature says cling to what you have, whether that's an old coat, a boyfriend, or a way of doing business," she says. A leader has to enjoy saying, "leave that behind."

SOURCE: Carol Hymowitz, "In the Lead," *The Wall Street Journal*, December 8, 1998, p. B1. (Copyright © 1998, Dow Jones & Company, Inc.)

MANAGERIAL BULLETIN

Leadership Practices and Attitudes (Competencies) Common to 62 Companies

The five core leadership attribute buckets:

"IQ" (Mental horsepower).

"EQ" (Emotional Intelligence).

"Know" (Business and technical acumen).

"Grow" (personal development).

"Ego" (Strong sense of self).

Next, the four core leadership practice buckets:

"Tell" (Giving direction).

"Sell" (Influencing others).

"Initiate" (Making things happen).

"Relate" (Building relationships).

SOURCE: George O. Klemp, "Leadership Practices and Attitudes (Competencies) Common to 62 Companies," in *Putting It Together* (Cambria Consulting, Inc., 1998).

becoming an effective leader. We, therefore, must emphasize that the potential for leadership may be assumed to be widely distributed among the general population, and a wide variety of leader behaviors may be effective in particular situations.[2]

What, then, must be taken into account by leaders who wish to be effective in their particular organization? What behavior works best under what conditions?

MANAGERIAL BULLETIN

Can Leadership Be Taught?

Leadership is no longer seen as the exclusive preserve of the inhabitants of executive row. The nurturing of "corporate Gandhis" has given way to a focus on developing leadership abilities among employees at all levels of our organizations. An executive, a manager, a supervisor, an hourly worker—all can learn to develop a vision for the future. All can learn to accept new responsibilities, to take risks, to build consensus and trust among subordinates and peers. Certainly not everyone has the potential of a Lee Iacocca. But everyone possesses innate leadership abilities to some degree and those abilities can be improved.

SOURCE: Chris Lee, *Training*, July 1989.

That is what we explore in this and the next chapter. We begin in this chapter with an analysis of leadership in general as the exercise of power and influence, then continue in Chapter 12 with the roles of formally appointed managers and their leadership choices.

Leadership as Influence

The core problem for leaders in organizations involves getting others to do what is necessary to accomplish the organization's goals. This is a complex process, because the goals as well as the means for accomplishing them are often unclear, subject to discussion or negotiation, and can change over time. A leader's boss (or bosses), peers, and subordinates all have ideas about what should be done and how to do it, and they are likely to try to get their ideas heard. Furthermore, leaders are only human and unlikely to know everything, so they need to be able to alter their views when others make good points.

Nevertheless, once goals are determined, leaders or managers must find a way to create the conditions that will cause (or allow) subordinates to work hard and to direct that work toward organizational ends. This may call for many different kinds of influence behavior aimed in many directions: negotiating a larger budget; getting other departments to deliver accurate and timely information; providing vision, direction, or training to subordinates; simplifying or complicating work; obtaining a deserved salary increase for someone, and so forth. All these activities—up, sideways, and down—ultimately are aimed at getting others, especially subordinates, to do what is necessary to accomplish successfully the work of the system being led.

Leadership is the ability to get men to do what they don't want to do and like it.

Harry Truman

As countless leaders have discovered countless times, this is more easily said than done. Subordinates don't always know how to work well, don't always work as hard as is necessary, and don't automatically care about the unit's or organization's success. The fact is, leaders are interdependent with many others, especially their followers. They have an effect on, and in turn are affected by, those with whom they must work. The key element is the *influence* the leader has on others and the *influence*

MANAGERIAL BULLETIN

Training Bosses to Use Influence, Not Raw Aggression, Improves Their Effectiveness

Coaching—as executive development has come to be called—is not new. But corporate shrinkage and the dawning era of flexible, decentralized management are making obsolete the idea that executives can expect to muscle their way to a career pinnacle and then coast until retirement. Increasingly, they are expected to be, in the words of the anthropologist Harvey Sarles, "autodidacts," or self-teachers and lifelong learners, whose performance will evolve and improve.

SOURCE: Barbara Presley Noble, "At Work: In Praise of Executive Coaching," *New York Times*, April 24, 1994, p. F23.

they have in return. For this reason we can think of leadership as a *process* in which the involved parties *influence* one another in particular ways. *Influence is any act or potential act that affects the behavior of another person(s).* Let's look at the implications of using the concept.

First, influence cannot happen in isolation from others; it takes at least two to "tangle," just as with interpersonal relationships. The person who wants to influence must find someone to influence. Second, if you think about it carefully, you will see that only in the most extreme situations could *one* person in an influence transaction have *all* the influence—that is, affect the other's behavior without being affected in turn by the other's reaction. The machinist who leaps to attention when the boss gives an order, the secretary who bursts into tears when feeling that a request to work late is unreasonable, the student who challenges an assignment due the day after vacation—all exert influence on the person trying to influence them.

Cooperating humbly, for example, affects the person who is asking for cooperation and "pulls" more of the same from him or her. As Gandhi showed so well in India, humble, passive noncooperation can have a profound influence on those giving orders. Even the person who follows directions he or she knows are wrong out of fear of being fired or punished has influence on the behavior of the tyrant, allowing further exploitation and mistakes, because the directions were not resisted.

We must be careful then to remember that influence succeeds in moving others in desired directions only when the *net* influence, the amount of A's influence on B compared with B's influence on A, is greater. In the classroom or on the job, students and workers can be less *or* more influential than teachers and supervisors. *Leadership is net influence in a direction desired by the person possessing it.*

To understand this process better, we need to look at various types of influence. One important aspect of influence is whether or not it is formal or informal, part of a job's definition or acquired in some other way. *Formal influence is influence prescribed for the holder of an "office" or a position in a particular social system.* It is influence *assigned* to a position. The coach of a team has formal influence in initiating practice sessions, selecting starting players and substitutes, and so forth. *Informal influence is influence not prescribed for the office holder but nevertheless affecting other members of the social system.* On the same team, for example, there may be several players whose advice other players and even the coach seek on such matters as techniques and strategy against opponents. Although by position the players have no special influence allotted or assigned to them, their knowledge or personal attractiveness, or both, give them influence anyway. Influence based on special knowledge is *expert* influence, while influence based on personal charm is called *charisma*.

In addition to the distinction between formal and informal influence (i.e., assigned or unassigned), we need to add the concepts of legitimacy and illegitimacy. Legitimate influence is exerted by a person who is seen as having the right to do so by those influenced. In other words, legitimate influence is *accepted as proper* by the person being influenced. Conversely, illegitimate influence is exerted by a person not seen as having the right to do so by those being influenced. Illegitimate influence is *not accepted as proper* by the person being influenced. The basis for considering an influencer as legitimate may be (1) a positive assessment of his or her personal qualities, such as competence, experience, and age and (2) the acceptance of the process (such as election, appointment, or automatic succession) by which the person acquired a role calling for the exercise of influence. Legitimacy will usually be limited to areas within the scope of the system and its goals. For example, most people will believe that the boss may legitimately give orders about how to sell a machine but not about where to go on vacation. But within the scope of the organization, orders, requests, and directions will be seen as proper when they come from someone who has acquired an office by an approved process or has personal qualities considered appropriate.

> To despise legitimate authority, no matter in whom it is invested, is unlawful; it is rebellion against God's will.
>
> Leo XII
> *Immortale Dei*
> November 1, 1885

On the other hand, even in the army—where soldiers are taught to "salute the uniform, not the man," suggesting that mere appointment to rank guarantees legitimacy—a soldier may refuse to follow direct orders under a variety of circumstances. To illustrate, if the commanding officer has disruptive personality characteristics or has acquired his office in objectionable ways, such as perceived favoritism, there may be rebellion. Furthermore, when influence is not seen as acquired legitimately, soldiers and other subordinates have many ways of subverting any orders from a person whose influence they do not accept, such as dragging their heels by following literally all rules in the books. Going passive is a common way of resisting what is seen as illegitimate influence.

Because having formal influence does not ensure legitimacy nor does having informal influence ensure illegitimacy, it is useful to combine the two categories into the four possible combinations, as shown in Figure 11–1.

By looking at the combinations, we can see the ways in which influence is exercised. *Formal-legitimate influence* is what is usually meant when people say "the boss has the authority" to enforce particular behaviors. *It is the influence both prescribed for the holder of an office in a social system and seen as his or her right to exert by the other members of it.* Many leadership activities in organizations involve formal-legitimate influence by someone who has been assigned a role with supervisory responsibilities and who can use organizational means to reward or punish subordinates. The right to hire, fire, promote, and adjust pay reinforces this kind of influence.

Because most people who accept jobs in an organization are reasonably willing to accept directions from their "boss" on job-related matters, legitimacy is often taken for granted and assumed to go with any formal role. During such times as the student strikes in the late 1960s and early 1970s or the rebellions of workers in France, it becomes evident that the legitimacy of those with formal organizational positions is precarious and rests upon the attitudes of the "followers." Students challenged the rights of professors to determine subject matter, give exams and grades, hire and fire colleagues; and they exerted influence on other activities that had traditionally been

FIGURE 11–1   *Examples of Types of Influence*

	Formal (assigned)	**Informal (not assigned)**
Legitimate (accepted as proper)	Boss gives work-related orders to subordinate: "Stop making widgets and begin making frammisses."	Respected colleague helps you solve a problem by showing you the proper order to make calculations.
	Teacher assigns an analytical paper, based on concepts in the text.	Basketball benchwarmer notices flaw in opponent's defense, convinces coach to alter offense.
Illegitimate (not accepted as proper)	Boss makes strong hints about subordinate's family life: "Send your son to a private school."	Co-worker threatens to beat you up if you continue to produce so much.
	Student put in charge of class discussion by instructor.	Fellow students ridicule you for asking questions in class, despite instructor's request for questions.

seen as part of faculty prerogatives. More recently, students have challenged college trustees about investments in companies using child labor, and challenged administrators about pay levels of building and grounds workers. Pressure from workers in several European countries has led to change in what were traditionally considered management's prerogatives. In several countries, workers must even be consulted for such decisions as plant location and new investments in equipment. Thus, the boundaries of legitimacy for decisions is changing. Furthermore, legitimacy, even for someone in a formal position, must be earned and may occasionally need renewal. At different times a formal leader may find legitimacy slipping away because of questions about competence or about the way in which the person is leading. Similarly, some subordinates may see the boss as legitimate while others don't. It is often the case that an appointed leader is perceived as legitimate by those with similar backgrounds and as illegitimate by those with backgrounds different from the leader's. A scientist might not, for example, accept the influence of an engineer as a project leader as readily as would another engineer. Since legitimacy is an attitude about a person by other persons, it can change just as do other attitudes. Nevertheless, much of the work of organizations is done because there is a considerable amount of legitimacy granted to those in formal positions; but that is by no means the only kind of leadership exerted.

A great deal of influence is based upon knowledge, expertise (whether perceived or real), or personal charm rather than position.[3] *This informal-legitimate influence by a member of a social system stands apart from the prescribed influence of his or her office but is accepted as within one's rights by the others in the system.* It is not predictable from organization charts but is essential to organizational functioning. Some people know things or behave in charismatic ways that others value, regardless of position, and are given influence accordingly. The most expert auditor in an accounting office may be consulted by other auditors and listened to even though he or she has no formal assignment to help others. The rewards and punishments available to this kind of influencer are more personal—that is, he or she can give or withhold important information or support in return for gratitude and respect.

Leadership in classroom groups is often of the "expert" kind, with the most knowledgeable member(s) of the group gradually becoming respected and listened to even when there is no formal leader. In fact, among many student groups there is a widespread student norm that no peer should give orders or directions to another student, so even those students put in leadership roles by a class exercise often hold back from giving directions.

Conversely, a fellow student making a "grab for power" will usually be resisted by other students. Sometimes such a person has quickly volunteered for a leadership role before others dare to and is allowed to take it despite feelings that "it isn't right"; in

MANAGERIAL BULLETIN

A Title Is No Guarantee of Power

And these considerations . . . hamstrung [Mayor] La-Guardia in his dealings with [Robert] Moses: Moses' popularity; Moses' immense influence with a governor and a legislature from whom the mayor constantly needed favors; Moses' ability to ram through the great public works that the mayor desperately wanted . . . scandal-free and in time for the next election. With good reason, he doubted whether anyone else could. The powers that the mayor possessed over Moses' authorities in theory he did not possess in practice. Political realities gave him no choice but to allow Moses to remain at their head. And the mayor knew it.

Moses knew it, too. After reading the bond agreements and contracts, LaGuardia dropped all further discussion of the authorities' powers. Moses never raised the matter again. But thereafter he treated La-Guardia not as his superior but as an equal. In the areas in which he was interested–transportation and recreation–Robert Moses, who had never been elected by the people of the city to any office, was thence forward to have at least as much voice in determining the city's future as any official the people *had* elected–including the mayor.

SOURCE: Robert A. Caro, *The Power Broker: Robert Moses and The Fall of New York* (New York: Alfred A. Knopf, © 1974).

that case, the student has *formal-illegitimate influence,* which may not last long, unless he or she is seen as helping the group reach its goals. Similarly, in organizations where members are accustomed to having considerable say in matters affecting them, the boss's decision to create a new position located between him or her and the others ("because the work load is too heavy for me") can result in resentment toward *whoever* is put in that new job and lead only to grudging cooperation. If that person, however, has the formal authorization to administer some organizational rewards and punishments, he or she may end up with considerable influence anyway.

Finally, *the person who acquires influence over others by personal access to some valued rewards or feared punishments is using informal-illegitimate influence.* Physical threats by a fellow worker can coerce compliance that would otherwise be refused, as can special relationships with higher-ups. In one New Hampshire school system, for example, by maintaining a close relationship with several powerful school board members, the music director forced principals to release students for weeklong band trips and to arrange schedules to suit his convenience. He thus obtained more influence over principals than was called for by his position or was seen as his right by them. Although he obtained compliance, he also created considerable resentment and was constantly criticized behind his back by the principals.

I must admit my management style was too simple sometimes.

Chinese track coach Ma Junren, after confirming that he occasionally beat up members of his world-class squad, *Newsweek,* April 3, 1995

Taking Initiative as an Act of Leadership

Have you ever found yourself in a room that was so hot and stuffy that you and other students were having trouble concentrating on the lecture or discussion? What do you do? Wait and hope the instructor will recognize the problem and call a break; or raise your hand, point out the difficulty, and suggest opening some windows and taking a break? Raising your hand could be an act of leadership. To wait for the designated leader (instructor) to act could mean missing an opportunity to make it a better class. Taking initiative might have the payoff of enhancing your influence (or status) but also involves the risk of being "shot down" by the formal leader of the class.

In the next chapter we examine the obligations and choices of those who have been formally appointed to managerial positions, that is, who are in a formal role. In this chapter we have been discussing the exercise of influence by anyone and have defined *leadership as influence*. We might also define leadership as those *actions that move a group toward its goals* (such as opening a window when the room is stuffy). The distinction between formal and informal leadership is a useful reminder that as group members and as subordinates anyone can exert influence (leadership)—and often should. In small work groups, it is important for all members to take initiative. Similarly, it can be important that a subordinate exert initiative in a staff meeting or a committee meeting and not just wait for all leadership to come from the designated manager or chairperson.

How People Are Influenced

There are three processes (not mutually exclusive) by which people are influenced—*compliance, identification,* and *internalization*.[4] The very same behavior (namely, doing what you are told to do by another person) can stem from any one or a combination of these processes.

Compliance amounts to doing something because of the costs of not doing it. You go along with the "order" on the outside, but inside you may feel resentment or resignation. Any leader's influence can rest on compliance, particularly where there is fear of punishment or a desire to gain some reward; this may be the only way in which an informal-illegitimate leader can exert influence. Where compliance is operating, leaders will be successful only as long as they have control over whatever it is followers need or want.

Identification occurs when you are influenced by someone because of the attractiveness of that person, because the person either is likable and has charisma or represents something to which you aspire (e.g., an important position). Formal, designated leaders or managers often exert influence because subordinates identify with them. They may also be legitimized by their subordinates through the same process.

Identification with a charismatic leader can dramatically affect behavior for people who want to believe in lofty goals that will somehow be ennobling. When such people see a leader as having a grand vision of what is possible and offering specific means for achieving their dreams, they identify with the leader and dedicate themselves to the cause. This can lead to extraordinary efforts by followers on behalf of the leader and, thus, unusually high organizational performance. That is why effective high-level executives spend so much time creating a vision or "story" about where they see their organization (or unit) going and then telling and retelling it to colleagues, subordinates, and outsiders.[5]

Ironically, it has been claimed that charismatic leaders only succeed because they make followers feel weak and dependent. But some charismatic leaders can make followers feel *more* powerful, *more* confident, and *more* capable, not less.[6] Followers come to see themselves as achieving their *own* goals through the leader, not as having the leader's goals forced on them. When this happens, influence through identification with the leader can spread to another mode, internalization.

Internalization, the third kind of influence, happens when leaders have the necessary expertise and values to be credible to their followers; they come to believe that what the leader suggests is in fact the best course of action for them. The leader's opinions are seen as valid and trustworthy. The effect is that followers internalize the leader's opinions, thus giving full legitimization to the leader—formally designated or not.

Managing Your Career: Silicon Valley Hybrid—A Boss Who Makes Others' Ideas Pay Off

At McKinsey, the emphasis was on getting the right answer, [Gregory Slayton, CEO of ClickAction, Inc.] says. But "Silicon Valley is all about the strength of your network. If no one answers your call, you can't get that answer implemented." . . .

To succeed as a Silicon Valley CEO, he says, requires more than "intellectual firepower." He considers himself an "implementer," whose successes have come mostly from other people's ideas. What is needed, he says, is the ceaseless drive to make things happen, the willingness to make a decision when you have only 10% of the information you would like to have, and the ability to forge trusting relationships.

That ability is critical in motivating the workers of the new economy, he says. "You have to get them interested in the greater cause you're pursuing," he explains. "If not, they're out there playing video games and trading on E*Trade."

SOURCE: Hal Lancaster, "Silicon Valley Hybrid: A Boss Who Makes Others' Ideas Pay," *The Wall Street Journal*, October 26, 1999.

. . . the ultimate paradox of social leadership and social power. To be an effective leader, one must turn all of his so-called followers into leaders.

David C. McClelland
Power: The Inner Experience

Over the long run, the most successful managers are those whose influence is based on credibility—that is, where the followers are convinced by the logic of the leader's ideas and requests and internalize the influence.

You can see how a combination of these factors can have different effects. Compliance may be necessary under certain conditions (e.g., an emergency or when the task is minor and implementation is easily enforced) but is difficult for a manager to sustain. Some people will do what you want strictly out of compliance and some because they identify with you or your position. To maximize your effectiveness as a leader, however, it is best to build credibility and reach people through internalization, so that they will do what is necessary because they want to.

Generating Employee Commitment

The important outcome of both identification and internalization is *commitment,* which is an attitude driven from within the person. You know when you are committed to something—a person, an activity, a belief—when your behavior is motivated by forces inside yourself and not from outside pressures, as with compliance. In the past, organizations have depended heavily on compliance and control to accomplish their goals; today more and more organizations are attempting to build employee commitment, which obviously has more long-lasting benefits. Leadership efforts have been directed to three major areas: the work itself, the relations among people, and the organization as a whole.

Approaches to building commitment to the work itself include both formal methods, such as work redesign, and informal ones, such as permitting employees a high degree of freedom to manage their own work procedures. Approaches to generating interpersonal commitment also have included formal and informal methods

Winning Strategies of Corporate Stars

Headhunters Neff and Citrin found America's top business leaders share these six principles:

1. Live with integrity, lead by example. "Integrity builds the trust in senior management that is . . . critical for high-performing organizations."

2. Develop a winning strategy or "big idea." "A successful leader must go to the company's roots and build on the things the organization truly does best."

3. Build a great management team. Great leaders hired managers "whose skills and experiences complemented their own, but whose passion, attitudes, and values were one and the same."

4. Inspire employees to greatness. "Communicate continuously, listen carefully, genuinely tolerate failure as a learning experience."

5. Create a flexible, responsive organization. "The best leaders have redesigned their organizations to make sure decisions can be made fast."

6. Use reinforcing management systems. "Compensation . . . must be consistent with and reinforce the values and strategy of the organization."

SOURCE: "In Search of Leadership: A Talk with Headhunters Turned Authors Citrin and Neff," *Business Week,* November 15, 1999, p. 172. (Copyright 1999 McGraw-Hill, Inc.)

such as planned team-building or informal encouragement of collaborative norms. Similarly, organizational commitment is developed in both formal and informal ways. The "transformational" leader, who inspires people to excel and articulates a meaningful vision for the organization, uses both ways to build employee commitment.[7] In Chapter 12 we introduce you to the concept of "developmental leadership," which is similar to that of transformational leadership, but which goes beyond it by spelling out practical applications in the workplace. It might interest you to know that the traits of the transformational or developmental leader are claimed to be more typically characteristic of women than of men. The implications of this for future organizational needs and for personal learning and opportunity are extremely important.[8] However, recent survey evidence raises questions about whether there are real differences between men and women managers:

> . . . a 15-year survey of 41,000 executives–25% of them female–at 5,000 companies shows that women are slightly more high-handed than the guys are when making decisions . . . Discovery Learning . . . came to that conclusion by investigating whether managers solve business problems autocratically–preferring to make unilateral decisions–or "inclusively . . ." [W]here an autocratic style was deemed appropriate, women chose "my-way-or-the-highway" 35% of the time, guys only 31.5% . . . "Did [women managers] make it to these levels because they operate more like men, or is there basically no difference?" . . . if your boss is a Ms., don't automatically expect her decision-making to be warm and fuzzy.[9]

Finally, it is important to recognize that, while the three areas of commitment discussed above tend to be related, they also exist independently of each other. Many workers are committed to their work and not to their colleagues or to the organization as a whole. And many employees are committed to their "team" and even to the organization and feel a very low level of identification with the work they are doing. Because there are a variety of combinations of the three dimensions, it is important for a manager to develop a diagnostic profile of the three as they fit his or her part of the organization. Such a diagnosis allows for a focused approach to

MANAGERIAL TOOLS

Gaining Commitment from Your Employees: Some Key Points

- For the *individual,* it depends on:

  1. Involvement.
  2. Choice.
  3. Meeting positive expectations.
  4. Feeling supported and valued.
  5. Need fulfillment.
  6. Feedback that facilitates improvement.
  7. Intrinsic satisfactions.
  8. Challenge and opportunities to grow.
  9. Being treated fairly.
  10. Affirmation of self-concept.

- In *interpersonal relationships,* it depends on:

  1. Mutual support, acceptance and reinforcement of self.
  2. Openness where needed and appropriate.
  3. Trust and confidence (mutual).
  4. Compatible styles:
     a. Similar or
     b. Complementary.
  5. Acceptance or appreciation of differences, or both.
  6. Opportunities to problem solve jointly.
  7. Willingness to manage conflicts.

- For a *group,* it depends on:

  1. Norms that support organizational goals.
  2. Cohesiveness around those norms.
  3. Rewards at a group level.
  4. Group being valued by organization.
  5. Acceptance of individual differences in abilities, preferences, and values.
  6. Ability to match member resources to any given task.

- For the *total system,* it depends on:

  1. The parts being aware of the whole.
  2. Groups being willing to accept each other's legitimacy and importance.
  3. Willingness of people to interact across group boundaries.
  4. Recognition of the importance of reciprocity.
  5. Appreciating the importance of diversity with respect to:
     a. Ideas and
     b. People.

SOURCE: Stephen L. Fink, *High Commitment Workplaces,* Quorum Books, 1992.

---

actions that will address problems of commitment where they exist. In the Managerial Tools box above, we have listed some of the key issues that pertain to employee commitment as they affect the individual, interpersonal relationships, group behavior, and the organization as a whole.

Power

The *capacity to exert influence is power.* (Often "power" and "influence" are used interchangeably.) People who have the ability to exert one or more of the four types of influence have power, which can be used toward the organization's ends or toward subgroup or individual goals, including those in direct opposition to organizational goals. As suggested earlier, no one is completely without influence, but some people have more net influence than others and hence more power.

Power is often perceived to be a bit "dirty," at least in the United States, something vulgar, but it is more than a set of sneaky tactics for grinding others into the dirt; *power in organizations is the ability to make things happen.*[10] Organizational work cannot be done without that ability, and managers need to understand it in order to bring together the people and resources to accomplish what must be done and to avoid the negative consequences of power differentials.

MANAGERIAL BULLETIN

Tyrants Beware

Nobody minds being subjected to the power of somebody who's genuinely interested in getting the job done and making more money and extracting maximum performance. But nobody wants to be told that they have to have their pencils sharpened and the erasers all facing in the same direction before they leave the office at night.

SOURCE: Michael Korda, "Psychodynamics of Power," *Mainliner*, March 1977.

MANAGERIAL BULLETIN

Rep. Bolling Takes His Leave of Power

It took me 32 years to realize that it's sometimes more important to have the trappings of power than power itself. If you've got a good-looking room with a nice chandelier, your colleagues may think you've got power.

Actually, all you've got is a chandelier and room. Washington is full of illusions like that.

SOURCE: Dennis Farney, *The Wall Street Journal*, January 1, 1982.

Sources of Power in Organizations

How, then, is power obtained by individuals in organizations? In general, The more legitimate one is perceived to be, the greater the likelihood of acceptance of one's attempts to influence, and the less resentment at going along.[11] Power goes to those who are seen as having a right to it. Conversely, the less legitimate forms of influence breed resistance and resentment, although they will probably enhance the power of someone who already possesses other kinds of legitimate influence.

Additionally, informal influence is often necessary for those with formal influence if they want more than drudging cooperation; when a formally designated leader does not have some knowledge seen as helpful by subordinates, it will be difficult to secure more than token compliance. As organizations become more complex and technically demanding, more people in leadership positions do *not* have the technical expertise necessary to gain influence beyond that of their own job description, making it hard for them to get full cooperation from those who know more than they do about some other aspects of the job. They must then find ways of gaining informal influence through their own personal attractiveness and their ability to make friendly relationships—or they must settle for a low-power position relative to their subordinates.

Perhaps the primary source of power is the ability to enhance the organization positively in relation to its "environment" or key problems.[12] Those who can help the organization achieve its goals by overcoming the most difficult, pressing, and dangerous problems are likely to acquire power. A marketing expert in a company that can sell everything it can make but cannot solve its production problems is less likely to gain power than the production engineer who can eliminate the bottlenecks. So it helps either to acquire skills that are (and will be) critical to the organization or to seek employment where the skills one has are most likely to be needed.

Management: When Young Managers Deliver the Pink Slips

Many 20-somethings are managers, and holding onto employees, not letting them go, is their main concern. But when pink slips must be delivered, these young bosses often have to deliver them. . . .

Managers have always had to dismiss underlings when their performance lagged or the company's profits sagged. Even Amazon.com and iVillage.com recently had to trim their staffs for economic reasons. . . .

But not so long ago, the bearer of bad tidings was usually an old pro, or . . . old enough to know how to cope with the emotions surrounding it. Today,

increasingly, the dirty work is done by people a few years out of college for whom management has mostly meant recruiting employees with stock options and playing the host at happy hours. . . .

Aside from the legal implications, young executives are often not equipped to handle the emotional side of firings.

SOURCE: Charles Butler, "Management: When Young Managers Deliver the Pink Slips," *New York Times,* February 16, 2000, p. 10. ©2000 The New York Times Company.

Furthermore, it helps to do things that are not routine, that are unusual or extraordinary in the organization. A person who performs critical tasks in a way that is already established and routinized will receive less power than a person who develops new methods or procedures, starts a new unit or task, creates a new project or product.[13] That is why those who are organizationally ambitious do not like to be the second or third person in a job; they would prefer to be the first to do a job, so they can most easily leave their mark. And in any job they move into, they often seek early changes in something, even office layout or decor, to show that they intend to do things differently.

That suggests a third important aspect of power acquisition: It is not enough to be doing extraordinary, critical activities; one's efforts must be visible and recognized. Power goes not just to those who do well, but to those who are also *seen* to do well.[14] (In fact, some cynics claim that appearance is all, though it is hard to sustain power when one does not actually produce.) Those who want power must find ways to achieve recognition. Among other things, it is a political process.

This can happen in many ways. A well-written and well-timed report can help promote visibility, as can a well-presented oral report at a meeting. The opportunity to make a presentation to higher-ups creates a natural chance for "showing one's stuff" and for demonstrating the importance and relevance of the work done. Similarly, serving on committees, often seen as a nuisance, is a chance to show others besides one's boss what one can do. "Doing one's homework" before meetings often helps both to make a good impression and to lead to more responsibility and thus power within the committee. Those who want power look for responsibility, for chances to demonstrate ability to get things done.

Through committee work or social contacts, power seekers make connections with one or more people higher in the organization. A higher-up who thinks a person shows promise might become a kind of "sponsor" who will look after the aspirant's career, help create opportunities, and build reputation. Also, when people are perceived as "having a friend or friends in high places," then others may defer to them or seek them out even without direct intervention on the powerful person's part.

Because power is a social process of influencing others to act, it comes in part from being able to do things for others that obligate them to be helpful in return by fulfilling the norm of reciprocity.[15] Thus, the person seeking power needs to find ways to be helpful to others in the organization. Volunteering to handle unpleasant

Are You More of a Street Fighter or a Jekyll and Hyde?

Most bosses think they do a pretty good job of keeping their subordinates happy. Don Bibeault has no such illusions. "I'm not a jolly fellow who's fun to be with," . . . "I'm extremely dedicated and determined, and I don't have time to sugarcoat problems. If that's considered abrasive behavior, so be it."

[He claims] that being a street fighter is the only way he could be effective. His harsh style helped him revive or liquidate 11 companies . . . as a turnaround specialist. But it did lead to occasional confrontations.

SOURCE: Tony Lee, "Are You More of A Street Fighter or a Jekyll and Hyde?" *The Wall Street Journal*, June 11, 1996, p. B1.

Is Craig Weatherup Too Nice for PepsiCola's Own Good?

The chief executive of PepsiCo Inc.'s global beverage arm is widely regarded by employees as a benevolent boss. . . .

One school of thought has it that Pepsi can never beat an increasingly aggressive Coca-Cola Co. without a certain ruthlessness in the executive suite. "What's needed at Pepsi is some basic brutality because when you're dealing with killers that's the only thing that will help you prevail. . . .

"It staggers me that for whatever reason being nice is seen as being inconsistent with being tough," says [Weatherup]. [His] argument is this: If you're a visionary but you're mean, employees won't follow you.

SOURCE: Nikhil Deogun, "Pepsi's Mr. Nice Guy Vows Not to Finish Last in Battle with Coke," *The Wall Street Journal*, March 19, 1997, p. B1.

tasks, finding ways to make others' jobs easier, and doing favors whenever possible are all ways of creating obligations, which can be collected on when needed. That is exactly how politicians, who have to be interested in power, build it.

Another way of looking at this is in terms of control of key rewards and punishments in the organization. Power reflects the ability to give rewards or punishments in order to get others to do what one believes needs to be done.[16] The more a person has access to controlling rewards and punishments, the greater his or her power.[17] Thus, a person who can give the formal rewards or use the formal punishments of an organization—hiring, firing, promoting, adjusting salary, allocating choice assignments or space, giving recommendations, and so forth—*and* give informal rewards or punishments, such as help, information, and liking, will have the most power. Just what the rewards and punishments are depends on the organization and the perceptions of those in it; but whatever it is that people value or fear, those who control it will have power to influence behavior. Attention to what the rewards are to those in the organization, who manages them, and which departments or units currently get them in greatest proportion, can aid in determining how to get control of them. At the very least, power seekers figure out what rewards they already control so that they can more wisely use them to create obligations or induce cooperation when needed. One common accessible reward (even at lower levels of the organization) is finishing, on time, work that someone else needs and is waiting for. That builds gratitude—or, as it is called in some organizations, *chits*—which can be "cashed in" when needed.

"That Report Is on My Coffee Table"

Many of your readers . . . have aspirations of becoming wealthy and powerful. If they succeed, however, I hope their egos will not require offices with private saunas and push-button controls. If one is important and powerful, the right people know it. If not, handpainted china will not change it.

With the economy in a depression, dividends being omitted, and millions unemployed, it is embarrassing to read about the conspicuous consumption and crystalline egos of America's top executives. What we need are offices that look like offices, not living rooms.

SOURCE: From a letter to the editor of *The Wall Street Journal* by Sam Bosch, January 28, 1982.

One interesting aspect of the kind of power that is associated with rewards is the power obtained by helping to relieve people's anxieties (reduce their tensions). "Got a problem? Go see Joe. He'll help you work it out." In fact, when this kind of power is carried to an extreme, unusually high expectations can be imposed on the holder and may even put a strain on that person's ability to retain that power.

Pfeffer[18] points out the power one obtains by being seen as someone who can reduce uncertainty in an otherwise chaotic situation. Given the nature of organizations today, this source of power is undoubtedly on the increase. Most people have a limited tolerance for uncertainty (or ambiguity); the person who can help to reduce that uncertainty is likely to attract a following. It is not unlike the following of any person who is viewed as "having the answers."

None of the methods described provide for easy access to power; in fact, sheer willingness to work hard is almost always a requisite for acquiring power. As should be clear by now, hard work alone may not be sufficient—it is necessary to work at critical, unusual tasks with or for people who recognize what you are doing—but without hard work it is extremely difficult to acquire power. Furthermore, A desire for power with little genuine concern for the well-being of the organization and for other members can be very destructive to the organization—and even to the power seeker.

Consequences of Possessing Power

Regardless of the source of power, its possession tends to lead toward certain consequences, not all positive. These can be stated in the following propositions:[19]

1. The more power attributed to a person, the more he or she is the recipient of:
   a. Communication.
   b. Solicitous behavior.
   c. Deference by others seeking power.

This proposition suggests that those with power will be deferred to and that, when those with less power are in the presence of powerful persons, they will address comments to them more than to one another. Large discrepancies in power between individuals, however, can interfere with successful work. If subordinates do not have sufficient power, they often will not be able to get their work done, because they can't get the resources or responses they need. This in turn reduces the leader's power. Furthermore, large power gaps often lead to avoidance of the high-power person by the low-power person and to distorted communications—telling the powerful person what one thinks that person wants to hear. Any powerful person will have to

MANAGERIAL BULLETIN

Bite Your Tongue When Evaluating Your Boss?

In a study at an insurance company, managers were more positive about upward feedback when their employees signed their name to upward appraisals. But the opposite was true for the employees. They rated their manager's leadership style more positively when they were held accountable for their opinions. They liked the process better and were more truthful only when their views were kept anonymous.

SOURCE: Leo F. Brajkovich, "How Truthful Should You Be When Evaluating Your Boss," (a research translation of a study by David Antonioni), *Academy of Management Executive* 9, no. 4 (1995).

MANAGERIAL BULLETIN

CEO Disease: Egotism Can Breed Corporate Disaster—and the Malady Is Spreading

Pampered, protected, and perked, the American CEO can know every indulgence. The executive who finally reaches the top of a major corporation enters an exclusive fraternity. The CEO's judgment and presence are eagerly sought by other captains of industry and policymakers. CEOs zip around the world in private jets and cash the heftiest personal paychecks in industry. They take home 85 times what the average blue-collar worker makes, unlike their counterparts in Japan, where the ratio is closer to 10 to 1.

It is a job that can easily go to one's head—and often does.

SOURCE: *Business Week,* April 1, 1991

be keenly aware of this problem and work hard to find ways to make less powerful people feel comfortable enough to tell the truth. Without accurate communications (and probably multiple sources), a powerful person will lose touch with actual feelings and is likely to make mistakes.

2. The more a person is treated as though he or she has power, the greater will be his or her self-esteem.

Feeling deferred to, powerful people have a tendency to begin to view themselves as important, which enhances how they feel about themselves. Not surprisingly, then, people who are powerful tend to seek one another out. Power breeds more power. Thus,

3. The more power attributed to a person, the more that person will tend to identify with others who also have power.
4. Those with high-attributed power are attracted to and communicate more with others with high-attributed power than with those who have low-attributed power.

Many political leaders have been known to shift their attention and allegiance from their constituencies to their fellow politicians. The same thing can happen in an organization, especially as people climb increasingly higher in the hierarchy. Are you familiar with instances in which an emergent social leader in a group was appointed formal leader by the system, thus enhancing his or her degree of influence?

MANAGERIAL BULLETIN

Charmed Forces: Army's "Baby Generals" Take a Crash Course in Sensitivity Training

"Each and every one of you has something that makes you a jerk. Some of you have more than one. I know. I've talked to you . . . work on losing that ugly part of your personality."

[Lt. Colonel Olsen] suggests that doubters ask their spouses what he's talking about: "They know, and they're dying to tell you." . . .

Gen. Burnette warns that "The first deadly sin of the general officer is arrogance. "Bask in the glow—and get over it." "You'll find," says another lecturer, "there aren't a whole lot of people who will tell you the truth anymore."

SOURCE: Thomas E. Ricks, "Charmed Forces," *The Wall Street Journal*, January 19, 1998, p. A1.

Very often the individual is then seen to "change"; he or she is seen as less friendly to "us mere workers" and as playing up to the big bosses. This frequently happens as people find themselves in new leadership roles, having influence over people in areas never before experienced.

In fact, one of the dangers of superiors having great power differentials over subordinates is that they begin to perceive any successes as due to their own skills and to discount the capacities of the subordinates. Great power differentials lead to overestimates by the powerful of their own contributions and to blindness to the contributions of others.[20]

By examining these propositions, you can see why it is often said that power corrupts. The entire constellation of behavior and relationships that follow from the possession of influence generates a cycle in which people with high power tend to become more and more differentiated form those with low power, even though each is dependent upon the other. The person with power has it only because it is given by others; it ends the moment those who are doing the giving choose not to do so. A leader is a leader only so long as there are followers. It certainly raises the question of who really possesses the power, the one who leads or those being led.

> There go my people. I must find out where they are going so I can lead them.
>
> Anonymous

Another consequence of power for someone new to a position is the likelihood of being closely observed by subordinates about where the leader's loyalties and priorities will be, how open they can be, how friendly and close the leader will allow them to be, and the like. Such early "testing" is often symbolic: The test is not direct, and the leader's reactions are carefully scrutinized for favorable and unfavorable signs of what is to come. A leader who is unaware that such testing is inevitable can make inadvertent mistakes that are hard to live down, sending messages that discourage future openness or cause resentment about assumed attitudes of superiority.

Consequences of Not Possessing Power

Although too much power can indeed be corrupting, so can too little. Because power is needed to make things happen in organizations—being without it means

The Bureaucrat Gets the Last Word

Ed Garvey was scheduled to make a business trip and needed a cash advance. He went to the controller's office to get the necessary signature on a form in order to receive the cash. Mr. Pomeroy, an administrative assistant, was the person whose signature Ed needed. But first Ed had to get past Mrs. Arnold, the secretary and receptionist in the controller's office. The Conversation went like this:

Ed: I'd like to see Mr. Pomeroy for just one minute. I need his signature for a cash advance.

Mrs. Arnold: Mr. Pomeroy is very busy, so you'll just have to wait. Please sit over there.

Ed: Mrs. Arnold, I really have to get back to my office. Could you ask Mr. Pomeroy if he could take a minute to sign this?

Mrs. Arnold: Well, I hate to interrupt him, but I'll see if he can take a moment. (Goes into Pomeroy's office and returns after about two minutes.) He'll see you, but you may have to leave the form here.

Ed goes into Pomeroy's office and explains that this trip was a last-minute thing and he was under time pressure. The conversation went like this:

Pomeroy: You know that at least 24 hours is required for approval of a cash advance.

Ed: I know, but I don't have 24 hours before I have to leave. I need the cash advance today.

Pomeroy: Well, I don't know if I can take it upon myself to sign this. If I break the rules for you, I could end up with endless requests like this from others.

Ed: Look, this is an exceptional situation. The rules don't cover every situation.

Pomeroy: I know, but I do have a job to perform.

Ed: Would you get into trouble if you signed it?

Pomeroy: No, but I believe in following proper procedure, Mr. Garvey.

Ed: I do too, but sometimes other things are more important than rules. Is there someone over you I can go to?

Pomeroy: I don't think that will be necessary. I'll make the exception this time, Mr. Garvey, but please try to give me the proper notice in the future.

Ed: That's very nice of you, Mr. Pomeroy. Thank you.

When Ed walked out, he had the signature, but he felt like he bought it with his soul.

---

insufficient resources, information, and support—managers who lack it have difficulty being effective. The manager who does not know what is going on, can't get the needed budget, and is not backed by higher-ups will inevitably be resisted by subordinates. Why should they cooperate with someone who can't deliver?

As a result, managers who are in positions that yield too little power (or who fill their positions ineptly and lose what power they had) tend to:

1. Overcontrol subordinates, try to make them cooperate.
2. Become petty tyrants, taking out their frustration on anyone they can dominate.
3. Become turf-minded and rules-oriented, carving out a fiefdom where they can reign supreme. [21]

In this way, powerlessness also corrupts, since managers who become so dominating are seldom effective. Their attempts to find someone on whom to exercise power only increase the resentment of their victims, causing even stronger attempts at domination, more resistance, and so on. Without the proper tools, few managers can be successful.

Currencies Frequently Valued in Organizations

Inspiration-Related Currencies

Vision	Being involved in a task that has larger significance for unit, organization, customers, or society.
Excellence	Having a chance to do important things really well.
Moral/ethical correctness	Doing what is "right" by a higher standard than efficiency.

Task-Related Currencies

New resources	Obtaining money, budget increases, personnel, space, and so forth.
Challenge/learning	Doing tasks that increase skills and abilities.
Assistance	Getting help with existing projects or unwanted tasks.
Task support	Receiving overt or subtle backing or actual assistance with implementation.
Rapid response	Quicker response time.
Information	Access to organizational as well as technical knowledge.

Position-Related Currencies

Recognition	Acknowledgment of effort, accomplishment, or abilities.
Visibility	The chance to be known by higher-ups or significant others in the organization.
Reputation	Being seen as competent, committed.
Insiderness/importance	A sense of centrality, of "belonging."
Contacts	Opportunities for linking with others.

Relationship-Related Currencies

Understanding	Having concerns and issues listened to.
Acceptance/inclusion	Closeness and friendship.
Personal support	Personal and emotional backing.

Personal-Related Currencies

Gratitude	Appreciation or expression of indebtedness.
Ownership/involvement	Ownership of and influence over important tasks.
Self-concept	Affirmation of one's values, self-esteem, and identity.
Comfort	Avoidance of hassles.

SOURCE: A. R. Cohen and D. L. Bradford, *Influence without Authority* (New York: John Wiley & Sons, 1990).

Some Currencies of Influence

Often people see themselves as having little power, because they do not occupy some formal position of power. But Cohen and Bradford[22] point out that "people also underestimate their power, because they aren't creative in seeing connections between what they have and what someone else wants." These connections are like "currencies," which serve as a basis of exchange: "I give you my time, and you give me appreciation." "I generate ideas, and you feel empowered to act in ways that I, in turn, value." Managers have a vast array of currencies to influence their subordinates, their peers, and their bosses. Students don't even begin to recognize the cur-

Guide to Managing Your Boss—Or Anyone Else You Don't Control

- Understand your boss and the forces surrounding him or her:
  Boss's goals and objectives.
  How boss is rewarded.
  Pressures on boss:
  - From his or her boss.
  - From the organization.
  - From the environment.
  Boss's power (capacity to mobilize resources).
  Boss's strengths, weaknesses, blind spots, and hot buttons.
  Boss's managerial style—preferred degree of:
  - Control.
  - Information received and shared.
  - Formality.
  - Openness.
- Work to make your boss's life easier:
  Aid in accomplishing boss's goals.
  Increase boss's visibility and reputation.
  Pick up tasks boss doesn't like or isn't good at.
- Tie your requests/preferences to boss's /organization's goals; show how giving you what you want will help achieve the goals.

- Ask boss for evaluation of how you can perform better:
  If boss is uncomfortable, offer self-appraisal to ease discussion.
- Keep boss informed:
  With frequency preferred by boss.
  With level of detail preferred by boss.
  In form preferred by boss:
  - Oral?
  - Brief reports?
  - Extensive reports?
  - Executive summary?
- Work to demonstrate dependability; keep your word.
- Reward boss whenever he or she manages in way you prefer:
  Many bosses feel underappreciated.
  Public praise increases boss's reputation, aiding obtaining of resources.

SOURCE: Based on J. J. Gabarro and J. P. Kotter, "Managing Your Boss," *Harvard Business Review*, January–February 1980; and Allan R. Cohen, "How to Manage Your Boss," *Ms. Magazine*, February 1981.

rencies they have to influence their instructors, ranging from nods of the head during a lecture to high levels of performance on papers or exams. The Managerial Tools Chart above, shows a variety of currencies that are valued in organizations. Although many are not likely to fit your present circumstances, you might explore the chart and possibly discover some influence currencies you do in fact possess and never realized you have. Also, try using the Personal Application Exercise at the end of the chapter.

Liking versus Respect

It is not uncommon for those who have power to be less well liked; as noted in the group chapters, the group members who contribute most to getting tasks accomplished are usually most respected but seldom most liked. Informal task leaders often have to trade liking for respect; while occasionally someone can get both, most often: The more a leader strives for popularity, the less effective he or she becomes as task leader. Also, the more the leader strives to maintain task leadership, the more he or she will lose popularity.[23] Can you think of any conditions where these propositions would not be true? How important each factor is in comparison with the other depends on the nature of the situation and the person involved in the leadership role. When a strong task leader brings a group through a very difficult situation, popularity may soar, at least for awhile.

All leaders have to struggle with the question of how close they can be with their followers. Can a leader also be a friend? If so, does this still allow him or her to push them into working harder? Or, if the leader remains distant, will the followers still feel the loyalty and commitment necessary to put forth sufficient effort?

Falling Stars—Twilight of the Gods: CEO as American Icon Slips into Down Cycle

"This whole drive toward empowerment," says Pillsbury's [CEO] Mr. Walsh, has meant that CEOs have to cast off their big-shot image in order to communicate with their troops. "You need to engage people on a one-on-one basis and really work hard to make them feel part of the enterprise," he says. "Great ideas usually come from deep in the organization. They don't come from CEOs."

SOURCE: Ellen Joan Pollock, *The Wall Street Journal*, January 5, 1999, p. A1.

Conflicting Demands on Politicians

It is a horrendously difficult mandate this—to remain in the people's eyes (1) a down-to-earth representative who understands them because he is one of them and (2) a leader to whom they can look up because he is somehow well above the rest of the pack in knowledge, mysteriously endowed with superior strengths and talents, a person who can be trusted to guard, to decide, to lead . . . in short, I suppose, a parent.

SOURCE: Meg Greenfield, "The 'Just Folks' Pantomine," *Newsweek*, October 10, 1994, p. 78.

For some situations and people, the task maintenance function must take priority over social maintenance; in other situations and for other individuals, the opposite might be true. The important thing to keep in mind is that there is more than one option and that there may be some trade-offs in each.

But *why* does this dilemma occur? Why is it so difficult to mix these functions? For one thing, not many people are really good at both; as a result, the task leader is likely to be someone who has the best skills or abilities related to the task (as it should be), and the social leader is often the most outgoing person in the group. If that's the case, then other group members tend to become dependent upon the task leader and may even see him or her as superior to the rest of the group. While this may generate respect for that individual, it also tends to breed resentment.

Furthermore, because people are social beings and usually have other interests in addition to interest in working well—or will retreat into socializing when tasks become unpleasant or might lead to conflict—task leaders occasionally have to refocus attention back to getting the task done. As a result, when the task leader pressures others into working, they may feel grateful for the direction but also may feel resentful, annoyed, and resistant to the task.[24] This sequence of events is not inevitable and may be overcome when it leads to group success, but it occurs frequently enough to warrant particular attention. We have also found it to be characteristic of a great many work groups in our classes. Does it apply to your own experience?

There is yet another problem. With a few exceptions, most people have the greatest difficulty being totally honest or giving directions to those to whom they feel closest. When someone else is emotionally close, people feel the risk is great that the relationship will be harmed by saying negative things or giving directions. Thus they find themselves unable to ask much of close friends. A few people, however, find that when they build close, supportive relationships, they can be both demanding

The Pentagon "Club" Closed Ranks to Shut Out Resor

Some defense officials sympathetic to Mr. Resor do feel, however, that he contributed to his own troubles by an unwillingness or inability to deal with the petty intrigues that are, after all, a cornerstone of any self-respecting bureaucracy.

"There was no major conspiracy to undermine Stan; it just happened, and he helped," said one. "You needed someone who could go to these little empires that have been built up and say, 'What are your priorities, what are the major issues, what are you doing?'

Stan just waited for people to come to him, and very few did."

A top defense official said in exasperation: "This is a very tough place. There's a lot of power; a lot of money at stake. In comes Stanley Resor—a very decent gentleman, somewhat old-school, not a self-serving type in any way.

"He was entirely wrong for the job."

SOURCE: Bernard Weinraub, *New York Times,* March 18, 1979, copyright © 1979 by The New York Times Company. Reprinted by permission.

and caring—and be cared for and receive demands in return. This kind of openness allows closeness with subordinates without harming productivity, but it requires high skill and mutual commitment and probably only works where both boss and subordinate have roughly equal expertise.

The Use and Abuse of Power

In general, it should be apparent by now that leadership can be an exciting opportunity to use power or influence for getting work done; but it can be abused. You have undoubtedly known or heard about people in power primarily to serve their own ends, and usually at the expense of others.

David McClelland distinguishes between *personal* power and *socialized* power, the former referring to self-serving uses (or abuses) and the latter to uses that consider the effects (usually benefits) on others.[25] Sometimes it's difficult to make a clear distinction between the two, especially when a leader claims to be acting for the benefit of others yet engages in behavior that reflects anything but the best of motives.

Any act by a person in power that pressures another person to behave in ways that violate that person's sense of personal worth is a form of manipulation. At best, it's insensitive; at worst, it's a form of violence. Today's organizations are paying increasing attention to these kinds of issues, including the specific problem of sexual harassment in the workplace. Laws and policies are being developed, in part because of pressures from the courts, that are designed to protect individuals from sexual harassment in their jobs. What was once looked on as harmless teasing has come to be recognized as a humiliating abuse of power, unacceptable and unprofessional, as well as illegal. How long it will take to educate organizational leaders and managers, university professors, and the general public to understand such abuses and take action to prevent them remains to be seen. However, it is important for *you*—as a future manager and as someone who will possess power—to appreciate the ethical burdens of your job and the kinds of actions you might be required to take in living up to those ethics.

The Opportunity to Empower Others

In the coming years, the effectiveness of leaders/managers will be measured as much by the performance of their subordinates as by their own performance. It will be the job of the leader—of a team, a department, or a company—to *empower* others to

Unmourned Departure

"[Departing chairman of Coopers & Lybrand, Eugene Freedman] rubs a lot of people wrong," . . . "He's a very aggressive person and very capable. But my guess is, there's no love for him."

"He's a legend in his own mind."

According to partners and former partners, Mr. Freedman gave himself big raises when profits flagged. They say he lived in the grand manner befitting a movie mogul, not the head of a public accounting firm, that he sidelined rivals and surrounded himself with hordes of minions. And they say Mr. Freedman used the power of his office to suit his personal agenda and to punish those who stood up to him.

SOURCE: Alison Leigh Cowan, "Unmourned Departure at Coopers," *New York Times,* January 17, 1994.

Chainsaw!

He Anointed Himself America's Best CEO, but Al Dunlap Drove Sunbeam into the Ground

Sunbeam investors knew that Dunlap's arrival meant that tough medicine would soon be administered. And at precisely 9 A.M. on Monday, July 22, 1996, when Dunlap marched into the penthouse boardroom at Sunbeam headquarters in Fort Lauderdale, the anxious group of executives gathered around the table knew it, too. Dunlap wasted no time on introductions. Like George C. Scott in the movie Patton, he began by delivering a spellbinding, if sometimes disjointed monologue on himself and the company. "You guys are responsible for the demise of Sunbeam!" Dunlap roared, tossing his glasses onto the table. "I'm here to tell you that things have changed. The old Sunbeam is over today. It's over!" . . .

The men gathered around the conference table were stunned by Dunlap's attack. "It was like a dog barking at you for hours," recalled Richard L. Boynton, president of the household-products division. "He just yelled, ranted, and raved. He was condescending, belligerent, and disrespectful." . . .

Almost all his executives believed these goals were impractical. Dunlap, however, refused to acknowledge the near-impossibility of meeting them. Instead, he began putting excruciating pressure on those who reported to him, who in turn passed that intimidation down the line. People were told that either they met their goals or another person would be found to do it for them. Their livelihood hung on making numbers that were not makeable.

In Dunlap's presence, knees trembled and stomachs churned. Underlings feared the torrential harangue that Dunlap could unleash at any moment. At his worst, he became viciously profane, even violent. Executives said he would throw papers or furniture, bang his hands on his desk, and shout so ferociously that a manager's hair would be blown back by the stream of air that rushed from Dunlap's mouth. "Hair spray day" became a code phrase among execs, signifying a potential tantrum. . . .

"I have thousands of resumes from people who would work here for free," Dunlap would scream, inches from his victim. "You are being paid to work here, and you can become rich because I've given you all these options. And you're letting me down. I'm working hard for you on the Street, and you're letting me down."

SOURCE: John A. Byrne, "Chainsaw!" *Business Week,* October 18, 1999, p. 128. (Copyright 1999 McGraw-Hill, Inc.)

perform at their best. Simple rewards and punishments won't do the job, at least over the long run; it will take efforts at employee involvement, shared purposes or vision, and, in general, a spirit of collaboration heretofore known in few organizations. Even as you consider the situational options available to the leader, keep in mind that in most cases any choice that fails to empower others is likely to be a poor one. Coercive approaches, while occasionally necessary and sometimes effective for the short run, rarely sustain positive effects for the long run.

> In the day of the knowledgeable workforce, when no single individual has a monopoly on talent and answers, good subordinateship cannot consist only of constant agreement with the boss. Bosses cannot afford to send in the clones; they must create, value, and work with strong individuals who have the knowledge the boss does not; and both must learn to blend views rather than always fight to win or compromise away strength.
>
> David Bradford and Allan Cohen
> *Power Up*

KEY CONCEPTS FROM CHAPTER 11

1. Leadership is mostly situational, rather than determined by personality traits.
2. Leadership is an influence process with subordinates, peers, and colleagues. Even subordinates are not totally without influence; thus, leadership is net influence.
3. Influence is an act or potential act that affects the behavior of another person(s). Types of influence:
   a. Formal: prescribed by office or position.
   b. Informal: based on expertise or charisma.
   c. Legitimate: influencer seen by influenced as having the right to do so.
   d. Illegitimate: influencer seen by influenced as not having the right to do so.
   e. Types *a* and *b* can each combine with *c* or *d* when examining influence.
4. People can be influenced through:
   a. Compliance: fear of influencer.
   b. Identification: attraction to influencer.
   c. Internalization: belief in influencer's beliefs.
5. Importance of employee commitment to:
   a. The work itself.
   b. The relationships with others.
   c. The organization as a whole.
6. Power is the capacity to exert influence, to make things happen.

7. Power is based on:
   a. Greater legitimacy.
   b. Ability to enhance organization in relation to key problems.
   c. Doing new activities rather than routine.
   d. Visibility, recognition.
   e. Creating obligations through helpful acts.
   f. Controlling rewards and punishments.
   g. Reducing uncertainty.
8. The greater one's power, the more one receives:
   a. Communication.
   b. Solicitous behavior.
   c. Deference.
   d. Self-esteem.
   e. Close observation in new situations.
9. Powerlessness often leads to:
   a. Overcontrol.
   b. Petty tyranny.
   c. Rule orientation and turf-mindedness.
10. Currencies of influence.
11. It is difficult for those with power to gain both respect and liking:
    a. Task orientation often breeds resentment.
    b. Closeness to followers may constrain task orientation.
12. The use and abuse of power.
13. Empowerment of others.

PERSONAL APPLICATION EXERCISE

Assessing Your Influence Currencies
As we pointed out in the chapter, you probably have more influence on others than you realize. You may not fully appreciate the behavior—"currencies"—you can offer that are valued by friends, family members, instructors, and others. The following exercise is designed to help you assess your currencies and thereby develop a picture

of the ways in which you influence others and how you might even increase that influence.

We want you to start by identifying *two* people in each of *three* categories: (1) friends, (2) family members, and (3) instructors. (Refer to the example below as a guide.) Then list the currencies you can offer that are valued by *both* individuals in each category and assign a value on a scale of 1 to 10 indicating the importance of that currency to each person, with the higher numbers reflecting greater importance.

You should find similarities (closer numbers) and differences (numbers further apart) between the individuals in a category, and you certainly should find some major differences in the currencies of the different categories. In the example, the numbers reflect a closer friendship with B than with A, because the currencies of "caring" and "support" are more highly valued by B. In the family category, the currency that counts more with the father than the mother is "success," while the opposite is true for the "dependency" currency. In the instructor example, "listening quietly" will work better in accounting class than in organizational behavior (OB), while the opposite will be true for "offering opinions."

If the example were you, can you see how your behavior could be different in the different situations and in relation to the different individuals? This kind of diagnostic process could be a valuable way for you to strengthen your interpersonal power. It could be especially useful in a work environment, where the career stakes are high.

EXAMPLE

Friends	A	B	Family	Mother	Father	Instructors	Acctg.	OB
Caring	5	8	Love	10	8	Listening		
Support	5	10	Pride	6	7	quietly	9	4
Feedback	6	6	Dependency	8	3	Asking		
Help	8	6	Success	5	10	questions	7	6
Knowledge of sports	2	9	Doing chores	9	9	Good work	10	10
Humor	10	7				Offering		
						opinions	3	9

SUGGESTED READINGS

Agor, W. H. "The Logic of Intuition: How Top Executives Make Important Decisions." *Organizational Dynamics,* Winter 1986, pp. 5–18.

Bass, B. M. *Leadership and Performance Beyond Expectations.* New York: Free Press, 1985.

Bateman, T. S., and S. Strasser. "A Longitudinal Analysis of the Antecedents of Organizational Commitment." *Academy of Management Journal* 27 (1984), pp. 95–112.

Bennis, W., and B. Nanus. *Leaders: The Strategies for Taking Charge.* New York: Harper & Row, 1985.

Caro, R. *The Power Broker.* New York: Alfred A. Knopf, 1974.

Cobb, A. T. "An Episodic Model of Power: Toward an Integration of Theory and Research." *Academy of Management Review,* July 1984, pp. 482–93.

Conger, J. A. and R. N. Kanungo. "Toward a Behavioral Theory of Charismatic Leadership in Organizational Settings." *Academy of Management Review* 12, no. 4 (1987), pp. 637–47.

Conger, J. A., and R. N. Kanungo. "The Empowerment Process: Integrating Theory and Practice." *Academy of Management Review,* July 1988, p. 474.

Deaux, K. "Authority, Gender, Power, and Tokenism." *Journal of Applied Behavioral Science,* January–February–March 1978, pp. 22–26.

Dobbins, G. H., and S. J. Platz. "Sex Differences in Leadership: How Real Are They?" *Academy of Management Review,* January 1986, pp. 118–27.

Dumaine, Brian. "What the Leaders of Tomorrow See." *Fortune,* July 3, 1989.

Farmer, Steven M.; John M. Maslyn; Donald B. Fedor; and Jodi S. Goodman. "Putting Upward Influence Strategies in Context." *Journal of Organizational Behavior,* January 1997, pp. 17–42.

Fink, S. L. *High Commitment Workplaces.* Westport, CT: Quorum Books, 1992.

Gabarro, J. J., and J. P. Kotter. "Managing Your Boss." *Harvard Business Review,* January–February 1980, pp. 97–100.

Gault, Stanley; Linda J. Wachner; Mike H. Walsh; David W. Johnson. "Leaders of Corporate Change." *Fortune,* December 14, 1992.

Heller, T. "Changing Authority Patterns: A Cultural Perspective." *Academy of Management Review,* July 1985, pp. 488–95.

Howell, J. P., and P. W. Dorfman. "Leadership and Substitutes for Leadership among Professional and Nonprofessional Workers." *Journal of Applied Behavioral Science* 22, no. 1 (1986), pp. 29–46.

Huey, John. "America's Most Successful Merchant." *Fortune,* September 23, 1991.

———. "Finding New Heroes for a New Era." *Fortune,* January 25, 1993.

———. "Where Managers Will Go." *Fortune,* January 27, 1992.

Kiechel, Walter III. "The Leader as Servant." *Fortune,* May 4, 1992.

King, D., and B. Bass. *Leadership, Power, and Influence.* Lafayette, IN: Herman C. Krannert Graduate School of Industrial Administration, Purdue University, 1970.

Kotkin, J. "Mr. Iacocca, Meet Mr. Honda." *Inc.,* November 1989, pp. 436–53.

Kotter, J. P. *The General Managers.* New York: Free Press, 1982.

———. *Power and Influence.* New York: Free Press, 1985.

Liden, R. C., and T. R. Mitchell. "Ingratiatory Behaviors in Organizations Settings." *Academy of Management Review* 13, no. 4 (1988), pp. 572–87.

Malone, Thomas W. "Is Empowerment Just a Fad? Control, Decision Making, and IT." *Sloan Management Review,* Winter 1997, pp. 23–35.

Mangham, Iain. *Power and Performance in Organizations.* New York: Basil Blackwell, 1988.

McGregor, D. *Leadership and Motivation.* Cambridge, MA: MIT Press, 1966.

Pfeffer, J., and G. Salancik. "Who Gets Power and How They Hold on to It." *Organizational Dynamics,* Winter 1977.

Quinn, Robert E., and Gretchen M. Spreitzer. "The Road to Empowerment: Seven Questions Every Leader Should Consider." *Organizational Dynamics,* Autumn 1997, pp. 37–50.

Reichers, A. E. "A Review and Reconceptualization of Organizational Commitment." *Academy of Management Review* 10 (1985), pp. 465–76.

Sarman, Colin. "Looking for Tomorrow's Leaders," *Management Today,* August 1997, p. 5.

Sayles, L. *Leadership: What Effective Managers Do and How They Do It.* New York: McGraw-Hill, 1979.

Schlesinger, L. A., and B. Oshry. "Quality of Work Life and the Manager: Muddle in the Middle." *Organizational Dynamics,* Summer 1984, pp. 4–19.

Sellers, Patricia. "What Exactly Is Charisma?" *Fortune,* January 15, 1996, pp. 68–75.

Stewart, Thomas. A. "Get with the New Power Game." *Fortune,* January 13, 1997, pp. 58–62.

Taylor, Alex, III. "Iacocca's Last Stand at Chrysler." *Fortune,* April 20, 1992.

———. "Success Depends on Leadership." *Fortune,* November 18, 1991.

Trevino, L. K. "Ethical Decision Making in Organizations: A Person-Situation Interactionist Model." *Academy of Management Review,* July 1986, pp. 601–17.

Tichy, N., and M. A. Devanna. *The Transformational Leader.* New York: John Wiley & Sons, 1986.

Walton, R. E. "From Control to Commitment in the Workplace." *Harvard Business Review* March–April 1985, pp. 77–84.

Whyte, G. "Escalating Commitment to a Course of Action: A Reinterpretation." *Academy of Management Review* 11 (1986), pp. 311–21.

Zand, Dale E. *The Leadership Triad: Knowledge, Trust, and Power.* New York: Oxford University Press, 1997.

Leadership

Managerial Functions and Styles

Carly Fiorina's Challenge

Fiorina must recalibrate HP's vaunted culture, dubbed the "HP Way." Founders Bill Hewlett and David Packard were renowned for emphasizing teamwork and respect for co-workers. But in recent years, that has translated into a bureaucratic, consensus-style culture that is at a sharp disadvantage in the Net-speed era. "They have this ready, aim-aim-aim, fire culture," says Bain & Co. consultant Vernon E. Altman, who has worked with HP. "These days, it has to be aim, fire, re-aim, re-fire." Disposing of the bad habits while retaining the good shouldn't be a problem," says Fiorina, who plans to use a scalpel and not a machete. "Our people are very proud and smart. So, first, you reinforce the things that work," she says, "and then appeal to their brains to address what doesn't."

As a leader, she has a personal touch that inspires intense loyalty. She's known for giving balloons and flowers to employees who land big contracts. When Lucent was spun off from AT&T in early 1996, Fiorina stayed up all night with Comptroller Jim Lusk and other employees to make sure the prospectus for the stock offering was perfect. And it's not just business: When the wife of a senior Lucent executive fell ill recently, Fiorina helped make sure he got medical advice, doctors, and emotional support. "I think the world of Carly. She's a great leader," says Nina Aversano, president of North America for Lucent's global service-provider business.

"Chess Guy"

By late 1997, employees were crying out for stronger direction. . . . HP's workers thought the company needed an infusion of new thinking and more customer focus. Stunned, [former CEO] Platt tried to take action, say insiders. [He] lambasted managers about the need to be more creative. But the speech backfired. Rather than being energized by Platt's talk, many executives grumbled that Platt was asking them to fix HP's ailments when he was the problem. What they needed was decisive leadership. Says a consultant who worked with Platt at the time: "Lew is a man of great integrity, but he seemed like a chess guy in a video-game world."

SOURCE: Peter Burrows with Peter Elstrom, "Carly Fiorina's Challenge Will Be to Propel Staid Hewlett-Packard into the Internet Age without Sacrificing the Very Things That Have Made It Great," *Business Week*, August 2, 1999, p. 76. (Copyright 1999 McGraw-Hill, Inc.)

. . . "when it finally comes down to it, leadership is more than a set of tools and choices; *who you are* is the most important consideration as to whether anyone will want to follow you."

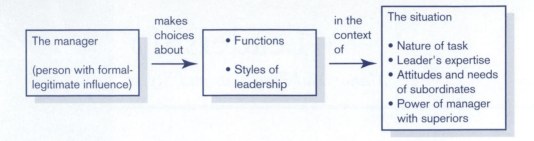

FIGURE 12–1   *Illustration of Managerial Choices Discussed in This Chapter*

Managers as Formal-Legitimate Leaders: Managerial Choices

Chapter 11 looked at how to use power and influence to get organizational work accomplished, regardless of organizational position. But the kinds of problems discussed there are especially applicable to those who have been assigned a managerial role with formal-legitimate influence.

While formally appointed managers, like peers who have acquired influence, need to balance relationships with work, they have a more complex set of choices that arise from holding a position organizationally defined as "above" the group. The responsibility and authority that go with the position impose their own set of considerations: What functions should the manager perform, with whom, and when; what style of leadership should be used; how are such decisions affected by the tasks to be accomplished, the manager's relative power and expertise, and the needs of subordinates? This chapter will address these crucial questions. Figure 12–1 shows the sequential relationship among the chapter's variables.

In 1999, Lew Platt was the formal corporate leader of Hewlett-Packard. However it would appear from the *Business Week* article (see the chapter-opening Managerial Bulletin "Carly Fiorina's Challenge") that his legitimacy (i.e., the extent to which his subordinates accepted his influence fully) depended in part on his ability to redefine his role and his leadership style in the face of mounting criticism. As you proceed through this chapter, you will see how a leader's choices about roles and style need to consider a variety of situational factors. In Platt's case, a major factor was related to the attitudes and needs of subordinates (as seen in Figure 12–1). The ultimate failings of Platt could be attributed in large part to his inability to change his role and his style as circumstances demanded. His attempts were not credible.

Managerial Functions

We begin by reviewing the set of functions that every manager must perform, which we introduced in Chapter 1. Here we will look more closely into these functions.

The manager's functions fall into three related groupings. One group, *interpersonal,* involves building and maintaining contacts and relationships with a variety of people located both inside and outside his or her organizational unit. A second group, *informational,* involves gathering and disseminating information inside the unit and to and from the external environment. The third group, *decision making,* involves making a range of decisions pertaining to internal operating practices and to exchanges with other units of the organization as well as the outside world.[1] (See Figure 12–2.)

As may be evident from the above, these groupings are interrelated; in accomplishing one function, the manager often will make progress on another. For example,

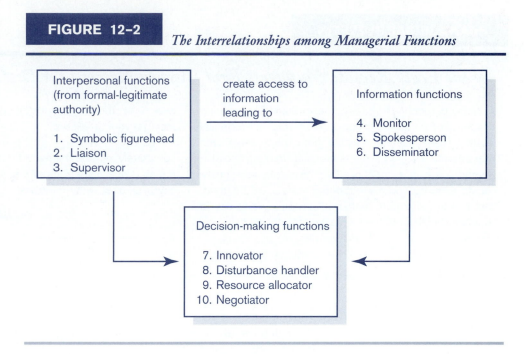

FIGURE 12–2 *The Interrelationships among Managerial Functions*

while building a relationship with the manager of another unit of the organization, the manager typically will be gathering and sharing information. Furthermore, the information a manager gains while carrying out an informational function may be crucial to his or her capability in carrying out the decision-making functions effectively. Let us now consider these interrelated functions in greater detail.

The Interpersonal Functions

The manager relates to people both within and outside of his or her own subsystem. Students of leadership often concentrate on the internal relationships of managers and think of their relationships with "outsiders" as nonessential or peripheral to the job. But some of the most important activities in which a manager engages involve building relationships with other people than subordinates.

One such function is that of *symbolic figurehead*. It entails *carrying out certain social, legal, inspirational, and ceremonial duties that simply go with being the head of an organizational system.* The manager's function is largely representational, serving to symbolize his or her organization to the rest of the world. The higher in the organization a manager's position, the greater will be the time spent in the symbolic figurehead function.

Closely related to this function is that of *liaison*. In carrying out the liaison function, the manager *gives and receives information and favors in order to learn what is going on elsewhere that can be useful within the unit.* Making contacts with people and then maintaining them are important activities, time-consuming but necessary if the manager is to stay informed on organizational politics, on new opportunities, on changes in demand for the organization's outputs, and so forth. Furthermore, the contacts make it possible to exchange other favors when necessary, facilitating internal operations.

The remaining interpersonal function is that of *supervisor,* a function one readily associates with managing. It entails *hiring, training, motivating, evaluating, and rewarding subordinates.* In carrying out this function, the manager tries to find a way to blend individual needs and concerns with the organization's goals, so the subordinates remain committed to doing what is necessary to meet the system's objectives.

The interpersonal functions in which the manager relates to relevant others serve to give him or her an important advantage:

In the Lead: Remote Managers Find Ways to Narrow the Distance Gap

To stay in touch with her scattered staff, Gale Hiering Varma, vice president of human resources at Prudential Institutional schedules specific "connection times" with her secretary. . . . To avoid endless phone tag, she also schedules phone meetings with her four vice presidents. She also tries to respond quickly. . . . "The greatest mistake a remote manager can make is to say to themselves, 'I'm too tired to make that phone call,'" . . . Employees need quick answers to job problems . . . and those who are at remote locations "can't simply walk down the hall to your office and stand there until they get your attention."

"All the technology in the world," however, can't completely replace the need for face time, especially at the start of a management job, when you are trying to establish trust with employees.

SOURCE: Carol Hymowitz, "Remote Managers Find Ways to Narrow the Distance Gap," *The Wall Street Journal,* April 6, 1999, p. B1. (Copyright © 1999, Dow Jones & Company, Inc.)

Through [them] the manager gains access to privileged information, and he emerges as the "nerve center" of his organization. He alone has formal access to every subordinate in his own organization, and he has unique access to a variety of outsiders, many of whom are nerve centers of their own organizations. Thus the manager is his organization's information generalist, that person best informed about its operations and environment.[2]

Informational Functions

The interpersonal functions then lead to *informational functions,* which channel information into and out of the manager's unit. By serving as a *monitor* of information from sources within and outside of the unit, the manager keeps up-to-date on the operating climate. The activities *include designing ways of collecting information (formally and informally), reading reports, questioning contacts and subordinates, observing others' activities, and so forth.*

In turn, the manager has the function of *disseminator,* passing relevant information to subordinates. Because the manager will often be the only one in a unit with access to some information, this job is important and requires good judgment in terms of what information to pass along and to whom. It requires such activities as *telling, announcing, memo writing, and telephoning.*

In addition to the internal dissemination function, there is an important *spokesperson* function, transmitting information outside the unit. This includes *informing, liaison contacts who influence the unit, lobbying, announcing, and so forth.*

Decision-Making Functions

As a consequence of formal position and access to information, the manager performs several functions that involve making strategic decisions for the unit.

The *innovator* function calls for initiating and designing changes in the way the unit operates. In carrying out this task. the manager *diagnoses trends, envisions possibilities, plans improvements, invents programs and other solutions,* and, in general, *promotes innovation.* This is at the heart of leadership, seeing what needs to be changed, whether it is direction, methods, activities, or relationships.

A related decision-making function is that of *disturbance handler.* Here the manager takes charge and makes decisions when nonroutine disturbances or interpersonal conflicts call for responses that individual subordinates cannot devise. The manager functions as the generalist problem solver, putting out fires as they arise either as a result of subordinates' inability to anticipate and handle difficulties or as a consequence of innovations. The lower the level of a manager in the organizational hierarchy, the greater will be the time spent on disturbance handling and other decision-making functions. The need at lower levels of an organization is for maintaining the daily work flow, so these functions are predominant there.

Another decision-making function is that of *resource allocator.* The manager parcels out his or her unit's resources through a series of decisions on how members will spend time, materials, and funds, as well as how they can utilize formal-legitimate influence. Resource allocation involves *deciding among proposals, controlling subordinate latitude, setting priorities, authorizing expenditures, and so forth.*

Finally, the manager serves as *negotiator* for important decisions involving other people inside and outside the organization. Negotiating involves *bargaining, trading, compromising, collaborating, avoiding, and other similar activities.*

Typically, the negotiating function builds upon several of the other managerial functions. In representing the unit, the manager serves as *symbolic figurehead* and *spokesperson,* summarizing the organization's views. The negotiation will result in *resource allocation,* as something is given up or obtained from outside.

In brief, the 10 functions comprise the job of the formal-legitimate officeholder:

> The manager must design the work of his organization, monitor its internal and external environment, initiate change when desirable, and renew stability when faced with a disturbance. The manager must lead his subordinates to work effectively for the organization, and he must provide them with special information, some of which he gains through the network of contacts that he develops. In addition, the manager must perform a number of "housekeeping" duties, including informing outsiders, serving as figurehead, and leading major negotiations.[3]

The 10 managerial functions differ on the basis of whether their focus is internal or external, or both. A manager "stands between his organizational unit and its environment,"[4] and his functions include looking outward to what is happening in other parts of the total organization and the environment as well as downward at what subordinates do.

While each of these functions is important, it is not always imperative that only the manager carry them out. Within an organization there may be individuals who can contribute to or do some of the particular functions more effectively than the manager in charge. Subordinates can take responsibility in these areas as well as managers give it. If, for example, a manager is not very effective at public speaking when carrying out the spokesperson function, he or she may want to delegate some of the necessary activities to a good speaker on the staff. Similarly, it may be appropriate for a staff member to initiate delegation by offering his or her services and not merely waiting for the manager to give it.

Those activities, however, that require special current information to perform well may not be easily delegated unless others have high access to such special information. Nevertheless, most managers are flooded with demands for their time and attention and must choose carefully which roles and functions to emphasize. There is seldom enough time to stay in contact with all information sources, inspire and direct all subordinates, cope with all disturbances and needs for innovation, and so forth. The choice constantly has to be made between another 15 minutes working on a problem in the office, a quick stroll through the plant to get a feel for morale, or an early arrival at a meeting with other executives in order to pick up some scraps of information about an upcoming crisis. The way in which the manager chooses to spend time determines his or her relative emphasis on the 10 roles, all of which are necessary and demanding. Success as a manager depends in part on the ability to choose correctly among roles and on the capacity to perform each of the roles well when necessary, as well as on the ability to get appropriate help.

Remember too, that everything the leader does or does not do is scrutinized and sends important messages about what matters. For example, asking for help in decision-making—or ignoring it—has symbolic meaning to others in the organization about how much initiative to take, how much they are valued, what information to pass on, how committed to be, and so on.

We have been looking at the nature of leadership as an influence process and at the various roles and functions a manager must fill. We turn now to a look at *how* a manager should do his or her job and under what conditions particular functions and styles are appropriate.

How Leadership Is Exercised; Alternative Styles

Situational Leadership

There are many ways to categorize leadership styles. One familiar classification distinguishes among autocratic, democratic, and laissez-faire approaches; another contrasts directive, supportive, participative, and achievement styles; yet another might compare "strictly business" with human relations approaches; the traditional paternalistic or charismatic style has been contrasted with the routinized bureaucratic and the more fluid "organic-adaptive," the transactional with the transformational, and so on. Different writers have different schemes with differing labels for and theories about the effectiveness of each style. Because each of the schemes offers interesting shadings of description, there are overlaps among them; and because most leaders seldom use the same style in all situations, we have developed a way of describing leadership style without using any one set of labels. We believe that this allows greater flexibility in talking about style and greater accuracy in identifying its component parts. We spell out several underlying dimensions along which leaders can differ in carrying out their functions. Each leadership style is composed of a combination of positions along each of these dimensions. The particular labels for styles are less important than an understanding of the choices leaders can make in how they perform their roles.

As in the chapters on interpersonal relations, we assume that each person is likely to have a *preferred* leadership style, which he or she will opt for whenever possible, but that this should be tempered by what is *appropriate* to the organizational situation. We will be as explicit as possible about which leadership behavior is called for under which circumstances, though the possibilities are complex.

There are five dimensions we use to describe how a leader might carry out his or her leadership functions:

1. Retaining control versus sharing control.
2. High task concern versus low task concern.
3. High person concern versus low person concern.
4. Explicit versus implicit expectations (degree of structure provided).
5. Cautious versus venturous.

Retaining versus Sharing Control

One of the most central dimensions of leadership style involves the degree of control exerted over the behavior of others. Control pervades organizational life. It can operate overtly or subtly; a manager can appear to be sharing control but actually retain it, as when opinions are asked but not accepted unless they fit a predetermined decision. Conversely, it can appear to be retained but actually shared, as when the manager insists on the final decision but gives great freedom to subordinates in choosing methods of analysis or implementation. You can ask some of the following questions in trying to analyze degree of control.

FIGURE 12–3   *The Continuum of Leadership Behavior*

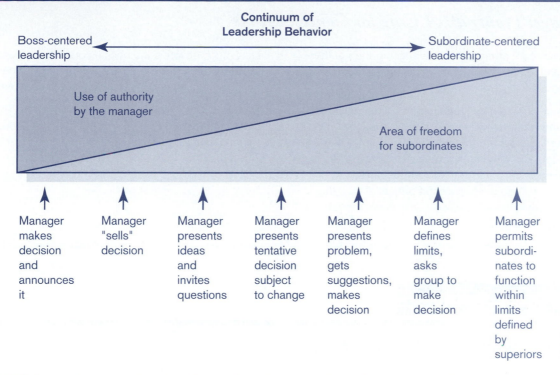

SOURCE: Reprinted by permission of the *Harvard Business Review*. An exhibit from "How to Choose a Leadership Pattern" by Robert Tannenbaum and Warren Schmidt (May/June 1973). Copyright © 1973 by the President and Fellows of Harvard College; all rights reserved.

> If you have a question, don't be afraid to raise it; if it doesn't fit my answer, I'm sure you can rephrase it!
>
> *Anonymous cynic about leadership*

How much latitude is given to others to make their own decisions, to vary from standard procedures, rules, and regulations? How much discretion do they have before they have to consult with or get a decision from their manager? How many people are included and from what ranks? Does the manager use group meetings or one-to-one relationships? How much information is shared with them? How free are they to question advice or orders or to initiate ideas? Is work delegated to others or carried out by the manager? What kind of work is delegated, important or routine? What decisions are made together? How closely are they supervised; are they constantly watched, or is their performance only checked periodically? In short, are they encouraged to try to influence the way work is done? For any particular problem, the amount of control retained by the manager can vary considerably—from decisions made autonomously by the manager, to those where subordinates are consulted, to those made jointly *with* subordinates, and, finally, to those delegated completely to subordinates. Figure 12–3 shows the choices a manager can make about how much influence to share with subordinates.

As you consider the options in the chart, remember that there are both short-term and long-term implications for which option will work best. *To the extent that the*

Manager's Journal: A Cure for Control Freaks

Executives concerned about maintaining their authority without going overboard should ask three basic questions:

- Which subordinates require close and constant observation? New hires, of course, must be watched closely enough to make sure they can do the job. But once an employee has proved his competence, it's time to loosen the reins.
- At what stage of an assigned project should the boss get involved? Answer: Only when the project is off target.

- How much power is the boss emotionally prepared to delegate? It serves no purpose to delegate control if you're such a perfectionist that you can't find it within yourself to trust your subordinates.

Effective managers exercise control, but ineffective ones often overdo it.

SOURCE: Mortimer R. Feinberg, "A Cure for Control Freaks," *The Wall Street Journal,* July 7, 1997, p. A18. (Copyright © 1997, Dow Jones & Company, Inc.)

Ready, Willing, and Too Little Used

We know what to do, but we need skills and authority to do it.

That's what many of 9,144 workers said in an attitude survey by benefits consultant Watson Wyatt Worldwide.

Well over 80% of the polled respondents said they know their employer's goals and their duties. But only

38% said they get needed information or regular performance feedback, and only 55% hold power to make decisions to satisfy customers.

SOURCE: Albert R. Karr, "A Special News Report about Life on the Job—and Trends Taking Shape There," *The Wall Street Journal,* August 26, 1997, p. A1.

effectiveness of a decision depends on the ongoing commitment of subordinates, a manager should share the control of that decision. We referred in Chapter 11 to transformational leadership and the importance of building employee commitment. We emphasize it here, even though the idea of situational leadership views a manager's choice in terms of a particular set of circumstances, because more and more situations require a long-term perspective and thus push the decision-making process in the direction of employee involvement.

High Task Concern versus Low Task Concern

While getting the work done is the essence of any leader's role, more or less attention can be paid to quantity of output, quality of work done, meeting deadlines, meeting output, expectations of other subsystems, or improving performance in general at any particular time. Managers can vary from constant preoccupation with output to negligible concern over it (see Figure 12–4).

A manager can put production ahead of all other considerations–the feelings and safety of subordinates, their learning and development, the maintenance of equipment, and the reactions of customers or other members of the organization. At the

FIGURE 12–4 *The Leadership Grid*

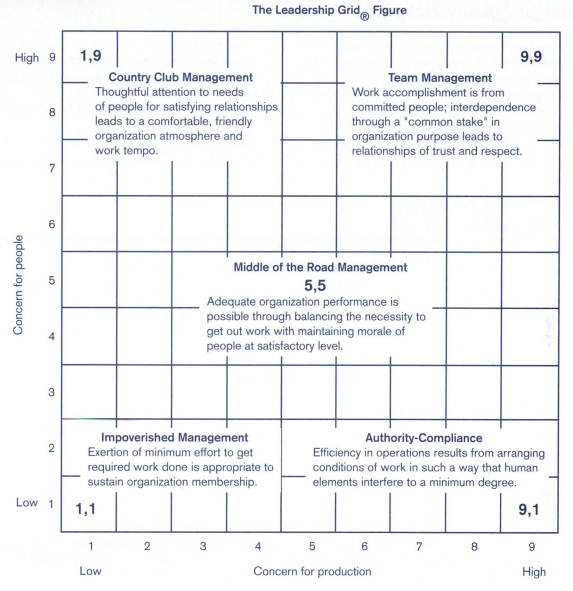

The Leadership Grid® Figure

1,9
Country Club Management
Thoughtful attention to needs of people for satisfying relationships leads to a comfortable, friendly organization atmosphere and work tempo.

9,9
Team Management
Work accomplishment is from committed people; interdependence through a "common stake" in organization purpose leads to relationships of trust and respect.

Middle of the Road Management
5,5
Adequate organization performance is possible through balancing the necessity to get out work with maintaining morale of people at satisfactory level.

Impoverished Management
Exertion of minimum effort to get required work done is appropriate to sustain organization membership.

Authority-Compliance
Efficiency in operations results from arranging conditions of work in such a way that human elements interfere to a minimum degree.

1,1
9,1

Concern for people — High 9, 8, 7, 6, 5, 4, 3, 2, Low 1

Concern for production — 1 2 3 4 5 6 7 8 9, Low ... High

SOURCE: The Leadership Grid ® Figure from *Leadership Dilemmas–Grid Solutions,* by Robert R. Blake and Anne Adams McCanse (formerly the Managerial Grid Figure, by Robert A. Blake and Jane S. Mouton). Houston: Gulf Publishing Company, p. 29. Copyright © 1991, by Scientific Methods, Inc. Reproduced by permission of the owners.

other extreme, a manager can be relatively indifferent to task accomplishment, either out of negligence, oversecurity, or a belief in allowing subordinates to learn for themselves from their own mistakes. Some managers try to wring every last drop of production from employees, while others do not stress production unless it falls below acceptable minimum levels.

Focus on task is often contrasted with focus on the morale and welfare of people doing the task, although they need not be contradictory. For example, the supervisor of the credit department in a bank had to see to it that at least one employee

Points for Effective Delegation

- Delegation is not abdication; you must manage it.
- Be clear about the assignment; check whether it is understood.
- Be clear about what results you expect, standards of performance.
- Be clear about known boundaries:
  How much authority is granted, over what issues.

Budget allowed, if any.
Territories to stay out of, political sensitivities.
- Establish mutually agreed checkpoints—frequency of contact, data, indicators.
- Agree on how much and what kind of information you want.
- Agree about how much help you will give.

Expecting Individual Initiative

No climbing of faddish 40-foot-high obstacle walls for [Genentech CEO Raab] or his executives. He never reads management books, because they bore him (he has a bachelor's degree in fine arts from Colgate). He dislikes meetings: "When you get more than three people in a room, it becomes tiring. A meeting is not the environment where you make strong decisions." He preaches that a CEO should select the best employees he can find and then leave them alone, coming to their aid only when they ask. When they fight him, Raab approves. He says he avoids promoting overly ambitious people to top spots, "because they won't tell me to go to hell, and I want people to speak up when they disagree."

SOURCE: Gene Bylinsky, "Got a Winner? Back It Big," *Fortune,* © March 21, 1994. Time, Inc. All rights reserved.

stayed late each Friday to complete certain forms. At first he made a list on which he arbitrarily rotated the assignment. When the employees complained, he adopted a method that gave them more say over the decision and led to a more satisfactory solution that both provided coverage and allowed employee choice. It is often possible, therefore, to maintain a high level of task concern without necessarily sacrificing the involvement and feelings of those affected.

High Concern for People versus Low Concern for People

As with concern for the task, the degree of a manager's concern for people may vary at any time with regard to such matters as consideration for the personal feelings and attitudes of others, subordinates' preferences when assigning work, providing a supportive working climate, how open about admitting feelings, and how close to allow others to be. Some managers focus all their attention on the effects of actions on the morale of those in their units, while others ignore it completely; clearly there are many options in between these extremes.

Although the grid shown in Figure 12–4 might be viewed as a guide to situational options, its authors do not favor that. Their own position, contrary to those who advocate situational leadership, is that there *is* a best way to lead—namely, with a high emphasis on both task and people in virtually all situations.[5] As we look to the

FIGURE 12–5   *The Hersey–Blanchard Situational Leadership Model*

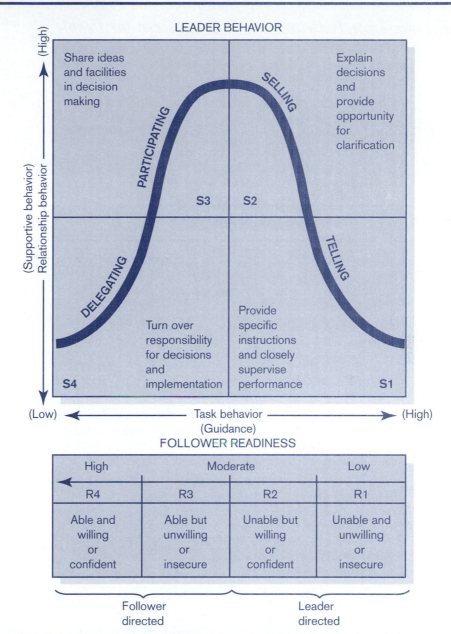

SOURCE: P. Hersey and K. H. Blanchard, *Management of Organizational Behavior: Utilizing Human Resources,* 5th ed. (Englewood Cliffs, NJ: Prentice-Hall, 1988), p. 171. The original model published in the first edition in 1969 used the label *maturity* instead of *readiness.* Copyrighted Material from Leadership Studies, Inc. Used by Permission. All Rights Reserved.

future, it appears that they may be correct, perhaps not for all but certainly for most organizational decisions. Contrast this with the Hersey–Blanchard and Ohio State models in Figures 12–5 and 12–6, in which the managerial choices are clearly linked to situational factors. The greater follower readiness for taking responsibility, the more voice they should be given. You might think about this relationship in the context of your instructor's leadership style in the classroom.

Bottom Line Indicator of High Concern for People

Working for many clients, Vernon Hills, Ill., consultant Barrett said, he has found that the quality of an employer's toilet paper is a litmus test. "Find a reason to visit the washroom and check out the toilet paper," he advised job seekers. "Is it soft and cushy or rough and gritty? Soft paper is a good sign. If the company cares enough to show some interest in (and spend the money on) your personal 'bottom line,' then it is probably a worker-friendly environment."

SOURCE: Sue Shellenbarger, "Work and Family: The Care and Feeding (and the Avoiding) of Horrible Bosses," *The Wall Street Journal,* October 20, 1999, p. B1.

FIGURE 12–6   *The Ohio State Leadership Dimensions*

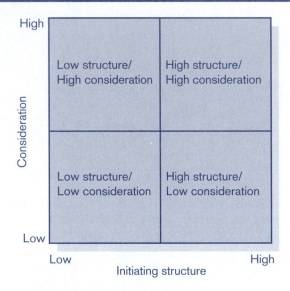

SOURCE: W. A. Randolph and R. S. Blackburn, *Managing Organizational Behavior* (New York: McGraw-Hill/Irwin, 1989); based on concepts in J. K. Hemphill, *Leader Behavior Description* (Columbus: Ohio State University Press, 1950).

Explicit versus Implicit Expectations (Degree of Structure Provided)

Leaders can be explicit about their expectations by using formal organizational procedures and rules or by personal communications with subordinates. The method chosen may make a difference to subordinates; some may prefer predetermined rules, regulations, and procedures, so they can master them in advance or refer to the written word when they have questions. Others may prefer spontaneous case-by-case discussion of expectations, so they can react to those expectations on the spot in a give-and-take discussion. Although formal procedures are usually intended to cover as many contingencies as possible, obviously no preestablished system can, in fact, anticipate them all. To understand degree of structure, you might ask: How clear is the leader about what is expected of each individual? Are detailed methods of working spelled out? Are desired results made clear? Are rewards clearly related to job performance, generally related, or not apparently related? Do rewards relate to short-term or long-term performance, and is there agreement in advance on the criteria? How frequently and directly is feedback given to subordinates? Is the basis for feedback known in advance? How specified are the rules for advancement?

Cautious versus Venturous

The final dimension addresses how venturesome the leader's actions and decisions are. How much risk is involved in decisions? How willing is the leader to make decisions that involve high risk? How entrepreneurial is the leader? How often does the manager go beyond preexisting arrangements? How visible is the leader willing to be to other parts of the organization and its environments? In other words, how bold is the leader? As you will see, the degree of boldness demanded of a leader varies from one situation to another.

Contingencies: Factors Involved in Determining Appropriate Leadership Choices

While it is probably easier to analyze what makes particular leadership styles effective than it is to actually *be* a good leader, there are a bewildering array of factors to keep in mind. We isolate a number of situational aspects that should be taken into account in making appropriate leadership choices, but it is not possible to account for every contingency. Some of the important factors follow.

Nature of the Task Situation

Some jobs (although a diminishing proportion) are very stable and predictable, their processes are not subject to rapid technological change, the need for their output is established and constant, and rapid decisions are not necessary. All elements necessary for good performance are known and well defined. Each job is discrete and essentially repetitive. Under these conditions, it is not especially effective to give great autonomy to subordinates. The more predictable the nature of the task situation, the more appropriate will be tight control, explicit expectations, formal standardized procedures, and cautiousness as leadership choices. The converse is true for work that is less predictable in nature.[6] The less predictable the nature of the task situations, the more appropriate will be shared control, less explicit expectations, informal procedures, and risk-taking.[7]

Work that is inherently stressful or frustrating because of its difficulty calls for more consideration. Under conditions of stressful work, high person-concern by the leader results in greater satisfaction.[8] Paying attention to needs of individuals may be done by providing greater structure or greater freedom; either can be a response to the person's needs.

Expertise of the Leader (as Compared with the Competence of the Subordinates)

A factor often related to the rate of change in the nature of the job is the amount of expert knowledge of the work possessed by the formal leader. When the leader clearly knows a great deal more about the work than any other members of the unit, whether through technical expertise or knowledge of the organization and its environment and their demands, it is costly to spend a lot of time asking for opinions, improvising methods, and sharing control. The greater the differential knowledge of the leader, the more appropriate will be unilateral control.[9]

For example, small businessmen or leaders active in the entrepreneurial role often are so invested in what they are doing (emotionally even more than financially) and so immersed in their vision of what is possible that they literally can do any job in the organization better than anyone else. In those situations high task concern and low sharing of influence is probably appropriate, if not inevitable.

Missing the Boss: Not All Workers Find Idea of Empowerment as Neat as It Sounds

Some Hate Fixing Machines, Apologizing for Errors, Disciplining Teammates; Rah-Rah Types Do the Best

Beverly Reynolds thought she wanted to be an empowered factory worker. But after nine months at Eaton Corp.'s small forge plant here, where empowerment is a near-religion, she had enough and left for another job. Though she liked the idea of being her own boss, she hated the headaches that came with it—fixing broken machines and having to learn a wide variety of jobs. She says her co-workers "weren't standing watching me, but from afar, they were watching me." She found that stressful, even though they were kind and willing to help her. "As it turns out, it just wasn't for me at all," she says.

Nor is it for many others—though you would never know that, to listen to the advocates of empowerment. It is sweeping through American factories, usually through creation of self-directed work teams and other organizational changes designed to push responsibilities down to the factory floor. The idea has obvious appeal: What better way to tap into workers' brains as well as their brawn than to encourage them to think on the job, to bring to it a greater sense of professionalism and self-motivation and to feel committed to the company's success?

So, this effort to "white-collarize" the factory has been adopted by 40% of U.S. manufacturers, estimates Richard Florida, a professor at Carnegie Mellon University in Pittsburgh. And many workers do prefer empowerment to old-style, narrowly defined tasks. Jan Biggerstaff, now a 39-year-old quality-support specialist at the Eaton plant, began working here when it first opened. But when Eaton started requiring a lot of overtime during a boom a few years ago, she faltered. "We were working seven days a week," she complains. So, she left for a job at a unionized machine shop. But, she says, "I hated it." The hours were better, but she couldn't get used to having a boss breathing down her neck again. She returned to Eaton.

Yet many working people aren't suited to the empowerment system. They balk at the subtle control mechanisms often used. They simply want to put in their eight hours and be done with it. Empowerment is "best for people who are very group-oriented—and it helps to be the real rah-rah, sis-boom-bah type," Prof. Florida says.

Eaton's 106 employees here are expected to enforce rules themselves. If someone misses too much work or picks fights with co-workers, other members of the production team are supposed to point out the problem. "They say there are no bosses here," says Randy Savage, a longtime, devoted employee, "but if you screw up, you find one pretty fast." Indeed, with everyone watching everyone else, it can feel like having a hundred bosses.

The plant's emphasis on fitting into the group can seem almost cultish: Worker mishaps that might hamper production or tarnish the plant's reputation are considered an affront to everyone and can prompt a sort of communal confession.

When one team of Eaton workers unwittingly made and passed through a batch of 1,200 faulty parts, they went before everyone to discuss what happened and how it could have been avoided. Even though no one was fired over the mistake, that procedure may seem harsh. But it is mild compared with something also tried at the plant: putting the offenders in front of the work force, then having everyone vote on whether to keep them.

"We did that twice real early in our history," says Tom Gothard, the plant manager. Both cases, he says, involved men accused of abusing Eaton's overtime guidelines. Both kept their jobs, but such meetings were stopped. "You run self-direction by trial and error," Mr. Gothard says, "and we decided that that didn't work." But it did underscore a point he stresses: If you're honest about mistakes, you need not fear discussing them.

Alexander M. Cutler, president and chief operating officer of Cleveland-based Eaton, concedes that such a workplace is demanding. "The admission ticket for this kind of responsibility is accountability and not everyone necessarily wants accountability." Some people think they want to be self-directed but discover they can't live up to their part of the bargain. Indeed, the nonunion plant has an employee turnover rate of about 10% a year, one of the highest in Eaton's 155 factories. While that includes a small number promoted to jobs in other Eaton plants, most are people who quit.

Mr. Gothard attributes the high turnover partly to the nature of the work: It's "hot, heavy, dirty," he says. At the core of the factory are giant forge presses, towering

Continued

machines that stamp hot steel into various shapes. The thumping of the presses is so loud that workers communicate via hand signals, and they use long tongs to handle the glowing parts, most of which are sent to other Eaton plants to be shaped into truck-transmission gears.

But the turnover is remarkable in light of the elaborate winnowing process used in hiring: Only about one in 10 applicants is offered a job, and promising candidates go through a grueling series of as many as 13 interviews. The final interview is typically conducted by a group of workers off the factory floor. Many jobs are filled through employees' recommendations of relatives or friends, but even people with such connections are subjected to the full barrage of interviews. And workers are careful about endorsing people because the failure of that person, if hired, might reflect badly on themselves.

The plant also strives to avoid the trappings of a traditional factory hierarchy. People such as Mr. Gothard aren't called managers, for instance, but rather "vision supporters." Everyone, including front-office people, wears the same blue uniforms. And newly hired workers aren't put through a probationary period; that would violate the emphasis on trust. "It also smacks of something negotiated with unions," says Mr. Gothard, who notes that despite the high turnover, the plant won a company trophy for its top quality.

As in any workplace, some people try to work around the system. They find subtle ways to resist policies they dislike—such as the daily locker inspections, which are part of a general cleanliness campaign. Workers take turns checking the locker rooms and noting the individual lockers that are smudged with oil as well as problems such as hangers left on the floor. Poor ratings are posted on a lunchroom bulletin board and are one factor in calculating everyone's annual bonus. One worker concedes he doesn't note any problems when he checks the lockers. "I say to myself: I'm empowered—and I ain't doing this," he says.

Similarly, some workers refuse to speak at meetings called to point out problems with a co-worker's performance. They consider this refusal a silent message to their co-worker that they don't like what is going on. And others say they would never go in front of the rest of the work force to apologize for a mistake.

Some people do well with all the physical aspects of the work, but fall short by other measures—such as their communications skills. With workers expected to sort out problems among themselves rather than have managers intervene, strong interpersonal skills are vital.

Ernest Gordon, who had spent a decade in a unionized auto plant and impressed people at Eaton in his job interviews, lasted only six months at the plant here. Co-workers say he was constantly clashing with those around him. He was sent to a counselor to talk about controlling his anger but walked out of the session. "They should have judged me on my job performance, not on how I interact with the teammates," Mr. Gordon says. He adds that he liked much about the plant, such as the absence of time clocks; everyone reports their hours, including overtime, on an honor basis—widely considered the ultimate sign of trust between management and workers. But Mr. Gordon didn't like the frequent meetings and emphasis on communication. For instance, new workers are required to give speeches before new employees and managers and to attend training seminars about saying "we," never "I" or "you," when being critical, to avoid sounding accusatory.

"I'm not talkative, and coming from a [union] shop, you tend to mind your own business," Mr. Gordon says. He also thinks that after he offended a few longtime employees, they worked quietly to get him fired—and that without a union to protect him, they could do so more easily. Plant managers deny there was a campaign against Mr. Gordon.

In any event, the work itself can be frustrating. Steve Bowerman recently tried for two hours to get one of the big presses to work correctly. He pulled apart die holders, put out small fires that flared up when hot metal fell into grease, and wiped up specks of graphite and water that sprayed everywhere, even on his teeth. "In other factories, if something goes wrong, I'd say I'm not worried; it's the foreman's job to worry about that," says the 45-year-old, whose cap bears the slogan: "This is what old looks like." But at Eaton, "you feel more responsible for what you're doing—and that makes you nervous." He and his teammates eventually got the machine working.

Nobody has to watch Mr. Bowerman to ensure he will fix the machine as quickly as possible; every minute it is idle means fewer parts produced on his shift—for everyone to see. Indeed, a hallway off the factory floor is devoted to charts for each production team, showing parts produced compared with pieces of scrap generated. These numbers are central to the workers' lives: They define who has the strongest team, who will win special awards and who gets to brag at lunch time.

In return for their efforts, workers get an average of $13.64 an hour—less than many of the area's union

Continued

Missing the Boss: Not All Workers Find Idea of Empowerment as Neat as It Sounds   Continued

workers but enough to attract applicants in a region with a chronic labor shortage. For many, the main lure is Eaton's benefits package, which includes health insurance, a retirement plan, a bonus program, and tuition reimbursement. And while many factories hire temporary workers as a screening technique, everyone Eaton hires becomes a permanent employee immediately.

But to many workers, the discipline process is a pain. It still bothers Mark Dixon, who has worked at the plant since it opened in 1989 and says his job is the best he has ever had. Recently, one of his two teammates, Brian White, was fired for missing too many days of work. The team did what it was supposed to do: Its members first held meetings to try to deal with the issue themselves. But such sessions can be uncomfortable.

In this case, Mr. Dixon heard about Mr. White's fights with his girlfriend and other personal problems. No matter how much Mr. Dixon tried to say he was only trying to help, such meetings are still a form of highly visible criticism, and everyone else in the plant also quickly hears about it. "I'd rather a 'vision supporter' dealt with stuff like that," Mr. Dixon says. And Mr. White, for his part, admits missing a lot of work. But he thinks his good performance over five years should have allowed him more leeway in light of his recent personal problems.

The episode was particularly painful for Mr. Gothard, the plant manager, who acknowledges Mr. White was once a star employee. "It tears at all my emotions that I wasn't able to get through to that young man," he says, sitting in his modest office. It also underscores that empowerment is no panacea. "It takes a huge amount of maturity to be a self-directed worker," he says. It can be taught, he adds, but the worker has to want to learn it.

SOURCE: Timothy Aeppel, "Missing the Boss," *The Wall Street Journal*, September 8, 1997, p. A1. (Copyright © 1997, Dow Jones & Company, Inc.)

MANAGERIAL BULLETIN

Everyone Clear?

Everyone will now be mobilized . . . and all boys old enough to carry a spear will be sent to Addis Ababa. Married men will take their wives to carry food and cook. Those without wives will take any woman without a husband. Women with small babies need not go.

Those blind, those who cannot walk or for any reason cannot carry a spear are exempted. **Anyone found at home after receipt of this order will be hanged.**

SOURCE: Haile Selassie I, Emperor of Ethiopia, upon invasion by Italy, 1935.

Not only is unilateral control more effective when the boss knows more, but failure to exercise it can lead to employee frustration. People hate to be asked their opinion when the person asking already knows the answer, especially if the opinion is less expert and cannot change the asker's conclusions. A leader may occasionally wish to give an assignment to someone less skilled in order to help develop that person, but in that case the objective is growth, not necessarily the best product. In general, a good rule of thumb is, "If you know the answer and what you plan to do, do not ask a subordinate's opinion." If you ask, you risk creating feelings of being manipulated, which decreases trust and, in turn, accuracy of communications upward. This does not rule out the potential value of allowing subordinates to ask questions in order to understand what is intended or to express their concerns about your planned action. Such airing of concerns can allay their doubts and build their belief in your decision in ways that will facilitate its implementation.

MANAGERIAL BULLETIN

First among Equals

[Pfizer President] McKinnell hasn't abandoned his hard-charging ways. He fosters bare-knuckle debates among colleagues. As a finance specialist, he is data-driven and "very analytical." McKinnell's mantra: "I believe that all of us are smarter than any of us."

Much as he listens to colleagues, McKinnell doesn't wait for the group to decide before he acts. A trade association staffer who has seen him working with groups of drug executives says he has at times "gotten ahead of the consensus." McKinnell's view: "that's what a leader does." A Pfizer associate adds something that already seems obvious: He doesn't suffer fools gladly.

SOURCE: Joseph Weber, "Leading Pfizer's Raid: "I'm Usually On Target," *Business Week,* November 22, 1999, p. 52.

MANAGERIAL BULLETIN

Reality Bites at Raytheon

How Its Can-Do Culture Kept Problems from Coming to Light

One well-connected defense consultant in Washington just completed a competitive analysis of Raytheon's culture. He concluded that Raytheon executives tended to be "passive aggressive." Afraid of being blamed if something went wrong, they managed cautiously yet tended to overreact when ordered to do something by [former Chairman and CEO] Picard. And some feared Picard, who had "not just a hot temper but was unpredictable." Moreover, two former Raytheon managers, who were among the company's top 25, allege that Picard set an aggressive, demeaning tone. They say he left executive vice presidents and others waiting for hours outside his office. It was a formal ambience in which executives were also publicly dressed down. Picard "created fear and self-doubt in people; they were afraid to tell him the truth," says one former executive.

Yet Picard has plenty of defenders. Skelley, one of Picard's closest confidantes, agrees that he has a temper and could certainly be a tough manager. But he says Picard also engendered intense loyalty among his top people. Adds former U.S. Senator Warren Rudman, a Raytheon director for the past nine years: "It may be that the culture played a role, but I don't think anyone is blameless in this." As for Picard, he says: "He's tough, he's fair, he's a tremendous patriot, and he's always pushing for excellence."

SOURCE: Geoffrey Smith, with Victoria Murphy, "Reality Bites at Raytheon," *Business Week,* November 15, 1999, p. 78. (Copyright 1999 McGraw-Hill, Inc.)

On the other hand, sharing control and soliciting opinions is appropriate for situations where the workers have knowledge equal to or greater than the leader, as is often the case for jobs requiring high technical input. In an information-oriented service economy, as is increasingly the case in the United States, there are more and more situations where each subordinate knows something that the boss does not. The director of a research lab, for example, usually supervises PhD specialists who know much more about some aspects of problems than the director does; tight control and formal procedures would be self-defeating. The newness of the Internet and World Wide Web has, in many instances, turned experience and expertise upside down; leaders who cannot acknowledge that for some issues a non-college technical whiz may have valuable knowledge can cause severe blockage.

GE Is No Place for Autocrats, Welch Decrees

General Electric Co. can no longer tolerate autocratic, tyrannical managers.

So said chairman and chief executive John F. Welch Jr., who has cracked his share of heads, in his letter to shareholders in GE's annual report . . . a promising future is "an easy call" for a leader who "delivers on commitments—financial or otherwise—and shares the values of our company." For that person, the prospect is "onward and upward," he declares.

The second type of leader, one who doesn't meet commitments and doesn't share values, is "not as pleasant a call, but equally easy," he says. Such personnel are soon gone, is the implication.

Leaders who miss commitments but share the values "usually get a second chance, preferably in a different environment" within the company, he declares.

But the fourth type is "the most difficult for many of us to deal with. That leader delivers on commitments, makes all the numbers, but doesn't share the values we must have. This is the individual who typically forces performance out of people rather than inspires it: the autocrat, the big shot, the tyrant. Too often all of us have looked the other way," tolerating these "'Type 4' managers because 'they always deliver'—at least in the short term."

But these days, "in an environment where we must have every good idea from every man and woman in the organization, we cannot afford management styles that suppress and intimidate," he declares.

SOURCE: James C. Hyatt and Amal Kumar Naj. Printed by permission of *The Wall Street Journal,* March 3, 1992. Dow Jones & Company, Inc. All Rights Reserved Worldwide.

Attitudes and Needs of Subordinates

The amount of challenge or routine in a job often attracts people whose motivations match job requirements. When subordinates enjoy problem solving and difficult assignments, are dedicated to the work, and enjoy independence (i.e., are operating on higher-level needs), different leadership choices are called for than when they are passive, dependent, and threatened. In general, The greater subordinates' needs for autonomy and independence, the less tight control by the leader is appropriate, and vice versa.[10]

Less independent subordinates, however, call for greater control and explicitness of expectations. The (decreasing number) of subordinates who are more dependent, more extrinsically motivated, and/or have relatively low ability, prefer high direction from their bosses. Those who have high ability and/or are intrinsically motivated want to participate in decision making and do not like to be controlled.[11]

As suggested in Chapter 7 on individual motivation, while close supervision of those operating on low-level needs may be productive in the short run, there are organizational and human consequences for satisfaction and learning, which also need to be taken into account. This connects to the issue of concern for people versus concern for task. Some researchers have claimed that high concern for both is always most effective, and, in general, either concern is ignored only at the leader's peril.[12] But in some situations, at least temporarily, one should probably take precedence over the other.

For those organizational members who have high needs for independence and love challenging tasks, high person-concern may be a bit superfluous. Leaving them alone to get on with the work, in a cordial way, can be very effective. At the other extreme, with subordinates who are operating on survival needs, warmth and support may not be necessary (although much appreciated if given).

Most organizational members, however, will be affected by a wider range of needs, including those for social approval, and will be quite responsive to a supportive climate. Where the work itself is not especially challenging or intrinsically fascinating but those doing it are not threatened about survival, high concern for people along with high concern for task is appropriate.

Leader's Upward Influence

For convenience we have been talking about "the leader" as if it were always one person with formal-legitimate influence and sufficient power to do whatever is needed. But the actual power of the leader or of those aspiring to perform leadership functions is a very important factor in determining appropriate leadership style. Even the supervisor or manager who is formally and legitimately in that position will have varying amounts of influence with subordinates, superiors, and peers. Leaders who have considerable influence with their superiors, for example, can take more risks in the decisions they make, vary more from formal procedures, and receive greater support from subordinates than those who do not. The greater the "upward" influence of a leader, the less it is necessary to share control with subordinates.[13] Effective shared influence, however, is likely to increase the upward influence of a leader, because it can yield a solid support base when trying to persuade superiors. The leader who does not have clout with higher-ups or other outsiders must be cautious in changing formal procedures and spend time building support among subordinates in order to have a stronger base of influence; thus, more sharing of control and concern for people is appropriate. A common mistake for leaders of dissident groups is to become so caught up in fighting higher-ups with power that group members are ignored or not given much say; in a showdown the group members may not stand solidly behind the leader because they have not been "brought along."

Any leader with low legitimacy must worry about similar problems. It is not very effective to go around barking orders if those who are supposed to follow them do not accept your right to issue them. If legitimacy will not or cannot be conferred from an organizational superior, then it must be earned; involving others, giving warmth and support, and taking low risks are then most appropriate. A successful risky decision can break through to a new level of respect from subordinates; a failure can cause a bad case of terminal influence.

The power of the leader and his or her relationship with subordinates also affect the appropriateness of task concern. Leaders with high power and good relationships who are responsible for structured jobs are most effective when task oriented. Ironically, in the opposite conditions (low power, poor relationships, and low structure), task orientation is also appropriate. It is only when these conditions are moderate that predominant person-concern seems to work best. In sum, Task-oriented leaders do best in situations that are highly favorable or highly unfavorable for exerting influence, while person-concerned leaders do best in moderately favorable conditions.[14]

In some settings an organization's traditions and culture will not legitimize influence when it is attempted in a style considered inappropriate. Faculty members in universities, for example, who are relatively independent, do unstructured work, and have relatively high power often only accept administrator influence when administrators do not behave in a controlling, cold way. Conversely, in some companies anything less than a gruff set of orders given as commands will be seen as weak and therefore unenforceable. In either type of organization, stylistic choices are limited by member willingness to give power only to those using particular influence modes.

All authority belongs to the people.

Thomas Jefferson

Carrots over Sticks

As a manager, Bill Prince bulldozed his way through problems, projects and—when they got in his way—people. He was demeaning to subordinates and disdainful of bosses, and as a result his fast-track career at BellSouth ground to a halt.

But Mr. Prince is proof that, on occasion, a leopard can change his spots. With the help of an understanding boss and a program that forced him to face his deficiencies, Mr. Prince changed his style. Now 54 years old, he has started his own business with an eye toward expansion and is even starting other businesses, something he says he would never have risked before for fear of alienating his staff. "I went through life thinking I was a top manager and couldn't understand why I didn't become a vice president," he says. "As it turned out, I had some blind spots in my management style that I wasn't aware of."

It's the eternal management conundrum: Are employees motivated more by fear or affection? For decades, bullying managers ruled American business. "It's my way or the highway" was their anthem. But in the information age, products increasingly come not from an assembly line but from employees' heads. And with workers job-hopping fearlessly in a talent-short market, managers are finding that showing a more compassionate side works better.

When Mr. Prince joined BellSouth in 1964 after graduating from college, the only thing that seemed to matter was results. After 15 years, he had become a middle manager and part of the company's high-potential development program by turning around underperforming organizations in a dozen cities. But he says he did it in a "brusque and unfeeling manner," firing people in droves. And those he sacked may have been the lucky ones: Survivors were treated coldly, praised infrequently and publicly demeaned for mistakes.

Eventually, Mr. Prince's career bogged down. Others got promotions he felt he deserved, and he grew bitter toward higher management. "I didn't always treat them with the respect I should have," he says. When a general manager didn't fire an employee for a security violation, as he had recommended, Mr. Prince went to the manager's boss to suggest disciplinary measures—for the GM. "I had low tolerance for executives who wouldn't deal with summary judgment when I felt we needed it," he says.

After 30 years with the company, Mr. Prince found himself in an executive support situation, headed nowhere. So he quit in 1994 and joined A&A Services, a telecommunications-services outsourcing firm owned by Art Hall, a former BellSouth colleague. He started as a senior consultant and was named executive director within 90 days.

But Mr. Prince's tough-guy management style had not changed. Mr. Hall recalls driving home from a seminar and asking if Mr. Prince would be able to respect

Continued

With so many possible stylistic choices to make and so many situational factors to take into account, it is hard for an aspiring leader to sort out what to do when. For example, in general, Less influence should be shared when subordinates are unconcerned about or unaffected by the decision and when they have less expertise than the manager. Greater sharing of influence should be used when subordinates' support and cooperation is needed, their knowledge is essential, or their commitment is necessary, because they must carry out the decision.[15]

Still other factors need to be taken into account. If time is short and a decision must be made, the leader should use the least participatory (most controlling) style suitable to solve the problem. If, however, the development of subordinates is very important, then the most participatory (least controlling) style that fits the problem should be used.[16]

Finally, the style exhibited by managers will be influenced by the managerial function (or role) they emphasize or concentrate their energies on. For example, managers whose situation requires them to concentrate on developing external relationships and monitoring what is happening in the environment are likely to have less time to supervise their subordinates and, hence, will be less controlling.

him as boss. Mr. Prince responded, "That's up to you," according to Mr. Hall.

Mr. Prince acknowledges he didn't show Mr. Hall the proper respect. "It was like, 'Just get out of my way and I'll get the sales and profits,'" he says.

Employees complained that Mr. Prince pushed too hard and treated them rudely, Mr. Hall recalls, "People were saying, 'This guy is toxic.'" So Mr. Hall called Mr. Prince in for a talk, offering to find him a program that would help him change his behavior. Mr. Prince got the message: "If I didn't want the help, he'd arrange a graceful exit."

The cure was an intensive leadership-development program run by Atlanta psychologist Robert L. Turknett. He put Mr. Prince through a battery of tests and sought assessments from 22 former bosses, peers, and subordinates going back 15 years. "He had a bull-in-a-china-shop approach to managing people," Mr. Turknett concluded. "He essentially saw people as instruments to get things done through, but didn't concern himself with their feelings."

Mr. Prince learned that people saw him as overly frank and often offensive. Nonverbal signals were also a problem. "I could look at you and you would know you were an inch tall," he says. He traced some of this behavior to a broken home. "It instilled in me a hard-nosed disposition," he says. "I was going to do whatever it took to survive."

Fortunately, he was also a man of strong will. He started making a list of desired behaviors: Treat employees the same as clients, don't go home with any relationships still damaged, take responsibility for your own actions. "I always said, 'That's just the way I am,'" he says. "Bob told me that being hard-nosed was a choice."

Mr. Turknett gave him homework: Focus on one person for a week, stressing the positive things that person has done. Write the things you value about the person. "He would come back and say, 'It's like a miracle; he's like my best buddy—he'll do anything for me,'" Mr. Turknett recalls. After the initial program, Mr. Prince returned monthly for 90 minutes of coaching and feedback.

Now, as the CEO of his own company, Mr. Prince is careful to focus on fixing the problem, not condemning the person who made the mistake. "Ten years ago, I probably would have glared at that person, gritted my teeth to indicate how upset I was with them personally," he says. "And I would have done it in front of other people."

Mr. Hall confirms that the change in Mr. Prince's approach was dramatic. "When I asked him where do you want to go to lunch, he said, 'Where do you want to go, Art?'" Mr. Hall says. "Before that, no matter what, he wanted to make the decision."

SOURCE: Hal Lancaster, "Given a Second Chance, a Boss Learns to Favor Carrots over Sticks," *The Wall Street Journal*, November 30, 1999, p. B1. (Copyright © 1999, Dow Jones & Company, Inc.)

However, they may also need to develop more explicit operating procedures so that their units present a consistent face to that outside world.

Making Choices

As you can see, there is a lot to take into account in deciding an appropriate style. What is appropriate will vary not only in an overall way, but also from situation to situation, person to person, time to time. It is no wonder that some managers are tempted to just do what comes naturally, whether it fits or not, and let the chips fall where they may. In fact, one leading leadership theorist, Fred Fiedler,[17] has argued that managers cannot really change their styles through training (and implicitly, by choice), so they should concentrate on getting into the situations that happen to fit their natural style. While it is clear that human beings are not infinitely malleable and cannot constantly and continually shift gears—and if they could, might badly confuse those around them—it seems overly pessimistic to conclude that no choice is possible. While there would never be time to examine *every* situation for the factors in it before having to decide how to lead, it is possible to step back from decisions periodically, go through the analysis we have explained, and roughly

FIGURE 12-7   *Making Choices (Leadership Style)*

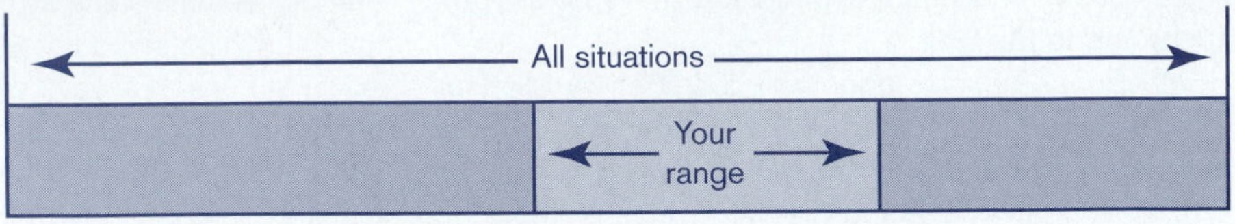

Adapt your style to fit the particular situation
or
Choose a situation that your style fits or
to which you can adapt (with training if needed).

determine if (1) your usual leadership style generally fits the situations you are in, (2) there are particular variations in situations that call for a different style than your usual one, and you might more readily adjust when those situations arise, (3) you sometimes face situations calling for a leadership style you are not comfortable with, and, therefore you need to practice acquiring the necessary skills or behavior, or (4) you want to get out of situations that demand behavior you cannot or do not want to learn (see Figure 12–7).

In Chapter 9 we talked about interpersonal competence as an important part of a manager's range of abilities, and we paid particular attention to the importance of developing a wide range of interpersonal styles in order to meet the demands of complex work situations. Successful leadership requires the same kind of mastery but with a special emphasis upon those interpersonal skills that enhance your influence and power in an organization. The wider the range of leadership styles available to you, the better able you are to exercise appropriate choices in a given situation.

As increasing numbers of employees have higher levels of education, a stronger belief in the appropriateness of having a say in the way things are run, and a desire for meaningful challenging work, managers are being pushed to use more participative styles. Pressure from below for more of a voice is a common phenomenon in many contemporary organizations. When it comes from subordinates who indeed have their own expertise to contribute, genuine participation is quite appropriate.

In general, Leadership that fully involves those being led in decision making ("participative," "employee-centered") is most effective under the following conditions:

a. Decisions are nonroutine.
b. Nonstandardized information is flowing in or must be gathered through subordinates.
c. Actions are not being taken under severe time pressure.
d. Subordinates feel the need for independence, are intrinsically motivated, see participation as legitimate, are competent, have needed expertise and can work without close supervision, will take the organization's goals into account, can affect the implementation of decisions by acceptance or rejection of them, and therefore need to be committed to the decisions.[18]

Under these conditions, where it is not enough to merely have subordinates going through the motions, leaders must find a way to "capture subordinates' hearts," gain their full commitment to doing what is needed. This calls for an across-the-board effort by leaders, as discussed in Chapter 11.

Nevertheless, many managers struggle with the issue of how to balance an emphasis upon "getting the job done" with the importance of fully involving employees in the process of decision making. The question seems to be, "How much time

Five Main Reasons Managers Fail: In Many Cases, Their Setbacks Are Self Made

Failure. It's every manager's terror. . . .

Whatever the reason for the career fall, it's considered shameful and scarring. So much so that managers who fail on the job often spend more time hiding the fact than examining why it happened.

Yet nearly every manager trips as he or she moves up the corporate ladder. . . .

[A] survey . . . found that the executives managed to spring back because they were able to admit failures, instead of blaming others, and then move on. Many changed employers or careers after a setback. . . .

[Most] often, managers contribute to their own career falls—usually through one of a handful of causes:

Inability to get along

Failure to adapt

The "me only" syndrome

Fear of action

Unable to rebound

SOURCE: Carol Hymowitz, *The Wall Street Journal,* © May 2, 1988. Dow Jones & Company, Inc.

The Front Lines: Jane Biering Tells Managers at Staples to Lead by Listening

It's amazing how much your employees know about your operation. It's equally amazing the sense of belonging they experience at the rare companies in which management acts on their cues.

Mere symbols—a suggestion box, say, or special parking privileges for the employee-of-the-month—accomplish nothing. Getting real ideas from employees demands buoyantly open-minded leadership and the eradication of intimidation. So Ms. Biering regularly assembles employees at all job levels, encouraging them to sound off.

There's a new world facing managements, a world of fickle customers, dispirited employees, and demanding technologies. Today's manager must listen as well as lead, collaborate as well as control, nurture as well as manipulate.

Are you thinking what I'm thinking? Does it take a woman to deliver this kind of corporate sensibility? Is the club of hierarchical male leadership becoming an anachronism?

SOURCE: Thomas Petzinger, Jr., "Jane Biering Tells Managers at Staples to Lead by Listening," *The Wall Street Journal,* March 15, 1996, p. B1. (Copyright © 1996, Dow Jones & Company, Inc.)

can I afford to spend informing and discussing matters with my employees if it cuts into valuable work time?" Or the question might be phrased in sharper terms, like "Who's running the show, me or my workers?"

The Problem of Heroic Models

What causes these concerns, even when the conditions for greater participation are clearly present? One explanation is that American managers have heroic images about leadership.[19] Raised on such heroic models as the Lone Ranger riding to the rescue to leave the silver bullet in the nick of time, American managers assume that

MANAGERIAL BULLETIN

99 Days: Manzi Quits at IBM, and His Many Critics Are Just Delighted

As CEO, Mr. Manzi unleashed an intense and mercurial personality. He could be friendly, boyishly charming, and smart. Then, without warning, he could turn paranoid and sarcastic, blaming others for mistakes he'd made himself, many former colleagues say.

"He's not a good person," says Steven Crummey, an early Lotus executive and one of the few willing to say, for publication, what many others say in private. "He doesn't care about anybody other than himself. He's rude, arrogant and condescending."

"Jim just turns on you, and you go from his buddy, being invited to his home, to being absolute scum."

SOURCE: Laurie Hays, "99 Days: Manzi Quits at IBM," *The Wall Street Journal,* October 12, 1995, p. 1.

leadership requires knowing all the answers, taking on the whole department's burdens, and being responsible for everything going right. Although having all the answers was possible and likely in simpler times, thereby making overcontrolling styles appropriate, such conditions are increasingly rare. Yet managers cling to old models out of feelings of great responsibility and misguided notions about what leaders are supposed to do. Even management students carry these heroic assumptions around; as soon as a student is selected to be manager of a classroom task group, members expect the manager to be instantly enlightened, and the manager often starts acting as if special expertise was magically conferred, or worrying because "the answers" are no clearer to him or her than when just an ordinary group member!

The heroic assumptions lead to two alternative models: the *manager-as-technician* and *manager-as-conductor.* Technicians try to have all the answers, just as they did when they were doing the work they are now managing. Their focus is on the technical content of the job; people problems are often seen as a nuisance, preventing "real work." Manager-conductors also feel overresponsible for their unit's success but try to maneuver their subordinates into arriving at the answer the conductor has already worked out. Conductors most often talk about being participative, while carefully constraining participation. Too often "participation" is limited to allowing subordinate discussion without decision-making responsibility. Both conductors and technicians are preoccupied with control of subordinates, to see that "everything is done right," but it is exactly this overcontrol that tends to demotivate subordinates and reduce their commitment.

By working extraordinarily hard, outstanding heroic managers can be quite effective, even when all the conditions are not appropriate for their styles, but they must run faster and faster to stay ahead of their subordinates.

A "post-heroic" model, more appropriate to the conditions fitting participative styles, has been called the *manager-as-developer* or shared-responsibility leadership. Bradford and Cohen[20] formulated this model as a result of working with managers who realized that the more traditional models were no longer fully effective. The manager-developer's basic orientation is to be concerned about seeing to it that problems get solved and work gets done in ways that develop subordinates' capacities for and commitment to sharing responsibility for the unit's success. To be effective, the manager-as-developer must accomplish the following major tasks:

1. Work with direct subordinates as a team to collectively share responsibility for managing the unit.
2. Determine and gain commitment to a common, tangible vision of the department's goals and purposes.

Managing Your Career: A Founder's Lesson: Market Reality Matters More than a Mission

In today's Silicon Valley, [Umang Gupta] concluded, companies that are built around the vision of a single founder will falter unless he surrounds himself with a savvy team. "No individual is smart enough to figure out all the technological moves," he says. "Bill Gates and Larry Ellison have done it, but they also built organizations that can react to change."

Companies need a lot of people who have great antennae that can sense changes in the market, he says. He didn't have those people at Gupta, or he wasn't listening to them. "Decisions can't be based just on what the founder knows or his gut feels," he says.

SOURCE: Hal Lancaster, "A Founder's Lesson: Market Reality Matters More than a Mission," *The Wall Street Journal,* November 2, 1999, p. B1.

3. Work on the continuous development of individual subordinate skills, especially in the managerial/interpersonal areas needed to be an effective member of the shared responsibility team.
4. Establish mutual influence relationships with everyone, including subordinates, who must be willing to push back when the manager is wrong, which in turn forces that manager to be frank and demanding.

The post-heroic leader, then, seeks to develop in subordinates the willingness and ability to share the responsibility for departmental success. The manager must shape subordinates into a powerful, cooperative, hardworking, dedicated, and responsible team.

> These . . . activities reinforce each other. A shared responsibility team is the instrument for tackling core problems and a venue in which members can influence each other (and the leader). A tangible vision pulls members above their parochial interests toward a common purpose and thereby aligns individual interests with the interests of the larger group. The vision serves as a standard for strategic decision making, coordination, and control. Greater ability to mutually influence each other is necessary for consensus decision making, for coordination, and control, and for member, leader, and team development. . . . The leader encourages members to take on more of the leadership functions, freeing the leader to spend more time on the lateral and upward aspects of leadership. None of this is easy to do, but the results are worth the effort.[21]

We are not suggesting that technical and conducting skills are not an important part of a manager's repertoire. Quite the contrary; these are often the very skills needed to establish credibility and to move the system. We *are* suggesting that in this day of knowledge-based work, managers must broaden their repertoire to include developer skills. They need to know such things as:

1. How to create the conditions and atmosphere that promote employee growth.
2. When *not* to manage an activity. (See Managerial Tools on delegation on p. 288.)
3. How to provide support and guidance to subordinates without taking over the task.
4. How to help people learn from their mistakes. (Learning to give constructive feedback is essential.)
5. Biting their tongues while subordinates struggle to master new skills.
6. How to talk about departmental goals in a way that provides meaning and inspires extraordinary effort.

Your Career Matters: Out of Tragedy at War, Lessons for Leaders on the Job

Who will want to follow you again after you launched the "friendly fire" that killed two young American soldiers? Lots of people, Ralph Hayles is discovering, and they're willing to pay handsomely for the opportunity.

"Don't always try to be a hero," Mr. Hayles counsels business clients, many of them managers of restaurants and retail stores who insist on leading all fights on the front lines. Overplaying your role as a hands-on manager can "lead to the 'big mistake.'"

SOURCE: Robert Johnson, "Your Career Matters: Out of Tragedy at War, Lessons for Leaders on the Job," *The Wall Street Journal*, March 9, 1999, p. B1.

Vision

Strong leaders articulate direction and save the organization from change via "drift." They create a vision of a possible future that allows themselves and others to see more clearly the focus to take.

SOURCE: Rosabeth Moss Kanter, *The Change Masters* (New York: Basic Books, 1977).

Because vision is so important, it isn't just the responsibility of top management, but of every manager throughout the organization. The larger vision must be retranslated at each level and connected closely to the specific work of that unit. Even when an organization has a well-formulated and accepted overall vision, each unit must determine its special, unique contributions, and have a way of describing the unit's work to give it as much significance as the whole organization's purpose.

SOURCE: Allan R. Cohen and David L. Bradford, *Power Up* (New York: John Wiley & Sons, 1998).

The role is not unlike that of an effective teacher. It is not a role easily come by, but the positive consequences of effective developer efforts tend to be long lasting and increase the quality of the work environment for all employees. Think about some of the best instructors you've had. Did they just present technical information? Did they manage the class in a highly controlled manner, carefully leading students to conclusions known to the instructor in advance? Were they sensitive to students' needs for autonomy and for opportunities to learn from their own mistakes? Chances are the best teachers you had were the ones who had competencies in all three areas: they had the technical knowledge that commanded your respect; they knew how to sequence material and manage the learning process in ways that enhanced learning; and they knew when and how to give students room to learn in their own ways. Teachers who depend exclusively on one set of skills or one style tend to be limited in their effectiveness. Think about the effect on you of these different kinds of leadership in the classroom. The effect will be similar with respect to managers in the work setting.

Of course, even within highly changing organizations, there are likely to be situations where the developer style is not appropriate. For example, time becomes an important factor when the environment demands rapid responses or when the leader feels rushed and pressured. Ironically, unless the need for decisions is ex-

The New Post-Heroic Leadership

The few corporate chiefs who saw all this [exponentially increasing change] coming declared themselves "transformational" and embraced such concepts as "empowerment," "workout," "quality," and "excellence." What they didn't do–deep down inside–was actually give up much control or abandon their fundamental beliefs about leadership. As James O'Toole, a professor and leadership expert, puts it, "Ninety-five percent of American managers today say the right thing. Five percent actually do it."

The pressure is building to walk the talk. Call it whatever you like: post-heroic leadership, servant leadership, distributed leadership, or, to suggest a tag, virtual leadership. But don't dismiss it as just another touchy-feely flavor of the month. It's real, it's radical, and it's challenging the very definition of corporate leadership for the 21st century. . . .

As the power of position continues to erode, corporate leaders are going to resemble not so much captains of ships as candidates running for office. They will face two fundamental tasks: first, to develop and articulate exactly what the company is trying to accomplish, and second, to create an environment in which employees can figure out what needs to be done and then do it well. . . .

Post-heroic leaders don't expect to solve all the problems themselves. They realize no one can deal with the emerging and colliding tyrannies of speed, quality, customer satisfaction, innovation, diversity, and technology. Virtual leaders just say no to their egos. They are confident enough in their vision to delegate true responsibility, both for the tedium of process and for the sweep of strategic planning. And they are careful to "model," or live by, the values they espouse. In a distinction that has been around for a while but is now taking on new meaning, they are leaders, not managers.

'Visioning' Missions Becomes Its Own Mission

Every Marriott hotel boasts a different one, signed by the bellhops, clerks and maids. Avis Inc. has 150, all hanging on a wall at corporate headquarters. Hundreds of workers at a Houston metalworking company carry credit-card sized versions in their shirtpockets and wallets.

They're "mission" statements, and they're fast becoming the latest management mania. . . . The result: a proliferation of "missions," "visions," "values" and the like, emblazoned on annual reports, factory walls and–companies hope–the psyches of their workers. It's the new groupthink: If we state our goals, we're more likely to meet them.

tremely urgent, it may be most functional to talk through decisions thoroughly when they are most pressing and important; it requires great skill to prevent premature closure of discussion when the wolf, real or imagined, is at the door.

Subordinate readiness is also a crucial issue, only briefly mentioned earlier. Sometimes a subordinate is not as yet competent to handle certain matters. A leader who fails to consider the "state of readiness" of employees with respect to sharing leadership responsibilities can easily create more problems by pushing this approach than by exercising more unilateral control. Under conditions where employees prefer to

MANAGERIAL BULLETIN

Leaders Acknowledge Vision's Importance, but Who's Buying?

Nevertheless, we have come to praise vision, not to bury it. As much as it is scorned, it is critical to success today. ["Developing Global Ability."] A recent worldwide survey of 2,664 upper-level line managers [by Douglas Ready, International Consortium for Executive Development Research, 1997] indicated that they ranked "actualizing a tangible vision" as their highest need for effective leadership." They also reported that they were not very skilled at doing it, which may account for some of the skepticism.

SOURCE: David Bradford and Allan Cohen, *Power Up*, John Wiley & Sons, 1998.

have the legitimate leader give the orders and feel the need for close supervision, participative leadership is likely to be highly dysfunctional.

Thus, When decisions are routine, actions are being taken under severe time pressure, information is standardized, and subordinates are dependent, more controlling forms of leadership are appropriate.[22] But to complicate the matter further, within any one organization the conditions surrounding each decision may vary. For example, subordinates may accept being controlled on some issues but not on others; some issues need immediate decisions, while others can be discussed at great length, and so forth. Effective leadership fits not only the general situation but also the particular circumstances of each decision. That requires great flexibility and responsiveness, as well as a genuinely exploratory attitude on the part of the manager who is trying to decide how much participation by subordinates is appropriate and when.

It may not always be possible, however, to adjust your behavior to the demands of the situation. As yet there are no agreed-upon limits to human flexibility. Individuals vary in their ability to change behavior; it may well be that when you face a situation demanding a style that is not natural to your personality, the best option is to find another person to do it, change jobs, or work at restructuring the situation to fit your strengths. Your own capacity to learn new behavior is thus an additional factor to consider when choosing a leadership style.

Similarly, the same factors that determine leadership *style* also can affect which managerial functions should be emphasized. When the environment demands rapid responses and considerable attention, the manager is likely to spend more time on external functions, such as spokesperson and negotiator, and less on the internal ones, such as supervisor. Conversely, when the manager's subordinates have less expertise than is needed to perform their tasks and only the manager can supply what is missing, greater emphasis may be placed internally on coaching and training. Again, however, individual capacity for flexibility serves to limit how easily a manager can *choose* what to do.

Leadership and Values

Unfortunately, leadership is not just a matter of deciding what will work and whether you can do it. The fundamental question has to do with how you personally feel about the exercise of power. Many people, including students who want to become managers, try to gain power through leadership roles at every opportunity and look down on anyone who is not interested in constantly enhancing power. For such power seekers, it would be worthwhile to spend some time thinking about their

MANAGERIAL BULLETIN

Never Too Late to Learn

Some human resource directors have come to think that all executives should be assigned [external] coaches when they are promoted to new levels of responsibility, whether they clearly need it or not . . . As companies shrink, they demand more effort, inspiration, and versatility from everyone who remains, down to the novices and apprentices. An executive who obstructs that creativity, innocently or not, ought to get coached—or get out.

SOURCE: Lee Smith, "The Executive's New Coach," *Fortune*, December 27, 1993.

motives in wanting power and the uses to which they intend to put it when a fair measure has been acquired.

On the other hand, many others, including even a few management students, fear leadership and its burdens and consequently refrain from exercising more than passive influence. Although some influence is inescapable, because even silence has consequences on other system members, such "power avoiders" either define themselves as helpless and powerless or backpedal when responsibility hovers near. "It's good to have a leader because then I'll have someone to blame when things go wrong" is the widely held counterfoil to the belief that "no game is worth playing if I'm not the captain" (or at least struggling to become the captain's replacement). Those who shy away from leadership might profitably contemplate the costs of anyone holding back his or her full strength and what the world would be like if everyone played it so safe.

The values question arises in another way. Even if a controlling, task-centered, "authoritarian" leadership style works best in some situations with some people, do you want to: (1) put yourself in such situations; (2) accept the conditions as fixed, rather than trying to change them, so that other styles become more appropriate; (3) focus on short-term results rather than long-term development of subordinates; or (4) live with the consequences of a society in which people who may currently work best under an authoritarian style are kept dependent, passive, and submissive? Are you willing to do what is necessary to maximize productivity regardless of the human costs?

Conversely, if a more influence-sharing, person-centered developer style is appropriate to get the work out, would you be willing to give up some control to get the best results? Could you respond to those you work with in a genuinely warm and supportive way, even when you would prefer that they do what you want without questioning everything? Could you risk your own job by allowing others the optimal amount of influence?

Trying to follow a contingency model as a manager does not automatically make that leadership role easier; even when you figure out *what* to do and whether you can do it, you still have to decide whether you *want* to do it. The garden of roses we never promised you is unfortunately strewn with thorns, and there is no simple way through it. There are hard choices at every turn.

Implications for Choosing Jobs and Career Planning–Personal Values and Ethics

As diagrammed in Figure 12–7, we believe that people are both malleable and limited in how much they can modify their competencies and values. This has implications for choosing a career, a particular organization, and a job. A professor has a great deal of autonomy and control over his or her activities and work schedule, needs to be constantly engaged in exploring new ideas and challenging old ones, and must be able to deal in abstract conceptualizations and communicate ideas effectively. Someone heading for an academic career needs to be comfortable in a system that places high value on ideas for their own sake and not just on immediate practicality. That individual also needs to be reasonably competent and interested in conducting research, teaching, and engaging in theoretical discourse. Given training, could your interests and values allow you to adapt to this role successfully and happily?

Similarly, many salespeople must interact with a wide range of customers, some politically liberal and some very conservative. This may mean that the salesperson must set aside, even deny, personal beliefs in the interest of maintaining a good relationship with the customer. Can you keep your mouth shut, or are you a person who must speak your mind on such value-laden topics as religion, politics, abortion, communism, and the like? The head of an advertising agency once said, "If you take a job with us, you must *believe* that the aspirin we advertise is the best, even though they are all made of essentially the same ingredients." Would such an organizational demand be one you could accept comfortably?

Sometimes, organizations get into trouble financially and operationally, and only drastic and unilateral action can save the day. Decisions must be made quickly, often on less than complete data. People may have their job assignments changed or even be fired. The decision maker in such a situation must live with being the one who "hurts" people, albeit to save the organization and other people, and the one who is often chastised, vilified, or hated. Not everyone can handle this role.

Earlier we talked about some of the ethical burdens of being a leader. If part of your ethical beliefs is the notion that it is wrong to hurt people, yet you have to take actions on behalf of the many that may hurt the few, you may find that you either have to live with that tension or get out of the role altogether. Have you ever heard the expression, "That person needs firing"? This is a handy way to avoid the responsibility for the act by translating it into a need of the employee. However, such a "need" (i.e., to be fired) doesn't appear in anyone's theory of motivation. In fact, there is no way to avoid your personal values when you exercise leadership.

As you consider your career and look for a job, consider the roles that you will find energizing because they challenge you yet do not exceed your range of adaptability in terms of competency and personal values.

Furthermore, when it finally comes down to it, leadership is more than a set of tools and choices; *who you are* is the most important consideration as to whether anyone will want to follow you. Are you trustworthy, dedicated, caring? Do you exercise good judgment? Are you out for only yourself or committed to the organization and its goals? Your *character* matters, not just your techniques. Set your learning agenda accordingly!

KEY CONCEPTS FROM CHAPTER 12

1. Manager's interpersonal functions create access to information, which leads to informational functions, allowing for decision-making functions.
2. Preferred leadership style should be tempered by what is appropriate to the situation.
3. Dimensions of leadership style; degree of:
   a. Control retained.
   b. Task concern.
   c. Person concern.
   d. Explicitness of expectations.
   e. Caution.
4. Appropriate leadership style determined by:
   a. Nature of the task situation.
      (1) If routine, needs control, explicitness, and standardization.

(2) Stressful tasks need high person concern.

b. Expertise of the leader.
   (1) The greater the expertise, the greater the appropriateness of control.

c. Attitudes and needs of subordinates.
   (1) The greater the subordinate need for independence and ability, the less appropriate is tight control.
   (2) If subordinates' survival is not threatened and work is not unusually challenging, high task and people concern appropriate.

d. Leader's upward influence.
   (1) The greater the leader's upward influence, the less the need to share control.

e. Leader's power with subordinates.
   (1) Person concern best with moderate power and relationships.
   (2) Task concern best with high or low power and relationships.

f. Organization's culture.

g. Need for subordinate commitment.
   (1) The greater the need, the more control should be shared.

h. Time pressure.
   (1) The greater the time pressure, the less appropriate is shared control.

i. Importance of subordinate development.
   (1) The greater the importance of subordinate development, the more control should be shared.

j. Managerial functions needed.

k. Leader's personal values and adaptability.

5. Participative leadership methods most appropriate when:
   a. Decisions nonroutine.
   b. Information nonstandardized.
   c. Low time pressure.
   d. Subordinates independent, intrinsically motivated, see participation as legitimate, are competent, will consider organizational goals, can affect the implementation.

6. General models of leadership:
   a. Heroic:
      (1) Manager-as-technician.
      (2) Manager-as conductor.
   b. Manager-as-developer/shared responsibility leadership.

7. Implications for own choice of job and career; no escape from values.

PERSONAL APPLICATION EXERCISE

Assess Leadership Style of Professors

Instructors are classroom managers. Like any leaders, they need to generate high performance from their "direct reports." As such, they have to be *technical experts* in the sense that they possess knowledge and information to be passed on to students; they have to be *conductors* in the sense that they plan, schedule, and conduct classes within specific time boundaries to achieve specific goals; and they have to be *developers* in the sense that they promote a learning environment that stimulates student learning and growth. Most professors pay a lot of attention to the first two (i.e., they focus heavily on making sure they provide students with all the information related to their subject matter that they can possibly cover within a given semester). The focus is on content. Some also pay equal attention to such matters as classroom atmosphere, responsiveness to students' needs, helping students see connections to their future career goals, encouraging students to take initiative and responsibility for their own learning, and so on.

Below you will find an instrument that describes a "developmental instructor." Fill it out on a favorite professor. You can obtain a single score, up to 100, of the extent to which a given instructor fits the developmental role. Note items that are most important to you. Also, consider the *context.* Some kinds of courses require more or less of a given role (expert, conductor, or developer) depending on the subject matter, class size, level of the course, and so on. Finally, identify your most and least favorite instructors and see how *your needs* as a student fit *their styles* as classroom managers. This analysis might give you some insight into your potential preferences for how you want to be "managed" on a job, as well as the style of management you yourself are likely to adopt.

Instructor as Developer Instrument

Evaluate the extent to which your instructor does the following:

CIRCLE YOUR ANSWER

	Very Little				Great Extent
1. Helps students think about or plan career choices.	1	2	3	4	5
2. Gives students freedom to determine the details of how they do an assignment.	1	2	3	4	5
3. Encourages feedback from students about his or her own performance as an instructor.	1	2	3	4	5
4. Gives challenging assignments.	1	2	3	4	5
5. Shows concern for students' well-being.	1	2	3	4	5
6. Allows students to influence activities in the classroom.	1	2	3	4	5
7. Encourages students to help each other.	1	2	3	4	5
8. Insists on high standards for performance.	1	2	3	4	5
9. Gives students timely and honest feedback on their performance.	1	2	3	4	5
10. Gives students latitude to make and learn from mistakes.	1	2	3	4	5
11. Tries to see the merits of a student's ideas when they differ from his or her own.	1	2	3	4	5
12. Inspires students to give their best efforts.	1	2	3	4	5
13. Coaches students in ways that help them to perform better.	1	2	3	4	5
14. Genuinely *listens* to students and their ideas.	1	2	3	4	5
15. Explains how assignments are exciting or challenging.	1	2	3	4	5
16. Encourages students to develop *new* skills and abilities.	1	2	3	4	5
17. Allows students to take initiative on tasks without having to check with him or her (the instructor).	1	2	3	4	5
18. Helps students to constructively confront differences of opinion among themselves.	1	2	3	4	5
19. In discussions, encourages students to express honestly how they *feel* about issues.	1	2	3	4	5
20. Speaks enthusiastically about career goals.	1	2	3	4	5

Total points (add the numbers circled) _____

SUGGESTED READINGS

Bass, B. M. *Leadership & Performance Beyond Expectations.* New York: Free Press, 1985.

Bass, Bernard M. "From Transactional to Transformational Leadership: Learning to Share the Vision." *Organizational Dynamics,* Winter 1990, pp. 19–31.

Behling, O., and C. F. Rauch, Jr. "A Functional Perspective on Improving Leadership Effectiveness." *Organizational Dynamics,* Spring 1985, pp. 51–61.

Bennis, W. G., and B. Nanus. *Leaders.* New York: Harper & Row, 1985.

Blake, R. R. and A. Adams McCanse. *Leadership Dilemmas–Grid Solutions.* Houston: Gulf Publishing, 1991.

Block, P. *The Empowered Manager.* San Francisco: Jossey-Bass Publishers, 1987.

Bradford, D. L., and A. R. Cohen, *Power Up: Transforming Organizations Through Shared Leadership.* New York: John Wiley & Sons, 1998.

Cotton, J. L. et al. "Employee Participation: Diverse Forms and Different Outcomes." *Academy of Management Review* 13, no. I (1988), pp. 8–22.

Dienesch, R. M., and R. C. Liden. "Leader-Member Exchange Model of Leadership: A Critique and Further Development." *Academy of Management Review,* July 1986, pp. 618–34.

Donovan, Hedley. "Managing Your Intellectuals." *Fortune,* October 23, 1989.

Driscoll, J. W. "Trust and Participation in Organizational Decision Making as Predictors of Satisfaction." *Advanced Management Journal,* March 1978, pp. 44–56.

Farnham, Alan, "Mary Kay's Lesson in Leadership." *Fortune,* September 20, 1993.

Fiedler, F. "The Trouble with Leadership Training Is That It Doesn't Train Leaders." *Psychology Today* 6 (1973), p. 23.

Fiedler, F., and M. Chemers. *Leadership and Effective Management.* Glenview, IL: Scott, Foresman, 1974.

Field, R. H. G. "A Critique of the Vroom-Yetton Contingency Model of Leadership Behavior." *Academy of Management Review,* April 1979, pp. 249–57.

Gardner, J. *On Leadership.* New York: The Free Press, 1990.

Goleman, D. "Leadership That Gets Results," *Harvard Business Review,* March–April (2000), pp. 78–90.

Graeff, C. L. "The Situational Leadership Theory: A Critical View." *Academy of Management Review,* April 1983, pp. 285–91.

Griffin, R. "Task Design Determinants of Effective Leader Behavior." *Academy of Management Review,* April 1979, pp. 215–24.

Helgesen, S. *The Female Advantage.* New York: Doubleday, 1990.

Hinckley, S. R., Jr. "A Closer Look at Participation." *Organizational Dynamics,* Winter 1985, pp. 57–67.

Hofheinz, Paul, "Europe's Tough New Managers." *Fortune,* September 6, 1993.

Hunt, J., and L. Larson. *Contingency Approaches to Leadership.* Carbondale: Southern Illinois University Press, 1974.

Hunt, J. G. *Leadership: A New Synthesis.* Newbury Park, CA: Sage Publications, 1991.

Kanter, R. M. *The Changemasters.* New York: Simon & Schuster, 1983.

Kanter, R. *Men and Women of the Corporation.* New York: Basic Books, 1977.

_____. "Dilemmas of Managing Participation." *Organizational Dynamics,* Summer 1982, pp. 5–27.

Kaplan, R. E. "Trade Routes: The Manager's Network of Relationships." *Organizational Dynamics,* Spring 1984, pp. 37–52.

Kiechel, Walter, III. "A Hard Look at Executive Vision." *Fortune,* October 23, 1989.

Kouzes, J. M., and B. Z. Posner. *Credibility.* San Francisco: Jossey-Bass Publishers, 1993.

_____. *The Leadership Challenge.* San Francisco: Jossey-Bass Publishers, 1987.

Kuhnert, K. W., and P. Lewis. "Transactional and Transformational Leadership: A Constructive/Developmental Analysis." *Academy of Management Review* 12, no. 4 (1987), pp. 648–57.

Levin, I. M. "Vision Revisited." *Journal of Applied Behavioral Science* 36, no. 1 (March 2000), pp. 91–107.

Locke, E. A.; D. M. Schweiger; and G. P. Latham. "Participation in Decision Making: When Should It Be Used?" *Organizational Dynamics,* Winter 1986, pp. 65–79.

Luthans, F.; S. A. Rosenkrantz; and H. W. Hennessey. "What Do Successful Managers Really Do? An Observation Study of Managerial Activities." *Journal of Applied Behavioral Science* 21, no. 3 (1985), pp. 255–70.

"Management Focus: Take Me to Your Leader." *Economist,* June 2, 1990.

McGill, Michael E., and John W. Slocum, Jr. "A Little Leadership, Please?" *Organizational Dynamics,* Winter 1998, pp. 39–49.

McGregor, D. *The Human Side of Enterprise.* New York: McGraw-Hill, 1960.

_____. *Leadership and Motivation.* Cambridge, MA: MIT Press, 1966.

_____. *The Professional Manager.* New York: McGraw-Hill, 1967.

Milgrim, S. "Behavioral Study of Obedience." *Journal of Abnormal and Social Psychology* 67 (1963), pp. 371–78.

Mintzberg, H. *The Nature of Managerial Work.* New York: Harper & Row, 1973.

Mockler, R. J. "Situational Theory of Management." *Harvard Business Review,* May–June 1971, pp. 146–55.

Morgan, G. *Images of Organization.* Newbury Park, CA: Sage, 1986.

_____. *Riding the Waves of Change.* San Francisco: Jossey-Bass Publishers, 1988.

Peters, T. *Thriving on Chaos.* New York: Alfred A. Knopf, 1988.

Powell, Gary N. "One More Time: Do Female and Male Managers Differ?" *Academy of Management Executive* 4, no. 3 (1990), p. 74.

Ragins, Belle Rose. "Diversified Mentoring Relationships in Organizations: A Power Perspective." *Academy of Management Review* 22 (1997), pp. 482–521.

Sargent, A. *The Androgynous Manager.* New York: AMACOM, 1981.

Sashkin, M. "Participative Management Is an Ethical Imperative." *Organizational Dynamics,* Spring 1984, pp. 4–22.

Sayles, L. R. *Managerial Behavior.* New York: McGraw-Hill, 1964.

Sember, Ricardo. "Managing without Managers." In Peter J. Frost, Vance F. Mitchell, and Walter R. Nord, *Organizational Reality.* 4th ed. New York: HarperCollins, 1992, pp. 104–12.

Shamir, Boas; Eliav Zakay; Esther Breinin; and Micha Popper. "Correlates of Charismatic Leader Behavior in Military Units: Subordinates' Attitudes, Unit Characteristics, and Superiors' Appraisals of Leader Performance." *Academy of Management Journal* 41 (1998), pp. 387–409.

Shankar Pawar, Badrinarayan, and Kenneth K. Eastman. "The Nature and Implications of Contextual Influences on Transformational Leadership: A Conceptual Examination." *Academy of Management Review* 22 (1997), pp. 80–109.

Tannenbaum, R., and W. Schmidt. "How to Choose a Leadership Pattern." *Harvard Business Review* 51, no. 3 (1973), pp. 1–10.

Tichy, N. M., and E. Cohen. *The Leadership Engine.* New York: Harper Business, 1997.

Tichy, N., and S. Sherman, *Control Your Destiny or Someone Else Will.* New York: Doubleday, 1993.

Vaill, P. *Managing as a Performing Art.* San Francisco: Jossey-Bass Publishers, 1989.

Vroom, V. "Can Leaders Learn to Lead?" *Organizational Dynamics,* Winter 1976, pp. 17–28.

Yammarino, Francis J.; Alan J. Dubinsky; Lucette B. Comer; and Marvin A. Jolson. "Women and Transformational Contingent Reward Leadership: A Multiple-Levels-of-Analysis Perspective." *Academy of Management Journal,* February 1997, pp. 205–22.

Yukl, G. A. *Leadership in Organizations.* 3rd ed. Englewood Cliffs, NJ: Prentice-Hall, 1994.

Intergroup, Interorganizational, and Intercultural Relations

Chapter

13

Cyberspace Inc.: More Companies Cut Risk by Collaborating with Their "Enemies"

Many Internet Operations Co-Invest in Bid to Ensure at Least a Slice of Success; The Real Giants Just Devour

If the 1980s brought a slew of joint ventures, and the 1990s ushered in loads of cross-border alliances, the digital revolution is taking business relationships to a new plane, blurring corporate identity even further. Some of the leading technology and Internet firms are creating Internet "ecosystems." . . . They evolve together, sometimes linked by cross-holdings, and continually pull more companies into their orbits. . . .

[T]he phenomenon seems to be spreading.

Why? One theory is that you cooperate to expand the market, then you can compete to divide it. "We're at a stage where there's a transformation of the economic infrastructure. It's too big a problem for any one company to solve. So you cooperate to create value." . . .

However, most companies are struggling to figure out just how to "divide" the pie. In one breath, Internet strategists make nice about co-evolution. In the next, they declare that the Internet is a land grab, and it is winner take all. It is all of the above, really, as companies spread their bets in a world where technology is changing rapidly and business models are often untested.

"My view is, you don't try to be too smart. If you own a piece of all the players, then if the pie grows, no matter who succeeds you succeed."

More than anything, what may motivate the blend of competition and collaboration is a strong sense that it is still very early in the game.

SOURCE: Bernard Wysocki, Jr., "Cyberspace Inc.: More Companies Cut Risk by Collaborating with Their 'Enemies,'" *The Wall Street Journal,* January 31, 2000, p. A1. (Copyright © 2000, Dow Jones & Company, Inc.)

> "While conflict can be costly . . . in some cases it is a necessary part of achieving full consideration of legitimately differing viewpoints."

The Basis of Inherent Conflicts

Because virtually every large organization requires some division of labor, it is usually necessary to have departments, branches, divisions, units, teams, and so forth to accomplish the various tasks. Helping the individual subsystems do their parts and ensuring that their work is integrated toward the goals of the organization as a whole is a key way in which a manager determines the system's overall effectiveness. When the organization has groups doing tasks that differ in terms of complexity, rate of change of the technology used, skills needed, length of time it takes to complete the task, and so forth, then the job of coordinating the subunits becomes a major managerial undertaking.

The kinds of differences that often lead to conflicts among groups are often just a reflection of how the organization conducts its business. These are *inherent conflicts*, ones that are just there. This chapter is about how to understand and manage these natural differences in ways that are constructive, healthy, and in the best interests of the organization as a whole.

In general, The more differentiated the tasks necessary to accomplish the organization's work, the more appropriate it is to create separate subsystems for doing each task. And as you might expect, Each subunit works best when organized in a way that fits the demands of its task.[1] The subunit's structure, personnel, operating style, reward system, and leadership should be matched to its particular tasks. In other words, When the background factors and required system "fit" the unit's goals, it is most likely to be effective; when the emergent system also fits, it is even more likely to be effective. Even when subunit organization is not perfectly matched to task, there is a tendency for the group to acquire an identity that is at least partly reflective of the type of work it does, the skills needed to do it, who the members are, the technology involved, the rate of change in the group's environment, and what behavior the organization rewards.

An increasing number of manufacturing companies are using teams on the shop floor to solve problems and maintain quality standards, even to act like minibusinesses. These teams have been known to develop their own distinctive ways of working, reflecting the particular combination of people, tasks, and interaction patterns that occur. In some cases, they have even given themselves names, created group T-shirts, and generally made it known to other teams that they see themselves as different and special. This is not really surprising. Work groups tend to develop a group concept, which they strive to maintain and enhance.[2]

People naturally gravitate into groups that reinforce their values. Most voluntary groups form on that basis, and their cohesiveness can be directly attributed to the fact that membership serves to reinforce basic personal values. While work groups in most organizations do not form on a voluntary basis, it is safe to say that, The more differentiated a work group's task, the more likely will members be recruited who share *common background factors*. These may include education, professional identity, ethnic grouping, race, religion, common interests, and so forth. The more similar are members' background factors, the clearer the group's emergent identity will tend to be. Because the division of labor is based on specialized task and skill areas in most organizations, work groups at all levels of the system tend to be composed of people with similar backgrounds, at least in regard to a given skill area.

Rewards can have an especially potent effect on group identity. Different units responsible for different tasks are often rewarded for different behavior. For example, employees responsible for production processes are rewarded for making sure that products *do not deviate* from prescribed standards, whereas those in a research and development function are often rewarded for *experimenting* with *deviations* from previously established standards. Rewards that differentially reinforce behavior serve also to reinforce distinct group identities. Consequently, without strong organizational rewards for cooperation among such differentiated groups, it becomes difficult to achieve satisfactory integration of functions where needed.

Interviewer: Did you have national anthems?

2,000-Year-Old Man: It was very fragmented. It wasn't nations; it was caves. Each cave had a national anthem.

Interviewer: Do you remember the national anthem of your cave?

2,000-Year-Old Man: I certainly do; I'll never forget it. You don't forget a national anthem in a minute.

Interviewer: Let me hear it, sir.

2,000-Year-Old Man: [Singing]: Let them all go to hell except cave 76.

The 2,000-Year-Old Man
Album by Carl Reiner & Mel Brooks

Furthermore, The more cohesive the group, the clearer and more strongly felt the identity is likely to be to group members.[3] As you may recall, in Chapter 4 we offered a number of propositions on the factors that increase a group's cohesiveness, including common values and goals, a common enemy, high required interactions, and low interactions required outside the group.

We suggested that the more cohesive the group, the more closely members would conform to the group's norms. Thus, when a group emergent system that is attractive to members develops out of what is required to get the work done, the group's way of doing things is likely to be seen by members not only as appropriate but also as extremely desirable and valuable. The *group's* "self-concept" becomes worth protecting.

Variations in Group Identity

What are some of the ways in which group identities may differ? How do differing emergent systems compare with one another? You will already have observed many groups in cases, in class, and at work, and have seen that they have different ways of doing things. To examine the reasons groups sometimes have difficulty working together, we need to suggest a few important dimensions on which work groups often differ, to add to those discussed in Chapter 6 on group effectiveness.

Time Horizon

One important way group members in organizations may differ is in their view of time. Certain kinds of tasks tend to call for a relatively short-term time horizon, and others call for a long-term time horizon. These task "demands" transcend the fact that we all have different preferences for work pace. Basic research, for example, is not a process that can easily be hurried along, and it tends to require a rather distant time horizon. Competitive sales, on the other hand, normally calls for rapid decisions and a series of short-term checkpoints on the way to long-range objectives. The time horizon tends to be shortest for those tasks that require immediate feedback and have outcomes that can provide such feedback; the time horizon tends to be longest for those tasks where relevant outcomes and, consequently, sources of feedback are more delayed.[4] You can see how people in a sales division of a company can measure their successes in terms of immediate sales and how inevitable it is that they

Aetna Hopes for Breath of New Life from Acquisition, but Some Fear U.S. Healthcare May Suffocate under Insurer's Staid Culture

"[T]he two companies should emerge stronger, and perhaps far stronger, than each currently is."

Smoothing Over Cultural Differences

Other analysts aren't so sanguine, noting that the merger is hardly an ordinary one. . . . the deal could be doomed by cultural differences. "Aetna is a staid old insurance culture," while U.S. Healthcare is scrappy and aggressive . . . "No doubt about it: There will be more than one meeting in which people from U.S. [Healthcare] will be frustrated with people from Aetna."

Aetna Vice Chairman Richard Huber himself acknowledges the importance of culture issues. "Even for companies with very similar cultures, [combining them] is a challenge." . . . "Most old-line insurers have been seen as sluggish and slow to make decisions. Over the last year or so, we've tried to bring in a greater sense of urgency and we've had some success in trying to teach this elephant to dance."

SOURCE: Ben Winslow; Leslie Schism; and Elyse Tanonye, "Aetna Hopes for Breath of New Life from Acquisitions," *The Wall Street Journal*, April 3, 1996, p. B4.

would operate out of a relatively short time horizon. If, however, such sales commit other divisions of the system to delivery times that are incompatible with their own time horizons, some degree of conflict is bound to ensue. Research and development people, for example, may find such commitments impossible to meet and foreign to their concepts of how their work should be carried out. Each group is likely to deal with time issues in its own way and believe in the "correctness" of its procedures and assumptions. Since time is so much a part of everything in organizational life, it is often taken for granted. Groups with different time horizons frequently have difficulty understanding one another.

Are you a person who gets to meetings on time or even early? Or, perhaps, a person who is habitually late? Groups' and departments' attitudes toward time also differ in this respect, with some likely to start and stop meetings right on time while others are much more casual about how rigidly people are expected to stick to schedules. Because attitudes toward time often take on a connotation of good and bad, such differences can create tension. Imagine five researchers strolling into a meeting at 4, 6, and even 12 minutes after 2 P.M. with production personnel, who all arrived 3 minutes before 2!

Different countries also have differing attitudes toward time, a point we discuss further in the last section of this chapter.

Perspective on the Task

Some units have jobs that keep members narrowly focused on one aspect of the work. An extreme example would be on an assembly line, where the workers tighten bolts on the same parts all day long, never getting to see the end product or even some of the subassemblies. Contrast that task to one like custom carpentry; the perspective of each is very different with respect to the scope of the task.

The broader the perspective on the task, the greater will be member awareness of task group interdependencies and the greater will be concern for the total effort.[5] Normally, the higher a unit is in the hierarchy, the greater the likelihood of members seeing the "big picture"—that is, the overall relation of subunits and their connections to organizational goals. Members of lower-level units often focus only on their particular set of tasks, with less sense of the context in which they are operating. But this difference in perspective is not limited to differences in hierarchical level. It can vary with the unit's required interactions with outside subsystems. The greater the number of interactions required with other subsystems, the broader is a subsystem's task perspective likely to be.[6]

Because breadth of perspective can vary, different units can place different priorities on organizational goals. And subunit goals can seem more important than overall goals to a group with limited perspective. Thus, there can be distinct differences among groups in perspective on tasks.

To broaden employees' perspectives, more and more companies are redesigning tasks in ways that expand worker responsibilities for carrying through several stages of a job. In addition, workers are being given increasing responsibility for managing and coordinating work activities individually and in groups. Many problems associated with a narrow task perspective are solvable through direct modification of the way in which the work is carried out, as discussed further in Chapter 14.

Professional Identity

If you ever get the chance, talk to a design engineer about his or her priorities; do the same with people in sales, financial operations, and human resources. Ask each group about their perceptions of the other groups. What you are likely to discover are some very fundamental differences in how each profession sees itself, its priorities, its importance to the total organization, and the qualities of the other groups. The very nature of the sales activity places a high premium on being able to make commitments to customers that the company can honor. This usually places heavy time pressures on the production end of the process. The very nature of the design function places a high premium on constant refinement, even if it takes more time to get the product finished. When these two sets of priorities collide, we have an *inherent conflict* that is a reflection of the background factors of the parties involved. Ironically, such conflicts are not all that undesirable, because the conflicting views are both usually legitimate. It is a manager's job to balance those views in ways that benefit the total organization and not to allow one side to dominate the other at the expense of the organization. In the example given, it is important to deliver a product with needed features, but also important to do so within a reasonable time. In a healthy organization, these differences are managed and do not become occasions for internally destructive consequences. But they do require attention and some skill on the part of a manager to keep things from deteriorating into win-lose or lose-lose battles. Unfortunately, the history of some interprofessional relations has been less than collaborative, as with some union–management relations.

Attitudes toward Authority and Internal Structure

As you may recall from the chapters on leadership (11 and 12) and group effectiveness (6), the amount of control and participation in a group should be related to the group's needs in accomplishing its tasks. Groups where expertise is widely distributed and needed for the solution of complex, changing problems require a more participative, free-wheeling, noncontrolling style of operation than those where task requirements are clear and expertise strongly differentiated.

Furthermore, over time groups develop quite different notions about the proper style of leadership, the appropriate amount of latitude for individual decision making and involvement, and for allowable amounts of initiative. Can you see how groups that differ along these dimensions might view one another with less than full approval?

In many high-tech companies today, there is a growing problem around the management of computer experts. Similar to research and development people, the computer engineers and scientists get so heavily involved in their work that they ignore the usual organizational rules about specific hours, dress, reporting relationships,

"Soul Wars"
How MCA's Relations with Motown Records Went So Sour So Fast

Cultures Clash and Egos, Too; Even the Great Conciliator Can't Stop a Nasty Blowup

The final blowup happened not at Motown Records' digs at the funky corner of Sunset and Vine, nor in the gleaming tower of MCA Inc.'s corporate headquarters in Universal City. Nor did it occur in the cobbled alley-ways of Boston's financial district, where the investment firm of Boston Ventures keeps its offices.

No, the summit meeting was called, by MCA's legendary chieftain Lew Wasserman, at a neutral site: the hushed, sylvan folds of the Hotel Bel-Air, where swans glide and tasteful elegance prevails.

It was there, late last month, when hopes of a settlement were highest, that things got really ugly.

Lionized for decades as Hollywood's greatest deal-maker, the 78-year-old Mr. Wasserman is a master at building bridges, at seeing the big picture. He can rise above the dust and flailing elbows of petty business disputes to bring people together.

But he couldn't save this meeting. It collapsed in a heap of tempers—including a scene with his own long-time president, Sidney J. Sheinberg, angrily facing off against Motown President Jheryl Busby. By the time Mr. Busby left the meeting, recalls one observer, "he

looked like he'd been shot." MCA's break with the whiteshoe Boston investment firm, with whom it had agreed just three years earlier to acquire and resurrect the famous black record label, seemed final.

Boston Ventures and MCA exchanged proposals and counterproposals—Motown and Boston Ventures wanted to renegotiate the contract, with a shorter term and a lower fee—but negotiations went nowhere. In fact, the partners were speaking different languages. Boston Ventures' style was deliberate and methodical. These former bankers were always coming up with flow charts and statistical analyses. At MCA, on the other hand, "we schmooze," says an MCA official. "We're renegotiating all the time with artists. But Boston Ventures was—well, strange." . . .

MCA may be flexible when it negotiates with actors and singers, but on a corporate level, it's known as the most intractable company in Hollywood. At MCA, a deal's a deal, and it's considered dishonorable to try to wiggle out. The sanctity of contracts is reinforced by the abundance of lawyers at the company. It's a cliché in Hollywood that at MCA, "litigation is a profit center." . . .

In a press release, Motown accused MCA of treating it like a "Third World country," and *Black Radio Exclusive* magazine editorialized that MCA was

Continued

and general work habits. The dilemma for top management is how to allow these employees the freedom and latitude that suits them and fosters their productivity without incurring the resentment of other groups whose work style is more in line with traditional management practices. Is it possible to have two (or even more) different sets of rules for employees in the same organization? Here is where the emergent norms of a subpart of the total organization may be highly functional for that group's work, but be dysfunctional for total system harmony. As you will see a little further on, this problem can proliferate into intergroup stereotyping and rivalries, which are potentially damaging if they are not managed constructively.

Interpersonal Orientation

One further way in which group identities differ is in their orientation to interpersonal relations. Groups vary in terms of whether they value closeness or distance, openness or politeness, seriousness or kidding, and so forth. Members who have arrived at some agreement on how people should relate to one another often think that members of other groups with different orientations are strange or unlikable. Others are "too pushy and effusive" or "too cold," "too blunt" or "too indirect," "too pompous" or "too frivolous," depending on the group to which one belongs.

"tarnishing the image" of an important black symbol. Matters like this were particularly sensitive since Japan's Matsushita Electric Industrial Co. had acquired MCA last January for more than $6 billion. Some national black leaders had attacked the Japanese as racist, and Matsushita didn't want any trouble. Motown hired Washington lobbyists to approach Matsushita directly, infuriating MCA.

Meantime, Mr. Busby, listening to MCA's refrain that this was a matter between MCA and Boston Ventures—that the beef wasn't with Motown—was angry. He felt like an invisible man and sent out a statement saying he felt "disrespected."

Boston Ventures says it often heard MCA executives deny requests by pointing helplessly to "the Tower." Finally, last month, the Tower got involved. Mr. Wasserman wrote a letter to Boston Ventures' Mr. Thompson, saying he wanted to work things out. Mr. Thompson agreed, but cautioned that the final decision rested with Motown. . . .

When Mr. Wasserman stood up, he was statesman-like. He said that even the worst of marriages can be repaired, that everyone had made mistakes—including MCA—and that they were all there to work things out.

Mr. Busby took the floor. A man who doesn't hide his emotions and uses New Age terms like "the next millennium," Mr. Busby talked about his vision for Mo-town and how MCA had let him down. MCA had realized its dream when it had delivered the company to the Japanese for the shareholders—why wouldn't they let him accomplish his? He didn't think the situation was resolvable. The MCA executive thought he was getting long-winded.

Mr. Sheinberg interrupted.

"Okay, you're a dreamer," Mr. Sheinberg told Mr. Busby, according to people who were there. "You're a visionary. But let me give you a dose of reality." Then, according to participants at the meeting, Mr. Sheinberg spoke in cold anger for 10 minutes, saying that MCA had put in more money than Boston Ventures had—deferring payments, transferring the contracts of artists, lending money—so how could he talk about Boston Ventures financing his dream? He said that MCA had released Mr. Busby from his contract to go to Motown in the first place, that if the parties didn't settle now they never would, that they would go to court and fight a long and expensive battle.

Visibly upset, Mr. Busby said he guessed there was nothing to talk about and walked out onto the garden patio. Mr. Wasserman closed the meeting, and everyone filed out in stunned silence.

Whatever the emergent orientation, "the way our group relates to people" comes to be seen as the best or only way for sensible people to deal with one another.

In one company a department made up of highly educated people with similar outside interests tended to socialize a great deal during nonworking hours and were openly friendly even during working hours. Individuals who were not a part of that group developed a very distorted picture of the group, seeing it as a bunch of goof-offs who did not care about their work or the company. The fact that the department was one of the most productive in the company didn't seem to change the perception. Obviously, the perceivers were finding the behavior of this department to be a threat to some aspect of their self-concepts. Furthermore, it reflected a frequently observed tendency for members of one group to interpret the behavior of another group according to their own norms and values, which, unfortunately, leads to further misperceptions.[7]

This matter is even more complicated when there are intercultural differences. Globalization is accompanied by inevitable misunderstandings and misinterpretations stemming from fundamental differences in beliefs, values, ethical considerations, and overall ways of doing business. The negotiation style of a Saudi businessman is governed by different ground rules from that of the typical American business leader. As a result, the American is likely to misjudge and mistrust the Saudi, unless he or she is sensitive to these differences. Doing business in Latin

MANAGERIAL BULLETIN

Imposing a Hierarchy on a Gaggle of Techies

As the No. 2 executive at Sun Microsystems Inc., Carol Bartz brushed aside many tentative offers to run a company, everything from a two-person start-up to a $250 million concern. She liked her job at Sun, and "I lacked that male-dominant gene," she said, "the one that says you have to be CEO, like the one that says you don't ask for directions."

One has to wonder, then, why she said yes when a search committee from Autodesk Inc. came calling. This was, after all, a company known as a theocracy of hackers, where a cabal of counterculture senior programmers took their dogs to work and tried to reach a consensus on strategy through endless memos sent by electronic mail.

But any honeymoon with Autodesk's fractious programmers was bound to be short-lived. Employees accustomed to consensus decision making have chafed at the top-down management Ms. Bartz installed (the company added five vice presidents and other lower executives). Senior programmers promoted to some of those management positions have found themselves uncomfortable playing boss to former peers.

In fact, there seems to be a great deal of confusion in the wake of all the changes. Some people have been told they'll be redeployed but have not been told to whom they'll report. Others who always helped decide what features to include in each new product, resent having management making such decisions.

If the programmers continue to grumble, Ms. Bartz's moves get applause from the sales and marketing side of Autodesk, which has long resented laboring in the shadow of the techies.

"From a sales perspective it's just nice to have a leader, someone to set priorities," said Rex Johnson, manager of major United States accounts. "It's nice to have someone who understands both sides, someone who understands technology but someone who has also talked to customers" . . .

SOURCE: Lawrence M. Fisher, *New York Times,* November 29, 1992. Copyright © 1992 by The New York Times Company. Reprinted by permission.

America has posed many problems for Americans, who typically want to "get down to business," while the Latins prefer to spend some time (often more than the American can tolerate) building a more social relationship (talking about family, personal interests, and so on). These differences can be a source of enrichment to the workplace, but all too often they tend to create barriers to cooperation across organizational boundaries. We explore these issues further in the latter part of this chapter.

The Stranger

The Stranger within my gate,
He may be true or kind,
But he does not talk my talk—
I cannot feel his mind.
I see the face and the eyes and the mouth,
But not the soul behind.

The men of my own stock,
They may do ill or well,
But they tell the lies I am wonted to,
They are used to the lies I tell;
And we do not need interpreters
When we go to buy and sell.

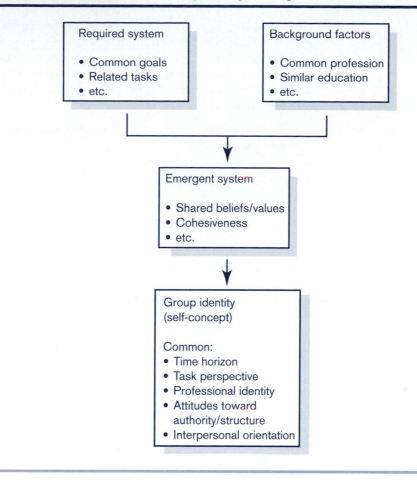

FIGURE 13–1   *How Group Identity Develops*

Required system

- Common goals
- Related tasks
- etc.

Background factors

- Common profession
- Similar education
- etc.

Emergent system

- Shared beliefs/values
- Cohesiveness
- etc.

Group identity
(self-concept)

Common:
- Time horizon
- Task perspective
- Professional identity
- Attitudes toward
  authority/structure
- Interpersonal orientation

> The men of my own stock,
>
> Bitter bad they may be,
>
> But, at least, they hear the things I hear,
>
> And see the things I see;
>
> And whatever I think of them and their likes
>
> They think of the likes of me.
>
> *Rudyard Kipling*

Summary

Thus, in terms of attitudes toward (1) time, (2) authority, and (3) structure, (4) perspective on tasks, and (5) interpersonal orientation, organizational subsystems can and do differ. Each develops its own identify in coping with the tasks assigned to it. That identity is the group equivalent of individual self-concept; the more cohesive the group, the greater the members' commitment is to preserving and enhancing its identity and the more likely members are to see the group's way of doing things as correct, valuable, and superior to other groups' ways. Finally, insofar as group organization should follow from and be appropriate to the group's tasks, The more differentiated a subsystem's tasks, the more effective it will be when its identity (or way of operating) is also differentiated from the identities of other subsystems (see Figure 13–1).

The Price of Appropriate Differentiation: Problems Arising from Strong Group Identity

Unfortunately, however, The clearer and more distinct a subsystem's identity, the greater the difficulty in coordination with other subsystems when their tasks are interdependent.[8] Insofar as differentiated groups carry on interdependent tasks, there is a need for coordination among them. And the greater the degree of interdependence, the more important is the coordination. In order for there to be effective intergroup coordination:

1. Each group must be aware of its own functions in relation to those of other groups.
2. Each group must be willing to maintain communication links with the other groups.
3. Each group must be willing to accept the legitimacy of the needs of the other groups.
4. Each group must be willing to meet its own needs within the framework of the total system.

But a group with a sharply differentiated identity is likely to resist any form of coordination that conflicts with its identity. The extent of a group's resistance to coordination with other groups will be directly related to the degree to which the required interactions conflict with the group's basic norms, ideals, and values.

Just as with individuals and relationships, To the extent that a group perceives a relationship with another group as enhancing its own identity, it will strive to develop and maintain that relationship. To the extent that a group perceives a relationship with another group as in some way threatening its own identity, it will strive to resist or avoid that relationship. In those instances in an organization where the nature of the task *requires* a working relationship between any two groups, these propositions become extremely important. The more an intergroup relationship requires activities and interactions that are compatible with the identities of the groups involved, the more effective will that relationship be; the more it requires activities and interactions that are contradictory to the identities of either or both groups, the more that relationship will be a source of conflict.

Once a group has developed a strong identity, there is a tendency to see any rival (or potential rival) group in predictably distorted ways. Members of a differentiated cohesive group with a strong sense of its own identity will show the following tendencies:[9]

1. Perception of their own group as "better" than the other group.
2. An upgrading of their own ideas and a downgrading of the other group's ideas.
3. An overestimation of their own competence and an underestimation of the competence of the other group.
4. Overvaluation of their own leader(s) and undervaluation of the other group's leader(s).
5. Avoidance or limiting of interactions and communications with the other group.
6. Distortion of information about the other group in ways that cast the other group in an unfavorable light.
7. Mistrust of the members of the other group.

Perhaps you can recognize some or all of these tendencies from your own experience. Intergroup rivalries in school, competing gangs in the neighborhood, and organized team sports are all familiar examples. More troublesome, of course, are situations involving race relations, political and military conflicts, and the like.

Crossing Wires: "Period of Adjustment" Faces AT&T and TCI, 2 Very Different Sorts

Zeglis, Cable Firm's Hindery Embody Sharp Contrasts in Companies' Cultures

[Chairman and Chief Executive Michael] Armstrong, is hoping that new talent and new ways will be good for the century-old telephone giant. "I don't expect conformity," he says. "The meetings . . . are not only low-key 'hail fellow' meetings. Probably half the time, someone is yelling at me. We pound the table. I don't think there has been enough of that in the company."

From the looks of things, more table-pounding could be in store. It won't be easy melding a TCI culture of swagger and hand-shake deals into one of the most by-the-book organizations on the planet. AT&T has established procedures for everything, from cutting deals to buying office supplies. It's a culture that Mr. Armstrong is trying to change. At TCI, independent thinking is encouraged, and executives tend to be far more informal. . . .

Some TCI executives bristle at what they perceive as AT&T's bureaucratic ways and preoccupation with performance data. AT&T insiders make no apologies. "We believe in God, but everybody else brings numbers," says one AT&T veteran.

Mr. Armstong acknowledges the differences. He says it isn't uncommon to call a meeting "and two people will show up from TCI and five times that many people show up from AT&T." He says AT&T could use some TCI influence on brevity, but adds that TCI, in turn, could use some AT&T influence on "conduct and quality." . . .

Mr. Armstrong says the two sides can learn from each other, but each will have to bend. "One of the challenges is to bring these styles together," the CEO says. "Everything is not bad at AT&T. . . . But we have been too slow at this company and we are going faster."

SOURCE: Leslie Cauley and Rebecca Blumenstein, "'Period of Adjustment' Faces AT&T and TCI," *The Wall Street Journal*, February 17, 1999, p. A1.

Prejudice feeds on limited and distorted information, strengthening the intensity with which the prejudiced beliefs are held and making the possibilities of misunderstanding and escalated conflict even greater.

Even when contradictory data are present, people tend to maintain stereotyped perceptions. The individual member of that group who behaves differently from what the stereotype suggests is always the "exception to the rule"; the individual who happens to behave according to the stereotype simply confirms its "validity." In our current era of social change, in which minorities and women are moving into more positions heretofore inaccessible to them, they face this kind of problem. Kanter[10] calls this "double jeopardy" and finds that it places incredible stress on those who experience it. In short, the consequences of intergroup stereotyping include damaging effects on both group relations and individuals in the organization. We comment further on this issue later when we discuss the management of diversity.

Prejudice and war are more dramatic and dangerous manifestations of the tendency to misperceive other groups. But even within formal organizations, these tendencies occur whenever two working units find themselves interdependent and in conflict. The conflict creates uncertainty and anxiety; often rumors develop about what one or another group is doing or plotting, which heightens the antagonism, causes "retaliation" in advance ("preemptive strikes" in military jargon), which in turn further angers the other group and "confirms" their worst suspicions. The more either or both groups see the conflict as a threat to group identity, the more evident these tendencies become and the more difficult it is to achieve resolution.

Group Status

We have been examining the sources of group identity as they follow from task differentiation and showing how the differentiation can lead to difficulties. But another aspect of a group's identity is important for understanding coordination problems.

It is inevitable that in assigning jobs to various subsystems an organization confers differing amounts of legitimate influence to groups. Some subsystems are expected to give orders to and initiate interaction with others; other subsystems are expected to wait for initiatives from subsystems doing different jobs. This allocation of influence is usually based on the flow of work, although it may not have a very explicit rationale. Whatever the reasoning behind the particular way power is allocated, The more *legitimate power* a group has within the system, the more freedom it has to initiate actions and the more that other less powerful groups are dependent upon it to initiate actions.[11] The marketing department in one firm might have the right to decide what products will be tested and sold, while the production department has to go along despite its reservations. In another organization, the financial group might be given the power to exert control over operating departments to ensure adequate returns. But the formal-legitimate power of groups is not the only determinant of influence. The informal social system, as usual, has an important part to play.

Informal Group Status in the System

We pointed out in Chapter 11 that influence in an organization is based on both formal position and informal status, the latter being determined by a variety of factors, including education, social status of a given profession or occupation, special abilities, "whom you know," how important the work is to the over-all organization, and seniority. Just as some individuals in an organization seem to carry more informal influence than they have been formally assigned, because they have been around for a long time or do a very special kind of work, it is not unusual for a particular subsystem to possess informal influence and status that far exceed what is formally designated to it.

A common example of this is the case of technical staff in industry. While they do not normally possess the designated formal authority of line people who are responsible for the operations of the firm, their special expertise and advanced degrees often give them an informal status that carries a great deal of influence with top management. Or, it may lead them to *see* themselves as higher status and therefore as having more influence than they are formally assigned. It becomes an intergroup problem when line people and staff people compete for influence and control because legitimacy is in dispute. Take the case of efficiency experts coming into a department to study its operations and make recommendations for improving that department. It doesn't take much imagination to see how the outside experts can be seen as the "enemy," since they pose the threat of carrying more influence than the organizational chart indicates. Similarly, within a university, power is delegated from the board of trustees to the administration; but informal status is attributed to the faculty, who are seen as the backbone of the educational process. Who carries the most weight and with whom? Struggles around this kind of issue can generate great tension and serious questions about what outcomes are functional for the *total* system as opposed to any one of the competing subsystems.

Groups that possess expertise crucial to the success of an organization often have considerable power attributed to them by other groups whose status in the power hierarchy is lower. Consequently, one of the interesting paradoxes of organizational life is that groups with special power (especially when it is not related to the structural hierarchy) tend to be envied, resented, and yet paid extra deference by other, less powerful groups. It is typical of the tension between "haves" and "have nots."[12]

The more *informal status* a group has within the system, the more freedom it has to initiate actions and the more other lower-status groups are dependent upon it to initiate actions.[13] With the exception of the *source* (formal versus informal) of influence, this proposition is a repeat of the previous one. When a group has both legitimate power and informal status (e.g., a medical staff running a hospital, engineers with advanced degrees managing a manufacturing company), one major source of intergroup conflict is eliminated. But most large organizations tend to promote people on the basis of demonstrated managerial competence, which may or may not have anything to do with technical expertise. High-status *professionals* often tend to view "mere administrators" as having less status and therefore as not legitimately able to control the professionals, even though the organization chart assigns the administrators formal authority.

In short, the existence of the two important sources of influence frequently results in incongruencies in intergroup relations. These incongruencies exist when a group possesses higher legitimate power than other groups but lower informal status, or vice versa. An incongruency between legitimate power and status tends to result in confusion about which group can exercise the greater freedom to take actions that affect the other and which group "has the right" to initiate interactions with the other.[14] Can the university faculty decide to limit class sizes without considering the registration, cost, and facility problems that such an action poses? Can the administration decide to expand the university for financial reasons without obtaining faculty consent? Can the quality control expert stop production over the protests of the production manager? And when serious conflicts occur, how can one group initiate action without in some way affecting the identity of the other group?

Social Diversity and Intergroup Relations

The management of diverse professions and varied educational backgrounds of employees has long been known to practicing managers. Similarly, most managers today are becoming increasingly conscious of the impact of employee social backgrounds on behavior and attitudes in the workplace. Differences in race, sex, age, and ethnicity are now becoming challenges for creative management, management that successfully *integrates* the work activities carried out by employees with such widely diverse backgrounds.

This diversity often gets played out in the relations among groups of employees in the same organization. The attitudes, perceptions, and problems that exist among groups in society are frequently carried into the work setting and create barriers to cooperation among groups that need to work together. Many nurses (mostly women) react to doctors (traditionally men) in part from their perceptions as women reacting to men; young high-tech engineers often discount the opinions of older engineering managers because of the age difference; many white professional managers find it difficult to defer to the opinion of an African-American counterpart even when that person is obviously competent. These are all background attitudes that people bring into their organizations; they add to some of the already present intergroup problems. A competent manager needs to be sensitive to the *sources* of intergroup attitudes, especially when they are totally outside management's sphere of control.

Choosing between Conflict and Cooperation

For the manager, whether or not to attempt to do something about subsystems in conflict depends on an assessment of the functionality of the dispute for the total organization. While conflict can be costly, as in the above example, in some cases it is a necessary part of achieving full consideration of legitimately differing viewpoints. Without conflict among subsystems, the total needs of the organization might be ignored in favor of the highest-status subsystem's needs or be pushed aside by the more

The Angry Voices at Kidder

Kidder . . . has become the target of several sex-, age-, and racial-discrimination charges that could slow its turnaround.

Women . . . complain that Kidder . . . has been an often hostile place to work . . . the executives who ran the division froze them out of top jobs, paid them less than male counterparts, and subjected them to verbal harassment. . . .

Kidder denies that it discriminates against women. . . .

Kidder is far from unique on Wall Street in its alleged insensitivity to certain categories of employees, especially women. The Street has long been a bastion of white males, especially young white males.

SOURCE: Leah Nathans Spiro, *Business Week,* February 1, 1993.

powerful subgroups. Allowing or even encouraging conflict by greater differentiation of group ways of working may be the only way to achieve some balance among subsystems, each of which would like to maximize its own effectiveness, regardless of the consequences for the whole organization. Remember the rationale for the matrix organization in Chapter 2? Balanced decisions often require conflicts over issues.

For example, while the survival of a company might depend on rapid sales pricing decisions, it may also be crucial for the company to maintain a reputation for quality products and service. If the quality control, engineering, and service departments all took the same short-term view as the sales department and exercised very little control over their individual employees in order to speed up decisions, they might get along better with sales but shortchange long-term quality. Only if the respective subgroups are properly differentiated, encouraged to fully express their respective points of view, and allowed to struggle with the trade-offs between keeping prices down and quality up will a proper balance be achieved.

Where intergroup problems surface as wasteful conflict, they need to be approached in terms of reducing conflict and building cooperation; where problems are created by disproportionate dominance of one subsystem, they need to be treated with measures to further differentiate subgroups and/or increase open conflict among the groups.[15] In short, conflict can be a result of genuine differences in group values, reflected in disputes about desired system goals, in which case they may be functional and necessary for the total system. Without thorough discussion, the total system may be harmed. On the other hand, when conflict is a result of the group identification that often occurs with differentiated groups and goes beyond legitimate disagreements into stereotyping, sniping, and sabotaging, it can be very dysfunctional for the total system. Energy is used that could be better focused on the actual tasks.

Similarly, cooperation can be functional or dysfunctional for the total system, depending on whether it reflects genuine integration of efforts or covering up of disagreements that need to be aired to arrive at balanced decisions. And as noted in Chapter 2, there are times when it is not possible to produce functional consequences for all subsystems as well as for the total system. Imperfection is a price that must often be lived with in a complex organization.

Types of Interdependence

The importance of intergroup cooperation versus conflict depends on the degree and kind of interdependence of the work groups involved.[16] If, for example, the work of each subsystem contributes to the productivity or welfare of the total

MANAGERIAL TOOLS

Sports Illustrations of Group Interdependencies

Pooled

Baseball companies . . . loosely coupled . . . include the classic sales organization, made up of high-performing soloists. Also . . . aggregations of basic researchers, in which each individual independently pursues his or her own line of inquiry—as happens with university professors.

Serial

Football companies . . . "long-linked" technologies; . . . production processes involve a complex of discrete steps, tightly coupled in serial (and sometimes parallel) order . . . example is . . . mass assembly line.

Reciprocal

Basketball companies . . . tightly coupled but less than tightly hierarchical . . . depend more on member interaction than on managerial direction. Examples . . . [are] think-tank consulting firms . . . creative advertising agencies, . . . state-of-the-art computer manufacturers. . . . [They] resemble (sets of) autonomous work teams: . . . self-organizing and highly flexible.

SOURCE: From Robert Keidel, "Baseball, Football, and Basketball: Models for Business," *Organizational Dynamics,* Winter 1984, pp. 15–18.

system, but is not directly related to that of the other, there are very few, if any, coordination issues. This is called *pooled interdependence.* The various subdivisions of a large department store (housewares, sporting goods, clothing, and so forth) might be a familiar example of pooled interdependence. Each can try to maximize its own sales effectiveness without hurting other units.

However, if the work is carried out in such a way that one group cannot begin its task until another has completed its work, then you can see the critical nature of interdependence. This type is called *serial interdependence;* it is typical of assembly line operations, construction companies, printing firms, and even health services where treatment at one point in the system depends on diagnostic tests at an earlier point in the system.

The most complex kind of interdependence occurs when work groups need to exchange information on a continuing basis. This is called *reciprocal interdependence.* In the development of plans for a new car model, for example, it is necessary for designers, engineers, market researchers, and production experts to exchange information and ideas over and over so the final product is both innovative and sound.

You can probably see for yourself how the manager's job will vary with each of the three kinds of situations described. In the case of pooled interdependence, a manager needs to make sure that each of the various groups maintains a satisfactory level of output but need not worry that one group is holding up the work of any other. With serial interdependence and reciprocal interdependence, the task is more complex and difficult. In fact, very few modern-day work patterns have the simplicity of pooled interdependence alone; a great many have elements of all three types.

You can appreciate by now just how important it is for a manager to understand and develop competence in dealing with intergroup relations. Whether the fostering of the conflict or cooperation is called for, it is important that the manager understand the need for differentiated subsystems, the likelihood of their developing diverse identities or cultures, and the need for methods to resolve wasteful conflict when greater coordination is needed to achieve serial or reciprocal interdependence. Similarly, managers should know some methods to achieve greater differentiation when too much harmony is creating imbalances.

For example, one of the major international oil companies established foreign regional divisions, each of which was to attempt capture of a significant portion of a regional market. At the same time, the company headquarters insisted upon having final say on prices of products to new customers. Problems occurred when regional salespeople needed rapid decisions in order to make a sale and were delayed by the policy of checking back with headquarters. The regional people felt that they were in the best position to know the local scene and ought to be able to take action as that scene demanded; the headquarters people insisted that their perspective was more worldwide and that they were in a better position to evaluate the going price on the world market. Both groups were right, but neither could acknowledge the legitimacy of the other's viewpoint. The longer the conflict went on, the more it got complicated with stereotypes, sabotage, miscommunications, and the like.

We describe how the issue was resolved later in this chapter when we discuss approaches to intergroup problems. Do you think you could come up with some approaches of your own? It could be useful then to try to compare your approach with the one used in the actual situation.

Foundations of Intergroup Cooperation

How, then, can cooperation be built when it is necessary? As you study the following proposition on the foundation of intergroup cooperation, see if you can recognize their parallel from the chapters on group behavior. In fact, the fundamental proposition is almost identical in both cases.

The more frequent the interaction between any two groups, the greater the tendency to cooperate with each other. However, as in the case of interactions among members of a group, it is important to qualify the above proposition. To the extent that there is frequent and open information flow among groups in a system, common goals are more likely to develop.[17] And add to this proposition the following one: The more that groups recognize and accept common goals, the more likely they are to cooperate.[18]

These propositions are basic to the effective management of all intergroup relations in an organization. To the extent that managers use a "divide and rule" approach by preventing open exchanges of information among working units, they risk intergroup competition and conflict, possibly to the serious detriment of the total system. Where task interdependence necessitates cooperation, bringing key managers together frequently and encouraging constant flow of communications among various interdependent work units increase the likelihood of ongoing cooperation and goal achievement.

Since we also know that The more groups share a common source of threat, the more likely they are to cooperate, it becomes crucial for a manager to avoid becoming that "common source of threat." The common source of threat obviously must be the *outside* competition. Here is where an effective manager can mobilize cooperative effort by making certain that any source of threat serving to bind groups together lies *outside* the system and does not have divisive effects inside the system.

There are three additional propositions that help to complete the foundation for intergroup cooperation:

1. The more groups share common responsibility for problem solving and for decision making, the more likely they are to cooperate.
2. The more groups are able to establish joint memberships, the more likely they are to cooperate.
3. The more groups are willing to share and discuss their perceptions of each other, the more likely they are to cooperate.[19]

The Norm of Reciprocity

For the propositions just stated to be translated into effective strategies for managing intergroup operations, the various groups involved need to recognize the significance of their interrelationships. Each needs to recognize that its own identity can be enhanced by its contribution to another group, and each needs to recognize the obligations for a return contribution. This kind of "fair exchange" principle increases *mutual* functionality and also is functional to the system. This is part of the "norm of reciprocity" discussed in Chapter 10, and it is often considered to be a critical factor in maximizing interdependence.[20]

An example of this norm in operation occurs in many business schools where several groupings of faculty, each from a different discipline, make decisions on curriculum content. With respect to each group's sense of its own importance, it might be functional for it to dominate the decisions, but that would lead to an imbalanced program. The finance people would push for more finance courses, the marketing people for more marketing courses, the behavioral scientists for more organizational behavior courses, and so forth. If the faculty can establish a norm of reciprocity, then it is possible for each group to enhance the other, with the net result being a broad and balanced set of courses and a program that is functional for the school and the students.

On the other hand, if the groups are too understanding of the others they may not demand the proper time for their own subject! Reciprocity can also become a form of "you scratch my back and I'll scratch yours," or "live and let live," which avoids tough priority decisions by giving everyone a bit of the goodies, deserved or not. It can be as dysfunctional to a total system to secure false peace as to fight endless battles.

Methods for Maximizing Intergroup Cooperation

When greater cooperation is called for, several techniques can help foster it. Listed next are six basic strategies for maximizing intergroup cooperation. These approaches are both preventive and curative—that is, each may serve as a means of establishing intergroup cooperation from the start or as a means of resolving intergroup problems or conflicts that have already developed. Obviously, the more these strategies are in operation, the fewer problems are likely to develop; but few, if any, organizations are free from intergroup problems no matter how well they implement these approaches.

The six strategies are as follows:

1. Overlapping or multiple group membership.
2. Liaison or linkage people.
3. Joint task forces.
4. Joint group meetings.
5. Job exchanges across groups.
6. Physical proximity.

Let's examine each of these approaches and see the advantages and disadvantages of each. Keep in mind that different situations call for different strategies and also that combinations of two or more of the approaches are often appropriate. Each of the six strategies is directly or indirectly derivable from the propositions stated in the previous section.

Overlapping or Multiple Group Memberships

In most organizations, it is not unusual to be a member of more than one work group at any given time. A department manager, for example, is a member of both his or her own department and that group of people identifiable as department heads. (In a linking-pin organization, this is formalized in its structure.) Managers also may be assigned to a committee or task force to represent the interests of their own department on some matter of planning, policy, budget decisions, and so forth. This type of multiple group membership has the obvious advantages of keeping the several groups in contact with one another, helping the manager to coordinate efforts of the different groups, helping him or her to see various perspectives, time horizons, and styles of operating, as well as facilitating a total system perspective. In all these respects, such an approach is functional.

One of the problems, however. is the fact that multiple group membership can trap a person between the norms or goals of conflicting groups. For example, a committee or task force will tend to develop its own identity as it continues to meet. All members become subject to the emergent norms and pressures of the "new group" and may, at times, be faced with the dilemma of choosing between the interests of their "home group" and those of the "new group." To the extent that they maintain absolute loyalty to the interests of the home group ("We'll get every dollar we can for our department no matter how hard we have to fight"), they may hang up the new group; insofar as they succumb to the pressures and influence of the new group ("We have to cut our budget for the sake of the other departments"), the home group can accuse the manager of forsaking the department.

This dilemma may be further complicated by the fact that the more frequently the individual meets and interacts with the members of both groups, the more difficult the loyalty bind becomes. Remember, this often tends to occur in the absence of other sources of interaction between members of the two groups, in which case the individual (manager, in our example) is the principal link between the groups. As a manager be comes more aware, via committee membership, of the legitimacy of the views and needs of other groups and interacts more frequently with the members of the committee, greater mutual liking and respect will develop. The individual becomes most acutely aware of this loyalty bind when: (1) attempting to explain and defend each group's position to the other group and (2) each group increases pressure on the individual to hold firm and maintain loyalty.

In addition, the more the individual representing a group embodies the norms and values of that group, the greater will be the bind in the face of conflicting pressures. And the more *cohesive* that group is, the more pressure it will exert to take an unyielding position.

In short, the multiple group memberships generally experienced by managers in large organizations can serve important functions in maintaining intergroup interdependence, but they also have built into them some serious obstacles related to conflicting pressures from the different groups. Some of the difficulties, however, can be offset by implementing additional approaches for intergroup interactions.

Liaison or Linkage People

Over the years as organizations have faced increasing complexities and uncertainties, it has become more important for them to be able to process information and make decisions rapidly. The classical chain of command has become obsolete in many areas of work. It simply cannot manage the demand for flexibility and responsiveness to change and uncertainty. It has become imperative for groups in a system to maintain a constant and open flow of important information. As a result, heavy demands are made on managers to serve as the critical information links for the various subunits of the system, But managers have their limits and, in modern society, can easily suffer from overload problems.

One important development that has occurred in response to this problem is the creation of liaison or linkage people for the groups in the organization. These individuals, or sometimes groups of individuals, are not normally identified with any one operational unit nor do they carry any specific task responsibilities. Their role is simply (and it may not be so simple) to coordinate the efforts of various work groups, to facilitate the necessary exchanges of information, and to help keep each unit apprised of the related activities of other units.

The advantages of utilizing liaisons who are not identified with existing work groups lie in their relative neutrality with respect to group pressures, their immunity from the sanctions of any single group, and their relative freedom to move back and forth in the system as the task demands it. One disadvantage, of course, lies in their lack of legitimate "clout" to make things happen. However, through demonstrated competence, they can develop a great deal of informal influence.

Linking people and groups works best when their emergent norms and attitudes toward time, structure, authority, and so forth fall approximately halfway between those of the groups being linked. If either group sees the linking people as too similar to the other group, the rejected group members are likely to feel ganged up on or misunderstood.

Joint Task Forces

The creation of a joint task force composed of members of different work groups, even groups that have experienced some conflicts, tends to be a very powerful and effective way of breaking down sharp lines between groups (see Chapter 3 for notes on task forces). Each member of the task force enters the new group with the security and support of members of the old group, but it generally follows that the interactions among the members across old group lines tend to generate liking and respect that eventually supersede old group differences. Certainly some loyalty binds will be experienced, and certainly the old group will never quite be the same. But the payoff in terms of greater productivity, mutual group enhancement, and a wider perspective for all individuals can more than compensate for the loss of "the way it used to be."

Joint Group Meetings

Meetings of total groups with one another go even further than joint task forces to break down barriers. Obviously, a small task force can get more work done, but there are times when it is appropriate for all the members of two or more work groups to meet together in a face-to-face situation. If there has been a history of conflicts between the groups, for example, it is likely that each has built up stereotypes of the other. Because stereotypes tend to be maintained in the absence of real data and direct contact, the logical step is to bring the groups together in a setting that will facilitate interaction. Under such circumstances, groups normally find it difficult to maintain the stereotypes and the related conflicts, although sometimes stereotypes can get worse.

> Remember the oil company situation described earlier? The regional people who wanted decision-making authority over prices had developed very negative stereotypes of the headquarters people who wanted final say, and vice versa. Because they were several thousand miles apart and had never even met each other, with the exception of a few top level managers, it was inevitable that their differences and their stereotypes would become fixed.
>
> The strategy that was employed as a first step to resolving the conflict was for each group to state explicitly its perceptions of the other and then to begin sharing these perceptions in a series of meetings designed to force a great deal of direct interaction. As you might guess, the stereotypes did not hold up for very long; the members of both groups began to perceive each other as individuals and to both like and respect one another. The joint meeting provided the necessary vehicle for the groups to recognize and accept their interdependence.
>
> Because meetings of all the members were too expensive and time-consuming to hold very often, they created several joint task forces whose purpose it was to stay on top of problems and decisions affecting both groups. They also agreed to have certain individuals serve as liaison persons whose job it was to maintain a constant and rapid flow of information from the region to headquarters and back.

Designed to Promote Harmony, Some Workshops Leave Race and Gender Divisions

In 1988, Lucky Stores wanted to find out why more women and minority-group employees were not being promoted. So the company held a workshop to increase sensitivity among its store managers. As part of an exercise common in such sessions, the supervisors were asked to mention stereotypes they'd heard about women and minority-group members.

"Women cry more," one said.

"Women don't have as much drive to get ahead," volunteered another manager.

"Black females are aggressive," said a third.

"The workforce would not perform for a black female manager," added a colleague.

The idea was to expose potential prejudice and to deal with it. But to management's horror, notes from this session later turned up as evidence in a sex-discrimination lawsuit arguing that female employees were not being promoted by the Dublin, California, grocery chain. The employees won the suit last August, in part because the court determined that some stereotypes mentioned at the sessions amounted to management bias. "We hadn't known what went on in those meetings, but hearing them say this confirmed that's what they thought of us," said Diane Skillsky, a bookkeeper at Lucky's in Redwood City, California, who stands to share more than $90 million in damages with about 20,000 other women.

The Lucky case is but one example, albeit an extreme one, of the potential pitfalls in corporate efforts to embrace "diversity training" programs intended to foster harmony in increasingly diverse workforces.

Even as businesses like the Flagstar Companies, owner of the Denny's restaurant chain, embark on such programs in the wake of discrimination charges, progressive organizations are finding that tackling issues like race and gender is a delicate undertaking. Among the problems: confrontational trainers who accuse employees of bigotry or pit them against each other, resentment by employees who feel left out of the process, and a sense among many executives that training sessions alone are inadequate.

"I've seen diversity trainers go into companies with wrecking balls, and they leave a mess," said Kate Butler, a management consultant in New Jersey. . . . A July 5 cover story in *The New Republic* criticized the "diversity industry" for charging millions of dollars for programs that don't always "solve the problems they purport to address." . . .

Some experts would like to see company trainers move away from the approach of categorizing employees. A few trainers have been known to say that all Asians don't like to look the boss in the eye or that Hispanic employees prefer working in groups. . . . Jeffrey A. Sonnenfeld, director of the Center for Leadership and Career Studies at Emory University, is troubled when he sees employees taught that different groups have different characteristics. Why not teach that each employee is different, he asks.

In a recent study of several diversity programs coauthored with Catherine Ellis, Professor Sonnenfeld concluded that simply replacing "negative" stereotypes with "positive" stereotypes can be equally divisive. In other words, it is just as damaging to say that all members of a certain group have an aptitude for high-tech work as it is to say that they are aloof toward their coworkers. Both stereotypes raise barriers against looking at workers as individuals.

SOURCE: Kathleen Murray, "The Unfortunate Side Effects of 'Diversity Training,'" *New York Times*, August 1, 1993. Copyright © 1993 by The New York Times Company. Reprinted by permission.

Whereas previously the managers were carrying the burden of all the problems and complaints and were consequently caught in the middle, the use of the listed strategies for promoting intergroup cooperation ultimately removed a very dysfunctional load from the managers' backs.

Job Exchanges across Groups

Some organizations increase cooperation by having people from different departments exchange jobs. It is difficult to appreciate another person's position until you've had a chance to walk in his or her shoes. Judgments about the behavior of other people are usually made from outside the situation. If that situation happens to involve the other person's membership in another group, judgment can be colored by previous perceptions of that group. Also, it may be difficult to understand how it feels to be a member of that other group. By exchanging members, chances are increased that members of each group can appreciate the needs and operations of the other. It has the same kind of benefits as a cultural exchange.

Physical Proximity

Perhaps all too obvious, but certainly not to be overlooked, is the importance of physical distance in the relations between groups. If two work groups are in different buildings, the chances for interaction are minimal during the normal working hours. The best that can be hoped for is linkage people, joint task forces, occasional joint meetings, and the like. But sometimes there is simply no substitute for frequent ongoing exchanges, both task related and of a social nature. None of the previous approaches allows much room for emergent social interactions among the members of the different groups. Each strategy is task related and has limited time boundaries. To the extent that two working groups are co-located, interactions are likely to develop that will enhance intergroup cooperation and minimize intergroup conflict. Perhaps each of the other approaches is a poor approximation of this one, but necessary because of the great variety of organizational constraints that dictate physical separation (e.g., job specialization and the technology of the work). However, all too often managers overlook the obvious: The physical placement of people at work can have a major effect upon their performance. The physical proximity of working groups can be a significant factor in establishing their cooperation.

Creating Intergroup Cooperation across International and Regional Cultures

With all economies becoming increasingly global, managers must deal with identity differences, not only among groups within their organization, but also among organizations, among regions of their home country, and throughout the world.[21] Managers must deal with groups and individuals from other countries who operate from a different cultural framework, and must travel to or live in different countries all around the world. We turn next to an exploration of some of the ways cultures differ, describing how they differ and the implications of those differences for management.

An understanding of cultural differences and skill in adapting to various cultures can be crucial for personal and organizational effectiveness. Consider the following experience of a professor while teaching managers who were candidates for the MBA degree in Sri Lanka:

> I grew up at a time when it was common for middle-aged females to be referred to as "girls," especially by men, but also by other women. However, given more recent developments in the United States, I had come to appreciate the disrespect that calling adult females "girls" entails, and as I approached teaching in a rather traditional Southwest Asian culture, I was careful to refer to the females in the MBA program as "women." Feeling good about my own awareness and sensitivity, I was taken aback when after the third class, several of the male students came to me asking why I was "insulting our ladies" in the class by referring to them as "women"! Discussion brought out the fact that in their culture the word "woman" was used in reference to the servant women employed in the households of university-educated professionals. The females of the class were "ladies."

This experience reflects at least three dimensions that often differ among cultures: connotations of words, relationships between men and women, and directness of

The Cross-Cultural Work of Geert Hofstede

In a major research project conducted in the late 1960s and early 1970s, Geert Hofstede surveyed the beliefs and values of 116,000 IBM employees from 40 different countries. The research produced four basic dimensions of national culture.

1. *Power Distance*—the degree to which members of a society accept the unequal and hierarchical distribution of power.
2. *Uncertainty Avoidance*—the degree to which a society feels threatened by uncertainty and deals with it by avoidance, formal rules, intolerance of deviant behavior, and holding to absolute truths.
3. *Individualism versus Collectivism*—the degree to which a society emphasizes self-reliance and independence versus social connectedness and interdependence.
4. *Masculinity versus Femininity*—the degree to which a society emphasizes assertiveness and

acquisition of material goods versus the support and nurturance of others.

The Hofstede dimensions help to explain how interpersonal differences are often reflections of cultural differences. For example, an American who is high on individualism might have difficulty dealing with a Japanese counterpart who tends to be high on collectivism. Similarly, an American or Canadian who is likely to be low on the dimension of power distance may be uncomfortable with the high level of power distance accepted by someone from a Latin American country, where there have been more autocratic traditions.

For those interested in studying Hofstede's work, we suggest beginning with "Motivation, Leadership and Organization: Do American Theories Apply Abroad?" in *Organizational Dynamics*, 1980, vol. 9, pp. 42–63.

---

expression or confrontation of differences. We turn now to a discussion of these and other cultural dimensions. But first, a warning: No culture produces totally uniform behavior, so beware of assuming that any generalization is true of all individuals, classes, or groups from any country.

Some Dimensions of Culture

1. The Connotations of Words

In the previous anecdote, the MBA class attached a connotation to the word *woman* that never crossed the professor's mind. As we explained in Chapter 10, such unexpected misunderstandings are always possible among people of different cultures. Even the English language, widely used by businesses throughout the world, receives different connotations in different cultures.

In some cultures (especially in Asia), it is considered impolite to say "no" directly. Consequently, a "yes" may not mean "yes" the way it might in North America. It may mean "maybe," or "I'll try," or even "I wish I could." The failure to do what a "yes" promised does not evidence a lack of responsibility or dishonesty; it is probably evidence of that person's politeness and the underlying cultural standard.

2. Directness of Expression and Confrontation of Differences and Conflict

In the United States, people often pride themselves on "calling a spade a spade" or "telling it like it is." In contrast, many other cultures take pride in being considerate of others' feelings by being much less direct. Japanese managers would seldom directly say "no" to a subordinate's proposal. Instead, the supervisor raises questions that indicate how to reshape the proposal to gain approval. This save the proposer from losing face and eventually can lead to acceptance of a modified proposal.

Imagine the reaction of someone from a more direct culture, ignorant of the Japanese way, when he or she doesn't get a direct answer. The questions and the lack of a definite yes or no might easily be interpreted as indecisiveness when the Japanese are merely behaving appropriately within their culture.

Fortunately for the professor in Sri Lanka, the MBA students were ready to confront more openly than was characteristic of their culture. Otherwise he might easily have continued to "insult" the ladies, especially if he failed to notice the class members' subtle reactions to his behavior.

3. The Relationship between Men and Women

The behavior of the men in Sri Lanka reflected a culture in which men have higher status than women, are expected to protect and defend them, and are more assertive than women.

Such a patriarchal relationship has been characteristic of many cultures throughout the world, including North America. However, differences exist even among patriarchal cultures. Thus, in Muslim cultures and the Japanese culture women are outwardly more subservient than are women in Western cultures even though all the cultures are patriarchal.

Imagine the complexities when men from more egalitarian cultures deal with or meet women from more patriarchal cultures or the difficulties for women business people in those cultures.

4. Orientation toward Time

North Americans and many Northern Europeans think of the clock as running and speak of time as flying. A literal translation of the same phrase in Spanish suggests that time walks. This reflects the difference between the orientation to time common in the United States and that of many other cultures of the world, including Native Americans. Generally, North Americans and Northern Europeans value time, seek to save it, and are concerned about wasting it by not being punctual. Other cultures take time as it comes.

How would you feel as a customer if you had an appointment with a supplier and the supplier kept you waiting for 30 minutes? In many places in the world, such a lack of punctuality would not stir up negative feelings. It would be viewed in some cultures as a North American might view being 5 minutes late. But 5 minutes late might be seen by a punctual German or Dutch businessperson as very rude. You can see what kind of misunderstanding could occur when individuals who count time by the minute interact with individuals from cultures for whom time is relatively unimportant.[22]

5. Distribution of Power/Emphasis on Rank

Cultures differ significantly in their attitudes toward others with power. Some expect directive, even autocratic, leadership patterns while others prefer more participative, egalitarian patterns, or industrial democracy.

In many cultures, managers dare not offer suggestions to their superior lest he (and it is likely to be a he in most countries) feel insulted by their apparent disrespect for his position and his personal competency. This reflects a strong cultural emphasis on respect for authority, position, and even age. Participation in decisions by individuals from many levels, departments, and ranks is seen as disrespectful and even morally wrong. To base influence on expertise and logical persuasion, as team and matrix structures require, rather than on position and rank, would smack of the manager abdicating his or her role.

During World War II a number of United States soldiers, captured by the Japanese, received additional punishment and even torture because they refused to bow to their captors and in other ways failed to fulfill Japanese cultural expectations that the less powerful show respect and deference for those in power, although Japanese business is changing in regard to hierarchy. (See Managerial Bulletin).

Not so many years ago a lower-ranking individual in a U.S. corporation would put on a suit coat before entering the department manager's office, address the manager by last name, and even remain standing throughout the conversation unless explicitly invited to take a chair. While such outward expression of respect for position and age is not common today in the United States, it would be found elsewhere in the world.

6. Emphasis on Individualism versus Group Orientation

Another way that cultures differ is in the relative emphasis on individual rights versus group needs. United States managers often value self-reliance, individual achievement, and competitiveness. Many cultures will emphasize much greater concern for the group and will expect the individual to subordinate his or her personal gain to the well-being of the family, the work group, the organization and the wider society. An arranged marriage for the purpose of developing a political or economic alliance perhaps epitomizes, in Western eyes, the placing of collective interests ahead of individual interests.

The Japanese have an expression, "The nail that sticks up gets hammered down." This captures the social disapproval attached to someone who personally seeks the limelight or is inappropriately given it by a supervisor. Thus, a manager from a country where individualism is prized could easily make a mistake by publicly praising an individual's performance in Japan. In a group-oriented culture, praise should go to the group rather than to the individual, or possibly to the senior member as representing the group, but certainly not to a younger member, however competent and effective he or she may be.

Also management is likely to find that group pay incentives will be more suitable in a group-oriented culture than piece work or other incentive systems based on individual performance.

7. The Relative Importance of People and Relationships, and Quality of Work-Life

In some cultures, such as Denmark, concern for people and relationships and for the quality of life weigh more heavily than does the acquisition of material things (i.e., "the bottom line") in the United States.[23] While these value orientations are not either/or categories, but instead a matter of emphasis and importance attached to each cluster of values, the implications for doing business in one culture or another are significant.

For example, in many cultures, managers as well as employees expect to have their weekends free. While they expect to work hard for the scheduled 40 hours of the work week, they do not find it reasonable to take time away from family life by working 60 to 70 hours per week, as is common in many U.S. companies. A manager from the United States, working in such a culture, needs to redefine what constitutes a hardworking, loyal employee from that which may apply in the United States and the rest of North America. This can be difficult for a manager who is strongly committed to business-first attitudes.

These are seven dimensions on which cultures can differ. There are others, including the use of personal space; uncertainty avoidance; attire, including degree of physical exposure (nudity); forms of address; and public expressions of affection (movies from the United States showing couples kissing are shocking, even disgusting, for some cultures).

Consequences of Cultural Unawareness

Anyone who has been a member of a group for a long time will tend to take the group's ways of doing things for granted. Because culturally determined customs and norms are typically behavioral patterns with which members of a culture have

MANAGERIAL BULLETIN

Just Wait until Young Teller-San Tells Old Chairman-San "Get Lost"

Will Japanese corporate etiquette ever be the same?

Dai-Ichi Kangyo Bank, the world's largest bank, has ordered its employees to stop the practice of addressing one another differently depending on rank.

In most Japanese organizations, a subordinate wouldn't dream of addressing his boss in the way that most people here call one another in everyday life, "Tanaka-san" or "Watanabe-san," for instance. Employees are usually indoctrinated in hierarchical forms of address that in the West are confined to the military.

Thus, when a subordinate addresses a senior in Japan, he says *kacho* (section chief) or *bucho* (department head); if he uses the senior's name, it's always with the title, as in "Tanaka-kacho." Similarly, subordinates are always addressed by name plus a suffix that indicates they are of lower rank or age, like "Tanaka-kun."

But now Dai-Ichi Kangyo is trying to change all that. Employees are to address one another the same way regardless of age, rank, or sex—last name, plus *san,* the Japanese equivalent of Mr., Miss, or Mrs.

The idea is "to promote open and free communication" within the bank, says Akiyoshi Shoji, the public-relations bucho, who is now just plain Shoji-san.

A few other companies, including Sony Corp., Kao Corp., and Shiseido Co., already practice *san-zuke,* as

it's called. But banks are among the most conservative of Japanese organizations, and Dai-Ichi Kangyo is one of the most conservative banks. Bank of Tokyo, which has a tradition of being more international, is apparently the only other major bank to eschew hierarchical forms of address.

Dai-Ichi Kangyo's new *kaicho,* or chairman, Kunji Miyazaki, waxes eloquent about the change: "We're getting rid of the class system. We're treating people equally. We're imitating America."

But for employees of long standing, the change is going to take some getting used to. "I would hesitate to call the chairman Miyazaki-san," says one senior manager.

Companies that already practice san-zuke say it encourages communication and discourages the extreme title-consciousness and obsession with the organization chart that's typical in Japanese firms.

But it also takes some of the fun out of being promoted. Says a recently appointed Dai-Ichi Kangyo bucho: "Some of my fellow buchos think it's not fair. We just got named bucho, and we'd like to be called bucho for a while."

SOURCE: Urban C. Lehner. Reprinted by permission of *The Wall Street Journal,* © April 24, 1992, Dow Jones & Company, Inc. All Rights Reserved Worldwide.

grown up, awareness of these dimensions is often quite limited. Actions are typically undertaken without a lot of conscious attention. The possibilities of violating the customs, mores, and values of another, not well-understood culture are great. Furthermore, because a particular culture's position on any dimension becomes for that culture the "right" way to do things—the way things "ought" to be done—personal insult, uncomfortable misunderstandings, and damage to interpersonal relationships can happen all too easily. Yet, if work is to get done effectively, such consequences must be minimized, and this requires developing cross-cultural skills.

Developing Cross-Cultural Skills for Working in Another Country

Learning how to handle yourself in a new and different culture is a long-term process. It starts with developing an awareness of cultural differences. It means learning about another perspective on life, other ways of thinking and acting, and an appreciation for different beliefs and values. Reading about culture, in general, as you have just been doing, is one step to that end. Seeking to identify attributes of your own culture is another. Talking to international students on campus to learn what struck them about your country when they first arrived, and even now, would give you insight into your culture as well as theirs.

A second step is to learn about the history and culture of the country you are traveling to, or think you may want to travel to someday. Exhibiting some knowledge of

MANAGERIAL BULLETIN

Europeans and North Americans: The Little Differences That Don't Go Away

Dealing with Western Europeans as trading partners and collaborators has become an everyday matter for great numbers of U.S. business people. Many of us see Europeans as old allies, cousins in democracy, distant relatives of the people who refashioned America in waves of immigration. We assume that they are very much like ourselves.

In many respects we are right. However, there are some noteworthy differences of values and attitudes that affect our relationships with Europeans, especially when we are working with them on a face-to-face or on a day-to-day basis. Experiencing each other with our guard down, we encounter "those little differences that don't go away."

Handling these differences can go a long way to cement the kind of business relationships that North Americans are beginning to discover as more important in other parts of the world than they seem at home. North Americans are often surprised to learn that business talk is not as all-pervasive with Europeans as it is with us. They often insist on nonbusiness topics when sharing meals or in informal situations. Themes may range from small talk about everyday things to big talk about philosophy, culture, art, and politics.

Since Europeans are likely to give us occasions to do this, we can take advantage of such times with stimulating cultural conversations. Sometimes we do this spontaneously by comparing our food, our homes, and other visible elements of our cultures. Less often—maybe because it's more delicate—we touch on contrasting values and perceptions about how life is or ought to be. Unexplored, these issues can contribute to false stereotypes about each other and over time create negative feelings that erode our trust in each other.

Language guides and travel books provide information to take some of the hazards out of coming to understand others, but they rarely do enough. To fill this gap, we have developed a schema called "How Europeans and Americans Can Misunderstand Each Other." It outlines some common attitudes that become friction points between us if we don't pay attention to them. Talking over these comparisons helps both U.S. and European business people to examine their attitudes and reactions toward each other.

When you bring up these topics, remember that no single segment of North American culture possesses all of the behaviors described in the schema as "American," nor does any one European ethnic group have those titled "European Behaviors." In sharing this tool with you, we do not presume to read the mind of any one person of either culture area. We are simply highlighting differences that have been cited as recurring misperceptions. On some items you will agree with your partners; on others, disagree. In some cases you will join forces to disagree with the author. The important thing is that such discussions help you to know each other better. Any cultures can be compared on these dimensions.

HOW EUROPEANS AND AMERICANS CAN MISUNDERSTAND EACH OTHER

American Behaviors	Americans See Their Own Behavior as	Europeans See American Behavior as	European Behavior	Europeans See Their Own Behavior as
Trust more readily	Constructive	Naive childishness	Trust less readily	Realism
Make many friends	Friendly, open	Superficial, insincere	Have fewer close friends	Discretion, depth
Smooth over differences	Cooperative, democratic, practical	Lack conviction, depth	Dispute differences	Refining the truth through dialectic.
Collaborate easily	Others will join you if it is in their interest. Common interests dominate. Conspiracies are evil.	Containing hidden agendas	Collaborate cautiously	Others will block you. Conflicting, territorial interests, conspiracies are normal.

Continued

American Behaviors	Americans See Their Own Behavior as	Europeans See American Behavior as	European Behavior	Europeans See Their Own Behavior as
Be optimistic and express optimism	Life is rich.	Foolishness	Be cautious, express reservations	Resources are limited.
Seek opportunity	The right time is now.	Aggressivity	Act out of purpose	The right time will show itself.
Mix business and pleasure	Life is a continuum.	Never stop doing business, workaholics	Separate business and private life	Everything has its time, place.
Think out loud, brainstorm	The more ideas, the better the product or solution.	Scatterbrained, undisciplined	Prepare what you say	Be accountable for your words.
Behave spontaneously	Free, creative	Irresponsible, immature	Behave logically, rationally	Mature, responsible
Decentralized politics	People can solve their own problems.	Chaotic, unreliable	Centralized politics	Controls and limits balkanization, assures everyone is cared for.
Do it, theorize later	We're being practical.	Rationalization, error prone	Theory before action	Do it right.
Create open information flow	Enables the relationship.	No substance	Guarded information flow, indirection	Enables the relationship.
Take pride in accomplishment	One becomes someone through doing things.	Petit bourgeois	Take pride in one's self and one's group	Maintain dignity by living out one's calling.
Attack because of the result	Getting things done is what counts.	Unprincipled, small-minded	Attack because of the process	Correctness and style are paramount.
Base authority and hierarchy on accomplishment	Positions exist as long as they are practical and functional.	Poor judges of character	Accept hierarchy as based in the nature of things	Position is based on the kind of person one is. Noblesse oblige.
Avoid differentiating female and male roles	We are trying to be more fair and egalitarian.	Debasing both women and men	Differentiate male and female roles	Both men's and women's roles have their own prestige.
Treat children as adults	Making choices helps them grow up.	Children are loud and intrusive, delinquent	Discipline children	Discipline creates character.
Put freedom and initiative first	Respecting the individual	Socially irresponsible	Put duty and obedience first	Respecting the common good
Forgive mistakes	Trying is what counts—you will get there.	Over-reaching themselves. Imposters	Avoid mistakes	Mistakes are often irreparable.
Consume	Being alive, moving, spirit filled	Wastefulness, quantity over quality. Meaninglessness	Be frugal	Strive for quality, not quantity.
Civil violence	Personal or moral failure	Lawless, undisciplined culture	Political violence	Conflict of group interests

SOURCE: George Simons International, © 1992. All rights reserved. Reprinted by permission. For more information, contact George Simons International, The Galleria Office Park, 740 Front Street, Suite 335, Santa Cruz, CA 95060 USA, 408-426-9608. Many of these ideas are reflected in David Miller's excellent book, *Painted in Blood*.

a country's history and exhibiting a genuine interest in its traditions, art, and histori-cally important sites can endear you to the citizens of that country. Inquire about im-portant social customs and traditions of the country. Ask questions directly about the cultural dimensions discussed above and others that you encounter in your reading.

As you learn about a culture before you go, a third step is to decide how you might adapt your own behavior. Would you be particularly punctual, as you'd need to be if you went to Switzerland? Would you need to modify your attire in any way, such as wearing only conservative suits if you were going to a very proper country or wearing only ankle-length skirts if going to a Muslim country? While thinking along these lines, you may also consider behaviors that you would not be comfortable adopting because they would force you to violate your personal values.

It is hard to be both culturally sensitive and true to one's own values. For exam-ple, in a culture that emphasizes deferring to authority and seniority, how would you deal with a much older boss you think is making a big mistake? Do you speak up to pursue efficiency, or keep quiet to be adaptive? Generally, it is probably better to be oneself, yet alert to learning from one's mistakes, than to be so on guard against making a mistake that one is stiff, unnatural, and lacking spontaneity. Many cultures make allowances for the "strange behavior" of "foreigners." You can decide how best and how much to adapt before reaching the country, but you should con-tinue to consider your decisions after you arrive.

Fourth, observe how things are done locally and try to be a "participant ob-server," paying attention to how your behavior is being received. The cues may be subtle and nonverbal, but they can reveal a violation of some cultural norm, and thereby suggest possible further adaptation.

A useful fifth step is to find someone from the culture to act as cultural advisor—someone from whom you can learn about the culture and who will give you feed-back when you unknowingly step on cultural toes.

Finally, remember that you are a guest in the country and approach the experi-ence with an attitude of inquisitiveness and a desire to learn about the country and its culture, rather than being judgmental because their ways differ from what you are used to. However different, their ways probably work for that country, even if they might be viewed as less effective than the pattern at home. Stay observant, open-minded, flexible, and courteous.

Dealing with Regional Cultures within Your Own Country

What we have said about cultures of different countries applies to a degree to dif-ferent regions of most countries. Each can have its distinct regional culture. If you are from North America, you may have heard Californians described as laid back, New Englanders as reserved, and Southerners as gracious and hospitable. Histori-cally, New York City has had a reputation for being very brusque, with individuals getting right down to business without wasting much time on social amenities. In contrast, in Texas, historically it was seen as necessary to develop a relationship be-fore doing business. As you travel around the United States or do business with in-dividuals from other parts of the country, some use of your awareness of cultural differences and some application of the cross-cultural skills discussed above will be appropriate.

Diversity within Organizations

Groups, regions, and countries all exhibit their own identities or cultures. Individu-als do also, due to their racial background, ethnic heritage, socioeconomic class, and gender. Consequently, within a single organization in North America, one can be working cross-culturally.

Although it is important to avoid stereotyping and thereby fail to notice individ-uals who are different from the group(s) they have been part of, when joining an

Computer Chip Project Brings Rivals Together, but the Cultures Clash

Foreign Work Habits Get in Way of Creative Leaps, Hobbling Joint Research

Life can be tough out here on the frontier of international business cooperation. Just ask Matt Wordeman.

Mr. Wordeman, an International Business Machines Corp. research scientist, works at the heart of one of the most ambitious cross-cultural business projects ever attempted. Three competing companies from three continents—Siemens AG of Germany, Toshiba Corp. of Japan, and IBM—are trying to develop a revolutionary computer memory chip together. The Triad, as they call themselves, has been working for a year at the IBM facility in this small Hudson River Valley town on research scheduled to last until at least 1997. The undertaking is cutting-edge, both in technology and in the scope of its cross-cultural cooperation.

Initially, some organizers wondered whether more than 100 scientists from competitive, culturally diverse backgrounds could work together on such a large project. They were right to worry.

Meeting Etiquette

At East Fishkill, Siemens scientists were shocked to find Toshiba colleagues closing their eyes and seeming to sleep during meetings (a common practice for overworked Japanese managers when talk doesn't concern them). The Japanese, who normally work in big groups, found it painful to sit in small, individual offices and speak English: some now withdraw when they can into all-Japanese groups. IBMers complained that the Germans plan too much and that the Japanese—who like to review ideas constantly—won't make clear decisions. Suspicions circulate that some researchers are withholding information from the group.

The human issues raised in this venture offer lessons not just for the three prominent firms involved, but for companies in a wide variety of businesses across the globe. . . .

In theory, bringing together scientists with diverse backgrounds to design such an advanced technology is supposed to generate creative leaps, yielding new approaches and dazzling discoveries . . . "For example," says cultural anthropologist Edward T. Hall, "Americans tend to look at objects. The Japanese look at spaces between objects. If you can relax and let everyone be himself, you can get a lot of strengths from that."

No problem, thought IBM: after all, the company hires people from all over the world. Mr. Wordeman says he figured he had plenty of experience working with foreigners, even those lacking English language skills.

"But most of those people had studied in the U.S.," he says. "They tend to become very Americanized very quickly. What's different this time is that there are entire groups of people who came with their own company ties. People have been able to stay more separate . . . we don't trust each other entirely.

A disappointed Mr. Wordeman says he hasn't seen the kinds of technical leaps he had hoped for. If it weren't for the financial savings implicit in such a joint research venture, he says, he thinks IBM could do the work more easily on its own.

Mr. Rodeman and other Triad participants emphasize that, despite the huge extra effort required, the project isn't in trouble. Work is on schedule—even a bit ahead in parts—and they are finding ways to overcome communications problems, they say. Members of all three teams say they have learned huge amounts, both about technology and about cooperating with outsiders. They say it is far too soon to evaluate successes and failures, and that the hoped-for technological leaps still may emerge.

But they agree that cooperation has come much harder than anyone imagined. Part of the problem was a businesslike effort to get a quick start on the daunting microchip technology. International joint ventures need to pay early attention to team-building and understanding various approaches to work, says Nancy Adler, a professor of management at Montreal's McGill University. Otherwise, cultural differences quickly switch from opportunities to obstacles: "They are used to explain problems rather than solve them. People say, 'We missed the deadline because those Japanese are so slow.'"

Needed: Joint Training

That is precisely what happened with the Triad companies.

Toshiba gave employees its normal course on working and living abroad. But, says Takaaki Tanaka, a Toshiba human-resource expert in New York, "We should have done more cooperative efforts with human-resources people from Siemens and IBM, to develop joint training programs."

Siemens briefed employees on what it calls America's "hamburger style of management." American managers, Siemens says, prefer to criticize subordinates

Continued

Computer Chip Project Brings Rivals Together, but the Cultures Clash   Continued

gently. They start with small talk: "How's the family?" That is the top of the hamburger bun. Then Americans slip in the meat—the criticism. And they exit with encouraging words—more bun.

"With Germans," says Alf Keogh, an Irishman who does cross-cultural training for Siemens, "all you get is the meat. And with the Japanese, it's all the soft stuff—you have to *smell* the meat."

The project's planners tried to address cultural differences by stipulating all work would be done in English and by creating mixed research teams of employees from all three companies. That basic plan, which seemed an obvious starting point for working together, became the first obstacle.

"My biggest problem is the English language," says Motoya Okazaki, a Toshiba researcher, who had been a student of foreign languages and cultures before coming to East Fishkill. "It took me almost one year to learn to communicate slightly well."

The Toshiba researchers also faced the biggest adjustment problem in terms of corporate culture. They are accustomed to working together in big tank-like rooms, which they compare to classrooms. By overhearing conversations, everyone knows what others are doing—from research to family problems. Senior people constantly look over subordinates' shoulders. "They live in a sea of information," says Mr. Hall, the anthropologist.

Toshiba wanted such a system here. But IBM's building already was cut up into a maze of small offices. To save time, the Japanese finally agreed to keep it that way, knocking out a few walls to improve communication.

"For us," explains Toru Watanabe, a senior Toshiba researcher, "very important information exchanges are handled in informal situations—just after finishing lunch,

while relaxing and discussing baseball. We say, 'I have a new idea, what do you think?' but here, you have to go to someone's office and say, 'Do you have a minute?' Small talk doesn't come naturally."

The Germans had difficulty adjusting to their American work space, too. In Germany, Siemens people say, no one would be asked to work in a windowless office; in East Fishkill, Siemens engineers learned to their horror, most of the offices are windowless. Office doors have narrow panes of glass so that visitors can see before entering whether occupants are busy; German and Japanese researchers, not accustomed to this, sometimes hang their coats over the glass, annoying IBMers. Equally annoying to some of the foreign visitors is IBM's strict no-smoking policy, requiring them to go outdoors in any weather if they want to light up.

Then comes the delicate question of how to make suggestions. Siemens engineer Klaus Roithner says he spent days analyzing IBM's pilot manufacturing system and then made some gentle proposals for improving it. IBM colleagues first told him to be more specific, he says; then they accused him of simply wanting to do things the Siemens way. Concluding that IBMers don't like outside suggestions, he finally resorted to amateur psychology. Nowadays, he says, "I indirectly suggest an idea to IBM engineers, and let them think they have come up with it themselves."

Also, Mr. Roithner says, deep corporate rivalries may be at work. "I have never been reluctant to share secrets," he says. "But I have had the feeling that this problem exists. Here you are working in a team, but you are still employed by your mother company. Some people still have to think, 'Don't tell too much about your company secrets.'"

Continued

organization, each person brings some cultural background experienced at home and while growing up. While we will have been influenced by the regions of the country in which we grew up, we will have also been influenced by our racial and ethnic origins (Native American, African-American, Spanish-speaking American, Asian-American, and Euro-American with roots in Poland, Germany, England, France, Italy, Scandinavia, Ireland, Greece, etc.).

Furthermore, we differ as to gender. Females experience a different culture than do males, whatever their racial and ethnic origins, because throughout the modern world the roles of men and women differ and female and male children are raised in subtly different ways. As we have mentioned throughout this book, women and men *tend* to differ in interpersonal style, in managerial style, in thought processes (relative emphasis on intuition versus analytical/rational processes), and in values (particularly in terms of the importance attached to relationships versus status and

For the first few months of the Triad project, the researchers say, everyone was on best behavior—and having fun. People spoke slowly and carefully to one another, making extra efforts to be understood. But with time, people fell into more normal speech and behavior patterns. The honeymoon ended; little slights were felt. The three groups grew more isolated, and some Japanese in particular began speaking less English.

"They do read English all day, but most of their communication now will be done in Japanese," says Mr. Wordeman. "People will talk if you seek them out, but there is very little casual chatting and dropping in the office across company lines—whereas there is a great deal of that kind of contact within each of the three companies."

"I see it most often at 7 or 8 in the evening," says Mr. Roithner, the German engineer. "The American engineers are gone. Most of the German engineers are gone. And half the Japanese engineers are in the aisles, talking. You can see that real work is going on—unplanned and informal."

The separation has prevented the hoped-for big creative leaps that researchers call Aha! effects. "I wish I had a good example of breaking through that and coming up with a great new idea, but unfortunately that hasn't happened very much," says Mr. Wordeman. He adds, however, that the engineers themselves are extremely talented, and this has permitted them to overcome disappointments and wasted time, keeping the project on track . . .

After-Hours Socializing

"It takes time to get to know one another," says Mr. Hall, the anthropologist. "One thing that seems to work across all three cultures is to go out and get drunk together."

But project organizers also were reluctant to push after-hours socializing, and now, in their second year of the project, Triad researchers tend to spend free time with colleagues from their own countries.

"For the Germans and the Japanese, this is a big adventure," says Mr. Abernathey. "But for the U.S. people, this is their home. They have school-board meetings, PTA meetings, and other activities."

One effort at cross-cultural schmoozing, a softball game, backfired.

"The Americans and Japanese know this game well, but the Germans don't," explains Mr. Roithner of Siemens. Determined to measure up in the new sport—"highly motivated," as he puts it—he hit the ball and raced for first. He beat the throw, but made the mistake of hitting the base stiff-legged, fracturing his hip. A Japanese co-worker took him to the hospital. An American colleague lent him a laptop computer to use at home. The cross-cultural softball project was canceled.

One small consolation: Mr. Roithner found what he calls "the perfect doctor." Why was he perfect? "He spoke German—he had studied in Switzerland. It is hard to explain where something hurts in a foreign language."

SOURCE: E. S. Browning. Reprinted by permission of *The Wall Street Journal*, © May 3, 1994, Dow Jones & Company, Inc. All Rights Reserved Worldwide.

power).[24] Diversity within organizations is increasing rapidly. The world of management in North America is no longer inhabited only by white, Euro-American males. The ability to respect, know, and work with a wide range of diverse individuals has become an important skill for effectiveness in working in one's own country as well as working internationally.

Implications for Organizational Change

As you will see in Chapter 14, groups can be important leverage points for bringing about change in an organization. The need for change often is related to the general issue of system interdependence and specifically to problems of intergroup cooperation and cooperation among individuals from diverse social groupings. Any of the strategies for increasing cooperation represents a significant intervention into the system, whether utilized to resolve an existing conflict or as a means of minimizing the potential for future conflict. Even organizational change efforts that are not directly intended to affect the relationships among work groups more often than not do have some important impact on them. As you read through the chapter on organizational change, it would be useful to keep in mind the basic propositions related to intergroup cooperation and see how they relate to the basic concepts and strategies for change.

KEY CONCEPTS FROM CHAPTER 13

1. The more differentiated the tasks necessary to accomplish the work, the more appropriate it is to create subsystems.
2. Variations in group identity.
    a. Attitudes toward time, authority, and structure.
    b. Perspective on the task, including professional identity.
    c. Interpersonal orientation.
3. Intergroup coordination depends on
    a. Awareness of own function in relation to others.
    b. Maintenance of communication links with others.
    c. Acceptance of legitimacy of the needs of others.
    d. Willingness to meet own needs within the framework of the total structure.
4. The degree of resistance to the above is related to resulting conflict with the group's basic norms, ideals, values.
5. Problems with strong group identity.
    a. Seeing one's group as better than other(s).
    b. Seeing one's ideas as better than other(s).
    c. Overestimation of own competence.
    d. Overvaluation of one's leader(s).
    e. Avoidance of interaction with other group.
    f. Distortion of information about other group.
    g. Mistrust of the members of the other group.
6. Groups may have formal or informal status.
7. Groups may have legitimate or illegitimate power.
8. Diversity of backgrounds contributes to intergroup conflict.
9. Cooperation and conflict may be either functional or dysfunctional to the total system.
10. Types of interdependence:
    a. Pooled.
    b. Serial.
    c. Reciprocal.

11. The foundation of intergroup cooperation.
    a. Frequent interactions.
    b. Frequent and open information flow.
    c. Development and acceptance of common goals.
    d. Sharing a common source of threat.
    e. Shared common responsibility.
    f. Ability to establish joint memberships.
    g. Willingness to share and discuss perceptions of each other.
12. The norm of reciprocity maximizes interdependence.
13. Methods for maximizing intergroup cooperation:
    a. Overlapping or multiple group membership.
    b. Liaison people.
    c. Joint task forces.
    d. Joint group meetings.
    e. Job exchanges.
    f. Physical proximity.
14. Creating intergroup cooperation across cultures; dimensions of culture
    a. Connotations of words in same language.
    b. Directness of expression/confrontation of differences.
    c. Relationship between men and women.
    d. Orientation toward time.
    e. Distribution of power/emphasis on rank.
    f. Individualism versus group orientation.
    g. Relative importance of people, relationships, quality of work life.
    h. Other.
15. Developing cross-cultural skills for working in other countries, regions, even within own organization.
    a. Develop awareness of differences.
    b. Learn the specific culture.
    c. Decide how you plan to adapt.
    d. Be participant-observer; note cues to your impact.
    e. Find a local to be your cultural advisor.
    f. As a guest, stay open to learning.

PERSONAL APPLICATION EXERCISE

The Public Conversation

As indicated in this chapter, the basic barrier to resolving conflicts between groups is that neither really understands the other. Whether some kind of resolution would occur with such understanding often remains unknown. An approach to building mutual understanding between groups that has been found to be very effective, even when there has been a long history of conflict, and even hostility, was developed some years ago by Laura Chasin and Carol Becker at the Family Institute of Cambridge, Massachusetts.[25] They call their approach a Public Conversation. It is a way of structuring a discussion, normally conducted in a public forum, to facilitate genuine listening on the part of the parties and, consequently, a better understanding and appreciation. It does not change the positions but often prevents the differences from escalating into more serious and damaging outcomes. The process involves having each party respond one at a time, with no interruption from the other, to each of three questions. Both respond to a given question before moving on to the next. The questions are as follows:

1. What has been your history with the issue, how did you get interested in it, and what has been your involvement with it?
2. What is at the heart of the matter for you, the central issue as it relates to your beliefs and/or values?
3. What are the gray areas, the uncertainties, the mixed feelings that complicate your position on the issue?

While the originators of this approach have used it in relation to major public issues (e.g., abortion), it can also be used to handle major organizational conflicts in which people are divided over issues such as proper business ethics and social responsibility. One of the authors of this book successfully helped members of a family business deal with the touchy issue of succession, in which the older and younger generations were nearly at war over control of the business.

At some point you may find yourself in a heated argument with another student or group. If the quality of listening is really bad and feelings are building to an explosive level, try stepping back from the situation and, perhaps with the help of a third party, using the Public Conversation model to break the stalemate. If you happen to be a third party to an argument between two of your friends or classmates, you might try jumping in and suggesting the use of this approach. It is something that you will ultimately find useful as a managerial tool. Even if it doesn't resolve the conflict, it will certainly give all parties a more informed perspective on the situation.

SUGGESTED READINGS

Alderfer, C. P. "Group and Intergroup Relations." In *Improving Life at Work,* ed. J. R. Hackman and J. L. Suttle. Santa Monica, CA: Goodyear Publishing, 1977.

Brett, Jerome M., and Tetsushi Okumura. "Inter- and Intracultural Negotiation: U.S. and Japanese Negotiators." *Academy of Management Journal* 41 (1998), pp. 138–52.

Chen, Chao C.; Chen Xiao-Ping; and James R. Meindl. "How Can Cooperation Be Fostered? The Cultural Effects of Individualism-Collectivism." *Academy of Management Review* 23 (1998), pp. 285–304.

Copeland, L., and L. Griggs. *Going International.* New York: Random House, 1985.

Dalton, D. R., and W. D. Todor. "Unanticipated Consequences of Union-Management Cooperation: An Interrupted Time Series Analysis." *Journal of Applied Behavioral Science* 20, no. 3 (1984), pp. 253–64.

Fedor, Kenneth J., and William B. Werther, Jr. "The Fourth Dimension: Creating Culturally Responsive International Alliances." *Organizational Dynamics,* Autumn 1996, pp. 39–53.

Finkel, Lee M., and Harry Kaminsky. "Teaching Managers to Mediate Win-Win Solutions." *Employment Relations Today,* Spring 1991, pp. 71–78.

Fisher, R., and W. Ury. *Getting to Yes: Negotiating Agreement without Giving In.* Boston: Houghton Mifflin, 1981.

Gercik, P. E., *On Track with the Japanese.* New York: Kodansha International, 1992.

Gibson, Cristina B. "Do They Do What They Believe They Can? Group Efficacy and Group Effectiveness across Tasks and Cultures." *Academy of Management Journal* 42 (1999), pp. 138–52.

Hall, E. T., *The Hidden Dimension.* Garden City, NY: Doubleday & Company, 1966.

_____. *The Silent Language.* Garden City, NY: Doubleday & Company, 1959.

Harris, P. R., and R. T. Moran. *Managing Cultural Differences,* 2nd ed. Houston, TX: Gulf Publishing, 1987.

Kabanoff, Boris. "Analyzing Organizational Conflict Using a Model Based on Structural Role Theory." *Human Relations,* November 1988, pp. 841–70.

Lentz, S. S. "The Labor Model for Mediation and Its Application to the Resolution of Environmental Disputes." *Journal of Applied Behavioral Science* 22, no. 2 (1986), pp. 127–40.

Lewicki, R. J., *Negotiations,* 2nd ed. New York, NY: McGraw-Hill/Irwin, 2000.

Lewicki, Roy J.: Stephen E. Weiss; David Lewin. "Models of Conflict, Negotiation, and Third Party Intervention: A Review and Synthesis." *Journal of Organizational Behavior,* May 1992, pp. 209–52.

Pondy, Louis, R. "Overview of Organizational Conflict: Concepts and Models by Louis R. Pondy; Reflections on Organizational Conflict." *Journal of Organizational Behavior,* May 1992, pp. 255–61.

Saavedra, Richard; P. Christopher Earley; Linn Van Dyne. "Complex Interdependence in Task-Performing Groups." *Journal of Applied Psychology,* February 1993, pp. 61–72.

Schopler, J. H. "Interorganizational Groups: Origins, Structure, and Outcomes." *Academy of Management Review* 12, no. 4 (1987), pp. 702–13.

Sheppard, Blair H. "Conflict Research as Schizophrenia: The Many Faces of Organizational Conflict." *Journal of Organizational Behavior,* May 1992, pp. 325–34.

Smith, K. K. "An Intergroup Perspective on Individual Behavior." In *Perspectives on Behavior in Organizations,* ed. J. R. Hackman, E. E. Lawler, and L. W. Porter. New York: McGraw-Hill, 1977.

Smith, Kenwyn K.; Valerie M. Simmons; Terri B. Thames. "'Fix the Women': An Intervention into an Organizational Conflict Based on Parallel Process Thinking." *Journal of Applied Behavioral Science,* 1989, pp. 11–29.

Stephens, Gregory K., and Charles R. Greer. "Doing Business in Mexico: Understanding Cultural Differences." *Organizational Dynamics,* Summer 1995, pp. 39–55.

Walton, R. E. "Third-Party Roles in Interdepartmental Conflict." *Industrial Relations* 7 (1967), pp. 24–43.

Yeung, Irene Y. M., and Rosalie L. Tung. "Achieving Business Success in Confucian Societies: The Importance of Guanxi (Connections)." *Organizational Dynamics,* Autumn 1996, pp. 54–66.

Initiating Change

Change

It's not that the business environment is changing. Change is the business environment. And it's not that every company is undergoing change. Change has overtaken every company. Creating change, managing it, mastering it, and surviving it is the agenda for anyone in business who aims to make a difference.

Even change has changed. The idea of "change programs" is mocked as "flavor-of-the-month" corporate faddism. "If you come in and announce, 'Here's the next change program,' you're dead," says U.S. West's Bob Knowling, a seasoned change agent. "You've just painted a target on your chest."

Instead of an external program, change today is intrinsic to business, an integral expression of how any successful business operates. It has escaped the narrow confines of human resources—or any other department or function—and become an issue of personal responsibility.

You can find people who make change today throughout the organization. They are change agents—but only as a way of working, not as a discrete job. They have real jobs, real work—and driving change is built into how they do their jobs. Creating change is a skill. But getting things done and moving the business is the passion.

SOURCE: Charles Fishman, "Change," *Fast Company*, April–May 1997.

"People resist change for a *reason,* and a manager's task is to try to identify those reasons and, where possible, to plan the change so as to reduce the negative effects and to correct misperceptions."

This chapter deals with the general topic of organizational change, discussing the issues related to identifying the need for change, various approaches to the issues, and specific methods and techniques designed to implement change in an organization. The chapter also provides an overview of the entire book by referring to the various perspectives and concepts presented in the previous chapters as they prove to be relevant to the issue of change.

How Do You Know When Change Is Needed?

People usually decide to make a change when things are not going the way they would like. From the perspective of a manager, the need for change usually occurs when there is a problem related to *productivity, satisfaction,* and/or *development* in the system. It may be that output has fallen below expected levels, that an atmosphere of discouragement has emerged, that clients are protesting slow service, that people in the system are not learning and developing needed skills and abilities, or some combination of these. Even when the need for change is identified or is being driven from above, too often managers close their eyes and hope that the pressure for it will go away, resulting in managers becoming the passive victims of the change rather than masters of it. We assume that as managers you will want to lead change rather than be paralyzed by it.

This chapter provides concepts and tools to help you assume a more activist stance. Unfortunately, it is exceedingly difficult to manage change in order to produce desired results. Most people, groups, and organizations have remarkable resiliency and, like the toy rubber punching clown, tend to return to the starting point as soon as the pressure is off. Furthermore, because of the interdependence of subsystems, a change in one place often pops up unexpectedly elsewhere, as shown in Chapter 2. It is not surprising that many people who have launched change projects give up in frustration and wonder why they did not "leave well enough alone."

> We trained hard—but it seemed that every time we were beginning to form up into teams, we would be reorganized. I was to learn that later in life we tend to meet any new situation by reorganizing, and a wonderful method it can be for creating the illusion of progress while producing confusion, inefficiency, and demoralization.
>
> Petronious Arbiter
> 66 AD

As a member of an organization, it is not easy to change something in a desired direction without (1) eventual reversion to the previous state, (2) consequences somewhere in the organization that you did not anticipate, or (3) negative outcomes cropping up that you did not intend.[1]

Throughout the book, problems with change at different levels of the organization have been *implicit* in the analytical tools presented. For example, the social system conceptual scheme, indicating connections between consequences of the emergent system and alterations in the required system or background factors, points toward various focal points for change efforts.

We turn now to an *explicit* overview of the strategy for initiating and managing change. No single chapter, book, or course can make you an expert on managing change. We look at how changes, even those aimed at technical processes, often create positive or negative consequences for the people in the organization. Because it takes people to perform the internal transformation processes of the organization, their reactions to changes are of great interest. We offer guidelines on changing behavior in ways that produce the least resistance and greatest chance of

Old, Top-Down Change Model Not Working

Most leadership strategies are doomed to failure from the outset. As people have been noting for years, the majority of strategic initiatives that are driven from the top are marginally effective—at best. Corporate reorganizations are even more common than new strategies, but how many reorganizations actually produce companies that are dramatically more effective than they were before? Throw in mergers and acquisitions: Look at all of those that have failed. The traditional model of change—change that is led from the top—has a less-than-impressive track record.

SOURCE: "Old Top-Down Change Model Not Working," *Fast Company*, May 1999.

How to Deal with Changes Imposed on You from Above

- Diagnose the company/unit's competitive position; are the changes driven by current or anticipated competition?
- If so, how do the proposed changes try to address the external problem?
- Ask your manager, and anyone else who might know, what the rationale is for the changes. Listen carefully rather than arguing with answers you don't like.
- What skills will be needed to be effective when the changes are implemented? Where you have relevant skills, make them visible. Where you do not, decide what you could learn that might make you more valuable—to your current (or future!) employer.
- Think about how to prepare yourself for unanticipated problems that could arise from the change. Work to head off the problems or be ready to jump in if they bring a crisis.
- Try not to get paralyzed; stay open to learning and don't hope to become invisible. Continue to do your current job enthusiastically.

If You Need a Crisis, Invent One

"Organizations don't change until external catastrophes bring them near the edge of annihilation. This is unfortunate, because at that point, they are usually low on cash resources and have cynical, demoralized personnel."

"The secret of successful change," explains [Symmetrix, Inc., chairman George B.] Bennett, "seems to be to create self-inflicted catastrophes so as not to have the threat imposed externally. These can usually be created by setting aggressive, external threat-based goals and then demanding that they be attained in aggressively short time-frames."

SOURCE: Andrew K. Sanoval Strausz, "Reinventing America," *Business Week*, December 1993.

implementation and continuation. We try to give you a sense of the various points at which a manager can intervene to accomplish goals, the variety of tools available for making desired changes, tools appropriate for solving various kinds of problems, and where in the organization they should be applied.

Why Shake-Ups Work for Some, Not for Others

Laying off workers is supposed to improve profits and cut costs. But many companies that slash furiously still perform poorly—and can't figure out why.

A new study by Wyatt Co. sheds light on this persistent corporate paradox by explaining why downsizing succeeds at some companies but fails at many others. . . . The study also offers some of the first concrete evidence that management behavior during cutbacks—such as the way employees are treated—can affect a company's financial performance.

RESTRUCTURING RIGHT

These practices were rated among the most effective in helping businesses attain their restructuring goals, according to a Wyatt Co. survey.

Practice	% Terming It "Very Effective"	% Who Used It
Creating restructuring project teams	64	56
Small-group meetings with employees	63	65
Involving employees on task forces	60	60
One-on-one counseling on early retirement	52	63
Briefings for managers and supervisors	51	74
Eliminating low-value work	51	58
Conducting team-building activities	45	61
Total-quality-management initiatives	41	68
Developing a restructuring communications strategy	41	63

SOURCE: Gilbert Fuchsberg. Reprinted by permission of *The Wall Street Journal,* © October 1, 1993, Dow Jones & Company, Inc. All Rights Reserved Worldwide.

Where to Start

One way to think about starting points for change is implicit in the organization of this book—by the numbers of people involved. Change may be aimed at the individual, pair, small group, two or more groups, the total organization, or at leaders themselves. The target for change efforts will depend upon a number of factors.

1. Where is the tension in the system?
2. How interconnected is the unit having the problem with other organizational units?
3. To what extent does the organization operation as a hierarchy?
4. Where in the system is there the most readiness for change?

Where Is the Tension?

It is often easier to get people to change when they are experiencing a moderate amount of discomfort. Those who are content with the way things are will resist changes that might increase tension; those who are suffering a great deal sometimes cling to the status quo because it is the only certainty they can identify. In classroom task groups, for example, you may have noticed that those individuals who are satisfied with the grades they are receiving resist efforts to change the way the group makes decisions, allocates work, and so on. At the other extreme, perhaps surprisingly, members who are very upset with their performance also may resist change. They often seem to freeze in unproductive patterns, repeating the same fruitless behavior, even though it does not help. A poor performer may continue to miss many classes or not prepare for discussions, even though it is clear from outside that change would be helpful. Have you ever seen someone who is worried about failing a math course continue to avoid doing practice problems? Great tension can create as much resistance to change as lack of it does. Thus, the system with the greatest need or the greatest pain is not always most receptive to change efforts. In general, those who are experiencing moderate discomfort and tension are most amenable to change.[2] But without discomfort of some kind, the sense of being on some kind of "burning platform," there will be no readiness. The tension can then serve as an impetus for change rather than as a signal for defensiveness.

How Interconnected Is the Problem Unit with Other Organizational Units?

Although ultimately all parts of an organization are interrelated, some units are relatively independent compared to others.

As you remember from Chapter 13, units in an organization might have only pooled interdependence, where they are connected only by being part of the same organization; serial interdependence, where one unit's work depends on receiving work from another; or reciprocal interdependence, where units need one another to do each one's work. The less "coupled" or linked units are to one another, as in pooled interdependence, the easier it will be to make changes without regard to consequences for other parts of the organization. For example, a research and development laboratory located miles away from the main offices and plant of a manufacturing company can probably change rules on dress and working hours more easily and with fewer repercussions than could the assembly department at the plant. When an organizational unit is relatively independent because of location, power, structure, or task, changes are easier to implement. Thus, The greater the autonomy of an organizational subsystem, the more readily can changes be implemented and the less will changes there cause problems for the rest of the organization.[3]

To What Extent Does the Organization Operate as a Hierarchy?

In strongly hierarchical organizations where control tends to be tight and top-down, changes that do not have the support of those at the top of the organization are likely to be short-lived. While problems requiring change may be showing up only at lower levels of the organization, changes below will have effects on higher levels, so the support of those with the formal legitimate power must be acquired. It is disheartening and a waste of time to initiate change efforts that are squashed just as they begin to work because higher-ups are made uncomfortable by them. The more hierarchical the organization, the higher the change efforts have to be aimed, or legitimized. In turn, the greater the autonomy of the subunit, the less important will be support from higher levels in the organization.[4] We should note, however, this does not imply that change in nonhierarchical organizations is necessarily *easier* to bring about; support from the top is almost always helpful. When those who have to change receive clear, unambiguous messages from the top about the reasons for and inevitability of change, they are more likely to go along with it.[5] Clear support reduces the tension that arises from ambiguity or lack of clarity. And top-level enthusiasm about the vision of the exciting way things will be when the change is implemented can carry people past the rough spots in getting there. This does not mean, however, that change automatically works best when driven from the top. Beer, Eisenstadt, and Spector[6] found that major change programs were more likely to succeed when they began as experiments in peripheral areas of the organization

Vision

MANAGERIAL BULLETIN

Walk the Talk, Talk the Talk, and Change Is Still Tough

One longtime middle manager . . . listens to [Sears CEO Brennan's] message of change, then watches as her boss spends his time golfing and politicking . . .

The problem is, we often want change, but not if it hurts . . .

Change takes time—a long time at big companies. Change also requires a well articulated vision,

something more than the desire for profit. And a network of compensation systems, human resource policies, and, most important, sound business plans to support the vision.

SOURCE: Keith H. Hammonds, "Why Big Companies Are So Tough to Change," *Business Week,* June 17, 1991.

than when top management decreed their importance. Many change efforts are designed to free those at lower levels to take initiative and come up with ideas for change. This is increasingly the way to get greater innovation. At every level there are likely to be people with knowledge of better ways to do things, and empowering them—with appropriate support as needed—accelerates change.

Where Is the Most Readiness and Receptivity to Change?

From one point of view, starting points are not so important, because a change in any one aspect of the organization is likely to affect other possible starting points anyway. For example, say you are trying to get Bill, who is uncooperative, to make a greater work contribution. The difficulties are caused by his attitude toward the individually oriented reward system and your controlling leadership style. You can begin trying to change his attitude by having conferences with him to show him the consequences of his negative feelings. But as soon as he begins to respond, your leadership style will be affected, and the reward system will somehow have to respond to his new behavior. Conversely, if you start by changing the reward system to encourage his cooperation more directly, his attitudes are likely to change accordingly, and you will be able to lead in a different, perhaps less controlling way. Nevertheless, it is worth thinking through the questions of *leverage:* Where would a change effort yield maximum payoff for the effort? As a manager it is useful to follow the principles of judo; rather than going against the resistance, go with it, so a small amount of effort results in a relatively large amount of movement.

To initiate change, first try to determine where there is already inclination for movement in the desired direction and then start with the aspect of the problem that is least likely to be directly resisted.[7] In the preceding example, it may well be easier to start with changing the reward system in a way that encourages and pays off for cooperation than to lecture at Bill, who already feels angry.

In analyzing the point of greatest leverage, it can be helpful to look at the functionality or dysfunctionality to the system of the behavior in question and the degree to which it is subject to change. The possible combinations are represented in Figure 14–1.

Resistance to Change

People do not necessarily resist change. We need only note how quickly people accepted the Internet, which has changed shopping and communication patterns a

MANAGERIAL BULLETIN

American Express Chairman Golub Has Unusual View of Timing of Cutbacks

"You can either cut costs when there is a clear and present danger or you can do it when people feel good about the way things are going," Mr. Golub asserted. "But it's much harder when you're in trouble: the world is looking at you, and you don't have much time."

When he was asked when was the best time to cut costs, he replied, "always . . . Change will never be easier than it is right now . . ." He believes that change makes change possible: "An organization's capacity to change increases as you succeed."

SOURCE: G. Bruce Knecht, "American Express Chairman Golub Has Unusual View of Timing of Cutbacks," *The Wall Street Journal,* October 6, 1994, p. B10.

MANAGERIAL BULLETIN

Embrace Resisters

"Just because someone resists you doesn't mean you're right and they're wrong . . . There's often information in resistance. People get so involved in their change efforts, when they encounter resistance, they immediately make the other people the problem."

SOURCE: Mark Maletz, as quoted in Charles Fishman, "Change," *Fast Company,* April–May 1997.

FIGURE 14–1   *A Way of Diagnosing Where to Attempt Change*

	Functional	Dysfunctional
Easily Subject to Change	A. Support existing behavior	C. Concentrate efforts
Not Easily Subject to Change	B. Protect the behavior	D. Box off the person or problem

SOURCE: From a lecture presented by Steven J. Ruma, June 1971. Bethel, Maine.

great deal, to realize that people in fact often embrace change. The issue is what people *perceive* to be the effect of change. People resist change when they perceive the consequences as negative. While individuals will differ in how ready they are to anticipate negative consequences, and even though their reasons may appear illogical or even wrong to an outsider, people are not automatically resistant to change. People resist change for a *reason,* and a manager's task is to try to identify those reasons and, where possible, to plan the change so as to reduce or eliminate the negative effects and to correct misperceptions. Let us now examine some common reasons why people resist change and what a manager might do to reduce the negative consequences—and even enhance the positive consequences.

Jack Welch's Lessons about Change

Change has no constituency. People like the status quo . . . When you start changing things, the good old days look better and better.

You've got to be prepared for massive resistance.

Incremental change doesn't work very well in the type of transformation GE has gone through. If your change isn't big enough, revolutionary enough, the bureaucracy can beat you. When you get leaders who confuse popularity with leadership, who just nibble away at things, nothing changes. . . .

Another big lesson: You've got to be hard to be soft. You have to demonstrate the ability to make the hard, tough decisions—closing plants, divesting, delayering—if you want to have any credibility when you try to promote soft values. We reduced employment and cut the bureaucracy and picked up some unpleasant nicknames, but when we spoke of soft values—things like candor, fairness, facing reality—people listened.

If you've got a fat organization, soft values won't get you very far. . . .

Every organization needs values, but a lean organization needs them even more. When you strip away the support systems of staffs and layers, people need to change their habits and expectations or else the stress will just overwhelm them. We're all working harder and faster. But unless we're also having more fun, the transformation doesn't work. Values are what enable people to guide themselves through that kind of change.

To create change, direct, personal, two-way communication is what seems to make the difference: exposing people—without the protection of title or position—to ideas from everywhere, judging ideas on their merits. You've got to be out in front of crowds, repeating yourself over and over again, never changing your message no matter how much it bores you. You need an overarching message, something big but simple and understandable. Whatever it is, every idea you present must be something you could get across easily at a cocktail party with strangers. If only aficionados of your industry can understand what you're saying, you've blown it.

SOURCE: "Jack Welch's Lessons for Success," *Fortune*, January 25, 1993, excerpted from *Control Your Destiny or Someone Else Will*, by Noel M. Tichy and Stratford Sherman. Copyright © 1993 by Noel M. Tichy and Stratford Sherman. Used by permission of Doubleday, a division of Bantam Doubleday Dell Publishing Group, Inc.

Change May Seem Threatening

Change usually means moving from the known to the unknown, from relative certainty to relative uncertainty, from the familiar to the unfamiliar. Obviously, if you like the status quo, you will not feel any desire to leave it. But often, even when you are not all that happy with things as they are, you feel some resistance to giving them up, in part because of uncertainty that the change will be an improvement. Furthermore, if you had a hand in building or creating the present situation—which might include the physical setting in which you live or work, the relationships that have grown, the routines and procedures for work, and so on—you would be hard put to give it up easily. Even a long-awaited promotion means a change, which in turn means giving something up in order to move on. In short, *change requires letting go of the past and present in order to move on into the future.*

A particular proposed change may or may not be perceived by an individual as threatening. The perception is a unique product of that person's self-concept and the situation he or she faces. What looks like an exciting opportunity to you may look more like a loss of everything important to the person next to you. Many managers seem to overlook that simple idea and are puzzled by the fact that not all their employees instantly perceive the merits of a change they (the managers) have thought through for some time and in some detail. Trying something new may feel risky; one is more willing to take a risk when perceived threat is low. While change always involves some degree of risk, a manager's attention to fears of the unknown can reduce the degree of potential threat that others may attribute to the change.

Riots on the Menu at [British] Private Prison That Left Out Chips [French Fries]

Staff . . . had been trying to cultivate a taste for finer cuisine among inmates. The prison's in-house professional caterers offered coq au vin, served with steamed vegetables. They served cod in parsley sauce with new potatoes. . . .

[A] prisoner said senior prison managers repeatedly warned cooks to stop serving "fancy food." He said the final straw was the decision to serve steak with new potatoes and carrots instead of chips.

More than 50 prisoners staged a sit-in protest. Their anger was assuaged only when David Brooke, the prison director, ordered a fry-up of bacon, chips, and beans . . .

SOURCE: Ian Burrell, *The Sunday Times of London,* August 29, 1993.

And my father . . . often told of an old parishioner of his who, in the course of a meeting, rose to his feet and declared, "Oh, no. Mr. Reid. We've tried change, and we know it doesn't work."

Alastair Reid
"Reflections" (Scotland)
New Yorker, October 5, 1981

Finally, change is sometimes resisted just because the ideas are new and people haven't had a chance to get used to them or don't fully understand their implications. Often the person initiating change has been working on the issues for a long time and assumes that everyone else understands them equally well; the initiator's early struggles to accept the need for the changes and the time it took to become familiar with the issues may long be forgotten when a "plan" is presented to others for the first time. In such cases, information, education, and time alone can often take care of the resistance. That is why effective change managers "plant seeds" early, to allow ideas to germinate and become familiar.[8]

It's an odd paradox. People want to grow, but they often resist some of the very changes that will enable them to grow. Organizations must develop, but they seem to fight continuous battles within themselves—often dragging others who did not initiate the change kicking and screaming into the future, a future that may even be an improvement over the past. The resistance can come from anywhere in the organization, above, below or laterally.

But is all that kicking and screaming necessary? Perhaps you can expect some resistance to change whenever it occurs, but there are ways to minimize it. Common to all of these is that they increase the degree to which people feel *control* over the events that affect them. To the extent that one has a sense of control over a situation, it will be perceived as less threatening.

Change Can Mean Direct Loss

It is safe to assume that anyone will resist change who thinks that the changes will make him or her look bad or lose power, income, status, privileges, conveniences, friends, and the like. For example, there is inevitable awkwardness in learning new skills, and resistance may just reflect anticipated embarrassment at having to go through learning something new. In such cases, it is important to provide the necessary training and emotional support for any awkwardness while learning.

MANAGERIAL BULLETIN

The President Has a Will—but No Way

In 1992, when Minoru Makihara became president of Mitsubishi Corp., Japan's powerful trading company and flagship of the nation's biggest *keiretsu,* observers thought the group was ready for serious change. . . .

The remaking of the Mitsubishi *keiretsu* never happened. Today, many of its key companies are deeply troubled. They need to plunge into radical restructuring, place a greater emphasis on profits, and put an end to the cross-subsidies that drain the resources of member companies. While this has been obvious for years, only now are Mitsubishi's managers showing the least sign they're ready for action. Somehow, there has been a serious disconnect between Makihara's vision and what he has been able to achieve.

Western Edge

His dilemma perfectly represents the plight of Japan's top bosses. In terms of brainpower, experience, and an understanding of world markets, managers such as Makihara, Taizo Nishimuro of Toshiba Corp., and Hiroshi Okuda of Toyota Motor Corp. are among the best corporate chiefs on the planet. But they have been cruelly misplaced in a Japan that cannot tolerate the unemployment and social upheaval that wholesale restructuring would entail. And because Japanese corporate culture places so much stress on building consensus and saving face, even world-class bosses often struggle vainly to impose their visions on the organizations they theoretically run.

SOURCE: Brian Brenner, "Commentary: The President Has a Will but No Way," *Business Week,* March 15, 1999.

Another example is those who perceive, correctly or not, that changes will cause them to become less central or influential. Except for those few people who may be feeling overburdened by power and responsibility, most people will not welcome changes that reduce their clout, even though the change might be good for the organization. It is hard to be selfless when one's own influence is at stake.

In these situations, negotiations with those affected may be necessary, with concessions made wherever possible. Face-saving devices may have to be invented for those whose status or clout cannot be preserved. Many organizations find it easier to preserve people's titles, salaries, or other symbols of status than to add insult to injury by removing all traces of former influence. Of course this sometimes gives the wrong message to others, who assume that nothing has changed, but with care it may be possible to preserve dignity while significantly altering degree of influence.

"... I LOVE PROGRESS, BUT I HATE CHANGE!"
From a letter to the president of Amherst College from an alumnus, on whether to allow women to join fraternities.

Amherst Alumni Bulletin
June 1980

Change Can Disrupt the Social System

Managers attempting change sometimes forget that there are emergent *social* systems, which will also be affected by even "pure" technological changes or other alterations in the required system. A new set of machines for producing a product with less manual labor may force new social groupings, violating existing friendships and relationships. This can create resistance aimed at the machinery or at the management, apparently irrationally, since physical "working conditions" are improved. Those involved may seem to be "unappreciative" when what is troubling them is their discomfort at altered relationships. Often those affected do not even consciously realize the source of their resistance or may feel embarrassed to state it directly.

Furthermore, even if a change is accepted by those directly affected, one must not overlook those who may be affected indirectly, those elsewhere in the system who are interdependent with the changed unit.

> A large corporation decided that it would have increasing problems if junior managers were not given more developmental training by their supervisors. The president of the company made an impassioned speech to all executives, explaining how important long-term development of subordinates was to the company. Even those executives, however, who were very positive about training subordinates soon found out that their annual bonuses depended only on the quarterly profitability of their units. Since developing subordinates required allowing them latitude to make mistakes that could affect short-term profits, all such activities were soon given mere lip service. Not until the executive bonus system was revised to reward developmental activities along with profits did serious developmental activities begin.
>
> Similarly, in one of the first management training programs, International Harvester developed an excellent human relations program for supervisors; by its completion supervisor attitudes were measurably different. When they got back on the jobs, however, many of their bosses ridiculed their learnings, because the more considerate behavior taught in the program violated the organization's norms for leaders. Within six months not only had the new behavior disappeared but supervisors were less satisfied and effective than before the training.

This lesson has had to be learned and relearned: To produce lasting changes, related subsystems must also be altered to support the initial changes.[9] Subsystems that will be most affected by changes and/or have the most power over the changing subsystem require attention, also. Using stakeholder analysis (see Managerial Tools and Figure 14–2 on pp. 358 and 359) can help identify related subsystems; others can be pinpointed by a review of background factors and the required system.

Although many situations, such as certain kinds of reengineering involving dramatic changes in organizational processes supported by information technology,[10] may not allow for the involvement of those expected to change in determining or shaping the change, it is well established that changes requiring the cooperation of those being changed are most likely to succeed when they are allowed to participate in the change process.

In general, The most effective way to ensure that change is implemented with minimal resistance is to involve those affected by it in determining what it should be.[11] Even the collection of data is best done in collaboration with those who will be affected by the changes. If those affected are involved in diagnosis of the data and formulation of proposed solutions, successful implementation is more likely. Even the lowest-level workers may have important contributions to make to solve an organizational problem of which they are a part; an elegant solution imposed from above but not "owned" or accepted is not so elegant after all. The world's wastebaskets are filled with brilliant but unused recommendations.

There are many situations, however, where full participation is not possible or appropriate. If, for example, the problem is with employees who are incapable of improving their own performance even after training and they must inevitably be replaced, participation is probably not very appropriate, even though it might be desirable from the employee's point of view. When the necessary changes involve an opposing group(s) or individual(s) already committed to using illegitimate power to resist the changes, offer of involvement probably will be perceived as weakness and

FIGURE 14–2   *Stakeholder Analysis Diagram for Eliminating Grades in Courses Outside Majors*

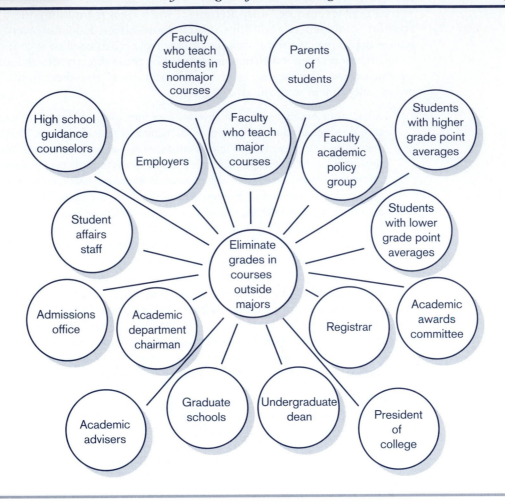

taken advantage of or as a trick and resented.[12] As suggested in earlier chapters, Participation and collaboration call for some basic level of trust in order to work; caution, distance, and legalistic negotiations are more appropriate when there is very low trust and/or high suspicion.[13] Can you think of other situations where participation of those affected by the change would not be effective in achieving implementation?

Perhaps the first factor to remember in beginning change efforts is that Diagnosis should precede action.[14] This point sounds obvious but is nonetheless important. Because those in managerial positions are often harassed and results oriented, they sometimes let impatience push them toward attempting solutions before the problem is clear. By now you have analyzed many problems where there were multiple, often hidden, causes for dysfunctional behavior. In organizations, as in life, there is seldom one simple, obvious cause for human problems. Inevitably some way of collecting data about the dimensions of the problem requiring change is necessary. Whether by interview, observation, questionnaire, or analysis of records, data on the social system aspects of the problem should be gathered and analyzed before solutions are determined. This is also a central tenet of the quality movement, too often ignored.

Finally, one more related factor in beginning a change effort is Plans ought to be tentative and subject to alteration as feedback is received.[15] Working out every detail of a change in advance, then plowing ahead regardless of responses along the way, is

Stakeholder Analysis

A very useful tool for assessing interdependence and planning for the effect of a change on all affected subsystems is called *stakeholder analysis.* For any change attempt, there will be a number of parties (individuals, groups, or organizations) who have a stake in the outcome. Often the number of stakeholders is far greater than is at first apparent; the manager of a regional office in a federal agency was astounded when, using this tool, she identified 236 stakeholders on a key issue she was trying to resolve. As an aid to visualizing the concept, start by placing a brief label for the change in the center of a blank page, and draw a circle around it. Then, one at a time, add spokes linked to each possible stakeholder. (See example in Figure 14–2 using a proposal to eliminate grades in courses outside majors.)

Once all the possible stakeholders are identified, then go back and try to determine the following for each:

- What exactly are their stakes in the issue?
- What are their needs/desires in relation to the issue?
- What are their resources in relation to the issue? Information? Allies? Funds or supplies?

- Exactly how will they be affected by the change? Finances? Relationships with others? Status? Influence? Reputation?
- Is their cooperation/goodwill necessary, desirable, or unimportant?

Having done this kind of analysis for each stakeholder, do the same for yourself. What do you bring to the issue? Then prioritize those stakeholders most necessary for your success. Your attention should first be directed to figuring out what you can offer them from your resources that would fit with their needs or desires, in return for whatever you need from them. Before initiating action, however, try to trace through *all* the possible implications for all the stakeholders and plan accordingly. This can be tedious, but it saves a great deal of aggravation later. Too many good change ideas have been sunk because the well-intentioned person driving change did not anticipate who would be affected and how to deal with them.

While this kind of diagnosis does not tell you what to do, it helps to prevent glaring omissions and unanticipated consequences. There are enough unpleasant surprises in organizational life without those you create for yourself by poor diagnosis and planning!

a fairly good recipe for creating unnecessary resistance. Most people do not like to feel powerless, overwhelmed, and ignored; if their legitimate objections and observations are belittled because they do not fit the master plan you have developed, they are unlikely to help make the changes successful. Again, this sounds obvious; but people with a vision, as you will be when you want to change something, often treat every negative reaction as a nuisance, rather than as helpful data necessary for achieving a *workable* plan. In this sense you should *welcome* resisters because they are bringing important information you need to be effective. You might not want to assemble them all in the same room, since they might reinforce one another, but you certainly can benefit from their reactions as a way to reduce some of your blind spots and to make necessary modifications in your plans. The process itself also tends to help increase needed cooperation.

The Forms Resistance Can Take

Resistance does not always show up as direct defiance or refusal to go along. In some ways, that is the easiest form to deal with, because it is on the surface and informs you as to what you have to do to gain acceptance. If acceptance by resisters isn't possible after carefully listening to them, then finding ways to work around them becomes the challenge. It is a visible challenge, however, and can sometimes just be allowed expression without stopping the change process.

How Ford.com Gets in Gear

Thor Ibsen Offers Insight on Running an Internet Initiative within a Large Organization

In 1997, Thor Ibsen became Ford's first full-time Internet sales-and-marketing strategist. Since then, he's built a 100-member team and established ford.com as one of the auto industry's most progressive Web sites. "We are constantly thinking about how to combine the best of both worlds—the flexibility of the Net and the power of Ford Motor Co.," Ibsen says. *Fast Company* asked for his advice on running an Internet initiative within a large organization.

Balance Outsiders with Insiders

In putting together Ford's Internet team, Ibsen made sure it included both Net-savvy outsiders and well-connected Ford insiders. The outsiders would push the team toward technology solutions and new business models. The insiders, meanwhile, would give the team credibility within Ford and would help it work efficiently within the company's structure. "You've got to allow institutional knowledge into the team, and let people develop familiarity with the Net as they go," Ibsen says. "The results are incredible."

Hire Only People Who Are Comfortable with Change

When hiring inside Ford, Ibsen and his colleagues look for candidates who are risk takers and have a vision for change. "There are some questions that are strong signals to us in job interviews," says Jeff Liedel, 33, the team's director of technology at the eConsumer Group. "Things like, 'Who am I going to report to?' or 'Can I see an org chart?' or 'What is my job description?' We don't know the answers. Everyone here reports to everyone else."

Don't Get Busted by Budgets

Ibsen wants his group to have all the freedom it takes to develop new Web applications as the market demands. Working with Kim Plummer, 29, the Consumer Connect Group's finance manager, he has established a rolling budget plan for his group, which means that although he doesn't have access to an infinite sum of money, he can decide throughout the year how he wants to spend the resources that he does have. "The worst thing I could do is have these guys manage against artificial restrictions," Plummer says. "There's no reason that they should have to think on an annual cycle, because that's not the way the Internet works."

Avoid Battles over Status

Ibsen points out that at any company, when two executives who are close in status discuss an initiative, it often devolves into a face-off. "Each one tries to show that he is the sheriff, and nothing gets done," he says. "We don't like face-offs. So we send a less-senior person who's not in the running to be sheriff." It's not unusual for a member of Ibsen's group to present a new idea to a Ford executive who is four steps up the hierarchy. "I might set someone up with a phone call saying this guy's an expert, and he's going to make his case. It gets the red tape out of the way, and that person can really make progress because he or she won't threaten anyone's status."

Campaign at Every Level

Ibsen acknowledges that high-level backers are important to any corporate Internet group. But, he says, "If you don't get support from the working lieutenants and line managers, you won't be able to deliver on your projects, and then your top-level support will quickly vaporize." Ibsen and his colleagues spend as much time getting buy-in from mid-level managers as they do courting senior VPs and divisional chiefs. "We have to hit people at all levels to make change happen here," he says.

SOURCE: Scott Kirsner, "How Ford.com Gets in Gear," *Fast Company*, January/February 2000, p. 128.

More difficult is the kind of resistance that takes on disguises. Sometimes it is just passive, not arguing but foot-dragging and taking forever to respond. "We're working on that" becomes a way to stall and can be hard to counteract without close working contact and a large infusion of energy and resources.

Where the Cadre Sets the Pattern; At AT&T Credit, Organizational Snarls Were Tackled by the Rank and File

AT&T Credit is in turmoil . . . The unit, with $2.5 billion in assets and 300,000 customer accounts, has been re-jiggering job titles, responsibilities, and bonus plans. . . .

Yet the staff is energetic rather than panicked. One reason: Every aspect of the new structure, from the description of the president's job to the decor, was designed by the workers.

"These people rebuilt this company from the ground up and that gives them a sense of ownership." . . .

AT&T Credit's route to this system proves that . . . the Japanese process of bottom-up consensus management can apparently work in at least one American corporate culture.

SOURCE: Claudia H. Deutsch, *New York Times,* June 30, 1991.

Another more camouflaged form of resistance takes on the language and appearance of the change, but nothing really happens. People adopt the required jargon, mouth the words, and pretend to be enthusiastic, but have merely slapped new labels on old wine (or whine, as the case may be). Managers who do not want to give real voice to those below will talk about participation, empowerment, and team processes endlessly, but still keep all the important decisions from the group. Others will talk about appreciative inquiry, active listening and authenticity, but continue to try to manipulate what they reveal and what they respond to. It is undoubtedly far easier to change vocabulary than actual behavior!

Finally, the most insidious form of resistance is covert sabotage. People really angry and frustrated have been known to deface property, destroy records, provide customers with defective or rotten products—perhaps helped along by subtle mistakes in producing the products—or just "lose" important information or material. Ignore resistance at your own peril, no matter how irritating it is that others do not understand how wonderful you are trying to make organizational life.

The Importance of Power for the Person Desiring Change

To sustain lasting change it is seldom enough to be officially in charge of the person or group that is the object of change. Even a boss giving direct orders cannot guarantee that they will be obeyed, or obeyed in a wholehearted way that makes them work. Many managers have discovered too late that they did not have nearly as much ability to guarantee cooperation as their title and job description seemed to imply. Imagine how much more difficult it is, then, to achieve change when you are in a relatively low power position, either because those you want to change are above you or do not report to you directly, or because, even if they do, you have few resources at your command to force compliance.

Because power is neither guaranteed by formal position (as you recall from Chapter 11) nor prevented by lack of formal authority, it is useful to inventory the sources of power available to you. What information, resources, or support do you command that would be desirable to your change targets? What can you provide for them that would make the need for change more apparent or the problems associated with changing easier to bear? How hard will it be for you to gain access to whatever is needed? Will you be able to proceed with implementation whether or not the person or group resists?

> To do his job well, any CEO must function and please those above him, such as his board, just as he must please those beneath him, or nothing will work. You've got to get consensus from both groups before you act. They're both watching you, and it's essential that you get their tacit approval, for the right reasons. Time spent making sure that what you're doing is well understood makes the chances for success much greater.
>
> Source:
> Steven Weiner
> *The Wall Street Journal,* August 31, 1984

After making a careful diagnosis of the changer's power relative to the change, a fundamental choice can be made. Initial attention can be focused on a vision of the future state desired, or on the problems with the way things are now. Although it is almost always useful to provide an image of the more desirable future, it is probably less necessary to start with that when you are relatively powerful. The greater the change initiator's relative power, the more change can begin with a focus on current problems as opposed to a vision of the future. When dealing with those who can easily refuse to cooperate, it becomes increasingly necessary to work on creating an attractive vision of what might be possible at a future date far enough away to reduce immediate threat.[16] This is the social science version of "catching more flies with honey than with vinegar." Once the vision is created, it is possible to begin to work backward from it, identifying the steps that would be needed to get to that desirable future state and a timetable for implementing each one.

Relative power affects tactics in another way. The lower the power of the change initiator, the more it is necessary to look for allies, carefully building support among those who do control vital resources and those who will be needed to implement the change effectively.[17] Changes that are directly under the control of the change initiator and within his or her job description require less extensive establishment of connections. Even there, however, if the cooperation of subordinates will be needed to make the change work well, efforts to sell them (or allow them enough say to sell themselves) will be necessary.

Inexperienced organizational members often underestimate the possibilities for accomplishing change when they cannot order it. They fail to identify the potential resources they can bring to bear on an issue: information, special services or priority services given to needed allies, recognition and praise, the chance to show others how they can look good to higher-ups by cooperating, potential new relationships, and so forth. You don't have to control others' salaries and promotions to gain cooperation; careful diagnosis of what you can offer and how that matches with what they need or desire will be necessary, however. Being in a lower-power position seldom means a total lack of potential power.

Similarly, it is also important to note that those in high-power positions are not obligated to use coercion every time they want change. Although sheer coercion or threats may be necessary in situations where there is great urgency and other tactics would not be practical, it is foolish to win a battle and lose the war. If the act of coercion causes anger and desire for retaliation, those who have been forced to change may well find ways to sabotage on the next issue or to undermine the changer. Greater power allows for pushing harder and for more explicit change efforts, but Change should always be initiated with the minimum amount of pressure necessary to accomplish the objectives.[18] Because pressure usually breeds counterpressure, its use in excess of what is mandatory just invites problems.

FIGURE 14–3   *Action–Research Cycle*

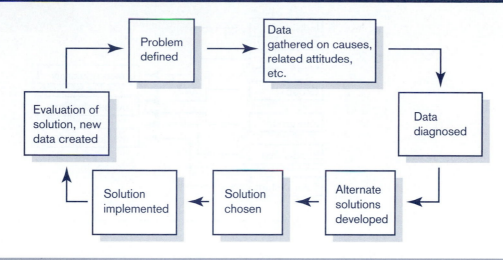

The Action–Research Model

The tentativeness and diagnostic activities called for above suggest that an action–research methodology is most appropriate for a planned change effort. Action–research begins with an identified problem. Data are then gathered to allow a diagnosis, which can produce a tentative solution, which is then implemented with the assumption that it is likely to cause new or unforeseen problems, which will, in turn, need to be evaluated, defined, diagnosed, and so forth. Thus, action–research methods assume a constantly evolving interplay between solutions, results, and new solutions. Figure 14–3 depicts the flow of steps in the model.[19]

This model is a general one applicable to solving any kind of problem in an ongoing organization. Many variations of this kind of problem solving model have been adopted by the quality movement, each using slightly different names or sequences, but all depend on a sensible definition of the problem and the collection of relevant data. To do that, however, requires some preliminary way of thinking about diagnosis, which can help sort out the root causes and interconnections among the complex factors likely to underlie any interesting problem. To help you organize the way you think about change problems, we show how the social system conceptual scheme used throughout the book can provide a useful diagnostic framework for organizational change. We already noted that problems of productivity, satisfaction, or development can occur in any one or more subsystems of the total system (see Figure 14–4).

Diagnostic Aids

Let's examine some procedures for tracing a problem back to its sources. Suppose, for example, a work group is having productivity problems because of insufficient resources. Efforts to improve member relationships might feel good but would probably be to no avail and, in fact, could complicate the problem even further. Or suppose a manager is overloaded with work and cannot keep up with the pressure. It could easily be assumed that the wrong person has been chosen for the job when the problem is the way work is organized. You can probably think of many examples of

FIGURE 14-4 *Change Problems Can Occur in Any Subsystem*

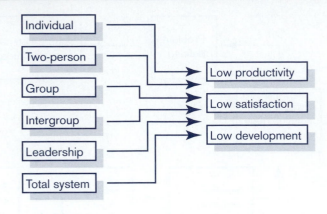

how a misdiagnosis could lead to inappropriate and even destructive consequences. Remember, a symptom can have many possible causes; any physician can attest to the dangers of treating symptoms without knowing the underlying causes. It is the same for a manager who is attempting to make changes intended to eliminate a problem and/or to improve the system; treating the symptom without understanding the problem can easily lead to an amputation when an antibiotic would do.

The social system conceptual scheme provides one useful way of sorting causes of problems into manageable categories. Problems always surface in the emergent system (by definition), but their cause(s) may be in the background factors, required system, *or* emergent system. For example, failure of a team to solve its problems effectively may be due to a lack of proper technical training for the job (background factor), unclear task requirements (required system), or decision-making processes that ignore valuable member contributions (emergent system). One way to approach a diagnosis of a change problem, then, is to sort the factors leading to it into the social system categories used throughout the book—background factors, required system, and emergent system.

In general, these categories should be examined sequentially for establishing a plan of attack. Background factors tend to set limits on both the required and emergent systems. Obviously it is useless to require people to behave in ways that are outside their range of competencies and then expect them to perform adequately. Nor is it sensible to establish output levels for the organization or one of its subunits that demand resources not present in the system and then expect adequate performance. For any organizational function, it is possible to list numerous background factors that place direct constraints upon both the required and emergent systems. What this line of reasoning suggests is that The first point of attack on any problem calling for change is a consideration of the background factors.[20]

If you have established that there are appropriate and adequate resources and that these are combined in ways suited to the organizational tasks, *then* you can move to examine the required and emergent systems with some degree of confidence that therein lies the cause(s) of the problem.

Because emergent behavior is governed by complex factors normally outside the direct control of a manager, strategies aimed at various aspects of the emergent systems tend to be complex, uncertain, and time consuming. Consequently, it makes sense to look next at the required system—at such matters as task definitions, work

What the Experts Forgot to Mention about Team–Based Management

Lauded by business gurus as a time-tested model of team-based management, XEL Communications swears by that now-trendy concept—and still struggles with its complexities every hour of every day.

- Tasks like adding new people get harder, not easier
- Supervisors are sorely missed—but not for the reasons you'd expect
  [Resolving day to day disputes]
- Team building doesn't go neatly from one stage to the next
- Managers need skills no MBA program—or traditional company—will ever teach them:
  Diplomacy
  Not allowing someone else's monkey, or problem, to jump on your back
  Make sure teams don't take too much into their own hands

- Employees, too, need skills they never had before:
  Math and statistical process control
  Assertiveness or ambition; learn a variety of skills and be willing to perform many tasks
- The standard systems for managing people go out the window:
  Need skill-based pay, merit increases based on a combination of team performance and peer reviews, profit-sharing
- A leader doesn't need to be a supervisor
- Teams alter everyone's knowledge about what's going on—which is felt most keenly at the top:
  Give up a measure of control

SOURCE: Excerpted from John Case, *Inc.*, September 1993.

allocation, work patterns and routines, and who reports to whom. A manager is in a position to act directly upon these factors. The required system tends to be the most directly and immediately within the control of management.

Again we remind you of the possible importance of the involvement of those most directly affected by the change effort. Emergent systems can sabotage required systems; people who resent changes in their required work patterns can be very inventive about undermining the objectives of the change. Therefore, even though it is more direct and perhaps easier to change the required system, do not overlook possible consequences in the emergent system.

Furthermore, a direct action at one point in the organization tends to reverberate at other points. For example, it may seem simple enough to redefine an individual's job if the diagnosis calls for that; however, that redefinition might affect a task relationship, thus calling for a realignment of roles. Again there seems to be no way to poke the system at point A without producing some reactions at points B and C.

If you as a manager can determine that you have the appropriate resources (background factors), task definitions (required system), and personal leadership style, then you can more confidently look for the sources of a problem in the emergent system (see Figure 14–5). It is similar to a physician ruling out several diagnoses before arriving at a final one. The importance of such a process of elimination is that strategies for change in the emergent system normally require in-depth data gathering and long-range procedures, and they often generate the greatest resistance. Thus, interventions on the emergent system ought to be undertaken with caution when other options are not appropriate.

While it is impossible to offer definite diagnoses of the causes of emergent human problems out of their unique contexts, Figure 14–6 has illustrative examples of causes of problems often associated with the various-size subsystems. It shows some possible causes of problems within each subsystem with variations for whether the

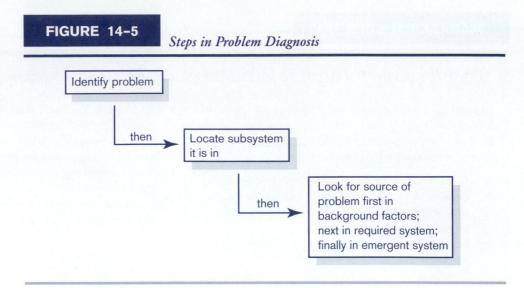

FIGURE 14–5   *Steps in Problem Diagnosis*

cause is in the background factors, required, or emergent system. The examples of causes are meant to indicate possible diagnoses, not instant answers. More important is the process of examining the underlying issues in a systematic way. Here is an example of how the chart might be used:

> A student group is having difficulty in producing high-quality case analyses despite seemingly endless hours of effort. Clearly some change is needed. Looking across Figure 14–6 in the row corresponding to the "group" subsystem, you can see that several possibilities exist: (1) The group may simply lack the intellectual resources to do the work (background factors); (2) the task requirements may not have been adequately explained to the members (required system); or (3) the group may have failed to develop the kinds of working processes that result in good analysis (emergent system). Obviously, all three of these factors may be operating, and each demands a different kind of remedy.

This rough guide to diagnosing the causes of organizational problems can help you focus on where action is needed. How to overcome each difficulty is not always obvious even after it is identified. We turn now to a brief survey of widely used change methods as a way of suggesting the range of approaches developed in the constant struggle by managers to maintain effective organizations.

Methods of Organizational Change

Because there is an endless variety of change methods available to managers and organizational experts, we can only discuss a limited number in this chapter. What we have chosen to do is to provide examples of strategies aimed at the background, required and emergent systems, and at the various-size groupings (individual, two-person, and so forth). Thus, we have organized the remainder of the chapter into three main sections: (1) change methods related to background factors, (2) those that focus on the required system, and (3) those that address the emergent system most directly. Within each section we offer examples of methods that focus on each size subsystem. Also, to facilitate the presentation and organization of the material in each section, we provide a chart to serve as a map for our discussion (See Figure 14–7 on the opposite page and Figures 14–8 and 14–9 on pp. 376 and 382).

FIGURE 14-6			
Possible Underlying Causes of Organizational Problems Requiring Change			

(1) When the Locus of the Problem Is:	and (2) the Source of the Problem is in the:		
	Background Factors	**Required System**	**Emergent System**
	then (3) the Causes Might Be:		
Individual	Poor match of individual with job; selection or promotion problem.	Task too easy or too difficult; poor job definition.	Job fails to fulfill range of needs; little chance for learning.
Two-person	Personality clash; conflict in basic styles, values, and so forth.	Poor role differentiation and/or integration in job description.	Misunderstandings; failure to deal with differences in preferences; unresolved feelings.
Group	Insufficient resources; poor group composition; bad physical setup; wrong behavior rewarded.	Task requirements poorly defined; role relationships unclear or inappropriate.	Poor working process in one or more of the 11 areas related to effectiveness.
Intergroup	Status and power conflicts of two professions; physical distance.	Conflict on task perspective; required interaction contary to background factors.	Conflicting group styles; dysfunctional competition.
Leadership	Poor selection and promotion decisions; poor training and preparation.	Overload of responsibility; inappropriate reporting procedures.	Individual not liked and/or respected; in conflict with other sources of power.
Total system	Geographic setting; limited labor market; physical conditions.	System goals inappropriate or poorly defined; inappropriate output levels.	General climate of malaise, suspicion, anxiety, pressure, and so forth.

FIGURE 14-7	
Methods of Changing Background Factors	

Method of Change	Focal Point
1. Personnel changes	Individual Two-person relationship Group Leadership
2. Training and education	Individual Group Leadership
3. Technology and work layout	Any level
4. Incentive plans	Individual Group
5. Background culture	Total system

Methods for Changing Background Factors

Figure 14–7 shows five general methods of change that deal directly with background factors; the focal point of each method is also identified. The focal point is not to be confused with the parts of the system that might be affected by the change; it simply refers to the place where the direct action is taken. The overall effects of any change action can spread to many subsystems of the organization.

Personnel Changes

One of the crucial background factors in any work situation is the personal histories and resultant attitudes of the individuals concerned. Some change strategies are

Uniting the Federal Lords at Citicorp; Chairman Reed Reins in a Me-First Culture That Brought a Banking Giant to the Brink

Citicorp's culture . . . encouraged bravado and hubris and brought the bank to the brink during the recession.

"We were like a medieval state . . . The king and his court might declare this or that, but the land barons went and did their thing." . . .

"We have gone from feudalism to a nation-state . . . We are all running the same company." . . .

The old culture . . . emphasized autonomy, internal competition, and risk taking and allowed Citicorp to become the most aggressive and innovative player in a stodgy industry.

But that culture also produced a strangling duplication of efforts . . .

". . . now . . . it is better to surface problems early. If I screw up, my name is on the line."

And if peer pressure wasn't enough, Mr. Reed changed the way bonuses would be calculated to emphasize teamwork . . . "Remuneration is not a bad way to influence people's thinking." . . .

"It's not easy to change 25 years' worth of culture in a company . . . there has been change at the top. But further down, is everyone being as friendly and collegial as we are at the top? Probably not yet."

SOURCE: Saul Hansell, *New York Times*, January 16, 1994. Copyright © 1994 by The New York Times Company. Reprinted by permission.

aimed at having an effect on what individuals bring to the situation and on which individuals are in the situation. The most direct way of affecting that is to replace individuals whose backgrounds cause difficulties with others who have appropriate skills, attitudes, and experiences.

Although this method has been used at least since Adam and Eve were removed for failing to follow direct orders, it is not uncomplicated in practice. Firing or displacing people can cause difficulties in a variety of ways. The insecurity level of others may be raised, leading to greater defensiveness or decreased morale (though in some cases to improved performance); unions may form or react negatively; legal problems may develop; work may be fouled up until a suitable replacement is found, brought in, and prepared, and so forth. Furthermore, there is no automatic guarantee that the replacement will be more suitable than the predecessor. Nevertheless, at times the wrong person(s) is in a job that is otherwise well designed, and only replacement will solve the problem. If that is so, then the original selection procedures may need examination and attention to reduce the likelihood of the same problem arising again.

In some instances, the problem may be related more to a poor *combination* of people in a two-person relationship, in a group, or in a superior-subordinate relationship. The individuals involved may be perfectly competent for their work, but when put together, they produce dysfunctional behavior. Obviously, one option is to fire one or more individuals, but a more functional option in terms of organizational resources is to recombine the people into more compatible groupings or pairs. The diagnosis of "personality clash" fits this example; there can be basic values or style differences that are not likely to be resolved.

Another approach that many organizations have used is a system of executive assessment (often using elaborate psychological tests) to identify leadership potential. Assessment centers, where individuals go through a series of activities and organizational simulations while being closely observed, spread rapidly as a way of trying to improve predictions about future managerial performance. It is not uncommon to find key decisions about promotion based upon these techniques. While their validity has been called into question by many organizational experts, these approaches have met with enough success to warrant their continued utilization.

If the Shoe Doesn't Fit, Look Elsewhere

Since [Tenneco CEO] Walsh arrived, "there's a lot more opportunity here for everybody—except people who can't be flexible, people who have no tolerance for ambiguity." . . .

To communicate what the new boss wants, McDonald says, consistency is critical: "You walk the walk as well as talk the talk. You structure the environment to foster the changes." But not everyone sees the logic. "You hear a lot or rationalization: 'This is just the flavor of the month, so I don't have to do it. This was good enough before. Maybe the problem isn't me; maybe it's with all of you.' When that happens, we say: 'You may be right. Some other organizations out there aren't embracing this. Maybe you'd be happier with them.' It used to be you fired people because they'd messed up a deal or lost some money. Now they have to go if quality isn't the most important thing to them."

SOURCE: John Huey, "Managing in the Midst of Chaos," *Fortune*, © April 5, 1993. Time, Inc. All Rights Reserved.

Firms Address Workers' Cultural Variety; the Differences Are Celebrated, Not Suppressed

Harvey Einstein, a merchandising manager, is one of about 75 Avon managers who have spent three weeks in seminars . . . "I had always considered myself just another pleasant guy," he says. The epiphany came when members of a mixed group were asked to write on a blackboard what occurred to them when they thought "white male"—and "the word 'bastard' popped up on the board." The shock made him reexamine his behavior, he adds, taking seriously, for example, that women don't want to be called girls.

SOURCE: Joliel Solomon, *The Wall Street Journal*, February 10,1989.

Training and Education

Other ways have been developed to change individual perceptions, attitudes, or skills. A great deal of what goes on in organizational training programs is aimed at the individual, with the assumption that improved knowledge or attitudes will be translated into organizational payoff. Programs designed specifically to change individual behavior and interpersonal skills have been widely offered within organizations and by outside consultants, universities, and training firms, and are a huge business.

Many organizations pay particular attention to the training and development of their managers. They institute leadership training programs that focus upon learning managerial skills considered vital to effective leadership. Some of these programs operate on a year-round basis in the form of inservice education, and many occur in the form of intensive workshops designed to focus upon specific skills and methods. When successful, such programs can have a significant effect upon the competence that a manager brings to his or her job, with obvious implications for the emergent behavior of people under that manager.

For example, training in achievement motivation was developed by psychologist David McClelland. His research indicated high correlation of need for achievement with entrepreneurship, so he and his associates developed a training program they claimed could alter individual motivation. McClelland subsequently determined that effective managers, unlike entrepreneurs, require high needs for socialized power coupled with high inhibition of their purely personal interests. He then developed ways of training to increase that kind of motivation.

In an attempt to increase behavioral effect, aimed at improving a person's interpersonal competence, a method called "sensitivity training" or "T-(for training) groups" was developed. In an unstructured group setting, participants learn about the basic dynamics of how groups work, receive feedback on their own behavior in the group and its impact on others, and have the opportunity to practice new behaviors in a controlled situation. Although the original T-group is now seldom used, many variations have developed. Some have focused more on what goes on within each individual member so that self-concept and the personal system are clarified or altered. Others have concentrated on group process phenomena, attempting to improve the ability of individuals to understand, predict, evaluate, and change the way groups work. Still others have worked on particular aspects of behavior, like the use of power and influence, leadership skills, listening ability, and giving and receiving feedback.[21]

There are many other variations of training activities designed to enhance management capacities, such as changing attitudes and behavior through intense sessions. Workshops to help people learn to value diversity, deal with stress, communicate or negotiate more effectively, be more entrepreneurial, influence without authority, and just about any organizationally valuable skill imaginable are being offered within companies and at hotels and conference centers all around the world. Many of these programs are tied to assessments of existing competencies, including formal questionnaires filled out by subordinates, peers, and managers. This kind of 360-degree feedback can be helpful in guiding the learning of any individual.

Insofar as these kinds of training utilize experience-based methods, they often have strong emotional effects on the participants. But these individually oriented techniques suffer from some of the same difficulties of traditional training programs. First, even when measurable changes occur during training, they often fade out back on the job if not supported there. Second, new knowledge that for any reason cannot be utilized can be very frustrating, leading to anger, decreased morale, or even departure from the organization for anticipated greener pastures. Third, those who receive such intense training experiences and like them often become impatient with nonparticipants who do not sympathize with or cannot understand the participant's enthusiasm. Some rivalry can result between the "elite" few who are in the know and the "unenlightened masses." Thus, an individual may bring to the work situation some new behaviors that are functional for a situation *outside* the work setting but dysfunctional to others on the job.

Every Manager a Teacher: Ford Rolls Out New Model of Corporate Culture

If you teach a Ford manager how to sell fish, will it help sell more cars and raise Ford Motor Co.'s stock price? Ford's new chief executive officer, Jacques Nasser, thinks it will—along with prodding managers to do more community service and having them spend 100 days at a time tackling cost, quality or other challenges.

It's all part of a major initiative by Mr. Nasser to overhaul Ford's management culture. His goal is to change the nation's No. 2 auto maker from a lumbering bureaucracy to one that responds quickly to consumer needs and is rewarded with the kind of high stock multiples that smart growth companies enjoy.

Oddly enough, growth and serving consumer needs haven't traditionally been goals in Detroit. "It's a terrible industry any way you look at it—economic value added, return on sales, market capitalization," says Noel Tichy, a University of Michigan business professor and consultant who helped develop the Business Leadership Initiative program with Mr. Nasser two years ago. BLI, as it is know, is all the buzz at Ford these days. The CEO wants all 350,000 of Ford's employees—who together control 20% of the company's shares—to act more like owners and entrepreneurs and less like bean counters, engineers, or hourly workers.

To that end, 55,000 Ford managers are being trained in the basics of business, learning what terms like "shareholder value" mean and what they can do to affect it. Those managers also are being assigned to successive "100-day projects" attacking costs or other problems. . . .

Another hallmark of BLI is that instead of hiring consultants to lead the training sessions and projects, Mr. Nasser is drafting the company's managers to do the teaching—with each level of executives instructing the level below. Managers are given a BLI manual, but they can also personalize the lessons. . . .

Rolling out the program has stirred some controversy, even among Ford's 200 most senior executives. "One night, a group of them was resisting the idea of teaching shareholder value themselves, and I asked what the average annual compensation in the room was—$600,000?" Mr. Tichy says. "And I said, 'If you people are afraid to teach shareholder value, you don't deserve a job.'" After a silence, one of the participants spoke up: "Leadership is a contact sport. Let's shut up and get on with it."

What's more, Mr. Nasser himself took the lead in teaching his views, says David Murphy, Ford's director of human resources, which "left other executives with no bloody excuse." Indeed, the 51-year-old Mr.

Nasser's own passion for leadership training—and the chances that he could be at Ford's helm for 15 more years—have reinforced the seriousness of BLI for company employees. Part of the goal, he says, is to reintroduce the feeling of pride and proprietorship that an owner has about a business. He knows that feeling well. As a teenager in Australia, he failed in a bicycle business and in a car-repair venture before succeeding in the coffeehouse business.

Another initially controversial element was that during the three-day, off-site training, each group carried out a half-day community-service project. Ford's point is that a company can be successful only if the broader community is successful. The projects also were meant to serve as team builders. They included painting houses and hospitals, landscaping a hospice, reclaiming parks, and the like. Some managers resisted this idea. In the Detroit area, some even phoned radio talk shows to complain. Others wrote to Mr. Nasser. In Europe, says Cary Wilson, director of electronics engineering, "people said, 'We pay taxes for this service.'"

"It was a challenge to us," acknowledges Mr. Murphy, the human resources director. "Jac encouraged people to try it, and some of the resisters did try it and wrote back saying, 'This is great.'" . . .

Ford estimates that the BLI program cost between $30 million and $40 million in its first year, and it does carry some risks. Lots of companies try to overhaul their corporate cultures, and lots of management consultants get rich selling culture change how-to books and leading off-site team-building exercises. In the end, many CEOs find the programs get shrugged off.

Culture-change gurus say Mr. Nasser's BLI may have more staying power than most, in part because Ford managers themselves have a big stake in the teaching. Another reason is that the 100-day projects are being incorporated into Ford's operations around the world. The message is that "it's not just three days of school—it's real life," Mr. Murphy, the human-resources director, says. "Otherwise, the half-life of these things would be less than two days."

Lastly, participation in BLI is being woven into the company's compensation and performance-review process, Mr. Nasser says. Last year, Ford began targeting underperformers in a buyout program. Those managers who lose their ardor for the BLI program are likely to be shown the door.

SOURCE: Robert L. Simison, "Ford Rolls Out New Model of Corporate Culture," *The Wall Street Journal*, January 13, 1999, p. B1. (Copyright © 1999, Dow Jones & Company, Inc.)

Yet another trend is to make training available through technology so that individuals can learn at their computer, on their own time. While convenient, it is not yet easy to have the same in-depth effect on the individual. Another variation is *action learning,* where managers not only learn new concepts but also work on actual projects and try to both solve company problems and develop new skills.

Technology and Work Layout

Another background factor that can be changed to affect behavior is technology and/or work layout. Although all too often changes in technology ignore the consequences for social interaction, some sophisticated change efforts have consistently altered the existing technology to result in more satisfactory relationships and productivity. For example, both Saab and Volvo have experimented with the assembly line, reducing the monotony, isolation, and repetitiveness of work in an effort to allow group pride and interaction around whole tasks. These experiments were extremely expensive, involving huge capital expenditures, but were undertaken because of labor force shortages and difficulties, which hampered production. In fact, the companies were facing staggeringly high rates of absenteeism—up to 20 percent daily—and employee turnover of 100 percent per year! The high education rates and generous unemployment benefits in Sweden had led to a widespread unwillingness to do boring, repetitive work. Thus, Saab and Volvo were virtually forced into being inventive at altering jobs and the assembly line to make work more satisfying. American and Japanese car manufacturers have subsequently tackled the need to make work more interesting. As the world car market has become more competitive, however, the lower productivity of the Volvo and Saab plants threatens their continued existence.[22]

Another series of experiments emanated from researchers at the Tavistock Institute in London. The method and organization of mining coal was changed to a more satisfying pattern of interaction and work, again allowing workers to gain the satisfaction of completing a whole task. Similar changes were made in weaving sheds in India. These large-scale changes in technology were made with explicit social system results in mind and have been quite successful. Called "sociotechnical" design, many work arrangements have been dramatically altered to simultaneously optimize both productivity and satisfaction.

A technological or work layout change need not be so elaborate in order to have substantial effects on emergent behavior. In a classic technological change, waitresses and cooks who were always fighting about unclear orders, differing priorities, and mistakes began to get along much better when a rotating spindle on which written orders could be clipped was introduced. Orders had been called out by the waitresses, leading to frequent arguments about whether the waitress actually made the order, in what sequence the orders had come in, whether the cooks had forgotten what was said, and the like. Each side thought the other was stupid. The spindle allowed both automatic sequencing and easy visual grouping by the cooks, so they could get all of an order together at the same time.[23] Thus, a problem that seemed to be wholly within the individuals involved was solved by a mechanical device that altered interaction patterns to fit existing attitudes and allowed differences to be easily checked and settled. Another simple change action can be the physical relocation of interdependent work groups to facilitate information flow, a method discussed in the previous chapter. Similarly, offices can be rearranged to facilitate interaction among those who need to work together more closely.[24]

Technological changes can be very potent in yielding positive results but are often expensive, demand extensive revisions in the required system, and lead to unpredictable emergent behavior. As many organizations have discovered with dismay, a change that looks simple and could be helpful may produce an unanticipated series of negative reactions in many related subsystems. Few companies, for example, have easily made the transition from a manual accounting system to a computerized

Managing Your Career: "Re-Engineering" Authors Reconsider Re-Engineering

The concept was compelling: To survive global competition, companies had to radically redesign work, combining fragmented tasks into streamlined processes that saved time and money.

Re-engineered work usually required fewer workers and far fewer managers. Managers resisted, stymying many re-engineering efforts. We've learned how to do the redesign. But the redesign, as brilliant as it may be,

doesn't get results because of managerial thought and ideology. Either top management isn't aligned behind the change, or others are threatened by a loss of power.

SOURCE: Hal Lancaster, "Managing Your Career: 'Re-Engineering' Authors Reconsider Re-Engineering," *The Wall Street Journal,* January 17, 1995, p. B1.

one, even though great benefits were anticipated. The people who had to make the new equipment work often reacted with less than enthusiasm. Current discussions about "the office of the future," featuring interlinked computers and managers who enter data at the keyboard, often sound as naïve about the human factors as did early discussions about computers for accounting purposes. Of course, in the last few years desktop PC's have become so widespread that few managers can any longer avoid touching keyboards. Similarly, great claims have been made for reengineering, using information technology to allow, for example, "one-stop shopping" for customers or clients, but the benefits have often been minimized by resistance of affected employees and managers. The wise manager tries carefully to predict likely consequences of any change in technology or layout before beginning!

Incentive Plans

An organization's reward system is a background factor that can have a great impact on behavior when altered but requires considerable thought first. People in organizations tend to do what will be rewarded (in the currency they value, which usually includes, but is not limited to, pay) and tend not to bother doing what goes unrewarded, even though it may be appropriate to the organization's goals. Therefore, dramatic changes in behavior often can be accomplished through this indirect mechanism. Careful applications of the principles of behavior modification developed by B. F. Skinner have produced some dramatic results in a few organizations.[25] It is not always easy, however, to be certain just what factors organizational members will consider to be rewarding, so what particular changes to make may not be obvious. And performance is not always easy to measure accurately enough to be able to effectively reward changes in it, as organization behavior modification requires. Numerous incentive schemes, including pay for performance, pay for quality, forced rankings, and peer review, have faltered because they either did not fully anticipate the behaviors that would result from how productivity was calculated and rewarded or take into account the existing social patterns and their value to organizational members. New pay schemes often work better on paper than in practice!

An individual incentive plan that fosters competition among cohesive group members may well be sabotaged by resentful members. In our classes, for example, if we force students to rate each other's contributions to group products and insist that all members not be given the same grade, many groups devise clever ways of "beating the system" by rotating grades among members, using the minimum grade spread allowed, giving only one member a different grade on each project, and so

MANAGERIAL BULLETIN

The Dangers of Incentives Causing Misfiring

[Auerbach on one of the major reasons behind the Boston Celtics' long-term success]: We don't give bonus clauses in contracts. When we give a guy a contract, we give him everything he is worth in salary. We don't pay him for great statistics. We pay him for winning. That is why, when we have a big lead, our top guys don't mind coming out and letting the bench guys come in and play. On other teams, they have all of these incentive clauses, and their big guys don't want to come off the floor. They want to stay on for garbage time so they can build up their stats and make the incentive bonuses in the contract. It's a stupid way to do business. Our players never have to worry about that, and we don't get involved in petty arguments over playing time.

SOURCE: Will McDonough, "Saying Isn't Believing Here," *Boston Globe,* April 13, 1986. Reprinted courtesy of the *Boston Globe.*

forth. When the groups feel cohesive, an accurate grade reward for individual effort is worth less to them than the preservation of harmony. The same can be true at work, when the reward is in dollars.

Furthermore, change in the reward system for any one subsystem inevitably has consequences for those in other subsystems. Therefore, even when localized changes produce desired results, the organizational ramifications may create difficulties. If one group, for example, responds to a new incentive-pay system by increasing production considerably, thereby earning pay perceived by others as "too high," the original change may end up being scuttled despite its effectiveness.

Also, only a few executives are likely to have sufficient power to avoid difficulty among subgroups by changing the reward system for the entire organization. When the power is available, it can allow executives to foster desired behavioral changes without any apparent efforts to change behavior, and thus avoid the usual resistances.

> The Merit rating nourishes short-term performance, annihilates long-term planning, builds fear, demolishes team work, and nourishes rivalry and politics.
>
> W. Edwards Deming

Background Culture

The final background factor we discuss is the culture of the organization—that is, the customary way of doing things, the attitudes and values that are "in the air" affecting everyone. (See Management Tools on corporate culture in Chapter 3.) Although ultimately any lasting systemwide behavioral change must affect the organization's culture, the overall culture is the most resistant aspect of any social system. The organization's attitudes about authority and how it should be used, interpersonal style, conflict, and so forth, condition and affect all other changes—even what is seen as possible to change—and, therefore, require special attention. The approach to changing the organization's culture, however, may have to begin with changes in areas that are more directly manageable. But any change effort benefits from being considered in terms of its effects on the overall culture of the organization and planned to either fit that total picture or change crucial aspects of it.

Changing the Culture to Foster Speed and Learning

How Are You Changing Dun & Bradstreet's Corporate Culture?

For a market leader like D&B, the approach in the past was to take action once management was sure they were right. But today the speed of the marketplace won't allow that luxury. The issue is no longer whether you're right. I'm working every day to convince my colleagues that at any moment in time, no matter how hard we try, we're always going to be wrong. The important thing is not to be right but to get "righter" faster than any competitor. It's OK to fail, and if you do, fail fast and learn fast.

A side benefit of this approach is that you won't have time to misspend much money. In the past, we said, "We're a big company, so we want big ideas. We want to be very careful, spend a lot of money and time on big projects." What we're doing now is planting many seeds. We'll help the ones that grow. My No. I priority for changing our corporate culture is to introduce adaptive behavior for every employee. . . .

We recognize the agents of change in our company as heroes.

Bob Weissman
CEO

SOURCE: Diane Coryell, Editor, *The Babson Bulletin,* Spring 1994 issue, "The New CEO." Reprinted with permission.

Deep Thinkers: Soul-Searching at Time Warner

Levin created a Values & Human Development Committee on the board to come up with a set of values for Time Warner. Now that the world's largest media company knows what it's about, it's making sure its minions know, too.

The new gospel will be spread by a video and a forum for 1,000 executives. For a hotbed of creative media types, the statement is pretty dry stuff—to wit, "strive to be the world's most respected and successful media company." Says one co-author, Atlantic Group chief Val Azzoli: "It seems obvious, but it had never been written down." Now Levin will see if Time Warner is as good at corporate culture as it is at pop culture.

SOURCE: Robert Siklos, "Soul-Searching at Time Warner," *Business Week,* March 29, 1999, p. 6.

Roger Harrison, for example, found in his consulting work in Europe that change efforts based on open expression of feelings were often resisted by executives from companies with cultures that strongly discourage such "emotionality." He developed new methods for altering behavior in conflict situations, utilizing negotiations about role obligations. These methods were more compatible with the organizational backgrounds from which the executives came.[26]

If, however, openness about feelings would have been functional for the organization, his methods would have had little effect on changing the culture that forbids that type of communication. Some other way of affecting the culture, rather than adapting to it, would be necessary—perhaps beginning with an intense group experience for the top executives, which might directly question existing beliefs and attitudes. But, as noted, direct attempts to change attitudes often increase resistance.

For example, a large French company decided to develop the leadership skills of its middle managers and help them learn to be more effective around the world. But

FIGURE 14-8   *Methods of Changing the Required System*

Method of Change	Focal Point
1. Revision of job descriptions and work relationships	Individual
Reporting relationships	Interpersonal
Task role assignments	Intergroup
Managerial responsibility; direct communication	Leadership
	Group
2. Job modification	Individual
Job narrowing	Two-person relation
Job enlargement, rotation	Group
Job enrichment	
3. Quality circles; problem-solving teams;	Group
employee involvement;	Leadership
process teams; self-	
managing teams	
4. Alternative work schedules	Individual
5. Work from home	Individual
6. Reformulation of work objectives	Total system

problems arose when the non-French outside trainers tried to teach managers to deal directly with interpersonal conflicts that block team effectiveness. The managers were extremely uncomfortable with the ideas presented because the company culture was conflict-avoidant, with an emphasis on being "nice." This created a dilemma for trainees: they couldn't directly express their disagreements with the trainers because that would also violate their deeply embedded cultural beliefs. The conversations about leadership were thus strained and disguised, despite the trainers' attempts to openly discuss the difficulties.

Ultimately, changing an organization's culture may require efforts along several fronts, utilizing a variety of approaches and supported from the top of the hierarchy. Because such efforts are expensive, require deep commitment from top executives who may not be fully comfortable with what behavior is required of them in a changed culture, and take several years to filter through the organization, you can see why such changes are difficult and rare.

Of course, one factor that determines the culture of any organization is its location or setting. A manufacturing plan located in South America may produce the same products as a similar plant in the United States, but the behavior of people in the respective settings will be very different because of obvious differences in the cultures of the two geographic areas. Even regional differences within the United States often determine differences in the culture of the same kinds of organizations in the different locations. For example, the rapid impersonal pace of a big-city environment tends to carry over into any system located there. Move that system to a rural area, where the pace is slower and the prevailing attitudes of people are different, and some very obvious differences within the organization itself may be observed.

Methods for Changing the Required System

Figure 14–8 summarizes the different approaches we discuss in this section.

Revision of Job Descriptions and Work Relationships

Job descriptions and organizational work relationships are two important determinants of behavior and interactions, and are often a starting place for change efforts. Examining a job description to see if responsibilities are clear, sufficient information is available, boundaries are sufficiently well defined, organizational authority is adequate, job activities needing interaction or coordination with others are spelled out,

Quality Circles/Problem-Solving Teams/Employee Involvement Groups/Process Teams/Self-Managing Teams

Spurred on by Japanese successes, many countries tried variations of Quality Circles, allowing (or sometimes requiring) teams of employees to periodically discuss ways of improving quality, or productivity. Often the teams are taught formal problem-solving methods, statistical and logical, then asked to track and solve quality problems. In some variations, the teams pick the problems to work on, while in others they are assigned. Often the groups are natural work teams, though sometimes they are assigned or voluntarily form across areas and/or levels. This is a formalized method of tapping employee talent and, if properly managed, can produce startling results, reducing defects, need for rework, and unnecessary work procedures. Care has to be taken to include and support supervisors, to be clear about management expectations, and to ensure management willingness to alter practices leading to quality problems; but it can be done. Where there are unions, they must be included in the planning, usually through joint labor–management committees. Interestingly, many proponents of Quality Circles attribute their success to the use of statistical techniques and do not appreciate the motivational impact of bringing employees together and allowing them to influence the way work is done. In some organizations, excellent results have been obtained without using statistical methods; in others, Quality teams using statistics have been abandoned because they were not properly managed and led to trivial results, then disenchantment. Many other organizations have incorporated the group participation and statistical tools into Total Quality Management systems. The descendants of the original quality centers give greater autonomy to the teams, making them responsible for many functions including repairs, estimating, purchasing—even hiring. These self-managing teams must be carefully developed and trained.

SOURCE: L. A. Schlesinger, *Quality of Work Life and the Supervisor.* (New York: Praeger Publishers, 1982) and B. A. Stein, *Quality of Work Life in Action: Managing for Effectiveness.* (New York: American Management Association, 1983).

and then making appropriate changes, can result in markedly different behavior. A person who is not sure of what to do may perform so badly that he or she appears to be totally incompetent. With responsibilities clarified, the same person may be able to do excellent work. On the other hand, tight, unambiguous job descriptions can inhibit innovation even while increasing predictability.[27] Similarly, changing who a person or group takes orders from can make a substantial difference in job performance. Changing the organizational level at which decisions are made, whether closer to the actual problem or closer to the top of the organization, also can have a significant effect on behavior. Some firms have tried to find ways to enable direct communication without using the "chain of command," such as allowing anonymous e-mail or voice mail messages to go to top management.[28]

These techniques of job analysis, centralization or decentralization of decision making, and similar restructuring have great appeal to managers because they appear to be rational and logical; there is no doubt that such structural changes can positively affect performance. But blueprints do not a bluebird make; human beings are remarkably inventive at getting around formal directions and plans. Organization charts and job descriptions, even when clear and relatively sophisticated, cannot take all contingencies and relationships into account. A certain amount of goodwill is necessary to effectively implement any structure. And, conversely, even a sloppy, illogical structure can be made to work if those involved want it to. The attitudes people bring to the situation affect their response to any formal structure. Nevertheless, insofar as the structure determines interactions and these in turn lead to positive feelings, structural changes can affect attitudes as well as be affected by them. When lack of clarity or poor utilization of resources within the organization is at the heart of a behavioral problem, the methods described above can be extremely useful.

Forget Empowerment, This Job [at Monarch Marking Systems] Requires Constant Brainpower

Most companies, [the CEO and Vice President of Operations] reasoned, treat worker-involvement programs as corporate cure-alls—turnarounds in a pill. They design these programs so broadly they can accomplish nothing specific. Worker teams dream up pie-in-the-sky solutions. Team meetings result mostly in more team meetings. . . .

First, [VP] Schneider identified every variable in the plant that could be readily measured—162 metrics in all—and declared that no problem-solving team would be created except to improve a specific metric. There would be no open-ended initiatives. Even more important, teams were charged with executing their own solution, in toto, to the point of working out any necessary changes with other departments and making arrangements with vendors. Combining ideation and implementation would motivate people to think hard for the most practical solution. "Go make it happen, then tell us about it," he told the teams. Finally, he decreed no team would last beyond 30 days. "It's a project," he said, "not a process." . . .

Along the way, however, crisis hit. When first assigned to come up with a more efficient assembly process for a hand-held bar-code reader, Ms. Winters and several other journeymen rebelled. Mr. Schneider feared their recalcitrance would spread through the plant. "This team could shut the whole thing down!" he told Mr. Schlaegel. The workers were called to a conference room. "You will do this," Mr. Schlaegel said.

Finding themselves alone with a problem and a deadline, the thinking came with startling ease. They knew it was ridiculous to build a two-pound product on a mechanical conveyor belt, for instance. By eliminating it they could face each other around a large workstation and simply pass around the product by hand. Anyone could easily talk to anyone, and anyone who got ahead could help anyone who fell behind. By the time it was over they had reduced the square footage of their assembly area 70%, cut work-in-progress inventory by $127,000 and slashed past-due shipments 90%—in addition to doubling productivity. . . .

Ms. Winters, her teammates and Messrs. Paxton, Schneider, and Schlaegel received the first "work-force excellence" award from the National Association of Manufacturers.

"Empowering" workers only patronizes them; brain work should be a duty, not an indulgence. In addition, brain work requires rules—the fewer the better, but enough to assure that ideas turn into action.

SOURCE: Thomas Petzinger, Jr, "The Front Lines: Forget Empowerment, This Job Requires Constant Brainpower," *The Wall Street Journal,* October 17, 1997, p. B1.

Job Modification

Job requirements can also be the focus for change when the required activities, interactions, and attitudes are too difficult or too simple for the people in the system. Work that asks more of people than they are capable of giving may need to be broken into less complex or less demanding activities, so others can do part of what is needed, or rules and procedures may need to be established in order to simplify decision making.

> In recent years, for example, a number of ways have been developed to make physicians' jobs less demanding, so they can best utilize their expertise. The physician's assistant and nurse practitioner were new roles carved out of the total job of diagnosing and treating patients, to free the doctor from the more routine but time-consuming aspects of the job. The physician's assistant may be trained to treat certain common, non-serious problems like colds, coughs, and so forth, and to recognize more serious conditions that must be seen by the doctor.

In the same way, assembly lines and other routinized forms of doing work can be used to make a job simple enough for a relatively unskilled person to do. Carried to the extreme, some jobs can be broken down into such simple repetitive activities

Are Saner Workloads the Unexpected Key To More Productivity?

After trimming fat, cutting layers, re-engineering and otherwise bending, folding, spindling and mutilating the work force, where can employers turn to wring out new productivity gains? A few big ones are tapping an unlikely source: employees' frustration over their outsize workloads.

The buzzword that's at work here is "work redesign," and it has BankAmerica, Hewlett-Packard, and a handful of other employers tapping employees' yearning for better balance in life as a motivator for overhauling the way work gets done. In the process, they're pushing work-life initiatives to a new level, with promising early results.

Managers start with a daring leap: asking employees how their jobs could be changed to make their work and personal lives better. "We want to know," a BankAmerica executive told employees, "all the dumb things we do."

Unlike re-engineering, this bottom-up strategy demands that any gains in time or efficiency be shared with employees, usually by giving them more control over their work or more flexibility in hours. Employees typically respond with a torrent of ideas on improving how work is done. In effect, employees' angst serves as a source of energy for streamlining work.

There's plenty of angst out there over work-life balance. About 40% of U.S. workers say workloads are excessive, and about the same proportion are bothered by excessive pressure on the job, based on surveys of more than 400,000 employees by International Survey Research, Chicago. One-third found it very difficult last year to balance work and personal duties, up from 28% in 1997.

Of course, an employer has to be willing to devote lots of time and energy to redesign and to follow up on employee suggestions. Efforts so far are scattered, mostly experimental and not easy to replicate. . . .

In another sign that work-life initiatives are increasingly a two-way street, employers are tying such popular programs as flexible scheduling to meeting work goals. . . .

Pursuing this dual agenda is something good managers do instinctively. All the projects hold promise for making the workplace a more humane and efficient environment.

SOURCE: Sue Shellenbarger, "Are Saner Workloads the Unexpected Key to More Productivity?" *The Wall Street Journal,* March 10, 1999, p. B1.

---

that machines can perform equally well. When trained personnel are scarce or very expensive and unemployment high so that few alternatives exist for employees, such methods can be effective.

On the other hand, overly mechanical, simple work can lead to boredom, lack of commitment, alienation, or sabotage, and the most elaborate change efforts have been geared to countering these effects. As mentioned in Chapter 7, a variety of ways have been invented to try to make work more interesting in the hopes of gaining improved performance and satisfaction. Job rotation, enlargement, and enrichment are all ways of making work more challenging. While the technology may remain the same, work is divided differently to provide more variety, challenge, and satisfaction, which hopefully lead to greater productivity. Similarly, work is increasingly assigned to teams, with far more decision-making responsibility, increasing both autonomy and accountability.

In the 1970s a number of activities involving job modification and revision of work relationships were described as efforts to improve *quality of working life.* Problems similar to those faced in Sweden—absenteeism, turnover, alienation, and boredom— led a number of firms to experiment with reorganization of work to give more responsibility to employees, to build team cooperation in working on identifiable complete tasks or products, to eliminate conventional supervision (creating self-supervising, autonomous work groups), and in general to try to foster both greater satisfaction and productivity. Many different experiments have been lumped together

More Companies Experiment with Workers' Schedules

Bending some previously rigid rules, big companies are offering more employees flexible work schedules. . . .

Some of the country's major corporations are conducting experiments in flexibility on hundreds of workers with all kinds of abilities and needs. The companies are pushing flexible work arrangements down through the ranks as a kind of shock treatment for stressed-out workers. . . .

[W]ork goals and criteria for success must be made clear. Responsibility for performance and team effort must be shifted to employees. . . . [T]alking about personal or family needs in the workplace . . . play[s] a big role in employees' ability to pitch in when flexible scheduling situations demand it.

SOURCE: Sue Shellenbarger. Reprinted by permission of *The Wall Street Journal,* © January 13, 1994, Dow Jones & Company, Inc. All Rights Reserved Worldwide.

under the "quality of work life" label, however, so the general category is hard to define. It does seem to indicate renewed attention to worker feelings about work, reflecting evidence that organizations ignore their employees at their own peril.[29]

Through the 1980s and 1990s, attention to worker satisfaction as opposed to productivity came and went—usually depending on employment levels and availability of skilled labor—but increasingly both productivity and satisfaction are taken into account.

Alternative Work Schedules

For many years most people worked on a fixed five-day, 40-hour schedule. Considerable supervisory energy went into enforcing starting and stopping times, trying to prevent tardiness (which was considered to be undisciplined and a waste of valuable work time). But partly as a result of the organizational need to pay more attention to employee preferences and partly because organizations don't always need all employees at the traditional hours, there has been a rapid spread of innovative work schedules in the United States, Europe, and Japan.

The majority of companies now allow many employees to choose their own starting and stopping times within specified ranges, provided that they complete 8 hours a day or 40 hours a week. This option, called *flexible working hours,* allows individuals to balance personal needs with those of the organization. Organizational benefits include higher morale, decreased short-term absenteeism, virtual elimination of tardiness, and, in some cases, increases in productivity. Disadvantages are occasional difficulties in communications or getting people together for meetings as well as some discomfort on the part of traditional supervisors who do not know how to plan and evaluate work they are not always physically present to observe. The individual employee gains flexibility in terms of family needs, often major savings in daily travel time (by avoiding rush-hour traffic), and enhanced self-esteem from being trusted by the company to manage one's own time. Employees almost universally approve of flexible working hours when given the chance to try it even if they choose to work the same hours as before.

The *compressed week* is a different schedule variation that does not usually permit flexibility, but does allow for a full week's work to be completed in less than five days by working longer days. Either the organization only remains open for four days or, more commonly, employees are scheduled for differing four- (or three-and-a-half-) day patterns such that there is greatest coverage on the busiest days. Compressed week arrangements can result in more efficient use of plant and equipment, availability of employees at odd hours (e.g., it is easier to attract night-shift employees if they can have three consecutive days off), higher productivity, and greater satisfaction. The compressed week, however, is usually quite unattractive to women with school-age children (and, as child-rearing practices change, to men who want to spend time with their children) and to older employees who may tire more easily working longer hours.

Another schedule variation being used more frequently is permanent part-time work, sometimes combined with job sharing. Permanent part-time means that not only does the individual work part-time but does so at a job that is part of a career with proportional pay and benefits, rather than low hourly wages. It is like other work, only for less than 40 hours a week, and may be divided up during the week at the mutual convenience of the individual and the employer. Job sharing is a variation of permanent part-time where two (or more) people share one full-time job, again by dividing working hours in a mutually convenient way.

Both of these variations can lead to greater productivity, availability of talented employees who would not otherwise be willing or able to work, and coverage at odd hours when full-time employees are not available. For example, one insurance company has "mother's hours," 10 A.M. to 2 P.M., which attracts women with school-age children who would not be willing to work all day but are very capable and potential future full-time employees.

All of these alternative arrangements, when carefully planned, can help companies improve morale and productivity at little cost. But they must be chosen in a way that fits the timing needs of the existing (or potential) workforce and delivers employees at times when the company needs them. Otherwise, this kind of change in the required system can worsen morale problems and hinder productivity.[30]

Work from Home

With the increased availability of access to technology in the home, allowing some people to work from home at least some of the time is another kind of scheduling change. It can allow people to be more productive, save hours commuting, and reduce space needs for the company. There needs to be careful attention to just how much face-to-face time is required, reliable technology, and clear agreements about work expectations, but in the right situation, both the company and employees win.

Reformulation of Work Objectives

Every individual and combination of people in an organization work toward certain objectives. Those objectives in turn fit into the broader framework of the total organization's objectives. Often the specific objectives at one level of the system may be out of phase or incongruent with those at another level and/or with those of the total system. This kind of problem calls for a reformulation of organizational objectives at one or another level in order to reestablish the necessary congruence for system interdependence. The focal point of such an approach may begin at any level, but it must also touch directly upon all others.

A specific approach called *management by objectives* was developed a number of years ago. Its broad philosophy states in essence that worker and manager performance can best be evaluated in terms of their degree of success in meeting specifically defined organizational objectives. These objectives (1) pertain directly to and may be defined by each individual in the system, (2) demand coordination at a group and intergroup level, and (3) must be reflective of the overall organizational goals. When utilized effectively, management by objectives can be an important vehicle for encouraging individuals to take responsibility for their own performance and provides them with the measuring sticks to do that.

The method requires each employee to set concrete, measurable objectives for some time period and then negotiate agreement on these with the employee's supervisor. Performance then is judged by how close to the objectives the individual comes within that time period, rather than on more intangible personal characteristics or

| FIGURE 14–9 | *Methods of Changing Emergent Factors* |

Methods of Change	Focal Point
1. Counseling/coaching	Individual
	Leadership
2. Third-party consultation	Two-person relation
	Intergroup relations
3. Task group training, team building	Group
4. Intergroup confrontation	Intergroup relations
5. Survey feedback	Total system
6. Executive planning and confrontation sessions	Total system

global judgments about the person's worth. The process of defining and agreeing upon objectives represents an attempt both to plan effectively and to generate commitment on the part of the employee to reach the goals.

The principle of management by objectives is sensible and almost inevitably practiced in some form or other, even if not formally adopted; however, its practice can be difficult or abused. If performance is to be judged by agreed-upon objectives, then the objectives stated must somehow be measurable; this can eliminate some important but not easily defined variables. The more specific are the objectives, the more easily is performance measured but the more likely it is that subtle factors will be ignored. Furthermore, many managers use management by objectives without first securing the initiative and agreement of both those who are judging and those who are to be judged by the objectives. If the subordinates are not really committed to the objectives on which they will be judged, their performance is not likely to be as effective as it might otherwise be.

Methods for Changing the Emergent System

In one sense, all change is ultimately aimed at the emergent system. It is in emergent behavior that problems present themselves and require attention. However, some change strategies begin by directly attacking emergent behavior, even if ultimate solutions demand attention to background factors and/or the required system. Figure 14–9 refers to several different approaches to change in emergent factors.

Counseling/Coaching

Many organizations provide individual help to employees who may be experiencing difficulties in handling work demands or who may be generally unhappy in their work. The physical and/or psychological pressures of a given type of work can often prove to be highly stressful; counseling is one tool to help an individual learn ways of handling tensions and, whenever possible, of minimizing their adverse consequences. When a problem is more directly related to interpersonal or social factors, the counseling is likely to focus on the individual's behavior, self-concept, and general attitude. Presumably, the use of counseling as a method of organizational change pertains to emergent behavior—that is, problems the work situation brought out in the individual. Some organizations also offer Employee Assistance Programs—help for problems that employees *bring* to the situation (e.g., personality problems, alcoholism, and marital difficulties); more places advise such individuals about where they can get help from outside resources.

In a more positive way, individual counseling or coaching as a vehicle for leadership development can be a potent source of change. Many executives rely heavily upon the support and guidance of a trusted colleague, specialist, or consultant. Through such a process, the individual manager can become more aware of his or her own goals, develop increased managerial competence, and learn how to maintain an integration of his or her personal beliefs and values with the goals of the organization.

Third-Party Consultation

An extension of the counseling process occurs when two people encounter difficulties in working together and seek the help of a third party to resolve the issue(s). This technique has been in existence for a very long time; examples include friends helping friends, marriage counseling, and clergy offering advice to prospective marriage partners. (Of course, when the help is not requested, it might be called *third-party interference.*) In a work setting, the helper might be a peer, a supervisor, or some other objective person. The choice of third-party consultant should be dictated by the demands of the situation and the mutual preferences of the two people needing the help.[31] The style of the third party can range form nondirective listening, to formal mediation where the parties are separated until the mediator works out an agreement, to experts who give strong advice.

Even when there is no problem as such, there is usually room for improvement in any working relationship. In this regard, a manager always has the option, possibly even the obligation, and, hopefully, the skills to help subordinates to improve their productivity, satisfaction, and development by improving their work relationships. Such a proactive stance is more likely to facilitate a healthy work environment than would the more passive attitude of waiting until a problem occurs before taking action.

Increasingly, intergroup problems are being addressed through the use of third parties, using arbitration, where the third party judges and makes a decision about a disputed issue, or mediation, where the third party works actively between the groups to find a mutually satisfactory solution.

Task Group Training: Process Consultation and Team Building

Out of the experiences of T-groups (mentioned earlier) have developed several variations of task group training or team building. In most of these methods, people who work together on a day-to-day basis are directly taught to work together more effectively. A team-building effort might examine the ways in which the group members collaborate or compete, the way they make decisions, the way they set agenda items, the amount of openness with which members relate to one another, and so forth. The person introducing change might observe regular meetings and make observations about the group's process or might take the group away for a working retreat where processes are directly examined.

Alternatively, the team may undergo a variation of Outward Bound or other outdoor activity, experiencing interdependency and trust solving nonbusiness problems.

The most sophisticated versions of team building, however, do not assume that all the problems arise from the group's emergent behavior, but may be traced back to background factors, such as the company's culture and reward system or to the required system and the way in which it determines influence and interactions. The advantage of team-building efforts is that, once changes are accepted by the group, group members themselves can reinforce the new patterns of behavior, and individuals are not left isolated as they might be after T-group or other such forms of training. A team that has developed sufficient levels of trust will be able to work on whatever problems arise, in a self-correcting way that allows for changes in structure or technology, as well as changes in member behavior.[32]

Even a successful team-building effort, however, can still create problems for members of adjoining subsystems or with those higher in the organizational hierarchy. The team that works well together may ignore outside interests and demands or see as inferior other groups that do not seem to be working so well. This can cause resentment or jealousy, creating problems in other parts of the system.

Intergroup Confrontation

As you might expect, methods also have been developed for dealing with problems between groups. In Chapter 13 you were introduced to some of the kinds of issues that lead to conflict between groups; reemphasized here are those methods that work on finding ways to resolve conflicts between groups. Several mechanisms for structurally interweaving group members have been invented to allow diffusion of group boundaries, thereby lowering rivalry and commitment to each group's own preferred way of doing things. Direct exchanges of members, a new linking group made up of some members from each of the original groups, whether individually elected or selected by all groups together, and the utilization of independent judges or arbitrators are all ways of resolving difficulties between groups. Joint labor-management committees, created to foster and supervise quality of work life projects, are a widely publicized example of creating a new linking group to allow for cooperation. These committees usually have an equal number of union and management members.

The inherent problem with these kinds of solutions is that those who form a new, supposedly independent group are likely to maintain allegiance to their own group and therefore have difficulties dealing with each other. Alternatively, they may link together into an independent system, which then has trouble getting support from the individual groups. A more direct way of trying to deal with feelings among group members has its roots in the T-group but is more structured and controlled. In the *intergroup confrontation laboratory,* groups exchange their collective opinion about how they see themselves and how they think the other group sees them and then work on the accuracy and stereotyping contained therein. Though risky and highly charged, this method can break through mutual hostilities, particularly when there are not fundamental value differences between the groups but only inaccurate perceptions.[33]

Many variations have been developed where groups in conflict are brought together to attempt to find common ground. These often involve asking people for their vision of the distant future and then seeking agreement that can frame subsequent discussions. When direct confrontational methods work, whether between individuals or groups, it is because increased and more accurate communication is an appropriate solution to a problem involving some form of misperception. At other times, however, increased accuracy of communication can lead to further distancing among the involved parties, especially when it becomes clear that there are fundamental value differences that cannot be negotiated away. In general, The more the problems among subsystems are based on value differences, the more appropriate are methods that involve arms-length, formal, and legalistic negotiations, rather than greater openness and trust.[34] When differing subsystems have high suspicions of each other and little trust, the most that can be hoped for is some kind of agreement to demarcate territories, live and let live within those boundaries, and then formulate specific rigid and observable contracts on a point-by-point basis as needed. It is naïve to try to shortcut this process by methods that encourage openness, honesty, and vulnerability. Similarly, when problems can be resolved by better understanding and clarity, it is "paranoid" to be willing only to deal in legalistic and distinct contractual terms.

The methodology for dealing with any two subsystems in conflict is worth spelling out in some detail:

1. The first phase of conflict resolution calls for a thorough understanding of each party's position. This can only be done if differences are brought out and made explicit, even at the risk of polarization, rather than minimized and papered over. The more clearly and dramatically differences are stated, the greater are the chances that individual members of each subsystem will begin to raise questions about the strength and clarity of their group's positions. Furthermore, unless subsystem members feel that they have had a chance to state their posi-

tion clearly and be understood by conflicting subsystems, they will find it hard to acknowledge the possibility of not being 100 percent right.

2. Once differences are looked at in bold relief, then the opposing subsystems can begin to point out perceived inaccuracies in other group perceptions. As noted earlier, where differences are great and value-based, tough bargaining leading to contractual relationships is appropriate. It is vital to have a contract for each side to do specific activities under particular conditions, composed in a way that allows each to observe whether the terms of the contract are being honored. If, however, the differences are not fundamental and based on values, a more direct and trusting collaboration can be developed. Any attempt to minimize a genuine set of differences may lead very rapidly toward each side believing that the other is behaving suspiciously, and then the conflicts are quickly renewed.[35]

Another variation is to ask each party to answer three questions:

1. What is your history with this issue?
2. What about this issue hooks you or is really problematic?
3. What are the gray areas for you?

This can free groups to examine their own assumptions and then problem-solve in a less polarized atmosphere. (See Personal Application Exercise at the end of Chapter 13.)

Survey Feedback

There's a paradox in all change efforts. On the one hand, those efforts aimed at changing subsystems suffer from the problems mentioned many times by now—namely, unintended consequences for other subsystems in the organization. On the other hand, efforts aimed at changing the *total* organization (particularly when it is a large and complex one) often are so general and impersonal that they have very little effect on day-to-day behavior within a given subsystem. Ideally then, the total change effort has to deal somehow with that paradox. A method is needed that first collects data about total system problems at a given time, allows diagnosis by those at the head of the organization about priorities in solving the problems, and then tackles problems in order of importance. One useful way of approaching such total system change is the survey-feedback method developed at the University of Michigan. A lengthy questionnaire on employee attitudes and perceptions of the organization is administered, tabulated, and the anonymous (with respect to individuals) results fed back by departments. When followed with specific action plans in each department, utilizing some of the methods described earlier, this can be an effective way to begin a total system change effort.[36] Some quality efforts have adopted variations of survey research to do system diagnosis and intervention.

Executive Planning and Confrontation Sessions

Another method, pioneered by Richard Beckhard[37], is called the *confrontation meeting*. A large cross section of organizational executives is brought together for a concentrated period, such as one day, assigned to small work groups, and asked to develop lists of organizational problems needing solution. When the groups have reported their lists, priorities are set for working on problems, various groups are given the responsibility to work on them, and deadlines are set for producing proposed solutions. Again, considerable follow-up is needed, utilizing some of the methods described earlier, such as team building, process consultation, or individual counseling; but this kind of "shock treatment" can be an excellent catalyst for generating energy to produce change. These methods and other comparable ones all follow on a somewhat more grand scale the general action–research cycle described earlier.

At General Electric, a variation was developed called Work-out, which brought together a large cross section of a division to identify useless procedures and practices,

MANAGERIAL BULLETIN

Planning Surprises

"Traditional" strategic planning is less relevant today . . . because everybody's planning horizon is shrinking rapidly.

I herewith propose a new measure, "the Mean Time between Surprises" (MTBS), and a set of propositions ("Surprise" is defined as any unpredicted event that materially affects the decision being made):

1. The MTBS has been dropping steadily.
2. The surprises are not simply *not* predicted but unpredictable.
3. The number of people or groups able to create a surprise has been growing steadily.

These ideas take on greater urgency when we consider another measure: "the Mean Time to Make Decisions" (MTMD), which leads to several more propositions:

1. When MTBS is less than or equal to MTMD, an organization loses its ability to function effectively.
2. Proposition 1 describes the situation at most organizations most of the time.
3. The main determinant of MTMD is organizational design and structure, not intent, policy, or management style.

SOURCE: From "Surprise, Surprise" by Barry A. Stein, president, Goodmeasure, Inc., May 1983.

quickly develop proposals, and make decisions on the spot. This methodology spread to other companies and other problems; sometimes suppliers or customers are included, both to get first-hand data on problems and to include them in problem solving.

The underlying assumption of such change attempts is that the collection of data around problems or even the generation of lists of problems acts as a disconfirming and *unfreezing* process, which creates sufficient tension to motivate commitment toward change. However, if our earlier proposition about the greatest change following moderate amounts of tension is valid, then, in some organizations, methods that produce less tension may be called for. As suggested earlier, methods that utilize "vision building" can be used when data about current problems might prove so overwhelmingly threatening that they would paralyze action. It can also be used when there is insufficient tension in the present circumstances to arouse the desire to make needed long-term changes.

Another variation of this type of method is called *open system planning*. It involves top executives in thinking through the organization's relationships with its various environments and then developing a plan to maximize the effectiveness of each subsystem's transactions with its dominant environment(s).[38] Strategic planning systems also attempt to position the firm in relation to environmental opportunities and organizational strengths. The better schemes help top management work through the human, organizational, and procedural changes necessary to implement the strategy.

All such total organization methods run the danger of mobilizing considerable enthusiasm for change all at once and then creating frustration when the actual results take a long time, which inevitably they do. Aroused expectations that are unmet may be considerably more dysfunctional than never raising expectations in the first place. Whether one is willing to take that risk is very much a matter of personal desires. Nevertheless, if organizations are to remain adaptive, they must find ways of gaining commitment to whatever changes are necessary to keep the organization working toward its goals.

Words That Can't Be Set to Music

Mission statements—those distilled essences of corporate goals—will never be confused with works of Donne or Shakespeare. Yet they have caught on, becoming poetry to executives' ears, so much so that 86 percent of American corporations have their own carefully worded, neatly printed, widely disseminated statements. . . .

Many executives hail their statements as magic potions that help inspire corporate turnarounds. But others acknowledge that such documents fall flat and end up forgotten just months after corporate leaders trumpeted the statements. . . .

"The vast majority are not worth the paper that they are written on and should not be taken with any degree of seriousness.

"[But] it's the glue that holds [Johnson & Johnson] together. The message is the ability to produce business results, not at any cost, but within our value system."

SOURCE: Steven Greenhouse, "Words That Can't Be Set to Music," *New York Times*, February 13, 2000, p. 4. © 2000 New York Times Company.

Change Must Be Managed

As is implied in all that has been stated so far, change must be actively managed. It is not enough to see a problem and decide what the solution will be; the tough issue is how to get there from where you are. In addition to careful diagnosis and excellent selection of solutions, the process of moving to the desired state requires special attention, especially for changes of any complexity. When large-scale change is involved, it is helpful to create a special structure for managing the transition—a high-level steering committee or advisory group that can link the changes to wider organizational goals, help overcome barriers or resistance, and anticipate connections to related subsystems.[39] Even when the change desired is not so vast, it is important to pay attention to what is and should be happening as you move from here to there. How will the change targets react? How are they feeling about the changes? Do they need extra support while they are learning new skills? Do the original plans make sense in light of new data? Is the pacing of the changes appropriate? How are others not directly involved being affected by the change? Do they have enough information about it to avoid rumors and negative fantasies?

Someone or some group needs to worry about and deal with these kinds of questions; your job as the manager of change is to do it or set up a mechanism for doing it. Many wonderful ideas have been killed off because no one managed the process of implementing them. Part of a good action plan is to think through these kinds of issues in advance insofar as possible, and then be ready to adapt and bend as you proceed. Effective masters of change combine a steadfast vision of where they are going and a willingness to be flexible along the way.[40] None of this happens by accident; change must be carefully managed.

An Overview of Organizational Change

We suspect that it might be a difficult task for you to develop an overall perspective on organizational change. The problems are many and complex, the procedures for diagnosis are loaded with uncertainties and pitfalls, and the methods of change are too complicated and varied to organize into a handy package. We hope that, by using

MANAGERIAL BULLETIN

Driving at High Speed while Changing Tires

"The toughest part is designing a new organization while you operate the old one. You can't slam dunk the new way. You have to run the two systems in parallel," [says Noel Tichy, professor and consultant].

SOURCE: John Huey, "Managing in the Midst of Chaos," *Fortune,* April 5, 1993.

MANAGERIAL BULLETIN

Not Coping with Change

U.S. executives are not well prepared to handle changes and, as a result, tend to resist them and cling to the status quo, according to "Hesitant at the Helm: American Executives in a Sea of Change," a study by The Gallup Organization in conjunction with Proudfoot Change Management.

"Only 1 percent of the total sample say they employ a formal change management structure. . . ."

[T]he majority of respondents (79%) describe the pace of change in their organization as "rapid" or "extremely rapid," but only 47 percent say they are very confident of their company's capability for handling change.

SOURCE: "U.S. Executives Deemed 'Hesitant at the Helm,'" *Quality Digest,* November 1993. Quality Digest © 1993 QCI International, PO Box 882, Red Bluff, CA. 96080, (800) 527-8875.

the social systems conceptual scheme as a framework for the chapter, we helped you to appreciate the importance of asking many questions before arriving at a diagnosis of a problem and before selecting a change method that will be *appropriate* to the situation.

All too often when change is needed, the presence of tension or anxiety makes it difficult to go through a systematic, careful series of diagnostic steps. It seems easier, perhaps even desirable, to grab the first "treatment" that comes along. That is why in the history of organizational change there have been many sales pitches for one or another magic "elixir." Got a problem? Use Dr. Fixit's All-Purpose Employee Productivity Kit. While this may sound exaggerated, it is more the rule than the exception to find advocates of particularized methods touting claims of success no matter what the change problem. We caution you as prospective managers to maintain some degree of scientific skepticism; this is what can make the difference between an ordinary manager and an outstanding manager.

> To a child with a hammer, everything looks like a nail.

Ultimately, however, no matter how astute you are as an observer of organizational culture, norms, and behavior or how shrewd at assessing organizational change techniques, you will be making choices that reflect your own values, your best assessment of what consequences you are willing to live with. We wish you valid predictions, good judgment, and informed choices in your managerial career.

The Best Laid Plans: Many Companies Try Management Fads, Only to See Them Flop In Practice, Trendy Theories Often Need Rejiggering to Get Intended Results

Process reengineering, benchmarking, total quality management, broadbanding, worker empowerment, skill-based pay. The labels abound when it comes to the trendy remedies executives are using to try to breathe new life and competitive fires into their companies.

But while these approaches may promise more motivated workforces and greater productivity, the results often fall far short. When this happens, companies find they must sharply modify, abandon, or find antidotes to programs that bring sweeping changes to organizational and human-resource management.

SOURCE: Fred R. Bleakley, *The Wall Street Journal*, July 6, 1993.

KEY CONCEPTS FROM CHAPTER 14

1. Need for change when problems occur with respect to production, satisfaction, and/or development.
2. A manager can be the passive victim of change, or its initiator and planner.
3. Target for change depends on following factors:
   a. Tension in the system.
   b. Interconnection of the problem person or groups with other units.
   c. The organization's hierarchy.
   d. Place or point with most readiness for change.
4. Considerations in regard to target:
   a. Those experiencing moderate discomfort and tension are most amenable to change.
   b. The more autonomy in the subunit, the easier to implement change.
   c. The more hierarchical the organization, the higher the change effort will have to be aimed.
   d. The more autonomy in the subunit, the less important will be support from higher levels.
   e. Start where resistance is least likely.
   f. Diagnosis should precede action.
      (1) Is the behavior functional or dysfunctional?
      (2) Is it easily or not easily subject to change?
5. Resistance to change by key stakeholders:
   a. People do not automatically resist change. They do so for reasons (however unclear and "illogical").
   b. People resist change when they perceive the consequences as negative, such as:
      (1) Perceived general threat from the unknown and from uncertainty.
      (2) Pain of letting go of the past with which one identifies.
      (3) Lack of control over what is happening (aggravated by not having time to get used to a new idea or plan).
      (4) Direct loss of:
         (i) "Face."
         (ii) Competency (relevant skills).
         (iii) Power and influence.
         (iv) Income, status, privileges, conveniences, friends, etc.
      (5) Disruption of the social system.
         (i) Technological changes often affect relationships.
         (ii) Pressure from other subsystems (interdependent).
   c. Resistance can be minimized by:
      (1) Providing accurate information and answers to questions.
      (2) Ownership through participation in diagnosis and implementation planning.
      (3) Reduction of direct negative impacts where possible and providing support, such as training, to help individuals to adapt.
      (4) Allowing people time to get used to an idea.
      (5) Utilizing the minimum amount of force possible.

(6)   Being responsive to developments as the change is implemented (flexible and open to feedback).

d.   The forms resistance can take.

6.   The changer's power relative to key stakeholders, an important consideration:

a.   Influences whether to emphasize current problems or to present a vision of the future.

b.   Influences need to look for allies.

c.   Influences the possibility of resorting to coercion in times of urgency.

d.   Should be used sparingly.

e.   Is not essential to gain cooperation, exert influence, and initiate change.

7.   Action–research cycle:
Constantly evolving interplay between solutions, results, and new solutions. Problem defined; data gathered on causes, related attitudes, and the like; diagnosis of data; alternative solutions developed; solution chosen; solution implementation; evaluation of solution; new data created; and redefinition of the problem(s).

8.   Identification of problem:

a.   Locate subsystem it is in.

(1)   Look for source of problem:

(i)   First in background factors.

(ii)   Next in required system.

(iii) Finally in emergent system.

9.   Methods of changing background factors:

a.   Personnel change.

b.   Training and education.

c.   Technology and layout.

d.   Incentive plans.

e.   Background culture.

10.   Methods of changing the required system:

a.   Revision of job descriptions and work relationships.

b.   Job modification.

c.   Quality circles; problem-solving teams; employee involvement; process teams; self-managing teams.

d.   Alternative work schedules.

e.   Work from home.

f.   Reformulation of objectives.

11.   Methods of changing the emergent system:

a.   Counseling.

b.   Third-party consultation.

c.   Task group training: team building.

d.   Intergroup confrontation: Dealing with two subsystems in conflict through understanding of each other's position; pointing out of perceived inaccuracies in other group's position.

e.   Survey feedback.

f.   Executive planning and confrontation sessions.

12.   Change must be managed.

PERSONAL APPLICATION EXERCISE

Making a Responsible Change from Below

Think about your own college or university. Is there any change that would benefit learning or student life? For example, would you like to see a course added, a group you belong to change its norms, class times made more convenient, registration smoother, rooming assignments using different priorities, student government more responsive, new teaching methods used—or some other change? Pick one and do an analysis of how to go about getting the change made.

Start by specifying just what the change should be, and why it would be beneficial. Then do a stakeholders' analysis. Just who has a stake in this change, and how would they be affected? Do you need each one (or group) on your side? What would have to happen for those who have to be won over to be willing to implement your change? Are there particular potential allies whom you can line up to help you?

What is your power to affect this change? Can you control it or do you have to line up support?

What resistance would you expect to find? What are the likely causes of it? What could you do to overcome the resistance?

Where could you start? Can you think of a small pilot or experiment that might be easier to sell? Can you find a way to demonstrate the benefits from the change? Will you spell out a vision of how things might be or point out what the problems are in the current situation?

Once you have done the basic analysis, jot down a provisional plan. Find someone you trust to discuss it with. Expect your plan to change, so try not to get defensive at the response you get. Perhaps you might test the plan with your instructor in this course, or any other instructor who you sense might have an interest in the issue. You may have to go back and use ideas learned in other parts of this course; everything you have studied can be helpful in diagnosing the causes of the problem you have identified—and in planning for how to change the situation.

We encourage you to set out to implement your plan—but not to do it in a way that makes those whom you want to change become *more* resistant! The doctors' Hippocratic oath is relevant here; if you can't "cure" the patient, at least do no harm! But this is a good way to put your course learnings to work. Good luck.

SUGGESTED READINGS

"A Conversation with Peter Senge: New Developments in Organizational Learning." *Organizational Dynamics,* Autumn 1998, pp. 33–43.

Alted, Brent B.; Charles C. Snow; and Raymold E. Miles. "Characteristics of Managerial Careers in the 21st Century." *Academy of Management Executives* 10 (1996), pp. 17–27.

Amabile, Teresa. M., and Regina Conti. "Changes in the Work Environment for Creativity during Downsizing." *Academy of Management Journal* 42 (1999), pp. 630–40.

Arthur, Michael B., and Denise Rousseau. "A New Career Lexicon for the 21st Century." *Academy of Management Executives* 10 (1996), p. 28.

Basler, Franklin C., Jr., and Anne B. Breslin. "Using Simulation to Assure Fit and Avoid Resistance." *Journal of Quality and Participation,* December 1990.

Brousseau, Kenneth R.; Michael J. Driver; Kristina Eneroth; and Rikard Larsson. "Career Pandemonium: Realigning Organizations and Individuals." *Academy of Management Executives* 10 (1996), pp. 52–66.

Buhler, Patricia. "Vision and the Change Process in the 90s." *Supervision,* January 1993.

Cantor, Bill. "Organizational Development for the Communication Professional—A Reality Check." *Communication World,* October 1993.

Coch, L., and J. R. French, Jr. "Overcoming Resistance to Change." *Human Relations Journal* 1 (1948), pp. 512–32.

Cohen, A. R. "Crisis Management: How to Turn Disasters into Advantages." *Management Review,* July–August 1982.

Cooper, A. C., and C. G. Smith. "How Established Firms Respond to Threatening Technologies." *Academy of Management Executive* 6, no. 2 (1992), pp. 56–69.

Cutcher-Gershenfeld, Joel; Ellen Ernst Kossek; and Heidi Sandling. "Managing Concurrent Change Initiatives: Integrating Quality ands Work/Family Strategies." *Organizational Dynamics,* Winter 1997, pp. 21–37.

Davis, Tim R. V. "Open-Book Management: Its Promise and Pitfalls." *Organizational Dynamics,* Winter 1997, pp. 7–20.

Deal, T., and A. Kennedy. *Corporate Culture.* Reading, MA: Addison-Wesley Publishing, 1982.

Delbecq, A. L., and P. K. Mills. "Managerial Practices That Enhance Innovation." *Organizational Dynamics,* Summer 1985, pp. 24–34.

Denison, D. R. *Corporate Culture and Organizational Effectiveness.* New York: Wiley, 1990.

Dunphy, Dexter, and Doug Stace. "The Strategic Management of Corporate Change." *Human Relations,* August 1993.

———. "Transformational and Coercive Strategies of Planned Organizational Change: Beyond the O.D. Model." *Organization Studies,* 1988.

Eby, L. T., D. M. Adams; J. E. A. Russell; and S. H. Gaby; "Perceptions of Organizational Readiness for Change: Factors Related to Employees' Reactions to the Implementation of Team-based Selling," *Human Relations* 53, no. 3 (March 2000), pp. 419–42.

Eden, D. "OD and Self-Fulfilling Prophecy: Boosting Productivity by Raising Expectations." *Journal of Applied Behavioral Science* 22, no. 1 (1986), pp. 1–14.

Fiol, C. M., and M. A. Lyles. "Organizational Learning." *Academy of Management Review,* October 1985, pp. 803–13.

Frohman, Alan L. "Igniting Organizational Change from Below: The Power of Personal Initiative." *Organizational Dynamics,* Winter 1997, pp. 39–53.

Garrity, Rudolph B. "Total Quality Management: An Opportunity for High Performance in Federal Organizations." *Public Administration Quarterly,* Winter 1993.

Gault, Stanley; Linda J. Wachner; Mike H. Walsh; and David W. Johnson. "Leaders of Corporate Change." *Fortune,* December 14, 1992.

Gordon, G. G. "Industry Determinants of Organizational Culture." *Academy of Management Review* 16, no. 2 (1991) pp. 396–415.

Greenwood, Royston, and C. R. Hinings. "Understanding Radical Organizational Change: Bringing Together the Old and New Institutionalism." *Academy of Management Review* 21 (1996), pp. 1022–54.

Hammonds, Keith H., and John Templeman. "Managing for Quality: Where Did They Go Wrong?; Grill-to-Grill with Japan." *Business Week,* October 25, 1991.

Hawley, J. A. "Transforming Organizations through Vertical Linking." *Organizational Dynamics,* Winter 1984, pp. 68–80.

Head, Thomas C., and Peter F. Sorenson. "Cultural Values and Organizational Development: A Seven-Country Study." *Leadership & Organization Development Journal,* 1993.

Henkoff, Ronald. "Companies That Train Best." *Fortune,* March 22, 1993, pp. 111–20.

Huey, John. "Nothing Is Impossible." *Fortune,* September 23, 1991.

Jenks, R. S. "An Action-Research Approach to Organizational Change." *Journal of Applied Behavioral Science* 6 (1970), pp. 131–50.

Jick, Todd. "Accelerating Change for Competitive Advantage." *Organizational Dynamics,* Summer 1995, pp. 78–82.

Kaplan, R. E.; M. M. Lombardo; and M. S. Mazique. "A Mirror for Managers: Using Simulation to Develop Management Teams." *Journal of Applied Behavioral Science* 21, no. 3 (1985), pp. 241–54.

Kerr, J., and J. W. Slocum. "Managing Corporate Culture through Reward Systems." *Academy of Management Executive* 1 (1987) pp. 99–107.

Kiechel, Walter III. "Facing Up to Denial." *Fortune,* October 18, 1993.

Kimberly, J. R., and R. E. Quinn. *Management Organizational Transitions.* New York, NY: McGraw-Hill/Irwin, 1984.

Kirkman, B. L., and B. Rosen. "Powering Up Teams." *Organizational Dynamics,* Winter 2000, pp. 48–66.

Kolodny, H. F., and B. Dresner. "Linking Arrangements and New Work Designs." *Organizational Dynamics,* Winter 1986, pp. 33–51.

Manz, Charles C.; David E. Keating; andAnne Donnellon. "Preparing for an Organizational Change to Employee Self-Management: The Managerial Transition." *Organizational Dynamics,* Autumn 1990.

Martin, P. Y.; D. Harrison; and D. DiNitto. "Advancement for Women in Hierarchical Organizations: A Multilevel Analysis of Problems and Prospects." *Journal of Applied Behavioral Science* 19, no. 1 (1983), pp. 19–34.

McClelland, D. C. *Power: The Inner Experience.* New York: Irvington, 1975.

McKendall, Marie. "The Tyranny of Change: Organizational Development Revisited." *Journal of Business Ethics,* February 1993.

Michael, R. "Organizational Change Techniques: Their Present, Their Future." *Organizational Dynamics,* Summer 1982, pp. 67–80.

Miner, John B. "The Expanded Horizon for Achieving Entrepreneurial Success." *Organizational Dynamics,* Winter 1997, pp. 54–67.

Mome, Mark A., William McKinley; and Vincent L. Barker III. "Organizational Decline and Innovation: A Contingency Framework." *Academy of Management Review* 23 (1998), pp. 115–32.

Nadler, D. A. "Consulting with Labor and Management: Some Learnings from Quality-of-Work-Life Projects." In *The Cutting Edge,* ed. W. W. Burke. San Diego: University Associates, 1978.

Nicholson, Nigel. "Career Systems in Crisis: Change and Opportunity in the Information Age." *Academy of Management Executives* 10 (1996), pp. 40–51.

Nystrom, P. C., and W. H. Starbuck. "To Avoid Organizational Crises, Unlearn." *Organizational Dynamics,* Spring 1984, pp. 53–65.

Pascale, R. T., and A. G. Athos. *The Art of Japanese Management.* New York: Simon & Schuster, 1981.

Peters, M., and V. Robinson. "The Origins and Status of Action Research." *Journal of Applied Behavioral Science* 20, no. 2 (1984), pp. 113–24.

Reichers, A. E. "A Review and Reconceptualization of Organizational Commitment." *Academy of Management Review,* July 1985, pp. 465–76.

Rice, B. "Measuring Executive Muscle." *Psychology Today,* December 1978.

Rigg, Michael. "Vision and Value: Key to Initiating Organizational Change." *Industrial Engineering,* June 1992.

Riplay, Robert E. "The Innovative Organization and Behavioral Technology for the 1990's." *SAM Advanced Management Journal,* Autumn 1992.

Schein, Edgard H. "Career Anchors Revisited: Implications for Career Development in the 21st Century." *Academy of Management Executives* 10 (1996), pp. 80–88.

Schein, E. H. *Organizational Culture and Leadership.* 2nd ed. San Francisco: Jossey-Bass, 1992.

Schneider, Benjamin; Arthur P. Brief; and Richard A. Guzzo. "Creating a Climate and Culture for Sustainable Organizational Change." *Organizational Dynamics,* Spring 1996, pp. 7–19.

Schwenk, C. R. "Information, Cognitive Biases, and Commitment to a Course of Action." *Academy of Management Review,* April 1986, pp. 298–310.

Senge, Peter, et al. *The Dance of Change.* New York: Doubleday, 1999.

Snow, Charles C.; Scott A. Snell; Sue Canney Davison; and Donald C. Hambrick. "Use Transnational Teams to Globalize Your Company." *Organizational Dynamics,* Spring 1996, pp. 50–67.

Stewart, Thomas A. "Allied-Signal's Turnaround Blitz." *Fortune,* November 30, 1992.

Sutton, R. I.; K. M. Eisenhardt; and J. V. Jucker. "Managing Organizational Decline: Lessons from Atari." *Organizational Dynamics,* Spring 1986, pp. 17–29.

Van Eynde, Donald F.; Allan Church; Robert F. Hurley; and W. Warner Burke. "What OD Practitioners Believe." *Training & Development,* April 1992.

Walton, R. "A Vision-Led Approach to Management Restructuring." *Organizational Dynamics,* Spring 1986, pp. 4–16.

Wilkins, A. L., and W. G. Dyer, Jr. "Toward Culturally Sensitive Theories of Culture Change." *Academy of Management Review* 13, no. 4 (1988), pp. 522–33.

Cases

Cases in this book not otherwise noted were prepared by, or with the help of, various individuals under the guidance of the authors. We are grateful to these individuals and organizations for their assistance. For reasons of preserving the anonymity of the organizations involved in the cases, we list the individuals' names below and gratefully acknowlege their contribution in this matter.

Andrea de Anguera
M. M. Ashraff
Barbara A. Corriveau
C. J. Crimmins
Kimberly Dalzell
Mary Ellen D'Antonio
Stephen P. Day
Mary L. Hynes
Stephanie L. Lavigne
Steve Lippman

Judith H. Long
E. Thorn Mead
Donna S. Miller
Gary Mongeon
The New Hampshire
Andrew R. Nichols
Robert V. O'Brien
Judith Pearson
Barbara Ready
Lauren Ready

Tetsuo Saitoh
Paul B. Samuels
Sandra Seiler
Ellina Tsirelson
Jane C. Vogt
Richard Weber
David Whall
Charles E. Winn

Case Titles

1. Atlantic Store Furniture
2. Back to Bickering
3. The Bagel Hockey Case
4. Baksheesh
5. Banana Time Case
6. Bangles
7. The Barbara Dibella Case
8. Beauty Classics, Inc.
9. Bill Michaels
10. Blair, Inc.
11. Bob Chen
12. The Brady Training Program
13. Bully or Victim?
14. Carpax Company and Phyllis Copeland
15. Chris Cunningham
16. Conscience or the Competitive Edge? (A)
17. Conscience or the Competitive Edge? (B)
18. The Consolidated Life Case: Caught between Corporate Cultures
19. Consumer Materials Enterprises, Inc. (Consummate Corporation)
20. Contract Negotiations in Western Africa: A Case of Mistaken Identity
21. David Shorter
22. Dilemma at Devil's Den
23. Electronics Unlimited
24. Estella Rios: Performance Problems at the Toll Authority
25. Evergreen Willows
26. The Forgotten Group Member
27. Fujiyama Trading Company, Ltd.
28. Grace Pastiak's "Web of Inclusion"
29. Growth at Stein, Bodello, & Associates, Inc.
30. Intel in China
31. Isabel Stewart
32. Jane Costello
33. Jim Donovan (A)
34. Jim Donovan (B)
35. Kate Cooper
36. Kingston Company
37. L. E. S., Inc.
38. Low Five
39. Management Diversity in the Large Corporation
40. Marilyn Adams (A)
41. Marilyn Adams (B)
42. A Matter of Ethics
43. The Misbranded Goat
44. The Montville Hospital Dietary Department
45. 3M's Occupational Health and Environmental Safety Division and Their Action Teams
46. Olivia Francis
47. A Particle of Evidence
48. Phil Daniels
49. Professional Exchange Service Organization (PESO)

ATLANTIC STORE FURNITURE

Atlantic Store Furniture (ASF) is a manufacturing operation in Moncton, New Brunswick. The company, located in an industrial park, employs about 25 people, with annual sales of about $2 million. Modern shelving systems are the main product, and these units are distributed throughout the Maritimes. Metal library shelving, dislay cases, acoustical screens, and work benches are a few of the products available at ASF. The products are classified by two distinct manufacturing procedures, which form separate sections of the plant. (See Exhibit 1 for ASF's organizational chart.)

The Metalworking Operation

In the metalworking part of the plant, sheet metal is cut and formed into shelving for assembly. The procedure is quite simple and organized in an assembly-line method. Six or eight stations are used to cut the metal to the appropriate length, drill press, shape, spotweld, and paint the final ready-to-assemble product. The equipment used in the operation is both modern and costly, but the technology is quite simple.

The metalworking operation employs on average about 8 or 10 workers, located along the line of assembly. The men range in age between 22 and 54 and are typically francophone Canadians. Most have high school education or have graduated from a technical program. The men as metalworkers are united by their common identity in the plant and have formed two or three subgroups based on common interests. One group, for example, comprising the foreman and three other workers, has season tickets to the New Brunswick Hawks home games. Another group bowls together in the winter and attends horse races in the summer months.

The foreman's group is the most influential among the workers. The men in this group joined the company at the same time, and James Savoie, the foreman, was once a worker with the three other men in the group. The group ccharacteristically gets to the lunch counter first, sits together in the most comfortable chairs, and punches the time clock first on the way out of work. Conrad LeBlanc, another group member, has a brother who plays professional hockey in the NHL and he frequently describes the success of the team and his brother's large home.

The metalworkers as a group operate on one side of the plant and work at a very steady pace. The demand for the products in this section is high and the production is usually constant. The group adjusts well to changes in the order requests and the occasional overtime pressures. The salespeople on the road provide a constant flow of orders, to the point where there is a small backlog of requisiton to be filled. The products vary in size and style but for the most part they are standardized items. A small amount of work is performed on a customized basis.

Woodworking Operations

The woodworking operation differs considerably from the metalworking operation. It is a new addition to the plant and has had some success. It is separated from the metal production unit by a wide sliding door.

The organizaiton of the wood shop is haphazard, because the majority of its work is customized. Some areas are organized to produce standard products like screening, but the majority of the woodworking section is organized around a particular project. Typically, tools, equipment, and supplies are left in the area of the partially completed projects. Custom cabinets and display cases are made for large department and retail stores. A small line of products is produced as a regular line while the rest of the products are custom designed. The flow of work is basically steady in the shop, but there are stages when the work orders become intermittent. Though the appearance of the woodworking shop is quite disorganized and messy, reflecting the nature of the operations, the workers in this section of the plant see themselves as real craftsmen and take considerable pride in their work. Typically, two or three projects are in process simultaneously along with the normal run of standard products. The metalworkers store some of their completed units in the woodworking area, to the dislike of the woodworkers and to the disorganization of the section.

Unlike the metalworkers there is a distinct hierarchy among the woodworkers based on seniority and ability. Sam Kirby is the quick-tempered but fiercely loyal foreman; most of the full-time woodworkers have come through apprenticeship programs or have similar backgrounds to the metalworkers'. Most are middle-aged anglophone Canadians and, beyond an occasional after-work beer at the local tavern, they do not spend time together. Through Kirby's persistence, an apprenticeship program within the company has produced a number of good carpenters. This section of the company, though still relatively young, has

EXHIBIT 1   *Partial Organizational Chart for Atlantic Store Furniture*

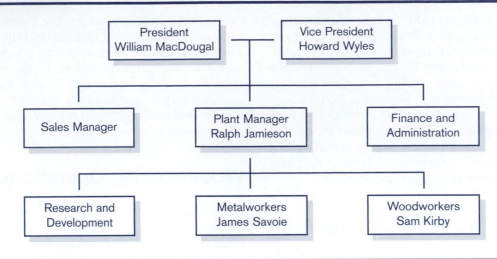

produced good work and has a reputation for quality craftsmanship.

The morning coffee break for the woodworkers follows that of the metalworkers. Lunch hour is staggered by 20 minutes as well. Only a minimal amount of interaction occurs between the woodworkers and metalworkers, as there tends to be rivalry and competition between the two groups.

Recent Events

The supervisor who oversees these two sections of the plant (plant manager) is Ralph Jamieson, a production engineer from a local university. As plant manager he reports to the vice president. At the time of his hiring, ASF had not developed the woodworking section of the plant. Jamieson's work at the university became integrated into the production line when he discovered a method of galvanizing the metal product in final stages of production. He spends a good deal of his time in the metalworking operaton, planning and discussing problems in production with the foreman, James Savoie. Laboratory research is another occupation assigned to Jamieson, who enjoys experimenting with new methods and techniques in design and fabrication of metal products. Jamieson and Savoie are good friends and they spend a good deal of time together both on and off the job. James Savoie is quite happy with the way his operation is running. His boisterous, good-humored attitudes have created a very good rapport with his men and absenteeism is minimal.

A recent personnel change that has occurred within ASF is the addition of two new salesmen who are on the road in New Brunswick and Nova Scotia. Their contribution to the company is most notable in the metalwork area. They have placed many orders for the company. The new sales incentive program has motivated these people to produce, and their efforts are being recognized.

Sam Kirby, the woodworking foreman, blew up at Jamieson the other day. Some metalworkers had pushed open the sliding doors with an interest in storing more excess shelving units in the woodworking area, without seeking Kirby's advice or permission. Sam is a hothead sometimes and has become quite annoyed with all the intergroup rivalry between the metalworkers and the woodworkers. Storage space has been a sore point between the groups for the last six months or so, ever since the metalworkers became very busy. Jamieson and Howard Wyles, the vice president, were asked to settle the problem between the two shops and decided that the metalworkers were only to enter the woodworking shop if absolutely necessary and with consent of the foreman.

This last incident really upset the fellows in the woodworking shop. The woodworkers feel intimidated by the metalworkers, who are taking space and interrupting their work. They grumble among themselves about the shouting and joking from the francophone assembly lines next door.

In a later conversation, Kirby and Jamieson smoothed things over somewhat. It was explained to Kirby that it was the metalworkers who were really turning out the firm's work and that they needed the extra space. The area that metalworkers want to use is not really needed by the woodworkers; rather, it is simply an area around the perimeter of the room, by the walls.

Kirby did not like Jamieson's response, knowing full well his commitment to the metalworking operations. With this decision, the metalworkers proceeded to use the area in the woodworking shop and never missed an opportunity to insult or criticize the woodworkers in French. The effect of the situation on the respective groups became quite obvious. The metalworkers became increasingly more jocular and irritating in their interactions with the woodworkers. The woodworkers grew resentful and their work pace slowed.

The infighting continued and became of concern to the president and vice president. For example, the large sliding doors separating the shops were too hastily closed one afternoon on a metalworker who was retreating from a practical joke he was playing on a woodworker. The resulting injury was not serious but it did interrupt a long series of accident-free days the company had been building up. This incident further divided the two groups. Meetings and disciplinary threats by management were not enough to curtail the problems.

The woodworkers were now withdrawing all efforts to communicate. They ate lunch separately and took coffee breaks away from the regular room. Kirby beccame impatient to complete new products and to acquire new contracts. He urged management to hire personnel and to solicit new business. The work atmosphere changed considerably in the woodworking shop as the workers lost their satisfying work experience. Much of the previous friendly interaction had ceased. Kirby's temper flared more frequently as small incidents seemed to upset him more than before. After-work get-togethers at the tavern were no longer of much appeal to the men.

The metalworkers were feeling quite good about their jobs as the weeks passed. Their orders remained strong as demand continued to grow for their products. The metalworkers complained about the woodworkers and demanded more space for their inventory. The metalworkers were becoming more cohesive and constantly ridiculed the woodworkers. The woodworkers' concern for the job decreased as back orders filled up and talk of expansion developed for the metalwork operation.

Just as the metal shop became more confident, there were more difficulties with the woodworking shop. The woodworkers were completing the final stages of an elaborate cabinet system when information came regarding a shipping delay. The new store for which the product was being built was experiencing problems, causing a two- or three-month delay before it could accept the new cabinet system. Kirby was very disturbed by this news, as his woodworkers needed to see the completion of their project and the beginning of a new one. The predicament was compounded somewhat by the attitude of the metalworkers, who heard of the frustration of the woodworkers and added only more jeers and smart remarks. Morale at this stage was at an all-time low. The chief carpenter, an integral member of the woodworkers, was looking for a new job. One or two of the casual workers were drifting into new work or not showing up for work they had. Contracts and orders for new products were arriving but in fewer numbers, and casual workers had to be laid off. Defective work was beginning to increase, to the embarrassment of the company.

Management was upset with the conditions of the two operations and threatened the foreman. Kirby was disturbed at the situation and was bitter about the deteriorating state of the woodworking shop. Despite many interviews, he was unable to replace the head carpenter, who had left the company attracted by a new job prospect. Efforts to reduce the intergroup conflict were tried but without success.

The president of ASF, William MacDougal, was alarmed with the situation. He recognized some of the problems with the different operations. One operation was active and busy while the other section worked primarily on project work. The organization was designed, he thought, with the normal structure in mind. The men in the company, he thought to himself, were very much of the same background and what little diversity there was should not have accounted for this animosity. As president, he had not developed a culture of competition or pressure in the company.

The disorganization and chaos in the woodworking shop was alarming, and there was very little that could be done about it. Kirby had been discussing the problem with the president, trying to identify some of the alternatives. This had been the third meeting in as many days, and each time the conversation drifted into a discussion about current developments in Jamieson's metalworking pursuits. James Savoie had told the president he felt that there was too much worrying going on "over there"! Plans for expanding the building at ASF were developing at a rapid pace. The president felt that more room might alleviate some of the problems, particularly with respect to inventory, warehousing, and storage.

Kirby became enthusiastic about the prospects of some relief for his side of the operation. He was very much aware of the fact that the performance of his operation was quite low. The president of the company felt satisfied that the woodworking concern was going to improve its performance. One or two new contracts with large department stores inspired an effort to improve the operation.

The men in the woodworking section became somewhat more relaxed. A few positive interactions between the woodworkers and metalworkers became evident. One afternoon about two weeks after the disclosure by the president of the new plant development, Kirby observed blueprints for the new expansion. The plans had been left on Jamieson's desk inadvertently and, to the surprise of Kirby, revealed full details of the expansion for the new building. Kirby sat down and examined the details more carefully and recognized that the woodworking area was not to be included in the expansion plans.

Kirby left the office in a rage and stormed into the president's office to demand an explanation. Kirby shouted that he had changed things around in the woodworking shop on the promise of more room and possibility of expansion. The president shook his head and apologized; he explained Kirby was going to be told nothing could be done. The market demand was simply not that great for wood products. Kirby left the office and went straight to his car and drove off.

2 | BACK TO BICKERING

AURORA, IL.–Rich Clausel helped lead a factory-floor revolution at the Caterpillar Inc. construction-equipment plant here. Under a much-touted program, he and other workers helped plan everything from purchasing machinery to reorganizing the excavator assembly line.

"For the first time, I felt when I went to work, I made some difference," Mr. Clausel says. The plant's efficiency, meanwhile, improved sharply.

But now the employee-involvement program is a victim of a bitter battle between the company and the United Auto Workers union. Advocates of employee involvement fear other companies may follow Caterpillar's example, particularly as they struggle with a weak economy.

Employee involvement became a near-religion in industrial America during the 1980s as Rust Belt companies sought to become competitive in world markets. But with so many workers now worried about losing their jobs, "these programs are under siege," says Tom Raleigh, a consultant who helped initiate Caterpillar's. The widening gulf between labor and management at Caterpillar was highlighted Friday, as the company said it will impose most of the remaining terms of its final contract offer to its 14,500 UAW employees.

Union hard-liners say the moral of the story is never to give up the adversarial relationship. Ron Carey, president of the Teamsters, says employee-involvement programs aim to "diminish the presence of the union." Adds Ed Sadlowski, a Steelworkers official in Chicago: "I haven't seen quality work life put an extra slice of bread on anybody's plate." Caterpillar, he says, provides "a simple lesson we should have learned a long time ago: not to trust management."

Issue: Pattern Bargaining

At Caterpillar, company-union cooperation ran smack into a dispute over pattern bargaining, the practice of negotiating similar contracts across an industry. Caterpillar considered it an albatross. "Is it worth signing a contract that won't allow you to be globally competitive?" asks Caterpillar Chairman Donald Fites.

But now Caterpillar may be burdened with a new albatross. J. Clayton Lafferty, a consultant who advised managers and workers at the Aurora plant, says the death of the employee-involvement program could damage the company's competitiveness. Months after the latest strike ended last April, its

workers "are angry and scared," says Bob Ross, a union member who helped oversee the program. One employee won't talk to his foreman; he uses cue cards to answer questions.

That is the sort of environment Caterpillar had before it created its highly successful program. In negotiating 10 contracts between 1955 and 1982, the company weathered eight strikes. When Mr. Clausel was hired in 1971, he says, the shop floor was like a "playground." Workers came in drunk or stoned on drugs. Union stewards spent much of their time trying to keep the company from firing chronic absentees.

Tensions exploded in 1982. Buffeted by a deep recession and foreign competition, the company demanded concessions from its workers. The union struck for 205 days. The agreement that ended the bitter walkout called for both sides to explore a new kind of relationship.

In the spring of 1986, Caterpillar and UAW officials gathered at an inn in St. Clair, Michigan. Guided by Delmar "Dutch" Landen, a former General Motors Corp. executive, they sought ways to make employee involvement work. Participants were heartened by the cooperative spirit, particularly given the long history of acrimony. "I'm getting worried," a union official told the executives. "I'm agreeing too much with you guys." The result was the Employee Satisfaction Process–introduced at all of Caterpillar's major U.S. plants.

Aurora was an ideal place for an ESP program. The workforce was maturing both in age and in the realization that with increasing foreign competition, the easy days for American companies and their workers were over. And Aurora had a head start, kicking off employee-involvement programs even before getting official blessing by the company and the union.

At first workers viewed the program with suspicion. "Why do they want our help now?" wondered Bob Thorpien, a 20-year veteran. But like many others, he was slowly won over. With the plant managers behind this and other such programs, employees found they could change their work lives.

Mr. Thorpien suggested training classes for workers new to his gear-making area; he ended up teaching the two-hour sessions. He became such a big booster that he persuaded the company to erect a banner at the plant's entrance announcing: "Quality People Working Together."

Mr. Clausel's team in the press shop–the *What Ifs*–spent six months redesigning the parking lot. The site of numerous accidents, it "bugged the hell out of me," he says. With ideas of what worked at local malls and grocery stores, the workers drew up blueprints. The company redid the lot.

Later Mr. Clausel was invited to share his team's ideas with a team at a company plant in Decatur, Illinois. "It gave me satisfaction thinking you were more than just a welder or machine operator," he says.

At home Mr. Clausel read about employee-involvement programs, and managers and hourly workers would call or stop by his house to chat. He soon moved from being a team leader to joining a dozen company and union "facilitators" who managed the growing number of ESP teams. That was a full-time job that took him off the assembly line.

Unlikely Friendships

Friendships bloomed between people who had long gone their separate ways. A group of workers in the gear area invited their foreman to their annual pig roast. Some workers found a new sense of self-worth in their ability to solve problems. "When we went to [team] meetings, there wasn't any such thing as union and management," says Wayne Jacobson, a field engineer. With half the 2,200 UAW members taking part, Aurora's teams increased to 110 last year from about 20 in 1987.

The paint line became a showcase. When its workers visited dealers, they heard gripes about the dull yellow finish on the plant's tractors. The teams spent months overhauling the process, changing the paint and the paint guns. The result: better paint coverage and a glossy finish praised by dealers and customers.

"The whole idea of doing something and doing something right became foremost," Mr. Clausel says. In April and May 1989, his What Ifs avoided $2,000 in costs. The Cat Scanners, a team in the paint area, saved $19,500. A Team called Wheel Do It saved $72,213. Total savings from 241 ideas in the two months: $4,912,432.

The Aurora plant, already a model within Caterpillar, hired Mr. Lafferty's Plymouth, Michigan, consulting firm to help take ESP to the next step. The facilitators administered the firm's self-evaluation tests, which helped workers identify their strengths and weaknesses. But they also told a disturbing story. Getting promotions, many said, came from stroking a higher-up or knowing the right person. Staying out of trouble meant hiding from responsibility.

In addition Mr. Clausel and John Smith, a plant official, conducted workshops for hourly, salaried, and management employees. They hoped to show that bad attitudes hurt the quality of jobs and products. Union and management both had faults, they

conceded, but the culture wouldn't change until people stopped pointing fingers and attacked problems.

It worked. Perennial problems such as defects and downtime dropped as the two gurus worked with employees. Mr. Clausel was invited to speak at other companies, including Mack Trucks Inc., Sky Chefs Inc., and the local Earthmover Credit Union. Peoria headquarters selected Aurora as one of the plants to start the tortuous route of applying for the Malcolm Baldrige National Quality Award. One tally showed that employees' ideas at Aurora alone saved $13 million over three years.

ESP even became a marketing tool as Caterpillar boasted to customers of improvements in quality, productivity, and employee relations. Steve Ames, a Caterpillar salesman in Hammond, Indiana, noticed the difference as workers escorted customers on plant tours. "There was a real willingness to recognize that this is a paying customer—and we want to keep him in the fold," he says.

In Peoria two chairmen, first Lee Morgan and then George Schaefer, pushed for better relations with the UAW. But in 1990 Donald Fites became chairman, with a new agenda, reorganizing the company into profit centers and mounting a drive to hold down costs. Ominously for the UAW, one way to slow the rise in costs would be to end pattern bargaining.

To Mr. Fites, taking on the UAW was a matter of long-term survival. Caterpillar had fought back the challenge of rivals such as Komatsu Ltd. of Japan. Caterpillar was No. 1 in its industry in the world, exporting 36 percent of its 1991 sales of $10.18 billion. But the 58-year-old chairman found it senseless to be tied to a contract modeled after Deere & Co., the company's U.S. competitor, or—even worse—the automakers. His number crunchers figured a Deere-like contract would raise Caterpillar's UAW wage and benefit costs 26 percent. He was ready to give a 17 percent wage-and-benefit increase and thought it generous.

The UAW Demands

That wasn't all. The UAW was also demanding a voice on which parts are made in-house and which are bought from outside suppliers. And it wanted Caterpillar to declare itself neutral in any future UAW organizing drives. To the UAW, it was a matter of saving good union jobs. To Mr. Fites, it was more like a power-grab. "How much is it worth to be able to manage your own company?" he asks.

The contention abruptly halted Caterpillar's extraordinary turnaround in labor relations. On November 5, 1991, a day after launching a strike at two

Caterpillar plants in downstate Illinois, the UAW suspended ESP activities. Mr. Clausel got the word as he conducted a workshop. "I felt like I'd been shot," he says. Three days later, Caterpillar locked out workers in Aurora and East Peoria in retaliation for the union's partial walkout.

Mr. Clausel used his spare time to write a 10-page critique of management-labor relations at Caterpillar. Both sides, he wrote, "believe in power, greed, and winning at all costs." He mailed his paper to local and national officials of the company and the union. He also reached Mr. Fites by phone to find out how it all might end. He got his answer on April Fool's Day: Caterpillar announced it would replace strikers who didn't return to work. To Rich Atwood, a UAW official who had helped create ESP in 1986, that announcement was a "death blow" to the program.

Torn between their company and their union, several ESP leaders, including Mr. Clausel, crossed the picket lines. After being jeered as he drove into the plant with other workers, Mr. Clausel hid in the back of the van on the way out. After two days, he joined the strikers—and both sides were angry at him. The UAW eventually censured him, prohibiting him from ever running for union office. The company played down his concern over the demise of ESP. Alan Rassi, the Aurora plant manager, says the disappointment of people such as Mr. Clausel reflects their loss of "a pretty glamorous job."

Us against Them Again

Two weeks after Caterpillar threatened to hire strikebreakers, the union ended the strike, and the workers returned to the plants under company-imposed conditions. The old us-against-them attitude was back.

Worker complaints, down sharply under the employee-involvement programs, ballooned. In Aurora, grievances in the final stage before arbitration are up to 336 from 22 before the lockout. Union officials who once pushed cooperation canceled joint programs and urged their members to join in a work-to-rule campaign to slow production. And they handed out new ESP buttons: "Employees Stop Participating."

Mr. Thorpien, who was elected financial secretary of the local union in 1990, couldn't stand to look at his banner. "How could a company with workers so loyal think of throwing us out like a worn-out pair of shoes?" he asks. And Mr. Ross, the union's ESP leader, is back running a machine. The ESP offices and meeting rooms are empty.

In Detroit and Peoria union and company executives who once bragged about their new ties accused

each other of arrogance. "I firmly believe if the Lord said, 'You're walking down the wrong path,' they'd [still] walk it to the end," says Bill Casstevens, the UAW's secretary-treasurer.

Caterpillar executives say the union's withdrawal forced the company to officially cancel ESP in September. But they say ESP was just one program among many. "We still have a lot of cooperative efforts going on in our plants every day," Mr. Fites says.

Indeed Caterpillar executives contend that productivity and quality are higher now than before the strike. In an interview in his Peoria office, Chairman Fites pulls out charts tracking the gains. "That's the real story of what's going on in Aurora," he says. Executives suggest they no longer need a formal program. In Aurora, managers say foremen will take the lead in encouraging worker suggestions.

Apparent Company Gains

On paper the company does appear to have come out ahead. Compared with a pattern contract, the conditions it imposed on its returning strikers would save it up to $80 million in wages and benefits alone after three years. That dwarfs a UAW official's estimate that cooperation saved the company up to $50 million through workers' suggestions at facilities around the country.

But the results are far from in. The company's strategy "sounds like it's really an attempt to go around the union, and we know from past experience it doesn't work," says Michael Rosow, executive vice president of the Work in America Institute, of Scarsdale, New York, which encourages labor-management cooperation. The union is making noises about another strike if President-elect Clinton signs legislation banning permanent replacement of strikers. Moreover, there is doubt that worker trust can be restored.

Not long ago Mr. Clausel dreamed that the Aurora plant would become another Saturn—the GM auto plant powered by labor-management cooperation in Spring Hill, Tennessee. Now, he dreams of quitting. "All you see are people doing the minimum to get by," he says.

He has returned to a job on the plant floor, working on a paint line on the second shift. Like others, he is baffled at the way the union and the company tossed aside six years of progress on the factory floor. On Labor Day, Mr. Clausel walked into his spare bedroom and threw out most of his material on employee involvement. He filled two 30-gallon trash bags.

3   THE BAGEL HOCKEY CASE

The Cafeteria for the Toronto Training Academy (TTA) was located on the first floor of the school's main residential hall. The cafeteria was open seven days a week. It consisted of a short-order grill, a salad and delicatessen bar, a soda fountain, and a hot-meals counter, although the latter was not operated on weekends. It was heavily utilized by the students and by others during the week for food and as a social center. On weekends its use was rather limited, since many TTA students were commuters and others left campus for the weekend. What business there was tended to come in spurts due in part to the use of the building for special workshops and other group activities.

During the weekend the cafeteria employed a different crew of workers than during the week. All seven of the weekend employees were students except for the cashier, who was a housewife in her mid-30s. Two of the employees were attending high school; the senior student supervisor was from a two-year business college, and the remaining three workers were from TTA.

Ernie Slim, the senior student supervisor, had been employed at the cafeteria for four years, a long period of employment for the cafeteria, and had worked his way up from grill attendant to his supervisory position. He was a shy, friendly character who rarely worked directly with the public but spent most of his time in the back room making food preparations for take-out and banquet orders. Henry Delano, the junior student supervisor, was more personable with the customers, often standing and chatting with them. He spent most of his day walking around overseeing the other employees, sometimes helping them when they found themselves bogged down with orders, or working the grill and fountain positions by himself while others took breaks. Having had no previous experience before beginning the job, Henry was often forced to rely on employees below him to explain tasks.

Two male students usually worked the grill, and during slow hours of the day were required to work in the dishroom. Two female students worked the fountain and deli bar and during slow hours bused cafeteria tables. The cashier's job only required her to attend the register and at the end of the day determine the total income. This position was always occupied (even during weekdays) by an older, more mature woman.

All worked under the general regulations of the cafeteria, which required that all employees be neatly and cleanly attired. Females were to wear hairnets and blue smocks over skirts, while males had to wear white work shirts and paper hats. Sideburns were not permitted to extend below the ear lobe, and beards were not allowed. Mustaches had to be neat and closely trimmed, not extending beyond the width of the upper lip. Good sanitary practices were expected of all employees, and the regulations included the statement: "Loud talking, singing, whistling, or horseplay will not be tolerated." A pay differential was established, depending upon the individual's position, time employed, and whether the student had purchased a meal ticket. Weekend and weekday employees were on the same wage scale, and the pay range for grill and fountain employees was between the minimum wage and 30 percent higher, while the supervisors received double that of the employees. Except for the supervisors, the job was not considered a very desirable one; and, in fact, it had been a last resort choice by every weekend employee.

Since the cafeteria was open from 12:30 to 7 on weekends, only one shift of workers was needed. All weekend employees worked on an eight-hour day and were allowed a half hour for dinner and given a 15-minute coffee break. These breaks were given at the discretion of the supervisors, but employees felt free to ask for them if they thought business was slow enough.

Scheduling, hiring, and firing were all done by the cafeteria manager, Mrs. Laraby, a middle-aged woman who had been manager for five years. She worked a 40-hour week, Monday through Friday, and rarely came into the cafeteria on weekends unless there was a special banquet to be set up. As manager she encouraged a relaxed working atmosphere but expected each employee to be responsible for his or her job and to strictly observe the regulations of the cafeteria. Although she was firm about what she expected of her workers, Mrs. Laraby was willing to listen to any problems encountered by the employees. As a result, they respected Mrs. Laraby and felt comfortable enough in her presence to joke with her, although they were careful not to whenever her boss was around.

Grill products were of the hamburger and hot dog variety; the fountain's main business was ice cream cones; the deli bar served salads, desserts, and cold sandwiches, most of which had been made during the week and were now in the "staling" process. All beverage machines were self-service. A customer passed down the food line and paid the cashier located at the end of the line.

EXHIBIT 1   *Cafeteria Layout*

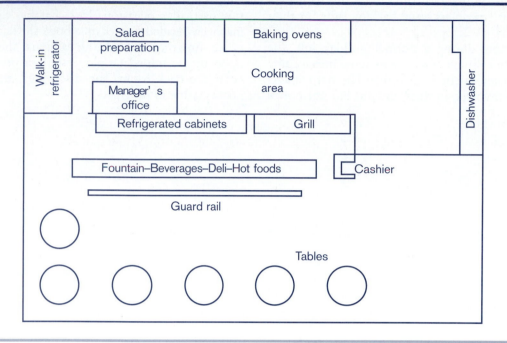

During the weekends no large-quantity food preparation was done, leaving the large kitchen area desolate and open to all employees. This large back room was blocked from the customer's view by walls that separated it from the food service area. (See Exhibit 1.)

All employees performed the essential tasks that their jobs demanded of them, but without much enthusiasm. The working atmosphere was extremely relaxed and lenient, and, since the work was menial, there was a flexible setup in which almost everyone could operate in another's position. Frequently the fountain person helped out the grill individual, and vice versa. However, a large portion of the working day passed with only a few customers trickling in. There was little opportunity to converse with friends coming through the food line, as was commonplace during the weekdays. This left the employees with much idle time.

The employees were close in age and shared common interests. Many friendships were formed. Supervisors were treated as equals and joked and fooled around with the others. In the back room (kitchen) as time allowed, the male employees—including the supervisors—often engaged in a game of floor hockey, using brooms as sticks and a stale bagel as a puck. The crew also participated in other sports. One was "baseball" played with a spatula and a hard-boiled egg. Another was "king of the eggs." This game was particularly

popular with the female employees. The idea was to find the "king egg" in a batch of hardboiled eggs destined to be used eventually in egg salad. The game required two players. Each chose an egg; then one party held her egg firmly in one hand while the other person used her egg to hit the immobile egg. The player whose egg withstood the impact without cracking was declared the winner and continued to challenge any other potential players. Of all the games, only baseball ruined any appreciable quantity of usable food.

There had never been any crackdown attempts on this behavior, which occurred only on weekends when the large kitchen was not in use and no older supervisors or managers were present.

Participation in these events was left up to the individual, but the usual participants included the three male student workers and the supervisor. The fountain girls took part in games such as the egg cracking less frequently, while the cashier never participated in any events but read during long intervals between customers. The general attitude of all employees toward these tournaments was favorable except, as a fountain employee put it, "when you get stuck doing all the work while the others are out back having fun." On occasion when employees were engaged in these tournaments, business picked up in the food service area. Then the one or two individuals left attending the fountain or grill were swamped with orders, finding it impossible to leave their jobs and notify the others in the back room of the customer influx. It placed a lot of pressure on these workers, and if this happened it meant that customers waited a long time for their orders.

One Sunday during a normal midday lull, the three men and the supervisor were deep into a game of bagel hockey in the back room. The participants were totally involved in their fun and did not notice that there was an influx of customers, that the other attendants were overwhelmed at both grill and fountain, and that the cashier was busy at her register. On this particular occasion, Mrs. Laraby, the cafeteria manager, decided to pick up a book she had left in her office. Entering through the cafeteria, she first came upon the swamped employees; then proceeding to enter the back room, she discovered an exuberant hockey game in progress!

4   BAKSHEESH

It was the middle of the night. My legs and neck ached as I stood up in the aircraft, but as a young man about to start his first expatriate assignment, I was thrilled to be in East Africa. Outside the air was hot. The terminal building was floodlit against the night sky. A small crowd of people moved out toward the aircraft, eager to meet relatives who had been to Europe on business or expats back for another tour of duty, and to receive supplies of fresh food, newspapers, and other goods from Europe.

The general manager of the local company, Mr. Lagarde, stood there on the tarmac to welcome me. He was French, in his early 50s, and had spent the last 15 years as an expatriate in Africa moving from country to country every three or four years. He seemed friendly enough and spoke to me in fatherly tones. I was far younger than he and had only worked one year for the company. I thought that he might resent my university background and early promotion to line responsibility overseas, but I also realized that he desperately needed a willing subordinate to manage an investment program to rebuild the company's facilities, which had fallen into disrepair.

The local company marketed oil products in the country and used its storage facilities in the port for transshipment to neighboring countries as well. The oil storage tanks, which sat between the small two-story office block and the Red Sea, had been built in 1936, but since the closure of the Suez Canal they had been little used. The company had run down its operations and was only just profitable. It was wholly owned by one of the oil majors but was fully autonomous in day-to-day operations. With about 100 local staff and 3 expatriates, it was too small to receive much attention from the parent company other than an annual review of the business plan. In 1983, an unexpected upturn in business had put new demands on the facilities, which no longer met the appropriate safety standards. I was sent out for 18 months or so with a mission to patch up the damage and update the facilities where necessary.

To meet my objectives, storage tanks, pumps, and pipework would need to be replaced section by section in order to keep the depot operational. The work would have to be done by local contractors, as the company only employed a small maintenance crew of semiskilled workers. I would depend on these contractors to do their work properly and finish on time. I was pleased when, in the first couple of weeks, a number of them came to see me in my office. As they had no offices and ran their business from their cars, they would turn up at any time and sit outside waiting

for me to arrive. They would come in, usually alone, introduce themselves, and sit down. I explained to them that each section of the work would need to be bid for and that I would contact them soon.

Saïd Guedi must have been the fifth such contractor to come and see me. He told me that his firm had worked for my company for many years and hoped that we would have a long and fruitful relationship. He reached into his pocket and pulled out a gold chain which he held out to me as a "gift for my lady."

I was shocked. I had imagined this scene many times but felt unable to respond. This was "baksheesh," not a bribe relating to a particular job or contract but a token offering which, he hoped, would win him my favor. Eventually, I thanked him but explained that I could not accept his gift, which, in any case, was not necessary. He replied, "But your predecessor took my gifts."

Suddenly I felt quite alone. I had assumed that my colleagues would turn down baksheesh, but now I wasn't sure. I said no again, led him out of my office, then sat back and thought about my position. I was flattered that my position justified such treatment but upset that he thought I might accept his gift. I realized that I would have to establish a position of principle in order to avoid this problem in the future.

I felt unsure that I could trust anyone within the company. Guedi had made me realize that my expatriate colleagues could possibly be taking bribes. A couple of days later, the general manager came into my office and asked me to consider a particular contractor for a forthcoming job, explaining that he had been "recommended by a minister." He was probably quite honest and his story was probably true, but I had a lingering doubt in my mind. I never told him what had happened with Guedi and, more generally, we never discussed the subject of bribery.

Two months or so later I had settled down in both the country and the company. I had moved into a small apartment in town away from my colleagues but close to a number of other expatriates. I had a small jeep to get me around and had built up an active social life. I did have some problems when the port police began to stop and search the jeep on my way into work every day, but I had learned to be patient and they gave up after a week. I later found that Guedi had arranged this "stop and search" to put me in my place. Other contractors had apparently heard that I was "clean" and I got no more offers of baksheesh.

At work, things were going well and I had established a good rapport with the clerical staff and the manual labor out in the depot. Some of them, in fact, seemed more able and enthusiastic than the local managers. These able young men were being managed by four local managers who could barely read and write. Among the four was a man called Ismail Farah. He was the ring-leader and had ambitions of being promoted to the post of operations manager, a job which had always been done by an expatriate. Previous general managers had considered him for the post but none had recommended him, despite the company's declared policy of promotion for nationals wherever possible. I wondered why.

Before leaving for Africa I had been told that two of the last three general managers had had nervous breakdowns which had caused them to be repatriated, but I was also told that these were caused by "age" in one case and "marital problems" in the other. The standard of living of the expats in the country was not high, but there was no particular hardship to explain why two previously successful managers should crack up in that way. I had been told that one of them would come to the office at night and work through the company's accounts. On one occasion, he was found sitting on the floor in tears by his secretary when she arrived in the morning. If life outside the company was not responsible, what within it could cause this level of anxiety?

Late one night I stood on the quay in the port, watching our men couple up hoses to a tanker which had to discharge oil into the storage tanks. As I looked down the quay, I could see someone walking up toward me. It was Ismail. He came up and we chatted for a few minutes before he started to tell me about his career and how he had been overlooked for promotion. I pointed out that I had not discussed his position with the general manager but that the company would promote nationals whenever possible. It was a weak reply but it was honest.

Ismail was reportedly the most talented of the four local managers, but I didn't know him well enough to form any other opinion. He seemed pleased that I would discuss the matter with him and hoped that we would "be good friends." He started to talk about the past, about how the country had broken away from colonial rule, and about the company's development through that time. Eventually he started to talk about the first of the general managers who had had a nervous breakdown. He smiled and appeared to mock the man's misfortune. "That man was trouble to me. He was a racist and he was weak. He treated us like children so we behaved like children. We would make mistakes in our work that he could never find and it drove him crazy."

I was stunned. I must have looked quite shocked because he went on to say, "Don't worry, you'll be all right; you're my friend." This time I went to see the general manager. We talked about Ismail and his past, which, it transpired, had been well documented in appraisal reports. He had the support of a minister within the government, which prevented us from firing him. There was nothing we could do.

Eventually I had come to terms with both internal and external threats and had learned to be cautious in my dealings. I had good working relationships with a number of contractors and no problems dealing with the local authorities. When the chief of port police came to see me in my office, I assumed that his visit was a courtesy call.

He sat down and, after a few minutes' discussion, started to explain that his mother was ill and needed medical care which he could not pay for until he received his pay at the end of the month. "Could you, as a personal favor, lend me the money until the end of the month?" I had had similar requests before and knew that the story was almost certainly a fabrication. "I'm sorry; I would help you if I could, but I have no money in this country." He leaned across the desk and beckoned me forward so that he could whisper into my ear: "But I know that you have money here, I have seen your account file in the bank." I felt quite sick. I had lied and he knew it.

Although his request was clearly extortion, I felt guilty. I stood up, told him that he must have made a mistake, and led him out of my office. Later that day I went to see the bank manager. As upset about the leak in confidential information as I was, he gave me an overdraft so that from that day on I never did have any money in the bank.

As work in the port depot progressed, we decided to invest in a small office block out at the airport to house the aviation manager and the 15 staff responsible for fueling European Airlines as they stopped over en route to and from the Indian Ocean. It would be a small, single-story, Arab-style building designed by a young French architect, a resident in the country, who reckoned that it would cost about $200,000 to build. Five contractors had bid for the construction work and I had awarded the contract to the lowest bidder, subject to planning approval being granted. To get the approval, the architect had completed the necessary forms and submitted them in the company's name to the Ministry of Public Works six weeks beforehand. We hadn't received any reply in writing when Abdi Issa, officer in charge of planning at the Ministry, called me on the phone. "I have a few queries about the drawings you submitted with the planning application forms for your new airport office. Nothing serious, the sort of thing we should discuss around the table. Could you come in and see me tomorrow morning in my office?" Now what? I wondered.

5 BANANA TIME CASE

This paper undertakes description and explanatory analysis of the social interaction which took place within a small work group of factory machine operatives during a two-month period of participation observation.

My fellow operatives and I spent our long days of simple, repetitive work in relative isolation from other employees of the factory. Our line of machines was sealed off from other work areas of the plant by the four walls of the clicking room. The one door of this room was usually closed. Even when it was kept open during periods of hot weather, the consequences were not social; it opened on an uninhabited storage room of the shipping department. Not even the sounds of work activity going on elsewhere in the factory carried to this isolated workplace. There were occasional contacts with outside employees, usually on matters connected with the work; but, with the exception of the daily calls of one fellow who came to pick up finished materials for the next step in processing, such visits were sporadic and infrequent.

The clickers were of the genus punching machines; of mechanical construction similar to that of the better-known punch presses, their leading features were hammer and block. The hammer, or punching head, was approximately 8 inches by 12 inches at its flat striking surface. The descent upon the block was initially forced by the operator, who exerted pressure on a handle attached to the side of the hammer head. A few inches of travel downward established electrical connection for a sharp power-driven blow. The hammer also traveled by manual guidance in a horizontal plane to and from, and in an arc around, the central column of the machine. Thus, the operator, up to the point of establishing electrical connections for the sudden and irrevocable downward thrust, had flexibility in maneuvering his instrument over the larger surface of the block. The latter, approximately 24 inches wide, 18 inches deep, and 10 inches thick, was made like a butcher's block, of inlaid hardwood; it was set in the machine at a convenient waist height. On it the operator placed his materials, one sheet at a time if leather, stacks of sheets if plastic, to be cut with steel dies of assorted sizes and shapes. The particular die in use would be moved, by hand, from spot to spot over the materials each time a cut was made; less frequently, materials would be shifted on the block as the operator saw need for such adjustment.

Introduction to the new job, with its relatively simple machine skills and work routines, was accomplished with what proved to be, in my experience, an all-time minimum of job training. The clicking machine assigned to me was situated at one end of the row. Here the superintendent and one of the operators gave a few brief demonstrations, accompanied by bits of advice, which included a warning to keep hands clear of the descending hammer. After a short practice period, at the end of which the superintendent expressed satisfaction with progress and potentialities, I was left to develop my learning curve with no other supervision than that afforded by members of the work group. Further advice and assistance did come from time to time from my fellow operatives, sometimes upon request, sometimes unsolicited.

The Work Group

Absorbed at first in three related goals of improving my clicking skill, increasing my rate of output, and keeping my left hand unclicked, I paid little attention to my fellow operatives save to observe that they were friendly, middle-aged, foreign born, full of advice, and very talkative. Their names, according to the way they addressed each other, were George, Ike, and Sammy. George, a stocky fellow in his late 50s, operated the machine at the opposite end of the line; he, I later discovered, had emigrated in early youth from a country in southeastern Europe. Ike, stationed at George's left, was tall, slender, in his early 50s, and Jewish; he had come from eastern Europe in his youth. Sammy, number-three man in the line and my neighbor, was heavy-set, in his late 50s, and Jewish; he had escaped from a country in eastern Europe just before Hitler's legions had move in. All three men had been downwardly mobile in occupation in recent years. George and Sammy had been proprietors of small businesses; the former had been "wiped out" when his uninsured establishment burned down; the latter had been entrepreneuring on a small scale before he left all behind him to flee the Germans. According to his account, Ike had left a highly skilled trade which he had practiced for years in Chicago.

The Work

It was evident to me before my first workday drew to a weary close that my clicking career was going to be a grim process of fighting the clock, the particular timepiece in this situation being an old-fashioned alarm clock that ticked away on a shelf near George's machine. I had struggled through many dreary rounds with the minutes and hours during the various phases of my industrial experience, but never had I been confronted with such a dismal combination of working conditions as the extra-long workday, the infinitesimal cerebral excitation, and the extreme limitation of physical movement. The contrast with a recent stint in the California oil fields was striking. This was no eight-hour day of racing hither and yon over desert and foothills with a rollicking crew of "roustabouts" on a variety of repair missions at oil wells, pipelines, and storage tanks. Here there were no afternoon dallyings to search the sands for horned toads, tarantulas, and rattlesnakes or to climb old wooden derricks for raven's nests with an eye out, of course, for the telltale streak of dust in the distance, which gave ample warning of the approach of the boss. This was standing all day in one spot beside three old codgers in a dingy room looking out through barred windows at the bare walls of a brick warehouse, leg movements largely restricted to the shifting of body weight from one foot to the other, hand and arm movements confined, for the most part, to a simple repetitive sequence of place the die–punch the clicker–place the die–punch the clicker, and intellectual activity reduced to computing the hours to quitting time. It is true that from time to time a fresh stack of sheets would have to be substituted for the clicked-out old ones; but the stack would have been prepared by someone else, and the exchange would be only a minute or two in the making. Now and then a box of finished work would have to be moved back out of the way, and an empty box brought up, but the moving back and the bringing up involved only a step or two. And there was the half hour for lunch and occasional trips to the lavatory or the drinking fountain to break up the day into digestible parts. But after each momentary respite, hammer and die were moving again: click–move die–click–move die.

I developed a game of work. The game developed was quite simple, so elementary, in fact, that its playing was reminiscent of rainy-day preoccupations in childhood when attention could be centered by the hour on colored bits of things of assorted sizes and shapes. But this adult activity was not mere pottering and piddling; what it lacked in the earlier imaginative content, it made up for in clean-cut structure. Fundamentally involved were: *(a)* variation in color of the materials cut, *(b)* variation in shapes of the dies used and *(c)* a process called "scraping the block." The basic procedure which ordered the particular combination of components employed could be stated in the form: "As soon as I do so many of these, I'll click some brown ones." And with success in attaining the objective of working with brown materials, a new goal of "I'll get to do the white ones" might be set. Or the new goal might involve switching dies.

Informal Social Activity of the Work Group: Times and Themes

I began to take serious note of the social activity going on around me; my attentiveness to this activity came with growing involvement in it. What I heard at first, before I started to listen, was a stream of disconnected bits of communication that did not make much sense. Foreign accents were strong, and referents were not joined to coherent contexts of meaning. It was just "jabbering." What I saw at first, before I began to observe, was occasional flurries of horseplay that were so simple and unvarying in pattern and so childish in quality that they made no strong bid for attention. For example, Ike would regularly switch off the power at Sammy's machine whenever Sammy made a trip to the lavatory or the drinking fountain. Correlatively, Sammy invariably fell victim to the plot by making an attempt to operate his clicking hammer after return to the shop. And as the simple pattern went, this blind stumbling into the trap was always followed by indignation and reproach from Sammy, smirking satisfaction from Ike, and mild paternal scolding from George. My interest in this procedure was at first confined to wondering when Ike would weary of his tedious joke or when Sammy would learn to check his power switch before trying the hammer.

Most of the breaks in the daily series were designated as "times" in the parlance of the clicker operators, and they featured the consumption of food or drink of one sort or another. There was coffee time, peach time, banana time, fish time, Coke time, and, of course, lunch time. Other interruptions that formed part of the series but were not verbally recognized as times were window time, pickup time, and the staggered quitting times of Sammy and Ike. These latter unnamed times did not involve the partaking of refreshments.

My attention was first drawn to this times business during my first week of employment when I was encouraged to join in the sharing of two peaches. It was Sammy who provided the peaches; he drew them from his lunch box after making the announcement, "Peach time!" On this first occasion, I refused the proffered fruit but thereafter regularly consumed my half peach. Sammy continued to provide the peaches and to make the "Peach time!" announcement, although there were days when Ike would remind him that it was peach time, urging him to hurry up with the midmorning snack. Ike invariably complained about the quality of the fruit, and his complaints fed the fires of continued banter between peach donor and critical recipient. I did find the fruit a bit on the scrubby side but felt, before I achieved insight into the function of peach time, that Ike was showing poor manners by looking a gift horse in the mouth. I wondered why Sammy continued to share his peaches with such an ingrate.

Banana time followed peach time by approximately an hour. Sammy again provided the refreshments—namely, one banana. There was, however, no four-way sharing of Sammy's banana. Ike would gulp it down by himself after surreptitiously extracting it from Sammy's lunch box, kept on a shelf behind Sammy's work station. Each morning, after making the snatch, Ike would call out, "Banana time!" and proceed to down his prize while Sammy made futile protests and denunciations. George would join in with mild remonstrances, sometimes scolding Sammy for making so much fuss. The banana was one that Sammy brought for his own consumption at lunch time; he never did get to eat his banana but kept bringing one for his lunch. At first this daily theft startled and amazed me. Then I grew to look forward to the daily seizure and the verbal interaction which followed.

Window time came next. It followed banana time as a regular consequence of Ike's castigation by the indignant Sammy. After "taking" repeated references to himself as a person badly lacking in morality and character, Ike would "finally" retaliate by opening the window that faced Sammy's machine to let the "cold air" blow in on Sammy. The slandering which would, in its echolalic repetition, wear down Ike's patience and forbearance usually took the form of the invidious comparison: "George is a good daddy. Ike is a bad man! A very bad man!" Opening the window would take a little time to accomplish and would involve a great deal of verbal interplay between Ike and Sammy, both before and after the event. Ike would threaten, make feints toward the window, then finally open it. Sammy would protest, argue, and make claims that the air blowing in on him would give him a cold; he would eventually have to leave his machine to close the window. Sometimes the weather was slightly chilly and the draft from the window unpleasant, but cool or hot, windy or still, window time arrived each day. (I assume that it was originally a cold-season development.) George's part in this interplay, in spite of the "good daddy" laudations, was to encourage Ike in his window work. He would stress the tonic values of fresh air and chide Sammy for his unappreciativeness.

Themes

To put flesh, so to speak, on this interactional frame of times, my work group had developed various "themes" of verbal interplay, which had become standardized in their repetition. These topics of conversation ranged from an extreme of nonsensical chatter to another extreme of serious discourse. Unlike the "times," these themes flowed one into the other in no particular sequence of predictability. Serious conversation could suddenly melt into horseplay, and vice versa. In the middle of a serious discussion on the high cost of living, Ike might drop a weight behind the easily startled Sammy or hit him over the head with a dusty paper sack. Interaction would immediately drop to a low comedy exchange of slaps, threats, guffaws, and disapprobations, which would invariably include a 10-minute echolalia of "Ike is a bad man, a very bad man! George is a good daddy, a very fine man!" Or, on the other hand, a stream of such invidious comparisons as followed a surreptitious switching-off of Sammy's machine by the playful Ike might merge suddenly into a discussion of the pros and cons of saving for one's funeral.

"Kidding themes" were usually started by George or Ike, and Sammy was usually the butt of the joke. Sometimes Ike would have to "take it," seldom George. One favorite kidding theme involved Sammy's alleged receipt of $100 a month from his son. The points stressed were that Sammy did not have to work long hours or did not have to work at all, because he had a son to support him. George would always point out that he sent money to his daughter; she did not send money to him. Sammy received occasional calls from his wife, and his claim that these calls were requests to shop for groceries on the way home were greeted with feigned disbelief. Sammy was ribbed for being closely watched, bossed, and henpecked by his wife, and the expression, "Are you man or mouse?" became an echolalic utterance, used both in and out of the original context.

Serious themes included the relating of major misfortunes suffered in the past by group members. George referred again and again to the loss by fire of his business establishment. Ike's chief complaints centered round a chronically ill wife who had undergone various operations and periods of hospital care. Ike spoke with discouragement of the expenses attendant upon hiring a housekeeper for himself and his children; he referred with disappointment and disgust to a teenage son, an inept lad who "couldn't even fix his own lunch. He couldn't even make himself a sandwich!" Sammy's reminiscences centered on the loss of a flourishing business when he had to flee Europe ahead of the Nazi invasion.

There was one theme of especially solemn import, the "professor theme." This theme might also be termed "George's daughter's marriage theme," for the recent marriage of George's only child was inextricably bound up with George's connection with higher learning. The daughter had married the son of a professor, who instructed in one of the local colleges. This professor theme was not in the strictest sense a conversation piece; when the subject came up, George did all the talking. The two Jewish operatives remained silent as they listened with deep respect, if not actual awe, to George's accounts of the Big Wedding, which, including the wedding pictures, entailed an expense of $1,000. It was monologue, but there was listening, there was communication, the sacred communication of a temple, when George told of going for Sunday afternoon walks on the Midway with the professor or of joining the professor for a Sunday dinner. Whenever he spoke of the professor, his daughter, the wedding, or even of the new son-in-law, who remained for the most part in the background, a sort of incidental like the wedding cake, George was complete master of the interaction. His manner, in speaking to the rank-and-file of clicker operators, was indeed that of master deigning to notice his underlings. I came to the conclusion that it was the professor connection, not the straw-boss-ship or the extra nickel an hour, that provided the fount of George's superior status in the group.

6   BANGLES

Leela Patel was standing by her machine as she had for eight hours of each working day for the past six years. The shop floor was clean and well lit if noisy and hot. Leela was happy; she had many friends amongst the 400 or so women in the workforce. Most of them were of Indian origin like herself although Asian women formed less than a fifth of the female workforce. Leela was a member of a five-girl team that was responsible for one part of the production process. There are several such teams, none wholly Asian but some, like Leela's, predominantly so. Each team reports to a supervisor, usually male and of English origin. Leela saw the supervisor approaching, accompanied by Janice Watkins, the shop steward.

"Hello, Leela; we've come to explain something to you." It was Bill Evans, the supervisor. "You must have heard about the accident last month when one of the girls caught a bangle in the machine and cut her wrist. Well, the Safety Committee, which Janice here is a member of, has decided that no one will be allowed to wear any bangles, engagement rings, earrings, or necklaces at work. So I'm afraid you'll have to take off your bangles."

Leela, as was her custom, was wearing three bangles, one steel, one plastic, and one gold. All the married Asian women wore bangles, and many of the English girls had also taken to them. Leela always found herself feeling nervous in front of any manager. "I'm sorry, but I cannot take off my bangles; I am a Hindu wife; the bangles are important to my religion."

"Come on, Leela," Janice interrupted. "It isn't just for safety reasons you know; we are processing foodstuff. If that plastic bangle shattered and a piece was found in the product, the company could be in a lot of trouble."

"Don't make a fuss, Leela. I've already had to shout at Hansa Patel and Mira Desai. Why can't you all be like Meena Shah. She didn't mind taking her bangles off; neither did the English girls."

Leela could see Bill was very angry, so almost in tears, she removed the bangles. When the two had moved off, however, she replaced the gold bangle and carried on with her work.

On the bus home that night, all the conversation among the Asian girls was about bangles. Some of the girls, mainly those from East Africa, thought it was a lot of fuss about nothing. However, many of the girls were very worried. The more militant among them chastised those who had submitted and removed their bangles. The less militant decided to talk to their husbands.

One week later, Mr. Jones, the personnel manager, was consulting the regional race relations employment advisor (RREA), Mr. Mason.

"I'm staggered by the response which this simple, common-sense restriction on the wearing of jewellery has brought. The first day after the ban, all of the English girls had removed their bangles and so had some of the Asian girls, but within two or three days all the Asian women were wearing bangles again—some more than ever before. I have had several deputations from them protesting the ban, not to mention visits by individuals on the instruction of their husbands. The strength of this discontent has prompted me to talk to you. Jewellery constitutes both a safety and a hygiene hazard on this site, so it must be removed. At the same time, we can't afford any work stoppages and we don't want to dismiss any of our employees."

A few days later, Mr. Mason had arranged for Mr. Singh from the local Council for Community Relations to talk to Mr. Jones and other managers at the company as well as members of the site Shop Stewards Committee.

Mr. Singh explained that in his opinion there were no obstacles arising from *religious* observance preventing the implementation of the rule. However, the bangles do have a custom base which is stronger than the English tradition base for wedding rings. "The bangles are a mark not only of marriage but of the esteem in which a wife is held by her husband. The more bangles and the greater their value, the higher her esteem and the greater her social standing. The tradition also has religious overtones, since the wearing of bangles by the wife demonstrates that each recognises the other as 'worthy' in terms of the fulfilment of their religious obligations. This position is further complicated in that women remove their bangles if they are widowed, and some fear that the removal of bangles may lead to their husbands' deaths."

During an informal discussion among several shop stewards the following day, the issue of the bangles was raised.

"What do you think we should do, Frank? We could hold a meeting with some of the Asians or call in the area official to deal with it. These girls feel very strongly, you know."

"Yes, I know, but they're being silly really. Jewellery is a safety hazard. We've had several accidents, and I was on the safety committee that decided on the ban. We're their representatives, and we have to decide what is in their best interests. As for calling in the area officials, haven't we got enough problems with them already? That new bloke is a bit of a militant; ever since he took over last year, we've had nothing but changes—new procedures, new agreements, closed shop, dozens of meetings. I don't think we need to bother him with this one. Anyway, he's always going on about how little the Asians participate in the union. He's arranging talks on trade unionism for them in the community hall, with guest speakers and interpreters. I don't suppose many will turn up. No, I think we should leave this to management. We're on the same side anyway with this issue."

The next few weeks were an anxious time for Leela. She wore a single bangle every day. Sometimes the supervisor made her take it off. Other times she managed to hide it under her sleeve. The initial arguments amongst the Asian girls had been resolved. The girls who felt strongly about the bangles had persuaded the others that solidarity was essential. Leela was sure that she would have to lose her job, and her husband supported her even though her income was needed.

Soon after the ban was imposed, Leela and her husband attended a meeting held by an organisation called the Asian Advisory Committee (AAC). This organisation was set up to help members of the Asian community and held regular meetings locally.

Mr. Pathak, the chairman of the AAC, listened to complaints of bullying by supervisors as well as to the fears of the Asians that they would have to give up their jobs if the ban continued and was effectively enforced. Mr. Pathak had visited the company several

years earlier when the AAC was being formed in order to try to establish a communication link. His lack of success was not confined to this company.

"Why haven't you got your union to represent you over these problems?" Mr. Pathak asked one protesting lady.

"The union isn't interested. It was a shop steward who told me to take my bangle off. They don't want to represent us. All they want is our money."

After several weeks and further consultations with the shop stewards, Mr. Jones decided that the ban on the wearing of bangles and dangling exterior jewellery would have to be enforced. It was decided to permit the wearing of wedding rings, sleepers for pierced ears, and wrist watches. Within a few days, he was talking to the RREA again.

"Mr. Mason, I'm afraid we need your help again. It looks like we're going to have a mass walkout of all our Asian women. I'm not sure what to do. I've received a letter from the chairman of some Asian association protesting the ban and asking for it to be lifted while we talk to them. I'm not going to lift the ban—it's supported by the employee representatives, and I'm afraid that if I talk to this Asian Advisory Committee, they'll turn out to be a bunch of militants who'll cause all sorts of trouble. I don't know what the union will think if I allow its members to be represented by an outside body."

Mr. Mason had never heard of the AAC.

7 **THE BARBARA DIBELLA CASE**

NOTE: DO NOT READ *this case until directed to do so by your instructor. It has been set up as a Prediction Case so you can test your analysis by answering questions before reading the entire case.*

Part I

Barbara DiBella began work in Spartan Corporation's management trainee program immediately after graduating from college with a major in marketing. Spartan had recruited her very vigorously as part of its affirmative action efforts to increase the number of women in management positions. While Barbara had had work experience in summer jobs, this was her first full-time position. In the trainee program Barbara would be assigned to the various departments of the corporation for periods of six weeks to six months so that she could receive an introduction to the complete scope of the organization's activities and also meet the key people. While assigned to each department she would be under the direct supervision of the department manager.

Paul Platowski was the corporation's marketing manager. He had joined the firm just seven years ago, following completion of an MBA program, and had progressed very rapidly to his current position of power and prominence. He, too, had gone through the management trainee program, following which he had selected marketing for his initial permanent assignment.

As Barbara's training assignment to the marketing department approached, she became increasingly apprehensive. Her fellow trainees and graduates of previous years' trainee programs told her many stories of Paul's interest in and involvement with young women in the trainee program. Barbara heard of no fewer than three former trainees with whom the grapevine said Paul had been or was intimately involved. Two of the three had excellent positions in the marketing department, and the third was progressing quickly in one of the product groups. The grapevine also indicated that Paul had sought relationships with two other women trainees but had been rejected. One of these women was mired in an undesirable field sales job and the other had left Spartan.

The manager of the accounting department, whom Barbara did not know particularly well but to whom she was assigned just prior to her rotation through marketing, warned her to be careful of Paul. He said he wouldn't be surprised if top management had

stalled the marketing manager's rise at its current level until he "cleans up his act."

Barbara was also concerned about her upcoming contact with Paul because he seemed to always have his arm around women when he was with them in the halls, at lunch, and at social gatherings.

Discussion Questions

1. What do you predict will happen next? Why?
2. What can Barbara do to prepare herself for her training in the marketing department?

Part II

On the first day of her assignment in marketing, Barbara had an early morning meeting with the department manager, as was typical when a trainee entered a new department. Paul welcomed her to his office by putting his arm around her and ushering her to a seat on the couch, where he joined her. Paul was extremely warm and animated in their conversation, telling Barbara he was impressed by her credentials. He promised that her stay in marketing could be an exciting, challenging experience and that a permanent position and unequalled career progress were possible if things worked out. Paul explained her first assignment, which Barbara recognized to be the most exciting she had had by far. After inviting and responding to Barbara's questions and explaining some of the mechanics of the department, Paul wrapped up the meeting by urging her to come to him at any time with questions, problems, or concerns. With that he helped her up from the couch and again put his arm around her as they walked toward the door of his office.

Barbara emerged from the meeting with mixed emotions. On the one hand she was elated about the assignment she had and the description of how the department operated. On the other hand, she was frightened by the prospect of Paul's desire for an intimate relationship with her. She was clear that both personally and professionally she did not want a romantic relationship with her boss. It seemed to her than any short-term benefits would be more than outweighed by long-term consequences.

Barbara decided she would keep her relationship with Paul strictly business. She would work very hard at her marketing assignments, but would keep the relationship cool and impersonal. She planned to take full advantage of the opportunity that Paul and his department offered for professional development, but be very sure that she was not drawn into the complexities of a personal relationship.

As Barbara considered her future with Paul, she rehearsed in her head a conversation in which she would tell him that she was very interested in an intense professional relationship, but totally uninterested in any kind of intimate relationship. Ultimately, though, she decided against actually having that talk with Paul. She would avoid the chance for things to get personal, but she would not confront the issue directly with Paul.

Discussion Questions

1. What do you predict will happen next? Why?
2. Should Barbara talk with Paul about her noninterest in an intimate relationship with him? Why?

Part III

Over the next couple of months Barbara became more and more comfortable with her relationship with Paul. In fact, as she thought back to her first days in the marketing department, she almost couldn't remember what she had been so upset about. She was working very hard at her assignments and producing work that Paul acknowledged to be top quality.

There had been a few occasions when her plan for keeping the relationship with her boss businesslike had been tested. For example, he had invited her to accompany him on a two-day trip for the presentation of a marketing plan at one of the key subsidiaries, but luckily the deadline of another project was close enough that she was able to beg off. A couple of times at the beginning Paul had asked her to go to lunch, but again she had been able to use the press of work as an excuse for declining. She had dealt with Paul's touching by simply keeping her physical distance from him, joking about him "keeping his hands off the merchandise," and choosing a chair rather than the couch when meeting with him in his office.

Overall, Barbara was feeling very good about her situation in marketing and the early threat of a personal relationship with Paul had become a nonissue.

Discussion Questions

1. What do you predict is going to happen? Why?
2. Do you approve or disapprove of the way Barbara handled herself?

Part IV

As time passed Barbara noticed that her assignments began to take on a certain sameness. Paul did not seem to be giving her anything new to do. There was nothing wrong with the work she was given—it was interesting and important—but it was not particularly challenging anymore because she had done it several times before. She decided to set up a meeting with Paul to discuss her concerns. Paul had some difficulty finding a time for them to meet but ultimately found 15 minutes to "squeeze her in." during the meeting he was continually interrupted by phone calls and questions from his secretary. In response to Barbara's concerns Paul said he was sorry to hear she was dissatisfied, but he also indicated that it was really too late to get into anything very new because she had only one month left in the marketing department. Barbara decided to raise the issue of a permanent position in marketing. Paul responded by suggesting that they hold off on any decision about that until she had completed her other assignments and knew what else was available. Rather abruptly Paul stood and thanked Barbara for coming in and walked to the door to discuss something with his secretary.

Discussion Questions

1. Why do you suppose Paul seems so cold to Barbara and not eager to have her work for him?
2. What do you predict will happen next? Why?

BEAUTY CLASSICS, INC.

Preparing for the Internship Debriefing

Sabrina Hill was elated but concerned as she reviewed her notes and diary. Tomorrow, December 14, 1992, she was to make a presentation to the internship committee; her goal tonight was to prepare herself for the 15-minute oral session. All exams were completed and this was the last course requirement for graduation from Nashville University. Professor Williams assured her that the committee was sympathetic, but she was apprehensive that the committee really wouldn't understand why her internship had failed. Although she felt confident that her diary (Appendix A) was adequate as an activity report, she worried that it didn't explain satisfactorily why the internship into which she had so positively ventured had turned so negative in such a short time. She had always considered herself an able communicator, ready and willing for the business world. Now she had her doubts. She had never before experienced such a humiliating incident.

True, she had been overcommitted, embarking on an internship at the same time she was working as a part-time waitress and completing the four additional courses necessary to finish her marketing degree program. However, she had known she had needed the business internship experience for her resume. In fact, she had eagerly anticipated the challenge of the Beauty Classics, Inc., internship because it was an opportunity to put her creative ideas to work.

Although Beauty Classics, Inc. (BCI), was founded and operated by African-Americans, Sabrina did not recall any great apprehension because she had always believed people should be judged based on who they were, not on their race. Since Sabrina had not attended an ethnically and racially diverse high school, and her college experience so far had been only moderately diverse, she had been excited by the prospect of learning about people with different ethnic backgrounds from her own while simultaneously obtaining valuable work experience. Coming from an upper-middle-class background and attending a relatively expensive private university did not mean that her limited exposure to other peoples and cultures was synonymous with intolerance.

Internship Requirements

The internship requirement that she spend 15 hours per week at the company had not at first appeared onerous. Her tasks were to (1) keep a weekly diary; (2) develop a company history and brief marketing prospectus; and (3) complete a project for the company.

Before the semester began, Beauty Classics management and Professor Williams had discussed three potential internship projects. These were: (1) reviewing distributor programs and incentives; (2) analyzing sales to the company's largest customer, Wal-Mart; and (3) managing a Christmas party for needy minority children in the immediate neighborhood of the BCI factory. Which project she would work on would depend on how the first few weeks of the internship proceeded. Professor Williams assured her that if none of these projects seemed to fit her needs and those of the company, his relationship with the principals of the company was such that a mutually rewarding project could be established.

The Company

Sabrina's first three weeks of her internship were devoted to discovering how Beauty Classics had achieved its magnitude of success. Her initial meeting with the company founders did not impress her. The situation seemed quite chaotic. A number of people interrupted Professor Williams as he introduced her to the company founders, Dr. and Mr. Exeter. Moreover, the company's facilities did not reflect, in her opinion, a successful business enterprise. Her report of the company history and the company's marketing prospects (Appendix B) was, however, incomplete due to the abrupt termination of the internship on October 27.

Sabrina leafed through her report. She jotted some additional notes in the report's margin, quoting from a 1985 press release:

> Edward Exeter [according to press clippings] flamboyant and jovial, model for black entrepreneurs

Then she reviewed her preliminary evaluation (Appendix C), which she had shown Professor Williams earlier in the week. The evaluation was based on her diary and on her opinions of what had happened. At the meeting at which she gave the evaluation to Professor Williams, he had given her a partial transcript of a debriefing session he had conducted at Beauty Classics, Inc. (Appendix D).

Sabrina knew that her final internship grade depended on tomorrow's oral presentation. Could she adequately explain what she had learned from the experience? She recognized that the postpresentation question-and-answer session would be critical. "What types of questions will the Internship Committee ask me?" Sabrina wondered.

Appendix A

EXCERPTS FROM SABRINA HILL'S DIARY—SEPTEMBER 2 TO NOVEMBER 2, 1992

September 2

I went to Dr. Williams' office this morning to explain why I missed his night class, the opening class of the semester. I had to go into work at Pepper's; hopefully they aren't going to be inflexible with my schedule this coming semester. Anyway, something good came out of the whole deal. We discussed what I was going (or wanted) to do after I graduate in December. I've been kind of worried about getting a job since I basically have no experience. He asked what I would like to do and I told him I could see myself in the fashion industry.

It turns out that there is an internship available at Beauty Classics, Inc., an ethnic fashion accessories company. Professor Williams explained that Beauty Classics, Inc., is the largest minority-owned business in town, and that it manufactures and sells fashion accessories, such as scarves, hairpins, and costume jewelry, aimed primarily at the black and Hispanic markets. He said they wanted a marketing intern to work on one of several projects. Professor Williams asked if I would like to take it. Of course I would! He explained it is going to take up a lot of my time and might be difficult to schedule since I already have a job. I know I can do it though, plus the experience will be worth it. Oh yeah, one more thing—I think I am going to be the only white person in the company. I am not too worried about that since I see people as who they are not by the color of their skin. I am kind of nervous about how they will accept ME, though.

September 4

Dr. Williams took me out to Beauty Classics, Inc., this afternoon. It was strange because I had a hard time deciding what to wear. I wanted to dress nicely, but not too nice. I felt that a business suit would be out of place. I wondered if I worried about it because it was a black-owned company. I don't think I have a negative attitude toward working out there but I am afraid they will have negative feelings toward me.

Beauty Classics, Inc., is located in a neighborhood known for its high crime rate. I am glad I have a beat-up car so I won't have to worry about leaving it there. I also think it will be good because it fits in with the rest of the cars on the lot. I don't want the people who work here to think I am a spoiled rich college student out here slumming or something.

Once we arrived at BCI I could not help but wonder at what I had gotten myself into. It seemed to me that the "factory" looked like an old bowling alley. Dr. Williams said that it in fact was that. Once inside I could not help but stare at the walls and interior of the place. It was like going into a time warp, back to the 1960s and 1970s. Everything was dated—the pictures, the carpeting, the furniture. There were also advertising posters on the walls and photographs of a handsome black couple with different celebrities from that time, such as Aretha Franklin and Tina Turner.

Dr. Williams pointed out one of the ad posters and told me that the model was Alexis Exeter. She is absolutely gorgeous! Dr. Williams also gave me a little more background about the company as we waited. Mr. and Dr. Exeter started the company, and their adopted daughter, Alexis, works with them. Mr. Exeter is in a wheelchair and he uses the company conference room as his office.

Finally we got to go into the conference room and I met the people who were going to be my new employers. It was awkward, I'm not going to deny it. Mr. Exeter is quite a character. He is a big man with long, slick, curly hair. He wore a jump suit and a lot of gold. Not at all what I expected, but he did seem excited at the prospect of me working there, and I have to admit that I am excited too. His wife, Dr. Daisy Exeter, is going to be a tough one to figure out. She didn't say much to me and I caught her looking at me in a way that made me very uncomfortable. I would guess that the Exeters are in their late sixties. Alexis, on the other hand, appears to be pretty normal. In person, she is not as beautiful as in the poster, but she is extremely attractive. She's a little taller than me, about five-seven, and I would guess about 32 or 33 years old. It seems I will be working mainly with her. She has a bunch of different ideas for a project, but they seem to be mostly short term. She did not mention any of the projects that Dr. Williams had discussed with me. I'm not sure that any one of her projects will fulfill my internship requirements.

Mr. Exeter offered to pay me. Dr. Williams said that it's strictly up to the client. Interns are not required to be paid. I was offered $5.00 per hour. I wonder if it would be better if I did not get paid because they would have less control over me. It's hard to turn the money down though, especially since I am so poor, so I don't think I will.

One thing that kind of gave me the creeps was when Mr. Exeter mentioned my looks. I guess he thinks I am attractive, but it seemed out of place for him to say something about it. Maybe that's why his wife put up a little attitude in front of me. Who knows?

September 8

I am going out to BCI five mornings a week from 9 A.M. until noon. It will be all right for me to take one morning off and make up my time on Friday afternoons. That little leeway will be nice when I need time off during the week to catch up on school. So anyway, I went out there this morning and Alexis showed me around the building. The place is in a run-down condition, and the people seem kind of run-down as well. No one in the manufacturing area even looked at me as I went through. Alexis introduced me to people but they would not look me in the face. It was the strangest feeling. I felt that they all had cast an immediate judgment on who I was and what I was like. It made me mad because I did not feel that I should be judged based upon the color of my skin any more than they should by theirs. But I walked through and acted like I did not notice any of the undertones. I wonder if that is how black people feel when they are with all white people. I guess I got my first taste of what it must be like to be a minority.

Thankfully, the people in the front part of the building treated me much differently. The three salesmen and the secretary made it a point to be friendly to me. I appreciated it more than they could imagine. My desk is back by the salesmen. It is the first cubicle and desk that I have ever had! I like the feeling of having my own phone and place to put my stuff. Even if it is old and small, I can consider it my own.

Week of September 14

My duties so far are not very clear to me. Alexis had me read up on the company. I looked through some magazines, at advertising and articles, to get a better understanding of what the industry is and how BCI does business. The magazines that hit their black target market are *Ebony, Sophisticate, Jet,* and *Essence,* and a trade publication, *Shop Talk.* I brainstormed some ideas for advertising and wrote down some questions I had about the company and their products.

One of their key product lines is hair-care fashion accessories, including combs, hairnets, hair ribbons, and hair clips. The products used by their customers are much different from the ones Caucasians use. I did not realize just how much. Even the terms used to describe how they style hair are different. When Blacks straighten their hair they call it a perm; I am used to a perm being used to curl hair. Black hair gets damaged because of the chemicals used to style their hair, so heavy oils must be used for conditioning. This then requires special clips and combs. My hair is as opposite as it can be from black hair—bone straight and fine.

Alexis asked if she could touch it so I asked if I could touch hers. It felt like something out of a movie, two people experiencing something new that is so common to each other. I am going to like Alexis. I do feel sorry for her because she has so much work to do all of the time. Everyone in that place brings things to her to get done. She is also the mediator between Mr. Exeter and the rest of the company.

Week of September 21

It has been a while since I put an entry into this journal. I am so frustrated out at that place. Mr. Exeter has been "using" me to do things simply because I am white, and I do not appreciate it at all! I spend a lot of time in the conference room. His wife, whom he always addresses as Dr. Exeter, doesn't say very much. Mr. Exeter has me call places because I have a "white" voice and he wants me to try to get accounts that he feels he hasn't been able to get because he is black. I am not a salesman—I have not been trained to do that type of work and it is ludicrous for him to think that I can get accounts because of the color of my skin.

He even had me try to call Ross Perot. I felt like the biggest idiot, trying to get a presidential candidate on the phone for my boss. I am seriously beginning to doubt the mental stability of Mr. Exeter. Yesterday he broke out in song during the meeting. He also recited a poem and a prayer. I had to write down what he was saying and then type it up for him. The looks being passed across the table should have been on videotape. No one changed facial expression but the eye contact among all of us was very descriptive.

There was an all-employee meeting today. I tried to hide in the back but it didn't work. Everyone in the company attended—an hour and forty-five minutes of wasted time! Nothing was accomplished, nothing except an embarrassing moment for me. Mr. Exeter wanted everyone to go around the room and introduce themselves. So much for me hiding in the back! When it got to be my turn he had me come up front and announced that I was going to be their new international model. I was shocked, and I didn't say anything—at all. But it seems preposterous that he would want me to model because I would not attract the market he is after. Honestly, it was flattering, but I don't think I would want my face associated with this product. That may sound like a harsh thing to say but it is how I feel about it. Their product line is low-quality and the advertising they use is poor. Not that I have ever modeled and have some type of image to uphold, but still I don't want to do it.

I think I made a huge judgment error today. Alexis was out for the day and she did not leave me anything to do. So I walked into the conference room to get something to do, or to be excused for the day. Well, Mr. Exeter decided there and then that Alexis was not doing her duty with me, and he was going to "take me under his wing." Uh oh! I guess I will be attending the daily production meetings from now on.

Every morning the senior people meet in the conference room to discuss production and sales issues. The three Exeters are almost always there; other managers join them as different issues arise. I do believe that these meetings are a waste of time in most aspects. Granted there is a need for them, but not every day for three hours! Mr. Exeter likes to ramble on and on. I do think he just likes to hear himself talk. It is a power trip for him, something to build up his ego.

Week of October 5

It is interesting to talk to the salesmen. Walter is flashy and outspoken. He has a daughter my age and is very opinionated about how she should act and whom she should date. I am outspoken toward him too, and I don't think he knows how to take it. I think deep inside he likes that I am not afraid to tell him how I feel about situations. He believes that since he is male he is superior. He is beginning to get the idea, however, that I was raised in a similar (male chauvinistic) household and do not want any part of it now. He understands my position on certain situations, and I understand his, but we agree to disagree. We do have friendly, heated debates on topics like women in executive positions, men in the home, women in politics, etc. It is fun to get his perspective on issues.

Monroe is a lot different than Walter. He more or less goes with the flow, doesn't take a side, but pipes up on everything. He is very sincere and always willing to help me. If I have a question about anything I ask Monroe. His answers are usually longer than I would like, but he does explain things well. Monroe is full of questions for me, too. His questions are more personal, mostly about how I feel about black issues. I tell him truthfully, and he respects that. I believe a friendship is building between the two of us.

Albert is kind of a strange one. He is very quiet and, well . . . odd. He appears to be nervous all of the time, fidgeting and not looking in my eyes. He asked if I have any friends that he could go out with. I said no, and I hope he doesn't take it personally. It is just that I do not think any of my friends would date a black man. I would not either. Which might be a bad thing to say, but I think it is honest. Monroe asked if I would or have ever dated a black man, and I said no. My reason is that it would cause problems if the relationship developed. I also brought up the fact that many, if not most, black people would not date a white person. It is not that I think there is anything

wrong with it, but it would not be a personal choice of mine.

It is neat how Walter, Monroe, and Albert treat me. They think I am helping the company, and I really want to. There is so much potential to be reached, but right now the barriers are too high. It seems that the salesmen like that I am working there. Does that make sense? I think they look at me as a symbol of white people, and that since I accepted the job it gives them hope that others may feel the way I do.

I do not think I am prejudiced. I do not want to be judged, nor do I feel it is my place to judge. This may come from my upbringing, but where I lived there were not too many people different from me. In fact, there was just one black person in my high school. I do worry, though, that I may appear to be prejudiced. Therefore, I worry about how I act or what I say, which may give the appearance of prejudice. It is kind of Catch-22. Although, I must say that I can already feel that I am more comfortable around black people, mostly because I think they will accept me as well. I think a lot of racial separation comes from a fear on both sides of not being accepted. But people should be intelligent enough to know that there is more to a person than the color of their skin. It's time to put stereotypes aside. It is interesting to me, though, that at BCI, some of the stereotypes do show. Many of the employees are lazy. But I think that some of it comes from poor management as much as anything else. I do believe that if those people were challenged to do more, and had an incentive to do more, they would. Right now they are paid minimum scale and do not receive any additional compensation or awards for excellent performance.

Week of October 12

I have been playing secretary to Mr. Exeter for the past couple of weeks. It is driving me insane. I have to go to the production meetings and take minutes. Mr. Exeter also has me get his coffee and juice. I don't mind doing it, after all, he is in a wheelchair. But I can't help wonder why he is doing it? Is it because I am white? He has a secretary whose job it is to do these things, but he insists that I do them. I do not want to rock the boat so I do not say anything about it. I did ask if I could be excused from the production meetings twice a week in order to work on the Christmas party project. Mr. Exeter took this quite personally. He felt that I did not appreciate being allowed into his "inner sanctum." In all honesty, I did not feel that my time was being spent well. I explained that it was simply that I had other projects to complete, but it was impossible when I spent every minute in the conference room. He then agreed that I could have two mornings a week to work independently. Hurrah!

One thing that I cannot handle is his breakfast. Every single morning he has his secretary microwave a Polish sausage in a hot dog bun. Every morning! But he does not eat it very quickly, and when it gets cold I get the honor of heating it up—about three times a day. When he eats I almost get sick, he smacks and talks with his mouth full even as food flies out. It is the most disgusting thing. I have to turn away and tune out when he takes bites out of that thing.

Week of October 19

Mr. Exeter told me he was dropping my Christmas project, but he changed his mind again in about fifteen minutes. I am glad he reconsidered because it is something I really want to do. I have been in touch with area businesses to donate toys and I have arranged to have some kids to the factory for a Christmas party. I want each of them to send a letter with their "wish list" and I will make sure each gets a gift from their list. The day will include a Santa, breakfast, games, a matinee, and toys. Hopefully, I will be able to enlist enough help from people within BCI. Dr. Exeter suggested that Alexis help me get other business support because the area's black businesses may be more willing to work with her. It amazes me that every aspect of their life and business dealings revolve around being black or white!

October 27

I am still in shock over what happened today. I called in to say that I could not come in and that I would make up the time on Friday. This is something that I have done since the start of the internship, and is part of our initial agreement. Well, Mr. Exeter decided today that it was not acceptable. He started yelling at me through the conference phone where I knew the entire staff could hear both sides of the conversation. I tried to explain, calmly, why I could not make it in. He was very upset. He told me he was going to show me how he did business in his part of town, and not to forget that he was on Ross Perot's side. Crazy talk! He said some other cruel and insensitive things, and I got extremely upset. Mr. Exeter screamed at me to get in there right now, and hung up the phone. I was stunned.

I called Dr. Williams and asked what I should do. He told me to wait until tomorrow and he would handle it. I should have listened. Instead, I tried to pull myself together and handle it on my own. I do not know what it was that Mr. Exeter said or what he did that caused such a reaction in me, but I wanted to fight him on my own terms. Bad idea, because at that point I couldn't stop crying. Which is the most frustrating thing for me to admit because I believe that women should have every opportunity to reverse the stereotype that they will break down and cry when something goes wrong. It was a very humbling experience. I hope I have learned how to handle myself better in the future.

Anyway, I went in to BCI as Mr. Exeter ordered. As I entered the conference room where the production meeting was taking place, Mr. Exeter had everyone give me a round of applause for making it in. I think they were in shock, as was I. Based on what I had rehearsed on my way over, I said, "Good morning, Mr. Exeter. I cannot be here this morning." He proceeded to announce that I looked hung over. I explained that I had been up most of the night completing a paper, and did not shower before coming in. He told me to leave, and then said something else, but I did not hear him because I was walking out. I was so frustrated! I think that all of the pressure of two jobs and my last semester at school, together with the "uniqueness" of my situation at BCI, finally caught up with me. I did not realize how much I was being drained.

I went to a side room and hand-wrote a letter to Mr. Exeter. Mistake number two! The letter basically said that I was sorry if there was any misunderstanding, but it was my belief that it was okay for me to make up missed time later in the week. I could not resist writing that I thought he handled the situation poorly and cruelly. I also explained, in detail, why I couldn't work this morning. I also expressed my opinion that I was doing a good job for him and his company—that I did everything expected of me and more. I wrote, "This is only an internship for me; school is still the most important thing to me." I also told him I felt that a letter was the only way he would listen to what I was saying because whenever I opened my mouth he told me to be quiet.

I learned a valuable lesson. Never write (or never send) a letter because it is there in black and white. A letter can be read over and over to many people. Mr. Exeter was furious. He called my poor professor and chewed him out for about a half hour. He said he couldn't understand why a white person had been sent out in the first place. Slap!

Needless to say, my internship is no longer. I am going to miss the people I worked with, and I am worried that I won't have a successful internship to bolster my resume.

November 2

I waited almost a week before going back to BCI. I was worried that I wouldn't even be able to get my personal possessions from my desk. But I was amazed at the turnaround Mr. Exeter had taken. He apologized and said that I could use him for a reference. He said I did a good job in his company and wished me every future success. I didn't know how to take it, and wondered about his motives. It may have been genuine sentiments, but I suspect it was because he did not want to lose contact with the university. I guess I will never know.

It was very special to me though, when I went in that last time, that people were sad to see me go. Sandra, the secretary, gave me her phone number and asked if I would like to get together some time. Albert came out and asked if I would come back and say "hi" to the guys. I did, and they were sincerely sorry that I was leaving. Monroe said that I could have done a lot of good for the company; Walter said it was definitely BCI's loss. That made me feel so good. It was one of those situations where you do not realize how much people like you until you leave.

My experience being the only nonblack person in a company taught me many things. I realized that even though I believe everyone is equal, I acted differently at first because I did not know if they thought the same. I was incredibly intimidated, but after a couple of weeks it didn't matter any more. They didn't care, and neither did I. Hopefully, I left that company with a better understanding of how little difference there really is between white and black people because I know that I learned that out there. I also learned things from a business standpoint that related to my college course. All in all, it was an experience I will never forget.

Appendix B

INTERNSHIP REPORT BY SABRINA HILL FOR PROFESSOR WILLIAMS

Beauty Classics, Inc. (BCI), is a manufacturer of fashion accessories whose principal target market is ethnic blacks. The company produces a variety of products marketed for use solely by professional hair and beauty consultants as well as products sold to consumers through retail channels. Products are marketed nationally, using national magazine advertising and regional and local television and radio spots. The company actively participates in national and regional trade shows and workshops for beauticians.

BCI was organized as a Tennessee corporation in October 1969. It began as a beauty supply house that purchased manufactured products and distributed these in Nashville and the surrounding region. Initial shareholders were Edward Exeter and Daisy Exeter, husband and wife. (Background information for these two founders are [sic] contained in Exhibit 1.)

Shortly after beginning business, the Exeters began manufacturing products, using their own brand name,

in their home. Company sales the first year were $24,000. The peak sales year was 1985, with gross sales of over $13 million achieved. In 1986 the Exeters invested large sums in other ventures, including cosmetics, better jewelry, and African clothing and art. None of these businesses were successful; the dilution of BCI's financial and human resources led to BCI losing sales and market share. BCI's sales forecast for the year ending December 31, 1992, is $4 million.

BCI has a unique "window of opportunity" to capture market share in the ethnic fashion accessories market within the next decade. The 1992 sales project was to capture a 1 percent share of this market; the company has products with a strong brand name, and a doubling of sales within a 3- to 5-year period is possible. This is particularly true since the company recently added Wal-Mart stores to its customer list.

The primary target market, ethnic blacks in the United States, contains approximately 31 million persons. A potential secondary market of Hispanic Americans currently has 22 million people. Combined, the two markets have over $435 billion in purchasing power. These markets are younger and growing more rapidly than the majority population. The average black per capita expenditure on fashion accessories is $23 to $25 annually. Hispanic consumption is somewhat less, but sociological and economic factors suggest this will increase. Both markets exhibit strong brand loyalty and a predisposition to purchase products produced and sold by their respective ethnic businesspeople. These markets are concentrated in urban areas which permits the focusing of marketing efforts.

Three distinct sets of competitors exist:

1. Black-owned companies whose efforts are directed primarily at the ethnic population
2. White-owned companies with the same target markets
3. Large fashion products companies with specific product lines targeted at ethnic markets.

While black-owned companies in total dominate the market, as a group they have proven to be inferior competitors. Many have severe financial problems. The larger fashion products companies apparently did not achieve projected results, and seem to be reducing their ethnic marketing efforts.

Three style or fashion submarkets currently exist. Competitive products are slightly different to address different perceived consumer needs for these styles. BCI management believes that its products are in several ways superior to those of its competitors and that these differences are noticed by consumers.

EXHIBIT 1   *Brief Biographical Sketches of the Two Principals*

EDWARD EXETER

Mr. Exeter graduated from Pennsylvania State University in 1962 with a B.S. degree in Business Administration. He served 15 years in the U.S. Army, and was promoted to the rank of Captain before leaving the service to start Beauty Classics, Inc. Mr. Exeter has received numerous civic and business awards, including Small Businessman of the Year and Manufacturer of the Year, and was recognized for outstanding achievement by *Black Enterprise* magazine. He is listed in "Who's Who among Black Americans" and is a member of the NAACP.

DAISY EXETER

Daisy Exeter is a graduate of several prominent fashion programs in the United States and France, and studied at Temple University. She received an honorary doctorate from Atlanta University. Dr. Exeter was a sales representative with Johnson Beauty Products (a prominent manufacturer of ethnic health and beauty products) for the years prior to founding BCI.

Appendix C

SABRINA HILL'S ASSESSMENT OF THE BCI INTERNSHIP

My internship work became increasingly demeaning and condescending. I was constantly embarrassed by Mr. Exeter's remarks, especially ones that I considered racial. The "production" meetings were a means through which Mr. Exeter exercised control, not only over me but over the entire staff. I was not the only one who was the butt of his cruel remarks; perhaps my skin was too thin.

I will never forget "the event." As usual, Mr. Exeter was on the speaker phone when I called in, and the entire staff KNEW what he said to me and my responses to him. When I walked into the conference room, and Mr. Exeter had those present give me a round of applause for showing up, I was incredibly angry at those "turncoats," those who had been my friends. I realize now that they had no other choice.

It is foolhardy to suggest that I was objective about what happened. What perplexed me the most was trying to decide if I felt like an outsider because I was only an intern, or if it was more a racial and/or sexual issue. Dr. Williams asked me specifically if it was my lack of socialization to the company, or were there really racial and sexual difficulties. I just don't know.

I'm sure I didn't handle Mr. Exeter with any great skill, but I'm not sure any intern could have handled it better. I think a black student would have fared even worse.

Mr. Exeter, despite any previous success, is currently a poor manager. All decisions in the company had to be approved by him; he took days, even weeks, to approve even the simplest request. Maybe his leadership abilities were once outstanding, and he deserved the awards he had won. But now his actions are nothing more than a struggle for power and control. His employees do as they are told, and have an appearance of respect for Mr. Exeter, but I am convinced that they tolerate his moods because they need the jobs. I'm sure they all agree that someone else could more capably run the business.

I am concerned that I haven't met with Alexis. I don't know what she thinks. I felt hurt that Alexis seemed to ignore me after the first couple of weeks, but looking back on it, she was just overwhelmed with work. She provided me with all the company background material, and encouraged me to follow through on the project. But Alexis was really the mediator between Mr. Exeter and the rest of the company. Did I undermine her?

Appendix D

TRANSCRIPT OF DEBRIEFING MEETING NOTES (TRANSCRIBED FROM AUDIOTAPE)

The debriefing meeting was held on November 20, 1992, in the Beauty Classics, Inc., Conference Room. Present were Edward Exeter, CEO; Dr. Daisy Exeter, Executive Vice President; Alexis Exeter, Director of Marketing; and Professor A. Williams, Professor of Marketing, Nashville University.

Professor Williams: I wish we were able to complete the internship, but it is unlikely that Sabrina wants to do it.

Edward Exeter: She was doing a good job for us. I'm sure the Christmas party is going to be a big success. Is there anyone else that could help Alexis?

Professor Williams: I don't think it's possible to get anyone at this late date. Even if there were a student that could assume the internship, it's not possible that this person could come in and take over. There's just not enough time.

Alexis Exeter: I still can't figure out what happened. She was right in the thick of things, privy to all the decision making.

Edward Exeter: She just didn't understand how hard we work. We were paying her $5.00 per hour, which is more than we start our production line at.

Professor Williams: Perhaps that was one of the problems. As I mentioned way back in August when we discussed the internship, it's not usual practice to pay an intern. In fact, our experience is that paid internships are usually less satisfactory because the company then treats the intern as an employee.

Daisy Exeter: Excuse me! We don't ask for charity. Whenever someone does something for us they get paid.

Professor Williams: Well, that's just the point. Interns usually take up an awful lot of company time. Most companies get a completed project, but the cost to them is a great deal of time spent.

Edward Exeter: She had tremendous privileges here. Learning how our system worked. The production meetings are the way we run this company.

Professor Williams: As I explained several times, the intern has certain requirements that the college imposes. Sometimes completing these seems to interfere with what the company expects.

Edward Exeter: But we had great plans for Sabrina. She and Alexis were to model our new international line.

Professor Williams: Sabrina felt that recording the notes of the production meeting wasn't productive.

Edward Exeter: That's gratitude! I put her in a position very few people are privileged to see—what our concerns are and how we make decisions—and she's ungrateful.

Daisy Exeter: Young people just don't seem to want to work nowadays.

Alexis Exeter: No, I don't think Sabrina . . .

Edward Exeter: Well, it's over and done with. We sure could use some help around here. I hope Sabrina learned a lot, and that she understands how difficult it is for a minority business to exist. But, she'll probably be happier working in an environment without blacks.

Professor Williams: I don't think . . .

Edward Exeter: It's over with. But we'd like an intern for the spring. This time we want a black.

(The discussion continued over spring internship possibilities. No further direct mention of Sabrina Hill's internship occurred.)

BILL MICHAELS

Bill Michaels is the project manager of a group of engineers at XYZ Engineering Services Company. As a results of the current financial slowdown of the New England economy, Bill is in the process of downsizing his project. Luckily there is room for excess engineering personnel in another department within the company. Obviously, Bill wants to retain the best and the most competent engineers as well as to continue a long history of team work and cooperation within the project. His dilemma is what to do about Ann Thomas, a relatively new and extremely capable engineer.

The Company

XYZ Engineering Services Company was founded and sponsored by 17 large corporations in 1962 for the purpose of providing them with engineering services. A group of engineering and support personnel with valuable knowledge and experience was assembled. All the engineers were male with a limited support staff of female secretaries and male technicians.

The company grew to include six engineering projects, each overseen by a project manager and four lead engineers who managed specific engineering functions. The engineers reported to the lead who reported to the project manager.

Bill Michaels

Bill Michaels joined the company in 1975 as an engineer. He worked on several different projects with many engineers and has risen in the company to the position of lead mechanical engineer and then to project manager. Bill puts a high value on technical competence and is also very much aware of the need for a close and cooperative relationship among engineers in order to produce the highest level of service to the customer. Over the years, Bill has put together a great group of male engineers who understand each other and the needs of the company. A close working relationship has developed among the men. Bill takes great pride in the integrated approach that he and his engineers provide to the customer.

Corporate Culture

At XYZ Engineering Services Company, the subject of sexual harassment has been dealt with on a relatively superficial level by the Human Resources Department. The problem has never really come up for Bill Michaels and his group, since they are all male and they have a limited amount of contact with the female secretaries. Bill's group is made up of highly technical men who have developed a camaraderie with each other. They spend a great deal of their day in each other's offices working together on a proposal for a customer or developing the best engineering approach to a problem. They have grown to know each other very well, and they trust each other as engineers as well as friends. This close-knit group is very loyal to the company and to each other. When they are not discussing business, they generally talk about the Boston Red Sox, the New England Patriots, the new model of Mazda RX-7 sports car, or the latest high-tech toy on the market. Sometimes they engage in off-color joke telling or they use language that might be considered crude by the general population, but they confine it to their own inner circle of fellow engineers. There is no harm intended, and it is all in the spirit of fun and serves as a way to relieve stress.

In October of 1991, the talk of the office turned to the Clarence Thomas confirmation hearing. Anita Hill had made some shocking accusations of sexual harassment against the Supreme Court nominee, Clarence Thomas. Every day the conversation at XYZ Engineering Services Company turned to the hearing and the extreme discomfort the men in Bill's group felt at the possibility of ever having to defend themselves against a sexual harassment allegation. Lurking behind the engineers' lunchroom debates about sexual harassment was mass confusion over how they should conduct themselves. The consensus among Bill's group of engineers was that they were lucky not to have to worry about the problem, since they were all men.

Ann Thomas

In January of 1992, Bill Michaels had an opening for a new engineer. He posted the job internally and had seven qualified applications: six men and one woman. Ann Thomas was by far the most technically capable of the applicants. She had excellent recommendations from her previous manager. Bill felt that Ann was the best choice for the job, and the lead engineer agreed that she should be selected to fill the opening.

Ann Thomas had worked as a systems engineer for another project in XYZ Engineering Services Company for the past three years. She was the only woman in the project, but seemed to get along well with the other engineers. Her manager had only good reports from the customers as well as from her associates. All of her evaluations were outstanding.

Ann felt that very often the men acted inappropriately in her presence. She didn't appreciate the joke telling and she felt that some of her fellow engineers made comments that were degrading to women. Ann kept her feelings to herself, thinking that she had to avoid making waves in order to get along in a male-dominated profession. Ann was disappointed in herself for compromising her strongly held beliefs about appropriate behavior at the workplace. She was eager for the opportunity to start a new position, and she vowed to herself that she would never again let a single questionable act or remark go unchallenged.

The New Job

The engineers working in Bill Michaels' group welcomed Ann Thomas warmly. They knew from talking with her former colleagues that Ann was a good engineer and that she "fit in" well. Ann jumped into her new job with enthusiasm and high spirits until she saw the pictures of the bikini-clad woman on the desk of one of the engineers. She immediately marched into Bill Michaels' office and complained about the pictures. Bill saw to it that the pictures were promptly removed. Three days later, Ann overheard a group of engineers joking around in their customary crude manner, and she reported to Bill that she was offended. Before Bill could address this complaint, Ann was in his office again. She was extremely upset by a comment from her lead engineer. "You did a great job getting those prints from Joe," he said. "I never had such luck. It must be because you're a woman. You can just show a little leg and get what you want." Bill Michaels had to address this serious problem.

Tense Environment

Bill handled the situation with the individuals who were involved, but it was clear from the tension in the office that the word had spread to the rest of the group. The engineers' attitude toward Ann was noticeably different. Their warm and friendly welcome had turned into an attitude of caution. During the next several months, there were no more complaints from Ann; however, Bill noticed that the male engineers were avoiding Ann and excluding her from their inner circle. Ann continued to perform her technical responsibilities, and she never let her work suffer, but Bill was concerned about the effect that this new "walking on egg shells" environment would have on the integrated engineering approach.

When the time came for Bill to decide which engineers would be transferred to the other project, he was faced with a difficult decision regarding Ann Thomas.

The information for this case was obtained from Mr. Burton L. Davis, a recent employee of Blair, Inc.

Burton Davis started work last September as a mechanical engineer in the Engine and Motor Division of the Blair Company, a large multiple-industry corporation. The division, with 400 employees, was the principal employer in Midland. Formed four years ago, the division designed and manufactured small gasoline combustion engines used in lawnmowers, motor scooters, snow throwers, portable saws, and power plants. Recently the division has begun to turn out small electric motors. Division sales were currently $6 million.

Davis, seven years out of Purdue, had previously worked as an automotive engineer for two major automobile manufacturers and had excellent references from both. His salary at Blair was $950 per month.

He found that the engineering offices were new, of modern design, and air-conditioned. Supporting personnel in drafting, machine shop, and laboratory were adequate, and excellent physical facilities were available. Fringe benefits were at or above the industry level. For instance, Davis was promised a two-week vacation before completing a full year of service. His moving expenses were paid in full, in addition to $500 for an earlier trip to locate suitable housing. His travel expenses also had been covered when he came to Midland to interview the division chief engineer, Charles Lyons, and the corporate executive personnel director.

Burton Davis was assigned to the design and development department (see Exhibit 1 for partial organization chart). Four of the six other engineers had no work experience with other employers (which was also true of the chief engineer) and had been with the company from 2 to 13 years.

Davis was assigned a numbered space in the main parking lot and was given a decal for his car window. Only the first three rows in this lot were reserved by number. Employment was high at the time, and the only space available was one vacated by a draftsman who had just resigned (see Exhibits 2 and 2A).

Davis soon noticed that more than half of those who parked in the two parking areas adjacent to the engineering offices were people he would not have expected to have more favorable parking locations than the engineers (see locations 6A and 6B, Exhibit 2A). Talking with his fellow engineers, he found they also thought it strange and had been irritated about it for some time.

The following personnel parked in these areas where space was reserved by name: C. Lyons, B. Swensen, J. Schomer, G. Tully, J. Barmeier, W. Wright, L. Stewart, S. Bonura, T. Michaels, V. Doran, and H. O'Brien. O'Brien was a disabled draftsman who used crutches—all agreed he deserved this location. Most engineers also agreed that Barmeier should park there; although his title was chief draftsman, he functioned almost as an assistant chief engineer and had been with the company for 20 years.

The engineering group felt strongly that Wright, Stewart, Bonura, Michaels, and Doran should not have parking privileges in a more desirable area than their own. Wright, assistant chief draftsman, supervised three drafting checkers and was seen constantly at Barmeier's elbow. The engineers called them "the Bobbsey twins." Stewart supervised some 20 draftsmen. In the engineers' view, his job consisted mainly of handing out timecards and paychecks. Draftsmen were allocated among the engineers and rarely changed assignments. Stewart usually asked the engineers to fill out job-rating sheets for the draftsmen, since he had no basis for appraising their performance. Bonura supervised several office clericals. Michaels of the machine shop and Doran of engine shop were called "supervisors," but the engineering group felt that *foremen* was a more accurate term.

Arnold Jensen (eight years with the company) and Paul Cooper (two years with Blair and two with Ellington Electronics) told Davis they were glad to find someone else concerned about this situation. Other engineers agreed but were reluctant to make an issue of it. One of them told Davis he might be considered a "rabble-rouser" if he talked too much about it.

From what Davis could determine, everyone had parked in the main lot until a few years back. Then two sections of grass were removed to make the small parking areas (6A and 6B in Exhibit 2A).

Since there wasn't room to include Lyons, Swensen, Schomer, Tully, Barmeier, and all the engineers, Lyons said that, rather than draw a line among them, he would not have any of the engineers park there. Instead, all "direct" supervisors were given reserved slots, which just filled the space in the new area. Some engineers felt that Barmeier may have influenced this decision. Technically the engineers were not "direct" supervisors, although they might have as many as 10 people (draftsmen, typists, and so on) working under their control at one time.

Davis knew that every company had irritations with which one learned to live. However, as the

EXHIBIT 1 *Partial Organization Chart: Engine and Motor Division*

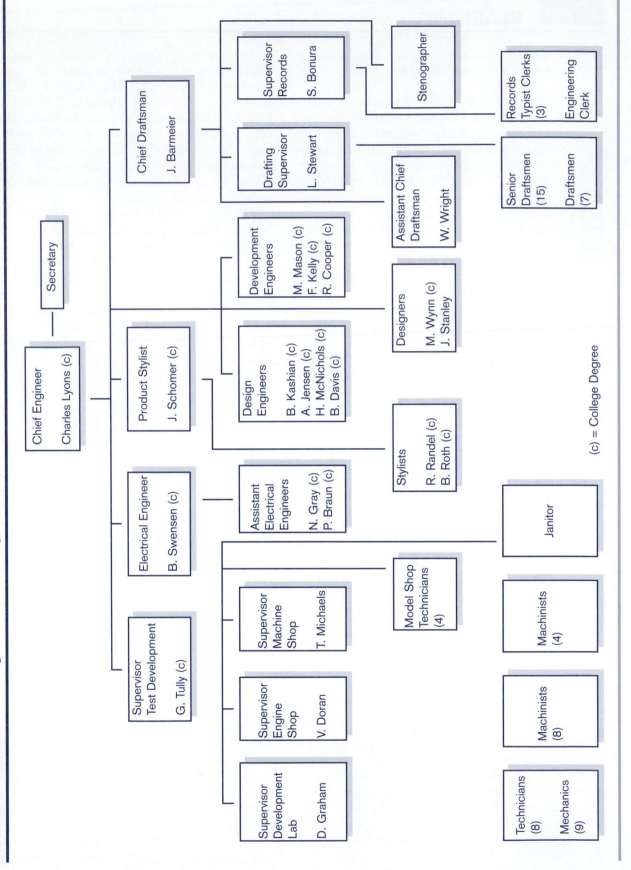

EXHIBIT 2   *Index to Plant Layout in Exhibit 2A*

1.   Main office door—visitors only.
2.   Division administration.
3.   Entrance—all administrative and engineering employees.
4.   Entrance—factory employees.
5.   Entrance—engineering labs (not an employee entrance).
6.   Parking—engineering personnel, reserved by name.
7.   Parking—administrative personnel, reserved by number.
8.   Parking—most of the engineers, reserved by number.
9.   Parking—most of the draftsmen, reserved by number.
10. Parking—Burton Davis, reserved by number.
11. Engineering gate—open all day.
12. Truck loading dock.
13. Paved empty space (could park 8 cars).
14. Storage area (could park 10 cars).
15. Storage area (could park 5 cars).
16. Storage area (could park 10 cars).
17. Parking—supervisor of development lab, later, also, supervisor of test and development.
18. Parking—engineering station wagon and pickup truck.

weather grew worse, he walked through the unpaved gravel lot (which developed many holes in winter), plodded along the street (there was no sidewalk), and still halfway from the entrance, watched others drive in, park near the engineering offices, and enter before he reached the door.

Other things began to disturb him about his position. He found that Barmeier and Wright, without his approval, changed drawings he had released from engineering.

There were three blank boxes on each engineering drawing. The draftsman would initial the "drawn by" space; the checker, the "checked by"; and the engineer, the "approved by." Lyons usually also initialed the last box, which provided room for two sets of initials. A few months after Davis had started work, Wright started erasing the engineer's initials from the "approved" box, entered his own, and told the engineers to initial after the checker's in the middle box. Jensen and Davis immediately told Wright that he could put his own initials after the checker's since he was supposed to be the checker's supervisor and they were the engineers in charge of the project. Davis told Wright, "If you feel otherwise about it, let's go to Lyons right now." Wright immediately agreed to initial after the checker.

Sometime after this incident, a sign reading "Authorized Personnel Only" appeared on the door to the blueprint records storage room where Bonura and the clerks worked. Barmeier told the engineering group that the purpose of this was to avoid disturbing the overworked print girls and that the sign applied to all draftsmen and engineers. Although the engineers protested, Barmeier refused to change his stand. Lyons came by during the argument and moved the group into the conference room. The engineers explained that they often needed information from a tracing; a quick glance was enough before returning it to the file. Under the new system, they would have to order a print and wait to get the information. Lyons agreed with the engineers. Davis, Jensen, and Cooper were particularly pleased. Jensen said later, "At last *we* won something around here."

It gradually became apparent to Davis that Lyons planned most of the engineering for his engineers. When assigning a new project, he would suggest the handling of it in such detail that all chance of creative or original work was eliminated. He frequently went out in the drafting room and told layout draftsmen how he wanted things done. Sometimes he even failed to bring the responsible engineer in on the discussion.

No engineering meetings were held. The only regular meeting was a "production" meeting for which the division manager and his plant manager came to Lyons' office. Lyons was the only engineer in the meetings, although he often stepped out to get a drawing or to get a question answered from a design or developmental engineer whose project was under discussion at the time. On the rare occasions when an engineer *was* called into the meeting, it was without any advance warning, so he was frequently unable to furnish the desired information on the spot. Barmeier, Wright, and Bonura sat in on all meetings. Since these were the only regular conferences, discussion inevitably went beyond production problems and dealt with new products and plans as well. The sales manager and the corporate director of engineering attended some of the meetings. To find out what was going on, the engineers

EXHIBIT 2A

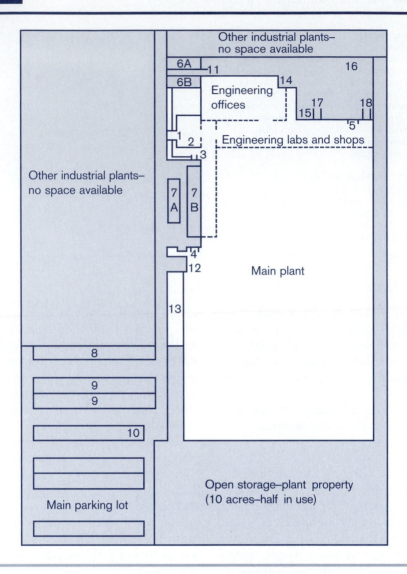

relied on the grapevine or were forced to ask Barmeier, Wright, or Bonura. They rarely talked with Lyons except when he was giving them ideas on how he thought they should do their jobs.

Dissatisfaction grew among the engineers, although several still felt there was nothing to be gained by "stirring things up." Davis felt that if Lyons realized the extent of the developing morale problem, he would try to do something about it.

One evening he had an opportunity to talk to Lyons alone. He made it clear that he thought the situation was becoming critical. He told Lyons what he thought were the main points: the generally low status of the engineers and the feeling they had that they were not given enough responsibility. Davis pointed out that the parking situation was one of the main symbols of the engineers' status, since it was a visible method of ranking. Lyons seemed uncomfortable throughout the discussion but said that he would think about it. Davis told Lyons that he was speaking only for himself but was sure his feelings were shared by most of the others. On leaving, Davis gave Lyons a reprint of an article on morale and suggested it might be of value.[1]

As months passed no perceptible changes were made.[2] George Dunlop was hired to supervise the

---

[1] A portion of the article is reproduced in Exhibit 3.
[2] During this period, Burton Davis typed a memo and circulated it informally among individuals in the division (see Exhibit 4).

EXHIBIT 3

Indicator Area	High Morale Exists When—	Low Morale Exists When—
1. The company	Lines of responsibility and authority are clear; coordination good; line staff teamwork generally productive; organization structure is flexible; managers can get to right official when necessary.	Authority overlaps; organizational structure is too complex; company has too many layers of review; communication breakdowns are frequent; reorganizations don't add up; committees interfere.
2. Company-division practices	Good rapport exists among managers; agreements are honored; people know where they stand and how they are doing; policies are clearly and quickly communicated; reward system is fair and current.	There's too much paperwork; managers have to beat the system; excessive rivalry exists among the departments; deadlines don't mean a thing; it is hard to get needed information; ideas die on vine.
3. Decisions	Decisions are tied in well to polices and plans; managers get chance to participate in decision making; delegation is adequate; bad decisions are withdrawn when necessary; accountability is clear.	Decisions are too slow, poorly timed; subordinate has little chance to participate in the making of decisions; delegation is meager; decisions unduly influenced by tradition; real issues are evaded.
4. Leadership	Staff meetings are well run and produce results; boss keeps subordinates informed of policies and plans affecting them; people know the scope of their responsibilites; boss shows dignity and fairness.	Assignments and orders of boss are unclear; people have to work without knowing policy limitations; boss sets unreasonable deadlines; too many attempts are made at regimentation; standards fall.
5. Group climate	Team takes pride in its performance; people will go to bat for each other; professional aims, standards are high; grievances of a member are heard; overall quality of group output is high grade.	Too many cliques exist; favoritism is shown some; work output is inadequate; one person dominates the group; bickering is common; there are recurrent rule violations; professional standards are low.
6. Job conditions	Managers find sufficient challenge in their jobs; abilities of people are utilized well; employees able to express their views; performance standards are realistic; workers get recognition when deserved.	It's difficult to get a job done; ideas put aside too often, too fast; people have to break rules to get action; boredom and restlessness are prevalent; pay scales lag behind the rates in other firms.
7. Status	Job privileges are modest but good; management is receptive to people's views; talents are utilized; employees enjoy higher status in community because of their association with the company.	Favored few get recognition; opportunities for development are restricted; criticisms far exceed compliments; people must look out for themselves; firm has too many dead-end jobs.

engineers with the title of "chief, design and development" and with the design and development engineers and the designers reporting to him. They had formerly reported directly to Lyons. (Dunlop parked in the engineering lot; Tully was moved to the rear with Graham, area 17 on Exhibit 2A–actually a more desirable spot, only 10 feet from a door.) Before Dunlop arrived Lyons held a meeting with all salaried personnel to explain the decision to bring in a man from outside. He said that he thought the position could have been filled from within the company but that Edward King, the corporate director of engineering, thought that a man with considerable experience was needed. Davis considered it interesting that Lyons was only 34.

Dunlop was 48 years old and had worked as an executive engineer for National Motors, for Burling Aircraft, and for Duval Manufacturing. Lyons mentioned that people might wonder why a man with his background would come here. He explained that Dunlop liked small towns and enjoyed this type of work and that money was not that important to him. Davis commented later to Jensen that "executive engineer" at National Motors meant a big job and that Dunlop must have had a real setback somewhere along the way. The engineers considered it significant that Dunlop was placed in charge of seven engineers with the draftsmen and technicians still reporting to others. Moreover, Barmeier was still next to Lyons with no

EXHIBIT 4

Office Memo

ENGINE AND MOTOR ENGINEERING SECTION

To: "Supervisory" personnel

Subject: Fitness Program

Going along with the present Washington administration's emphasis on hiking as a means of improving the fitness of the American people, it is suggested that those Blair employees now parking near the building exchange parking places with the engine and motor section *engineers.* The engineers are in splendid shape from their long hikes and feel that it is only fair to share this conditioning. After a suitable "build-up" period, a rotation system will be worked out to ensure the retention of all the fitness benefits.

The Personnel Department

---

intermediary. They also noted that Dunlop had not been given the title of assistant chief engineer.

Several engineers with long experience with the firm believed they should have been candidates for the job. Other engineers thought Dunlop might become a useful go-between for them. They saw that Barmeier took care of *his* people and Tully took care of *his.* Perhaps the engineers now had someone to put in a few good words for them. Dunlop seemed, at first, to be a much better administrator than Lyons. At least, the engineers felt he "talked a good game." They began to tell him about things they felt needed improvement or correction. But after two months it became apparent that Dunlop had not recommended any changes to Lyons. It appeared to Davis and others that he was loathe to tell Lyons anything that might be disturbing. The engineers felt that he was "running scared."

Davis suggested to Jensen and Cooper that talking to Dunlop was not unlike a session with a psychiatrist. You talked about your problems and felt better even though nothing really changed. Whenever anyone returned from a talk with Dunlop, a colleague would ask, "Did you have a nice couch session?"

As the small group talked about their problems, the situation became almost unbearable to Davis. There was considerable talk of other jobs, and occasionally one of the men would have an interview with

another firm. Finally, Davis, Jensen, and Cooper decided to approach Lyons in a group. They had decided that they would all leave anyway unless changes were made. This "group action" was distasteful to them, but they felt that it was the only way to get Lyons to realize he had a real problem to face. There seemed to be little to lose.

Following are some of the comments made by the engineers and Lyons as they talked in the chief engineer's office one evening after work:

Engineer: We feel a little silly talking about this, but since it does bother us and affects our morale, we feel you should know.

Engineer: The parking position ranks everyone, whether or not you believe it does.

Lyons: Where you park doesn't have anything to do with the way I rank you.

Engineer: We feel that as highly paid college graduates who actually do the creative work we should rank above "assistant chief draftsmen" and "foremen."

Engineer: Specifically, we feel that we should rank ahead of Wright, Stewart, Bonura, Doran, and Michaels.

Lyons: Do you feel you are better than those people?

Engineer: In terms of working for this company, yes. We would certainly be harder to replace. In any case, ranking is inevitable; we would like to think that you agree with us on where we rank.

Lyons: You know that you make much more money than those people, don't you?

Engineer: Yes, which is another reason for keeping the other symbols of rank in the same order.

Engineer: Salary is not a problem. We do not feel overpaid or underpaid in our present job.

Engineer: Whether or not *you* feel this is a problem, the fact that *we* do feel it is a problem *makes* it a problem, by definition.

Engineer: The fact that parking ranks us in status actually affects our job efficiency as it relates to others. We have more trouble "getting things done" if we don't have the status to back it up.

Engineer: Saying that status symbols are unimportant doesn't make them go away. We live with status symbols all the time; unless they are distorted from the way most people expect to see them, they go unnoticed. Only when the symbol system gets out of line does it become a problem. This means that to have a smoothly functioning organization, an administrator has to consider status symbols and make every attempt to allocate them as his subordinates expect him to.

Engineer: Doran and Michaels are foremen, no matter what fancy names they are called. Stewart is the drafting supervisor and should rank under us, but Barmeier and Wright are doing engineer work. If you want to rank them above us, that is your decision, but their titles should be changed. A chief draftsman and his assistant should never rank above any engineer. The situation is similar to the army, where a master sergeant may have many years of experience and be valuable, but he does not outrank the greenest second lieutenant.

Engineer: We note that you have the closest space to the door in the lots near engineering, and the division manager has the space closest to the door in the administration lot. Isn't it logical that the number two ranking people have the next spaces, and so on down the line? That's the way almost everyone looks at it.

Engineer: We don't care *where* we actually park. The question is *who* parks where. If everyone had the same long walk, there would be no problem.

Engineer: Locating our parking spaces more conveniently without changing the relative status of the spaces will be no solution at all.

Lyons: But where can I find more parking space?

Engineer: We think there are a number of areas that could be used, but some effort would be required. There is unused space in front of the plant [13 in Exhibit 2A], or space could be made available by moving some of the stored materials from the area east of engineering [14, 15, and 16 in Exhibit 2A]. Even if you can't find space for improved parking for everyone, engineers should park in that lot. Not necessarily the three of us, but *engineers*.

Engineer: The fact that you don't or can't trust us with more responsibility affects our morale and job interest also.

Lyons: But I do give as much responsibility as possible.

Engineer: But you act as if you don't really trust us.

Lyons: It's not that I don't trust you; it's just that I want to see the job done right.

As the talk ended, Lyons appeared to be disturbed and concerned. He said that he would think about what had been said and would see if there was anything that he could do.

Nevertheless, the three engineers were sure that Lyons had not really understood them. In spite of their emphasis on "not where, but *who*," they sensed that the chief engineer believed that all they wanted was better, closer parking places. They felt he didn't understand their desire for more responsibility, either; he seemed to think they had all the responsibility they had a right to expect. They agreed that his comment on "doing the job right" demonstrated how little effect they had had.

They predicted that any solution Lyons might devise would be unsatisfactory. They wondered if they should take any other steps or just wait and hope that Lyons had more understanding than they suspected. They realized that if the solution was unsatisfactory it was the end of the road. They could hardly start the process all over again.

Neil Abramson prepared this case under the supervision of Professor J. J. DiStefano solely to provide material for class discussion. The authors do not intend to illustrate either effective or ineffective handling of a managerial situation. The authors may have disguised certain names and other identifying information to protect confidentiality.

Ivey Management Services prohibits any form of reproduction, storage or transmittal without its written permission. This material is not covered under authorization from CanCopy or any reproduction rights organization. To order copies or request permission to reproduce materials, contact Ivey Publishing, Ivey Management Services, c/o Richard Ivey School of Business, The University of Western Ontario, London, Ontario, Canada, N6A 3K7; phone (519) 661-3208; fax (519) 661-3882; e-mail cases@ivey.uwo.ca.
Copyright© 1991, Ivey Management Services
Version: (A)1992-08-24

Bob Chen prepared himself for his meeting with David Shorter, Practice Director of the New Enterprise Group at James-Williams. In a few minutes, Bob might feel it necessary to resign from James-Williams. Bob had no other job to go to, and with a recession looming, it might be hard to find other employment. Nevertheless, Bob felt that his career was at stake if he was not firm.

The New Enterprise Group at James-Williams

The New Enterprise Group was a division of James-Williams located in Toronto. James-Williams was one of the six largest public accounting firms in Canada with 400 partners practicing in 30 Canadian cities. James-Williams was the sole Canadian member of James-Williams International, which provided audit, tax consulting and other services to individuals, private businesses and governments in the Americas, Europe, the Middle East, Africa, Asia and the Pacific.

The New Enterprise Group had been set up seven years ago to provide service to smaller growth companies managed by entrepreneurs. David Shorter had been the Practice Director for the past four years. James-Williams believed that companies with gross annual revenues of between $5 and $100 M were often neglected as potential customers by Canadian public accounting firms because of their small size. Yet these companies had need of a variety of services that could be provided by James-Williams and these companies would pay high fees for their relative size.

When these companies had grown beyond gross revenues of $100 M, their business could be transferred from the New Enterprise Group to the main auditing and consulting services of James-Williams and a solid relationship would exist. This was an important consideration in a mature industry where public accounting firms competed on service, reputation, and price. Often, it was a long-term relationship that kept a client with a public accounting firm. These relationships enabled partners of the public accounting firms to have such an intimate knowledge of their clients' activities that they could anticipate problems and become indispensable to their clients' planning process.

The New Enterprise Group provided a range of consulting services geared to the needs of growing entrepreneurial companies. In addition to accounting and auditing services, the partners acted as principal business advisors. Client companies were particularly interested in corporate finance, tax consulting, and the problems of acquisition and divestiture. Consulting was also available on strategic planning, developing business plans, marketing, human resource management, and information systems.

The New Enterprise Group was organized as a collegial system of partners who managed their own clients and activities within the performance objectives established by James-Williams, and under the general supervision of the Practice Director who was also a partner (see Exhibit 1). Staff members below the partner level were organized on the staff system. A staff usually consisted of one or two senior staff accountants and several intermediate or junior staff accountants under a manager. A partner would have one, two, or three managers and several staff reporting to him/her.

Most of the staff were either chartered accountants or in the process of becoming chartered accountants. Usually, staff would be hired out of business school as junior staff accountants and would work on staff over a two-year period while they studied for their chartered accountant examinations. At the beginning of their second year, they were promoted to intermediate staff accountants at which level they remained until they passed the chartered accountant exams. At the beginning of their third year, they wrote their exams, and, if they passed, they were promoted to senior staff accountants. If they did not pass, which was fairly common, they would have another year to prepare for a final chance at the exams.

EXHIBIT 1 *James-Williams: The New Enterprise Group Organizational Chart*
(Reporting relationships prior to Bob Chen's reassignment to tax)

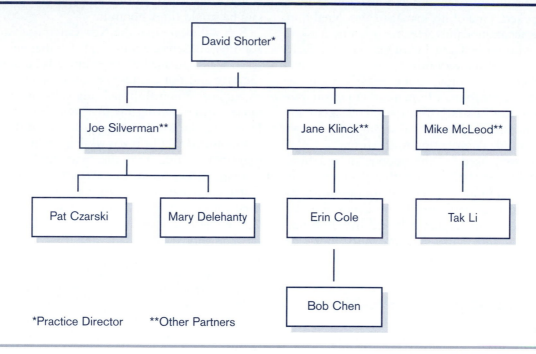

*Practice Director   **Other Partners

The normal promotion process at James-Williams was for staff to remain as senior staff accountants for two years while they developed a consulting specialty of their choice. Then they might be promoted to manager and supervise six to nine staff. Most partners were selected from the ranks of the managers after they had been with the firm for ten to eleven years.

Bob Chen's Background at James-Williams

Bob Chen was born in Hong Kong and came to Toronto as a high school student for Grade 13. He graduated with a Bachelor of Commerce from Queen's University in Kingston. At Queen's he achieved an overall grade point average of 75%[1] and was the treasurer of the Chinese Students' Society. He was recruited for James-Williams in the spring of his final year at Queen's, and began as a junior staff accountant at the New Enterprise Group in the following September.

Early in his final year at Queen's, Bob's father, living in Hong Kong, suggested he find a job in Canada because Hong Kong would revert to the People's Re-

public of China in 1997. His father believed Bob's future would be better in Canada. Bob applied to a number of major Canadian public accounting firms and was told to re-apply if he was able to obtain landed immigrant status. These companies did not seem to realize that it was very hard to obtain landed immigrant status unless one had a job offer.

One firm, James-Williams, offered Bob a job. He accepted. Afterwards Bob felt very loyal to the company because their offer had made it possible for him to remain in Canada.

In September after graduation, Bob started with James-Williams in the New Enterprise Group as a junior staff accountant, doing accounting work and studying for his chartered accountant exams which were scheduled for two years hence. In the following fall he was promoted to intermediate staff accountant as was standard for all second-year staff at James-Williams. During his first two years with the New Enterprise Group, Bob worked under the supervision of several managers including Tak Li and a partner named Lara Witmer. Due to turnover of staff in the New Enterprise Group during those years, Bob was attached for various job to a number of managers and partners. About the time that Bob was scheduled to write his C.A. exams, he learned that Lara Witmer had been asked to leave the firm. Bob would be assigned

---

[1] In Canada the grade point system follows the British model. At Queen's a 75 average is a B+ and is considered evidence of high achievement.

to work for Jane Klinck under the project supervision of Erin Cole.

In the New Enterprise Group Bob was seen as quiet and soft-spoken. One of his managers described him as "shy and accommodating. He does what he is asked to do and a bit more. Casual requests get immediate results." He was also a very private person whose politeness often meant not saying exactly what he wanted out of a situation or from another person. His civility may have masked from his colleagues his strongly felt desire for success and strongly held views about his possible contribution to the firm.

Bob was well liked by the people around him. Some partners and staff thought that Bob was fairly outgoing and had much better oral communications skills than previous staff from Hong Kong hired by the company. His colleagues believed that Bob had good potential with James-Williams and hoped he would stay with the company.

The Beginnings of a Problem

Early in his employment at James-Williams, Bob decided he would like to specialize as a tax consultant. He knew that the normal procedure at James-Williams was for intermediate staff to wait until they had passed their chartered accountant exams before approaching the Practice Director with indications of their specialization interests. However, tax was a very popular choice and some intermediate staff in the New Enterprise Group went to David Shorter before they had passed their exams so that David would have enough time to find them assignments in their preferred areas.

Nine months after joining the New Enterprise Group, Bob met formally with David Shorter when David reviewed Bob's annual performance appraisal. Bob's impression of the meeting was that David had agreed to see what he could do to further Bob's interests. Bob expected that he would receive some tax assignments over the next year while he was studying for his chartered accountant exams, but no such assignments materialized.

In September, Bob wrote his exams and, in December, he received the good news that he had passed on his first attempt. The following January David Shorter called Bob in for an interview during which he congratulated Bob on passing his C.A. exam and asked what Bob would like to specialize in. Bob again asked for an assignment to tax, but David told him that he wasn't ready for tax because his auditing skills were not strong enough. David asked Bob to work as a senior auditor for a year in order to provide a

stronger base for his tax specialization. David also asked Bob to consider the idea of specializing in Hong Kong–based entrepreneurial companies. Bob said he would think about it.

Bob was aware that the New Enterprise Group had a shortage of senior auditors. He felt that he was being asked not to pursue his career interests because of this shortage and not because of any weakness he had as an auditor. When Bob had originally mentioned his interest in tax during his first interview with David, David said he would see what he could do and had not indicated that Bob was weak in auditing. This also suggested to Bob that the main problem was the shortage. "I wanted to choose tax but I had the feeling that the partners didn't want me to because of the need for continuity in audit. I was maybe the only C.A. under Jane Klinck. Partners want qualified C.A.'s on their jobs. Maybe Jane didn't want me to go to tax."

Bob was also aware that he had a reputation for doing what he was told. He tried to anticipate the needs of his supervisors and his clients, and he worked extra hard to accommodate their wishes. Partly this was his natural tendency, but he also felt a strong loyalty to the firm for hiring him and thereby providing a way for him to stay in Canada. Now he wondered if David thought he would not make a fuss if he was held back in auditing for another year. "I did not usually express myself. I wondered if he thought I was too easygoing and would do whatever he wanted."

When David reviewed his annual performance appraisal in June after Bob had passed his C.A. exams, Bob again asked David for an assignment to tax. And again David refused, indicating that Bob needed more experience in audit. Bob did not accept this judgement and felt that he had once again been too easygoing and had failed to express himself forcefully enough.

Therefore, in late June, Bob approached David once more and after extensive discussion got David to compromise that if Bob would agree to stay in audit for the year, David would arrange to send Bob on a three-year tax training program. Bob initially agreed, but when he talked to friends in tax, they told him that the course would not teach him tax. Becoming a tax consultant required hands-on experience and the opportunity to deal with the tax problems of real companies in real situations. "I initially agreed, but decided later that it wasn't a good compromise because I wouldn't learn tax technique."

Once again Bob approached David with his concerns and David finally agreed to assign Bob to Joe Silverman, a tax consultant, in September as long as Bob agreed to finish his current audit work and was willing to accept one major audit assignment in January and February. Bob agreed and David made the arrangements for transferring Bob to Joe's tax group starting in September.

The Softdisk Audit

On July 10, soon after this series of conversations with David Shorter, Bob was approached by Mike McLeod, another partner in the New Enterprise Group, to be the senior on an audit of the Softdisk Computer Company. The audit would require Bob's full time attention in September and October. Bob was extremely wary. He believed if he accepted the Softdisk audit, he would have very little opportunity to specialize in tax for the entire year. The problem, as Bob saw it, was that it now looked as if he might be required to do audit for six of the next eight months. He was currently doing an audit of a film company for his present managing partner, Jane Klinck. This audit had been scheduled for completion in early July, but the company's books were a mess and Bob thought he might have to continue on that job through August. In August, he would have to begin an interim audit of Softdisk. The Softdisk audit would occupy September and October. Then in January and February, he was required to do another major audit for Jane Klinck as part of his agreement with David. This left November and December for tax work, but December was a slow month due to Christmas. It didn't seem fair to Bob. He had friends who had also passed their C.A. exams and had been transferred directly into the Tax Department at James-Williams's main group in Toronto without having to agree to any further auditing responsibilities.

Consequently, Bob decided not to do the Softdisk audit. He told Mike McLeod that he would help out because there were no other senior auditors currently available in the New Enterprise Group. He went to the physical inventory at Softdisk in mid-July because no one else seemed to be available. At the time, he told Jane's staff manager, Erin Cole, that he would not do the Softdisk audit even though he went to observe the physical inventory.

Mike had tried to entice Bob into the audit by indicating the possibilities of learning about tax because of the intricate tax situation at the company. Bob talked about these possible advantages with others and decided that Softdisk was not as good an opportunity as Mike was describing. For one thing, Softdisk's tax complexities had been sorted out the year before by a senior tax manager, and Bob would sim-

ply be following the procedures developed at that time. Yet the situation wasn't risk free. Bob did not have adequate expertise in tax yet, and he was concerned that if he did encounter a difficult problem and made a serious mistake, he would be blamed and it would damage his career.

Bob tried to break the news gently that he would not be doing the Softdisk audit. He approached Tak Li, who now worked for Mike McLeod as a manager, and told Tak that he did not want to do the job. He also told Pat Czarski, a manager reporting to his new managing partner, Joe Silverman. Somehow the message did not seem to get through to Mike McLeod and over the next week Mike would stop Bob in the halls or in the men's room and ask if Bob had made a decision, or if Bob had any reservations that Mike could help him resolve. Mike seemed to be convinced that Bob would eventually take the job. Bob began to feel trapped. Since David Shorter had gone on vacation, he could not help sort out the situation. "I knew that Mike was quite influential in the New Enterprises Group because he had many bigger clients. He was persuasive and forceful. I wondered, 'Why is this happening to me? Why is he so determined to make me give in and take this job? Why is he going around to other partners and managers trying to get them to persuade me? He wants me to bow on this issue and I don't want to.'"

The final straw for Bob was a meeting called by Mike, including himself, Pat, Tak and Bob on July 20. Bob felt that the sole purpose of the meeting was to coerce him into taking on the Softdisk audit. After hours of pressure, Bob said he would do the job, just to end the meeting. However, he felt that he had been unfairly treated in the meeting and that he did not have to honour his agreement. "I felt isolated, like it was three against one."

Other Factors

After his meeting with Mike, Pat, and Tak, Bob reviewed his situation and prospects. He knew that he had offended Mike McLeod. He had heard from Jane Klinck that he had also offended Joe Silverman who was scheduled to be his new managing partner in tax. Bob did not feel that he had a career potential with the New Enterprise Group any more.

In addition, the New Enterprise Group did not seem committed to supporting his desire to become a tax consultant. They appeared more concerned with their shortage of senior auditors. Bob felt less inclined to be loyal to a company which was not loyal to him.

Bob felt that he had the security to find another job. He had his chartered accountant designation. He was a Canadian citizen. He had money saved and his family would support him if he got into financial difficulties. He also had contacts from a management recruiting company that had tried to hire him for another company after he passed his chartered accountant exams. He decided to resign and told Jane of his intention. She discouraged him from acting rashly and convinced him to at least talk with David Shorter again when he returned from vacation on July 24. "Jane seemed to be shocked when I said I was thinking of resigning. She said, 'But you're usually so easy going!' I thought maybe they were picking on me because I'm easy going and never complain."

A Final Meeting with David Shorter

Bob expected no miracles from David before his upcoming meeting of July 24. He expected David to tell him that he was doing good work and to ask him to stay. He also expected David to ask him to do the Softdisk audit and to "tough out" the situation. Although Bob was prepared to listen, he thought he might have to resign unless David was willing to work out an acceptable alternative for him. Bob hoped David could come up with something. In the final analysis, Bob did not really want to leave. He just wanted to do tax.

12   THE BRADY TRAINING PROGRAM

Introduction

"Well, I'm very happy you've accepted, Bill," said Dick Hubbard. "You are the type of person we believe will succeed here. You scored very well on the computer-aptitude test and seem to be very personable. Our next training class starts a week from Monday. I trust you can relocate by then; I've bumped another candidate in order to accept you."

Dick Hubbard shook hands with his new employee and directed him toward Brady Company's nursing office. Accepting the training position with the Information Systems Department was a big change for Bill Flynn, and he hoped he could meet the challenge. Flynn's only prior experience had been in computer sales. Because of this, Bill lacked technical expertise and felt as though he were flying by the seat of his pants. However, he seriously wanted to succeed in the computer field, so he decided to leave his sales position after only one year. Although he considered the technical aspects of computers to be quite uninteresting and difficult to learn, Bill was determined that they were a hurdle he would overcome. Flynn turned down two sales positions for the opportunity to gain some hands-on programming analysis and hardware experience. His goal was to build a solid technical foundation from which to launch his career by investing at least two years in the technical side of the computer field.

Initial Orientation

Things seemed to be happening very quickly. While speaking with the company nurse, Bill learned he could rent a room from her until he was able to find an apartment. In a matter of three hours, he had changed jobs and arranged to relocate. He drove home that day somewhat pleased with himself while wondering what the near future held in store.

The first day on the job soon arrived. The new training group consisted of 11 people, 3 women and 8 men. Most of the members agreed that it would be a tough year, but well worth it by year's end. Each trainee had received a letter with a generous starting salary for the first year; after 12 months and completion of all the required courses, the trainee was to receive a promotion and a 50% raise. Bill's letter named the following February 14 as the promotion date.

The orientation was administered by Al Gavin. He was one of three bosses the trainees were to report to

and be reviewed by. Al was in charge of computer room operations, where the trainees were to work. The other two bosses were Dick Hubbard, the program coordinator, and Mark Toner, the department manager.

Al explained that the trainees would work eight-hour days and be rotated among the three shifts, spending approximately four months on each shift. The majority of the trainees were quite surprised, for until then, they had not heard any mention of night shift work. Al stated:

> Each trainee must complete all four training courses offered by the department. Each course will last for three months and be taught by department personnel. Two-and-a-half hour classes will be held Monday through Friday. Trainees are not to help one another. We are looking for people who can solve problems on their own. Besides, you are competing for the same positions; helping others could hurt your chances. All assistance is to be asked of the course instructor. All course assignments are to be handed in on time. A late or poorly completed assignment could mean termination. Each trainee will be reviewed after every project and judged eligible or ineligible to continue. We are determined to raise the productivity of software design, and if you survive, you will be a valuable contribution.

There were many surprised faces among the group. The trainees had not been aware of the competition for department positions. They were still not sure of the degree of competition when they left the orientation.

After the orientation the trainees seemed somewhat wary of one another, and for the most part they kept to themselves. All were attending the first course and engaged in very little discussion about the material. While working in computer operations, they constantly competed with one another.

The First Month

Bill was able to make two friends that first month. The first was Harry Andrews, a family man with three young children. Harry was 30 years old and one of four former schoolteachers in the midst of a career change. Bill and Harry shared a similar sense of humor and enjoyed one another's company. It always broke the tension.

The second friend was Bob Hackey. Bob was a member of the last training class and had just been promoted. He was 25, which was only two years older than Bill. Bill and Bob were very interested in sports and planned to go skiing together.

Bill was really struggling to complete the last assignment for the first course. It seemed to be about three weeks' worth of work but had to be completed in 10 days. Harry noticed the problem Bill was having and offered to help. They secretly met outside of work at Bill's new apartment. Harry's assistance got Bill on the right track, and he was able to complete the project on time. He vowed to help Harry in any way he could. The day after the assignment was due, there were two less members in the training class. Barbara Green, who always looked as though she were in a cold sweat from the daily pressure of the training program, had decided to quit. Another member, Glenn Reed, had submitted his assignment a day late. The following day he was asked to leave class by Mark Toner and was terminated from the training program.

A Study Group Forms

Upon finding out about Glenn, Harry and Bill decided to meet at Bill's apartment on a biweekly basis to discuss problems and share ideas and discoveries. The very next week, Bob stopped over to see Bill while he and Harry were working on an assignment. They decided to break for a beer, and work crept into the conversation. Bob offered the following:

> You two had better stick together, but be very careful—don't let anyone know that you help each other. Share your ideas, but do separate work. The course instructors will look for too many similarities among trainee's projects. You can't trust any of these people. They want to see how much you can take. There are nine left in your class and only three or four positions for you to fill. You are all very well qualified for the open positions. Each of you was selected from over 120 applicants. But being qualified is not enough. They will be very tough on you and apply extreme pressure to expose any possible weakness. They don't want to keep all of you, just the toughest three or four. Management maintains an extremely competitive environment among the department's systems analysts. They feel it improves quantity and quality of output. The competition can get very tiresome and rough, so they want to identify the tougher competitors as soon as possible.
>
> Yours is only the third training group. We are an experiment to see if they can produce almost perfectly homogeneous systems people who are superior to those they are able to hire from outside. It may cost their staff members valuable time, but they make it up by having trainees operate their computer on all shifts at a very low rate of pay. That's another reason for having a few extra trainees around.

> Former trainees can be your worst enemies. They feel part of a select group that has made it through the program. The more that enter their ranks, the smaller a fish each one becomes. They will keep an eye on you and report any flaws that they think they notice. I don't mean to sound like such a malcontent. Fact is, I've located a very good position, and I plan to leave. My new employer was very excited to hire someone who had completed the Brady training program. The program has an extremely good reputation and deservedly so. Nowhere else can you learn so much, so fast. Many area businesses have heard of Brady's well-developed systems department. The computer vendor uses Brady as a model site. Some of the companies have even hired people that have either quit or washed out of the training program. They have had extremely good luck with them and find that they have had to spend very little time and expense on further training. These companies jump at the opportunity to hire someone who has completed the Brady training program. You'll see; soon you will be receiving daily calls from area placement firms.

The Study Group Expands

During the second course, Bill held a party for all the trainees at his apartment. He invited his two roommates and many of their friends. Bill was afraid that a party consisting of the training group alone might not be much fun. Cathy Moore, one of the two remaining women trainees, struck up a friendship with Bill's roommate, Rick, and they began to spend quite a lot of time with one another. As a result Bill and Harry were having trouble concealing their meetings. Since Cathy was one of the sharpest trainees and she and Bill also were becoming quite good friends, Bill thought she should be part of the help sessions. Harry agreed, and they made the offer to Cathy, who was happy to join.

As the second course was drawing to a close, the pressure was mounting. Bill, Harry, and Cathy were all struggling. They were saddled with another large project to be completed in a very short amount of time.

Bill was working the third shift and arrived four hours early to spend some time on his project. His arrival surprised two of the other trainees; Chris Peck and Harold Breen were in the process of printing multiple computer files. Bill noticed that they were nervous and trying to hide something, so he checked the printouts. They were listings of the current project assignment as completed by several members of the previous class. Chris and Harold were upset and pleaded with Bill not to report them. Bill assured them that he had no intention of reporting anyone. He told them: "Listen, you guys, I'm relieved to find that I'm not the only one who is struggling here. We're all in trouble but refuse to admit it to one another. I don't have to tell you what a great help these printouts can be. Could you give me a copy of each of them?"

Chris and Harold got the copies for Bill. The next day he presented them to the study group, explaining that he could not divulge his source until the end of the training program. The members decided to split the completed projects among themselves and to study them for useful ideas, style, and problem-solving methods. They met two days later to share their discoveries. The three had found many good ideas along with quite a few poor ones. They were surprised to find that some of the former trainees who were very condescending to them were not as sharp as they were led to believe. Each member agreed to use the ideas only as reference, to keep the information in the strictest of confidence, and to complete their own individual work. They had learned more in those two days than in the previous three weeks.

The study group members submitted their projects on time but felt as though they were just keeping their heads above water. Two more people were let go the day after the project was due, but all the study group members had survived. Cathy was now the only woman remaining.

An Opportunity

During the seventh month of the program, Bill and Harry were in their second month on the third shift. They would work from midnight to 8 A.M. and then have to attend a two-and-a-half-hour class during the day. They had three morning classes and two afternoon classes per week. Each trainee worked every other weekend. Almost all the trainees were present in the computer room every weekend, working on completing their project assignments.

On one particular third shift, about 3 A.M., Bill was delivering some computer printouts when he noticed that Mark Toner's office door was left ajar. The only people in the building were another trainee and a night watchman occasionally passing through. On impulse, Bill let himself into the office and closed the door. Mark's desk was not locked, and Bill decided to have a look through it. Quickly, he found the training program files. He couldn't believe the risk he was taking, but rationalized that not knowing what his reviewers thought of him could be a larger risk. He nervously opened the files. There was a long review form for each trainee, and Bill read all of them. Each form had four duplications of the same review crite-

ria. As trainees progressed through the program, the form would follow them. They were judged on their ability to grasp and apply concepts, quality of work, attitude, compatibility, promptness, appearance, and competitive ranking among the other trainees. While reviewing an individual's performance, an instructor could read about the trainee. Bill noticed that many of the first reviewer's comments had been duplicated by the second reviewer.

Bill's review was much better than he had anticipated. It did mention some doubt about his willingness to become part of the departmental organization. He wondered why this supposed weakness had not been pointed out to him. He felt uneasy and vulnerable.

The next day Bill told Harry and Cathy about his discovery. They couldn't believe he had done it. When asked why, Bill had trouble explaining; he had never done anything like that before. Bill also told them about Victor Lawton's review. Victor was very well liked by all three of the study group members. He'd been married just over a year, and his wife was about to have their first child. It was written on Victor's review that he was a candidate for firing, so they decided to ask him to join them. Victor gladly accepted. The study group now consisted of four of the seven remaining trainees.

Building Goodwill

Bill had joined the company softball team, of which Al Gavin was the manager. They got to know one another outside of work and became fairly good friends. Bill really liked Al. He decided to build a better rapport with the other two bosses, although he was not very fond of either of them.

Mark Toner was an avid outdoorsman and had many fishing pictures on his office walls. Bill was originally from Vermont and still owned a cabin up in the mountains. He loved to fish and considered himself as somewhat of an expert. He slowly broke into conversations with Mark about fishing. Soon they were trading stories, and Bill showed Mark some pictures of one of his very successful fishing trips to the cabin. They made tentative plans for a trip to Bill's cabin for the following year. However, Bill had no intention of ever fishing with Mark.

Dick Hubbard's position called for occasional trips to Brady Company's Latin American operations. He was attempting to learn Spanish. Bill had spent a year in Colombia, South America, while in college. He spoke fluent Spanish and decided to use it to his advantage. He often conversed with Dick and acted more than happy to help Dick with the language. Dick was very interested in Bill's experiences in

Colombia and, again, Bill acted more than happy to discuss them.

Some of the trainees expressed their displeasure with Bill's constant contact with the three bosses, but Bill only cared about the opinions of the study group members. He asked them what they thought. None of them seemed to mind; and Harry said, "Each one of us must do whatever we think it takes to complete the program." Bill gave them the following explanation:

> I have mixed emotions about my actions. At times I feel pretty underhanded, but I know the actions are justified. My back is against the wall; I can't afford not to complete this training program. I just quit my last job after only one year. I don't want to appear as though I can't stick with anything. Besides, I'm really interested and want to learn as much as I possibly can. By Brady's standards, I may be cheating a little bit, but I'm learning while I do it. I fully intend to finish in spite of these people. If anyone is going to win this game, I'm going to make sure it's me!

Making It

The group agreed that each individual was playing a game of self-preservation. They felt that their chances of survival were greatly increased by the help they gave one another.

The final project for the third course was an extremely large assignment to be completed in 10 days. Everyone was working at a nerve-wracking pace. By now Bill was feeling more comfortable with his ability to complete the projects on time. He submitted the project a day early. Victor was the only one to be late handing in the project, because he had been very sick with the flu and had fallen behind. He submitted his project two days after it was due. The next day's class was interrupted by the department secretary, who notified Victor Lawton and Harold Breen that Mark Toner wanted to speak with them during the next break. They did not return after the break, and the instructor announced that they had been let go.

The remaining five employees were all of similar caliber. They wondered if more firing would take place and, if so, who would be next. No one dared to ask management. They knew that they were marketable by this point, but all were determined to prove they could finish the training program.

On February 14, shortly after the fourth and final course ended, five of the original trainees were still present. They were Bill, Harry, Cathy, Chris Peck, and Mike Sears. What seemed to be a very long year for Bill had ended in success. He had attained the tools he had set out to acquire.

What Next?

Bill had been interviewing for about a month. He had made some very interesting contacts but had held off until the program was over. After hearing Mark's comment, he decided to pursue them more seriously. He had only taken two days of vacation time in the last year. He asked his bosses if he could take a week of vacation time he had saved. "I've pushed myself very hard all year and could use a rest before digging into a new assignment," he explained. He spent the entire week interviewing in Boston. Two positions were particularly interesting, and he met with each prospective employer twice. They expressed considerable interest in him and had much to offer. Both firms were large computer manufacturers, with a position open in their in-house systems departments. They both offered more than ample facilities and made Bill feel as though they really wanted him to be a part of their teams. Bill liked the idea of working for a computer manufacturer. He felt that almost all aspects of the industry would be available to him in one location. If he got his foot in the door and worked very hard, he should be able to select from many possible career paths.

Upon his return Bill was notified that his review would take place on Thursday of the following week. By then, he had received written offers of employment from both of the companies that he was interested in. The salaries were higher than he expected to receive from Brady. That day Bill had lunch with all three bosses. As they finished their meal, Dick Hubbard said, "We're very impressed with your performance in the training program. By the manner in which you have progressed and improved throughout the year, we know that you can handle this business. We want you to be a part of our team. Welcome to the department!"

Bill turned to Dick and told him of the offers he had received and how interested he was. Dick exclaimed, "We'll better those offers; stay with us! How much are they for?" Bill gave them the figures, and they immediately made a counteroffer. To that, Bill replied, "I would like to go home and give it some serious thought. I'll let you know tomorrow."

BULLY OR VICTIM?

WEST POINT, N.Y.–Col. James Hallums, a veteran of two wars, had seen lots of nasty skirmishes in his career. But he thought his combat days were behind him when he arrived to instill a "warrior spirit" in the leadership department of the U.S. Military Academy here.

He was wrong. Soon, some subordinate academic officers would rise up in open revolt, and eventually some female faculty members would complain that he was sexist.

This was hard for a tough infantry officer to take. West Point, though a college, is still part of the Army and the colonel expected to be obeyed. This insurrection was all insubordination and nonsense, in his estimation, and he fought back.

Yet today Col. Hallums, who once seemed assured of a promotion to general, finds himself pilloried as a bully–and out of the Army, his 30-year-career brought to an ugly end.

He was brought to the academy out of worries that the venerable institution had lost its military and disciplinary edge. But late last year, after a tumultuous one-year stint and a rancorous investigation of his actions by academy superiors, he lost his post as head of the leadership department, sacked for "abusive leadership."

Among the charges against him: that he harassed some of his female subordinates by lecturing them about their personal lives and showed a gender bias because he was so gung-ho about combat forces, and under Army rules, women are excluded from ground combat roles. Yet, Col. Hallums, whose supporters say he sometimes showed a clumsiness around women professionals, had been maverick enough to favor giving women a role on the front lines.

His supporters, a number of West Point women among them, remain bitter about his treatment, and use a military metaphor to describe what befell the colonel: ambush. They contend that the same divisive culture wars that have been raging in the corridors of U.S. education, religion and the workplace have now broken out in the military. Col. Hallums, a soldier of the Old School, had been plenty good enough to lead men into deadly combat and win medals of valor. But, supporters say, he didn't pass muster with the "weenie" element of the modern Army. Too gruff, blunt, and demanding for the academics around him; too proud of his warrior past. He was, they charge, drummed out of the service for being politically incorrect.

Detractors have another version. They say the colonel was a bullying loudmouth who went out of his way to offend and humiliate certain of his subordinates. He treated his post like an infantry command, running roughshod over the academy's academic mission. In the end, critics say Col. Hallums proved himself a macho, oafish officer out of step with the reality of a peacetime Army whose purpose is now more complicated than storming a machine-gun nest–and whose culture now includes technicians and managers as well as warriors like himself.

More neutral observers wonder whether he wasn't simply what one calls "the wrong man for the wrong times." But neutral observers are hard to find.

"What West Point did to Col. Hallums is sordid," says retired Col. Robert Seigle, an ardent supporter of the colonel. But Brig. Gen. Fletcher M. Lamkin Jr., dean of West Point's academic board, defends the academy's decision, saying Col. Hallums was undone by his style, not his politics. "Abusive leadership has no place in the Army," the general says.

The polarized sides in this fracas do agree on one thing: The culture war isn't over, and it is a fight for the Army's soul and future. Indeed, the West Point skirmish follows a host of sexual abuse and harassment charges that have bedeviled the military in recent months. In one high-profile case involving a number of drill sergeants at Aberdeen, Md., affairs took an even more divisive turn this week when four female soldiers recanted rape allegations against superiors–saying they had been pressured by overzealous Army investigators.

Moreover, the Hallums matter, and its handling, points to a long-simmering debate within West Point itself. "In the last 30 years, West Point has had an intellectual crisis as to whether it's a military academy or an Ivy League college," says retired Lt. Gen. Richard Trefry, a West Point graduate and former inspector general of the Army who also has served as an academy adviser.

The bad blood left behind and the handling of the matter remain so controversial that few in the academy would speak on the record about it. But interviews with insiders, and details in a West Point investigator's report and scores of other government documents, paint the picture of a culture war at West Point.

When this all began, Col. Hallums was seen as a solution, not a problem. In 1990, Col. Seigle, then commander of the 18th Aviation Brigade at Fort Bragg, N.C., wrote a fierce letter to West Point's commanders to complain that "for those of us out in the Army, the product you're putting out doesn't measure up." Specifically, he said the leadership department needed a genuine warrior in charge, not a mild academic in uniform.

Complaints from commanders of hotshot combat brigades resonate in the Army. And Col. Seigle was articulating a frustration that had been bubbling within the Army's ranks for years. The criticism hit home at the academy, in the midst of its own soul-searching about, among other things, a rise in the flameout rate of West Point graduates who leave the Army. When an academy committee began looking for a chairman of what is formally called the Department of Behavioral Sciences and Leadership, it turned to Col. Hallums.

The colonel was known throughout the Army as a tough infantry commander from the West Point class of '66, on which the Vietnam War fell heavily. As a young lieutenant, he had fought in the battle of Hue and twice was decorated for valor. At age 24, he became one of the youngest company commanders in the elite 101st Airborne Division there.

A decade later, his brigade commander, one Col. Colin Powell, evaluated him as "a forceful, tough leader as well as a brilliant staff officer" with "a great enthusiasm and love for the Army." He called James Hallums a general in the making.

Col. Hallums's Army career included an unusual six additional tours in six different countries. He advised the military of El Salvador—and then went to Harvard to co-author a monograph critical of how the U.S. handled guerrilla war there. He led a sensitive mission in Honduras and then served on the front lines of the drug war in Bolivia.

When the West Point post came up, Col. Hallums recalls being "practically ordered" to take it. He was shipped off to Vanderbilt University to earn the doctorate he needed to burnish his academic credentials. He reported to the academy in the summer of 1995 for what normally would have been a posting of five years or more. The real plum: a brigadier general's rank upon retirement from West Point and the Army.

Col. Hallums, given his considerable command experience, figured he was ready for anything. Besides, he had bagged what seemed like a helpful degree, in sociology. But West Point's leadership department had few similarities to his familiar terrain.

Housed in the faux-Gothic fortress of Thayer Hall, it was proud of its academic atmosphere and consensus management. Many of its permanent faculty members, though Army officers, are essentially tenured professors—and view themselves with the same independence. Col. Hallums was shocked by his initial meetings as the department prepared for fall 1995 classes. He recalls encountering what he considered "a visceral antimilitary feeling."

Other arrivals from the regular Army felt the same way. Col. Michael Anderson, a senior instructor who had led an infantry battalion at Fort Lewis, Wash., was stunned to hear his experiences derided by some

academics as mere war stories. "I was told that professional experiences I had in my operational assignments had no place in the leadership course I taught," he later wrote in a memorandum to Brig. Gen. Lamkin, the dean.

Col. Hallums set out, in his words, "to bring the department back into the Army." This proved no simple matter. Small and energetic, his normal communication is a bellow—a trait some faculty interpreted as macho aggressiveness. He ended the practice of calling superiors by their first names; he wanted to be addressed as "Colonel Hallums." On the first day of classes, he ordered officers to wear their "Class A" uniforms, the equivalent of business suits; before, they had dressed in military sweaters and slacks.

The sniping began soon enough. Col. Anderson, in his memo to Gen. Lamkin, said some officers cracked "that Col. Hallums just wanted to show off his war medals and display the contrast with the rest of the faculty with little to no combat experience." Another groused that Col. Hallums, in his insistence on more formal uniforms, "obviously had no identity outside the military," according to a memo by Lt. Col. Randall Chase that became part of the investigation. He is a career artillery-man and another department member.

The new chairman also irked faculty members by judging them, in part, by their fitness for combat, viewing this as relevant to their role of training future military leaders. At age 53, he was a hard-body fitness nut whose two-hour daily regime alternated weightlifting with running. He amused himself by showing others he could undulate chest muscles beneath his shirt.

Several younger officers welcomed this new approach, especially those fresh from combat units. Maj. Christopher Putko, former battery commander in the premier 82nd Airborne Division, based at Fort Bragg, later told investigators in a written statement that the new chairman had been "a breath of fresh air" in a department mocked by other faculty as "touchy-feely."

But the handful of lieutenant colonels who served as permanent faculty were appalled—and began resisting. Among these senior officers, one in particular stood out: Michael Hughes, who taught psychology and counseling and, after an earlier stint in the infantry, had embarked on a military career in counseling. In a memo written during the investigation, Lt. Col. Chase noted that at one autumn meeting Lt. Col. Hughes said "someone needed to tell Col. Hallums that this was not his department, but theirs and the academy's." (Lt. Col. Hughes, like all of Col. Hallums's departmental critics, declined to be interviewed for this story.)

Meanwhile, Col. Hallums gave his subordinates some ammunition. He called in the department's civilian female teachers and asked if they had any romantic entanglements he should know about. Early in September, Barbara Hunter later recalled, the colonel told her she was expected to serve at West Point "for the long haul and that I couldn't be expected to get married and move." Unaware that she was divorced, the colonel, a married man with three daughters, told her he thought people who divorce lack commitment. A few days later, Col. Hallums had a similar conversation with civilian professor Patricia Rooney.

One senior faculty member, Lt. Col. Gayle Watkins, learned of these conversations and criticized them. Col. Hallums sent an apology down the chain of command; he says he doesn't recall hearing any other objections to his behavior during the entire academic year. But there would be some, dumped in one load at the end of the year. "I didn't realize they were keeping book on me," he later said.

On Sept. 8, Col. Hallums, while working out, learned from a junior faculty member, Special Forces Capt. Kevin Berry, that the lieutenant colonels were being openly critical of him. Such dissent was common in the old leadership department, but Col. Hallums saw it as improper in a military unit—his unit. He told his executive officer, Lt. Col. Chase, that senior faculty members "were saying things that in any unit he had ever been in would have been seen as disloyal," the XO later wrote in a memorandum.

Col. Anderson, who as the department's electives director supervised several of the dissident lieutenant colonels, tried to head off the looming confrontation between the chairman and faculty. On Sept. 29, he sent a blunt warning memo to Lt. Col. Hughes and others that Col. Hallums wasn't to be trifled with: "He does not want to be one of your colleagues," the memo said.

More provocatively, Col. Hallums insisted the department's attitude, not his, must change. In January, he found a line of cadets waiting to file course change slips. What branch are you going into, he asked one. "Infantry," came the answer. Responded a pleased Col. Hallums: "Go to the head of the line."

But he confounded those who would later portray him as sexist by selecting a woman, Maj. Deirdre Dixon, for a departmental plum: directing its core course on military leadership. It was, Col. Anderson later noted, a position that "traditionally goes to the most dynamic officer in the department." Maj. Dixon herself was a physical fitness buff—and also a master parachutist.

In February 1996, Col. Hallums directly confronted the dissenters. As the meeting began, his tone was chillier than the winter fog rolling off the Hudson River just downhill from his office.

As Lt. Col. Hughes later recalled, Col. Hallums told the three unhappy lieutenant colonels he was tired of their criticism. They said they were just doing their jobs. At this, Col. Hallums blew his stack. "Don't you get it?" he shouted, according to several accounts. "The only correct response to a decision I make is silence and obedience on your part. I don't want your input, just your absolute obedience."

Red-faced, he leaned across the table and said, through clenched teeth, "Do you understand me, lieutenant colonels?" he made each answer in turn: "Yes, sir."

Col. Hallums left the meeting having decided that the three officers had lost touch with the Army and with soldiering. But the next day Lt. Col. Hughes sent an upbeat memo to his immediate supervisor, Col. Anderson, detailing five steps he was taking to get with the program. Among other things, he said he would volunteer to help with cadets' military training. "I am really hitting it!" he concluded.

Yet a guerrilla war was under way. The more resistance Col. Hallums met, the more he acted as if he were still an infantryman in the field where soldiers breathe, eat, and sleep together—and where commanders are obeyed instantly. One March day, he thought little of changing into running clothes while talking to Lt. Col. Hughes in his office, though he says he did first ask permission. Lt. Col. Hughes, himself an infantryman, took deep offense. "I felt very awkward," he would later formally complain. "It was intended to be a 'power session' where he clearly was in control."

In May, as the academic year ended, the department held a formal dinner at nearby Nicole's Restaurant to say farewell to junior faculty members moving on to new assignments. Col. Hallums had ordered the officers to wear their dress-blue uniforms. Maj. Putko, a departing psychology teacher, stood with his souvenir guidon, a small black-and-gold departmental pennant, and said he would follow Col. Hallums into battle without hesitation, the highest praise one warrior can bestow on another. Yet for some of the senior academics there, this was more goading. They weren't heading into combat; they were trying to teach psychology, sociology, and leadership to undergraduates.

Four days earlier, in fact, at a year-end cocktail party aboard the academy superintendent's yacht, Lt. Col. Hughes had unburdened himself to another senior West Point officer, who took the allegations to the office of Brig. Gen. Lamkin.

On May 15, Lt. Col. Hughes delivered a seven-page, single-spaced memorandum to Gen. Lamkin. It charged Col. Hallums with "abusive leadership" saying that, among other things, he had feared the colonel might strike him at the explosive February meeting. He recounted the scene in which Col. Hallums had lectured him while changing into exercise clothes. Col.

Hallums also made women feel uncomfortable, the lieutenant colonel alleged further, by walking through the department in a sleeveless shirt and Spandex shorts. Gen. Lamkin immediately began his inquiry.

In the following days, Gen. Lamkin said in an interview, he was flooded with complaints. Ms. Hunter and Ms. Rooney, two of the department's three civilian female professors, filed sworn statements formally accusing Col. Hallums of sexism. Ms. Hunter cited his denunciation of those who divorce as "gender discrimination." Ms. Rooney said the colonel's September conversation with her had "implied that as a woman, my career shouldn't come first. This is sexism." (The third female civilian professor filed a dissent saying she had found Col. Hallums to be supportive.)

A sworn statement by Capt. Sharon Bowers said that, in February, Col. Hallums showed off his biceps and invited her to touch them. "In retrospect, I believe this was sexual harassment," she said.

Lt. Col. Joseph Napoleon LeBoeuf, one of the three senior officers confronted by Col. Hallums at the February meeting, summarized his concerns in a sworn statement. Because women aren't allowed in ground combat, he argued, "Colonel Hallums' glorification of the combat arms . . . translates into a program that is being perceived as exclusionary of women." In addition, he said, the colonel was "insensitive to our feelings." Though he and his colleagues were technically subordinate, he added, "it was hardly the way we expect to be treated."

Several other department members, both junior and senior, filed sharply different views. Capt. Berry, the Special Forces officer, said Col. Hallums was in touch with the ordinary soldier and "has a 'grunt in muddy boots' way of looking at issues." Col. Anderson, who in effect was deputy department head, said in a sworn statement, "I suspect these complaints against Colonel Hallums are a conspiracy to overthrow him."

Then came a wave of sworn statements from West Point's "tactical officers," who actually command cadets that others teach. In their view, an officer they respected was being torn down by professors they saw as "weenies."

More than a dozen of these young hard chargers formally questioned their superiors' actions. "I would serve anywhere with Colonel Hallums," stated Capt. David Duffy, a Special Forces officer. Tactical officers believe, said Capt. Robert Roggeman, "he has improved the command climate."

Even female tactical officers supported the colonel. Capt. Trese LaCamera, a military-intelligence specialist, said he "always made me feel as though I were part of the team and no different because I am a woman." Capt. Cheryl Solomon, a military-police officer, said, "I would gladly serve in his command."

But inside Thayer Hall the atmosphere was poisonous. "The climate is crazy in the department," Maj. Dixon, who had gotten a plum promotion from Col. Hallums, told investigators. Her conclusion: The colonel "has worked only with men before, and I think he just isn't educated on how to work with women."

In late May Col. Hallums offered to resign but Brig. Gen. Lamkin dissuaded him by saying, the general recalls, "Whoa, you're not a quitter. Let's see what the facts are."

On June 10, Col. Dennis Hunt, head of West Point's law department, found Col. Hallums guilty of sexual harassment under Army Regulation 600-20, not for seeking sexual favors but for creating "an intimidating, hostile or offensive environment." He was also adjudged to have belittled the Army's support branches. "Many in the department perceive that he disdains the non-combat arms, and by implication, female officers," the investigator wrote. He also said the colonel chewed out his subordinates "far too often."

Col. Hunt recommended that Col. Hallums be retained but counseled. "Fairness suggests he be given an opportunity to put things right," he wrote. He also recommended that Col. Hallums be ordered to remove all athletic gear from his office, "never appear at his office in exercise clothes and cease all posing, flexing and making body-oriented comments."

But West Point's superintendent, Lt. Gen. Daniel Christman, rejected that recommendation and removed Col. Hallums from his post, effectively forcing him to retire.

On Jan. 24, Col. Hallums left the Army. Significantly, Gen. David Bramlett, who had headed the original search committee that selected Col. Hallums, sponsored his retirement ceremony–not at West Point but at the 101st Airborne's post at Fort Campbell, Ky. "Jim Hallums went where the Army sent him and he did his duty," the four-star general said at the ceremony. Facing the colonel, he added, "Your example stands for all of us."

West Point has a new leadership department chairman, Col. Charles "Casey" Brower, a member of the academy's history department and a former military aide to President Reagan. Col. Hallums says he isn't bitter, but offers: "Vietnam was tough but I would say that one year at West Point was the only bad time I had in the Army."

CARPAX COMPANY AND PHYLLIS COPELAND

Doug Singer sat back in his chair and reflected on how so much had gone so terribly wrong in such a short period of time. Only 3 months earlier, the opportunity at Carpax, a rapidly growing manufacturer of specialty steel products, had seemed to provide just the kind of boost his career needed. He had not thought twice about tendering his resignation at Tenntex, even though he had spent 10 very good years there. The position of advertising director with young, rapidly growing Carpax was exactly what Doug had been looking for. Or so he thought. Now he wasn't at all sure he had made the right decision.

He was sure that the cause of his current problems originated with one person—Phyllis Copeland—but his best course of action was not at all obvious. Doug had been told by some of his co-workers that in spite of Phyllis's blatantly poor job performance, she was known to wield a lot of power. A few had expressed the opinion that if either Doug or Phyllis had to leave the company, Doug might very well be the one to leave.

As Doug tried to identify alternatives for dealing with the situation, he reflected on Carpax's corporate culture. The "good old boy" atmosphere seemed to be a throwback to an earlier era. He smiled as he remembered his wife's reaction the first time he mentioned what he termed the "Bubba Boys" to her. But the more he told her, the less amused she had been.

Doug realized that most of what he knew about Phyllis was based on hearsay, but when he considered the number of apparently objective and reliable sources who had said essentially the same things, he concluded that at least some of it had to be true. Doug's new colleagues were candid in sharing what they knew about Phyllis's work history. With this information, Doug compiled the following summary of Phyllis's association with Carpax.

Background

About 6 years earlier, Mr. Rodney Hauck (owner of a local CPA firm and personal friend of Carpax Company's CEO and founder, Justin Broadrick) had phoned Broadrick about a personal problem. It concerned Phyllis Copeland, Rodney Hauck's receptionist and secretary, who had been in his employ for about a year and a half.

Phyllis Copeland, an attractive woman in her late twenties, was a single parent and sole support of an adolescent daughter. She had been deserted by her second husband and her emotionally charged divorce provided a compelling opportunity for an affair with her close associate at work. In fact, Doug Singer was told that Copeland and Rodney Hauck had become the talk of East Ridge and the country club set.

East Ridge was a small town of 25,000. The word going through the rumor mill at Hauck's CPA firm was that Mrs. Hauck had issued an ultimatum to her husband: "Get rid of Phyllis Copeland or else." Rodney Hauck leveled with Phyllis Copeland and set the stage for her dismissal. Unfortunately for Hauck, Phyllis did not accept discharge quietly. Rumor had it that she sensed an opportunity to use the situation to enhance her career, and she took it. It was a common assumption that Phyllis had issued a thinly veiled threat: "Make me a better deal, or I'll make this termination tough" (translation: "Look out for a sexual harassment complaint and its attendant publicity").

Founded some 10 years before Singer joined the company, Carpax was experiencing major growth. The company had been started by a small group of entrepreneurs utilizing imported technology that, until then, had not been precisely duplicated in the United States. Sales-driven and free-spirited, the company was taking advantage of an open market and enjoying extraordinary success, both financial and in terms of market share. Carpax was now the largest employer in East Ridge, employing over 2000, with corporate offices at three different sites in the community. In addition to the manufacturing facility in East Ridge, there was another on the West coast and one in Europe. Carpax maintained numerous regional sales offices in the United States and Europe.

To the average East Ridge resident, the high-profile Carpax seemed to provide a golden opportunity to get on a fast-track career path. It was *the* place to work, even for secretarial, clerical, and production employees, since there were few other attractive employment opportunities locally. Carpax's senior management (the founding group) were the social elite of East Ridge; quick money had catapulted them to that position. Carpax was also a model of a high-tech environment: impressive offices, corporate jets, and generous expense accounts.

Carpax's founding group effectively managed the business, but stories of their excesses and indiscretions in personal matters were legendary. As local gossip had it, almost every Carpax senior officer, and many other managers, had affairs with their secretaries and other female associates. In fact, the word in East Ridge was that Carpax considered it a corporate perk to have an affair with your secretary. Doug Singer had heard of these personal entanglements for years prior to joining Carpax. It seemed to be common knowledge that the firm had a very macho, sexist culture. There were no women in the firm above middle management, nor were there any known plans for recruiting or promoting women to those positions. Doug was concerned about the firm's reputation, but the opportunity for professional advancement at Carpax seemed too good to pass up.

Justin Broadrick had been a friend of Rodney Hauck's for many years. The Haucks and Broadricks frequently socialized with each other. Justin and Rodney had graduated form East Ridge High School together and had remained in the community ever since. They had even engaged in some early business ventures together. When Rodney Hauck confessed his plight regarding Phyllis Copeland, Justin Broadrick rallied to the aid of his friend. Of course he would provide a position for Ms. Copeland.

Phyllis Copeland was hired at Carpax and assigned to the senior vice president of marketing, John Baker, whose executive secretary had recently moved to another city. This was quite a promotion for Phyllis from her former receptionist-secretary position in Mr. Hauck's small CPA firm. Copeland, who possessed few credentials, seemed to realize that the new position was an unusual opportunity. She commented to a co-worker in an adjoining office that for the first time in her life, she might be able to buy a little house.

Phyllis Copeland was assigned routine secretarial and administrative duties. But from the outset, it was clear to everyone in the department that she was not qualified; she lacked the education and the experience to handle the job. Even very basic tasks were confusing to her, and customers as well as co-workers were struck by her obvious incompetence. Correspondence for which she was responsible routinely contained grammatical, spelling, and punctuation errors. Her telephone communication skills were equally deficient; she handled calls in an unprofessional, even bored manner. Although Copeland's responsibilities were soon absorbed by her more competent fellow employees (John Baker just bypassed her when he handed down work assignments), she retained her executive secretarial position. To no one's surprise, it was soon widely reported that Baker and Phyllis were having an affair.

Although the Carpax culture was tolerant of their personal relationship, Phyllis's co-workers found it difficult to tolerate Phyllis's own attitude and behavior, which were causing an acute morale problem. The situation was compounded by Phyllis's introverted personality—she appeared almost aloof to everyone in the department, operating in isolation from every other person with the exception of John Baker, on whom she lavished extraordinary attention. Casual peer exchanges were rebuffed with icy indifference. Even the simplest request from anyone other than Baker was ignored, giving co-workers the impression that she regarded her relationship with Baker as the last word in job security.

In time, it became obvious to even the most casual observer that Phyllis had no real duties left. She read books and wandered about the halls. Several times, co-workers found her taking a nap in Justin Broadrick's office when he was away. At the same time, her relationship with John Baker developed an openness that seemed flagrant to her co-workers, even by Carpax standards. Extended trips with Baker in his car and long personal lunches became the rule. Additionally, the two occasionally spent the entire afternoon behind the closed doors of John Baker's office. The crowning blow was John Baker's own contentious divorce, exacerbated by detailed testimony regarding Phyllis Copeland's role. Embarrassing details of the company culture and atmosphere at Carpax became part of the court records. An incensed Justin Broadrick called John Baker in for a conference. In the interest of department morale, John Baker agreed to end the affair. In addition, the two concurred on the necessity of transferring Phyllis to another area of the company, preferably to another location in town, away from the main headquarters office.

Baker and Broadrick also agreed that the transfer had to be perceived as a promotion, because they felt that there was no way to predict what action Phyllis might take—even an embarrassing sexual harassment complaint was not out of the question. Following considerable deliberation, they decided to make Phyllis a manager in the advertising department, located several blocks away from Baker's office.

Wallace Baird, the advertising director, reported to John Baker. Wallace was not originally hired by John Baker, but was assigned to him as the result of a corporate restructuring. Wallace had started with Carpax several years earlier, when the company was still quite small. Wallace's performance as advertising director proved to be more troublesome with each passing year. His reputation was that of an underachiever at the limit of his promotability. His organizational skills and productivity were poor.

John Baker was beginning to feel some pressure from top management as a result of Wallace's poor performance. But John confided to a colleague that even though Phyllis wasn't capable of bringing about any improvements in the advertising department, at least she could funnel inside information from the department to him—maybe even disclose some of Wallace's more spectacular failures. As stated to his

FIGURE 1   *Advertising Department Relationships under Wallace Baird*

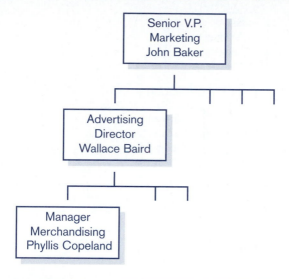

colleague, he also believed that she could not significantly damage the department, since it was already performing poorly. At any rate, she would be out of his way. And with Baird insecure in his position, he would be unlikely to resist the assignment of Phyllis to his staff. So Phyllis was appointed manager of merchandising (see Figure 1).

Soon after Phyllis Copeland's promotion to management status, it became apparent to those in her new department that she had no understanding of the work requirements of her new position. She acted as though "management" was synonymous with indolence, as though she no longer had to do anything. Unmanageable and untouchable, Phyllis proceeded to establish herself in the advertising department. By using veiled threats to exercise her connections with John Baker and, if need be, Justin Broadrick, she thwarted even mild attempts by Wallace Baird to discipline or direct her.

Shortly after Phyllis's arrival, Wallace Baird's morale began a perceptible decline. Subsequently, everyone in the department noticed that he had begun to completely defer to Phyllis Copeland. He seemed to have turned over the departmental reins to her. In less than a year, the advertising department was in shambles. (Baird would later tell friends that he thought letting Phyllis run the department would be a sure prescription for her failure.)

Finally, John Baker was called to a conference with Justin Broadrick. This time, the good-old-boy network was showing signs of wear-and-tear. The confusion in

the advertising department was beginning to cost the company considerable market share. John Baker received his ultimatum: "Get the advertising department straightened out, or else." A search was begun for a new advertising director. John Baker, who knew that his own reputation—and possibly even career—had been damaged by the situation, told a confidant that he realized he needed to hire a no-nonsense person to replace Wallace Baird. The question remained, however: "How would Phyllis fit into the new picture?"

The Current Situation

Doug Singer, the new advertising director, came to Carpax from Tenntex, a major customer of Carpax's. With 10 years of related experience under his belt, Doug viewed the position with Carpax as a major career opportunity. His first week on the job, however, revealed some frightening realities. First and foremost, Doug realized the organizational structure was practically nonexistent. He would have to rebuild from scratch. Since Phyllis had joined the department, three key employees had left, apparently demoralized and disgusted with the whole situation, according to those who remained.

Phyllis Copeland quickly sensed potential trouble as a result of the appointment of her new boss, Doug Singer. Having had no performance demands placed on her throughout her employment at Carpax, Phyllis was now suddenly expected to become a productive

FIGURE 2   *Advertising Relationships under Doug Singer*

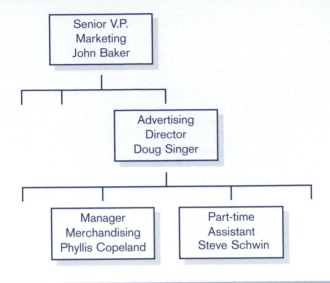

employee. Her first response, apparently in hopes of securing him as an ally, was an overt sexual advance. Doug was unresponsive.

Although John Baker was no longer having an affair with Phyllis, they continued to have extended telephone conversations at work, with Phyllis making no attempt to conceal this contact. Doug realized he had a major personnel problem.

Desperate to make headway in the rebuilding of the advertising department, Doug Singer decided to look for a part-time employee, someone to run interference while he dug through the reams of undone and botched projects. He wanted an outsider who wasn't suffering from the poor morale that permeated the department.

Steve Schwin, a junior marketing major at East Ridge College, was a bit older and more mature than most of his classmates. One of Steve's fraternity brothers who was employed at Carpax part time alerted him to the opening. Steve joined Doug Singer's department (see Figure 2) and made immediate and significant contributions. Young and career-oriented, he worked hard and performed well beyond his credentials. Doug recognized Steve's talents and sensed an opportunity to groom a key manager.

Within a few weeks, Steve was given projects that would have normally been assigned to the merchandising manager. They were completed promptly and accurately. Steve's performance did not go unnoticed by Phyllis. Her reaction to Doug's increasing reliance

on his new, young assistant was to do even less work than she had previously. Before long, Phyllis's attendance also began to fall drastically. In one month she was absent 11 days, without bothering to call in. It was clear to Doug that Phyllis had no intention of performing even the most routine of tasks.

Morale in the department continued to fall. The other workers in the department resented Phyllis's very presence. Doug often overheard cutting remarks made about Phyllis. He was certain the remarks were usually meant for him to hear and that his associates in the department expected something to be done very soon. As an experienced manager, Doug knew that he had to resolve this crisis by taking definite action.

Doug did not expect the human resource department to provide much assistance to him. Carpax had emphasized sales and, to a lesser extent, manufacturing functions during its years of rapid growth. The human resource function was not well developed, providing few guidelines and little expertise to operating managers. In fact, modern human resource management techniques were presently nonexistent at Carpax. Doug knew this situation would have to change if Carpax was to survive.

Knowing Phyllis's history in the company, it was unclear what course of action had the best chance of success. Well aware of Phyllis's role in the departure of his predecessor, Wallace Baird, Doug was determined not to let the same thing happen to him.

CHRIS CUNNINGHAM

Elizabeth Stover was the president of Stover Industries, an amalgamation of several small companies in the electrical parts industry. She and her husband had inherited one of the group of companies from her father-in-law. Mrs. Stover, an engineer, elected to run the company while her husband pursued a separate career as a dental surgeon. In addition to the original inheritance, Mrs. Stover had purchased three other companies to make the present Stover Industries. Mrs. Stover was only 31 years old. She was a dynamic individual, full of ideas and drive. In the space of a year, she had welded Stover Industries into a profitable organization known for its aggressiveness.

Mrs. Stover integrated the four companies into a unified organization by welding the individual managements into one unit. Some individuals were let go in each organization as it was purchased and became part of Stover Industries. In several other instances, executives of the newly purchased companies resigned because of difficulties in working for such a young and driving boss. The four plants continued as individual manufacturing units of the company and together employed approximately 475 production workers. Some problems arose in integrating the individual sales staffs, since the original companies had been competing with each other. Consequently, the salesmen had overlapping territories. This was gradually being worked out; but the salespeople were permitted to keep their own old customers, making it next to impossible to assign exclusive territories to each salesperson.

The sales staff included 17 men and the sales director. The sales director had been with the original Stover Company as sales manager. He knew Elizabeth Stover well and was able to work as her complacent subordinate. Most of his time and energy was devoted to routine direction and coordination of the sales team. Although a trusted lieutenant of Mrs. Stover, the sales director was not much more than titular head of the sales force. Mrs. Stover provided the active leadership.

Mrs. Stover had personally hired Chris Cunningham, a college classmate, as a salesperson for the organization. Chris shared some of Mrs. Stover's drive and enthusiasm and, in a short time, had justified Mrs. Stover's choice with a sensational sales record. In terms of sales performance, Chris Cunningham's record left little to be desired.

Yet Chris represented a thorny problem to Mrs. Stover. The problem, as outlined by Mrs. Stover, appeared to her to shape up in the following fashion:

I hired Chris because we knew and admired each other in our college days. Chris was always a leader on campus, and we had worked well together in campus affairs. Chris was just the kind of person I wanted in this organization—a lot of drive and originality, combined with tremendous loyalty. The way I operate, I need a loyal organization of people who will pitch right in on the projects we develop.

Chris has already been proven a top-notch performer and will probably be our best salesperson in a year or two. Could one ask for anything better than that?

Here is where the rub comes in. Chris is the sort of person who has absolutely no respect for organization. A hot order will come in, for example, and Chris will go straight to the plant with it and raise hell until that order is delivered. It doesn't make any difference that our production schedule has been knocked to pieces. The order is out, and Chris has a satisfied customer. Of course, that sort of thing gets repeat business and does show well on Chris's sales record. But it has made running our plants a constant headache. It is not only the production people who have felt the impact of Cunningham on the operations. Chris gets mixed up with our engineering department on new designs and has even made the purchasing department furious by needling them to hurry supplies on special orders.

You can just imagine how the rest of the organization feels about all this. The other salespeople are pretty upset that their orders get pushed aside—and are probably a bit jealous, too. The production people, the engineers, the purchasing agent, and most of the rest of the staff have constantly complained to me about how Chris gets in their hair. On a personal level, the staff say they like Chris a lot but that they just cannot work with such a troublemaker in the organization.

I have talked to Chris many times about this. I have tried raising hell over the issue, pleading for change, and patient and rational discussion. For maybe a week after one of these sessions, Chris seems like a reformed character, everyone relaxes a bit, and then bang—off we go again in the same old pattern.

I suppose that in many ways Chris is just like me—I must admit I would probably be inclined to act in much the same way. You see, I have a lot of sympathy for Chris's point of view.

I think you can see now what my problem is. Should I fire Chris and lose a star salesperson? That does not make too much sense. In fact, Chris is probably the person who should be our sales director, if not immediately at least in a few years. But without the ability to get along with the organization, to understand the meaning of "channels" and "procedures," Chris is not only a valuable and talented addition to the company, but a liability as well. Should I take a chance on things eventually working out and Chris getting educated to the organization? Should I put on a lot of pressure and force a change? What would that do to Chris's enthusiasm and sales record? If I just let things go, then, there is a real danger to my organization. My executives will think I have given Chris the green light, and they will transfer their antagonism to me. I certainly cannot afford that.

CONSCIENCE OR THE COMPETITIVE EDGE? (A)

The plane touched down at Bombay airport precisely on time. Olivia Jones made her way through the usual immigration bureaucracy without incident and was finally ushered into a waiting limousine, complete with uniformed chauffeur and soft black leather seats. Her already considerable excitement at being in India for the first time was mounting. As she cruised the dark city streets, she asked her chauffeur why so few cars had their headlights on at night. The driver responded that most drivers believed that headlights use too much petrol! Finally, she arrived at her hotel, a black marble monolith, grandiose and decadent in its splendour, towering above the bay.

The goal of her 4-day trip was to sample and select swatches of woven cotton from the mills in and around Bombay, to be used in the following season's youthwear collection of shirts, trousers, and underwear. She was thus treated with the utmost deference by her hosts, who were invariably Indian factory owners, or British agents for Indian mills. For 3 days she was ferried from one air-conditioned office to another, sipping iced tea or chilled lemonade, poring over leather-bound swatch catalogues, which featured every type of stripe and design possible. On the fourth day, Jones made a request which she knew would cause some anxiety in the camp. "I want to see a factory," she declared.

After much consultation and several attempts at dissuasion, she was once again ushered into a limousine and driven through a part of the city she had not previously seen. Gradually, the hotel and the Western shops dissolved into the background and Jones entered downtown Bombay. All around was a sprawling shantytown, constructed from sheets of corrugated iron and panels of cardboard boxes. Dust flew in spirals everywhere among the dirt roads and open drains. The car crawled along the unsealed roads behind carts hauled by man and beast alike, laden to overflowing with straw or city refuse—the treasure of the ghetto. More than once the limousine had to halt and wait while a lumbering white bull crossed the road.

Finally, in the very heart of the ghetto, the car came to a stop. "Are you sure you want to do this?" asked her host. Determined not to be fainthearted, Jones got out of the car.

White-skinned, blue-eyed, and blond, clad in a city suit and stiletto-heeled shoes, and carrying a briefcase, Jones was indeed conspicuous. It was hardly surprising that the inhabitants of the area found her an interesting and amusing subject, as she teetered along the dusty street and stepped gingerly over the open sewers.

Her host led her down an alley, between the shacks and open doors and inky black interiors. Some shelters, Jones was told, were restaurants, where at lunchtime people would gather on the rush mat floors and eat rice together. In the doorway of one shack there was a table which served as a counter, laden with ancient cans of baked beans, sardines, and rusted tins of a fluorescent green substance that might have been peas. The eyes of the young man behind the counter were smiling and proud as he beckoned her forward to view his wares.

As Jones turned another corner, she saw an old man in the middle of the street, clad in a waist cloth, sitting in a large tin bucket. He had a tin can in his hand with which he poured water from the bucket over his head and shoulders. Beside him two little girls played in brilliant white nylon dresses, bedecked with ribbons and lace. They posed for her with smiling faces, delighted at having their photograph taken in their best frocks. The men and women moved around her with great dignity and grace, Jones thought.

Finally, her host led her up a precarious wooden ladder to a floor above the street. At the top Jones was warned not to stand straight as the ceiling was just 5 feet high. There, in a room not 20 feet by 40 feet, twenty men were sitting at treadle sewing machines, bent over yards of white cloth. Between them on the floor were rush mats, some occupied by sleeping workers awaiting their next shift. Jones learned that these men were on a 24-hour rotation, 12 hours on and 12 hours off, every day for 6 months of the year. For the remaining 6 months they returned to their families in the countryside to work the land, planting and building with the money they had earned in the city. The shirts they were working on were for an order she had placed 4 weeks earlier in London, an order of which she had been particularly proud because of the low price she had succeeded in negotiating. Jones reflected that this sight was the most humbling experience of her life. When she questioned her host about these conditions, she was told that they were typical for her industry—and for most of the third world, as well.

Eventually, she left the heat, dust, and din of the little shirt factory and returned to the protected, air-conditioned world of the limousine.

"What I've experienced today and the role I've played in creating that living hell will stay with me forever," she thought. Later in the day, she asked herself whether what she had seen was an inevitable consequence of pricing policies that enabled the British customer to purchase shirts at £12.99 instead of £13.99 and at the same time allowed the company to make its mandatory 56 percent profit margin? Were her negotiating skills—the result of many years of training—an indirect cause of the terrible conditions she had seen?

Once Jones returned to the U.K., she considered her position and the options open to her as a buyer for a large, publicly traded, retail chain operating in a highly competitive environment. Her dilemma was twofold: Can an ambitious employee afford to exercise a social conscience in his or her career? And can career-minded individuals truly make a difference without jeopardizing their future?

17   # CONSCIENCE OR THE COMPETITIVE EDGE? (B)

Olivia Jones described her subsequent decision as follows:

"The alternatives for me were perfectly clear, if somewhat unrealistic: I could stipulate a standard of working conditions to be enforced at any factory employed, and offer to pay an inflated price for merchandise in an effort to fund the necessary improvements. This would mean having to increase the margins in other sections of the range and explaining to my controller exactly why prices had risen.

"There was, of course, no guarantee that the extra cash would make its way safely into the hands of the worker or improve his working conditions. Even exercising my greatest faith in human nature, I could see the wealthy factory owner getting increasingly fatter and some other keen and able buyer being promoted into my highly coveted position!

"I could refuse to buy from India. This would mean I would have to find alternative sources at equally low prices to justify my action. There was always Macau, where I knew conditions were worse if anything, or Hong Kong, where conditions were certainly better, from what I had seen, but prices were much higher. I had to ask myself if I would truly be improving the plight of the workers by denying them the enormous orders that I usually put through their factories. Or would I simply be salving my own conscience by righteously congratulating myself at not dealing in slave labour? Doubtless my production schedule would be snapped up eagerly by the next buyer who was hungry for cheap labour and fast turnaround.

"I could consider speaking to the powers that be and ask their advice. After all, the group was proud of its philanthropic reputation and had promoted its charity work and sponsorship of various causes, including Wimbledon Football Club and Miss World. This in mind, I approached my line manager, who laughed at my idealistic naivety and made it quite clear that I should hold my tongue if I knew what was good for me.

"It seemed I had but two choices. Either I quit the company and look for an employer which would be more responsible in its attitude toward sourcing merchandise, or I could continue to buy as before, but aware of the consequences and exercising a conscience wherever possible. I won't bother to list my excuses for opting for the latter choice.

"I believe that there is no solution, no generalization which can be used as a precedent in this type of scenario. I don't know to this day what action I could have taken to improve the lives of those individuals whom I felt I had compromised.

"Every day, in various work situations, employees, and specifically managers, come up against questions of conscience versus the status quo. It may be that you are encouraged to show prejudice against an individual or group of employees due to their race, colour or clique; maybe your boss asked you to lie to camouflage an embarrassing error and insinuate that the fault lies with someone else; maybe your employer's policy requires you to screw a client or a supplier to close a deal and maintain the bottom line.

"Each case is different and demands its own evaluation. Each man and woman must draw their own set of rules and regulations to suit their own situation and conscience.

"It takes brave individuals to jeopardize their careers for a cause but it is thanks to those who do take a stand that great feats of humanitarian work are successfully undertaken and completed. We should all evaluate the choices that are open to us and be true to ourselves. Let your conscience be your guide within the realms of reality.

"The most important lesson that I learned from the episode was that, above all, you have to learn to live with the choices that you make."

18   THE CONSOLIDATED LIFE CASE: CAUGHT BETWEEN CORPORATE CULTURES

Part I

It all started so positively. Three days after graduating with his degree in business administration, Mike Wilson started his first day at a prestigious insurance company–Consolidated Life. He worked in the policy issue department. The work of the department was mostly clerical and did not require a high degree of technical knowledge. Given the repetitive and mundane nature of the work, the successful worker had to be consistent and willing to grind out paperwork.

Rick Belkner was the division's vice president, "the man in charge" at the time. Rich was an actuary by training, a technical professional whose leadership style was laissez-faire. He was described in the division as, "the mirror of whoever was the strongest personality around him." It was also common knowledge that Rick made a [huge salary] while he spent his time doing crossword puzzles.

Mike was hired as a management trainee and promised a supervisory assignment within a year. However, because of a management reorganization, it was only six weeks before he was placed in charge of an eight-person unit.

The reorganization was intended to streamline work flow, upgrade and combine the clerical jobs, and make greater use of the computer system. It was a drastic departure from the old way of doing things and created a great deal of animosity and anxiety among the clerical staff.

Management realized that a flexible supervisory style was necessary to pull off the reorganization without immense turnover, so they gave their supervisors a free hand to run their units as they saw fit. Mike used this latitude to implement group meetings and training classes in his unit. In addition, he assured all members raises if they worked hard to attain them. By working long hours, participating in the mundane tasks with his unit, and being flexible in his management style, he was able to increase productivity, reduce errors, and reduce lost time. Things improved so dramatically that he was noticed by upper management and earned a reputation as a "superstar" despite being viewed as free spirited and unorthodox. The feeling was that his loose, people-oriented management style could be tolerated because his results were excellent.

A CHANCE FOR ADVANCEMENT

After a year Mike received an offer from a different Consolidated Life division located across town. Mike was asked to manage an office in the marketing area. The pay was excellent, and it offered an opportunity to turn around an office in disarray. The reorganization in his present division at Consolidated was almost complete, and most of his mentors and friends in management had moved on to other jobs. Mike decided to accept the offer.

In his exit interview, he was assured that if he ever wanted to return, a position would be made for him. It was clear that he was held in high regard by management and staff alike. A huge party was thrown to send him off.

The new job was satisfying for a short time, but it became apparent to Mike that it did not have the long-term potential he was promised. After bringing on a new staff, computerizing the office, and auditing the books, he began looking for a position that would both challenge him and give him the autonomy he needed to be successful.

Eventually, word got back to his former vice president, Rick Belkner, at Consolidated Life that Mike was looking for another job. Rick offered Mike a position with the same pay he was now receiving and control over a 14-person unit in his old division. After considering other options, Mike decided to return to his old division, feeling that he would be able to progress steadily over the next several years.

ENTER JACK GREELY; RETURN MIKE WILSON

Upon his return to Consolidated Life, Mike became aware of several changes that had taken place in the six months since his departure. The most important change was the hiring of a new divisional senior vice president, Jack Greely. Jack had been given total authority to run the division. Rick Belkner now reported to Jack.

Jack's reputation was that he was tough but fair. It was necessary for people in Jack's division to do things his way and "get the work out."

Mike also found himself reporting to one of his former peers, Kathy Miller, who had been promoted to manager during the reorganization. Mike had always "hit it off" with Kathy and foresaw no problem in working with her.

After a week Mike realized the extent of the changes that had occurred. Gone was the loose, casual atmosphere that had marked his first tour in the division. Now, a stricter, task-oriented management doctrine was practiced. Morale of the supervisory staff had decreased to an alarming level. Jack Greely was the major topic of conversation in and around the division. People joked that MBO now meant "management by oppression."

Mike was greeted back with comments like "Welcome to prison" and "Why would you come back here? You must be desperate!" It seemed like everyone was looking for new jobs or transfers. Their lack of desire was reflected in the poor quality of work being done.

MIKE'S IDEA: SUPERVISOR'S FORUM

Mike felt that a change in the management style of his boss was necessary to improve a frustrating situation. Realizing that it would be difficult to affect his style directly, Mike requested permission from Rick Belkner to form a Supervisor's Forum for all the managers on Mike's level in the division. Mike explained that the purpose would be to enhance the existing management training program. The forum would include weekly meetings, guest speakers, and discussions of topics relevant to the division and the industry. Mike thought the forum would show Greely that he was serious about both his job and improving morale in the division. Rick gave the OK for an initial meeting.

The meeting took place, and 10 supervisors who were Mike's peers in the company eagerly took the opportunity to "blue sky" it. There was a euphoric attitude about the group as they drafted their statement of intent. It read as shown in Exhibit 1.

The group felt the memo accurately and diplomatically stated their dissatisfaction with the current situation. However, they pondered what the results of their actions would be and what else they could have done.

Part II

An emergency management meeting was called by Rick Belkner at Jack Greely's request to address the "union" being formed by the supervisors. Four general managers, Rick Belkner, and Jack Greely were at that meeting. During the meeting it was suggested the forum be disbanded to "put them in their place." However, Rick Belkner felt that, if "guided" in the proper direction, the forum could die from lack of interest. His stance was adopted, but it was common knowledge that Jack Greely was strongly opposed to

the group and wanted its founders dealt with. His comment was, "It's not a democracy and they're not a union. If they don't like it here, then they can leave." A campaign was directed by the managers to determine who the main authors of the memo were so they could be dealt with.

About this time Mike's unit had made a mistake on a case, which Jack Greely was embarrassed to admit to his boss. This embarrassment was more than Jack Greely cared to take from Mike Wilson. At the manager's staff meeting that day, Jack stormed in and declared that the next supervisor to "screw up" was out the door. He would permit no more embarrassments of his division and repeated his earlier statement about "people leaving if they didn't like it here." It was clear to Mike and everyone else present that Mike Wilson was a marked man.

Mike had always been a loose, amiable supervisor. The major reason his units had been successful was the attention he paid to each individual and how they interacted with the group. He had a reputation for fairness, was seen as an excellent judge of personnel for new positions, and was noted for his ability to turn around people who had been in trouble. He motivated people through a dynamic, personable style and was noted for his general lack of regard for rules. He treated rules as obstacles to management and usually used his own discretion about what was important. His office had a sign saying "Any fool can manage by rules. It takes an uncommon man to manage without any." It was an approach that flew in the face of company policy, but it had been overlooked in the past because of his results. However, because of Mike's actions with the Supervisors' Forum, he was now regarded as a thorn in the side, not a superstar, and his oddball style only made things worse.

Faced with the fact that he was rumored to be out the door, Mike sat down to appraise the situation.

Part III

Mike decided on the following course of action:

1. Keep the forum alive but moderate its tone so it didn't step on Jack Greely's toes.
2. Don't panic. Simply outwork and outsmart the rest of the division. This plan included a massive retraining and remotivation of his personnel. He implemented weekly meetings, cross-training with other divisions, and a lot of interpersonal "stroking" to motivate the group.
3. Evoke praise from vendors and customers through excellent service and direct that praise to Jack Greely.

EXHIBIT 1

TO: Rick Belkner

FROM: New Issue Services Supervisors

SUBJECT: Supervisors' Forum

On Thursday, June 11, the Supervisors' Forum held its first meeting. The objective of the meeting was to identify common areas of concern among us and to determine topics that we might be interested in pursuing.

The first area addressed was the void that we perceive exists in the management training program. As a result of conditions beyond anyone's control, many of us over the past year have held supervisory duties without the benefit of formal training or proper experience. Therefore, what we propose is that we utilize the Supervisors' Forum as a vehicle with which to enhance the existing management training program. The areas that we hope to affect with this supplemental training are: (a) morale/job satisfaction; (b) quality of work and service; (c) productivity; and (d) management expertise as it relates to the life insurance industry. With these objectives in mind, we have outlined below a list of possible activities that we would like to pursue.

1. Further utilization of the existing "in-house" training programs provided for manager trainees and supervisors (i.e., Introduction to Supervision, E.E.O., and Coaching and Counseling).
2. A series of speakers from various sections in the company. This would help expose us to the technical aspects of their departments and their managerial style.
3. Invitations to outside speakers to address the forum on management topics, such as managerial development, organizational structure and behavior, business policy, and the insurance industry. Suggested speakers could be area college professors, consultants, and state insurance officials.
4. Outside training and visits to the field. This could include attendance at seminars concerning management theory and development relative to the insurance industry. Attached is a representative sample of a program we would like to have considered in the future.

In conclusion, we hope that this memo clearly illustrates what we are attempting to accomplish with this program. It is our hope that the above outline will be able to give the forum credibility and establish it as an effective tool for all levels of management within New Issue. By supplementing our on-the-job training with a series of speakers and classes, we aim to develop prospective management personnel with a broad perspective of both the life insurance industry and management's role in it. Also, we would like to extend an invitation to the underwriters to attend any programs at which the topic of the speaker might be of interest to them.

cc: J. Greely
     Managers

The results after eight months were impressive. Mike's unit improved the speed of processing 60 percent and lowered errors 75 percent. His staff became the most highly trained in the division. Mike had a file of several letters to Jack Greely that praised the unit's excellent service. In addition, the Supervisors' Forum had grudgingly attained credibility, although the scope of activity was restricted. Mike had even improved to the point of submitting reports on time as a concession to management.

Mike was confident that the results would speak for themselves. However, one month before his scheduled promotion and one month after an excellent merit raise in recognition of his exceptional work record, he was called into his supervisor's, Kathy Miller's, office. She informed him that after long and careful consideration, the decision had been made to deny his promotion because of his lack of attention to detail. This did not mean he was not a good supervisor, just that he needed to follow more instead of taking the lead. Mike was stunned and said so. But before he said anything else, he asked to see Rick Belkner and Jack Greely the next day.

THE SHOWDOWN

Sitting face-to-face with Rick and Jack, Mike asked if they agreed with the appraisal Kathy had discussed with him. They both said they did. When asked if any other supervisor surpassed his ability and results, each stated Mike was one of the best, if not *the* best they had. Then why, Mike asked, would they deny him a promotion when others of less ability were approved? The answer came from Jack: "It's nothing personal, but we just don't like you. We don't like your management style. You're an oddball. We can't run a division with 10 supervisors all doing different things. What kind of a business do you think we're running here? We need people who conform to our style and methods so we can measure their results objectively. There is no room for subjective interpretation. It's our feeling that if you really put your mind to it, you can be an excellent manager. It's just that you now create trouble and rock the boat. We don't need that. It doesn't matter if you're the best now, sooner or later, as you go up the ladder, you will be forced to pay more attention to administrative duties and you won't handle them well. If we correct your bad habits now, we think you can go far."

Mike was shocked. He turned to face Rick and blurted out nervously, "You mean it doesn't matter what my results are? All that matters is how I do things?" Rick leaned back in his chair and said in a casual tone, "In so many words, yes."

Mike left the office knowing that his career at Consolidated was over and immediately started looking for a new job. What had gone wrong?

Epilogue

After leaving Consolidated Life, Mike Wilson started his own insurance, sales, and consulting firm, which specialized in providing corporate-risk managers with insurance protection and claims-settlement strategies. He works with a staff assistant and one other associate. After three years, sales averaged over $7 million annually, netting approximately $125,000 to $175,000 before taxes to Mike Wilson.

During a return visit to Consolidated Life three years after his departure, Mike found Rick Belkner and Jack Greely still in charge of the division in which Mike had worked. The division's size had shrunk by 50 percent. All of the members of the old Supervisors' Forum had left. The reason for the decrease in the division's size was that computerization had removed many of the people's tasks.

Note: The authors thank Duncan Spelman and Anthony Buono for their helpful comments on this text.

19   CONSUMER MATERIALS ENTERPRISES, INC. (CONSUMMATE CORPORATION)

Introduction

Paul Rubin, a summer intern at Consumer Materials Enterprises, Inc. (Consummate Corporation), had just spoiled David Gold's day by reporting severe tensions in David's unit. Consummate Corporation (a large, highly profitable manufacturer of consumer products located in Atlanta) had been running a series of week-long seminars for its management staff designed to accelerate their interest in worker satisfaction. David Gold, 35, manager of Consummate Corporation's refill packaging unit, had recently returned from one of the company's seminars. At that time he had been the manager of the refill packaging unit for about a year and had been feeling good about the progress he had made in solving the department's problems. But now Paul had given him reason to worry.

An engineer by training, David had worked his way up through the company to his present position over a period of 13 years. David was an intelligent, thoughtful person with a dry sense of humor, who managed in a low-key, unaggressive way. He was very accepting of what other people thought, a good listener, and a believer in being supportive of the people who worked for him. When he first started with Consummate Corporation, David had been more aggressive and had tried to cut into the permissive culture of the company. Early in his career, in an attempt to shape things up in their units, he and a group of other supervisors had made a 14-point proposal, containing what they thought were not very radical suggestions. For example, they proposed that all employees be required to be present at the beginning and end of the time they were paid for, that work breaks be reasonable in length, that production logs be filled out as per the rules, and so forth.

To his amazement these proposals were rejected, and David and his cosponsors were told at that time that they had to become more understanding of the people who worked for them. Since that time David had made an effort to "soften up" on his employees and had developed a quiet, restrained approach to managing people.

Now he wanted to make a start on improving employee satisfaction in his department and thought he should start with his own immediate subordinates. Satisfied that earlier production problems were under control, he wanted to create the atmosphere of "one big happy family." But suddenly after the visit from Paul Rubin, a summer intern, he had found that there was more tension among his staff than he had realized, and he was wondering how to proceed.

Background of Refill Packaging Unit

The product manufactured by Consummate Corporation required many refills. The refill packaging unit performed all of the various packaging operations associated with getting the refills ready for final shipment and sale. An assembly-line operation was set up where the previously manufactured refills were slipped into cardboard boxes by machines, grouped together in packages, and then loaded by hand into cardboard cases.

The refill packaging unit was considered to be one of the lowest status units in Consummate Corporation. The manufacturing of products and refills required a high level of sophistication, but putting the refills into boxes did not. The packaging operation itself did not have a significant impact on profits, though high and growing demand for refills required a high daily volume.

Many of the jobs in the packaging unit were entry-level positions. New employees were typically sent to packaging first and, if they showed promise, were moved out of the unit into the manufacturing units. The same procedure held true for many of the supervisory jobs. Newly hired supervisors would often start in refill packaging and, once they had proven themselves, would be moved into more sophisticated supervisory jobs in the other units of the company.

Because the refill packaging unit was used as an entry-level place for new employees, it experienced a relatively high turnover rate into other positions within the corporation. The people who stayed in the refill packaging unit were seen by others as not holding much future promise and therefore were looked upon as the organization's "losers."

The refill packaging unit was part of a wider organization culture considered to be one of the "softest" human relations programs in all of industry. The company, by long-standing policy, would turn itself inside out for its employees.

The traditional policies and practices elsewhere in the building housing the refill packaging unit were even softer than in the rest of the company. For example, it was not uncommon to have people organize their breaks so they could leave a half hour or more before their shift was over. Many breaks were allowed employees during their shifts, and it was not uncommon to "shut down a line" right in the middle of a shift to hold a meeting. Even people caught stealing might not be fired; it was believed by many supervisors to be nearly impossible to get any employee fired, regardless of how legitimate the reason.

Because of the need to produce around the clock and some absenteeism, production operators were given the opportunity to work a great deal of overtime; as a result, some took home as much or more money than their supervisors. Many employees, because of the extensive overtime, worked under supervisors from more than one shift and thus were able to see and compare the different supervisory styles that existed across work shifts.

The organizational structure of the refill packaging unit is shown in Exhibit 1.

David Gold had three people reporting directly to him: Jim Whiting, the general supervisor for maintenance (new to the unit); Bill Dane, the general supervisor for production (with whom he was particularly close); and Kevin Flynn, the statistical analyst. The unit operated three shifts around the clock. Members of these shifts did not rotate; in other words, those on the first shift always worked days (7 A.M. to 3 P.M.), the second always worked 3 to 11 P.M. and the third always worked 11 P.M. to 7 A.M.

Each shift was required to leave the production lines set up and equipped to make it easier for the next shift to get started. Aside from this activity, there was low interdependence among shifts and supervisors.

Each shift had two or three production-line supervisors. These supervisors were responsible for several production lines. Each individual production line had a crew chief, who helped the supervisors keep the lines running smoothly and on schedule, and eight operators.

The general supervisors worked mostly when the first shift was present and for about two hours each day of the second shift, but they did not usually have direct daily contact with the third shift.

As a result of this lack of direct face-to-face contact with all three work shifts, a lot of "memos" were passed around to supervisors from the general supervisors and between shift supervisors themselves.

The production supervisors were a mix of college-hired people and experienced, up-through-the-ranks old-timers. The maintenance crew and its supervisor were all skilled tradesmen (mechanics and electricians), and as such, no college graduates were hired for these jobs.

Exhibit 2 shows the backgrounds of the supervisors in the refill packaging unit.

First Off-Site Meeting

In the process of assessing the current situation in the refill packaging unit, David Gold reflected back on a two-and-a-half-day, off-site meeting he had held six months ago with the supervisors in his unit.

He called the meeting because there were many problems in the area he had recently taken over. Production was below target, safety rules weren't enforced, work areas weren't kept clean, and there was too little cooperation across shifts and between production and maintenance supervisors. Several of the long-term supervisors had resisted very strongly going to the first off-site meeting. The person who was most vocal in complaining was Kathy Flamme, 40, married, with one child, an experienced supervisor, and known as the "Blonde Bomber" behind her back. Kathy argued that the company should not require anyone to leave home overnight and should not require people to put in extra time or work on weekends (the meeting had continued through Saturday morning). Kathy clearly demonstrated that she resented the time away, didn't think it was fair, didn't want to invest any extra time and energy in so-called seminars, and in general didn't think there was anything she needed to learn. Although Kathy was the loudest of the long-term supervisors (old-timers), most of the others had voiced similar kinds of complaints as well.

At the meeting David Gold responded to supervisor complaints about not knowing what he wanted with a clear statement of his goals for packaging. He told the supervisors that this was a new era and the long-term supervisors (the people who had been in the unit for several years) were going to have to be more professional, more effective in involving workers, managing more participatively, and learning new skills ("the old ways will no longer work"). Time also was spent discussing the general sloppiness of the work areas, failure to clean up around the machines, and passing machines along to the next shift with everything out of place and disorganized. In essence David Gold told his supervisors that they were going to have to become more committed to their jobs.

The supervisors who had been with the packaging unit of the company for several years felt that their job experience wasn't being valued by upper management and that they had never received the recognition they deserved. They worked very hard, their production quotas were almost always met, and they felt they ought to be recognized for their efforts.

EXHIBIT 1 *Structure of the Refill Packaging Unit*

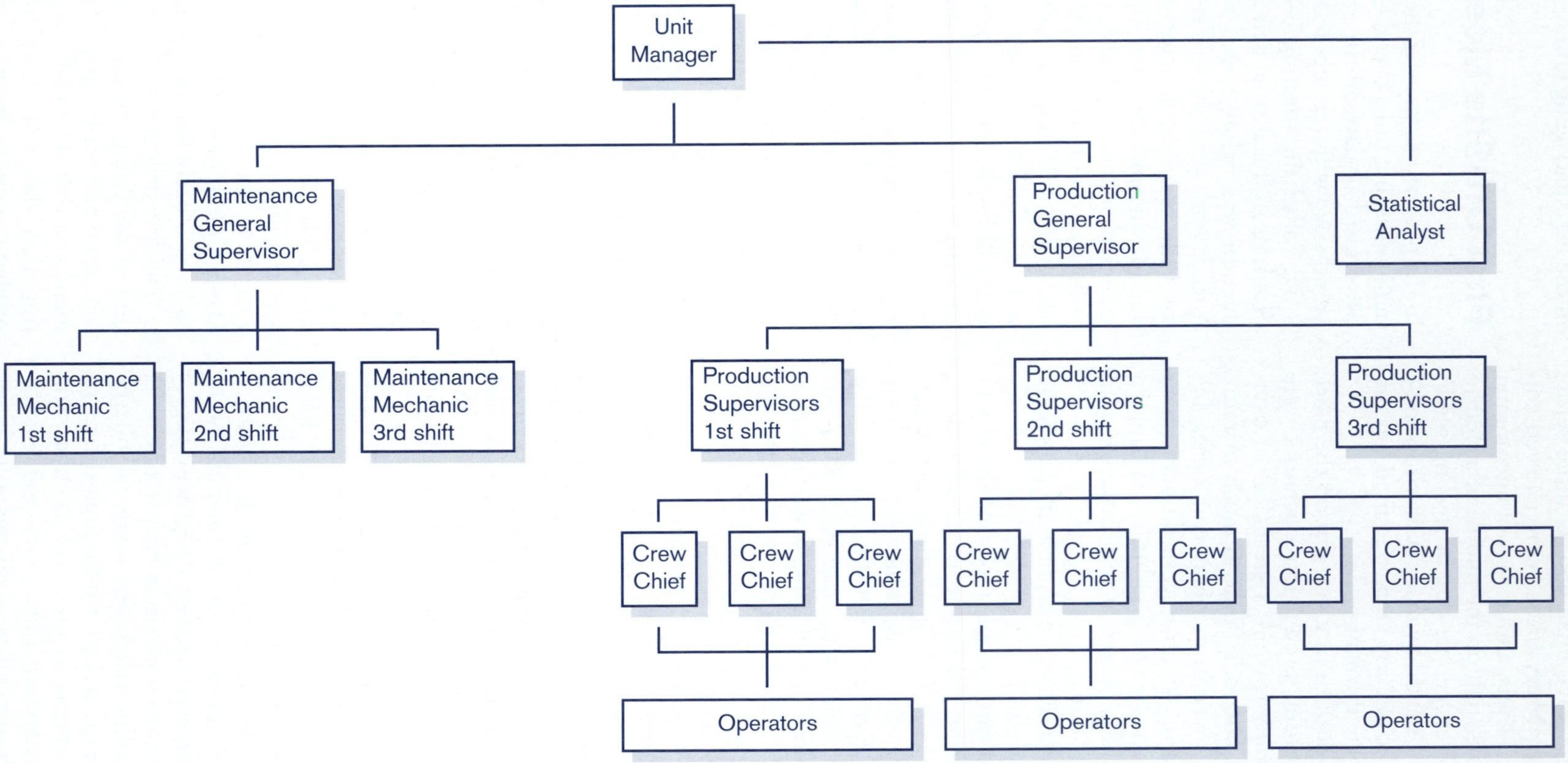

EXHIBIT 2 *Background Information on Refill Packaging Unit Supervisory Personnel*

Supervisor Name	Education	Race	Age	Number Years with Company	Number Years Packaging Unit	Position	Work Shift
David Gold	College	White	35	13	1	Manager, refill packaging.	–
Bill Dane	College	White	35	13	3	General supervisor, production.	–
Jim Whiting	HS	White	40	20	1	General supervisor, maintenance.	–
Kevin Flynn	HS	White	41	25	4	Statistical analyst.	–
Roosevelt Barnes	College	Black	23	new	8 months	Production supervisor.	1st
Kathy Flamme	HS	White	40	22	5	Production supervisor.	1st
Sheldon Levy	HS	White	58	14	14	Production supervisor.	1st
Dot Stewart	College	White	22	new	5 months	Production supervisor.	2nd
Liza Stone	College	Black	22	new	5 months	Production supervisor.	2nd
Richard Scott	HS	White	55	20+	4	Production supervisor.	3rd
Ed Tudor	HS	White	42	20	1	Production supervisor.	3rd
Ray Burr	HS	White	60	20	4 months	Production supervisor.	3rd
Charlie O'Reilly	HS	White	29	8	2	Production supervisor.	2nd
Ann Smith	College	Black	35	5	2 months	Personnel production.	–
Ted Marker	College (while working at the company)	White	28	6	4 months	Supervisor trainee.	1st
Paul Rubin	College student	White	20	–	2	Summer management trainee.	Rotating shifts

It was also discovered at this meeting that it was the supervisors' perception that in the company "you're not supposed to make waves" and that they could not really challenge the general supervisors and David Gold. They also perceived that initiative wasn't particularly welcomed in the past, and so they felt they should just stick to their work, do what they were told, and ignore everything and everybody else.

This behavior on the part of the line supervisors had served to confirm David Gold's and the two general supervisors' suspicions about the competence and professionalism of these people. They now saw the supervisors as having tunnel vision. Thus, a circular, self-defeating cycle was discovered to be operating, where supervisors behaved as if they were all wearing blinders because they felt that they were ignored and looked down upon, and as a result Gold's team became even more suspicious of the competence of the supervisors and gave them even less recognition.

In addition, the line supervisors expressed many feelings of powerlessness. They felt constrained by what they perceived to be the company's reluctance to get rid of low-performing employees, by the strength of the Employee Association, by the rapid turnover out of the packaging unit, and by the lack of

confidence that supervisors on other shifts and in other parts of their building would support their dealings with employees or management. One story that appeared to confirm the supervisors' belief that they couldn't really fire anybody concerned Kathy. Kathy had once challenged an employee, who she was certain was stealing refills by hiding them in his pants. When stopped, he refused to show her what he had and later claimed it was a dirty book, which he didn't want to show to a female supervisor. Eventually, a vice president excused the employee from the accusation of stealing because there was no proof, and the employee had stayed on.

Part of the consequence of the general attitude of the supervisors was that there were problems with achieving coordination among maintenance and production supervisors on the same shift and across shifts. They were not telling each other what they were doing or had done.

As a result of this lack of communication, very large assumptions were made about what other people were doing, thinking, and feeling on different shifts. At the off-site meeting, many instances were revealed. For example, a supervisor would say, "I saw X when I came in on my shift. He was finishing up his shift, and he let

---

EXHIBIT 3   *Summary of Issues among Subgroups*

How College Inexperienced See Selves	How College Inexperienced See Experienced Old-Timers	How Experienced Old-Timers See Selves	How Experienced Old-Timers See College Inexperienced	How Senior Management Sees College Inexperienced	How Senior Management Sees Experienced Old-Timers
Bright, quick, ambitious, want to learn and grow; like to make own mistakes, yet want guidance from Bill Dane, who isn't available without effort.	Don't want to try anything new. "Did it 6 years ago, and it failed then."	Know the ropes. Get production out, reliable.	Can't trust them. Crybabies—always running to Bill Dane.	Ambitious, energetic, creative.	Valuable. Reliable, dedicated.
Become bored when things are running smoothly.	Willing to help us but upset when advice not followed.	Care about job, dedicated, put in extra time when needed.	Wet behind the ears.	Project-oriented. More open.	Knowledgeable. Less mobile, less flexible, more defensive, expectations too low.
Open, willing to deal with problems on job, but eager for session to work things out fully.	Know many tricks. Have ways of dealing with crew chiefs that work for them but affect the work of our lines.	Know how to keep our mouths shut.	Have no respect for us and our ways.	Protective, lack of depth, need more detail knowledge.	More people-oriented— more loyal to their "hourlys."
	Threatened by us.	Don't need to have everything spelled out. Willing to deal with problems on job—don't feel it necessary to go away in special sessions.	Don't really care about job—just want to make a big impression to get ahead.	Expectations too high. More promotable.	

Note: See Appendix for specific comments made by members of each group, as recalled by Paul Rubin.

---

people walk out early and never said a word about it. If he's going to take that attitude, well then, to hell with him." Then X would respond, "Wait a second, I didn't let people walk off the shift; so-and-so had a medical thing, so he was going downstairs to the nurse. Why didn't you ask me in the first place?" There were a lot of uncontested assumptions circulating about people on different shifts, and the supervisors would use incidents they observed to confirm their prejudices about one another without doing much testing to see whether what they were observing was really as they perceived it to be.

Out of these discussions at the off-site meeting, a number of commitments were made. As a result of these commitments, production had improved considerably, general housekeeping was much better (machines were being cleaned at the end of each shift), relationships between production supervisors and the maintenance supervisors had improved markedly, there seemed to be more direct communication across shifts, and the supervisors' general understanding of the goals of the packaging unit appeared to be much clearer.

David Gold was pleased with the progress. He knew many felt they were moving in the right direction. Now he felt it was time to move toward real teamwork. He wanted overall commitment to one another and to the unit and wanted to create the feeling of being "one big happy family."

Decision to Hold a Second Off-Site Meeting

David decided to schedule another off-site meeting of all refill packaging unit supervisors.

About 10 days after he had announced the arrangements for the second off-site meeting, Paul Rubin, a college student who was spending the summer observing the department, arranged for an appointment. Rubin was visibly upset and informed Gold that the problems in the department were alarming. As a "naïve student," Rubin had managed to make friends with almost all of the supervisors, and they had talked freely with him. He described the situation in the units as "grim" and told Gold about the tension and hostility between the newly hired college graduates and the older experienced supervisors. Exhibit 3 is a summary of what Rubin had learned and told Gold.

David was rather surprised and had to figure out what to do about the unexpected tension among his staff members.

Appendix

Selected comments were made to Paul Rubin by the three groups—management, experienced supervisors, and new supervisors at Consummate's refill packaging unit.

VIEWS ON MANAGEMENT: OLD-TIMERS

"Why should we have to go away? My family will be upset . . . What's the point anyway? We don't want to be friends with the people we work with. I don't want to mix my personal life with my work life, so what's the point of it . . . These meetings management calls are a big waste."

"People who voice opinions have them brought back up to them later. I got penalized for talking at the last meeting. Everything you say around here gets back to the managers. We can't address issues like working hours, taking breaks, wearing safety glasses, and getting rid of deadweight employees."

"I don't trust anybody . . . I won't give my comment on things; I've learned to keep my mouth shut about things . . . What's said at these meetings gets passed on to the 'hourlys'; nothing is kept private. There are only two guys I can trust [old-timers from the same shift]."

"We can't deal with the bad actors . . . If they did their paperwork, there might be a chance that we could get rid of them . . . but at the top someone will give them a second chance, and they'll be back on the floor the next day laughing at you. We'd have a better unit if we had tougher rules . . . It's not doing us any good to keep bad people on, but we can't take a hard stand as supervisors or we'll get in trouble if we do."

"I haven't seen any changes under the new management . . . It seems like Gold and the general supervisors are always on a pedestal. They dictate how things are to be done, and we don't have a say at all. There are some hard feelings going around about Dane [general supervisor, production]. People say he's a hard-ass and doesn't make it very clear what it is he really wants from us."

"I wish we could get rid of the stiffs [low-performance people]. Maybe at this next meeting I'll mention it again."

"If you create waves here, it's all over . . . The crew chiefs run the show, not Dane or the supervisors . . . The second shift gets a lot of static from upstairs. Gold is a little Caesar . . . I don't see the general supervisors or the other supervisors too often; we just communicate through memos, you know . . ."

VIEWS ON OTHER EXPERIENCED SUPERVISORS: OLD-TIMERS

"We know the ropes, know how to get the numbers out [make production quotas], and we *care* about our jobs. We're willing to put in extra time where needed, . . . and we don't need everything spelled out for us."

"We're willing to deal with problems on the job as they come up; we don't feel it's necessary to have to go away in a special session to do this."

"We're more dedicated to our jobs than the young ones . . . We're reliable; you can count on us to get the numbers out on schedule."

"It looks like we're becoming a dying breed around here. I don't like the feeling . . . Maybe by hiring all these college kids they're trying to tell us something, you know what I mean?"

From Richard Scott (third shift): "That Kathy . . . she's always off someplace having breakfast with her boyfriend when she could come in and find out from me how the night shift has gone."

From Kathy Flamme (first shift): "I know Richard hates me. I hear he's always saying really nasty things about me behind my back . . . Then he expects me to come in early to meet with him and discuss things— no way!"

VIEWS ON COLLEGE-HIRES: OLD-TIMERS

"You can't trust them to do what they've agreed to do . . . They don't want to listen . . . They can't keep their mouths shut."

"These college kids are a bunch of wise-asses who are still wet behind the ears. They spend all of their time sucking up to Bill Dane [general supervisor, production]. While he's too smart to fall for it, they are constantly writing him notes or talking to him, telling him what's going on. Supervisors aren't supposed to do that . . . You shouldn't go running to the general supervisor every time you have a problem."

Ted Marker's [supervisor trainee] presence is costing us supervisors overtime pay. Can he or can't he run his own line? They say he has to wait a year, to train first, yet they give him a line when they're short on supervisors. He has a luxury we didn't have . . . He can step back and watch without having any responsibility to a line or crew."

"You can't trust the college supervisors to keep their mouths shut and to listen . . . They resent our advice . . . They're really cocky, and they're not concerned with who's in their way; they're just concerned about climbing the ladder to big success."

"They're always trying to make a big impression on David and the general supervisors. Instead they should pay more attention to getting the numbers out" (meeting production quotas).

"They strike me as being a bunch of crybabies . . . They're always running to Bill Dane about one thing or another. Bill has probably had it up to here with them and their complaining."

VIEWS ON MANAGEMENT: COLLEGE-HIRES, INEXPERIENCED SUPERVISORS

"I'm on the first shift, and we have all the bosses working with us. As a result they tend to make all of our decisions for us. We'd like more responsibility on our shift. The second and third shifts have the luxury of being able to make their own decisions."

"Bill Dane [general supervisor, production] is very arrogant in the way in which he writes notes . . . He gets his point across very strongly."

"David Gold appears not to care; he acts very casual when being informed about what's going on in his department but gets quite upset if he's not kept informed. He doesn't give support . . . or much of any response . . . He shows no emotion whatsoever."

"There's very little consistency up there . . . Some carry out what management tells us to do at a meeting, but others don't."

"Bill Dane writes vicious notes . . . He seems not to like one-on-one conversations . . . He spends a lot of time defending the first shift . . . I'm not really sure what he's thinking most of the time."

"The second shift is blamed for everything . . . When we're supposed to meet with the first shift, they don't show up; they won't stay around to meet with us because it's an intrusion on their time, they say."

"I'm not clear as to what's expected of us—how we should meet our goals and expectations, how our performance is measured. David needs to tell us what he expects of us . . . We always have to ask for meetings. Bill and David should be taking the initiative here, not us."

"You seldom get praised for your work, and when you do there's always a twist added to it—a sort of hidden criticism added in to balance it out."

"Bill's style makes you feel defensive immediately. Bill just says 'wrong,' but doesn't give suggestions for how something should be done."

"I'm not getting the direction I need . . . I'm told, 'Make your mark,' but I don't know how."

"Bill overreacts; he doesn't think before giving instructions. If you say something to him that he doesn't like, he's on you all the time . . . Even for petty things . . . he gets charged up . . . You can't argue with him."

"David delegates to Bill Dane and Jim Whiting . . . He won't involve himself in the petty stuff, which is reasonable, but it also restricts communications with him."

VIEWS ON FELLOW COLLEGE-HIRES

"I'd like to see us be more honest with each other; everyone gives criticism so indirectly that you're not really sure what is actually meant by them."

"We work well together, but oftentimes Charlie [old-timer—second shift] gets in our way."

"Four of us were brought in at about the same time, five months ago. I guess in the past they've brought in college supervisors one at a time. Maybe four at the same time is too strong a dose for these old farts around here."

From Roosevelt Barnes (first shift): "Dot [second shift] doesn't trust me—I don't know why. She gets very upset with me at times; in fact, right now we're not even speaking to each other . . . She thinks she can tell me off whenever she feels like it . . . I resent that attitude, and I told her off last time."

VIEWS ON OLD-TIMERS: COLLEGE-HIRES

"Our relationships could be better. I, myself, have had several clashes with Kathy [same shift]. We have very different outlooks. She's tough on people; my style is looser. Also I have ideas I'd like to try out. She's opposed to making any changes whatsoever. We've had several disagreements in front of others . . . I've said what I had to say and walked away from it. I'm very direct, and as a result I've been told by other supervisors to 'bite my tongue.' I've been told several times that Kathy says stuff about me behind my back."

"We have different styles—they're more laid back, don't like to rock the boat; they want to keep things exactly as they are forever. All of us have had run-ins [between the experienced and the inexperienced]. The older supers give too much power to the crew chiefs—they let them run the show. As for myself, I don't feel I should have to do somersaults just because the crew chiefs tell me I should."

"Kathy's shift [first shift] leaves at 2:30; our people complain about having to be there from 3 to 11."

"The experienced supervisors say, 'We just want to share our knowledge with you'; but they get very mad if you don't always follow their advice."

"There are a lot of 'systems' the old-timers have with the crew chiefs, which is OK except it gets in the way of my job. The problem is how do I tell them this without their feeling I'm attacking them . . . They know ways around things, shortcuts . . . but their shortcuts cause me to have to scramble to cover my behind."

"When you want to try out a new idea, the old-timers say, 'Why bother; they tried that six years ago and it didn't work then.' I get the impression that they feel we don't respect them and their ways of getting things done."

CONTRACT NEGOTIATIONS IN WESTERN AFRICA: A CASE OF MISTAKEN IDENTITY

Peter Janes, a young member of Eurojet's Contracts Department, was on his way to Saheli in French-speaking Western Africa to work on the complicated negotiations involved in selling a jet airliner to the Saheli government. He was not altogether thrilled with the assignment and hoped it would be a quick deal, since financing seemed to be available for it. Janes, educated in law, had experience in contract negotiation in India, the Philippines, Saudi Arabia, and most recently, Australia. At 27 he was one of the younger members of the department but was seen as trustworthy, with a high degree of motivation. If successful, it would be the first deal he had brought to closure on his own. But he had serious doubts about the project's feasibility or desirability. Furthermore, he had no desire to become a Francophone Africa expert within the company. In addition, Janes had left behind what seemed to be the beginning of a great relationship in Australia and he wanted to get back to his girlfriend.

The Company

Eurojet, based in the UK, was one of the larger diversified aircraft manufacturers. It had developed a special jet for third-world operations, able to operate from hot, high-altitude airfields, including unprepared strips. However, orders were hard to come by because of the difficulties in third-world financing and the poor financial condition of regional airlines. The company was therefore delighted to learn that its regional sales executive in Saheli, Mr. Ali Osaju, had found a potential sale in his country's desire for a presidential aircraft, along with its need for reliable regional air transport.

The sale looked even more likely when it was discovered that the government export/import bank had a substantial budget available for Saheli, making financing of the multimillion dollar aircraft feasible. It would be necessary to arrange an international commercial bank loan for Saheli as well. The potential of the airliner to earn revenue through regional transport was considered important in securing the loan.

The Negotiating Team

In December 1987 the Saheli government announced that it was ready to begin detailed negotiations.

According to Eurojet policy, negotiations were conducted by the Contracts Department in close cooperation with sales and internal specialist functions. Peter Janes, having just spent three-months based in Australia working across South-East Asia on specialist leasing packages, with only four days off in the last six months, was assigned to the team because of his third-world experience and his ability to speak French. He had been with the company for about two years but had no experience in Africa.

Ali Osaju was a highly placed African of Middle-Eastern origin, educated in Europe, with a background in aviation. He had joined the company at about the same time as Janes. Osaju had no previous experience in selling high-tech capital goods but had many good connections. He was seen as invaluable to the company because of his African background combined with his European education. He had been developing local contacts in Saheli by spending a week there every two or three months over the past two years.

The Negotiating Policy

The company's negotiating policy inevitably led to what was referred to as the "two-headed monster approach." The sales representative was responsible for initial discussions and for overall relations with the customer. The contracts representative was responsible for negotiating concrete offers and signing contracts and finance agreements on behalf of the company. This double approach led to varying degrees of tension between the members of particular teams as well as between the departments in general. Sales was particularly aggrieved that contracts operated on a worldwide basis rather than a regional one.

Working on a team where both parties have important roles to play required considerable sensitivity. In his two years of working at Eurojet, Peter Janes was looked on by the sales people as a considerate and skilled negotiating partner. He was not likely to lose a contract which they had spent years developing because of cultural clumsiness. Nevertheless, he walked a very narrow line, as it was his role to say no to all the wishes of the customer which were not feasible from the company's perspective. As this was to be his first solo contract negotiation and Ali Osaju's first sale with the company, they shared a similar personal motivation for closing the deal.

The Negotiation: The Early Days

Eurojet was not the only company trying to sell a jetliner to Saheli. The Russians, who had had considerable influence on the country since its independence 20 years earlier, were very much present trying to sell their aircraft and sabotage the deal with Eurojet. Janes and Osaju frequently received strange phone calls in their hotel rooms and were aware that all their telephone calls were bugged. Once, Janes returned to his room to find that his briefcase had been tampered with. In addition, another European company with a number of contracts in surrounding countries was trying to arrange a deal.

The main negotiating point of the team was to propose that the Sahelis accept one airplane that could be converted from a regional airliner to a VIP presidential jet. The Sahelis had originally wanted a specially designed VIP jet, which would have cost an extra $10 million and would never be used other than for the president. The negotiations moved extremely slowly. Janes and Osaju spent hours waiting to see officials and chasing administrative papers from one office to another. They became aware that no one official wanted to be responsible for making the decision, to avoid being blamed should things go wrong.

The two men spent many hours debating strategy in the bar of the hotel. Janes objected to Osaju telling him what to do. Osaju objected to Janes making issues too complicated for the client. The relationship was a very tense one. They both felt they were getting little support from head office. They also thought that the circumstances they were working in were very difficult.

Peter Janes began to feel he was in a no-win situation. He realized that the negotiating process could go on for months, and he knew that another colleague had already begun to take over his activities with multiorder prospects in Australia. Conditions at the hotel were not that comfortable, and both he and Osaju were paid on a salary-only basis. There were no overseas allowances.

The lack of support from headquarters was a problem for both the negotiators. Communications were difficult, as they felt they could not talk freely over the telephone because of being bugged. Furthermore, they did not feel that their contacts at headquarters could begin to understand the finer points of the negotiation difficulties. They did learn from headquarters that they were considered to be moving too slowly in making the deal.

There were constant discussions on finance, spare parts, configuration, certification, and training. All the legal and technical documents had to be translated from English to French, causing many minor but significant misunderstandings. In one case, the standard contract in the UK called for the Saheli government to waive its "sovereign immunity" and "contract in its private rather than its public capacity." However, Saheli had adopted the Napoleonic Code from France and had no equivalent legal concepts. The courts in the UK had a very limited right to hear actions against the Crown and they assumed that this element of the law held true for all countries. The Saheli negotiators listened with polite disbelief to these explanations and sent a telegram to the president saying "Sahelian sovereignty is being threatened."

Janes and Osaju decided on a very basic strategy of patience and a friendly, open manner. Establishing trust and preserving individual and corporate credibility were recognized as being vital. They placed great emphasis on simplifying the bureaucratic process. Two months of negotiating passed with no commitment in sight.

Eurojet management were beginning to show a lack of confidence in the deal. Peter Janes had committed the company to $1,000,000 of expenditure to fit an airliner to the Saheli's specifications and deliver it on time, yet saw no formal contract nor any evidence of the loan money. On the Saheli side, there was considerable nervousness about the commercial sovereign loans from the international banks.

Peter Janes had adapted himself to local culture as much as he could. Although his natural inclinations would have been to get things done quickly, deal with business first, and make friends later, he was aware that that was not how business deals were made in Saheli. So he had spent many hours making friends, going to people's houses and walking round their businesses and factories. On one such occasion, he was walking round a factory with one of his friends holding his hand as was the custom for Sahelian male friends to do. To his horror, a group of foreign diplomats came toward them on their tour of the factory. Janes was aware of an almost superhuman effort on his part not to let go of his friend's hand and keep his own relaxed, even as he felt the rest of his body stiffen with tension.

Janes continued to make his daily round of visits to offices and homes, establishing himself as open, as trustworthy, and as trying to express complex legal and technical terms in a simple way. He began to be aware of a warming of perceptions toward him. Up until then he had felt that the Sahelian officials were always guarded, on the defensive in the presence of Eurojet's legal commercial representative. He thought that this was because it was his role to say "no." In the third month of the negotiations, he received an extremely encouraging sign. A source close to the president had recently been quoted as saying "He (Janes) doesn't say 'yes' very often, but when he says 'yes,' he means 'yes.'" This was the sign that he and Osaju had been waiting for, a sign that his credibility had been established and they could now begin to deal with some of the more sensitive issues in the negotiation.

Mistaken Identity?

Most meetings in Saheli began with extended conversations about everyone's family and general social subjects. It was not uncommon to go to a meeting and find 20 people in the room, friends and relations of the person who had arranged the meeting. It was considered extremely rude not to go around the room greeting and chatting with everyone, so that even the first stage of saying hello in a meeting could take one or two hours.

On one of these occasions, Peter Janes was introduced to the son of the presidential pilot, a nine-year-old soccer fanatic. Janes had last played soccer at university, but he was a great fan and was amused to find in this nine-year-old extensive knowledge of all the international teams. The father told his son that Janes played soccer himself, which Janes took to be a bit of fun. Thereafter he was always introduced as "Mr. Janes, the great footballer" and had many affable conversations with the father and son about playing soccer. It soon became clear that the son, having listened with awe to Jane's extensive explanations about the game, decided that he played for CEDEX, the national team.

The first inkling Janes had that this matter had gone beyond a family joke was when the head of the local television station sought an invitation to meet him and immediately brought the conversation around to soccer. In order to avoid embarrassment, Janes was careful to sidestep questions—his training as a lawyer was not for nothing—by saying "CEDEX is doing fine" or "No, I'm not playing as much soccer as I used to." He was very careful neither to deny nor to affirm the misunderstanding of his playing for CEDEX, but the situation began to make him extremely uneasy.

Conversations with complete strangers became increasingly bizarre. Janes at first thought his hosts were having a laugh at his expense, but he then began to suspect that there was something more important at stake than making him feel foolish. The minister of protocol invited him to be the guest of honor at the local Cup Final. His new visa was returned to him as a "Visa de Courtoisie" or diplomatic visa. Several times he tried to bring the subject up with the pilot-father, but his attempts were always met with a big guffaw, a slap on the back, and some remark about "the great footballer!"

Janes was increasingly upset about further references to his career as an international soccer player. He did not understand how anyone could take him as a professional player for an international team when he spent all his time negotiating the sale of aircraft with government officials. He imagined daily what it would be like to phone his boss at home to try to justify the loss of the contract by explaining that he had misled people into thinking that he was a famous soccer player.

He was unwilling to embarrass people by saying they were wrong, but he was equally uncomfortable not striking down the myth—perhaps it served some purpose. His status as an international soccer player was apparently much greater than that of a young lawyer and perhaps he needed that "little extra" to justify his power in negotiating and signing the contract. It was relatively easy to give indirect answers to questions, thus salving his conscience and protecting his strangely acquired status. Nonetheless, alluding to his legal training, Janes had said to Osaju, "I can put my hand on my heart and say 'I have not told a lie' but I don't feel comfortable. We have worked so hard for credibility I would hate a silly issue like this to backfire on us." At the time they had agreed to laugh off the matter, as the people involved were not main players in the negotiations.

The issue came to a head one day when Peter Janes had a chance meeting in the lobby of the hotel with an important Saheli minister and his counterpart from a neighboring country, with whom Eurojet was very keen to do business. To Janes's horror, the two launched into an enthusiastic and serious discussion about potential dates for a tour of West Africa by CEDEX. Maybe now, he thought, he had better set the record straight.

Epilogue

Peter Janes continued to make noncommittal replies and managed to avoid any further serious problems. Although greatly disturbing to him personally, the soccer question was a non-issue in terms of the negotiations. Fortunately for Janes, he could discuss his feelings about the situation with Ali Osaju and so relieve some of his own tension by laughing about the absurdity of it.

After 10 months of intense negotiations, the deal was almost called off by the negotiating team at the last minute. They had spent days retranslating the French contract back into English and then sitting beside a Sahelian typist who did not speak English, saying each word to her phonetically so that she could type it. They both had had very little sleep in order to get the contract finished in time. When they finally went with the Attorney General to the president's office to sign the contract, they were kept waiting for several hours as usual. During that time, the Attorney General reread the French contract and discovered numerous spelling mistakes in it. He then declared that he could not give it to the president in its present condition and that the signing would have to be delayed for another week.

Osaju and Janes both hit the wall—literally. It was the last straw. While Osaju threw books and papers, Janes strode around the room shouting that unless they signed immediately, he was withdrawing Eurojet's approval of the contract. The Attorney General stood his ground, and Osaju and Janes stormed off to the hotel. They could scarcely believe what they had done after almost a year's worth of friendly and meticulous negotiating. Janes went to sleep, exhausted after the last 10 days of work and the loss of the contract.

He was awakened four hours later to be informed that the Attorney General was waiting to see him. He was escorted to an office across the road where he found the Attorney General in his shirtsleeves sitting at a typewriter, carefully changing all the spelling mistakes himself. He wanted Peter to initial all the changes so that he would feel confident that no substantial changes were being made in the contract. The contract was signed the next day.

Despite Eurojet's advice, the aircraft was not handled by the national airlines but kept under the president's control and thus rarely used. Debt servicing soon became a problem and one year later the aircraft was quietly and informally repossessed. Eurojet offered to resell the aircraft, but the Saheli government balked at authorizing the sale.

Osaju spent one more year in Africa and was then promoted to the Far East, where he was made Regional Sales Director. Janes was promoted to another project in early 1983, where he continued to work for the next four years.

DAVID SHORTER   **IVEY**

Neil Abramson prepared this case under the supervision of Professor J. J. DiStefano solely to provide material for class discussion. The authors do not intend to illustrate either effective or ineffective handling of a managerial situation. The authors may have disguised certain names and other identifying information to protect confidentiality.

Ivey Management Services prohibits any form of reproduction, storage or transmittal without its written permission. This material is not covered under authorization from CanCopy or any reproduction rights organization. To order copies or request permission to reproduce materials, contact Ivey Publishing, Ivey Management Services, c/o Richard Ivey School of Business, The University of Western Ontario, London, Ontario, Canada, N6A 3K7; phone (519) 661-3208; fax (519) 661-3882; e-mail cases@ivey.uwo.ca.

Copyright© 1991, Ivey Management Services
Version: (A)1992-08-24

David Shorter sat back in his chair and thought about what he should say to Bob Chen when they met in a few minutes. Three weeks ago when David had left for holiday, he had regarded Bob as an up-and-coming member of the James-Williams team. David had seen Bob as a solid performer who wanted a career at James-Williams and who could be developed over time into a manager and perhaps eventually into a partner. David had even thought that Bob could help attract to James-Williams some of the new entrepreneurial Hong Kong companies that were coming to Toronto. Now David heard from Bob's managing partner, Jane Klinck, that Bob was threatening to resign.

David's First Day Back

David thought about the steady stream of people who had been in to see him this first morning back in the office. Jane Klinck was worried and upset. She felt that Bob was acting "crazy" and that there might be some sort of personality conflict between Bob and Mike McLeod. She hoped that David would be able to sort out the problem and find a solution that would keep Bob in the company. Mike McLeod had been in to see David, too. Mike was a fairly new partner who attracted a lot of business to James-Williams. He felt that he had not only been through the proper channels to have Bob assigned to the Softdisk Computer audit, but that he had been extremely patient with Bob. Mike said the other partners were shaking their heads about his behaviour, wondering why he was being so patient when it was standard procedure for

partners to make such an assignment. Joe Silverman had been in as well. Joe was the tax partner Bob would report to starting in September, just five weeks from now. Joe hotly protested Bob's behaviour: "We can't have staff refusing assignments! Bob is way out of line! The customers must come first and this behaviour sheds a poor light on Bob. If he doesn't take the Softdisk job, he should be fired!"

The New Enterprise Group at James-Williams

David Shorter was the Practice Director of the New Enterprise Group at James-Williams. James-Williams was one of the six largest public accounting firms in Canada with 400 partners practising in 30 Canadian cities. James-Williams was the sole Canadian member of James-Williams International which provided audit, tax, consulting and other services to individuals, private businesses and governments in the Americas, Europe, the Middle East, Africa, Asia and the Pacific.

The New Enterprise Group had been set up seven years ago to provide service to smaller growth companies managed by entrepreneurs. David had been the Practice Director for the past four years. James-Williams believed that companies with gross annual revenues of between $5 and $100 M were often neglected as potential customers by Canadian public accounting firms because of their small size. Yet these companies had need of a variety of services that could be provided by James-Williams and these companies would pay high fees for their relative size. When these companies had grown beyond gross revenues of $100 M, their business could be transferred from the New Enterprise Group to the main auditing and consulting services of James-Williams and a solid relationship would exist. This was an important consideration in a mature industry where public accounting firms competed on service, reputation and price. Often, it was a long-term relationship that kept a client with a public accounting firm. These relationships enabled partners of the public accounting firms to have such an intimate knowledge of their clients' activities that they could anticipate problems and become indispensable to their clients' planning process.

The New Enterprise Group provided a range of consulting services geared to the needs of growing

James-Williams: The New Enterprise Group Organizational Chart
(Reporting relationships prior to Bob Chen's reassignment to tax)

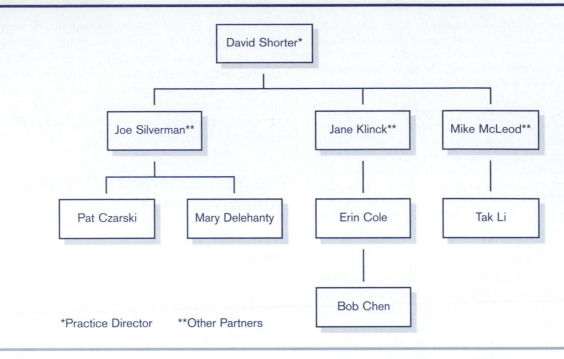

*Practice Director   **Other Partners

entrepreneurial companies. In addition to accounting and auditing services, the partners acted as principal business advisors. Client companies were particularly interested in the subjects of corporate finance and tax consulting, as well as the problems of acquisition and divestiture. Consulting was also available on strategic planning, development of business plans, marketing, human resource management, and information systems.

The New Enterprise Group was organized as a collegial system of partners who managed their own clients and activities within the performance objectives established by James-Williams, and under the general supervision of the Practice Director, who was also a partner (see Exhibit 1). Staff members below the partner level were organized on the staff system. A staff usually consisted of one or two senior staff accountants and several intermediate or junior staff accountants under a manager. A partner would have one, two or three managers and several staff reporting to him/her.

Most of the staff were either chartered accountants or in the process of becoming chartered accountants. Usually, staff would be hired out of business school as junior staff accountants and would work on staff over a two-year period while they studied for their chartered accountant examinations. At the beginning of their second year, they were promoted to intermediate staff accountants at which level they remained until

they passed the chartered accountant exams. At the beginning of their third year they wrote their exams, and, if they passed, they were promoted to senior staff accountants. If they did not pass, which was fairly common, they would have another year to prepare for a final chance at the exams.

The normal promotion process at James-Williams was for staff to remain as senior staff accountants for two years while they developed a consulting specialty of their choice. Then they might be promoted to manager and supervise six to nine staff. Most partners were selected from the ranks of the managers after they had been with the firm for ten to eleven years.

Bob Chen's Background with the New Enterprise Group

Bob Chen was born in Hong Kong and came to Toronto as a high school student for Grade 13. He graduated with a Bachelor of Commerce from Queen's University in Kingston. At Queen's he achieved an overall grade point average of 75 percent[1] and was the treasurer of the Chinese Students Society.

---

[1]In Canada the grade point system follows the British model. At Queen's a 75 average is a B+ and is considered evidence of high achievement.

He was recruited for James-Williams in the spring of his final year at Queen's, and began as a junior staff accountant at the New Enterprise Group in the following September.

Bob was seen as quiet and soft-spoken. One of his managers described him as "shy and accommodating. He does what he is asked to do and a bit more. Casual requests get immediate results." He was also a very private person whose politeness often meant not saying exactly what he wanted out of a situation or from another person. His civility may have masked from his colleagues his strongly felt desire for success and strongly held views about his possible contribution to the firm.

Bob was well liked by the people around him, most of whom viewed him as Westernized. Some partners and staff thought that Bob "was fairly outgoing for an Oriental" and had much better oral communications skills than previous staff from Hong Kong hired by the firm. His colleagues believed that Bob had good potential with James-Williams and hoped he would stay with the firm.

Previous Contacts between David and Bob

Two years after joining the firm, Bob wrote his chartered accountant examinations and in the following December learned the good news that he had passed. He was transferred as an audit senior to Jane Klinck, because the partner Bob had previously reported to was leaving the company. Bob was to report to Erin Cole who was the manager working under Jane.

Early in the new year, David Shorter followed his usual custom of having one-on-one meetings with staff who had passed their examinations and been promoted to senior staff accountant positions. The purpose of the meetings was not only to congratulate them on their success, but also to begin to identify their interests in professional specialization so that David could plan appropriate assignments for them within the New Enterprise Group. New assignments were usually announced after the annual performance appraisal in May, and were effective by September.

When he met with Bob in January, David was pleased with Bob's success because he had thought that Bob was a solid, but average performer and might not pass his examination the first time he wrote it. Now David decided that Bob might have higher potential within the New Enterprise Group and suggested that Bob might like to work to build a practice around attracting entrepreneurial, Hong Kong–based companies to use the New Enterprise Group's services. David explained, "One of our goals is to build up our business with Hong Kong companies. Up to now, we haven't had much success because most Hong Kong money has been invested in real estate. Now, however, Hong Kong money is being invested in businesses which are in the New Enterprise Group's target market."

To be able to attract a Hong Kong practice, Bob would have to build up his auditing skills for another year, because audit was the initial function which brought companies to the New Enterprise Group and stimulated their interest in other consulting services. David remembered that he had two goals in suggesting further auditing experience for Bob. First, the New Enterprise Group had a shortage of senior auditors for this year. Second, he felt that Bob was a "keeper" who could have a long and mutually valuable future with the firm. Bob's auditing skills needed strengthening since he had done very little auditing in his first two years. David had seen previous staff with similar limitations fail as both managers and partners, because without auditing experience they could not understand the practical nature of most business problems. David noted, "Without more seasoning, he would not be as valuable to us. He would get weeded out as a technician."

But Bob had other ideas; he indicated to David that now that he had his C. A. designation, he wanted to develop a specialization in tax. He was open to the idea of developing a Hong Kong practice, but in the meantime he wanted an assignment that would teach him tax. David told Bob that he didn't believe Bob was ready for a tax assignment, because tax was a practical discipline that needed the ability to find creative tax solutions to business problems. Without a firm grounding in audit, staff had a tendency to quote tax regulations, rather than use the tax regulations to the advantage of their clients. "I didn't think he was ready and believed that his chargeable activity time would fall. I was under pressure to keep up the chargeable activity time of all staff." David thought that by the end of the interview he had convinced Bob of the soundness of his argument and that Bob had agreed to defer his request for a tax position.

In May, Jane conducted Bob's annual performance appraisal during which time Bob repeated his request for an assignment in tax. Her reply was similar to David's earlier commentary. Jane told Bob that she thought he needed another year of auditing work. "He had one year of decent audit work with me, but his junior year had not been enlightening in the area of audit. I thought he agreed that his junior year had not been productive in the area of audit." Jane asked David to review the performance appraisal because Bob had only been transferred to her in December. When David met with Bob in June, Bob again asked for an assignment in tax. David said no, reiterating his earlier argument that Bob needed more auditing experience. He added that Jane supported this recommendation. It was both David's and Jane's opinion that Bob was only now doing his first and second comprehensive audits. Bob seemed to accept this judgement, though he did not appear to be satisfied by it.

Over the next month, Bob requested and received two more interviews with David to request a tax assignment. David was pleased to talk with Bob because he felt that Bob's concern showed he was highly interested in his career and also highly committed to James-Williams. At the first meeting, David offered the compromise that if Bob would continue as an auditor for a year, then David would send Bob on a comprehensive three-year tax training program that was a much prized opportunity among tax consultants. "I offered to send him on this expensive course fully funded by the firm if he would agree to wait another year for a tax assignment." Bob seemed initially to agree but then asked for another meeting. At the second meeting, David finally agreed to assign Bob to a tax partner, Joe Silverman, to work in tax starting in September. "I told him that even though he could make the move into tax in September, he'd have to do some audits during his first year in tax. The firm needed to take advantage of his auditing skills as a senior. It would also keep his activities time up." Bob agreed to the conditions and David left for holidays shortly after.

Events Occurring during David Shorter's Absence

David Shorter left the New Enterprise Group to attend a Partner Development Program and for holidays at the beginning of July. During this time, Mike McLeod realized his upcoming need for a senior auditor for an important account, the Softdisk Computer Company. Softdisk's year-end required that the audit had to be done in September and October. The audit would fully occupy the time of the senior auditor during those two months. In order to make preparations for the job, the senior auditor had to be assigned to the audit by the end of July at the latest. It was more desirable for the senior auditor to be in place by July 13 in order to attend the client's physical inventory being conducted on that date. This would also provide an opportunity for the client and senior auditor to meet each other and work together prior to the actual audit.

Mike found that Bob Chen was the only senior auditor in the New Enterprise Group who might be available in September and October. Policy in the New Enterprise Group was to use internal staff as senior auditors whenever possible because the cost for hours of internal staff was less than if an auditor had to be "rented" from another division of James-Williams. Also, it would be easier for Mike to manage someone from inside the New Enterprise Group.

Since the actual audit work was to be conducted in the fall, Bob would be "officially" working for Joe Silverman in tax. Mike approached Joe Silverman and his manager, Pat Czarski, to see whether he could use Bob Chen for the audit. Joe and Pat told him that Bob was to be assigned to Joe's other manager, Mary Delehanty, who was away on holiday. But Joe and Pat thought it was a very good idea to assign Bob to the audit. The arrangements for Bob to be transferred to Joe had only been made in June and there was no tax work available for him. Further, with Mary on holiday, it was unlikely that she could find tax work for Bob to do in September and the Softdisk audit would keep Bob's billable hours at an acceptable level until they could use his services effectively.

With this approval, Mike approached Bob on July 10. He asked Bob to take the Softdisk audit and provided Bob with information on the company. In particular, Mike wanted Bob to know that the Softdisk audit would fit in with Bob's career path in tax. The audit would include international multi-jurisdictional tax issues, tax problems concerning research and development being done in Quebec, and a high technology emphasis much valued by staff who worked in the New Enterprise Group. The tax issues were so complex and interesting that the audit had been supervised last year by a tax partner who was now in New York. Mike reassured Bob that this partner would be available for consultation if Bob had problems. Further, once Bob had done the audit, he would have first call on any further, special tax work which might be required by Softdisk. Mike suggested that Bob should contact Dominick Sousa, a manager in the New Enterprise Group who had acted as senior auditor for Softdisk last year, to confirm these details.

Mike also noted that because the prior year's work with Softdisk had been a first audit by James-Williams, extra efforts had been taken. Therefore Bob would benefit from a better planning package being in place and a high client commitment for the second year. In addition, two James-Williams staff members from last year's audit would be carried over to Bob's team, further strengthening the continuity. Finally, Mike assured Bob that Mike and Tak Li would also be available to assist as needed. Altogether, he sought to assure Bob that taking on this audit would be consistent with his professed career objectives.

It was Mike's impression that Bob had agreed to do the Softdisk audit once he had confirmed the information Mike had given him with "due diligence." He didn't refuse. Basically, he did not say yes, but he said, "Yes, I'll consider it and will talk to the people." I was led to believe that he would seriously consider it and I got the impression he would do it. I thought we had a reasonable exchange and that we were both being open with each other." Bob agreed to attend the physical inventory conducted on July 13. The key contact at Softdisk was also of Chinese origin, liked Bob, and was pleased to have him for the audit.

Then Mike heard from Pat Czarski and from his own manager, Tak Li, that Bob had told them privately that he did not intend to do the audit. Given that Mike had thought the matter settled, he was shocked by this turn of events. He was especially surprised because Bob's attendance at the physical inventory sent a clear signal to Mike of Bob's acceptance of the assignment. Over the next week when Mike saw Bob in the office corridor or in the washroom, he checked if Bob was planning to do the audit and got the impression that Bob was still agreeable to the arrangements made earlier. But then he would hear more secondhand reports from Pat and Tak that Bob was not planning to do the audit. So Mike decided to be more direct. "I guess that I precipitated a crisis from Bob's perspective. I said, 'Don't BS me. Tell me up front. What are you going to do instead?' We had frequent contact in the hallways. I would ask him if he had a chance to talk to Dominick Sousa. But Bob wouldn't say anything about it." At this point, Mike decided that Bob was not being straight with him. He asked Pat and Tak to act as agents to see how Bob was reacting to the Softdisk project. "They would report one day that he was committed. Then the next day he had thought about it and wasn't committed any more."

This situation frustrated Mike immensely. His parents had lived in Hong Kong while Mike was growing up. His sister still lived there. "I have a better than average knowledge of cultural differences between Canadians and people from Hong Kong. I thought I was being effective." Mike decided an open discussion was necessary and wondered if Bob had not understood what a developmental opportunity the Softdisk audit was for furthering his professed career interest in tax consulting. Mike needed a fast and firm resolution to the problem because an auditor had to be in place by the end of July. If Bob would not do the job, then Mike would have to borrow a senior auditor from another James-Williams office, and the time pressure to brief such a replacement adequately would be extreme.

Mike decided to call a meeting with Bob, Pat, and Tak for July 20. "I didn't want a fight but I wasn't going to take any BS. Tak and Pat weren't getting the same story that I was. Bob was telling them 'no' and me 'maybe.' I wanted to get all four of us in a room and finally get some straight answers. I was going to tell Bob, 'You want to be a tax consultant. Well, here is the opportunity.'"

On July 19, Bob met with Jane and asked for her help. Jane had supported Bob at partners' meetings and he felt she was an ally. Bob told Jane that he wanted to refuse the Softdisk job. He said he was concerned that the amount of planning time required for the Softdisk audit would interfere with a complex audit he was currently doing with a film company. He was afraid he might have to take leave from the film company audit. Jane asked if scheduling was his only concern. "Bob told me there was a bigger problem than scheduling. He didn't want to do the audit. He said he couldn't work for Mike but he wouldn't say why." Jane told Bob that he was crazy and not to do anything rash.

On July 20, Mike, Pat, Tak and Bob met for three hours. Most of the discussion centered around Mike's re-emphasizing how the Softdisk job fit with Bob's career goals in tax consulting. "I kept dragging Bob back to the career goals he said he had and showing him that if he was serious about tax then this was an opportunity. I answered all of his objections. Pat, Tak and I left the meeting once again thinking that Bob agreed to do the job."

Meanwhile, Joe Silverman had heard about the situation and started to have doubts about the desirability of Bob joining his tax group in the fall. Since he had never worked with Bob, he approached Jane and asked for more information. Joe said the grapevine was giving him a poor impression of Bob. In Joe's view, not only was it out of line for staff to refuse assignments from partners, but also the clients' interests were the number one concern of the firm. Yet Bob did not seem to be acknowledging either of these values. If Bob would not do the Softdisk audit, then Joe thought Bob should be forced out.

Jane agreed with Joe. She was shocked by Bob's behaviour and felt, as Bob's key backer in partners' meetings, very unhappy to be caught in the middle. She called Bob into her office and told him that both Mike and Joe were furious. She told Bob that his behaviour had put him in a bad position with Joe, who was to be Bob's new managing partner. Joe was very client-oriented and was unlikely to give Bob the benefit of the doubt, because he had never seen Bob's hard work first-hand. "I told him that it didn't seem to be the right time for taking a stand. He said he believed it was a serious enough problem to resist. He was willing to leave the firm rather than work with Mike on the audit. I was shocked. I thought he enjoyed working for the firm and that he saw himself as having a good, long-term career here. I don't know if he had a personal problem about working with Mike. I've talked to Mike and he doesn't know either."

On Sunday night, July 22, Bob phoned Pat to say that he would not do the Softdisk audit. Pat informed Mike who washed his hands of the matter and obtained another senior auditor from the Richmond Hill office of James-Williams.

On the morning of July 23, Bob came to see Jane. He said he would have to resign because he could not work for Mike. He also said he realized he had ruined his relationships with the partners and could not expect good performance appraisals even if he did do the audit. Jane told him he was crazy to throw away his career at James-Williams. Jane thought that maybe he was right about getting a poor performance appraisal because Joe "was fit to be tied," but she suggested that Bob wait and talk to David who was returning from holiday the next day. Perhaps David could transfer Bob since David had a high opinion of Bob's worth to the company.

David's Decision

David Shorter returned from vacation on July 23. His first day back he met with Jane Klinck and Mike McLeod, who briefed him about the trouble with Bob. He also met with Joe Silverman who came to express his outrage about Bob's behaviour.

On July 24, David sat at his desk thinking. Bob would be here in a few minutes. David had some decisions to make. He knew that Bob was threatening to resign rather than do the Softdisk audit. He knew that both Mike and Joe were furious, but if Bob worked hard in the future, he did not think that Joe would give Bob poor performance appraisals. He knew that Jane had a high opinion of Bob and could not understand what was causing Bob to act this way.

David knew he had to make a decision that balanced the needs of all the people involved. On the one hand, Bob had offended some fairly important partners with whom David had to work and maintain good relationships. David was under no illusion that he could tell these partners what to do or think. They were all partners together, and they decided together. Besides, David agreed with them that it was inappropriate to let an employee with the capacity and the time to do a job refuse it. The Softdisk job also looked like a good opportunity for someone who wanted to specialize in tax. David did not know why Bob had turned it down.

On the other hand, Bob was a valuable employee given his skills and his potential for helping the New Enterprise Group attract business from Hong Kong investors. In addition to his knowledge, as reflected by his passing the uniform C.A. exam on his first attempt, he spoke and wrote Chinese fluently, skills relevant to James-Williams's stated goal of attracting Hong Kong business. That objective was one reason why the James-Williams office had been opened in Hong Kong. Yet the office had not done well and was now closed, so David was uncertain of the importance of Bob to the Canadian strategy.

There was the possibility of a transfer. The "Tower" (James-Williams's main group in Toronto) had been requesting that seniors interested in specializing in tax be transferred to them because they anticipated a future demand for tax specialists. Maybe that was what Bob was hoping for. David suspected that some of Bob's friends had been transferred to the Tower without any audit responsibilities and that Bob had been comparing notes with them.

David was sure of one thing. He did not want to offend the other partners in the New Enterprise Group. Perhaps he could persuade Bob to stay, and do the job, and then start tax work. Bob was an emotional kind of guy. Maybe David could get him to see reason.

DILEMMA AT DEVIL'S DEN

My name is Susan, and I'm a business student at Mt. Eagle College. Let me tell you about one of my worst experiences. I had a part-time job in the campus snack bar, The Devil's Den. At the time, I was 21 years old and a junior with a concentration in finance. I originally started working at the Den in order to earn some extra spending money. I had been working there for one semester and became upset with some of the happenings. The Den was managed by contract with an external company, College Food Services (CFS). What bothered me was that many employees were allowing their friends to take free food, and the employees themselves were also taking food in large quantities when leaving their shifts. The policy was that employees could eat whatever they liked free of charge while they were working, but it had become common for employees to leave with food and not to be charged for their snacks while off duty as well.

I felt these problems were occurring for several reasons. For example, employee wages were low, there was easy access to the unlocked storage room door, and inventory was poorly controlled. Also, there was weak supervision by the student managers and no written rules or strict guidelines. It seemed that most of the employees were enjoying "freebies," and it had been going on for so long that it was taken for granted. The problem got so far out of hand that customers who had seen others do it felt free to do it whether they knew the workers or not. The employees who witnessed this never challenged anyone because, in my opinion, they did not care and they feared the loss of friendship or being frowned upon by others. Apparently, speaking up was more costly to the employees than the loss of money to CFS for the unpaid food items. It seemed obvious to me that the employees felt too secure in their jobs and did not feel that their jobs were in jeopardy.

The employees involved were those who worked the night shifts and on the weekends. They were students at the college and were under the supervision of another student, who held the position of manager. There were approximately 30 student employees and 6 student managers on the staff. During the day there were no student managers; instead, a full-time manager was employed by CFS to supervise the Den. The employees and student managers were mostly freshmen and sophomores, probably because of the low wages, inconvenient hours (late weeknights and weekends), and the duties of the job itself. Employees were hard to come by; the high rate of employee turnover indicated that the job qualifications and the selection process were minimal.

The student managers were previous employees chosen—by other student managers and the full-time CFS day manager—based upon their ability to work and on their length of employment. They received no further formal training or written rules beyond what they had already learned by working there. The student managers were briefed on how to close the snack bar at night but still did not get the job done properly. They received authority and responsibility over events occurring during their shifts as manager, although they were never actually taught how and when to enforce it! Their increase in pay was small, from a starting pay of just over minimum wage to an additional 15 percent for student managers. Regular employees received an additional nickel for each semester of employment.

Although I only worked seven hours per week, I was in the Den often as a customer and saw the problem frequently. I felt the problem was on a large enough scale that action should have been taken, not only to correct any financial loss that the Den might have experienced but also to help give the student employees a true sense of their responsibilities, the limits of their freedom, respect for rules, and pride in their jobs. The issues at hand bothered my conscience, although I was not directly involved. I felt that the employees and customers were taking advantage of the situation whereby they could "steal" food almost whenever they wanted. I believed that I had been brought up correctly and knew "right" from "wrong," and I felt that the happenings in the Den were wrong. It wasn't fair that CFS paid for others' greediness or urges to show what they could get away with in front of their friends.

I was also bothered by the lack of responsibility of the managers to get the employees to do their work. I had seen the morning employees work very hard trying to do their jobs, in addition to the jobs the closing shift should have done. I assumed the night managers did not care or think about who worked the next day. It bothered me to think that the morning employees were suffering because of careless employees and student managers from the night before.

I had never heard of CFS mentioning any problems or taking any corrective action; therefore, I wasn't sure whether they knew what was going on, or if they were ignoring it. I was speaking to a close friend, Mack, a student manager at the Den, and I mentioned the fact that the frequently unlocked door to the storage room was an easy exit through which I had seen different quantities of unpaid goods taken out. I told him about some specific instances and said that I believed that it happened rather frequently. Nothing was ever said to other employees about this, and the only corrective action was that the door was locked more often, yet the key to the lock was still available upon request to all employees during their shifts.

Another lack of strong corrective action I remembered was when an employee was caught pocketing cash from the register. The student was neither suspended nor threatened with losing his job (nor was the event even mentioned). Instead, he was just told to stay away from the register. I felt that this weak punishment happened not because he was a good worker but because he worked so many hours and it would be difficult to find someone who would work all those hours and remain working for more than a few months. Although the incident was reported by a customer, I still felt that management should have taken more corrective action.

The attitudes of the student managers seemed to vary. I had noticed that one in particular, Bill, always got the job done. He made a list of each small duty that needed to be done, such as restocking, and he made sure the jobs were divided among the employees and finished before his shift was over. Bill also "stared down" employees who allowed thefts by their friends or who took freebies themselves; yet I had never heard of an employee being challenged verbally, nor had anyone ever been fired for these actions. My friend Mack was concerned about theft, or so I assumed, because he had taken some action about locking the doors, but he didn't really get after employees to work if they were slacking off.

I didn't think the rest of the student managers were good motivators. I noticed that they did little work themselves and did not show much control over the employees. The student managers allowed their friends to take food for free, therefore setting bad examples for the other workers, and allowed the employees to take what they wanted even when they were not working. I thought their attitudes were shared by most of the other employees: not caring about their jobs or working hard, as long as they got paid and their jobs were not threatened.

I had let the "thefts" continue without mention because I felt that no one else really cared and may even have frowned upon me for trying to take action. Management thus far had not reported significant losses to the employees so as to encourage them to watch for theft and prevent it. Management did not threaten employees with job loss, nor did they provide employees with supervision. I felt it was not my place to report the theft to management, because I was "just an employee" and I would be overstepping the student managers. Also, I was unsure whether management would do anything about it anyway—maybe they did not care. I felt that talking to the student managers or other employees would be useless, because they were either abusing the rules themselves or were clearly aware of what was going on and just ignored it. I felt that others may have frowned upon me and made it uncomfortable for me to continue working there. This would be very difficult for me, because I wanted to become a student manager the next semester and did not want to create any waves that might have prevented me from doing so. I recognized the student manager position as a chance to gain some managerial and leadership skills, while at the same time adding a great plus to my resume when I graduated. Besides, as a student manager, I would be in a better position to do something about all the problems at the Den that bothered me so much.

What could I do in the meantime to clear my conscience of the "freebies," favors to friends, and employee snacks? What could I do without ruining my chances of becoming a student manager myself someday? I hated just keeping quiet, but I didn't want to make a fool of myself. I was really stuck.

Mike Craig, an economics major from Laurentian University, was employed by the Department of Agriculture for the last three years at the government offices for this department in the downtown area of Hamilton, Ontario. His work was assessed as above average and his ability to organize and present work efficiently as noteworthy. His job involved preparing reports and statistics based on current trends and developments in farm management. Mike had a number of colleagues with whom he worked on a cooperative basis, each supplying the others with pertinent data for their studies. The organizational hierarchy under which he worked was a traditional bureaucratic structure; supervisors tended to be formal and impersonal, and there was strict adherence to procedure. It was within this environment that Mike performed his research and administrative activity.

Mike's role was very clearly defined: He was assigned a supervisor to whom he reported directly. His research work was submitted at various intervals, but current progress was frequently examined. While there was cooperative effort among the workers, there was very little enthusiasm for the work. The challenge seemed to be missing from the required task, for seldom were the results of his research implemented into a strategy for action. Instead much of the work was collated with other material for government reports and sent to Ottawa.

Mike had been dissatisfied with his job for about six months. He felt he had nowhere to go in this government position; and, since he was still single and without family responsibility, he thought it was time to look for a more challenging job. He therefore watched the newspaper for an interesting position and consulted a Toronto placement agency for opportunities in that capital city. His interests as he described them to an interviewer were in joining a growing and dynamic company, possibly a young company looking for people to train as managers in an expanding operation.

Eventually, the placement agency in Toronto uncovered an opportunity for Mike in a Willowdale firm called Electronics Unlimited. The company was new and growing in the field of electronic equipment for the home and office. It had a growing sales and distribution network, with a production operation to follow in the near future. The product line the company distributed was broad and served both the industrial and commercial markets. There were many new and innovative developments in this field and in this organization. For example, the Willowdale plant was organizing for a more sophisticated warehousing and distribution operation, and plans were forthcoming for a fully integrated marketing department.

Frank Wilson, the personnel manager, interviewed Mike Craig for the opening at Electronics Unlimited. Mike was immediately impressed not only with the organization but by the personal style of Frank Wilson, who as a manager appeared innovative and progressive. He was quite empathetic to Mike's predicament and understood the value of growth opportunities in any company. Also, the discussion on money and potential for moving up in the organization seemed very promising. Wilson further discussed the young company's need for energetic managers with ambitious goals for achievement. As he suggested, "We have outlets to develop, contacts to be made, people to recruit, and many more activities that will challenge a young college graduate."

Mike was very excited about his meeting with Frank Wilson and his application with the company. He felt sure that Wilson liked him and would offer him a job with the company. The situation, too, he thought, would be a complete change from his current position and a welcome relief from the routine. For the first time in three years, Mike was enthusiastic about his life and the prospects it held for him.

The job offer came three weeks later, and he accepted the position with a substantial increase in salary. He was due to begin in early September, and he proceeded to resign from his present position and to find an apartment in Toronto.

The first two months on his new job were a real learning experience, as Mike Craig made himself acquainted with the people and the situation. Three other recent college graduates were hired from the area. One of these was John Corrigon, a marketing major from the University of Western Ontario and a very aggressive, outgoing individual. The other two co-workers, Jim Manus and Harry Brown, had degrees from McMaster in engineering and were studying for the MBA degree in the evening. (See Exhibit 1.) The four new employees to the company all seemed to hit it off well at the start.

At a small convention room in a local motel, the four new staff members got together with the personnel director, Frank Wilson, for an introductory training program. The group met the staff and reviewed general policies and procedures of the company. Actually, the procedure manual was quite thin. Slides and promotional material were the extent of the information on the company. The meeting was more a

EXHIBIT 1			*Background Information on the New Employees*			

Name	Age	Marital Status	Education	Work Experience	Personal Interests	Career Goals
Mike Craig	27	Single	BA Econ., Laurentian U.	Dept. of Agriculture (3 years)	X-country skiing, bridge.	Management, small mfg. co.
John Corrigon	24	Single	B Comm. Marketing, U. of Western Ontario.	Sales rep., Procter & Gamble.	Water skiing, squash.	Marketing manager.
Jim Manus	26	Married, 2 children	Professional engineer (P. Eng.).	Engr. dept., City of Windsor.	Lacrosse, racquet sports, computer games.	Manager, mfg. and/ or R&D.
Harry Brown	25	Single	Professional engineer (P. Eng.).	National Electronics (1.5 years).	Tennis, golf.	R&D.

casual get-together that largely addressed the plans of the company for the next few years. Frank Wilson and other staff were heartily enthusiastic about the prospects of making it big in the electronics field. The company was described by them as young and dynamic and one that encouraged and welcomed new ideas. "We are looking for opportunists, staff that will design their own future," he continued. "We encourage open and frank communication and dialogue." He sounded impressive and exciting, and expectations were high when the meeting ended.

Afterward, on their own, the new group convened to a local tavern for informal talks on their prospects with the new company. John Corrigon seemed to lead the group as the conversation began to flow.

"Well, I think the opportunities look good here," said John. "Frank Wilson tells me that 'the sky is the limit for those that can produce.' Their freewheeling structure and interpersonal style seem interesting to me. They don't seem to be hung up on formal channels of communication. Talking to the boss seems like talking to an old friend. I think that sales and marketing could really be exciting. At P&G we got good training, but the opportunity for advancement seemed somewhat limited. I am looking forward to bigger and better things here."

Mike Craig spoke of his experience with the department of agriculture and the low level of challenge to the work. "I am looking forward to more opportunities to get involved with decision making at a management level. Frank Wilson has also suggested to me a growth opportunity with Electronics Unlimited. They are really banking on this market developing quickly over the next little while. I am looking forward to meeting customers and being delegated responsibility in the

near future. I guess I would like to move cautiously at first though."

Harry Brown had moved here from Quebec where, as he suggested, the political climate was worrisome. National Electronics also had been a growing firm, but when the headquarters moved to Winnipeg he decided to look in the Toronto area for a job. He was a quiet, reserved type who seemed caught up in his world of research and development.

"What about you, Jim," said John Corrigon, "you worked with the City of Windsor. What kind of job was that?"

"Mostly routine work of one sort or another," said Jim. "It was a job at the time when there were very few jobs to be had. I like Toronto and the challenge of this new position. We, too, were plagued with red tape and bureaucracy."

Corrigon ordered more refreshment, and the conversation continued.

"John Mitchell graduated three years ahead of me at the University of Windsor," continued Jim, "so I know him a little from college days. He is really an ambitious guy. He recruited me when he was in Windsor recently and really sold me on coming to Toronto. He has got big plans for the company and good ideas in the electronics field."

The talk continued and was dominated by Corrigon and Manus who, as it turned out, played college football against each other. A few hours passed and the group broke up with arrangements for another session of this kind.

For the first six months, the four young men were expected to get acquainted with the firm's operation and make themselves available to do reports and other tasks required by the managers. Mike Craig and

John Corrigon became involved with the distribution and sales side of the organization. Their first task was to generate a report on potential users of electronic equipment in the area on a commercial basis. Their guidelines were to examine demographic trends, store openings, potential volumes, and customer needs. The existing group had made some contacts in this area, but a thorough report and strategy were required. The managers of various departments indicated they would be available for consultation and inquiries. Craig felt very confident about this new assignment. His economics background provided him with all the knowledge to complete a thorough analysis of the area and, though he and Corrigon kept each other informed about their activities, they worked independently in different areas. Their plan was to meet before the date of submission and review their efforts.

Mike followed a steady pattern of work in the next week, confining much of his efforts to written material and research. *Stats Canada, Financial Post* survey of markets, and other books were among his sources of information. He gained confidence as the time passed. Corrigon, on the other hand, to avoid duplication spent much of his time out of the office and in the field. He visited people and talked to them of their needs and requirements. When he was in the office, he frequently visited the executive offices to gather information and to learn about the operation. Mike, for his part, had conversed with the managers only at lunch. He also would take work home with him at night and on weekends. Many of the avenues he was pursuing were of great interest to him, and he wanted to follow them through in what was now becoming a lengthy report.

Craig and Corrigon met at the end of the month just prior to their submission to management. (See Exhibit 2.) It was a brief meeting and involved Corrigon flipping through Craig's typed pages of report material. Then, behind closed doors on the Friday afternoon, two of the managers, Flemming and LeBlanc, discussed the research and activities with the two new employees. The meeting took most of the afternoon, a rather formal atmosphere prevailing throughout the early part of the encounter. Later, however, over coffee the meeting became more relaxed. Jerry Munroe, the president, came in for a moment and exchanged casual comments with the group. It seemed as though Corrigon had gotten to know Jerry, since they were on a first-name basis. Much of the discussion centered around Corrigon's ideas. He quoted names of people in key locations and presented an understanding of the needs and requirements of the area. Corrigon did not hesitate to initiate discussion and, when necessary, to focus the direction of the meeting. Craig, on the other hand,

spoke infrequently and made vague references to his written report, his confidence dwindling as the time passed. Mike was continually forced to confirm by figures much of what Corrigon was expressing in his ideas and proposals. At the conclusion of the meeting, a short summary was sketched out by Flemming and LeBlanc on a flip chart, summarizing much of what Corrigon had suggested.

Mike Craig left the office that afternoon somewhat dismayed by the results of the meeting. He felt Corrigon had dominated the discussion and not contributed his ideas in their pre-meeting discussion. He thought over the way Corrigon was so much at ease with managers and of the way they responded to him. Ideas and action were clearly becoming the bywords of this company.

In the next few weeks, many of the major ideas of the meeting were broken down into smaller areas of focus; both Craig and Corrigon were left alone on their job without too much direction. The managers continued to hurry through one task after another. Potential customers were given full details of the company aspirations, and frequently Corrigon was asked to entertain customers and show them the operations. His aggressive and outgoing style seemed most suited to this task. Craig was given small reports to make and was generally left to muddle in the details. He would ask Corrigon for support from time to time on some of the matters, but seldom could he sit him down long enough for a meaningful exchange of ideas or plans. At the bimonthly meetings, Corrigon was never short of a comment or an idea for a particular project.

The manufacturing side of Electronics Unlimited was now coming on line for full production. Harry Brown and Jim Manus were working well under Rafuse and Mitchell in their departments. They had settled in their own offices and were very productive in their field, developing changes and ideas for the product line. Both Rafuse and Mitchell were satisfied with the new employees, particularly since they provided current ideas for their work. They had already been invited to Montreal to visit the main plant and production operation.

Flemming and LeBlanc continued to make good use of Corrigon and Craig, who were busy on the marketing side of the operation. However, nothing was clearly defined in this company. John Mitchell, for example, frequently provided data and reports for Paul LeBlanc on distribution networks for the area. The organization was run on a flexible pattern of interactions and responsibilities.

Corrigon continued his aggressive style and developed an excellent rapport with Jim Flemming. They were in the process of hiring salespeople for the field, and Corrigon was given an opportunity to conduct

EXHIBIT 2   *Organizational Chart*

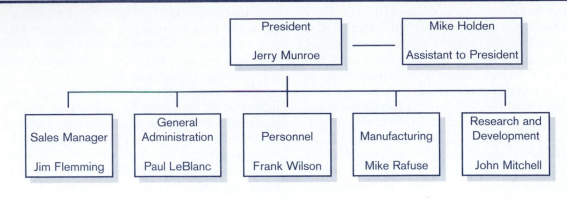

the interviewing and initial screening. Craig, on the other hand, seemed always ready for more reports and analyzing data, largely because he had not been asked to take other responsibilities.

Mitchell and Rafuse also had begun to take advantage of Craig's report writing. By now, however, Craig had had enough and become quite discouraged at these frequent requests. He began to wonder just what he was going to be expected to do on this "dynamic job." This uncertainty bothered him.

At the same time, Corrigon was now beginning to annoy him with his abrasive style. He would ask for information and request of Craig routine jobs a secretary could do. Craig resented these requests but, in the interest of the company, would complete the tasks despite the fact that increased effort at establishing rapport with the sales manager, Flemming, produced no results.

After six months on the job, Craig had still not found it a satisfying experience. He was determined not to give up, however, and proceeded to present lengthy and detailed studies of market trends and other reports that would help the company. All the managers took advantage of his services to the point where Craig was frequently working on weekends.

Corrigon, well on his way to organizing a sales staff, also requested a lengthy analysis of sales potential for the company. Craig had worked himself into a position of complete frustration. He didn't feel he was there just to write reports but rather to become more involved with managing the company. He felt he was receiving little recognition for his contribution, while Corrigon and the other two engineers were progressing much more rapidly.

Craig's frustrations turned to anger as he became more disenchanted with his job at Electronics Unlimited. One day he refused to write a report for Corrigon, which earned him a sharp rebuke from Flemming. This upset him, and he felt he had to redeem himself.

The company had been growing and stabilizing in the months that had passed. The retail outlets had been contacted and connections organized to complete the network of distribution. New products had been developed by the company and were marketed in an effective manner. The administrative staff had been growing to meet the requirements of the production and sales force. An incentive system for the sales force had been designed in the Willowdale office and had received wide recognition throughout the company. Corrigon was instrumental in this effort and was appropriately rewarded for his contribution. A small achievement award was presented to Corrigon for his part in the design of the plan that had been implemented. The award was presented to him at an office get-together.

The event further deflated Craig's self-image in the growing company. What little spirit or camaraderie that had existed between the four original employees who had arrived together had been lost by this time. Mike Craig had retreated into a gloomy silence, anticipating a difficult time in an upcoming evaluation that had been announced.

Notice had come to the desks of the respective employees that they would be evaluated in the next month by the managers. It would be a formal evaluation and one that would take place in their offices over coffee. It would be verbal and based on discussion, rather than a written document channeled through personnel.

Craig looked glum as he peered up from his desk after reading the memo, one of the first of its kind. Corrigon, in his usual attitude and cockiness, suggested that he would have to get the boss a bottle of good Scotch but that he really didn't have much to worry about.

Craig had less secure feelings about the whole procedure. He had this terrible feeling that the whole thing was going to be poorly handled. In a brief discussion with Flemming one afternoon, he made inquiries about the method of evaluation, pointing out the traditional function of personnel administration. Flemming laughed at this idea, responding that around here they worked to get things done and did not worry too much about who did the evaluation!

The evaluation day arrived and Craig was assigned to Rafuse, the person he felt was least involved with his work. The interview and discussion went smoothly but not very cordially. There were many silent moments during the course of the interview, and he went away feeling that his work was regarded as less than satisfactory. Rafuse had hinted that the company's interest lay in more outgoing individuals. Craig was left with mixed feelings about the company and his future!

Indeed, Craig felt the time had come for a confrontation with the management of the company, and he proceeded to make an appointment with the personnel officer for a lengthy discussion about his future. He felt he might be able to get some straight answers from Frank Wilson, but he knew that he was taking a chance in finding out the worst. Some hard discussions would follow.

24 ESTELLA RIOS: PERFORMANCE PROBLEMS AT THE TOLL AUTHORITY

When the personnel director of the Toll Authority (TA) asked Estella Rios to take the position of supervisor in the accounting unit, she was delighted. Rios had just finished her fourth year with the TA and was pleased with her progress. She had spent her first two years on a computer aided design project, and had subsequently moved to a design unit team where she helped the deputy commissioner of the TA handle all the intergovernmental transactions necessary to issue bonds for financing new state road and bridge construction. Rios's work had brought her into contact with many people in other state agencies and private firms in the northeast. She had even worked with people in the governor's office. The new offer was concrete evidence that her career was taking off.

Rios was 31 years old. A second-generation Hispanic whose parents emigrated from the Dominican Republic to New York City when she was 10, Rios was bright and ambitious. After earning a degree in civil engineering from a state university in New York, she worked for two years in the design unit of New York State's Department of Transportation (DOT), where she made good use of her recent training in computer aided design. She loved the technical side of things, but also had ambitions to become involved in management. The work force at DOT was mature (average age 49) and 81 percent white male. Rios knew she would have to earn further credentials if she wanted to move into management, and she had completed half of an executive MBA program at a college in Albany when she was offered the toll authority job in another northeastern state. Although Rios had felt some misgivings about leaving DOT and going to a different state government, and had not been happy about interrupting her work on the MBA, she had felt that the move would be a step up.

Rios didn't take long to say she'd be happy to transfer to the TA's accounting unit. The promotion meant a 13 percent pay increase and a little more flexibility in her schedule. Rios would now be on the Financial Division's management team, which would give her a bigger window on the organization and its environment. At 31, Rios was eager to do and know more. This new job looked like a solid opportunity.

A Sketch of the Toll Authority

The TA was created as a nonprofit, financially self-supporting organization by the state legislature to serve the public. It collected all the revenue from state toll roads and bridges and used its revenue to build and repair roads and bridges and supplement federal and county funding for infrastructure projects within the state. Through a legislative quirk, the TA also handled the retirement funds for all 960 of its employees. The retirement funds alone exceeded $230 million. TA employees earned slightly more than their counterparts in state agencies and slightly less than their counterparts in the private sector. Most TA employees felt that job security was good and that benefits were excellent; in addition most regarded their jobs as acceptable in terms of workload and quality of work life.

The accounting department kept track of the TA's money, held the retirement funds in high interest-bearing accounts, and occasionally embarked on a bond issue to raise funds for capital investment projects. The TA also audited the local toll offices across the state. The TA was frequently under fire from the state legislature, which believed the TA should hand the management of its revenues over to the State Division of the Budget, an organization that the legislature could influence directly. Thus the work of the accounting unit was vital to the TA's success not only financially but also politically, since internal financial problems could result in a loss of political legitimacy.

Rios would be supervising the work of fourteen accountants and auditors—seven in the central office, four in the northern regional office, and three in the southern regional office. The accounting unit kept track of all revenue and expenditures and made sure the TA's money was invested to ensure a maximum rate of return. Some of the small "accounts," the little toll bridges in the state's southern townships, were the hardest to manage. Rios was told that some of those townships had, over the years, been known to skim a portion of the revenue by keeping it off the books. Field audits conducted by TA accountants were supposed to detect problems and prevent irregularities, but the audits were not always effective. The local field offices were protective of their turfs, and auditors from the central office were not welcomed with open arms. Joanna Rice, personnel director at the TA, hoped that Rios would be able to improve relations with the field.

Although Rios had confidence in her abilities (her previous job with the TA had made her familiar with the TA's accounting and auditing procedures and she had a strong quantitative background), she knew that a few eyebrows had been raised when she was brought in to supervise the accounting unit. In the past, the promotions had always come from within, and a seasoned accountant had been rewarded with the supervisor's position. Rios, who was not an accountant, knew that many would feel she had gotten the job because she was a female minority. It was no secret that the TA had been criticized by the Governor's Office of Employee Relations for having a work force in which minorities and women were underrepresented. She knew she would have to earn her legitimacy with good performance.

Enter Ted Barlow

After about a month on the job—in early January—Rios faced her first real challenge: Glenn Streck, director of the financial unit at The Dunns Memorial Bridge, called Rios to complain about the way the team leader for the annual audit of the Bridge's offices had conducted the audit. The team leader's name was Ted Barlow, a name that would surface often as the months went by.

BARLOW'S BACKGROUND

Barlow, who worked as field auditor and funds accountant in the central office, had joined the Toll Authority during a time of expansion. Because salaries in the private sector were slightly higher, competition for qualified accountants and auditors had always been difficult for the TA. For entry-level accountants, the state required a bachelor's degree, with at least 18 hours of credit in accounting courses. Most of the accountants in Rios's unit were field auditors, and most had secured their jobs by going to night school and studying accounting. Barlow, who had graduated from the state university system with an accounting major, came to the TA with four years' experience with a manufacturing company. He was very bright, and fundamentally competent.

Despite his credentials, Barlow was the most controversial and talked-about person in the unit, and he had a reputation for being close to controversial issues. Even his friends in the agency said that his work had sometimes suffered in the past because of all the union issues he became involved in. Four years before Rios came to the TA, Barlow had been elected as an officer in the Public Employees Federation, the union that represented most TA employees. Barlow served in that position for two years. In his first year, the TA set a new record for the number of grievances filed by employees: 26. The annual average was 16. No one accused Barlow of being directly responsible for the high number of grievances, but he was heavily involved in some of the hearings that took place as part of the grievance process. Some colleagues complained to the Personnel Department that Barlow was leaving agency work unfinished because of his union-related activities. The Personnel Department tried to deal with the issue diplomatically, not wanting to upset the already strained relationships between union officers and the agency's management. Eventually, the storm passed, without anything having been said to Ted Barlow or other members of the union committee. Although some TA workers regarded Barlow as a champion of employee rights and interests, others were highly critical, claiming that he was sometimes "disloyal" to the agency. At the time of Rios's promotion, Barlow was no longer an officer of the union, but he remained closely connected to the union leadership and was frequently consulted on labor-management issues.

THE DUNNS MEMORIAL BRIDGE INCIDENT

The general thrust of Streck's complaint about Barlow's handling of the Dunns Memorial Bridge audit was that he was guilty of "insensitivity and pushiness." Specifically, Streck claimed that Barlow had given the unit insufficient lead time to prepare for the audit and then had asked for almost random information, giving Streck's people little opportunity to explain themselves.

The day after hearing Streck's complaint, Rios talked to Barlow about the incident:

Rios: Ted, I received a call yesterday from Glenn Streck at Dunns Memorial. He had some concerns about the way the field audit was handled. In fact, he was pretty unhappy about it. He said that your team had given his people very little notice and then pushed them through the audit. He didn't think you had given him enough opportunity to answer questions and explain things. I was pretty concerned about his call.

Barlow: Well, let me help you understand what's happening. Streck's office isn't covered with glory to begin with. He has been written up twice in three years for being out of compliance with some basic stuff, and, yeah, he gripes about not having enough notice. We go out of our way not to give those people much notice, because they will cook the books if they have time. We like to come in fast and hard and find out what's going on. I let him answer our questions. He oughta buy me a beer for not writing him up. We found some stuff. The books looked better this year so we gave them some verbal advice and reprimands and let it go. Gee, talk about getting off easy. Streck should have called you and said me and my team were the greatest.

> To: Ted Barlow
>
> From: Estella Rios
>
> Date: February 20, 1993
>
> Subject: Notification of Substandard Work
>
> I have talked with you previously about problems with your work. Again, your work has caused problems with our audits and reports with the state. Your work on the Queller account has caused a $34,788 shortfall in interest revenue.
>
> If there are any more troubles with your work, as one who must account to the citizens for their money, I will have to take action to protect those resources. Please take more care. If you are having any problems with your workload or assignments, please come in and talk to me about them.

Rios: Well, OK. I just hope we weren't out of line in anyway. We're under heavy scrutiny, and our personnel director keeps asking me what I'm doing to improve relations with the field offices.

Barlow: It's going OK. We have to keep a grip on these characters or we'll have real scandals on our hands. Believe me, it's not all bad when the field offices complain about the way we treat them. We get too cozy and we're not doing our jobs.

Barlow's responses seemed reasonable and intelligent to Rios, and she felt reassured.

THE QUELLER TURNPIKE INCIDENT

In mid-February Barlow's name came up again, this time in a memo from the office of the state controller. Barlow was in charge of revenue management for the Queller Turnpike. An audit by the controller's office showed that funds had been left in lower interest-yielding accounts and had run up a shortfall of $34,788 in a 2-year period compared with what an optimal investment policy would have returned. The memo included a reprimand for such "negligent handling of the public trust," and, of course, a copy was sent to the TA's commissioner, Hyde Randall. Fortunately, this incident escaped the notice of the local media; however, by the end of the month, the problem had cost Rios more than one sleepless night. Rios again called Barlow in and had a chat about the Queller account. Barlow responded that the TA must take some responsibility for the problem. The workload of the accountants was too heavy, and their responsibilities too diverse. Barlow put it this way:

> You have to realize that this kind of thing has happened before and it'll happen again. We have too many things to do. We do the field audits on all the offices in the state, and at the same time, they keep a gun at our heads and tell us we have to manage the retirement funds. The financial markets are volatile. It would take a couple of full-time fund managers to stay on top of where the money ought to be each minute. If I didn't have access to some pros in New York City who give me free advice, we would do a lot worse on where the money should go when the markets change direction. Listen, I'm not the one that could be left out to dry on this issue. The TA isn't exercising "due diligence" in managing retirement funds. If you want details, I can supply them.

Rios's instincts told her that the Queller incident might be symptomatic of deeper problems, so she decided to keep careful records. She felt strongly that Ted might be trying to cover up for his own poor performance. He always seemed to have reasonable explanations about complaints or problems, but Rios was becoming uncomfortable. Immediately after her conversation with Barlow about the Queller funds, Rios sent a follow-up memo to him and put a copy in the file. She also made a note to herself to pursue the issue with various managers at the TA. The memo, the text of which is above, did not mention any of the points Barlow made in his defense. Rios was not convinced that his defense was valid.

The Whistle Blower Incident

Rios decided to do some research on Barlow's history. She began talking to people and looking through the files. The personnel file on Ted Barlow recorded an incident Rios had heard about, but never understood. About a year earlier, the TA had received an unfavorable report during an audit by the State Controller's Office. Some money in the employee retirement fund had been mismanaged, resulting in an estimated loss of $160,000 of potential interest revenue. No funds had been stolen. As in the Queller case, the loss had resulted from keeping funds in low interest-bearing accounts for too long. Before the organization had time to react, the story was leaked to the press.

There were strong indications that Ted Barlow was responsible for the press leak. The journalist who had written the article about the mismanagement of funds was a good friend of his, and Ted had been quoted as making some "very critical comments" about the situation. Of the employees with knowledge of the information that had been leaked, only Barlow had had continual access to the facts of the case as it developed. All of the others had been on vacation at least part of the time.

The personnel file contained a report by one of Barlow's co-workers claiming that the day before a newspaper report appeared revealing some of the facts of the case, Ted had been overheard talking on the telephone about those same facts. This sequence, as well as the knowledge that Ted was the only one with full access to the facts, was enough to convince Ted's supervisor that there was a strong case against Ted. Although the supervisor never confronted Ted about the situation directly, he wrote a memo to file in which he stated his belief that Barlow was the source of the leak. When someone from another unit asked Ted about the rumors, Ted neither confirmed nor denied them. He simply said, "Whatever you think is fine, but you can't prove anything in a court of law, and you and I both know that the law protects anybody who makes this kind of stuff public anyway."

Even if Ted's responsibility for the press leak could be substantiated, he would probably be shielded from any disciplinary action by state and federal legislation protecting whistle blowers. In fact, Rios suspected that the report of the press leak incident included in Barlow's file was illegal and that Barlow could take action against the TA for the material in the file. Rios was not even sure how the documents got there. She learned by talking to people in the legal office that top management had told people to "stay away from Barlow and take no recriminating actions." She made a note to discuss the issue with the Toll Authority's chief counsel. She also had some frustration about the TA's role in the situation. Commissioner Randall was outraged that the problem had been made public before he had a chance to investigate it, but Rios felt that such problems probably *should* become public

before all the damage could be controlled by internal management. She also had the impression that the TA, while not "punishing" Barlow, probably shunned him, at least unofficially. That behavior was hardly professional or helpful. It provided support for Barlow's apparent opinion that the leadership of the TA could not be trusted.

Barlow and the Toll Authority System

Rios, however, was more worried about Barlow's use of information than she was about the TA's use of information. Barlow had been heard to say that he knew "where the bodies are buried around here," implying that if some kind of action were taken on his performance, he could retaliate because he knew where people were vulnerable. This threat concerned Rios, whose knowledge of the TA's history was so limited. Barlow seemed to Rios to take a very political view of issues. For him, controversies seemed reducible to who had power. Those who had power would prevail over those who did not.

Rios also wondered about the truth of Barlow's charges that employees in other units were "milking their jobs" and doing substandard work. She wanted to make her unit more results-oriented, and she wanted to reward merit. But how did her standards compare with those of other departments? She wasn't sure. When she looked at Barlow's work, he did seem to have real performance problems, but when she talked to him about his performance, he blamed the system for most of his difficulties, saying that the system set people up to fail or make mistakes. The other accountants had neither Ted's problems nor his strengths. They seldom discussed the big issues he brought up. They audited the field offices, managed the funds, and turned in their reports. They made fewer mistakes, and were more positive about the system, but Rios felt they had fewer ideas on how to improve the process.

Apparently, Barlow really did know a lot about state government and the informal network of relationships and information that people used to get work done and make decisions. Some of his claims might have been bluster, but some had been substantiated by the homework Rios did. People stepped lightly around Barlow. He intimidated them, with his technical knowledge (most people, even in the accounting department, were only slightly computer literate) and he had an uncanny memory for details. He also seemed to know at least half the people in the state legislature. In the spring of 1992, the TA's legal staff was officially reprimanded by the Division of the Budget for their handling of a suit brought against the TA by a private contractor. While working on a new bridge, the contractor's son had been killed by a car. (The TA had responsibility for traffic control on all toll road and bridge construction sites.) When the suit was filed, the response from the TA's Legal Department had been slow, which only made matters worse. During this time, Barlow had told several people in the TA about conversations between the contractor and staff members in the attorney general's office. From all Rios could determine from her own sources, his reports were accurate and current. Ted Barlow had an effective information network.

Barlow and Routine Job Performance

As the weeks and months passed, Ted Barlow continued to be a challenge to Rios. More performance problems surfaced. Rios, a stickler for deadlines, didn't like getting work handed to her at the last minute. During her first month as supervisor she had shortened the deadline for monthly audit reports by 2 days. She wanted more time to review them before passing them upstairs. Barlow, however, continued to get his reports in at the last minute, usually only one day before Rios had to send them on. In addition, although Barlow's reports were usually insightful and provided helpful recommendations and posed thought-provoking questions, they were quickly written and sometimes lacked basic details. Rios had a strong personal reaction to what she considered "inconsiderate and unprofessional behavior" on Ted's part. She spotted Ted one afternoon by the water cooler and told him he had to be more careful about deadlines. Ted put the blame on people from the field, claiming that they were often late in giving him the information he needed to complete the reports. Rios became irritated and impatient.

In January, her first month on the job, Rios had met with Barlow to discuss his "insensitive, pushy" work on the Dunns Bridge audit. Rios recorded the date and subject of the meeting in her planner. The Queller case hit the fan in February. In March, another monthly audit report had prompted a phone call from the controller's office complaining that a small section of data was missing. Later in March, Ted had missed an important meeting with people from the accounting office of the Jameson Turnpike. Rios covered for him. Ted also missed a March meeting

with a productivity team from another agency; his excuse was that the team had not set up a definite appointment time with him. Rios noticed that he was clearly unprepared for a monthly briefing in early April. In addition, Ted could be disruptive in meetings. Always talkative and verbally aggressive, recently he had been even more aggressive, trying to dominate discussions more often and growing impatient when decisions did not go his way. Rios often agreed with the positions he took, but was frustrated by his lack of diplomacy.

Barlow's performance record was not totally negative; it also contained some pluses. In his file was a February letter from Grace Hendricks, a manager at the State Insurance Fund, thanking Ted for his "very professional handling" of an audit conducted on another state agency, an audit that required special cooperation from the TA. When the governor's office sent a consulting team to interview people in public agencies and identify new ideas for streamlining work and improving services, Barlow, according to the team leader, came up with better suggestions than anyone else interviewed at the TA.

Another plus concerned Ted's training of a new accountant during the first quarter. Rios's brief chat with the new employee revealed a positive assessment of Barlow's work and his knowledge of accounting and auditing procedures. No one disputed Barlow's technical proficiency. He had been one of the first auditors to take a laptop computer into the field to conduct an audit, and he was often the person audit teams conferred with on technical problems.

Rios had no doubts about Barlow's abilities, but she felt that he was currently running on intelligence and experience, not on consistency and motivation. The accounting unit had recently added three people to its staff, and Rios had been instrumental in getting the new hires. The new employees often conferred with Barlow on technical issues, and Rios was worried about his influence on them. She knew his advice and expertise were solid, but feared that the negative effect of his example and attitude would outweigh any positives.

Insights from the Field

In April, Rios was faced with the task of submitting her unit's performance evaluations, due at the end of the month. The other thirteen ratings were not going to be too difficult, but Ted Barlow's was. Rios decided to get some input from Barlow's co-workers, and chose the five who knew him best, the members of his audit team. Following are the points made by Barlow's co-workers that Rios thought most relevant to the case.

1. Ted was a "knowledgeable guy" and "very bright," but his work was "spotty." Sometimes his audits were thorough, and sometimes sloppy. As one co-worker said, "On a good day, Ted is as sharp as anyone in the unit; on a bad day, he would help everyone by staying home. Fortunately, he still has more good days than bad days." (Three of the five team members were surprised that Ted had not had some kind of disciplinary action taken against him.)

2. The past supervisor was nice, but not strong-willed enough to try to change Ted's habits, which had been developed over years under weak supervision. It was easier to look the other way, at least in the short run. People *had* looked the other way, and as a consequence, the unit seemed to have lost a sense of mutual accountability. One employee said, "I don't think we care enough about each other and our work to really hold one another accountable."

3. Rios was clearly perceived as more "results oriented" than the former supervisor had been. Three employees said that they sensed pressure was mounting in the organization to improve performance and prevent costly errors, but this new emphasis would require better management and lots more feedback on how people were doing in their jobs.

4. Everyone agreed that Ted had been a good contributor "at times" to the TA and that he frequently provided valuable technical information, but that over the past 6 months his work had been noticeably weak.

5. Ted had never raised the issue of personal problems, but the word in the department was that he was going through an ugly divorce and custody battle. Ted was known as a guy who liked to have a drink after work, and sometimes at lunch. Two people volunteered that Ted had recently returned pretty "high" from a birthday luncheon for a friend in another unit, and that at other times he seemed to be "under the influence" while at work.

6. Shortly before Rios's arrival, Barlow had taken all of his accrued sick leave over a 2-month period, but several people reported that Barlow had been seen around the community during that time "functioning well."

Time to Decide

Although Barlow's co-workers had not explicitly said so, Rios had the impression that Barlow was drinking heavily on a regular basis. The drinking issue was a particularly troublesome one. Substance abusers in the public sector had more protection than those in the private sector. For example, the Supreme Court had ruled that federal employers can only dismiss an alcoholic "who refuses treatment, or repeatedly fails in treatment." No one, to Rios's knowledge, had ever broached the issue with Barlow. She suspected that if drinking were affecting Barlow's performance, she had a legal, as well as ethical, responsibility to take the initiative and offer help through the Toll Authority's employee assistance program. On the other hand, she was wary about how to approach Barlow. He knew the law and the TA's culture better than she did. If she handled things wrong, Barlow might be able to take legal action.

Very soon Rios would have to submit formal performance evaluations on all the workers under her supervision, including Barlow. The TA's policy was to dismiss employees who received overall ratings of under 2.3, unless there were extenuating circumstances. Unit managers, such as Estella Rios, had the authority to set up short-term periods of probation for employees who received unsatisfactory ratings, but these arrangements had to be approved by the division manager. Unit managers were not allowed to dismiss permanent salaried employees. They could recommend dismissal, but the action had to be taken by the director of personnel. Barlow had just completed his fifth year with the TA. His performance ratings for the previous four years are listed in Table 1. (The TA hired new employees in May, which meant that they were not given a performance evaluation until they had been on the job for a year.) Average ratings for TA employees correlated with their tenure are given in Table 2.

Not only did Rios have to decide what rating to give Barlow, but, as required by the TA, to write a memo to him explaining the rationale behind the rating given. The performance evaluation for Ted Barlow was the most difficult task that Rios had faced in her new position.

TABLE 1

Summary of Ted Barlow's Performance Ratings for the Years 1989–1992

	CATEGORIES						
Year	#1	#2	#3	#4	#5	#6	Average
1989	3	3	4	3	2	3	3
1990	3	3	3	3	3	3	3
1991	3	3	4	3	3	3	3.1
1992	3	3	4	3	3	3	3.1

Scale: Rating of 1 = unacceptable
          Rating of 5 = ideal

Categories:
1. Level of knowledge in required field
2. Effectiveness in working with others
3. Degree of initiative and self-directedness
4. Consistency and dependability in doing quality work
5. Willingness to share skills and information
6. Overall effectiveness

TABLE 2

Average TA Employee Ratings Correlated with Number of Years with Company

Year	Average Overall Rating	% in Unacceptable Range
10	4.2	0
9	4.1	0
8	4.2	0
7	4.1	0
6	4.1	0
5	3.9	2
4	3.6	0
3	3.5	4
2	3.3	17
1	2.9	26

EVERGREEN WILLOWS

Evergreen Willows, a new convalescent home, had been in operation for several months. The large one-story building, which had been specially constructed for its purpose, was divided into two identical wings designated A and B. In the center of the building, separating the wing, was a large living room, chapel, offices, and a middle wing, which included the kitchen, patients' dining room, and employees' dining room. A and B wings consisted of a nurse's station in the center with a corridor of patients' rooms to each side (see Exhibit 1).

Each nurse's station served the patients for its wing, and each was under the direction of a charge nurse. Other nurses and nurse's aides worked under the charge nurse. From the opening day, each wing had been staffed separately. The director of nurses had assigned the more experienced, older aides to A wing, where she planned to locate sicker patients. She assigned the less experienced aides to B wing, which was to have patients who were more ambulatory. Except on rare occasions, A-wing staff did not work on B wing or B-wing staff on A wing.

The day shift on B wing consisted of one charge nurse and four nurse's aides. Normally the charge nurse was Jenny, a young registered nurse who had had no previous experience as a charge nurse before working at the home. On her days off, she was replaced by Sue, a licensed practical nurse who worked part-time. The nurse's aides had rotating days off each week so that, except when someone was sick and had to be replaced, the same aides were usually on duty at the same time. The B-wing aides were of similar age and experience, having been hired at the same time. All lived in the local community and tended to see one another socially after hours.

Jenny's duties as charge nurse included dispensing medications, keeping charts and records up-to-date, and supervising the work of the aides. Actual patient care was the responsibility of the aides. Most of the B-wing patients were at least partially ambulatory. Caring for them involved assisting them in bathing, dressing, walking, and feeding, or what nurses call "activities of daily living." The aides also liked to visit the lonelier patients whenever time permitted. A number of the patients wandered around during the day, and it was often necessary for the aides to look for them, which consumed a great deal of time, considering the size of the building. Jenny, in giving her medications, ranged all over the building in search of patients and was not always to be found on the wing.

From the opening of the home, Jenny had found there was barely enough time in the day for the work she had to do. She did not give detailed instructions to the aides, and they developed their own routines in caring for the patients. One new aide even said that "it took me weeks before I felt I knew what I was supposed to be doing." Usually, they would separate by corridor, each doing the work they saw needing to be done. All helped in passing out breakfast and dinner trays, feeding patients, and in answering lights when a patient called for assistance. All of the B-wing aides kept busy, although sometimes there were complaints by some who felt they were "getting stuck" with the more unpleasant jobs because no one else would do them.

Nonetheless, the atmosphere on the wing was friendly. The aides often spoke of how much they enjoyed the patients. While most of the aides had not sought a job working with older patients, even those who might have preferred a job in a hospital caring for younger patients soon discovered that the "old folks" were interesting people. Consequently, there was much friendly contact between patients and aides as well as among aides and among patients. The patients enjoyed the atmosphere, although sometimes their families worried about the way they were allowed to wander about.

In contrast, A-wing patients were for the most part bedridden and required more actual nursing care. In fact, if a patient on B wing took sick, the home's policy was to transfer that patient to A wing where there was a larger staff/patient ratio. The staff consisted of a charge nurse, Elizabeth, and two or three RNs or LPNs and six aides. The charge nurse took care of duties at the nurse's station and drug room, while the other nurses dispensed drugs and did treatments. The nurse's aides did patient care. Many of the patients were unable to walk or stand and helping them up to a chair involved heavy lifting. Fewer patients than on B wing were dressed, most wearing johnnies and bathrobes, and most remained in their rooms. Many of the patients who were confined to their rooms rang for the aides frequently throughout the day, often for only minor requests.

Elizabeth was an older, more experienced nurse than Jenny and supervised the aides working under her in a strict manner. Each morning the aides were paired in teams of two and assigned to 16 specific patients. The assignments were standardized, and the A-wing aides usually worked systematically and on a schedule to complete their work. There was little change from day today, and patients were generally taken care of at the same time each day and were accustomed to this. Working in teams of two gave each aide someone to assist her when lifting was necessary.

EXHIBIT 1   *Evergreen Willows Floor Plan*

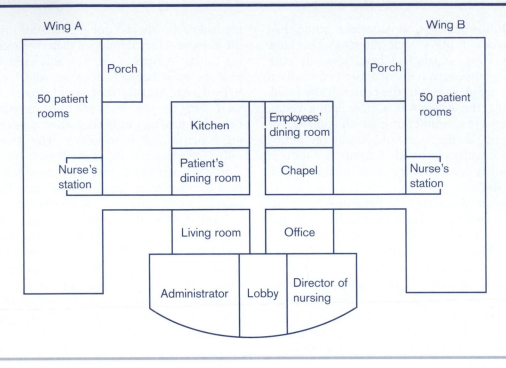

Assignments included patients located far apart on the floor, but aides usually cared only for the patients on their assignment sheets. When another patient asked for assistance, they would often answer, "Wait until your nurse gets here." Elizabeth kept a close watch on her aides and was very critical of the work they did. Sometimes she could be heard over the intercom saying something like, "Girls, there are five lights on A wing." She insisted that the girls maintain a professional relationship with the patients. While the atmosphere on the wing was far from homey, the sick patients received good technical care and their families felt a good deal of confidence in the quality of care provided on A wing.

The administrator and the director of nurses were cheerful and apparently well liked by the nursing staff. They appeared at meetings held approximately every other week for in-service educational training or to update employees on issues of importance. Their response to the work done by the nurses and the aides was favorable. However, they were rarely seen on the wings, and they delegated a great deal of responsibility to the charge nurses.

After several months the director of nurses announced at one of the inservice meetings that aides would now have assignments alternating them between the two wings. While she felt completely satis-fied with the performance of both wings, she felt the aides should be more versatile and experienced with all types of patients.

When this new plan went into effect, a series of problems began to develop between the head nurses and aides of the two wings. B-wing aides on A wing found themselves answering lights not belonging to their own patients and falling behind in their own scheduled work. While working on one corridor, an aide would often forget those patients on the other corridor assigned to her, and those patients frequently had their lights on and unanswered for long periods. They complained to the head nurse when they had to wait. Thus, the B-wing aides were under constant criticism from Elizabeth, but when they tried to talk to her they found she was not listening.

The help Elizabeth had from the other nurses allowed her more free time than Jenny had. She often was seen laughing and talking with the other nurses, but she did not socialize with the aides.

When on their own wing, the B-wing aides now found they had to do even more work than usual. Most of the aides from A wing were lost on B and needed much help in caring for the B-wing patients. Nothing was written down, and Jenny was too busy or not around to help them; so the responsibility of orienting them fell to the B-wing aides.

Stating that there was "nothing to do" on B wing, a few of the A-wing aides took frequent coffee breaks. The regular aides from B wing could not find them when they needed help or did not have the time to go to the employees' dining room to get them. One incident on B wing occurred when an aide was assisting a patient to bed, and the patient slipped to the floor. There was no one nearby, nor did anyone answer the emergency light when the aide called. The aide had to leave the patient to get help. When this situation was reported to Jenny, she reprimanded the A-wing aide who was not on the floor where she was supposed to be and recommended to the director of nurses that she be fired. It was the decision of the director that she "should be entitled to a second chance." The situation did not improve.

A great deal of resentment developed among the nursing staff. Several of the aides, including those considered to be the best workers, quit or began looking for other jobs. The attitude of the administrator and director of nurses was one of little concern. In the words of the director of nursing: "We have many applicants for each vacancy. Anyone can be replaced. Our turnover rate of employees here is better than in most nursing homes."

26 THE FORGOTTEN GROUP MEMBER

Frank Rasmussen put down the telephone receiver and leaned back in the comfortable swivel chair. He put his hands behind his head, interlocked his fingers, and raised his feet onto the desk. The traffic on University Avenue three floors below him was heavy but he was not really thinking about it. He thought of Janet Simpson, who had just called. She had sounded frustrated and even somewhat defiant. "I cannot fathom why the other group members are against me. I know that you have assigned a group project, but I would like to request permission to do an individual project."

His course outline stated that Business 388 was "heavily group-oriented," and his consent to Janet's request would essentially contradict the conceptual approach he had chosen. He could do it, using the rationale he had proposed so often, that the organization needs to be as flexible as possible in trying to meet the needs of individual members. Either way, there seemed to be a catch. He was not sure at this point how to address the problem.

The Setting and Environment

The University of Ontario School of Business and Economics caters to approximately 1000 students. It has acquired an enviable reputation in the province of Ontario and normally has to turn down numerous applications each year, even though the minimum average percentage required for entry is 83 percent.

Students are exposed to larger classes and a general management program in the first two years of their Bachelor in Business Administration (B.B.A.) program. Classes are smaller in the third year and number 35 on average. Courses are "functional" in orientation and involve areas such as human resources, marketing, production operations, finance, and accounting.

Some of the classes in the third year are run on a group basis. These entail group discussions in class as well as out-of-class group assignments. It is optional for the instructor to have a group-oriented class, but in the last five years departments have been urging instructors to have some measure of group work to increase interaction and interpersonal skills.

Frank Rasmussen teaches Organizational Behaviour and he believes in the benefits of group work. He particularly espouses use of the "classroom as organization" model proposed by Cohen,[1] although this is modified to suit the purposes of the class. Thus, members of the class are designated employees of the "Enterprise Corporation." They receive a mission statement and a job description which they have to sign (Exhibits 1 and 2). Duties include task assignments such as completion of a case analysis by the group as well as maintenance issues such as helping peers in the group. A group facilitator is also selected and the system in this respect varies from semester to semester. There could be a structured set of procedures such as having candidates for the position submit to interviews by Rasmussen. This particular semester saw the facilitator being chosen by the group itself.

Whatever the mode of selection, the facilitator is charged with coordination of the group's activities. Many meetings are held out of class and the facilitator sets the time and place based on input from the members. He/she informs all concerned about meetings and other plans, and then generally initiates activities when members gather together. The participation mark for the course is 20 percent of the total. Rasmussen awards members a number of points out of ten and the facilitator is responsible for the other half. In addition, the instructor scores the facilitator out of twenty and criteria for judging include response of the group in terms of readiness for in-class discussions as well as the quality of the group assignment. As invariably happens, some groups have problems, e.g., the free-rider effect, and the facilitator could then be partially evaluated on how well the situation is handled.

The students who enter the business programme and succeed until third year are high achievers and are marked by the desire to do the best that they possibly can. Group members try to give their optimum and facilitators normally strive for the best group possible. Students aim for A's because they realize the impact that a record such as this could have on their ultimate careers. There is a competitive environment and group work, including facilitating, is taken very seriously. In addition, although it may appear to be a minor point, Rasmussen hands out an award at the end of the semester for the best group and peer pressure is such that there is always a notable effort by each group to claim the prize.

The Enterprise Corporation consequently uses an autonomous group conceptual base. Rasmussen attends meetings whenever invited and if his schedule

---

[1] Allan R. Cohen, "Beyond Simulation: Treating the Clasroom as an Organization," Exchange, September 1975, vol. 1, no. 3.

EXHIBIT 1	*The Enterprise Corporation: Mission Statement*

What is an organization? Is the University of Ontario School of Business and Economics an organization? Perhaps it goes without saying, but the buildings, the concrete and mortar do not constitute an organization. These are but facades and the actual organization encompasses people who are working together toward the attainment of a common goal.

Similarly, the Enterprise Corporation consists of you and me, all reaching for the same objective, i.e., to experience the best education possible within the context of this course. Consequently the primary goals of our corporation are:

- To be adequately prepared for class discussions, by completing the necessary readings
- To complete the assignments
- To attend sessions to the best of your ability
- To strive for the highest grade possible
- To take part in class discussions

These can be considered the task issues of the corporation. The maintenance issues involve the goals of:

- Contributing to the efforts of the group
- Attending group meetings
- Striving for a cohesive group, while not falling prey to groupthink
- Assisting the group manager in the managerial functions of planning, leading, and coordinating

You are an integral part of our organization. Your signing of the job description form indicates that you accept the basic tenets of this corporation. Your input is valuable. Given the nature of our venture, it is imperative that you understand the aims of the organization and realize the important part that you, as an individual—with unique perspectives, ideas and criticisms—will play.

In this mission statement, I take the opportunity to welcome you to a different experience. I would ask that, during our time together, you try to carry out the Enterprise Corporation's prime objective, that you try to enjoy our sessions. Once this is achieved, we may then learn something from them.

EXHIBIT 2	*The Enterprise Corporation: Job Description*

Position Title: Group Member
The group member will be responsible for:

- Regular attendance on the job.
- Informing the group manager when attendance is not possible. This should be done prior to the start of the specific session.
- Taking part in group discussions.
- Contributing to the best of his/her ability in making the group case hand-in a success.
- Contributing to the best of his/her ability in making the oral presentation a success.
- Contributing to the cohesiveness of his/her group.
- Putting the best possible effort into the individual project.
- Supporting the group manager and Enterprise manager wherever possible.

I agree to the above and will endeavour to give of my best to the Enterprise.

Signed:

_____   _____   _____
GROUP MEMBER   GROUP MANAGER   ENTERPRISE MANAGER

Date:

_____   _____
                                              Section Designation

allows. Otherwise the facilitator and the group determine their own schedules and plans in respect of the course. The final product involves completion of the group assignments to the best of the group's ability and also the development of tenets which would allow for a cohesive group. Rasmussen's telephone numbers at his office and home are given to members in case anyone wishes to reach him. He stresses, however, that the outlook of the organization is such that groups should at first attempt to address problems on their own. He could be *informed* but he generally expects that most problematic issues would be handled at the group level. If this is not possible, the facilitator would discuss the problem with him.

The Semester Begins

Frank Rasmussen left his office and headed to the classroom which was on the same floor. He was in high spirits as was usually the case when he was going into a class for the first time. He looked forward to meeting the new crop of third-year Business Honours students and as the excitement mounted he quickened his pace. What were they going to be like this time around? Would he have an enthusiastic group or would the twelve-week session be lukewarm? Third year marked the students' introduction to group work and sometimes his "classroom-as-organization" model could be a shock to students who had been conditioned to think of university life as a series of lectures. He had had positive results with the model, however, and continued to look forward to implementing it. The model provided for an interactive class and even when there were problems in groups, he had learned something about the group dynamics process.

He strode into the classroom and looked around. The class list indicated 34 students. The faces appeared to be stamped with the expression reminiscent of each new class and reflected anticipation. They seemed to be saying to him "O.K. buddy, let's see what you're like."

He gave a brief opening talk outlining the course objectives and method of grading. This was followed by a request to the class to complete a one-page questionnaire. The questions elicited information about work experience, hobbies, as well as attitudes concerning group work. The rest of the class was spent in introductions and discussion. Each participant introduced himself/herself and briefly described the worst job he/she had experienced. The "pits," as one student described it, was working on a racing track and having to clean up after the horses in full view of the crowd. Needless to say, some very colourful moments were offered.

Rasmussen guided the discussion and selected the factors which made the job the worst. Together they determined that issues such as leadership, job design, culture or power, and politics contributed to the negative effects, and he tied the topics into the course material for the semester.

Later that evening, he fed the information provided by the students into a home-made software programme which focused on a mix of male/female, similar work experience and hobbies. The result was the formation of groups, each consisting of five to seven members. As he completed the process, he thought that he would opt for group selection of facilitators. Members would consequently have to decide whom their facilitators would be.

The second session began with the announcement of the groups. This was punctuated by comments such as, "Oh yeah!" and "Oh no!" The newly formed groups were then asked to select a facilitator by the third session and to communicate this information to the instructor. Rasmussen then initiated a discussion about group dynamics and went through the stages that groups experience such as forming, norming, storming, and performing. There were encouraging responses from participants as the oral analysis of the case for that day began. The case was entitled "Full Speed Ahead."

Third Week of the Semester: Meeting with Rasmussen

"I guess we can begin our meeting." Rasmussen normally met with facilitators at least three times for the semester and this day marked the first meeting with the Business 388 class.

"Can each facilitator begin with a verbal report of how the group is functioning?"

The seven members each presented a short report indicating that everything was going fine. This was to be expected as it had been proven with past classes that problems did not develop this early. One facilitator brought up the issue, however, of an unusually shy group member. The assembled group brainstormed and came up with ideas to deal with the point. It was agreed that the facilitator should invite the member to discuss his opinions at the outset of each session and that other members should be privately asked to be as supportive as possible. On the surface, the groups seemed to be going through the forming stage in an inconspicuous manner. Although Rasmussen did not know it, however, the group led by Christine Spencer was already beginning to experience some problems which would ultimately fall onto his plate.

Christine Spencer's Group: The First Group Meeting (End of Week One)

Christine's group consisted of five members. There were two other females, Diane Stuart and Janet Simpson. The male complement consisted of Steve Raison and Mike Thanakos.

The group started out in high spirits and most seemed eager to tackle the group project. The first meeting was called by Christine who coordinated the schedules and selected a suitable time. The meeting was held through mutual agreement at Steve's house since it was close to the university. The group met at four o'clock when no one had classes. The first "order of business," as Christine put it, was to exchange telephone numbers and timetables. Christine also brought up the issue of whether or not they should meet briefly prior to the start of each class to discuss the case for that day. The group consensually agreed that it would not be feasible. Rasmussen had said that he would normally allow for fifteen minutes of class time so that groups could discuss among themselves the major issues of the case. It was decided that the task of each group member was to have the case prepared through "reading and reflecting." They talked among themselves for a while longer.

The session ended with everyone agreeing that Christine would contact each member before the next meeting. She returned to her campus residence and stretched out on her bed for a "pick me up" rest as she called her half-hour catnaps. The meeting went well, she thought, and her mind focused on the group members. She tried to formulate in her mind the impressions she had garnered from their actions, and demeanour in and out of class, as well as from the brief biographies she had requested from each member.

INDIVIDUAL MEMBERS

Steve Raison

Steve seems to be a nice guy, thought Christine. He had worked in the Cooperative programme promoted by the School of Business and Economics and had been attached to a managerial accounting firm for the past two work terms. He appeared eager to get the group project going and wanted to have the best product. He seemed to be good at the computer and had already begun talking about the design for the cover of the case analysis, as well as the type font, and the fact that he "could have the analysis sparkle by using a new laser printer."

Diane Stuart

Christine perceived Diane as a quiet, perhaps even shy individual. She hardly said anything, but always had a sensible answer if she was asked a question. Her major was marketing and her placement on the Dean's Honour Roll since the start of university marked her as a good student. Christine got the idea that Diane was capable of solid work and wondered why she appeared so withdrawn. Christine attributed this to the fact that she was slightly overweight.

Mike Thanakos

What a clown, thought Christine. After the first ten minutes of the meeting, Mike had said "Well, I guess we can all go now. . . . " He gave the impression that

he was in the group only because it was required. When Christine had posed the question of possibly getting together before each class, he had blurted out "What!" Actually, the remark seemed to be both a question and an exclamation, and she was taken aback by its vociferousness. Mike worked on a "normal programme" basis, meaning that he did not participate in the co-op program. He did not have a major and the response to Christine's questionnaire in this regard was, "I'll choose. There's still lots of time." Sure, she thought.

Janet Simpson

At first, Christine did not think that Janet would attend the meeting. Almost a half-hour had gone by before she appeared. "Sorry" she had said, "you know how it is when you're working part-time." She seemed quite rushed and a little out of breath. Christine recalled Janet's answers to her questionnaire. "I am presently working at two part-time jobs, two days per week, four hours per day. I hope that I can attend all the meetings." Under the question about extracurricular activities, Janet had enigmatically stated, "Spending time with my boyfriend." She was a Human Resources major and had stated that she "just managed to get by." At least we have the H.R. in common, thought Christine.

Christine Spencer

Christine thought about herself in relation to the group. She saw herself as a meticulous, organized individual who tried to give her best in anything she did. She was a Human Resources major and really enjoyed the area. She had told the group that she was a people person who saw herself in a senior H.R. position "within the next five to seven years." She also resolved to win the Best Group Prize that Rasmussen was offering.

Fifth Week of the Semester: The Second Group Meeting

The group case hand-in, due the last week of classes, was the primary topic on the agenda. Rasmussen had continued to mention it in the class, and the group thought that it was time to get started. They were required to analyze a case and decide among themselves what aspect each would handle. The group case was worth 25 percent of the mark and that figure could be raised or lowered through peer evaluation.

Mike thought that discussion of this item was premature. "We have other assignments. Do we really need to devote time to the case project so early? We should leave it until later. I'm sure we can whip it up in two weeks, man."

"Well, the case has been assigned. I have other projects too and I don't think we should leave major items until the last minute. Believe me, two weeks would be the last minute." It was surprising to hear Diane speak up like this but she clearly had the support of Steve and Christine.

"O.K. already! Just give me the executive summary: I can handle that." Mike laughed loudly as he said this and the group laughed with him.

"You can handle the title page, Mike. What about that?" Christine joined in the good-natured ribbing.

"Gee Chris, that's just about my speed. You've got a deal."

"Did anyone see Janet lately? Is she coming to the meeting?" Steve seemed concerned that all members were not present.

"I spoke with her on campus two days ago and she said she would be here. I guess she's just late," explained Christine.

The meeting went on for approximately three hours. There was much discussion that evening, and not all about the case. Mike insisted on telling the "latest" jokes including his knock-knock specialties.

"Knock, knock."

No one answered. Finally, Diane responded.

"Who's there?" she answered wearily.

"Amos."

"Amos who?"

"A mosquito bit me." Mike laughed the loudest.

"Knock, knock."

"I'm only saying this so you'll be quiet, Mike." "Who's there?" Steve was sounding exasperated.

"Andy."

"Andy who?"

"And he bit me again."

The group all broke into laughter. They spent the rest of the time assigning various parts of the case. Janet was given the Justification and Implementation sections since these were left over and she had not shown up. The group went to Wolf's university pub after the meeting.

Later that evening, Christine called Janet on the telephone.

"Christine! I'm sorry. I left work and began heading to the meeting. I met Sean, my boyfriend, who had a midterm project to hand in tomorrow and he needed some help with the proofreading and corrections. I'm helping to put him through school and we plan to get married after we graduate, you know. Anyway, before we knew it a few hours had passed and I thought it was too late to come." Janet did not seem to mind when she was told about the sections assigned to her and Christine ended the conversation by telling her about the date for the next meeting.

The Semester Progresses

The members of the group became more familiar with each other during discussion of the cases in class. They usually reviewed the major issues in groups before Rasmussen initiated the class discussion. The instructor would normally spend a few minutes in each group during this time. When he came to Christine's group, he asked how everything was going. Christine smiled warmly and replied that things could not go any better.

She reflected on that remark during her "thinking period" that afternoon, just before her catnap. The group seemed to be coming together and operating cohesively, all things being equal. Mike's performance was still lukewarm, however. Whenever they discussed cases in class, he seemed ill-prepared. Christine would usually admonish him by saying "Oh Mike, you really should read the case." Mike would usually start the discussion by talking about the football game to be played that evening, or the concert the night before. The group would chime in and Christine would bring them back on track with an, "O.K. guys, back to work."

And then there was Janet. Diane had privately remarked that she thought it odd the way Janet would address Mike as "Michael." Whenever the group discussed a case during class, Janet would generally be prepared. When it came to bantering and just talking as friends, she would be very quiet.

Janet Simpson

It was a particularly bad day for Janet She had two projects due, one for Marketing and the other for Production Operations. She had been pushing herself academically as well as in the job. Earlier, she was working at the restaurant and had delivered an order of stir-fried shrimp to Table 4. The customer in the suit had virtually sputtered with indignation. "You have the wrong order, miss. Besides, I am quite allergic to shrimp and the odour of this dish is upsetting me." Other customers had heard as did the manager and she was reprimanded. She broke into tears at the waitresses' station.

That night she thought about her own situation. She tried her best. Sean seemed to be overly demanding lately and she wondered if the commitment they had made to each other could last—should last. She worked at the two part-time jobs for his sake. In addition, she had to keep up with her courses. Then there was the Organizational Behaviour group. What was wrong with them anyway? Did they not like her? They seemed to get along so well together and she got the impression that her presence was merely an intrusion. Could they not see that she was just a human being trying her best at all the many activities in her life?

Seventh Week of the Semester: The Third Group Meeting

Christine had called the meeting for seven o'clock since this time appeared suitable to all. Janet was working that night and could not attend. However, a meeting at any other time would conflict with both Steve's and Mike's schedule. Consequently, she decided this was the best alternative.

They discussed the first drafts of the sections assigned to each individual. Changes were made across-the-board and these included adjustments to the Justification and Implementation sections that Janet had handed in. Mike's section looked like a sea of red when they were finished with it.

Christine tried a number of times that night to reach Janet by telephone. She thought that Janet would be finished by then. There was no answer.

Eighth Week of the Semester: The Classroom Incident

The members of the group had found themselves sitting in the first row next to each other in Rasmussen's class. Mike and Diane were engaged in conversation prior to the beginning of this class. They were early and as Janet took her seat in the last row, she thought it more beneficial to read the case rather than talk with the two members of her group. She couldn't help but overhear their conversation, though.

"Hey, Di, did you see Chris last night? She was dancing up a storm in the aisles, no less—at the Frozen Ghost gig!" Mike laughed and recalled the event for Diane.

"Well, I prefer a more dignified existence than our beloved leader. I sat quietly and took in the music."

Steve and Christine walked into the classroom, along with some other members of the class.

"Look who I had to pick up from the sidewalk and drag to class, guys. Steve was just about ready to collapse. He had a better time than even little old me last night," Christine teased.

"Yeah! Well I partied after the party."

They laughed. They had not seen Janet until she greeted them from the other side of the room.

Tenth Week of the Semester: The Cafeteria Incident

It was 11:30 A.M. and Janet was just leaving after her accounting class. She had missed breakfast and decided to go to the cafeteria to pick up an order of fries.

After emerging from the queue, she looked for a table and much to her surprise she saw her Human Resources group sitting together. She approached the table but they did not notice her. They were busily engrossed in discussion of the group case.

"You guys didn't say you were having a group meeting," blurted Janet.

They looked surprised.

"Well . . . why not join us?" invited Christine. Janet did but hardly said anything.

A similar incident happened the next week. Janet inadvertently came across her group (with the exception of Mike, who was absent). Again they invited her over, saying that they just happened to run into each other.

Seventh Week of the Semester: An Appeal to Professor Rasmussen

Janet decided that she had to discuss the events with Professor Rasmussen. She explained the situation to the instructor.

"I try my best. I hold down two jobs, but I still devote quality time to my courses. I know I can do well, but the group does not seem to like me. They have formed their own little clique and I seem to be excluded from that circle. The situation is affecting me emotionally and I know it will affect my grade. I need this course. I can do it. And I don't need the emotional hassle."

Rasmussen thought it would be best for him to speak with Christine. At the next class he asked her about the progress of her group.

"Well, I have no specific complaints. Everything seems to be working out well. Our group members generally contribute to the best of their abilities."

"How is Mike coming along? You had mentioned that he had a heavy course load."

"Okay, I guess. At least he makes an effort."

"What about Janet?"

"I was not really going to bring up Janet's situation, but since you ask, I will fill you in. I know that she is quite busy with her courses and part-time jobs. As a result, she has not really had the opportunity to become part of the group. We meet each other on campus and in fact have been having spontaneous meetings about our case analysis. We are all pretty well a cohesive group in that respect. As facilitator of the group, I realize I have a responsibility to Janet. I've tried to phone her on a number of occasions to fill her in on our meetings. But there never seems to be anyone home. Once I was passing by the discount store where she works and dropped in there to try to catch her, but she was actually working at the restaurant that evening. If you want to know the truth, I was going to keep everything quiet and have Janet share in whatever mark the group obtained."

The next day Rasmussen received a telephone call from Janet.

"I know that your class is group-oriented but I find it difficult to work with a group that excludes me and worse, doesn't like me. The whole situation is disturbing me more than you can imagine. Would you consider letting me do an individual case instead of the group analysis? I promise I will do the best I can and I think I will be more motivated. I would not have to worry about the likes of Christine and her buddies."

27　FUJIYAMA TRADING COMPANY, LTD.

Mr. R. Nara, executive vice president of Fujiyama American Corporation (hereafter referred to as FAM), was sitting in his office in New York, recalling the day a year ago when FAM first hired an American MBA as a future manager of the company.

FAM's parent company, Fujiyama Trading Co., Ltd. (hereafter referred to as FTC), is one of the Japanese "sogo-shosha," usually translated as "general trading companies," a distinctly Japanese business enterprise. Unlike specialized trading firms, which limit their activities to specific types of products on a limited geographic basis, the sogo-shosha handles every kind of product and conducts import, export, and offshore transactions worldwide, as well as trade within Japan.

Characteristics of the sogo-shosha are: a great number of items traded; vast sales with small profit margins; worldwide office and information networks; a large number of highly skilled employees of many nationalities; intimate acquaintance with the law, business practices, trading procedures, customs, and languages of many countries; central position in diversified groups of companies and close ties with many other companies; central roles in the Japanese economy; and growing importance in international trade.

FTC, one of the leading sogo-shosha in Japan, had a total of 8,400 staff members, including 1,400 employed in foreign countries who devoted themselves to customer service through international trade, development, and processing of natural resources overseas, as well as to distribution, financing, and many other areas.

The company transferred staff members on planned rotation through a variety of jobs to help younger staff members develop into well-rounded employees capable of handling all facets of the company's business. These transfers were made not only within FTC's domestic divisions but also to overseas offices and subsidiaries.

FAM is FTC's wholly owned (100 percent shares) subsidiary and contributes a growing percentage (currently over 15 percent) to FTC's overall business. FAM, with 12 offices in the United States, has literally become an American sogo-shosha. At any given moment, FAM's divisions are engaged in the import and export of thousands upon thousands of different commodities and products. Simultaneously they may be working on such diverse ventures as the creation and organization of a consortium of enterprises from different countries to search for and develop new energy or mineral resources. Several may be involved, in unison, in planning and coordinating the construction of ports, plants, or pipelines. Still another division may be guiding an American firm in its first attempt at creating an international market for its products.

FAM's New York head office had 100 Japanese staff members and 200 American staff members. Among the American staff, about 30 were male employees and the remaining were female employees, all of whom were engaged in clerical jobs. In order for the company to meet equal opportunity commitments, some of the top managers of FAM had discussed the hiring of Americans as prospective managers. In other words, in order to avoid trouble and to get government business, it was decided that the company should have a certain percentage of American managers among the total officers of the company.

Mr. Nara, 47, office manager of the New York head office, was in favor of starting and developing this program of hiring prospective American managers. He had spent 25 years with the parent company, including 8 years in the United States as office manager in Los Angeles and 2 years in Argentina. As such he was interested in management in different cultures and had studied it himself. After one year as an executive vice president, he asked the personnel department to find American MBAs suitable as future managers. He commented:

> Through my long experience of working overseas, I have always recognized the differences of managerial cultures. As you are well aware, the American society is based upon individualism, free mobility, and less human-oriented organizations, which has resulted in a very unique and efficient organization. However, it is not necessarily true that this type of organization can function well under any culture and society.
>
> The Japanese organization, of course, is based on the peculiar Japanese value system. In a word it is often said that America is individual oriented, while Japan is group oriented. In America, personal responsibility is always emphasized, and one's authority and responsibility are clarified. I think that the job description, for example, comes from this idea. The reason why job descriptions have not been developed in Japan as a basis of personnel or organizational administration is because of differences of culture and social value systems.
>
> In Japanese organizations authority tends to be a vague concept, which makes it somewhat hard for each individual to take clear responsibility. Sometimes responsibility is regarded as an ambiguous concept by the Japanese manager. The process of Japanese decision

making is very much like consensus building, which makes it harder to determine who should take final responsibility.

The basic principle of Japanese organization is not an authoritarian command, but wa [harmony], which is achieved by mutual consideration. The "group-oriented" tendency of Japanese people is related to such Japanese management practices as lifetime employment and seniority systems. These practices reflect the Japanese concept of household, which holds that the high-born and powerful have an obligation and a social responsibility to protect the less fortunate and less powerful.

Under such practices, the future of all employees depends upon the performance of the company as a unit. Therefore, in Japan, more than in America, management and employees cooperate in working toward the goal of a successful company. We often say "spirit of belonging" or "love for the company" to express our loyalty, which is the outcome of the above-mentioned atmosphere. In short, for the Japanese people, corporate life does not only mean the profit center but also the social unit where one achieves emotional satisfaction.

As such, the people we want are those who can demonstrate skill at building good personal relationships and performing so-called team work. When we hire college students, for example, observation of their personality takes priority over their special knowledge, such as accounting, economics, marketing, and so forth. Therefore, we usually hire college students as soon as they graduate and train them. After joining a company, the college graduates usually find themselves initially spending some time working and learning in two or three departments in the company. This on-the-job training continues for a couple of years, during which they gain a wide range of experience in all aspects of the company operation.

Because of such differences about the concept of the business community, I don't believe that American managers would work efficiently or happily if we hired them away from other companies. If we really want an American to manage our organization, we have to train him by on-the-job training and keep him with the company for a long time in order for him to feel loyalty.

I do not deny that, in any society, organizations must be established on the basis of the value system which prevails in that society for the organization to survive and develop in that society. It is easy to say, but hard to do. I can easily imagine that Japanese staff would not be able to work efficiently here, if they have to work in the type of working environment as in the United States. This will result in unfavorable performance of the company, which I, as a manager, have to avoid. Therefore, the very crucial thing is, I believe, how to find the meeting point.

Of course, it is necessary for us to be somewhat Americanized, but at the same time, it is also necessary for the Americans to be Japanized, if they want to work for such a company as ours. In other words, we will preserve our basic Japanese system, which is a very good system, but make the proper adaptations to operating in America.

To begin, Mr. Nara ordered the establishment of Japanese-language classes, opened a library with a lot of books about Japan, and offered flower arrangement classes in the company. These programs were offered for the purpose of raising the American staff's sense of belonging to the company and letting them understand various aspects of Japan. Every program was operated at the company's expense. These programs were very well received by the American employees.

Although these programs were offered mainly for the lower-level staff, Mr. Nara thought of having MBAs join them when they were hired to let them understand Japan. Mr. Nara intended after this to send MBAs to Japan for several years so they could learn and experience the Japanese managerial way, business customs, ways of thinking, and so forth, and then to send them back to the United States. By doing so, Mr. Nara believed that MBAs would understand how to bridge the gap between two cultures and function better as international managers.

Upon receiving the order from Mr. Nara, the staff of the personnel department, who had just been brought from Japan to establish that department, began to contact several business schools, which were supposed to be interested in Japan, to inform them of the company's desire to hire MBAs. As a result of this, FAM had 15 inquiries, and the personnel staff had an interview with each of them. At that time, the company policy was to hire one or two MBAs on a trial basis. The personnel department picked five students who seemed to be interested in working for a Japanese company and left the final decision to Mr. Nara. Through personal interviews, Mr. Nara decided to hire two prospective MBAs.

Mr. Karl Smith was one of the two hired. He had gone to a small college in Maine that reflected and stressed the traditional "Yankee" values of independence, hard work, and self-reliance. After college he continued his education by studying for an MA in international relations at City College of New York. Following this, he took a job with the Savings Bank Life Insurance Company in New York but continued to study Middle East politics at night. Finally he enrolled full-time in the MBA program and joined FAM at the age of 27. At that time, he described himself as follows:

> My personal goal is to become a top manager in a large corporation. Power, status, luxury, and quick decision making . . . that's the life for me. For this purpose, I'll face up to any difficulties and not run away from them.

I don't mind if my whole life revolves around business. I am an aggressive type of person and feel bad if someone gets ahead of me.

The MBA program was a great program that emphasized basic principles of management. I found their emphasis on such ideas as clear job descriptions and individual accountability, as well as on promotions based on merit, compatible with my philosophy that the rewards of life should go to those who perform the best. The program was just the starting point for my career goals. They gave me some of the skills I will need to be a success!

Mr. Nara made a comment on his decision to hire Karl:

He was more enthusiastic than the others. He personally was interested in Arab countries, and he was a member of a study group about Arab politics with other MBA students at the university. Some of them are actually working over there now.

The passion for one specific thing, which is not necessarily inside the realm of work, is also very important. I remember hiring a guy who was a great college baseball player in Japan, and this led me to feel that he would demonstrate self-discipline, loyalty, and commitment to the company. I have recently seen many young people who don't know what their goals are or even what they would like to do. The person who is vague about these things is useless. If one has devoted himself to a specific thing, it would be possible for him to demonstrate loyalty and commitment to the company for a long time. As a matter of fact, Karl told me that he had a passion for hunting with bow and arrow. I heard that he even makes his own bows and arrows, which is really a specialty.

I also saw another reason for my decision. As you are well aware, Arab countries have a tremendous amount of Eurodollars because of sales of oil, and they are trying to industrialize with their earnings. We have technology and knowledge about how to industrialize. There exists a great possibility for us to win big projects in those countries. In such a situation, if we hired Karl, he will be able to provide us with some valuable information. That is why I have come up with the final decision.

Mr. Nara thought that Ferrous Metal Products Division would be best fitted for Mr. Smith and assigned him to this division as the immediate subordinate of Mr. Y. Kato, who was an assistant manager of the division.

As usual with the Japanese trading company, most college graduates find themselves spending time in two or three departments after joining a company, to develop their general knowledge. Thereafter, they begin to specialize. Since the commodities handled vary tremendously, it is necessary for the company to have a specialist in the particular commodity to respond to the customer's needs.

Mr. Nara had been dealing with the exporting of steel products since he joined the company. During the 25 years he had spent in this business, he had brought up many subordinates, a number of whom had become managers of overseas offices themselves. Almost all 120 overseas offices handle steel products. It can be said that Mr. Nara has his subordinates all over the world. One of his subordinates, Mr. Kato, had spent his 15 years with the company in the business of selling steel products. During this period while he had had several trips overseas, he had never worked in any of the company's overseas offices. At the beginning of January, he was transferred to the FAM New York office as an assistant manager of the Ferrous Metal Products Division. He recalled the first impression he had when he joined the New York office:

When I was working in Japan, whenever I was not too busy, I used to take subordinates, sometimes including female employees in section, to the bar to have a talk with them over glass of beer. It was very useful to talk to them in an informal place out of office to get to know them. Sometimes they complained about company policy or customers, and sometimes they consulted about personal matters. I believe these relationships were very basis of my management style. I don't think I can manage people without knowing them. Interpersonal relationship between subordinates and myself was that of support and dependence, instead of dominance and submission. However, when I first came here, I was really shocked with American people's practical and businesslike way of thinking. I couldn't see any warm human relationships. For example, every female employee leaves office exactly at five o'clock. When one female clerk was working most hard the other day, other female clerk sitting next to her never helped at all, even though she did not have any work to do because of boss's absence. These kinds of things never happen in Japan. If I ask female employee to work overtime, she willingly did it. When someone was very busy, others gave help. I think this is way it's supposed to be.

However, this does not happen here as in Japan, and in this way. New York office is not comfortable place to work. I am not criticizing company policy about hiring MBAs, because I am loyal and also respect Mr. Nara. But, having American MBA assigned to department is personally unpleasant for me. I've just arrived in this country and I am not good English speaker, so I have hard time dealing with American people. If I cannot communicate well, it's going to be embarrassing to them and me as well.

Mr. Smith joined Mr. Kato's division one month after Mr. Kato was transferred to New York. Mr. Smith quickly learned the steel business through the instruction given him by the other employees and through his inherent aggressiveness and enthusiasm. In the course of teaching the business to him, his peers tried to get him involved in their jobs as well. He had the impression that he was receiving special attention, and he felt pleased that the other managers apparently recognized his knowledge of Arab countries. On the contrary, Mr. Smith's peers were merely trying to make him understand how the Japanese organization works utilizing a group approach.

In October the company had to send someone to Saudi Arabia for finalizing the business negotiation of exporting steel products to a certain engineering company there. Mr. Kato's boss suggested sending Mr. Smith to Saudi Arabia, because he thought that this opportunity might give Mr. Smith incentive and motivation. However, Mr. Kato wanted to conclude this business deal without any trouble, and he felt that a Japanese staff member could work more cooperatively with the Japanese staff of Jedda than Mr. Smith could. Furthermore, Mr. Kato thought that Mr. Smith was not yet really ready to represent the company, having observed Mr. Smith's everyday behavior in the office. However, keeping in mind his boss's suggestion, he reluctantly decided to send Mr. Smith, taking into account his abundant knowledge of Arab countries.

At Jedda International Airport, Mr. Smith was welcomed by a staff member of FTC's Jedda office, who had been informed of his arrival beforehand. The staff member spoke to him:

> How do you do, Mr. Smith? How was your trip? If you are not tired, I'd like to have lunch with you and talk about the upcoming business negotiation. Also I can tell you about some of the people you are going to meet; that might be helpful to you. By the way, I used to work as a subordinate of Mr. Nara before and he took very good care of me. How is he doing lately? . . .

Mr. Smith, on the other hand, was surprised with the man's coming to the airport to see him. He thought to himself:

> Gee, I don't understand why he came to the airport to see me, when he must have been very busy with his own job. I could go to my hotel or the company office or luncheon meeting without any help. It is a waste of his time, an unnecessary expense, and surely not a professional way to conduct business when time is short.

Karl spoke courteously with the staff member but kept the conversation on pleasantries and got away from him as soon as he could. This left the staff member feeling very perplexed. He could not understand why Karl asked so few questions of a business nature, nor why he left so abruptly after they reached the Jedda office. He wondered if he had said something that violated American customs, such as mentioning his past association with Mr. Nara (to which Karl had hardly responded). He certainly felt bad that he had been of so little assistance to Mr. Smith.

Besides his original business negotiation, Karl was supposed to meet Mr. Henry Bodwell, his friend from the MBA program, who held an important position in a Saudi Arabian company. When they met, Karl got some confidential information from Mr. Bodwell, which was that Freedman Construction, Inc., of the United States had undertaken a big project for the government of Saudi Arabia. The project was to develop a big outer harbor at Jedda, including construction of berths, highly developed mechanical loaders and unloaders, and many infrastructures. In total, it would amount to about $100 million.

For the steel divisions of FTC and FAM, this type of project was one of the most desirable ones. Since the division earns profit on a commission basis (usually 2.5–3 percent of steel price, which is about $300 per ton) in accordance with the quantity handled, big projects that allow the division to deal with large quantities of steel (15,000–20,000 tons for this project) are always sought by everybody in the division.

Almost all of the people and agencies interested in this project thought that nobody had yet successfully undertaken this project, because the press release was not yet scheduled. Knowing this information, Karl thought there existed the possibility of his selling a large quantity of Japanese steel products to Freedman, Inc., if he approached the firm before anybody after he got back to New York. On the way back to New York, he was excited about this.

> I'm the one who found out about this project. I can take the initiative and responsibility, also. I must finalize this project independently at any cost. This is a damn good opportunity to demonstrate my knowledge about the Arab countries and my confidence in carrying out new business. If I make it, my status in the company will be well established, and I will be relied upon by my fellow employees and my bosses as well. The company should appreciate this, and my status will rise. Since I was not familiar with the steel business, I have had to be passive in most cases; however, from now on, I will be able to be more active and assertive.

After getting back to New York, he reported to Mr. Kato about his original business and quietly started approaching Freedman, Inc.

When he was asked by Mr. Kato or his fellow workers what he was doing, he used to say that it was not important and he never talked much.

I'm not going to disclose this opportunity to anyone until I've made real progress. If I do, it will be talk, talk, talk, and more talk. Time will be lost, and more than likely someone outside the company will hear about it. If I carry the ball myself, the company will get the jump on other companies, I'll establish my capability and credibility, and everyone will gain an unexpected dividend. As Professor Chandler used to say, the way to get a job done right is to assign it to one man and then hold him responsible for results.

In November Karl succeeded in making contact with a vice president of engineering for Freedman, Inc. Karl's strategy was to influence the design specifications written by Freedman's engineering department. He believed that if he could convince Freedman of the superiority and competitiveness of the quality and price of Japanese steel, then they would write the design specifications in a manner that ensured the acceptability, and even favored the use, of Japanese steel. Karl knew it was important that the specifications not rule out the use of Japanese steel in favor of steel from some other country, and he also knew that in Mr. Kato's experience Japanese steel mills would nominate Fujiyama (FTC) as the exclusive negotiator in appreciation for its efforts in attaining "good" specifications.

Karl's discussions with the Freedman vice president were successful. However, there was one condition; namely, the approval of the specifications by the Saudi government. Time was urgent, because Freedman had to send the design drawings containing the specifications to the Saudi government in two weeks.

Karl knew that personal connections were very crucial for doing business in Saudi Arabia; therefore, he believed that he had to hold direct negotiations with some suitable person in the Saudi government. Keeping in mind the time element involved to prepare the necessary data, Karl believed that he had to fly to Jedda immediately. He felt sure that he could make an appointment with the "key" men of the Saudi government through the cooperation of Mr. Bodwell, and then, through "person-to-person" negotiations, have them accept the desired specifications.

Therefore, he went to Mr. Kato and told him all about the project and the necessity of getting an approval from the government of Saudi Arabia. He asked Mr. Kato for permission to make the trip to Saudi Arabia at once. Mr. Kato was very surprised with this and said:

Why have you done this all by yourself so far? As you know, we are not manufacturing steel products; therefore, you are supposed to ask about the possibility of getting such a quantity of steel products from Japan first of all. And you have not gotten any approval from the Tokyo office as to this project. Nor have you ever consulted our two offices in Saudi Arabia. If you keep going with this project without cooperation with offices in Saudi Arabia, they will lose face toward Tokyo office, as will others. You are supposed to know that the overseas offices can get commission as a certain percentage of business transactions around the office area. The more the office is involved in the business, the more commission it can get ... This time, I think you had better stay in office and ask the staffs in Saudi Arabia to negotiate with the person in the government ...

Mr. Smith was very much disappointed with Mr. Kato's decision and said:

Maybe you don't know, but personal connections are very important for conducting business over there, and I have that connection. I need no coordinator. This is a project that will be very beneficial to the company; if necessary, I'll ask offices in Saudi Arabia for help myself. I must have permission to go over there.

In order to decide anything, in Japanese business society, people are expected to lay the groundwork and achieve consensus among everybody involved before taking any action. Mr. Kato was very dissatisfied with Mr. Smith's taking action on his own and finally told Mr. Smith: "As long as you work for Japanese company, you are supposed to understand the Japanese way."

Very much disappointed with Mr. Kato's words, Mr. Smith went to Mr. Nara's office, told him all about what was going on, and complained:

I'll have to leave New York for Jedda at once to get approval from the government of Saudi Arabia. I already have a personal connection, which is a "must" over there for this kind of negotiation. I want to do this even at the risk of losing my job. Since you have influence over the staff of the steel division in Saudi Arabia, you can take care of them. However, I have to go there as soon as possible. Please let me go!

Mr. Nara thought about the impact on everybody and of all the offices that would be affected by his saying yes or no. Whichever his decision, it must be made immediately.

Last fall, Tellabs Inc., a maker of sophisticated telephone equipment, received an important order that would have to be completed by the end of the year. Instead of simply posting overtime notices, as would happen in many factories, Grace Pastiak called a meeting of the plant's workers.

"I knew that it was getting into the holiday season and many of the people would have family demands," said Mrs. Pastiak, director of manufacturing for one of three operating divisions.

Standing on a ladder in the middle of the plant, she spoke to the workers. "I gave them some choices," she said. "I said we could tell marketing we could only do half. We could bring in contract labor, or we could shift some production outside. After we talked about it, they said, 'Go for it' and that's what we did." The workers readily put in overtime to get the job done on time.

Mrs. Pastiak appears to be not just another plant manager. Instead of writing memos or limiting her discussions to one or two lieutenants, she prefers a more personal approach. She communicates directly with her people on the plant floor, trying to infect them with a zeal for producing high-quality products. And she fiddles endlessly in search of a better production set-up.

It is a style that Judy B. Rosener, a professor at the University of California at Irvine, calls "interactive leadership" and that some researchers have suggested is distinctive to women. The female managers who exhibit it, Professor Rosener wrote in a December article in the *Harvard Business Review,* "encourage participation, share power and information, enhance other people's self-worth, and get others excited about their work."

Sally Helgesen, a journalist and author of the book *The Female Advantage—Women's Ways of Leadership,* says the phenomenon affects the configurations of their staffs. She concludes that women tend to form flat organizations, rather than hierarchies, that emphasize frequent contacts among staff members and the sharing of information. She calls these networks "webs of inclusion."

An Evolving Role

The developments, these researchers say, are an outgrowth of women's evolving role in the workforce. While earlier generations of female executives seemed to delight in proving they were tougher than any man,

"a second wave of women," Professor Rosener wrote, "is making its way into top management not by adopting the style and habits that have proved successful for men, but by drawing on the skills and attitudes they developed from their shared experience as women."

Grace Pastiak, who at the age of 35 is one of the rare female managers in manufacturing, may be representative of this new generation. But she says her style stems from reading and courses rather than from her orientation as a woman. "I don't think it is gender-specific," she said.

"I have the bias that people do better when they are happy," said Mrs. Pastiak, who attributes her style in part to her education in sociology and early jobs in social work. "The old style of beating on people to get things done does not work."

In fact, whether this more nurturing management style is more distinctive to women than to men is a controversial issue. Indeed, Professor Rosener's article touched off a spirited discussion in a subsequent issue of the *Harvard Business Review.*

One woman who is free to run a business as she chooses, Barbara Grogan, the owner of Western Industrial Contractors, a heavy-equipment moving company in Denver, said: "Women do lead and manage differently. There is no real hierarchy in my office, and we never have meetings. Nobody controls information and power. We just make it happen."

Ross Webber, a professor of management at the Wharton School of the University of Pennsylvania, thinks there is a general drift away from a hierarchical, military-style management style. "In the broadest-brush terms, the decline of the hierarchy as a source of power, and an emphasis on the ability to build coalitions, is the central management trend of the past 25 years," he said. "As such, it has been a helpful trend for women managers."

For her part, Mrs. Pastiak, as the supervisor of a workforce of 170 people, provides a test case of whether the factories can work effectively without relying on the traditional rigid command structure.

Although high-ranking women are found in abundance in the professions and in important staff positions in large corporations, fewer have moved into jobs of authority in manufacturing. "It may be a supply-side problem," Professor Webber observed. "Women do not want to manage in blue-collar, union situations."

There is a culture of flexibility and innovation at Tellabs that has probably permitted Mrs. Pastiak to go further with soft management methods than might have been possible in more tradition-bound companies.

Founded in 1974, Tellabs employs 2,100 in a nonunion shop and has annual sales of about $200 million, which means it is still tiny to be competing with the likes of AT&T, Northern Telecom, Siemens, NEC, and Fujitsu.

The company operates at the intersection of the communications and computer industries. It produces products for the big long-distance and regional telephone companies as well as concerns that have their own telephone and data communications systems. A typical product is an echo canceler, which blocks out the mysterious third voice that can be a nuisance during long distance calls.

Committed to Training

Mrs. Pastiak is regarded by both her bosses and subordinates as an effective manager, and the numbers seem to back this up. She meets production targets 98 percent of the time, compared with an industry standard that she puts near 96 percent. And it is a record she keeps without seeming to be preoccupied with the output, attendance, and cost reports that are the production manager's staples.

Instead, she is a champion of worker empowerment, worker education, and Japanese quality methods. She takes two full days each month, for example, to teach a course in what the company calls Total Quality Commitment—a task that she believes most male managers in her position would assign a subordinate.

Speaking to factory workers gathered in a conference room, she bubbles with enthusiasm as she goes over her personal formula for improving quality by systematic problem solving. An astute instructor making sure her students get the message, she repeatedly focuses their attention: "What is the purpose? What is the process? And what is the payoff?"

About a dozen workers are taken at a time from their usual task of assembling circuit boards to attend the hour-long sessions. Mrs. Pastiak considers it time well spent, despite the loss of production time. "I cannot think of anything more important that I should be doing than empowering people," she said in the flat twang of a native of northern Illinois. "I want people to have a sense of accomplishment."

Not that production is neglected. Sitting in her corner office, Mrs. Pastiak reaches for a thick red binder filled with documents listing output by shift. "I get daily reports on what we shipped and weekly reports on other key measures," she said.

But she says the staff's development means she does not need to spend as much time studying reports. "The stronger the teams become, the less they need you," she said.

Worker Self-Reliance

That throws more of the problem solving to workers on the factory floor, said Tom Sharpe and Tim Murphy, two of her subordinates. "We get daily reports on why things did not ship," said Mr. Sharpe. "Usually it is for a reason out of our control. If it is within our control, we fix it and then cut the boss in on what we have done."

The proof of the production line's self-reliance: its ability to fill 98 percent of its orders. "In another plant, something may need to be done, but people say, 'That's not my job' and the order goes unfilled," Mrs. Pastiak said. "Around here the attitude is 'what do we have to do to get the order to the customer.'"

Mrs. Pastiak said it helps if top management reinforces this every-person-matters mentality. Even though the recession has cut orders, no production workers have been laid off. Instead, workers have shifted to four-day weeks until orders pick up. (The company reported a loss of $968,000 for the first quarter, compared with a profit of $2.54 million last year.)

Most of Mrs. Pastiak's subordinate managers are men, many of whom say she manages differently than men in senior roles. Duane Dhamen, a project manager, said in referring to the head of another division, "he talks to one or two key people and lets the information filter down to the ranks." By contrast, Mrs. Pastiak "puts a stronger focus on the team and open communications," he said.

Another manager, David Gladstein, said: "If Grace left tomorrow, we would still be a team, at least for a while. But with a different individual, it could change."

Mrs. Pastiak did not know a capacitor from a resistor when she came to work at Tellabs as a buyer in 1977.

At that time, recalls Michael J. Birck, a former Bell Laboratories engineer who was one of the founders of Tellabs and remains its president, sales growth was rapid, but it was clear the company's manufacturing operations were dragging it down. "We had a 35.8 percent gross margin in 1985, which is no way to survive," he said, "At that level we could not invest enough in new products to grow." The aim was at least 45 percent before taxes and depreciation and interest costs.

In addition, there were serious quality problems, a significant threat in an industry that emphasizes reliability. "Mike Birck went into one of our stockrooms

EXHIBIT 1 *A Big Gap between the Sexes*

Finance, insurance and real estate	49.9%	2,089,000
Services*	49.2%	4,757,000
Wholesale and retail trade	43.5	2,078,000
Agriculture	27.4%	95,000
Manufacturing	26.4%	2,544,000
Mining	25.0%	112,000
Construction	13.2%	1,042,000

*Includes repair services; personal services, except private household; entertainment and recreation services; and professional services.

SOURCE: Women's Bureau, Department of Labor, 1990.

and checked some of our products," recalled Edward McDevitt, a vice president. "Only 70 percent of the samples he chose performed to specs."

Rather than try to solve the problems by shifting production overseas, as some companies have done, Mr. Birck asked Mr. McDevitt to start applying Japanese manufacturing methods, like just-in-time inventory control and statistical quality control. Mr. McDevitt, in turn, chose Mrs. Pastiak to lead a pilot project in the Lisle factory in mid-1986.

"I knew that Grace was good at teaching and training, and I knew she would move any roadblocks in her way," he said.

Under the new process, individual workers were trained to inspect their own work and given the right to shut down production until errors were corrected. Rather than working on parts of a product, like

welders on an automobile assembly line, workers were organized into teams. Each team assembles a product from beginning to end, and each member of a team is trained to do multiple jobs.

The pilot project was successful. Work-in-process inventory went down 80 percent. The time it took to fill an order went from 22 days to two. Financial margins improved as well. Last year the company, whose shares are traded over-the-counter, reported that its gross margin had widened to 44.9 percent.

While the project was under way, Mrs. Pastiak spent most of her days on the factory floor, changing the way the circuit boards were assembled, soldered, and tested. She rearranged so many machines that the maintenance crews would try to hide when she came around. "They would say, 'That woman is moving furniture again,'" Mrs. Pastiak recalled.

The success of the pilot led to companywide use of the technique and to Mrs. Pastiak's promotion to director of manufacturing in 1987, making her the highest-ranking woman line executive in the company. (Among staff jobs, women hold the titles of general counsel and the head of a software development project.)

A Few More Hurdles

Grace Swanson met Robert Pastiak at Tellabs. "He actually worked for me for awhile, which was interesting," she said.

They have two small children: Annie, who is 2½ years old and Brian, 17 months. Mrs. Pastiak said she drops the children at a day care center in the morning and picks them up in the evening. She concedes it is a less-than-ideal arrangement.

Nevertheless, being part of a two-income couple may also have given her more latitude to act than her male peers. "I may have more freedom to innovate, because my paycheck is not the sole support of the family," she said.

Still, even at Tellabs, some of her female colleagues doubt that a woman can go to the very top. They said that in general the men who control manufacturing companies need to become more comfortable with women as colleagues—and their styles—before they begin bestowing vice presidential titles on women.

"It is a comfort-level thing," said Diana Kreitling, a former manufacturing supervisor who is now in marketing. "Most of the male managers are in their mid-40s to 60s, which is about half a generation ahead of us. Their real concern is, 'Can I tell this joke? Can I go golfing with her? What about business trips?'"

Changes came hard at Stein, Bodello, & Associates, Inc. (SBA). Following a move to a new location and an upgrading of both the business and project management functions, some unhappiness had developed in the ranks of middle management.

Stein, Bodello, & Associates was a consulting civil engineering firm founded by Dan Stein. It was located in the Midwest, employing 100 people in four branch offices. The business had grown rapidly, especially in recent years. In the past three years, business volume had grown from $4 million to $10 million annually. As Dan Stein explained, "The firm is committed to growth."

The firm was managed by four principals: the senior partners, Dan Stein and Joe Bodello, and two junior partners, John Lahey and Robert Waters. The senior partners were both in their mid-50s, with over 30 years of experience in the field. Dan Stein was the founder of the firm. He had both a BS and an MS in engineering and had presented more than 20 professional papers over the years. An engineer's engineer, he was oriented to the practical end of the business. He liked to keep abreast technically of the projects in which he was the principal in charge and enjoyed making technical input into solutions; he would rather be an engineer than a manager. As a businessman he was conservative and didn't like to take risks. He was sensitive and on several occasions asked what image, such as an older brother or friend, he portrayed to younger employees, most of whom were under 40.

On the other hand, he did not walk around the office to socialize. If he was seen away from his desk, it was because he was on his way out of the building or asking an engineer a technical question about one of his projects. Because principals in the firm were required to have high chargeable ratios for billable work, just as did the staff, they found it hard to find "free time" to socialize with their employees. Likewise, they found it hard to find time to be participative leaders or to take on more management responsibility.

Joe Bodello had joined the firm shortly after its founding. He also was a professional engineer but had become more of a businessman and was treasurer of the firm. His management style was quite strict. He spent some time walking around the office, usually visiting engineers twice a day to maintain visibility.

The junior partners had been with the firm for 15 years and had become vice presidents. John Lahey was a professional engineer with 20 years of experience. He was a good practical engineer and managed in a participative, trusting style. He usually mixed with employees at lunch. Robert Waters was not an engineer but had a degree in an engineering-related field. He was an aggressive go-getter. His style was "strictly business," and though he was willing to chat with employees and occasionally would sit and socialize, he was usually too busy to do so. Both vice presidents, however, were regarded as easygoing.

The board of directors, composed of Stein, Bodello, and Lahey, had overall responsibility for management of the firm. However, if an issue didn't meet with Stein's approval it had little chance of being passed. There was also a management committee comprised of the four partners. It functioned as an advisory group to the board of directors to deal with matters of business management, including internal operations, marketing, and profitability. It was a forum for discussion of policy and company goals. In addition, there was a personnel committee comprised of Stein, Bodello, and a senior associate, which functioned as an advisory group to the board of directors on matters of personnel management.

When the firm was young, Stein and Bodello had performed all the functions of the business from field work to engineering to report writing. As the firm grew they gradually had to give up various activities; first the field work and then some of the engineering. However, they continued to want to be involved in the engineering whenever possible. In recent years the senior staff associates and senior-level employees, who were project managers, had the responsibility for seeing projects through to completion. (See Exhibit 1 for an approximate organization chart.) Occasionally, more experienced junior staff also would function as project managers. This included detailed budget tracking, management of personnel assigned to the project, client relationships, approving invoices for billing, and overall projection direction.

Although project managers had a high level of responsibility, they were not provided with all the tools they believed they needed to manage the projects. One issue was whether salary levels or ranges for employees should be made available to the project managers for use in controlling budgets. Dan Stein, as president, was reluctant to make this information available. He explained that he was uncomfortable with allowing staff members to know one another's salaries, because he did not wish to be confronted. Nevertheless, what each employee earned probably was no secret among the project managers and engineers. Other members of the management committee disagreed with Stein and had been trying to persuade him to make the information available.

EXHIBIT 1   *Approximate Organization Chart*

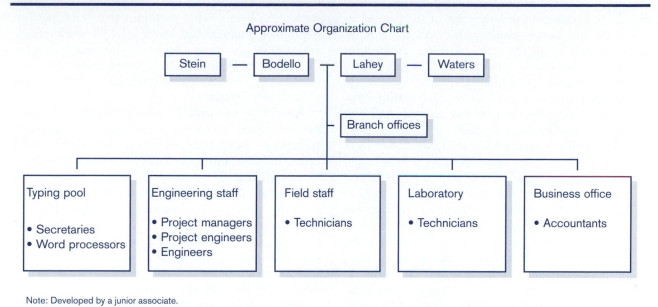

Approximate Organization Chart

Note: Developed by a junior associate.

What budget information was accessible to the project managers was obtained by asking the accounts manager for the data. This usually was provided as a lump-sum figure. Many times the information given to the project manager was late, incomplete, or incorrect. The accounts manager had many other things to do besides developing this type of information. The data was often incorrect due to incorrect recording of labor-hours. This frequently would not be discovered until the bills had been made out or until after they had been sent. Engineers were reprimanded when the budgets were significantly overrun, and it reflected poorly on their ability to control budgets. As a result, many project managers were frustrated. The issue was often a topic of conversation at lunch or around the office, and the management committee heard rumors about the frustrations and problems with controlling budgets from a few of the more senior employees.

Stein, Bodello, & Associates had formulated a plan whereby partners' stocks would be sold to senior-level employees and associates according to a prearranged formula. The purpose of this was to provide a mechanism for selling the company to employees, provide value to the stock, and provide incentive to younger engineers. Senior staff had recognized this potential and therefore were interested in maintaining SBA as a comfortable place to work, as well as maintaining its growth and profitability.

During the past year an MBA was hired to manage the business office; changes in business and accounting procedures had followed. The computer, purchased two years earlier, was put to use for word processing and financial accounting, which previously had been done manually. Getting the computer system in operation, working out the bugs, and making it useful had been a long, tiring, and frustrating process. Additional staff were hired, procedures formalized, accounts receivable collection tightened, and productivity and profitability stressed by management in the new procedures that were instituted.

Frequent memos announced these changes on short notice. The memos dealt with such issues as time-sheet reporting and charging telephone calls to a project by computerized methods. In some instances, the staff made jokes about the triviality of the requests—for example, charging file clerks' time to the project. One of the real issues, however, was that these memos appeared without any discussion about the reason the changes were being made and without any prior request for suggestions.

Often, only a few weeks after a change had been implemented, the staff reverted to its "old" ways or chose to forget about the new procedure. In many cases changes were being made by support staff personnel who were responsible for purchasing materials, and so on. However, those changes usually had an impact upon the technical staff, who never had an opportunity to provide input.

In one case several senior associates and staff became quite angered when each employee suddenly was assigned an employee number for accounting purposes. Comments about the loss of the old "homey," informal atmosphere were common. Employees remembered the early years of the firm when it was one big, happy family with direct access to all the principals by all the staff. However, as the firm had grown, the senior principals had become more and more removed from the staff. One person commented that instead of insisting on high-quality engineering as in the past, the firm was now satisfied with "adequate" engineering at a profit.

As its growth continued, the firm outgrew its facilities, and a decision was made to move to new, larger quarters. The new building was owned by Stein and Bodello through a realty trust, and the company leased space in the building. Although relocation was rumored for some time, only a few people knew of the actual plans until about two months before the move. Layout of the new facility, office assignments, and space allocations were kept secret. The responsibility for the new office layout belonged to Stein. After all, this was his project. Extensive renovations were required in the building to make it look good, but corners were cut and many things were missed in the new layout. The result was that the new office was less efficient than the old facility in terms of productivity, even though the building was larger.

The old building layout had evolved after many years. There was a common secretarial area centrally located in the middle of the building, and the business office was physically separated from the engineering staff in another part of the building. The principals' offices were adjacent to the common area, and their door opened into the area. Engineering staff, both senior and junior, were located in somewhat larger, two-person offices, each with a door for privacy if needed. Some of the offices were also adjacent to the common area, while the others were clustered along the corridors that led to the common area. Individuals were generally free to decorate and set up their offices as they pleased, and many had worked evenings and weekends doing just that (e.g., painting or building shelves). There was a sense of harmony in the environment, and morale was high. Older employees described it as homey, informal, and a place where you were treated as one of the family.

The new office reflected the "open space" concept. The partners' offices were for the most part isolated in one corner of the building, while senior engineers were given enclosed offices adjacent to a common area where the engineers, secretaries, and accounting personnel were located. The senior staff shared what amounted to good-size single offices. The accounting staff and secretaries occupied large open areas, but with minimal separation between work areas. They complained that the area was too noisy and distracting. The engineers occupied space in the rear of the common area. The section was divided into four-person work areas by movable partitions that were five feet high. Each engineer had his own 8-by-8 work cubicle with a table providing a separation between engineers. The engineers frequently complained about the noise, distractions, and absence of privacy. (See Exhibit 2 for old and new layouts.)

Allocation of space for nontechnical work (on a per-individual basis) was clearly larger; draftsmen, technicians (who were seldom in the office), secretaries, and accounting staff had more space to work in than engineers. The new space for each engineer was smaller than the space he had left in the old building, even though the overall building was larger. One engineer stated it was clear that "those who were doing the work, who were the backbone of the organization, who were putting out the projects, got the least desirable space." One senior employee said that he was concerned because the employees had no say in changes that affected them and their future. In this view his office, which he shared with another senior employee, was too small for productive work. In comparison to the area allotted to the nontechnical employees, especially to the chief draftsman, his allocation was small; and his status seemed to have been lowered. He went on to explain that the draftsman, along with Stein, had allocated the space. When this senior person questioned Stein about the size of the shared office, Stein told him that, "if you cleaned out some of your books and shelves, the office wouldn't be so crowded."

When plans for the building were being developed, an employee petition had been circulated requesting that a shower be installed because many employees came in from the field and wanted to shower before changing into office attire. The petition was sent to Stein. The shower was not installed, and no reasons were ever given. This seriously affected morale. Employees who used to stay late to work on a problem began staying only until the end of eight hours. The traditional Friday gatherings after work at the Fish House for a few drinks stopped even though the Fish House was still only a few blocks away. Some isolated attempts to revive the tradition were unsuccessful.

The Ad Hoc Committee

Shortly after the move, a group of senior-level employees on their own formed an ad hoc committee to address issues of employee concern and make them known to the management committee. The ad hoc committee intended to discuss specifics, such as office

EXHIBIT 2

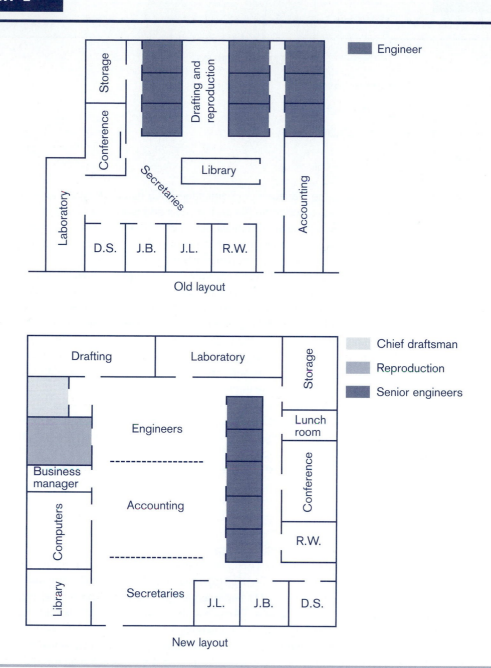

layout, space allocation, and project management, and to recommend concrete courses of action.

Members of the ad hoc committee were well respected both within and outside of the organization; they formed the core of the project management group. Mike, one of the cochairs of the committee, was 36 years old and had a doctorate in engineering. He handled both business and engineering matters and had a good rapport with Dan Stein. Bob, the other cochair, was 34, with a master's degree in engineering.

He headed one facet of the engineering section and was on good terms with John Lahey. Both men were associates.

Other members of the committee were all project managers. Larry had been with the firm for five years. He was well respected but was considered a radical. Responsible for the formulation of the ad hoc committee, he was on good terms with Robert Waters. Bruce also was considered a radical. He was very vocal and complained often. Nonetheless, in his six years

EXHIBIT 3

MEMORANDUM

To: Management Committee

From: The Ad Hoc Committee

Subject: Committee Organization

Date: June 17

Over the past few weeks, the management committee (MC) has been made aware of a certain amount of dissatisfaction on the part of Stein and Bodello employees in general, and senior staff in particular. The initial response of the MC, as transmitted to the senior staff through John Lahey, has been positive and directed toward reducing specific sources of tension (e.g., working-space arrangements).

In an effort to carry forth this encouragement from the MC into productive action, the undersigned have constituted themselves into the ad hoc committee (TAHC). The intent of TAHC is to assist the MC in implementing the administrative policies necessary to maintain Stein and Bodello's profitability in a manner consistent with traditional "family" atmosphere. The means to accomplish this goal will be to develop recommendations to the MC concerning administrative matters and to provide an organization and a cadre of middle-level line managers who will be responsible for implementing procedures authorized by the MC.

We recognize that the growth of our firm has led to some loss of personal contact between principals and staff. Although we may regret this change in the "personality" of our firm, bemoaning this fact will not change it. We believe that middle-management resources can be developed to compensate for the loss of "personal touch" with principals and to take on increased responsibilities within the firm.

TAHC is composed of senior technical staff (i.e., those who deal with clients and have a line responsibility for execution of engineering projects). Staff department heads have not been included, but their experience, opinions, and involvement will be diligently solicited on issues affecting their area of responsibility.

Responding to needs identified by TAHC members and to the request transmitted from the MC through John Lahey, TAHC proposed to address the following matters as the first orders of business: (1) improvement of the work space and (2) accuracy and timeliness of time sheets. TAHC members have agreed to volunteer their time for this effort, meeting after work biweekly or as often as necessary to make progress. Any requests and recommendations developed by TAHC would be set forth in writing for consideration by the MC; further discussions between the MC and TAHC cochairs might take place at the monthly luncheon meetings held on the day of projection meetings.

The members of TAHC wish to retain the quality of work produced and the quality of working conditions that have always been associated with SBA, and we are prepared to act accordingly. In return we request only that the MC accord us recognition and its full support. TAHC has already begun work on the two priorities listed above.

with the firm, he had become well respected for his engineering ability. He also had a good rapport with Dan Stein. Tony was quiet and easygoing. He had been with the firm for five years and got along well with Dan Stein. Paul was moderate and easygoing. In his three years with the firm, he had developed good relationships with Dan Stein and Joe Bodello.

The committee decided that the way to proceed was through written memos. Face-to-face meetings with Dan Stein were judged to be useless because "he would have no time to waste discussing such matters." The first memo sent to the management committee stated what the ad hoc committee was trying to achieve (see Exhibit 3) and requested that the management committee formally recognize the ad hoc committee. This was never done, although one junior partner told the committee verbally that in his judgment its formulation was a good idea and he hoped that it would be made use of. Stein's response was that any memos should be sent to him, as president, first. Those issues he agreed with would be given to the proper people for implementation; there was "no need to waste management time on something I've already agreed to." Those issues that he disagreed with would be discussed.

The committee initially sent several memos to the management committee on various issues. Management responded by issuing a memo to staff directing that some of the recommendations be implemented. Nothing was heard regarding other items. Subsequently, the committee decided it was time to address the concerns about office layout and space. To employees, this was a major issue. While it would require some expenditures to redo the job, the ad hoc committee felt that changes in this area would help to restore efficiency, productivity, and morale.

The ad hoc committee did not want to be perceived as a threat to management and to Stein in particular. It wanted to be seen as a valuable resource and to be used to formulate worthwhile recommendations. At the same time, it did not want to waste its time making suggestions if sensitive ones were going to be ignored without discussion. They had to decide how to proceed.

30 ## INTEL IN CHINA   **IVEY**

Charles Tang, newly appointed manager of marketing programs of Intel China, had just emerged from an emotionally charged meeting with Yong Lui, an account manager in Tang's division. The meeting, attended by Lui's direct supervisor, Qing Chan, was convened by Tang to discuss Lui's feelings regarding a decision Tang had made to discontinue a project that had been assigned to Lui by his previous supervisor. Despite what Tang considered to be sound business logic supporting his decision, Lui's resistance left Tang wondering whether there were extenuating factors he needed to consider. Tang also wondered whether the blow-up with Lui was an isolated incident, or whether it signalled deeper organizational or communication problems in his newly acquired division.

Intel

In the mid-1960s, Intel introduced the world's first microprocessor, sparking a revolution in the technological industry. Intel was an unequivocal success story—its strategy of "driving new technology, serving global markets, and increasing customer preference for the Intel brand, while delivering excellent financial results to our stockholders" had served them well over the years. By 1996, driven by strong sales of the Pentium® processor, Intel was on their seventh consecutive year of record earnings of both sales and revenue, and had reached the US$20 billion in revenues milestone. 1997 was another year of record revenues (an increase of 20 percent) and record net income of almost US$7 billion, up 35 percent over 1996. However, 1998 brought weaker than anticipated demand

for personal computer (PC) products, which led to lower first quarter revenue and earnings. Dr. Andy Grove, the founder and enigmatic leader of Intel, referred to first quarter 1998 results as "disappointing," and stated that the "PC industry seems to have gotten ahead of itself, building more product than customers wanted." First quarter 1998 revenue of US$6 billion fell seven percent; net income and earnings per share declined 36 percent from the first quarter of 1997. The company widely expected revenue for the second quarter of 1998 to be flat, and year-to-date performance during the year had reflected this expectation.

Intel's global mission was nothing short of being the "pre-eminent building block supplier to the new computing industry worldwide." Thus, a major part of Intel's strategy was their commitment to creating microprocessors that the software of the next millennium could tap into. Concurrently, Intel followed a strategy of encouraging the developments of software engineers so they could push the envelope in software design to ensure that users would receive the benefits of the most advanced hardware Intel was developing. To help strengthen the Pentium® brand name, Intel focused on emerging markets with programs that stimulated demand for Intel products. Intel had succeeded tremendously in their branding campaign, and was considered one of the world's top 10 brands. Indeed, in 1997, over half (56 percent) of Intel's revenue was generated outside of the U.S., with the Asia-Pacific region and Japan accounting for almost a third of Intel's revenue. In 1999, Intel considered China to be their single most important market.

Intel People's Republic of China (PRC)

Intel PRC Corporation established a representative office in China as early as 1985; however, it was not until 1993 that Intel felt the time was right to more fully enter the Chinese market with the establishment of two wholly-owned foreign enterprises. The first, Intel Architecture Development Co., Ltd. (IADL), was responsible for the sales, marketing, and development of Intel's products and services in China. IADL's 250 employees were located in 13 offices throughout China; however, the Shanghai office with 100 employees and the Beijing office with 80 were the largest. The second,

Intel (China) Technology Co. Ltd., was the entity of Intel's assembly and testing plant operations.

IADL employed more than 80 engineers who worked with local and multinational software vendors to develop innovative consumer and business applications to PC users in China. IADL's charter was to "accelerate technology adoption in the PRC by providing technical and marketing support to local software developers." Initiatives included a developer support program, which included seminars, matchmaking events, training and conferences for Chinese software engineers and a donation of more than RMB$1.5 million of Pentium II processor-based development systems to assist leading Chinese software developers in bringing advanced software to local and international markets.

IADL's mandate was critical to Intel's growth, as senior management was aware that regardless of their research and development (R&D) expenditures, without software applications that could take advantage of the latest hardware developments, the user would not receive the advantage from that innovation. Thus, according to Tang, Intel's role in China was to act as a matchmaker, bringing all pieces of technology together to help China's PC users to understand how computing could help them in a comprehensive way. Tang explained that Intel looked at technology from a "total solution standpoint."

> By the time we start developing a new chip, we're already looking at what applications it will support and what solution it provides to the user. Thus, by the time the chip is ready to go into market, the platforms, the solutions are all ready so it is co-ordinated. This way, we're all moving forward and everybody wins.

By 1999, Intel had become involved in "just about every operation in the IT industry in China" and were aggressively marketing Intel-branded products throughout the country. Though still at its early stage of development, China's computer market had been growing twice as fast as the world average, and was poised to become the second-largest computer market in the world by the end of the century. With its large population and fast economic growth, China's potential was extremely attractive to multinationals. As a global leader, Intel was well-positioned to capitalize on this opportunity and Charles Tang was one of the most important players in advancing Intel's presence in China.

Charles Tang

Tang had not returned to China since his departure eight years prior and his home country had changed dramatically during that time. Beijing had undergone a rapid period of extensive growth and the ubiquity of shiny modern buildings and presence of so many foreign firms was a shock to Tang. However, despite the changes in Beijing that he saw, Tang had the advantage of being previously exposed to the reality of life in Beijing, which could overwhelm many expatriates—the crowded streets, the pungent aromas emanating from the street markets, traffic congestion, punishing heat, and air quality, for example. Tang commented that he had known of other Chinese nationals who had returned to the mainland, and despite the fact several months had elapsed, they still did not feel comfortable being in China and never really could adjust to life there after having lived in the U.S. or Europe. Though he initially felt "like a tourist," after having spent just one weekend wandering through the street markets, alleyways and pathways through the heart of Beijing, he was convinced he had made the right decision and had not looked back since.

Tang was one of the first three employees who were transferred to China from other Intel sites in 1993 to more firmly establish Intel's operations on the mainland. Tang gained experience in many areas, including a two-year stint in Shanghai to help establish Intel Architecture Laboratory there. During his time there, Tang established Intel's software developer support program—an integral part of Intel's China strategy. The account managers (AMs) in Tang's department played a critical role in this support effort. Their prime mandate was to forge and nurture relationships with prestigious Chinese software developers and vendors. By 1999, Tang reported directly to the president of Intel PRC and oversaw critical areas such as government relations, as well as industry and community programs, which included donations to many of the top universities in China to support research and teaching activities, as well as donations of equipment, upgraded on an annual basis.

The scope of Tang's development projects ranged from the grassroots community level such as a program that would sponsor Chinese high school students to attend a popular international science and technology fair in the U.S., to investigating strategic investment opportunities. Tang also played a leading role on Intel's corporate advisory board, a body that was comprised of some of the most prominent Chinese influencers, both from the IT industry and academia. The board's broad mandate was to "spearhead industry programs by working with trade associations and industry leaders to influence the development of programs throughout the region to promote indigenous development of the industry by transferring Intel's acquired experience and expertise locally."

Yong Lui

Yong Lui was one of four AMs, each of whom had individual projects in addition to their primary responsibility. According to Tang, an AM's required skill set included the ability to interact as an Intel ambassador with senior managers and owners of the software firms that Intel was developing relationships with. This involved effectively communicating Intel's IT strategy, "not from a technical viewpoint but rather from a strategic perspective," while ensuring full customer satisfaction on a daily basis. Another critical strategic component of the AM's responsibilities lay in their ability to consistently recognize the possibilities of advancing the mutual interests of IADL and their clients—a key part of Intel's strategy in China. An AM's ability to exceed their clients' expectations was predicated on their effectiveness in mobilizing Intel's internal resources, which involved extremely strong people skills and the ability to consistently demonstrate a mature, professional, and diplomatic manner.

The Issue

When Tang took over Intel's Beijing division, he was eager to familiarize himself with the operation of each department, and to aid him in this, he reviewed the files of each employee to understand their roles. Using his best judgment, Tang reassigned work as he deemed necessary, to ensure that each employee was working both individually and within a team, toward advancing the strategic goals of the department, thus, Intel in China. The same rationale was behind a reassignment of various departmental managers, and in the process, Tang reassigned the AMs under Qing Chan, a Beijing native. Though she had worked for a multinational before joining Intel, this was her first managerial position.

Thus, Tang's attention was drawn to Lui's project upon reviewing Lui's employee file. Though Tang felt the basic concept behind the project to be sound, he felt that it had expanded to such an extent from that which was initially proposed that it was not reasonable to expect that Lui could realize the project's goals without it interfering in his primary duties of servicing his account base. The scope of the project had mushroomed in part due to the perspective of Lui's previous supervisor who, according to Tang, was a very ambitious person who "approached everything on a grand scale with massive goals."

Initially, the project assigned to Lui was the creation of a manual providing local software vendors with tips on running their enterprise, such as marketing various software products or how to manage or set up distribution channels, for example. However, Lui approached the project with such unchecked zeal that it quickly transformed from a manual to a book form, with a chapter dedicated to comprehensive business planning issues, beginning with such basics as how to incorporate a business in China, sourcing venture capital, and the development of a comprehensive marketing plan tailored for software products, for example.

Tang described the project as a "portable MBA-type book, covering essentially every topic a software company would need to know to do business in China." This was such an ambitious project, and Tang estimated it could take up to one year to complete, not including the two months of research Lui had already conducted. Thus, upon review of the file, Tang concluded that Lui, a new and relatively young employee, without significant exposure to the business world or the software industry, did not have the background or expertise for this type of book. Tang felt that the project would be better suited to a writer who specialized in issues in the software industry. Given that there were many other projects that could be assigned to Lui, which were of a more appropriate scope and focus, Tang instructed Chan to inform Lui that work on the project was to be halted immediately, and that Lui should be assigned a new project.

However, when Chan informed Lui of Tang's decision to cancel the project, Lui "totally rejected her," and he was not willing to even listen to the rationale behind the decision. Chan turned to Tang for assistance as she was at a loss as to how to reconcile Tang's demand with Lui's desire to continue with the project and his agitated state that it had been cancelled. Tang decided that given Lui's reaction, the best course of action was to bring them all together, and he scheduled a meeting as soon as he could to resolve the issue. Tang was conscious of handling the situation in such a way that did not undermine Chan's authority, as he felt that the empowerment of direct supervisors was critical. On the other hand, Chan confessed she was confounded by Lui's reaction.

Lui's Perspective

During his brief history with Intel, Lui had dedicated himself to exceeding his client's service expectations. Indeed, Tang readily acknowledged that Lui had excelled at developing relationships with senior management in the companies in his assigned account base. Tang agreed that this was no small feat, as Tang's client base included some of China's most influential software firms, and in some cases had been so successful that he had created strong *guanxi* with senior management at those firms. *Guanxi* was the basis on which business in a Chinese context thrived. Loosely translated as "relationships," *guanxi* was such an integral part of doing business in China, that it was essentially impossible to do without it. Thus, when *guanxi* was established, it was protected at great cost as it was widely considered to be the single most important factor in a successful business transaction. Its value in a Chinese business context could not be underestimated.

Lui's success, therefore, in the realm of his primary duties was indisputable; however, he also applied himself equally to conducting research for his project and took ownership of it very seriously. Upon hearing that Tang had cancelled his project, he voiced his opinion immediately to Chan, saying that the two months of work he had conducted on his project was "wasted." Moreover, it was Lui's strong contention that Tang had altered not only one of his projects, but the essence of his responsibilities in one broad stroke, without due consideration, undermining his efforts to date. Lui continued:

> This is typical of expat managers—they come along and don't really care about what the workers are doing. They don't show respect and change the workplace according to their whim without providing explanation, and without warning.

Lui felt that Tang had caused him to "lose face." The concept of "face" in Asian cultures was roughly analogous to "respect" in Western cultures and permeated every level of Chinese interpersonal relations on both a personal and professional basis. If someone had caused another to "lose face," it could result in irreparable damage to the interpersonal relations between those two parties.

Tang's Perspective

Though he had heard through Chan that Lui was very upset, Tang was previously unaware of the extent to which Lui felt he had "lost face." Tang was thus largely unsure of how his actions could have affected Lui at such an emotional level, and he took a few moments to consider his perspective on the situation. Tang acknowledged that Lui was successful in establishing strong relationships with his clients. However, Lui won various concessions for his clients through a demanding style toward his colleagues and a single-mindedness of purpose. Another talent that Tang acknowledged Lui brought to his AM position was his ability to "think big." However, Lui's assertive manner was not commonly found in traditional Chinese workplaces, and some of his colleagues, both

within his department and throughout other departments in which Lui relied on, were uncomfortable with Lui's level of zeal. Complicating the situation was Tang's assumption that Lui had not been formally indoctrinated to the Intel culture.

To demonstrate the Intel culture, Tang explained that Intel's employees throughout the world were characterized by their energy and youth, and thrived in a dynamic and creative environment. Tang further explained that in order to sustain intense levels of innovation, a degree of dissension and constructive criticism was encouraged. However, policies that helped advance Intel's 64,000 employees globally in the same direction were required. Tang explained a crucial part of Intel's culture—which was in place to achieve this end—the "disagree and commit" philosophy.

> If a consensus has been established that a particular course of action or a decision is appropriate, any individual employee would not only have to commit to that decision, but if he or she were responsible in any way in implementing it, this concept would dictate that they act as if they were in 100 percent agreement with the decision. This means that once the course of action had been decided, it should not be discernible who was for and who was against the decision before it was made. This is a condition of employment at Intel. It is the professional code on which I was brought up at Intel.

However, given Lui's reaction, Tang wondered whether he had communicated to Lui, and potentially his other employees, the quintessential role that this philosophy played in Intel's culture.

Tang reflected upon what other factors he should consider in analysing Lui's behavior beyond his inexperience and apparent ignorance of Intel doctrine, and considered potential underlying cross-cultural issues that might help to explain Lui's behavior and at the same time increase his understanding of all his employees. Tang had grown up in China and pursued his undergraduate degree in China, yet had received a graduate degree from study in the U.S. and had as well almost a decade of Western experience. Thus, he found himself in a precarious balance between two cultures. This created a rather unique situation for Tang—internally, he was perceived as an expatriate, yet because of his precise fluency in Mandarin and obvious comfort in Chinese culture, Tang felt he was perceived externally as a local Chinese.

Tang—An Expatriate or a Local?

When Tang first returned to China, when meeting with local government officials, he had a difficult time in persuading them that he was directly authorized to make decisions. First, at 33, he was significantly younger than most senior managers at multinationals in Beijing. Second, most often local Chinese did not hold positions of such power in multinationals.

To establish his credibility externally, Tang used a clever and effective technique. When Tang first met with the officials, he noticed that when he proffered his opinions directly, many of the local officials did not have confidence that Tang was empowered to make decisions. After trying a more direct approach, when a decision was consequently required, Tang told the officials that "I should check with my boss" but offered his decision in the interim. In subsequent meetings, it became clear to the local officials that Tang's "boss's" decision correlated precisely with Tang's personal decision, time and time again. Thus, in time, he succeeded in establishing his credibility.

On other occasions, when he encountered a reticence among senior external managers or officials, he used another technique, equally effective. Tang would say, "I'll see if I can set up a meeting with my boss to discuss this issue, but may I have some background information to impart to him on which he can base his decision?" This would allow Tang to obtain the required information on which to base his decision, which he would disclose at the following meeting. In these ways, Tang artfully managed his credibility as a local Chinese with external stakeholders. However, internally, Tang was perceived as an expatriate, as he had been transferred from Intel in the U.S. after a long term of employment there, and had pursued his postgraduate studies in the States.

Tang was aware that being perceived as an "outsider" could undermine his ability to persuade his department that they were all a part of the same team. Complicating the issue was not only Tang's expatriate status (one of the few at the time), but as an expatriate, Tang received a superior pay and benefit package to local (Chinese) employees. Tang saw how he had advanced in relation to his employees as "just going through a different process to get to where we are, but now we're all at the same place—part of the Intel team." According to Tang:

> Work really doesn't have anything to do with whether you're an expatriate or local Chinese—it has to do with your ideas, how you understand strategy, technology and marketing—that's work. As long as you focus on that, and once your employees begin to focus on that, perceived differences really become a non-issue.

Tang dealt with the potential for conflict because of his rank or his experience in the U.S. by largely ignoring it, but Tang did not view this as an abdication of his responsibilities. On the contrary, Tang believed that by working hard and proving himself trustworthy, his employees would come to see that "we're all working together." According to Tang:

> How people look at you and how they feel about you has everything to do with how you make them feel about you. If you want to be seen as different, and if you want them to see you as different, they will. If you want to distance yourself from them, you can. However, if you want them to see you as one of them, they will.

Tang was cognizant of some basic tenets on which the foundation of organizational behavioral differences as generally found between Chinese and Western firms were based, and acknowledged that both his Western education and experience as well as his exposure to Eastern business cultures affected his interpretation of the situation he was facing with Lui. What challenged Tang also, with regard to managing Lui, was how much of a departure Lui's behavior was from what Tang considered to be a more traditional Chinese business culture. Thus, Tang wondered whether he should question some of his beliefs about Chinese communication patterns and organizational behavior. Had things changed drastically since he had been away or was Lui's behavior out of the ordinary?

Organizational Differences

DIFFERENCES IN COMMUNICATION PATTERNS BETWEEN THE EAST AND THE WEST

Generally speaking, Chinese organizational structures were more vertically layered than Western firms, resulting in dense reporting lines and bureaucratic administrative mechanisms. Moreover, Chinese organizations were most often led by a strong autocratic figure, who took an active role in daily operations as well as the strategic direction of the firm. Whereas in some Western firms the organizational structure, supported by cultural influences, encouraged a degree of dissension and disagreement to advance the firm's organizational effectiveness and strategic direction, generally speaking Chinese firms operated on a principle of unquestioning adherence to the direction as dictated by senior management.

However, in contrast to Eastern management style, in Tang's opinion, Western organizational and communication systems promoted a more open discussion between managers and their employees. Tang's management experience suggested to him that employees in the West had a higher propensity to be more open and possessed a greater willingness to listen to their bosses if they had established a track record of being reasonable and open-minded. In contrast, Tang felt there seemed to be more suspicion among employees toward their supervisors in an Asian business context, as they managed with a much more closed style.

Though Tang considered his management style to be a mixture of Eastern and Western characteristics, he felt that many Western management principles manifested themselves stronger. For example, he considered being open with his employees an integral part of managing, and indeed had succeeded in encouraging many of his employees to treat him as a confidante. On several occasions, he had been approached by members of his team and had held closed-door, one-on-one discussions regarding various aspects of their personal and professional lives. Tang was proud of the role he was able to take in acting in this capacity for his employees. On a broader level, Tang did his best to ensure that his employees' needs and concerns were addressed. For example, Tang ensured that his employees' salaries were commensurate with their responsibilities, and competitive as compared to other multinationals for employees working in a similar capacity. Tang considered actions such as this to be critical in establishing his employees' trust in him. It was actions such as this that reinforced Tang's belief that his employees were more comfortable approaching him than they may have been with an expatriate manager from North America or Europe given his cultural background.

The Decision

In this context, Tang was confounded by Lui's reactions. Why did he respond so emotionally and what could he now do about it? Lui was otherwise a promising employee who had forged valuable *guanxi* with his accounts, so Tang did not want to risk losing him. Moreover, on a personal level, Tang cared about the welfare of his employees and, thus, it was upsetting to him that he may have caused his employee some distress. Tang considered whether in light of Lui's emotional attachment to the project he should allow him to continue with it, as in the scheme of things it was a relatively short-term project. Or was there a way to modify the project, finding a compromise between his needs and Lui's desire to continue with the project? Tang was eager to have his employees contribute in such a way that would advance the strategic direction of his department, and felt strongly that whatever decision he made should be guided by that general principle. Tang knew that perhaps the easiest means to achieve this end would be to coerce Lui to follow the "disagree and commit" philosophy at Intel and redirect Lui's attention altogether to a more appropriate project. However, he was concerned about Lui's reaction to this move, given his emotional state.

Tang also considered the idea that perhaps this issue pointed to a larger one. Were the systems that facilitated vertical communication sufficient or should he consider implementing a more effective, more formal internal communications strategy? But Tang did not have time to consider this issue at the present moment—he glanced at his watch, jumped up, and hurriedly placed his laptop in his briefcase to rush to a meeting.

31   ISABEL STEWART

Isabel Stewart, 39, was a member of the partnership at Austin & March, one of Philadelphia's largest and most prestigious law firms. A graduate of Harvard Law School, Stewart worked in the tax department, a highly specialized legal area that had doubled in size during the 1980s. Stewart had been made a partner in 1987, despite a recent maternity leave and the fact that she was by a margin of several years the youngest associate to be promoted.

In 1990 Austin & March employed 300 attorneys and an equal number of support staff. Sixty-four lawyers at the firm—58 men and 6 women—had partner status. Clients included large corporations, financial institutions, and public agencies, as well as smaller privately owned businesses. During the late 1980s, the real estate and corporate departments had generated substantial business for the firm, but more recently volume in these areas had begun to decline, while the legal work connected with bankruptcy and litigation increased.

Isabel Stewart occupied a spacious office overlooking the river. Her annual compensation was larger than many of her peers due to the highly specialized nature of her work. Nonetheless Stewart was dissatisfied; in the last several months a more junior male lawyer had been able to secure what she regarded as better work. She was convinced that she was being excluded from the "big deal" cases and that her career would suffer as a consequence:

> I'm worried because I have the sense that I am losing ground to someone who has only been here a few years. We do some big transactions, with mega-bills, and I find myself competing for a chunk of those with the guy in the next office. There is a limited universe of high-profile deals, and he markets against me the way he would market against a competing firm. It's in his interests to get more of those deals and for me to get fewer—the more you get, the more money you make.
>
> The head of the department said I should just accept it: "He may always make more money than you, and to set yourself up in competition with him is a bad move, because you may lose." That really gets me riled! I work as hard. I'm smarter. I have been here for 10 years and I have cultivated those relationships for a long time, and I guess that I just think that people should be more loyal.

Personal and Career Background

Isabel Stewart graduated from college in 1977 with a degree in mathematics and from Harvard Law School in 1980. Stewart was married and had two young sons; her husband was a faculty member in the history department at Princeton.

At Harvard, Stewart had distinguished herself in tax courses, receiving an A+ in corporate tax law. Stewart joined the tax department at Austin & March after graduation.

As an associate, Isabel was able to work with a number of the firm's senior lawyers: "As a tax lawyer you work with people in other departments, and I had close working relationships with a lot of people in the firm," she explained. "I had a lot more contacts with other partners than most associates."

She did, however, find one of the two partners who ran the tax department difficult to work with. Ralph Egan was six years older than she, a specialist in corporate tax, and according to Isabel, a person who liked to be in control:

> On the surface Ralph is very gregarious. He doesn't scream or yell. But he likes to be right all the time. He has a reputation for being difficult.
>
> I worked with him a little at the very beginning. He asked me to research a question, so I went to the library, did the research, and wrote him a seven-page memo. He raked me over the coals when he saw it. "I don't want this; I want the equivalent of a Law Review article, with footnotes!" Then he took ideas out of my memo and used them as his own.

Later Isabel was approached by a young lawyer in another department about a corporate tax issue. It developed that they were going to have to get an opinion, for which a partner was needed. Isabel approached one partner, who said, "I don't know; ask Ralph." Knowing that problems might result from Egan's involvement, but wanting to remain in charge of the project, Isabel organized a meeting early in the process in order to circumvent any complications. She prepared both an analysis of the issue and recommendations regarding the opinion and solicited the approval of the partner from the other department. On the day of the meeting this partner was ill, but the meeting went well and Ralph Egan gave his approval. However,

> Six weeks later, when we were really down to the wire, Ralph called me and said, "I have some problems with this. I don't think we can get an opinion." The client was getting upset. I was looking like an idiot. And it turned out that all Ralph's issues were straw men.
>
> His approach is to get you out on a limb and then saw it off. He puts things off and it makes you look bad in front of other people. On the surface he was very pleasant about it. "Isabel, you've got to pay more attention to these things." This is after I had gotten everything lined up ahead of time, got him signed off early, had the partner from corporate in agreement, and still it didn't work. Then, later, I botched a couple of things he asked me to do because he made me so upset, feel so insecure. So that cut me off from a lot I wanted to do.
>
> A number of people have had problems with him. He's only six years senior to me, so I guess at the time I started he wasn't so secure himself. When I was made partner, he called me in and told me, "I didn't support you as a candidate, but that's all behind us. Welcome to the partnership." It seems like we get along but it's all below the surface. He seems so reasonable, so rational, that when you start screaming, you are the one out of control.

Isabel was made a partner on schedule, despite her maternity leave and the dissenting vote of Ralph Egan. At the time she was the youngest partner and one of only three women in the partnership. Isabel felt that she had done enough good work for a number of lawyers in the firm that there was sufficient support for the decision to promote her.

Although she had specialized in corporate tax, work in that area never materialized. "There were a lot of men who would get involved in the corporate department, but when I asked about it, people would say there isn't much of that work," Isabel recalled. "It was all very vague." Further, the one partner with whom Isabel did not get along did most of that work, and from the start she became much more heavily involved in other areas, such as partnership tax law. But in recent years corporate tax had become a major legal area, and Stewart was eager to get involved. She found herself hindered, however, by both a lack of hands-on experience and an unwillingness on the part of key people to include her in corporate tax transactions.

> I am missing big pieces of substantive knowledge that didn't get developed over the years. But I can work with associates who have the knowledge—I have the managerial and decision-making skills needed to understand it. But there is little reason to come to someone who is playing catch-up.

So I am looking for opportunities to jump in. This week, for example, for a company that was going public, there was a question on net operating losses that came up at the last minute. It's a classic corporate tax kind of question, so I did some work on it. That may happen again, but it is not going to be easy.

When asked why she was so intent on doing this kind of work, Stewart responded that in addition to the intellectual appeal, it was important work in career terms:

> Part of the appeal is that I have been shut out of it, and I don't like that. Damn it, I'm not going to let them do that to me! I'm going to prove that I can do it. It can be lucrative work for clients who can pay for the kind of planning and in-depth research we like to do. It's a big source of that kind of business. So being excluded from it is potentially harmful.

Stewart explained that although attracting new clients was desirable, corporate clients typically did not come in through the tax department.

> Corporate clients come in through the corporate department. I don't work on attracting new business, but it is going to become more and more of a prerequisite for becoming a partner. Certainly there is a reward system built around people bringing in business. No one tells you you have to bring in business—you are not under direct pressure from your boss. The pressure comes from the fact that if you don't bring in business, if you don't work on very high-profile, profitable cases, your compensation is going to suffer. That's the form the pressure takes: it's a piece of being a very well-respected, well-compensated partner.

Stewart was increasingly aware of the competition within the office for high-profile work, and she explained that she was trying to figure out how the process worked:

> There is not a God up there who says, OK, there are two people of equal ability and they each ought to get their fair share. It goes to the people who manage to pull it in. There is competition for clients both inside and outside the firm.
>
> I have been talking to people. Some people say I am imagining things. Others say I should just accept it.
>
> I may not play squash, or do the old boy stuff, but I think I am pretty easy to get along with. It's not that I have negative qualities—it's that I don't have positive ones—that high energy level and enthusiasm.

Isabel told the following anecdote to illustrate the kind of "positive" qualities she believed were required at Austin & March:

John, a fellow I know in another department, told me a story about a piece of work he had that he thought he would give to a friend of his, Steve. He knew Steve was in competition with another associate and had some catching up to do. So he went to his friend with the work, and his friend said, "Gee, I don't know if I can do it; I guess I can." John said, "Steve is my friend." I had the feeling that if he did it he was going to be doing me a favor, and I don't want him doing me favors just because he's my friend. So he went to Pete, the other guy. Pete goes, "Oh, yeah! That sounds great! I'd really like to do that." Pete perceived the work as an opportunity. Steve would do it, but as a favor. He perceived it only as something else that had to be done. So John gave the work to Pete. Then Steve got mad because he thinks he is competing with Pete.

So I thought about that and realize that I do favors, instead of, "Wow, that's a really interesting project; tell me about it." I had never thought of every project as an opportunity. I thought every project is something I have to do. I don't mind doing it; it's my work. But I didn't see it in terms of making the person feel that their work is fascinating, the most important thing I had to do.

I tend to do too many things, which means that things sit for awhile and I do it only at the last minute. I'm not right on top of things. I've also noticed that the guy next door has a clean desk. Something hits his desk, it's off his desk. He doesn't work on as many things, but he can be much more responsive. I was cultivating lots and lots and lots of contacts, thinking that the more goodwill I built up with more people, the better off I would be.

It doesn't matter how smart you are if you don't get the work out the right way. I thought if I did good work everyone would know it. Now I am trying to figure out the external things. This is not a place where people tell you much of anything.

Isabel Stewart talked at length about how she had been trained to behave, and she had gradually begun to realize that a different set of characteristics from those she had learned were required in her current milieu:

> If you look at the people who are successful here, one of the key characteristics is energy level. Just pure, raw energy, almost to the point of craziness. I have two little boys and they have that kind of run-around, crazy energy. There is a male model by which you attack your work; you go after it, you kill it. It's very different from the way I approach work. There is a frenetic style—just moving from one thing to another quickly, moving fast, jumping around the room, and working long hours.
>
> I think that that kind of style is what sells. That is what makes people comfortable. But women don't

approach work that way. If they did, they probably wouldn't make it, because they would be viewed as too hard to get along with. Women who behaved like that were filtered out years ago.

> I had a conversation just yesterday with two lawyers about another lawyer. What the men said was, "She's too aggressive. There's no softness to her. She backs people into corners and leaves them with no way out." What they really were saying was that she has bad judgment in managing situations. But would they be so bothered if she were a man? No. But with a woman they assume any negative traits are female, so she won't change.
>
> So we are left with a bunch of relatively passive women in the upper ranks. But now we are being measured against a standard that is much more male.

Isabel talked about how her own working style differed from that of her male colleagues. For her it was critical to study legal problems from both her and her client's point of view, and to provide the client with several options and an assessment of the relative value of each. The men at Austin & March, however, tended to propose one specific legal approach, and most often an approach in which they were personally invested.

> The guy in the next office—Mike Horn—is extraordinarily masculine in his approach. There is a right answer to a problem for everybody. I'll say, Wait a minute, that might make sense for this client, but mine has another set of problems. Mike doesn't tolerate that kind of ambiguity. There has to be a right answer.
>
> Well, the problem is that when one of the partners from the corporate department is working with both of us on the same issue but for different clients, it makes him nervous: "Gee, Mike thinks that there is an absolute right answer. Why is Isabel being so wishy-washy about it?"
>
> I may come up with a better answer more often, because I am willing to hand-craft a solution for a particular client, whereas he says, This is the right answer, and we'll do it this way for everybody!
>
> The other thing that goes on is that if someone brings a problem to me—and they basically don't have a problem—I look it over, and say, Well, there's this issue, and there's that issue, but I think basically that the way you've done it is one of several different ways to do it. There are three choices, all relatively equal; the client has chosen one, which may suit his business objectives a bit better, so I say, Fine, if that suits his business objectives, the others are not so much better from a tax point of view that it is worth switching him into one of the other two modes. But what Mike will do is, every single time, he'll switch it. Every time. It's, "You've got to do it my way!" They have to put their

mark on the transaction. It's like dogs—it's the peeing on the tree. You're marking out your territory: This is my tree!

But this too makes people uncomfortable when they deal with me. I'm not changing things enough. They think what a tax lawyer does is change things around—how come she doesn't make any changes? She must not be seeing things. Mike must be seeing more things, or understanding this better.

Most clients are more comfortable with the style they understand, and it is a very dominating kind of style. But I'm capable of being very definitive. If a client is uncomfortable with choices, I can move into that mode. "This is what we'll do." But one risk is, if you do things that way, you may end up in a power play with someone just like you on the other side. If you both come out with, "This is the way it's got to be!" you're going to end up with a clash. So I am more likely to get the lay of the land, get a sense of what the client wants me to do. Do they want me to present them with all the options and accompanying analysis?

When I deal with lawyers in this office, I always assume, which is probably a mistake, that they can tolerate the kind of analytic process that I'm going through, and that I should show them—we are on the same team, and there is no reason for me to hide that from view. We're all working together to get a particular solution for a particular client, and I ought to lay all my cards on the table. But I get the sense that many people here feel more comfortable with someone who imposes a structure on them. I don't know what to do about that.

When asked what she thought clients who were paying large sums for legal advice expected from their attorneys, both in terms of behavior and content, Isabel said that she was no longer certain:

What do clients expect? I don't really know. I thought they wanted someone with technical knowledge who could help them make a decision, not make it for them. These are sophisticated people who understand their business better than I do. I only understand a piece of it. I'm a specialist.

I had a conversation with a friend who is a professor. He was adamant that people want to be told what to do. They don't want their doctor giving them five choices. He hires people to make decisions.

I know what clients should want. I think you should go for the best outcome, and if it doesn't work, have a fall-back position. But do you really want to make everyone stand on their heads? It is easier for me to adjust my approach with clients after I get certain signals from them. Where I fall down is inside the office. I feel like I should be able to be honest, to let my guard down, to explain the process. But I get in trouble doing this.

There is one guy in the corporate department I don't get along with, and I'm beginning to realize that I

make him nervous. He's losing confidence in me. For example, last Thursday we had a conference with a client and it went very well. The client asked hard questions and I thought I answered them. But I also was supposed to have answers to lots of procedural questions. One of them was whether it takes 30 or 60 days to line up an appeal, but as the event is two years off I didn't bother with that one. I knew the client didn't care. But the other guy lashed out at me: "You don't know?" He seems motivated by fear. He comes from another firm and it seems to be cultural. With him you have to know all the answers. He was afraid I'd screw up.

We all have our own internal sense of risk assessment. We're dealing with situations where we are trying to figure out how the IRS will apply a particular rule to a particular situation. There aren't any answers. The relative risk assessment is a very subjective thing. Plus, it's one element in a business deal. Is it worth changing the business deal some way in order to get slightly better tax position? I would tend to tolerate more risk, or to see that the shades are very fine—"It's a bit better, but not much." I may be creating more tax risk because I am not willing to impose my will. I say, "It might be 5 percent better if you did this, but you make the choice, because you can better assess what it is going to do to the business deal."

I tend to look at the whole thing as pieces of one puzzle, whereas a man would tend to look at his one little piece, and say, "I can make this better."

I can understand changing certain kinds of behavior, being more aggressive, being on top of things, making everyone feel more important. Acting that way won't fundamentally change who I am or how I look at things. But with problem solving, I don't see any utility or benefit to doing things the male way. I tend to like my way!

Isabel acknowledged that another key area in which she differed from her male colleagues was in her ability to sell herself and to take personal risks in the process:

I have avoided a lot of things that would have done me good. I have always been very shy—in college I couldn't even talk to a professor—and it is uncomfortable for me to have lunch with clients or to insert myself into their life. It doesn't feel natural to me. If a client called me and said, "There is this group called Philadelphia Women in Real Estate; do you want to come?" I would say I was too busy. But I'm trying now to view things like that more as opportunities. I've been doing a lot of speaking. I gave a speech at a real estate institute, and unlike the old days I stayed after and tried to meet the people and make contacts.

One thing I have noticed is that the people who are very successful at marketing don't have very much self-awareness. People that do the best never question themselves. They just do it. The world is divided into people who like them and people who are jerks. It's very simple—you either like me, or you are a jerk! They don't worry about the jerks. But if I stick my neck out and nothing comes from it, I want to crawl into a hole and not get back out!

I know that I have set up blocks to certain kinds of work. Mike is able to get work off his desk, but when I get something new, I say, I'm not up to that right now. It is a resistance due to lack of confidence. Mike doesn't have that hurdle to get over.

We women coming into the professions and business wanted to be invisible, so we learned one kind of behavior in order to succeed at one stage. But this same behavior makes you fail at the next stage.

Isabel summarized what she perceived as her own career problems at Austin & March:

I was only 24 when I came to work here, and I probably wasn't a very mature 24. I'm still carrying the "immature me" image here with a lot of people. I could go to the firm across the street and not have that baggage, but here I can't get rid of it. Mike came in at 34 and was fully developed. He didn't have the ghosts. I was the youngest in my class and for two years the youngest partner. So that has affected people's sense of who I am.

For me the glass ceiling is an inability to project growth and development. With men, they can see the possibilities for growth and so they influence them to develop the positive qualities, to grow in certain ways. But they can't project the same way with women. They think our qualities are fixed because they are female ones.

I've changed, but people don't understand how much I have changed. Most partners remember me then. Success or failure now depends upon how those senior partners think of me, what is locked in their collective memory.

I could have left and joined another firm if I wanted to do more corporate tax work. But I feel loyalty and ties to my clients. I can't jump around just because I am building a career. Relationships are important.

I know I am not going to be happy saying, "I make a lot of money; I'll just do my stuff." No, it will really get to me. I have to find a way to use what I do to be successful.

See Appendix A for an interview with a senior male lawyer on the subject of career progression at firms like Austin & March.

Appendix A

INTERVIEW WITH JOHN SANFORD

John Sanford, 48, was a senior partner in the corporate department at another Philadelphia law firm,

Alden and May. Alden and May was similar in size and organization to Austin and March and tended to follow the same recruiting, hiring, and promotion practices. John Sanford, whose wife was a doctor and whose two daughters were recent college graduates, was particularly sympathetic to career problems faced by women.

The following excerpts are taken from a discussion with Sanford concerning what he believed were issues affecting women in firms such as his own.

On career paths in law firms: "Most lawyers come in as summer interns. During this time they are being wooed by the firm, with baseball games and visits to restaurants. A big chunk of the permanent staff comes from this group. During the first two years of employment associates have a 'major' and a 'minor,' in that they do work in two different departments. It is hoped that they will develop a single focus after 2 to 3 years. (Today's legal environment consists of a series of specialties—it is very unusual for a lawyer to be a generalist.)"

On women's career development: "The two senior women here came to the firm at a time when Harvard didn't even admit women to law school. In those days women lawyers typically did one of two things: they did trust and estate work or 'blue sky' filings. In either case they had very little client contact and certainly none with business clients. They did memo work, research, and maybe once in awhile might meet with a little old lady who needed her will drawn up. But certainly they would never meet with male clients. I think the attitude was, 'What? Women meet with male clients? Can women do this? Go out for a beer? What if they need to talk about baseball?' Often the expression of this would be much more subtle, but even today the fundamental question remains, 'How will they fit in?'

"For example, one prominent woman lawyer in town is a very successful litigator. She was recently in California on a vacation and met a man in his 60s who was talking about his legal difficulties. She said to him, 'I should be your lawyer. I win cases.' He stopped, and looked at her, and said, 'My, you are a very aggressive woman!' She was stunned. But that's how little perceptions have changed.

"Associates aren't expected to have billings, but—business-getting ability is a factor in their evaluation. It's a bit fuzzy. If they have some clients of their own, it would certainly indicate business-getting ability.

"The economics of law firms are that there needs to be work to support your salary. Either you are one of the partners who bring in work and then share it with the others—those partners are the most highly paid—or you are what is referred to as a 'support partner'—which means you do the work that supports the partners who bring in the work (i.e., you are a tax lawyer).

People in all the departments have tax issues. Another support area is trusts and estates, because clients who have businesses need to have their wills done. Also for every financing deal you need 'blue sky' lawyers who deal with the state security laws. So you don't need to bring in business to be a partner, but it's a precarious position to be in. If a big client leaves, then you have to find another niche."

On dealing with clients: "Some tax questions are unanswerable. But clients do not want to pay for lawyers who sit around and chew the fat. They prefer the approach of, 'Come right in and we'll deal with that question.' There is pressure from clients to be efficient. Some of them will look at every hour billed and ask us just what it is for. The clients from bigger companies have to answer for their own people.

"If it is early in the process and it appears that there is going to be a tax issue, you may call in someone from the tax department and say to the client, 'Let's let this person listen in so they get the story straight from you.' That is a more efficient approach because you catch the critical issues early.

"One of the things good client-getters have is antennae. They ask, What does the client want? With some it may be a certain result, regardless of the cost. Others want you to listen to their ideas first. It may be, 'No if's, just get it done!' But some people are real 'hands-on' clients who want to know all the ins and outs. But by far the most people want to know how to save money, time, or effort. The most successful relationships are those where I give them some choice. More than half would rather have choices.

"I like to involve the clients, give them an understanding of the process. It makes them better clients in the long run. Some of them are getting pretty good at the law after all of these years! The other way—just 'get it done'—is risky.

"At some point in the client relationship, it changes. You get to a point where you say, Let's go out for a beer. It's not going to change who you are, but the relationship changes. I'm still going to give you legal advice, even if the subject comes up outside the office. There's a moment—a beginning—when I decide that I will open my life to you a bit—I will trust you. At 10:00 at night I am going to tell you things, even if it's just jokes or anecdotes. I am the godfather to the children of two of my clients.

"You probably practice better law if you are able to listen better, if you have antennae—you can sense how the client is feeling. I can sense impatience. There is one client of mine who sends out an early warning signal I have learned to recognize. He doesn't know he is doing it, but it is clear to me, and I know we are near a breakdown point.

"Litigation may be a more transactional kind of law, but in most areas these are long-term, ongoing relationships."

Criteria for promotion: "The training here is quality, quality, quality. Every memo an associate does here is scrutinized. There can't be even a single typo. As an associate what is important is to demonstrate your technical skills—that is drummed into you. And even a single typo may prompt a partner to wonder what else may be wrong, what other mistakes you are making.

"Associates don't deal with clients. At that point in their career they are pleasing the partner. But once you are a partner, you must please the client—there is a definite shift. Pleasing the client is something you have to learn, a skill that is developed.

"Right now we have an associate who specializes in an area of tax law—a very minute area, part of pension law. She is from Brooklyn, and although she is very bright, she is not polished. But she is confident and cheerful. I find her very refreshing. She just had her review, which was excellent. But her salary and bonus were in the middle range. So she went to the head of her department and asked why, since her review was very high, why was her salary and bonus in the middle range? 'Well,' she was told, 'some people think you are too cheerful, too outgoing. And you are friends with one of the other associates who isn't that well regarded.' She had a great deal of difficulty telling me about this. I was appalled. But the fact is that the way to succeed in a firm this large is to be good at committee work, at politics. The firm is so big that you have to go through many levels to be recognized, and there is a type of person woven into the fabric of the organization who has a narrower view of life. They are the ones who will say, 'You aren't fitting in.' So, when she said to me, 'What does he mean?' I told her, 'Don't pay any attention to that garbage.' But in fact, confidence is seen as good, but overconfidence as bad—what does that really mean?

"Years ago I worked with a younger lawyer here who was terrific. I loved working with him. But he wasn't getting ahead, and even though I really hated doing it, I had to tell him: 'Cut your hair and stop wearing those flowered ties.' Now he's a partner. There is another associate here, a young woman—it's going to be easy for her. Her personality has no rough edges; she has the right kind of confidence in herself. It's like the typo in the memo—it's only one thing, but does it mean that there is something else? Something deeper?"

On women's problems: "I wonder if, for women looking back, being an associate wasn't really much easier than being a partner. It's like college, which you think is so rough you can't wait to get out, but then you find that the real world is much harder. As an associate you have one kind of anxiety—performing for partners—but as a partner those anxieties shift. It becomes life anxiety—getting an income. Access to clients, to boardrooms, networking. It's easier for men because they already have buddies who are established in business. How many women executives are there? The person a partner focuses on is the one who makes the key decision to hire a lawyer. A lawyer needs to get himself in a room full of people who hire lawyers.

"But even for men who are shy, or who are unprepared for the shift to selling that happens when they become partners; the world makes it easier for them. 'Oh, do I have to do that? Do I have to get clients? Well, I guess I'll call my roommate; he's the counsel at General Motors.' How many women have that kind of contact?"

JANE COSTELLO

In November 1983, Jane Costello was the youngest executive on the corporate staff at Chase, Beacon and Company, a large New York publishing company. As director of the new investor relations department, she was responsible for designing and implementing a program for improving communications between the company and its current and potential stockholders. Although she was only 31 years old, she had been chosen for the job in May 1982 because she had had several years of experience in the investment community.

Eighteen months into the job, Jane felt she had made important headway toward meeting the original goals of her department, but she wondered what she could do to convince senior management to take advantage of her particular skills when shaping corporate policy. During the previous summer she had written a memorandum to the chairman of the board, Hamilton Chase III, concerning questions that major investors had recently been asking about the company and had included her own recommendations for responding to the issues involved. The chairman's response had been immediate. Within 90 minutes of receiving her message, he had called a meeting. Present, in addition to Chase and Jane herself, were Russell Timm, the company's legal counsel; Rob Rittenhouse, the vice president of public affairs (to whom Jane reported); and Ted Page, the senior vice president for administration (to whom Rittenhouse reported).

Chase had questioned Jane closely about the exact wording of the investors' queries and had then spent the rest of the meeting talking with Timm and Page.

Several weeks later both Rittenhouse and Page told Jane that her memorandum to the chairman had been "more than a bit presumptuous," and that she "had overstepped her boundaries." It was not the first time they had criticized her style of communication with senior management.

Background

Jane Costello radiated self-confidence and enthusiasm whenever she spoke. Energetic and articulate, she dressed with the same flair that characterized her manner of speaking. There was a sparkle about her, a sense of drive and purpose. Anyone who had known her only since her arrival at Chase Beacon might have been surprised to hear her description of herself at age 20 when she graduated from college.

> I was shy and frightened. I didn't think a whole lot about myself in those days. When I did, it wasn't with much satisfaction.

At 17, Jane had looked forward to attending Earlham College in Indiana as a way out of a "claustrophobic" situation at home. But once there,

> I finished college in three years because I hated it so much. I was totally unequipped for being on my own. At college I took only English courses—I had no intellectual curiosity.

Jane decided to be a teacher: she sent applications to most of the public school systems in the state and accepted the first offer she received. It was from a high school in a small rural town about 50 miles outside of Indianapolis. She recalled:

> I didn't think of a job in terms of a career commitment. I didn't have any idea of what I had gotten myself into or what I planned to do with the rest of my life. I was there and I just did it, almost like a piece-worker in a factory.

To Jane's amazement, the school board found her teaching style objectionable and five months later, she was fired. Believing that her ability to type was all she could now rely on, she found a secretarial position in a state government office responsible for the state's pension funds. With the job came a salary which was $1,500 more than she had been earning as a teacher.

Despite the fact that her typing skills were really minimal, the professionals in her department responded to her enthusiasm.

> This job was a big deal to me. I was an active part of a busy office. To me, the stimulation was incredible and I was energetic. I came across as a real go-getter. Of course, I started from scratch. I had to ask people what a bond was because I didn't have any idea, and our office had responsibility for managing $200 million worth of bonds. But I had all this energy. I loved it there.

After six months she was spending about three-quarters of her time on nonsecretarial jobs. She talked with brokers. She was involved in decisions on stocks and bonds to be added or dropped from the pension fund. She met a number of Wall Street brokers when they came to Indianapolis on business.

As a result, she began to understand the complexities of the stock market. Three years later she decided to move again and to try for a job in New York City. She put her furniture in storage, sold her car, and moved to the Barbizon Hotel in Manhattan.

Once there, she called Wall Street brokers she had met in Indianapolis and after seven weeks she found a position as a research assistant with Houghton and Everett, investment bankers. Her salary was $21,000.

She also enrolled in evening courses at New York University Graduate School of Business.

After about six months on her new job, Jane called a meeting of the four security analysts whom she assisted and suggested that they give her more work to do. She recalled:

> They made some effort, but they were used to doing things themselves. Security analysts are independent individual performers. So I went to the head of the personnel department and asked some general questions about consulting which I thought might be a good place for me. He arranged a meeting with Rich Gehrig, one of the whiz kids. He was a senior vice president in the corporate finance department. I had an hour-long talk with Rich and he called the personnel department and told them he wanted me on his staff.

Jane described Houghton and Everett as a company that emphasized excellence.

> The company song is—you are the smartest people in the world. Their typical male associate is a Harvard MBA from the top 10 percent of his class. He is groomed for two or three years, travels, meets clients all over the country, while still serving in a support role. By the end of his second or third year he becomes a vice president. Most of the men who are vice presidents are making $100,000 by the time they are 30 or 31.

Like most brokerage companies, H&E had several specialized divisions. The corporate finance department, in which Jane worked, was one of them.

> I was taken on as an attachment to Rich Gehrig. He advised companies on how to handle their financial problems and I was his back-up person. Sometimes he would send me to the library for a week to learn everything I could about a whole industry. Then I would report back on what the key issues were so that he could pursue these with the client. I had a little office in the back and was still making $21,000, less than some of the secretaries.

A year after Jane started work, the corporate finance department was reorganized and this helped her gain more responsibility.

> With a bigger corporate finance department, I had a lot more flexibility. I let the people in the group know what I was willing to do and capable of doing, though still in a support role.
>
> That's usually the role of the associate: support. You're not going to go out much on your own to work with clients. But your days are your own and you are an individual performer. You work with one or two senior people at a time, and over the course of a year you work with a number of different people. You feel pretty independent because you're not strongly supervised,

you determine your own priorities and you're playing on a team but it's not cohesive. Everyone fits into the organization in an individual sort of way.

Three years later Jane had earned her MBA. In spite of this she had begun to feel that she was in a rut, going nowhere with the company. Around her, men with MBAs were being promoted to vice presidencies. She decided upon two courses of action: to send out résumés to other companies and to discuss the situation with Rich Gehrig.

> I had this incredible session with Gehrig. I told him I was sick and tired of being ripped off. "You guys are paying the new associates from Harvard $32,000 a year and I'm only getting $26,500. I have my MBA plus I've been with you for four years and I worked for several years before that. He said, "All right, I'll see what I can do." He went to the president of the company. He not only got me a raise to $35,000 but all the vice presidential privileges as well—use of the officers' dining room and the potential of earning 30–40 percent of my salary as a member of the officers' bonus pool.

Jane was not immediately named a vice president, however. She explained:

> It was the company's policy that the announcement of the new vice presidents was made after a board of directors meeting in June. Whether it was normal for people to get their privileges before the announcement, I didn't know. I wasn't actually told I would be made a vice president in June. I didn't know what to expect.

Before she could find out what would happen in June, Jane left the company. She had this to say about leaving Houghton and Everett:

> The implication that you are the best runs through the company so you have some very egotistical, high-powered people who think they are gods. I wasn't aware of that at the beginning, but once I was, it was a real challenge to try to compete because I'm a very competitive person. But I couldn't win. If I was ever going to be vice president, I knew it would be a second-level sort of thing. That's when I started thinking there are places where corporations can use people like me.
>
> I realized I didn't know anything about good management because Houghton and Everett was not managed like a standard corporation. The whole scene just wasn't for me. I am a process person. I think in terms of organizing resources to meet objectives. Planning, implementing, evaluating—that's the way my mind works.
>
> Then, too, I had begun to realize my potential. Business school had a lot to do with making me realize that I am a bright, capable person.

In January 1982 even before she met with Gehrig, she had sent her résumé to all Fortune 500 companies with headquarters in New York. This happened to coincide with Chase Beacon's search for a director of investor relations, and Rob Rittenhouse, vice president for public affairs, invited her for an interview. After several meetings with Jane, Rittenhouse recommended her to the chairman, Hamilton Chase III. At the time Chase felt strongly that the position should be filled by an older and more experienced person, preferably a company veteran. He told Rittenhouse to continue his search. More than 100 interviews later, Rittenhouse advised Chase that Jane was still the best candidate. She was offered the job and accepted it immediately.

Chase, Beacon and Company

Chase Beacon was one of the oldest, largest, and most respected publishing houses in the United States. (Annual operating revenues in 1982 were $1.4 billion, a growth of 10.5 percent over 1981.) Founded in the 1890s by two magazine publishers, the company established its early reputation by publishing technical journals for scientists and engineers. By 1930, it was publishing 15 magazines. In the 1940s, the company added works of fiction, nonfiction, and educational texts. During the 1950s expansion continued with the addition of paperback books, a highly acclaimed scientific encyclopedia, and specialized periodicals in the fields of medicine, art, architecture, and the social sciences.

In the 1960s and early 1970s, Chase Beacon acquired two companies in the information systems industry, five radio and television stations, a number of special interest book clubs, and several established news, sports, and fashion magazines. Each acquisition was brought into one of the company's operating divisions. (In 1982 the company had eight divisions: Domestic Books; International Books; Specialized Periodicals; General Audience Periodicals; Educational Texts and Services; Radio and Television; Information Services; and Book Clubs.) Although corporate management set overall company policy, each division president was virtually autonomous. He ran his division as an independent profit center. Division presidents had considerable prestige and influence within the company.

Hamilton Chase III became chairman of the board, chief executive officer, and president of Chase Beacon in 1982. He was the fourth member of the Chase family to hold these positions, and Chase Beacon was still considered a "family business" by some of its older executives, many of whom had been with the company for their entire careers. In 1982 seven of the eight division presidents had been with Chase Beacon since the 1950s. The company employed 12,000 people and was considered a leader among U.S. corporations in the area of social responsibility. It had begun a conscious effort to upgrade its women managers in the 1970s and by 1982, two women were corporate staff officers (a vice president and senior vice president), and others held important line positions.

The Investor Relations Department

Investor Relations was a new unit within the Department of Public Affairs, which included Internal Communications (employee newspapers) and the Contributions Department. (See Exhibit 1 for a partial organization chart.) In Jane's opinion there was a need to be met:

> I think the company finally realized that Wall Street people really do speak a different language. They think differently. It's not a whole new world for people like me. I don't make mistakes, through ignorance of the language, that a corporate person might make.

She believed that as a result her role had expanded.

> When I drew up my department plan, it included having the chairman make a number of speeches to bankers and large investors around the country. But he only wanted to do one or two speeches a year because he was concentrating on the internal affairs of the company. So although it wasn't part of my role as negotiated before I came here, I have become the company spokesman. My official job description doesn't reflect that. It's just something that happened.
>
> When they wrote my job description, they were hoping to hire somebody from inside the company, someone who would be a superb administrator, setting up meetings, knowing who was going to be there, what kind of people they were, what they were interested in, but not actually running the meetings as I do. It's a bit of an unusual situation, but I think my personal style has something to do with it. I'm an articulate person and I'm comfortable speaking to groups of 100 people or more.

Soon after Jane assumed her position, she was asked to make a speech at a lunch for the eight division controllers. This was her formal introduction to the organization. Rob Rittenhouse also introduced her to the eight division presidents, one by one. Beyond that it had been up to her to establish her own information network. She said:

> When an investor calls me up to get information, if I don't know the answer, I look in the company telephone directory to see who's in charge of that area and I make a call. Sometimes I call people up and introduce myself and ask them to lunch, but I don't have a lot of

time for that because I'm also setting up lunches with potential investors. But I want to keep in touch with marketing, with finance, with legal people.

I want to know everything that's happening in the divisions. In my field I have to know what our company's strengths are; its weaknesses; problems it's struggling with; opportunities for the future; management's ideas about what the company will look like in 10 years, and how they're going to get there.

I know what kind of information I need because securities analysts and investment people always ask the same kinds of questions. I know what their concerns are, and how they think.

Jane explained how the environment at Chase Beacon differed from what she had experienced in other jobs.

In the beginning I really didn't think I had to ask permission to do anything. In all my jobs I was an individual performer. Here they want team players. The corporate reality is that it's an authoritarian environment.

She described her working relationship with Rob Rittenhouse:

He's the kind of guy who lets the people reporting to him pretty much do their own thing. I don't think we understand each other on a personal level, however. He kids me about taking this job too seriously. During my first year, I worked 40 out of 52 Sundays. I only took 12 Sundays off. He wants me to care a little less.

When he hired Jane, Rittenhouse told her that the chairman would have preferred a man in his 40s or 50s for the job, had he been able to find such a person. Jane remarked:

So almost as soon as I came here I knew there had been resistance to hiring me. I was told *that* within 30 days so I would know what kind of resistance to overcome! The whole first year on the job, my boss spent a lot of time telling me to be less visible. I was told that I should "cool it" and not go too fast in the beginning, that I should try to "charm" people. He told me to be more charming, less threatening, to calm down, not to come on too strong, not to give somebody six ideas in a meeting but just to slightly suggest one. So as I met senior executives, he gave me tips on how to deal with each one.

Jane had not been at Chase Beacon for very long before she recognized that Rob Rittenhouse had been "extraordinarily disturbed" by a number of the initiatives she had taken. She had written letters to potential investors to accompany mailings from her department. In addition, she had written to several division presidents and to senior vice presidents on the corporate staff, asking for information and also setting up meetings between senior management people and potential investors. Rittenhouse had learned of these contacts indirectly, from other managers. Jane described his response:

Rob is a man who avoids confrontations. He has a difficult time giving negative feedback, but finally he said to me, "Listen, I want to see everything that comes out of your secretary's typewriter, for approval. I want you to advise me about whatever you do before you do it."

Jane attributed these early problems at Chase Beacon to her "lack of sensitivity to the power of the written word." She said:

Rob has told me that I have been perceived by the company as arrogant. I think my reputation came from the way I wrote. My memos weren't couched in a gentle enough tone. I wrote, "I think you should . . ." or "I want you to . . ." instead of "You might consider . . ." or "I'd like to suggest . . ."

Jane said that another problem was her own youthfulness.

I have been told since the day I joined the company that it would be terrific if I had some gray hairs. My boss and his boss tell me that if I had some gray hairs, management would probably like me a lot better.

I don't mean to say that I don't have other problems. I had lunch with the number-three man in the company today and he still calls me "dear." I changed my hairstyle this summer. Everyone here talked to me about that for weeks. They talk a lot about my clothes.

Jane's biggest concern was that top management was not using her as a resource person.

I need to interact with the division heads, plus the top six or eight people in the company, so that if an investor or a reporter asks me a question about Chase Beacon, I can go to the right place for information. They are prompt in giving me answers, but they aren't asking me questions to learn something useful for themselves. They don't involve me in long-range planning, where my knowledge of the financial community could be helpful. They don't ask me for advice on where the stock market is going—how they should manage their pension money. They don't use me as a consultant on the money market.

I've tried to send "alert" memos on what investors are asking about, but they feel that sort of thing is none of my business. It's probably a reflection of their perception of this department's role within the company. It may be a matter of my personal style.

At this point, I feel my best bet is still to keep testing the water, occasionally sending an "alert" memo, including—gently—a recommendation that might reflect that there is expertise here that might be called upon.

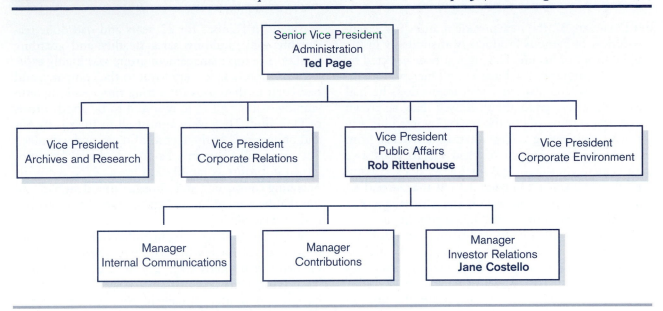

Jane said that she was learning how to communicate more effectively within the company by emulating Rob Rittenhouse.

> I defer to his authority and make him aware that I defer to his authority. I see the way he defers to the chairman, just by things like always ending a conversation or a memo with a question: "What do you think?" "Would you like me to follow up on this?" I end all my memos to Rob in the same way now.
>
> I've watched him very carefully. I see how he sits when he and the chairman and I are in a meeting, how he handles himself. I see how his personality changes, how he chooses his words. I feel his fear, his incredible fear—"What do you want?" "Do you mean this?"—Trying to pull out of the chairman what the chairman wants, making it clear with every sentence that he knows the chairman is the boss. I have watched that very carefully and picked up on it. It's not quite second nature to me yet, but it's getting to be, in terms of the way I react to him.
>
> All this is a super education. I have accepted that in order to be as extraordinarily effective in business and as successful as I plan to be, I have to be more sensitive. This is an important thing for me to learn, because it really does work. That's why it doesn't grate on me to do this. I accept the fact that I am in the learning phase. I realize that it compromises me, or forces me to change somewhat, but I have really accepted that this might make the difference between the people who are allowed to shoot up in the company without any resistance and those who aren't.

Jane discussed some of her goals for her department in the next year.

> I want to send corporate information to hundreds of people to tell them who we are. I want to redesign the annual report and our quarterly reports so that they are more informative. So far my recommendations in that area have not been accepted.
>
> Investor relations is very marketing oriented. I want to really sell the company image. I want to be more aggressive in getting our message out. I want to compete with every other company whose stock is sold in the market.
>
> I want to be more aggressive on staffing. An investor relations department for a company this size needs at least five or six professionals. We are only three and a half now and we're being reduced to two and a half in 1984. Management doesn't feel we need that extra person.

Jane also discussed her personal long-term goals.

> Wall Street people see corporate investor relations as a stepping-stone to a line position. In this company, I know the good divisions, who's good to work with and whom to avoid. I know where the company is expecting growth in the 1990s. In five years, I will be running a division. If it comes to the point where I can't move on a fast track here, I might go to law school. That probably is a good credential for a chief executive of the 1990s.

33   JIM DONOVAN (A)

Jim Donovan, 37, the new president and chief executive officer of Famous Products, was suddenly in the toughest spot of his life. Having just been selected by Omega Corporation, a huge conglomerate, to take over as president of their latest acquisition, he had been feeling very good about himself. Having grown up on "the wrong side of the tracks," worked his way through engineering college, earned an MBA from Harvard Business School, worked for 10 years as a management consultant and for 2 years as a successful president of a small company, he felt that he had arrived. The company he was going to manage was known throughout the world, had a good reputation, and would provide a good opportunity for visibility in the parent company. The pay would be the highest he had ever earned, and, while the money itself was not that important (though he'd be able to assure his wife and four children financial security), he enjoyed the indicator of success a high salary provided. And Jim was eager to manage a company with over 1,000 employees; the power to get things done on such a large scale was very attractive to him.

When Omega had selected him, they had told him that Don Bird, the current president of Famous Products, was close to retirement and would be moved upstairs to chairman of the board. Bird had been president of Famous for 22 years and had done reasonably well, building sales steadily and guarding quality. The top management group was highly experienced, closely knit, very loyal to the company, and had been in their jobs for a long time. As long-term employees they all were reported to be good friends of Don Bird. They were almost all in their early 60s and quite proud of the record of their moderate-sized but successful company. Famous had not, however, grown in profits as rapidly as Omega expected of its operating companies, and Omega's president had told Jim that he wanted Jim to "grab ahold of Famous and make it take off."

With this challenge ringing in his ears, Jim flew out to Milwaukee for his first visit to Famous Products. He had talked briefly with Don Bird to say that he'd be arriving Thursday for half a day, then would be back for good after 10 days in New York at Omega. Bird had been cordial but rather distant on the phone, and Jim wondered how Bird was taking Jim's appointment. "I've only got a few hours here," thought Jim. "I wonder how I should play it."

STOP: DO NOT READ *Case B until requested to do so by your instructor.*

JIM DONOVAN (B)

34

JIM DONOVAN (B)

When Jim pulled up to Famous Products' headquarters in his rented car, he noticed the neat grounds and immaculate landscaping. To his surprise, Don Bird met him at the door. Bird had on a very conservative blue business suit, black tie, black shoes, and white shirt. He peered out at Jim through old-fashioned steel-rimmed glasses and said, "Welcome to our plant. You're just in time for our usual Thursday morning executive meeting; would you like to sit in on that and meet our people?" Jim thought that the meeting would give him a chance to observe the management group in action, and he readily agreed, planning to sit back and watch for as long as he could.

Jim was ushered into the most formal meeting room he could remember ever having seen. The dark-paneled room was dominated by a long, heavy table with 12 high-backed chairs around it. Seven of the chairs were filled with unsmiling executives in dark suits.

Bird led Jim to the front of the room, indicated an empty chair to the left of the seat at the head of the table, then sat down in the place that was obviously his. Turning to the group, he said:

> Gentlemen, I want you to meet Mr. Donovan; but before I turn the meeting over to him, I want you to know that I do not believe he should be here; I do not believe he's qualified, and I will give him no support. Mr. Donovan . . .

35   KATE COOPER

My name is Kate Cooper. I am 31, a registered nurse with a bachelor's degree in nursing and 6 years of supervisory experience. I was charge nurse and then house supervisor in the medical/surgical wing of a large regional medical center and was in-service director in charge of continuing education and staff development in a geriatric nursing setting. In addition, I have been teaching nursing courses in the night program at a local technical school.

Ready for the next step in my career, I obtained the position of Manager of Adult Services for the twenty-bed adult psychiatric wing at Green Meadows Hospital. Green Meadows was a newly constructed forty-room community hospital for the care of acutely ill psychiatric patients. It was the twenty-third facility owned by Southern Hospitals Corporation (SHC), the largest chain of acute-care psychiatric hospitals in the country.

I felt excited about my new position. I saw it as a fine opportunity for career development in nursing, and the possibility of transferring to other facilities in the chain was a definite benefit in my eyes. I had many projects to complete before the planned opening of the hospital in 2 weeks, and I started my new position with high energy and enthusiasm.

My supervisor, Alan Jones, who hired me, was assistant administrator of the hospital. He had 1 year of previous experience as director of nursing at a fifty-bed acute-care psychiatric hospital. On my first day he encouraged me to "just dig right in and get started" organizing my department. I asked to see my job description and the hospital policy manual to become familiar with the organization employing me. Alan gave me a job description and explained that I was part of the "start-up" process. At this time there was no personnel handbook for employees.

One condition of employment I stipulated in accepting the job was that I be able to continue my schooling as a part-time graduate student working on my master's degree in nursing education. Alan Jones readily agreed to this condition, stating that he was a strong supporter of continuing education for all managers and staff.

In my opinion the first week I worked for Green Meadows consisted of many wasted hours. I learned on my own that my main task prior to the opening was to hire the patient care staff for my twenty-bed unit. I tried to line up interviews for nurses and mental health workers, since Alan Jones had told me to "go ahead and hire the personnel you need for your unit."

Peter Smith, manager of the eighteen-bed chemical dependency unit, had previously worked with Alan Jones at a psychiatric hospital 50 miles from Green Meadows. Peter had been hired by Alan along with two other managers from that location who had not yet arrived at Green Meadows. Peter was hiring staff for his unit, and he told me he wanted to interview the nurses and mental health workers also, since those employees would be working on his unit as well.

This request surprised me. I tried to find an organization chart and asked the hospital administrator, Doug Anderson, in passing one morning if he had one I could see. He jokingly asked me if I was serious. "After all," he said, "I think it is changing every day." I laughed at first, but my amusement was short-lived when no chart was forthcoming. Eventually, I came to visualize the organization chain as presented in Figure 1.

Doug Anderson had served as office manager in a small hospital in California. His wife, an occupational therapist, was also a part-time employee at Green Meadows. Two of Doug's hires were a personal friend from California, Leonard Snare, and Leonard's wife. Leonard's sole job qualification was certification to be a psychiatric technician, earned by attending workshops. His wife worked in the business office.

Construction work had progressed, and Green Meadows was ready for staff occupancy 1 week before the planned hospital opening. Although much remained to be done and things were still confused, I was excited about moving into my new office.

During the previous week Peter and I had hired our initial staff. I was worried my unit would not be ready to receive patients and had written a 5-day orientation program specific to the unit that included information I thought my patient care staff would find beneficial. I shared the orientation outline with Peter, who informed me that he would need 2½ days to teach the new staff members *his* program alone.

I was shocked and angered that he had planned this commitment for my staff: With one week left, both orientation programs could not be completed prior to opening. I asked Peter if his plan had been cleared with Alan Jones. Peter replied with a grin, "Of course. It was his idea." As a result, I sought out Alan and asked if he could meet on some neutral ground with the adult psychiatric and chemical dependency units. I told him that orientation to my department was just as important as orientation to Peter's department. Alan told me that Peter had his program all ready to

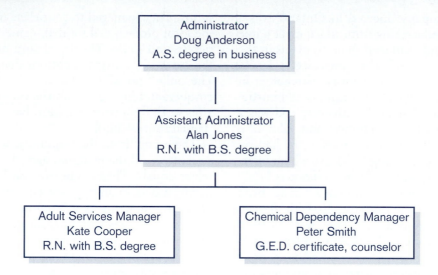

FIGURE 1   *Green Meadows Hospital Management Staff—Partial Organization Chart*

go and would only need "a couple of days" to present it. All of this left me feeling very frustrated.

I had other problems with Alan. Despite his having told me to go ahead and hire staff nurses and mental health workers, I later discovered he was hiring those people at the same time I was interviewing prospective employees. In addition, Alan had instructed me to assume the role of in-service director and write the staff orientation program. He told me that I would have to be the unit head nurse for the chemical dependency unit, although I told him that I thought the responsibilities would be too great due to my duties as the adult services unit manager. Alan's response to my doubts was his standard one in such situations: "You are tough, and I know you can handle it."

As a result of these and similar interactions with Alan, I became confused and frustrated by his lack of support and his behavior, which seemed inconsistent with directions he had given me. I was overwhelmed with the amount of work and responsibility. I was most frustrated and angered when additional tasks were "dumped" on me because I felt I had to complete the extra work as soon as possible in addition to doing my own work on the unit.

Alan apparently had difficult relationships with some other employees as well. Other female managers complained almost from the start that Alan needed to be "put in his place" for his sexist remarks and behaviors. Doug Anderson received reports indicating that Alan's behavior had been inappropriate on several occasions. Doug also heard second-hand that Alan was overstepping his responsibilities as assistant administrator and making policy statements contrary to Doug's positions.

This general employee dissatisfaction continued. Three months after the opening of the hospital Alan Jones strongly implied that I would have to quit school. He explained that he expected people to be there, saying that "to be a good manager you should be here all the time." I took issue with this and sought Doug Anderson's assistance. Doug had never been informed about my going to school and was unaware that I was even taking classes. Alan alone had approved my return to school to continue my education. Doug's response was simply to encourage me to speak with Alan again and "communicate better with him."

Feeling pressure on several fronts, I reached the limit of my tolerance with Alan Jones and handed in my notice of resignation. Alan Jones subsequently refused to speak with me. The manager of the chemical dependency unit told me that my timing was lousy, accused me of trying to create waves, and said I should put work as a priority over continuing my education.

KINGSTON COMPANY

The Kingston Company, located in Ontario, was a medium-sized manufacturing firm, which made a line of machine parts and marketed them to plants in the southeastern section of the province. Harold Kingston, the president and majority shareholder in the company, held a master of business administration degree from an American university and was a vigorous supporter of the usefulness and value of a graduate business education. As a result, he had on his staff a group of four young MBAs, to whom he referred as the "think group" or "troubleshooters."

The four members of the group ranged in age from the youngest at 23 to the oldest at 35, with the two intermediate members being 27. They were all from different universities and had different academic backgrounds. Their areas of interest were marketing, organizational behavior, operations research, and finance. All had been hired simultaneously and placed together in the think group by Mr. Kingston because, as he put it, "With their diverse knowledge and intelligence, they ought to be able to solve any of this company's problems."

For their first month on the job, the "Big Four," as they became known in the firm, familiarized themselves with the company's operations and employees. They spent a half day every week in conference with Mr. Kingston and his executive committee, discussing the goals and objectives of the company and going over the history of the major policy decisions made by the firm over the years. While the process of familiarization was a continuing one, the group decided after four weeks that it had uncovered some of the firm's problems and that it would begin to set out recommendations for the solution of these problems.

From the beginning the members of the group had worked long hours and could usually be found in the office, well after the plant had closed, discussing their findings and trading opinions and ideas. The approach to problem solving that they adopted was to attack each problem as a group and to pool their ideas. This seemed to give a number of different slants to the problems and many times helped clear away the bias that inevitably crept into each member's analysis.

Mike Norton, the finance specialist and the youngest member of the group, and Jim Thorne and Dave Knight, the operations research man and the behavioral management man, respectively, spent a lot of time together outside the work environment. They seemed to have similar interests, playing tennis and golf together and generally having a keen interest in sports. They managed to get tickets together to watch the local professional football games, and ice hockey tickets, and so on. The fourth and oldest member of the group, Cy Gittinger, did not share these interests. The only "sports" he played were shuffleboard and croquet; and he didn't join the other three too often after work for a beer in a local bar, since he also abstained from alcohol.

The group, from the beginning, was purposely unstructured. All the members agreed to consider themselves equals. They occupied one large office, each having a desk in an opposite corner, with the middle of the room acting as a "common." Basic decisions usually were made with the four men pacing about in the open area, leaning against the walls and desks, and either squeezing or bouncing "worry balls" of a rubber putty substance, used for cleaning typewriters, off the walls. The atmosphere was completely informal, and the rest of the firm kidded the members of the group about the inordinately large amount of typewriter cleaner used in the room when there were no typewriters to be seen.

While consensus was not required, the group members found that they were able to agree on a course of action most of the time. When they were unable to do so, they presented their differing opinions to Mr. Kingston, in whose hands the final decision rested. They acted in a purely staff capacity, and, unless requested to help a particular manager and authorized to do so by Mr. Kingston, they confined their reports to the president and his executive committee. Reports usually were presented in written form, with all four members of the group present and contributing verbal support and summation.

The group realized that working in close contact would result in strained relations on occasion, and the members agreed to attempt to express their feelings accurately and try to understand issues from the other members' points of view. Jokes about "happiness boys," "junior Baruchs," "peddlers," and "formula babies" were bandied about, and each of the four made a conscious effort to see the biases introduced by his field of interest. Attempts at controlling the discussion and establishing a leadership position were handled by pointing out the behavior to the individual involved.

However, as the months passed, there seemed to be a growing uneasiness in the relationship between Norton, Thorne, and Knight and the fourth member, Gittinger. The three brought their feelings out one day when they were playing golf. At the 19th hole over a drink, Thorne commented on the amount of time Gittinger spent talking to Mr. Kingston in his office. They all spent a great deal of time out of their office talking to managers and workers all through the plant, gathering data on various problems; but Thorne remarked Gittinger seemed to confine his activities to the upper levels of management far more than the others did. The other two had made the same observation but felt that it was really hard to put a finger on anything "wrong" about consulting with the president continually. They agreed that their fact-finding did not generally require as much time at higher levels as Gittinger was devoting; but when the point was brought up in subsequent discussion at the office, Cy explained that to get information from Mr. Kingston, he found an "indirect" approach, which entailed a certain amount of small talk, was most successful.

After the group had been functioning for 10 months, Kingston called them into a meeting with his executive committee and went through an appraisal of their performance. He was, he said, tremendously pleased that his think group had performed so well, and he felt vindicated in his belief in the potency of applying the skills learned in graduate business school. His executives added their words of praise. Then Mr. Kingston brought up a suggestion he said he and Cy Gittinger had been discussing for the past month and a half, to appoint one of the group members as a coordinator. The coordinator's job would be to form a liaison between Kingston and the executive committee on the one hand and the group on the other and also to guide the group, as a result of the closer ties of the coordinator with the management team, in establishing a set of priorities for different problem areas.

When Kingston had finished describing the proposal, which, it seemed, met with his and the committee's approval, Jim Thorne remarked that this procedure seemed to be unnecessary in the light of the previous smooth functioning of the group and began to explain that such a change would upset the structure and goals of the group. He was interrupted by Mr. Kingston, who said he had an important engagement. "We'll leave the working out of all the details to you men," he said. "We don't want to impose anything on you, and we have all agreed that you should be the ones to work out just how this new plan can be implemented." At this point the meeting ended.

As the group walked back to their office, Gittinger was the only one who talked. He wondered aloud who would be the most suitable man for the coordinator's job and repeated Kingston's words, citing the advantages that would accrue to the company with the creation of such a position. Since it was 4:45 P.M., they all cleared their desks and left the plant together, splitting up outside to go home.

At 6 P.M., Thorne called Norton to ask him what he thought about the developments of the afternoon. The latter expressed surprise, anger, and resentment that the decision had been made without the consultation of the group and remarked that Knight, to whom he had just been talking, felt the same way. The trio made arrangements to meet for dinner at their downtown athletic club at 7 P.M. that evening to discuss the situation.

37   L. E. S., INC.

Background

L. E. S., Inc., is a large U.S. company engaged in the manufacture and sales of a wide range of electrical products. Headquarters are in Ohio, with five regional sales and marketing offices. L. E. S. has 17 manufacturing facilities mainly concentrated in the Northeast, with newer plants in the Southwest. There is a national network of warehouses to service the U.S. market. The manufacturing operations are organized on a divisional basis: power and transmission, electrical components, and small appliances. There are three plants manufacturing electrical components, such as switches, sockets, and relays. One of these plants is L. E. S. (Clarksburg).

The site at Clarksburg consists of a manufacturing plant where low-cost, high-volume electrical components are assembled for the computer and electrical industry. Over the last three years, Clarksburg Plant has doubled its workforce in response to rapid sales growth. (See organization chart in Exhibit 1.)

There are six production sections:

Section 1—connector and cable assemblies.

Sections 2 and 3—switches, relays, and timers.

Sections 4 and 5—circuit board components.

Section 6—circuit breaker assemblies.

Sections 2 through 6 work two shifts, Section 1 operates three shifts, and each shift has its own supervisor. Half of the production operators have less than one year with the company. Only four section shift supervisors have more than two years' service, and only two of these have had any supervisory training.

KEY CHARACTERS

Manufacturing Manager

Martin Collins; MBA; age 44. Overall responsibility for Clarksburg Plant. Reports to the divisional vice president in Ohio. Martin has been manufacturing manager for six years, having been appointed to the position from a job at headquarters.

Production Manager

John Drummond; no formal qualifications; age 49. John has worked in the plant for 15 years, 4 as a supervisor, and the last 11 as a production manager. Responsible for the six production sections and their maintenance. This involves planning work schedules, dealing with day-to-day production issues, and the maintenance of equipment and a workshop to build and modify equipment according to plans drawn by the design department.

Quality Manager

Mike Peterson; degree in electrical engineering; age 43. Mike has worked in quality in the plant for the last 12 years, and he ensures that products meet quality standards by the inspection of finished products prior to dispatch to the warehouse. He also is responsible for the inspection of incoming new materials.

Engineering Manager

Chris Brooks; degree in electrical engineering; MBA; age 35. The only woman on the management team, she was recruited by the manufacturing manager, three years ago, from outside the company. She is responsible for the development of new products, the improvement of existing manufacturing methods, and technical problem solving in the production departments. There is also a responsibility for process control. Most of the projects relating to the former two activities are self-generated and important in maintaining the competitiveness of L. E. S. The production department relies heavily on the technical expertise of the engineering department in maintaining a smooth flow of operations.

Materials Manager

Rick Sweeney; experience; age 39. He has spent six years in this job. He plans production and ensures the required amount of materials are in stock to manufacture customer orders. Responsible also for implementing the manufacturing requirements planning (MRP) to optimize and control material inventories.

Design Manager

Bob Lemire; degree in mechanical engineering; age 30. Worked for L. E. S. (Clarksburg) for one year. He is responsible for the design of new equipment and the modification of existing equipment. This department works closely with the maintenance department.

TEAM OBJECTIVES

Objectives for each year are set at an annual seminar for the management team listed above. These objectives were identified by the manufacturing manager and agreed to by the team after a brief discussion. Extracts from the annual plan show the main priorities of the company this year:

> We are in a very competitive era in which we must reduce costs to survive. Part of this activity is increasing

EXHIBIT 1 *Organization Chart L. E. S., Inc. (Clarksburg): 236 Employees*

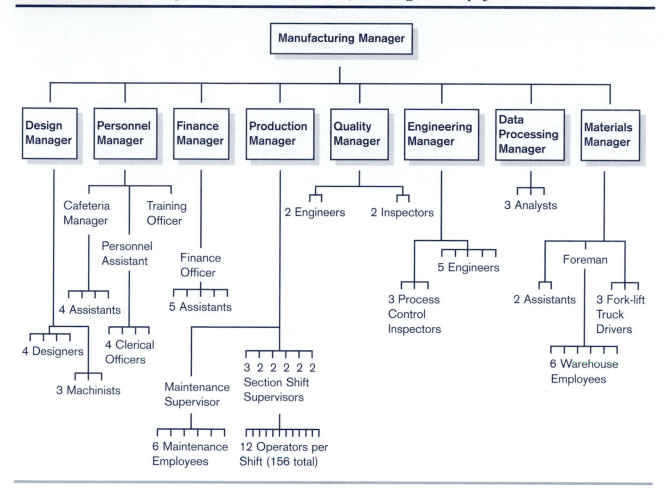

productivity through the introduction of more efficient manufacturing activity. Specifically, this involves the introduction of new equipment and processes, the modification of existing equipment, and the more effective use of that equipment to improve output, quality, and reduce wastage.

It is extremely important to our overall success that we carry out our activities on a team basis. The company will only maintain and improve its product leadership through commitment to a team effort.

Currently, a number of production problems exist in the plant, resulting in late deliveries to customers. These problems have been identified by the management team as:

1. A high scrap rate: 15 percent of wasted products and materials over all sections.

2. Section 1 being fully utilized, 24 hours a day. This results in no leeway in meeting excess demands.

3. Quality problems, requiring products to be reworked to meet quality standards.

Last week, the memorandum shown at the top of the next page was sent.

The Management Meeting

Martin Collins (manufacturing manager): "Thanks for coming. As you know, we have a number of problems that we need to resolve if we are to improve productivity levels and meet current and future market demands. We need to improve manufacturing efficiency, and there are two main problems we need to consider: One, productivity is falling. We have more people but they seem to be less effective. Second, there are a number of projects that have not and will not be completed in the time scale we would like them to be.

MEMORANDUM

From: M. Collins   To: J. Drummond
                                    M. Peterson
                                    C. Brooks
                                    R. Sweeney
                                    B. Lemire

MANUFACTURING MEETING

As you are aware, we have a number of problems affecting plant performance. I have organized a meeting for next Monday, 2 P.M., to assess the situation and identify some solutions to our problems. This situation is reaching a critical point and we need to take action fast. Please ensure that you attend.

"In today's climate we cannot afford to continue like this. We need to address these issues—and fast! Perhaps we can start by assessing the current situation."

"The problem is, we've just got too much to do," said John (production manager). "We've got to produce more and more with the same number of sections. Section 1 is running to capacity, 24 hours a day, seven days a week. We need more equipment. Maintenance and design are working on improving our existing equipment, but it's a slow job with the breakdowns they keep having to deal with. Bob and I have discussed this and agree it would help us both."

Bob (design manager) nodded in agreement.

"I don't think it's only that, John; we have got quality problems as well, which need to be ironed out," said Chris (engineering manager).

"We can't afford to buy more equipment until we've dealt with our existing problems," said Martin. "The emphasis is on cost reduction as well as on maintaining our market share."

John replied, "The other problem is that half the employees only started with us less than a year ago, so they haven't much experience. The supervisors haven't much idea about work scheduling, as most of them have had no training in supervision. I have to keep on their backs all the time to make sure they get the job done."

"Why don't we get the personnel department down to look at the possibility of training those who need it?" asked Chris. "We could use training as a base for increasing individual efficiency."

"When do you think we have time to take them off production?" John replied. "We have enough trouble meeting targets with everyone working."

"That's true," said Martin.

"Give me some more operators and I might have the time," added John.

"I think it would be worthwhile looking at equipment and staffing implications, as well as at operator and supervisor competence," said Chris. "It's no use saying we need more operators until we know we are utilizing the people and equipment we've got—effectively."

"It's an idea. I'll get personnel to look into the possibilities; after all, its job is to assess staffing needs," said Martin.

"The other problem is that we are not focusing on quality and volume of output for each particular product." Chris paused. "The operators do, but no one else does. We are all more concerned with our own individual functions—we see things in a compartmentalized way, rather than focusing on the product as a whole."

"Yes," agreed Mike (quality manager). "Take quality. Chris and I provided a procedure and control chart for supervisors to work to—but it won't work unless we have some formal mechanism for the engineer, the process control technician, and the supervisor to modify it for each line. There seems to be a lack of communication between these people at the shop floor level, no matter how we try to encourage it."

"I agree," added Chris. "There seems to be a number of solutions to problems that have been improvised or implemented by various people—supervisors, maintenance, quality engineers, and engineers who just happened to get involved. Because these aren't documented, the next person to deal with the problem is unaware of them and has to start dealing with the problem from scratch. We need some formalization of procedures and problem solving."

"It would certainly help," said Mike.

"Look, I've said before that we need to be more flexible in production," said John firmly. He turned to Mike. "You know what it was like when we first started: there were no written job descriptions; everyone knew what they were doing and did it—we had no problems then."

"But things have changed," said Mike.

"We just got bigger," replied John. "So we need to be more flexible—I'm sure Rick would agree; we were talking about it yesterday."

"Sure," said Rick (materials manager), "and Martin is always saying we need to be more flexible."

"I accept that in our business we need to be able to adapt quickly to customer demands if we are to remain competitive; but we can still have structure and flexibility . . ." began Chris.

"Is that what you learned on your business course?" interrupted John. "Well, Mike knows that production can only be effective if we've got that space to maneuver. He's worked with us for 12 years and knows we've had some very good workers who have come up with some creative solutions."

"Well . . . I suppose so," Mike reluctantly agreed.

"That's fine," said Chris. "But because those solutions aren't documented or formalized, we get changes on changes that can mask the original problem. One of the supervisors was telling me yesterday that they rarely get the same maintenance person dealing with problems in her section. When they eventually arrive, they do something—go away—and no one is any the wiser. When the next problem occurs, it's a different maintenance employee who starts again. She says it's the same on other sections and that the maintenance people can't wait to get back to their workshop to get on with their job there. That is one area that would benefit from formalization . . ."

"My maintenance department personnel do their jobs!" interrupted John.

"They do see themselves as a 'cut above the rest,' John," said Mike.

"They have an important job to do," replied John. "They like things as they are."

"But it takes them time to deal with any problems because they are not thoroughly familiar with the detail of that particular section," said Chris. "They've no allegiance to a product."

"Look, I'll say it again—we need to be flexible," said John.

"Well, there is something in that. What about the problem we have with the overrunning of projects?" asked Martin. "It's particularly a problem in engineering and in quality."

"I'm glad to hear it's not only production having problems!" said John, in a loud aside to Rick. "Guess an MBA doesn't give you all the answers!"

Ignoring this comment, Chris began, "My engineers are just as frustrated as we are that they can't meet the deadlines. Their jobs are becoming frag-

mented, and they are having to move from one task to another because of the day-to-day problems that arise. This obscures the more long-term projects, and it's only the urgent jobs that get attention. The conflict arises because the same people are dealing with long-term improvement projects and day-to-day problems, and the latter have to take precedence. What do you think, Mike?"

"I agree. We have the same problems and for basically the same reasons," replied Mike. "We can't concentrate on long-term quality problems because of the day-to-day ones . . ."

"We are here to get the product out, Mike," interrupted John. "That's got to be our priority. We need to meet customer orders."

"Yes, but don't forget we also have to retain those customers and meet the quality specifications. We need to consider the medium to long-term, as well," said Martin.

"We really need to look at how to balance the two and minimize the conflicting demands. Mike and I have been discussing the problem and think it may be useful to separate development and day-to-day problems." Chris looked at Mike for support.

"That's impossible!" retorted John.

"It can be done," replied Chris. "We need to develop a team approach. A small development group could be established to deal with medium to long-term projects. We could organize production on a team basis, each section having a team consisting of the appropriate shift supervisor or supervisors, someone from maintenance who would have a permanent assignment to that section, an engineer, and quality input."

"One quality inspector could cover each product group," added Mike.

"We would need more staff for that," said Rick, "and John and I have more than enough problems to deal with without trying to get a team to work together!"

"Anyway, we need more operators, not engineers and quality people—it's *producers* we need," said John.

"It would give us more time to study our quality problems . . ." began Mike.

Martin said, "It would also need more money and an immediate cost increase."

Mike looked around the group. "Well, . . . maybe it is a nonstarter." He looked apologetically at Chris.

Chris tried again. "I believe we should be looking at the way we are organized and staffed. We are obviously going wrong somewhere, and I don't believe it's all based on technical problems. I'm sure we could run more efficiently, even if we only reorganized our existing resources. We also need to stress the importance of quality; the operators can't be very motivated when they see such a high scrap rate—that we are doing little about."

"The only way I'll produce more is with more operators," said John.

Chris gave up, feeling frustrated that no one was open to the points she was making.

"Okay," said Martin. "I'll get personnel to look at staffing levels. Can you liaise with them, John, and report back to our next meeting? I'll also get them to look at the supervisors' training needs, although I doubt we'll have time to release them. Meanwhile, let's try and solve some of those quality problems."

The meeting finished.

Chris caught up with Mike outside. "What happened, Mike? I thought we'd agreed to push for the team approach?"

"There isn't much you can do when John gets started," said Mike. "Anyway, things aren't going to change."

"Not if we all take the short-term expedient view," replied Chris. "Martin knows we need to do something but he's not sure what. We could have put forward those alternatives we discussed—I thought you were all for them?"

"I was . . ." said Mike.

38 | LOW FIVE

I'm desperate. I've never been so frustrated in all my life. The new basketball coach benched me for the whole game yesterday, just one day after I tried to help her see what her coaching was doing to the team. I had fully promised to support her methods, yet she went ahead and kept me out of the entire game the next day, without saying a word to me. That's the first game I have not started in three years at Burke College. Can't she see how badly she's hurting the whole team? All of us are incredibly upset with her. I'm so frustrated I can hardly keep from bursting into tears. It's not like me to be so emotional.

Let me get hold of myself and tell you what's happened. My name's Paula, and I'm a cocaptain of Burke College's varsity women's basketball team. This year we got a new coach, Shirley Sharpe. She's 23 and was hired by the athletic department this summer to fill a position that never existed at Burke before but was very much needed. Burke's a 1,500-student coed liberal arts school, and women's sports are on the upswing. Shirley was appointed as the full-time coach of both women's varsity soccer and women's varsity basketball. She's a lanky six-footer who arrived at Burke in late August from Westbrook State College, where she played on a strong women's soccer team that won a national championship. She had also been a basketball All-American in high school but surrendered her game to soccer early in her college career. Stepping into a college coaching position, she appeared to be enthusiastic but also skeptical of her new venture. We were also unsure of what we should expect from her.

The soccer season started, and the several new freshmen had respectable soccer backgrounds and skills. On the other hand, many of the veterans and upperclassmen had little, if any, soccer knowledge. This forced Shirley to start with the basics. She showed patience and confidence, using her experiences as a soccer player to teach valuable lessons and eventually work her way up to teaching more difficult drills and plays.

Throughout the season the team was impressed and encouraged with her coaching skills and knowledge. The team's final record was not as successful as we had hoped, but we saw a bright future. Shirley expressed that a lot of good things had happened during the season, and she was excited about next year. She often spoke about the high school games she traveled to and from, talking with prospective soccer players and promising recruits.

Soccer ended, and basketball was about to begin. Having lost no team members to graduation, the nine returning basketball veterans were extremely excited and optimistic about the upcoming season. Although we girls only had a 9–12 record the previous year, we lost most of our games in the first half of the season before Christmas and were powerful and dominant in the latter half. We had favorable attitudes and confidence in our team's play and performance. We had been well conditioned, which allowed us to capitalize on our weaker opponents. We worked hard and had become very effective together. Our team had several strengths, such as pushing the ball down the court to score on a fast break and pressing our opponents to steal the ball. As players we believed in this strategy and felt our own individual talent was being utilized, which was rewarding to ourselves as well as to our team as a whole. The . . . season concluded on a successful note, with two great team effort victories in back-to-back Friday night and Saturday night games. During the last game, every player on our team made the scorebook, and I was even honored so much as to receive a ball signed by my teammates after scoring my thousandth (1,000) point. In addition, I was selected to the second team All-New England. We all knew I never would have achieved this without our team's cohesiveness and ability to work together. The mood of our team could not have been higher! We were so pleased to end the season in such a positive way, knowing that every game we had ever played was filled with heart and desire. We were psyched for the next year, knowing that we had the talent and ability to win many of those games we had lost. We were upset the season had to come to an end, but we were very cheerful and confident about the year to come.

The next basketball season finally arrived, and the new coach, Shirley, controlled the court. The first few practices were encouraging. They were filled with many conditioning exercises and sprints. Our team wasn't actually fond of sprints; but we realized if we wanted to be good, we had to work hard. After several practices the coach finally introduced the offense she wanted our team to use. It was different in the sense that it was a motion offense, rather than an offense with any set plays. A motion offense or freelance play style of basketball is more conducive to individuality and permissiveness, and it operates without floor balance or other objectives than to get the ball through the basket. A freelance team learns by doing. Initiative is the by-product of such an offense, and scrimmage and more scrimmage is the key to this brand of basketball. Furthermore, pattern play requires mechanical conditioning and the coordination of five players into a team. Each player is mentally and physically conditioned to her individual responsibilities, which coordinate her with other team members.

Floor balance is the foundation of pattern basketball, repetition of drills and more drills is its key, and teamwork is its ultimate goal. In addition Shirley also set us up into a zone press to use against our opponents. We went through it a few times, but were unhappy when we found Shirley not supplying specific instructions of where to go or how our trap would actually work effectively.

After a couple of weeks, our team found practices to be of less intensity. We weren't forced to do any sprints, and often during practice we saw ourselves doing little, if any, actual running. While trying to work through this new offense, several players commented that it was like a "zoo." Players were running every which way without actually knowing where the ball was or where it should have been. Frustration was developing. The one fullcourt press we had, compared to the six effective half- and full-court traps we had in the past year, just didn't seem to do the job. Collectively, we began talking outside of practice, expressing our concern. Thinking of the opponents we had to face, we felt we could do things differently, which would be more effective. We saw that the individual skills of our players weren't being used to their maximum, and that a lot of talent was being wasted. One girl, Cheryl, who was small but very fast, had proven time and time again to be an extremely good defensive player, coming up with steal after steal, especially on all the trap variations; but Shirley saw none of this. With the one unorganized trap we had now, Cheryl felt useless and unconfident. Others, who were known for having a strong game underneath the boards, felt their ability to get position and score baskets was being overlooked.

Finally, after several weeks, we felt something should be done. As cocaptain, I approached the coach. (The other captain was out due to injury.) I expressed to our coach that we found her new ways to be difficult and thought things were less effective than they should be. Afterward, the coach briefly told the whole team that we just had to work through it and give it time. She said this type of offense had proven several times to be effective and had won several NCAA championships. Besides, the JV team she once coached had picked it up in two weeks, and her 13- and 14-year-old boys' team developed it with no problem after a short while. We knew it wouldn't necessarily work for us just because it worked for others, but we agreed to give it another try. A couple more weeks went by, and practices never seemed to accomplish much more. We didn't feel coached. Shirley would sit up on the top bleacher while we were playing one-on-one or doing some other drill, and she would constantly be writing in her notebook while observing our performance. One player said she felt "paranoid" by constantly being watched and written about. The coach never came out to criticize or compliment our plays or moves. Oftentimes when Florence, the part-time assistant coach, was there, the two of them got together and spoke quietly as they watched. Our team expressed to each other our uneasiness.

One night we scrimmaged with the faculty. It was a messy game with people running every which way. After the game one of the staff players, Mr. Swift, approached me and another player and asked, "Were you playing with an offense?" He said that there were lots of open shots, but we never took them. We replied that Shirley wanted the ball to be worked around again and again so that we could waste as much of the 30 seconds that we were allowed before shooting. A few days later, another faculty member who had played asked me what the hell we were doing out there. He also said, "That lady [the coach] doesn't know a thing." He said there were openings after openings to shoot but no one did.

After three games, we had lost two and won one. The first game we lost was a game I felt we definitely should have won, especially since we were up a good 10 points the entire game until the last three minutes, when we didn't score at all. The other team pressed us and we were helpless in getting around it. Nothing was done and the coach offered no plays to conquer our difficulty. The other game we lost was played without Shirley ever calling a timeout. She felt there was no need for one even when the other team began to walk away with the victory. This made several players very upset. After this particular game, several of us expressed the need for a team meeting. We had been hesitant right along, because we knew we had to give Shirley a fair chance. I and a few others had played for her on the soccer team and thought she had been a great soccer coach. We had grown to like her but now felt we had to do something to preserve our basketball team as well as ourselves. We felt Shirley had been given a fair chance, and now we wanted her to actually know our feelings and possibly suggest to her a few things that were effectively done in the past. Our team couldn't decide on a time everyone could make, so we decided to think about it on the two-hour ride home. Although we had the next day off, I said the sooner the meeting, the better. The coach said she was very busy the next day with soccer recruiting and everything else. Another player also heard her say to the assistant coach that she "didn't want the meeting if it was what she expected."

Once at home, the coach finally decided to hold the meeting two days later, after the next practice.

The next day on our day off, the injured captain who hadn't gone to the game the night before learned of the situation. She suggested to me that we and a couple of others get together that night and have a beer and talk things over. We talked about the different things that had happened all season and expressed our negative feelings and unhappiness. We were frustrated because our coach objected even to doing certain things we felt capable of and confident with. Although Shirley felt our team's skills were weak, she didn't push us at practice or encourage us to improve. Our team didn't even have shooting practice. Instead, Shirley shied away from these weaker skills, saying she would prefer it if we didn't do them. I felt we had never been given the opportunity to show our ability. The coach disagreed with doing things we had done in the past, thinking they were unnecessary or not effective. Sitting at the pub, I wished we could do the weave and the Celtics drill—two drills that we missed and thought to be beneficial. I was concerned about the meeting, because I saw Shirley as taking it personally and likely to become defensive.

The next day, while having practice before the team meeting, much to our surprise we found ourselves being told to do the weave and throw baseball passes—which was the main idea of the Celtics drill. I saw no connection with the night before and welcomed the change. Practice this day had gone well. We had a good feeling about it for the first time in weeks. This improvement in practice made it difficult for us to actually start the meeting, since we had just finished the new drills that we had wanted to suggest to the coach.

Finally Cheryl began by telling of the success we had last year with several different presses. She expressed that it wasn't right to compare the years, but asked if there was any way our team could possibly have different zone press versions that we knew to be very effective. The coach replied, "No!" She saw no need for several presses and said, "If you can't do one, how can you do six?" Cheryl, the defensive specialist, was shocked and went on to say that she felt "useless out there" and that she was receiving no direction. Shirley once again said we had to give it time and believe in it because it had been proven to be effective. I then tried to express that our team had a real concern about our performance. We knew we were better than we had been performing and wanted to do something about it before it was too late. I said we had trouble seeing the value in the offense, especially since it wasn't proving to be effective for our team. During the games after a few times down the court, the other teams knew exactly what was happening. They stole the ball while Burke did nothing to change pace or give variety.

Uneasiness was seen growing on Shirley's face, and once again she replied that there was no way our team could do anything else, especially if we couldn't even do this. She said she saw us with less skill than she expected, and now she would have to go back to basics. She said we just didn't understand how it should work and refused to learn.

As captain, I tried to say something else, but Shirley quickly responded with, "Don't analyze everything I say." Shirley was clearly defensive, and I tried to defend myself as well as explain the team's position. As a result both Shirley and I became more angry with one another, causing the gap between us to grow wider. As the meeting continued, it was obvious that something needed to be done before the conflict got worse. Cheryl added that many girls played basketball for years and were very committed to it. She said that in many cases the girls who also had played soccer did so to be in shape for basketball. Cheryl went on to say that we were willing to give more than Shirley expected from us. Shirley said she felt we were still trying to play under our previous coach and would not accept change. She said we had to be willing to have faith in her as a coach. It was important for us to have confidence in her ability to do what's best. We agreed, but time and time again things were never done when we thought they should be. Another player, Karen, went on to ask about not calling a time-out during that one particular game. The coach said she had reasons for it. When asked what reasons, she said she wouldn't explain because if she did, it would take over an hour. She did go on to say that she didn't see our team as being "rattled" out on the court and didn't see a timeout as necessary. Karen went on to say, "Oh—but they scored 10 points in a row, and we just kept turning the ball over!" It was obvious that Shirley was not enjoying this meeting. She and Florence concluded it by saying that as players we have to be willing to go along with them. Shirley said the offense had proven itself time and time again, and we had to have faith in her to know what was right.

We left; later, several players said that the meeting was a waste and accomplished nothing. We knew, however, we had to make the best of it because we had a tournament to play in the next two days.

The next day, Friday, was the opening round of the tournament. The coach called and had left a message for me to go to the gym early so she could talk to me. However, I didn't receive the message until later, because I had a previously scheduled appointment. When I did arrive at the gym, Shirley said she would talk to me after our game.

Our team lost, and after the game I sat patiently in Shirley's office, waiting for her to come up. When Shirley finally arrived, she also had Florence right at her side. Shirley sat down at her desk, and Florence pulled up a chair. As the two of them faced me (I was sitting in the corner), Shirley pulled out her notebook, which had everything written down that she wanted to say. Looking down, Shirley began by saying that she was disappointed with me for having the attitude I did as a captain. Shirley was very defensive and said that the team and I started the season great, but now I was the one resisting the change and constantly analyzing everything she did and said. Shirley continued that my influence had a negative effect on everyone else, and as a result it was affecting my own individual performance as well as the team's. I retaliated by saying I realized that as a coach Shirley had her own philosophies and styles, but as a new coach walking into a new situation with a large group of veterans, she herself had to be open to the team's feelings and suggestions. She couldn't take from our team everything we had confidence in, especially since it had worked in the past with the very same people. Shirley further said that it wasn't right for me to analyze her. I saw this as Shirley's resentment of someone questioning her knowledge. I replied that as a player playing under Shirley first in soccer and now basketball, I saw Shirley to be more relaxed and comfortable with soccer and also more knowledgeable with the game of soccer than with the game of basketball. Shirley immediately objected, saying I had no right even to question or judge her knowledge or capability as a coach. Once again, she stated that she had spent years studying the game. I questioned the difference between studying the game and actually coaching it. Both Shirley and Florence argued that my statement showed how little I knew about the game.

As the conflict escalated, I tried to tell Shirley that in all honesty the team and I weren't attacking her personally. We were concerned about basketball, something we valued so much. I further said it had been difficult for the team to approach Shirley because not only was she quiet and low keyed but we had also grown to like and respect Shirley as a person. We just wanted her to realize that just as much as our team had to be willing to change and adapt to the new situation, she did, too, and we were willing to help her. I said it was hard because Shirley wasn't allowing our players to do what we felt we did best, such as run a fast break or press effectively. I also told Shirley that she had to see my view as a captain, too—as one whom the players were friends with and one whom they were coming to and complaining to. What was I to do? I had to be allowed to express the team's feelings without Shirley thinking they were only mine. I said that there was no communication between Shirley and anyone, and it was definitely needed.

Eventually Shirley said that she wanted to keep the problem from spreading and that she intended to treat it as though it were cancer, in the sense that it was a problem that could be controlled with radiation, before it got any worse and spread. In addition I could not understand Florence. Florence was also a new coach this year, and she coached the first-year varsity field hockey team. Throughout the first hockey season, I always heard good reports of Florence. She was 27 years old and had been the head field hockey coach at Lincolnsberg University for the past three or four years. Her players found her friendly and personable. I knew Florence had experience coaching a varsity college team and wished she had been more open to the situation. Florence just seemed to side with Shirley.

Throughout the hour-long conference, I saw that Shirley had become very offended. I also felt that I had been attacked by both Shirley and Florence and that they refused to see anything from my point of view. I knew they wouldn't concede, but I needed to do something, so I promised them that I would make an honest effort to accept what Shirley said and did in games as right and that I would encourage the others to go along with it, too. I admitted that maybe I had been too negative and semihesitant to change but would try to improve the situation now. At the same time, I also said I hoped that they could try and see my position, too. I stressed to them that being the captain, I had the responsibility to go to the coach when players had concerns, whether they were good or bad.

After this meeting I felt as though Shirley had done a good job blaming the team's poor attitude and poor performance on someone. I didn't believe it could be all me, and I still questioned the two coaches' basketball knowledge. Why all the resentment, I asked? For a good 12 years I had played basketball competitively. I had been on one of the top high school teams in Massachusetts and had played with many of the best players in the state. I had been coached by several coaches who had received honors and awards as both players and coaches.

There was also another player on our Burke team, a freshman, who had her high school coach come to the game played earlier that evening. Her coach said that our team should just go out on the court and play our own game. This coach, who had coached with Florence in the past, couldn't believe she was a basketball coach because she knew "nil about the game."

That night, being very upset, I thought about what had to happen next. Possibly, I had been too unwilling to accept all these new philosophies, but I also knew that in 12 years I had been coached by some of the best; and, throughout those 12 years, I had never faced anything so unorthodox. I knew I gave my word to do my best, and I intended to keep it. I wanted my team to do well and to win. However, it wasn't just me who was questioning what was happening. Some of the others were wondering whether they wanted to play the second half of the season. They saw their efforts as useless, and they weren't getting any satisfaction. At this point I still saw Shirley as very unwilling to change, especially since she insisted she knew more than anyone on the court. Despairingly, I saw that I had to be the one to make the best of it.

The next day was the final day of the tournament. We had lost the night before by 30 points to a team that had beaten us last year by only 3 points. We had to play in the consolation game, and, although I believed our team could be more successful with other methods, I was determined to play according to Shirley's wishes. However, to my surprise, I did not start the game nor did I even play in it. Shirley said nothing. It upset me because this was the first time I had not begun a game while playing on this team in three years. It upset me even more to think that my coach did not have the intestinal fortitude to tell me why I didn't play, especially in light of the meeting we had had the night before. I couldn't understand my coach's logic.

I didn't know what to do next. After the game, I didn't go to Shirley because I didn't want to start anything else. Enough was enough. I knew there was no way I could go to the other staff in the department, those above Shirley, not only because they were unaware of the entire situation but because they were viewed by many as unresponsive to students' needs. They received little respect from athletes and deserved none. Furthermore, they were not promoters of women's athletics and didn't even seem concerned with the program. After this last episode, several players expressed to me that they couldn't believe what Shirley did. She was losing more and more respect. The girls said she had no right to bench me, and it wasn't fair to me or the team. They said I was expressing their feelings and not just my own.

Although we felt we would never go to the extreme of quitting—nor did we want to—the thought was still there. We enjoyed the game and loved the team. We wanted to fix things now to save the remaining two-thirds of the season.

Our team had to do something, but what? And me? What should I do? Unfortunately, the fun and enjoyment of the sport is gone. Shirley had taken the importance of basketball away. No longer does my heart hold the love I once had for this terrific game.

39

MANAGEMENT DIVERSITY IN THE LARGE CORPORATION

Walter Roberts was transferred from Boston Trust in Detroit, Michigan, where he functioned as Sales and Marketing Manager. Walter was actively recruited and promoted by Boston Trust in Boston, Massachusetts, to fill a newly created position as Marketing Director. This occurred while he was pursuing a juris doctor and masters in business administration. Upon completion of his JD and MBA, Walter relocated to Boston to occupy this position. He feels that his new department is leading a shift in the company to become more market-driven. In addition he is not only the highest ranking black officer in the company, but he is the only black manager in the entire company. Walter feels that he is paving the way for the future development of more black managers in the company. Even though he feels that he is highly qualified, he feels a great deal of resentment from all levels of employees that he either does not deserve the position because he did not work through the ranks in Boston or he must be a "yes man" to high-management levels in order to have been selected.

Description

Brian Nelson is Walter's immediate manager and he reports to him. Brian has been with Boston Trust in Boston and worked his way up the ranks since he received his MBA 10 years ago. It was not Brian's idea to have Walter transferred from Detroit. Since his arrival seven months ago, he has treated Walter in a distant, mistrusting manner. Walter has not found him to be an effective communicator. While he always claims to be too busy to meet with Walter, he always seems to have time for others. Without Walter's strong insistence that they periodically talk, Brian would not initiate these meetings. He will not take the time to provide feedback on Walter's performance.

Brian can be very moody and makes everyone aware of it when he is in a bad mood. He belittles people in meetings and in private, and unless you are in agreement with him or working to support his ego, you are perceived as a threat. These are some of the comments that he has made to Walter:

- When Walter asked him what he thought of a presentation he gave, Brian replied, "It was OK. Why do you ask? Are you insecure or something?"

- At a manager's meeting, in front of the attendees and Walter, he said, "He won't be here long; he won't make it past March."
- Brian has told other managers that Walter has been prescribing cures without knowing the illness, as a result of being asked to speak about his observations of the organization.
- Brian has mentioned a few times in meetings in front of Walter why a person in a similar position was fired and that he had better watch himself. (Walter's conduct had not warranted such a warning.)
- Finally, Brian teases women managers in particular at meetings and uses vulgarity toward them, yet they go along with it. Walter has been the only manager to stand up to him when he has either attacked him in meetings or has interfered in his department.

Calvin Mason is Regional Manager for the Northeast and Brian Nelson reports to him. Calvin is the person responsible for Walter's transfer to Boston. He was impressed with Walter's performance a few years ago when he was Regional Manager for the Southwest. Calvin is very bright, intuitive, and well educated, with a JD/MBA. He cares about people and believes in what the company stands for, which is quality and good service. Although Walter does not get many opportunities to talk to him, when he does, Calvin gives him some encouragement. He has said to Walter on a few occasions, "You will be the first black manager of a major city in this company." Calvin Mason evaluates employees on job performance and not on how hard they laugh at his jokes.

Boston Trust has offered financial services to the business community and individuals since 1874. The environment of the company is similar to that at AT&T. It is stodgy and most employees have been with the company 10 to 20 years. Boston Trust is one of the largest and most profitable financial services companies in the United States and, in particular, Boston. However, over the past six years, it has steadily been losing its market share.

Walter Roberts has come to you as a fellow manager to discuss the frustration that he feels in Boston Trust. How would you describe his situation and what types of things would you advise him to do in order to alleviate his problem?

40   MARILYN ADAMS (A)

I wasn't one of the best students in my class at Simmons, but when people asked me how I was doing in school, I would say I was doing terrifically, which was true as far as I was concerned. I knew what I wanted to get out of the MBA program and I think I learned as much as I could assimilate at the time, considering the other things that were going on in my life. I had an excellent study group, one that worked well because we were all very work-oriented, very sensible. We shared the load and didn't just do what each one especially liked. It taught me a lot about efficient usage of work time. I think a lot of the students expected too much, wanted too much handholding. I thought I should figure out the reasons why I was there and then use what was available. Maybe because I didn't have a college degree I wasn't hung up on grades. I had family problems that took a lot of time, I recruited really hard and I cut classes when I had to. I push a lot of things into my life and I've had to learn how to get the most out of my time.

Marilyn Adams had been out of high school for eight years and had worked at three different jobs when she began to think that an MBA might be worth the effort. She had, as she put it, "bypassed college for a lot of good reasons." Her family had been forced to ration their income carefully because of illness. Marilyn said, briskly:

I figured that I could get along without college better than my brother could. I was stronger, more sure of myself. I didn't need it and I told my parents to send him.

Not having been to college presented some problems, however, when she decided to look into graduate school. "But I don't give up easily," she said. Both Harvard and Simmons were willing to take the chance that her ability was up to the task. The shorter, more intensive program (eleven months as opposed to two years) at Simmons and its orientation toward women appealed to her:

I always felt that my mother had been trapped by marriage and children in a way I didn't want. She was very dependent and dissatisfied. Even though I got married about the time I started at Simmons, I never considered following her pattern. I wanted a career. I wanted—I want—independence. My husband and I divide all the expenses equally; we take turns doing the cooking; I borrowed to pay for school. I didn't want him to pay for it. We bought our house with a complicated arrangement that allows each of us to keep a portion in case of divorce and we both make payments on it. I made one

concession toward the marriage when I accepted the job I have now and I'm close to regretting that.

The job she had taken with a bank in the Midwest after graduation from Simmons had not been her first choice. She had liked her internship with a large bank in New York and would have accepted their offer of a permanent position if her husband had been able to locate in New York. His options, however, were narrower than hers and she had instead entered the management training program in the credit department of a bank in the city where he was employed. The first weeks had been "a big letdown." She said:

Even though I wasn't hysterical about it, I had worked hard at school. I had been busy all of the time. Ever since I started at this bank, I've just felt that I was adrift, adrift with no direction and with no ability to program myself at all. I just feel stuck. My path is being directed or decided upon by people who have no input from me. I was literally put in this big room with 40 other people two months ago and told nothing.

In every other job that I've had they at least said, "Well, gee, we really don't know what to do with you right now; why don't you read through the files?" You'd always been expected to do something. But I came here and we've had a couple of hours of talks each day from specialists in the bank, and we aren't expected to do anything else. No one even said, "Here are the files; look around." Just nothing. I sit at a desk in this big open area near the glassed-in offices of the two head guys. They can both see me and I can see them. The men in those offices along the windows tend to just sort of stare out at us when they're not doing anything. I feel I am being judged on nothing but my movements that they happen to see. My future could be determined by their idle looks.

Most of the trainees came into the bank between June and October, with another group entering from graduating college classes in January and a few drifting in throughout the year. Marilyn had started in September. There was little formal contact between the trainees who had been there a while and new recruits. "Some of the older trainees come in and just walk by me day after day as if I'm not here," Marilyn said. "When people sit at a desk next to yours and never say hello, you sure feel as if you don't belong." She continued,

The trainees were given an exemption exam the first week to see whether they needed the bank's accounting course or knew enough to do without it. I did badly on the test. That, of course, made me feel all the worse about myself and what I wasn't doing here. Pearson Baker, the vice president in charge of the training program, met with us and said that all of us who were going into the accounting course were being faced with the hardest thing that we'd ever do at the bank. He said, "We're going to expect you to really work your ass off." Well, it turned out that I had accounting three days a week, two hours a day; there's some homework, but that's it. The rest of the time I am sitting here again. The people who haven't had any accounting have some trouble, but for the rest of us it isn't any problem now that we're back in the swing of it. I know that it wouldn't pay to go in and say to anybody in charge that I want to do more. This is the way they run their program. They think they know what they're doing. Besides I can see that the likely alternative to nothing is the uninteresting public service work that some of the runty little trainees are doing. I don't want that so I just sit here seething and miserable.

I did notice that a few of the trainees—one guy who has a law degree and another who worked at Citibank—

are being given other things to do besides the accounting course. Not the public service junk either. That's really frustrating. I wonder if I'm already being lumped into the slow road and will I ever get off of it.

When I was hired, they said it was all up to me. You know, the old carrot-and-stick routine. That my path was going to be as fast as I could make it, and the better I performed, the faster I'd go. All I want is to have a chance to perform so that I can advance. And I feel that no one is giving me that chance. I just feel sick. My husband keeps asking me how it is at work and every night I say, "It's fine; it's just fine." That is, I did until yesterday. It wasn't like me but I just broke down and cried and cried. I told him, "It's just awful; I hate it. I've been there two months and it's just a big zero." He was upset. Usually I'm the one who tells him to stop worrying. Finally he suggested that maybe I could try calling one of my professors at Simmons to get some advice. I know they're busy and I'm not ready to go whining back to them yet, so I've been sitting here all evening thinking to myself, "Okay, what would they advise?"

When Marilyn Adams went back to the bank the day after her tearful breakdown, her first action, she reported later, was to look around at her co-workers, picking out the ones she thought were likely to advance sooner than the others. She realized that although she had noticed that a few of the trainees were being given extra projects, she had reacted only with anxiety and some jealousy:

> I remembered the class discussions at business school about how debilitating anxiety can be. It wasn't like me to be tense and worried and I think I hadn't realized what was happening to me until I found myself in tears. Now I figured it was time to do something besides worry and feel left out.
>
> I looked at those trainees that I thought were real comers in a new way. I figured that if I thought they were special, others would, too. I knew they were going to be moving up all right, but instead of letting it make me miserable, I thought maybe it could work for me. I wanted to make sure that when they were in a situation where they had to pick people for a team, they'd think I was good enough to be chosen. I looked for the brightest and the best and I began to say hello to them, asked them what they were doing, just easygoing and friendly. I began having lunch with them and then I found that two people walked home in the same direction I did. I'd walk with them and get to know them a little that way.

That week she and a group of 25 other trainees who had started at about the same time were assembled for a group picture and an introductory lecture before assignment to their next brief tour through the loan division. It was an interesting scene, she said.

> There were 10 or so women and about 15 men in the room waiting to get the picture taken before going on to the lecture. All the men stood up at the wall and let all the women have seats. I realized that it looked like dancing school and that I should think about where I wanted to align myself. I definitely didn't want to take a seat. The men were just looking over the girls sitting there making self-conscious conversation. I wanted the stars I had picked out to notice me. I stood up against the wall.

Although still unhappy about her nonproductive days at the bank, Marilyn began to feel a little better as she talked to the other trainees and sensed that most were uneasy:

> At least it wasn't me alone who was unable to figure out what to do. I still had the feeling that I had to do something to prove to those men in the glass cages that I was worth the money they were paying me . . .

It was well into November before Marilyn received a demanding assignment. She was asked to write the Senior Reports (SRs); these were comprehensive reviews of the companies that had requested substantial loans from the bank. Reviews were completed by junior staff at monthly intervals and forwarded to the senior officers to aid them in their loan decisions. One member of the trainees, generally considered superior in ability to the others, was selected each month to be in charge of the 10 or 15 trainees assigned to the task. He or she was responsible for their results and was expected to guide them in the preparation of the analyses of the companies requesting loans. She soon discovered that everyone assigned to do these reports was keyed up and worried about pleasing the vice president who checked and questioned the SRs before they were sent on to the senior executives:

> Mitchell, the senior VP, was tremendously picky and demanding. He asked difficult questions and expected a lot of the trainees. He looks sort of like a platinum nail and is just about as warm. I guess I was lucky that first month in getting Roger as my trainee captain. I was lucky, too, that I was no longer quite as depressed about the job because I don't know how I would have accepted his corrections earlier. It's hard to have someone tell you you did something wrong. Anyway it's hard for me to accept that kind of thing, and I was choking down my anger when Roger told me I should change a sentence. I found it really irritated me because I think I write pretty well. I couldn't help noticing, though, and being impressed by the graceful way he was doing it. I pretty much knew how to prepare those reports; he wasn't teaching me too much about that, but I realized I was getting a pretty good lesson in behavior. He would say things like, "This is a really good job and I hope you don't mind, but I have done a lot of work for this guy and I think you have to change this sentence to please him." Well, I still resented the corrections, but I was able to keep it to myself and not get bent all out of shape. And after a while I was able to see that most of his suggestions were valid and that pretty soon I was motoring along, doing the SRs much more easily.

By the next month, when a new trainee captain was put in charge, Marilyn was confident of her ability. The new captain hadn't Roger's finesse. She reported:

This guy, Jim, was putting a red pen all over my reports without explaining or justifying his changes, and I was just going berserk. But by this time I was pretty sure it wasn't just me-and-my-anxiety. I knew the other trainees enough by now to know that they were disturbed, too. It was unprecedented, but the trainees called a meeting with the idea of telling Jim what they thought. We all got together but then no one wanted to say anything. Everyone just sat there. I thought I might as well be the one to begin and I got up and said, "I feel I have not been happy with your leadership because you've been treating me like a two-year-old—as if I didn't know how to do good work." Then everyone else started talking and finally he got the message that one of us could be ahead of him in another situation and we'd never let him forget it. He toned things down.

What I learned from all that, though, is that I have a hard time with criticism and so does everyone else. I had responded better with Roger than with Jim, because Roger had made me feel that basically I was doing a good job and that the corrections were incidental.

Old Platinum Nail hadn't had any problem with my reports in the second month; his questions were minimal and that was satisfying. I was appointed the trainee captain the third month, and that was nice; that was very nice. I bent over backwards to give the people reporting to me the feeling that they were doing a good job so they'd like working for me. That wasn't easy because they didn't all do well. One guy in particular was just stupid. He worked hard, stayed late at night but just didn't get it. He didn't write good sentences and in fact a lot of the trainees had very bad grammar. This guy I mentioned would say things like, "Here's the dummy of the class asking another question," which would make me feel awful, just terrible. I also found that some of the people who had seemed easygoing in other office interaction were very different when they worked for you. They'd be pounding on your desk every minute refusing to change a thing. A lot of them would throw in everything but the kitchen sink in writing what was supposed to be a brief summary. Part of my job, as I saw it, was to keep each report down to the tight format that Platinum Nail wanted so the senior officers could get through them quickly.

Each trainee was expected to complete a credit analysis of six companies, consulting with and getting the approval of the trainee captain for each report. The completed report was read critically by the junior officer in charge and then sent to Mitchell. Marilyn commented:

> The junior officers read them very carefully because if there are any misrepresentations, they are the ones who

will be held responsible. Their credibility would be affected if Mitchell thought they had agreed to a rotten deal.

She explained that she had scheduled the report writing differently from the way it had been done earlier. She had specified that each trainee spend only two and a half days on each report to allow an adequate interval for typing and duplicating. With the basic reports ready in plenty of time for Mitchell's review, the trainees could then afford to use the lag time to do extra research on each company so that they would be fully prepared to discuss their reports with Mitchell. She said:

> It worked out well. Mitchell came up and he went through all the SRs and managed to say that I had done a good job. He even stopped in to see my department head, Pearson Baker, to tell him that I had done well. That was nice. Baker called me in and said, "Well, you managed to pull the wool over Mitchell's eyes. He actually thinks that you are very bright. His only problem is that he doesn't think you have a sense of humor." Well, Mitchell has the reputation of being totally humorless himself and Baker is no comedian either so I wasn't going to get into that with him. A few days later I bumped into Mitchell in the hall and I thought, "What am I going to do? Just make polite conversation or try to be funny?" So we just walked down the hall in dead silence. I told Baker later that I had decided not to yak it up with Mitchell because I was afraid that he might think that I was a piece of fluff. And he said, "Don't worry, Marilyn; no one would ever think you were a piece of fluff."
>
> I sensed from that and from his remark about "pulling the wool over Mitchell's eyes" that Baker was surprised that Mitchell found me smart. I don't think Baker ever thought I was anything until Mitchell stopped in to see him about me. If it had depended on him, I would never have been put in charge of the SRs. I had Fred Randolph, Baker's assistant, to thank for that. I had been making a point of talking to Randolph from the time I decided to pull myself together and begin doing something to help myself. I'd go in to see him, say hello, make little complaints, ask him questions. No one seemed to be paying attention to him—everyone just wanted to get Baker's ear. To tell the truth, I wasn't sure what Randolph was supposed to be doing, but I figured the way to help yourself is to maintain contact with everyone you can get to on top, see if you can impress them in some way. Randolph didn't seem to be too busy, he was approachable, and I found out later that it was he who recommended me as the SR leader and later suggested I do the Money Market Memo, which I really enjoyed.

Adams described the Memo as an internal "information sheet" about the money market sent to the bank's international branch offices. "It's a report on our perspective on the various money markets—how we've done in the past, what we expect in the next week." She was expected to attend a meeting once a week of the Money Market division and to learn all she could from the reports brought into that meeting. She found that keeping a clipping file of the pertinent information in the business publications was also necessary. Between the notes she took at the meeting and her other research, she was able to come up with a report once a week. She said:

> I enjoyed it; it was really good for me because it was demanding. I didn't know anything about money market research when I began, and doing it forced me to learn a lot. So much else here had no definite timetable; you were setting your own pace, your own style. This report had to be done and telexed out every week. It was something I had to do and I liked that. Preparing it had only recently become a job for our department, and I think I was only the third person to be chosen in the rotation of people who do it. Fred Randolph did me a favor in choosing me to lead the SR group and write the Memo. Doing these things brought me to Baker's attention.

Soon after she had begun writing the Money Market Memo, Baker asked her to take a prospective employee to lunch during an evaluative visit. Marilyn assumed that this was a courtesy lunch, but she made a point of stopping in to see Baker and thanking him for letting her get to know the prospective candidate. "I'm good at getting information from people. It's fun to try to find out what makes somebody tick." He seemed to like what I had to say and after that, he began using me a lot. She commented that she had only been asked to interview women candidates, which she viewed as a mistake because it allowed her little perspective on the candidate group as a whole. She did not plan to tell Baker what she thought, however, since she had heard recently that a woman in another division had complained about this practice to personnel and had been quickly reprimanded by Baker "for giving personnel a hard time." She commented:

> At this point in my career it's not time to tell Baker that the bank is too rigid. I did talk about it with Randolph the other day, though, and he agreed that my talking to men as well as women would be a good idea. It'll be interesting to see whether he'll do something about it, but it's not the time for me to say anything to Baker. He's the one who makes you or breaks you at my stage. He decides whether you sit around and rot or whether you move ahead fast. For instance I had to

learn how to exchange credit information with other banks—we find out about each other's customers, very discreetly, of course. A lot of people spend six to eight weeks doing that, but I went through it in three. I was pretty frustrated here at the bank at the beginning so I know how it must feel if you find yourself going really slowly all along. You're not marketable during the training period and you just have to put up with whatever they want you to do.

Although she knew other trainees criticized the training program and thought it could be improved, she had not made known her own feelings about it:

> I'm pretty careful not to make criticisms unless I can come up with concrete suggestions for changes. And at this point I can't think of any. It seems to me that more incentive for working hard and fast should be built in. I did go so far as to ask Baker recently whether any thought had been given to revising the training program. He said no; there were too many complications. All I know is there's a lot of inertia, a kind of lethargy that affects the whole bank. I don't really care because I'm working hard and I know it's been noticed favorably. A lot of the others complain about the training but at the same time spend a lot of time watching the clock.
>
> Mitchell has noticed me by now and has said he'd like to have me work for him. I recognize him as somebody who just cares about having good people around him—he's only loyal as long as you produce for him. But that's all right with me. I look for people who will bring me along because I'm worthwhile to them—not one person in particular but whomever I can find. Mitchell could be very helpful in getting me into the departments I'd like to learn more about. And I'm using my discussion time after the recruiting lunches to chat it up with Baker, try to make him feel I'm intelligent. My idea is to ask him to let me train in a division that's not usually part of the training program. No one ever asks for something like that, but I think he'll be amenable, that he'll feel it's worthwhile to make a deviation for me. That particular division deals with businesses that are risky and more exciting than the usual credit operations. They also have a reputation of hating women, no women, don't want women. But I think I know why.

She explained that the few women who had had any contact with that division had reached it after their training period, had no experience with such lending, and invariably had been dismissed very quickly. She thought that not all the men who were sent to the division were satisfactory either, but that less prejudice existed, and they were not judged as promptly. Allowing women to rotate through the division as part of the training session would accustom the division to women and at the same time would allow the women a chance to succeed or fail without such a high profile. "When you're sent out of a division after you're supposedly trained, it looks much worse than if you find out you're not well suited to a spot while training." She had planned her appeal to Baker; she said:

> I'll tell him that one of the reasons that women don't have a good reputation down there is that they get sent down after training. I'll ask him to send me as a rotation and if it doesn't work out, fine, no skin off our backs. I just would like the opportunity to give it a try. I've done good work for you, I'll tell him, and I know they take good people down there and I'd like to see if I can please them. It has a reputation as a hardworking area and I work best in that kind of environment. I guess I won't mention right now that that division has the reputation for requesting the best and the brightest and somehow that's almost never been a woman. It's a highly visible area of the bank that has always taken the Golden Boys. I want to be in there.

By the time Marilyn Adams had worked as a trainee for eight months, her attitude had changed appreciably from her distraught state two months after she had begun work. She smiled as she said:

> Sometimes I can hardly believe that I felt like that until I look around at the new trainees and see them just frothing with frustration and anxiety. Now when I look back at one paragraph in Baker's introduction to the training program, I can see that he looks at the whole process casually. He's just going to sit back and watch

the group, not really helping anyone very much, and see what comes out at the other end. He can afford to lose some. The bank isn't really interested in maximizing everyone's training opportunity. What seemed like a big waste of money to me in letting us flounder doesn't seem like it to them. As long as I was waiting for someone to tell me what to do, I was very unhappy. Once I realized it was up to me to just try to relax about it, do the best I could, look for chances to show what I could do, things worked out.

New Assignment

By midsummer Marilyn had had several seemingly casual conversations with Pearson Baker, during which she had made suggestions for changes in the training program. Before each of these encounters she had carefully written out the points she wanted to make known to him. Among them was her idea of routing women through the division that serviced unusual companies. Just before he left for his vacation, he asked her to prepare a memo outlining her suggestions. It was to be ready when he returned. She reported:

> Of course I had it beautifully typed and ready on his desk. The result was a talk with him that lasted 1½ hours and centered on me and my future.
>
> The next day he called me into his office and asked how I'd like to "take a flyer" in being assigned to that division I'd been longing to join. Wow! I start in just one week!

| 42 | **A MATTER OF ETHICS** |

NOTE: DO NOT READ *this case until directed to do so by your instructor. It has been set up as a Prediction Case so you can test your analysis by answering questions before reading the entire case.*

Part I

BACKGROUND

Miriam Simonov and Barbara DeGaulle were roommates and classmates in Prof. Klein's organizational behavior class. The class had been divided into three groups. Miriam and Barbara were in different groups, and Serge Oblomov, Miriam's ex-boyfriend, was in Barbara's group. (See Exhibit 1.)

Thorne Elliot was Barbara's group leader, and Gloria Bonifacio was Miriam's group leader. Thorne's group was made up of six rather aggressive individuals who took great pride in their academic performance. They were competitive in nature and worked hard to "beat" the rest of the groups in the class. Gloria's group, however, was composed of five people who were more relaxed about grades and did not see the situation as competitive. They set out only to achieve Bs on all of their papers and were satisfied when they did so.

UPSETTING EVENTS

Thorne's group worked for seven hours on the beginning stages of the first class paper. A copy of the draft was lying on Barbara's bed, and Miriam, her roommate, noticed it there. Out of curiosity, she read the other group's paper and then commented on it to Barbara. Thinking that the paper sounded like Serge's rather formal writing style, she told Barbara that she didn't like the paper and that the writing style was "too stiff." She also said that she couldn't believe it had taken Barbara's group seven hours to write, since it was only two pages long! Later, Miriam also commented to Serge that she had read the paper and again offered her opinion of it.

Both Barbara and Serge were angered by Miriam's actions and decided to tell the rest of their group about what she had done. They were upset, which Serge told Miriam the next time he saw her. She offered to apologize or write a letter of apology, but Serge said that it wasn't necessary and that he'd convey her apologies to the group.

The next night, over a pizza in the room, Miriam told Barbara about the funny conversation her group

| **EXHIBIT 1** | *Key Players* |

Thorne's Group	Gloria's Group	Notes
Serge Oblomov	–	Miriam's ex-boyfriend
Barbara DeGaulle	Miriam Simonov	Roommates
Thorne Elliot	Gloria Bonifacio	Group leaders

had had a few days earlier, before the incident, when Gloria had jokingly said, "We can get Miriam to spy on Thorne's group, since she and Barbara are roommates." Miriam thought the whole paper-on-the-bed incident was blown out of proportion, and she relayed the joking around as a demonstration of how unnecessary all the concern was. Miriam continued by saying she read the paper out of curiosity alone, since her group's paper was already done. Fearing some kind of misunderstanding, Miriam asked Barbara not to mention Gloria's joke to her group. Barbara, however, felt it was important to let them know and relayed the story to them.

Thorne and his group were extremely angry with both Gloria and Miriam. Despite Miriam's claims of mere curiosity and her puzzlement about why they could suspect her when her group's paper was already finished, Barbara and Serge remembered previous conversations with Miriam about her attitudes toward classwork, and they still questioned her motives for reading their paper.

Discussion Questions

1. Assess Miriam's actions in reading and commenting on the paper.
2. How might you explain the reactions of Thorne's group?
3. What alternative courses of action are available to Thorne's group to deal with their extreme anger?
4. What action would you recommend? Why?

STOP: DO NOT READ FURTHER *until instructed to do so.*

Part II

After considerable discussion, Thorne's group decided to write Gloria's group a letter. (See Exhibit 2.)

EXHIBIT 2   *Thorne's Group's Letter to Gloria's Group*

To the Members of Gloria's OB Group,

Although this memo may seem highly irregular in nature, our organization believes it is the most effective way of clearly expressing our position toward your group's current behavior.

This organization views "spying" on or an attempt to pry information regarding our current class projects as cheating, and as a potential infringement upon plagiarism laws and regulations. Any confusion regarding the definition of these terms or the punishments surrounding a guilty party should be clarified on pages 74 and 75 of the most recent *Undergraduate Handbook*.

Our organization has been made aware of the suggestions instructing your members to "spy on Thorne's group." Although these instructions may have been issued in jest, they pose a potential threat and may have indirectly resulted in an infringement of the above-mentioned school codes. Instructing a group like this is highly unorthodox.

During the course of the week, one of your group members failed to exercise self-control and allowed his or her eyes to wander. When confronted with the opportunity of reading and evaluating our work, he or she failed to recognize the potential dangers associated with proceeding. Examining the paper and exposing himself or herself to our ideas opened your entire group to charges of academic dishonesty.

As a sign of good faith and friendship, our organization has decided not to pursue the incident any further. However, we feel that the matter deserves our fullest attention. We offer several suggestions for rectifying the current atmosphere.

Although we are not concerned with what happens within the structure of your work group, we propose evaluating all of your current practices. Be certain they reflect wholesome and legal objectives agreed upon by all of the members. Remember, your individual actions are being evaluated on a group level.

Certain questions should be re-asked. Is the leadership style of your group operating effectively in a manner best suited for the group? Should you be so aggressive and openly competitive with the other groups? This incident indicates not.

Our group believes this incident resulted from the overly aggressive and competitive nature of your leadership style. Allowing the desire to outperform your classmates to become a guiding objective of the group is unproductive and as you have seen—dangerous.

Effective leadership requires management, not manipulation or intimidation, and must be cultivated by an individual who seeks the best interest of his or her group. Placing individual satisfaction and competitive desires first will not cultivate the intended goals and objective of the organizational behavior class.

It is important that we all understand the significance of discussions we have and the actions we take. In the real world, outside of Babson, we are responsible for everything we say and do. Sometimes our individual beliefs and actions are even associated with a group.

Correcting the immediate situation may require a well-thought-out apology signed by all of the individuals who feel they are involved.

We sincerely hope that we can overcome these early conflicts and work toward developing a less competitive relationship in the future.

Sincerely,
The Members of Thorne's OB group

cc: Prof. Klein

Discussion Questions

1. Assess the impact of this letter on Gloria's group.
2. Identify several alternative actions Gloria's group might take in response.
3. Evaluate the merits of each alternative and indicate which you would choose, explaining why.

STOP: DO NOT READ FURTHER *until instructed to do so.*

Part III

THAT EVENING

Prof. Klein was at home relaxing at the end of a very long day when he received a phone call from Gloria Bonifacio, group manager. She was extremely distraught and wanted to know what she and her group should do about "the letter." Klein didn't know what letter she was referring to. He suggested she read it to him, which she did; it was a letter from another group to hers, attacking her group's integrity; then she asked what she should do. As he thought about it, he remembered that just the night before, he had enjoyed dinner at the invitation of the group which had sent the letter and that as he was leaving, Thorne's group had mentioned they were having problems with Gloria's group, but didn't want to talk about it at dinner. Now Gloria was on the line, waiting for a response.

Prof. Klein suggested to Gloria that she and her group might learn a lot and contribute to others' learning if they would be willing to discuss the problems at the next class meeting. He reassured her that he would not leap to conclusions about what they had or had not done and that his interest was in fostering learning, not playing detective about whether the charges were true. He encouraged her to discuss with her group their own responses to the incident and to proceed thoughtfully.

Discussion Question

1. What do you think Gloria's group should do?

STOP: DO NOT READ FURTHER *until instructed to do so.*

Part IV

Gloria's group was extremely upset and angry; the members decided to send the following letter back to Thorne's group. (See Exhibit 3.)

As Prof Klein prepared for the next day's meeting of the class, he wondered what he could do to ensure that all the parties learn from what was obviously a highly charged situation.

Discussion Questions

1. How do you explain the reactions of Gloria's group?
2. What impact do you expect it will have on Thorne's group?
3. Assess Prof. Klein's reactions to the call from Gloria.
4. If you were in Prof. Klein's shoes, what would you do to facilitate a resolution of this situation that has developed between Gloria's and Thorne's groups?

EXHIBIT 3   *Letter from Gloria's Group to Thorne's Group*

To the Members of Thorne's OB Group:

We find it disappointing that your group has taken such an extreme step in this situation. You have made nothing more than innocent curiosity into an unnecessary game of slander. We hate to reduce the dialogue between our groups to letter writing, but we feel we must respond to your unfounded accusations.

One of the major points we have trouble with is the fact that you have gone to the formality of putting your thoughts down in writing, with a copy to Prof. Klein. You claim that "as a sign of good faith and friendship" you have decided not to make this an issue, but how can that be avoided now? It would have been much more effective if you had spoken with us informally as a group and discussed your feelings.

We do not want this to transcend to a personal battle. Therefore, in the future, we ask that you refrain from giving our group advice on how to operate (especially right after you say you have no interest in doing so). The preachy tone of your letter does nothing to alleviate any tension between our respective groups; in fact, it only serves to aggravate it.

In conclusion, we would like to state as strongly as possible that at no time did Gloria or anyone else ever attempt to "spy" on your group or even to imply that this should be done. Your inclusion of the definition of plagiarism implies that we are in some way conniving to "beat" everyone else on this project. The only grade we are concerned with is our own.

If you wish to address your concerns in a mature, adult manner, then feel free to contact us and we will set up a meeting. Otherwise, this matter can only be looked upon by us as a group of people taking themselves too seriously. Relax, and good luck on your grades.

Sincerely,

The Members of Gloria's OB group

cc: Prof. Klein

43 THE MISBRANDED GOAT

Last March I was approached by Fred Wilson, director of engineering of the eastern division of our parent company, about a job assignment that he hoped would interest me. Fred and I had never worked together, but each knew of the other's characteristics and accomplishments. Everyone with whom I spoke knew Fred as brash, impersonal, demanding, and short tempered. During our prejob negotiations, Fred (who had been drafted for this division about one year ago) confided to me that corporate had given him approval to do whatever was necessary to turn his division into a productive and efficient organization. He also explained that when he delved into the personnel statistics, he found that the group (with a few exceptions) had been formed with lower-quartile people. In order to upgrade the group, he immediately acquired a few key upper-quartile employees. Fred was offering me a new position reporting directly to him. His ultimate goal was to return to the northwest division with me as his replacement in the East.

On my first workday, Fred informed me that there were three "dumb ass" engineering managers working for me that he wanted replaced as soon as possible. Because of my recent arrival, I begged off for 30 days so I might become familiar with the division. Initially, I assumed that Fred was correct in the assessment of the three managers; but as time progressed one of the three (Ray) appeared to differ from the other two. Ray responded instantly to requests made of him, accepted any task that was put forth, and worked diligently to get good, justifiable solutions. My concerns for the job and the people influenced me to apply more than normal amounts of time observing their work habits and performance. At meetings and in discussions with other organizations, it became apparent that Ray had the respect and confidence of everyone on the program, with the exception of Fred.

During lunch with Fred one day, I asked him to explain his reasons for wanting to replace the three. His concerns regarding the other two were understandable, but I pursued his opinions on Ray. Fred considered Ray worthless and felt that all of the problems seemed to originate from Ray's area. His releases were usually late or incomplete, or both; he lacked the answers to important questions; and he was continually asking for more people, even though the manpower curve for the division was in the reducing mode.

After expressing himself very vividly, Fred tensely questioned my concerns about Ray. Listening to my observations, Fred became very upset. He ordered me to quit wasting time with Ray and to speed up the process of his replacement.

My next move was to check on Ray's background. Assessment of Ray's personnel folder revealed no negative statements. Actually, it was just the reverse. In his last 14 years of employment in our company, he had had a variety of engineering and management assignments. In every case, Ray's capabilities in design, management, and cooperation had been praised. This was later verified when I spoke to his previous supervisors.

Being thoroughly confused at this point, I decided to confront Ray. In the two-hour discussion that followed, Ray stated that Fred had informed him personally, prior to my arrival, that he was going to be fired. I asked Ray to explain his perception of Fred's reasoning. His story concurred with Fred's. His releases were late, even though he was working 40 to 50 percent overtime. He repeatedly requested additional personnel, and his area was the major origin of problems. He also had difficulty answering some of Fred's questions related to the early parts of the program. But Ray also pointed out that he had been assigned his area of responsibility only six months prior to Fred's arrival. Since the program was over four years old, the design problems had been created by managers that Ray had replaced. However, each time that he had used this reasoning, Fred had become more and more irate. Ray also expressed the feeling that his workload was considerably greater than in other areas. I closed the discussions with the promise that I would continue to work on the problem and that, in my opinion, the harassment was unjustified. I informed Ray that I appreciated the fine job that he was doing and requested that he continue his good performance.

Next I studied the workload in all areas and found evidence confirming Ray's analysis. I then shuffled available manpower so the capability was more evenly distributed. I explained to Fred that I had no plans to replace Ray and in fact thought that he was doing a creditable job. Fred became furious and made it quite clear that Ray's performance could reflect on me.

In the months that followed, Ray continued to do his tasks well. His group started meeting schedules and eventually eliminated the need for overtime. However, Fred continued his relentless badgering. In meetings and in the group, he continued to try to embarrass Ray, especially when I was present. To my amazement, Fred didn't apply the harassment to me. In fact, he seemed to give me more and more freedom and responsibility as time went on.

44   THE MONTVILLE HOSPITAL DIETARY DEPARTMENT

Introduction

Rene Marcotte briskly walked home from her part-time job with the Montville Hospital dietary department. "Mom," she said as she entered the house, "they may have to close down the hospital! The Montville Department of Health has just found the dietary department's sanitary conditions to be substandard. Mrs. DeMambro, our chief supervisor, said that we are really going to have to get to work and clean the place or the hospital is in trouble!"

The Hospital

As Rene continued to tell her mother about this latest event, she thought about her part-time job at the hospital, which she had had now for almost a year. Montville Hospital was a 400-bed community general hospital located in suburban Montville outside of New York City. Montville itself was a racially mixed community of low- and middle-income working families. However, Montville, along with most hospitals, was operating under severe financial pressure and needed constantly to find ways to reduce costs. It offered a range of medical services; but, due to the nature of the Montville population, it had an appreciable number of elderly terminal patients. The hospital was well thought of by the community both as a place of treatment and as a source of employment. Through the years it had received strong financial support from the community and had grown as the community had grown. It currently was building a new wing to keep up with expanding demand, and this added to its tight financial situation.

The Dietary Department

The dietary department, where Rene worked, was located in the wing that had been added during the previous expansion project a little more than 10 years ago. This department employed approximately 100 employees (mostly female) and was under the direction of Mr. Thomas Ellis, food service director. The department employed cooks, dieticians, and "kitchen workers" (of whom Rene was one). The department had two major responsibilities—namely, the planning, preparation, and serving of three meals a day to every patient and the operation of an employees' cafeteria. Since most of the patients required special diets, such as salt-free diets, the food for each was quite different, although cooked in a common kitchen.

Rene well remembered her initial contact with the department. When applying for a job, she was first "screened" by the hospital personnel office, then sent to be interviewed by Mrs. Kelley, the chief dietary supervisor, and, after a second interview by Mrs. Kelley, given a "tour" through the kitchen facilities by one of the supervisors. She never saw Mr. Ellis or Mrs. Johnston, the chief dietician. As she later learned, Mrs. Kelley did all of the hiring and firing, while salary and raises were determined by the payroll department. Rene felt as if Mr. Ellis were some kind of "god," when she eventually heard of his existence two weeks after starting work.

Upon being hired, Rene was put right to work with no formal instructions in standards or procedures. She, as was every other new employee, was expected to learn by watching others and asking her peers. Rene, who undertook the job with a deep sense of responsibility, well remembered one of the older kids saying to her, "Hurry up; you're taking too long; don't bother to clean up those spots of spilled soup."

Along with Rene, the majority of the employees were kitchen workers (diet aides, dishwashers, and porters). Ninety-five percent were female. Twenty-five were full-timers working 40 hours per week, and 50 to 60 were part-timers, as was Rene.

Ten years ago the dietary department was smaller and under the direction of one of the current dieticians. There were no food service director and no chief dietary supervisor positions. While the kitchen was centralized at that time, tray preparation was not. This was done in a kitchenette located on each floor of the hospital. The workers moved from floor to floor, serving food from bulk containers onto individual trays on each floor. The dishroom also was separated physically. When the new wing was built, everything was centralized into one location from which carts of setup trays were sent out to each floor. Now, only the diet aides went to the floors and only for the purpose of distributing and collecting trays from the patients.

THE FULL-TIME EMPLOYEES

The full-time employees were mostly older women (40 to 65 years of age) who had been working in the department for a long time; some for 15 to 20 years. All lived in Montville; most had a high school education; many were married, and most were helping to augment the family income so their children could be the first in their family to go to college. With few exceptions, they worked a morning shift from either 6:30 A.M. to 3 P.M. or 8 A.M. to 4:30 P.M.

Most of the women had worked in this organization back in the old days before the hospital expanded and the kitchen was rebuilt. They had many stories to tell about how it used to be and how much easier and less chaotic their jobs had been before the change. One woman, who had recently been reemployed, had worked in the same dietary department 20 years ago as a teenager. She was amazed at how different everything was and said how she felt she was in another world from the job she used to know and love 20 years ago. The women, however, took great pride in their work (many had been doing the same job for years). Each woman had her own assigned task, which she did every day, and there was little shifting around of positions. The dessert- or salad-makers never learned much about the work routine of the tray-coverers, silverware-sorters, or juice-setter-uppers. Every woman was set in a specific routine during a day's work. This routine was heavily controlled by the tight time schedule everyone had to follow. There was no fooling around, even though the working atmosphere was very congenial and everyone was on a first-name basis, including the supervisors. There was considerable conversation among the women while they worked; but it did not distract them from doing their jobs—perhaps because management required the workers to completely finish their assigned tasks before leaving for home, even if it meant working overtime, without extra pay.

There was a striking cross section of cultural backgrounds among these full-time employees. There were about equal numbers of whites, blacks, and Asians, and many were immigrants. Many spoke Spanish and very little English. Although a language barrier existed between many of the employees, feelings of mutual respect and friendliness were maintained. Malicious gossip due to racial or ethnic differences was uncommon, and the women helped each other when necessary to finish their jobs on time.

The women often expressed their concern about not getting their jobs done on time, especially when they were working the assembly line. This assembly line consisted of sending a tray down a belt, along which, at certain intervals, each worker put a specific item on the tray as designated by the menu for each patient. After each tray was completed, it was put in an electric cart with each cart containing trays for different floors of the hospital. The carts were then pulled (by men porters) into elevators and transferred to the designated floors. At this time, pairs of diet aides (not working on the line) were sent to the floors to deliver the trays to the patients. Speed and efficiency in delivering trays were very important. If the trays were sent up and then left standing for a long time before delivery to each patient, the food got cold and the dietary department received complaints directed at the dieticians. The complaints were relayed to the supervisor, who in turn reprimanded the diet aide(s) responsible for the cold food. This temporarily disrupted the very informal and friendly working relationship between the diet aides and their supervisor, whom they liked and respected, causing uncomfortable guilt feelings for the diet aides. As a result, reprimands were seldom necessary among the full-timers.

At the same time, the diet aides were expected to meet certain established standards governing such matters as size of portion, cleanliness of kitchen facilities, and cleanliness in food handling and preparation. At times, in fact rather often, the standards were overlooked under the pressure of time. For instance, if the line was to be started at exactly 11 A.M. and if by that time the desserts were not wrapped or covered as required by sanitary regulations, the line might begin anyway, and the desserts went to the patients unwrapped.

The full-time employees received pay raises designated by a set scale based on continuing length of employment. Starting salary was about average for this type of work. They were allowed a certain number of sick days per year as well as paid vacations (the length of which were based on the numbers of years of employment). The uniforms they were required to wear were provided (three per person) by the hospital and could be laundered free of charge at the hospital laundry service. Also, the workers paid very little money, if anything at all, for meals eaten at work. Technically, they were supposed to pay in full for meals, but seldom did because of lack of consistent control.

Work performance was evaluated on the basis of group effort. Individual effort usually was not singled out and rewarded in any tangible way. However, supervisors often would compliment an individual on how nice a salad plate looked or how quickly and efficiently a worker delivered the patients' trays. For instance, the woman who prepared fancy salad plates and sandwiches could take pride in the way they looked. Furthermore, the aides recognized that their work could affect a patient's well-being and therefore could be important, and sometimes a patient was a former hospital staff member or neighbor known by the aides. When delivering a tray, a diet aide might chat with a patient and discover particular likes or dislikes, which, when reported to the dietician, sometimes led to a revision in the patient's diet.

Extra care often was taken in arranging food on the tray in an attractive manner to please the patient. Sometimes this dedication produced minor problems, such as when a diet aide violated certain rules to do something extra for a patient or to promote her own version of efficiency in doing a task. This type of individual initiative (and creativity) was not encouraged. Management set down rigid guidelines for performing all tasks as the only correct way, since they had worked out for so many years. Any recommendations for changes in these techniques were approached with caution by management. The equipment also had changed little in the past decade.

THE PART-TIME EMPLOYEES

There were 50 to 60 part-time employees in the dietary department whose level of pay was appreciably less than that of the full-timers. They were divided into two teams (team A and team B); each team worked on alternate days of the week and on alternate weekends, a device adopted on the advice of some efficiency experts as a way of avoiding having to pay overtime to anyone. There was no specific supervisor for each team; instead, each might have one of two supervisors depending on the day and/or week. Two different shifts exist for the part-timers: 3:30 to 6:30 and 4 to 8 (the kitchen closed at 8 P.M.), but on the average all part-timers including Rene worked a 16-hour week. Their duties were the same as the full-timers, except that part-timers served and cleaned up after dinner instead of after breakfast and lunch. The majority of these workers were young, mostly high school age (16 to 18 years), working for extra money and because friends were working. Most had not worked in the hospital very long, because there was a constant turnover as individuals left to go to college, etc., but other kids were readily available to take their places. There were also several older women, working on a part-time basis, who had been with the organization for many years.

The part-timers' situation exhibited a striking contrast to that of full-timers. There were no permanent task assignments; each night a part-timer did something different, and the kids often asked to do this or that different task. As a group, the night shift was not as unified in spirit or congeniality as the day shift (full-timers). The younger workers tended to form cliques apart from the older women and gossip and poke fun at non–English-speaking workers.

Most of the teenagers also took their work much less seriously than did the older women (the full-timers), doing only what was required at the most minimal level. As was the case with the full-timers, they worked on a tight schedule and their working behavior was heavily controlled by it. However, they seemed more anxious to get their work done as soon as possible. Once they had finished, they were free to leave no matter what time it was at no loss of pay— that is, if everyone was finished at, say, 7:45 P.M., all could leave yet still be paid until 8 P.M. It was not uncommon for work areas to become messy, for hands to be left unwashed, and for food to be handled and touched even though it shouldn't be. They also tended to devise their own ways for doing the job, partially to promote efficiency and decrease the time needed for completion. It was not uncommon to hear a more experienced teenage part-timer tell a newcomer, "Oh, come on, we don't have to do it that way. Don't be so eager; relax and enjoy yourself." The supervisor seemed to have little control over the teenagers. They ignored her comments or talked back to her and continued doing things their own way. The working atmosphere was informal and friendly, with everyone on a first-name basis except for the supervisor. At times there was a high pitch of excitement among the kids as everyone kidded one another, sang songs, and generally socialized together. At times this led to mistakes being made, which infuriated the supervisor but didn't bother the kids, as they had little respect for her.

Conflict existed between the supervisor and the teenagers about wearing the required hairnets (especially the boys) and aprons and such procedures as not eating during work. They seldom took reprimands seriously, saying that they "hated their job" but needed the money. In general, however, these young diet aides did complete their required tasks in the time allotted, although the quality was often substandard. There was not a total lack of concern for quality because, if so, they would have lost their jobs, and they knew this; but quality was maintained most strongly only when "it didn't take too long."

There did exist some conflict between the older and younger workers during the night shift. The older women did not approve of the young people's attitudes, even though those older women who worked at night did not exhibit as much pride in their work as did their daytime counterparts. They resented the teenagers' new and different ways of doing jobs, as was especially evident when an older woman was assigned to work with a teenager for the evening.

THE MANAGEMENT

With regard to the management staff of the dietary department, there were several people involved. Mr. Ellis was the man to whom everyone else was ultimately responsible as the food service director. He was an older man, hired by the hospital about five years previously. A flashy dresser, he wore no uniform and spent most of the day in his office. He rarely talked to anyone in the department except the chief dietician and the chief dietary supervisor. He communicated to the rest of the employees by way of memos posted on a bulletin board in the kitchen. His memos usually contained instructions, telling the workers to change or improve some facet of their jobs. He also relayed messages down the ranks via the supervisors to the workers. About once a day he would walk through the kitchen in a very formal manner, apparently observing what was going on. The diet aides (and supervisors) became very conscious of their actions as he walked by, hoping they were doing everything right. When questioned about this man, the workers expressed feelings of curiosity mixed with an element of fear. The only time a diet aide came into direct contact with him was on payday, when she entered his office to receive her check after he signed it. One recently hired employee said that she thought that his main job was signing paychecks. There was obviously much confusion by workers concerning who this man really was. He was the mystery man of management to them.

A second management person was the chief dietician, Mrs. Johnston, a woman in her late 30s. Her job was mainly administrative in nature, acting as a consultant to the dieticians and assisting them when the workload was heavy or someone was out sick. She also helped out in the kitchen once in awhile if the kitchen staff was especially shorthanded. In general, however, she tended to remain relatively formal and distant from the workers, although, when she had suggestions to make, she often went directly to the workers instead of using memos. Her relationship with the four dieticians was informal and friendly, and she was highly respected by them for her technical excellence as a dietician.

The chief dietary supervisor, Mrs. Kelly (about age 44), was in charge of hiring and firing. She also was responsible for making up employee schedules week by week, especially those involving the scheduling of the part-time workers. Workers went to her with gripes and requests for favors and special days off. She was generally sympathetic to employee problems, having been one of them about six years ago before she became the chief supervisor. In general, she was relatively informal with the workers, although not on a first-name basis. The employees respected her, and her authority was rarely questioned or challenged by any of the workers. She seemed to be regarded as the real boss, rather than the two people who ranked above her.

These three people constituted the main power structure in the dietary department. They tended to keep to themselves socially as well as physically. They never ate with the workers and seldom communicated with them except about their work. If any changes, plans, or decisions were to be made, they were made by these three people, the final say being had by the food service director. The supervisors were then told of any new policy and expected to inform the workers and implement the change. The chief dietary supervisor (CDS) seemed to act as a middleman between the director and the workers. When she (or the director) felt that the workers were "sloughing off," a staff meeting would be called and she would exhort everyone to shape up. For instance, a meeting was called after an unusually large number of complaints were received about patients receiving cold food. The CDS said, "We are here to help these patients get well as best we can—they are sick and deserve the best possible care. They won't eat cold food, and that slows down their recovery. Keeping the food warm is more important than whether or not you want to hurry to get the day's work done."

Other members of the management staff included the supervisors, whose main responsibilities involved the diet aides and other kitchen workers. The supervisors, who in all cases were former diet aides, worked in the kitchen. They assigned jobs, made sure they got done, maintained discipline and order (hopefully), and helped out when needed. In general, they saw that everything ran smoothly. Altogether there were three supervisors, one of whom was part-time. They took turns covering the weekends and thus had contact with all employees, although they worked with one group most of the time.

The cooks and the dieticians were the other members of the department. The cooks' job was to prepare the food according to standard recipes and to put it on the serving line at meal times. They did their jobs efficiently and effectively. They kept to themselves, eating together and not mingling with the diet aides. The dieticians also kept to themselves both physically and socially. They had their own office and ate together. Little was seen of them by the workers; however, when approached, they seemed quite friendly.

The Current Problem

The state board of health makes periodic, unannounced visits to the dietary department to determine whether it meets certain sanitary standards. Although the hospital believes that the board of health interprets the regulations too strictly, there is little it can do except make efforts to satisfy any criticisms made by the inspectors.

In the past, the director of the dietary department managed to find out when the inspectors were coming and prepared for the visit by a frantic two- to three-day major clean-up campaign. Historically, this resulted in Montville passing the inspection.

However, over the past two or three months, the inspectors have become more successful in making their visits a complete surprise. Frantic efforts to clean up took place the last time during the brief time it took the inspectors to get from their car to the kitchen. As a result, the department recently failed the inspection and was given a limited amount of time to correct the situation or else face being shut down. The department did pass a reinspection, but only because a lot of extra pressure was put on workers to do extra cleaning during and after working hours (for overtime pay) for several days. If the organization should fail inspection repeatedly, it would be required to shut down indefinitely. The impact of this would be catastrophic for the hospital as a whole, since it must provide food for both patients and employees! Rene wondered what the hospital would do about the situation and how it might affect her job situation.

45   3M'S OCCUPATIONAL HEALTH AND ENVIRONMENTAL SAFETY DIVISION AND THEIR ACTION TEAMS

"Sure, I'd be happy to come tell you about our product development teams," said Robert Hershock, Vice President and General Manager of 3M's Occupational Health and Environmental Safety Division. However, on this day in 1992 as he made final plans for yet another presentation on the successful implementation of cross-functional teams in his division, Hershock was preoccupied by the most recent problems presented by his action teams. Increasingly, he was feeling that the individually focused performance and reward systems were threatening the team culture, but it was not clear what kinds of changes could and should be made there. Despite efforts that had been made to align the organization with the team system, pressures from middle management seemed to be gaining force. Hershock was beginning to worry that the team system he had worked so long and hard to get into place was susceptible to becoming bureaucratic.

Occupational Health and Environmental Safety Division

The Occupational Health and Environmental Safety Division (OH&ESD) is one of 3M's 42 divisions. 3M has gained a reputation as one of the United States' most innovative companies, and its $10.5 billion in annual sales (1988) came from products as diverse as office supplies and surgical preparation solutions. 3M boasted over 100 core technologies, R&D spending nearly double the average rate for the 50 largest U.S. companies, and more than $3 billion in sales from products introduced in the last five years. 3M employed 83,000 people throughout the world and international sales reached $4.4 billion in 1988. The company took pride in having developed a successful two-track career system, which allowed scientists to climb the corporate ranks alongside managers without leaving research and development.[1]

OH&ESD was quickly becoming one of 3M's most progressive divisions by transforming itself into a highly innovative division in a company whose reputation rode on innovation. OH&ESD manufactured products to help protect workers from workplace health and safety hazards. Respirators worn by workers exposed to gases, vapors, and particles—as in oil drilling and car painting—formed the largest share of

the division's products, but more recent products included insulating materials used in clothing and clean-room suits. The multimillion-dollar division recorded sizable increases in sales for 1989, but people were most proud of the fact that their division was once again generating 25 percent of sales from products introduced within the last five years.

HISTORY

In 1982, Robert Hershock returned to the United States from Switzerland, where he had been head of 3M operations, to become director of OH&ESD. When Hershock became general manager, OH&ESD was relying primarily on two products. One had been introduced in 1961, the other in 1972, and together they accounted for a major portion of the division's sales. OH&ESD was a 3M aberration: it suffered from a limited technology base. It had few products in development and was in what people at the division referred to as a "harvest mode." The climate in the early 1980s at OH&ESD reflected this situation. Most senior managers had either taken early retirement or transferred to other divisions.

The organization had been run autocratically by Hershock's predecessor. Directors of all the functional areas kept the strategy to themselves, and employees were given little responsibility. Barriers erected between functions were impregnable and people did not take risks. Despite Hershock's efforts, morale remained at a low throughout the division.[2]

By 1985 OH&ESD generated only 12 percent of its sales from products introduced in the last five years. Bob Hershock knew the division had to make dramatic changes.

THE MOVE TO TEAMS

"We fell into teams out of necessity," Hershock recounted, "and fear." The necessity was based on 3M's insistence that each division generate 25 percent of its revenues from products developed in the last five years. The fear? "My own," stated Hershock.

Hershock had been reading a lot about teams, and he witnessed how futile 3M's traditional approach to teams (Business Development Units, or BDUs) was at OH&ESD. Those teams were intended to chart new opportunities and new products within a particular area of the division's business, but they left people

---

[1]Russell Mitchell, "Masters of Innovation," *Business Week,* April 10, 1989, pp. 58–63. *3M 1988 Annual Report: Sustaining Profitable Growth.*

[2]Mitchell, "Masters of Innovation," p. 61.

EXHIBIT 1   *Occupational Health Division: Teams and Strategic Goals*

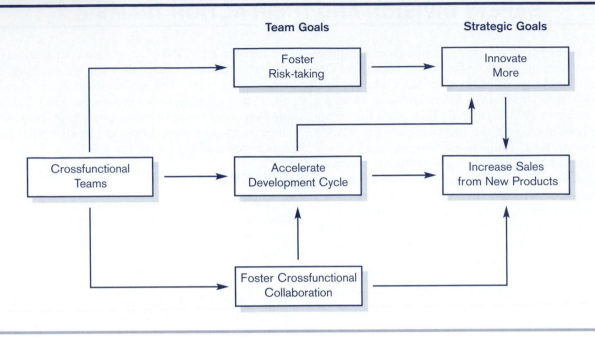

with a similar impression: 35 people gathered in a room, doing nothing but arranging their next meeting. Hershock wanted to capture the same orientation toward innovation that BDUs were intended to foster, but he sought to create a system agile enough to inspire risk-taking and personal involvement. (See Exhibit 1 for a map of Hershock's intended relationship between teams and strategic goals.) Together with the laboratory (research and development, product engineering) director and an external consultant, Hershock designed OH&ESD's Action Teams.

"To set up the teams," Hershock later recounted in an article highlighting the division's efforts for a 3M audience, "we had to do a tremendous amount of restructuring. (See Exhibit 2 for an organizational chart with action teams.) This created opposition from those people who were very structured and focused on their specific job responsibilities." The major opposition came from middle managers, who felt teams infringed on their authority and on the control they had over their direct reports. Teams threw the managers' responsibility into question, and managers saw a conflict between their goals and the goals of teams. Hershock discussed the painful transformation the division undertook, and he underscored a fundamental principle that would anchor action teams.

> Change like this is an evolutionary process, and there are a lot of problems to deal with. You can't expect to move from one system to another without some

complications . . . and without some people not buying in. I had to deal with a lot of fence guarding and parochialism . . . people saying, "This isn't my job; it's *their* job."

> My major irritation is people who put walls around a job description. What I'll say is, *"Hey, your job isn't process engineering manager or whatever; your job is to use your skill to do whatever is necessary to get the business moving in the right direction."* [3]

Even after extensive training, not everyone felt comfortable with teams and some people left the division. But action teams revived OH&ESD and inspired an additional organizational change. Laboratory, process engineering, and quality assurance were all placed in one building and united under one line of management.

Action Teams

Robert Hershock introduced teams to develop new products and to do so quickly. The traditional, serial approach to product development would not suffice. Hershock also set an ambitious goal for action teams: cut new product development time in half. With an emphasis on the timely introduction of new products,

---

[3]"OH&ESD Action Teams," *3M Manager: Special Report,* February 1988, pp. 6, 7. Second emphasis added.

EXHIBIT 2   *Simplified Organization Chart of OH&ES Division and Eurous Team*

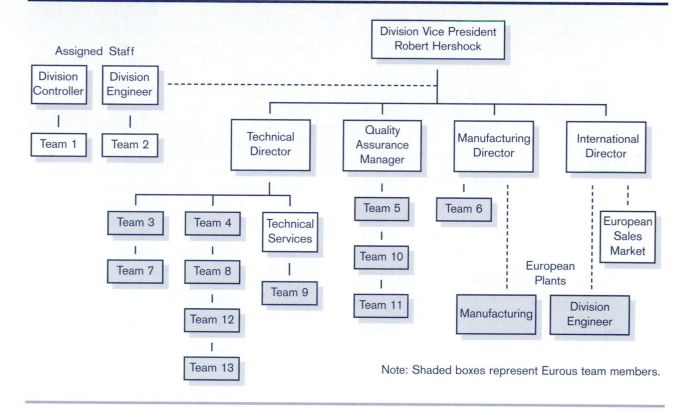

Note: Shaded boxes represent Eurous team members.

action teams were expected to accomplish several other objectives as well. By cutting across functions, teams would promote interdisciplinary cooperation and understanding. By focusing on new products with high potential, teams would create an innovative atmosphere at OH&ESD and increase the level of risk-taking. Teams would be formed around products with significant potential for growth, products which could boost the division's technology base and expand its array of new products (rather than product modifications or line extensions). Teams would rally people around a project, allow them to identify with a product, thereby instilling a sense of ownership and, as a result, inspire heightened commitment to quality. Teams would enable OH&ESD to respond to changing customer needs.

THE PLAN

Working with Charlie Cowman, director of the OH&ESD laboratory, and with a management consultant in the Twin Cities, Bob Hershock tried to think through the obstacles teams might encounter, and they tried to anticipate the support the division would need to provide if it were to accommodate teams. To

transform itself from a complacent, risk-averse, autocratic organization into an innovative, flexible, and daring one required forethought—and risk on Hershock's part. Hershock decided to introduce teams alongside the existing organizational structure, which would be left intact. Teams would take their ideas to the operating committee—Bob Hershock and the functional directors—who would designate resources to be provided by the functional managers. By maintaining the existing functional structure while introducing teams, senior management sought to balance control with risk. Instead of swinging back and forth between the team and the functional department, Hershock and his cohorts hoped to create an ongoing mixture of the two perspectives.

To introduce teams successfully, people had to be taught to operate within this new format without relying on the familiar practices derived from the traditional structure. People had to feel comfortable working together before they could approach projects with the risk-taking attitude Hershock sought to foster, an attitude of "Why not try? What do we have to lose?" OH&ESD focused its training on the personal and interpersonal foundations of becoming a team member, rather than on the formal group aspects usually emphasized. Instead of teaching people the steps in producing a team's mission, goals, and strategies, OH&ESD helped people understand the personal and interpersonal impediments to teamwork: concerns about acceptance and respect, stereotypes of other functional areas, and work style. Training taught people to become team members, empowering them to believe they could—and should—do whatever had to be done for the project, regardless of their individual background, position, or function.

FEATURES

The team system at OH&ESD had several features that ensured practical success. Although the division had as many as 40 development projects ongoing, it established teams around a limited number of those projects (11 at the beginning). Teams formed only around those products which had significant potential for growth. This allowed the division to focus its energy on the most promising projects and to support those teams properly. The first set of teams concentrated on projects previously identified, and it took some coaxing to get the first team leaders in place. However, the second generation of team projects, such as the Eurous, conformed to Hershock's intentions. To create a team, the person developing the product idea had to convince senior management that the product warranted a team. The product had to be worthy of the resources it would get, and it had to elicit participation from the professional ranks. Voluntary participation proved vital to OH&ESD's team system, as did the central figure, or champion. The champion was the team leader, the person with unswerving belief in the project who had to recruit team members to participate.

Membership on a team did not exempt an employee from doing his or her regular job—teams existed over and above normal responsibilities—so people would only volunteer, would only share in the commitment and risk, if they felt the project worthwhile. If they volunteered for the team, they were to do whatever was necessary for the project—and were told specifically not to think of themselves (or act) as representatives of their functional area. Team members "were turned loose in the organization to make a contribution." One team put this freedom to use when two team members, a design engineer and a manufacturing expert, developed specifications for the production machinery. Ordinarily this was the responsibility of the tooling engineer on the team; however, he was occupied with other pressing demands in another town. In order to meet team deadlines, the tooling engineer over the telephone guided the work performed by the other two.

All team members were provided with team training that focused on the personal and interpersonal challenges of teamwork and also provided team members the opportunity to learn how people from the various functions or departments tended to approach certain problems. Once a team was recruited and trained, they convened to establish their own goals, budgets, and deadlines.

Bob Hershock made sure that once a team was assembled, it received all the support from upper management it needed. Providing adequate support paradoxically required accurate information but limited reporting. Hershock believed that if the reporting became too formal, it distracted from the real work and the information became less accurate as presenters strove to look better to their superiors. He also believed that managers, when faced with formal reviews, tended to meddle; and the overall atmosphere became political and less trusting. To counter these tendencies, action teams reported progress quarterly, at an informal lunch meeting for all team champions with Bob Hershock and other senior managers. The lunch meetings fostered trust and encouraged champions to share good and bad news. It produced trust between teams and senior managers and convinced teams to approach managers whenever they encountered serious obstacles.

The mind-set that senior managers were there to help teams had been reinforced already through the role of sponsor. A person from Bob Hershock's senior management team was assigned to each action team as a sponsor whose role was not to monitor but to provide support. The sponsor did not run the team and did not monitor it on behalf of Hershock. Rather, the sponsor served as an advisor, mentor, and troubleshooter; most important, he or she could run interference and obtain resources the team was having trouble securing. The sponsor's attention reinforced the senior managers' commitment to teams, particularly in the eyes of team members, and it opened a channel of communication to the senior managers.

Team members and managers across the division were persuaded that these features of the action team system worked together to create a unique blend of commitment and control. Dave Braun, the team leader for the Eurous action team, typified the prevailing sentiment: "A chart of my team would need lines going everywhere to show that everyone reports to everyone."

RESULTS

OH&ESD introduced approximately 20 new products to the market starting in 1986, when the action team concept was first introduced. According to Charlie Cowman the division's success rate with action teams was 90 percent, with 9 out 10 products developed by the action teams introduced into the market on time and showing significant market potential. In 1992, 30 percent of the division's sales came from products developed in the last five years. The division reported that teams had in fact cut product development time in half. The estimated time to market for new products ranged from 4 months for products using an existing process to 24 months for a product with an entirely new process and new equipment. Hershock and Cowman were routinely being asked by the counterparts in other divisions to explain their process for achieving such results, and, increasingly, other companies were also calling to ask for Hershock's advice on using crossfunctional teams for product development.

Prospects were not always so positive, especially in the early days of action teams. To the surprise and initial shock of division management, teams spent far more money in the initial months of a project than under the traditional development procedure. Anxiety was relieved when data began to show that teams were only using funds sooner, while total expenditures for the duration of the development remained the same as before. The division benefited, however, because products were getting to market sooner and generating sales earlier than they would have under the traditional process. OH&ESD had found a way to accelerate its growth.

Pressures and Problems

In 1992 as action teams were busy making their contributions to the division's growth, there were still pressures that threatened the teams and several problems that Hershock felt needed to be addressed. Action teams had been introduced to jump-start product development. They had come at the expense of product maintenance, a necessary expense because the division needed new products. But now with so many new products, OH&ESD had to address issues other than product development. The same flexible thinking that had designated teams as a solution would be needed to determine the best system for maintaining the division's products—perhaps teams, perhaps a different solution.

Teams, in the words of one manager, "grease the skids and get the products out the door faster." That, he added, takes a lot of energy and drains people. Team members, he felt, could not be expected to sustain that level of intensity indefinitely. People at OH&ESD also worried about 3M's emphasis on big hits—like Post-it Notes. Once a team developed a product and introduced it, they moved on to another project. Some team members wondered if a team should be maintained to keep track of the product and make continual improvements. Perhaps, most ominous of all dangers to teams, and contrary to OH&ESD's past willingness to tolerate the managerial ambiguity teams entailed, thoughts were beginning to percolate of new regimentation—a new layer of management teams to collect information and report quarterly on teams.

Another dilemma had been created by the organization's philosophy and practice of accommodating the organization to the team process for developing new products. One of the accommodations made to the centrality of teams and the resultant discomfort of middle managers to being "out of the loop" and "out of the action" was to allow managers to join teams. The political concession ensured support for the teams but as a deviation from the team recruitment practice, it created some difficulties. Six of the team members on one of the most effective teams were direct reports of a manager who had demanded to be included on the team. Some of her direct reports felt that they would act differently if she were not a member of the team—that she inhibited candor and prevented them from doing what was best, even if it might displease her. Others did not feel at all inhibited and felt that her contributions were crucial. In their view, only by being on the team, they believed, could she truly understand the value of the work they were doing.

This was perhaps only a symptom of a broader dilemma teams posed for OH&ESD. Action teams had infused OH&ESD with dedication, commitment, effort, and daring, and a tangible result, growth. But were these only tenuous accomplishments of teams, in jeopardy because traditional structures are tenacious? Existing hierarchy, functional division of work, and promotion practices told people what they should expect, what they should pursue—managers' recognition and individual reward. One team member expressed a widely shared set of expectations:

> I'm a team player, but I want rewards to be individual. The rewards should be divided equally across the team, but they should be individual: promotions, salary raises, added responsibility, opportunity to lead your own team. The best way to achieve these rewards is to work as a team. But management has to be involved enough to know individual performance.

Bob Hershock and Charlie Cowman were proud of the positive response team rewards accorded to members and their spouses had received. Dinners and trips were applauded, and special gestures—roses sent to spouses of one team that worked overtime for an extended period—were deeply appreciated. As so many of their actions had done, senior managers again reinforced the message that teams were important. That message was so clear—OH&ESD had developed teams to such a stage—that people sought what they considered real rewards for their effort on teams. Reward meant promotion.

An internal audit of OH&ESD found that people did not consider action teams to be "career-enhancing." Several team members had expressed this concern. Teams relied on the willingness to complete whatever tasks had to get done to advance the project. To earn a promotion at 3M, however, people had to complete tasks at the level designated as worthy of their hierarchical station or above. Not only were people still thinking of real reward as that reflected in one's march up the hierarchy, teams could not deliver along that plane. How could each team member's actual contribution be measured accurately? Even if that were possible, what might be its impact on the cohesion teams were creating? Already some team members on the most effective action teams worried that only certain team members stood to gain individually for the collective risk the team had taken. What consequence would such concerns have for their behavior on teams?

The traditional structure raised dilemmas of monitoring and controlling teams in a related way. A functional manager, himself once a team leader, described the classic predicament of middle managers.

> Probably the toughest part about teams is management and how they accept it and what they feel their role is. It's a difficult assignment . . . to be manager in that kind of a system, particularly because you're held responsible for your area's developments and scale-ups and cost reductions, and you know, Charlie [Cowman] is telling you, "Get in control," and you've got this team over here. Now how am I going to get in control of the team without really getting actively involved? And so it's tough.
>
> It means that in the area that these teams operate in your group, you've got to give them some leeway and make sure that you communicate with the leader that the goal of the division is still your goal, and how you're going to accomplish it.

Middle managers felt squeezed. On the one hand, they were not to interfere with teams. They were told to let teams operate autonomously. Senior managers could praise the success of teams and talk about the latitude they allowed those teams. Yet senior managers still expected their direct reports in the functional lines to know and control what was happening at the working level. Still expected to control and monitor, middle managers remained the crutch for senior managers, providing the sense of control they sought. The autonomy and informal reporting teams enjoyed helped create strong teams, teams capable of monitoring and motivating themselves, but like the issue of reward, the success of action teams raised serious questions about the existing organizational structure.

Was it realistic to expect an environment free of intrusive control, an environment in which teams could flourish, but also an environment in which middle managers were capable of tracking and controlling whenever called upon? Unlike other organizations, as soon as OH&ESD introduced teams, it acknowledged the tension between teams and middle managers. Like the sudden spike in expenditures teams required, the division's awareness again helped it accommodate the tension rather than attempt to eliminate it by reverting to old approaches. One of the functional managers explained how he was dealing with the change:

> The other thing I've found real nice about it [the team system], is you're not embarrassed to say, "I can't keep track of every detail, every day, on every project," is you're not embarrassed to say to the person asking the question, "See the team leader because he'll be right up-to-date because that's his main function in life." So when I get a call from Charlie [Cowman] or another director saying "Where are we on this?" if I know, great. If I don't, I can give him a name of the person to call, or I could say, "I will have Harvey or Bob or somebody call you and give you a rundown on details or write a description of what's happening."
>
> From a communication standpoint, if the management of the division will allow people to know that I can't keep track of everything, but I'm confident in the people we've assigned, it's an easy way to get business done. Charlie [Cowman] may want some details, [but] I don't want to chase them down, [so I'll say,] "Harvey, tell Charlie what's going on," and I don't have to worry about it, and then [I would say to Harvey], "Tell me what you told Charlie, by the way."

The last sentence, said jocularly, reflects a degree of openness unthinkable at other organizations, but it also demonstrates how embedded the dilemma was. Perhaps it was more difficult and intractable than people at OH&ESD understood, but that too was questionable. Bob Hershock himself wondered if the interaction of teams and middle managers begged a fundamental question, "Why do you need middle management anyway?" How far would the accommodation need to go? How far could it go?

Jim Markham did not know what to do. The more he tried to analyze the problem, the murkier it became. Normally, Jim felt confident in counseling his students—both past and present—but this time it was different. Olivia Francis had been one of the best students he had ever taught in the MBA program. She was bright and curious, one of those rare students whose thirst for knowledge was uppermost in her reasons for being in the program.

She had never disclosed much about her family or her past to him, but he knew from her student file and information sheet, and from bits and pieces of conversations with her, that she had come from a poor, somewhat impoverished neighborhood in St. Louis and had earned her way through college on academic scholarship and part-time jobs. Upon graduation from the MBA program she left the Midwest, taking a job with a prestigious consulting firm in Los Angeles, and at the time he had felt sure she would travel far in her career. Perhaps that is why her phone call earlier that morning troubled him so.

Awaiting him on his arrival at the office was a message on his answering machine from Olivia. He returned her call and wound up talking to her for an hour. The salient portions of their conversation began to run through his mind again. What had struck him the most initially was the range and the depth of her emotions. He had never spoken to anyone in his life who had so much rage seething within them. After she had vented the rage, like air slowly being discharged from a balloon, she became almost apathetic, and her resignation to her situation almost frightened him—her only way out, as far as she could see it, was to find another job. Jim could not recall ever being in a situation where he felt he had absolutely no control over what happened to him, where his input was meaningless to the resolution of a problem he faced.

Olivia had stated that her first performance appraisal had been below average, and two weeks ago, her second appraisal was only average. She felt that she had worked hard on her part of the team's projects and believed her work was first rate. The only reason for the appraisals, as far as she could see, was that she was black. She was the only black on the team—in the whole office for that matter. Jim believed her when she said that her work was excellent, for her work had always been excellent as a graduate student and as a research assistant. He had attempted to get her to analyze the situation further, but it was like pulling teeth; she seemed emotionally worn out and just wanted out.

"Surely they gave you more feedback about your performance than that it was below average?" he remembered saying. All she would say is that they mentioned something about her attitude, not being a team player, that her work was technically exemplary, but that she was part of a team and that working with others was as critical as the nature of the work she did by herself. Olivia felt that this was a smokescreen for the fact that she had been dumped on the office by a corporate recruiter with an EEO quota to fill, and that they were trying to get rid of her by using subjective criteria that she couldn't really defend herself against. The frustration came back to Jim as he remembered probing her for more information.

"What was the tone of your manager in the feedback session?"

"Condescending, false sincerity; there was a lot of talk on his part of 'my potential.' It was humiliating, actually."

"How do the other people in your team act toward you? Are they friendly, aloof, or what?"

"Oh, they're friendly on the surface—especially the project leader—but that's about as far as it goes."

"Is the project manager the person who gave you this feedback?"

"No, she is under the group manager. He is a long-time company guy. But obviously she gives him her evaluation and impressions of me, so I'm sure that they both pretty much see issues regarding me eye-to-eye."

"Tell me more about the group manager."

"Mr. Bresnan? I don't know much about him to tell you the truth. He oversees five project teams, and each project manager reports to him. He comes in and gives a pep talk from time to time to us. Other than that I've never had occasion to really interact with him. He's always cracking jokes, putting people at ease. Kind of a 'Theory Y' type—at least on the surface."

"Do you ever go to lunch as a group?"

"Yes, they go to lunch a lot and they invite me along, but all they talk about are things I don't find very interesting—they're kind of a shallow bunch."

"What do you mean, shallow?"

"They could care less about real issues—their discussions range from restaurants to social events around town to recent movies they've seen."

"Does the project manager go to these lunches?"

"Yes, she comes and even plans parties after work too. Her husband is in the entertainment industry, a movie producer. Nothing big, documentaries and that type of thing, but they put on airs, if you know what

I mean. She is really gregarious and always wants to be of help to people, but she strikes me as putting on a front, a mask—obviously she isn't really sincere in wanting to help everyone 'be the best that they can be'; that's one of her little slogans by the way; after all, look what happened to me."

"Why do you think they're prejudiced against you?"

"Well, the poor appraisals for one thing—those are completely unfounded. They do other less obvious things too. Twice I've overheard some of them from behind cubicles relaxing and telling racist jokes about 'wetbacks.'"

"Is it just a few of them that do this? I can't believe all of them are racist."

"I don't know; I don't enter the cubicle and say, 'Hi guys, tell some more jokes!' But it isn't just one or two of them. Look, I obviously don't fit in, do I? It's lily-white in the office, and I'm not."

"What do they do that's work related that bothers you?"

"Well, when project deadlines get closer, their anxiety level increases. They run around the office, yell at secretaries . . . it's like a volcano building up power to explode. They worry and agonize over the presentation to the client and have two or three trial 'presentation runs' that everyone is required to go to. It's all so stupid."

"Why is that?"

"The clients always like what we produce, and with a few relatively small adjustments, our work is acceptable to the clients. So, it's like all that wasted energy was needless. We could accomplish so much more if they would just settle down and trust their abilities."

"How do you act when they are like this?"

"I do my work. I respond to them rationally. I turn my part of the project in on time, and it is *good* work, Professor Markham. I guess I try to be the stabilizing force in the team by not acting like they do—I guess I just don't find the work pressures to be all that stressful."

"Why not?"

"Oh, I don't know really. Well, maybe I do a little bit. I don't know if you know this or not, but my mother was a single parent with four kids. I was the oldest. She worked and I looked after the kids when I came home from school. She worked two jobs to provide for us, so I would be in charge of the smaller kids sometimes upwards of 9 o'clock at night. Doing your homework while taking care of a sick kid with the others listening to the television—that's stressful! These people at work—they don't know what stress is. Most of them are single, or if they are married, they don't have any kids. They all seem very self-centered, like the universe revolves around them and their careers."

"What kind of behavior at work seems to get rewarded?"

"I guess doing good work doesn't. What seems to get rewarded is being white, being more or less competent, and being interested in insipid topics. Professor Markham, don't you know of any firms that are more enlightened I can send my résumé to? I'm looking for a firm that will reward me for the work I do and not for who I am or am not."

Jim leaned back in his chair pondering what to do next. He had promised Olivia that he would call her back in a day or two with some advice. He sensed that he didn't quite understand her problem, that there was more to it than what appeared on the surface. But he just felt like he didn't have good enough data to analyze it properly. He decided to go for a walk around the neighborhood to clear his mind. As he opened the front door and gazed down his street, he suddenly realized for the first time that his neighborhood was lily-white.

47 A PARTICLE OF EVIDENCE

Mark King, monorator department manager for Blue Sky Research (BSR), was unable to fall asleep after getting home from work. An accident caused by one of his best operators had contaminated the building. Mark was afraid that the accident had been a result of the operator smoking marijuana on the unsupervised night shift. Although it was the middle of the night, the cleanup crew was still at work. Now Mark was struggling with what he should do the next day.

Blue Sky Research was a medium-sized company in the Southwest that produced chemicals and gases for a variety of industrial and military purposes. Monorators were a special kind of large-scale equipment used to manufacture and alter highly dangerous gases.

Mark King had been with BSR as the monorator department manager for five successful years. Under him in the department were his assistant manager, two chemists, and 14 operators. Mark enjoyed a comfortable, informal relationship with his subordinates and could usually be found joking with the monorator operators in his spare time. He was also very active on the company's tennis team. He took this time from his personal life not only because he loved the sport but also because many of the company's senior management played, and he saw this as a good way to make connections and build relationships with his superiors.

The monorator department's job was to operate the equipment 24 hours a day, six to seven days a week, and to perform necessary repairs. To accomplish this, employees worked three separate shifts. The first was composed of Mark, his assistant manager, the two chemists, and six operators. The second and third shifts consisted of four operators each. Mark gave the operators the responsibility to monitor the control board on the monorator and to correct all minor problems.

In order to repair the monorators, the operators had to enter the outer chamber, thus exposing themselves to the inhalation and/or contact with toxic residues created by the machines. The residue particles were so small and so potent that even with safety outfits and masks a certain amount of absorption was inevitable. In response to the medical hazards of the operator's job, which included the possibility of cancer developing up to 20 years later, the government had set maximum toxic absorption levels that an operator could be exposed to in a year. BSR had taken these restrictions one step further by setting its own maximum level at one-half that of the legal limit. If any employee exceeded this limit, he was temporarily assigned to another department where the exposure was minimal. The company monitored this absorption by requiring each employee to wear electronic devices clamped to body hair to measure the amount of residue absorbed internally through inhaling it or from contact with the skin. Urine and blood samples were periodically analyzed as additional safety tests.

Even with these thorough tests and precautions, BSR still felt the best protection for the employees was their own common sense. BSR believed that the only way the employees could act in a sensible and responsible way was to be educated about the dangers of residues and how to handle them. This philosophy led to the creation of an intensive four-day course, after which the participants had to pass an exam before being allowed to work in the monorator department.

As a result of this program, many employees conducted themselves in a much safer manner. A few were very nervous about the long-term consequences of working with chemicals that could cause cancer, but no one objected to those who were concerned and who avoided going in the chamber. Most were cautious; however there were still a reckless few that acted as if they thought residue could not hurt them because they could not see, smell, or feel the minute amounts. Such people did not stay very long in the department, as they soon exceeded their exposure limit and were transferred.

The monorator operators ranged in age from 20 to 26. They were all males and high school graduates; women were legally prohibited from working in the department because of the dangers of causing birth defects. Although the 14 operators were separated by shifts, they were able to interact while changing shifts, working overtime, and participating in outside activities, such as BSR's interdepartmental basketball tournament. They all got along very well and frequently went out "on the town" together at night.

Each operator had his own reasons for working in that department. Some were going to college at night and worked there because they could study at work (watching a control board does not take one's constant attention). Others worked there because they didn't have to do much but were well paid. They valued the overtime premiums possible from working late or double shifts. Still there were a few who wanted to learn about the field and hoped to move up in the company's ranks.

As operators spent more time in the department, they learned more about the monorator. The newer workers were informally introduced to the more technical maintenance problems by the more experienced operators. If they were interested in learning more about the equipment than what was necessary to perform their jobs, the more experienced operators were happy to teach them. This additional learning was not required of the operators but was encouraged by BSR and considered during evaluations for raises or promotions, or both.

As a whole, the operators took great pride in their ability to keep the monorator running, and even more pride in their individual output, or "volume/min." average. Every week each operator's volume/min. average was posted, and everyone tried to be on the top of the list.

Recently when BSR was building an additional monorator, the company hired a new operator: 26-year-old Bruce Altman. Bruce had a high school diploma and a natural aptitude for technical and electronic work. His father had owned an air-conditioning store, and in this environment Bruce had been able to develop and exercise his skills. Bruce fit in well with the other operators and the organization. As BSR proceeded to build the new monorator that Bruce was to operate, he watched and learned a great deal about the device and how it worked. Bruce became somewhat attached to this machine since he had helped to build it. He often stopped by BSR in his free time to see if everything was going well. He never asked for extra pay when he stayed to fix the equipment because he enjoyed it.

Bruce was respected by his peers as well as by Mark for his knowledge of the monorators and for his constant number-one ranking in volume/min. averages. He was also admired for his ingenuity in increasing the equipment's production rate. For example, he found that an ordinary screwdriver wedged in the seal at the top of the monorator altered the vacuum pressure and increased its efficiency. The other operators loved it when Bruce got a chance to "beat out" the scientists, whom they thought were nice but strange because the scientists wore long beards, flowered shirts, and love beads—despite being in their 50s. One instance of Bruce's ingenuity was that when he was on vacation, one of the monorators broke down and no one could figure out what was wrong, including the scientists. They ordered a complete overhaul to be conducted. The overhaul itself would only take a week, but they had to first scrub for a week to lower the toxicity level before anyone could spend any length of time inside the chamber to fix it. Bruce came back to work the day the overhaul was to begin on the washed-down chamber. He could not believe the scientists were going to waste a whole week fixing it; he went in the chamber and fixed it in two hours. The scientists were mostly amused by the progress of

Bruce and other operators, although occasionally they were a bit embarrassed.

BSR recognized how boring the operators' jobs could be and permitted them to bring reading material and other diversions to pass the time. This reading material consisted of everything from *The Wall Street Journal* to *Playboy*. As long as the monorators were in good working order, producing the expected amount, and safety requirements were being observed, the company was satisfied. Operators were usually left to themselves to do things their way. The managers only worked the first shift and were never there on the weekends. During these unsupervised hours, it was not uncommon for the operators to bring in a TV or radio, or occasionally even beer or marijuana. One operator claimed to the others he had seen even Mark drinking a beer in his parked car one lunch hour. The work seemed so easy most of the time that the operators didn't worry about any effects of alcohol or pot.

The managers were not stupid and suspected that the mice did play while the cat was away. However, they had no real evidence of the beer and marijuana and did not really see any point in researching the issue as long as it was kept under control. They did not want to jeopardize their rapport with the operators, nor did they want the operators rebelling against their authority. Both could result from accusing the operators of doing something that the managers were not sure was really going on.

Late one night Bruce and another operator were putting in some overtime. The two had been smoking pot, listening to the radio, and joking around. Suddenly one of the monorators broke down, and all meters read zero. Bruce put on his safety gear and went into the outer chamber to fix it, as he usually did. While working on the equipment, he accidentally dropped one of the valves on the floor. This valve connected to the inner tank of the machine and was highly contaminated. Instead of picking it up with the tongs as was always done, he used a piece of equipment not designed for that purpose. He placed the valve in a safety cart to take it to another lab for repair. As he pushed the cart out of the chamber, he ran over the spot where the part had fallen, contaminating the wheels of the cart with toxic residue. As he maneuvered the cart through the halls, the wheels contaminated the entire building, triggering the electronic "sniffer" alarm. It was later discovered that he had spent too much time in the chamber, a careless error, and had breathed in more vapor than his mask could filter. He would have to be temporarily transferred to another department.

When the night security guard heard the alarm, he immediately called Mark King at home. Mark then ordered an emergency cleanup crew to meet him at the plant. When Mark arrived, he went to the control room where Bruce and the other operator were sitting. Mark noticed a partially smoked joint sitting in the ashtray and inconspicuously put it in his pocket. He told the two operators to go to the chemical analysis center for an immediate absorption check. Then he supervised the decontamination of the plant.

Mark finally got home at 3:30 A.M. He tried to fall asleep, but it was futile. The question of what to do about Bruce was bothering him too much. Bruce was one of his best workers and was well liked by most everyone, including Mark. But Mark worried that if anyone ever found out he knew about the smoking, he'd be fired. Mark felt himself to be a fair man, giving his subordinates lots of room in which to work, but now he was caught between a rock and a hard place.

PHIL DANIELS

IVEY

Phil Daniels could not believe what had just happened. In a group meeting, in front of virtually everyone in the office, Phil's boss, Andre Trudel, had humiliated him. "This wasn't what I signed on for," Phil thought. "I'm not even doing the job I thought I was going to be doing." As he walked onto the elevator, he wondered what options were open to him. Considering that he was a summer student, and it was only mid-June, he had over two months before returning to school. He certainly did not want to eliminate the possibility of returning to the Rex Wallace Group full-time when he finished his degree.

History

It had been three years since Phil Daniels had first met Ryan Cassidy and his brother, Mark. Phil was in Toronto for a job interview for a summer position taking orders for a motorcycle parts supplier when he was involved in a car accident en route to a camping trip. As Phil waited for his car to be repaired, his uncle, Alan Daniels, invited Phil to check out his new office in Toronto. It was there that Alan introduced Phil to Ryan and Mark.

Ryan had left South Africa five years previously with nothing but the Canadian rights to the Lewis Personality Profiling System and $1000 in cash. The Lewis Personality Profiling System (LPS) was a behavioral assessment tool based on the DiSC methodology of

Professor William Moulton Marston, developed in the 1930s.[1] The LPS was widely used in South Africa and the rest of the world, and Ryan felt that he could create a successful business in Canada. He also hoped that by proving his competence and building the right network, he could acquire the U.S. rights as well. Within five years, LPS Canada generated $700,000 in revenues with six staff members, including his brother Mark as the national account manager. It was during this time that Ryan had entered into a partnership with Alan Daniels.

Ryan and Alan formed The Rex Wallace Group (RWG) as a 50–50 partnership. RWG owned the rights to the LPS and operated Rex Wallace Executive Search Consultants. It was felt that, due to the screening applications of LPS, there were synergies to be achieved in executive recruitment as well as a distinct competitive advantage.[2] Ryan's father had run an executive search firm in South Africa, and Ryan was excited by the opportunity for explosive growth.

Phil's First Summer

After his first year at the University of Western Ontario (UWO) located in London, Ontario, Phil needed a job for the summer. Even though he interviewed with the motorcycle parts supplier, he yearned to do something that would give him more corporate experience. After he first met Mark and Ryan, he hoped that they might have a job for him at RWG. He was very impressed by the charismatic brothers, as well as by the LPS. When they called to offer him a position that involved telemarketing and basic administrative duties, he readily accepted.

On his first day, Phil was introduced to the other members of the office, including Tina Mohr, the operations manager, and Jean-Paul Cote, the sales consultant. Phil discovered that Jean-Paul and Mark had recently complained that they did not have enough time to develop new leads because maintaining their existing accounts and following direct leads were consuming all of their time. For the remainder of the summer, Phil "cold-called" human resource professionals and generally helped out around the office:

> My first summer at RWG was incredible. I couldn't believe how much I learned. When I returned to UWO, Ryan and Mark wanted me to start up a division in

[1] DiSC stands for Dominance, Influence, Steadiness, and Compliance. The methodology stated that every personality was a combination of these four factors. RWG sold the software that generated the profiles, and acted as consultants to firms in human resources–related matters.

[2] Rex Wallace Executive Search Consultants used the LPS to help their clients screen candidates by first developing a benchmark profile for the job, and then matching candidates' personalities to this benchmark.

London, as time permitted, selling the LPS. Unfortunately, as I was trying to apply to the Richard Ivey School of Business and made school my priority, the opportunity never materialized.

Phil was confident that when he returned the following summer, he would be able to gain even more experience.

Phil's Second Summer

In the year between Phil's first and second summers, RWG grew considerably. The executive search division, originally just one consultant, now had three, and LPS had added a full-time staff member, Avery Johnson, to develop presentations and to handle any technical issues. Phil's role now had considerably more responsibility. Ryan asked him to perform a competitive analysis on RWG's direct and indirect competitors for both LPS and the Executive Search division. Phil received accolades for his work and was subsequently assigned to the Executive Search division full-time to conduct research. It was there that he struck up a friendship with Victoria White, one of the consultants, and with Avery.

Phil reflected on his second summer:

> Working in the RW Executive Search division was fascinating. I really enjoyed finding people whom I would subsequently match to jobs. Unfortunately, I also came to realize how arbitrary the recruiting process is. If the interviewer is put off by anything (your attitude, your appearance, your voice), it can seriously harm your chances of getting a job. Qualifications will only get you so far.
>
> Avery and I really bonded. It was nice to have someone in the firm my age. She was a very conscientious person, and that rubbed off on me. She really became my confidant, and vice versa. It was great having someone to vent to.
>
> It was also nice that RWG finally had some technical support. Now I could ask someone for computer help as opposed to being the go-to guy just because I was the youngest person in the firm. Avery really was representative of RWG's commitment to isolating their weaknesses and solving operational problems. In a fairly young organization, that's an important step.

A further example of this commitment to solving difficulties was the decision late in the summer to fire Jim Adams, the head of Rex Wallace Executive Search Consultants:

> I really liked Jim. From day one, he and I really got along. In my first summer, I would occasionally help him out as he was the only one running the show. As long as it didn't seriously compromise my other tasks, they let me help him, as it was good for RWG as a whole. When I wasn't working for him, we would chat all the time about sports and stuff. He was great, but he was rarely around. I assumed it was business.

Phil returned to UWO for his third year as an HBA candidate in the Richard Ivey School of Business.

Changes

Once again, RWG grew substantially in Phil's absence (see Exhibit 1). They expanded their offices, added a full-time receptionist and another LPS salesperson. The consulting division became a joint venture with Courtney Green, an experienced consultant who had run her own boutique firm for a number of years. Her partnership with RWG provided her with a wide customer base and the ability to provide a full range of services, including personality profiling and executive recruitment.

The executive search division had a new executive vice president, Andre Trudel. Andre was hired in mid-April with a mandate to make the executive search division profitable, which it had not been since its inception. Given low overhead costs (a portion of the office space and expenses incurred by RWG as a whole), and a commission and base salary compensation, the best way to do this was to increase revenues. Andre, who relocated from Montreal, had formerly been the general manager of a division of an international greeting card company, and had served as president of a marketing firm. Andre was a French Canadian (though fully fluent in English) and it was hoped that he would also help RWG with business development in Quebec.

One of Andre's first actions was to fire Judy Glenn, a consultant. Andre had noticed a lack of commitment on Judy's part, demonstrated by frequent absences, lateness and extended lunches. When he confronted her, Judy told Andre to talk to the clients in order to gauge their appraisal of her performance. When Andre did so, he was informed that one of Judy's accounts was so dissatisfied that they were considering dropping RWG. Judy was summarily dismissed, and Andre took over the account personally. This move left RW Executive Search Consultants severely understaffed.

Phil's Third Summer

Ryan contacted Phil in the spring to ask him to return for a third summer at RWG. He explained that there

EXHIBIT 1   *Rex Wallace Group Organization*

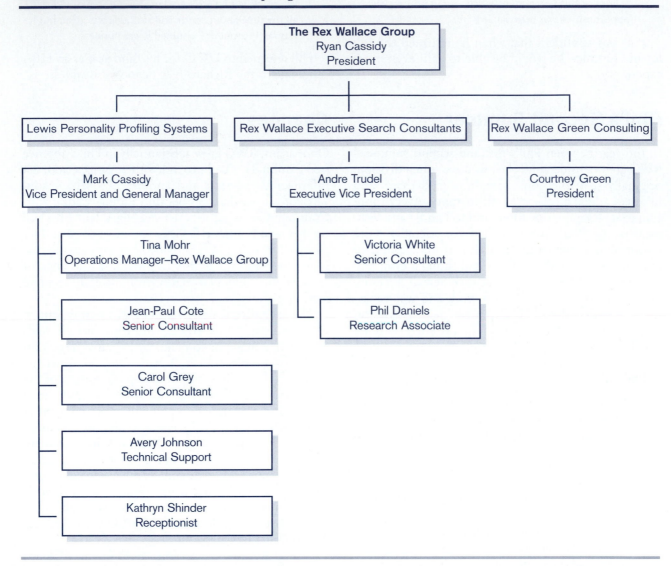

was a multitude of opportunities, and that Phil would have his choice. The options were clear. He could:

- Continue to do research for Rex Wallace Executive Search Consultants.
- Help with the marketing of a new retail product that RWG was developing.
- Assist in RWG's new management consulting division.
- Sell the LPS full-time.

Excited by the prospects for his future, Phil agreed to return to RWG for the summer, and indicated to Alan that his preference was to work in the consulting division.

MAY 4

Phil arrived at RWG on May 4, a day early, in order to get caught up on the changes, to see his old friends, and to start talking formally about his duties. He discovered that two of the suggested roles for him would not be possible. Given the nature of the LPS sales cycle, a four-month tenure would not be sufficient to develop any accounts. Additionally, the retail product did not require any assistance as the marketing had been outsourced. Disappointed that opportunities were disappearing, Phil was shocked when it appeared that the decision had been made for him:

> Andre seemed really enthusiastic about my arrival. He and I sat down and talked about how RW Executive

Search Consultants really needed me, and how Andre was not familiar with headhunting and how he hoped to learn a lot from me. He wanted me not only for research, but also to help him directly as he developed and implemented his vision for the company. I had met Courtney briefly, and she had told me that she was never informed of my impending arrival, and that she wished she had known, because she definitely could use a person of my calibre. I assumed at this point that I had no choice but to work for RW Executive Search, and I tried to make the most of it. There was no one I could talk to. Ryan was travelling at the time and would not be back for weeks. Going to my uncle (Alan) was not a consideration since he had no operational role in the company. Besides, I wanted to make it on my own.

Phil reported to work Monday morning and began working with Andre and, to a lesser extent, Victoria.

In his first week on the job, Phil was very impressed with Andre:

> Andre was a phenomenal guy to work for at first. He made a point to take me and Victoria out to lunch on my first day in order to welcome me to his team. No one at RWG had ever done that before. Andre was very open and kept me abreast of what direction he wanted to take the division in. I was really excited to be back, and I felt like a consultant to RW Executive Search Consultants. I was developing systems for tracking sales and improving communication to clients. I felt like this opportunity was really going to work out for me.

In Phil's second week, his opinion changed:

> As time passed, Andre seemed to grow generally less and less patient. At first, I was happy to help Andre with basic administrative tasks. I would write faxes and letters for him, and he would ask me for phone numbers. I thought this was a temporary thing, but it started happening with greater frequency. It was really frustrating, so I started teaching Andre how things worked at RWG, while trying not to be pretentious.
>
> RWG was a very entrepreneurial organization. Everyone did all the aspects of the job, when time permitted. Ryan, who was the president of the whole group, could always be seen making his own copies and faxes. He had set up his own database, and had a computer program that functioned as a rudimentary assistant. This philosophy trickled down through the entire firm. Everyone was self-reliant, and no one was considered someone else's personal assistant.
>
> Unfortunately, this was not Andre's way. He came from a big, hierarchical firm. He was used to having an assistant. He had been relying on Victoria until I came along, and he decided that I could fill this role. I became so exasperated that I started venting a lot to Victoria and Avery. I slowly tried to change Andre's habits. I set up a contact database for him, and explained that

it was quicker for him to look up an entry than to call me and have me do it. These same efficiencies could be exploited in correspondence. It made more sense for him to write a fax or letter than for him to tell me what he wanted, have me write it up and then submit it back to him for his signature. I really tried to get him "off my back," and get him to do things for himself so that I could concentrate on my other duties. Unfortunately, I lost a lot of credibility over the airport incident.

The Airport Incident

On the Thursday of his third week at RWG, Phil became ill. He came into the office and worked most of the day before Tina, who was in charge of the office, sent him home, after explaining the company policy that employees who were sick should stay home, lest others in the office catch the illness. She asked Phil to take Friday off if he was still sick. He did so, but had some documents faxed to him at home so that he could get something accomplished.

Monday morning, Phil was greeted with a very distressing voice-mail from Andre. He sounded agitated, and asked Phil what flight a placement candidate that he was scheduled to pick up at Pearson Airport was on.[3] Andre had been relying on Phil to make travel arrangements for candidates when necessary. Phil was horrified. He looked at his bulletin board and saw the itinerary pinned behind another document. He had forgotten to give it to Andre! When Andre called again a short while later, Phil gave him the information but not before Andre expressed his anger with Phil at his lack of competence. When Phil tried to explain, Andre hung up.

When Andre returned to the office later in the day, he explained to Phil that this performance was unacceptable. He also criticized the disorganization of Phil's office, stating that he could not find materials that he required while Phil was away. The next day, after he had cooled off, Andre handed Phil a list of his duties, and explained that, while he loved Phil's sense of initiative and insights, he would have to work on his organizational skills. Phil expressed his regret at what had transpired, and promised that this would never happen again.

To Phil, this incident was another example of how he was doing a job that he did not like. Organizational skills and attention to detail were not among his strengths. As the role increasingly required him to rely on these and less on his other skills, he became more frustrated with Andre for not letting him do the

---

[3]RWG often arranged transportation for candidates that they were placing for their clients. As a courtesy, consultants would meet the candidates at the airport and accompany them to the client's offices.

job to which he was assigned: candidate research and the development of the internal systems of RW Executive Search Consultants.

Office Relations

As it turned out, Phil was not the only staff member who had conflicts with Andre.

Victoria White had been employed with RWG for over a year before Andre was hired. His management style clashed with hers. He was condescending and berated her for leaving early (at 4:00 P.M.) regularly, even though this was a term of her contract. Victoria was a single mother, and often took hours of work home to complete after she had put her son to bed. She felt that her work was more effective after hours, as it involved contacting potential candidates, who tended to be much more open to conversation in their homes, rather than in their offices.

Victoria had worked in the search industry for over a decade, but was not considered for the position of managing RWG's search division. She was very good at her work, and had no aspirations for a more managerial role. She was very protective of Phil, and had talked to Andre about his often rude and condescending manner when communicating with him.

Victoria and Phil would often compare notes on Andre. Victoria disliked his manner and the way in which he talked to clients, as she felt that he was not concentrating on long-term relationships, but on making the immediate sale, much like a used-car salesman.[4]

Like most Ivey Business School students, Phil really wanted experience in the consulting industry. He was disappointed when the opportunity dissipated, and this feeling was enhanced when Courtney expressed a need for him. Courtney had, on a few occasions, asked Andre if she could "borrow" Phil when she had work that she felt he would find interesting. Andre allowed Phil to complete projects for Courtney, provided it did not interfere with the rest of his duties. Phil worked on three of these special projects. Courtney had expressed a high level of satisfaction with his

work and took the role of mentor. She would often talk to Phil about his plans for the future.

The Meeting

Every Tuesday morning, RWG held a group meeting to keep all the divisions informed about which clients needed what services. The attendees were Courtney, Andre, Victoria, Phil, Tina, Jean-Paul, and Mark. The meetings were generally informal, and when attendance became a problem for some of the consultants, Phil suggested that he take minutes and e-mail them to everyone. This idea was well liked, and Phil's minutes became regularly anticipated.

In mid-June meeting, Andre began with an overview of the accounts that he and Victoria were currently servicing. When he was asked about the status of one search, he shuffled through his papers, looking for information. Finding none, he turned to Phil for an update. When Phil denied having been given the assignment, Andre mumbled something about incompetence and berated Phil for his constant lack of organization:

> Phil, I can't believe you still haven't learned. The key to being successful is to be organized. You're going to go nowhere in life if you don't get it together.

When Phil tried to protest, Andre told him that his behavior was inappropriate, and that his job was to keep Andre organized at all times.

Phil sat through the rest of the hour-long meeting in silence, seething at his humiliation.

On his way back to his office, Phil poked his head into Avery's cubicle and asked her to meet him for a cigarette downstairs in 10 minutes. He was fuming. He stormed into his office, closed the door, shut his eyes and counted slowly to 10. He couldn't believe what had just happened. Andre had just completely humiliated him. "This wasn't what I signed on for," Phil thought. "I'm not even doing the job I thought I was going to be doing." As he walked onto the elevator to meet Avery downstairs, he wondered what options were open to him.

---

[4]There are two ways in which the executive search industry operates: contingency and retainer. A retainer-based firm takes a fee (calculated as a percentage of the candidate's salary) for finding a candidate to fill a particular position. Most contracts involve a guarantee that the headhunter will find another candidate at no extra charge if the original candidate is deemed unsuitable within a one-year period. Contingency-based search firms take a flat fee, fill a position and move on.

PROFESSIONAL EXCHANGE SERVICE ORGANIZATION (PESO)

Laura Smith was, in the words of her grandfather, "so upset she could spit." As she left October's Executive Committee meeting, she realized that the other three officers of the Professional Exchange Service Organization (PESO) wanted to avoid conflict. Even worse, she knew that most of the board members felt the same way. As Laura considered the upcoming board meeting, she was thinking, "I am going to push the board to do something. There is no way people will trust us when this gets public. This problem will not go away!"

Laura felt that a moral rule was being broken. She knew that it would hurt PESO's reputation when people learned that a board member was secretly living with an employee. Although she did not like to admit it, Laura Smith was also concerned about her personal reputation and credibility if it became known that she had information about a conflict of interest and had done nothing about it. Even worse, the entire matter was causing dissension and conflict among the employees. She had told the other officers that she planned to introduce an amendment prohibiting conflict of interest at the next board meeting and had asked them to join with her so the proposed amendment would be a recommendation from all of the officers. They had refused.

Organization History and Background

Laura Smith was vice president of Professional Exchange Service Organization (PESO), a nonprofit business cooperative located in the southeast United States. Members could exchange many different types of personal services through the cooperative at a price substantially lower than the market price. Almost any personal service, except those prohibited by law, was exchanged through the cooperative: catering, income tax preparation, housekeeping, baby-sitting, tutoring, landscaping, management consulting, data processing—you name it. Laura Smith, a business professor at the local university, had agreed to serve on the board because she felt that the organization was a great asset to the community. Many of PESO's members were low-income people who were happy to get the price breaks on services made possible by the co-op.

PESO, which had been started by a small group of people eight years earlier, had evolved over the years into a highly successful operation with about 400 active members. Members elected a Board of Directors, which set most of the policies. Decisions, other than the annual election of directors, were rarely taken to the full membership.

The rules for membership and pricing of services were complex. In addition, the organization had to collect and remit sales taxes on all services rendered. Because PESO had been so successful, the board had found it necessary to hire several people to maintain records, match providers and users of services, recruit and educate new members, and, in general, support day-to-day operations. In September 1992, the board had hired an executive director, David Jeffreys, at an annual salary of $33,000. He had been given a great deal of authority and responsibility, and he reported directly to the four officers of the Board of Directors. The Executive Committee was composed of the four officers and the executive director. It was empowered to act on behalf of the organization between monthly meetings of the Board of Directors. The Executive Committee met at least once monthly and sometimes more often. (See Figure 1 for reporting relationships.)

One of the reasons for hiring an executive director was to reduce the workload of board members, who as volunteers received no financial compensation. By October 1993, PESO had ten full-time employees and two part-timers. The annual budget was $280,000.

In general, board members were pleased with the performance of David Jeffreys. He was a hard worker, usually represented the agency well, took every advantage of free publicity, and was always looking for cost savings However, there were comments among members and staff that he was stubborn and not willing to discuss alternatives once his mind was made up.

The Secret

Laura had first become aware of the problem she brought to the October meeting in July of 1993. At that time a board member, Helen Black, had approached Laura in confidence. Helen had explained that she was a lesbian and that her life partner was Susan Holmes, an employee of PESO. In fact, Helen and Susan were now living together. However, Helen stressed that this information had to remain secret since there were state laws forbidding homosexuality

FIGURE 1   *Organization Chart—Professional Exchange Service Organization (PESO)*

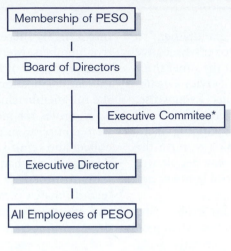

* The four officers and the executive
director make up the executive committee.
The executive director is a nonvoting
member of the committee.

and there were other legal issues concerning the children of both Helen and Susan. Helen Black explained to Laura that she was telling her about this matter privately since Laura was the only female officer of the cooperative.

Laura was surprised to learn that a board member and an employee were involved in a secret romance. She immediately told Helen that she believed this was a conflict of interest and that either Helen should resign from the board or Susan should resign from her paid position. However, Laura also said that she felt both Helen and Susan were valuable members of PESO and that she hoped neither of them would resign as members.

To Laura's surprise, Helen informed her that she did not intend to resign from the board, nor did Susan plan to resign from her paid position. "I was elected to this board by the membership because they trusted me to make decisions for PESO. I do not intend to let them down by leaving the board," declared Helen.

"But they did not know you had an intimate relationship with an employee when they elected you. I bet that most members would not vote for you now if they knew that you and Susan were lovers," responded Laura.

Helen insisted that there was no problem and kept repeating that neither she nor Susan would resign.

Helen felt that she and Susan had both earned the respect of the membership. She argued that a conflict of interest would only occur if she voted on matters directly affecting her partner. And, she explained to Laura, she intended to quietly abstain from discussing or voting on such matters.

"You must believe that there is some problem because you have chosen to tell me this," was Laura's reply.

"No, I do not believe there is a problem. Susan and I just wanted you to be aware of our relationship and why I would not be voting on any matter relating to Susan. I can see that you do not understand my purpose in giving you this information. I want to remind you that this information has been given in confidence and I expect you to honor that confidentiality."

Helen emphasized that, under no circumstances, should the executive director be told about the relationship. When Laura asked why, Helen expressed fear that Jeffreys would discriminate against her partner in some way.

Ethical Concerns

Laura didn't understand how Helen could fail to perceive that her relationship with Susan was a potential conflict of interest. She was angry because she believed that Helen and Susan were placing the agency in some jeopardy with their relationship. Public disclosure of this relationship could be interpreted in many ways, but Laura knew that people would regard the situation as negative.

Also, Laura was fairly certain that Jeffreys would be quite upset about the arrangement if he ever found out. She felt that if he knew that an employee had a romantic relationship with a board member, he would take matters into his own hands, probably in a way that would exacerbate the problem. David was very clear about reporting relationships, and he did not want staff members taking problems to the board. He wanted all staff matters to come to him, and then he would decide how and when to provide information to the Board of Directors or the Executive Committee.

Between July and October, Laura spoke with Helen four or five times and always urged her to resign from the board. She cited past situations where a conflict of interest had existed, such as the time last year that Helen voted for a raise for Susan and the time Helen argued against a proposed personnel policy that would have been less convenient for Susan's vacation. Helen replied that all staff members were underpaid and that the personnel policy was not fair. (The board had voted for the pay raise for all employees and for the new personnel policy.) Furthermore, Helen insisted that she had never told her partner about board actions or discussions. Laura was skeptical of that assertion; lovers usually share confidential information with each other. Laura and Helen were clearly at an impasse. Laura saw a moral problem; Helen did not.

Soon after Helen confided in Laura, she also privately told the other officers about the relationship. The officers of PESO had many private discussions about the potential for conflict of interest. All of the officers felt the conflict of interest was real, and wanted Helen to resign. Chester Clay, the president of PESO, became quite animated during one discussion with Laura and Joe Ryan, the board secretary. He exclaimed, "Helen and Susan want to have their cake and eat it, too."

Legal Concerns

The officers did not discuss the matter officially in Executive Committee meetings because Executive Director Jeffreys did not seem to be aware of the relationship between Helen and Susan. Finally, they decided to privately seek legal counsel regarding Helen and Susan's relationship.

"You need to talk to the two women and get them to listen to reason. Either Susan should quit her employment or Helen should resign as a board member

because this could look very bad for PESO if it becomes public. But you have to get this done privately because there is nothing you can do legally," said the attorney for the cooperative when he met with the officers one Saturday morning in mid-September in the back office at Chester Clay's furniture store.

According to the attorney, there were several reasons why PESO had no legal recourse. The first was that PESO's bylaws did not have any prohibition on conflicts of interest. Second, state statutes did not have any general prohibition against conflict of interest in private corporations. There were prohibitions against conflict of interest in public organizations and for those agencies which took government funds, but PESO did not take government funds. Finally, because the state did not recognize homosexual relationships as legal, there were no laws concerning such relationships or concerning conflicts of interests involving homosexual partners.

Although there was no legal solution to their problem, the officers still felt the potential for trouble was great if Helen remained on the board and Susan continued as an employee. There had been problems in the past about perceived preferential treatment of some members and alleged excessive board member involvement in the operation of PESO. Laura sensed that revelation of Susan and Helen's relationship could stir up those old resentments. Furthermore, she realized that the entire situation put the executive director in a tenuous position.

Laura thought that sexual orientation was not the issue. A romantic relationship between a board member and an employee was the issue.

Hurt Feelings

As Laura thought about the best way to manage the situation, she decided that a bylaw amendment to prohibit conflict of interest should be brought before the board. When she telephoned Helen to tell her about the proposed amendment, Helen was immediately angry and resentful. Helen insisted that her relationship with Susan was not a problem because neither Helen nor Susan did anything to harm the organization. Helen reminded Laura that she was not at liberty to tell the board about Helen's and Susan's relationship because the information had been given in confidence. She emphasized that her children and Susan's children could be harmed if this information became public. By the end of the conversation, Helen had become very angry and accused Laura of being homophobic and of harassing her.

Laura knew that she could introduce the amendment prohibiting conflicts of interest and almost certainly get it passed. However, even then Helen could remain on the board unless it was publicly disclosed that she had a personal relationship with an employee. If Laura disclosed the lesbian relationship and the potential conflict of interest, she would be "outing"* two people, subjecting them and their families to potential harassment. She felt that it was not ethical to disclose information that could be damaging and which had been given in confidence. On the other hand, she was convinced that if a board member and employee who were heterosexual had an on-going romance, she would follow the same course of action—i.e., urge the board member to resign. Furthermore, she reflected, any organization acting in the public interest should have a bylaw prohibiting conflict of interest.

The Turning Point

In late September the situation became more serious. David Jeffreys found out about the relationship. David was angry when he telephoned Laura. He said that he could no longer trust Helen Black. He feared she had told Susan about confidential board matters and he was angry that an employee, someone he supervised, might have significant influence with a board member. As he pointed out, he served at the pleasure of the Board of Directors and he felt caught in the middle between a board member and an employee he supervised. David told Laura that he was going to fire Susan as soon as he could accumulate enough documentation to prove that she did not adequately perform her job. Laura knew that Susan was a competent employee, but she also knew that the board had given Jeffreys the authority to hire and dismiss any employee so the decision would not come to the board. David also telephoned or met privately with the other three officers and told them the same things—that he was caught in the middle, that he did not believe Helen should remain on the board, and that he would fire Susan as soon as possible.

In early October, two discussions occurred which convinced Laura that she had to do something more to resolve this matter. She had contracted with Julie Frame, a long-time PESO member and employee, to wash her windows. During a work break, Julie brought up the romance.

"You know, Laura, I have always trusted you to do the right thing. That's the main reason I supported you for board membership. But I just don't understand why you allow Helen Black to stay on the board."

"What do you mean?" Laura replied. "Why shouldn't Helen be on the board? She is a great PESO volunteer and knows a lot about the organization."

Julie frowned and said, "Sure, Helen knows a lot. Susan Holmes tells her everything that goes on at PESO. And Susan gets all kinds of special treatment because her lover is on the board. Don't tell me that you don't know that they are lovers. If you don't know, you are one of the few people in this town who doesn't know what is going on between those two."

Laura sighed, "I didn't know that you knew."

"Most people know. And we know that Helen goes home and tells Susan what goes on in board meetings. Susan is always the first one to know about any board decisions that will influence us," responded Julie.

After Julie left, Laura thought about what Julie had said. She did not believe that Susan Holmes had special privileges or that she knew everything that happened in board meetings. But Julie's complaint caused Laura to realize that many employees and members knew about the relationship and were not happy about it.

The following week, Matt Owens, the service manager of PESO, phoned Laura and asked her to meet him for lunch. Matt and Laura had been friends before they were PESO members and Laura had recommended Matt for the PESO job. At lunch, Matt was blunt. He told Laura that all of the employees knew about the romance. He thought it was disruptive and damaging the productivity of PESO.

"How can a relationship between two people be so damaging to our services?" questioned Laura.

"Employees are choosing sides. Those who think that the executive director is more powerful and will get rid of Susan are on David's side. They try to give him any information about Susan or Helen which could be used against them. On the other side are those who do not like David; they are always running to Susan with information that she can give to Helen. They think that Helen will take information to the board which will undercut David's power."

Matt's analysis of what was happening did not surprise Laura. When Laura brought this up at the Executive Committee meeting on the second Monday of October, the other officers indicated that they wanted to avoid conflict and stressful situations. In general, the officers believed that most of the board members were not aware of Helen and Susan's relationship and they felt that the executive director should manage the dissension among the employees. The other three officers were not willing to have a recommendation come from the Executive Committee to the board concerning conflict of interest. Only Laura and David

---

*"Outing" is the term used for public disclosure of the homosexuality of another person who has not publicly acknowledged his or her sexual orientation.

Jeffreys wanted the committee to take a stand. The other officers wanted to continue to talk privately to Helen and urge her to resign.

"I have talked to Helen for three months. I am exhausted. She is not going to resign because she believes there is no conflict of interest. I believe this is a board problem," was Laura's sharp rejoinder. She was convinced that PESO should have a bylaw prohibiting conflict of interest. A bylaw might prevent future problems; Laura told the Executive Committee that she was going to introduce the amendment at the board meeting in 2 weeks. The proposed amendment would prohibit conflicts of interest and Laura would present it as her motion.

Laura was frustrated when she left the Executive Committee meeting. She felt she was letting all of the PESO members down by not acting on her knowledge of the potential conflict of interest. So far, she thought, the problem was confined to some disgruntled employees. But Laura knew that David Jeffreys felt a lot of pressure. What might happen next?

50 SANDRA LEE, PRINCIPAL OF SOUTH HEIGHTS PUBLIC SCHOOL (A)

Sandra Lee hit bottom in February 1998. She was physically and emotionally drained by her experiences as the new Principal of an inner city school. Her previous teaching career had been marked by stunning success—in fact, she had gained a wide reputation as a leading educational innovator. All of this had meant nothing when she encountered the brick walls of South Heights Public School. After six months in which she attempted to infuse the school with a new vitality, she could see few changes which had made a difference in the lives of her students. Indeed, the only significant change was a campaign to get rid of her launched by a group of disaffected teachers. Should she resign and go back to the classroom she so loved or should she forge ahead?

The South Side

South Heights Public School of the Sherwood School Board is located in a small city in southern Ontario. The city is only a short commute from Toronto, and is widely known as an automobile manufacturing centre in Canada. Most of the inhabitants either work at the auto plants or at the other manufacturing and service enterprises that support them. There is also a significant commuting population that arrives and then leaves the city on a daily basis.

The school is located on the "South Side", in an area that was once a commercial centre. Over the years the focus of commerce has shifted to suburban shopping centres. The only recent commercial developments have been some fast food restaurants and a few service businesses, but they come and go and do little to create any sense of prosperity or revival for the area.

The residences around the school have also been largely neglected. Most of these were originally constructed as row housing for the immigrants who came to work at the auto plants after WWII. As the families of these workers prospered and moved on to other areas of the city and the province, their homes were converted to low rent and subsidized housing. Most of the current residents were attracted to the area for this reason: It is one of the cheapest places to live in Ontario. The South Side is known locally as the "welfare zone" since most of the residents are dependent on some form of government support.

There is chronic unemployment of about 70 percent in the South Heights school area. Many of the families are headed by a single parent, mostly women, and some of these families are third and fourth generation welfare recipients. The South Side is only a step from the North Side but it is a world away in terms of economic and social status. People on the North Side generally own their homes, have new cars, send their children to college, and most important, are employed. This level of stability and material well-being is almost non-existent on the South Side because the residents are largely transients, who appear unable to find or keep jobs for any sustained period of time.

This transience in their working lives is also reflected in the family structures. Many of the single mothers are young and became mothers in their mid to late teens. They were forced into major family responsibilities quite abruptly and were ill-prepared for their new parental role. They often had no network of family and few friends to advise them or support them. The men who filled the family position of "father" often stayed only a short time. The combination of these conditions of early motherhood, absence of support networks, and replacement of the original spouse, created severe stresses. These were frequently expressed in violent confrontations among family members and often involved the children directly. Violence or threats of violence by parents and open defiance by children were commonplace methods of dealing with problems. This violent and defiant behaviour was frequently transferred to the school setting. Equally disturbing, many of the children came to school hungry, without haven eaten breakfast, and sometimes "with a bag of chips for lunch."

Another feature of the South Side culture was its association with drugs, violence and petty crime. Although the extent of this activity was less than what occurs in the worst areas of large cities, it further served to undermine the sense of security of children and parents.

South Heights Public School

Just as the South Side was neglected and run down, so was the school itself. Built in 1916 to serve children from kindergarten to grade 8, it was typical of the stolid and enduring institutional style of the times. With its brick walls and vaulting ceilings and windows, it was functional, but grey, drab and uninviting. Virtually nothing had been done over the years to renew the building, spruce it up, or even keep it very clean. The school stood as a metaphor for the whole South Side. It stood as a challenge to the educational system, much as the area was to the municipality, but there seemed no collective will to change or redeem either one.

The school's location and reputation frightened off most experienced teachers. South Heights was often a first posting for new teachers and administrators, a place "where you would pay your dues." It hadn't always been so—indeed, the school had a rich and proud history. Past students and teachers had fond memories of their days at South Heights and witnessed the continual neglect and decay of recent times with considerable regret.

One particular difficulty for the school was that a significant number of the parents had negative experiences when they were part of the school system. Many of them had been school dropouts and many others just turned off by formal schooling. In spite of this, most parents saw education as important for the lives of their children. The problem was that they did not know *how* to help their children be successful in school. Apart from this, given the conditions in which they lived, many parents were primarily concerned with survival. As a consequence, the parents did not get involved in the education process and did not particularly encourage school activities or interests for their children.

The school had such a poor reputation that it was continually rumoured to be closing. In fact, this was a focus of debate within the School Board: Should South Heights remain open or be closed? The School Board saw an aging school with a multitude of problems, and little else. As a result, very little was invested in the school to either improve or even maintain it. The result of all these forces was a school with little in the way of a future or hope.

An opportunity arose in 1997 to change this dismal picture. The Principal of South Heights was moving to another school and some senior officials of the Sherwood School Board saw this as a chance to intervene in this situation. The chair of the publicly elected School Trustees commented, "South Heights had become a dumping ground for bad teachers. I was determined to veto the appointment of anyone who wasn't going to change this place." In the end the choice was a young Vice-Principal who had gained a strong reputation for innovative programs for children with disabilities, but who had relatively little administrative experience for the type of situation she would encounter at South Heights.

The New Principal: Sandra Lee

Sandra Lee became the Principal of South Heights Public School in 1997, coming upon the scene amid the conditions previously described. She was not happy about being placed at South Heights. She was advised by friends and peers that South Heights would be a difficult situation to endure even for a short period of time. However, one did not turn down an administrative appointment. To do so would have effectively ended her career in administration. Since, in her own words, she was "very ambitious" about her career progress, she took the job. She came directly from a Vice-Principal position at a new model public school and the change to South Heights was far greater and more traumatic than she could ever have imagined.

Sandra's background in education was somewhat unusual in that her decision to become a teacher was taken later in life than most, after she had emigrated to Canada from Trinidad. She already had two children and she waited until her youngest was age two before she began her educational career. Sandra graduated from Teachers College as a special education teacher and embraced this as an anchor for her whole career. She had begun her practice teaching with mentally handicapped children and this early experience served to confirm her choice—this was what she wanted to do.

She spent the next 3 years working for the School Board on special education programs. Her specific focus at the time was children with developmental disabilities, which included children who were functioning at the lowest level within the educational system. Her goal was to discover ways that would really make a difference in their ability to learn and consequently in their quality of life. She also wanted to improve their status in the educational system and to attract many more competent educators into that part of the system. It was around this time that she developed what was to become an enduring foundation of her philosophy of education that, "there is always a way, you just have to find it."

Her time at the School Board Office was followed by another three-year stint developing diagnostic and training classes for the learning disabled. Her proudest accomplishment was a writing program for children with learning disabilities. This was a singularly successful activity which provided her with a high profile at the Board as well as with other educators from all over the continent who came to observe the program. This program reflected her belief that, ". . . every child could bring out their ideas in writing."

From this foundation arose the idea of a Writing Guild, where children in the regular school program would write and present their own work during Education Week. She envisioned children in each town and city presenting their work to parents and members of the community, with panels of authors and illustrators to give the children guidance. To make this happen, she enlisted the support of a socially and politically skilful Principal to co-chair the Writing Guild. This support enabled the writing program to be successfully implemented in schools across the Board.

The final three-year period prior to her appointment as Vice-Principal involved a combination of expanding and developing her educational programs and positioning herself for promotion in the system. First, she enrolled in and completed a Masters of Education degree. She also took a leadership course through the School Board during this time, a course which emphasized the importance of both vision and a team approach to leadership. Participants in these courses and, more important, her mentors at the School Board, began to persuade her that she could have a wider impact on the school system as a Principal or executive administrator than she could as a classroom teacher. Sandra finally succumbed to this advice and applied to be a Vice-Principal. She felt she was getting valuable support from senior Board administrators both for her programs and for her career moves. Whatever happened, Sandra was steadfast in her view that career moves would be taken only if they helped to promote programs she had developed for writing and for children with learning disabilities. Her application for Vice-Principal was successful and she was placed at Academy Hill Public School.

During her first year, Academy Hill was selected by the School Board as a pilot project for developing a cooperative learning program at the public school level. In this program children learned to work together in positive ways to build social and team skills. This provided a friendly environment for innovative programming. Quite conveniently, the Principal at Academy Hill was not very familiar with new program development, thus giving Sandra a fairly free rein. Once again her efforts were very successful and boosted her strong reputation for implementing new educational concepts. Indeed, she was gaining the attention and support of educators at the forefront of educational innovation and change.

Following her two-year stay at Academy Hill she took an internal Board transfer to Don Valley Public School. Her placement at Don Valley had been carefully planned to cultivate her administrative skills. Her new Principal worked with and managed people very well. She was advised by her mentors to observe and emulate those skills, with this note of caution: ". . . sometimes you go too fast. You think so far ahead and move so quickly, you leave people behind in the dust. We want you to learn that change takes time. You won't always have us around. . . ."

Welcome to South Heights Public School

Sandra's first visit to South Heights School was a horrifying experience. She arrived fresh from Don Valley, a new model suburban public school, and the contrast was shocking. The schools she had experience with were bright, happy places, that welcomed students and teachers alike. To Sandra, South Heights looked dark and depressing. It exuded an institutional atmosphere from its square box-like shape to its brick exterior. There was some grass but no flowers to be seen anywhere. The school may have once been appealing but now it seemed to be part of a world that years of modern education had passed by completely.

While the outside was forbidding enough, the inside was even worse. The paint on some of the walls appeared to be original and on others it was peeling in patches. The dominant colours were green, yellow, and burgundy and it created a drab and sombre effect. The classrooms were very spartan, containing little decoration beyond the desks and chalk boards. Classroom displays were neither colourful, nor eye appealing. Sandra found out later that decorations and other classroom embellishments were repeatedly stolen and any attempt to create a more appealing atmosphere had long been abandoned. The staff room was located in a former coal bin in the basement. Isolated from the rest of the school, it was more squalid than the rest of the school, although it was decorated in the same style.

Sandra not only was shocked but felt hurt and angry that a school would be allowed to deteriorate to such a state. Her first trip to South Heights was in early spring and she decided immediately that the first order of the day would be to clean and paint the place. The Board arranged for painting the school. Sandra enlisted family and friends and spent most of the summer sprucing up and decorating a new staff room. She also had murals painted in the school. The notion was to create "bright and happy" scenes and colours to relieve some of the interior gloom. Sandra admits that she did not have a clear strategy for improving conditions at the school beyond these initial steps. She essentially had no idea of what she should do next.

The first days of school had further surprises in store. Arriving early one morning, Sandra observed some parents waiting with their children in the schoolyard. She approached the parents, introduced herself and began with a few pleasantries. She could feel they were rather reticent and uncomfortable but she wanted to make contact and very shortly invited them inside for coffee. There was a brief hesitation and then one father blurted, "Lady, I don't want to have coffee with you. Just go to hell." Sandra had arrived at South Heights.

The confrontation with the parents foreshadowed what was going on throughout the school. In the halls, in the playground, in the classroom, students shouted incessantly at each other, and if shouting didn't resolve the issue, they slugged it out. Cathy, a first-year teacher who arrived at the same time as Sandra, described what she encountered: "I grew up in a big family, a protected world. My initial reaction in coming here was utter shock. When I was a kid, I wouldn't have looked at a teacher sideways. These children have grown up where they are not respected, they think it is normal, they don't know any different."

The staff knew the home life for most of the children reinforced this aggressive behaviour and the only responses the children seemed to understand were shouting even louder in return and using physical restraint to keep them in line. Some staff were shouting almost as much as the children! Sandra was appalled but the staff seemed hardly aware of their conduct. There were certainly many other school problems, no less discouraging, but these highly vocal confrontations seemed symbolic of a basic mistrust and resentment between the school and the families it was meant to serve.

Equally disturbing was how low standards had fallen in the school. Some staff were continually late for the start of their classes; others did not appear to have lesson plans prepared for their classes. The books in the school library appeared to be shelved on a random basis, and the library itself was closed as often as it was open. The school was not even kept clean; dust and dirt accumulated in the hallways and classrooms. Sandra felt she had to act quickly and she soon called a staff planning meeting. The purpose was to devise a plan, at least for the year, to give the staff a sense of mission.

The planning meetings were conducted as a series so that the task was not perceived as too formidable. The format utilized the cooperative group techniques that Sandra had learned at Academy Hill and Don Valley. This cooperative technique involved assigning roles to each group member so that each person had to interact with others in order to fulfil their roles.

This was intended to build team spirit as the plan was being developed.

The simple objective of the planning sessions was to identify what staff was doing that should be continued or expanded and what should be eliminated. A formal planning document evolved from these meetings identifying both positive and negative practices. Many of the items seemed to have Sandra's stamp on them but she insisted that the plan arose through consensus.

The central features of the school plan were grouped around the motto, "Together we light the way." This concept focused on teacher, student, and parent relationships that implied a partnership in the learning process. In keeping with this theme, other objectives were developed. These included an agreement that the learning process would be student-centred; focused on student needs, not teacher needs. It was also decided that teachers would make every effort to model appropriate behaviours for the students. This was obviously directed at eliminating aggressive verbal and physical confrontations among students, and between staff and students. However, it also included many other things, such as being on time, having lesson plans prepared for each class, standing at the door with a smile on your face and welcoming each student as they entered class, giving parents clear and detailed information on their child's progress on report cards, and generally taking personal responsibility for creating a good learning environment.

According to the plan, teachers were also expected to work together developing lesson plans so that both the content and consistency of instruction would improve. Teachers were responsible for the students' learning development, particularly their reading and writing skills. This presumably meant that teachers were accountable if a student's performance fell below some reasonable level of expectation.

Two months later, Sandra asked herself what had changed as a result of the school plan. In short, the answer was very little! The staff who had previously arrived late, and those who were unprepared, continued to do so. Those who engaged in verbal and physical confrontations with students continued this practice. She did take some comfort in the efforts of several new, enthusiastic teachers to implement the plan. She was also pleased that one of her initiatives to get parents more involved in the school was having some success. A group called "Parent Rap" was formed to bring parents and teachers together to discuss issues affecting the children. Unfortunately, just 3 parents were coming to the meetings on a regular basis.

Most senior teachers, however, were not cooperating with her attempts to change the school. Many of these teachers had not been to a professional development workshop in years, and were not simply sceptical toward her new approach to education, but were openly hostile and confrontational. Their opposition rested on the conviction that an authoritarian manner was the only thing that worked with these children. Further, their scepticism of new approaches had been strengthened by the failure of past efforts to make meaningful changes at South Heights.

Some of the confrontations with senior staff were quite unpleasant. For example, she refused to sign the report cards of one senior teacher because he wrote one or two words on each report card, rather than the detailed feedback they had agreed to provide to the parents. To the teacher this activity seemed pointless: "Would any of the parents bother reading this!" This teacher confronted her in the hallway and yelled at her in front of students and teachers. She told him quietly but firmly to go into her office. Once in her office he continued to yell and swept everything off her desk onto the floor. She received a visit the next day from an official of the teachers' union who said the problems she was having with this teacher could best be explained as ". . . a new female Principal trying to intimidate the males in the system." This situation was similar to other hostile confrontations with the librarian and a few of the senior teachers. She had only a vague knowledge of her rights as Principal to enforce standards, as standards had never been an issue in her previous experience.

Some of the senior staff had recently begun a campaign to have her dismissed, and tried to enlist other teachers and parents to their cause, in their words, "to save the children." A senior teacher who was sympathetic to Sandra's attempts to improve the school told her that the campaign was gaining momentum. She also confided to Sandra that she was not fully convinced of the ideas underlying the school plan.

Two events around this time brought her to an emotional low point in her life. Her father died suddenly, unexpectedly, at the beginning of December. No one close to her had ever died and the pain she felt was "absolutely unendurable." She did not look forward to returning to South Heights after the Christmas break. A second event shortly thereafter brought her to the point of resignation. One day in early February she asked a female custodian to clean something up. The custodian screamed and yelled that she had ". . . ridiculous expectations . . . the school was fine before you came here . . . why don't you go back to where you came from!" Sandra was crushed. It was the "first time in my career I had experienced racism." Equally bad, she realized that ". . . even the custodian felt she could lace into me."

She drove home in tears. She knew "this is it: I can't take this any more." Should she resign now as Principal of South Heights? She could quickly return to developing programs for children with learning disabilities; indeed, the School Board would welcome her back. On the other hand, the children of South Heights desperately needed her help. The pain of her failure to make a meaningful change in their lives was acute. But if she stayed, what could she do to transform South Heights?

Discussion Questions

1. What are the problems here?
2. What are the important aspects of the situation confronting Sandra Lee upon her arrival at South Heights?
3. Why has the plan failed?
4. What theories and concepts help to explain the events in this case?
5. Should Sandra Lee resign and return to the classroom? What are the implications for her career if she chooses to return to the classroom? If she chooses to press on?
6. If she chooses to stay and attempt to transform South Heights, what should she do? What are the reasonable alternatives? What course of action should she pursue? How should she implement these actions?

51   SICK . . . AGAIN (A)

Sick again! Selina Anderson sat looking at the message her secretary left on her desk: Jennifer called in sick today; sorry! Selina was disgusted. This was the second Monday in a row that Jennifer Tate called in sick. She seemed fine to Selina on Friday. Jennifer had been working on the Northeast Corporation account, which was now two days behind schedule, probably soon to be three days. To make matters worse, Mr. Bradley, the firm's managing partner, was particularly interested in the progress on the Northeast account.

During their Monday morning meeting, Selina had the unpleasant task of updating Mr. Bradley on the status of the Northeast account. She also informed him of Jennifer's untimely sick day. She told Mr. Bradley that she planned to talk to Jennifer when she returned to work concerning the many sick days she had recently taken. She would inform Jennifer that the next time she called in sick she would be given a written warning which would be included in her permanent file. Just as she had suspected, Mr. Bradley was not pleased to hear the news. He agreed with Selina that Jennifer needed a "good talking to." He pondered aloud that he was rather disappointed in Jennifer's poor attendance and bad attitude. It seemed to him that the rest of the staff was working harder than ever to get new clients and increase revenues and productivity.

Jennifer Tate had worked in the Accounting Department of Quantum Corporation for just under five years. She had started with Quantum when she was a senior in college, in an internship program which enabled students to get on-the-job experience. She had done such good work in the internship program that she was offered a position at Quantum when she graduated from college.

Quantum Corporation was a medium-sized consulting firm with six different locations in the New England and New York areas. It had been in the consulting industry since 1960, when its first office opened in Boston, Massachusetts. Business for Quantum had paralleled the Northeast economy and thus the 80s proved to be prosperous, while the early 90s saw a decline in both revenues and clients.

Jennifer worked in Quantum's Worcester, Massachusetts, office. The atmosphere here was friendly yet competitive. The staff accountants generally played office politics, which meant "brown-nosing" the partners and "shmoozing" the clients. They made every attempt to be recognized as partner material and hoped to get promoted in the process. Since business had been particularly stagnant, there had been a recent push by the partners to get new clients. Jennifer was a hard worker who always got her work done on a timely basis but took quite a few sick days in the process. Also, since she was a little on the quiet side, her ability to attract new clientele was merely satisfactory. Because she kept to herself and didn't go out of her way to talk to the partners, Jennifer had received only one promotion in her almost five years with the company.

Even though the partners didn't think Jennifer was a star, her manager Selina thought she was a hard worker who should be at a higher level. Selina knew the reason Jennifer wasn't at a higher level was because she didn't play "office politics." She also felt bad for Jennifer, who had no family except her husband. Since she had moved to Worcester from New York, Jennifer did not have many friends in the area. Her personal history was sad; it explained why she was so quiet and kept to herself most of the time. Jennifer was adopted as a baby and had never known her real parents. The couple that adopted her was older and had severe health problems. They died when Jennifer was 15 years old. She moved around a lot after their death, usually staying with different friends of her parents and even on occasion living in her car. Jennifer decided to go to a small college in Massachusetts to try to start a new life. She wanted to make new friends, be accepted, and prepare herself for a rewarding career upon graduation. It was at college that she met her soon-to-be-husband Mitch. Selina knew Jennifer's personal history and admired her courage and spirit in all of the adversities she had struggled through. She felt that Jennifer worked harder to get to where she was than many of the staff at Quantum who seemed to have everything handed to them on a silver platter. This was why Selina took Jennifer under her wing and became her mentor at Quantum.

This was also why Selina was not looking forward to talking to Jennifer about her absences. In her mind she had gone over and over what she would say to Jennifer and how Jennifer would respond. It was Wednesday when Jennifer finally returned to work. She seemed very nervous and uncomfortable and kept even more to herself than usual. If she had gone over it a thousand times in her mind, Selina would never have been prepared for Jennifer's explanation of her many recent absences. Jennifer told Selina the reason she was out so often was because her husband Mitch had been physically abusing her. She explained that they recently went through a difficult time having a new house built and that this frustration, coupled with problems at work, had made Mitch very stressed and irritable. The economy was hitting the banking business hard, which was the industry Mitch was employed in. He recently found out that his office might be forced to move to Hartford, or more likely, that he would be laid off. Also his salary was very low, and it seemed as though he was always getting passed over for promotions. Jennifer made considerably more money than Mitch, which hurt his pride and made him jealous and resentful of her.

Selina had heard of Jennifer's concerns about Mitch and his increasingly frequent temper tantrums. The staff accountants at Quantum had met Jennifer's husband at various social events the company sponsored. They thought he was domineering and possessive and didn't seem very comfortable in social situations. Jennifer had told her close friends at Quantum that Mitch had an "old school mentality" and believed that a woman's place was in the home; he expected Jennifer to have dinner ready every night when he got home from work and also for her to do all of the housework and bill paying, and so forth. He had come from a home where his mother was very subservient to his father, and he expected Jennifer to behave similarly.

Jennifer told Selina that Mitch had beaten her up rather badly this time and had even tried to kill her! Jennifer called the police and they made Mitch leave. Jennifer filed a restraining order and also called a lawyer to file for a divorce. She told Selina this was not the first time it had happened and she was sure if she stayed with him it wouldn't be the last. She was told the restraining order would be hard to enforce because she and Mitch still had joint possessions and if he wanted to talk to her about them, he could. Since the incident Mitch had been back to the house to get his things and asked Jennifer to take him back. He threatened her repeatedly that if she didn't take him back, he would continue to harass her until she changed her mind. True to his word, he called continuously on the phone until she took it off the hook. He then went to their house and tried to break in. She called the police, who took him away and reprimanded him.

When Jennifer spoke to Selina, she was very upset and not sure what to do or whom to turn to. She told Selina she would need a few days away from work to move out of the house and begin divorce proceedings. She also asked Selina not to tell any of the other staff accountants. Jennifer said she was worried for her safety and thought Mitch would probably call or come to Quantum looking for her. Since she had moved out of the house, work was the only place he would be able to find her. Jennifer asked Selina to think about any precautions Quantum could take until the divorce and the imminent danger of the situation was over.

Selina told Jennifer that she felt sick over what had happened to her. She felt very sympathetic that Jennifer had no family and few friends in the area to turn to. She thought that it was her place as her supervisor and friend to help in whatever way she could, especially as far as Jennifer's safety at Quantum was concerned. Selina assured Jennifer that a company like Quantum must certainly have policies and procedures for situations like this. Selina was sure that there were precautions that could be taken to ensure Jennifer's safety. She told Jennifer that she would confer with the managing partner, Mr. Bradley, and see what steps they should take.

SMOKESTACK VILLAGE, INC.

Thomas J. Bronston, chairman of the board of trustees and general manager of Smokestack Village, was worried about the developing problem between his employees and Karl Olson, the man he wished to have replace him as general manager.

Smokestack Village was a tourist attraction located near the Continental Divide in central Colorado. It offered visitors a large railroad museum and daily excursion rides on old railroad lines. The museum had over 40 steam locomotives on display and many other exhibits relating to the days of steam railroading. The excursion rides were operated during the summer and fall months over 26 miles of track winding through a valley high in the Rockies. It had been founded by Miles E. Smith, a semiretired railroad buff, with Mr. Bronston's assistance in arranging financing.

Mr. Smith served as general manager during the early years of slow growth. When he was unexpectedly killed in an automobile accident, Mr. Bronston tried to find someone to take care of the day-to-day operating responsibility. This included short-range planning, ordering supplies, handling the finances, and coping with "nosey federal inspectors." When unsuccessful in finding someone he considered satisfactory, he reluctantly took on the task himself. This meant closing up his own business as an investment counselor and moving from Denver to Grenoble, which was closer but still 45 miles from Smokestack Village.

He had been general manager for the past five years. During that time the museum had started running the excursion trains, and the many engines that had been sitting around the turntable rusting had been stored under cover during the winter and restored on a regular basis. Attendance had tripled over the five-year period. He now felt that it was time for "new blood" in management, and he was informally looking for a replacement. The long commute was also getting to him.

Assistant manager Jim Harris, 28, was in charge of restoration, painting, lawnmowing, and ticket sales. Working for him were three girls who sold tickets and staffed the exhibit cars. Also under his direction were five high school boys who worked around the locomotive displays, painting, restoring the engines to their original looks, lawnmowing, weeding, sweeping walks, and doing track work. Jim spent most of his day making sure the boys were working and not goofing off from what they considered to be "just a summer job in which you put in your 40 hours."

Contact between Harris's crew and a crew that operated the excursion trains was limited because of the physical layout of Smokestack Village (see Exhibit 1) and the jobs they did. This train crew spent the day either in the station or up the line, while the museum crew was working around the display engines a distance away.

Sven Olson was in charge of the train crew and was also the engineer on the train. Sven was a veteran of 50 years' service as an engineer for the Great Western Railroad, and he knew his business. The other employees used to joke that he knew more about railroads than they would ever have time to forget. At 75, he was still capable of working longer and harder than most of the other employees 55 years younger than he.

Ned Bronston, 17, the son of Mr. Bronston, was the fireman. He lived with Sven in the bunk car parked near the engine house. It was the first summer working at Smokestack Village for both of them, although Ned had spent many days at Smokestack with his father over the years.

Working with them were three other employees who had worked at Smokestack Village in the past. Bob Johnson, 30, had worked for the village for four years as conductor for the passenger train in the summer and in the office in the winter.

The brakemen were Al Stanhope, 18, and Peter Townshend, also 18. They had worked at Smokestack for the past two summers on the museum crew, and it was their first summer on the train.

The five of them became fast friends. They worked well together and enjoyed each other's company both during and after work. It was not unusual for them all to go out to dinner at the end of the day or sit around the bunk car half the night talking about railroads. Al and Peter kept sleeping bags at the bunk car and frequently stayed overnight.

Al, Peter, and Ned, with Sven's consent, traded jobs occasionally; Ned worked as brakeman while Al or Peter fired the engine. Frequently, Sven would allow the fireman to run the engine while he fired. Most railroads allowed this, and Mr. Bronston knew that with Sven in the cab, nothing could go wrong. The practice allowed for the training of future engineers. Mr. Bronston only asked that the train leave and arrive in the village on time. How this was to be done was left up to the five of them. They found it best to work as a team; each of them knew the other's job well enough from the practice of switching jobs to know what to expect from the others. Arguments were few and far between.

The day started for Sven and Ned at 8:30 A.M. Being fireman, Ned had many duties to tend to before the engine could be run that day. The fire had to be rebuilt from the day before, lubricators filled, water

EXHIBIT 1

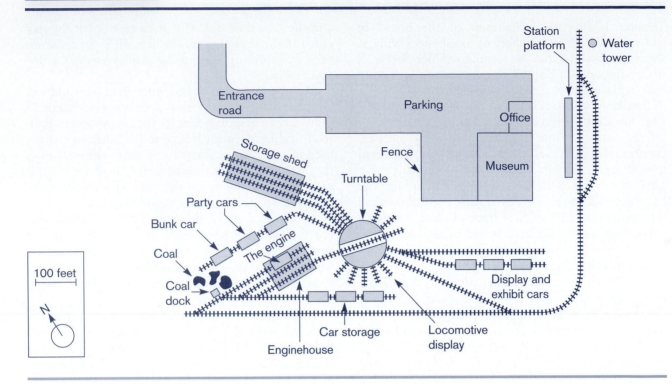

worked out of the cylinders, and the engine coaled. The coal dock was 75 yards from the engine house, and this gave Ned an opportunity to run the engine a bit. If he had time and the engine warranted it, he would polish the engine, wiping oil and cinders from the boiler and wheels.

While Ned was working on the engine, Sven would be preparing a sumptuous breakfast for the two of them. He would also boil a large pot of coffee for Bob, Al, and Peter, who would arrive at 10. Breakfast started at 9:30, and the train crew would join them at 10 for a half hour of railroad talk. The talk usually turned to girls, sports, and movies; the breakfast hour was enjoyed by all.

At 10:30 it was time to take the engine and passenger cars down to the station in preparation for the first run, leaving at 11. Mr. Bronston would be waiting on the platform for the train's arrival. He would climb into the cab to talk with Sven about the engine. He would inquire about whether the engine was running well, the coal supply was lasting, and any other details related to the operating department. Satisfied that all was going well, he would head back to his office.

Mr. Bronston felt that he had a responsible crew working on the train. There was an unstated understanding between him and the train crew that as long

as things went smoothly, he would not interfere in their routine. Sven worked hard with the train crew, drilling them on railroad procedures and safety measures. Running a railroad is serious business, and they all knew it. Fooling around could not be tolerated when 800 people were on the train. There were instances where local kids had tried to derail the train by placing ties and spikes on the track. Al and Ned had managed to catch the culprits, and they were turned over to the state police.

The arrival of the train back in Smokestack Village after the first trip marked the beginning of lunch for both the museum and train crews. Ned would buy lunch for Sven and himself and return to the engine. One of them stayed on the engine at all times. After eating, Sven would climb down off the engine and wander around talking with visitors, while other visitors would climb into the cab for a look around and maybe a chance to blow the whistle.

Two more trips would be made before the end of the day at 6 P.M. It took Ned about an hour to shut down the engine for the night. If the train crew was going out to dinner together, they would all pitch in to get the work done; otherwise Sven would start dinner for Ned and himself while Bob, Al, and Peter would head home for dinner.

There were times when the engine needed major repair due to some malfunction. When this happened, the museum crew would join the train crew in repairing the locomotive. Sometimes the work would take all night–nobody complained. It had to be done if the train was to run the next day. Sven and Ned would work with the crews until midnight and then retire. If they were to function the next day, they needed their sleep. The two of them put in the hardest day of all the employees.

Each morning at 3 A.M., Ned would wake up and go out to the engine to check the water level, steam pressure, and the fire, which was left burning from the day before. The engine had a habit of building up steam pressure when left unattended, and this led to difficulties the next morning, the worst being a boiler explosion.

In doing this Ned violated federal law, which requires that railroad employees not work more than 16 hours, followed by a 10-hour rest period. Ned was well aware of this law but chose to ignore it. Smokestack Village would have had to hire a night hostler to watch the engine, and this was costly. So he did it himself.

Employees turned in their time cards each Wednesday. They were to write down the hours they had worked and what they had done. Average pay for the museum and train crews was minimum wage. Bob earned a higher wage since legally the responsibility of the train and the hundreds of passengers was his, and his higher pay was justified. The train crew only put in for a 44-hour week, although 50 and 60 hours of actual work was not unusual. They never asked for pay for the nights they worked repairing the engine. Working on steam engines was considered a privilege. Al, Peter, and Ned spent many evenings working on one engine in the exhibit area that was their favorite. They had painted the engine and spent many hours hunting through the storage shed and spare parts boxcars looking for gauges, valves, and other parts to replace ones missing from the locomotive. They didn't ask to be paid for this.

The museum crew, for the most part, did the same thing with their time cards. They only asked for overtime when the work was not with the engines. They had a few pet projects that they also worked on after hours; for example, they had been painting the railroad name on the sides of the passenger cars, doing one side of one car an evening.

During the times when the two crews were working in the evenings, Jim Harris and Sven were never around. The evening projects were the idea of the employees involved, and they wished to do it on their own. Mr. Bronston, on his daily inspection tours of the grounds, would only offer suggestions on what might look better or more realistic. The final decisions were left up to the crews. The two groups stayed to themselves most of the time. The only time the two crews worked together was when the engine that Al, Peter, and Ned were working on had to be lettered. The museum crew stenciled the engine for the three of them to paint. The museum crew had offered to do the job, and the offer was gladly accepted. Once the job was done, the two crews went back to the original format of working by themselves.

The museum crew's attitude of it being "just a summer job" changed during the month of June. Once the lawnmowing and trackwork and other tasks were done, they were permitted to work on the engines, which was much more interesting and enjoyable to the point that they stayed late on their own time.

Sven had one son, Karl, 50, who lived in Wyoming. Karl was a successful mechanical engineer with a long list of patents to his credit. He had been involved in the production of a sound movie projector for a large camera producer, and his expertise had helped send a man to the moon. He had started many engineering consulting firms with clients like NASA, the armed services, the automobile industry suppliers, and railroads. He had sold his businesses over the past few years and was now in semiretirement, taking on consulting work out of his home when he wanted.

During the month of June, he made several trips with his wife Henrietta to Smokestack Village and the area to visit his father. He would ride in the cab of the engine, and Ned would sometimes let him sit in the fireman's seat. Karl considered this a privilege and was grateful to Ned. Sven and Karl got along quite well. Karl never interfered with Sven's work, realizing that he was in the presence of one of the best and most well-known engineers in the country.

It was not long before Karl was seen in the office with Mr. Bronston discussing Smokestack Village. Karl had many ideas on how to increase patronage at the museum. He knew some people in the TV advertising business, and he arranged for low-cost TV commercials to be aired in major cities of the area.

Karl started spending more and more time at the museum. Mr. Bronston, realizing that Karl had plenty of spare time that might be put to constructive use at Smokestack Village, asked him if he would be interested in becoming a trustee. Karl accepted the offer, and he and his wife moved into a local motel for an indefinite stay.

Prior to Karl's becoming a trustee, Mr. Bronston had asked Ned what he thought of Karl. Ned couldn't think of anything negative at the time and told his father that he would get the other employees' reactions. The museum crew didn't have much contact with Karl; only Jim knew who he was, and he thought Karl was OK. The train crew had only known Karl for a month at that point and didn't register any complaints about him, either. They knew that Mr. Bronston was looking for a replacement; but, since Mr. Bronston had left the operating department to them and didn't interfere, they didn't care who was the boss. In the next two weeks, they would all have reason to care after all.

Karl, now a trustee, began to make his appearance in the bunk car every morning at 9 to start issuing orders. The train crew started to grumble that they didn't need this intrusion in their morning routine. Karl no longer allowed the morning coffee break. The work that Al, Peter, and Ned did in the evenings was now to be done in the morning starting at 9. Ned, having to work on the engine, couldn't participate. Ned's work in the morning was under constant fire from Karl. As a result, the "extra bit" Ned did polishing the engine was neglected. Karl also ordered that the engine and train be ready in the station at 10:15 each morning. Sven and Ned were incensed at this. It meant getting up earlier and rushing breakfast on what they considered to be their own time. Sven was also told by Karl that when the engine was moved even a foot, he had better be at the throttle or Karl would find a new engineer. Ned was no longer allowed to run the engine to the coal dock, and the firemen were not allowed to run the engine on the mainline. At lunchtime, Ned could no longer leave the engine to get lunch for Sven and himself from the cafeteria in the station. They were both to stay on the engine at all times during the day. The conductor and brakemen were not subjected to the same restriction, and this caused hard feelings between the engine and train crews. When Sven had asked Karl how he was to get lunch, Karl told him to bring a sandwich with him in the morning. Sven told the four men he worked with to ignore Karl. Mr. Bronston had given Sven his orders and those were the ones to follow. Karl seemed careful not to give orders when Mr. Bronston was around.

The employees began to look around to see if Karl was watching and, if he was, to do it his way. Nobody dared cross him. But the trips allowed the train crew a chance to get away from Karl and do things their own way. Once the train left the station, they would stop looking over their shoulders to see if Karl was watching. Bob got in the habit of signaling Sven to start when Karl was nowhere in sight, while Al and Peter would walk the length of the train to see if Karl had gotten on while they weren't watching and, if so, tell the engine crew through a prearranged hand signal. If Karl was on the train, the trip would be slower and the whistle wasn't blown as much, which upset Sven because he felt that the people had paid for a train

ride and he was going to give them a ride they would never forget.

Mr. Bronston had told the employees that Karl had been made a trustee but had not made any mention of any authority that Karl might have when dealing with employees. The Smokestack Village board had 15 trustees on it. They were all known by the employees, and many of them came to Smokestack on weekends to look around. They frequently asked the employees how projects were coming but never ordered anyone around. For the most part they were fund-raisers for the organization and policymakers. On one trustee's visit, he asked one of the museum crew workers to wear cleaner clothes because the employees were in the limelight. It was the only incident where a trustee, other than Karl, confronted an employee all summer.

Karl had made it understood that anyone who didn't do as he said would be fired. The way he gave orders, the message was clear: "Do it my way, or you're out."

Morale hit bottom. Employees came to work at 9 and left at 5. Before, when the engine needed repair, Jim had asked who would like to stay late to help fix the engine, and the museum crew would head for the phone to call home to cancel dinner or their girlfriends to cancel dates. This was no longer true. Sven and Jim had to plead with the museum crew to stay, and they would agree only if it were understood that they were free to leave if Karl showed up. Ned and Al and Peter would stay, even if he did show, because they needed the engine. The time cards started to show exactly how many hours each employee worked. Fifty and 60 hours was not unusual, and the payroll was doubled with the overtime.

About two weeks after Karl's appointment as a trustee, Mr. Bronston was made aware of the payroll increase by his secretary Jean, who handled the payroll accounts. Jean, the employees' "second mother," offered no explanation, although she did know what was happening. Mr. Bronston decided to accept Sven's standing invitation for dinner in the bunk car with Ned and himself. The conversation that night finally turned to Karl. Sven related some of the incidents that made him angry with his son Karl. Ned, at Sven's insistence, let it be known that Karl was ruining a good working environment. Employees were rebelling by "misplacing" valuable locomotive tools and parts; painting and restoration work was slowing down, and little jobs, such as picking up trash, were not being done. If Mr. Bronston wanted the stenciling and lettering of the passenger cars finished, he would have to order it finished on Smokestack Village's time. Ned also stated that he and most of the other workers felt it difficult to follow two bosses. They were all at a loss about whose orders to follow: Karl's, as he was always around the grounds, or Mr. Bronston's, who was the boss even when he was working in the office.

Mr. Bronston thanked the two of them for dinner and got in his car for the 45-minute trip home. As he drove, he reflected upon the situation. Karl looked like a man capable of taking his place. He had plenty of spare time, which he was willing to devote to the village, and was a successful businessman with many connections in the railroad industry. Karl would make the village his life, something that Mr. Bronston didn't want to do. Living in Grenoble, a poor mill town, wouldn't bother Karl, as he didn't have any children and didn't much care what his wife thought. Ned had overheard Karl tell Sven that his wife had cancer, "so she'll be gone soon."

The present circumstances cast a doubt in Mr. Bronston's mind about whether he could entrust Karl with the museum. The next trustees' meeting would be in October. He knew he would have to stay on as general manager until then, when Karl might take the job. Now if he could figure out a way to keep peace until then . . .

53 ST INDUSTRIES, INC.

Stover Industries was an amalgamation of several small companies in the electrical parts industry. Elizabeth Stover and her husband had inherited one of the group of companies from her father-in-law. Mrs. Stover, an engineer, elected to run the company while her husband pursued a separate career as a dental surgeon. In addition to the original inheritance, Mrs. Stover had purchased three other companies to create the present Stover Industries. Mrs. Stover, at 31 years of age, was a dynamic individual, full of ideas and drive.

Chris Cunningham had been a salesperson for Stover Industries for about nine months. Chris had joined Stover Industries about three months after Elizabeth Stover, a college classmate, had become president of the company and had offered Chris a job. After talking to Mrs. Stover and hearing about her plans for the company, Chris had jumped at the opportunity to move from a large, reputable, but slow-moving company to Stover Industries, where the prospects, from being part of a small, aggressive organization, looked great.

After talking to Mrs. Stover at the time of hiring, Chris knew that she planned to integrate the four companies into a unified organization by welding the individual managements into one unit. Chris also knew that she was determined to remake the company from the rather complacent organization it had become into a dynamic, aggressive, and highly profitable business. In Chris's view, Mrs. Stover had accomplished a lot, although she had not moved as rapidly as Chris had expected her to. Several of the executives of the old companies, who obviously could not keep up with their new, young, and driving boss, had resigned, but others remained. Also, the question of sales territories had not been resolved. Many of the salespeople from the original companies still had their old customers, which meant that their territories often overlapped. Furthermore, the sales director, whom Mrs. Stover had known for a long time as the sales director of the original Stover Company, spent most of his time attending to routine matters. If it weren't for Liz Stover's own input, there would be no real sales leadership at all. Finally there were the people in production—who, in Chris's view, were far from dynamic.

Chris liked the job and had developed a good sales record. More than that, Chris felt that that record constituted a significant contribution to the progress the company was making. But there was one cloud in an otherwise satisfying nine months, which Chris expressed as follows:

> Every now and then, Liz seems to act like a different person, suddenly treating me as a child. When this happens, Liz usually gets very protective of the weak characters she still has working for her in production and starts telling me to baby them even though it's obvious that the company is going to suffer.
>
> Why, only last week, I had to push the purchasing agent to get some supplies that were needed to fill a special order that one of our best customers needed to complete a prototype. If I hadn't built a little bit of a fire under that guy, we would have missed the delivery date I promised and undoubtedly lost out on an order next year that will really benefit Stover. Most of the production people are still so used to the old complacent ways of doing things that the only way to ensure that Stover builds good customer relations is to directly insist that they show the kind of aggressiveness this company needs. I don't see how Liz puts up with them. I've tried asking them politely when we need to make a special effort, I've tried logical persuasion, and I've tried begging—but nothing seems to work except a little heat. So when Liz is in one of her protective moods, I back off, but I find that soon I have to begin to prod those people again.
>
> I don't understand this pattern in Liz. She wants to turn the company around and usually acts in a forceful manner but she seems to get sentimental about some of those old-timers in production every now and then and lets their feelings come ahead of what's best for Stover Industries—and this has me concerned. I like Liz; I think the company has a lot of potential, but I'm beginning to wonder if Liz has the stuff to make the tough decisions that a president has to make.

54   THE VIRTUAL ENVIRONMENT WORK TEAM

T. A. Stearns was a national tax accounting firm whose main business was its popular tax preparation service for individuals. Stearns' superior reputation was based on the high quality of its advice and the excellence of its service. Key to the achievement of its reputation were the superior computer data bases and analysis tools that its agents used when counseling clients. These programs were developed by highly trained individuals, usually lawyers and tax accountants who had picked up programming skills on the side.

The programs that these individuals produced were highly technical both in terms of the tax laws they covered and the code in which they were written. Perfecting them required high levels of programming skill as well as the ability to understand the law. New laws and interpretations of existing laws had to be integrated quickly and flawlessly into the existing regulations and analysis tools.

The work was carried out in a virtual environment by four programmers in the greater Boston area. Four work sites were connected to each other and to the company by e-mail, telephone, and conferencing software. Formal meetings among all of the programmers took place only a few times a year, although the workers sometimes met informally outside of these scheduled occasions.

The following paragraphs describe the members of the virtual work team.

Tom Andrews was a tax lawyer, a graduate of State University and a former hockey player there. At thirty-five years old, Tom had worked on the programs for six years and was the longest-standing member of the group. Along with his design responsibilities, Tom was the primary liaison with Stearns. He was also responsible for training new group members. Single, he worked out of his farm in Southern New Hampshire where in his spare time he enjoyed hunting and fishing.

Cy Crane, a tax accountant and computer science graduate of State University, was thirty-two years old, married with two children ages 4 and 6. His wife worked full time in a law firm in downtown Boston, while he commuted from his kitchen to his computer in their home in the Boston suburbs. In his spare time he enjoyed biking and fishing.

Marge Dector, tax lawyer, graduate of Outstate University, thirty-eight years old, was married with two children ages 8 and 10. Her husband worked full time as an electrical engineer at a local defense contractor. She lived and worked in her suburban Boston home, and she enjoyed golf and skiing.

Megan Harris, tax accountant and graduate of Big Time University, was 26 years old and single. She had recently relocated to Boston to take advantage of the wide range of opportunities in her field and to enjoy the beauty of New England. She worked out of her Back Bay apartment.

In the course of their work, these four people exchanged e-mail messages many times every day, and it was not unusual for one of them to step away from guests or children to log on and check in with the others. Often their e-mails were amusing as well as work-related. Sometimes they helped each other with the work, as for example, when a parent with a sick child was facing a deadline. Tom occasionally invited the others to visit with him on his farm, and once in a while Marge and Cy got their families together for dinner. About once a month the whole group got together for lunch.

All of these workers were on salary, which, according to company custom, each had negotiated separately and secretly with management. A major factor in their commitment to the job was its flexibility. Although they were required to check in regularly during every work day, they could do the work whenever they wanted to. When they got together, they often joked about the managers and workers who had to be in the office during specific hours, referring to them as "face timers" and to themselves as "free agents."

When the programmers were asked to make a major program change, they often developed programming tools called macros which would help them to do their work more efficiently. These macros greatly enhanced the speed at which a change could be written into the programs. Cy in particular really enjoyed hacking around with macros. For example, on one recent project, he became obsessed by the prospect of creating a shortcut that could save him a huge amount of time. One week after he had turned in his code and his release notes to the company, Cy bragged to Tom that he had created a new macro that had saved him eight hours of work that week. "The stripers are running," he had said, "And I want to be on the beach." Tom was skeptical about the shortcut, but after trying it out in his own work, he found that it actually did save him many hours.

T. A. Stearns had an employee suggestion program that rewarded employees for innovations that saved the company money. The program gave an employee five percent of the savings generated by their innovation over a period of three months. The company also had a profit sharing plan. Tom and Cy felt that the small amount of money that would be generated by a company reward would not offset the free time that they gained using their new macro. They wanted the time either for leisure or for other consulting, and furthermore, they agreed that because the money came out of profits, the money was really coming out of the employees' pockets anyhow. There seemed to be little incentive to share their innovation macro with management.

They also believed that their group could suffer if management learned about the innovation. They could now do the work so quickly that only three programmers might be needed. If management were to learn about the macro, one of them would probably lose their job, and the remaining workers would have more work thrown at them.

Cy and Tom decided that there was not enough incentive to tell the company about the macro. However, they were just entering their busy season and they knew that everyone in the group would be stressed by the heavy workload. They decided to distribute the macro to the other members of their group and swore them to secrecy.

Over lunch one day, the group set for itself a level of production that it felt would not arouse management's suspicion. Several months passed, and they used some of their extra time to push the quality of their work even higher. The rest of the time gained they used for their own personal interests.

Dave Regan, the manager of the work group, picked up on the innovation several weeks after it was first implemented. He had wondered why production time had gone down a bit, while quality had shot up, and he got his first inkling of an answer when he saw an e-mail from Marge to Cy thanking him for saving her so much time with his "brilliant mind." Not wanting to embarrass his group of employees, the manager hinted to Tom that he wanted to know what was happening, but he got nowhere. He did not tell his own manager about his suspicions, reasoning that since both quality and productivity were up he did not really need to pursue the matter further.

Then one day Dave heard that Cy had boasted about his trick to a member of another virtual work group in the company. Suddenly the situation seemed to have gotten out of hand. Dave took Cy to lunch and asked him to explain what was happening. Cy told him about the innovation, but he insisted that the group's actions had been justified to protect itself.

Dave knew that his own boss would soon hear of the situation, and that he would be looking for answers—from him.

THE WELL-PAID RECEPTIONIST

Harvey Finley did a quick double take when he caught a glimpse of the figure representing Ms. Brannen's salary on the year-end printout. A hurried call to payroll confirmed it. Yes, his receptionist had been paid $127,614.21 for her services last year. As he sat in stunned silence, he had the sudden realization that, since his firm was doing so well this year, she would earn at least 10 to 15 percent more money during the current fiscal year. This was a shock, indeed.

With a second call to payroll, Harvey found out that Ms. Brannen's salary had been approximately $112,000 the year before last and $100,000 the year before that. She had been well paid for some time, he concluded.

Background

Harvey began his career as a service technician for a major manufacturer of copy machines. He received rather extensive technical training, but his duties were limited to performing routine, on-site maintenance and service for customers. After a year's experience as a service technician, he asked for and received a promotion to sales representative. In this capacity, he established many favorable contacts in the business community of Troupville and the surrounding towns. He began to think seriously about capitalizing on his success by opening his own business.

Then, seven years ago, he decided to take the plunge and start his own firm. He was tired of selling for someone else. When he mentioned his plan to his friends, they all expressed serious doubts; Troupville, a city of approximately 35,000 people located in the deep South, had just begun to recover from a severe recession. The painful memories of the layoffs, bankruptcies, and plummeting real estate values were too recent and vivid to be forgotten.

Undeterred by the skeptics, Harvey was optimistic that Troupville's slow recovery would soon become a boom. Even though his firm would certainly have to be started on a shoestring, Harvey thought his sales experience and technical competence would enable him to survive what was sure to be a difficult beginning. He was nervous but excited when he signed the lease on the first little building. A lifelong dream was either about to be realized or dashed forever. Troupville Business Systems was born.

While he had managed to borrow, rent, lease, or subcontract for almost everything that was absolutely necessary, he did need one employee immediately. Of course, he hoped the business would expand rapidly and that he would soon have a complete and compe-

tent staff. But until he could be sure that some revenue would be generated, he thought he could get by with one person who would be a combination receptionist/secretary and general assistant.

The typical salary for such a position in the area was about $14,000 per year; for Harvey, this was a major expense. Nevertheless, he placed what he thought was a well-worded ad in the "Help Wanted" section of the local newspaper. There were five applicants, four of whom just did not seem quite right for the position he envisioned. The fifth applicant, Ms. Cathy Brannen, was absolutely captivating.

Ms. Brannen was a twenty-seven-year-old divorcée with one small child. Her resume showed that she had graduated from a two-year office administration program at a state university. She had worked for only two employers following graduation, one for five years and the most recent for two years. Since returning to her hometown of Troupville two months ago, following her divorce, she had not been able to find suitable employment.

From the moment she sat down for the interview, Harvey and Ms. Brannen seemed to be on exactly the same wavelength. She was very articulate, obviously quite bright, and, most important, very enthusiastic about assisting with the start-up of the new venture. She seemed to be exactly the sort of person Harvey had envisioned when he first began to think seriously about taking the big plunge. He resisted the temptation to offer her the job on the spot, but ended the hour-long interview by telling her that he would check her references and contact her again very soon.

Telephone calls to her two former employers convinced Harvey that he had actually underestimated Ms. Brannen's suitability for the position. Each one said without equivocation that she was the best employee he had ever had in any position. Both former employers concluded the conversation by saying they would rehire her in a minute if she were still available. The only bit of disturbing information gleaned from these two calls was the fact that her annual salary had risen to $15,900 in her last job. Although Harvey thought that the cost of living was probably a bit higher in Houston, where she had last worked, he wasn't sure she would react favorably to the $14,000 offer he was planning to make. However, he was determined that, somehow, Cathy Brannen would be his first employee.

Ms. Brannen seemed quite pleased when Harvey telephoned her at home that same evening. She said she would be delighted to meet him at the office the next morning to discuss the position more fully.

Cathy Brannen was obviously very enthusiastic about the job as outlined in the meeting. She asked all of the right questions, responded quickly and articulately to every query posed to her, and seemed ready to accept the position even before the offer was extended. When Harvey finally got around to mentioning the salary, there was a slight change in Cathy's eager expression. She stiffened. Since Harvey realized that salary might be a problem, he decided to offer Cathy an incentive of sorts in addition to the $14,000 annual salary. He told her that he realized his salary offer was lower than the amount she had earned on her last job. And, he told her, he understood that a definite disadvantage of working for a new firm was the complete absence of financial security. Although he was extremely reluctant to guarantee a larger salary because of his own uncertainty regarding the future, he offered her a sales override in the amount of two percent of sales. He explained that she would largely determine the success or failure of the firm. She needed to represent the firm in the finest possible manner to potential customers who telephoned and to those who walked in the front door. For this reason, the sales override seemed to be an appropriate addition to her straight salary. It would provide her with incentive to take an active interest in the firm.

Cathy accepted the offer immediately. Even though she was expecting a salary offer of $16,000, she hoped the sales override might make up the difference. "Who knows," she thought, "two percent of sales may amount to big money someday." It did not, however, seem very likely at the time.

Troupville Business Systems began as a very small distributor of copy machines. The original business plan was just to sell copy machines and provide routine, on-site service. More extensive on-site service and repairs requiring that a machine be removed from a customer's premises were to be provided by a regional distributor located in a major city approximately 100 miles from Troupville.

Troupville Business Systems did well from the start. Several important changes were made in the services the firm offered during the first year. Harvey soon found that there was a greater demand for the leasing of copy machines, particularly the large expensive models which he originally planned to sell. He also soon discovered that his customers wanted to be able to contract directly with his firm for all of their service needs. Merely guaranteeing that he could get the machines serviced was not sufficient in the eyes of potential customers. In attempting to accommodate the market, he developed a complete service facility and began to offer leasing options on all models. These changes in the business all occurred during the first year. Growth during that year was steady but not spec-

tacular. While sales continued to grow steadily the second year, it was early in the third year that Harvey made what turned out to be his best decision. He entered the computer business.

Harvey had purchased a personal computer soon after Troupville Business Systems was founded. The machine and its capabilities fascinated him, although he knew virtually nothing about computers. He was soon a member of a local users club, was subscribing to all the magazines, and was taking evening computer courses at the local university—in short, he became a computer buff. Harvey recognized the business potential of the rapidly growing personal computer market, but he did not believe that his original business was sufficiently stable to introduce a new product line just yet.

During his third year of operations, he decided the time was right to enter the computer business. He added to his product line a number of personal computers popular with small businesses in the area. This key decision caused a virtual explosion in the growth of his firm. Several key positions were added, including that of comptroller. By the fourth year of operations, computers produced by several other manufacturers had been added to Harvey's product line, and he had developed the capability of providing complete service for all products carried. His computer enterprise was not limited to business customers, because he quickly developed a significant walk-in retail trade. Rapid growth continued unabated.

During the first seven years of the company's existence, Cathy Brannen had proven truly indispensable. Her performance exceeded Harvey's highest expectations. Although her official position remained that of secretary/receptionist, she took it upon herself to learn about each new product or service. During the early years, Harvey often thought that she did a better job than he did whenever a potential customer called in his absence. Even after he acquired a qualified sales staff, Harvey had no concerns when Cathy had to field questions from a potential customer because a regular salesperson was not available. The customer never realized that the professional young lady capably handling all inquiries was "only" the receptionist.

Cathy began performing fewer sales functions because of the increased number of professional salespersons, but her secretarial duties expanded tremendously. She was still Harvey's secretary, and she continued to answer virtually every telephone call coming into the business. Since her office was in an open area, she still was the first to greet many visitors.

Cathy took a word processing course at a local business school shortly after joining the firm. As she began working with Harvey's first personal computer, she, too, developed into a computer aficionado and became the best computer operator in the firm.

The Current Situation

Harvey was shaken by the realization that Cathy Brannen had been paid over $127,000 last year. As he wondered what, if anything, should be done about her earnings, he began to reflect on the previous seven years.

Success had come almost overnight. It seemed as though Troupville Business Systems could do no wrong. The work force had grown at a rate of approximately 15 percent per year since the third year of operations. Seventeen people were now employed by the firm. While Harvey did acknowledge that some of this success was due to being in the right place at the right time, he also had reason to be proud of the choices he had made. Time had proven that all of his major decisions had been correct. He also could not overestimate Cathy's contribution to the success of the firm. Yes, certainly, one of the most important days in the life of the firm was the day when Cathy responded to his ad in the newspaper.

Success had brought with it ever-increasing demands on his time. He had never worked so hard, but the rewards were certainly forthcoming. First there was the new Jaguar, then the new home on Country Club Drive, the vacation home on the coast, the European trips . . . Yes, success was wonderful.

During these years Cathy, too, had prospered. Harvey had not thought much about it, but he did remember making a joking comment the first day she drove her new Mercedes to work. He also remembered commenting on her mink coat at the company banquet last December. Cathy had been dazzling.

Now that Harvey realized what he was paying Cathy, he was greatly disturbed. She was making over twice as much money as anyone else in the firm with the exception of himself. The best salesman had earned an amount in the low sixties last year. His top managers were paid salaries ranging from the high forties to the mid-fifties. The average salary in the area for executive secretaries was now probably between $22,000 and $25,000 per year. A good receptionist could be hired for under $20,000, and yet Cathy had been paid $127,614.21 last year. The sales override had certainly enabled Cathy to share in the firm's success. Yes, indeed.

As Harvey thought more and more about the situation, he kept returning to the same conclusion. He felt something had to be done about her compensation. It was just too far out of line with other salaries in the firm. Although Harvey was drawing over $200,000 per year in salary and had built an equity in the business of more than $1 million, these facts did not seem relevant as he pondered what to do. It seemed likely that a number of other employees did know about Cathy's compensation level. Harvey wondered why no one ever mentioned it. Even the comptroller never mentioned Cathy's compensation. This did seem quite odd to Harvey, as the comptroller, Frank Bain, knew that Harvey did not even attempt to keep up with the financial details. He relied on Frank to bring important matters to his attention.

With no idea of how to approach this problem, Harvey decided to begin by making a list of alternatives. He got out a piece of paper and, as he stared at the blank lines, overheard Cathy's cheerful exchange with a customer in the next room.

56 **WESTERN DISTRIBUTION CENTER, INC.**

Part I: The Problem

"This is a can-do company, a company that people are proud to work for," Mike Henley told himself. "Then why is it that we can't solve our safety problem? I love this company too. I am fully committed to it and to my people! But right now I certainly could use some inspiration. . . ."

Mike Henley was the middle-level manager responsible for daily operations in the regional distribution center of a major mail-order catalog company. The subsidiary was located in a small and cohesive community in which such traditional values as close-knit families and patriotism were highly regarded. Mike had been working for the company for 12 years, and many of his employees had been with the company for even longer. The company was run like a large and friendly family in which the norm was to work with diligence and enthusiasm. Employees were seldom fired.

Depending on the time of year, Mike supervised between 60 and 100 hourly and salaried associates (nonunion). Their duties were to receive, store, and ship merchandise advertised in the quarterly catalog. More specifically, the associates packed orders, hand-carried merchandise, ran a forklift operation, counted stock, stacked and opened cartons, and handled related paperwork. The company was known locally as a good, even inspiring place to work, and turnover was low.

In recent months Mike had become deeply concerned about an upward trend in the frequency of accidents in the facility. Injuries had been up over the same period last year, and fall and the December holidays—traditionally the busiest months of the year—were still to come. At the same time, cost reductions had become a special concern in the highly competitive mail-order business, and upper management had been urging middle-level supervisors to closely examine expenditures. Over recent years the average cost per injury at Western, including first aid, medical care, and time lost from work, had been high.

Mike was determined to reverse the trend for accidents. He decided to challenge himself, and his associates. Even though his busiest season was yet to come, involving more associates and more orders, he wanted to end the year with some improvement and, in the subsequent year, he wanted a major change.

Mike consulted his corporate organizational development people in the Chicago office, who suggested that he might want to use behavior modification and feedback techniques to influence associates to work more safely. The OD staff suggested that even though the company already had a highly positive culture, setting specific goals and carefully managing rewards could still have strong payoffs. Mike was a willing listener; he felt as though he had tried everything else without success.

However, the OD staff tried to temper his eagerness to get started right away. In fact, they cautioned him on several issues. For instance, to use these techniques effectively he would have to know exactly what the problem was. Also, he would have to make a commitment to involving and training the associates. Furthermore, if he wanted the program to be a success for more than just a few months, he would have to understand how behavior is maintained for the long term. The OD staff noted that the corporate culture would probably support the change, but that he must be careful not to challenge that culture by his efforts. After several detailed discussions with the staff, Mike decided to commit himself to taking a course on behavior modification techniques and to designing a "b mod" program to reduce the warehouse accident rate.

As he learned more about the theory of behavior modification, Mike decided to research systematically the causes of the accident rate. He wanted to "know exactly what the problem is." Initially, he nominated a representative team of workers and managers to study facility safety. Their job was to get answers to the following questions:

- Have conditions in the facility been unsafe?
- Have the workers lacked training in safety procedures?
- Is there some factor of human fallibility that contributes to the accident rate?

To answer these questions, the task force first tested workers on their knowledge of safety procedures: Each associate was interviewed by his or her immediate manager about safety procedures pertinent to their job. Next, through additional interviews and examination of records, a detailed review of the causes of previous accidents was assembled.

The results of this investigation indicated that workers' actual knowledge of safety procedures was extremely high. Accidents occurred most frequently when people "forgot" about safety, for example, when they were distracted from their task or were in a hurry. The task force's conclusion was that 97 percent of all accidents had been caused by mistaken acts, not by inadequate training or unsafe conditions.

Mike accepted the task force's analysis that it was people's behavior on the job that should be targeted for change. He believed that improving people's attention to issues of safety would translate into improved safety behaviors. He decided that his next step should be to design a program to motivate people to behave safely.

Questions for Discussion–Part I

1. Why has the OD staff cautioned Mike? Discuss the issues the staff has raised in light of what you know about application of behavior modification principles in the workplace.

2. What additional problems should Mike anticipate, if any?

3. How would you design the program? Consider each step, from diagnosis of the problem through implementation and follow-up.

4. Why should Mike use behavior modification instead of other approaches (for example, a change in leadership style or team building or employee training) to address this issue?

Part II: The Program

Students: PLEASE DO NOT READ *this part until asked to do so.*

First Mike concerned himself with getting his team to buy into the idea of using behavior modification. He invited an internal OD consultant to the plant to explain such programs and the evidence of their effectiveness. The consultant emphasized the positive aspects of behavior modification and worked for nearly 2 hours with the associates discussing thoroughly their concerns about the negative images and associations ("punishment," "manipulation," "shock treatment") they had with the term "behavior modification." The consultant's main theme was "empowerment": Knowing behavior modification empowers people to work more efficiently and effectively.

Subsequently, Mike and his team decided to run a 4-month pilot project for the remainder of the year. Based on what was learned in the pilot, the final implementation would take place in the next year, with continual monitoring in subsequent years. To emphasize that the goal of the project was safety and to focus people's attention on the fact that the project would be ongoing, Mike named his intervention the MAIM project: *m*easure, *a*nalyze, *i*mplement, and *m*aintain.

His study of behavior modification had convinced Mike that he would need to identify observable and quantifiable behaviors in order to effectively implement the program. His examination of current safety standards in the warehouse indicated a standard

operating procedure that was too vague to be really useful. Managers generally believed that their goal was "to work as quickly, accurately, and safely as possible." When pressed, a few remembered that the company policy handbook suggested that the safety standard was "to have fewer injuries than last year." Mike decided to set two new, specific goals. First, for the current year the target would be to not exceed the previous year's total number of chargeable injuries (which was 17). Second, for the subsequent year the goal would be to reduce the figure to zero, though an intermediate goal of 50 percent reduction would be acceptable.

Baseline information on current safety behavior was collected. This included the total number of accidents and the amount of lost time for accidents for the current and past year. The method of measurement Mike used for determining an annual injury rate is shown in Exhibit 1.

The MAIM team drew up a matrix of recent accidents which showed type of accident, location of the injury on the body, cause of the accident, time of occurrence, age and length of service of the injured, and job classification of the injured. Finally, the baseline data included the cost of the accidents to the department.

Mike met with Tom Alexander, the operations manager of the warehouse, to explain in detail how the program would work. Tom, who had a degree in operations management, had been with the company for 3 years. Together they reviewed current baseline performance, and Mike had no trouble convincing Tom to buy into the program based on the various payoffs that would result from improved performance. They discussed and agreed upon the behavioral emphasis of the program, the new safety performance goals, and various feedback methods. Together they determined that the best way to secure authorization from top management was to emphasize the projected performance improvements and the minimal funds outlay required to get the program off the ground. Subsequently, they did obtain this authorization.

Finding the best way to provide feedback to associates was a key part of Mike and Tom's discussion. For some time the two men discussed the merits of positive reinforcement of safe behaviors versus punishment of unsafe behaviors. Should the program use one or the other method, or perhaps both? They considered the corporate culture, the seriousness of the problem, and the long-term effects on their associates, and in the end decided to first attempt the project using positive feedback alone. They would provide a comprehensive list of positive-feedback components to their managers, and suggest to the managers that they each select from this list the kinds of reinforcement

EXHIBIT 1
Method of Measurement

This is a standard industry method for computing the injury rate at any particular week of the fiscal or calendar year for a company, or part of a company. For example, if a department with 75 employees has one injury in its first week, that extrapolates into a rate of 1 injury on average per week for the year. If after thirteen weeks there have been three injuries, that extrapolates into twelve injuries for the year. Obviously, choosing an appropriate reference year is crucial in determining this statistic.

$$\frac{\text{Number of injuries} \times \text{annual hours}}{\text{Hours of exposure}} = \frac{\text{Total department injury}}{\text{Frequency rate per hours worked}}$$

Example: After 1 week:

$$\frac{1 \text{ Injury} \times 156{,}000 \text{ annual hours (department)}}{3{,}000 \text{ hours of exposure (1 week)}} = 52 \text{ injuries on average per year}$$

Example: After 13 weeks:

$$\frac{3 \text{ Injuries} \times 156{,}000 \text{ annual hours (department)}}{39{,}000 \text{ hours of exposure (13 weeks)}} = 12 \text{ injuries on average per year}$$

Example: After 39 weeks:

$$\frac{5 \text{ Injuries} \times 156{,}000 \text{ annual hours (department)}}{117{,}000 \text{ hours of exposure (39 weeks)}} = 6.7 \text{ injuries on average per year}$$

TABLE 1
Potential Rewards

Pay in its various forms—salary, bonuses, stock options, benefits, perquisites.
Promotion, both upward mobility and transfers laterally into desirable positions.
Management praise.
Career opportunities, longer-term chances for growth and development.
Appreciation from customers and/or clients of the organization.
Personal sense of well-being, feeling good about oneself for accomplishing things.
Opportunity to learn, chances to expand one's skills and knowledge base.
Security, sense of job and financial security.
Responsibility, providing individuals with a sense of organizational responsibility.
Respect from co-workers.
Friendship of co-workers.

they would be most comfortable using. Table 1 shows the list of potential rewards used by Mike and Tom.

Despite the fact that "pay in its various forms" was on the list, such a strict budget was established that large monetary rewards were out of the question. Also, Mike and Tom planned to initiate a top-down, tiered approach, in which all managers would be responsible for providing feedback to those individuals on the organizational level immediately below them. In addition, they felt that all managers should emphasize the positive results of the program by posting performance on a daily basis where every associate could see it and by sending the results to their associates at home.

A schedule of reinforcement was also discussed. It was decided that during the first 2 weeks managers should reward associates with praise whenever a safe working procedure was being followed. This meant that during the first 2 weeks workers would frequently receive positive feedback. In weekly meetings during this period, managers would require supervisors to cite specific examples of how they had used positive reinforcement during that week. The managers in turn would reward the supervisors with praise. Gradually, as performance improved, less emphasis would be placed on direct personal praise, but performance feedback would continue.

Mike then scheduled several meetings involving Tom, the supervisors, and the team leaders in the warehouse. In the first meeting, the details of the program were reviewed. In the second meeting, basic principles of positive reinforcement were studied and role-plays simulating effective use of positive reinforcement were conducted. At the same time the principles of timing feedback were reviewed and application exercises were run.

The next step was to communicate all of this information to associates in a condensed form. The operations manager and supervisors met with the associates to explain the details of the program implementation and to tell them what the new goals would be. Questions and objections were handled at this time.

Once the implementation of the pilot program began, a safety performance information graph was posted in the warehouse on the wall across from the time clock. The graph was updated daily.

After the first month Mike distributed the following letter:

> To: All Catalog Associates:
>
> As you know, we are all making an all-out effort to reduce the number of accidents in our department. Our goal, of course, is to not have any more during the rest of the calendar year.
>
> The key to not having accidents is in working *safely*—lifting correctly, being very careful when using a knife, and always being on the alert for potential hazards. Having an accident is not a pleasant experience. If you've never had one, ask someone who has.
>
> We are glad to report that our department had no reportable accidents this past week. This shows that we're *thinking* and *practicing* safety. You are to be commended for your contribution toward decreasing our accident frequency rate. The line on the graph looks great going *down*, doesn't it?
>
> Keep up the good work!

The letter was signed by "Mike" and "Tom" and all of the other supervisors.

The information was also sent to the division director, the company safety manager, and to associates at their homes. Associates received the information at home after the first week of implementation, the third week, the sixth week, the tenth week, and once a month thereafter.

Questions for Discussion–Part II

1. What are the strengths and weaknesses of the MAIM program?
2. Estimate how much you believe the company should have invested in this program. How much do you think it did invest?

3. What else might Mike have done to maximize its chances of success?
4. Predict the results of the pilot project and the outcome of the project in the subsequent year.

Part III: The Results

Students: PLEASE DO NOT READ *this part until asked to do so.*

The result of the pilot project was that the trend toward an increase in injury frequency was reversed. In the first year of full implementation there was an improvement of 94 percent in the accident frequency rate, despite a 64 percent increase in orders processed and an 80 percent increase in merchandise handled. After 5 months of the following year, only one injury was charged. This happened in spite of the fact that there had been a 76 percent increase in orders processed, an 89 percent increase in the amount of merchandise handled, and an approximate 30 percent increase in the number of people in the department over the same period in the previous year.

Total investment in the project was approximately $3000, about $300 of which was materials and the rest salary.

An additional result of the program was that it served as a model for the application of behavior modification principles in other areas of the company. The same approach was used to modify safety procedures in manufacturing, receiving, and building and grounds, and significant positive results were achieved. The legal assistance department adapted the principles to reduce a 5-month correspondence backlog within 6 weeks.

Mike Henley had more than met his challenge, and his program eventually won a regional industry award for excellence in organizational change.

Questions for Discussion–Part III

1. The MAIM program achieved improved safety over a period of several years. What were the reasons for this success? What would be required to ensure continued success for the program?
2. What sort of corporate culture supports this kind of program?
3. Do you believe this success is typical of safety programs? From a behavioral standpoint, why do some safety programs succeed while others fail?
4. What do we learn from corporate success stories such as this one, as opposed to stories of corporate problems and failures? Under what circumstances are companies likely to keep their successes to themselves? to publicize them?

57   WHAT TO DO WITH BOB AND NANCY?

Dave Simpson was sitting at his desk wondering how the devil to handle this situation. In engineering school, they don't tell you what to do when you think two of your key subordinates are having an affair! Dave knew a lot about the relative conducting properties of metals, but what about the properties of people?

Dave was engineering manager of a division in a large corporation situated on the East Coast. The division was comprised of 3 engineering supervisors, 5 lead engineers, and approximately 55 engineers (see Exhibit 1). The past two years had seen several reductions in manpower due to a temporary decline in the business base. The remaining men and women in the organization were "cream of the crop," all hard workers with a professional attitude about their jobs; any deadwood was long gone. The division had just won a large contract, which would provide for long-term growth but would also require a heavy workload until new people could be hired and trained.

The work of the organization was highly technical and required considerable sharing of ideas within and between the individual groups. This need for internal cooperation and support had been amplified because the organization was still undermanned and staffing up.

Dave's previous secretary had transferred to an out-plant location just before the new contract award, and it had taken a long time to find a suitable replacement. Because of a general shortage within the company, Dave had been forced to hire temporary help from a secretarial service. After several months he found Nancy and felt very fortunate to have located an experienced secretary from within the company. She was in her mid-30s, attractive, had a pleasant disposition, and was very competent.

In the electronic design group was an enthusiastic, highly respected lead engineer named Bob. Bob and Dave had been close friends for several years, having started with the company at the same time. They shared several common interests, which had led to spending a fair amount of time together away from work.

Bob was struggling to get into management, and Dave's more rapid advancement had put a strain on the friendship. Dave had moved up from co-worker to being his boss and finally to being his boss's boss. Dave felt they could still be good friends at work, but he could not show Bob any favoritism. Bob understood the situation.

From Nancy's first day on the job, Bob began to hang around her desk. He would go out of his way to start conversations and draw her attention. This was not a surprise, since Nancy was attractive and Bob had gained a reputation over the years as being a bit of a "wolf." He was always the first on the scene when an attractive new female joined the program.

Before long, Bob and Nancy began eating lunch together. As time passed the lunch dates became a regular routine, as did their trips together to the coffee machine. Their conversations during the working day also became more frequent. Dave felt slightly concerned about the wasted time, but since the quality and quantity of their work was not suffering in any measurable way, he did not say anything to either person. Furthermore, it was not unreasonable for Bob to be having numerous conversations with her, since she had been instructed to provide typing and clerical support to the engineers whenever she had idle time. (Bob's section was temporarily looking for a secretary, and the engineers were developing several new documents.)

After a few months, Bob and Nancy introduced their spouses to each other, and the two couples began to get together for an increasing number of social gatherings. Bob and Nancy continued their frequent lunch dates, now leaving the plant for lunch and occasionally returning late. This was not considered a major rule infraction, if the lateness was infrequent and if the time were made up in the long run. This tolerance policy was generally respected by all, including Bob and Nancy. On balance, the company seemed to be receiving at least a full week's work from both of them, since they often worked late.

What also was going on (but Dave didn't learn about until later) was that Bob and Nancy were calling each other on the phone during the workday even though they worked in the same general area, just desks apart. They would wait until Dave had left the office and then chat on the phone. However, Nancy's work performance still was not visibly affected.

Of course, the internal grapevine was at work, and occasionally Dave would be asked about the situation between Bob and Nancy. "Do you know they've been seen having drinks together in the evening?" "Did you know Nancy was having marital problems?" "Does Bob's wife know what's going on?"

It was apparent that Bob and Nancy were starting to have an affair, but how serious it was and how long it would last wasn't known. They were being very careful around Dave, and almost all of what Dave knew was based upon second- and third-hand information and rumors. At this point, about four months after Nancy had started work, Dave did speak to Ron, Bob's supervisor, about it; but Ron was anxious to downplay the whole thing. He was willing to talk to

EXHIBIT 1   *Table of Organization*

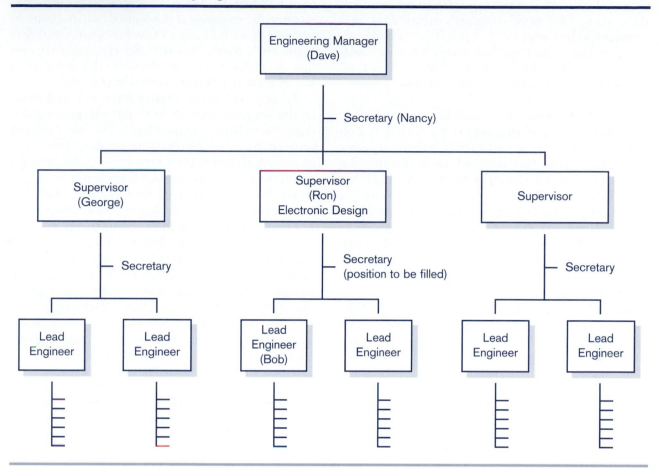

Bob about the late lunches but unwilling to discuss anything else. This seemed appropriate since, from the company's standpoint, employees' private lives were their own business. Ron was new to the organization, and this factor contributed to his reluctance to discuss a delicate issue.

Dave decided not to confront Bob directly. If their relationship were as close as it had been in years past, he might have spoken to Bob about the rumors going around; but during this period the friendship had further deteriorated. They were talking on a less personal level, and Bob was spending less off-hours time with old friends. Furthermore, Dave knew from previous discussions that Bob was particularly sensitive about private matters. "He probably wouldn't welcome my advice," thought Dave.

Dave did speak to Nancy about the need to be back in the office at the end of the lunch hour, but he had not made an issue out of it. Even though it was a definite annoyance when she was not there to answer the phone or type a memo, her performance had not

declined. Dave certainly did not want to bring up with Nancy the issue of an affair. He imagined what might arise: tears, defensive denial (much of what Dave thought was going on would be difficult to substantiate if Nancy were to challenge his assessment), and even potential legal ramifications if the situation were handled improperly. Bob and Nancy could claim that their reputations or careers had been damaged. (Dave also didn't want to raise this issue with Human Resources; it might permanently tarnish both of their records.)

During this same time frame, there was a dramatic change in Bob's personal appearance. Instead of his usual coat-and-tie attire, he started wearing open-front shirts and a beaded necklace. Although perhaps acceptable in some companies that had moved to casual dress, it certainly was out of place in the still conservative environment of the company. As a lead engineer, Bob directed and often presented to management the work of 12 other engineers. The custom was for all engineers and managers to wear a coat and tie, especially since they might be called upon with little notice to meet with a customer or higher management. Even though Bob's attire was considered unprofessional, there was nothing in the company's written dress code requirement to forbid it.

Up to this point there had been no serious violation of company rules by either Bob or Nancy, although rules were being bent and tolerance practices abused.

Then the situation took a turn for the worse while Dave was on a two-week company trip with Ron. Bob and Nancy used the opportunity to go out for a very long lunch. When they returned just before quitting time, George, one of the other supervisors, called Bob into his office and suggested that he "clean up his act." George told Bob that he was being foolish in chasing Nancy and that, among other things, he was jeopardizing his career opportunities with the company. Bob denied being anything more than friends with Nancy and politely told George to stay out of his private affairs.

When Dave returned from his trip and heard of the incident, he told Ron to reprimand Bob and make it clear to him that "his actions are unacceptable and that further long lunch periods will not be tolerated." Bob apologized, said he would make up the time and that it wouldn't happen again.

Dave spoke to Nancy, and she also promised that there would be no more long lunches. But this was not the end of their noontime outplant lunch dates, and before long, Nancy's husband Ted got involved. Ted was a salesman for the company and worked in the same building. He began to drop by at lunchtime to question the engineers about Nancy's whereabouts. In addition he started calling Dave after work, wanting to know when Nancy had left and expressing concern that she had not yet arrived home. This questioning was an unpleasant experience for everybody.

By now, the entire organization was well aware of the irregular relationship and was growing disrespectful of both Bob and Nancy. This was a difficult situation for the engineers. The attitude of the organization had always been very professional, and the success of each group depended upon teamwork and strong leadership from its lead engineer. Bob had been highly respected for his technical competence and ability to direct. In addition the members of his group knew Bob's family and had always considered him to be a good family man. Now this image had been destroyed. From a technical standpoint, Bob was still an excellent engineer and a vital resource on the new contract. But with the group's declining respect, Bob was becoming less effective as a leader. Bob's own engineers felt very uncomfortable about the situation. They believed that Bob's real interests at work were now more with Nancy than with them.

The situation had deteriorated to the point where total organization effectiveness clearly was being affected. Something had to be done to remedy this situation. But what to do?

WHO'S IN CHARGE? (THE JIM DAVIS CASE)

James Davis began his employment with Hereford National Bank in October. He had been hired away from an investment firm on the recommendation of Eric Johnson, vice president in charge of marketing. Mr. Johnson had heard through a friend at IDS, the company that Davis was employed by, that Jim was unhappy in his position there and thought of looking for employment elsewhere. Mr. Johnson felt that because of his experience in the investment world and in sales techniques (Davis had been a sales representative for IDS, helping people plan for their financial future and at the same time selling them the company's services), Davis could prove to be a valuable asset to his division. Since Jim was only 23 years old and had been out of school for two years, Johnson felt that he could offer him less of a salary than the job was worth and save some money. Davis was contacted and seemed interested. An initial interview was arranged, and both decided that Jim was suited to the job. He began working the following month.

Because he was not familiar with the bank and its operations, Jim was put through a five-week training session. It was very informal and consisted of exposure and practice in different areas of banking services. On November 2, Jim began in his new position. He was placed in charge of the Retirement Division. See Exhibit 1 for partial organization chart.

This division was a relatively new area for the bank. It dealt basically with IRA and Keogh retirement accounts. As acting head and sole employee of this division, Jim's job was to sell these services to the public as well as handle the administrative work. He was given a desk on the first floor, which he had to share with the coordinator for the branch managers, Allen Jones.

One of the first tasks to be performed was to transfer balances of certain savings accounts into IRAs (individual retirement accounts). Jim prepared all the calculations and got them entered. Two weeks later, calls started coming in from the people whose accounts had been transferred. They had all received notices that their accounts had a zero balance and wanted to know what was going on. Jim answered them that it was a clerical error and that their money was intact. Upon investigating the incident, he found that it was bank policy to issue statements whenever an account reached a zero balance. When all the money was transferred from savings to IRA, the savings accounts were left with a balance of zero. Jim tried to find out why this policy had not been explained to him; however, he could not get a straight answer. The problem was not a major one, though, and it had been cured rather easily, so he let it pass. The last thing he wanted was to start any bad relationships.

Over the next two months Davis accomplished a lot. The people he worked with on the first floor seemed to be more than friendly once they got to know him. They were always willing to help and give their advice if needed. Jim and Allen became good friends. They played racquetball twice a week and often had lunch together. Allen, like Jim, had been hired away from another firm. Currently working on his master's degree, Allen had been with the bank for three years as the branch manager coordinator. In this role all eight branch managers reported directly to him. Through Allen, Jim met the bank's branch managers. Allen frequently talked about the managers and the problems he had with them. It seemed that Allen was having trouble exerting authority over these managers. Jim always listened but never advised. He always made it policy not to discuss business matters with friends. To him it was just not a good idea.

In January, Jim was promoted to business development manager; until that time the bank had no business development department. To keep up with the competition, it was decided by the board of directors that one should be established. Business development dealt with the sales of bank services to the general public as well as all types of businesses. Johnson told Davis that he would have to keep up with the Retirement Division also, since there was not enough money to employ another person just for this role. Jim's salary was increased, and he was given an office on the third floor (with the other bank executives).

Within a week Davis saw that he had too much work to handle himself and made a request for a part-time secretary. Johnson told him that he would look for someone, but in the meantime Jim could make use of the administrative personnel on the first floor. "All you have to do is call and they will be happy to help out," Johnson said. "After all, that's all they are there for." Jim decided that although he really didn't want to, he would make use of this benefit. The next day he called down to ask two clerks to come up for an hour to classify and file some applications. He was referred to the supervisor, who rather impolitely asked him why he couldn't do it himself. "After all," she said, "it is your job." Infuriated, Jim went directly to Mr. Johnson to ask him what was going on. Mr. Johnson told him not to worry about it; he would have two people for Jim within the hour. No one showed up that afternoon; however, the next morning two clerks were waiting for Jim when he

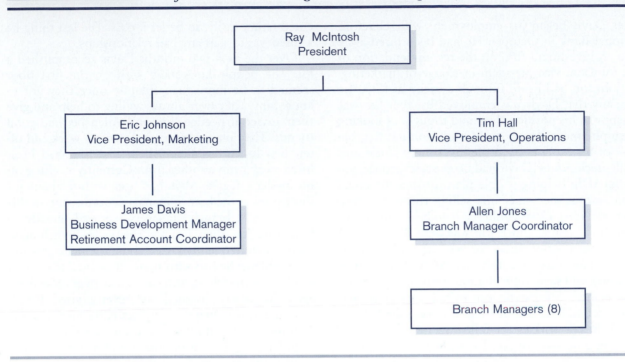

EXHIBIT 1   *Hereford National Bank Organizational Chart (partial)*

came into the office. A week later he had a part-time secretary.

Davis spent the next three months organizing a handbook on bank policy and sales techniques to be distributed to the branch managers. Johnson had told him that it would be the branch managers' job to carry out the policies handed down from development. Although the managers had never actually involved themselves in the sale of bank services in the past, it was in their job description. Johnson told Jim that it should be no problem and that the branch managers would cooperate in any way they could. Jim decided to play it safe, though, and not jump head-first into the situation.

He was playing racquetball with Allen the next evening, and although he didn't want to, he decided that he would ask Allen what he thought. After the game, Jim told Allen what was going on and what Mr. Johnson had said. Allen replied that although nothing had been said to him, he had heard something about it. "I don't know, Jim," Allen said slowly as he paused to take a sip of his drink. "You might have a little bit of a problem. You see, these branch managers have been here for a long time—Patty for 25 years. Out of the eight of them, only Ted Yurek has a college education; the rest have only been to high school. None of them have any sales skills, and somehow I don't think that they are going to like having to learn them. God

. . . I have a hard time keeping them in line . . . and I'm their boss." Jim told Allen that he thought this could be the case and asked him if he thought a training session would help. Allen replied that he thought it would be a good idea, and if Jim wanted to, they would sit down and analyze each manager individually so the training session could be tailored to the group. Jim gladly accepted. Each of the branch managers was notified that selling bank services was to become a major portion of their job and that Jim would keep them up to date on all developments.

The initial training session was scheduled for July 15. On July 1, Jim and Allen held a short, informal meeting for the branch managers. They handed out the handbooks, went over the goals of the program, and asked if there were any questions.

Patty Mathews raised her hand and spoke. "What is the situation with expense accounts . . . like . . . suppose we have to take a client out to dinner?" Jim and Allen looked at each other in surprise. Jim knew that his department did not have the money, nor would the bank allow it even if he did. "At this point," Jim responded, "I see no reason to have expense accounts; the people you will be dealing with won't be of that type. If, however, we feel that a dinner is needed to help close a sale, come and see me and we can decide." "Well," said Patty, "I don't see why we can't have expense accounts. All the executives do!" Allen pointed out that the only expense accounts the executives had was for when they were away from the bank on business. All employees are entitled to this privilege, and anyone who had reason could use it. This remark was, however, ignored by Mrs. Mathews. There were no more questions, and the meeting was adjourned.

On July 15, all the managers were scheduled to go through the training session that Jim and Allen had designed. They were all informed that they could use their expense accounts to get to and from the meeting location and that lunch was being provided by the bank. Jim and Allen had decided in advance that if all went well they would take the group out for drinks afterward. The session was scheduled to begin at 9 A.M. By 8:45 A.M. everyone was there with the exception of Patty Mathews. When she had not shown up by 9:30 A.M., Jim called her branch office and was told that she had called in sick. The training session went as planned, and both Allen and Jim were very pleased with the results.

Jim, however, was undecided about what to do about Patty Mathews. He had a feeling that she was not really sick, but he could not prove it. Even if he could, though, she had been with the bank longer than any other manager. He did not want to get on her bad side, since she carried a lot of weight with the other managers. Still, he refused to allow this situation to go by without some form of reprimand. Jim decided to consult both Allen and Mr. Johnson before acting on this situation.

Endnotes

Chapter 1

1. "Hot Seat in the Corner Office," *Business Week,* February 14, 2000, p. 8.
2. Michele Galen, "Work and Family; Companies Are Starting to Respond to Workers' Needs—and Gain from It," *Business Week,* June 28, 1993.
3. "Loyalty Ebbs at Many Companies as Employees Grow Disillusioned," *The Wall Street Journal,* July 11, 1986.
4. De'Ann Weimer, "3M: The Heat Is on the Boss," *Business Week,* March 15, 1999, p. B2.
5. Report on Watson Wyatt Worldwide study in "Commitment Pays," in "Work Week" column, *The Wall Street Journal,* January 11, 2000, p. 1.
6. "The War for Talent," McKinsey and Company Report, 1998.
7. Frederick M. Biddle, "Stock options Climb Far Down the Corporate Ladeer," *The Wall Street Journal,* January 18, 2000, p. A1.
8. See several issues of *Fast Company,* 1998–1999.
9. "Two-Thirds of 1811 Employees Reported Using Formal Teams to Do Work" in Work Week; "Teams Become Commonplace in U.S. Companies," *The Wall Street Journal,* November 28, 1995, p. A1.
10. Amanda Bennett, "The Chief Executives in Year 2000 Will Be Experienced Abroad," *The Wall Street Journal,* February 27, 1989.
11. Thomas A. Stewart, "Welcome to the Revolution," *Fortune,* December 13, 1993; and Daniel Coleman, "Why Managers Resist Machines," *New York Times,* February 7, 1988.
12. Keith H. Hammonds, "Work and Family; Juggling Both Is an Endless Struggle—and Companies Aren't Helping Much," *Business Week,* September 15, 1997, p. 96.
13. Much of this section is based on the research of Henry Mintzberg, reported in *The Nature of Managerial Work* and in "The Manager's Job: Folklore and Fact" in the *Harvard Business Review.* (See Suggested Readings at the end of this chapter for complete references.)
14. These activities or roles are described in more detail in Chapter 12.
15. A. R. Cohen, and B. A. Stein, "Task Forces in Management: A Key Development Tool," *The NABW Journal,* November–December 1980.
16. "A Brave New Darwinian Workplace," *Fortune,* January 25, 1993.
17. Michelle Colin, "The CEO Still Wears Wingtips; Does That Lead to the Top Remaining Overwhelmingly Female Face," *Business Week,* November 22, 1979, p. 81.
18. H. Mintzberg, "Planning on the Left Side and Managing on the Right," *Harvard Business Review,* July–August 1976.
19. R. P. Weathersby, "Ego Development," in *The Modern American College,* ed. A. W. Chickering (San Francisco: Jossey-Bass, 1981).
20. Copyright 1987 by Kenneth L. Murrell. Management and O.D., University of West Florida, Pensacola, Florida. Used with permission. This instrument may be freely used for educational/training activities. Systematic or large-scale reproduction or distribution may be done only with prior written permission of the author.

Chapter 2

1. R. Likert, *New Patterns of Management* (New York: McGraw-Hill, 1961).
2. These terms are our adaptations of the conceptual scheme of George Homans, elaborated more fully for small groups in Chapter 3.

Chapter 3

1. The balance of this chapter is our adaptation of the work of George C. Homans in *The Human Group* (New York: Harcourt Brace Jovanovich, 1950), and in *Social Behavior: Its Elementary Forms* (New York: Harcourt Grace Jovanovich, 1961).
2. This use of the concept of attitudes, based on Homans, is less restrictive than the traditional individual psychological definition.
3. Individual ideas about how members ought to behave, which are not widely held by the group, are not called *norms;* rather, they are *individual beliefs.*

4. See endnote 1, 1950 entry.
5. F. Steele, and R. S. Jenks, *The Feel of the Work Place* (Reading, MA: Addison-Wesley Publishing, 1977).

Chapter 4

1. G. C. Homans, *The Human Group* (New York: Harcourt Brace Jovanovich, 1950); and *Social Behavior: Its Elementary Forms* (New York: Harcourt Brace Jovanovich, 1961).
2. Ibid.
3. Ibid.
4. Ibid.
5. L. Festinger, S. Schacter, and K. Back, *Social Pressures in Informal Groups: A Study of a Housing Project* (New York: Harper & Row, 1950).
6. See notes 1 (1961 entry) and 5.
7. See note 1 (1961 entry).
8. M. Sherif, *Group Conflict and Cooperation: Their Social Psychology* (Boston: Routledge & Kegan Paul, 1967).
9. R. Blake, and J. Mouton, "Reactions to Intergroup Competition under Win-Lose Competition," *Management Science,* July 1961, pp. 420–25.
10. M. Sherif and C. Sherif, *Groups in Harmony and Tension* (New York: Harper & Row, 1953).
11. D. Cartright, and Z. Zander, *Group Dynamics: Research and Theory* (New York: Harper & Row, 1968).
12. See note 1 (1950 entry).
13. M. Deutsch, "The Effects of Cooperation and Competition upon Group Process," in *Group Dynamics: Research and Theory,* ed. D. Cartright and A. Zander (New York: Harper & Row, 1968).
14. See note 1 (1950 entry).
15. A. Zaleznik, C. R. Christensen, and F. J. Roethlisberger, *The Motivation, Productivity, and Satisfaction of Workers* (Boston: Harvard Business School, 1958).
16. D. F. Gillespie and P. H. Birnbaum, "Status Concordance, Coordination, and Success in Interdisciplinary Research Teams," *Human Relations* 33, no. 1 (1980), pp. 41–56.
17. I. Janis, *Victims of Groupthink* (Boston: Houghton Mifflin, 1972).
18. J. B. Harvey, "The Abilene Paradox: The Management of Agreement," *Organizational Dynamics* 17, no. 1 (1988), pp. 16–43.

Chapter 5

1. R. F. Bales, "Task Roles and Social Roles in Problem-Solving Groups," in *Readings in Social Psychology,* 3rd ed., ed. E. Maccoby. T. M. Newcomb, and E. L. Hartley (New York: Holt, Rinehart & Winston, 1958).
2. G. Homans, *The Human Group* (New York: Harcourt Brace Jovanovich, 1950).
3. ———, *Social Behavior: Its Elementary Forms* (New York: Harcourt Brace Jovanovich, 1961).
4. F. Roethlisberger and W. Dickson, *Management and the Worker (*Cambridge, MA: Harvard University Press, 1939).

5. See note 3.
6. See note 3.
7. A. Zaleznik, C. R. Christensen, and F. Roethlisberger, *The Motivation, Productivity, and Satisfaction of Workers* (Boston: Division of Research, Graduate School of Business, Harvard University, 1958).
8. See note 3.
9. See note 3.
10. See note 7.
11. Adapted from K. Benne and P. Sheats, "Functional Roles of Group Members," *Journal of Social Issues* 4, no. 2 (1948), pp. 41–49.
12. W. F. Whyte, *Street Corner Society,* rev. ed. (Chicago: University of Chicago Press, 1955).
13. The following formulation was originally suggested by one of our students, Nfor Susungi.
14. R. M. Kanter, *Men and Women of the Corporation* (New York: Basic Books, 1977).
15. See note 12.
16. This has its parallel in organizations, where members of groups associated with that company's important priorities (e.g., sales, engineering, and so on) tend to be highly influential.
17. P. R. Lawrence and J. Lorsch, *Organization and Environment* (New York: McGraw-Hill/Irwin, 1967).

Chapter 6

1. A number of years ago, Douglas McGregor, a leading organizational theorist, described 11 criteria of an effective working group. While his studies were specific to certain kinds of groups (mainly executives), the issues inherent in McGregor's criteria serve as a useful framework for this chapter. See D. McGregor, *The Human Side of Enterprise* (New York: McGraw-Hill, 1960).
2. R. F. Bales and E. F. Borgatta, "Size of Group as a Factor in the Interaction Profile," in *Small Groups,* ed. A. P. Hare et al. (New York: Alfred A. Knopf, 1955); and J. J. Seta, P. B. Paulus and J. K. Schkade, "Effects of Group Size and Proximity under Cooperative and Competitive Conditions," *Journal of Personality and Social Psychology* 98, no. 2 (1976), pp. 47–53.
3. G. A. Heise and G. A. Miller. "Problem Solving by Groups Using Various Communication Nets," *Journal of Abnormal Psychology* 46 (1951), pp. 327–35.
4. R. J. Steers, "Antecedents and Outcomes of Organizational Commitment," *Administrative Science Quarterly* 22 (1977), pp. 46–56.
5. D. J. Isenberg, "Some Effects of Time Pressure on Leadership and Decision-Making Accuracy in Small Groups," unpublished paper, Harvard University, 1979.
6. The original discussion by Tuckman appeared in the following article: B. W. Tuckman, "Developmental Sequence in Small Groups," *Psychological Bulletin* 63 (1965), pp. 384–99.
7. This discussion is adapted from Steven L. Obert, "The Development of Organizational Task Groups," PhD Dissertation, Case-Western Reserve University, 1979.

Chapter 7

1. "Howard Atkins and Joseph Wexler" case, copyright by President and Fellows, Harvard College.
2. C. Rogers, *On Becoming a Person* (Boston: Houghton Mifflin, 1961).
3. A. W. Combs and D. Snygg, *Individual Behavior* (New York: Harper & Row, 1959), p. 19.
4. Much of this section is based upon the concepts of A. H. Maslow, F. Herzberg, R. White, and D. McClelland. For references to the work of these authors, see Suggested Readings at the end of this chapter.
5. J. R. Hackman and G. R. Oldham, *Work Redesign* (Reading, MA: Addison-Wesley Publishing Co., 1980).
6. E. L. Lawler, *Pay and Organizational Effectiveness: Psychological View* (New York: McGraw-Hill, 1971); R. A. Guzzo, "Types of Rewards, Cognitions, and Work Motivation," *Academy of Management Review,* January 1979, pp. 75–86; C. C. Pinder, "Concerning the Application of Human Motivation Theories in Organizational Settings," *Academy of Management Review* 2 (1977), pp. 384–97; and M. S. Myers, "Who Are Your Motivated Workers?" *Harvard Business Review* 42 (1964) pp. 73–88.
7. B. F. Skinner, *Contingencies of Reinforcement* (New York: Appleton-Century-Crofts, 1969).
8. See note 7.
9. See note 6, Guzzo and Pinder entries.
10. See note 6, Lawler entry.
11. E. L. Deci, "The Effects of Contingent and Noncontingent Rewards and Controls on Intrinsic Motivation," *Organizational Behavior and Human Performance* 8 (1972), pp. 217–29.
12. D. C. McClelland, *The Achieving Society* (New York: Van Nostrand Reinhold, 1961).
13. For a more complete discussion of the issue, see W. C. Hamner and D. Organ, *Organizational Behavior* (Plano, TX: Business Publications, 1978), chap. 3.
14. See note 6, Lawler and Guzzo entries; and E. L. Lawler, *Motivation in Work Organizations* (Monterey, CA: Brooks/Cole Publishing, 1973).
15. See note 6, Lawler entry.
16. J. S. Adams, "Towards an Understanding of Inequity," *Journal of Abnormal and Social Psychology* 67 (1963), pp. 422–36.
17. See note 14, Lawler (1973) entry.
18. A. Lakein, *How to Get Control of Your Time and Your Life* (New York: Signet, 1973).

Chapter 8

1. A. Combs and D. Snygg, *Individual Behavior,* (New York: Harper & Row, 1959).
2. Justin Kruger and David Dunnings, "Unskilled and Unaware of It: How Difficulties in Recognizing One's Own Incompetence Lead to Inflated Self-assessment," *Journal of Personality and Social Psychology* 77, (December 2000), pp. 1121–34.
3. D. McGregor, *The Human Side of Enterprise.* (New York: McGraw-Hill, 1960), chap 3.

4. See note 3, Chap 4.
5. See note 1.
6. K. Vandivier, "Why Should My Conscience Bother Me?" in *In the Name of Profit,* ed. R. Heilbroner (Garden City, NY: Doubleday 1972), pp. 3–26, 28–31.
7. C. Rogers, *On Becoming a Person (*Boston: Houghton Mifflin, 1961).
8. See note 7.
9. See note 7.
10. H. H. Kelley and J. L. Michela, "Attribution Theory and Research," *Annual Review of Psychology* 31 (1980), pp. 400–405; and J. Jaspars, F. D. Fincham, and M. Hewstone, *Attribution Theory and Research: Conceptual, Developmental, and Social Dimensions* (London: Academic Press, 1983).
11. R. M. Kanter, *Men and Women of the Corporation (*New York: Basic Books, 1977), p. 166.
12. R. Harrison, "Defenses and the Need to Know," *Human Relations Training News* 6 (1962).
13. See note 7.
14. E. Goffman, *The Presentation of Self in Everyday Life* (Garden City, NY: Doubleday, 1959).
15. See note 14.
16. D. Nadler and E. Lawler, "Motivation: A Diagnostic Approach," In *Perspectives on Behavior in Organizations,* ed. J. R. Hackman, E. E. Lawler, and L. W. Porter (New York: McGraw-Hill, 1977), chap. 3.
17. I. B. Myers, *Gifts Differing* (Palo Alto, CA: Consulting Psychologists Press, Inc. 1980).

Chapter 9

1. Based on concepts presented in W. G. Bennis, D. E. Berlew, E. H. Schein, and F. I. Steele, *Interpersonal Dynamics,* 3rd ed. (Chicago: Dorsey Press, 1973), pp. 495–518.
2. F. Steele and S. Jenks,. *The Feel of the Work Place* (Reading, MA: Addison-Wesley Publishing, 1977).
3. Based on concepts developed by W. F. Hill, *Hill Interaction Matrix* (Los Angeles: Youth Study Center, University of Southern California, 1965).
4. C. Argyris, *Interpersonal Competence and Organizational Effectiveness* (Homewood, IL: Richard D. Irwin and Dorsey Press, 1962); and D. Moment and A. Zaleznik, *Role Development and Interpersonal Competence* (Cambridge, MA: Harvard University Press, 1963).

Chapter 10

1. K. Griffin and B. R. Patton, *Personal Communication in Human Relations* (Columbus, OH: Charles E. Merrill Publishing, 1974).
2. C. Rogers and R. E. Farson, "Active Listening," in *Effective Behavior in Organizations,* 1st ed. Ed. Cohen et al. (New York: McGraw-Hill/Irwin, 1976).
3. C. Rogers, "The Characteristics of a Helping Relationship," in *On Becoming a Person* (Boston: Houghton Mifflin, 1961), pp. 39–58.
4. R. E. Walton, *Interpersonal Peacemaking: Confrontations and Third-Party Consultation* (Reading, MA: Ad-

dison-Wesley Publishing, 1969); see note 3; and G. Egan, *Face to Face* (Monterey, CA: Brooks/Cole Publishing, 1973).

5. S. M. Jourard, *The Transparent Self,* rev. ed. (New York: Van Nostrand Reinhold, 1971); and J. Luft, *Group Processes* (Palo Alto, CA: National Press Books, 1970).

6. See note 3 and note 4, Egan entry.

7. This section, including Figures 10–5 and 10–6, is based on "Negotiating Strategically" by Roy J. Lewicki, in *The Portable MBA in Management,* ed. A. R. Cohen, Wiley. Both figures, © 1993, John Wiley and Sons, Inc., are reprinted by permission of John Wiley and Sons, Inc.

8. W. Bennis; D. Berlew; E. Schein; and F. I. Steele, *Interpersonal Dynamics,* 3rd ed. (Chicago: Dorsey Press, 1973).

Chapter 11

1. R. M. Stodgill, *Handbook of Leadership* (New York: Free Press, 1974).

2. D. McGregor, *The Human Side of Enterprise* (New York: McGraw-Hill, 1960).

3. J. R. P. French, Jr., and B. Raven, "The Bases of Social Power," in *Group Dynamics: Research and Theory,* ed. D. Cartwright and Z. Zander (New York: Harper & Row, 1960), pp. 607–23.

4. H. C. Kelman, "Processes of Opinion Change," *Public Opinion Quarterly,* Spring 1961, pp. 56–78.

5. T. J. Peters, "Symbols, Patterns, and Settings: An Optimistic Case for Getting Things Done," *Organizational Dynamics,* Autumn 1978.

6. D. C. McClelland, *Power: The Inner Experience* (New York: Irvington, 1975).

7. B. M. Bass, "Leadership: Good, Better, Best," *Organizational Dynamics,* Winter 1985, pp. 26–40.

8. See Judith Rosener, "Ways Women Lead," *Harvard Business Review,* November–December 1990, pp. 119–25, and the responses in the following issue, January–February 1991.

9. "Up Front, Executive Suite, Don't Mess with These Ladies," *Business Week,* February 28, 2000, p. 8.

10. R. M. Kanter, *Men and Women of the Corporation* (New York: Basic Books, 1977).

11. H. A. Simon, *Administrative Behavior* (New York: Free Press, 1957).

12. J. Pfeffer, "Power and Resource Allocation in Organizations," in *Psychological Foundations of Organizational Behavior,* ed. B. Straw (Santa Monica, CA: Goodyear Publishing, 1977); and *Power in Organizations* (Marshfield, MA: Pitman Publishing, 1981).

13. See note 10.

14. See note 10.

15. A. Gouldner, "The Norm of Reciprocity: A Preliminary Statement," *American Sociological Review,* April 1960, pp. 161–78; J. P. Kotter, *Power in Management* (New York: AMACOM, 1979); and A. R. Cohen, and D. L. Bradford, *Influence without Authority* (New York: John Wiley & Sons, 1990).

16. See note 15, Kotter entry.

17. J. R. P. French, Jr., and B. Raven, "The Bases of Social Power" in D. Cartwright and A. Zander, eds., *Group Dynamics, Research and Theory* (New York: Harper & Row, 1960), pp. 607–23.

18. See note 12, Pfeffer entry.

19. B. Berelson and G. Steiner, *Human Behavior: An Inventory of Scientific Findings* (New York: Harcourt Brace Jovanovich, 1964).

20. D. Kipnis, *The Powerholders* (Chicago: University of Chicago Press, 1976).

21. See note 10.

22. See note 15, Cohen and Bradford entry.

23. P. E. Slater, "Role Differentiation in Small Groups," *American Sociological Review* 20 (1965).

24. A. Zaleznik, "The Human Dilemmas of Leadership," *Harvard Business Review,* July–August 1963.

25. David C. McClelland, *Power: The Inner Experience* (New York: Irvington, 1975).

Chapter 12

1. The managerial functions described here are an adaptation of managerial roles described by Henry Mintzberg, *The Nature of Managerial Work* (New York: Harper & Row, 1973).

2. See note 1.

3. See note 1.

4. See note 1.

5. R. R. Blake and J. S. Mouton, "A Comparative Analysis of Situationalism and 9, 9 Management by Principle," *Organizational Dynamics,* Spring 1982, pp. 20–43.

6. F. A. Fiedler, *Theory of Leadership Effectiveness* (New York: McGraw-Hill, 1967). For an opposing view, see R. House, "A Path Goal Theory of Leader Effectiveness," *Administrative Science Quarterly,* September 1971, pp. 321–38.

7. J. J. Morse and J. W. Lorsch, "Beyond Theory Y," *Harvard Business Review,* May–June 1970, pp. 61–68; and P. Hersey and K. H. Blanchard, *Management of Organizational Behavior: Utilizing Human Resources.* 3rd ed. (Englewood Cliffs, NJ: Prentice Hall, 1977).

8. See note 6, House entry.

9. See note 6, Fiedler entry.

10. V. Vroom, "Some Personality Determinants of the Effects of Participation (Englewood Cliffs, N.J.: Prentice Hall 1960); and G. Strauss, "Some Notes on Power Equalization," in *The Social Science of Organizations,* ed. H. J. Leavitt (Englewood Cliffs, NJ: Prentice Hall, 1963); and note 7, Hershey and Blanchard entry.

11. See note 6, House entry.

12. R. Likert, *New Patterns of Management* (New York: McGraw-Hill, 1961) and see note 5.

13. D. C. Pelz, "Influence: Key to Effective Leadership in the First Line Supervisor," *Personnel* 29 (1952), pp. 209–17.

14. See note 6, Fiedler entry.

15. V. Vroom and P. Yetton, *Leadership and Decision Making* (Pittsburgh: University of Pittsburgh Press, 1973).

16. See note 15.

17. See note 6, Fiedler entry.

18. See note 15. Also R. M. Stogdill, *Handbook of Leadership* (New York: Macmillan/Free Press, 1974); and R. Miles and J. B. Ritchie, "Participative Management: Quality versus Quantity," *California Management Review,* Summer 1971 pp. 48–56.

19. D.L. Bradford and A. R. Cohen, *Managing for Excellence: The Guide to Developing High Performance in Contemporary Organizations* (New York: John Wiley & Sons, 1984).

20. See note 19.

21. David L. Bradford and Allan R. Cohen, *Power Up: Transforming Organizations through Shared Leadership* (New York: John Wiley & Sons, 1998).

22. H. W. Wilensky, "Human Relations in the Work Place" *Research in Human Industrial Relations,* 12th ed., ed. Conrad Arensberg (New York: Harper & Row, 1957).

Chapter 13

1. P. R. Lawrence and J. W. Lorsch, *Organization and Environment: Managing Differentiation and Integration* (Cambridge, MA: Division of Research, Graduate School of Business, Harvard University, 1967).

2. R. R. Blake, H. A. Shepard; and J. Mouton, *Managing Intergroup Conflict in Industry* (Houston: Gulf Publishing, 1964).

3. R. R. Blake and J. S. Mouton, "Reactions to Intergroup Competition under Win-Lose Competition," *Management Science,* July 1961, pp. 420–25.

4. See note 1; and A. K. Rice, "Individual, Group, and Intergroup Behavior," *Human Relations* 22 (1969), pp. 565–84.

5. See note 2.

6. J. W. Lorsch and P. R. Lawrence, *Managing Group and Intergroup Relations* (New York: McGraw-Hill/Irwin, 1972), pp. 285–304.

7. E. T. Hall and W. F. Whyte, "Intercultural Communication: A Guide to Men of Action," in *Readings in Managerial Psychology, 2nd ed.,* ed. H. J. Leavitt and L. R. Pondy (Chicago: University of Chicago Press, 1973).

8. See note 3.

9. See note 3; and R. R. Blake and J. S. Mouton, "Overevaluation of Own Group's Product in Intergroup Competition," *Journal of Abnormal and Social Psychology* 64, no. 3 (1962), pp. 237–38.

10. R. M. Kanter, *Men and Women of the Corporation* (New York: Alfred A. Knopf, 1977).

11. J. A. Seiler, "Diagnosing Interdepartmental Conflict," *Harvard Business Review,* September–October 1963.

12. L. D. Brown, "Toward a Theory of Power and Intergroup Relations," in *Advances in Experiential Social Processes* vol. 1. E. C. L. Cooper and C. P. Alderfer, (New York: John Wiley & Sons, 1978).

13. See note 11.

14. See note 11.

15. See notes 11 and 2; Joe Kelly "Make Conflict Work For You," *Harvard Business Review,* July–August 1970, pp. 103–13. R. T. Pascale, *Managing on the Edge* (New York: Simon & Schuster, 1991).

16. J. D. Thompson, *Organizations in Action* (New York: McGraw-Hill, 1967).

17. A. Gouldner, "The Role of the Norm of Reciprocity in Social Stabilization," *American Sociological Review* 25 (1960), pp. 161–78.

18. R. E. Walton and J. M. Dutton, "The Management of Interdepartmental Conflict," *Administrative Science Quarterly* 14 (1969), pp. 73–84.

19. See note 2.

20. See note 17.

21. N. J. Adler, *International Dimensions of Organizational Behavior* (Belmont, CA: Kent Publishing, 1986).

22. E T. Hall, *Dance of Life: The Other Dimension of Time* (New York: Anchor/Doubleday, 1984).

23. G. Hofstede, "Motivation, Leadership, and Organization: Do American Theories Apply Abroad?" *Organizational Dynamics,* Summer 1980.

24. D. Tannen, *You Just Don't Understand* (New York: William Morrow & Company, 1990).

25. Laura Chasin and Carol Becker, "Public Conversation Project," APA Presentation, August 15, 1992.

Chapter 14

1. W. Bennis, K. D. Benne, and R. Chin, eds., *The Planning of Change* (New York: Holt, Rinehart and Winston, 1964).

2. D. C. Basil and C. W. Cook, *The Management of Change* (New York: McGraw-Hill, 1974).

3. A. R. Cohen and H. Gadon, "Changing the Management Culture in a Public School System," *Journal of Applied Behavioral Science* 4, no. 2 (1978).

4. R. Beckhard, "The Confrontation Meeting," *Harvard Business Review* 45 (1967), pp. 149–55.

5. R. M. Kanter, *The Change Masters: Innovation for Productivity in the American Corporation* (New York: Simon & Schuster, 1983); and T. Peters and S. Waterman, *In Search of Excellence: Lessons from America's Best-Managed Corporations* (New York: Harper & Row, 1982).

6. M. Beer, R. A. Eisenstadt, and B. Spector, "Why Change Programs Don't Produce Change," *Harvard Business Review,* November–December 1990.

7. P. Lawrence, "How to Deal with Resistance to Change," *Harvard Business Review,* January–February 1969, p. 4; see note 1; and J. L. Franklin, "Characteristics of Successful and Unsuccessful Organization Development," *Journal of Applied Behavioral Science* 11, no. 4 (1976), pp. 471–92.

8. See note 5, Kanter entry.

9. R. Beckhard and R. T. Harris, *Organizational Transitions: Managing Complex Change* (Reading, MA: Addison-Wesley Publishing, 1977); W. Bennis, *Changing Organizations* (New York: John Wiley & Sons, 1966); and W. Bennis, *Organizational Development: Its Nature, Origins, and Prospects* (Reading, Mass.: Addison-Wesley Publishing, 1969).

10. M. Hammer and J. Ciampy, *Reengineering the Corporation: A Manifesto for Business Revolution* (New York: Harper Business, 1993); and T. H. Davenport, "Process Innovation," *Reengineering Work through Information Technology* (Boston: Harvard Business School Press, 1993).

11. See note 7, Lawrence entry; and see note 9, Bennis entries.

12. D. A. Nadler, "Managing Organizational Change: An Integrative Perspective," *Journal of Applied Behavioral Science,* April–May–June 1981, pp. 191–211.

13. R. T. Golembiewski, "Managing the Tension between OD Principles and Political Dynamics," in *The Cutting Edge: Current Theory and Practice in Organizational Development*, ed. W. Burke (San Diego: University Associates, 1978).

14. C. Argyris, *Intervention Theory and Method* (Reading, MA: Addison-Wesley Publishing, 1970).

15. See note 14.

16. See note 9, Beckhard and Harris entry.

17. A. R. Cohen and D. L. Bradford, *Influence without Authority* (New York: John Wiley & Sons, 1990); see note 5, Kanter entry; and D. Mechanic, "Sources of Power of Lower Participants in Complex Organizations," *Administrative Science Quarterly* 7, no. 3 (1962).

18. J. Kotter and L. Schlesinger, "Choosing Strategies for Change," *Harvard Business Review,* March–April 1979; and R. Harrison, "Choosing the Depth of Organizational Intervention," *Journal of Applied Behavioral Science* 6, no. 2 (1970), pp. 181–202.

19. R. Lipitt, J. Watson, and B. Westley, *The Dynamics of Planned Change* (New York: Harcourt Brace Jovanovich, 1958).

20. H. J. Leavitt and H. Bahrami, *Managerial Psychology,* 5th ed. (Chicago: University of Chicago Press, 1988).

21. L. P. Bradford, J. R. Gibb, and K. D. Benne, eds. *T-Group Theory and Laboratory Method* (New York: John Wiley & Sons 1964); and R. T. Golembiewski and A. Blumberg, *Sensitivity and the Laboratory Approach,* 3rd ed. (Itasca, IL: F. E. Peacock Publishers, 1977).

22. S. Prokesch, "Edges Fray on Volvo's Brave New Humanistic World," *New York Times,* July 7, 1991.

23. E. H. Porter, "The Parable of the Spindle," *Harvard Business Review* 40, no. 3 (1962).

24. F. Steele, *Physical Settings and Organization Development* (Reading, MA: Addison-Wesley Publishing, 1976).

25. H. W. Babb and D. G. Kopp, "Applications of Behavior Modification in Organizations: A Review and Critique," *Academy of Management Review,* April 1978, pp. 281–92; and E. J. Feeney, "At Emery Air Freight: Positive Reinforcement Boosts Performance," *Organizational Dynamics* 1 (1973), pp. 41–50.

26. R. Harrison, "When Power Conflicts Trigger Team Spirit," *European Business,* Spring 1972.

27. See note 5, Kanter entry.

28. Thomas Petzinger, Jr., "Two Executives Work Up Way to Make Pillsbury Listen," *The Wall Street Journal,* September 27, 1996, p. B1.

29. B. A. Stein, *Quality of Work Life in Action: Managing for Effectiveness* (New York: American Management Association, 1983); J. R. Hackman and J. L. Suttle, *Improving Life at Work* (Santa Monica, CA: Goodyear Publishing, 1977); and H. C. Carlson, "GM's Quality-of-Work-Life Efforts . . . An Interview," *Personnel,* July–August 1978.

30. A. R. Cohen and H. Gadon, *Alternative Work Schedules: Integrating Individual and Organizational Needs* (Reading, MA: Addison-Wesley Publishing, 1978).

31. R. Walton, *Interpersonal Peacemaking: Confrontations and Third-Party Consultation* (Reading, MA: Addison-Wesley Publishing, 1969); and E. H. Schein, *Process Consultation II* (Reading, MA: Addison-Wesley Publishing, 1987).

32. A. R. Cohen, S. L. Fink, and H. Gadon, "Key Groups Not T-Groups for Organizational Development," in *Consultants and Consulting Styles,* ed. D. Sinha (Delhi: Vision Books, 1978).

33. R. R. Blake, J. S. Mouton, and R. L. Sloma, "The Union–Management Intergroup Laboratory: Strategy for Resolving Intergroup Conflict," *Journal of Applied Behavior Science* 1, no. 1 (1965), pp. 25–57.

34. See note 12; R. E. Walton, J. Cutcher-Gershenfeld, and R. B. McKersie, *Strategic Negotiations: A Theory of Change in Labor-Management Relations* (Boston, Harvard Business School Press, 1994); and See note 13.

35. See note 31, Walton entry.

36. D. G. Bowers, "OD Techniques and Their Results in 23 Organizations," *Journal of Applied Behavioral Science* 9 (1973), pp. 21–43.

37. See note 4.

38. C. Krone, "Open Systems Redesign," in *New Technologies in Organizational Development* 2, ed. J. D. Adams (San Diego: University Associates, 1975).

39. See note 9, Beckhard and Harris entry; and R. M. Kanter and B. A. Stein, "Building the Parallel Organization: Creating Mechanisms for Permanent Quality of Work Life," *Journal of Applied Behavioral Science* 16, no. 3 (1980), pp. 371–88.

40. See note 5, Kanter entry.

Cases

Case 1. This case was prepared by Peter McGrady, Whitby, Ontario, Canada. Copyright © 1990 by Peter McGrady. Reproduced with permission.

Case 2. Robert L. Rose and Alex Kotlowitz, "Back to Bickering: Strife between UAW and Caterpillar Blights Promising Labor Idea." Reprinted by permission of *The Wall Street Journal,* © November 23, 1992, Dow Jones & Company, Inc. All Rights Reserved Worldwide.

Case 3. © Whittemore School of Business and Economics, University of New Hampshire.

Case 4. This case was written by Tom Delay, MBA, under the supervision of Susan Schneider, associate professor at INSEAD. It is intended to be used as a basis for class discussion rather than to illustrate either effective or ineffective handling of an administrative situation. Reprinted with the permission of INSEAD. Copyright © 1988 INSEAD, Fontainebleau, France. Revised 1992.

Case 5. Excerpted from Donald F. Roy, "'Banana Time,' Job Satisfaction, and Informal Interaction." Reprinted by permission of the Society for Applied Anthropology from *Human Organization* 18, no. 4 (Winter 1959–60), pp. 151–68.

Case 6. This case was prepared by Mr. Bob Lee of England, address unknown. We wish to give credit to Mr. Lee for providing this instructional case, so valuable in teaching about cross-cultural management.

Case 7. This case was prepared by Professors Duncan Spelman and Marcy Crary of Bentley College. It was originally published in an article entitled "Intimacy or Distance? A Case on Male-Female Attraction at Work" in the *Organizational Behavior Teaching Review* 9, no. 2, 1984. Copyright © 1984 by *The Organizational Behavior Teaching Society.*

Case 8. This case was prepared by Peggy C. Smith, Kathy Kargel, and Lester A. Neidell, the University of Tulsa. This case was written with the cooperation of management, solely for the purpose of stimulating student discussion. Data are based on field research in the organization and on the student diary developed as part of the internship requirement. All events and individuals are real, but names and locations have been disguised. Copyright © 1993 by the *Case Research Journal* and Peggy C. Smith, Kathy Kargel, and Lester A. Neidell.

Case 9. This case was prepared by Sheila R. Cizauskas, MBA. Copyright © 1994, Sheila R. Cizauskas. Reproduced with her permission.

Case 10. Copyright © J. L. Kellogg Graduate School of Management, Northwestern University. Reproduced by permission.

Case 11. Neil Abramson prepared this case under the supervision of Professor J. J. DiStefano solely to provide material for class discussion. The authors do not intend to illustrate either effective or ineffective handling of a managerial situation. The authors may have disguised certain names and other identifying information to protect confidentiality. Copyright © 1991, Ivey Management Services, Version: (A) 1992-08-24.

Case 12. This case was prepared by William Duckett under the supervision of Professor Allan R. Cohen for classroom discussion. Copyright © 1983, Babson College. Revised 2000. Reproduced with permission.

Case 13. Thomas E. Ricks, "Army at Odds: West Point Posting Becomes a Minefield for 'Warrior' Officer," *The Wall Street Journal,* March 13, 1997, p. A1. (Copyright © 1997, Dow Jones & Company, Inc.)

Case 14. This case was originally presented at the 1993 North American Case Research Association annual meeting. The authors' names and affiliations are withheld from publication in order to assure anonymity to the company and managers described here. All events and individuals are real, but names have been disguised. Copyright © 1995 by the *Case Research Journal* and the authors.

Case 15. This case was prepared by Todd Jick as an adaptation of an old case titled "Gregory Pellham." The author of that case is unknown.

Case 16. This case was prepared by Kate Button, journalist, and Christopher K. Bart, McMaster University, Canada. This case was written solely for the purpose of stimulating student discussion. All events and individuals are real, but names have been disguised at the request of the principals involved. Copyright © 1993 by the *Case Research Journal* and Kate Button and Christopher K. Bart.

Case 17. This case was prepared by Kate Button, journalist, and Christopher K. Bart, McMaster University, Canada. This case was written solely for the purpose of stimulating student discussion. All events and individuals are real, but names have been disguised at the request of the principals involved. Copyright © 1993 by the *Case Research Journal* and Kate Button and Christopher K. Bart.

Case 18. Reprinted by permission of the publisher from *Journal of Management Case Studies* 1986; 2:238–243, Copyright © 1986 by Elsevier Science Publishing Co., Inc. Authors: Joseph Weiss, Mark Wahlstrom, and Edward Marshall.

Case 19. This case was prepared by Allan R. Cohen. Copyright © 2000; Whittemore School of Business and Economics, University of New Hampshire. Reproduced with permission.

Case 20. This case was prepared by Gordon Anderson, MBA graduate 1988, and Christine Mead, Research Assistant, under the supervision of Professor Susan Schneider, as a basis for class discussion rather than to illustrate either effective or ineffective handling of an administrative situation. Reprinted with the permission of INSEAD-CEDEP. Copyright © 1993 INSEAD-CEDEP, Fontainebleau, France. All rights reserved.

Case 21. Neil Abramson prepared this case under the supervision of Professor J. J. DiStefano solely to provide material for class discussion. The authors do not intend to illustrate either effective or ineffective handling of a managerial situation. The authors may have disguised certain names and other identifying information to protect confidentiality. Copyright © 1991, Ivey Management Services, Version: (A) 1992-08-24.

Case 22. This case was prepared by Kim Johnson under the supervision of Professor Allan R. Cohen for classroom discussion. Copyright © 1986, Babson College. Reproduced with permission.

Case 23. This case was prepared Peter McGrady, Whitby, Ontario, Canada. Copyright © 1982 by Peter McGrady. Reproduced with permission.

Case 24. This case was prepared by Michael Thompson, Brigham Young University. The author thanks Daniel Hecht for assistance on an early draft of the case, which was written solely for the purpose of stimulating student discussion. Data are based on field research; all events are real, although the names of organizations, locations, and individuals have been disguised. Copyright © 1994 by the *Case Research Journal* and Michael Thompson and Daniel Hecht.

Case 25. © Whittemore School of Business and Economics, University of New Hampshire.

Case 26. This case was prepared by Franklin Ramsoomair of Wilfrid Laurier University. This case was originally presented at a workshop of the Eastern Casewriters' Association. It was written with the cooperation of the professor described, solely for the purpose of stimulating student discussion. All individuals and incidents are real, but names and data have been disguised. Copyright © 1992 by the *Case Research Journal* and Franklin Ramsoomair.

Case 27. From S. Fink, S. Jenks, and R. Willits, *Designing and Managing Organizations,* 1983, pages 464–73.

Case 50. Robert Ellis and Raymond Adamson wrote this case for the purpose of class discussion. It is not meant to illustrate either effective or ineffective management behaviour. The names of the main characters and other identifying information have been disguised to protect confidentiality. Copyright © 1998 Wilfrid Laurier University.

Case 51. This case was prepared by Ellen T. LeBoeuf. Copyright © 1993 by Ellen T. LeBoeuf. Reproduced with her permission.

Case 52. Copyright © 2000 Babson College.

Case 53. This case was written by Professor Robin Willits. It is based on the *Chris Cunningham* case, which was prepared by Todd Jick as an adaptation of an old case titled *Gregory Pellham* (author unknown).

Case 54. © 1999 by Rae André, Northeastern University. All rights reserved.

Case 55. This case was prepared by Roland B. Cousins, of LaGrange College. Management cooperated in the field research for this case, which was written solely for the purpose of stimulating student discussion. All individuals and incidents are real, but names and data have been disguised at the request of the organization. Copyright © 1992 by the *Case Research Journal* and Roland B. Cousins.

Case 56. This case was prepared by Rae André of Northeastern University. This case was written under a grant from the Minerva Education Institute, with the cooperation of management, solely for the purpose of stimulating class discussion. All events and individuals are real, but names and locations have been disguised.

Case 57. This case was prepared under the supervision of David L. Bradford, Lecturer in Organizational Behavior, as the basis of class discussion, rather than to illustrate either effective or ineffective handling of an administrative situation. Reprinted with permission of Stanford University Graduate School of Business, © 1983, Revised 2000, by the Board of Trustees of the Leland Stanford Junior University.

Case 58. This case was prepared by Danny J. Mainolfi under the supervision of Professor Allan R. Cohen for classroom discussion. Copyright © 1983, Revised 2000, Babson College. Reproduced with permission.

Index